Turkey

Tom Brosnahan
Pat Yale

LONELY PLANET PUBLICATIONS
Melbourne • Oakland • London • Paris

TURKEY

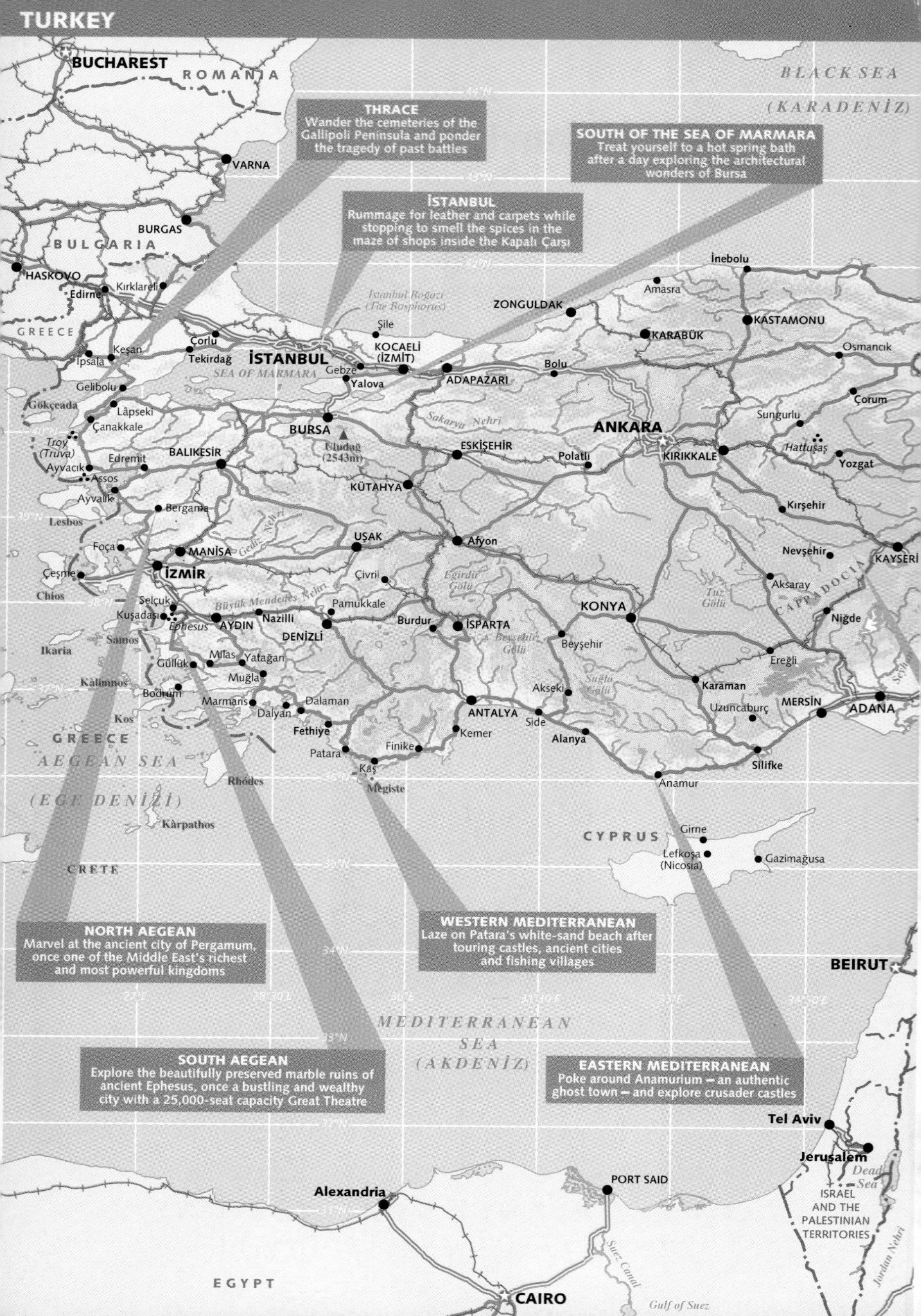

THRACE
Wander the cemeteries of the Gallipoli Peninsula and ponder the tragedy of past battles
SOUTH OF THE SEA OF MARMARA
Treat yourself to a hot spring bath after a day exploring the architectural wonders of Bursa
İSTANBUL
Rummage for leather and carpets while stopping to smell the spices in the maze of shops inside the Kapalı Çarşı
NORTH AEGEAN
Marvel at the ancient city of Pergamum, once one of the Middle East's richest and most powerful kingdoms
WESTERN MEDITERRANEAN
Laze on Patara's white-sand beach after touring castles, ancient cities and fishing villages
SOUTH AEGEAN
Explore the beautifully preserved marble ruins of ancient Ephesus, once a bustling and wealthy city with a 25,000-seat capacity Great Theatre
EASTERN MEDITERRANEAN
Poke around Anamurium – an authentic ghost town – and explore crusader castles
BUCHAREST
ROMANIA
BLACK SEA
(KARADENİZ)
VARNA
BURGAS
BULGARIA
HASKOVO
Edirne
Kırklareli
GREECE
İnebolu
Amasra
ZONGULDAK
KASTAMONU
KARABÜK
İstanbul Boğazı
(The Bosphorus)
Şile
Çorlu
Keşan
Ipsala
Tekirdağ
İSTANBUL
KOCAELİ
(İZMİT)
Gebze
Yalova
SEA OF MARMARA
ADAPAZARI
Bolu
Osmancık
Çorum
Gelibolu
Gökçeada
Lâpseki
Çanakkale
Troy
(Truva)
BURSA
Uludağ
(2543m)
Sakarya Nehri
ANKARA
Sungurlu
Hattuşaş
Yozgat
KIRIKKALE
Polatlı
ESKİŞEHİR
BALIKESİR
Edremit
Ayvacık
Assos
Ayvalık
KÜTAHYA
Bergama
Lesbos
Kırşehir
Gediz Nehri
UŞAK
Afyon
Foça
MANİSA
İZMİR
Çeşme
Chios
Çivril
Eğirdir Gölü
Nevşehir
KAYSERİ
Aksaray
Tuz Gölü
CAPPADOCIA
Niğde
Selçuk
Kuşadası
Ephesus
AYDIN
Nazilli
Büyük Menderes Nehri
Pamukkale
DENİZLİ
Burdur
İSPARTA
Beyşehir Gölü
Beyşehir
KONYA
Samos
Ikaria
Milas
Yatağan
Güllük
Muğla
Kàlimnos
Bodrum
Kos
Marmaris
Dalyan
Dalaman
Fethiye
ANTALYA
Kemer
Side
Akseki
Suğla Gölü
Alanya
Ereğli
Karaman
Uzuncaburç
MERSİN
ADANA
Seyhan
GREECE
AEGEAN SEA
(EGE DENİZİ)
Rhódes
Kàrpathos
Patara
Finike
Kaş
Megiste
Anamur
Silifke
CYPRUS
Girne
Lefkoşa
(Nicosia)
Gazimağusa
CRETE
BEIRUT
MEDITERRANEAN
SEA
(AKDENİZ)
Tel Aviv
Jerusalem
Dead Sea
ISRAEL AND THE PALESTINIAN TERRITORIES
Jordan Nehri
PORT SAID
Alexandria
Suez Canal
EGYPT
CAIRO
Gulf of Suez
44°N
43°N
42°N
40°N
39°N
38°N
37°N
36°N
35°N
34°N
33°N
32°N
31°N
27°E
28°30'E
30°E
31°30'E
33°E
34°30'E

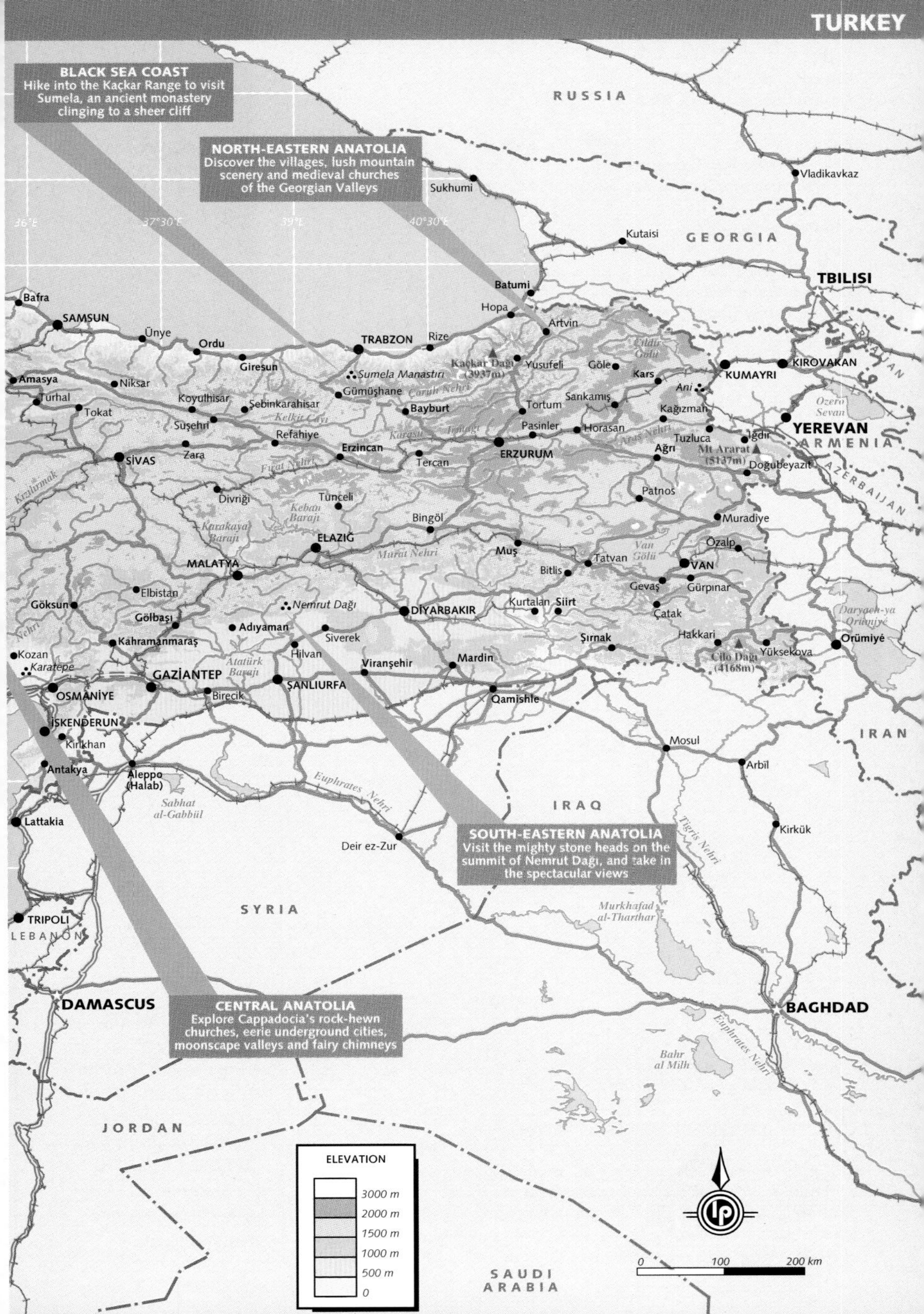
BLACK SEA COAST
Hike into the Kaçkar Range to visit Sumela, an ancient monastery clinging to a sheer cliff
NORTH-EASTERN ANATOLIA
Discover the villages, lush mountain scenery and medieval churches of the Georgian Valleys
SOUTH-EASTERN ANATOLIA
Visit the mighty stone heads on the summit of Nemrut Dağı, and take in the spectacular views
CENTRAL ANATOLIA
Explore Cappadocia's rock-hewn churches, eerie underground cities, moonscape valleys and fairy chimneys
RUSSIA
GEORGIA
ARMENIA
AZERBAIJAN
IRAN
IRAQ
SYRIA
LEBANON
JORDAN
SAUDI ARABIA
TBILISI
YEREVAN
BAGHDAD
DAMASCUS
Vladikavkaz
Sukhumi
Kutaisi
Batumi
Hopa
Artvin
Bafra
SAMSUN
Ünye
Ordu
Giresun
TRABZON
Rize
Kaçkar Dağı (3937m)
Yusufeli
Göle
Kars
KUMAYRI
KIROVAKAN
Amasya
Niksar
Sumela Manastırı
Gümüşhane
Ani
Turhal
Tokat
Koyulhisar
Şebinkarahisar
Bayburt
Tortum
Sarıkamış
Kağızman
Suşehri
Refahiye
Pasinler
Horasan
Tuzluca
Iğdır
Zara
Erzincan
Tercan
ERZURUM
Ağrı
Mt Ararat (5137m)
Doğubeyazıt
SİVAS
Divriği
Tunceli
Patnos
Bingöl
Muradiye
ELAZIĞ
Muş
Özalp
MALATYA
Tatvan
Bitlis
VAN
Gevaş
Gürpınar
Elbistan
Kurtalan
Siirt
Göksun
Nemrut Dağı
DİYARBAKIR
Çatak
Gölbaşı
Adıyaman
Siverek
Şırnak
Hakkari
Yüksekova
Orümiyé
Kahramanmaraş
Hilvan
Cilo Dağı (4168m)
Kozan
Karatepe
Mardin
Viranşehir
GAZİANTEP
ŞANLIURFA
OSMANİYE
Birecik
Qamishle
İSKENDERUN
Kırıkhan
Mosul
Antakya
Aleppo (Halab)
Arbil
Lattakia
Deir ez-Zur
Kirkük
TRIPOLI
Çoruh Nehri
Kelkit Çayı
Fırat Nehri
Kızılırmak
Keban Barajı
Karakaya Barajı
Murat Nehri
Van Gölü
Atatürk Barajı
Euphrates Nehri
Tigris Nehri
Sabhat al-Gabbūl
Murkhafad al-Tharthar
Bahr al Milh
Ozero Sevan
Daryaeh-ye Orūmīyé
36°E
37°30'E
39°E
40°30'E
ELEVATION
3000 m
2000 m
1500 m
1000 m
500 m
0
0
100
200 km

Turkey
6th edition – April 1999
First published – July 1985

Published by
Lonely Planet Publications Pty Ltd A.C.N. 005 607 983
192 Burwood Rd, Hawthorn, Victoria 3122, Australia

Lonely Planet Offices
Australia PO Box 617, Hawthorn, Victoria 3122
USA 150 Linden St, Oakland, CA 94607
UK 10a Spring Place, London NW5 3BH
France 1 rue du Dahomey, 75011 Paris

Photographs
Many of the images in this guide are available for licensing from Lonely Planet Images.
email: lpi@lonelyplanet.com.au

Front cover photograph
Delicious Turkish delight (John Hay)

ISBN 0 86442 599 6

Printed by SNP Printing Pte Ltd, Singapore

Contents – Text

Contents – Maps

INTRODUCTION

İSTANBUL

THRACE 250

SOUTH OF THE SEA OF MARMARA 274

NORTH AEGEAN TURKEY 301

SOUTH AEGEAN TURKEY 370

WESTERN MEDITERRANEAN TURKEY 438-9

EASTERN MEDITERRANEAN TURKEY 510

CENTRAL ANATOLIA 552

BLACK SEA COAST 650-1

EASTERN ANATOLIA

MAP LEGEND – SEE BACK PAGE

MAPS

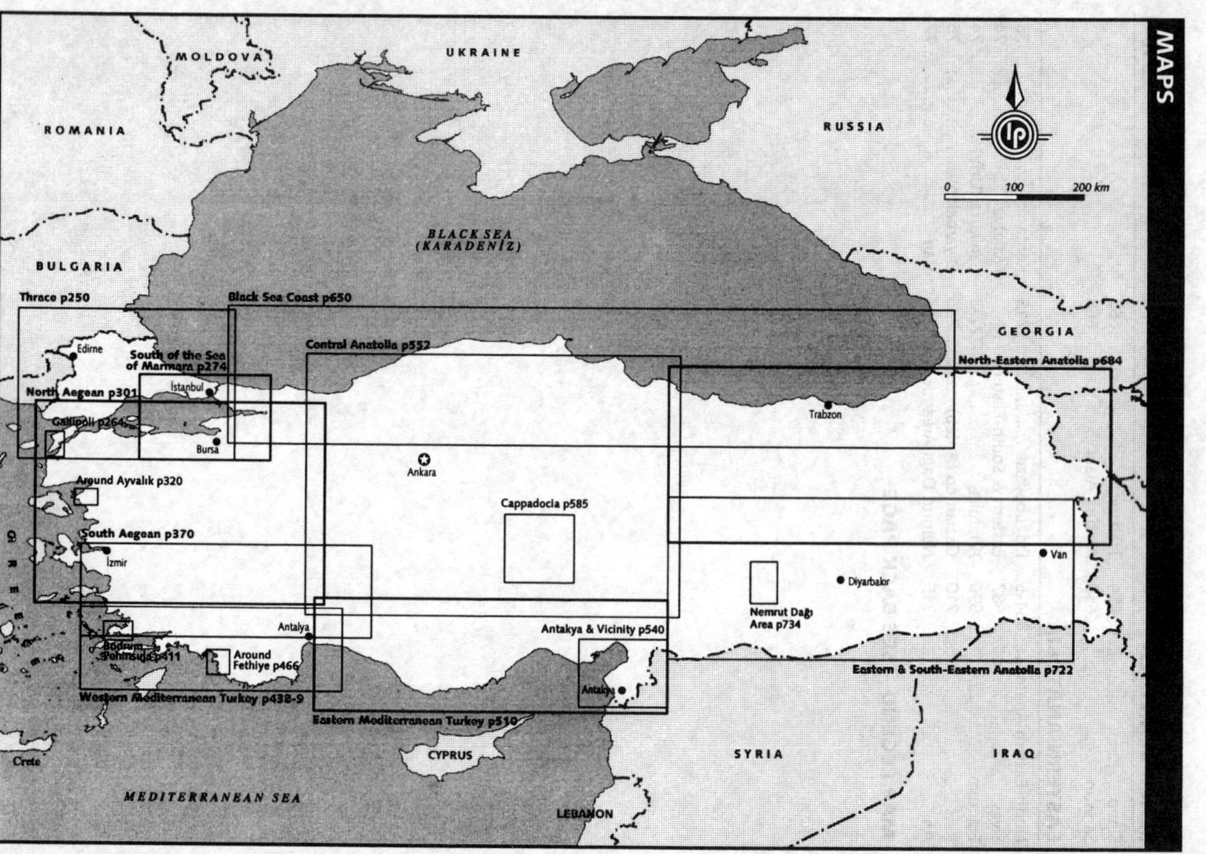

MOLDOVA
UKRAINE
ROMANIA
RUSSIA
0
100
200 km
BLACK SEA
(KARADENİZ)
BULGARIA
Thrace p250
Black Sea Coast p650
GEORGIA
Central Anatolia p552
Edirne
South of the Sea of Marmara p274
North-Eastern Anatolia p684
İstanbul
North Aegean p301
Trabzon
Gallipoli p264
Bursa
Ankara
Around Ayvalık p320
Cappadocia p585
South Aegean p370
Van
İzmir
Diyarbakır
Nemrut Dağı Area p734
Antalya
Antakya & Vicinity p540
Bodrum Peninsula p411
Around Fethiye p466
Eastern & South-Eastern Anatolia p722
Antakya
Western Mediterranean Turkey p438-9
Eastern Mediterranean Turkey p510
CYPRUS
SYRIA
IRAQ
Crete
MEDITERRANEAN SEA
LEBANON

The Authors

Tom Brosnahan

Tom Brosnahan was born in Pennsylvania, went to college in Boston, then set out on the road. He first went to Turkey as a US Peace Corps volunteer, teaching English and learning Turkish. He studied Ottoman Turkish history and language for eight years, but abandoned the writing of his PhD dissertation in favor of writing guidebooks.

Since then, his 35 guidebooks have sold nearly three million copies in 12 languages. Turkey is the result of more than a decade of experience and travel in the country.

Tom is also the author of Lonely Planet's guide to İstanbul and the Turkish phrasebook, and co-author of *Guatemala, Belize & Yucatán: La Ruta Maya, Mexico, Central America, New England* and other Lonely Planet guides.

Pat Yale

Pat Yale first went to Turkey in 1974 in an old van that didn't look as if it would make it past Dover. After graduating she spent several years selling holidays before throwing away sensible careerdom to head overland from Egypt to Zimbabwe. Returning home, she mixed teaching with extensive travelling in Europe, Asia, and Central and South America. A full-time writer now, she also helped update Lonely Planet's *Ireland, Dublin* and *Britain* guides.

FROM THE AUTHORS

Tom Brosnahan Updated information for travellers to Turkey is available on Lonely Planet's Web site (www.lonelyplanet.com) and on my Web site (www.infoexchange.com). Please send us your tips, suggestions and comments so that we can improve our books and help other travellers. If you have a question for which this book and our Web sites do not provide the answer, I'll be happy to try to answer it through my Web site.

I've made up an audio cassette to help you learn traveller's Turkish. If you're interested, please see the Turkish Language Guide chapter at the end of this book.

My thanks to Mr Selami Karaibrahimgil, director of the Turkish tourism office in New York City; Mr Mustafa Siyahhan of the Turkish Ministry of Tourism in Ankara; Mr Bülent Erdemgil, Press Counselor in the Turkish Embassy in Washington; Mr Ersan Atsür of Orion-Tour in İstanbul; Mr Süha Ersöz of the Esbelli Evi in Ürgüp; Ms Ann Nevans of the Hotel Empress Zoe in İstanbul; and, as always, the Turkish people (especially the cooks!) who made my research trips so enjoyable.

Pat Yale So many people deserve my thanks, but special mention must go to John Williams in Antakya; Adem Nakçı in Diyarbakır; Sedat Kiğili and friends in İstanbul; Mahmut Arslan in Kahta; the Durmuş brothers in Pamukkale; Özcan Arslan in Şanlıurfa; Sinan and Emanuelle Bayram in Selçuk; Penny Yeşilipek in Side; Remzi Bozbay in Van; and to all my Kapadokyan cronies, in particular Ahmet, Yasin, Tovi and Osman Diler in Avanos, and Dawn Köse, Mehmet Metin, and the two Mehmets at Safran Halı in Göreme. Letters from David Hays and Ted Rowliffe provided particularly helpful leads – and Ted and I are still recovering from the coincidence of our bumping into each other on the road! My travels would have been infinitely less enjoyable without the company of Blair, Caitlin and Sarah who accompanied me to Hakkari, and of Lesley Levene who saw more of the Aegean in 10 days than most people see in 10 visits.

Only those with an equal fear of dentists will understand how grateful I was to Ruth Lockwood for taking me to the dentist in Nevşehir and metaphorically holding my hand while I had my teeth put to rights – in the event, nothing like the fearful business it might have been (thanks to you too, Ahmet!).

This Book

From the Publisher

This sixth edition of Turkey was edited by Justin Flynn with assistance from Elizabeth Swan, Michelle Glynn, Martin Hughes, Alan Murphy, Thalia Kalkipsakis and Kirsten John. Cartography and design were coordinated by Leanne Peake with mapping assistance from Sonya Brooke, Trudi Canavan, Piotr Czajkowski, Derek Percival, Sarah Sloane and Maree Styles. Maree also helped with the final layout. The illustrations were drawn by Mick Weldon and Trudi Canavan.

Thanks to Maria Vallianos for the cover design, Dan Levin for the soft fonts, Paul Piaia for the climate charts, Quentin Frayne for his help on the Turkish Language Guide chapter and the readers' letters team for all their assistance.

THANKS
Many thanks to the travellers who used the last edition and wrote to us with helpful hints, advice and interesting anecdotes. Your names appear in the back of this book.

Foreword

ABOUT LONELY PLANET GUIDEBOOKS

The story begins with a classic travel adventure: Tony and Maureen Wheeler's 1972 journey across Europe and Asia to Australia. Useful information about the overland trail did not exist at that time, so Tony and Maureen published the first Lonely Planet guidebook to meet a growing need.

From a kitchen table, then from a tiny office in Melbourne (Australia), Lonely Planet has become the largest independent travel publisher in the world, an international company with offices in Melbourne, Oakland (USA), London (UK) and Paris (France).

Today Lonely Planet guidebooks cover the globe. There is an ever-growing list of books and there's information in a variety of forms and media. Some things haven't changed. The main aim is still to help make it possible for adventurous travellers to get out there – to explore and better understand the world.

At Lonely Planet we believe travellers can make a positive contribution to the countries they visit – if they respect their host communities and spend their money wisely. Since 1986 a percentage of the income from each book has been donated to aid projects and human rights campaigns.

Updates Lonely Planet thoroughly updates each guidebook as often as possible. This usually means there are around two years between editions, although for more unusual or more stable destinations the gap can be longer. Check the imprint page (following the colour map at the beginning of the book) for publication dates.

Between editions up-to-date information is available in two free newsletters – the paper *Planet Talk* and email *Comet* (to subscribe, contact any Lonely Planet office) – and on our Web site at www.lonelyplanet.com. The *Upgrades* section of the Web site covers a number of important and volatile destinations and is regularly updated by Lonely Planet authors. *Scoop* covers news and current affairs relevant to travellers. And, lastly, the *Thorn Tree* bulletin board, and *Postcards* section of the site carry unverified, but fascinating, reports from travellers.

Correspondence The process of creating new editions begins with the letters, postcards and emails received from travellers. This correspondence often includes suggestions, criticisms and comments about the current editions. Interesting excerpts are immediately passed on via newsletters and the Web site, and everything goes to our authors to be verified when they're researching on the road. We're keen to get more feedback from organisations or individuals who represent communities visited by travellers.

Lonely Planet gathers information for everyone who's curious about the planet – and especially for those who explore it first-hand. Through guidebooks, phrasebooks, activity guides, maps, literature, newsletters, image library, TV series and web site we act as an information exchange for a worldwide community of travellers.

Research Authors aim to gather sufficient practical information to enable travellers to make informed choices and to make the mechanics of a journey run smoothly. They also research historical and cultural background to help enrich the travel experience and allow travellers to understand and respond appropriately to cultural and environmental issues.

Authors don't stay in every hotel because that would mean spending a couple of months in each medium-sized city and, no, they don't eat at every restaurant because that would mean stretching belts beyond capacity. They do visit hotels and restaurants to check standards and prices, but feedback based on readers' direct experiences can be very helpful.

Many of our authors work undercover, others aren't so secretive. None of them accept freebies in exchange for positive write-ups. And none of our guidebooks contain any advertising.

Production Authors submit their raw manuscripts and maps to offices in Australia, USA, UK or France. Editors and cartographers – all experienced travellers themselves – then begin the process of assembling the pieces. When the book finally hits the shops some things are already out of date, we start getting feedback from readers, and the process begins again …

WARNING & REQUEST

Things change – prices go up, schedules change, good places go bad and bad places go bankrupt – nothing stays the same. So, if you find things better or worse, recently opened or long since closed, please tell us and help make the next edition even more accurate and useful. We genuinely value all the feedback we receive. Julie Young coordinates a well-travelled team that reads and acknowledges every letter, postcard and email and ensures that every morsel of information finds its way to the appropriate authors, editors and cartographers for verification.

Everyone who writes to us will find their name in the next edition of the appropriate guidebook. They will also receive the latest issue of *Planet Talk*, our quarterly printed newsletter, or *Comet*, our monthly email newsletter. Subscriptions to both newsletters are free. The very best contributions will be rewarded with a free guidebook.

Excerpts from your correspondence may appear in new editions of Lonely Planet guidebooks, the Lonely Planet Web site, *Planet Talk* or *Comet*, so please let us know if you *don't* want your letter published or your name acknowledged.

Send all correspondence to the Lonely Planet office closest to you:

Australia: PO Box 617, Hawthorn, Victoria 3122
UK: 10A Spring Place, London NW5 3BH
USA: 150 Linden St, Oakland CA 94607
France: 1 rue du Dahomey, Paris 75011

Or email us at: talk2us@lonelyplanet.com.au

For news, views and updates see our Web site: www.lonelyplanet.com

HOW TO USE A LONELY PLANET GUIDEBOOK

The best way to use a Lonely Planet guidebook is any way you choose. At Lonely Planet we believe the most memorable travel experiences are often those that are unexpected, and the finest discoveries are those you make yourself. Guidebooks are not intended to be used as if they provide a detailed set of infallible instructions!

Contents All Lonely Planet guidebooks follow the same format. The Facts about the Country chapters or sections give background information ranging from history to weather. Facts for the Visitor gives practical information on issues like visas and health. Getting There & Away gives a brief starting point for researching travel to and from the destination. Getting Around gives an overview of the transport options when you arrive.

The peculiar demands of each destination determine how subsequent chapters are broken up, but some things remain constant. We always start with background, then proceed to sights, places to stay, places to eat, entertainment, getting there and away, and getting around information – in that order.

Heading Hierarchy Lonely Planet headings are used in a strict hierarchical structure that can be visualised as a set of Russian dolls. Each heading (and its following text) is encompassed by any preceding heading that is higher on the hierarchical ladder.

Entry Points We do not assume guidebooks will be read from beginning to end, but that people will dip into them. The traditional entry points are the list of contents and the index. In addition, however, there is a complete list of maps and an index map illustrating map coverage.

There's also a colour map that shows highlights. These highlights are dealt with in greater detail in the Facts for the Visitor chapter, along with planning questions and suggested itineraries. Each chapter covering a geographical region begins with a locator map and another list of highlights. Once you find something of interest in a list of highlights, turn to the index.

Maps Maps play a crucial role in Lonely Planet guidebooks and include a huge amount of information. A legend is printed on the back page. We seek to have complete consistency between maps and text, and to have every important place in the text captured on a map. Map key numbers usually start in the top left corner.

Although inclusion in a guidebook usually implies a recommendation we cannot list every good place. Exclusion does not necessarily imply criticism. In fact there are a number of reasons why we might exclude a place – sometimes it is simply inappropriate to encourage an influx of travellers.

Introduction

In the minds of some first-time visitors the mention of Turkey conjures up media-generated visions of sultans and harems, oriental splendour and squalor, luxury and decadence, mystery and intrigue.

These inaccurate and outdated stereotypes quickly evaporate once you arrive in the country. The Turkish Republic is democratic, rapidly modernising, secular and western-oriented with a vigorous free enterprise economy. The Turks are quite friendly to foreign visitors, the cuisine is a savoury surprise, the cities are dotted with majestic old buildings and most of the countryside is as beautiful as a national park. And it's yours all for the lowest travel costs in Europe.

The history of Anatolia, the Turkish homeland, is incredibly long and rich. The world's oldest 'city', dating from 7500 BC, was discovered at Çatal Höyük near Konya. The Hittite Empire, mentioned in the Bible but little known in the west, rivalled that of ancient Egypt and left behind captivating works of art.

Many of the most famous sites from classical Hellenic and Hellenistic culture are not in Greece but in Turkey, including such cities as Troy, Pergamum, Ephesus, Miletus and Halicarnassus. Most modern Turkish cities have a Roman past and a good number are mentioned in the New Testament. The Seljuk Turkish Empire which ruled Anatolia in the 13th century could boast of greats like poet Omar Khayyam and Celaleddin Rumi, the poet, mystic and founder of the Whirling Dervishes.

The Ottoman Turkish Empire ruled the entire eastern Mediterranean, much of eastern Europe and North Africa for six centuries. The myriad customs, cultures, languages and religions of the sultan's vast domains came together in his capital of

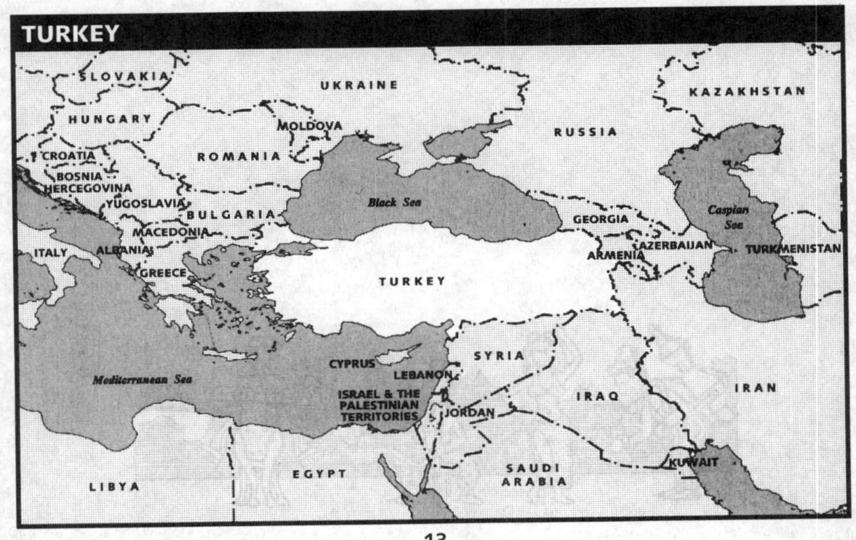

İstanbul, surely one of the world's most fascinating cities.

Though history and culture abound, there's plenty more to see and do. With more than 7000km of coastline, it's an excellent destination for water sports and yacht cruising, especially along the Mediterranean, which enjoys an average of 300 sunny days per year. Its highlands – which include Biblical Mt Ararat (5137m) – are scenic and varied, from the pine-clad alpine Kaçkar Dağları of the eastern Black Sea coast to extinct volcanoes such as Erciyes Dağı near Kayseri to the Toros Dağları along the Mediterranean coast. There are also many opportunities for hiking, white-water rafting, kayaking and skiing.

Turkey is a big country, but transport is usually easy and cheap, especially the marvellous far-flung system of comfortable buses.

Hoş geldiniz! (Welcome!) You're in Turkey. Sit down, have a glass of *çay* (tea), listen to the call to prayer from the minaret and get ready for a memorable journey.

Facts about Turkey

HISTORY

The history of civilisation in Turkey is astoundingly long, extending for almost 10,000 years.

Earliest Times

The Mediterranean region was inhabited as early as 7500 BC, during Palaeolithic (Old Stone Age) times. Around 7500 BC a Neolithic (New Stone Age) city had grown up at what's now called Çatal Höyük, 50km south-east of Konya. The early Anatolians developed fine wall paintings, statuettes, domestic architecture and pottery. Artefacts from the site, including the wall paintings, are displayed in Ankara's Museum of Anatolian Civilisations.

The Chalcolithic (Stone and Copper Age) period resulted in the building of a city at Hacılar, near Burdur, in about 5000 BC. The pottery here was of finer quality and copper implements, rather than stone or clay ones, were used.

Hittites – the Bronze Age

The Old Bronze Age (2600-1900 BC) was when Anatolians first developed cities of substantial size. An indigenous people now named the Proto-Hittites, or Hatti, built cities at Nesa or Kanesh (today's Kültepe) and Alacahöyük. The first known ruler of Kanesh was King Zipani (circa 2300 BC), according to Akkadian texts. As for Alacahöyük, 36km from Boğazkale (bo-AHZ-kahl-eh), it was perhaps the most important pre-Hittite city and may have been the first Hittite capital.

The Hittites, a people who spoke an Indo-European language, overran this area and established themselves as a ruling class over the local people during the Middle Bronze Age (1900-1600 BC). The Hittites took over existing cities and built a magnificent capital at Hattuşaş (Boğazkale), 212km east of Ankara near Sungurlu. The early Hittite Kingdom (1600-1500 BC) was replaced by the greater Hittite Empire (1450-1200 BC). The Hittites captured Syria from the Egyptians (1380-1316 BC), clashed with the great Rameses II (1298 BC), and meanwhile developed a wonderful culture.

Their graceful pottery, ironwork ornaments and implements, gold jewellery and figurines now fill a large section of the Museum of Anatolian Civilisations in Ankara. The striking site of Boğazkale, set in dramatic countryside, is worth a visit, as is the religious centre of Yazılıkaya nearby. The Hittite religion was based upon worship of a sun goddess and a storm god.

The Hittite Empire was weakened in its final period by the cities of Assuwa ('Asia'), subject principalities along the Aegean coast, which included the city of Troy. The Trojans were attacked by Achaean Greeks in 1250 BC – the Trojan

The Hittites artwork blossomed with their unique culture.

Time Line

7500 BC	Earliest known inhabitants; earliest human community at Çatal Höyük
5000 BC	Stone and Copper Age; settlement at Hacılar
2600-1900 BC	Old Bronze Age; Proto-Hittite Empire in central and south-eastern Anatolia
1900-1300 BC	Hittite Empire, wars with Egypt; the Patriarch Abraham departs from Harran, near Şanlıurfa, for Canaan
1250 BC	Trojan War
1200-600 BC	Phrygian and Mysian invasions, followed by the great period of Hellenic civilisation; Yassı Höyük settlement flourishes; King Midas and King Croesus reign; coinage is invented; kingdoms of Ionia, Lycia, Lydia, Caria, Pamphylia; Empire of Urartu
550 BC	Cyrus of Persia invades Anatolia
334 BC	Conquest of simply everything and everybody by Alexander the Great from Macedon
279 BC	Celts (or Gauls) invade and set up Galatia near Ankara
250 BC	Rise of the Kingdom of Pergamum (Bergama)
129 BC	Rome establishes the Province of Asia ('Asia Minor'), with its capital at Ephesus (near İzmir)
47-57 AD	St Paul's trips in Anatolia
330 AD	Constantine dedicates the 'New Rome' of Constantinople, and the centre of the Roman Empire moves from Rome to the Bosphorus
527-65 AD	Reign of Justinian, greatest Byzantine emperor; construction of Sancta Sophia, greatest church in the world
570-622 AD	Muhammed's birth; revelation of the Koran; flight *(hijra)* to Medina
1037-1109 AD	Empire of the Great Seljuk Turks, based in Iran
1071-1243 AD	Seljuk Sultanate of Rum, based in Konya; life and work of Celaleddin Rumi ('Mevlana'), founder of the Whirling Dervishes
1000s-1200s AD	Age of the Crusades
1288 AD	Birth of the Ottoman Empire, near Bursa
1453 AD	Conquest of Constantinople by Mehmet II
1520-66 AD	Reign of Sultan Süleyman the Magnificent, the great age of the Ottoman Empire; most of North Africa, most of Eastern Europe and all of the Middle East controlled from İstanbul; Ottoman navies patrol the Mediterranean and Red seas and the Indian Ocean
1876-1909 AD	Reign of Sultan Abdül Hamit, last of the powerful sultans; the 'Eastern Question' arises: which European nations will be able to grab Ottoman territory when the empire topples?
1923 AD	Proclamation of the Turkish Republic
1938 AD	Death of Atatürk

War – which gave the Hittites a break. But the *coup de grâce* came with a massive invasion of 'sea peoples' from various Greek islands and city-states. Driven from their homelands by the invading Dorians, the sea peoples flocked into Anatolia by way of the Aegean coast. The Hittite state survived for a few centuries longer in the south-eastern Taurus (Toros) Mountains, but the great empire was dead.

Phrygians, Urartians, Lydians & Others

With the Hittite decline, smaller states filled the power vacuum. Around 1200 BC the Phrygians and Mysians, of Indo-European stock, invaded Anatolia from Thrace and settled at Gordium (Yassı Höyük), 106km south-west of Ankara. This Hittite city became the Phrygian capital (circa 800 BC). A huge Hittite cemetery and a royal Phrygian tomb still exist at the site. King Midas (circa 715 BC), he of the golden touch, is Phrygia's most famous son.

At the same time (after 1200 BC), the Aegean coast was populated with a mixture of native peoples and Greek invaders. The region around İzmir became Ionia, with numerous cities. To the south was Caria, between modern Milas and Fethiye, a mountainous region with people who were great traders. The Carians sided with the Trojans during the Trojan War. When the Dorians arrived they brought some Greek culture to Caria, which the great Carian king Mausolus developed even further. His tomb, the Mausoleum, was among the Seven Wonders of the Ancient World. Of his capital city, Halicarnassus (modern Bodrum), little remains.

Further east from Caria were Lycia, a kingdom stretching from Fethiye to Antalya, and Pamphylia, the land east of Antalya.

As the centuries passed, a great city grew up at Sardis, in the Kingdom of Lydia, 60km east of İzmir. Sardis dominated most of Ionia and clashed with Phrygia. Lydia is famous not only for Sardis, but for a great invention: coinage. It's also famous for King Croesus, the world's first great coin collector. Lydia's primacy lasted only from 680 BC to 547 BC, when Persian invaders overran it.

Meanwhile, out east on the shores of salty Van Gölü (Lake Van), yet another kingdom and culture arose. Not much is known about the Urartians who founded the Kingdom of Van (860-612 BC), except that they left interesting ruins and vast, bewildering cuneiform inscriptions in the massive Val Kalesi (Rock of Van) just outside the modern town.

The Cimmerians invaded Anatolia from the west, conquered Phrygia and challenged Lydia, then settled down to take their place among the great jumble of Anatolian peoples. In 547 BC the Persians invaded and jumbled the situation even more. Though the Ionian cities survived the invasion and lived on under Persian rule, the great period of Hellenic culture was winding down. Ionia, with its important cities of Phocaea (Foça, north of İzmir), Teos, Ephesus, Priene and Miletus and Aeolia, centred on Smyrna (İzmir), had contributed a great deal to ancient culture, from the graceful scrolled capitals of Ionic columns to the ideas of Thales of Miletus, the first recorded philosopher in the west.

While the great city of Athens was relatively unimportant, the Ionian cities were laying the foundations of Hellenic civilisation. It is ironic that the Persian invasion which curtailed Ionia's culture caused that of Athens to flourish. On reaching Athens, the Persians were overextended. By meeting the Persian challenge, Athens grew powerful and influential, taking the lead in the further progress of Hellenic culture.

Cyrus & Alexander

Cyrus, emperor of Persia (550-530 BC), swept into Anatolia from the east, conquering everybody and everything. Though he subjected the cities of the Aegean coast to his rule, this was not easy. The independent-minded citizens gave him and his successors trouble for the next two centuries.

The Persian conquerors were defeated by Alexander the Great, who stormed out of Macedon, crossed the Hellespont (Dardanelles) in 334 BC, and within a few years had conquered the entire Middle East from Greece to India. Alexander, so it is said, was frustrated in untying the Gordian knot at Gordium, so he cut it with his sword. It seems he did the right thing, as the domination of Asia – which he was supposed to gain by untying the knot – came to be his in

Alexander the Great is renowned as an ingenious strategist and one of the most skilful generals in history.

record time. His sword-blow proved that he was an impetuous young man.

Alexander's effects on Anatolia were profound. He was the first of many rulers to attempt to meld western and eastern cultures (the Byzantines and the Ottomans followed suit). Upon his death in 323 BC, in Babylon, Alexander's empire was divided among his generals in a flurry of civil wars. Lysimachus claimed western and central Anatolia after winning the Battle of Ipsus in 301 BC, and he set his mark on the Ionian cities. Many Hellenistic buildings went up on his orders. Ancient Smyrna was abandoned and a brand-new city was built several kilometres away, where the modern city stands.

But the civil wars continued, and Lysimachus was slain by Seleucus (King of Seleucid lands from 305 to 280 BC), another of Alexander's generals, at the Battle of Corupedium in 281 BC. Though Seleucus was in turn slain by Ptolemy Ceraunus, the kingdom of the Seleucids, based in Antioch (Antakya), was to rule a great part of the Middle East for the next century.

Meanwhile the next invaders, the Celts (or Gauls) this time, were storming through Macedonia on their way to Anatolia in 279 BC where they established the Kingdom of Galatia. The Galatians made Ancyra (Ankara) their capital and subjected the Aegean cities to their rule. The foundations of parts of the citadel in Ankara date from Galatian times.

While the Galatians ruled western Anatolia, Mithridates I had become King of Pontus, a state based in Trebizond (Trabzon) on the eastern Black Sea coast. At its height, the Pontic Kingdom extended all the way to Cappadocia in central Anatolia.

Still other small kingdoms flourished at this time, between 300 and 200 BC. A leader named Prusias founded the Kingdom of Bithynia and gave his name to the chief city: Prusa (Bursa). Nicaea (İznik, near Bursa) was also of great importance. And in south-eastern Anatolia an Armenian kingdom grew, based at Van. The Armenians, a Phrygian tribe, settled around Van Gölü after the decline of Urartian power.

A fellow named Ardvates who ruled from 317 to 284 BC and was a Persian *satrap* (provincial governor) under the Seleucids, broke away from the Seleucid Kingdom to found the short-lived Kingdom of Armenia. The Seleucids later regained control, but lost it again as Armenia was split into two kingdoms, Greater and Lesser Armenia. Reunited in 94 BC under Tigranes I, the Kingdom of Armenia became very powerful for a short period (83-69 BC). Armenia finally fell to the Roman legions not long afterwards.

But the most impressive and powerful of Anatolia's many kingdoms at this time was Pergamum. Gaining tremendous power around 250 BC, the Pergamene king picked the right side to be on, siding with Rome early in the game. With Roman help, Pergamum threw off Seleucid rule and went on to challenge King Prusias of Bithynia (186 BC) and also King Pharnaces I of Pontus (183 BC).

The kings of Pergamum were great warriors, governors and also mad patrons of the arts, assembling an enormous library which rivalled that of Alexandria's. The Asclepion, or medical centre, at Pergamum was flourishing at this time and continued to flourish for centuries under Roman rule. Greatest of the Pergamene kings was Eumenes II (197-159 BC), who ruled an enormous empire stretching from the Dardanelles to the Taurus Mountains near Syria. He was responsible for building much of what's left on Pergamum's acropolis, including the grand library.

Roman Times

The Romans took Anatolia almost by default. The various Anatolian kings could not refrain from picking away at Roman holdings and causing other sorts of irritation, so finally the legions marched in and took over. Defeating King Antiochus III of Seleucia at Magnesia (Manisa, near İzmir) in 190 BC, the Romans were content for the time being to leave 'Asia' (Anatolia) in the hands of the kings of Pergamum. But the last king, dying without an heir, bequeathed his kingdom to Rome (133 BC). In 129 BC, the Romans established the province of Asia, with its capital at Ephesus.

An interesting postscript to this period is the story of Commagene. This small and rather unimportant little kingdom in east-central Anatolia, near Adıyaman, left few marks on history. But the one notable reminder of Commagene is very notable indeed: on top of Nemrut Dağı (Mt Nimrod), Antiochus I (68-38 BC) built a mammoth, cone-shaped funerary mound framed by twin temples filled with huge stone statues portraying himself and the gods and goddesses who were his 'peers'. A visit to Nemrut Dağı, from the nearby town of Kahta, is one of the highlights of a visit to Turkey.

Roman rule brought relative peace and prosperity for almost three centuries to Anatolia and provided the perfect conditions for the spread of a brand-new, world-class religion.

Early Christianity

Christianity began in Roman Palestine (Judaea), but its foremost proponent, St Paul, came from Tarsus in Cilicia, in what is now southern Turkey. Paul took advantage of the excellent Roman road system to spread the teachings of Jesus. When the Romans drove the Jews out of Judaea in 70 AD, Christian members of this Diaspora may have made their way to the numerous small Christian congregations in the Roman province of Asia.

On his first journey in about 47-49 AD, Paul went to Antioch, Seleucia (Silifke), and along the southern coast through Pamphylia (Side, Antalya) and up into the mountains. First stop was Antioch-in-Pisidia, today called Yalvaç, near Akşehir. Next he went to Iconium (Konya), the chief city in Galatia; Paul wrote a.. important 'Letter to the Galatians' which is now the ninth book of the New Testament.

From Iconium, Paul tramped to Lystra, 40km south, and to Derbe nearby. Then it was back to Attaleia (Antalya) to catch a boat for Antioch. His second journey took him to some of these same cities, and later north-west to the district of Mysia where Troy (Truva) is located; then into Macedonia.

Paul's third trip (53-57 AD) took in many of these same places, including Ancyra, Smyrna and Adramyttium (Edremit). On the way back he stopped in Ephesus, capital of Roman Asia and one of the greatest cities of the time. Here he ran into trouble because his teachings were ruining the market for silver effigies of the local favourite goddess, Cybele/Diana. The silversmiths led a riot, and Paul's companions were hustled into the great theatre for a sort of kangaroo court. Luckily, the authorities kept order: there was free speech in Ephesus; Paul and his companions had broken no laws; they were permitted to go freely. Later on this third journey Paul stopped in Miletus.

Paul got his last glimpses of Anatolia as he was being taken to Rome as a prisoner for trial on charges of inciting a riot in Jerusalem (59-60 AD). He changed ships at

Myra (Demre); further west, he was supposed to land at Cnidos, at the tip of the peninsula west of Marmaris, but stormy seas prevented this.

Other saints played a role in the life of Roman Asia as well. Tradition has it that St John retired to Ephesus to write the fourth gospel near the end of his life, and that he brought Jesus' mother Mary with him. John was buried on top of a hill in what is now the town of Selçuk, near Ephesus. The great, now ruined basilica of St John marks the site. As for Mary, she is said to have retired to a mountaintop cottage near Ephesus. The small chapel at Meryemana ('Mother Mary') is the site of a mass to celebrate her Assumption on 15 August.

The Seven Churches of the Revelation were the Seven Churches of Asia: Ephesus (Efes), Smyrna (İzmir), Pergamum (Bergama), Sardis (Sart, east of İzmir), Philadelphia (Alaşehir), Laodicea (Goncalı, between Denizli and Pamukkale) and Thyatira (Akhisar). 'Church' of course meant congregation, so don't go to these sites looking for the ruins of seven buildings.

The New Rome

Christianity was a struggling faith during the centuries of Roman rule. By 250 AD, the faith had grown strong enough and Roman rule so unsteady that the Roman emperor Decius decreed a general persecution of Christians. Not only this, but the empire was falling to pieces. Goths attacked the Aegean cities with fleets and later invaded Anatolia. The Persian Empire again threatened from the east. Diocletian (284-305 AD) restored the empire somewhat, but continued the persecutions.

When Diocletian abdicated, Constantine battled for succession, which he won in 324 AD. He united the empire, declared equal rights for all religions, and called the first ecumenical council to meet in Nicaea in 325 AD.

Meanwhile, Constantine was building a great city on the site of Hellenic Byzantium. In 330 AD he dedicated it as New Rome, his capital city; it came to be called Constantinople. The emperor died seven years later in Nicomedia (İzmit, Kocaeli), east of his capital. On his deathbed he adopted Christianity.

Justinian

While the barbarians of Europe were sweeping down on weakened Rome, the eastern capital grew in wealth and strength. Emperor Justinian (527-65 AD) brought the eastern Roman, or Byzantine, Empire to its greatest strength. He reconquered Italy, the Balkans, Anatolia, Egypt and North Africa and further embellished Constantinople with great buildings. His personal triumph was the Church of the Holy Wisdom, or Aya Sofya (Sancta Sophia), which remained the most splendid church in Christendom for almost 1000 years, after which it became the most splendid mosque.

Justinian's successors were generally good, but not good enough, and the empire's conquests couldn't be maintained. Besides, something quite momentous was happening in Arabia.

Birth of Islam

Five years after the death of Justinian, Muhammed was born in Mecca. In 612 AD, while meditating, he heard the voice of God command him to 'recite'. Muhammed was to become the Messenger of God, communicating his holy word to people. The written record of these recitations, collected after Muhammed's death into a book by his family and followers, is the Koran.

The people of Mecca didn't take to Muhammed's preaching all at once. In fact, they forced him to leave Mecca, which he did, according to tradition, in 622 AD. This 'flight' (*hijra* or *hegira*) is the starting-point for the Muslim lunar calendar.

Setting up house in Medina, Muhammed organised a religious commonwealth which over 10 years became so powerful that it could challenge and conquer Mecca (624-30 AD). Before Muhammed died two years later, the Muslims (adherents of Islam, 'submission to God's will') had begun the conquest of other Arab tribes.

The story of militant Islam is one of history's most astounding tales. Fifty years after the Prophet's ignominious flight from Mecca, the armies of Islam were threatening the walls of Constantinople (669-78 AD), having conquered everything and everybody from there to Mecca, plus Persia and Egypt. The Arabic Muslim empires that followed these conquests were among the world's greatest political, social and cultural achievements.

Muhammed was succeeded by caliphs, or deputies, whose job was to oversee the welfare of the Muslim commonwealth. His close companions got the job first, then his son-in-law Ali. After that, two great dynasties emerged: the Umayyads (661-750 AD), whose empire was based in Damascus, and the Abbasids (750-1100), who ruled from Baghdad. Both continually challenged the power and status of Byzantium.

The Coming of the Turks

The history of the Turks as excellent soldiers goes back at least to the reign of the Abbasid caliph Al-Mutasim (833-42 AD). This ruler formed an army of Turkish captives and mercenaries that became the empire's strength, and also its undoing. Later caliphs found that their protectors had become their masters, and the Turkish 'praetorian guard' raised or toppled caliphs as it chose.

The Seljuk Empire

The first great Turkish state to rule Anatolia was the Great Seljuk Turkish Empire (1037-1109), based in Persia. Coming from Central Asia, the Turks captured Baghdad (1055). In 1071, Seljuk armies decisively defeated the Byzantines at Manzikert (Malazgırt), taking the Byzantine emperor as a prisoner. The Seljuks then took over most of Anatolia and established a provincial capital at Nicaea. Their domains now included today's Turkey, Iran and Iraq. Their empire developed a distinctive culture, with especially beautiful architecture and design; the Great Seljuks also produced Omar Khayyam (died 1123). Politically, however, the Great Seljuk Turkish Empire declined quickly, in the style of Alexander the Great's empire, with various pieces being taken by generals.

A remnant of the Seljuk Empire lived on in Anatolia, based in Iconium. Called the Seljuk Sultanate of Rum ('Rome', meaning Roman Asia), it continued to flourish, producing great art and great thinkers until it was overrun by the Mongol hordes in 1243. Celaleddin Rumi or 'Mevlana', founder of the Mevlevi (Whirling) Dervish order, is perhaps the Sultanate of Rum's most outstanding thinker.

The Crusades

These 'holy wars', created to provide work for the lesser nobles and riffraff of Europe, proved disastrous for the Byzantine emperors. Although a combined Byzantine and crusader army captured Nicaea from the Seljuks in 1097, the crusaders were mostly an unhelpful, unruly bunch. The Fourth Crusade (1202-4) saw European ragtag armies invade and plunder Christian Constantinople. This was the first and most horrible defeat for the great city, and it was carried out by 'friendly' armies.

Having barely recovered from the ravages of the crusades, the Byzantines were greeted with a new and greater threat: the Ottomans.

Founding of the Ottoman Empire

In the late 13th century, Byzantine weakness left a power vacuum which was filled by bands of Turks fleeing west from the Mongols. Warrior bands, each led by a warlord, took over parts of the Aegean and Marmara coasts. The Turks who moved into Bithynia, around Bursa, were followers of a man named Ertuğrul. His son, Osman, founded a principality (circa 1288) which was to grow into the Osmanlı (Ottoman) Empire.

The Ottomans took Bursa in 1326. It served them well as their first capital city. But they were vigorous and ambitious and by 1402 they moved the capital to Adrianople

(Edirne) because it was easier to rule their Balkan conquests from there. Constantinople was still in Byzantine hands.

The Turkish advance spread rapidly to both east and west, despite some setbacks. By 1452, under Mehmet the Conqueror, they were strong enough to think of taking Constantinople, capital of eastern Christendom, which they did in 1453. Mehmet's reign (1451-81) began the great era of Ottoman power.

Süleyman the Magnificent

The height of Ottoman glory was under Sultan Süleyman the Magnificent (1520-66). Called the 'Lawgiver' by the Turks, he beautified İstanbul, rebuilt Jerusalem and expanded Ottoman power to the gates of Vienna in 1529. The Ottoman fleet under Barbaros Hayrettin Paşa seemed invincible, but by 1585 the empire had begun its long and celebrated decline. Most of the sultans after Süleyman were incapable of great rule. Luckily for the empire, there were very competent and talented men to serve as grand viziers, ruling the empire in the sultans' stead.

Süleyman I, sultan of the Ottoman Empire between 1520 and 1566, was also known as Süleyman the Magnificent or the Lawgiver.

The Later Empire

By 1699, Europeans no longer feared an invasion by the 'terrible Turk'. The empire was still vast and powerful, but it had lost its momentum and was rapidly dropping behind the west in terms of social, military, scientific and material progress. In the 19th century, several sultans undertook important reforms. Selim III, for instance, revised taxation, commerce and the military. But the Janissaries (members of the sultan's personal guard) and other conservative elements resisted the new measures strongly and sometimes violently.

For centuries, the non-Turkish ethnic and religious minorities in the sultan's domains had lived side by side with their Turkish neighbours, governed by their own religious and traditional laws. But in the 19th century, strong currents of ethnic nationalism flowed eastward from Europe. Decline and misrule made nationalism very appealing. The subject peoples of the Ottoman Empire revolted, often with the direct encouragement and assistance of the European powers. After bitter fighting in 1832, the Kingdom of Greece was formed; the Serbs, Bulgarians, Romanians, Albanians, Armenians and Arabs would all seek their independence soon after.

As the empire broke up, the European powers (Britain, France, Italy, Germany and Russia) hovered in readiness to colonise or annex the pieces. They used religion as a reason for pressure or control, saying that it was their duty to protect the Catholic, Protestant or Orthodox subjects from misrule and anarchy. The holy places in Palestine were a favourite target and each power tried to obtain a foothold here for colonisation later.

The Russian emperors put pressure on the Turks to grant them powers over all Ottoman Orthodox subjects, whom the Russian emperor would thus 'protect'. The result of this pressure was the Crimean War (1853-56), with Britain and France fighting with the Ottomans against the Russians.

In the midst of imperial dissolution, western-style reforms were proposed in an

Gazi Osman Paşa

Gazi Osman Paşa was born in 1832, to relatively poor parents in Tokat, but grew up to become one of Ottoman Turkey's most famous soldiers, serving in Thessaly, Crete, Bosnia-Herzegovina and Yemen. After a great victory in the Ottoman-Serbian War of 1875-76 he became a *paşa* (general).

During the Russo-Turkish War (1877-78), Russian forces crossed the Danube into Ottoman Bulgaria, headed for Pleven (Plevne). Osman Paşa, ordered to defend it, surrounded the town with earthworks and endured a five-month siege by a Russian force twice the size of his own. Attempting to fight his way out, he was taken captive with serious injuries, and treated as a hero by a Russian tsar astonished at his fortitude.

Equally impressed, Sultan Abdül Hamit II bestowed the title of Gazi (Conqueror) on him. Osman became commander-in-chief and then marshal of the Sultan's household.

Gazi Osman Paşa died in İstanbul in 1900 but there's hardly a Turkish town which doesn't commemorate him in a street name.

attempt to revive the moribund empire and make it compatible with modern Europe. Mithat Paşa, a successful general and powerful grand vizier, brought the young crown prince Abdül Hamit II (1876-1909) to the throne along with a constitution in 1876. But the new sultan did away both with Mithat Paşa and the constitution and established his own absolute rule.

Abdül Hamit modernised without democratising, building telegraph lines and railways, encouraging modern industry, and keeping watch on everything through an extensive spy network. But the empire continued to disintegrate, with nationalist insurrections in Crete, Armenia, Bulgaria and Macedonia.

The younger generation of the Turkish elite watched bitterly as the country fell apart, then organised into secret societies bent on toppling the sultan. The Young Turk movement for western-style reforms gained enough power by 1908 to force the restoration of the constitution. In 1909, the Young Turk-led Ottoman parliament deposed Abdül Hamit and put his weak-willed, indecisive brother Mehmet V ('Vahdettin') on the throne.

In its last years, though a sultan still sat on the throne, the Ottoman Empire was ruled by three members of the Young Turks' Committee of Union & Progress, named Talat, Enver and Jemal. Their rule was vigorous, but harsh and misguided, and it only worsened an already hopeless situation. When WWI broke out, they made the fatal error of siding with Germany and the Central Powers. With their defeat, the Ottoman Empire collapsed. İstanbul and several other parts of Anatolia were occupied, and the sultan became a pawn in the hands of the victors.

The victorious Allies had been planning, since the beginning of the war, how they would carve up the Ottoman Empire. They even promised certain lands to several different peoples or factions in order to get their support for the war effort. With the end of the war, these promises came due. With more promises than territory, the Allies decided on the dismemberment of Anatolia itself in order to get more land with which to satisfy the ambitions of the victorious countries. The choicest bits of Anatolia were to be given to Christian peoples, with the Muslim Turks relegated to a small land-locked region of semi-barren steppe.

The Turkish Republic

The situation looked very bleak for the Turks as their armies were being disbanded and their country taken under the control of the Allies. But a catastrophe turned things around.

Ever since gaining independence in 1831, the Greeks had entertained the

Megali Idea (Great Plan) of a new Greek Empire encompassing all the lands which had once had Greek influence – in effect, the refounding of the Byzantine Empire. During WWI, the Allies had offered Greece the Ottoman city of Smyrna. King Constantine declined for various reasons, even though his prime minister, Eleutherios Venizelos, wanted to accept. After the war, however, Alexander became king, Venizelos became prime minister again and Britain encouraged the Greeks to go ahead and take Smyrna. On 15 May 1919, they did.

The Turks, depressed and hopeless over the occupation of their country and the powerlessness of the sultan, couldn't take this: a former subject people capturing an Ottoman city and pushing inland with great speed and ferocity. Even before the Greek invasion, an Ottoman general named Mustafa Kemal had decided that a new government must take over the destiny of the Turks from the powerless sultan. He began organising resistance on 19 May 1919. The Greek invasion was just the shock needed to galvanise the people and lead them to his way of thinking.

The Turkish War of Independence lasted from 1920 to 1922. In September 1921 the Greeks very nearly reached Ankara, the nationalist headquarters, but in desperate fighting the Turks were successful in holding them off. A year later, the Turks began their counteroffensive attack and drove the Greek armies back to İzmir by 9 September 1922.

Atatürk

It won't take you long to discover the national hero, Kemal Atatürk. Though he died on 10 November 1938, his image is everywhere in Turkey – his picture is in every schoolroom, office and shop, a bust or statue (preferably equestrian) is in every park, quotations from his speeches and writings are on every public building. He is virtually synonymous with the Turkish Republic.

In Lord Kinross's best-selling biography *Atatürk: The Rebirth of a Nation*, Kemal is portrayed as a man of great intelligence and even greater energy and daring, possessed by the idea of giving his fellow Turks and their homeland a new lease of life. In contrast to many leaders, he had the capability and opportunity to realise his obsession almost single-handedly. His achievement in turning a backward empire into a forward-looking nation-state was extraordinary, and was taken as a model by Nasser of Egypt, Reza Shah of Iran and other leaders of neighbouring countries.

Early Years In 1881, a boy named Mustafa was born into the family of a minor Turkish bureaucrat living in Salonika – now the Greek city of Thessaloniki, but at that time a city in Ottoman Macedonia. Mustafa was smart and a hard worker at school. His mathematics teacher was so impressed that he gave him the nickname Kemal (excellence). The name Mustafa Kemal stuck with him as he went through a military academy and Harbiye, the Ottoman war college, and his career as an infantry officer.

Military Career He served with distinction, particularly in the Tripolitanian War (1911) when Italy seized Ottoman Libya, though he acquired a reputation as something of a hothead. By 1915 he was a promising lieutenant colonel of infantry in command of the 57th Regiment, one of many units posted to the Gallipoli peninsula.

Victory in the bitterly fought war made Mustafa Kemal even more of a national hero. He was now fully in command of the fate of the Turks. The sultanate was soon abolished and, after it, the Ottoman Empire. A Turkish republic was born, based in the region of Anatolia and eastern Thrace. The treaties of WWI, which had left the Turks with almost no country, were renegotiated.

Ethnic Greeks in Turkey and ethnic Turks in Greece were required to leave their ancestral homes and move to their respective ethnic nation-states; Greeks from İzmir moved into the houses of Turks in Salonika, whose owners had moved to İzmir, and so forth. Venizelos even came to terms with Kemal, signing a treaty in 1930.

Atatürk's Reforms

Mustafa Kemal undertook the job of completely remaking a society. After the republic was declared in 1923, a constitution was adopted (1924); polygamy was abolished and the fez, mark of Ottoman backwardness, was prohibited (1925); new, western-style legal codes were instituted, and civil (not religious) marriage was required (1926); Islam was removed as the state religion and the Arabic alphabet was replaced by a modified Latin one (1928). In 1930, Constantinople officially became İstanbul, and other city names were officially Turkified (Angora to Ankara, Smyrna to İzmir, Adrianople to Edirne etc). Women obtained the right to vote and serve in parliament in 1934.

Atatürk

The defence of Gallipoli, which saved Constantinople from British conquest (until the end of the war, at least), was a personal triumph for Mustafa Kemal. His strategic and tactical genius came into full play when circumstances put him at the heart of the battle and he correctly devined the enemy's strategy. He led with utter disregard for his own safety, inspiring his men with his heroism. A superior force of British, Australian, New Zealand and French armies and navies was fought to a standstill and finally forced to withdraw, and Mustafa Kemal became a popular hero.

Though he was promoted to the rank of *paşa* (general), the sultan and government were afraid of his brilliance and popularity, and sought to keep this 'dangerous element' in İstanbul under their control. When the war was lost and the empire was on the verge of being dismembered, Mustafa Kemal Paşa had himself posted to Anatolia as Inspector-General of the defeated Ottoman armies – the perfect post from which to begin his revolution.

Founding of the Republic On 19 May 1919, four days after a Greek army of invasion landed at İzmir, Mustafa Kemal Paşa landed at the port of Samsun. He reorganized the defeated Ottoman armies, and convened congresses to focus the will and energies of the people. His democratically established revolutionary government at Ankara held off several invading armies (French, Italian and Greek) with severely limited resources. Several times the whole tenuous effort neared collapse, and many of his friends and advisors were ready to ride out of Ankara for their lives. Kemal never flinched, always ready to dare the worst – and he succeeded brilliantly.

Atatürk's Legacy Many great revolutionary leaders falter or fade when the revolution is won. Atatürk lived 15 years into the republican era, and directed the country's progress with surprising skill and foresight. The forward-looking, westernised, secular, democratic nation-state you see today is his legacy, and his memory is truly sacred to the majority of Turks.

In 1935, Mustafa Kemal sponsored one of the most curious laws of modern times. Up to this time, Muslims had only one given name. Family names were purely optional. So he decided that all Turks should choose a family name, and they did. He himself was proclaimed Atatürk, or 'Father Turk', by the Turkish parliament, and officially became Kemal Atatürk.

Atatürk lived and directed the country's destiny until 10 November 1938. He saw WWII coming and was anxious that Turkey stay out of it. His friend and successor as president of the republic, İsmet İnönü, succeeded in preserving a precarious neutrality. Ankara became a hotbed of Allied-Axis spying, but the Turks managed to stay out of the conflict.

Recent Years

In its early years, Atatürk's Republican Peoples' Party was the only political party allowed. But between 1946 and 1950 true democracy was instituted, and the opposition Democratic Party won the election in 1950.

By 1960 the Democratic Party had acquired so much power that the democratic system was threatened. The army, charged by Atatürk to protect democracy and the constitution, stepped in and brought various Democratic Party leaders to trial on charges of violating the constitution. The popular Peron-like party leader, Adnan Menderes, was executed, though all other death sentences were commuted. Elections were held in 1961.

In 1970 there was a polite coup d'état again because the successor to the Democratic Party had overreached its bounds. High-ranking military officers entered the national broadcasting headquarters and read a short message, and the government fell.

Under the careful watch of those same officers, democracy returned and things went well for years, until political infighting and civil unrest brought the country to a virtual halt in 1980. On the left side of the political spectrum, Soviet-bloc countries pumped in arms and money for destabilisation and, it is claimed, supported Armenian terrorist elements who murdered Turkish diplomats and their families abroad. On the right side of the spectrum, fanatical Muslim religious groups and a neo-Nazi party caused havoc. In the centre, the two major political parties were deadlocked so badly in parliament that for months they couldn't even elect a parliamentary president.

The economy was near collapse, inflation was 130% per year, the law-makers were not making laws, and crime in the streets by the fringe elements of left and right was epidemic. The military stepped in again on 12 September 1980, much to the relief of the general population, and restored civil, fiscal and legal order, but at the price of strict control and human rights abuses.

The constitution was rewritten so as to avoid parliamentary impasses. In a controlled plebiscite, it was approved by the voters. The head of the military government, General Kenan Evren, resigned his military commission (as Atatürk had done) and became the country's new president. The old political leaders, seen by the new government to have been responsible for the breakdown of society, were tried (if they were thought to have committed crimes) or excluded from political life for 10 years, though many returned to politics before this time was up.

In 1983, elections under the new constitution were held, and the centre-right Anavatan Partisi (Motherland Party), the one less favoured by the military caretakers, won easily. The new prime minister was Turgut Özal, a former World Bank economist, who instituted economic liberalisations and precipitated a business boom which lasted through the 1980s.

Özal's untimely death in April 1993 removed a powerful, innovative but controversial force from Turkish politics and left a power vacuum which was filled by veteran politician Süleyman Demirel, a former prime minister who was elected president, and his protege, Professor Tansu Çiller, Turkey's first woman prime minister.

Telegenic, forthright and ambitious, Ms Çiller seemed a fitting symbol of progressive late 20th-century Turkish society, but frequent charges of opportunism, corruption and cronyism tarnished her image, and her intense antipathy to her right-of-centre rival Mr Mesut Yılmaz made a strong right-of-centre government coalition impossible. Turkey returned to its pre-Özal political condition: numerous parties with incompatible leaders, none with a reputation for honesty and efficiency, none able to claim more than about 21% of the electorate. (For more recent developments see under Political Parties in the following Government & Politics section.)

GEOGRAPHY

Most first-time visitors come to Turkey expecting to find deserts, palm trees and camel caravans. In fact, the country is geographically diverse, with snow-capped mountains, rolling steppe, broad rivers, verdant coasts and rich agricultural valleys.

It's interesting to note that Ankara, the country's capital, is at a latitude similar to that of Naples, Lisbon, Beijing and Philadelphia. The southernmost shore of Turkey is similar in latitude to Tokyo, Seoul, Gibraltar and San Francisco.

Distances

Turkey is big: the road distance from Edirne on the Bulgarian border to Kars on the Armenian one is more than 1700km. From the Black Sea shore to the Mediterranean coast it's almost 1000km. Now, 1000km on flat ground might take only one very long day to drive, but Turkey has many mountain ranges which can lengthen travel times considerably.

Geographical Statistics

Turkey is between 35° and 42° north latitude and 25° and 44° east longitude. It covers 779,452 sq km and has borders with Armenia, Bulgaria, Georgia, Greece, Iran, Iraq and Syria. The coastline totals almost 8400km – the Aegean coastline alone is 2800km long. As for mountains, the highest is Ağrı Dağı (Mt Ararat) at 5137m. Uludağ (Mt Olympus) near Bursa is 2543m high. During imperial times, snow and ice could be taken from Uludağ, sailed across the Sea of Marmara, and presented to the sultan in İstanbul to cool his drinks.

CLIMATE

Turkey has seven climatic regions. Climate graphs are on the following page; for temperature conversion, see the table at the back of the book. Going from west to east, here's the lay of the land:

Marmara

The Marmara region includes eastern Thrace from Edirne to İstanbul, with rolling steppe and low hills good for grazing, some farming and industry. The peninsula of Gelibolu (Gallipoli) forms the northern shore of the Çanakkale Boğazı (the Dardanelles or Hellespont).

On the southern shore of the Sea of Marmara are low hills and higher mountains (including Uludağ). The land is very rich, excellent for producing fruit such as grapes, peaches and apricots. Average rainfall is 668mm; temperature extremes are 40.5°C maximum and -16.1°C minimum. This is Turkey's second most humid region, with an annual average of 73% humidity.

Aegean

Fertile plains and river valleys, low hills and not-so-low mountains make up the Aegean region. The ancient river Meander, now called the Menderes, is a good example of the Aegean's rivers. When you see it from the heights of ruined Priene, you'll know where the word 'meander' comes from.

When travelling, the Aegean region presents constantly changing views of olive, fig and fruit orchards on hillsides, and broad tobacco and sunflower fields in the valleys. The maximum temperature is 42.7°C, the minimum is -8.2°C. Average humidity is 69%; average annual rainfall is 647mm.

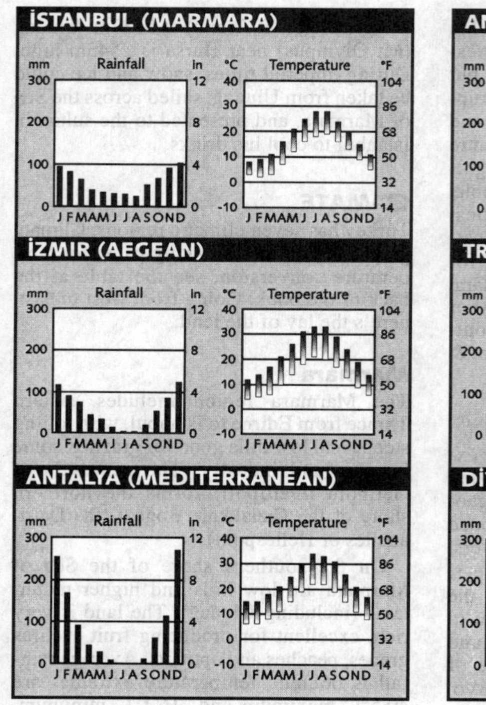

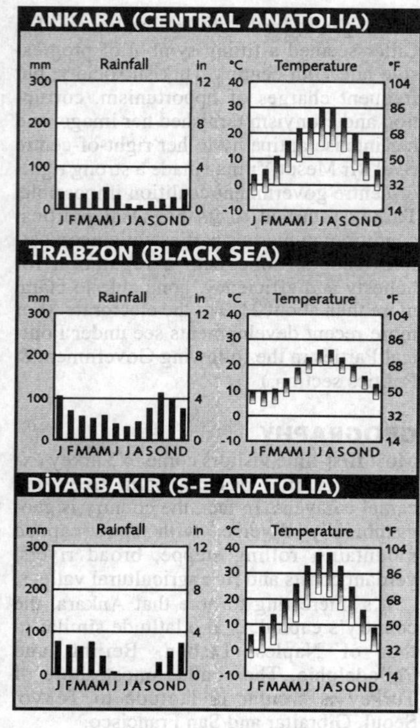

Mediterranean Coast

The Mediterranean coast is mountainous without much beach between Fethiye and Antalya, but then opens up into a fertile plain between Antalya and Alanya before turning into mountains again. All along the southern coast mountains loom to the north. The great Taurus range stretches all the way from Alanya east to Adana. Temperatures at Antalya are a few degrees warmer than at İzmir. The eastern Mediterranean coast is always very humid. The maximum temperature is 44.6°C, and the minimum is -4.6°C. Annual precipitation is 777mm; average humidity is 69%.

Central Anatolia

The Turkish heartland of Central Anatolia is a vast high plateau broken by mountain ranges, including some volcanoes with snow-capped peaks. The land is mostly rolling steppe, good for growing wheat and grazing sheep. Ankara's elevation is 900m above sea level. In summer Ankara is hot and dry; in winter it's chilly and often damp. Late spring and early autumn are perfect. The maximum temperature is 40°C, the minimum is -24.9°C. Annual rainfall is a low 382mm; average humidity is 62%.

Black Sea Coast

The Black Sea coast, 1700km long, has a climate you might not expect to find in this part of the world. Rainfall is two to three times the national average and temperatures are moderate. You will see hazelnut groves (on which the economy depends heavily), cherry orchards and tobacco fields. This is where cherries originated, getting their name in Roman times: the root word of 'cherry' is the Latin *cerasus* (Turkish: *kiraz)*. The cattle on the outskirts of every town provide milk, cream and butter famous throughout Turkey. At the eastern end of the Black Sea coast, the mountains come right down to the sea, and the slopes are covered with tea plantations. Rainfall and humidity are highest here. All in all, the Black Sea coast is like central Europe, but pleasantly warmer. The maximum temperature is 40.5°C, the minimum is -8°C. Annual rainfall is 781mm and average humidity is 72%.

South-Eastern Anatolia

The region of south-eastern Anatolia is of rolling steppe with outcrops of rock. The major rivers are the Tigris (Dicle) and the Euphrates (Fırat), both of which have their sources in Turkey. With 576mm of rain per year, it is very dry and hot in summer, with maximum temperatures reaching 46.5°C. Minimums are around -12°C. Average humidity, at 52%, is the lowest in Turkey. The climate produces bumper crops if there's water. The mammoth GAP hydroelectric project now provides irrigation water in abundance.

Eastern Anatolia

A mountainous and somewhat forbidding zone, this is a wildly beautiful region like no other in Turkey. The average temperature is a cool 9.5°C, but varies between a hot 38°C and a daunting -43.2°C. It's cold out here except from June to September. The rainfall is average for Turkey, about 560mm per year. The people are not as rich as in other regions, but they do well enough grazing sheep, growing wheat and producing a few other crops.

ECOLOGY & ENVIRONMENT

Turkey is one of those countries straddling the environmental dilemma. Much of the country still lives in the pre-pollution era of frugal living, home-made goods and dungcake fuel, but urban dwellers are well into the lifestyle of quickly changing fashion and disposable everything. Village dwellers are just leaving the era when environmental concern was not necessary, and urbanites are just discovering it as a major problem.

There is an environmental movement in Turkey and it is making some progress. Some cities attempt to recycle glass and metal and Bosphorus restaurants now seem to refrain from disposing of food waste right into the water. Sewage treatment plants are being built, but as these projects are expensive and Turkey is hardly a rich country, it will take time. At least vessels – including yachts – in Turkish waters are prohibited by law from emptying waste into the seas, though it still happens because of insufficient enforcement.

The best thing that you, the traveller, can do to help the cause of environmental protection in Turkey is to set a good example and encourage local efforts. Despite the insufficient number of rubbish bins, don't litter, and if you see others littering, suggest that they dispose of it properly. Complain to local tourism offices about litter on beaches or sewage near swimming areas. Ask for nonsmoking buses, even if it's plain that none exist on your route.

Remember that you're a guest in Turkey and that Turkey doesn't yet have anywhere near the financial resources or technical expertise – or force of public concern – for these issues as exists in western countries. A superior, preachy attitude may do more harm than good, but acting the part of environmental advocate may hasten the adoption of similar attitudes by the Turks.

FLORA & FAUNA

Once cloaked in dense forest, after a thousand years of woodcutting, Anatolia is now largely denuded. The government encourages conservation and reforestation, but the great forests will never return. The Mediterranean coast west of Antalya, the Black Sea area and north-eastern Anatolia still have forests of considerable size. Elsewhere, the great swaths of wild flowers which cover the rolling steppes in spring make fine splashes of colour.

Because of Turkey's temperate climate, domesticated plants such as apples, apricots, bananas, cherries, citrus fruit, cotton, date palms, grapes, sugar beet, sunflowers and tobacco thrive. The long roots of deliciously sweet *kavun* melons go deep into the dry soil of the Anatolian Plateau to find water. Turkey grows much of the world's supply of hazelnuts, and a large volume of pistachios and walnuts. Of the cash crops, cotton is king, and grains such as wheat and barley are important.

Turkey has similar animal life to that in the Balkans and much of Europe: bear, deer, jackal, lynx, wild boar, wolf and rare leopard. Besides the usual domestic animals such as cattle, horse, donkey, goat and several varieties of sheep (including the fat-tail), there are camel and water buffalo. (Though most yoghurt is made from cow's milk, that from sheep's milk is richer, and that from water buffalo's milk is richer still.)

Turkish shepherds are proud of their big, powerful and fierce Kangal sheep dogs which guard the flocks from hungry wolves. The breed is now controlled, and export is only allowed under licence. The same goes for the beautiful Van cats, with pure white fur and different-coloured eyes – one blue, one green.

Birdlife is exceptionally rich, with eagles, vultures and storks, as well as rare species such as the bald ibis, now nearly extinct except for a few birds which visit Birecik, between Gaziantep and Şanlıurfa, each year. In several parts of the country reserves have been set aside as *kuş cenneti* (bird paradises).

Turkey's coastal waters have rich varieties of fish, shellfish and other sea creatures, though overfishing and pollution are now serious problems.

GOVERNMENT & POLITICS

Parliament

Turkey is a parliamentary democracy. The Turkish Grand National Assembly (TGNA), elected by all citizens over 19 years of age, is the direct descendant of the congress assembled by Atatürk during the War of Independence to act as the legitimate voice of the Turkish nation in place of the sultan.

President & Prime Minister

The president, elected by the TGNA from among its members, serves for one seven-year term and is supposed to be 'above politics', and symbolise the nation. He or she is the head of state, with important executive powers and responsibilities. The true head of government, who decides its policies and directions, is the prime minister. However, recent presidents (Özal and Demirel) have informally expanded the powers of the presidential office and have been accused at times of having used the office with partisan effect.

The prime minister is appointed by the president to form a government, and thus is almost always the head of the party with the most seats in parliament.

The judiciary, though theoretically independent, has in many instances been influenced by current government policies.

Political Parties

Turkish democracy has had its ups and downs. Though the Turks are firm believers in democracy, the tradition of popular rule and responsibility is relatively short. Real multiparty democracy came into being only after WWII (compared to England's tradition of almost 800 years).

Mid-Century Atatürk's Republican People's Party (CHP) enjoyed one-party rule until after WWII, when multiparty democracy became a reality. In the first elections the CHP lost out to the right-wing Democratic Party (DP), which attempted to control the government as closely as the CHP had before the war by grabbing extra-constitutional power. The Turkish armed forces, which were entrusted by Atatürk's legacy as guarantors of the Turkish constitution, then intervened.

After the military intervention of 1960, the Democratic Party was banned, but its party faithful simply formed a successor, the similarly centre-right Justice Party (AP), and did as well in the elections against the centre-left CHP.

1960s Under the watchful eye of the military, the CHP and AP governed as a coalition until 1965, when the AP won a parliamentary majority on its own, and its leader, Süleyman Demirel, began his first term as prime minister. He stepped down at the insistence of the military in 1971 as left-right violence and parliamentary deadlock threatened public order.

1970s In 1973 a revivified CHP under Bülent Ecevit won election and formed a government, but was soon forced into coalition with the small far-right religious National Salvation Party (MSP).

During the 1970s the CHP and AP locked horns in parliament, both having around 40% of the votes. The smaller parties further out on the political spectrum thus gained inordinate influence – their few votes making the difference between winning or losing a parliamentary vote. The Islamic fundamentalist MSP led by Professor Necmettin Erbakan, the fascistic Nationalist Action Party (MHP), and the leftist Turkish Workers Party (TİP) all traded their support for control of various government ministries through which to push their agendas. The result was widespread civil violence and government paralysis.

1980s The bloodless military coup of September 1980 saw the dissolution of all former political parties and the exclusion from politics of their leaders (including Ecevit, Demirel and Erbakan). In the elections of 1983, the armed forces supported a new centrist party formed of their supporters, but the new centre-right Motherland Party (ANAP) led by Turgut Özal won.

Özal was a financial technocrat and former World Bank economist who had helped the military to revivify the economy after the 1980 intervention. His policies not only produced a boom in economic development, but also high inflation and charges of corruption. Throughout the decade his policies were challenged by several 'new' parties: the Social Democrat Populist Party (SHP), an heir to the CHP; the Democratic Left Party (DSP), another heir to the CHP led secretly by Ecevit, who was still under political exclusion; the True Path Party (DYP), successor to Demirel's Justice Party; and the Welfare (Refah) Party (RP), led by Mr Erbakan, successor to the religious MSP.

Late in 1989, Turgut Özal was elected to the presidency. He remained active in ANAP politics, however, running the country through figurehead prime minister Yıldırım Akbulut. This was against at least the spirit if not the letter of the constitution and raised eyebrows in political and military circles.

1990s In the hotly contested elections of February 1992 ANAP gained only about a third of the vote, losing the plurality to the durable Süleyman Demirel, back from political exclusion, and his DYP. The centre-right True Path formed an unlikely coalition with the centre-left SHP under Professor Erdal İnönü (son of general, prime minister and president, the late İsmet İnönü) to form a government.

Demirel brought a new vigour to the government after almost a decade of Motherland leadership.

With Özal's untimely death due to heart disease in April 1993, Demirel was elected to be the ninth president of the Turkish Republic. In June 1993, President Demirel asked Professor Tansu Çiller, the economics minister, to form a government, thereby making her Turkey's first woman prime minister.

Prime Minister Çiller earned high marks from international bankers for making progress in privatising Turkey's money-losing state enterprises, leftovers from the statist policies of Atatürk of 60 years ago. Despite her modest progress in this, the economy worsened as the government seemed to lack any strong, clearly defined economic plan – and it continued to run

Army Days

To the Turks, the army is an honourable institution with a long and glorious history. In a recent public opinion poll, the Turkish populace was asked which national institution they held in the highest regard, and the military won handily over parliament, the courts and the religious establishment.

The Turkish people trace their lineage all the way back to the ancient Turkish states in Dzungaria around 2000 BC, but the earliest great Turkic empire dependent upon military prowess was that of the Huns around 220 BC. Through the Göktürks (552-745 AD), the Avars (565-835 AD), the Uygurs (745-940 AD), the Karahanlıs (940-1040), the Ghaznavids (962-1187), the Great Seljuks (990-1157), and the Ottomans (1281-1922), Turkey's armed forces retained a central role in government and society. In other societies, such as the Arab and Mameluke empires, Turks formed the military caste.

Turkey was neutral during WWII, and the Turkish contingent with the United Nations forces during the Korean War was highly praised for its discipline, courage and tenacity.

To be a Turk is to be a soldier, at least at some point in life. In republican Turkey, every Turkish male is required to spend some months in the army, with very few exceptions. Despite it being an honourable duty, few Turkish men look forward to it. Conscientious objection is not an option.

Most men do their military service when they are 18. There are several ways in which the moment can be put off. Deferment is allowed, for example, if you are a student or if your brother is already doing his military service. But in practice, a young man over 18 who has not yet done his military service may find it almost impossible to get a job, as no employer wants his new employee to have to run off to the army for months.

Useful social as well as military purposes are served by army service. It's not unusual to see army troops doing clean-up or gardening duty at archaeological sites, or planting new forests.

The army has traditionally used compulsory military service as a mechanism for social leavening and cohesion. Young men from the comfortable, developed western provinces are often shipped off to serve in the rugged east, while country boys from poor eastern villages are posted to cosmopolitan İstanbul, İzmir, or the tourist resorts, giving both extremes a close-up view of the 'other' Turkey.

The recent PKK insurgency in the south-east has meant that being a Turkish soldier is not just a temporary interruption to a young man's career. Thousands of conscripts have come home in body bags.

huge deficits. Turkey's commercial, industrial, agricultural and tourism sectors boomed producing record profits, but the lira continued to slide in a constant devaluation against harder currencies.

In the summer of 1995 Çiller's government lost a vote of confidence in parliament when its coalition partner, upset over the government's unwillingness to raise the minimum wage, withdrew. September and October were one long political crisis as Çiller, now caretaker, attempted to form a new government, ultimately forming a new coalition with Mr Deniz Baykal of the Republican Peoples' Party (CHP) as foreign minister and deputy prime minister to take the country to early elections.

Islamist Interlude The elections of December 1995 were a wake-up call against politics as usual: the upstart religious-right

Welfare Party (RP) won a plurality of 21%, which was seen as a protest vote against the ineffective policies and tedious political wrangles of the mainstream Motherland Party (20%) and Çiller's True Path Party (19%). Professor Necmettin Erbakan, the RP leader, was given the mandate to form a coalition, but neither of the other big parties would join him.

In March 1996, President Demirel gave the nod to Çiller, the caretaker prime minister who formed a coalition with former bitter political rival Mesut Yilmaz of Motherland. The coalition predictably broke down soon after. Unable to avoid it any longer, in July President Demirel charged Professor Erbakan with the duty of forming a government, which he did, becoming prime minister by allying with none other than Professor Çiller.

Emboldened by political power, Prime Minister Erbakan and other Refah politicians tested the boundaries of Turkey's traditional secularism and westernism. Erbakan made triumphant visits to Iran and other aggressively Islamist countries, and reputedly received financial subsidies from them. Local politicians made Islamist gestures and statements which alarmed the powerful National Security Council, the most visible symbol of the military establishment's role as the caretaker of secularism.

In 1997 the Council let it be known that Refah's time was up. Erbakan was forced to resign the prime ministership and his party was dissolved for having flouted the constitutional ban against religion in politics. Mesut Yılmaz formed a coalition government which to date has operated within the military's secret guidelines.

Most secular, democratically minded Turks were not sorry to see Refah go, but neither were they happy with the precedent of the military establishment, charged by Atatürk to protect democracy, forcing a democratically elected government from office.

ECONOMY

Turkey has a strong agricultural base to its economy, being among the handful of countries which are net exporters of food. Wheat, cotton, sugar beet, sunflowers, hazelnuts, tobacco, fruit and vegetables are abundant. Sheep are the main livestock, and Turkey is the biggest wool producer in Europe.

However, manufactured goods now dominate exports and much of the economy. Turkey makes motor vehicles, appliances, pharmaceuticals, consumer goods and large engineering projects, and exports them throughout the region. Its export growth rate in recent years has been more than 25%, among the highest in the world.

However, the economy is still dragged down by the heavy weight of the 'state economic enterprises' (KITs), government controlled corporations subject to subsidies, political influence, payroll-padding and corruption. In 1994, six of the 10 largest corporations were KITs, refining and selling petroleum products and petrochemicals; generating and distributing electricity; making and selling salt, tobacco products and alcoholic beverages; and refining and marketing sugar. The government is also involved in the marketing of agricultural products including grain, hazelnuts and tea; in coal and steel production; in transportation and broadcasting and many other industries.

Tourism is now among the most important sectors of the Turkish economy, bringing in billions of dollars in foreign currency earnings.

There is still a large Turkish workforce in the industries of Europe, particularly those of Germany, which sends home remittances.

POPULATION & PEOPLE

Turkey has a population of approximately 60 million, the great majority being Sunni Muslim Turks.

Turks

The Turkic peoples originated in central Asia, where they were a presence to be reckoned with as early as the 4th century AD. The Chinese called them *Tu-küe*, which is perhaps the root of our word 'Turk'. They were related to the *Hiung-nu*, or Huns.

The normally nomadic Turks ruled several vast empires in Central Asia before being pushed westward by the Mongols. Various tribes of the Oğuz Turkic group settled in Azerbaijan, northern Iran and Anatolia.

At first they were shamanist, but at one time or another these early Turks followed each of the great religions of the region including Buddhism, Nestorian Christianity, Manichaeism and Judaism. During their western migrations they became more familiar with Islam, and it stuck.

Having begun their history as nomadic shepherds, the Turks used their skills with horses to become excellent soldiers. With the expansion of the Arab Empire into Turkish lands, the Turks used their renowned military prowess first to gain influence, and later to gain control. To this day most Turks are proud of their military traditions, while military prowess, courage and discipline are widely admired.

Kurds

Turkey has a significant Kurdish minority estimated at 10 million. Some ethnologists believe that the Kurds, who speak an Indo-European language, are closely related to the Persians, and that they migrated here from northern Europe centuries before Christ.

Turkey's sparsely populated eastern and south-eastern regions are home to perhaps six million Kurds and minorities of Turks, Armenians and others. Four million Kurds live elsewhere throughout the country, more or less integrated into greater Turkish society. (Yilmaz Güney's film *Yol (The Road)*, winner of the best film award at Cannes in 1982, explores the dilemmas of a Kurd from a traditional family integrated into modern, urban Turkish society. Unfortunately, the subtitles do not do the script justice, and anti-Turkish trailers were added by the foreign distributor.)

Though virtually all of the Kurds living in Turkey are Muslims and look physically similar to the Turks, they proudly maintain their Kurdish language, culture and family traditions.

Separatism Since the collapse of the Ottoman Empire, the Kurds have periodically aspired to their own ethnic nation-state with revolts. Some dream of a Greater Kurdistan encompassing the millions of Kurds in neighbouring regions of Iran, Iraq and Syria. Fearing that Kurdish separatism could tear the country apart, the government in Ankara pursued a policy of assimilation. Officially, there were no 'Kurds', only 'mountain Turks', and all were equal citizens of the republic. The Kurdish language and other overt signs of Kurdish life were outlawed.

In recent years the Kurdish question has come to the fore again. During the 1980s, Kurdistan Workers Party (PKK) guerrillas, based in neighbouring Syria, Iraq and Iran and supported clandestinely by the PLO, made hundreds of raids into south-eastern Turkey killing thousands of civilians and Turkish troops. The resulting military crackdown embittered many Turkish Kurds, but also brought the matter of Turks and Kurds to the national agenda. Some say Kurdish separatists fear that the vast South-East Anatolia Project (GAP) will bring prosperity to a historically poor region, thereby ruining their chances of ever founding an independent Kurdistan.

In 1988, Iraqi armed forces made a deadly chemical-weapon attack on the Iraqi Kurdish village of Halabja, sending thousands of refugees fleeing across the border to safety in Turkey. After the Gulf War of 1991, fearing similar attacks, three million Iraqi Kurds fled towards Turkey, threatening to overwhelm its eastern provinces.

The plight of the Kurds drew the attention of Europe and the USA, and resultant publicity led to a softening of Ankara's restrictions: Kurdish conversation and songs are now legal, and other measures such as Kurdish-language radio and TV broadcasts are being debated. But just as many Kurds are now beginning to imagine the delights of independence, their Turkish compatriots are imagining the disaster of the Turkish homeland dismembered. With the violent chaos of the former Soviet Caucasian republics and Yugoslavia in mind, one can only hope that the Kurds and Turks find some peaceful *modus vivendi*.

Other Islamic Peoples

Turkey's coasts are home to small ethnic or linguistic groups such as the Laz and Hemşin peoples along the Black Sea coast, and the Yörüks and Tahtacıs along the eastern Mediterranean coast.

Jews

The small Jewish community of about 24,000 people is centred in İstanbul (20,000), with smaller communities in Ankara, Bursa, İzmir and other cities. The Turkish Jewish community is the remnant of a great influx which took place in the 16th century when the Jews of Spain (Sephardim) were forced by the Spanish Inquisition to flee their homes. They were welcomed into the Ottoman Empire and brought with them knowledge of many recent European scientific and economic discoveries and advancements. In 1992 they celebrated 500 years of peaceful life among the Turks.

Armenians

The Armenians are thought by some to be descended from the Urartians (518-330 BC), but others think they arrived from the Caucasus area after the Urartian state collapsed.

Armenians have lived in eastern Anatolia for a thousand years, almost always as subjects of some greater state such as the Alexandrine empire, or of the Romans, Byzantines, Persians, Seljuks or Ottomans. They lived with their Kurdish and Turkish neighbours in relative peace and harmony under the Ottoman *millet* system of distinct religious communities. But when this system gave way to modern ethnic nationalism, they suffered one of the greatest tragedies in their history.

Rebellion As ethnic groups on the fringes of the empire rose in rebellion and won their independence, the Armenians followed. Unlike other peoples, however, the Armenians lived in the Muslim heartland, where they were sometimes a plurality but never a majority. (The tragic ethnic wars of the early 1990s in the former Soviet Union and Yugoslavia arose from similarly confused ethnic situations.)

By the 1890s there were frequent protests, rebellions and Armenian terrorist attacks on Ottoman government buildings and personnel, which were inevitably answered with ferocious repression by the police, army and populace. The revolutionaries hoped that if they triggered atrocities, the Christian powers of Europe would be persuaded to come to their aid, opening the way to independence. None of the powers, however, would allow any other to gain an advantage in the dismantling of the Ottoman Empire. Also, the tsar, like the sultan, did not want the creation of an independent Armenian state carved from his territory. The Armenians became the hopeless victims of their own small numbers, European power politics, and the Ottomans' alarm at the dissolution of their once-mighty country.

As the terrorist incidents continued, the Armenians' former Turkish and Kurdish neighbours turned against them violently. On 26 August 1896, Armenian revolutionaries seized the Ottoman Bank building in İstanbul, threatening to blow it up. Though they were unsuccessful, the incident provoked widespread massacres in the capital and elsewhere in which thousands of innocent Armenians died. The European powers raised their voices in protest, but again put no effective pressure on the sultan to stop the atrocities.

The restoration of the Ottoman constitution in 1908 provided a brief respite as all Ottoman peoples saw hope of living in harmony. But ethnic rivalries surfaced again quickly as Ottoman Bulgaria declared independence and Austria seized the former Ottoman provinces of Bosnia and Herzegovina. More Armenian demonstrations provoked more massacres at Adana in April 1909. Albania and Arabia rose in revolt.

War broke out with Italy, Bulgaria, Serbia and Greece. The Ottoman grand vizier was assassinated. The Ottoman Turks felt beleaguered on all sides.

WWI As WWI approached, a triumvirate of Young Turks named Enver, Talat and Jemal seized power. When war broke out, the Christian Orthodox Armenians of eastern Turkey were seen (with some justification) as being a 'fifth column' sympathetic to and aiding the advancing Russian army.

On 20 April 1915 the Armenians of Van rose in revolt, massacred the local Muslims, took the *kale* (fortress) and held it until the Russian army arrived. Four days after the beginning of the Van revolt, on 24 April 1915 (now commemorated as Armenian Martyrs' Day) the Ottoman government began the deportation of the Armenian population from the war zone to Syria. Hundreds of thousands of Armenians (mostly men) were massacred in the process, the rest (mostly women and children) were marched to Syria in great privation.

With the Russian victories a short-lived Armenian Republic was proclaimed in north-eastern Anatolia, and the victorious Armenians repaid defeated local Muslims with massacres in kind. But an offensive by the armies of Mustafa Kemal's Turkish nationalist Ankara government reclaimed Kars and Ardahan.

On 3 December 1920, the Ankara government concluded a peace treaty with the Armenian government in Erivan, now a Soviet republic. By the end of the war, the Armenian population of Anatolia had been reduced to a small minority, mostly in the major cities.

The Aftermath The Armenians who survived the cataclysm, and their descendants in the Diaspora, blame both the Ottoman government and the Turkish people as a whole for the tragedy, labelling it genocide. The Turks, while not denying that massacres occurred, deny that there was an official policy of genocide, claim that many Armenians were indeed traitorous, and that many if not most Armenian casualties were the result of civil war, disease and privation rather than massacre. Republican Turks dissociate themselves from the actions of the Ottoman government, pointing out that they themselves (or, more correctly, their parents and grandparents) fought to overthrow it.

Historians and pseudo-historians on both sides trade accusations and recriminations, dispute the actual number of casualties, the authenticity of incriminating historical documents, and the motives and actions of the other side. In the 1970s, Armenian terrorist assassinations of Turkish diplomats, their families, and innocent bystanders raised the level of recrimination and bitterness.

Armenians say they want the Turks to recognise and acknowledge the tragedy, and to provide compensation, perhaps even territory. Turks say they sympathise with the Armenians' loss, but that those who were responsible are long dead and those living today had nothing to do with it and cannot be held responsible, and thus compensation is inappropriate. It is an impasse likely to endure for generations.

Other Christian Peoples

As for Christian Turkish citizens, ethnic Greeks number fewer than 100,000 and live mostly in İstanbul. Assyrian Orthodox Christians, sometimes called Jacobites, trace their roots to the church founded by Jacob Baradeus, the 6th-century bishop of Edessa (today called Şanlıurfa). Their small community has its centre south of Diyarbakır, in and around Mardin and the Tür Abdin.

EDUCATION

The Turkish Republic provides five years of compulsory *ilkokul* (primary) and *ortaokul* (middle-school) education for all children aged from seven to 12 years. Secondary, *lise* (high school, *lycée*), and vocational or technical education is available at no cost to those who decide to continue. Specialised schools are available for the blind, the deaf, the mentally retarded, orphans and the very poor. There are also numerous licensed private schools, *kolej* (colleges, like high schools) and universities which charge tuition fees.

Turkey has 29 government-funded universities to which students are admitted through a central placement system. At Ankara's Middle East Technical University and Bilkent University, and at İstanbul's Boğaziçi (Bosphorus) University, English is the language of instruction.

ARTS

Ottoman Art

Art under the Ottomans was very different from art in the Turkish Republic. Until 1923 and the founding of the republic, all mainstream artistic expression conformed (more or less) to the laws of Islam, which forbade representation of any being 'with an immortal soul' (ie animal or human). Sculpture and painting as known in the west did not exist – with the notable exception of Turkish miniature painting, which was for the upper classes.

Instead of painting and sculpture, Islamic artists worked at arabesque decoration, faïence, filigree, geometric stained glass, gilding, pottery and metalworking, glass-blowing, marquetry, repoussé work, calligraphy and illumination, textile design (including costumes and carpets), horticulture and landscape gardening. Turks may have invented the art of marbling paper, which is still practised today. Ottoman architecture is outstanding.

The dome was one of many Byzantine designs adopted by the Ottomans.

Most of these arts reached their height during the great age of Ottoman power from the early 16th to the late 18th centuries. Turkish museums are full of examples: delicate coloured tiles from İznik, graceful glass vases and pitchers from İstanbul, carved wooden mosque doors, glittering illuminated Korans, intricate jewellery and sumptuous costumes.

By the late 19th century educated Ottomans were taking up landscape and still-life painting in European styles.

Literature before the republic was also bound up with Islam. Treatises on history, geography and science were cast in religious terms. Ottoman poets, borrowing from the great Arabic and Persian traditions, wrote sensual love poems of attraction, longing, fulfilment and ecstasy about the search for union with God.

Republican Art

Under the republic, Atatürk encouraged European-style artistic expression. The government opened official painting and sculpture academies, encouraging this 'modern' secular art over the religious art of the past.

In this century, Turkish artists and writers have been in touch with European and US trends in the arts. Some have followed slavishly, others have borrowed judiciously, mixing in a good portion of local tradition and inspiration. By the 1970s and 80s, Turkish painting had become vigorous enough to support numerous different local schools of artists whose work is shown by museums, galleries, collectors and patrons.

By the late 19th century some Ottoman writers were adapting to European forms. With the foundation of the republic, the ponderous cadences of Ottoman courtly prose and poetry gave way to use of the vernacular. Atatürk decreed that the Turkish language be 'purified' of Arabic and Persian borrowings. This, and the introduction of the new Latin-based Turkish alphabet, brought literacy within the reach of many more citizens. Several Turkish writers, including Nazım Hikmet, Yashar Kemal and Orhan Pamuk, have been translated into other languages and have met with critical and popular acclaim abroad.

Folk Arts & Crafts

Turkish carpet-making transcends the boundaries of folk art and fine art. Embroidery and lace-making are still practised in rural Turkey, as they have been for centuries. Primitive landscape painters once used horse-drawn wagons and carts as their venue; now it's the wood-panelled sides of trucks.

Turkish artisans also craft decorated wooden spoons, lathe-turned wooden items, lamps and stoves in tinplate, onyx and alabaster carvings, pottery and glass. Almost no one leaves the country without a blue-and-white *nazar boncuğu* (evil-eye charm), usually of glass but now also of plastic.

Music

There are many kinds of Turkish music, almost all of them unfamiliar to foreign ears. Ottoman classical, religious (particularly *Mevlevi)* and some folk and popular music uses a system of *makams*, or modalities, an exotic-sounding series of tones similar in function to western scales. In addition to the familiar western whole and half-tone intervals, much Turkish music uses quarter-tones, unfamiliar to foreign ears and perceived as 'flat' until the ear becomes accustomed to them.

Though Ottoman classical music sounds ponderous and lugubrious to the uninitiated, much Turkish folk music as played in the villages is sprightly and immediately appealing. *Türkü* music, of which you'll hear lots on the radio, falls somewhere in between: traditional folk music as performed by modern singers who live in the city.

The 1000-year-old tradition of Turkish troubadours *(aşık)*, still very much alive as late as the 1960s and 70s, is now dying out in its pure form – killed off by radio, TV, video and CDs. The songs of the great troubadours – Yunus Emre (1238?-1320?), Pir Sultan Abdal (16th century) and Aşık Veysel (died 1974) – are still popular, however, and are often performed and recorded.

Unfortunately, the sorts of Turkish music which are most easily comprehensible to foreign ears are the fairly vapid *taverna* styles, and the local popular songs based on European and US models. Though this music can be fun, it is also fairly mindless and forgettable. Perhaps the best is Adnan Ergil's series of audio cassettes entitled *Turkish Folk Guitar*.

Though the music of Europe and the USA played a predominant role in Turkish musical life for most of this century, the phenomenal growth and sophisticated development of local Turkish artists and recording studios has recently pushed

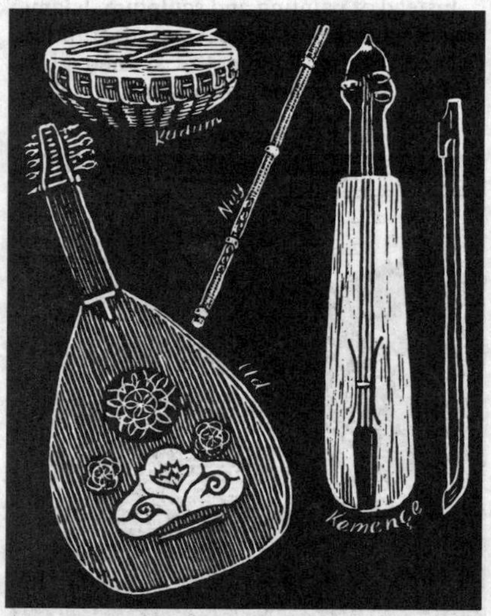

Some of the musical instruments used in classical Turkish ensembles.

Top of the Turkish Pops

Rock music in Turkey is as faddy and ephemeral as anywhere else. The flavour of 1998, for example, was **Tarkan**, the teenybop idol of Turkish pop who rocketed to fame on the back of his *Acayıpsın (You're Weird)* album in 1994 and has been riding high ever since.

But alongside the shooting stars there are also many well-established artists whose back catalogues remain as popular as those of the Stones and Springsteen. Queen of 1990s pop was **Sezen Aksu**, a singer-songwriter whose memorable melodies were typified by the 1991 album *Gülümse (Smile)*. Well enough established to take risks, she has since branched out with the more experimental *Işik Doğudan Yükselir (The Light Rises in the East)* which draws on Turkey's regional musical traditions.

Another long-established performer is protest singer **Zülfü Livaneli**, a singer and saz player who is also well known in Turkey as a columnist (for the daily newspaper *Milliyet*) with left-wing sympathies who was once was narrowly defeated for the post of mayor of İstanbul. Since Livaneli's music often incorporates western instrumentation, it's fairly accessible to non-Turkish audiences. His songs are often covered by other musicians, not least by his daughter Aylin, and he has recorded with Greek musicians Maria Farandouri and Mikis Theodorakis in an effort to heal one set of Turkey's political wounds.

More alien to western ears is the style of music known as *arabesk* which, as its name implies, puts an Arabic spin on home-grown Turkish traditions. The mournful themes (if not the melodies) of this music have led to its being compared to Greek *rembetika* and until the advent of independent radio and TV in the 1990s, the authorities kept arabesk off the air-waves, even conjuring up their own, more cheerful version in an attempt to undermine its power.

Until recently it wasn't at all cool to like a style of music associated, as the *Virgin Guide to World Music* put it, 'with gazinos and the sound systems of taxis'. However, arabesk now attracts a gay following which sits rather oddly alongside its more traditional macho audience. Playing to arabesk's traditional audience is the hugely successful Kurdish singer **İbrahim Tatlıses**, a burly, moustached former construction worker from Şanlıurfa whose life seems positively dull compared to those of arabesk's artier practitioners (see 'Urfa's Favourite Son' in the Şanlıurfa section).

In 1980, for example, **Bülent Ersoy's** music was banned following his sex-change operation. Once the ban was lifted, Ersoy started performing live again – only to be shot at by a member of the reactionary, neo-fascist Grey Wolves militia group for refusing to sing a nationalist anthem. Ersoy was last heard of arranging to have a baby with her new, much younger partner.

western music into a subsidiary role. Many western soloists and groups are popular in Turkey – everyone from the Spice Girls to Andrea Bocelli – but you will hear much more Turkish music.

Western classical symphony, chamber music, opera and ballet have a small but fiercely loyal following in Turkey. Government-funded orchestras, dance groups and opera companies, supported by visiting artists, keep them satisfied.

Film

Cinema appeared in Turkey just a year after the Lumière brothers presented their first cinematic show in 1895. At first it was only foreigners and non-Muslims who watched movies, but by 1914 there were cinemas run by and for Muslims as well.

The War of Independence inspired actor Muhsin Ertuğrul, Turkey's cinema pioneer, to establish a film company in 1922 and make patriotic films. Comedies and documentaries followed. Within a decade Turkish films were winning awards in international competitions, even though a mere 23 films had been made.

After WWII the industry expanded rapidly with new companies and young directors. Lütfi Akad's *Kanun Namına* (*In the Name of the Law*, 1952), Turkey's first colour film, brought realism to the screen in place of melodrama, and won first prize at the first Turkish film festival held a year later.

By the 1960s, Turkish cinema was delving deeply into social and political issues. Metin Erksan's *Susuz Yaz* (*Dry Summer*, 1964) won a gold medal at the Berlin Film Festival and another award in Venice. Yılmaz Güney, the fiery actor-director, directed his first film *At, Avrat, Silah* (*Horse, Woman, Gun*) in 1966, and starred in Lütfi Akad's *Hudutların Kanunu* (*The Law of the Borders*) after he had written the script.

The 1970s brought the challenge of television, dwindling audiences, political pressures and unionisation of the industry. The quality of films continued to improve, and social issues such as Turkish workers in Europe were treated with honesty, naturalism and dry humour. By the early 1980s, several Turkish directors were well recognised in Europe and the USA. Among current directors, Tunç Başaran, Zülfü, Halit Refiğ and Ömer Kavur are worth watching.

SOCIETY & CONDUCT

At first glance, much of Turkish society is highly Europeanised. Men and women march off to jobs in city offices and shops, farmers mount their tractors for a day in the fields, and bureaucrats belly up to typewriters and computer keyboards. But Turkish traditions are different from those of Europe, and glimpses of traditional attitudes and behaviour often come through.

Liberal western attitudes born of Atatürk's reforms are strongest in the urban centres of the west and along the coasts, among the middle and upper classes. Westerners will feel quite comfortable among these Turks, who look to western culture as the ideal, and accept the validity of other religious beliefs alongside their own.

The working and farming classes, particularly in the east, are more conservative, traditional and religious. There is a small but growing segment of 'born again' Muslims, fervent and strict in their religion but otherwise modern. Though always polite, these Turks may give you the feeling that east is east and west is west, and that the last echo of crusaders versus Saracens has not yet died away.

Hospitality is an honoured tradition in Turkey, from the shopkeeper who plies you with tea, coffee or soft drinks to the village family which invites you to share their home and meals for the customary three days. Commercialism has begun to corrupt traditional hospitality in tourist areas, producing the shady carpet merchant who lays on the friendliness with a trowel only to sell you shoddy goods at inflated prices. Don't let the carpet touts make you lose sight of true Turkish hospitality, which is a wonderful thing.

'While on a long bus ride from Pamukkale to Fethiye, we made a routine rest stop. I went to a nearby toilet where I noticed a scruffy-looking young boy sitting at the entrance. Afterwards I made my way back to the bus and took my seat. The bus pulled out of the rest stop and I noticed the boy running alongside it, trying frantically to get the driver's attention. The bus stopped and the boy immediately made his way towards me and handed me my money belt. I must have dropped it when entering the toilet. My money belt contained about UK£300, a credit card, about UK£30 worth of Turkish lira and my passport – a small fortune by Turkish standards and an absolute fortune to an eight-year-old boy – all of it untouched. Needless to say the boy was rewarded handsomely for his honesty. This gesture only served to remind me what a kind and generous country Turkey really is.'

Justin Flynn, Australia

The Hat Law

'Put on your hat.' Those were fighting words in Ottoman times, when a hat (defined as headgear with a brim) was seen as a Christian adornment by every self-respecting Muslim Turk. The brim on a hat interfered with Muslim prayer, in which the person performing it must touch the forehead to the ground. A hat was fit only for an infidel.

Many sayings attributed to the Prophet Muhammed praised the wearing of the turban, and the sheikh of a dervish order would symbolise his presence, if he needed to be somewhere else, by placing his turban in his accustomed seat.

Indeed, throughout Ottoman Turkey one's headgear was a recognised symbol of one's rank and role in life, as evidenced by Ottoman tombstones which often included a stylised headgear modelled in stone at the top, showing the social role of the deceased. Legal dress codes dictated certain items of apparel which might be worn by Muslim, Christian and Jew; a member of one group was forbidden – and usually didn't want – to wear the colours or styles of the others. To wear a hat was, for a Muslim, a symbol of apostasy, the highest crime in Islamic theology.

In early 20th century Turkey, most Muslim men wore maroon-coloured felt fezzes and had done so since this style of headgear had been introduced as a replacement for 'old-fashioned' turbans in 1829. However, as a young man growing up in Macedonia, Mustafa Kemal (Atatürk) had been laughed at for his fez and came to see it as exemplifying the backwardness of Ottoman Turkey.

Thus one of his first acts as president of the new Turkish Republic was to abolish the fez. The Hat Law, which was promulgated on 25 November 1925, outlawed the wearing of the fez, and required men to wear hats, brim and all, as the 'civilised head covering' of the new Turkish republic. The president of the republic always appeared in public wearing a variety of hats.

So sudden was the change that Turkey didn't have enough hats in store to cover all the heads now needing them. There was a rush to snap up second-hand bowlers, and unscrupulous European retailers took the opportunity to offload outmoded and wholly inappropriate hats on unsuspecting Turks. Reports exist of burly İzmir cobblers and blacksmiths going about their daily business clad in pink hats complete with feathers and ribbons. The press had a field day, too, with articles explaining how to wear these uncustomary items of apparel.

Coming in the midst of a year of social upheaval and rapid government-decreed secularisation, the Hat Law was vigorously resisted in conservative Muslim circles. Men who saw their Muslim identity being ripped from their heads rioted against the new law. Some refused point-blank to remove their fezzes. The government reacted even more vigorously, enforcing its edict and punishing anti-secular elements severely. Men were hanged in Erzurum, Giresun, Rize and Maraş. Others received hefty jail sentences.

Today, most Turks regard the fez as a souvenir fit for tourists locked in an overly romantic vision of Ottoman times. But many good Muslims still sidestep the hat issue by going bare-headed or wearing knitted ski caps. In certain parts of the country, traditional headgear survives, like the *puşu* (a cloth wrapped loosely around the head) in the Aegean region, and the *tarbuş* (a skullcap wrapped with a cloth) in the south-east.

For more on the Hat Law and the upset it caused, read Jeremy Seal's witty *A Fez of the Heart*.

Customs & Practices

Under the Ottoman Empire (from the 14th century to 1923), Turkish etiquette was highly organised and very formal. Every encounter between people turned into a mini-ceremony full of the flowery romance of the east.

Though the Turks have adapted to the informality of 20th-century life, you'll still notice vestiges of this courtly state of mind. Were you to learn Turkish, you'd find dozens of polite phrases – actually rigid formulas – to be repeated on cue in many daily situations. Some are listed in the Turkish Language guide chapter. Use one of these at the proper moment, and the Turks will love it.

Turks are very understanding of foreigners' different customs, but if you want to behave in accordance with local feelings, use all the polite words you can muster, at all times. This can get laborious, and even Turks complain about how one can't even get out the door without five minutes of politenesses. But even the complainers still say them.

Also note these things: don't point your finger directly towards any person. Don't show the sole of your foot or shoe towards anyone (ie so they can see it). Don't blow your nose openly in public, especially in a restaurant; instead, turn or leave the room and blow quietly. Don't pick your teeth openly, but cover your mouth with your hand. Don't do a lot of kissing or hugging with a person of the opposite sex in public. All of the above actions are considered rude.

'In Ankara I observed the ritual killing of a sheep on a traffic island. A man slit the sheep's throat and washed the blood away to the side of the road, hailed a taxi, put the carcass in the boot and went off! No one else but me seemed at all surprised. What a fascinating country!'

Dr L Massey, England

Lese-Majesty

At the beginning of the 20th century, the western image of the Ottoman Turks was of a decadent, sombre, ignorant and incompetent people. This western image, which replaced that of the 'Terrible Turk' once there was no longer a threat that Turkey would conquer Europe, was based on a little truth, a lot of politics, and a good dose of religious and ethnic prejudice.

Atatürk's success in holding off the Allied powers from dismembering Turkey, and his republican reforms, gave Turks a new, positive image of themselves as pro-European and modern in outlook.

Atatürk was the right man at the right time, and many Turks believe that without this particular man there is no way Turkey could be what it is today. Rather, it might have ceased to exist entirely; at the least, it might be like one of its Islamic neighbours, with less material and social progress, and no real grounding in democratic traditions. The Turks look around them at their Islamic neighbours and think themselves lucky to have had a leader of such ability and foresight.

This all means something to the visitor. There is a law against defaming the national hero, who is still held in the highest regard by most Turks (excluding the religious right); and similar laws against showing disrespect to other patriotic institutions such as the armed forces, the president, parliament, or national symbols such as the Turkish flag. You won't see cartoons or caricatures of Atatürk, and no one mentions him in jest. A slight or joke directed toward Atatürk, the Turkish flag, the Turkish Republic or any other national symbol may be interpreted as a serious case of lese-majesty, and should be avoided.

Mosque Etiquette Always remove your shoes before stepping on a mosque's carpets, or on the clean area just in front of the mosque door. This is not a religious law, just a practical one. Worshippers kneel and touch their foreheads to the carpets, and they like to keep them clean. If there are no carpets, as in a saint's tomb, you can leave your shoes on.

Wear modest clothes when visiting mosques, as you would when visiting a church. Don't wear tatty blue jeans, shorts (men or women) or any gear which worshippers might find outlandish. Women should have head, arms and shoulders covered, and wear modest dresses or skirts, preferably reaching to the knees. At some of the most visited mosques, attendants will lend you long robes if your clothing doesn't meet a minimum standard. Although the loan of the robe is free, a donation is appreciated.

Visiting Turkish mosques is generally very easy, though there are no hard and fast rules. Most times no one will give you any trouble, but now and then there may be a stickler for propriety guarding the door, and they will keep you out if your dress or demeanour is not acceptable.

Avoid entering mosques at prayer time (ie at the call to prayer – dawn, noon, mid-afternoon, dusk and evening, or 20 minutes thereafter). Avoid visiting mosques at all on Fridays, especially morning and noon. Friday is the Muslim holy day.

When you're inside a mosque, even if it is not prayer time, there will usually be several people praying. Don't disturb them in any way; don't take flash photos; don't walk directly in front of them.

Everybody will appreciate it if you drop some money into the donations box; chances are that the money actually will go to the mosque.

Body Language Turks say 'yes' (*evet*, eh-VEHT) by nodding forward and down.

To say 'no' (*hayır*, HAH-yuhr), nod your head up and back, lifting your eyebrows at the same time. Or just raise your eyebrows: that's 'no'.

Another way to say 'no' is *yok* (YOHK): literally, 'It doesn't exist (here)', or 'We don't have any (of it)' – the same head upward, raised eyebrows applies.

Remember, when a Turkish person seems to be giving you an arch look, they're only saying 'no'. They may also make the sound 'tsk', which also means 'no'. There are lots of ways to say 'no' in Turkish.

By contrast, wagging your head from side to side doesn't mean 'no' in Turkish; it means 'I don't understand'. So if a Turkish person asks you, 'Are you looking for the bus to Ankara?' and you shake your head, they'll assume you don't understand English and will probably ask you the same question again, this time in German.

There are other signs that can sometimes cause confusion, especially when you are out shopping. For instance, if you want to indicate length ('I want a fish this big'), don't hold your hands apart at the desired length, but hold out your arm and place a flat hand on it, measuring from your fingertips to the hand. Thus, if you want a pretty big fish, you must 'chop' your arm with your other hand at about the elbow.

Height is indicated by holding a flat hand the desired distance above the floor or some other flat surface such as a counter or table top.

If someone – a shopkeeper or restaurant waiter, for instance – wants to show you the stockroom or the kitchen, they'll signal 'Come on, follow me' by waving a hand downward and towards themselves in a scooping motion. Waggling an upright finger would never occur to them, except perhaps as a vaguely obscene gesture.

RELIGION

The Turkish population is 99% Muslim, mostly of the Sunni creed; there are groups of Shiites in the east and south-east. As non-Muslim groups make up less than 1% of the population, to talk about Turkish religion is to talk about Islam.

The story of Islam's founding is covered in the earlier History section.

Principles of Islam

The basic beliefs of Islam are these: God (Allah) created the world and everything in it pretty much according to the biblical account. In fact, the Bible is a sacred book to Muslims. Adam, Noah, Abraham, Moses and Jesus were prophets. Their teachings and revelations are accepted by Muslims, except for Jesus' divinity and his status as saviour. Jews and Christians are called 'People of the Book', meaning those with a revealed religion that preceded Islam. The Koran prohibits enslavement of any People of the Book. Jewish prophets and wise men, and Christian saints and martyrs, are all accepted as holy in Islam.

However, Islam is the 'perfection' of this earlier tradition. Though Moses and Jesus were great prophets, Muhammed was the greatest and last, *the* Prophet. To him, God communicated his final revelation, and entrusted him to communicate it to the world. Muhammed is not a saviour, nor is he divine. He is God's messenger, deliverer of the final, definitive message.

Muslims do not worship Muhammed, only God. In fact, *Muslim* in Arabic means, 'one who has submitted to God's will'; *Islam* is 'submission to God's will'. It's all summed up in the Ezan, the phrase called out from the minaret five times a day and said at the beginning of Muslim prayers: 'God is great! There is no god but God, and Muhammed is his Prophet'.

The Koran

God's revelations to Muhammed are contained in the *Kur'an-i Kerim*, the Holy Koran. Muhammed recited the *Suras* (verses or chapters) of the Koran in an inspired state. They were written down by followers, and are still regarded as the most beautiful, melodic and poetic work in Arabic literature, sacred or profane. The Koran, being sacred, cannot be translated. It exists in its true form in Arabic only.

The Islamic Commonwealth

Ideally, Islam is a commonwealth, a theocracy, in which the religious law of the Koran is the only law – there is no secular law. Courts are religious courts. In Turkey and several other Muslim countries, this belief has been replaced by secular law codes.

By contrast, Ayatollah Khomeini attempted to do away with secular law and return to the exclusive use of Islamic law in the Islamic Republic of Iran. In Saudi Arabia, religious law of the strict Wahhabi sect rules as well.

Religious Duties & Practices

To be a Muslim, one need only submit in one's heart to God's will and perform a few basic and simple religious duties:

- One must say, understand and believe, 'There is no god but God, and Muhammed is his Prophet'.
- One must pray five times daily: at dawn, at noon, at mid-afternoon, at dusk and after dark.
- One must give alms to the poor.
- One must keep the fast of Ramazan, if capable of doing so.
- One must make a pilgrimage to Mecca once during one's life, if possible.

Muslim prayers are set rituals. Before praying, Muslims must wash hands and arms, feet and ankles, head and neck in running water; if no water is available, in clean sand; if there's no sand, the motions will suffice. Then they must cover their head, face Mecca and perform a precise series of gestures and genuflections. If they deviate from the pattern, they must begin again.

In daily life, a Muslim must not touch or eat pork, nor drink wine (interpreted as any alcoholic beverage), and must refrain from fraud, usury, slander and gambling. No sort of image of any 'being with an immortal soul' (ie human or animal) can be revered or worshipped in any way.

Islam has been split into many factions and sects since the time of Muhammed. Islamic theology has become very elaborate and complex. These tenets, however, are still the basic ones shared by all Muslims.

LANGUAGE

The national language of Turkey is – naturally – Turkish. Turks don't expect any foreigner to know Turkish, but if you can manage a few words it will always be appreciated. For their part, they'll try whatever foreign words they know, usually English or German.

For the meanings of common terms used throughout this book, and Turkish words and phrases you might encounter on signs, refer to the Glossary at the back of this book. For a basic guide to Turkish and a list of useful words and phrases, see the Turkish Language Guide chapter, also at the back of this book.

Facts for the Visitor

SUGGESTED ITINERARIES

Any itinerary is an expression of interest, energy, time and money. You can see a lot of the country if you spend from six to eight weeks, but if your time is limited, here are some suggestions. These are *minimal* times.

Less than a Week (three to five days)
İstanbul, with an overnight trip to İznik and Bursa, or Troy and the Dardanelles. You might also take a day excursion by plane to Ephesus and return.

Basic One-Week Itinerary (seven to nine days)
İstanbul (two nights), Bursa (one night), Gallipoli and Troy (one night), Bergama, İzmir and Kuşadası (two nights), excursions to Ephesus, Priene, Miletus, Didyma; return to İstanbul (one night). Spend any extra time in İstanbul.

Two Weeks
Add an excursion from Kuşadası via Aphrodisias to Pamukkale and Hierapolis (one to two

Highlights of Turkey

There's a lot to see and do in Turkey. Here are some of the highlights to whet your appetite:

Turkish Architecture The great imperial mosques of İstanbul are perhaps the most famous image of Turkey. If you're at all interested in the art of architecture, Turkey is a treasure-house. Be sure to see the Süleymaniye, the Sultan Ahmet Camii and the Rüstem Paşa mosques in İstanbul; the Selimiye and Eski Cami in Edirne; and – way off the beaten track – the great Ulu Cami at Divriği, near Sivas.

Ancient Cities Unless your home country has hundreds of Greek and Roman archaeological sites, you'll enjoy strolling through Ephesus, Aphrodisias, Priene, Miletus, Didyma, Hierapolis, Termessos – the list seems endless. At the most spectacular sites (such as those named above), you'll see fine classical buildings, ancient inscriptions, intricate mosaics, and lots of other people. At the more remote sites, you may find yourself alone among picturesque tumbled-down marble temples, the only sound being that of the fragrant, soughing pines which surround you.

Water Sports Turkey's 7000km of coastline means that aquatic activity is a natural. The waters of the Black Sea are pretty chilly, but the Aegean and Mediterranean coasts are excellent from late April through October.

Museums Every city and town in Turkey has its museum, usually a mundane place with simple displays ... but the exhibits may be stone implements from the dawn of human history, Roman sculpture, Hellenic jewellery, Byzantine icons, Ottoman calligraphy, Turkish folklore, or all of the above. A number of Turkish museums are world-class, including İstanbul's Topkapı Sarayı, its archaeological museums, and the Türk ve İslam Eserleri Müzesi; Ankara's Anadolu Medeniyetleri Müzesi; the Antalya Müzesi; the Antakya Müzesi for its Roman mosaics; and Bodrum's Museum of Underwater Archaeology.

Hamams The Turkish bath, or hamam, is the direct successor to the Roman steam baths of two millennia ago. If you've never enjoyed a Turkish bath, you must do so in Turkey. You'll nights); also take a loop excursion to Ankara, Konya and Cappadocia. Visit the Hittite cities. If you have time left over, spend a day or two on the Turquoise Coast (Kaş, Antalya, Side, Alanya).

Three Weeks
Add a yacht cruise or coastal highway excursion from Kuşadası south to Bodrum (Halicarnassus), Marmaris, Fethiye, Kaş, Finike, Kemer and Antalya; or second-best, an excursion along the Black Sea coast. Another option is a tour to the south-east – Şanlıurfa, Mardin and Diyarbakır – which is best done at a time other than blazing-hot July and August.

Eastern Tour
A 14 to 21-day tour for mid-May to early October only: a circuit beginning in Ankara or Cappadocia going to Adıyaman and Nemrut Dağı (Mt Nimrod), Diyarbakır, Van, Doğubeyazıt and Mt Ararat, Erzurum, Kars, Artvin, Hopa, Rize, Trabzon, Samsun, Amasya and returning to Ankara via Boğazkale (Hattuşaş).

PLANNING

When to Go

Spring and autumn are best, roughly from April to June and from September to

Highlights of Turkey

never know how clean and refreshed you can feel until you do. All cities and most towns have public baths, often beautiful, historic Ottoman buildings.

Hiking Perhaps the best mountain hiking is in the Kaçkar Dağları along the eastern Black Sea coast near Ayder; or on the southern side of the range around Yusufeli. Try the walk from Fethiye to Ölüdeniz via the Ottoman Greek ghost town of Kayaköy, or a hike in the hills above Köprülü Kanyon near Side on the Mediterranean coast. The surreal valleys of Cappadocia make for fine hikes in the morning and evening when there's less heat and more golden light.

Skiing Turkish ski resorts are simple compared to those in Europe or North America. But if you visit Turkey in winter and simply have to get on a slope, the best facilities are at Uludağ, near Bursa. The slopes of volcanic Erciyes Dağı near Kayseri are convenient to Cappadocia, and new hotels at Palandöken near Erzurum anticipate increased interest in skiing the mountains of eastern Turkey.

Shopping İstanbul's Kapalı Çarşı has 4000 shops selling leather apparel and accessories, coloured tiles, brass and copper ware, antiques and fake antiques, old coins, carpets and kilims, meerschaum pipes and ornaments, silk scarves, perfumes and colognes – the list goes on. Many larger towns also have historic covered markets stuffed with Turkish treasures.

Yacht Cruising Whether you take a day-long excursion from Fethiye, rent a cabin for a three-day sail from Bodrum, or charter an entire *gulet* (traditional Turkish motor-sailer) for a week-long 'Blue Voyage' out of Marmaris, a journey by boat along the Aegean or Mediterranean coast will be among the most vivid memories of your trip.

Keyf *Keyf* is the Turkish art of quiet relaxation. Opportunities for it abound in Turkey. Sitting in the shade of a palm tree, sipping a drink, watching the sun set over the Aegean; enjoying a bracing glass of tea beneath a jasmine vine in the fresh morning air; stretching out in the warm sun on the deck of a boat headed for the ancient port of Knidos. That's keyf!

October. The climate is perfect on the Aegean and Mediterranean coasts then, as well as in İstanbul. It's cooler in Central Anatolia, but not unpleasantly so. Normally, there is little rain between May and October except along the Black Sea coast. If you visit before mid-June or after August, you may avoid the mosquitoes which can be a plague in some areas.

Most places to stay and restaurants in coastal resorts close from late October to early April, though a few remain open year-round.

The best months for water sports are July and August, but the water is fine in May, June, September and October too.

In the hottest months on the coasts you may have to take a siesta during the heat of the day between noon and 3 pm. Get up early in the morning, clamber around the local ruins, then after lunch and a siesta, come out again for *piyasa vakti* (promenade time) when everyone strolls by the sea, sits in a cafe, and watches the sunset.

If you plan a trip to eastern Turkey, go there in late June, July, August or September. As a general rule, you should not venture into the east before mid-May or after mid-October unless you're prepared, as there may be snow, perhaps even enough to close roads and mountain passes. Unfortunately, a tour of eastern Turkey in high summer usually includes passing through the south-east, which is beastly hot at that time.

See The Calendar section later in this chapter for further weather information and details of religious festivals and other special events.

Maps

Lonely Planet's *Turkey travel atlas* (126 pages, US$14.95) covers the entire country at a scale of 1:800,000 in a handy format which includes travel and transport tips in English, French, German, Spanish and Japanese, as well as colour photographs.

Of the British maps, the Bartholomew *Euromap Turkey* (two sheets) covers the country at 1:800,000 for about US$10 per sheet; the *AA/ESR Tourist Map Turkey* is also good, covering the entire country at 1:2,000,000; the south-west coast at 1:750,000; and includes street plans of İstanbul, İzmir and several tourist resorts.

Germany produces several good series, including the Reise und Verkehrsverlag's *Euro-Atlas* series which covers the country in two sheets, eastern and western Turkey at 1:800,000. They also have some city maps, including a detailed street plan of İstanbul in both map and atlas form; take your pick. Kümmerly + Frey has a fairly good sheet which covers the entire country, as does Hallwag.

Turkish-produced maps often lack detail or contain inaccuracies, so you'd be well advised to bring a good map from home. If you buy a Turkish one, try to get the Turkish Touring & Automobile Association's *East Turkey* and/or *West Turkey* at 1:850,000, for about US$5 each. They divide the country at Kayseri and do not show the railways. Don't trust these maps for back roads, though, particularly in the east.

For İstanbul, the useful *İstanbul A-Z Rehber-Atlas* is sold in many foreign-language and tourist-oriented bookshops for about US$10.

What to Bring

In the hottest months from mid-June to mid-September, you'll need light cotton summer clothes, and a light sweater or jacket for the evenings or to wear up on the Central Anatolian Plateau. You won't really need rain gear at all. You would do better to duck between the showers rather than haul rain gear during your entire trip just for a possible day or two of rain on the Black Sea coast.

In spring and autumn, summer clothing is still OK, but the evenings are cooler. If you plan to travel extensively in Central Anatolia (to Ankara, Konya, Cappadocia or Nemrut Dağı) after mid-October or before mid-May, pack a heavier sweater and perhaps a light raincoat.

Winter wear – for December to March – is woollens and rain gear. Though it doesn't get really cold along the Mediterranean coast, it does get damp, rainy and chilly in most of the country, including along the southern coast. İstanbul and İzmir get dustings of snow; Ankara gets more. Nemrut Dağı and the eastern region are frigid and covered in snow.

Formal or Informal? How does one dress in a Muslim country? In Turkey, men dress pretty much as they would for Europe; women should dress on the conservative side.

In the height of summer, no one will really expect men to have a coat and tie, even when visiting a government official. Women should avoid clothing that is particularly revealing.

For the rest of the year, Turks tend to dress formally in formal situations such as at the office or in a good restaurant or nightclub, but informally at other times. Neat and tidy dress is still admired here. Tatty or careless clothes, a sign of nonchalance or independence in other societies, are looked upon as tatty or careless in Turkey. T-shirts and shorts are the mark of the summer tourist.

Anyone can visit a Turkish mosque so long as they look presentable. Clothes must be neat – no shorts or sleeveless shirts on either men or women; women require skirts of a modest length (knees) and a headscarf.

RESPONSIBLE TOURISM

Tourism has made a huge economic and social impact on Turkey during the last two decades. While bringing in much-needed money to support local economies and workers, it has also fostered rapid and pervasive social change.

For example, until the 1970s it was frowned upon for a male and female to show affection in public; even a kiss or holding hands between husband and wife was illegal (though rarely enforced). Today many tourists go topless on Turkey's Mediterranean beaches, are photographed and appear on the front pages of national newspapers.

Likewise, public drunkenness used to be almost unheard of; today it is a growing problem.

The shock of this rapid cultural change may have encouraged the growth of Islamic fundamentalism as people seek a firm grounding amid bewildering novelty.

As a tourist, you should be sensitive to these currents and to the sensitivities of your Turkish hosts. See the sections on Ecology & Environment and Society & Conduct in the Facts About Turkey chapter, and also the Customs section in this chapter.

TOURIST OFFICES

Local Tourist Offices

Every Turkish town of any size has a Tourism Information Office run by the Ministry of Tourism and marked by the fan-like Hittite sun figure. Some are staffed by helpful people with more or less knowledge about the area; others are attended by those who see tourists as interruptions in their otherwise somnolent and comfortable daily routine. There may also be an office operated by the city or provincial government, or by a local tourism association (Turizm Derneği). Locations of all are given in the text.

If you need help and can't find an office, ask for the Belediye Sarayı (Municipality). They'll rummage around for someone who speaks some English.

Turkish Tourist Offices Abroad

Turkey has tourist offices in the following countries:

Australia
(☎ 02-9223 3055, fax 9223 3204, turkish@ozemail.com.au)
Suite 101, 280 George St, Sydney, NSW 2000

Canada
(☎ 613-230 8654, fax 230 3683)
Constitution Square, 360 Albert St, Suite 801, Ottawa, ON K1R 7X7

UK
(☎ 0171-629 7771, fax 491 0773, from 22 April 2000 ☎ 020-7629 7771, fax 020-7491 0773, eb25@cityscape.co.uk)
170-173 Piccadilly, 1st floor, London, W1V 9DD

USA
(☎ 212-687 2194, fax 599 7568, www.turkey.org/turkey)
821 UN Plaza, New York, NY 10017

VISAS & DOCUMENTS

Passport

Nationals of the following countries (partial list) can enter Turkey for up to three months with just a valid passport; a visa is not required: Australia, Belgium, Canada, Denmark, Finland, France, Germany, Greece, Holland, Iceland, Japan, New Zealand, Norway, Sweden and Switzerland.

Make sure your passport has at least three months' validity remaining, or you may not be admitted.

Visas

Nationals of Austria, Ireland, Israel, Italy, Portugal, Spain, the UK and the USA may enter Turkey after obtaining a multiple-entry sticker visa at the border or airport.

UK nationals should carry a cash UK£10 note (English, not Scottish) to pay for the visa.

Nationals of the USA must pay US$45 in cash for the visa.

Residence Permit

If you plan to stay in Turkey for more than three months, you might want to apply for an *ikamet tezkeresi* (residence permit). Contact a tourist office or tourism police office. You will need to show means of support: savings, a steady income from outside the country, or legal work within the country (see Work later in this chapter). Most people staying for a shorter period, or working without a valid permit (as short-term private tutors of English, for example), cross the border into Greece for a day or two every three months rather than bother with the residence permit.

Driving Licence & Permits

Drivers must have a valid driving licence; an International Driving Permit is useful, but not normally required. Your own national driving licence should be sufficient. Third-party insurance, such as a Green Card, valid for the entire country (not just for Thrace or European Turkey), or a Turkish policy purchased at the border is obligatory.

International Health Card

You need proof of vaccination against infectious diseases only if you are coming from an endemic or epidemic area.

Special Discounts

Holders of International Student Identity Cards (ISICs) are granted discounts of 25% to 33% on the admission fees at some museums. It's a good idea to show your student card before you show your money.

Students with ISICs get discounts of 10% on Turkish State Railways and on Turkish Maritime Lines ships. Turkish Airlines, which used to give good student discounts, does not do so any more. However, the airline offers a 10% 'family discount' to husband-and-wife couples, with or without children.

Turkey is part of Wasteels and Inter-Rail Youth discount schemes for rail. You'll save on train fares if you have one of these cards.

Those over 65 years of age receive free or discounted admission to some archaeological and historical sites and museums. Show your passport to prove that you are of the *Altın Yaş* (Golden Age).

EMBASSIES & CONSULATES

Turkish Embassies

Here are the details on Turkish embassies:

Australia
 (☎ 02-6295 0227, fax 6239 6592)
 60 Mugga Way, Red Hill, ACT 2603
Bulgaria
 (☎ 02-980 2270, fax 981 9358)
 Blvd Vasil Levski No 80, 1000 Sofia
Canada
 (☎ 613-789 4044, fax 789-3442)
 197 Wurtemburg St, Ottawa, Ontario KIN 8L9
Greece
 (☎ 01-724 5915, fax 722 9597)
 Vasilissis Georgiou B 8, 10674 Athens
UK
 (☎ 0171-393 0202, fax 393 0066, from 22 April 2000 ☎ 020-7393 0202, fax 020-7393 0066)
 43 Belgrave Square, London, SW1X 8PA
USA
 (☎ 202-659 8200, fax 659 0744)
 1714 Massachusetts Ave NW, Washington, DC, 20036

Embassies & Consulates in Turkey

Here are some of the foreign missions to Turkey:

Australia *(Avustralya)*
ANKARA EMBASSY
(☎ 312-446 1180, fax 446 1188)
Nene Hatun Caddesi 83, 06700 Gaziosmanpaşa
İSTANBUL CONSULATE
(☎ 212-257 7050, fax 257 7054)
Tepecik Yolu 58, 80630 Etiler, open from 8.30 am to 12.30 pm weekdays

Bulgaria *(Bulgaristan)*
ANKARA EMBASSY
(☎ 312-426 7456, fax 427 3178)
Atatürk Bulvarı 124, Kavaklıdere
İSTANBUL CONSULATE
(☎ 212-2269 0478, 269 2216)
Zincirlikuyu Caddesi 44, Ulus, Levent; take bus No 210 behind Sultanahmet tourist office to Beşiktaş, get out and take bus No 58/L, 58/1 or 58/2 to Zincirlikuyu, a 1½-hour trip.

Canada *(Kanada)*
ANKARA EMBASSY
(☎ 312-436 1275, fax 446 4437)
Nene Hatun Caddesi 75, 06700 Gaziosmanpaşa
İSTANBUL HONORARY CONSULATE
(☎ 212-272 5174)
Büyükdere Caddesi 107/3, Bengün Han, 3rd floor, Gayrettepe

France *(Fransa)*
ANKARA EMBASSY
(☎ 312-468 1154, fax 467 1489)
Paris Caddesi 70, Kavaklıdere
İSTANBUL CONSULATE
(☎ 212-243 1852, fax 249 9168)
İstiklal Caddesi 8, Taksim

Greece *(Yunanistan)*
ANKARA EMBASSY
(☎ 312-436 8861, fax 446 3191)
Ziya-ur-Rahman (Karagöz) Caddesi 9-11, 06610 Gaziosmanpaşa
İSTANBUL CONSULATE
(☎ 212-245 0596, fax 252 1365)
Turnacıbaşı Sokak 32, Ağahamam, Kuloğlu, Beyoğlu

Iran *(İran)*
ANKARA EMBASSY
(☎ 312-427 4320, fax 468 2823)
Tahran Caddesi 10, Kavaklıdere
İSTANBUL CONSULATE
(☎ 212-513 8230)
Ankara Caddesi 1/2, Cağaloğlu

Iraq *(Irak)*
ANKARA EMBASSY
(☎ 312-468 7421, fax 468 4832)
Turan Emeksiz Sokak 11, 06692 Gaziosmanpaşa
İSTANBUL CONSULATE
(☎ 212-230 2930/3, fax 234 5726)
Halide Edip Adıvar Mahallesi, İpekböceği Sokak 1

Netherlands *(Holanda)*
ANKARA EMBASSY
(☎ 312-446 0470, fax 446 3358)
Uğur Mumcu Caddesi 16, Gaziosmanpaşa
İSTANBUL CONSULATE
(☎ 212-251 5030, fax 251 9289)
İstiklal Caddesi 393, Tünel, Beyoğlu

New Zealand *(Yeni Zelanda)*
ANKARA EMBASSY
(☎ 312-467 9054, fax 467 9013, newzealand@superonline.com.tr)
Level 4, İran Caddesi 13, Kavaklıdere 06700 (PO Box/PK162 Kavaklıdere 06692)
İSTANBUL CONSULATE
(☎ 212-275 2989, fax 275 5008)
Maya Akar Center, 24th floor, Büyükdere Caddesi 100/102, Esentepe 80280

Syria *(Suriye)*
ANKARA EMBASSY
(☎ 312-440 9657, fax 438 5609)
Sedat Simavi Sokak 40, 06680 Çankaya
İSTANBUL CONSULATE
(☎ 212-232 6721)
Maçka Caddesi 59

UK *(İngiltere, Birleşik Krallığı)*
ANKARA EMBASSY
(☎ 312-468 6230, fax 468 3214)
Şehit Ersan Caddesi 46/A, Çankaya
ANTALYA CONSULATE
(☎ 242-247 7000, fax 247 7005)
Üçgen Mahallesi, Dolaplıdere Caddesi, Pırıltı Sitesi, Kat 1, İlit Sauna Karşısı
BODRUM CONSULATE
(☎ 252-316 4932, fax 313 0052)
Atatürk Caddesi, Adliye Sokak 12/C
İSKENDERUM CONSULAR AGENCY
(☎ 326-613 0361, fax 613 0364)
Catoni Maritime Agencies, Mareşal Çakmak Caddesi 28
İSTANBUL CONSULATE
(☎ 212-293 7545, fax 245 4989)
Meşrutiyet Caddesi 34, Tepebaşı, Beyoğlu
İZMİR VICE CONSULATE
(☎ 232-463 5151, fax 421 2914)
Mahmut Esat Bozkurt Caddesi, 1442 Sokak No 49, Alsancak
MARMARİS CONSULAR AGENCY
(☎ 252-412 6486, fax 412 5077)

Yeşil Marmaris Tourism & Yacht Management, Barbaros Caddesi 118
MERSİN VICE-CONSULATE
(☎ 324-232 1248, fax 232 2991)
Catoni Maritime Agencies, Çakmak Caddesi, Mersin Orta Okulu Sokak 3/B

USA *(Amerika Birleşik Devletleri, Amerika)*
ANKARA EMBASSY
(☎ 312-468 6110, fax 467 0019)
Atatürk Bulvarı 110, Kavaklıdere
İSTANBUL CONSULATE
(☎ 212-251 3602, fax 267 0057)
Meşrutiyet Caddesi 104-108, Tepebaşı, Beyoğlu
İZMİR CONSULATE
(☎ 232-441 2203, fax 441 2373)
Kâzım Dirik Caddesi, Atabay İş Merkezi 13/8, Pasaport, 35210

CUSTOMS

Upon entering the country, customs inspection is often very cursory for foreign tourists. There may be spot-checks, but you probably won't have to open your bags.

Arriving in Turkey

A verbal declaration is usually all you need; the major airports use the red and green channel system. You can bring in up to 1kg of coffee, 5L of liquor and two cartons (400) of cigarettes. Things of exceptional value (jewellery, unusually expensive electronic or photographic gear etc) are supposed to be declared and may be entered in your passport to guarantee that you will take the goods out of the country when you leave.

Vehicles Automobiles, minibuses, trailers, towed watercraft, motorcycles and bicycles can be brought in for up to three months without a carnet or triptyque (a customs licence allowing the temporary importation of a motor vehicle). See also Driving Licence & Permits in Visas & Documents earlier in this chapter.

Departing Turkey

It is illegal to buy, sell, possess or export antiquities! Read on.

You may export valuables (except antiquities) that have been registered in your passport on entry, or that have been purchased with legally converted money. For souvenirs, the maximum export limit is US$1000 of all items combined; if two or more similar items are exported, a licence may be required. Also, you may need to show proof of exchange transactions for at least these amounts. Save your currency exchange slips, and have them ready for the customs officer who will confront you after passport control, as you make your way to your departing flight.

Your bags may well be searched when you leave the country (both for customs and security reasons) and questions may be asked about whether or not you are taking any antiquities with you. Only true antiquities much more than a century old are off limits, not newer items or the many artful fakes. If you buy a real Roman coin from a shepherd boy at an archaeological site, can you take it home with you? Legally not. What happens if you get caught trying to smuggle out a significant piece of ancient statuary? Big trouble.

Turkey is one of those countries with treasure-troves of antiquities, some of which are smuggled out of the country and fed into the international contraband art market. The Turkish government takes vigorous measures to defend its patrimony against theft. Antiquity smuggling, like drug smuggling, is a dirty business. Don't do anything that makes you look like you're a part of it.

Arriving Home

British readers have written to warn that you should get official-looking receipts from Turkish shopkeepers for any expensive item you purchase to take home to the UK. British customs officers may expect you to underdeclare, asking 'What did you *really* pay?'. If you budge from your original price (as on the receipt), they'll read you the riot act and you'll have to cough up some duty. If you try to smuggle dutiable goods through the 'green' channel and are caught, they may offer you a choice: pay a fine equal to the price you paid for the goods abroad, or face criminal prosecution. In any country it is best to make a full and honest declaration to avoid expensive unpleasantness.

MONEY

Currency

The unit of currency is the Turkish *lira*, or TL, which was called the Turkish pound (LT) in Ottoman times. The lira is supposedly divided into 100 *kuruş* (koo-ROOSH), but inflation of roughly 70% to 100% per year has rendered the kuruş obsolete. Even a minor purchase of something costing under US$10 now takes several million liras. Soon the Turkish government will have to drop at least three, and possibly more zeros from the currency.

Coins are 1000, 2500, 5000, 10,000 and, as time goes on, ever higher denominations. Banknotes come as 10,000, 20,000, 50,000, 100,000, 250,000, 500,000, one million etc. With all those zeros, it's often difficult to make sure you're giving the proper notes – or getting the correct change. Beware of shopkeepers and taxi drivers who may try to give you a 50,000 lira note in place of a 500,000, or a 100,000 note instead of a one million.

When the government eliminates some zeros on the currency, the confusion will be far greater as old lira notes with all the zeros will remain in circulation with the new notes, at least for a time. Take your time and be sure of amounts.

Exchange Rates

With inflation at 100% in Turkey, the value of the lira drops daily. An exchange rate table is not provided as it would be prehistoric by the time you arrive.

Exchanging Money

Wait until you arrive in Turkey to change your home currency (cash or travellers cheques) into Turkish liras. Exchange offices in other countries (eg the UK, USA) usually offer terrible rates of exchange. When in doubt, check the foreign exchange listings in the business section of any important daily newspaper, or call a commercial bank. A proper tourist exchange rate will be only a few percentage points less than – and may well be better than – this published rate.

With the value of the Turkish lira constantly dropping, it's wise to change money every few days rather than all at once at the beginning of your visit.

You will always need your passport when you change travellers cheques in Turkey, and you may need it when you change cash as well.

Many tourist shops, travel agencies, expensive restaurants and most hotels accept foreign currency, though they often give bad rates of exchange. Most post office (PTT) branches will give you liras for foreign cash, but not always for travellers cheques.

Banks & Exchange Offices Banks are open from 8.30 am to noon and from 1.30 to 5 pm from Monday to Friday. Outside those times it can be difficult to change money, so plan ahead, and anticipate holidays such as Şeker Bayramı and Kurban Bayramı (see Business Hours and Holidays & Special Events later in this chapter).

It's a good idea to change some money when you enter Turkey – US$25 or US$50 at least. There are currency exchange desks that are open long hours, and also ATMs, at the major entry points to Turkey by road, air and sea. It's a good practice not to change money at the first exchange booth you encounter at an airport or other point of entry, as it may take advantage of its premier position to give a low exchange rate. Also, the clerk may attempt to take advantage of your confusion and jet lag by giving you less than you're supposed to get. Make sure the amount of cash you're given agrees with the amount shown on your exchange receipt.

Many banks will change money. Keep an eye out for a sign on or near the front door reading 'Kambiyo – Exchange – Change – Wechsel', which says it all. In the large cities, big banks have branches everywhere, even within 100m of one another, and exchange facilities may be limited to the more convenient branches. If a particular branch can't change your money, clerks will direct you to one that can.

In many cities, nonbank currency exchange offices handle much of the exchange business. They prefer to change cash – and may even require that it be US dollars or deutschmarks – but may change travellers cheques if you pressure them.

Procedures Changing money, either travellers cheques or banknotes, can often take anywhere from two to 20 minutes, depending upon the bank and how cumbersome its procedures are. Sometimes a clerk must type up a form with your name and passport number, you must sign it once or twice, then it must be countersigned by one or two bank officers before you get your money. Always take your passport when changing money at a bank and be prepared to wait a while. Currency exchange offices are generally much faster and more efficient than banks.

Commissions Some banks charge a fee for changing travellers cheques (though not for changing cash notes). To find out before you begin, ask *Komisyon alınır mı?* (koh-meess-YOHN ah-luh-NUHR muh, 'Is a commission taken?'). Sometimes the teller will scribble some figures on the back of the form, then pay out your liras several thousand short, saying this is a commission, but will give no receipt. Don't let them do this. It's your money they're keeping.

Travellers Cheques

Turkish banks, shops and hotels often see it as a burden to change travellers cheques (including Eurocheques) and may try to get you to go elsewhere. You must often press the issue. The more expensive hotels, restaurants and shops will more readily accept the cheques, as will car rental agencies and travel agencies, but not at good exchange rates. Generally it's better to change cheques to Turkish liras at a bank, although some banks may charge a fee (see the previous Commissions section).

Exchange Receipts Save your currency exchange *bordro* (receipts). You may need them to change back Turkish liras at the end of your stay, and to show to the customs officer if you've purchased expensive souvenirs such as carpets or jewellery. Turkish liras are worth less outside the country, so you won't want to take any with you.

ATMs

Automated teller machines (ATMs, cashpoints etc) are common in Turkish cities, towns and resorts. Virtually all offer instructions in English, French, German and Turkish, and will pay out Turkish liras as a cash advance when you insert your major credit card (especially Visa). The daily limit on payouts is the equivalent of about US$250 per day; the exchange rate at which the transaction is processed is usually among the best you can get.

Most machines also accept bank cash (debit) cards in principle, if not in fact. The specific machine you use must be reliably connected to one of the major cashpoint networks such as Cirrus or Plus Systems. Look for stickers with the logos of these services affixed to the machine. If the connection is not reliable, you may get a message saying that the transaction was refused by your bank (which may not be true), and your card will be returned to you. Try another machine.

ATMs also suffer from an insufficiency of telephone lines to foreign bank databases, and your transaction may not go through. Try in the evening, early morning, or on the weekend.

All major Turkish banks – Akbank, Garanti Bankası, Türkiye İş Bankası, Pamukbank, Yapı Kredi and Ziraat Bankası – and some smaller banks, have ATMs connected to the Visa system, allowing you to take cash advances on your Visa credit card. Akbank, Pamukbank and Yapı Kredi also claim to have the most machines connected to Plus Systems, so that you can withdraw money from your bank account with your bank cash card. I've found Yapı Kredi cashpoints to be the most convenient and reliable.

Credit & Cash Cards

Big hotels, car rental agencies and the more expensive shops will usually accept your credit card. Make sure in advance because not all establishments accept all cards. If you have American Express, Visa, Diners Club, MasterCard, Access and Eurocard, you're probably equipped for any establishment that takes cards. If you only have one or two cards, ask. Turkish Airlines, for instance, may accept only Visa, MasterCard, Access and Eurocard. The Turkish State Railways doesn't accept credit cards at present, but it may soon do so. A souvenir shop may accept all major cards.

An insufficient number of telephone lines connect Turkey to the international credit card databases, so it is not always possible to obtain approval for a charge. The best times to try are in the evening, early morning and on weekends.

A few shopkeepers may still require you to pay the credit card fee, from 3% to 7%, or the charges (up to US$10) for making credit card arrangements with a bank. They could assume that any price haggled is for cash.

International Transfers

The PTT in Turkey handles postal money orders, and this is fine for small amounts. For large amounts, you'd do better with a bank.

Banks can wire money in a matter of a day or two (usually), for a fee of US$20 to US$40 per transfer. Sometimes the transfer fee is a percentage of the amount transferred. Have your passport with you when you go to receive your money.

If you have a credit or bank cash card, why not just have someone at home dump some money into your card account? You should be able to draw on it several days later.

Black Market

There is no currency black market as the Turkish lira is fully convertible.

Security

See the section on Dangers & Annoyances later in this chapter.

Costs

All costs in this guide are given only in US dollars as prices in Turkish liras (TL) would be hopelessly out of date before the book even emerged from the printer.

In recent years, inflation has been 75% to 100% per annum, and the Turkish lira has been subjected to a slow, creeping devaluation which offsets this inflation and keeps the actual cost for foreign visitors low. You may find some of the prices in this guide to be higher or lower than the amounts you'll actually pay. The situation is volatile, and prices can fluctuate from month to month, or even week to week.

Turkey is Europe's low-price leader, and you can travel on as little as US$15 to US$20 (average) per day using buses and trains, staying in pensions, and eating one restaurant meal daily. For US$20 to US$35 per person per day you can travel more comfortably by bus and train, staying in one and two-star hotels with private baths, and eating most meals in average restaurants. For US$30 to US$70 per day you can move up to three and four-star hotels, take the occasional airline flight, and dine in restaurants all the time. If you have more than US$100 per person to spend, you can travel luxury class. Costs are highest in İstanbul and lowest in small eastern towns off the tourist track.

Here are some average costs:

Single/double room without bath in small pension – US$8 to US$20
Single/double room with bath in one-star hotel – US$18 to US$40
Three-course meal in simple restaurant – US$6
Loaf of bread – US$0.35
Bottle of beer (from a shop) – US$0.95
1L of petrol/gasoline – US$0.70 to US$0.90
100km by express train (1st class) – US$1.80 to US$2.20
100km by bus – US$2.25 to US$3
Local telephone call – US$0.15
Turkish Daily News – US$0.80

Price Adjustments Government entities such as the Turkish State Railways, Turkish Maritime Lines and the Ministry of Culture (which administers many of the country's

Commissions – A Colossal Ripoff

In recent years the practice of paying commissions to anyone who brings in business has gotten completely out of hand in Turkey. If a taxi driver recommends a hotel and takes you there, he gets a commission. If a shill leads you to a carpet shop, he gets a commission. If your pension owner books you on a tour, she gets a commission.

Commissions, or finder's fees, are a normal part of doing business in most parts of the world. But in Turkey the fee is not 2% or 3% as in many places, or even the 10% common in the travel industry. It's at least 20%, more usually 30% or 35%, and often as high as 50% or more.

This money comes directly out of your pocket, but buys you almost nothing.

Many legitimate businesses despise the rage for commissions as much as travellers do. Pension owners resent freelance shills bringing customers to their door and demanding huge commissions when it's probable that customers would have found their way to the pension in any case. Carpet shops resent having to charge ever higher prices in order to cover the huge commissions demanded by the same importunate shills who have badgered you endlessly on the street. Indeed, there have been many ugly incidents between shopkeepers and shills.

The commission ripoff has even become big business. Package tour operators bring plane-loads of tourists from Europe at tour prices below the price of round-trip airfare alone. The groups are put up in hotels which are virtual shopping malls, and every day of bus touring includes a stop of several hours at a shop. The tour company regularly makes far more money from commission mark-ups on purchases than from the tour fee. (If tour participants were to seek out independent shops by themselves, they'd find all prices significantly lower.)

What to do? It's simple: don't go into a shop accompanied by anyone. Make your own reservations for special activities and events. Buy your own tickets. Sign up for a tour at the tour operator's office, not at your pension or hotel. Don't let anyone 'claim' you as their commission bait.

In some situations you needn't worry too much about commissions, as when a legitimate travel agency arranges a plane or train ticket for you (the normal 10% commission is included in the ticket price), or when you ask a pension owner to call ahead to a pension in the next town as a favour. Remember, most businesses resent the commission badgers as much as you do.

museums) may set prices at the beginning of the year, and then adjust them only every three or four months – if at all – throughout the year. Thus a two million TL museum admission ticket might cost you US$6 in January, but only US$4 or even US$3 later in the year. For this reason, many prices in this guide must be looked upon as approximate.

Private enterprises tend to adjust prices more frequently and many in the travel industry such as Turkish Airlines, Turkish Maritime Lines international routes, rental car firms and the more expensive hotels quote prices not in liras but in US dollars or in deutschmarks.

Tipping

Restaurants In the cheapest places tipping is not necessary, though some people do leave a few coins in the change plate. In more expensive restaurants, tipping is customary.

Some places will automatically add a *servis ücreti* (service charge) of 10% or 15% to your bill, but this does not absolve you from the tip, oddly enough. The service charge goes into the pocket of the *patron* (owner). Turks will give around 5% to the waiter directly, and perhaps the same amount to the head waiter.

If service is included, the bill may say *servis dahil* (service included). Still, a small tip is expected. In any situation, 5% to 10% is fine. Only in the fancy foreign-operated hotels will waiters expect those enormous 15% to 20% US-style tips. In the very plain, basic restaurants you needn't tip at all, though the price of a soft drink or a cup of coffee is always appreciated.

Hotels In the cheapest hotels there are few services and tips are not expected. In most hotels a porter will carry your luggage and show you to your room. For doing this he'll expect about 2% or 3% of the room price. So if your room costs US$30, give about US$0.60 to US$1. For any other chore done by a porter, a slightly smaller tip is in order.

Taxis Taxi drivers may look for a tip from you (especially on trips to the airport), but that's only because you're a foreigner and foreigners tip taxi drivers. Turks don't tip taxi drivers, though they often round off the metered fare. Thus, if the meter reads 916,000TL, it's quite common to give the driver one million. Conversely, if the fare is slightly more than a million TL, the driver may happily accept one million and wave off the extra coins.

A driver of a *dolmuş* – a cab or minibus that departs only when all seats are filled – never expects a tip or a fare to be rounded upwards.

Hairdressers In barbershops and hairdressers, pay the fee for the services rendered (which goes to the shop), then about 10% to the person who cut your hair, and smaller tips to the others who provided service, down to the one who brushes stray locks from your clothing as you prepare to leave (5% for that).

Hamams In a *hamam* (Turkish bath), there will be fees for the services, and in baths frequented mostly by Turks these will be sufficient. In tourist-oriented baths these prices may be an order of magnitude higher (US$20 instead of US$2!), in which case you may assume that service is included.

If staff in a nontourist bath approach you as you are leaving, share out 20% to 30% of the bath fees among them.

Sleeping Cars If you take a sleeping compartment on a train, the porter will come around near the end of the trip, request an official service charge of 10% of the sleeping car charge, give you a receipt for it, and hope for a small additional tip of around 5%.

Other Situations There are other situations in which a tip is indicated, but these must be handled delicately. For instance, at a remote archaeological site, local guardians may unlock the gate and show you around the ruins. The guardians will probably have official admission tickets, which you must pay for. If that's all they do, that's all you pay. But if they go out of their way to help you, you may want to offer a tip. They may be reluctant to accept it, and may refuse once or even twice. Try at least three times. They may well need the money, but the rules of politeness require several refusals. If they refuse three times, though, you can assume that they truly want to help you only for friendship's sake. Don't press matters further, for this will insult their good intentions.

In many of these situations, a token gift will be just as happily received as a cash tip. If you have some small item, particularly something distinctive from your home country, you can offer it in lieu of money.

Bargaining

See the section on Shopping later in this chapter.

Taxes & Refunds

There is a Value Added Tax (VAT) on most goods and services in Turkey. When leaving the country, tourists can claim the VAT paid on larger purchases. (See Value Added Tax under Shopping later in this chapter.)

POST & COMMUNICATIONS

Postal and telegraph services in Turkey are handled by the Posta Telgraf office, usually known as the PTT (peh-teh-TEH, *posta, telefon, telgraf*). However, the telephone service has been privatised. To find a PTT, look for the distinctive yellow signs with black 'PTT' letters. For hours of operation, see Business Hours later in this chapter.

Letter boxes and postal vehicles are yellow as well. Every town has a PTT, usually close to the main square. Go there to buy stamps, send letters, faxes and telegrams, or to make telephone calls if no other phone is available. It's best to post letters in the post office slots rather than in a letter box. The *Yurtdışı* slot is for mail to foreign countries, *Yurtiçi* is for mail to other Turkish cities and *Şehiriçi* is for mail within the city.

Many of the larger train stations and *otogars* (bus stations) in Turkey have their own branch PTTs.

Count your change carefully when buying stamps. Short-changing foreigners is common in some PTTs.

Anyone asking for stamps for Australia will invariably be asked *Avusturya Avustralya?* (Austria or Australia?) The two words are quite similar in Turkish, and every clerk's response is automatic. Get used to it.

Sending Mail

Express Mail The PTT operates an express mail, courier-type service called *acele posta servisi* (AH-jeh-leh POHSS-tah sehr-vee-see) or APS, which competes with international express carriers such as DHL, Federal Express and United Parcel Service. If you must have something reach its destination fast, ask for this. Don't confuse this courier service with the traditional *ekspres* (special delivery) service, which is slower.

Parcels To mail packages out of the country, or to receive dutiable merchandise, you must have your package opened for customs inspection, and you may have to endure a bit of frustrating red tape. Have paper, box, string, tape and marker pens with you when you go.

If you want to be sure that a parcel will get to its destination intact, send it by APS, an international courier service (DHL, Fedex, UPS) or at least *kayıtlı* (by registered mail).

Receiving Mail

Addresses Turkish postal addresses are usually written with the name of the main street first, then the minor street and then the name and number of the building. For example:

Bay Mustafa Adıyok
Geçilmez Sokak, Bulunmaz Çıkmazı
Lüks Apartımanı No 23/14
80200 Tophane
İSTANBUL

In this example, *Bay* means 'Mr'; for 'Mrs', 'Ms' or 'Miss', use *Bayan*, pronounced like the English phrase 'buy an ...'. The next line has the name of a largish street, 'Geçilmez Sokak', followed by the name of a smaller street, alley, or dead end, 'Bulunmaz Çıkmazı', which runs off it. The third line has the name of an apartment building, 'Lüks Apartımanı'. As for the numbers, the first one, '23', is the street number of the building; the second, '14', is the apartment or office number within the building. The district, 'Tophane', comes next, then the city. *Kat* in an address means floor, as in Kat 3, '3rd floor' (4th floor up if you count street level as the 1st floor).

The address can be written more simply when the desired building is on a large, well-known street. For example:

Bay Mustafa Adıyok
Büyük Caddesi No 44/10
80090 Taksim
İSTANBUL

In some cases, the district of the city is put at the beginning of the second line, eg 'Taksim, Büyük Caddesi No 44/10'. In any case, you've got to be familiar with the district names to find a certain address.

Turkey has a system of five-digit *posta kodu* (postal codes). Use the postal code if you have it.

Poste Restante If you are having mail sent, have it addressed this way:

(Name)
Poste Restante
Merkez Postahane
(District)
(City, Province)
TURKEY

Merkez Postane means Central or Main Post Office, which is where you should go to pick up your mail, passport in hand. The poste restante desk often keeps more limited hours than others, and may close for lunch.

Telephone

Turkey's country code is 90. You pay for a call on Türk Telekom's network with a *telekart* debit card, a credit card or, in a few older phones, a *jeton* (zheh-TOHN, token). Calls are measured in usage units, each of which costs about US$0.10; a local call of several minutes' duration costs one usage unit.

Cards 'Telekart' telephone debit cards are sold in shops and kiosks near public phones in values of 30, 60, 100, 120, or 180 telephone usage units. In general, a 30-unit card is sufficient for local calls; 60 for a short, domestic intercity call; 100 for a domestic intercity call of moderate length or a short international call; and the higher-value cards for longer domestic or international calls. Some newer phones also accept Visa and Mastercard/Eurocard/Access cards.

Kontürlü Telefon Some shops and kiosks have *kontürlü* telephones, that is, a phone with a meter attached. You make your call, the owner reads the meter and charges you accordingly. The cost of the call depends upon what the phone's owner charges for each unit (*kontür*) on the meter, so ask *Bir kontür kaç lira?* (How many liras does a unit cost?) It can vary from US$0.05 at a kiosk to US$0.15 (that is, three times as much) in a four-star hotel. Shop around.

Long-Distance Calls For inter-city calls, press '0' (zero), area code and local number. For international calls, press '0' twice, then the country code, area code and local number. For instance, to call 555 5555 in London, press 00 44 171 555 5555. For Melbourne, press 00 61 3 5555 5555. For New York, press 00 1 212 555 5555. Be patient; it can take as long as one minute for the connection to be made.

Rates for local and intercity domestic calls are moderate, but international calls can be quite expensive: almost UK£1 per minute to the UK, US$3 per minute to the USA, and even higher to Australia. Reduced rates are in effect from midnight to 7 am, and on Sunday. Beware of hotel surcharges, which can be as high as 100%. Perhaps the best strategy is to make a quick call, give the other person the telephone number and a time at which you can be reached, and have them call you back.

If you make an international call from a Türk Telekom telephone centre, be sure to get a receipt. Fiddling the bills is common as you see no meter and can't tell what a call will cost. Clerks are less willing to fiddle with an official receipt with an amount and their name on it.

Country Direct In theory, you can call one of the numbers below toll-free from Turkey to access your home telephone company, which may have cheaper rates. In practice, the call often doesn't go through.

Australia	☎ (00-800) 61 1177
Canada (Teleglobe)	☎ (00-800) 1 6677
France (Telecom)	☎ (00-800) 33 1177
Germany (PTT)	☎ (00-800) 49 1149
Ireland	☎ (00-800) 353 1177
Italy	☎ (00-800) 39 1177
Japan (IDC Direct)	☎ (00-800) 81 0086
Japan (IDC)	☎ (00-800) 81 0080
Japan (KDD)	☎ (00-800) 81 1177
Netherlands (PTT)	☎ (00-800) 31 1177
UK (BTI)	☎ (00-800) 44 1177
UK (Mercury)	☎ (00-800) 44 2277
USA (AT&T)	☎ (00-800) 1 2277
USA (MCI)	☎ (00-800) 1 1177
USA (SPRINT)	☎ (00-800) 1 4477

Telephone Etiquette Turks answer the phone by saying *Alo?* (from 'hello'), a word which is defined in Turkish dictionaries as 'Word said when answering the telephone' because it is never used otherwise. Turks may also say *Buyurun!* ('at your service'). When speaking to a Turk in whatever language, he or she is liable to say *hah!* now and then. This means 'yes', 'I agree', 'all right' or 'just so'.

Fax

Turks are addicted to fax machines. Most businesses including hotels, car rental companies and airlines have them. If you must make reservations in advance, this is the fastest and often the cheapest way. Usually you can send a fax in English, German or French and the recipients will have someone translate it and reply in the same language.

Though you can send a fax from one of the Türk Telekom phone centres, it's usually much quicker and easier – and usually not much more expensive – to send it from your hotel.

Email & Internet Access

Major cities and tourist centres all have cybercafes. Many small hotels and pensions around the country have Internet services which you can use for a fee to send and receive email. CompuServe has nodes (9600 bps) in Ankara (modem 312-468 8042) and İstanbul (modem 212-234 5168). America Online's İstanbul node is 212-234 5158 (28,800 bps).

Internet Resources

Lonely Planet's award-winning Web site at www.lonelyplanet.com is a rich resource for travellers. Here you can research your trip, hunt down bargain air fares, book hotels, check on weather conditions. You'll also find succinct summaries on travelling to most places on earth, postcards from other travellers and the Thorn Tree bulletin board, where you can ask questions before you go or dispense advice when you get back. You can also find travel news and updates to many of our most popular guidebooks, and the subWWWay section links you to the most useful travel resources elsewhere on the Web.

Also check out the information and Turkey travel tips and updates provided by Tom Brosnahan, the coordinating co-author of this guide book, at www.infoexchange.com.

There are many other Web sites dealing with Turkey. Most offer glacial download, browser-crashing complexity, mediocre information, and vigorous sales pitches. A few exceptions, all bilingual (Turkish and English) are:

www.turkishdailynews.com – the *Turkish Daily News* site has current information, weather and, in the classifieds section, ads for rental apartments, jobs as English teachers and translators etc

www.milliyet.com/e/ – *Milliyet*, a prominent national daily newspaper, provides news in slightly rickety but ambitious English

www.turkey.org – as might be expected, the official Turkish government site is rather dry, with full texts of government communiqués and speeches, but also visa, passport, consular and economic information, email addresses of Turkish diplomatic missions, and useful links to other sites related to Turkey

BOOKS

Everyone from St Paul to Mark Twain and Agatha Christie has written about Turkey. The books mentioned below have not been published in all countries by the same publisher, so publication information is not given. The titles used for some books may even change from country to country. Bookshops and libraries index books by author and title, so you should be able to locate those that are available in your country.

Lonely Planet

Besides this guide to Turkey, Lonely Planet has other titles which may assist you.

Istanbul city guide has expanded information on Turkey's largest city, plus many maps and walking tours.

Turkish phrasebook is truly a language survival kit, as it contains words and phrases useful to real-life situations as you travel. Besides including all the common words and phrases needed during travel, it covers the unmentionable situations in which you need to know the word for tampon or condom.

Turkey travel atlas covers the entire country at 1:800,000 in a handy format which includes travel and transport tips in

English, French, German, Spanish and Japanese, as well as colour photographs.

Travel with Children by Maureen Wheeler provides comprehensive information about what you can do to prepare yourself and enjoy your trip, wherever you may be travelling.

Guidebooks

This book was written to tell you just about everything you'd need to know on a first or even subsequent trip to Turkey. Other excellent guides exist, however, each with its own special interest.

For the literary minded, *Istanbul – a traveller's companion* (1987) by Laurence Kelly is a delight. The editor has combed through the writings of two millennia and collected the choicest bits, by the most interesting writers, relating to Byzantium, Constantinople and İstanbul. History, biography, diary and travellers' observations are all included.

Otherwise, the most interesting travel guides on Turkey are those published by the Redhouse Press of İstanbul. Founded under the Ottoman Empire as part of a US missionary effort, the Redhouse Press now does an admirable job of publishing dictionaries, guidebooks and general works designed to bridge the gap between the Turkish and English-speaking realms. Some of the Redhouse guides have been translated into German, French and Italian. Though only a few Redhouse books turn up in bookshops outside Turkey, you'll find them readily within the country itself, in decent editions at moderate prices. A good example of a Redhouse work is *Religious Sites in Turkey* (1997) by Anna G Edmonds.

Travel

The published diaries and accounts of earlier travellers in Turkey provide fascinating glimpses of Ottoman life. One of the more familiar of these is Mark Twain's *Innocents Abroad*. Twain accompanied a group of wealthy tourists on a chartered boat which sailed the Black Sea and eastern Mediterranean more than a century ago. Many of the things he saw in İstanbul haven't changed much.

A Fez of the Heart by Jeremy Seal is the account of the author's recent journeys throughout Turkey in search of Turks who still wear the fez. Despite its unfortunate title it's a witty, entertaining inquiry into resurgent Islam and what it means to be a 'modern' Turk.

Tim Kelsey's *Dervish* is a more sobering account of a similar journey which grows darker the further east he travels.

In *The Turkish Labyrinth: Atatürk and the New Islam*, journalist James Pettifer examines the pressures on modern Turkey as it struggles to cope with population movements, the Kurdish war and the growth of Islamic fundamentalism.

Neal Ascherson's *Black Sea* is a long essay on that region by the talented *Observer* journalist. *A Traveller's History of Turkey* by Richard Stoneman is also worth a look.

History

The Ottoman Centuries by Lord Kinross covers the greatness of the empire without weighing too heavily on your consciousness.

Professors Stanford and Ezel Kural Shaw's excellent and authoritative *History of the Ottoman Empire & Modern Turkey* comes in two volumes. Volume One is *Empire of the Gazis: The Rise & Decline of the Ottoman Empire 1280-1808*; Volume Two is *Reform, Revolution & Republic: The Rise of Modern Turkey 1808-1975*.

The Emergence of Modern Turkey by Bernard Lewis is a scholarly work covering Turkey's history roughly from 1850 to 1950, with a few chapters on the earlier history of the Turks.

Gallipoli by Alan Moorhead is the fascinating story of the battles for the Dardanelles, which figured so significantly in the careers of Atatürk and Winston Churchill, and in the histories of Australia and New Zealand.

The Harvest of Hellenism by FE Peters details Turkey's Hellenic heritage. *Byzantine Style & Civilisation* by Sir Steven Runciman is the standard work on the later Roman Empire.

General

Biography *Atatürk, The Rebirth of a Nation* by Lord Kinross (JPD Balfour) is essential reading for anyone who wants to understand the formation of the Turkish Republic and the reverence in which modern Turks hold the father of modern Turkey. It's well written and more exciting than many novels. The US edition is *Atatürk: A Biography of Mustafa Kemal*.

For a fascinating look into the last years of the Ottoman Empire and the early years of the Turkish Republic, read İrfan Orga's *Portrait of a Turkish Family*. First published in 1950 and recently republished with an afterword by the author's son, it's an absorbing portrait of a family trying to survive the collapse of an old society and the birth of a new one.

Anthropology For a good overview of life during the great days of the empire, look in a library for *Everyday Life in Ottoman Turkey* by Raphaela Lewis.

Archaeology *Ancient Civilisations & Ruins of Turkey* by Ekrem Akurgal is a detailed and scholarly guide to many of Turkey's ruins 'from Prehistoric Times until the End of the Roman Empire'. The book has 112 pages of photographs and is a good, readable English translation of the original. This is the best handbook for those with a deep interest in classical archaeology.

George Bean (1903-77) was the grand old man of western travel writers on Turkish antiquities. His four books with maps, diagrams and photos cover the country's greatest wealth of Greek and Roman sites in depth, but in a very readable style. These four works were written as guidebooks to the ruins. They contain plenty of detail, but not so much that the fascination of exploring an ancient city or temple is taken away.

If you'd like to go deeply into a few sites, but not make the investments of time, energy and money necessary to cover the entire coast from Pergamum to Silifke, just buy Bean's *Aegean Turkey*. It covers İzmir and its vicinity, Pergamum, Aeolis, sites west of İzmir to Sardis, Ephesus, Priene, Miletus, Didyma, Magnesia on the Menderes River and Heracleia.

Other books by George Bean include:

Lycian Turkey (1978), which covers the Turkish coast roughly from Fethiye to Antalya, and its hinterland.

Turkey Beyond the Meander (1980), which covers the region south of the Menderes River, excluding Miletus, Didyma and Heracleia (covered in ***Aegean Turkey***) but including sites near Bodrum, Pamukkale, Aphrodisias and Marmaris, and to the western outskirts of Fethiye.

Turkey's Southern Shore (1979), which overlaps with ***Lycian Turkey*** a bit, and covers eastern Lycia, Pisidia and Pamphylia, or roughly the coast from Finike east to Silifke.

Besides these archaeological guides, you'll find shorter, locally produced guides on sale at each site. Most include colour photographs but of varying quality. The text, however, is often badly translated, or else doesn't go into much depth. Look closely before you buy.

Food *Eat Smart in Turkey: How to Decipher the Menu, Know the Market Foods & Embark on a Tasting Adventure*, written by Joan & David Peterson, is a delightful in-depth look at the history, practice and enjoyment of Turkish cuisine.

Fiction Everybody knows about Agatha Christie's *Murder on the Orient Express*, and so they should. It has some scenes in Turkey itself, though most of the train's journey was through Europe and the Balkans. In any case, it helps to make vivid the 19th-century importance of the Turkish Empire.

Among Turkish authors, the one with the world-class reputation is Yaşar Kemal, whom some compare to Kazantzakis. Kemal's novels often take Turkish farming or working-class life as their subject matter, and are full of colourful characters and drama. There are translations in English (done by Kemal's wife) of *Memed, My*

Hawk and *The Wind from the Plains* and several others.

Orhan Pamuk is a young Turkish novelist who now has a worldwide following. *The White Tower* and *The Black Book* are his two best known works translated into English, with *New Life* (1997) gaining recognition.

Many modern 'harem' novels trade on the romance (real or wildly imagined) of the sultan's private household. Most are facile. The exception is *The Bride of Suleiman* (1981) by Aileen Crawley. The author, who lives in Northern Ireland, has written a historically faithful and absorbing fictionalised account of the relationship between Hürrem Sultan ('Roxelana') and her husband Süleyman the Magnificent, greatest of the Ottoman sultans. She brings alive the life of the Ottoman Empire during its golden age.

Arts & Crafts *Turkish Traditional Art Today* by Henry Glassie (1993) is truly a masterful, scholarly, detailed yet superbly entertaining survey of traditional Turkish arts such as calligraphy, carpet-weaving, pottery, metal and woodworking.

Dictionaries Several companies publish Turkish-English pocket dictionaries, including Langenscheidt and McGraw Hill.

For a more detailed dictionary, look to *The Concise Oxford Turkish Dictionary*. Similar in scope and easier to find in Turkey is the *Redhouse Küçük Elsözlüğlu* (Small Hand Dictionary) this 702-page work on thin paper was actually intended for Turkish students learning English, but it does the job well when you graduate from the pocket dictionary.

Turkish Grammar by Geoffrey L Lewis is the best general grammar. If a grammar book can be said to read like a novel, this one does.

However, the most useful thing to have is not a dictionary, but a good phrasebook. (See Lonely Planet earlier in this section.)

Bookshops

Major cities and most of the resort towns have bookshops which sell some foreign-language books, newspapers and magazines. See each city section for details.

FILMS

Perhaps the most famous movie about Turkey is *Midnight Express*, a politically motivated, anti-Turkish diatribe in which a convicted drug smuggler is magically transformed into a suffering hero (see the 'Midnight Express' boxed text in the Thrace chapter for more information). Virtually all of the 'Turkish' actors in the movie were of Greek or Armenian extraction; funding was provided by cinema magnate Kirk Kerkorian. Controversial director Oliver Stone created a visually striking and emotionally chilling story in this early work by playing fast and loose with the facts. An entire generation of intelligent cinema-goers never questioned its overt racism.

The classic suspense-comedy *Topkapi*, with Peter Ustinov and Melina Mercouri, is much more fun to watch, as is the James Bond thriller *From Russia With Love*, set in İstanbul.

For years various producers have been discussing a film biography of Atatürk – a dramatic story if ever there was one – but actors and directors approached about the film are often put under extreme pressure by anti-Turkish elements not to participate. Anything but positive coverage of the national hero is certain to be greeted with strong disapproval from the Turkish government.

NEWSPAPERS & MAGAZINES

Local daily newspapers are produced by up-to-date computerised methods in lurid colour. Of prime interest to visitors is the *Turkish Daily News*, an English-language daily newspaper published in Ankara and available for purchase (US$0.80) in most Turkish cities where there are tourists. It is the cheapest source of English language news in print.

The big international papers such as the *International Herald Tribune, Le Monde, Corriere della Sera, Die Welt* etc are on sale in tourist spots as well, but are much more expensive (US$2 for the *International Herald Tribune*). Check the date on any international paper before you buy it. If it's more than a day or two old, look elsewhere.

Large-circulation magazines including *The Economist, Newsweek, Time, Der Spiegel* and the like, are also sold in tourist spots.

If you can't find the foreign publication you want, go to a big hotel's newsstand or check at a foreign-language bookshop.

RADIO & TV

Radio and TV broadcasting is both public and private.

TRT, for Türkiye Radyo ve Televizyon, is a quasi-independent government broadcasting service modelled on the BBC. Western classical and popular music, along with Turkish classic, folk, religious and pop music, are played regularly on both AM (medium-wave) and FM channels. TRT-TV broadcasts in colour from breakfast time to midnight on four TV channels.

Short news broadcasts in English, French and German are given on national radio each morning and evening. TRT's Tourism (Holiday) Radio broadcasts news and historical, geographical and social information about Turkey in the same three languages from 7.30 am to 12.45 pm and 6.30 to 10 pm in major tourist areas.

A variety of independent commercial broadcast and cable stations provide Turkish musical and variety programs. The familiar Los Angeles-made series and many of the films are dubbed in Turkish. Occasionally you'll catch a film in the original language.

The BBC World Service is often receivable on AM as well as on short-wave. The rest of the AM band is a wonderful collection of Albanian, Arabic, Bulgarian, Greek, Hebrew, Italian, Persian, Romanian and Russian.

In addition to the Turkish TV channels, many of the larger and more expensive hotels have satellite hook-ups to receive European channels, with programmes mostly in German, but often including the European service of CNN, NBC Super-Channel, and/or the BBC.

VIDEO SYSTEMS

Turkey uses the European-standard PAL standard for its TV and video. If your home country uses SECAM (France) or NTSC (North America) and you buy a Turkish video cassette, it will not play properly on your home equipment, even if it is made to be played in a VHS video cassette recorder/player.

PHOTOGRAPHY

Colour print film costs about US$8, plus developing, for 24 exposures. It's readily available and easily processed in city photo shops, as are E-6 process slide films such as Ektachrome, Fujichrome and Velvia, but Kodachrome slide film is rarely found, and cannot be developed in Turkey.

Still cameras are subject to an extra fee in most museums; in some they are not allowed at all. For use of flash or tripod, you must normally obtain written permission from the staff or the appropriate government ministry (not easy). Video fees are usually even higher, thereby denying Turkey the free publicity which would be provided by thousands of home videos being shown around the world by happy returned travellers.

Do not photograph anything military, whether or not you see signs reading *Foto çekmek yasak(tır)* or *Fotoğraf çekilmez* (No Photography).

In areas off the tourist track, it's polite to ask *Foto çekebilir miyim?* ('May I take a photo?') before taking any close-ups of people.

TIME

Turkish time is East European Time, two hours ahead of Coordinated Universal Time (UTC/GMT), except in the warm months, when clocks are turned ahead one hour. Daylight saving ('summer') time usually begins at 1 am on the last Sunday in March, and ends at 2 am on the last

Sunday in September. When it's noon in İstanbul, Ankara or Erzurum, the time elsewhere is:

city	winter	summer
London	10 am	10 am
Paris, Rome	11 am	11 am
Perth, Hong Kong	6 pm	5 pm
Sydney	8 pm	7 pm
Auckland	10 pm	9 pm
Los Angeles	2 am	2 am
New York	5 am	5 am

ELECTRICITY

Electricity in Turkey is supplied at 220 volts, 50 cycles, as in Europe. *Fiş* (FEESH, plugs) are of the European variety with two round prongs, but there are two sizes in use. Most common is the small-diameter prong, so if you have this you'll be fine. The large-diameter, grounded plug, used in Germany and Austria, is also in use, and you'll find some *priz* (PREEZ, outlets or points) of this type. Plugs for these won't fit the small-diameter outlets.

If you have to rig an adaptor, electrical shops have the necessary parts at reasonable prices.

WEIGHTS & MEASURES

Turkey uses the metric system. For those accustomed to the British-US systems of measurement, conversion information can be found at the back of this book.

LAUNDRY

Getting your *çamaşır* (chahm-mah-SHUR, laundry) done is a simple matter. At any hotel or pension, ask at the reception desk, or go directly to a housekeeper. They'll quickly find someone to do laundry. Agree on a price in advance. The classier the hotel, the more exorbitant their laundry rates. Even so, the rates are no higher than at home.

Allow at least a day to get laundry done. It may be washed in a machine or by hand, but it may be dried on a line, not in a drying machine. In summer, drying takes no time at all. If you wash a T-shirt at 10.30 am in İzmir and hang it in the sun, it'll be dry by 11 am.

By the way, the word çamaşır also means 'underwear' in Turkish. This can be confusing at times.

Kuru temizleme (koo-ROO tehm-eez-lem-MEH, dry-cleaning shops) are found here and there in big cities, usually in the better residential sections or near luxury hotels.

Service is similar to that in Europe and the USA: fast service takes an hour or two if you're willing to pay 50% more; otherwise, overnight or two-day service is normal practice. Prices are moderate to expensive, and you'll save money by taking the garments there yourself rather than having the hotel staff do it.

HEALTH

Travel health depends on your predeparture preparations, your day-to-day health care while travelling and how you handle any

Hit the Internet

Lonely Planet provides up-to-date information for travellers on health issues on the Internet. For all you need to know about pre-departure planning, keeping healthy, women's health and diseases and ailments, go to www.lonelyplanet.com.au/health/health.htm. Lonely Planet's site can also direct you to other relevant on-line health information.

The US Public Health Service's Centers for Disease Control and Prevention in Atlanta, Georgia, can also provide current health information through the three Internet sites it maintains.

The CDC site is at http://www.cdc.gov/travel/travel.html. Look for the Middle East region. You may also be interested in the item called Information Networks and Other Information Sources.

There's more information available by file transfer protocol (ftp) at ftp.cdc.gov, and at the CDC Gopher site at gopher://gopher.cdc.gov/ under Traveler's Health.

medical problem or emergency that does develop. While the list of potential dangers can seem quite frightening, with a little luck, some basic precautions and adequate information, few travellers experience more than an upset stomach. However, if you do happen to get sick the information on various diseases may be useful.

It's worth mentioning that highway traffic accidents claim thousands of lives annually in Turkey. See Driving in the Getting Around chapter for more details.

Predeparture Preparations

Immunisations Plan ahead for getting your vaccinations: some of them require more than one injection, while some vaccinations should not be given together. Note that some vaccinations should not be given during pregnancy or to people with allergies – discuss with your doctor.

It is recommended you seek medical advice at least six weeks before travel. Be aware that there is often a greater risk of disease with children and during pregnancy.

Record all vaccinations on an International Certificate of Vaccination, available from your doctor or government health department.

Legally, there are no vaccination requirements for entry into Turkey. Discuss with your doctor, but vaccinations you should consider for this trip include the following (for more details on the diseases, see the individual entries later in this section):

Diphtheria & Tetanus Vaccinations for these two diseases are usually combined and are recommended for everyone. After an initial course of three injections (usually given in childhood), boosters are necessary every 10 years.

Polio Everyone should keep up-to-date with this vaccination, which is normally given in childhood. A booster every 10 years maintains immunity.

Hepatitis A The hepatitis A vaccine (eg Avaxim, Havrix 1440 or VAQTA) provides long-term immunity (possibly more than 10 years) after an initial injection and a booster at six to 12 months. Alternatively, an injection of gamma globulin can provide short-term protection against hepatitis A – two to six months, depending on the dose given. It is not a vaccine, but is ready-made antibody collected from blood donations. It is reasonably effective and, unlike the vaccine, it is protective immediately; however, because it is a blood product, there are current concerns about its long-term safety. Hepatitis A vaccine is also available in a combined form, Twinrix, with hepatitis B vaccine. Three injections over a six-month period are required, the first two providing substantial protection against hepatitis A.

Typhoid Vaccination against typhoid may be required if you are travelling for more than a couple of weeks in most parts of Asia, Africa, Central and South America and Central and Eastern Europe. It is now available either as an injection or as capsules to be taken orally.

Cholera The current injectable vaccine against cholera is poorly protective and has many side effects, so it is not generally recommended for travellers. However, in some situations it may be necessary to have a certificate as travellers are very occasionally asked by immigration officials to present one, even though all countries and the WHO have dropped cholera immunisation as a health requirement for entry.

Hepatitis B Travellers who should consider vaccination against hepatitis B include those on a long trip, as well as those visiting countries where there are high levels of hepatitis B infection, where blood transfusions may not be adequately screened or where sexual contact or needle sharing is a possibility. Vaccination involves three injections, with a booster at 12 months. More rapid courses are available if necessary.

Rabies Vaccination should be considered by those who will spend a month or longer in Turkey especially if they are cycling, handling animals, caving or travelling to remote areas, and for children (who may not report a bite). Pretravel rabies vaccination involves having three injections over 21 to 28 days. If someone who has been vaccinated is bitten or scratched by an animal, they will require two booster injections of vaccine; those not vaccinated require more.

Tuberculosis The risk of TB to travellers is usually very low, unless you will be living with or closely associated with local people in high risk areas such as Asia, Africa and some parts of the Americas and Pacific. Vaccination against TB (BCG) is recommended for children and young adults living in these areas for three months or more.

Malaria Medication Antimalarial drugs do not prevent you from being infected but kill the malaria parasites during a stage in their development and significantly reduce the risk of becoming very ill or dying. Expert advice on medication should be sought, as there are many factors to consider, including the area to be visited, the risk of exposure to malaria-carrying mosquitoes, the side effects of medication, your medical history and whether you are a child or an adult or pregnant. Travellers to isolated area in high risk countries may like to carry a treatment dose of medication for use if symptoms occur.

Health Insurance Make sure that you have adequate health insurance.

Travel Health Guides If you are planning to be away or travelling in remote areas for a long period of time, you may like to consider taking a more detailed health guide.

CDC's Complete Guide to Healthy Travel, Open Road Publishing, 1997. The US Centers for Disease Control & Prevention recommendations for international travel.

Travellers' Health, Dr Richard Dawood, Oxford University Press, 1995. Comprehensive, easy to read, authoritative and highly recommended, although it's rather large to lug around.

Travel with Children, Maureen Wheeler, Lonely Planet Publications, 1995. Includes advice on travel health for younger children.

There are also a number of excellent travel health sites on the Internet. From the Lonely Planet home page there are links at www.lonelyplanet.com/weblinks/wlprep.htm#heal to the World Health Organization and the US Centers for Disease Control & Prevention.

Other Preparations Make sure you're healthy before you start travelling. If you are going on a long trip make sure your teeth are OK. If you wear glasses take a spare pair and your prescription.

Though Turkey manufactures most modern prescription medicines, don't risk running out of your medicine. If you take a drug regularly, bring a supply. Take the prescription or better still part of the packaging showing the generic rather than the brand name (which may not be locally available). It is wise to have a legible prescription or letter from your doctor with you to show that you legally use the medication.

Basic Rules

Food & Water Travellers in Turkey experience a fair amount of travellers' diarrhoea ('the Sultan's Revenge'). Any experienced traveller knows that getting sick from food is mostly by chance, but there are still a few things you can do to improve your chances.

Nutrition

If your food is poor or limited in availability, if you're travelling hard and fast and therefore missing meals or if you simply lose your appetite, you can soon start to lose weight and place your health at risk.

Make sure your diet is well balanced. Cooked eggs, beans, lentils and nuts are all safe ways to get protein. Fruit you can peel (bananas, oranges or mandarins for example) is usually safe (melons can harbour bacteria in their flesh and are best avoided) and a good source of vitamins. Try to eat plenty of grains (including rice) and bread. Remember that although food is generally safer if it is cooked well, overcooked food loses much of its nutritional value. If your diet isn't well balanced or if your food intake is insufficient, it's a good idea to take vitamin and iron pills.

In hot climates make sure you drink enough – don't rely on feeling thirsty to indicate when you should drink. Not needing to urinate or small amounts of very dark yellow urine is a danger sign. Always carry a water bottle with you on long trips. Excessive sweating can lead to loss of salt and therefore muscle cramping. Salt tablets are not a good idea as a preventative, but in places where salt is not used much, adding salt to food can help.

Dining Precautions Choose dishes that look freshly prepared and sufficiently hot. You can go into almost any Turkish kitchen (except in the very posh places) for a look at what's cooking. In fact, in most places that's what the staff will suggest, the language barrier being what it is. Except for grilled meats, Turkish dishes tend to be cooked slowly for a long time, just the thing to kill any errant bacteria. But if the dishes don't sell on the day they're cooked, they might be saved.

As for grilled meats, these may be offered to you medium rare. They'll probably be all right, but if they really look pink, send them back for more cooking (no problem in this). The words you'll need are *biraz daha pişmiş* (beer-ahz da-HAH peesh-meesh) for 'cooked a bit more', and *iyi pişmiş* (ee-EE peesh-meesh) or *pişkin,* (peesh-KEEN) for 'well done'.

Beware of milk products, and dishes which contain milk that has not been properly refrigerated. Electricity is expensive in Turkey, and many places will scrimp on refrigeration temperature. If you want a *sütlaç* (rice pudding) or some such dish with milk in it, choose a shop that has lots of them in the window, meaning that a batch has been made recently. In general, choose things from bins, trays, cases, pots etc that are fairly full. If you make a point of eating some yoghurt every day, you'll keep your digestive system in excellent condition.

Drinking Precautions Drink bottled spring water whenever possible. It's sold everywhere in clear plastic bottles in sizes of one-third of a litre, 1.5L and three litres. Check the date of manufacture on the bottle, and don't buy water that's been around for a while as it may taste of the plastic. Check that the seal of the bottle hasn't been tampered with.

Tap water in Turkey is chlorinated, but it is not certain to be safe, and it rarely tastes good.

A roadside *çeşme* (CHESH-meh, fountain or spring), may bear the word *içilmez* (eech-eel-MEHZ, 'not to be drunk'), or *içilir* (eech-eel-LEER, 'drinkable'), or *içme suyu* (EECH-meh soo-yoo, 'drinking water'), or *içilebilir* (EECH-eel-eh-bee-LEER, 'can be drunk'), but I'd avoid these if possible unless you think you really know what's upstream from them.

Alternatives to spring water include *maden suyu*, naturally fizzy mineral water, and *maden sodası* (or just *soda*), artificially carbonated mineral water. The latter just has bigger bubbles, and more of them, than the former. Both come from mineral springs, and both are truly full of minerals. The taste is not neutral. Some people like it, some don't. It's supposed to cleanse your kidneys and be good for you. Packaged *meyva suyu* (fruit juice), soft drinks, beer and wine are usually safe to drink.

Water Purification The simplest way of purifying water is to boil it thoroughly. Note that at high altitude water boils at a much lower temperature, so germs are less likely to be killed, – boil it for longer in these environments.

Consider purchasing a water filter for a long trip. There are two main kinds of filter. Total filters take out all parasites, bacteria and viruses and make water safe to drink. They are often expensive, but they can be more cost effective than buying bottled water. Simple filters (which can even be a nylon mesh bag) take out dirt and larger foreign bodies from the water so that chemical solutions work much more effectively; if water is dirty, chemical solutions may not work at all. It's very important when buying a filter to read the specifications, so that you know exactly what it removes from the water and what it doesn't. Simple filtering will not remove all dangerous organisms, so if you cannot boil water it should be treated chemically. Chlorine tablets (Puritabs, Steritabs or other brand names) will kill many pathogens, but not some parasites like giardia and amoebic cysts. Iodine is more effective in purifying water and is available in tablet form (such as Potable Aqua). Follow the directions carefully and remember that too much iodine can be harmful.

Medical Problems & Treatment

Self-diagnosis and treatment can be risky, so you should always seek medical help. Although we do give drug dosages in this section, they are for emergency use only. Correct diagnosis is vital.

Antibiotics should ideally be administered only under medical supervision. Take only the recommended dose at the prescribed intervals and use the whole course, even if the illness seems to be cured earlier. Stop immediately if there are any serious reactions and don't use the antibiotic at all if you are unsure that you have the correct one. Some people are allergic to commonly prescribed antibiotics such as penicillin; carry this information (eg on a bracelet) when travelling.

Medical Services Medical services are fairly well distributed in Turkey, though they are often very basic and sometimes inept. Some doctors in the larger cities speak English, French or German, and have studied in Europe or the USA. Your embassy or consulate may be able to recommend a good doctor or dentist (see Embassies earlier in this chapter).

You can find good doctors and dentists in Turkey's big cities, as well as *hastane* (hahs-tah-NEH, hospitals) and *klinik* (klee-NEEK, clinics). Government-supported hospitals are called *devlet hastanesi*, and you can find them by following the standard international road sign with a large 'H' on it. See the chapter or section about each city for details.

Clinics run by the Red Crescent (Kızılay, the Turkish equivalent of the Red Cross) are marked by a red crescent. *İlk yardım* on one of these signs means 'first aid', which may or may not be competent; a *sağlık ocağı* is a simple dispensary. All hospital and clinic costs are controlled by the government, and are quite low, even at private hospitals.

In every city and town of any size you will see signs marking the medical offices of doctors and giving their specialities.

A *tıbbi doktor*, medical doctor, might specialise in *dahili*, internal medicine; *göz hastalıkları*, eye diseases; *kadın hastalıkları*,

Medical Kit Check List

Following is a list of items you should consider including in your medical kit – consult your pharmacist for brands available in your country.

- ☐ **Aspirin** or **paracetamol** (acetaminophen in the US) – for pain or fever.
- ☐ **Antihistamine** – for allergies, eg hay fever; to ease the itch from insect bites or stings; and to prevent motion sickness.
- ☐ **Antibiotics** – consider including these if you're travelling well off the beaten track; see your doctor, as they must be prescribed, and carry the prescription with you.
- ☐ **Loperamide** or **diphenoxylate** – 'blockers' for diarrhoea; **prochlorperazine** or **metaclopramide** for nausea and vomiting.
- ☐ **Rehydration mixture** – to prevent dehydration, eg due to severe diarrhoea; particularly important when travelling with children.
- ☐ **Insect repellent, sunscreen, lip balm** and **eye drops**.
- ☐ **Calamine lotion, sting relief spray** or **aloe vera** – to ease irritation from sunburn and insect bites or stings.
- ☐ **Antifungal cream** or **powder** – for fungal skin infections and thrush.
- ☐ **Antiseptic** (such as povidone-iodine) – for cuts and grazes.
- ☐ **Bandages, Band-Aids (plasters)** and other wound dressings.
- ☐ **Water purification tablets** or **iodine**.
- ☐ **Scissors, tweezers** and a **thermometer** (note that mercury thermometers are prohibited by airlines).
- ☐ **Syringes** and **needles** – in case you need injections in a country with medical hygine problems. Ask your doctor for a note explaining why you have them.
- ☐ **Cold** and **flu tablets, throat lozenges** and **nasal decongestant**.
- ☐ **Multivitamins** – consider for long trips, when dietary vitamin intake may be inadequate.

gynaecological ailments or *çocuk hastalıkları*, paediatric (children's) ailments. An *operatör* is a surgeon.

By the way, half of all the physicians in Turkey are women. If a woman visits a male doctor, it's customary to have a companion present during any physical examination or treatment. There is not always a nurse available to serve in this role.

Care in provincial Turkish hospitals is sometimes not of the highest standard in terms of comfort, convenience or facilities. But medical care often depends upon the particular staff members (doctors and nurses) involved. The quality varies. The lower staff echelons may be low paid and trained on the job. As a foreigner, you will probably be given the best possible treatment and the greatest consideration.

For minor problems, it's customary to ask at an *eczane* (edj-zahn-NEH, pharmacy) for advice. Sign language usually suffices to communicate symptoms, and the pharmacist/chemist will prescribe on the spot. Even 'prescription' drugs (except the most dangerous or addictive ones) are often sold without a prescription.

Environmental Hazards

Heat Exhaustion Dehydration and salt deficiency can cause heat exhaustion. Take time to acclimatise to high temperatures, drink sufficient liquids and do not do anything too physically demanding.

Salt deficiency is characterised by fatigue, lethargy, headaches, giddiness and muscle cramps; salt tablets may help, but adding extra salt to your food is better.

Anhidrotic heat exhaustion is a rare form of heat exhaustion that is caused by an inability to sweat. It tends to affect people who have been in a hot climate for some time, rather than newcomers. It can progress to heatstroke. Treatment involves removal to a cooler climate.

Heatstroke This serious, occasionally fatal, condition can occur if the body's heat-regulating mechanism breaks down and the body temperature rises to dangerous levels. Long, continuous periods of exposure to high temperatures and insufficient fluids can leave you vulnerable to heatstroke.

The symptoms are feeling unwell, not sweating very much (or at all) and a high body temperature (39° to 41°C or 102° to 106°F). When sweating has ceased, the skin becomes flushed and red. Severe, throbbing headaches and lack of coordination will also occur, and the sufferer may be confused or aggressive. Eventually the victim will become delirious or convulse. Hospitalisation is essential, but in the interim get victims out of the sun, remove their clothing, cover them with a wet sheet or towel and then fan continually. Give fluids if they are conscious.

Hypothermia Too much cold can be just as dangerous as too much heat. If you are trekking at high altitudes or simply taking a long bus trip over mountains, particularly at night, be prepared.

Hypothermia occurs when the body loses heat faster than it can produce it and the core temperature of the body falls. It is surprisingly easy to progress from very cold to dangerously cold due to a combination of wind, wet clothing, fatigue and hunger, even if the air temperature is above freezing. It is best to dress in layers; silk, wool and some of the new artificial fibres are all good insulating materials. A hat is important, as a lot of heat is lost through the head. A strong, waterproof outer layer (and a 'space' blanket for emergencies) is essential. Carry basic supplies, including food containing simple sugars to generate heat quickly and fluid to drink.

Symptoms of hypothermia are exhaustion, numb skin (particularly toes and fingers), shivering, slurred speech, irrational or violent behaviour, lethargy, stumbling, dizzy spells, muscle cramps and violent bursts of energy. Irrationality may take the form of sufferers claiming they are warm and trying to take off their clothes.

To treat mild hypothermia, first get the person out of the wind and/or rain, remove their clothing if it's wet and replace it with dry, warm clothing. Give them hot liquids – not alcohol – and some high-kilojoule, easily digestible food. Do not rub victims: instead, allow them to slowly warm themselves. This should be enough to treat the early stages of hypothermia. The early recognition and treatment of mild hypothermia is the only way to prevent severe hypothermia, which is a critical condition.

Jet Lag Jet lag is experienced when a person travels by air across more than three time zones (each time zone usually represents a one-hour time difference). It occurs because many of the functions of the human body (such as temperature, pulse rate and emptying of the bladder and bowels) are regulated by internal 24-hour cycles. When we travel long distances rapidly, our bodies take time to adjust to the 'new time' of our destination, and we may experience fatigue, disorientation, insomnia, anxiety, impaired concentration and loss of appetite. These effects will usually be gone within three days of arrival, but to minimise the impact of jet lag:

- Rest for a couple of days prior to departure.
- Try to select flight schedules that minimise sleep deprivation; arriving late in the day means you can go to sleep soon after you arrive. For very long flights, try to organise a stopover.
- Avoid excessive eating (which bloats the stomach) and alcohol (which causes dehydration) during the flight. Instead, drink plenty of noncarbonated, nonalcoholic drinks such as fruit juice or water.
- Avoid smoking.
- Make yourself comfortable by wearing loose-fitting clothes and perhaps bringing an eye mask and ear plugs to help you sleep.
- Try to sleep at the appropriate time for the time zone you are travelling to.

Motion Sickness Eating lightly before and during a trip will reduce the chances of motion sickness. If you are prone to motion sickness try to find a place that minimises movement – near the wing on aircraft, close to midships on boats, near the centre on buses. Fresh air usually helps; reading and cigarette smoke don't. Commercial motion-sickness preparations, which can cause drowsiness, have to be taken before the trip commences. Ginger (available in capsule form) and peppermint (including mint-flavoured sweets) are natural preventatives.

Prickly Heat Prickly heat is an itchy rash caused by excessive perspiration trapped under the skin. It usually strikes people who have just arrived in a hot climate. Keeping cool, bathing often, drying the skin and using a mild talcum or prickly heat powder or resorting to air-conditioning may help.

Sunburn In Turkey you can get sunburnt surprisingly quickly, even through cloud. Use a sunscreen, a hat, and a barrier cream for your nose and lips. Calamine lotion or aloe vera are good for mild sunburn. Protect your eyes with good quality sunglasses, particularly if you will be near water, sand or snow.

Infectious Diseases

Diarrhoea Simple things like a change of water, food or climate can all cause a mild bout of diarrhoea, but a few rushed toilet trips with no other symptoms is not indicative of a major problem.

Dehydration is the main danger with any diarrhoea, particularly in children or the elderly as dehydration can occur quite quickly. Under all circumstances fluid replacement (at least equal to the volume being lost) is the most important thing to remember. Weak black tea with a little sugar, soda water, or soft drinks allowed to go flat and diluted 50% with clean water are all good. With severe diarrhoea a rehydrating solution is preferable to replace minerals and salts lost. Commercially available oral rehydration salts (ORS) are very useful; add them to boiled or bottled water. In an emergency you can make up a solution of six teaspoons of sugar and a half teaspoon of salt to a litre of boiled or bottled water.

You need to drink at least the same volume of fluid that you are losing in bowel movements and vomiting. Urine is the best guide to the adequacy of replacement – if you have small amounts of concentrated urine, you need to drink more. Keep drinking small amounts often. Stick to a bland diet as you recover.

Gut-paralysing drugs such as loperamide or diphenoxylate can be used to bring relief from the symptoms, although they do not actually cure the problem. Only use these drugs if you do not have access to toilets – eg if you *must* travel. For children under 12 years these drugs are not recommended. Do not use these drugs if the person has a high fever or is severely dehydrated.

In certain situations antibiotics may be required: diarrhoea with blood or mucus (dysentery), any diarrhoea with fever, profuse watery diarrhoea, persistent diarrhoea not improving after 48 hours and severe diarrhoea. These suggest a more serious cause of diarrhoea and in these situations gut-paralysing drugs should be avoided.

In these situations, a stool test may be necessary to diagnose what bug is causing your diarrhoea, so you should seek medical help urgently. Where this is not possible the recommended drugs for bacterial diarrhoea (the most likely cause of severe diarrhoea in travellers) are norfloxacin 400mg twice daily for three days or ciprofloxacin 500mg twice daily for five days. These are not recommended for children or pregnant women. The drug of choice for children would be co-trimoxazole (Bactrim, Septrin or Resprim) with dosage dependent on weight. A five day course is given. Ampicillin or amoxycillin may be given in pregnancy, but medical care is necessary.

Two other causes of persistent diarrhoea in travellers are giardiasis and amoebic dysentery.

Giardiasis is caused by a common parasite, *Giardia lamblia*. Symptoms include stomach cramps, nausea, a bloated stomach, watery, foul-smelling diarrhoea and frequent gas. Giardiasis can appear several weeks after you have been exposed to the parasite. The symptoms may disappear for a few days and then return; this can go on for several weeks.

Amoebic dysentery, caused by the protozoan *Entamoeba histolytica*, is characterised by a gradual onset of low-grade diarrhoea, often with blood and mucus. Cramping abdominal pain and vomiting are less likely than in other types of diarrhoea, and fever may not be present. It will persist until treated and can recur and cause other health problems.

You should seek medical advice if you think you have giardiasis or amoebic dysentery, but where this is not possible, tinidazole (Fasigyn) or metronidazole (Flagyl) are the recommended drugs. Treatment is a 2g single dose of tinidazole or 250mg of metronidazole three times daily for five to 10 days.

Fungal Infections Fungal infections occur more commonly in hot weather and are usually found on the scalp, between the toes (athlete's foot) or fingers, in the groin and on the body (ringworm). You get ringworm (which is a fungal infection, not a worm) from infected animals or other people. Moisture encourages these infections.

To prevent fungal infections wear loose, comfortable clothes, avoid artificial fibres, wash frequently and dry yourself carefully. If you do get an infection, wash the infected area at least daily with a disinfectant or medicated soap and water, and rinse and dry well. Apply an antifungal cream or powder like tolnaftate (Tinaderm). Try to expose the infected area to air or sunlight as much as possible and wash all towels and underwear in hot water, change them often and let them dry in the sun.

Hepatitis Hepatitis (*sarılık*, SAH-ruh-luhk) is a general term for inflammation of the liver. It is a common disease worldwide. There are several different viruses that cause hepatitis, and they differ in the way that they are transmitted. The symptoms are similar in all forms of the illness, and include fever, chills, headache, fatigue, feelings of weakness and aches and pains, followed by loss of appetite, nausea, vomiting, abdominal pain, dark urine, light-coloured faeces, jaundiced (yellow) skin and yellowing of the whites of the eyes. People who have had hepatitis should avoid alcohol for some time after the illness, as the liver needs time to recover.

Hepatitis A is transmitted by contaminated food and drinking water. You should seek medical advice, but there is not much you can do apart from resting, drinking lots of fluids, eating lightly and avoiding fatty foods. **Hepatitis E** is transmitted in the same way as hepatitis A; it can be particularly serious in pregnant women.

There are almost 300 million chronic carriers of **hepatitis B** in the world. It is spread through contact with infected blood, blood products or body fluids, for example through sexual contact, unsterilised needles and blood transfusions, or contact with blood via small breaks in the skin. Other risk situations include having a shave, tattoo or body piercing with contaminated equipment. The symptoms of hepatitis B may be more severe than type A and the disease can lead to long term problems such as chronic liver damage, liver cancer or a long term carrier state. **Hepatitis C** and **hepatitis D** are spread in the same way as hepatitis B and can also lead to long-term complications.

There are vaccines against hepatitis A and B, but there are currently no vaccines against the other types of hepatitis. Following the basic rules about food and water (hepatitis A and E) and avoiding risk situations (hepatitis B, C and D) are important preventative measures.

HIV & AIDS Infection with the human immunodeficiency virus (HIV) may lead to acquired immune deficiency syndrome (AIDS), which is a fatal disease. Any exposure to blood, blood products or body fluids may put the individual at risk. The disease is often transmitted through sexual contact or dirty needles – vaccinations, acupuncture, tattooing and body piercing can be potentially as dangerous as intravenous drug use. HIV/AIDS can also be spread through infected blood transfusions; some developing countries cannot afford to screen blood used for transfusions.

The best course is to buy a new *şırınga* (syringe) from a pharmacy and ask the doctor to use it.

Fear of HIV infection should never preclude treatment for serious medical conditions.

Intestinal Worms These parasites are most common in rural, tropical areas. The different worms have different ways of infecting people. Some may be ingested on food such as undercooked meat (eg tapeworms) and some enter through your skin (eg hookworms). Infestations may not show up for some time, and although they are generally not serious, if left untreated some can cause severe health problems later. Consider having a stool test when you return home to check for these and determine the appropriate treatment.

Sexually Transmitted Diseases Gonorrhoea, herpes and syphilis are among these diseases; sores, blisters or rashes around the genitals and discharges or pain when urinating are common symptoms. In some STDs, such as wart virus or chlamydia, symptoms may be less marked or not observed at all, especially in women. Syphilis symptoms eventually disappear completely but the disease continues and can cause severe problems in later years. While abstinence from sexual contact is the only 100% effective prevention, using condoms is also effective. The treatment of gonorrhoea and syphilis is with antibiotics. The different sexually transmitted diseases each require specific antibiotics. There is no cure for herpes or AIDS.

Typhoid Typhoid fever is a dangerous gut infection caused by contaminated water and food. Medical help must be sought.

In its early stages sufferers may feel they have a bad cold or flu on the way, as early symptoms are a headache, body aches and a fever which rises a little each day until it is around 40°C (104°F) or more. The victim's pulse is often slow, relative to the degree of fever present – unlike a normal fever where the pulse increases. There may also be vomiting, abdominal pain, diarrhoea or constipation.

In the second week the high fever and slow pulse continue and a few pink spots may appear on the body; trembling, delirium, weakness, weight loss and dehydration may occur. Complications such as pneumonia, perforated bowel or meningitis may occur.

Insect-Borne Diseases

Leishmaniasis, Lyme Disease and typhus are also insect-borne diseases that occur in Turkey, but they do not pose a great risk to travellers. For more information on them see Less Common Diseases later in this section.

Malaria This serious disease is spread by mosquito bites. If you are travelling in endemic areas it is extremely important to avoid mosquito bites and to take tablets to prevent this disease.

Overall, the risk of malaria is very small, and most travellers will not need to take precautions. Officially, malaria is present in south-eastern Anatolia from Mersin on the Mediterranean coast eastward to the Iraqi border, but the highest danger is in the muggy agricultural area called Çukurova north of Adana, and in the newly irrigated areas around Şanlıurfa, where the incidence of malaria has skyrocketed from 8600 cases in 1990 to approximately 100,000 cases in 1995.

If you just pass through these areas, or spend most of your time in cities, the danger is lower; but if you plan to spend lots of time in rural areas and camp out in this region, you're at significant risk and should take appropriate precautions – consult your doctor.

Symptoms range from fever, chills and sweating, headache, diarrhoea and abdominal pains to a vague feeling of ill-health. Seek medical help immediately if malaria is suspected. Without treatment malaria can rapidly become more serious and can be fatal.

It's unlikely that medical care will not be available, but if it isn't, malaria tablets can be used for treatment. You need to use a malaria tablet which is different from the one you were taking when you contracted malaria. The standard treatment dose of mefloquine is two 250mg tablets and a further two six hours later. For Fansidar, it's a single dose of three tablets. If you were previously taking mefloquine and cannot obtain Fansidar, then other alternatives are Malarone (atovaquone-proguanil; four tablets once daily for three days), halofantrine (three doses of two 250mg tablets every six hours) or quinine sulphate (600mg every six hours). There is a greater risk of side effects with these dosages than in normal use if used with mefloquine, so medical advice is preferable. Be aware also that halofantrine is no longer recommended by the WHO as emergency standby treatment, because of side effects, and should only be used if no other drugs are available.

Travellers are advised to prevent mosquito bites at all times. The main messages are:

- wear light-coloured clothing
- wear long trousers and long-sleeved shirts
- use mosquito repellents containing the compound DEET on exposed areas (prolonged overuse of DEET may be harmful, especially to children, but its use is considered preferable to being bitten by disease-transmitting mosquitoes)
- avoid perfumes or aftershave
- use a mosquito net impregnated with mosquito repellent (permethrin) – it may be worth taking your own
- impregnating clothes with permethrin effectively deters mosquitoes and other insects

Cuts, Bites & Stings

See Less Common Diseases for details of rabies, which is passed through animal bites.

Bedbugs & Lice Bedbugs live in various places, but particularly in dirty mattresses and bedding, evidenced by spots of blood on bedclothes or on the wall. Bedbugs leave itchy bites in neat rows. Calamine lotion or Stingose spray may help.

Everyday Health

Normal body temperature is up to 37°C (98.6°F); more than 2°C (4°F) higher indicates a high fever. The normal adult pulse rate is 60 to 100 per minute (children 80 to 100, babies 100 to 140). As a general rule the pulse increases about 20 beats per minute for each 1°C (2°F) rise in fever.

Respiration (breathing) rate is also an indicator of illness. Count the number of breaths per minute: between 12 and 20 is normal for adults and older children (up to 30 for younger children, 40 for babies). People with a high fever or serious respiratory illness breathe more quickly than normal. More than 40 shallow breaths a minute may indicate pneumonia.

All lice cause itching and discomfort. They make themselves at home in your hair (head lice), your clothing (body lice) or in your pubic hair (crabs). You catch lice through direct contact with infected people or by sharing combs, clothing and the like. Powder or shampoo treatment will kill the lice and infected clothing should then be washed in very hot, soapy water and left in the sun to dry.

Bites & Stings Bee and wasp stings are usually painful rather than dangerous. However, in people who are allergic to them severe breathing difficulties may occur and require urgent medical care. Calamine lotion or a sting relief spray may help and ice packs will reduce the pain and swelling. There are some spiders with dangerous bites but antivenins are usually available. Scorpion stings are notoriously painful and in some parts of Asia, the Middle East and Central America can actually be fatal. Scorpions often shelter in shoes or clothing.

Cuts & Scratches Wash well and treat any cut with an antiseptic such as povidone-iodine. Where possible avoid bandages and Band-Aids, which can keep wounds wet.

Jellyfish Avoid contact with these sea creatures, which have stinging tentacles – seek local advice. Dousing in vinegar will de-activate any stingers which have not 'fired'. Calamine lotion, antihistamines and analgesics may reduce the reaction and relieve the pain.

Ticks You should always check all over your body if you have been walking through a potentially tick-infested area as ticks can cause skin infections and other more serious diseases.

If a tick is found attached, press down around the tick's head with tweezers, grab the head and gently pull upwards. Avoid pulling the rear of the body as this may squeeze the tick's gut contents through the attached mouth parts into the skin, increasing the risk of infection and disease. Smearing chemicals on the tick will not make it let go and is not recommended.

Snakes To minimise your chances of being bitten always wear boots, socks and long trousers when walking through undergrowth where snakes may be present. Don't put your hands into holes and crevices, and be careful when collecting firewood.

Snake bites do not cause instantaneous death and antivenins are usually available. Immediately wrap the bitten limb tightly, as you would for a sprained ankle, and then attach a splint to immobilise it. Keep the victim still and seek medical help, if possible with the dead snake for identification. Don't attempt to catch the snake if there is a possibility of being bitten again. Tourniquets and sucking out the poison are now comprehensively discredited.

Less Common Diseases

The following diseases pose a small risk to travellers, and so are only mentioned in passing. Seek medical advice if you think you may have any of these diseases.

Cholera This is the worst of the watery diarrhoeas and medical help should be sought. Outbreaks of cholera are generally widely reported, so you can avoid such problem areas. *Fluid replacement is the most vital treatment* – the risk of dehydration is severe as you may lose up to 20L a day. If there is a delay in getting to hospital, then begin taking tetracycline. The adult dose is 250mg four times daily. It is not recommended for children under nine years nor for pregnant women. Tetracycline may help shorten the illness, but adequate fluids are required to save lives.

Leishmaniasis This is a group of parasitic diseases transmitted by sandflies, which are found in many parts of the Middle East, Africa, India, Central and South America and the Mediterranean. Cutaneous leishmaniasis affects the skin tissue causing ulceration and disfigurement, and visceral leishmaniasis affects the internal organs. Seek medical advice, as laboratory testing is required for diagnosis and correct treatment. Avoiding sandfly bites is the best precaution. Bites are usually painless, itchy and yet another reason to cover up and apply repellent.

Lyme Disease This is a tick-transmitted infection which may be acquired throughout North America, Europe and Asia. The illness usually begins with a spreading rash at the site of the tick bite and is accompanied by fever, headache, extreme fatigue, aching joints and muscles and mild neck stiffness. If untreated, these symptoms usually resolve over several weeks but over subsequent weeks or months disorders of the nervous system, heart and joints may develop. Treatment works best early in the illness. Medical help should be sought.

Rabies This fatal viral infection is found in many countries, including Turkey. Many animals can be infected (such as dogs, cats, bats and monkeys) and it is their saliva which is infectious. Any bite, scratch or even lick from an animal should be cleaned immediately and thoroughly. Scrub with soap and running water, and then apply alcohol or iodine solution. Medical help should be sought promptly to receive a course of injections to prevent the onset of symptoms and death.

Tetanus This disease is caused by a germ which lives in soil and in the faeces of horses and other animals. It enters the body via breaks in the skin. The first symptom may be discomfort in swallowing, or stiffening of the jaw and neck; this is followed by painful convulsions of the jaw and whole body. The disease can be fatal. It can be prevented by vaccination.

Tuberculosis (TB) TB is a bacterial infection usually transmitted from person to person by coughing but which may be transmitted through consumption of unpasteurised milk. Milk that has been boiled is safe to drink, and the souring of milk to make yoghurt or cheese also kills the bacilli. Travellers are usually not at great risk as close household contact with the infected person is usually required before the disease is passed on. You may need to have a TB test before you travel as this can help diagnose the disease later if you become ill.

Typhus This disease is spread by ticks, mites or lice. It begins with fever, chills, headache and muscle pains followed a few days later by a body rash. There is often a large painful sore at the site of the bite and nearby lymph nodes are swollen and painful. Typhus can be treated under medical supervision. Seek local advice on areas where ticks pose a danger and always check your skin carefully for ticks after walking in a danger area such as a tropical forest. An insect repellent can help, and walkers in tick-infested areas should consider having their boots and trousers impregnated with benzyl benzoate and dibutylphthalate.

Women's Health

Gynaecological Problems Antibiotic use, synthetic underwear, sweating and contraceptive pills can lead to fungal vaginal infections, especially when travelling in hot climates. Fungal infections are characterised by a rash, itch and discharge and can be treated with a vinegar or lemon-juice douche, or with yoghurt. Nystatin, miconazole or clotrimazole pessaries or vaginal cream are the usual treatment. Maintaining good personal hygiene and wearing loose-fitting clothes and cotton underwear may help prevent these infections.

Sexually transmitted diseases are a major cause of vaginal problems. Symptoms include a smelly discharge, painful intercourse and sometimes a burning sensation when urinating. Medical attention should be sought and male sexual partners must also be treated. Remember that in addition to these diseases, HIV or hepatitis B may also be acquired during exposure. Besides abstinence, the best thing is to practise safe sex using condoms.

Pregnancy It is not advisable to travel to some places while pregnant as some vaccinations normally used to prevent serious diseases are not advisable during pregnancy (eg yellow fever). In addition, some diseases are much more serious for the mother (and may increase the risk of a stillborn child) in pregnancy (eg malaria).

Most miscarriages occur during the first three months of pregnancy. Miscarriage is not uncommon and can occasionally lead to severe bleeding. The last three months should also be spent within reasonable distance of good medical care. A baby born as early as 24 weeks stands a chance of survival, but only in a good modern hospital. Pregnant women should avoid all unnecessary medication; vaccinations and malarial prophylactics should still be taken where needed. Additional care should be taken to prevent illness and particular attention should be paid to diet and nutrition. Alcohol and nicotine, for example, should be avoided.

TOILETS

In most public conveniences you are asked to pay a small fee of US$0.10 to US$0.20. Virtually every hotel above the lowest class, most apartments, many restaurants, train stations and airports have the familiar raised-bowl commode toilet. The Turkish version is equipped with facilities for washing the user's bottom (always with the left hand): a spigot and can on the floor nearby or, much more conveniently, a little copper tube snaking up the back and right to the spot where it's needed. As washing is the accustomed method of hygiene, toilet paper – used by Turks mostly for drying – is considered a dispensable luxury and may not be provided. In the government-rated hotels there should be paper. In public toilets, if there's no attendant, there will be no paper. It's a good idea to carry enough paper or tissues with you at all times.

You may also meet with the traditional flat 'elephant's feet' toilet, a porcelain or concrete rectangle with two oblong footplaces and a sunken hole. Though daunting, it has much to recommend it: doctors say that the squatting position aids in the swift and thorough accomplishment of the business at hand; and since only your shod feet contact the vessel, it is more sanitary than bowl toilets.

So much for science. The first time you use it, you'll feel awkward (and older readers have found it difficult to arise from the squat). Don't despair. Think of the generations of magnificent Ottoman sultans and gracious harem ladies who did it this way. Take a tip from them: don't let all of the stuff fall out of your pockets when you squat.

Sometimes the plumbing is not built to take wads of paper, and the management will place a wastepaper basket or can next to the toilet for used paper. Signs in Turkish will plead with you not to throw the paper down the toilet. If the toilet doesn't flush when you pull the handle, use the usually provided bucket or plastic container of water to do the job.

Serviceably clean public toilets can be found near the big tourist attractions. In other places, it depends. Look first. Every mosque has a toilet, often smelly and very basic, but it may be better than nothing, depending upon the urgency of nature's call.

WOMEN TRAVELLERS

Ms Pat Yale, my assistant in the preparation of this guide, gives this advice to women travellers in Turkey:

Attitudes to Women

As in most Muslim countries, western women travellers often attract the sort of attention they never would at home. Since Turkey is basically friendly and welcoming, much of this attention will be perfectly pleasant. (Though one black female traveller wrote to say that she was stared at by everyone, all the time, as Turks are not used to seeing black people.) Inevitably, however, some of the attention won't be, and many women write to Lonely Planet complaining about verbal and physical harassment.

Social Customs

If you want to avoid problems, it helps to understand – and perhaps follow – Turkish social custom. Things may be easing up in the big cities, but in general young women don't go out shopping without friends or mother. College-aged women usually stroll with friends; they look purposeful, ignore catcalls and don't walk on lonely streets after dark. Physical contact between women and men outside their immediate family is taboo. Even smiling at a man can be misconstrued as flirtation.

Countermeasures

That said, it's very difficult to lay down hard and fast rules that will protect you. Obviously how you dress has some bearing on the problem, particularly as you travel further east to areas where most women are still covered up. However, I have been groped when clothed from head to toe. At the very least keep your torso, legs and upper arms covered – no shorts or skimpy T-shirts.

Wearing a wedding ring and carrying photos of a husband and children can be helpful ... and who's to stop you inventing some even if they don't exist? Wearing dark glasses to avoid eye contact can also be helpful.

If approached by a Turkish man in circumstances that you don't appreciate, you could try ignoring him. You could also try saying *Ayıp!* (ah-YUHP) which means 'shameful', but some men won't take kindly to being called shameful when they're sure you'll find them irresistible.

On the Road

Ironically the habitual segregation of Turkish society can actually help tourist women. Men and unrelated women are not expected to sit beside each other on public transport, and you'll often see an extraordinary rigmarole going on to separate the sexes on crowded dolmuşes.

When you buy a bus ticket, the ticket agent will automatically put you next to another woman or leave the other seat empty. Some buses even have single seats near the driver set aside for women. That said, we have received letters from women who have been hassled by bus conductors, especially on night buses. If anything like that happens to you, it would be a good idea to complain loudly to the bus conductor and/or the driver. You should certainly complain when you reach your destination. If you don't, you risk adding substance to the belief that western women don't mind these things.

Women should avoid sitting in the front seat of a taxi next to the driver if at all possible. The driver may believe it is an invitation to greater intimacy. It is not advisable for women to hitchhike in Turkey, especially alone. (See Hitching in the Getting Around chapter.)

At the Hotel

When it comes to finding a hotel, women travellers may have to accept that the cheapest flea-pits may not be the best places to stay. It's not that anything will happen to you in them; more that it's hard to feel comfortable in a place where conversation in the lobby invariably comes to a halt every time you cross the threshold. If men bang on your door at night, make your annoyance known in the morning before you leave.

In Restaurants

When looking for somewhere to eat, the magic word to look out for is *aile*, meaning wife, or husband and wife, or family. Restaurants often have a separate *aile salonu* and tea gardens may also have a *aile* section. Disliking the idea of segregation, western women often ignore these areas, especially as aile salonus are often less immediately inviting than the main dining rooms. However, if you're alone they do offer you protection and indicate that you want to be treated with respect.

Love & Marriage

It would be easy to run away with the idea that every approach made by a Turkish man to a western woman is harassment. In fact many Turkish men are extremely charming and countless women fall in love during their trip. There's nothing wrong with that, of course, except that there have been some cases of tourist women giving large sums of money to their lovers, to pay for visas and air tickets out of Turkey that never materialise. However starry-eyed you may be, you should never forget the safe sex message, especially in the resort areas where promiscuity is commonplace.

Safety

It's important to remember that most female tourists would be at much greater risk of serious assault in their home countries than in Turkey, where social taboos against sexual assault and rape remain strong. But as Turkish society takes on western ways, the bad comes along with the good. A particularly nasty multiple rape and murder, involving tourists near Alanya in 1995, shocked the Turkish public and announced to all that western-style crime was starting.

A Final Word

Whatever happens, try not to get paranoid and let stupid hassles ruin your trip. Provided you dress and behave sensibly, most men will treat you hospitably, with kindness and generosity.

GAY & LESBIAN TRAVELLERS

Though not uncommon in a culture which traditionally separated men and women in society, overt homosexuality is not socially or legally acceptable in Turkey. While not strictly illegal, laws prohibiting 'lewd behaviour' are often used to suppress it. Even so, it exists openly at a small number of gay bars and clubs in big cities and resorts. Be discreet.

For more information, surf to www.qrd.org/qrd/www/world/europe/turkey.

DISABLED TRAVELLERS

Turkey has severely limited accessibility for disabled travellers. Though local people will go out of their way to help a disabled traveller get around, with few exceptions the arrangements are ad hoc.

Airlines and the top hotels and resorts have some provisions for wheelchair access, and ramps are beginning to appear (ever so slowly) in a few other places. But you should still expect general difficulty.

A good source of information on accessible travel is the Royal Association for Disability and Rehabilitation (RADAR) (☎ 0171-250 3222, from 22 April ☎ 020-7250 3222), 12 City Forum, 250 City Road, London EC1V 8AF, UK.

SENIOR TRAVELLERS

Seniors are welcomed and respected in Turkey, and sometimes receive discounts at hotels, museums and other tourist sites. Use your passport as proof of age.

TRAVEL WITH CHILDREN

For lots of practical information and advice on how to make travel as stress-free as possible, for both children and parents, consult Lonely Planet's *Travel with Children* by Maureen Wheeler. It is a complete guide to what to take, being on the road, health issues and also includes stories of other people who have travelled with their children, including in Turkey.

Your *çocuk* (child) or *çocuklar* (children) will be very well received in Turkey and, given the high Turkish birthrate, they'll have lots of company.

Child safety seats are available from all large, and many small, car rental companies at a small extra daily charge. It's best to request a child seat in advance, when you reserve your car.

Disposable *bebek bezi* (baby diapers) are readily available for *bebek* (infants). The best brand is Ultra Prima, sold in pharmacies according to the baby's weight in kilograms. A packet of 24 costs about US$6.

Ultra-pasteurised milk is sold everywhere. Some baby foods in individual jars may also be found, but it's usually better to rely on the willingness and ingenuity of hotel and restaurant staff to make up special dishes for small children. You might also want to carry a small portable food mill, on sale in pharmacies and children's products shops at home, to puree vegetables, fruits and meats.

The larger hotels and resorts can arrange for *kreş* (daycare) and baby-sitting services; the seaside resorts often have extensive children's play and activity equipment. Public parks sometimes have basic play equipment.

The market for childhood products and services is not as elaborately developed in Turkey as in Europe or the US, but Turks are handy at improvising anything which may be needed for a child's safety, health or enjoyment.

DANGERS & ANNOYANCES

Turkey is a safe country relative to most of the world; however, if you plan on travelling in the east, read the warning about Kurdish activity at the start of the Eastern Anatolia chapter.

Street crime is not a big problem in Turkey – yet. You may feel safer here than at home, but don't let this lull you into complacency. Take the normal travel precautions.

Police

The blue-clad officers, both men and women, are part of a national force designated by the words *Polis* (poh-LEES) or *Emniyet* (ehm-nee-YEHT, security). They

The Turkish Knockout

There is a small but significant danger of theft by drugging. Thieves befriend travellers, usually single men, and offer them drinks which contain powerful drugs which cause the victims to lose consciousness quickly. When the victims awake hours later, they have a terrible hangover and have been stripped of everything except their clothes.

The perpetrators of this sort of crime, who are usually *not* Turkish, often work in pairs or trios. They befriend you and travel with you, perhaps even for a day, two, or more. One report was of foreign (non-Turkish) thieves from a Middle Eastern country befriending a British subject and riding by bus with him across the country to İstanbul. The thieves offered him a soda in Gülhane Parkı. When the victim awoke, his camera, wallet and passport were gone, as was his luggage from the hotel where they were all staying.

Another team – Turks this time – works out of Ankara's otogar. They look for travellers on their way to Cappadocia and start a conversation. They mention that, by coincidence, they're going to Ürgüp as well. They buy their own tickets and join you on the bus. When you arrive at your destination, they break open a container of *ayran* (the yoghurt drink), they each take a sip, then they offer it to you. How they get the drugs in after they drink is a mystery, but the effect on the victim is powerful and virtually immediate. One sip knocks you out for half a day.

A variation perpetrated by impatient thieves is to offer you the drink (tea, soda, whatever) on the bus, you 'fall asleep', and they get off at the next town with all your gear.

This scheme is difficult to defeat, as Turks are generally very hospitable, and it is a Turkish custom to offer visitors drinks. Here are some things you can do to protect yourself:

control traffic, patrol highways and attend to other police duties in cities and towns. Under normal circumstances you will have little to do with them. If you do encounter them, they will judge you partly by your clothes and personal appearance. If you look tidy and 'proper', they'll be on your side. If you're dressed carelessly, they may subject you to bureaucratic tedium.

Other blue-clad officers with special peaked caps are called *belediye zabıtası*, municipal inspectors or market police. These officers are the modern expression of an age-old Islamic custom of special commercial police who make sure a loaf of bread weighs what it should, that 24-carat gold is indeed 24 carats, that scales and balances don't cheat the customer. You'll see these officials patrolling the markets and bazaars, and if you have a commercial problem they'll be glad to help, though they may not speak much of a foreign language.

Soldiers in the standard Turkish army uniforms may be of three types. Without special insignia, they're regular army. With a red armband bearing the word 'jandarma', they're gendarmes, a paramilitary police force charged with keeping the peace, catching criminals on the run, stopping smuggling etc. In rural areas the jandarma may be the only local police force. If the soldiers have white helmets emblazoned with the letters 'As İz', plus pistols in white holsters connected to lanyards around their necks, they're Askeri İnzibat, or military police who keep off-duty soldiers in line.

Most of these soldiers are draftees inducted into the enormous Turkish army, put through basic training, and sent out to make-work jobs that are usually pretty unexciting. They look ferocious – life in the Turkish army is no joke – but basically they are hometown boys waiting to get out. Every single one of them can tell you the precise number of days he has left to serve. Any request from a foreign tourist for help or directions is usually received as though it were a marvellous privilege.

The Turkish Knockout

- If you are a single male traveller, be suspicious of pairs or trios of other males (usually aged 18 to 28 years) who befriend you, whether Turkish or foreign. Be especially suspicious if they ask you where you are going, then travel with you.
- If you are at all suspicious of new-found friends, eat and drink only from your own supplies or those bought fresh in sealed containers from the hand of a waiter or shopkeeper. (It's possible to inject drugs into a sealed container using a syringe through the seal.) True Turkish friends may offer to pay for drinks to satisfy the requirements of traditional hospitality. They needn't deliver the drinks themselves.
- If your new travelling companions insist on staying with you at the same lodging, start thinking of how to get away. Suggest that you want to take their picture as a souvenir, and see how they react. If they've got mischief on their minds, they won't like the idea of photographic evidence.
- If you must, cite 'allergy' *(alerji)* as your reason for not accepting a drink. Or 'accidentally' spill the drink. And if your new 'friends' accuse you of insulting their generosity, get out of the situation quickly – to the police if necessary. If there is no police station near, try a bank or other location with a security officer.

A variation was described by a female reader who claims that an over-friendly local in the village of Tevfikiye (next to Troy) drugged her husband in the course of a 'friendly' evening of drinking with them, in order to get her alone and pressure her for sex.

Theft & Robbery

Theft is not much of a problem, and robbery (mugging) even less, but don't let Turkey's relative safety lull you. Take normal precautions. As is the case in every country, foreign travellers may be targeted by criminals.

Precautions include keeping track of your wallet or other valuables on crowded buses and trains and in markets; not leaving valuables in your hotel room, or at least not in view; and not walking into unknown parts of town when nobody else is around. There are isolated reports of bags being quietly slashed in İstanbul's Kapalı Çarşı, and of distract, bump-and-grab thefts in similar crowded places in the major cities.

Actually, the biggest danger of theft is probably in dormitory rooms and other open accommodation where other foreigners can see what sort of camera you have or where you stash your money.

Gassing happens mostly on trains in the Balkans (ie not in Turkey) when thieves spray anaesthetic gas into your train compartment as you sleep, then enter and relieve you of all your belongings. One reader of this guide, suitably alerted to the danger of gassing, left the compartment window open a bit (it was a cold night) and tried to stay awake, but the gas worked anyway and the thieves stole all his valuables.

In İstanbul there's a nightclub shakedown racket aimed at single men. Here's how it works: you're strolling along İstiklal Caddesi or Cumhuriyet Caddesi in the evening. You stop to look in a shop window. A well-dressed man or a couple of men approach and chat about this and that. They offer to buy you a drink in a nightclub nearby. You're given a seat next to some 'girls', and even if you protest at this point, it's too late. They say the girls' drinks are on your bill. If you resist paying an amount which conveniently equals the entire contents of your wallet, you are escorted to the back office and convinced forcibly to pay up. Moral: single men should not accept invitations from unknown Turks in large cities without sizing the situation up very carefully.

Disputes

In general, Turks view foreigners as cultured, educated and wealthy – even if many foreign visitors don't deserve such a view. This means that you will sometimes be given special consideration, jumped to the heads of queues, given the best seat on public transport etc.

Thus, in a dispute, if you keep your cool and act dignified, you will generally be given the benefit of the doubt. If it is thought you have powerful friends, you will definitely be given that benefit.

It's difficult to imagine a dispute involving a foreigner coming to the point of blows, as Turks are slow to anger. Don't let it happen. A Turk rarely finds it necessary to fight, but if he does, he wants to win, *whatever* the cost. Knowing that horrible things could happen, bystanders will pull two quarrelling men apart, even if they've never seen them before.

In the case of women travellers in disputes with Turks, you should know that Turkish men are incredibly offended at any insults to their manhood, and will retaliate. Insults to them can include being shouted at or browbeaten by a woman who is not (in their eyes) unquestionably of a higher social status. In general, keep it all formal.

Lese-Majesty

There are laws against insulting, defaming or making light of Atatürk, the Turkish flag, the Turkish people, the Turkish Republic etc. Any difficulty will probably arise from misunderstanding.

At the first sign that you have inadvertently been guilty of lese-majesty, be sure to make your apologies, which will be readily accepted (see the 'Lese-Majesty' boxed text in the Facts about Turkey chapter).

Natural Hazards

Earthquakes Turkey sometimes has bad earthquakes. The big quakes only seem to hit every eight or 10 years, but the same thing happens in many parts of the world, so it's up to Allah.

Undertows & Riptides At some of the swimming areas, particularly in the Black Sea near İstanbul, this is a real danger. Undertows can kill you by powerfully pulling you beneath the surface, and a riptide does the same by sweeping you out to sea so that you exhaust yourself trying to regain the shore. There may be no signs warning of the danger. Lifeguards may not be present, or may be untrained or not equipped with a boat. Don't trust luck. You can't necessarily see these hazards or predict where they will be.

In either situation, remain calm, as panic can be fatal. Don't exhaust yourself by trying to swim straight back to the beach from a rip, because you'll never make it. Rather, swim to the left or right to escape the rip area, and make for land in that direction. These dangers are usually a problem only on long stretches of open-sea beach with surf. In coves and bays, where waves are broken or diverted by headlands, you probably won't be in danger.

Insects, Snakes & Other Animals Turkey has mosquitoes, scorpions and snakes. You will not see many of them, but be aware, as you tramp around the ruins on the Aegean and Mediterranean coasts in particular, that such beasts do live here and may be nearby, at least in summer. There are also wild boar and wolves about, though you won't encounter these unless you hike deep into the bush.

The Imperial Auto

As a pedestrian, give way to cars and trucks in all situations, even if you have to jump out of the way. The sovereignty of the pedestrian is unrecognised in Turkey. If a car hits you, the driver (if not the law courts) will blame you. This does not apply on a recognised crossing controlled by a traffic officer or a traffic signal. If you've got a 'Walk' light, you've got the right of way. Watch out, all the same. Know that every Turkish driver considers you, a pedestrian, as merely an annoyance. A dispute with a driver will get you nowhere and may escalate into an even bigger problem.

Cigarette Smoke

If you're offended by cigarette smoke, you will have some unpleasant moments in Turkey. Though the local cancer prevention society fields a brave effort to stop smoking, this is the land of aromatic Turkish tobacco and smoking is a national passion. The movement for nonsmoking areas in public places is gaining ground, but it will be a long battle.

By law, no smoking is allowed on domestic airline flights, or on city or intercity buses (except for the driver, who may smoke!). Trains are supposed to have nonsmoking carriages, but the prohibition is often ignored.

Noise

Noise is a source of great annoyance in cities and larger towns. Choose hotel rooms keeping noise in mind.

Among the most persistent and omnipresent noises is that of the call to prayer, amplified to ear-splitting levels. In the good old days before microphones and amplifiers, it must have been beautiful to hear the clear, natural voices of the muezzins calling from a hundred minarets, even before dawn, when the first call is given. Now you hear a cacophony of blaring noise five or more times a day. If there's a minaret right outside your hotel window, you'll know it.

Also, Turks are addicted to nightlife and think nothing of staying up until 1 or 2 am in the middle of the week, so watch out for highly amplified bands and singers. Nightclub noise is particularly insulting when you have spent good money to upgrade your accommodation only to find that the better the hotel, the louder its nightclub. In some resorts (such as Bodrum), atomic-powered discos rock the entire town until dawn, making sleep virtually impossible. Indeed, the governor of Muğla, the province in which Bodrum is located, typified the problem: when confronted with a noise complaint, he responded 'If they don't like noise and nightlife, why did they come to Bodrum?'

When in doubt, ask *Sakin mi?* (sah-KEEN mee, 'Is it quiet here?').

Air Pollution

Winter heating furnaces in Ankara and İstanbul, which used to create severe pollution problems from the burning of lignite (soft coal), have largely been converted to natural gas, as have taxis. But lignite is still burned in medium-sized and smaller cities, creating moderate pollution. If you find your nose running, your eyes watering and itching, and your head aching, that's the pollution. The heating season lasts from 15 October to 1 April. In summer there is some pollution from cars, but it's no worse than in other big cities.

BUSINESS HOURS

The following are opening hours in Turkey:

Archaeological Sites
Sites are open from 8 or 9 am to 5 or 6 pm (some later) every day, with no break for lunch.

Banks
Open from 8.30 am to noon and 1.30 to 5 pm from Monday to Friday.

Covered Markets
İstanbul's Kapalı Çarşı and covered markets in other cities are open from Monday to Saturday from 8 am to 6.30 pm.

Grocery Shops & Markets
Open from Monday to Saturday from 6 or 7 am to 7 or 8 pm. On Sunday most markets close, though one or two grocers stay open in each neighbourhood.

Mosques
Most are open all the time. If a mosque is locked, there is usually a *bekçi* (guardian) with a key somewhere nearby. Avoid visiting mosques at prayer time (at or within 20 minutes after the call to prayer). Avoid visiting on Friday, the Muslim holy day, particularly in the morning.

Museums
Museums open from 8.30 or 9.30 am to noon or 12.30 pm, then (in some cases) they close for lunch, reopening at 1 or 1.30 pm and remaining open until 5 or 5.30 pm, perhaps later in summer. Museums are closed on Monday, with the exception of Topkapı Palace in İstanbul which is closed on Tuesday.

Offices
Government and business offices may open at 8 or 9 am, close for lunch, and reopen around 1.30 pm, remaining open until 4 or 5 pm. During the hot summer months in some cities the working day begins at 7 or 8 am and finishes at 2 pm. Also, during the holy month of Ramazan the working day is shortened.

Post Offices
Main post offices in large cities tend to be open every day from 8 am to 8 pm for most services (stamp sales, telephone jeton and card sales, telegrams, fax etc), and the telephone centres may be open until midnight. However, windows may be open only from 8.30 am to noon and 1.30 pm to 5 or 6 pm for other services such as poste restante and parcel service. Smaller post offices have more limited hours: 8.30 am to 12.30 pm and 1.30 to 5.30 pm, and may be closed part of Saturday, and all day Sunday.

Restaurants
Most restaurants serve food continuously from 11 am to 11 pm or later. Many open early (6 or 7 am) for breakfast. The exceptions are a few restaurants in bazaars, business and financial districts which serve primarily office workers and serve only lunch.

Shops
Open Monday to Saturday from 9 am to noon and 1.30 or 2.30 pm to 6 or 7 pm or even later; many don't close for lunch.

Tourist Offices
Usually open Monday to Friday from 8.30 am to noon or 12.30 pm, and 1.30 to 5.30 pm, longer in summer in popular tourist locations.

THE CALENDAR

Religious Festivals

The official Turkish calendar is the western, Gregorian one used in Europe, but religious festivals are celebrated according to the Muslim lunar Hijri calendar. As the lunar calendar is about 11 days shorter than the Gregorian, the Muslim festivals arrive 11 days earlier each year.

Actual dates for Muslim religious festivals are not completely systematic. Rather, they are proclaimed by Muslim authorities after the appropriate astronomical observations and calculations have been made, and then the civil authorities decide how many days should be public holidays. To help you know what's going on, the approximate dates of all major festivals for the near future are listed below.

Muslim days, like Jewish ones, begin at sundown. Thus a Friday holiday will begin on Thursday at sunset and last until Friday at sunset.

For major religious and public holidays there is also a half-day vacation for 'preparation', called *arife*, preceding the start of a festival. Shops and offices close about noon, and the festival begins at sunset.

Friday is the Muslim Sabbath, but it is not a holiday. Mosques and baths will be crowded, especially on Friday morning. The day of rest, a secular one, is Sunday.

Only two religious holidays are public holidays: Şeker Bayramı and Kurban Bayramı.

Ramazan The Holy Month, called Ramadan in other Muslim countries, is similar in some ways to Lent. For the 30 days of Ramazan, a good Muslim lets *nothing* pass the lips during daylight hours: no eating, drinking, smoking, or even licking a postage stamp.

A cannon shot, and these days a radio announcer, signal the end of the fast at sunset. The fast is broken traditionally with flat pide bread if possible. Lavish dinners are given and may last far into the night. Before dawn, drummers circulate through town to awaken the faithful so they can eat before sunrise.

During Ramazan, restaurants may be closed from dawn to nightfall, and in conservative towns it's bad form for anyone – non-Muslims included – to smoke, munch snacks or sip drinks in plain view. Business hours may change and be shorter. As non-Muslims, it's understood that you get to eat and drink when you like, and in the big cities you'll find lots of nonfasting Muslims right beside you, but it's best to be discreet and to maintain a polite low visibility.

The 27th day of Ramazan is **Kadir Gecesi**, the Night of Power, when the Koran was revealed and Muhammed was appointed the Messenger of God.

The fasting of Ramazan is a worthy, sacred act and a blessing to Muslims. Pregnant or nursing women, the infirm and aged, and travellers are excused, according to the Koran, if they feel they cannot keep the fast.

Şeker Bayramı Also called Ramazan Bayramı or İd es-Seğir, this is a three-day festival at the end of Ramazan. *Şeker* (shek-EHR) is sugar or candy. During this festival children traditionally go door to door asking for sweet treats, Muslims exchange greeting cards and pay social calls, and everybody enjoys drinking lots of tea in broad daylight after fasting for Ramazan. The festival is a national holiday when banks and offices are closed and hotels, buses, trains and planes are heavily booked.

Kurban Bayramı The most important religious and secular holiday of the year, Kurban Bayramı (koor-BAHN, sacrifice) is equivalent in importance to Christmas in Christian countries.

The festival commemorates Abraham's near-sacrifice of Isaac on Mt Moriah (Genesis 22; Koran, Sura 37). In the story, God orders Abraham to take Isaac, the son of his old age, up to Mt Moriah and sacrifice him.

Abraham takes Isaac up the mountain and lays him on the altar, but at the last moment God stops Abraham, congratulates him on his faithfulness, and orders him to sacrifice instead a ram tangled in a nearby bush. Abraham does so.

Following the tradition today, 2.5 million rams are sacrificed on Kurban Bayramı in Turkey each year. For days beforehand you'll see herds of sheep parading through streets or gathered in markets. Every head of a household who can afford a sheep buys one and takes it home. Right after the early morning prayers on the actual day of Bayramı, the head of the household slits the sheep's throat. It's then flayed and butchered, and family and friends immediately cook up a feast. A sizeable portion of the meat is distributed to the needy, and the skin is often donated to a charity; the charity sells it to a leather products company.

Lots of people take to the road, going home to parents or friends. Everybody exchanges greeting cards. At some point you'll probably be invited to share in the festivities.

Kurban Bayramı is a four-day national holiday which you must plan for. Banks may be closed for a full week, though one or two branches will stay open in the big cities to serve foreigners. Transportation will be packed, and hotel rooms, particularly in resort areas, will be scarce and expensive.

Minor Festivals During minor religious festivals mosques are illuminated with strings of lights, and special foods are prepared.

Regaip Kandili This is the traditional date for the conception of the Prophet Muhammed. You'll see packets of small, sweetish *simit* bread rings, wrapped in coloured paper, for sale on the streets.

Miraç Kandili This is the celebration of Muhammed's miraculous nocturnal journey from Mecca to Jerusalem and to heaven astride a winged horse named Burak.

Berat Kandili This festival has various meanings in different Islamic countries.

Mevlid-i Nebi The 12th of the Hijri month of Rebi ul-evvel is the anniversary of the Prophet's birth (in 570 AD). There are special prayers and foods, and mosque illuminations.

Holidays & Special Events

The following is a month-by-month list of holidays and special events in Turkey.

January It's rainy and cold throughout the country in January, with high air pollution in the cities – not usually a pleasant time to visit. Eastern Turkey is in the icy grip of winter; Ankara and the rest of the Anatolian Plateau may be covered in snow.

Religious Festivals
: Ramazan, the holy month which changes lots of schedules, is from 8 December 1999 to 7 January 2000. Kadir Gecesi, the Night of Power, is celebrated on 15 January 1999 and 4 January 2000. Ramazan is followed by the three-day celebration of Şeker Bayramı from 8 to 10 January 2000.

New Year's Day
: 1 January – a public holiday. Decorations in shops, exchanges of gifts and greeting cards, make it a kind of surrogate Christmas, good for business.

Camel-Wrestling Festival
: Mid-January – held in the village of Selçuk, next to Ephesus, south of İzmir.

February In February it rains almost everywhere and is chilly and cheerless. The only fun to be had is indoors or at the ski slopes on Uludağ near Bursa, in the Beydağları mountains near Antalya, on Erciyes near Kayseri, or at Palandöken near Erzurum.

Kurban Bayramı
: 22 to 26 February 2002.

March Still rainy in most of the country, though there may be some good periods on the south Aegean and Mediterranean coasts. It's still bitterly cold in the east.

Kurban Bayramı
: The four-day holiday which disrupts Turkish schedules for a week, is celebrated from 28 March to 1 April 1999, 16 to 20 March 2000 and 5 to 9 March 2001.

Çanakkale Victory Days
: 12 to 19 March – celebrates the successful defence of the straits at the beginning of the Gallipoli campaign in WWI.

April April can be delightful throughout the country, except in the east, where it's still cold. There may be some rain, but in any case the wild flowers will be out on the Anatolian Plateau. The waters of the Aegean and Mediterranean are approaching a comfortable temperature for swimming. The south-east (Gaziantep, Şanlıurfa, Mardin and Diyarbakır), so torrid and parched in high summer, is very pleasant now, but there may still be snow on top of Nemrut Dağı. April is when the bus tours begin in earnest.

Manisa Power Gum Festival
: 20-30 April – when a traditional remedy called *mesir macunu* or *kuvvet macunu* (power gum), said to restore health, youth and potency, is concocted and distributed in Manisa, near İzmir.

National Sovereignty Day
April 23 – is the big national holiday, when the first Grand National Assembly, or republican parliament, met in Ankara in 1920. It's also Children's Day, an international children's festival, with kids from all over the world, held in Ankara.

Anzac Day
April 24-25 – is commemorated with a dawn ceremony at Gallipoli.

May May usually brings perfectly beautiful weather throughout the country, with little chance of rain, though it's still chilly out east. May is a good month to visit the hot, dry south-east.

This month begins the tourist season in earnest, and also includes important public holidays. Sound and light shows begin at the Sultan Ahmet Camii (Blue Mosque) in İstanbul and last until October. In Konya, the javelin-throwing game of *cirit* (jirid), played on horseback, takes place every Saturday and Sunday until October.

Mevlid-i Nebi
The Prophet's birthday, is celebrated on 23 May 2002.

Selçuk Ephesus Festival of Culture & Art
1st week in May – at Selçuk, south of İzmir, features folk dances, concerts and exhibits, some in the Great Theatre at Ephesus.

Youth & Sports Day
19 May – held to commemorate Atatürk's birthday (1881).

29 May
In İstanbul, celebrations remember the conquest of the city from the Byzantines in 1453.

June The weather is perfect throughout the country, but getting hot. There is little rain except along the Black Sea coast.

Mevlid-i Nebi
The Prophet's birthday, is celebrated on 26 June 1999, 15 June 2000 and 4 June 2001.

International Mediterranean Festival
1st week in June – takes place in İzmir usually at this time.

Traditional Kırkpınar Oiled Wrestling Competition
2nd week in June – held at Edirne and Festival of Troy at Çanakkale, on the Dardanelles near Troy.

Kafkasör Festival
3rd week in June – in a *yayla* (alpine pasture). It takes place near Artvin in north-eastern Turkey and is a true country festival featuring local dances, crafts, foods, and fights between bulls in rut.

International İstanbul Festival of the Arts
Late June-Mid-July – this is a world-class festival, with top performers in music and dance, and special exhibitions.

July The weather is hot, the sky is always blue, the sea water is warm, and everything is crowded with holidaymakers, both Turkish and foreign.

International İstanbul Festival
This continues until mid-July.

Denizcilik Günü (Navy Day)
1 July – when mariners, ships and various maritime pursuits are celebrated.

Nasreddin Hodja Celebrations
5-10 July – (in Akşehir, Nasreddin Hodja's traditional birthplace) are held in honour of the semi-legendary, humorous master of Turkish folklore legends and tales.

Folklore & Music Festival
7-12 July – at Bursa, this is one of Turkey's best folk-dancing events of the year; the Bursa Fair (trade & tourism) starts about the same time.

August It's hot, sunny and crowded. This is the best time to be in eastern Turkey, when the weather is fine and crowds are smaller than along the western beaches. Sound and light shows begin at the Anıt Kabir, Atatürk's mausoleum, in Ankara.

Special Mass
15 August – at the House of the Virgin Mary (Meryemana) near Ephesus celebrates the Assumption of the Virgin Mary. The Catholic archbishop of İzmir says mass.

Çanakkale Troy Festival
15-18 August – at Çanakkale, with folk dances, music, tours of Mt Ida and Troy.

Haci Bektaş Veli Commemoration
Mid-August – at the town of that name in Cappadocia.

İzmir International Fair
20 August-9 September – for three weeks the city's hotels are packed and transportation is crowded. The fair has amusements, cultural and commercial-industrial displays.

Zafer Bayramı
30 August – commemorating the decisive victory at Dumlupınar of the republican armies over the invading Greek army during Turkey's War of Independence in 1922. Towns and cities celebrate their own Kurtuluş Günü (Day of Liberation) on the appropriate date commemorating when Atatürk's armies drove out the foreign troops during July and August 1922.

September The weather is still hot and fine, moderating a bit towards the end of the month. Swimming is still wonderful, crowds are still fairly heavy, and the bus tours begin to make a comeback. Sound and light shows continue at the Anıt Kabir in Ankara. The İzmir Fair goes on until 9 September.

Regaip Kandili
Celebrated on 21 September 2001 and 13 September 2002.

Bodrum Culture & Art Week
1-9 September – featuring Turkish classical music concerts in Bodrum Castle, art exhibits and water sports shows.

Kurtuluş Günü (Liberation Day)
9 September – in İzmir, with lots of parades, speeches and flags.

Cappadocia Festival
15-18 September – a grape harvest and folklore festival highlighting the 'fairy chimneys' and underground cities of Cappadocia.

Culinary Contest
22-30 September – in Konya.

Diyarbakır Watermelon Festival
Mid or Late September – one year, everybody was disappointed because the prize-winning watermelon weighed in at a mere 32kg. A bad year, they said – no rain.

October The weather is perfect again, and crowds are diminishing, though bus tours start again, after a lull in high summer. The rains begin around mid or late October. There may also be freak snowstorms on the Anatolian Plateau. Sound and light shows are supposed to continue in İstanbul at the Sultan Ahmet Camii – check in advance.

Religious Festivals
Regaip Kandili – 15 October 1999 and 6 October 2000; Miraç Kandili – 25 October 2000, 14 October 2001 and 3 October 2002; Berat Kandili – 21 to 22 October 2002.

'Golden Orange' Film & Art Festival
1-9 October – held in Antalya, with a competition for best Turkish film of the year. There are other exhibits.

Turkish Troubadours' Week
21-29 October – held in Konya, where bards continue the traditional poetic forms hold contests in repartee, free-form composition and riddles.

Cumhuriyet Bayramı (Republic Day)
29 October – commemorates the proclamation of the republic by Atatürk in 1923. It's the biggest civil holiday, with lots of parades and speeches.

November The weather is very pleasant, with cool to warm days and chilly nights, but one must dodge the rain. If your luck holds, you can have a marvellous late-year beach holiday.

Religious Festivals
Berat Kandili – 23 and 24 November 1999, 12 and 13 November 2000 and 1 and 2 November 2001; Miraç Kandili – 5 November 1999. Ramazan is from 28 November to 27 December 2000, 17 November to 16 December 2001 and 6 November to 5 December 2002.

Anniversary of Atatürk's Death
10 November – the most important day of the month, it is the day Atatürk died in 1938. At precisely 9.05 am, the moment of his death, the entire country comes to a screeching halt for a moment of silence. Literally everything stops in its tracks (you should too), just for a moment. Car horns and sirens blare. In schools, in the newspapers (the names of which are normally printed in red, but are all in black on this day), on radio and TV, the national hero's life and accomplishments are reviewed.

December The weather is chilly throughout the country, though milder along the Mediterranean coast. You must expect some, perhaps heavy, rain. There are few visitors; some museums close some exhibits for renovation. In rare years, the warmth and pleasantness of a good November will stretch into early December.

Religious Festivals
The holy month of Ramazan starts in November and lasts until 27 December 2000, 16 December 2001 and 5 December 2002. Kadir Gecesi, the Night of Power, is commemorated

on 24 December 2000, 13 December 2001 and 2 December 2002. Şeker Bayramı is from 28 to 30 December 2000, 17 to 19 December 2001 and 6 to 8 December 2002.

Camel Wrestling
: All Month – at various locations in the province of Aydın, south of İzmir.

St Nicholas Festival
: 6-8 December – commemorative ceremonies are held in the 4th-century church of St Nicholas, the original Santa Claus, in Demre.

Mevlana Festival
: 14-17 December (approximately) – honouring Celaleddin Rumi, the great poet and mystic who founded the Mevlevi order of Whirling Dervishes, held in Konya. Hotel space is tight, so try to pin down a room in advance, or be prepared for a room below your normal standard.

ACTIVITIES

Water Sports

Water sports are big in Turkey because of the beautiful coasts and beaches. Yachting, rowing, water-skiing, snorkelling, scuba diving and swimming are well represented. Because of the many antiquities in the depths off the Turkish coasts, scuba diving is regulated. Diving shops in Marmaris, Bodrum and other coastal towns can provide details. Turkish divers are very safety conscious, so bring your diving credentials to dive to the depth you want to explore.

Mountain Climbing

Dağcılık (DAAH-juh-LUHK, mountain climbing) is practised by a small but enthusiastic number of Turks, and Turkey has plenty of good, high mountains for it. *The Mountains of Turkey* by Karl Smith is a good guide.

Skiing

There is decent skiing on Uludağ, near Bursa, at a few resorts in the Beydağları mountain range near Antalya, on Mt Erciyes near Kayseri, and at Palandöken on the outskirts of Erzurum. Uludağ and Palandöken have a range of accommodation from moderate to expensive. Ski facilities are rather basic by European or US standards, but the snow can be good and may last well into spring, especially at Palandöken. Lift fees are usually included in your accommodation package.

Cycling

Cycling through Turkey is possible, and mostly delightful. For details, see the Getting Around chapter.

WORK

You can extend your time in Turkey by getting a job. Most people who do this teach English at one of the many private colleges or schools in İstanbul or Ankara. Others work at one of the publication offices such as at the *Turkish Daily News*.

It's best to obtain a *çalışma vizesi* (work visa) from the Turkish embassy or consulate (in person or by mail; it takes about three weeks) in your home country before you leave. Submit the completed visa form, your passport, two photos of yourself, your proof of employment (a contract or letter from your employer) and the required fee. Your passport will be returned with the visa stamped inside.

If you're not at home and you want a work visa, apply for it outside Turkey. The Turkish consulate in Komotini in Greece, a 10-hour overnight bus ride from İstanbul, is used to such requests. It usually grants the visa within a few hours. If you plan to make a special trip, check to make sure the consulate will be open and issuing work visas when you arrive. Your own consulate or a Greek consulate may be able to tell you (see Embassies earlier in this chapter).

Once you arrive in Turkey on a work visa, you must obtain a 'pink book', a combined work permit and residence permit, from the *Yabancılar Polisi* (Foreigners' Police). In İstanbul they're in Cağaloğlu behind the İstanbul Valiliği on Ankara Caddesi. Your employer may do this for you. If not, apply with your passport, two more photos, and the US$40 processing fee. They should have your pink book ready in two or three days. The pink book, which takes over from the visa in your passport, is renewable every year, as long as you show proof of continued employment.

If you can't provide proof of employment (ie if you're working illegally), you may still be able to get a three-month residence permit if you can show bank deposits in Turkey totalling more than about US$200. You may or may not be able to renew a three-month permit, at the whim of the officer.

When all else fails, leave the country for a day or two to Greece, Bulgaria or Cyprus, and get a new 90-day tourist visa as you return to Turkey. This may only be possible a few times, however, as the immigration officer will become suspicious of too many recent Turkish stamps in your passport.

ACCOMMODATION

Camping

Using your own equipment and bedding, it is sometimes possible to sleep on the roof of a pension or hotel, or camp in the garden, for a minimal fee of US$2 to US$4 per person, which includes use of bathing and other hotel facilities. The fancier camping grounds near seaside resorts and in Cappadocia may have all facilities – showers, shops, swimming pools, gardens – but charge almost as much as cheap hotels.

Camping outside recognised camping grounds by the roadside is often more hassle than it's worth as the police may come and check you out, the landowner may wonder what's up, and curious villagers may decide that they'd rather sit and watch you than the *Dynasty* reruns on TV.

Hostels

As the lowest priced hotels and pensions are already rock-bottom, there is no extensive system of hostels in Turkey. The term *yurt* (hostel or lodge) or *öğrenci yurdu* (student hostel) usually defines an extremely basic and often dingy dormitory lodging intended for low-budget Turkish students from the provinces who are attending university classes. These are not normally affiliated with the International Youth Hostel Federation, and often they are not conveniently located near the major sights, though they may open their doors to foreign students in the summertime. Tourism offices have details.

Hotels

The cheapest hotels in Turkey are rated by each local municipality. These are the basic places that provide bed, heat, light and water. They are used mostly by working-class Turkish men travelling on business. Virtually all hotels above this basic standard are rated by the Ministry of Tourism according to a star system. One-star hotels are just a step above the cheap places rated by the municipalities. At the top, rating five stars, are the international-class places, such as the Hiltons, Hyatts, Kempinskis, Ramadas and Sheratons.

Budget Lodgings in this group are priced from US$4 per bed in a small town up to US$20 or US$30 for a double room in a large city. For Turks, these are the *otels* (hotels) used by farmers in town for the market, workers in town looking for a job, or the *pansiyons* (pensions) used by working-class families on holiday at the seaside. Not surprisingly, the most difficult place to find a truly cheap, good, low-budget room is İstanbul. In most other cities good, cheap beds can be found fairly easily. In out-of-the-way villages the price for a bed is surprisingly low, and the bedbugs are free.

Rooms priced less than about US$10 do not usually have a private shower or toilet in the room, but may have a *lavabo* (sink). Above that price, in small towns you may get private facilities. Cold-water showers are usually free, as they should be. Hot-water showers may cost between US$1 and US$2 in lodgings where a fire must be built in the hot-water heater. If there is solar water-heating, hot showers are often free. With solar water-heating, plan to shower in the evening when the water is hottest, rather than in the morning.

At the lowest prices, the rooms will be quite bare and spartan, but functional. Hotels may quote prices per bed rather than per room. For privacy, you may have to pay for all of the beds in the room. If you find used sheets on the bed, request clean ones; the owner has got to change them sometime, and it may as well be for you. Say *Temiz çarşaf lazım* (teh-MEEZ chahr-SHAHF lyaa-zuhm, 'Clean sheets are necessary').

Mid-Range Turkey has lots of modern and comfortable hotels rated at one to three stars by the Ministry of Tourism. Facilities in this range include lifts, staff capable of speaking a smattering of German, French and English, rooms with a private shower or bath and toilet, perhaps balconies from which you can enjoy the view, and maybe guarded car parks. Prices in this range are from US$20 to US$90.

A one-star hotel will have these facilities and little else, and will price its double rooms with a bath at around US$20. A two-star hotel will probably have a restaurant and bar, a TV lounge, obsequious staff, and some pretensions to decor and architecture. Double rooms with a private bath would be priced from US$25 to US$60.

A three-star hotel may provide colour TVs and minibar refrigerators in all guest rooms, and may have haughty multilingual staff, a swimming pool, nightclub, pastry shop, or other special facilities as well. Double rooms with a bath would be priced from US$40 to US$90. Fairly prosperous Turks look upon a hotel room in this range as quite luxurious accommodation.

Top End Hotels at the top end are priced from US$90 to US$250 or more for a double room.

Hotels of an international standard, such as the Hiltons, Sheratons, Kempinskis, Inter-Continentals, Hyatts, Swissötels etc, are rated at five stars and are mostly found in the largest cities (İstanbul, Ankara, İzmir) and in the most famous tourist destinations (Antalya, Cappadocia). Just below the international chains in luxury are the Turkish chain hotels such as Dedeman, Merit and others, rated at four or five stars. These hotels sometimes provide almost the same degree of luxury as some of the top places, but at prices around 20% to 40% lower.

Besides these expensive places, Turkey has a number of smaller, very comfortable hotels where you'll enjoy more personal and attentive service at much lower prices. These four-star luxury hotels may not have swimming pools, health clubs, ballrooms and convention centres, but they have most of the comforts an individual traveller would normally require. Prices for a double room range from US$90 to US$150.

Boutique Hotels In some tourist towns old Ottoman mansions, caravanserais or other historic buildings have been refurbished or even completely rebuilt and equipped with modern conveniences. Charm, atmosphere and history are the attractions here, and they are provided in abundance at prices ranging from US$75 to US$175 for a double room, breakfast included. Because of their unique character, these hotels may not be rated according to the star system although most would rate three or four stars if they were.

Choosing a Hotel

The following are some points to watch.

Inspect the Rooms For budget and mid-range accommodation, don't judge a hotel by its facade, tell the reception clerk you'd like to see a room. A staff member will invariably be appointed to show you one or several rooms.

In the mid-range Turkish hotels there is a tendency to put money into the lobby rather than into the rooms, and so looking at the lobby does not give you an accurate idea of the quality of the guest quarters.

Know the Price Prices should be posted prominently at the reception desk. Sometimes the posted prices will be more than what the proprietor actually expects to get for a room. Unless the hotel or pension is obviously quite full and very busy, you may be able to haggle for a lower price.

Please keep in mind when you haggle that pension and cheap hotel owners must be able to make some money to stay in business. A few travellers make a habit of haggling forcefully even if the price (say, US$3 for a tidy bed with clean sheets in a safe dorm room) is already rock bottom. This may only lead to unpleasantness and even bitterness. It certainly doesn't promote understanding between Turks and foreigners. If the price represents good value for money, it's best to pay it with a smile.

Whether you haggle or not, make sure you understand the price. Is it per bed (*beher yatak*, beh-HEHR yah-TAHK) or per room (*oda fiyatı*, OH-dah fee-yah-tuh)? Is breakfast (*kahvaltı*) included (*dahil*) or excluded (*hariç*)? Is there an extra fee for a hot shower (*duş ücreti*, DOOSH urj-reh-tee)? Is the tax included (*vergi dahil*, vehr-GEE dah-HEEL)? It usually is (and should be) except at the most expensive hotels.

Beware of Noise Turkish cities and towns are noisy places, and you will soon learn to choose a hotel and a room with quiet in mind. In this guide I have done some of the work for you by recommending mostly the quieter places, but you will have to be aware when you select your room. The front rooms in a hotel, those facing the busy street, are usually looked upon as the most desirable by the hotel management, and are sometimes priced higher than rooms at the rear. Take advantage of this: take a room at the back. Ask for *sakin bir oda* (sah-KEEN beer oh-dah, 'a quiet room') and pay less.

Water Pressure In some cities, and particularly in summer, water may be cut off for several hours at a time, though many hotels have roof tanks which do away with this problem. The other problem with water pressure is when the pressure remains high, but the fixtures are not in good repair, and the toilet tinkles all night.

Hot Water Except in the fanciest hotels, do not trust hot water to come out of the left-hand tap and cold water out of the right-hand one. In the same bathroom, the sink may be marked correctly and the shower incorrectly. Open both taps and let them run full force for a minute or so, close them, then open one and next the other to see what you get. If both are cold, let them run a few minutes more and check again. Still cold? Now it's time to complain to the management.

Every desk clerk will say, 'Yes, we have hot water', but when you try to take a shower the new fact may be, 'Ah, the furnace just this minute broke down!'

Lifts The button marked 'Ç' (*çağır,* call) brings the lift to you. 'G' is for *gönder* (send), and if you push this one, you'll send the lift to the end of its run (usually to the ground floor). A little illuminated 'M' means the lift is *meşgül* (engaged); wait until the light goes out before pushing 'Ç'. If there's a little illuminated 'K', it means the car is *katta* (positioned at your floor). 'Z' or *zemin* in lift parlance means ground floor; this is the button to push to get there. If you push '1', you'll end up on the 1st floor above ground level. If the ground floor button is not 'Z' it's probably 'L' for *lobi.*

Electricity Electricity may go off for short periods in some locations.

Except in the more expensive hotels, your bedside lamp will never have more than a 25-watt bulb in it. Apparently Turks don't read in bed. However, you may find a *gece lambası* in your room, a low-wattage bulb, perhaps even one in a lurid colour, perhaps high on the wall, meant to give an eerie glow to the room so that you need not sleep in total darkness.

Unmarried Couples Unmarried couples sharing rooms usually run into no problems, even though the desk clerk sees the obvious when taking down the pertinent information from your passports onto the registration form. By law, Turkish men are forbidden to share rooms with women to whom they are not married, and if there is a doubt must produce a marriage certificate. The cheaper the hotel, the more traditional and conservative its management tends to be. Very simple hotels which are clean and 'proper' want to maintain their reputations. If you look clean and proper, and act that way, there should be no trouble.

continued on page 102

FOOD

EDDIE GERALD

Turkish cuisine is at the heart of eastern Mediterranean cooking. It demands fresh ingredients and careful preparation. The ingredients are often simple but of high quality. Turkish farmers, herders and fishers bring forth a wealth of superb produce from this agriculturally rich land and its surrounding seas. Turkey is one of only seven countries on earth which produces a surplus of food.

For help in reading the menu and identifying Turkish dishes, refer to the Turkish Language Guide chapter at the back of this book.

The variety of dishes found in restaurants is not as great as that found in home kitchens. And when you'd like a change from grilled lamb, you'll rarely find an Indonesian, Mexican, Indian or Japanese restaurant just around the corner. Despite the extent of the Ottoman Empire the Turks did not trade extensively with other nations during the 18th and 19th centuries and never received an influx of foreign populations and cuisines. This is changing, though. Some Chinese restaurants have opened, Japanese ones are sure to follow, and you can now – for better or worse – get authentic Yankee hamburgers and pizza in the larger cities and resorts.

Kosher Food

Turkey's small Jewish community lives in the largest cities. Some kosher food is available to them, but there are virtually no kosher restaurants, groceries or butchers serving the traveller.

Saving Money

Always know the price in advance. Though menus bearing prices have become common in many resorts, they are uncommon in the rest of Turkey. Prices may be posted on the wall (all in Turkish). The prices of certain items, such as fresh whole fish, may depend upon the daily market, and may be negotiable. Whatever the case, if you have no idea of the price, you may be overcharged.

Order as you eat. There is no need to order your entire meal at the beginning, except perhaps in the international hotels. It's fine to order an appetizer or two, sit and talk, and order your main course later.

Don't overeat with your eyes. Turkish restaurants often have elaborate displays of available dishes. Resist the temptation to try six things.

Eat bread. Turkish sourdough bread is fresh, delicious, plentiful and cheap. Many Turkish dishes are served with savoury sauces; dip and sop your bread and enjoy.

Don't accept any plate of food which you have not specifically ordered. For example, in İstanbul's Çiçek Pasajı, near Galatasaray Square, itinerant vendors may put a dish of fresh almonds on your table. They're not a gift. They'll show up on your bill at a higher than average rate. If you haven't ordered it, ask *İkramiye mi?* ('Is it a gift?') or *Bedava mı?* ('Is it free?'). If the answer is no, say *İstemiyorum* ('I don't want it'), or settle on a price if you do.

Be sure you receive an itemised restaurant bill (it's customary), and check it for errors. Restaurant waiters are not usually the world's star mathematicians; and widespread tourism has brought with it the sin of bill-fiddling, virtually unknown before 1980. By the way, the traditional Turkish practice of figuring the bill, then turning it over, folding it in half and writing the total on the back has the look of a rip-off. It's not necessarily so, but you should feel no embarrassment in opening the bill, redoing the addition, and questioning any items, including obscure *kuver* (cover) and *servis* (service) charges. If you don't get an itemised bill, by all means ask for one.

Places to Eat

Restaurants

Restoran/Lokanta (restaurants) are everywhere, and most are open early in the morning until late at night. Most are inexpensive, and although price is always some determinant of quality, often the difference between a US$6 meal and a US$15 meal is not great, at least as far as flavour is concerned. Service and ambience are fancier at the higher price.

In any restaurant in Turkey there is a convenient *lavabo* (sink) so that you can wash your hands before eating. Just say the word and the waiter will point it out.

Also, if you're a woman or are travelling with a woman, ask for the *aile salonu* (family dining room, often upstairs) which will be free of the sometimes oppressive all-male atmosphere to be found in many cheap Turkish eateries.

Many Turkish waiters have the annoying habit of snatching your plate away before you're finished with it. This may be due to a rule of eastern etiquette which holds that it is impolite to leave a finished plate

EDDIE GERALD

You are unlikely to go hungry in Turkey as restaurants are open everywhere. Food preparation in a Turkish restaurant like this is sometimes carried out before your eyes.

sitting in front of a guest. If a waiter engages in plate-snatching, say '*Kalsın*' ('Let it stay').

Full Service

This is the familiar sort of restaurant with white tablecloths and waiter service. It may be open for three meals a day, and will probably be among the more expensive dining places. They usually serve spirits, wine and beer, and are sometimes called *içkili* (literally, 'serving drinks') because of this. (See under Drinks later in this section.)

Hazır Yemek

Literally, 'ready food', these are sometimes arranged as *self-servis* cafeterias. Although all restaurants offer some dishes prepared in advance, these places specialise in an assortment of dishes, prepared in advance, kept warm in steam tables. Usually no alcoholic beverages are served, but occasionally, if you order a beer, the waiter will run to a shop nearby and get one for you.

Decor may be nonexistent and the letters on the front window may only say 'Lokanta', but the welcome will be warm and the food delicious and cheap.

With your meal you will receive as much fresh bread as you can eat, for a nominal charge.

Kebapçı & Köfteci

Two other sorts of restaurants are the *kebapçı* (keh-BAHP-chuh) and *köfteci* (KURF-teh-jee). A kebapçı is a person who cooks *kebap* (roast meat). A köfteci roasts *köfte*, meatballs of minced (ground) lamb made with savoury spices. Though they may have one or two ready-food dishes, kebapçı and köfteci restaurants specialise in grilled meat, plus soups, salad, yoghurt and perhaps dessert.

Kebapçıs can be great fun, especially the ones that are *ocakbaşı* (oh-JAHK bah-shuh, fireside). Patrons sit around the sides of a long rectangular firepit and the kebapçı sits enthroned in the middle, grilling hundreds of *şiş kebap* and *şiş köfte*, which is köfte wrapped around a flat skewer. *Adana köfte* (ah-DAHN-nah) is the same thing, but spicy hot. The chef hands them over as they're done, and they are eaten with flat bread, a salad and perhaps *ayran* (ah-yee-RAHN), a drink of yoghurt mixed with spring water. Alcoholic beverages are not usually served.

Pideci

For those on an adventurer's low budget, the *pideci* (Turkish pizza place) is a godsend. Ask *Buralarda bir pideci var mı?* ('Is there a pideci around here?').

At a pideci, the dough for flat bread is patted out into an oblong boat shape, dabbed with butter and other toppings, baked in a wood-fired oven, cut into strips and served. It's fresh, delicious, inexpensive, sanitary and nutritious. As for toppings, say *peynirli* (pehy-neer-LEE) for cheese, *yumurtalı* (yoo-moor-tah-LUH) for eggs, *kıymalı* or *etli* for minced lamb. In some parts of Turkey a *pide* (pizza) with meat is called *etli ekmek*. Alcoholic beverages are usually not served in pidecis.

TOM BROSNAHAN

Slicing döner to make Bursa, or İskender, kebap.

Pastane

Pasta in Turkey is pastry, not noodles, which are usually designated by some Turkicised Italian name such as *makarna or lazanya*. Turkish *pastanes* (pastry shops) generally have supplies of *kuru pasta* (dry pastry) such as biscuits of various sorts, and *yaş pasta* (moist pastry) meaning cakes, crumpets, and syrup-soaked baked goods. Soft drinks are served, and tea and coffee are sometimes available. Some pastanes serve *baklava*, the many-layered nut-and-honey sweet; others leave this to separate shops called *baklavacıs*.

Most pastanes serve breakfast, either from their normal stock or as a *komple kahvaltı* (kohm-PLEH kahvahl-TUH, breakfast) of bread, butter, honey or jam, egg, olives, cheese and coffee or tea. In Kars, out by the Armenian frontier, you can have great gobs of the excellent local honey to mix with butter and spread on fresh bread.

Büfe & Kuru Yemiş

Other than restaurants, Turkey has millions of little snack stands and quick-lunch places known as *büfe* (bew-FEH, buffet). These serve sandwiches, often grilled, puddings, portions of *börek* (bur-REHK, flaky pastry), and perhaps *lahmacun* (LAHH-mah-joon), an Arabic soft pizza made with chopped onion, lamb and tomato sauce.

A *kuru yemiş* (koo-ROO yeh-MEESH) place serves dried fruits and nuts and about a dozen other good things. Prices are displayed in kilograms.

İstanbul's Mısır Çarşısı (Egyptian Market) in Eminönü has several kuru yemiş shops which also sell *pestil* (pehs-TEEL), fruit which has been dried and pressed into flat, flexible sheets (sometimes called 'fruit leather' in English). Odd at first, but tasty, it's a home-made village product made from *kayısı* (apricots), *dut* (mulberries) and other fruits.

Hotel Restaurants

These, in general, do not offer good value in Turkey. You may want to have breakfast in a hotel restaurant for convenience (or because breakfast has been included in the room price), but most other meals

OLIVIER CIRENDINI

GLENN BEANLAND

GLENN BEANLAND

Top Left: *Çay* (tea), the national drink of Turkey, is traditionally served in tulip-shaped glasses.

Top Right: Tables in Turkish restaurants often have decorative metal ornaments like this which also keep food warm while you're eating.

Bottom: Turkish 'dolma' (stuffed vine leaves or vegetables) are prepared in a variety of delicious ways.

EDDIE GERALD

PETER PTSCHELINZEW

PAT YALE

Top: The produce at the fishmarket near Galata Bridge in İstanbul is fresh and cheap.

Middle: A welcome alternative to kebaps and pide – fresh fruit on sale at the Balık Pazar, on İstiklal Caddesi, İstanbul.

Bottom: Giant loaves on sale in the back streets of Malatya, in eastern Anatolia.

EDDIE GERALD

PAT YALE

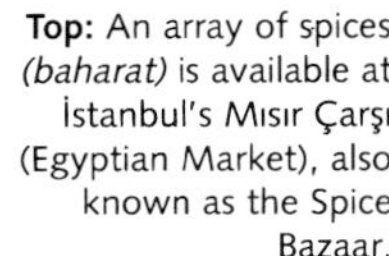

PAT YALE

Top: An array of spices *(baharat)* is available at İstanbul's Mısır Çarşı (Egyptian Market), also known as the Spice Bazaar.

Middle: Rows of sausages in Afyon, a town normally associated with clotted cream and Turkish delight.

Bottom: Stuffed vine leaves are a popular *meze* (hors d'oeuvre) in Turkish restaurants.

ALL PHOTOGRAPHS BY EDDIE GERALD

Top: Pickles on wheels in Sultanahmet, İstanbul.

Middle: Selling chestnuts, near Galata Bridge, İstanbul.

Bottom: Bread is cheap, filling and convenient and this vendor, in İstanbul's Sultanahmet area, is open for business.

The waters off Turkey's extensive coastline yield an abundance of fresh fish.

should be taken in independent, local places. There are exceptions, of course, as in those remote towns where the one good hotel in town also has the one good restaurant.

Meals

For words of common foods, see the Turkish Language Guide chapter at the back of this book.

Breakfast

In a hotel or pastry shop, komple kahvaltı consists of fresh, delicious *ekmek* (ek-MEHK, Turkish bread) with jam or honey, butter, salty black olives, sliced tomatoes and cucumbers and cheese, as well as *çay* (CHAH-yee, tea). In my experience, Turkish bread and tea are usually fresh and good, but the other ingredients are often of poor quality or stale.

You can always order a *yumurta* (yoo-moor-TAH, egg). Soft-boiled is *üç dakikalık* (EWCH dahk-kah-luhk), hard-boiled is *sert* (SEHRT) and fried eggs are *sahanda yumurta* (sah-hahn-DAH yoo-moor-tah). Bacon is extremely difficult to find as any pork product is forbidden to Muslims.

When breakfast is included in the room rate, the desk clerk will say *Kahvaltı dahil* (kah-vahl-TUH dah-HEEL).

After a week or so of standard Turkish breakfasts (and a few bad ones), I generally do what many working-class Turks do. I go to a lokanta for breakfast and have a bowl of hot soup which, with lots of fresh bread, makes quite a delicious breakfast for a very low price. If that's not for you, try a lokanta or pastane serving *su böreği* (SOO bur-reh-yee), a many-layered noodle-like pastry with white cheese and parsley among the layers, served warm.

Hot, *sıcak süt* (suh-JAHK sewt, sweetened milk) is also a traditional breakfast drink, replaced in winter by *sahlep* (sah-LEHP), which is hot, sweetened milk flavoured with tasty *Orchis mascula* (orchid-root) powder and a sprinkle of cinnamon.

A Taste of Honey

As you journey around Turkey you will no doubt spot the lines of blue and white beehives lined up by the roadside, tended by their careful owners in space-age beekeeper suits.

Turkish honey comes in several delicious varieties which are well worth sampling. First, there's *çam balı* (CHAHM bah-luh), a pine-scented honey from young forest growth which is rich, dark and full-flavoured. One variation is *siyah çam balı,* black-pine honey, with a rich deep flavour and a colour which is almost as dark as molasses.

Then there's *portakal*, or orange-blossom honey, which is very light-coloured and thin textured, with a light, sweet flavour. *Akasya balı* comes from locust-tree blossom. Slightly darker and more flavoursome is *çiçek*, or flower honey. Finally there's *oğul balı,* or virgin honey, which is the very first honey from a new swarm.

A popular Turkish breakfast consists of half a loaf of bread with a pat of butter which you mix with honey and then spread on the bread. In western Turkey, Marmaris is a particularly good place for sampling honey. In eastern Turkey, Kars is definitely the place to venture.

Lunch

Lunch is called *öğle yemeği.* In summer, many Turks wisely prefer to eat a big meal at lunchtime and a light supper in the evening.

Dinner

The evening meal can be a repeat of lunch, a light supper, or a sumptuous repast. In fine weather the setting might be outdoors.

DRINKS

Nonalcoholic Drinks

When waiters ask *İçecek?* or *Ne içeceksiniz?*, they're asking what you'd like to drink. You will find the usual range of soft drinks. Shops and restaurants often sign exclusive distribution contracts with one company or the other, so you will find either Coke or Pepsi but rarely Coke and Pepsi. Turks just order *kola* and take what comes.

Fruit juice is a favourite refresher, and can be excellent, though there are also numerous watery, sugared juice imitations.

See the Turkish Language Guide chapter at the back of this book for the names of Turkish drinks.

Water

Turks are connoisseurs of good *su* (water) and stories circulate of old people able to tell which spring it came from just by tasting it. Spring water is served everywhere, even on intercity buses. The standard price for a 1.5L bottle of any brand, sold in a grocery, probably chilled, is around US$0.75. If you order it in a restaurant there will be a markup of 100% to 300%.

Tap water is supposedly safe to drink because it is treated, but it's not as tasty or as trustworthy as spring water. (For more information on water, see Food & Water in the Health section earlier in this chapter.)

Tea & Coffee

The national drink is not really Turkish coffee as you might expect, but çay. The Turks drank a lot of coffee when they owned Arabia, because the world's first (and best) coffee is said to have come from Yemen. With the collapse of the Ottoman Empire, coffee became an imported commodity. You can get Turkish coffee anywhere in Turkey, but you'll find yourself drinking a lot more çay.

The tea plantations are along the eastern Black Sea coast, centred on the town of Rize. Turkish tea is hearty and full-flavoured, traditionally served in little tulip-shaped glasses which you hold by the rim to avoid burning your fingers. (If you need a lot, order a *duble*, which may come in a drinking glass.) Sugar is usually added; milk is often available, though milk in tea is a foreign custom. If you want your tea weaker, ask for it *açık* (ah-CHUK, clear); for stronger, darker tea, order *koyu or demli* (dark).

For a real tea-drinking and talking session, Turks go to an outdoor tea garden and order a *semaver* (samovar) of tea so they can refill the glasses themselves, without having to call the *çaycı* (CHAH-yee-juh, tea waiter).

Traditional herbal teas are infusions such as *adaçay* (island tea), made from coastal sage, and *ıhlamur* (linden-flower tea), perfumed and soothing. *Papatya çayı* is camomile tea.

A few years ago a brand-new beverage, *elma çay* (apple tea) was introduced, and it caught on quickly. Tourists love it as much as Turks

KIMBERLY GRANT

The humble glass of çay is the centre of many a Turkish conversation. It's almost impossible for travellers to avoid drinking it, and why would you want to? It's delicious.

do, and you may even see street vendors selling packets of it for tourists to take home with them. It's caffeine-free and slightly tart, with a mild apple flavour. There are other, similar fruit-flavoured teas as well. Surprisingly, the list of ingredients yields no mention of fruit, only sugar, citric acid, citrate, food essence and vitamin C.

As for Turkish *kahve* (coffee) you must order it according to sweetness – the sugar is mixed in during the brewing, not afterwards. You can drink it *sade*, without sugar; *az*, if you want just a bit of sugar; *orta*, with a middling amount; *çok* or *şekerli* or even *çok şekerli*, with lots of sugar. Nescafé is readily found throughout Turkey but tends to be expensive, often around US$0.70 per cup.

Alcoholic Drinks

Strictly observant Muslims do not touch alcoholic beverages at all, but in Turkey the strictures of religion are moderated by the 20th-century lifestyle.

In resorts popular with foreigners, virtually every restaurant may serve alcohol. In the big cities, restaurants above a certain price range may do so. In mid-sized cities and towns, there is usually at least one restaurant where alcohol is served so that the local movers-and-shakers can get together over long dinners with drinks. In a few religiously conservative cities such as Konya, very few restaurants serve alcoholic beverages, and those that do are so debased as to confirm the opinions of the conservative majority.

Beer

A local company with a European brewmaster is Efes Pilsen, which makes light and dark beer claimed by many to be Turkey's best. The light is a good, slightly bitter pilsener. Tuborg, a Danish company, makes *beyaz* (bey-AHZ, light or pale) and *siyah* (see-YAH, dark) beer in Turkey under licence. Marmara is another lager, not easily found.

Restaurants and shops usually sign exclusive contracts with beer companies to feature their brand, so you rarely get a choice. Except in the most expensive places, you might as well just order 'bira' and you'll get whatever they have.

Beer is available in returnable bottles, and also in disposable cans at a higher than average price. You'll save money, get better flavour, and not contribute to the litter problem if you buy bottled beer.

Wine

Turkish wines are drinkable and cheap. Doluca (DOHL-oo-jah) and Kavaklıdere (kah-vakh-LUH-deh-reh) are the favoured brands, making good table wines as well as several varietals, such as the Villa Doluca line. Kavaklıdere's serviceable wines include the premium Çankaya (white) and Dikmen (red), and the medium-range wines named Kavak (white and red) and Lal (rosé/blush). Tekel, the government alcoholic beverages company, also makes wines.

Strong Liquor

The favourite ardent spirit in Turkey is *rakı* (rah-KUH), an aniseed-flavoured grape brandy similar to the Greek ouzo, French pastis and

Arab arak. Turkish rakı is made by Tekel. The standard is Yeni Rakı. Kulüp Rakısı is somewhat stronger, with a bit more anise. Altınbaş is the strongest and most expensive, with the highest anise content.

It's customary (but not essential) to mix rakı with cool water, half-and-half, perhaps add ice, and to drink it with a meal, or at least some *çerez* (nibbles, snacks).

Tekel also makes decent *cin* (JEEN, gin), *votka* and *kanyak* (kahn-YAHK, brandy). When ordering kanyak, always specify the *beş yıldız* or *kaliteli* (five-star or quality) stuff, officially named Truva Kanyak. The regular kanyak is thick and heavy, the five-star much lighter. There is a Tekel *viski* (VEES-kee, whisky) named Ankara. You might try it once. Vermouth is *vermut*.

For after-dinner drinks, better restaurants will stock the local sweet fruit-brandies, which are nothing special.

Imported spirits are available from shops in the larger cities and resorts. Though they are much more expensive than local drinks, they may not cost much more than what you'd pay at home. Hotels and restaurants usually mark up the prices of imported spirits hugely.

continued from page 92

ENTERTAINMENT

İstanbul, Ankara and İzmir have opera, symphony, ballet and theatre. Every Turkish town has at least one cinema and one nightclub with live entertainment.

The seaside resorts throb every warm evening to the sounds of seemingly innumerable clubs and discos.

SPECTATOR SPORT

Football (soccer), basketball and wrestling are the favoured sports. Every city of any size has a large football stadium which fills up on match days.

The famous oiled wrestling matches, where brawny strongmen in leather breeches rub themselves down with olive oil and grapple with equally slippery opponents, take place each June in Edirne (see the 'Oiled Wrestling' boxed text in the Thrace chapter). Another purely Turkish sight is the camel-wrestling matches held in the province of Aydın, south of İzmir, in the winter months. Konya is the setting for *cirit*, the javelin-throwing game played on horseback.

SHOPPING

Most shops and shopping areas close on Sunday. For details, see the Business Hours section earlier in this chapter.

Haggling

For the best buy in terms of price and quality, know the market. Spend some time shopping for similar items in various shops, asking prices. Shopkeepers will give you pointers on what makes a good *kilim* (flat-woven mat), carpet, meerschaum pipe or alabaster carving. In effect, you're getting a free course in product lore. This is not at all unpleasant, as you will often be invited to have coffee, tea or a soft drink as you talk over the goods and prices.

You can, and should, ask prices if they're not marked, but you should not make a counter-offer unless you are seriously interested in buying. No matter how often the shopkeeper asks you, 'OK, how much will you pay for it?', no matter how many glasses of tea you've drunk at their expense, don't make a counter-offer if you do not plan to buy. If the shopkeeper meets your price, you should buy. It's considered very bad form to haggle over a price, agree, and then not buy.

Some shopkeepers, even in the 'haggle capital of the world' (İstanbul's Kapalı Çarşı), will offer a decent price and say, 'That's my best offer'. Many times they mean it, and they're trying to do you a favour by saving time. How will you know when they are, and when it's just another haggling technique? Only by knowing the market, by having shopped around. Remember, even if they say, 'This is my best offer', you are under no obligation to buy unless you have made a counter-offer, or have said, 'I'll buy it'.

It's perfectly acceptable to say a pleasant goodbye and walk out of the shop, even after all that free tea, if you cannot agree on a price. In fact, walking out is one of the best ways to test the authenticity of the shopkeeper's price. If they know you can surely find the item somewhere else for less, they'll stop you and say, 'OK, you win, it's yours for what you offered'. And if they don't stop you, there's nothing to prevent you from returning in half an hour and buying the item for what they quoted.

If any shopkeeper puts extraordinary pressure on you to buy, walk out of the shop, and consider reporting the shop to the Market Police (see the information on belediye zabıtası under Police in the Dangers & Annoyances section earlier in this chapter).

Value Added Tax

Turkey has a Value Added Tax (VAT), called Katma Değer Vergisi or KDV, added to and hidden in the price of most items and services, from souvenirs to hotel rooms to restaurant meals. Most establishments display a sign saying *'Fiatlarımızda KDV Dahildir'* ('VAT is included in our prices'). Thus, it is rare that the VAT is added to your bill separately, and you should be suspicious if it is.

There is a scheme where tourists can reclaim the amount paid in VAT on larger purchases such as leather garments, carpets etc. Not all shops participate in the scheme, so you must ask if it is possible to get a KDV İade Özel Fatura (keh-deh-VEH ee-ah-DEH err-ZEHL fah-too-rah, 'Special VAT Refund Receipt'). Ask for this during the haggling rather than after you've bought. The receipt can – in principle – be converted to cash at a bank in the international departures lounge at the airport (if there is a bank open, which there usually isn't), or at your other point of exit from Turkey. Or, if you submit the form to a customs officer as you leave the country, the shop will (hopefully) mail a refund cheque to your home after the government has completed its procedures (don't hold your breath though).

To increase your chances of actually getting the refund, make a photocopy or two of the KDV İade Özel Fatura in advance and, when you're leaving Turkey, take along a stamped envelope addressed to the shop where you bought the goods. Have the KDV form and the photocopy stamped by the customs officer at the airport, then mail the photocopy from the airport to the shop. Enclose a note requesting refund of the tax and giving your address to which the refund cheque should be sent. In some cases it can take as long as four months for the cheque to arrive. Keep the other photocopy for your own records.

Shipping Parcels Home

If practicable, carrying your parcels with you is the best idea, as you may escape extra duty payments when you return to your home country; parcels arriving separately may be dutiable. If you decide to ship something home from Turkey, don't close up your parcel before it has been inspected by a customs or postal official, who will check to see if you are shipping antiquities out of the country; take packing and wrapping materials with you to the post office. Wrap it very securely and insure it. Sending it by *kayıtlı* (registered mail) is not a bad idea, either. Unless you buy from a very posh shop, it's best to ship your own parcels. Several readers have had the sad experience of buying a beautiful kilim and agreeing to have the shopkeeper ship it, only to discover that the kilim shipped was not the one bought, but a much cheaper item.

Alabaster

A translucent, fine-grained variety of either gypsum or calcite, alabaster is pretty because of its grain and colour, and because light passes through it. You'll see ashtrays, vases, chess sets, bowls, egg cups, even the eggs themselves carved from the stone.

Antiques

Turkey has a lot of fascinating stuff left over from the empire: vigorous peasant jewellery, water-pipe mouthpieces carved from amber, old Korans and illuminated manuscripts, Greek and Roman figurines and coins, tacky furniture in the Ottoman Baroque style. However, *it is illegal to buy, sell, possess or export any antiquity*, and you can go to prison for breaking the law. All antiquities must be turned over to a museum immediately upon discovery. (See Departure under Customs earlier in this chapter for details.)

Ceramics

The best Turkish ceramics were made in İznik and Kütahya in the 17th and 18th centuries. These tiles from the great days are now museum-pieces, found in collections throughout the world.

Today most of the tile-making is done in Kütahya in the Aegean hinterland. For the very best ceramics, you must go there (see Kütahya in the Northern Aegean Hinterland section of the North Aegean Turkey chapter for more information on buying ceramics). Souvenir shops will also have attractive, handmade tiles, plates, cups and bowls. They're not really high-fired so they're vulnerable to breaks and cracks, but they can be quite attractive and useful even so.

continued on page 108

TURKISH CARPETS

NEIL WILSON

Turkey is famous for its beautiful carpets and kilims and wherever you go you'll be spoilt for choice as to what to buy. Unfortunately, the carpet market is very lucrative and the hard-sell antics of some dealers and their shills have tended to bring it into disrepute, putting many visitors off venturing into the shops. Also, with the tourism boom, carpet prices in Turkey have risen so much that it may actually be cheaper to buy your Turkish carpet at home. Indeed, we've heard one story of a man who bought up old kilims in the Paris flea market, had them cleaned, then brought them to Turkey to sell to tourists at high prices – creative recycling!

If you have it in mind to buy a carpet, browse in your local shop before coming to Turkey. This will give you some idea of prices and will acquaint you with the various designs so you can shop more knowledgeably when in Turkey.

An Age-Old Art

Turkish women have been weaving carpets for a very long time. These beautiful, durable, eminently portable floor coverings were a nomadic family's most valuable and practical 'furniture', warming and brightening the clan's oft-moved homes.

The oldest known carpet woven in the Turkish double-knotted *Gördes* style dates from between the 4th and 1st centuries BC.

It is thought that hand-woven carpet techniques were introduced to Anatolia by the Seljuks in the 12th century. Thus it's not surprising that Konya, the Seljuk capital, was mentioned by Marco Polo as a centre of carpet production in the 13th century.

Traditional Patterns

Traditionally, village women wove carpets for their own family's use, or for their dowry. Knowing they would be judged on their efforts, the women took great care over their handiwork, hand-spinning and dyeing the wool, and choosing what they judged to be the most interesting and beautiful patterns.

The general pattern and colour scheme of old carpets was influenced by local traditions and the availability of certain types of wool and colours of dyes. Patterns were memorised, and women usually worked with no more than 18 inches of the carpet visible. But each artist imbued her work with her own personality, choosing a motif or a colour based on her own artistic preferences, and even events and emotions in her daily life.

In the 19th century, the European rage for Turkish carpets spurred the development of carpet companies. The companies, run by men, would deal with customers, take orders, purchase and dye the wool according to the customers' preferences, and contract local women to produce the finished product. The designs might be left to the women, but more often

ALL PHOTOGRAPHS BY EDDIE GERALD

Top: A kaleidoscope of colours waiting to be turned into the finest of Turkish carpets.

Middle: Wool stocked in cupboard of rug mender, Sultanahmet area.

Bottom: Rug mender, Sultanahmet area.

TURKISH TOURISM

NEIL WILSON

Bold geometric Anatolian designs have been popular for many centuries.

TOM BROSNAHAN

GLENN BEANLAND

When buying a carpet, take your time and shop around. Wherever you go you'll be spoilt for choice.

ALL PHOTOGRAPHS BY TOM BROSNAHAN

Top: Carpet shop owners in Turkey are always willing to show you their wares.

Middle: A cosy place for a catnap at the Kapalı Çarşı (Grand Bazaar), İstanbul.

Bottom: A woman presides over a carpet shop in Side on the Mediterranean Coast.

were provided by the company based on the customers' tastes. Though well made, these carpets lost some originality and spirit of the older work.

Even carpets made today often use the same traditional patterns and incorporate all sorts of symbols which can be 'read' by those in the know. At a glance two carpets might look identical, but closer examination reveals the subtle differences that give each Turkish carpet its individuality and much of its charm.

Carpet Weaving Today

These days the picture is more complicated. Many carpets are made not according to local traditions, but to the dictates of the market. Weavers in eastern Turkey might make carpets in popular styles native to western Turkey. Long-settled villagers might duplicate the wilder, hairier and more naive *yörük* (nomad) carpets.

Village women still weave carpets but most of them work to fixed contracts for specific shops. Usually they work to a pattern and are paid for their final effort rather than for each hour of work. A carpet made to a fixed contract may still be of great value to its purchaser. However, the selling price should be lower than for a one-off piece.

Other carpets are the product of division of labour, with different individuals responsible for dyeing and weaving. What such pieces lose in individuality and rarity is often more than made up for in quality control. Most silk Hereke carpets are mass produced but to standards that make them some of the most sought-after of all Turkish carpets.

Fearing that old carpet-making methods would be lost, the Ministry of Culture now sponsors a number of projects to revive traditional weaving and dyeing methods in western Turkey. Some carpet shops will have stocks of these 'project carpets' which are usually of high quality with prices reflecting that fact.

Kilims, Sumaks & Cicims

A good carpet shop will have a range of pieces made by a variety of techniques. Besides the traditional pile carpets, they may offer double-sided flat-woven mats such as kilims. Some traditional kilim motifs are similar to patterns found at the prehistoric mound of Çatal Höyük, testifying to the very ancient traditions of flat-woven floor coverings in Anatolia. Older, larger kilims may actually be two narrower pieces of similar but not always identical design stitched together. As this is now rarely done, any such piece is likely to be fairly old.

Other flat-weave techniques include *sumak*, a style originally from Azerbaijan in which coloured threads are wrapped around the warp. *Cicims* are kilims with small, lively patterns embroidered on top of them.

Carpets From Other Countries

As well as Turkish carpets, many carpet shops sell pieces from other countries, especially from Iran, Afghanistan and from the ex-Soviet Republics of Azerbaijan, Turkmenistan and Uzbekistan. If it matters that yours is actually from Turkey, bear in mind that Iran favours the single knot and Turkey the double knot. Turkish carpets also tend to have a higher pile, more dramatic designs and more varied colours than their Iranian cousins. Some Iranian sumaks are decorated with naive animal patterns, encouraging shopkeepers to call them 'Noah's Ark carpets' although they have absolutely nothing to do with the Bible story.

A CARPET BUYER'S PRIMER

The bad news is that there are no short cuts when it comes to learning about carpets. To ensure you get a good buy, you'll have to spend time visiting several shops and compare prices and quality. It's also worth taking a look in the department stores at home before you leave. That way, you'll know what's available and for what prices at home.

That said, when deciding whether to buy a particular carpet, it might help to follow some of the guidelines below.

A good-quality, long-lasting carpet should be 100% wool (*yüz de yüz yün*): check the warp (the lengthwise yarns), weft (the crosswise yarns) and pile (the vertical yarns knotted into the matrix of warp and weft). Is the wool fine and shiny, with signs of the natural oil? More expensive carpets may be of a silk and wool blend. Cheaper carpets may have warp and weft of mercerised cotton. You can tell by checking the fringes at either end – if the fringe is of cotton or 'flosh' (mercerised cotton) you shouldn't pay for wool. Another way to identify the material of the warp and weft is to turn the carpet over and look for the fine, frizzy fibres common to wool, but not to cotton. But bear in mind that just being made of wool doesn't guarantee a carpet's quality. If the dyes and design are ugly, even a 100% woollen carpet can be a bad buy.

Check the closeness of the weave by turning the carpet over and inspecting the back. In general, the tighter the weave and the smaller the knots, the higher the quality and durability of the carpet. The oldest carpets sometimes had thick knots, so consider the number of knots alongside the colours and the quality of the wool.

Compare the colours on the back with those on the front. Spread the nap with your fingers and look at the bottom of the pile. Are the colours brighter there than on the surface? Slight colour variations could occur in older carpets when a new batch of dye was mixed, but richer colour deep in the pile is often an indication that the surface has faded in the sun. Natural dyes don't fade as readily as chemical dyes. There is nothing wrong with chemical dyes, which have a long history of their own, but natural dyes and colours tend to be preferred and therefore fetch higher prices. Don't pay for natural if you're getting chemical.

New carpets can be made to look old, and damaged or worn carpets can be rewoven (good work, but expensive), patched or even painted. There's nothing wrong with a dealer offering you a patched or repainted carpet provided they point out these defects and price the piece accordingly, but it would be dishonest to offer you cheap goods at an Inflated price. But some red Bokhara carpets will continue to give off colour even though they're of better quality than cheap woollen carpets which don't.

Look at the carpet from one end, then from the other. The colours will differ because the pile always leans one way or the other. Take the carpet out into the sunlight and look at it there. Imagine where you might put the carpet at home, and how the light will strike it.

In the end the most important consideration should be whether or not you like the carpet. It's all very well to pluck some fibres and burn them to see if they smell like wool, silk, or nylon or to rub a wet handkerchief over the carpet to see if the colour comes off, but unless you know what you're doing you're unlikely to learn much from the exercise – and you may well end up with a irate carpet seller to deal with!

Pricing & Payment

When it comes to buying, there's no substitute for spending time developing an 'eye' for what you really like. You also need to be realistic about your budget. These days carpets are such big business that true bargains are hard to come by unless there's something (like gigantic size) that makes them hard to sell for their true value.

Prices are determined by age, material, quality, condition, demand in the market, the enthusiasm of the buyer, and the debt load of the seller. Bear in mind that if you do your shopping on a tour or when accompanied by a guide, the price will be hiked by up to 35% to cover somebody's commission.

It may be wiser to go for something small but of high quality rather than for a room-sized cheapie. Another way to make the money stretch further is to opt for one of the smaller items made from carpet materials: old camel bags and hanging baby's cradles opened out to make rugs; sofras or rugs on which food would be eaten; decorative grain bags; cushion covers; even the bags which once held rock salt for animals.

Some dealers will take personal cheques, but all prefer cash. An increasing number of shops take credit cards but some require you to pay the credit card company's fee and the cost of the phone call to check your creditworthiness. A few dealers will let you pay in instalments.

All this is a lot to remember, but it'll be worth it if you get a carpet you like at a decent price. It will give you pleasure for the rest of your life.

continued from page 103

The real, old İznik tiles from the 16th and 17th centuries qualify as antiquities and cannot be exported. If you go to İznik, you will find a reviving tile industry on a small scale. Some of the items are quite pretty and reasonably priced.

Avanos, in Cappadocia, is a centre for simple but attractive red clay pottery, made from deposits taken from the neighbouring Kızılırmak (Red River).

Copper

Gleaming copper vessels will greet you in every souvenir shop you peep into. Some are old, sometimes several centuries old. Most are handsome, and some are still eminently useful. The new copperware tends to be of lighter gauge; that's one of the ways you tell new from old. But even the new stuff will have been made by hand.

'See that old copper water pipe over there?' my friend Alaettin asked me once. We were sitting in his cluttered, closet-sized shop on İstanbul's Çadırcılar Caddesi, just outside the Kapalı Çarşı. 'It dates from the time of Sultan Ahmet III (1703-30), and was used by the *Padişah* (sultan) himself. I just finished making it yesterday.'

Alaettin was a master coppersmith, and had made pieces for many luminaries, including the late Nelson Rockefeller. His pieces might well have graced the sultan's private apartments – except that the sultanate was abolished in 1922. He charged a hefty price for his fine craftwork but not for the story, which was the gift-wrapping, so to speak.

Copper vessels should not be used for cooking in or eating from unless they are tinned inside: that is, washed with molten tin which covers the toxic copper. If you intend to use a copper vessel, make sure the interior layer of tin is intact, or negotiate to have it *kalaylamak* (tinned). If there is a *kalaycı* shop nearby, ask about the price of the tinning in advance, as tin is expensive.

Inlaid Wood

Cigarette boxes, chess and *tavla* (backgammon) boards and other items will be inlaid with different coloured woods, silver or mother-of-pearl. It's not the finest work, but it's pretty good. Make sure there is indeed inlay. These days, alarmingly accurate decals exist. Also, check the silver: is it silver, or aluminium or pewter? Is the mother-of-pearl actually 'daughter-of-polystyrene'?

Jewellery

Turkey is a wonderful place to buy jewellery, especially antique. None of the items sold here may meet your definition of 'chic', but window-shopping is great fun. Jewellers' Row in any market is a dazzling strip of glittering shop windows filled with gold. In the Kapalı Çarşı, a blackboard sign hung above Kuyumcular Caddesi (Street of the Jewellers) bears the daily price for unworked gold of so-many carats. Serious gold-buyers should check this price, watch carefully as the jeweller weighs the piece in question, and then calculate what part of the price is for gold and what part for labour.

Silver is another matter. There is sterling silver jewellery (look for the hallmark), but nickel silver and pewter-like alloys are much more common. Serious dealers don't try to pass off alloy as silver.

Leather & Suede

On any given Kurban Bayramı (Sacrifice Holiday), more than 2.5 million sheep get the axe in Turkey. Add to that the normal day-to-day needs of a cuisine based on mutton and lamb and you have a huge amount of raw material to be made into leather items.

Shoes, bags, cushions, jackets, skirts, vests, hats, gloves and trousers are all made from soft leather. This is a big industry in Turkey, particularly in and around the Kapalı Çarşı in İstanbul. So much leather clothing is turned out that a good deal of it will be badly cut or carelessly made, but there are lots of fine pieces as well.

The only way to assure yourself of a good piece is to examine it carefully, taking time. Try it on just as carefully; see if the sleeves are full enough, if the buttonholes are positioned well, if the collar rubs. If something is wrong, keep trying others until you find what you want.

Made-to-order garments can be excellent or disappointing, as the same tailor who made the ready-made stuff will make the ordered stuff; and will be making it fast because the shopkeeper has already impressed you by saying 'No problem. I can have it for you tomorrow'. It's better to find something off the rack that fits than to order it, unless you can order without putting down a deposit or committing yourself to buy (this is often possible).

Leather items and clothing are standard tourist stuff, found in all major tourist destinations.

Meerschaum

If you smoke a pipe, you know about meerschaum. For those who don't, meerschaum ('sea foam' in German; *lületaşı* in Turkish) is a hydrous magnesium silicate, a soft, white, clay-like material which is porous but heat-resistant. When carved into a pipe, it smokes cool and sweet.

Over time, it absorbs residues from the tobacco and turns a nut-brown colour. Devoted meerschaum pipe smokers even have special gloves for holding the pipe as they smoke, so that oil from their fingers won't sully the fine, even patina of the pipe.

The world's largest and finest beds of meerschaum are found in Turkey, near the city of Eskişehir. Miners climb down shafts in the earth to bring up buckets of mud, some of which contain chunks of the mineral. Artful carving of this soft stone has always been done, and blocks of meerschaum were exported to be carved abroad as well. These days, however, the export of block meerschaum is prohibited because the government realised that exporting uncarved blocks was the same as exporting the jobs to carve them. So any carved pipe will have been carved in Turkey.

You'll marvel at the artistry of the Eskişehir carvers. Pipes portraying turbaned paşas, wizened old men, fair maidens and mythological beasts, as well as many pipes in geometrical designs, will be on view in any souvenir shop.

Pipes are not the only things carved from meerschaum these days. Bracelets, necklaces, pendants, earrings and cigarette holders all appear in souvenir shops.

When buying, look for purity and uniformity in the stone. Carving is often used to cover up flaws in a piece of meerschaum. For pipes, check that the bowl walls are uniform in thickness all around, and that the hole at the bottom of the bowl is centred. Purists buy uncarved, plain pipe-shaped meerschaums that are simply but perfectly made.

Prices for pipes vary, but should be fairly low. Abroad, meerschaum is an expensive commodity, and pipes are luxury items. Here in Turkey meerschaum is cheap, the services of the carver are low-priced, and nobody smokes pipes. If you can't get the pipe you want for US$10 to US$20, or at least only half of what you'd pay at home, then you're not working hard enough.

Getting There & Away

AIR

İstanbul's Atatürk airport is the country's busiest. Other international airports are at Adana, Ankara, Antalya, Dalaman (between Marmaris and Fethiye) and İzmir.

Turkish Airlines (Türk Hava Yolları or THY, symbol TK) has nonstop flights serving most major cities in Europe and New York. Other routes serve the Middle East, North Africa and the Far East.

İstanbul Airlines (symbol IL) has flights between Turkey and Austria, Belgium, Denmark, France, Germany, Holland, Ireland, Israel, Italy, Norway, Russia, Spain, Sweden, Turkish Cyprus and the UK.

The fares stated here are subject to change, but they'll give you an idea of what to expect. For more details of air travel to/from Turkey see the Getting There & Away sections under individual Turkish destinations.

Greece

Olympic Airlines and Turkish Airlines share the Athens-İstanbul route, offering at least two flights per day in summer. Fares for the 70-minute flight are US$255 one way, US$386 for a round-trip excursion (fixed-date return) ticket.

Western Europe

Both Turkish Airlines and İstanbul Airlines fly to Turkey from many points in Europe. Most Turkish Airlines flights go to the airline's hub in İstanbul, while İstanbul Airlines flies nonstop from Europe to cities such as Adana, Antalya, Dalaman and İzmir. İstanbul Airlines' fares tend to be lower than those of the major carriers, but flights are less frequent, perhaps only once a week.

The normal one-way fare from London to İstanbul is UK£250 (US$425) and up, but there are fixed-date return (excursion) fares as low as UK£175 (US$300). British Airways and Turkish Airlines fly the route nonstop, and most other European airlines do it with one stop.

Don't neglect the European and Turkish charter lines such as Condor (German) and Air Alfa (Turkish), which fly to Turkey from more than a dozen European centres, often for round-trip fares as low as US$225.

Recently some European and Turkish tour operators have been selling complete tours priced below normal airfares. They make up the difference by lodging tour participants in hotels attached to shopping centres, and by depositing participants in shops during each day's touring, then collecting huge commissions on any purchases. These tours can be great bargains if you take advantage of the cheap flight and perhaps some of the hotels, but avoid the shopping. An alternative would be to do your own shopping, away from the tour.

WARNING

The information in this chapter is particularly vulnerable to change: prices for international travel are volatile, routes are introduced and cancelled, schedules change, special deals come and go, and rules and visa requirements are amended. Airlines and governments seem to take a perverse pleasure in making price structures and regulations as complicated as possible.

You should check directly with the airline or travel agent to make sure you understand how a fare (and ticket you may buy) works. In addition, the travel industry is highly competitive and there are many lurks and perks.

The upshot of this is that you should get opinions, quotes and advice from as many airlines and travel agents as possible before you part with your hard-earned cash. The details given in this chapter should be regarded as pointers and are not a substitute for your own careful, up-to-date research.

Middle East

Middle Eastern flights by Turkish Airlines include the following weekly nonstop flights to/from İstanbul: two from Bahrain, three from Beirut, two from Dubai, five from Kuwait, four from Tehran, three from Tripoli and four from Tunis.

Details of the most popular services to İstanbul from various Middle Eastern cities follow.

Amman Turkish Airlines and Royal Jordanian share the traffic, with about three flights per week. The nonstop 2½-hour flight costs US$310 one way. An İstanbul Airlines round-trip excursion ticket costs about US$388.

Cairo EgyptAir and Turkish Airlines have at least one flight per day between them, charging from US$355 to US$398 one way. It costs from US$408 to US$450 for a round-trip excursion ticket on the nonstop, two-hour flight.

Damascus Syrian Arab Airlines and Turkish Airlines make the 2½-hour flight two days per week and charge from US$240 to US$278 one way and from US$300 to US$326 for a round-trip excursion.

Nicosia (Turkish Side) Turkish Airlines operates nonstop flights connecting Ercan airport (ECN) in Nicosia (Lefkoşa in Turkish) with Adana (four flights weekly), Ankara (five flights weekly), Antalya (one flight weekly), İstanbul (daily, twice daily in summer, US$200 round-trip excursion) and İzmir (four flights weekly).

İstanbul Airlines flies nonstop from Nicosia to Antalya and İstanbul.

Tel Aviv El Al Israel Airlines and Turkish Airlines share the traffic with daily nonstop flights to and from İstanbul for US$333 one way and US$369 for a round-trip excursion. Turkish Airlines also has nonstop flights at least weekly between Tel Aviv and Ankara, Antalya and İzmir.

Azerbaijan & Georgia

Turkish Airlines runs flights from İstanbul nonstop to Baku, and nonstop to Tblisi, four days per week.

The USA

Airlines Turkish Airlines operates daily nonstop flights in summer on the New York-İstanbul route, and daily service from Chicago (nonstop three days per week). Delta Air Lines also flies nonstop daily. All of the major European airlines offer one-stop service.

Coach-class New York to İstanbul excursion fares sometimes dip below US$500 in winter, and even the fares for the Los Angeles to İstanbul route can get as low as US$570 or so. It's worth noting that November and early January are particularly cheap times to travel. Summer excursion fares are more likely to be US$650 to US$950.

Consolidators Consolidators, also known as 'bucket shops', buy blocks of seats at wholesale prices from major airlines and then sell them to the general public at retail, often at significant discounts. They're the ones who put those small advertisements in newspaper and magazine travel sections boasting of low fares. Though some are incompetent or crooked, most consolidators are quite legitimate companies.

You can often buy consolidator tickets from your travel agency, which will put its own markup on the ticket, but it'll still be cheaper than a standard fare. In general, buying through a travel agency is usually a bit more expensive, but it helps to avoid the less reliable consolidators.

Whether you buy your ticket through a travel agency or direct from the consolidator, be sure to pay for it with a credit card. If for some reason your ticket or flight does not materialise, you can then legally refuse to pay the credit card charge. If you pay in cash or by cheque and the consolidator goes bankrupt or disappears, your money is gone.

Air Travel Glossary

Baggage Allowance This will be written on your ticket and usually includes one 20kg item to go in the hold, plus one item of hand luggage.

Bucket Shops These are unbonded travel agencies specialising in discounted airline tickets.

Bumped Just because you have a confirmed seat doesn't mean you're going to get on the plane (see Overbooking).

Cancellation Penalties If you have to cancel or change a discounted ticket, there are often heavy penalties involved; insurance can sometimes be taken out against these penalties. Some airlines impose penalties on regular tickets as well, particularly against 'no-show' passengers.

Check-In Airlines ask you to check in a certain time ahead of the flight departure (usually one to two hours on international flights). If you fail to check in on time and the flight is overbooked, the airline can cancel your booking and give your seat to somebody else.

Confirmation Having a ticket written out with the flight and date you want doesn't mean you have a seat until the agent has checked with the airline that your status is 'OK' or confirmed. Meanwhile you could just be 'on request'.

Courier Fares Businesses often need to send urgent documents or freight securely and quickly. Courier companies hire people to accompany the package through customs and, in return, offer a discount ticket which is sometimes a phenomenal bargain. In effect, what the companies do is ship their freight as your luggage on regular commercial flights. This is a legitimate operation, but there are two shortcomings – the short turnaround time of the ticket (usually not longer than a month) and the limitation on your luggage allowance. You may have to surrender all your allowance and take only carry-on luggage.

Full Fares Airlines traditionally offer 1st class (coded F), business class (coded J) and economy class (coded Y) tickets. These days there are so many promotional and discounted fares available that few passengers pay full economy fare.

ITX An ITX, or 'independent inclusive tour excursion', is often available on tickets to popular holiday destinations. Officially it's a package deal combined with hotel accommodation, but many agents will sell you one of these for the flight only and give you phoney hotel vouchers in the unlikely event that you're challenged at the airport.

Lost Tickets If you lose your airline ticket an airline will usually treat it like a travellers cheque and, after inquiries, issue you with another one. Legally, however, an airline is entitled to treat it like cash and if you lose it then it's gone forever. Take good care of your tickets.

MCO An MCO, or 'miscellaneous charge order', is a voucher that looks like an airline ticket but carries no destination or date. It can be exchanged through any International Association of Travel Agents (IATA) airline for a ticket on a specific flight. It's a useful alternative to an onward ticket in those countries that demand one, and is more flexible than an ordinary ticket if you're unsure of your route.

No-Shows No-shows are passengers who fail to show up for their flight. Full-fare passengers who fail to turn up are sometimes entitled to travel on a later flight. The rest are penalised (see Cancellation Penalties).

On Request This is an unconfirmed booking for a flight.

Air Travel Glossary

Onward Tickets An entry requirement for many countries is that you have a ticket out of the country. If you're unsure of your next move, the easiest solution is to buy the cheapest onward ticket to a neighbouring country or a ticket from a reliable airline which can later be refunded if you do not use it.

Open Jaw Tickets These are return tickets where you fly out to one place but return from another. If available, this can save you backtracking to your arrival point.

Overbooking Airlines hate to fly empty seats and since every flight has some passengers who fail to show up, airlines often book more passengers than they have seats. Usually excess passengers make up for the no-shows, but occasionally somebody gets bumped. Guess who it is most likely to be? The passengers who check in late.

Point-to-Point Tickets These are discount tickets that can be bought on some routes in return for passengers waiving their rights to a stopover.

Promotional Fares These are officially discounted fares, available from travel agencies or direct from the airline.

Reconfirmation At least 72 hours prior to departure time of an onward or return flight, you must contact the airline and 'reconfirm' that you intend to be on the flight. If you don't do this the airline can delete your name from the passenger list and you could lose your seat.

Restrictions Discounted tickets often have various restrictions on them – such as needing to be paid for in advance and incurring a penalty to be altered. Others are restrictions on the minimum and maximum period you must be away, such as a minimum of 14 days or a maximum of one year.

Round-the-World Tickets RTW tickets give you a limited period (usually a year) in which to circumnavigate the globe. You can go anywhere the carrying airlines go, as long as you don't backtrack. The number of stopovers or total number of separate flights is decided before you set off and they usually cost a bit more than a basic return flight.

Stand-by This is a discounted ticket where you only fly if there is a seat free at the last moment. Stand-by fares are usually available only on domestic routes.

Transferred Tickets Airline tickets cannot be transferred from one person to another. Travellers sometimes try to sell the return half of their ticket, but officials can ask you to prove that you are the person named on the ticket. This is less likely to happen on domestic flights, but on an international flight tickets are compared with passports.

Travel Agencies Travel agencies vary widely and you should choose one that suits your needs. Some simply handle tours, while full-services agencies handle everything from tours and tickets to car rental and hotel bookings. If all you want is a ticket at the lowest possible price, then go to an agency specialising in discounted tickets.

Travel Periods Ticket prices vary with the time of year. There is a low (off-peak) season and a high (peak) season, and often a low-shoulder season and a high-shoulder season as well. Usually the fare depends on your outward flight – if you depart in the high season and return in the low season, you pay the high-season fare.

Australia

There are direct flights from Australia to İstanbul offered by Malaysian Airlines (via Kuala Lumpur and Dubai) and Singapore Airlines (via Singapore and Dhahran) with round-trip fares for about A$1800. Cheaper are Middle Eastern Airlines, Gulf Air and EgyptAir with round-trip fares for about A$1600. There are also connecting flights via Athens, London, Rome, Amsterdam or Singapore on Thai International, British Airways, Olympic, Alitalia, KLM, Turkish Airlines and Qantas.

All these airlines regularly have specials (usually during the European low season of mid-January to the end of February and the start of October to mid-November) with most offering fares for A$1400 or less. Usually these specials must be booked and paid for reasonably quickly.

If you can get a cheap fare to London, you might do well once you're there to look for a cheap flight to Turkey.

LAND

Greece

From Greece, the major road goes to Ferai (Greece) and İpsala (Turkey), then to Keşan and east to İstanbul or south to Gallipoli, Çanakkale and the Aegean coast.

To the north, the road goes to Kastaneai (Greece) and Pazarkule (Turkey), 7km south-west of Edirne on the Meriç River (mehr-EECH, Maritsa), 2km past the Turkish village of Karaağaç, a border post originally meant to serve the railway line. The problem here is that the Greeks have declared the border area a military zone and do not permit anyone to walk in it without a military escort, so you will probably have to take a Greek taxi (US$6, two minutes) to the actual border, which is midway in the 1km-wide wasteland which separates the two border posts. On the Turkish side, you can walk to and from Pazarkule. These small border posts are open during daylight hours.

From Pazarkule, or from the nearby train station, you will probably have to take a Turkish taxi (US$5, 15 minutes) into town as there is not much traffic and hitching is not too easy, though you may be lucky.

If you are crossing from Turkey into Greece, do so as soon after 8 am as possible in order to catch one of the few trains or buses from Kastaneai heading south to Alexandroûpolis.

Lonely Planet's *Greece* guide covers the country thoroughly.

Bulgaria

If you're travelling overland from Bulgaria see the Edirne section in the Thrace chapter for border-crossing and travel details. Lonely Planet's *Eastern Europe* guide includes coverage of Bulgaria.

Georgia

The Turkish-Georgian border crossing at Sarp is now open to all travellers, not just to Turks and Georgians. For details see the Black Sea Coast chapter.

Iran

If you hope to travel in or through Iran, contact the Iranian embassy or consulate in your home country before leaving for Turkey, and check on visa requirements. It is usually easier and better to apply for the essential Iranian visa before leaving home.

It may take anywhere from a week to a month or more to obtain a visa. You may first have to obtain a visa for the country you will enter when you leave Iran; you may be asked to show a bus or airline ticket out of Iran. Be prepared for some bureaucratic hassles. See the Visas & Embassies sections in the Facts for the Visitor chapter, and contact your embassy in Ankara for details on availability and requirements for visas.

The border crossing may take as little as one hour. You may be asked to pay an unofficial fee (a bribe) by the Iranian officials. The Bank Melli branch at the border changes cash dollars or pounds or travellers cheques into Iranian rials (tomans). It may not change Turkish liras, but you may be able to exchange liras at banks further into Iran.

For full information on travel in Iran, see the Lonely Planet *Iran* guide.

Syria

Syrian visas are not normally issued at the border, but this depends partly upon your nationality and partly upon current regulations. One reader reports that border hassles are less if you cross by train rather than bus.

If you plan to travel to Syria and other countries in the Middle Eastern region, plan ahead and obtain the necessary visas in your home country. If you apply in İstanbul or Ankara, you may need a letter of recommendation from your home embassy or consulate.

Lonely Planet's *Jordan & Syria* is the guidebook to have when you enter the country.

Bus

Turkish bus companies operate frequent passenger services from all neighbouring companies, and even some in western Europe.

Athens For a bus to İstanbul, go to the train station (OSE Hellenic Railways Organisation, Plateia Peloponisu), from which the buses depart.

Varan Turizm (☎ 1-513 5768) in Athens operates daily buses to and from İstanbul via Thessaloniki, as does Ulusoy (☎ 1-524 0519, fax 524 3290), also at the Peloponese train station. The trip takes about 20 hours and costs about US$65 from Athens, US$40 from Thessaloniki, one way.

Elsewhere in Europe Several Turkish bus lines, including Ulusoy and Varan/Bosfor, offer services between İstanbul and some Central European cities such as Frankfurt, Munich and Vienna. One-way tickets range from US$85 to US$140 – so there's little savings over a cheap air ticket.

Syria, Jordan, Israel & Egypt For details of bus services to/from Syria and other Middle Eastern countries see the Antakya Getting There & Away section in the Eastern Mediterranean Turkey chapter. Get your visas in advance to hasten formalities.

Train

Few travellers choose to travel to Turkey by train these days. Excursion airfares are often lower than international rail fares, and the flight takes only hours, not days. Even the bus is usually faster.

Central Europe At the time of writing there are no direct trains between western or central Europe and Turkey. To travel from Munich to İstanbul, for example, you must change trains in Vienna and again in Belgrade; or Budapest and Niš, a journey of close to 40 hours. There is a daily direct train service between Budapest and İstanbul (*Balkan Express*, 31 hours) and Bucharest and İstanbul (*Bucharest-İstanbul Express*, 17 hours).

Greece The daily Thessaloniki-İstanbul passenger train takes 16 to 18 hours to cover the 850km. Almost a century ago, under the Ottoman Empire, it took 13½ hours. The bus covers the distance in greater comfort in about half the time.

Armenia The railway line from Ankara to Erzurum goes on to Kars but at the time of writing the Turkish-Armenian border is closed.

Iran In the past there has sometimes been a train between Turkey and Tehran, but it has not run for some years, and was not running at the time of writing.

Car

Car ferries (see the following Boat section) from Italy and Cyprus can shorten driving time considerably, but at a price. No special car documents are required for visits of up to three months. The car will be entered in the driver's passport as imported goods, and must be driven out of the country by the same visitor within the time period allowed.

Do not drive someone else's car into Turkey. At the least, it might end up on your passport as imported goods, meaning you won't be able to leave the country without it. At worst, it may be full of hidden contraband.

Normally, you can't rent a car in Europe and include Turkey (or many other Eastern European countries) in your driving plans. If you want to leave your car in Turkey and collect it later, the car must be put under customs seal (usually a tedious process).

For stays of longer than three months, or for any other information regarding car travel in Turkey, contact the Türk Turing ve Otomobil Kurumu (Turkish Touring and Automobile Association) (☎ 212-282 8140, fax 282 8042), Oto Sanayi Sitesi Yanı, Seyrantepe, 4 Levent, İstanbul.

The E80 highway goes through the Balkans to Edirne (see Edirne in the Thrace chapter) and İstanbul, then onward to Ankara.

Insurance Your Green Card third-party insurance must be endorsed for all of Turkey, both European and Asian, not just the European portion (Thrace). If it is not, you will be required to buy a Turkish insurance policy at the border.

BOAT

Luxury cruise ships frequently dock at İstanbul during Aegean or Mediterranean cruises, and fast ferryboats bring people here from other parts of Turkey.

Other Parts of Turkey

Turkish Maritime Administration (Türkiye Denizcilik İşletmeleri), also called Turkish Maritime Lines (TML) operates car and passenger ferries from İstanbul eastward along the Black Sea coast and southward through the Aegean to İzmir, as well as car and passenger ferry services in the Sea of Marmara.

Car Ferry Car and passenger ferries save you days of driving. Even if you have no car, they offer the opportunity to take mini-cruises along the Turkish coasts. Room on these ships is usually in hot demand, so reserve as far in advance as possible through one of TML's agents (see later), or directly with the İstanbul Karaköy office by fax.

İstanbul to İzmir İstanbul-İzmir car ferry services operates each weekend all year, departing İstanbul's Sarayburnu dock on Friday at 3 pm, arriving in İzmir on Saturday at 9 am. Departure from İzmir is on Sunday at 2 pm, arriving in İstanbul on Monday at 9 am.

One-way fares (per person) range from Pullman seats for US$35 to deluxe cabin berths for US$150; a two-berth, B-class cabin would cost US$160 a double. Should you want to use your cabin as a hotel room on Saturday night in İzmir, the cost ranges from US$45 a double for the cheapest cabin to US$165 a double for deluxe, with a two-berth, B-class cabin costing US$95.

Meals are extra, at US$7 for breakfast, US$15 for lunch and US$15 for dinner. The fare for a car is US$60 one way, less than half that for a motorcycle.

İstanbul to Trabzon Car ferries operate each week from early June to mid-September, departing from İstanbul on Monday at 2 pm, stopping briefly in Sinop, arriving in Samsun on Tuesday at 6.30 pm and departing at 8.30 pm, arriving in Trabzon on Wednesday at 9.30 am.

The boat continues to Rize, returning to Trabzon and departing on the return voyage to İstanbul at 4.30 pm on Wednesday. The returning ferry stops briefly at Giresun, Samsun and Sinop, arriving back in İstanbul on Friday at 2 pm.

Per-person fares between İstanbul and Trabzon are US$35 for a Pullman seat, US$50 to US$160 for cabin berths; meals cost US$7 for breakfast, US$15 for lunch or dinner extra. Cars cost US$56; motorcycles, US$25.

Catamaran & Fast Car-Ferries Fast catamaran passenger and car ferries connect İstanbul's Yenikapı seabus port with Yalova (near İznik and Bursa) and Bandırma where you can catch a train to İzmir. See the relevant sections for details.

There is also a traditional (meaning slow) car ferry service every half-hour between Gebze (Eskihisar docks), on the coast east of Üsküdar, and Topçular, east of Yalova on the Sea of Marmara's southern shore. A similar car ferry shuttles between Hereke and Karamürsel, further east. The drive (or bus ride) east around the Bay of İzmit is long, boring, congested and the scenery's ugly. Take one of these ferries instead.

Other Countries

Comfortable car ferry services operate between Italian and Greek ports and several Turkish ports, though not to İstanbul.

Turkish Maritime Lines Turkish Maritime Lines (Denizyolları, or TML) operates comfortable car and passenger ferries departing from Venice on Wednesday afternoon, arriving in İzmir midday on Saturday; departing İzmir on Saturday evening, and arriving in Venice on Tuesday at noon.

Per-person one-way Venice-İzmir fares range from US$215 to US$240 for a Pullman seat to US$600 for a berth in a luxury cabin; the fare for each of two berths in an air-con B-class cabin with shower and toilet is US$390 in the busy summer months; three meals and port tax are included in these examples. A car costs US$260 one-way.

Another TML service operates in summer, departing Brindisi, Italy around noon on Tuesday, Wednesday, Friday and Saturday, arriving in Çeşme, on the following evening around suppertime; departing Çeşme late in the evening on Wednesday, Thursday, Saturday and Sunday, arriving in Brindisi at breakfast time two days later.

Per-person one-way Brindisi-Çeşme fares range from US$155 for a Pullman seat to US$402 for a berth in a luxury cabin; the fare for each of two berths in an air-con B-class cabin with shower and WC is US$236 in the busy summer months; three meals and port tax are included in these examples. A car costs US$228 one-way.

Contact TML at the following addresses:

Brindisi
(☎ 831-568 633) Carso Garibaldi SpA, 19 72100 Zacmari, Brindisi Italy

İstanbul
(☎ 212-249 9222, fax 251 9025)
Türkiye Denizcilik İşletmeleri, Rıhtım Caddesi, Karaköy

İzmir
(☎ 232-421 1484, fax 421 1481)
Türkiye Denizcilik İşletmeleri Acenteliği, Yeniliman, Alsancak

London
(☎ 0171-923 3230, fax 923 3118, from 22 April 2000 ☎ 020-7923 3230, fax 020-7923 3118) Alternative Holidays Ltd, 146, Kingsland High St, London E8 2NS
(☎ 0181-211 7779, fax 211 8891, from 22 April 2000 ☎ 020-8211 7779, fax 020-8211 8891) Pasha Travel Ltd, 9 Grand Parade, Green Lane, Harringay, London N4 1JX

Venice
(☎ 41-522 9544, fax 520 4009)
Bassani SpA, Via 22 Marzo 2414, 30124 Venezia

Med Link Lines Med Link Lines operates two ferries, the *Poseidon* and the *Maria G* on the route Brindisi-Igoumenitsa-Patras-Çeşme from June to September. Fares tend to be lower than on TML, and there are reductions for students travelling in Deck, Pullman or C-class cabins (four to eight beds).

Departures from Brindisi are on Tuesday, Wednesday and Saturday, from Çeşme on Monday, Thursday, Friday and Sunday.

Contact MLL at the following addresses:

Brindisi
(☎ 831-52 76 67, fax 56 40 70)
Discovery Shipping Agency, 49 Corso Garibaldi, 72100 Brindisi, Italy

Çeşme
(☎ 232-712 7230, fax 712 8987)
Karavan Shipping, Belediye Dükkanları 3, by the harbour

Cologne
(☎ 221-257 3781, fax 257 3682)
Viamare seetouristik, Apostelnstrasse 9, 50667 Köln, Germany

Igoumenitsa
(☎ 665-26833, fax 26111)
Eleni Pantazi, 8 December St No 27, Greece

Patras
(☎ 061-62 30 11, fax 62 33 20)
George Giannatos, Othonos Amalias St 15

Poseidon Lines Poseidon operates ferries between Bari, Italy and Turkey during the summer tourist season. Contact Poseidon's booking centre (☎ 080-521 0022, fax 521 1204), Morfimare, Corso de Tullio 36/40, 70122 Bari, Italy.

Greek Islands

With the boom in Turkish tourism, the traffic from the Greek Islands to the Turkish mainland is intense in the warm months. From time to time, the Greek government issues regulations designed to make it difficult for travellers to go from Greece to Turkey. You may have to contend with these.

Previous efforts have included making it difficult to obtain information on boats to Turkey: the law stated that only one sign no greater than a piece of typing paper could be displayed, and only in the window of the agency selling tickets. In general it is very difficult to obtain information on transport from Greece to Turkey while in Greece. The best in the Athens area is to be had from the ferry offices at the port in Piraeus.

Greek regulations may require that passengers on trips originating in Greece must travel on Greek-flag vessels, which means that you may not be allowed to hop aboard a convenient Turkish vessel for your trip from the Greek Islands to the Turkish mainland. (If you've come over from Turkey for the day, you may return on the Turkish boat.)

The most recent regulation raised port taxes for travellers to Turkey to unconscionable heights – several times the actual boat fare. The Turkish government and tourism sector – and travellers – protested at once. The Greek taxes were lowered, but are still unconscionably high, about US$25 per person on some crossings.

There are numerous regular ferry services: in the North Aegean, Lesbos-Ayvalık and Chios-Çeşme; in the South Aegean, Samos-Kuşadası, Kos-Bodrum and Rhodes-Bodrum; in the Western Mediterranean, Rhodes-Marmaris, Rhodes-Fethiye and Kaş-Kastellorizo. The cheapest, most frequent and convenient are Samos-Kuşadası and Rhodes-Marmaris. The most expensive and hassled is Lesbos-Ayvalık.

The procedure is this: once you've found the ticket office, buy your ticket a day in advance. You may be asked to turn in your passport the night before the trip. The next day, before you board the boat, you'll get it back.

Cyprus

You should be aware that relations between the Greek Cypriot-administered Republic of Cyprus and the Turkish Republic of Northern Cyprus (TRNC) are not good, and that the border between the two regions will probably be closed. Also, if you enter the TRNC and have your passport stamped you will later be denied entry to Greece. The Greeks will reject only a stamp from the Turkish Republic of Northern Cyprus, *not* a stamp from Turkey proper. Have the Turkish Cypriot official stamp a piece of paper instead of your passport.

Kyrenia (Girne in Turkish) and Taşucu, near Silifke, are connected by daily hydrofoil and car-ferry services. See the Taşucu section in the Eastern Mediterranean Turkey chapter for details.

LEAVING TURKEY

Turkey levies a tax of about US$12 on visitors departing by air. The tax is customarily included in the cost of your ticket.

Don't have any antiquities in your luggage. If you're caught smuggling them out, you'll probably go to jail.

Getting Around

Turks love to travel, a legacy perhaps of all those centuries spent racing across the steppes on fast ponies. Turkey's elaborate public transport system meets their needs, and will meet yours as well. The intercity bus system is a marvel, with big, modern coaches going everywhere, all the time, at reasonable prices. The railway network, though limited and ageing, is useful on a few major routes. Turkish Airlines connects all the major cities and resorts.

AIR

Domestic Air Services

Turkish Airlines Türk Hava Yolları (THY, Turkish Airlines; symbol: TK), the state-owned airline waiting reluctantly for privatisation, has the major route network in Turkey. When you fly THY, ask about the 10% discount for couples or parent(s) with child(ren) travelling together, and discounts for youth (aged from 12 to 24 years), seniors (60 years and over), and those on their honeymoon or wedding anniversary.

THY flights serve these cities and towns: Adana, Ağrı, Ankara, Antalya, Balıkesir, Batman, Bodrum, Dalaman, Denizli, Diyarbakır, Edremit, Elazığ, Erzincan, Erzurum, Eskişehir, Gaziantep, Isparta, İstanbul, İzmir, Kahramanmaraş, Kars, Kayseri, Konya, Malatya, Muş Samsun, Siirt, Sinop, Sivas, Şanlıurfa, Tokat, Trabzon and Van. Hubs are İstanbul and Ankara; to go from Dalaman to Diyarbakır, for example, you will connect at İstanbul or Ankara.

İstanbul Airlines İstanbul Hava Yolları (İstanbul Airlines, symbol: IL) operates a few flights between its namesake city and Adana, Ankara, Antalya, Bodrum, Dalaman, Erzurum, Gaziantep, İzmir, Kars, Trabzon and Van, as well as on international routes to Austria, Belgium, Denmark, France, Germany, Holland, Ireland, Italy, Spain, Turkish Cyprus and the UK. The domestic flights are essentially feeder operations for international routes, so most flights operate only once or twice per week.

Prices are usually lower than those of THY. You can make reservations through the reservations centre (☎ 212-509 2121, fax 593 6035) in İstanbul at Firuzköy Yolu No 26, Avcılar and buy tickets at the airport. (See each city section for details on each local office.) Discounts include 10% for families, youth fares (12 to 24 years), and seniors over 60 years of age.

Check-in Procedures

It's a good idea to get to the airport *at least* 45 minutes before domestic flight departure to allow time for security checks and normal confusion. Signs and announcements are not always provided or understandable, so you need to keep asking to make sure you end up at the proper destination.

Security

Pack anything which can be construed as a weapon (a pocket knife or screwdriver, for example) in the luggage you will check-in, *not* in your carry-on luggage.

As you approach the airport perimeter, your bus or taxi may be stopped and spot-checked by police. On a bus, your passport and ticket may be inspected.

As you enter the terminal, your luggage must go through an x-ray machine. Before you leave the terminal police will frisk you for weapons and your hand baggage will be searched. If you haven't packed potential weapons in your checked luggage, declare them, don't wait until the officer finds them.

As you approach the aircraft, all passengers' luggage will be lined up, and you will be asked to point out your bag. It will then be put on board. This is to prevent someone from checking in a bag with a bomb inside it, then not boarding the plane. If you forget to point out your bag to the baggage handler, it may not be loaded on board and may be regarded with distrust, or even destroyed.

BUS

The bus and the *dolmuş* (minibus) are the most widespread and popular means of transport in Turkey. Buses go literally everywhere, all the time. Virtually every first-time traveller in Turkey comments on the convenience of the bus system.

The bus service runs the gamut from plain and inexpensive to comfortable and moderately priced. It is so cheap and convenient that many former long-distance hitchhikers opt for the bus. The six-hour, 450km trip between İstanbul and Ankara, for example, costs only US$15 to US$24, depending on the bus company.

Though bus fares are open to fierce competition among companies, and even to haggling for a reduction, the cost of bus travel in Turkey usually works out to be around US$2.25 to US$2.75 per 100km – a surprising bargain.

The best companies, offering smooth service at a higher than average price on national routes are Kamil Koç, Metro, Ulusoy and Varan. Many other regional companies offer varying levels of service, some quite good, others less so.

Otogar

Most Turkish cities and towns have a central bus station called variously *otogar*, *otobüs garajı*, *otobüs terminalı* or *şehir garajı* (city garage), depending upon the city. Besides intercity buses, the otogar often handles dolmuşes to outlying districts or villages. A few small towns have only a collection of bus line offices rather than a proper station.

Otogars are often equipped with their own PTT branches, bank or currency exchange offices, ATMs, telephones with international service, restaurants, snack stands, pastry shops, tourism information booths as well as left-luggage offices (*emanet*).

Buying Tickets

Though you can often just walk into an otogar and buy a ticket for the next bus out, it's wise to plan ahead. At the least, locate the companies' offices and note the times for your destination a day in advance. This is especially important along the south-east Mediterranean coast and the east, where long-distance bus traffic is less frequent than in other parts of the country.

Some bus companies will grant you a reduction on the fare if you show your ISIC student card. This may not be official policy, but just an excuse for a reduction – in any case you win.

The word for 'tomorrow', very handy to know when buying bus tickets a day in advance, is *yarın* (YAHR-uhn). Bus departure times will be given using the 24-hour clock, eg 18.30 instead of 6.30 pm.

When you enter an otogar you'll see lots of people and baggage, buses and dolmuşes, and rows of little ticket offices. Touts will invariably approach asking where you're bound; it's better to ask for any information at the ticket counters.

Competition on some routes is stiff. In most cases, more than one company will run to your desired destination; the cities and towns served by the company will be written prominently at that company's ticket office.

Once you've bought a ticket, getting a refund can be difficult, though it's possible. Exchanges for other tickets within the same company are easier.

Seat Selection Plan your seat strategy. Don't leave it up to the ticket agent. All seats are reserved, and your ticket will bear a specific seat number. The ticket agent often has a chart of the seats in front of them, with those already sold crossed off. Look at the chart, and indicate your seating preference.

Preferable seats are in the middle of the bus; seats over the wheels are liable to be cramped and will give you a rough ride. You also want to get a seat on the side of the bus which will not get full sun. Turks, it seems, are constitutionally opposed to air draughts of any strength, even (or perhaps especially) on a sweltering hot day. The ventilation or air-con system of the bus may be efficient,

The Fez Bus

If you don't want to travel on the local buses, the Fez Bus offers a hop-on, hop-off service which works its way around the most popular parts of Turkey: namely from İstanbul along the Aegean coast and the Mediterranean coast as far as Antalya, then inland to Eğirdir, Konya, Cappadocia and back to İstanbul via Ankara. Buses go every other day at quiet times, but daily in high season. A variety of passes are available. The Flying Carpet 12-day pass costs US$165 (US$147 under-28s); the Turkish Delight two-month pass costs US$180 (US$164 under-28s); and the Silk Road season pass costs US$213 (US$197 under-28s).

Fez also organises tours of the Black Sea area, and tours to Nemrut Dağı from İstanbul or Cappadocia. In winter 12-day set tours replace the hop-on, hop-off service (US$428 for 11 nights).

You can book on the Fez Bus at the Sultan Tourist Office, Akbıyık Caddesi, Terbıyık Sokak 3, Sultanahmet, İstanbul (☎ 212-516 9024, fax 517 1626), or through branches of STA Travel in Britain and Australia.

The advantage of using Fez is that you're taken from door to door and never have to drag your luggage about with you. The couriers will also help you with booking your accommodation and onward travel on the bus. On the other hand, you'll be travelling with other tourists, thus missing out on some of Turkey's famous hospitality.

but it may not be activated. On a 3½-hour summer afternoon trip from Ankara to Cappadocia, for instance, you'll be too warm if you're on the right-hand (western) side of the bus, while the seats on the left (eastern) side will remain comfortable.

You may want to avoid sitting near the driver as drivers are still allowed to smoke on intercity buses.

About Bus Travel

A bus trip in Turkey is usually a fairly pleasant experience, if it's not too long. Buses are big, modern and comfortable.

Once en route, your fellow passengers will be curious about where you come from, what language you speak, and how you're enjoying the country. It's polite to exchange at least a few sentences.

Shortly after you head out, the *yardımcı* (assistant, also called the *muavin*) will come through the bus with a bottle of lemon cologne with which to refresh their *sayın yolcular* (honoured passengers). They'll dribble some cologne into your cupped hands, which you then rub together, and then rub on your face and hair, ending with a sniff to clear your nasal passages. You may not be used to the custom, but if you ride buses in Turkey much you will get used to it quickly, and probably love it.

Water is provided at no charge on virtually all buses. Signal to the yardımcı and ask *Su, lütfen* ('Water, please').

You can also join in my fresh-air campaign. Summon the yardımcı/muavin and say *çok sıcak!* ('choke' suh-jahk, 'It's very hot'). Indicate the ventilation system and say *Havalandırma açın!* (hah-vah-lahn-duhr-MAH ah-chun, 'Open the ventilation system'). If you can't manage that, just point to it here, in the book, and let the yardımcı read it. Sometimes this works.

Stops will be made every 1½ hours or so for the toilet, snacks or meals and the inevitable *çay* (tea). At some stops children rush onto the bus selling sweets, nuts, sandwiches and the like, or a waiter from the teahouse (buses always stop at a teahouse) may come through to take orders. Most people, however, welcome the chance to stretch their legs.

Keep your bus ticket until you reach your absolutely final destination. In some cases, companies have *servis arabası* (sehr-VEES ah-rah-bah-suh, service cars) – a minibus service that will shuttle you from the otogar into the city at no extra charge, provided you can show a ticket for the company's line.

'My two companions and I stepped off a bus near Bergama and were just about to file into a taxi when an English guy jumped into OUR taxi and yelled 'Follow that bus!'. We just thought he accidentally left something on his seat. Later that day we bumped into him and he told us that the bus had sped off with his luggage still aboard. He explained that he had tremendous difficulty in getting the bus to pull over and spent a small fortune in taxi fares. We all laughed and had a couple of beers before hitting the ruins together.'

Tanya Campbell, Australia

Dolmuş or Minibus

A dolmuş (DOHL-moosh, 'filled') is a Turkish minibus (*minibüs* or *münübüs*), Fiat taxi, or huge old US car serving as a shared cab.

A dolmuş departs as soon as every seat (or nearly every seat) is taken. You can catch one from point to point in a city, or from village to village, and in some cases from town to town.

Though dolmuşes on some routes operate like buses by selling tickets in advance (perhaps even for reserved seats), the true dolmuş does not. Rather, it is parked at the point of departure (a town square, city otogar or beach) and waits for the seats to fill up.

The dolmuş route may be painted on the side of the minibus, or on a sign posted next to the dolmuş, or in its window; or a hawker may call out the destination. When the driver is satisfied with the load, the dolmuş heads off.

Fares Fares are collected en route or at the final stop. Often the fare is posted on the destination sign, whether it's on a signpost or in the vehicle's window. If it's not, watch what other passengers to your destination are paying and pay the same, or ask. Though passengers to intermediate stops sometimes pay a partial fare, on other routes the driver (or the law) may require that you pay the full fare. In either case, prices are low, though slightly more than for a bus on the same route.

Dolmuş Etiquette If your stop comes before the final destination, you may do some shuffling to ensure that you are sitting right by the door and not way up the back. Also, a woman is expected to sit with other women whenever possible. If this is not possible, she should choose a side seat, not a middle seat between two men, for her own comfort and 'protection'. If a man and a woman passenger get into the front of a car, for instance, the man should get in first and sit by the driver (contrary to everything his mother taught him about letting the lady go first), so that the woman is between 'her' man and the door. This is not a gesture against women, but rather the opposite, to show respect for their honour.

Collection of fares will begin after the car starts off, and the driver will juggle and change money as he drives. If you're still not sure about your fare, hand over a bill large enough to cover the fare but small enough not to anger the driver, who will never have enough change and will not want a large bill. Should there be any doubt about fares or problem in payment (rare), you can always settle up at the last stop.

To signal the driver that you want to get out, say *İnecek var* (ee-neh-JEK vahr, 'Someone wants to get out') or *Sağda* (SAAH-dah, 'On the right', meaning 'Please pull over to the kerb'.) Other useful words are *durun* (DOOR-oon, stop) and *burada* (BOO-rah-dah, here).

TRAIN

Turkish State Railways (TC Devlet Demiryolları, TCDD or DDY) runs services to many parts of the country on lines laid out by German companies which were supposedly paid by the kilometre. Some newer, more direct lines have been laid during the republican era, shortening travel times for the best express trains.

Alas, TCDD trains are the poor cousins in Turkey's transport mix. In the past few decades millions have been poured into highways and airports, but very little into the railroad network. Passenger equipment has a distinctly 1960s look to it, with many holes, patches and cigarette burns since then.

It's not a good idea to plan a train trip all the way across Turkey in one stretch as the country is large, and the cross-country trains are slower than the buses. For example, the *Vangölü Ekspresi* from İstanbul to Lake Van (Tatvan), a 1900km trip, takes almost two full days – and that's an express! The bus would take less than 24 hours, the plane less than two hours. Train travel between Ankara and İstanbul is fast and pleasant, however.

Whenever you take an intercity train in Turkey, you'd do well to take only *mavi tren* (blue train), *ekspres* or *mototren* trains. These are fairly fast, comfortable, and often not too much more expensive than the bus. On *yolcu* (passenger) and *posta* (mail) trains, however, you could grow old and die before reaching your destination.

Note that Turkish train schedules indicate *stations*, not cities; the station name is usually, but not always, the city name. Thus you may not see İstanbul on a schedule, but you will see Haydarpaşa and Sirkeci, the Asian and European stations in İstanbul. For İzmir, the stations are Basmane and Alsancak.

Top Trains

Here are the top trains running on the most important routes. Not all station stops are noted; use a map to estimate if a particular train might go to your destination. All trains are daily unless otherwise noted, and all schedules and fares are subject to change.

Anadolu Ekspresi This nightly *kuşetli* (couchette) and coach train between **Ankara** and **İstanbul** (Haydarpaşa) via Eskişehir hauls Pullman (US$6.50) and couchette (US$8) cars. It departs Ankara and İstanbul at 10 pm and arrives at 7 am.

Ankara Ekspresi Sleeping compartments on this nightly all-sleeping-car express between **Ankara** and **İstanbul** (Haydarpaşa) cost US$25/40 a single/double. It departs Ankara and İstanbul at 10.30 pm and arrives in the other city at 7.35 am.

Başkent Ekspresi The *Başkent* (Capital) *Ekspresi*, pride of the Turkish State Railways, departs **İstanbul** and **Ankara** at 10.30 am and makes the run to the opposite city in seven hours, the fastest train of all. It's an air-conditioned, super-1st-class day train between İstanbul (Haydarpaşa) and Ankara with Pullman seats, video, and meals served at your seat, airline-style. The fare is US$12 or US$9 for students.

Boğaziçi Ekspresi The *Boğaziçi* (Bosphorus) *Ekspresi* is a comfortable if faded 1st class Pullman-car train costing US$6.50 between **İstanbul** (Haydarpaşa) and **Ankara**, departing each city at 1.55 pm, and arriving in the other at 10 pm.

Çukurova Ekspresi The *Çukurova Ekspresi* departs **Ankara** daily at 8.10 pm hauling one-class coaches, couchette cars and sleeping cars to **Mersin** and **Adana** (arrives 8.18 am). The return trip departs from Adana at 7.15 pm and arrives in Ankara at 8.05 am. One-way tickets between Ankara and Adana or Mersin cost US$10/12 in a coach/couchette. Fares in a sleeping compartment cost US$24/42/58 for one/two/three people.

Doğu Ekspresi Though this train departs from **İstanbul** (Haydarpaşa) on time at 11.55 pm, it is usually late thereafter on its long trip via **Ankara, Sivas, Erzincan** and **Erzurum** to **Kars** near the Armenian border. It is a long (about 45 hours) and not particularly pleasant trip, but it is certainly cheap, costing only US$18/13 in 1st/2nd class. There are coaches only, no sleeping accommodation. See also Yeni Doğu Ekspresi, later.

Fatih Ekspresi Named after Mehmet the Conqueror (Fatih), this is a night train departing **İstanbul** (Haydarpaşa) and **Ankara** at 11.30 pm, arriving in the opposite city at 7.10 am, otherwise similar to the *Başkent* in comfort, speed and price.

Güney-Vangölü Ekspresi This train departs **İstanbul** (Haydarpaşa) each evening at 8 pm, and departs **Ankara** (5.55 am), **Kayseri** (2.32 pm), **Sivas** (6.48 pm) and **Malatya** (1.20 am) before arriving at **Elazığ Junction**. East of the junction, the train continues as the *Vangölü* (Lake Van) *Ekspresi* to **Tatvan** (arrives 2.30 pm), or the *Güney* (Southern) *Ekspresi* to **Diyarbakır** (8.25 am) and **Kurtalan** (east of Diyarbakır, arrives 12.05 pm), depending upon the day.

For the Van Gölü eastbound, board in İstanbul on Monday, Wednesday or Saturday, or in Ankara, Kayseri or Sivas on Tuesday, Thursday or Sunday.

For the *Güney*, board in İstanbul on Tuesday, Thursday, Friday or Sunday, or in Ankara, Kayseri or Sivas on Monday, Wednesday, Friday or Saturday.

These trains haul sleepers and 2nd-class coaches. A one-way 1st/2nd-class ticket from Ankara costs US$12/9 to Tatvan and US$10/7 to Diyarbakır. The fare in a sleeping car is from US$20/37/52 for one/two/three people.

İç Anadolu Mavi Tren This coach and couchette train departs **İstanbul** at 11.50 pm via **Kütahya** (6.10 am), **Afyon** (8.02 am) and **Konya** (noon) to **Karaman** (1.40 pm), for US$10; couchette US$12.

İstanbul-Ankara Mavi Tren 'Blue Trains' are comfortable expresses with 1st-class Pullman-style seats only. The **İstanbul-Ankara** Mavi Tren departs each city at 1 pm, arrives in the other at 8.11 pm. The one-way fare is US$9. The *Ek Mavi I* departs at noon and arrives at 7.35 pm; the *Ek Mavi II* departs at 9 pm and arrives at 6.20 am.

İzmir Ekspresi This nightly coach train departs **İzmir** (Basmane) at 6 pm, arriving in **Ankara** at 9.17 am; departure from Ankara is at 6.15 pm, arriving in İzmir at 9.35 am. The one-way fare is US$6/5 in 1st/2nd-class.

İzmir-Ankara Mavi Tren The nightly coach and sleeping car *Ankara Blue Train* departs **İzmir** (Basmane) at 7.40 pm, arriving in **Ankara** at 9.45 am. The *İzmir Blue Train* departs Ankara at 9.50 pm, arriving in İzmir at noon. The one-way fare is US$7; sleeping compartments cost US$10 for one person, US$18 for two people, US$26 for three. A set menu dinner on board costs from US$6 to US$10.

Marmara Ekspresi Take one of the several daily fast *hızlı feribot* (car ferries) from İstanbul's Yenikapı docks to Bandırma to catch the *Marmara Ekspresi*, a motor-train which departs **Bandırma** each afternoon at 3 pm, reaching **İzmir** (Basmane) by 9.15 pm, for US$3. The return train departs İzmir (Basmane) at 8 am, arriving in Bandırma at 2.12 pm, connecting with a fast car-ferry to **İstanbul** (Yenikapı).

Meram Ekspresi The *Meram Ekspresi* departs **İstanbul** (Haydarpaşa) daily at 7.30 pm via **Kütahya** (1.55 am) and **Afyon** (4 am), arriving in **Konya** at 8.10 am. The İstanbul-Konya fare is US$8/5 in 1st/2nd class; for sleeping compartments, total fares are US$20/38/56 for singles/doubles/triples.

Pamukkale Ekspresi The *Pamukkale Ekspresi* departs each night from **İstanbul** (Haydarpaşa) daily at 6.30 pm, via **Kütahya** (12.46 am), **Afyon** (2.20 am), **Isparta** (6.14 am), **Burdur** (7.40 am), **Eğirdir** (8.03 am), arriving in **Denizli** at 9.10 am. İstanbul to Denizli fares are US$8/5 in 1st/2nd class; for sleeping compartments, total fares are US$20/38/56 for singles/doubles/triples.

Toros Ekspresi This train departs from **İstanbul** (Haydarpaşa) on Tuesday, Thursday and Sunday at 8.25 am and heads for the south-east, stopping in **Eskişehir** (Enveriye, 1.55 pm), **Afyon** (5.40 pm), **Konya** (10.10 pm), **Adana** (4.50 am) and finally **Gaziantep** (11.40 am). On the return trip, it departs Gaziantep at 2.40 pm, Adana at 9.45 pm, Konya at 4.55 am, Afyon at 9.02 am and Eskişehir at 12.35 pm, to arrive in İstanbul (Haydarpaşa) at 5.54 pm. Fares from İstanbul are US$7 to Konya, US$10 to Adana and US$13 to Gaziantep. A sleeping car between İstanbul and Gaziantep costs US$20/25/28 a single/double/triple, total fare.

Vangölü Ekspresi See *Güney/Vangölü Ekspresi*, earlier.

Yeni Doğu Ekspresi The newer, faster cousin of the *Doğu Ekspresi* (see earlier), the *Yeni Doğu* runs from **İstanbul** (Haydarpaşa) to **Kars** in about 33 hours, departing İstanbul's Haydarpaşa station on Tuesday, Thursday and Saturday at 1.30 pm, arriving in **Ankara** at 9 pm and then leaving at 9.10 pm for **Sivas** (6.40 am), **Erzurum** (6.10 pm) and Kars (10.20 pm). On its return, the train departs Kars at 8.30 am, Erzurum at 12.40 pm, Sivas at 11.45 pm and Ankara at 10.20 am, arriving in İstanbul (Haydarpaşa) at 5.30 pm. Tickets between Ankara and Erzurum cost US$10 for a 1st-class seat, or US$18/30 for a single/double berth in a sleeping car. To go all the way from İstanbul to Kars costs only US$20/15 in a 1st/2nd-class seat, or US$30/55 in a single/double sleeping compartment.

Buying Tickets

Most seats on the best trains, and all sleeping compartments, must be reserved. As the best trains are popular, particularly the sleeping-car trains, you should make your reservation and buy your ticket as far in advance as possible. A few days will usually suffice, except at holiday times (see The Calendar section in the Facts for the Visitor chapter). Weekend trains, between Friday evening and Monday morning, seem to be the busiest.

If you can't buy in advance, check at the station anyway. There may be cancellations, even at the last minute.

Though Turkish State Railways now has a computerised reservations system, it is usually impossible to book sleeping-car space except in the city from which the train departs. You can buy tickets at the train station, at some PTTs (post offices) in the major cities, and at some travel agencies.

Turkish words useful in the train station are given in the Turkish Language Guide chapter at the back of this book.

Classes of Travel Most of the best trains, and the short-haul *mototrens* (motor-trains) and rail-buses now have only one class of travel. Coaches on the top trains (*Başkent* and *Fatih Ekspresi*, *Mavi Tren*) usually have Pullman reclining seats; the normal expresses usually have European-style compartments with six seats. The very slow trains – and those in the east – often have 1st and 2nd-class coaches with compartments.

Sleeping accommodation is of three classes. A couchette wagon has six-person compartments with seats which rearrange into six shelf-like beds at night; you sleep with strangers. *Örtülü kuşetli* means the couchettes have bedding (sheets, pillows and blanket), and there may be only four beds per compartment, so two couples travelling together can get an almost private compartment. A *yataklı* wagon has European-style sleeping compartments capable of sleeping up to three people. Price depends upon the number of occupants: per person cost is lowest when three people share and is highest if you want a compartment all to yourself.

Discounts & Passes Inter-Rail passes are valid on the Turkish State Railways' entire network; Eurail passes are not valid on any of it.

Full fare is called *tam*. Round-trip (return) fares, called *Gidiş-Dönüş*, are discounted by 20%. *Öğrenci* or *talebe* (student) fares discounted by 20% to 30% are offered on most routes (show your ISIC). If you are under 26 years of age or over 55, you can buy a Tren-Tur card which allows you one month's unlimited rail travel. Ask at Sirkeci Station in İstanbul, or at the Ankara Garı. *Aile* (families), meaning a married couple travelling with or without children, are entitled to a 20% to 30% discount; disabled persons get 30% off and press card holders are entitled to 50% off.

Cancellation Penalties If you decide not to travel and you seek a refund for your train ticket up to 24 hours before the train's departure, you must pay a cancellation fee of 10% of the ticket price. Within 24 hours of departure the fee rises to 25%. After the train has departed the fee is 50%.

CAR

Having a car in Turkey, whether owned or rented, gives you unparalleled freedom to enjoy the marvellous countryside and coastline. If you can manage it, car travel in Turkey is rewarding despite the drawbacks.

Road Rules

In theory, Turks drive on the right and yield to traffic approaching them from the right. In practice, Turks drive in the middle and yield to no one. You must accustom yourself to drivers overtaking you on blind curves. If a car approaches from the opposite direction, all three drivers stand on their brakes and trust to Allah.

The international driving signs are there but are rarely observed. Signs indicating *otoyols* (motorways, expressways) are green. Maximum speed limits, unless otherwise posted, are 50 km/h in towns, 90 km/h on highways; and 130km/h maximum, 40 km/h minimum on otoyols.

As there are only a few divided highways and many two-lane roads are serpentine, you must reconcile yourself to spending some hours sniffing the stinky diesel exhaust of slow, seriously overladen trucks. At night you'll encounter cars without lights or with lights missing; vehicles stopped in the middle of the road; and oncoming drivers flashing their lights just to announce their approach.

Driving Permits

You don't really need an International Driving Permit (IDP) when you drive in Turkey, despite what some travel books say. Your home driving licence, unless it's something unusual (say, from Upper Volta), will be accepted by traffic police and by car rental firms. If you'd feel more secure against bureaucratic hassle by carrying an IDP, you can get one through an automobile club in your home country. Always carry your normal license as well.

Road Safety

Turkey has one of the highest motor vehicle accident rates in the world, with about 7000 deaths a year, and tens of thousands of injuries. The government, media and several private groups have undertaken a vigorous driver education safety campaign, urging motorists to tame the 'Trafik Canavarı' ('Motoring Monster') within them, to drive considerately and at a safe speed; but it may be years before the campaign has an effect.

Turkish drivers are not particularly discourteous out on the highway, but they are impatient and far from cautious. They drive at high speed. They have an irrepressible urge to overtake you. To survive on Turkey's highways, drive very defensively, avoid driving at night, and *never* let emotions affect what you do.

Road Conditions

The quality of Turkish highways is passable. The Türkiye Cumhuriyeti Karayolları (Turkish Republic Highways Department or TCK) undertakes ambitious improvements constantly, but despite its efforts most roads still have only two lanes, perhaps with overtaking lanes on long uphill grades. Otoyols run from the Bulgarian border near Edirne to İstanbul and Ankara, and south from İzmir to Aydın.

In eastern Turkey, with its severe winter, roads are easily destroyed by frost, and potholes are a tyre-breaking nuisance any time of year.

The expressways are often busy but not impossible; the lesser highways can be busy or pleasantly traffic-free. City streets are usually thronged.

In the cities *düzensizlik* (disorder) is universal. In addition to the customary and very appropriate *Allah Korusun* ('May God Protect Me') emblazoned somewhere on every Turkish car, bus and truck, imagine the additional motto *Önce Ben* ('Me First').

Fuel

Fuel stations are everywhere, operated by some familiar international companies (BP, Shell, Mobil) and unfamiliar Turkish ones (Türk Petrol, Petrol Ofisi). Many never close, others stay open long hours, so refuelling is usually no problem. All the same, it's a good idea to have a full tank when you start out in the morning across the vast spaces of central and eastern Anatolia.

Most accept credit cards in payment, though they may not be able to get approval for your charge due to insufficient telephone lines.

Benzin (petrol/gasoline) comes as *normal, süper* and *kurşunsuz* (the last being unleaded). Normal costs about US$0.80 per litre (US$3 per US gallon); süper, about US$0.82 per litre (US$3.10 per US gallon); kurşunsuz, about US$0.87 per litre (US$3.30 per US gallon). *Dizel* (diesel) costs about US$0.55 per litre (US$2.08 per US gallon).

Some stations give a free car wash when you fill your tank.

Spares & Repairs

Turkey's equivalent of the Automobile Association (UK) and American Automobile Association (USA) is the Türkiye Turing ve Otomobile Kurumu (Turkish Touring & Automobile Association, TTOK) (☎ 212-282 8140, fax 282 8042), Oto Sanayi Sitesi Yanı, Seyrantepe, 4 Levent, İstanbul. It is useful for driving aids (maps, lists of repair shops, legal necessities) as well as for repairs and advice on repairs.

Spare parts for most cars may be available, if not readily so, outside the big cities. European models (especially Renaults, Fiats and Mercedes-Benz) are preferred, though ingenious Turkish mechanics contrive to keep all manner of huge US models – some of them half a century old – in daily service.

If you have a model with which Turkish mechanics are familiar, repairs can be swift and very cheap. Don't be afraid of little roadside repair shops, which can often provide excellent, virtually immediate service, though they (or you) may have to go somewhere else to get the parts. The Sanayi Bölgesi (industrial zone) on the outskirts of every city and town has a row of repair shops.

It's always good to get an estimate of the repair cost in advance. Ask *Tamirat kaç para?* ('How much will repairs cost?'). For tyre repairs find an *oto lastikçi* (tyre repairer). Repair shops are closed on Sunday, but even so, if you go to the repair shop district of town (every town has one: ask for the *sanayi bölgesi*) and look around, you may still find someone willing and able to help you.

Traffic Police

Trafik Polisi in black-and-white cars (usually Renaults) and blue uniforms set up checkpoints on major highways in order to make sure that vehicle documents are in order, that you are wearing your seatbelt, and that vehicle safety features are in working condition. They busy themselves mostly with trucks and buses, as that is where lies the greatest possibilities for supplemental income. They'll usually wave you on, but you should slow down and prepare to stop until you get the wave.

If you're stopped, officers may ask for your car registration, insurance certificate and driving licence. They may ask you to turn on your headlights, hoot your horn, switch on the turning signals and windscreen wipers etc, to see that all are working properly. They'll certainly ask your nationality, and try to chat, because one of the reasons you (an 'exotic' foreigner) have been stopped is to break the monotony of checking trucks. If they seem to be requesting money, refuse to understand.

Rental

Renting a car is expensive, but gives you freedom. If you share the cost among several people, renting can be reasonable.

Minimum age is generally 19 or 21 years for the cheapest cars, 24 for some larger cars, and 27 for the best. You must pay with a major credit card, or you will be required to make a large cash deposit.

Cars may be rented in Adana, Alanya, Ankara, Antalya, Bodrum, Bursa, Çeşme, Dalaman, Fethiye, Gaziantep, İstanbul, İzmir, Kemer, Kuşadası, Marmaris, Mersin, Samsun, Side and Trabzon from the larger international rental firms (Avis, Budget, Dollar, Europcar, Hertz, Inter-Rent, Kemwel and National) or from smaller local ones. Rentals may also be picked up in most other cities by prior arrangement.

Avis has the most extensive and experienced network of agencies and staff, and the highest prices. Some firms will be happy to deliver your car to another place, or arrange for pick-up, at no extra charge; others will charge you.

You should not be afraid to try (with caution) one of the small local agencies. Though there is no far-flung network for repairs and people in these places have little fluency in English, they are friendly, helpful and charge from 10% to 20% less than the large firms, particularly if you're willing to haggle a bit.

The most popular rental cars are the Fiat 124 (Serçe), a small four-passenger car with limited space and power; Fiat 131 (Şahin), more powerful and comfortable; Fiat 131SW (Kartal), still more powerful and comfortable; and Fiat Mirafiori (Doğan), big enough for five. Of the Renaults, the 12TX is similar to the Fiat 131, but more economical with fuel; the Renault 9 is larger and more powerful, the 12 STW, better still. All of these cars have standard gear shift. Only the most expensive cars (big Fords, Mercedes etc) have automatic transmission and air-conditioning.

Costs Rental cars are moderately expensive in Turkey, partly due to huge excise taxes paid when the cars are purchased. Total costs of a rental arranged on the spot in Turkey during the busy summer months, for a week with unlimited kilometres, including full insurance and tax, might be from US$300 to US$600. Ask your travel agent to shop around, or to set up a fly-drive arrangement.

If you rent from abroad before arriving in Turkey, the Collision Damage Waiver (CDW) is usually included in the all-inclusive price quoted to you. The CDW is not a bad thing to have, because a renter is liable not merely for damage, but for rental revenue lost while the car is being repaired or, in the case of a stolen car, until the car is recovered.

The normal CDW does not cover damage to the car's glass (windscreen, side windows, head and tail lamps etc) nor to its tyres. Yet another charge of US$3 to US$5 per day is required to pay for this. If you do not pay this charge and encounter these misfortunes, it's usually best and cheapest to arrange for repair or replacement yourself, en route.

Note that many travellers do not need the personal injury insurance that's offered by the rental company. Your health insurance from home may cover any medical costs of an accident.

Kısmet & Kader

Many local drivers, it seems, believe in *kısmet* (luck) and *kader* (fate). If Turkish drivers, careering along slippery highways in cars with smooth tyres and accelerator pedals flat to the floor and their minds engaged in heated conversation, swerve to avoid an errant sheep and crash into trees, that's kısmet, and it can't be helped.

Moderating speed, getting better tyres, wearing safety belts or paying attention to the road are a waste of time and money, as kader, your fate, is already written in Allah's big book. The Grim Reaper will get you if he's going to, no matter what you do. So why bother?

Whether because of kısmet and kader or not, Turkey's highway accident rate is among the highest in the world. In the last decade around 80,000 people have lost their lives, and a million have been injured in traffic accidents, most often because of driver error. On Turkey's highways in the average day, 15 people are killed. Almost every family in the country has been touched by the tragedy.

If you drive, be extremely cautious and defensive. When travelling by bus, it's good to give preference to the better companies with newer equipment, better trained and more experienced drivers, and stricter policies regarding vehicular safety.

When you look at a rental company's current price list, keep in mind that the daily or weekly rental charge is only a small portion of what you will actually end up paying, unless it includes unlimited kilometres. The charge for kilometres normally ends up being higher, per day, than the daily rental charge. By the way, the 15% Value Added Tax (KDV) should be included in the rental, insurance and kilometres prices quoted to you. It should not be added to your bill as an extra item.

Any traffic fines you incur will be charged to you. Normally, the company charges your credit card.

Safety & Accidents Child safety seats are usually available from the larger companies for about US$5 per day if you order them at least 48 hours in advance.

If your car incurs any accident damage, or if you cause any, do not move the car before finding a police officer and asking for a *kaza raporu* (accident report). The officer may ask you to submit to an alcohol breath-test. Contact your car rental company within 48 hours. Your insurance coverage may be void if it can be shown that you were operating under the influence of alcohol or other drugs, were speeding, or if you did not submit the required accident report within 48 hours.

MOTORCYCLE

You can bring your motorcycle to Turkey and have a fine time seeing the country. Spare parts will probably be hard to come by, so bring what you may need, or rely on the boundless ingenuity of Turkish mechanics to find, adapt or make you a part. Or else be prepared to call home, have the part flown in, and endure considerable hassles from customs.

BICYCLE

Though Turks use bicycles primarily as utilitarian vehicles to go short distances, long-distance bicycling for sport is being introduced by foreign cyclers. You can cycle pleasurably through Turkey, though you may want to bring your own bike, as renting and selling good bikes isn't yet widespread.

The pleasures are in the spectacular scenery, the friendly people, the easy access to archaeological sites and the ready availability of natural camping sites both official and unofficial. The best routes are those along the coasts, particularly the western Mediterranean coast between Marmaris and Antalya. You may be wheeling merrily along, be overtaken by a truck loaded with fruit, and handed some on the run by the laughing children who have just picked it. Some of the best routes are the unpaved coastal roads not marked on many maps.

On the minus side, you must watch out for the occasional inattentive driver: have a rear-view mirror on your bike. Also, maps available in Turkey are sometimes incorrect on such things as grades and altitudes, so search out a suitable map before leaving home (see Maps in the Facts for the Visitor chapter).

As a cyclist, you may find your relations with Turks somewhat extreme. Along the road, some children not used to cyclists may toss stones. This is often more of an annoyance than a danger, and as cyclists become more familiar sights it should subside. In hotels and pensions, and on those occasional bus and train rides, you may find people so accommodating and helpful in storing your valuable cycle 'safely' that lights, carriers and reflectors may get damaged unintentionally, so supervise and say *yavaş yavaş* (yah-VAHSH yah-VAHSH, 'slowly') frequently.

Whenever you stop for a rest or to camp, the rural staring squads of the curious will appear, instantly, as if by magic. You may find, like the royal family, that constant scrutiny, even if friendly, can be wearisome.

You can usually transport your bike by air, bus, train and ferry, sometimes at no extra charge.

Here are some tips on equipment and repairs. You cannot depend upon finding spare parts, so bring whatever you think you may need. Moped and motorcycle repair shops are often helpful, and if they can't do the repairs they will seek out someone who can. High-pressure pumps are not yet available in Turkey; fuel-station pumps may or may not go to 90 psi (high pressure). Inner tubes of 69cm by 3cm are available, but not everywhere; most of the tubes sold are larger, and they won't fit 69cm by 2.5cm rims because of the large valve seat. Be prepared for frequent chain maintenance because of the effects of dust, sand and mud.

HITCHING

Hitching is never entirely safe in any country in the world, and we don't recommend it. Travellers who decide to hitch should understand that they are taking a potentially serious risk.

If you must *otostop* (hitch), Turkish custom requires that you offer to pay for your ride, though these days some drivers pick up foreign hitchers for the curiosity value. The amount is more or less equivalent to the bus fare on the same route. (Say *Borcum kaç?*, bohr-JOOM kahtch, 'How much do I owe you?' as you prepare to get out.) Overcharging hitchers has not been a big problem.

Long-distance hitching, though possible in Turkey, is not all that common. The bus and minibus network is so elaborate and cheap that most people opt for that, figuring that if bus fares must be paid, bus comforts might as well be enjoyed. Private cars are not as plentiful as in Europe, and owners here are not as inclined to pick up hitchers.

Short-distance hitching is somewhat different. As the country is large and vehicles not so plentiful outside the towns, short-distance country hops are the norm. If you need to get from the highway (where the bus dropped you) into an archaeological site (Troy, Patara or wherever), you hitch a ride with whatever comes along. Again, private cars are the least amenable, but delivery vans, heavy machinery, oil tankers, farm tractors etc are all fair game. You should still offer to pay for the ride; in most cases your offer will be declined (though appreciated), because you are a 'guest' in Turkey.

The signal used in hitching is not an upturned thumb. In Turkey, you face the traffic, hold your arm out towards the road, and wave your hand and arm up and down as though bouncing a basketball.

Women Hitchers

When it comes to women hitching, Turkey is like the rest of the world, perhaps a bit more so: it is seldom done, and you really should not do it, especially alone. Except in an emergency, a Turkish woman would rather die than hitch; she'd feel like she was offering herself to every man in every car that picked her up. With buses so cheap, why set yourself up for hassles?

Two women hitching together is a bit safer, but avoid vehicles with more than one or two men in them. If you're determined to hitch, take the normal precautions: don't accept a ride in a car or truck which is already occupied by men only (especially if it's only one man, the driver). Look for vehicles carrying women and/or children as well as men. Act appreciative and polite, but cool, dignified and formal. Avoid hitching across long, empty spaces, and never hitch at night.

BOAT

Türkiye Denizcilik İşletmeleri (Turkish Maritime Administration), also called Turkish Maritime Lines (TML) operates car and passenger ferry services from İstanbul eastward along the Black Sea coast and southward along the Aegean coast, as well as passenger services in the Sea of Marmara and shuttle services across the Dardanelles and the Bay of İzmit. These services may be privatised in the near future, in which case terms of service may change.

Ferry

Car and passenger ferries save you days of driving. Even if you have no car, they offer the opportunity to take mini-cruises along the Turkish coasts. Room on these ships is usually in hot demand, so reserve as far in advance as possible through one of TML's agents, or directly with the İstanbul Karaköy office by fax.

İstanbul to İzmir The İstanbul-İzmir car ferry service operates each weekend throughout the year, departing İstanbul's Sarayburnu dock each Friday at 3 pm and arriving in İzmir on Saturday at 9 am. Departure from İzmir is on Sunday at 2 pm, arriving in İstanbul on Monday at 9 am.

One-way fares (per person) range from Pullman seats for US$35 to deluxe cabin berths for US$150; a two-berth B-class cabin would cost US$160 a double. Should you want to use your cabin as a hotel room on Saturday night in İzmir, the cost ranges from US$45 a double for the cheapest cabin to US$165 a double for deluxe, with a two-berth, B-class cabin costing US$95.

Meals are extra, at US$7 for breakfast, US$15 for lunch and US$15 for dinner. Fare for a car is US$60 one way and less than half that for a motorcycle.

İstanbul to Trabzon Car ferries operate each week from early June to mid-September, departing from İstanbul on Monday at 2 pm, stopping briefly in Sinop, arriving in Samsun on Tuesday at 6.30 pm and departing at 8.30 pm, arriving in Trabzon on Wednesday at 9.30 am.

The boat continues to Rize, returning to Trabzon and departing on the return voyage to İstanbul at 4.30 pm on Wednesday. The returning ferry stops briefly at Giresun, Samsun and Sinop, arriving back in İstanbul on Friday at 2 pm.

Per-person fares between İstanbul and Trabzon are US$35 for a Pullman seat, US$50 to US$160 for cabin berths; meals cost US$7 for breakfast, US$15 extra for lunch or dinner. Cars cost US$56; motorcycles are US$25.

Catamaran & Fast Car-Ferries Fast catamaran passenger and car ferries connect İstanbul's Yenikapı seabus port with Yalova (near İznik and Bursa) and Bandırma where you can catch a train to İzmir. See the relevant sections for details.

There is also a traditional (meaning slow) car ferry service every 30 minutes between Gebze (Eskihisar docks), on the coast east of Üsküdar, and Topçular, east of Yalova on the Sea of Marmara's southern shore. A similar car ferry shuttles between Hereke and Karamürsel, further east. The drive (or bus ride) east around the Bay of İzmit is long, boring, congested and the scenery is ugly. Take one of these ferries instead.

LOCAL TRANSPORT

Airport

Transport to and from each airport in Turkey is covered within the Getting Around section on each city.

Bus

Turkish cities have lots of buses, but they are usually crowded to capacity. Buses run by the city government often have (*city-name*) *Belediyesi* (municipality) marked on them. Most municipal buses now work on a ticket system, and you must buy a ticket (*otobüs bileti*, or simply *bilet*, bee-LEHT) in advance at a special ticket kiosk. These kiosks are at major bus termini or transfer points; some shops may sell them as well, and scalpers may hang around bus stops selling them for a marked-up price.

In some cities, notably İstanbul, private buses called *halk otobüsü* (peoples' bus) operate on the same routes as municipal buses. They're usually older buses, and painted somewhat differently. They accept either cash fares or tickets, and follow the same routes as city buses.

Dolmuş

Dolmuşes, minibuses or sedans, operate in many cities, and are usually faster, more comfortable and only slightly more expensive than the bus (and still very cheap). Intracity dolmuş stops are near major squares, terminals or intersections, and you'll have to ask: (name of destination) *dolmuş var mı?* (DOHL-moosh VAHR muh). If you are in Eminönü in İstanbul, for instance, and you want to get to Taksim Square, you ask, *Taksim dolmuş var mı?* Someone will point you to the dolmuş stop on the eastern side of the Yeni Cami.

Once you know a few convenient routes, you'll feel confident about picking up a dolmuş at the kerb. In the larger cities, stopping-places are regulated and sometimes marked by signs with a black 'D' on a blue-and-white background reading *Dolmuş İndirme Bindirme Yeri* (Dolmuş Boarding and Alighting Place).

A true city dolmuş has a solid-colour band, usually yellow or black, painted horizontally around the car just below the windows. Sometimes taxis with a black-and-yellow chequered band operate like the dolmuş. You've got to be careful. If you climb into an empty car, the driver might assume (honestly, or for his own benefit) that you want a taxi, and will charge you the taxi fare. Always ask, *Dolmuş mu?* (dohl-MOOSH moo? 'Is this a dolmuş?') when you climb into an empty car.

Taxi

Taxis in most cities have digital meters and routinely use them. If yours doesn't, mention it right away by saying, *Saatiniz* (saa-AHT-EE-NEEZ, 'Your meter'). The starting rate is about US$1. The average taxi ride costs from US$2 to US$4 during the day time, 50% more at night.

With the flood of tourists arriving in Turkey, some taxi drivers – especially İstanbul's many crooks-on-wheels – have begun to demand flat payment from foreigners. In some cases the driver will actually offer you a decent fare, and will then pocket all the money instead of giving the owners of the cab their share. But most of the time such drivers will offer an exorbitant fare, give you trouble, and refuse to run the meter. Find another cab and, if convenient, report them to the police.

A woman should not sit in the front seat next to the driver unless there is no other available seat. The driver may misunderstand the gesture as an invitation to greater intimacy.

Ferry & Sea Bus

Public intracity sea transport is by ferryboat and *deniz otobüsü* ('sea bus' catamaran).

Traditional ferries steam up, down and across the Bosphorus and the Bay of İzmir, providing city dwellers with cheap, convenient transport, views of open water and (in summer) fresh cool breezes.

Sea bus catamarans are faster enclosed craft which ply certain routes heavily used by commuters.

These are not nostalgic transport but vital elements of each city's transport system. You should take the ferry in each city at least once, sipping tea while enjoying the cityscapes from the decks. The ferries can be crowded during rush hours but there's always air and scenery; and while buses sit trapped in noisy traffic the ferries glide through the water effortlessly, at speed.

TOURS

As Turkey's tourist boom continues, the number of companies offering guided tours of cities or regions expands. A travel agency and tour operator of long standing and excellent reputation is Orion-Tour (☎ 212-248 8437, fax 241 2808, oriontour@compuserve.com, www.orion-tour.com), Halaskargazi Caddesi 284/3, Marmara Ap, 80220 Şişli, İstanbul. Orion's multilingual staff can arrange almost any sort of travel in Turkey, from flight reservations and airport transfers to guided tours and yacht cruises.

Along with legitimate operators, the shifty ones are moving in, so you should be extremely careful when choosing a tour company.

The actual tour you get depends greatly on the competence, character and personality of your particular guide; but it's difficult to pick a tour by guide rather than company, so you must go by the reputation of the tour company.

The best course of action is to ask at your hotel for recommendations. Other foreign visitors may be able to give you tips about which companies to use and which to avoid. Watch out for the following rip-offs: a tour bus that spends the first hour or two of your 'tour' circulating through the city to various hotels, picking up tour participants; a tour that includes an extended stop at some particular shop (from which the tour company or guide gets a kickback); a tour that includes a lunch which turns out to be mediocre.

Most of the time, it is a lot cheaper and quicker to see things on your own by bus, dolmuş, or even taxi. Tours can cost from US$20 to US$40 per person; you may be able to hire a taxi and driver for the entire day for less than that, after a bit of haggling.

İstanbul

For many centuries this city was the capital of the civilised world. Even though in 1922 Ankara became the capital of the newly proclaimed Turkish Republic, İstanbul continued to be the Turkish metropolis. It remains the country's largest city (with about 12 million residents) and port, its business and cultural centre and the first destination for Turkish and foreign tourists alike.

Although İstanbul has yielded some of its pre-eminence to up-and-coming towns such as Ankara, İzmir and Antalya, it remains, without doubt, the heartbeat of the Turkish spirit. The Turks are proud of Ankara, their modern, 20th-century capital, but it is İstanbul, the well-worn but still glorious metropolis, which they love. Its place in the country's history, folklore, commerce and culture is unchallenged.

No matter how you arrive in İstanbul, you'll be impressed. The train skirts the southern coast of the Thracian peninsula, following the city walls until it comes around Seraglio Point and terminates directly below Topkapı Sarayı (Topkapı Palace). Buses come in along an expressway built on the path of the Roman road. Flying in on a clear day may reveal the great mosques and palaces, the wide Bosphorus (Boğaziçi) and the narrower Golden Horn (Haliç), all in a wonderful panorama.

But nothing beats 'sailing to Byzantium' – gliding across the Sea of Marmara while watching the slender minarets and bulbous mosque domes rise on the horizon. Even Mark Twain, who certainly had control of his emotions, waxed rhapsodic in his *Innocents Abroad* on the beauties of arriving by sea. Today, though fumes from fossil fuels may obscure the view, it's still impressive – and the pollution is much less than it was only a few years ago thanks to the widespread use of natural gas for heating and taxi fuel. If you take the boat-train from İzmir via Bandırma, or the ferry from Yalova, you'll approach the city by sea.

HIGHLIGHTS

- Gaping at the incredible gems in the Treasury of the Topkapı Sarayı
- Hearing the echoes of centuries in the vastness of the Aya Sofya
- Feeling the sacred stillness of the Sultan Ahmet Camii (Blue Mosque)
- Getting lost amid the 4000 shops of the Kapalı Çarşı (Grand Bazaar)
- Seeing the glittering 14th-century Byzantine mosaics in the Kariye Müzesi (Chora Church)
- Cruising up the Bosphorus past Ottoman castles and palaces

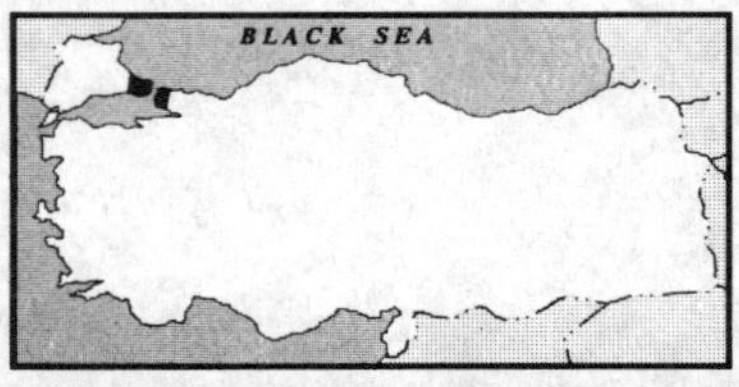

İstanbul has grown ferociously in the past two decades, and now sprawls westward beyond the airport, 23km from the centre, northward halfway to the Black Sea, and eastward deep into Anatolia. And it is crowded. However, both the Bosphorus, the strait which connects the Black Sea and the Sea of Marmara, and the narrower Golden Horn, a freshwater estuary, help to create a sense of openness and space. More than that, the Bosphorus provides an uncrowded maritime highway for transport to various sections of the city. For several thousand years before the construction of the Bosphorus Bridge in 1973, the only way to go between the European and Asian parts of the city was by boat. The second Bosphorus bridge, named Fatih Köprüsü, north of the first one at Bebek/Beylerbeyi, was finished in 1988. A third bridge, further north, is planned, and a metro is being developed.

HISTORY

With a past spanning 3000 years, the greatest part of İstanbul's fascination comes from its place in history and the buildings that remain from ancient times. Here's a quick summary of its past to help you to distinguish a hippodrome from a harem.

1000-657 BC
Ancient fishing villages on this site.

657 BC-330 AD
Byzantium, a Greek city-state, later subject to Rome.

330-1453 AD
Constantinople, the 'New Rome', capital of the Later or Eastern Roman (Byzantine) Empire – reached its height in the 12th century.

1453-1922
İstanbul, capital of the Ottoman Turkish Empire – reached the height of its glory in the 16th century.

1922-84
Ankara becomes the capital of the Turkish Republic. İstanbul continues to be the country's largest city and port, and its commercial and cultural centre.

1984 to the Present
İstanbul begins to enjoy a renaissance as 'Capital of the East'. A new municipal government undertakes vast schemes to modernise and beautify the city and attract international business operations. New parks, museums and cultural centres are opened, old ones are restored and refurbished.

Early Times

The earliest settlement, Semistra, was probably around 1000 BC, a few hundred years after the Trojan War and in the same period that kings David and Solomon ruled in Jerusalem.

It was followed by a fishing village named Lygos, which occupied Seraglio Point where Topkapı Sarayı stands today. Later, around 700 BC, colonists from Megara (near Corinth) in Greece settled at Chalcedon (now Kadıköy) on the Asian shore of the Bosphorus.

Byzantium

The first settlement to have historic significance was founded by another Megarian colonist, a fellow named Byzas. Before leaving Greece, he asked the oracle at Delphi where he should establish his new colony. The enigmatic answer was, 'Opposite the blind'. When Byzas and his fellow colonists sailed up the Bosphorus, they noticed the colony on the Asian shore at Chalcedon. Looking to their left, they saw the superb natural harbour of the Golden Horn on the European shore. Thinking, as legend has it, 'Those people in Chalcedon must be blind', they settled on the opposite shore, on the site of Lygos, and named their new city Byzantium. This was in 657 BC.

The legend might as well be true. İstanbul's location on the waterway linking the Sea of Marmara and the Black Sea, and on the 'land bridge' linking Europe and Asia, is still of tremendous importance today, 2600 years after the oracle spoke.

Byzantium submitted willingly to Rome and fought Rome's battles for centuries, but got caught supporting the wrong side in a civil war. The winner, Septimius Severus, razed the city walls and took its privileges in 196 AD. When he relented and rebuilt the city, he named it Augusta Antonina.

Constantinople

Another struggle for control of the Roman Empire determined the city's fate for the next 1000 years. Constantine pursued his rival Licinius to Augusta Antonina, then across the Bosphorus to Chrysopolis (Üsküdar). Defeating his rival in 324 AD, Constantine solidified his control and declared this city to be 'New Rome'. He laid out a vast new city to serve as capital of his empire, and inaugurated it with much pomp in 330 AD. The place which had been first settled as a fishing village more than 1000 years earlier was now the capital of the world, and would remain so for almost another 1000 years.

The Later Roman, or Byzantine, Empire lasted from the re-founding of the city in 330 AD to the Ottoman Turkish conquest in 1453, an impressive 1123 years. Much remains of ancient Constantinople, and you'll be able to visit churches, palaces, cisterns and the Hippodrome during your stay. In fact, there's more of Constantinople left than anyone knows about. Any sort of excavation reveals streets, mosaics, tunnels, water and sewer systems, houses and public buildings. Construction of a modern building may be held up for months while archaeologists investigate – an unmitigated disaster to a modern real-estate developer!

The Conquest What westerners refer to as 'The Fall of Constantinople' was to Muslims 'The Conquest of İstanbul'. Though the Byzantine Empire had been moribund for several centuries, the Ottomans were quite content to accept tribute from the weak Byzantine emperor as they progressively captured all the lands surrounding his well-fortified city. By the time of the Conquest, the emperor had control over little more than the city itself and a few territories in Greece.

When Mehmet II, 'the Conqueror' *(Fatih)*, came to power in 1451 as a young man, he needed an impressive military victory to solidify his dominance of the powerful noble class. As the Ottomans controlled all of Anatolia and most of the Balkans by this time, it was obvious that the great city should be theirs. Mehmet decided it should be sooner rather than later.

The story of the Conquest is thrilling, full of bold strokes and daring exploits, heroism, treachery and intrigue. Mehmet started with the two great fortresses on the Bosphorus. Rumeli Hisarı, the larger one, was built in an incredibly short four months on the European side. Anadolu Hisarı, the smaller one on the Asian side built half a century earlier by Yıldırım Beyazıt, was repaired and brought to readiness. Together they controlled the strait's narrowest point.

The Byzantines had closed the mouth of the Golden Horn with a heavy chain to prevent Ottoman boats from sailing in and attacking the city walls on the northern side. In another bold stroke, Mehmet marshalled his boats at a cove (now covered by Dolmabahçe Palace) and had them transported overland on rollers and slides, by night, up the valley (where the Hilton now stands) and down the other side into the Golden Horn at Kasım Paşa. He caught the Byzantine defenders completely by surprise and soon had the Golden Horn well under control.

The last great obstacle was the mighty bastion of land walls on the western side. No matter how heavily Mehmet's cannons battered them by day, the Byzantines would rebuild them by night and, come daybreak, the impetuous young sultan would find himself back where he'd started. Then he received a proposal from a Hungarian cannon founder named Urban who had come to offer his services to the Byzantine emperor for the defence of Christendom against the infidels. Finding that the emperor had no money, he went to Mehmet and offered to make the most enormous cannon ever. Mehmet, who had lots of money, accepted the offer, and the cannon was cast and tested in Edirne.

The first shot, which terrified hundreds of peasants, sent a huge ball 1.5km, where it buried itself 2m in the ground. The jubilant sultan had his new toy transported to the front lines and set to firing. A special crew worked hours to ready it for each shot, for every firing wrecked the mount, and the gun had to be cooled with buckets of water.

Despite the inevitability of the Conquest, the emperor refused surrender terms offered by Mehmet on 23 May 1453, preferring to wait in hope that Christendom would come and save him. On 28 May the final attack began, and by the evening of the 29th Mehmet's troops were in control of every quarter. The emperor, Constantine XI Dragases, died in battle, fighting on the walls.

Mehmet's triumphant entry into 'the world's greatest city' on the evening of 29 May is commemorated every year in İstanbul. Those parts of the city which did not resist his troops were spared, and their churches guaranteed. Those that resisted were sacked for the customary three days, and their churches turned into mosques. As for Sancta Sophia, the greatest church in Christendom (St Peter's in Rome, though larger, was not begun until 1506), it was converted immediately into a mosque.

İstanbul

The Ottoman Centuries Mehmet the Conqueror began at once to rebuild and repopulate the city. He saw himself as the successor to the glories and powers of Constantine, Justinian and the other great emperors who had reigned here. He built a mosque (Fatih Camii) on one of the city's seven hills, repaired the walls and made İstanbul the administrative, commercial and cultural centre of his growing empire.

Süleyman the Magnificent (1520-66) was perhaps İstanbul's greatest builder. His mosque, the Süleymaniye (1550), is İstanbul's largest. Other sultans added more grand mosques, and in the 19th century numerous palaces were built along the Bosphorus: Çirağan, Dolmabahçe, Yıldız, Beylerbeyi and Küçük Su.

As the Ottoman Empire grew to include all of the Middle East and North Africa as well as half of Eastern Europe, İstanbul became a fabulous melting pot. On its streets and in its bazaars, people spoke Turkish, Greek, Armenian, Ladino, Russian, Arabic, Bulgarian, Romanian, Albanian, Italian, French, German, English and Maltese. The parade of national costumes was no less varied.

However, the most civilised city on earth in the time of Süleyman eventually declined, as did the Ottoman Empire, and by the 19th century it had lost some of its former glory. But it continued to be the 'Paris of the East' and, to reaffirm this, the first great international luxury express train ever run, the famous *Orient Express*, connected İstanbul with Paris.

Republican İstanbul Atatürk's (1881-1938) campaign for national salvation and independence was directed from Ankara. (For more detailed information see The Turkish Republic in the Facts about Turkey chapter.) The founder of the Turkish Republic decided to get away from the imperial memories of İstanbul and to set up the new government in a city which could not easily be threatened by gunboats. Robbed of its importance as the capital of a vast empire, İstanbul lost much of its wealth and glitter. From being the East's most cosmopolitan place, it relaxed into a new role as an important national, rather than international, city.

During the 1980s İstanbul began to reassume something of its former role. Easier to live in than Cairo or Beirut, more attractive than Tel Aviv, more in touch with the Islamic world than Athens, it is fast becoming the 'capital' of the eastern Mediterranean again.

ORIENTATION

İstanbul is divided from north to south by the Bosphorus, the wide strait connecting the Black and Marmara seas, into *Avrupa* (European) and *Asya* (Asian) portions. European İstanbul is further divided by the Golden Horn into Old İstanbul (Eski İstanbul, sometimes called the Old City) to the south and Beyoğlu (BEY-oh-loo) to the north.

Three days is the minimum time necessary for a meaningful visit to this city; a week is better. The sights below are organised with the most important and accessible sights first, and the lesser ones after.

Eski İstanbul

The Old City is ancient Byzantium/Constantinople İstanbul, called Stamboul by 19th-century travellers. It's here, from Seraglio Point (Sarayburnu) jutting into the Bosphorus to the mammoth land walls some 7km westward, that you'll find the great palaces and mosques, hippodromes and monumental columns, ancient churches and the Grand Bazaar, called the Kapalı Çarşı (Covered Market). The best selection of budget and mid-range hotels is also here, with a few top-end places as well.

Beyoğlu

North of the Golden Horn is Beyoğlu, the Turkish name for the two ancient cities of Pera and Galata, or roughly all the land from the Golden Horn to Taksim Square. Here you'll find the Hilton, the Inter-Continental, the Hyatt and other luxury hotels; airline offices and banks; the European consulates and hospitals; and Taksim Square, the hub of European İstanbul.

Under the Byzantines, Galata (now called Karaköy, KAHR-ah-keuy) was a separate city built and inhabited by Genoese traders.

Under the sultans, the non-Muslim European population of Galata spread up the hill and along the ridge, founding Galata's sister city of Pera. In modern times this part of the city has been the fastest growing and has stretched far beyond the limits of old Galata and Pera. The name Beyoğlu still refers to just those two old cities. Beyoğlu is good for a walking tour, especially along İstiklal Caddesi, formerly known as the Grande Rue de Péra.

Eski İstanbul and Beyoğlu are connected by the Galata Köprüsü (Galata Bridge) at the mouth of the Golden Horn. Just east of the bridge are the docks for Bosphorus ferries.

Asian İstanbul

The Asian part of the city, on the eastern shore of the Bosphorus, is of less interest to tourists, being mostly dormitory suburbs such as Üsküdar (EU-skeu-dahr, Scutari) and Kadıköy (KAH-duh-keuy, Chalcedon). One landmark you'll want to know about is Haydarpaşa Station (Haydarpaşa İstasyonu), right between Üsküdar and Kadıköy. This is the terminus for Anatolian trains, which means any Turkish train except the one from Europe via Edirne. If you're headed for Ankara, Cappadocia or any point east of İstanbul, you'll board at Haydarpaşa.

The Bosphorus

The Bosphorus is lined with more suburbs, some of which are quite charming and worth a walk around. You should plan to spend at least one day exploring the strait.

INFORMATION

Tourist Offices

There are Ministry of Tourism offices at Atatürk airport (☎ 663 6363, fax 663 0793) in the international arrivals area, at the north-western end of the Hippodrome in Sultanahmet (Map 7, ☎ 518 1802, fax 518 1802), open from 9 am to 5 pm daily, and at Sirkeci train station (Map 4, ☎ 511 5888).

In Beyoğlu, there is an office at the Karaköy Yolcu Salonu (Karaköy International Maritime Passenger Terminal) (Map 3, ☎ 249 5776); another in Elmadağ in the Hilton Hotel arcade (Map 2, ☎ 233 0592), just off Cumhuriyet Caddesi, two long blocks north of Taksim Square on the right-hand side of the street (open from 9 am to 5 pm, closed on Sunday). Yet another office is in the regional Directorate of Tourism (Map 3, ☎ 243 2928, fax 252 4346), more or less opposite the British consulate general at Meşrutiyet Caddesi 57, Tepebaşı.

Automobile Club

The Türk Turing ve Otomobil Kurumu (Turkish Touring & Automobile Association) (☎ 280 4449 or 282 7874), Birinci Oto Sanayi Sitesi Yanı, Dördüncü Levent, about 7km north of Taksim Square, provides information on car insurance and import permits, and has a breakdown service and repair facilities. The association and its longtime director, Mr Çelik Gülersoy, have been prime movers in efforts at historical restoration and beautification in İstanbul and several other Turkish cities.

Foreign Consulates

For details of the many consulates in Turkey, see the Facts for the Visitor chapter.

Money

For general information on banks, see the Money section in the Facts for the Visitor chapter. Remember that you can usually change money (preferably cash) at PTT branches; see the following Post & Communications for locations. Currency exchange booths at Atatürk airport's international arrivals area are open whenever flights arrive.

Most bank ATMs allow withdrawals only in Turkish liras, but the larger branches of Türkiye İş Bankası will usually allow you to withdraw money via ATMs in US dollars as well, which is useful if you're trying to build up your dollar reserves for travel to another country. An alternative is to withdraw liras and convert them to dollars at a nonbank *döviz bürosu* (currency exchange office) offering good selling rates for dollars.

İstanbul has an ever-growing number of döviz bürosus. They offer faster service than banks, longer opening hours, and usually do not charge a commission. The rates are worse at offices heavily used by tourists, such as those in Sultanahmet; better rates are offered in Taksim, the side streets of the Grand Bazaar, Şişli, Eminönü, and other areas where Turks change money.

Entel Döviz (Map 4, ☎ 513 8284), on Ankara Caddesi opposite Sirkeci station, gives decent rates of exchange. A nearby alternative is Koçkaya Döviz (☎ 522 5353), Muradiye Caddesi, Kale İş Hanı 12.

Bamka Döviz (Map 2, ☎ 253 5500), Cumhuriyet Caddesi 23 near Aydede Caddesi, two blocks north of Taksim across the boulevard from Pizza Hut, is open every day from 8 am to 8 pm. Çetin Döviz (Map 2, ☎ 252 6428), İstiklal Caddesi 39, Beyoğlu, across from the French consulate, a block off Taksim, does not offer as good a rate as Bamka. Fast Forex (Map 3, ☎ 293 0024), Meşrutiyet Caddesi 22, Galatasaray, near the British consulate, has English-speaking staff. The cheapest rate in town is at Aktif (☎ 230 1961), on the western side of Şişli Meydanı, 2km north of Taksim, but there's usually a long queue.

Post & Communications

İstanbul's *Merkez Postane* (Main Post Office) is several blocks west of Sirkeci train station on Mevlana Caddesi. It's always open, though special services have shorter hours, such as poste restante (8.30 am to 12.30 pm, and 1.30 to 5.30 pm). The phone and fax centre is open all the time. There are PTT branches near Taksim Square at Cumhuriyet Caddesi, Taksim Gezi Dükkanları, on İstiklal Caddesi in Galatasaray, in Aksaray and in the Kapalı Çarşı near the Havuzlu Lokantası.

The telephone area code for European İstanbul is 212. This code applies to all numbers given in this chapter which do not include an area code. The area code for Asian İstanbul is 216.

Internet Resources

You can check your email at several backpackers' hostels and cafes in Cankurtaran, south of Sultanahmet, including the Orient Youth Hostel (Map 7) and the Mavi Guesthouse (Map 7) (see Places to Stay); and at Yağmur Cybercafe (☎ 292 3020, anu@citlembik.com.tr), located near the American consulate general, in the Çitlembik Apartıman building (2nd floor), Şeyh Bender Sokak 18, Asmalımescit, Beyoğlu.

Travel Agencies

Travel agents on the northern side of Divan Yolu in Sultanahmet specialise in budget flights, but can also arrange bus and train tickets. Don't use them as your only source of information, though, as some of their prices can be artificially high.

The fancier travel agencies and airline offices are in the districts called Elmadağ and Harbiye, north of Taksim Square along Cumhuriyet Caddesi between the Divan Oteli and İstanbul Hilton Hotel (Map 2).

A travel agent/tour operator which gives good service with English-speaking staff is Orion-Tour (☎ 248 8437, fax 241 2808), Halaskargazi Caddesi 284/3, Marmara Apartımanı, Şişli, about 2km north of Taksim. Orion (pronounced OR-yohn in Turkish) can arrange flights, cruises (including private or group yacht charters), transfers to and from the airport, city tours of İstanbul and other major cities, and private or group tours anywhere in Turkey.

Bookshops

In general, the place to find foreign-language books is in Beyoğlu on İstiklal Caddesi, between Galatasaray and Tünel squares.

Robinson Crusoe (Map 3, ☎ 293 6968), İstiklal Caddesi 389, has fiction, general-interest, and many books (including Lonely Planet) about Turkey in English and, to a lesser extent, in French and German.

Dünya Aktüel (Map 3, ☎ 249 1006), İstiklal Caddesi 469, which also operates shops at the Hilton, Holiday Inn and Swissôtel hotels, has Turkish, French and English books and periodicals.

Metro Kitabevi (☎ 249 5827), İstiklal Caddesi 513, sells guidebooks and maps in English, French and German. The nearby ABC Kitabevi (☎ 293 1629), on Tünel Square, has a few books, but mostly language-learning aids.

Pandora (Map 3, ☎ 243 3503, H.Sonmez@info-ist.comlink.apc.org,www.ftz.org/info-ist/pandora), Büyükparmakkapı Sokak 3, off İstiklal Caddesi, has a good collection of books (including Lonely Planet) in English on Turkish and Ottoman history and literature.

Firnas Bookstore (Map 3, ☎ 244 5446), at No 5 in the Avrupa Pasajı between Meşrutiyet Caddesi and Sahne Sokak off Galatasaray Square, stocks dictionaries of many languages and some travel guides.

Türk-Alman Kitabevi (Map 3, ☎ 244 7731), İstiklal Caddesi 481-487, Tünel, near the Swedish consulate, sells German-language books (mostly religious and language-learning materials).

In Sultanahmet, several shops along Divanyolu facing the Hippodrome carry maps and guides, often at premium prices. Aypa (Map 7, ☎ 516 0100), Mimar Mehmet Ağa Caddesi 19, behind the Sultan Ahmet Camii (Blue Mosque), has a small selection of guides, maps and magazines in English, French and German.

Karum (☎ 241 7988), Akkavak Sokak 19/21/1 Nişantaşı, has a good selection of art books, art prints and posters.

Remzi Kitabevi (☎ 234 5475), Rumeli Caddesi 44, Nişantaşı, is a top quality general English language bookshop with a wide selection on all subjects. Another Remzi shop (☎ 282 0245) is in the Akmerkez Shopping Centre (see Shopping Centres under Shopping later in this chapter).

See also Old Books, Maps & Prints in the Shopping section.

Libraries

The American Library (☎ 251 2675), next to the American consulate general at Meşrutiyet Caddesi 108, Tepebaşı, has been scaled back to a reference library due to government budget cuts. It's open Monday to Friday from noon to 4 pm.

The British Council Library (☎ 252 7474 ext 115, 118 or 119), İstiklal Caddesi 151-253, Beyoğlu, two flights up in the Örs Turistik İş Merkezi building, is open Tuesday to Friday from 10.30 am to at least 5.30 pm (later some nights) and on Saturday from 9.30 am to 2.30 pm.

The Women's Library (☎ 534 9550), just east of St Stephen's Church on the southwestern side of the Golden Horn, is open from 9 am to 5.30 pm; closed Sunday. The library (Kadın Eserleri Kütüphanesi ve Bilgi Merkezi Vakfı), housed in a historic building, acts as a women's resource centre, with a programme of cultural and special events of interest to women.

Laundry

If you don't do your own laundry, ask for prices at your hotel. Alternatives in Sultanahmet (Map 7) include:

Hobby Laundry (☎ 513 6150) Caferiye Sokak 6/1, Sultanahmet, in the Yücelt Interyouth Hostel opposite Aya Sofya. Posted hours are 9 am to 8 pm every day, actual hours may be different. The charge is US$1.50 per 1kg to wash (minimum 2kg), US$1 per 1kg to dry, but 'dry' can mean dampish. Attendants take your clothes and run the machines.

Active Laundry, Dr Emin Paşa Sokak 14, off Divan Yolu beneath Arsenal Youth Hostel, charges the same.

Sultan Laundry, İncili Çavuş Çıkmazı 21, opposite Hotel Nomade and around the corner, same rates.

Vardar Laundry, in a side street opposite the Gülhane tram stop and Gülhane Parkı entrance, same rates.

İstanbul has numerous *kuru temizleme* (dry-cleaning shops), usually open every day except Sunday from 8 am to 7 pm. Bring items in early for same-day service. Two blocks westward uphill from the southern end of the Hippodrome in Sultanahmet is Doğu Expres (☎ 526 0725), Peykhane Sokak 61 (also called Üçler Sokak). In Tepebaşı, try Reforma Kuru Temizleme (Map 3, ☎ 243 6862), Meşrutiyet Caddesi 131, near the Büyük Londra Oteli.

Medical Services

For details of health concerns in Turkey, see the Health section in the Facts for the Visitor chapter. You should contact your country's consulate in İstanbul or embassy in Ankara (see Embassies & Consulates in the Facts for the Visitor chapter). They may have advice about suitable doctors, dentists, hospitals, and other medical care. İstanbul has several private hospitals which provide good quality care at low government-controlled prices. These include:

Alman Hastanesi
(Map 3, ☎ 293 2150) Sıraselviler Caddesi 119, Taksim, a few hundred metres south of Taksim on the left-hand side, with German administration

American Hospital
(☎ 231 4050, fax 234 1432)
Güzelbahçe Sokak 20, Nişantaşı, about 2km north-east of Taksim

Florence Nightingale Hospital
(☎ 231 2021) Abidei Hürriyet Caddesi 290, Çağlayan, Şişli, about 4km north of Taksim

Intermed Check-up Centre
(☎ 225 0660) Teşvikiye Caddesi, Bayar Apt 143, Nişantaşı, about 2km north of Taksim

International Hospital
(☎ 663 3000) İstanbul Caddesi 82, Yeşilyurt, west of the centre on the shore near the airport

La Paix ('Lape')
(☎ 246 1020) Hastanesi, Büyükdere Caddesi 22-24, Şişli, with French administration

Emergency

In case of hassles, stolen or lost documents and the like, you might get some help from the Tourism Police (Map 7, ☎ 527 4503), Yerebatan Caddesi 2, Sultanahmet, opposite Yerebatan Saray (the 'Sunken Palace' cistern). They have some multilingual staff and experience with foreigners.

If you have a personal crisis – financial, physical, psychological, emotional – and need someone to talk to, dial the İstanbul Blue Line on ☎ 638 2626. Multilingual staff will help you to find a solution.

Turkey has national emergency numbers which can be dialled from any phone without charge:

Ambulance	☎ 112
Fire	☎ 110
Police	☎ 155

Admission Hours & Days

Most museums are closed on Monday, but Topkapı Sarayı and several others are closed on Tuesday, the Kariye Müzesi (Chora Church) on Wednesday, and the Maritime Museum on Wednesday and Thursday. Dolmabahçe Palace is closed on both Monday and Thursday. The Kapalı Çarşı is closed on Sunday.

Major tourist-target mosques are open all day, every day. Avoid visiting these mosques right after the call to prayer (wait 30 minutes) and on Friday morning and noon (the Muslim Sabbath), when congregations assemble for prayers and sermons. Smaller mosques are usually open only at prayer times, and you may only be able to visit after a prayer is finished and before the doors are locked.

Holders of an International Student Identity Card are admitted free or at reduced rates to sites controlled by the Ministry of Tourism and Ministry of Culture.

OLD İSTANBUL

In the Old City, Topkapı Sarayı is right next to Aya Sofya, which is right next to the Sultan Ahmet Camii, which is right on the Hippodrome, which is right next to the Yerebatan Saray, which is only a few steps from the museum complex, which is right next to Topkapı Sarayı – phew! You can spend at least two days just completing this loop. Start with the palace, which is among the world's great museums.

continued on page 160

Okmeydanı
Kurtuluş
Halıcıoğlu
Kulaksız
Hasköy
Piyalepaşa
Eyüp Sultan Camii
Feshane
EYÜP
Rahmi M Koç Müsesi
Ayvansaray
Balıkhane
Old Galata Bridge
Aynalıkavak Kasrı
MAP 3
MAP 8
Avcı Bey
Balat
Kasım Gösim
Church of St Stephen
Bayrampaşa
To Uluslararası İstanbul Otogar & Edirne
Edirnekapı
Hızır Çavuş
Draman
Kasımpaşa
Tepebaşı
Kariye-i Atik
Katip Muslihittin
Golden Horn (Haliç)
Our Ecumenical Orthodox Patriarchate
Fener
Karagümrük
Derviş Ali
Abdülezel
Hatice Sultan
Beyceğiz
Çarşamba
Selimiye Camii
MAP 4
Atatürk Bridge
Ulubatlı
Topkapı Cannon Gate
Fatih Camii
Zeyrek
Küçükpazar
Sandemir
To Atatürk Airport
Emniyet
Demirtaç
Rüstempaşa
FATİH
Vefa
Süleymaniye Camii
EMİNÖNÜ
Mevlanakapı
Çapa
Saraçhane
Tahtakale
Şehremini
Fatih Anıtı Parkı
Molla Hüsrev
St Polyeuchtos Church Ruins
Saraçhane Park
Kalenderhane
Mercan
MAP 6
Sururi
Aksaray
İstanbul Üniversitesi
Süleymaniye
Fındıkzade
Balaban Ağa
Tayahatun
Kapalı Çarşı
Altımermer
Laleli
Beyazıt
Haseki
Nişanca
Emin Sinan
Gedik Paşa
Kocamustafa Paşa
Yenikapı
Kadırga
Silivrikapı
Cerrahpaşa
Küçük Ayasofya
Şehsuvarbey
Kumkapı
Yenikapı Fast Car Ferry & Seabus Port
Belgratkapı
Mustafa Paşa
Sea of Marmara (Marmara Denizi)
To Yedikule
Silahtarağa Caddesi
Çevre Yolu
Karaağaç Caddesi
Kumbarahane Caddesi
Feshane Caddesi
Hasköy Caddesi
Mutfakkapı Caddesi
Piyale Paşa
Rami-Edirnekapı Caddesi
Eyüp Sultan Bulvarı
Demirhisar Caddesi
Balat Vapur Iskelesi Caddesi
Mürsel Paşa Caddesi
Savaklar Caddesi
Topkapı Edirnekapı Caddesi
Fevzi Paşa Caddesi
Evliya Çelebi Caddesi
Bahriye Caddesi
Tersane Caddesi
Yavuz Selim Caddesi
Haliç Caddesi
Yeni Çevre Yolu
Adnan Menderes Bulvarı
Akşemsettin Caddesi
Macar Kardeşler Caddesi
Ragıp Gümüşpala Caddesi
Sobacılar Caddesi
Londra Asfaltı
Turgut Özal Caddesi
Tatlıpınar Caddesi
Guraba Hastanesi Caddesi
Akdeniz Caddesi
İtfaiye Caddesi
Atatürk Bulvarı
Aqueduct of Valens
Mevlanakapı Yolu
Saray Meydanı Caddesi
Başvekil Caddesi
Oğuzhan Caddesi
Mevlanakapı Caddesi
Ahmet Vefikpaşa Caddesi
Ordu Caddesi
Yeniçeriler Caddesi
Altımermer Caddesi
Kızılelma Caddesi
Haseki Caddesi
Cerrahpaşa Caddesi
Namık Kemal Caddesi
Hayriye Tüccarı Caddesi
Gedikpaşa Caddesi
Çifte Gelinler Caddesi
Hekimoğlu Alipaşa Caddesi
Vidin Caddesi
Kocamustafa Paşa Caddesi
Langa Caddesi
Küçük Langa Caddesi
Kennedy Caddesi
A Nafiz Gürman Caddesi
Sahil Yolu
Hacı Hamza Mektebi Sokak
Hoca Kadın Caddesi

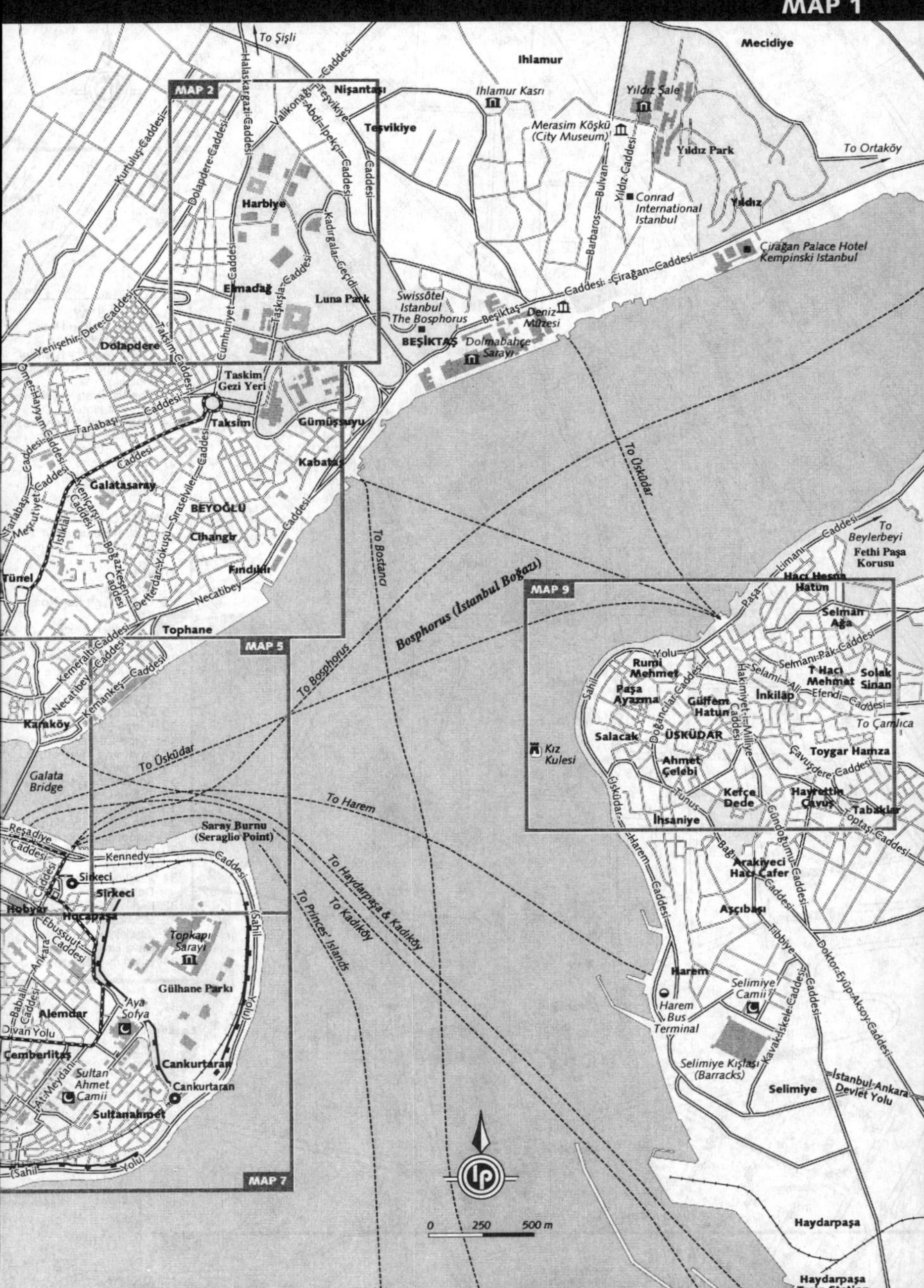

To Şişli
Ihlamur
Mecidiye
MAP 2
Nişantaşı
Teşvikiye
Ihlamur Kasrı
Yıldız Şale
Merasim Köşkü (City Museum)
Yıldız Park
To Ortaköy
Harbiye
Conrad International Istanbul
Yıldız
Çırağan Palace Hotel Kempinski Istanbul
Elmadağ
Luna Park
Swissôtel Istanbul The Bosphorus
Deniz Müzesi
Dolapdere
BEŞİKTAŞ
Dolmabahçe Sarayı
Taskim Gezi Yeri
Taksim
Gümüşsuyu
Kabataş
To Üsküdar
Galatasaray
BEYOĞLU
Cihangir
To Bostancı
To Beylerbeyi
Fethi Paşa Korusu
Tünel
Fındıklı
Bosphorus (İstanbul Boğazı)
MAP 9
Hacı Hesna Hatun
Selman Ağa
Tophane
MAP 5
Rumi Mehmet
Hacı Mehmet
Solak Sinan
Paşa Ayazma
Gülfem Hatun
İnkilâp
To Bosphorus
Karaköy
To Çamlıca
Salacak
ÜSKÜDAR
Kız Kulesi
Toygar Hamza
To Üsküdar
Ahmet Çelebi
Galata Bridge
To Harem
Kefçe Dede
Hayrettin Çavuş
Tabaklar
İhsaniye
Saray Burnu (Seraglio Point)
Arakiyeci Hacı Cafer
Sirkeci
To Haydarpaşa & Kadıköy
Hobyar
Hocapaşa
To Kadıköy
Aşçıbaşı
To Princes' Islands
Topkapı Sarayı
Gülhane Parkı
Harem
Selimiye Camii
Harem Bus Terminal
Alemdar
Aya Sofya
Çemberlitaş
Cankurtaran
Selimiye Kışlası (Barracks)
Sultan Ahmet Camii
Selimiye
Sultanahmet
MAP 7
0 250 500 m
Haydarpaşa
Haydarpaşa Train Station

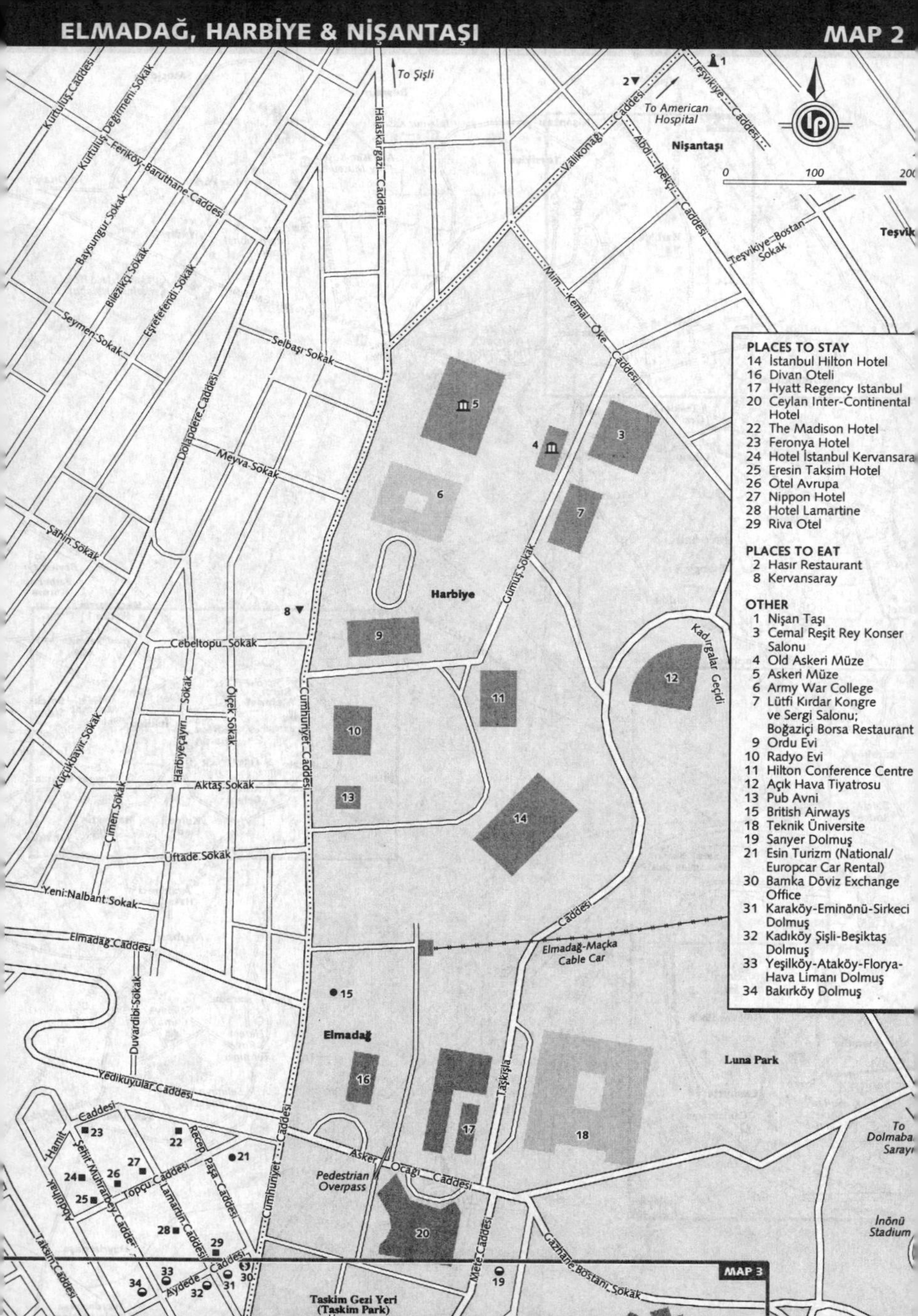

To Şişli
To American Hospital
Nişantaşı
Harbiye
Elmadağ
Luna Park
Teşvik
To Dolmabahçe Sarayı
İnönü Stadium
Taskim Gezi Yeri (Taşkim Park)
Pedestrian Overpass
Elmadağ-Maçka Cable Car
MAP 3
Kurtuluş Caddesi
Kurtuluş Değirmeni Sokak
Feriköy-Baruthane Caddesi
Baysungur Sokak
Bilezikçi Sokak
Eşrefefendi Sokak
Seymen Sokak
Selbaşı Sokak
Dolapdere Caddesi
Meyva Sokak
Şahin Sokak
Cebeltopu Sokak
Küçükbayır Sokak
Harbiyeçayırı Sokak
Ölçek Sokak
Aktaş Sokak
Çimen Sokak
Üftade Sokak
Yeni Nalbant Sokak
Elmadağ Caddesi
Duvardibi Sokak
Yedikuyular Caddesi
Cumhuriyet Caddesi
Halaskargazi Caddesi
Valikonağı Caddesi
Teşvikiye Caddesi
Abdi İpekçi Caddesi
Teşvikiye-Bostan Sokak
Mim Kemal Öke Caddesi
Gümüş Sokak
Kadırgalar Caddesi
Kadırgalar Geçidi
Taşkışla
Asker Ocağı Caddesi
Mete Caddesi
Gazhane Bostanı Sokak
Hamit Caddesi
Şehit Muhtarbey Caddesi
Topçu Caddesi
Lamartin Caddesi
Recep Paşa Caddesi
Abdülhak
Taksim Caddesi
Aydede Caddesi
0
100
200

PLACES TO STAY
14 İstanbul Hilton Hotel
16 Divan Oteli
17 Hyatt Regency Istanbul
20 Ceylan Inter-Continental Hotel
22 The Madison Hotel
23 Feronya Hotel
24 Hotel İstanbul Kervansara
25 Eresin Taksim Hotel
26 Otel Avrupa
27 Nippon Hotel
28 Hotel Lamartine
29 Riva Otel

PLACES TO EAT
2 Hasır Restaurant
8 Kervansaray

OTHER
1 Nişan Taşı
3 Cemal Reşit Rey Konser Salonu
4 Old Askeri Müze
5 Askeri Müze
6 Army War College
7 Lütfi Kırdar Kongre ve Sergi Salonu; Boğaziçi Borsa Restaurant
9 Ordu Evi
10 Radyo Evi
11 Hilton Conference Centre
12 Açık Hava Tiyatrosu
13 Pub Avni
15 British Airways
18 Teknik Üniversite
19 Sanyer Dolmuş
21 Esin Turizm (National/ Europcar Car Rental)
30 Bamka Döviz Exchange Office
31 Karaköy-Eminönü-Sirkeci Dolmuş
32 Kadıköy Şişli-Beşiktaş Dolmuş
33 Yeşilköy-Ataköy-Florya-Hava Limanı Dolmuş
34 Bakırköy Dolmuş

EDDIE GERALD

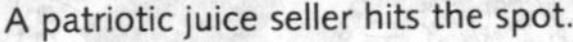

A patriotic juice seller hits the spot.

TOM BROSNAHAN

EDDIE GERALD

Pigeon-food seller with accomplices.

EDDIE GERALD

For a shoe shine guaranteed to impress.

İSTİKLAL CADDESİ
Dolapdere Caddesi
Dilbaz Sokak
Bocurgat
Kasımpaşa Akarcası Sokak
Caddesi
Tennure Sokak
Şamancı Ferhat Caddesi
Ömer Hayyam Caddesi
Düğün Sokak
Kurdele Sokak
Akkiraz Sokak
Kalyoncu Kulluğu Caddesi
Kara Kurum Sokak
Şahin Sokak
Sakızağacı Caddesi
Genis Yokuş Sokak
Çukur Sokak
Peşkirci Sokak
Dereotu Sokak
Kurtuluş Sokak
Paşa Bakkal Sokak
Bekir Sokak
Eski Çeşme
Dernek Sokak
Bilgü Sokak
Simitçi Sokak
Fakir Sokak
Narçıl Sokak
Fıçıcı Apti Sokak
Gümüş Küpe Sokak
Camii
Emin
Keramet Sokak
Tarlabaşı
Abanoz Sokak
Bayram Sokak
Daracık Sokak
Balık Sokak
Kalyoncu
Topçekenler
Büyük
Yeşilçam Sokak
Balo Sokak
Kameriye
Sahne
Nevizade Sokak
Aynalı Çeşme Caddesi
Bahriye
Fırını Sokak
Sipahi
Arslan Sokak
Hamalbaşı Caddesi
Duduodalan Sokak
Sokak
Meydanı
Aşıklar
Neva Sokak
Tepebaşı
Caddesi
Turnacıbaşı Sokak
Kartal Sk
Galatasaray
Yeniçarşı Caddesi
Akarsu Sokak
Acar Sokak
Gazeteci Erol Dernek
Kuloğlu
Başağa Çeşmesi Sokak
Turnacıbaşı
Çivici Sokak
Tepebaşı Caddesi
Kallavi Sokak
Tarlabaşı Caddesi
Tozkoparan Mezarlık Sokak
Meşrutiyet
Eskiçiçekçi Sokak
Hayriye Sokak
Ankan Sokak
Tatlı Sokak
Camadan Sokak
Çatma Merdiven Sokak
Nuruziya Sokak
Bostancıbaşı Caddesi
Çukurcuma Caddesi
Akarca Sokak
Balyoz Sokak
Orhan Adli Apaydın Sokak
İstiklal
Postacılar Sokak
Tomtom Kaptan Sokak
Tali Sokak
Hayratçı Sokak
Tepebaşı
Kuytu Sokak
Asmalımescit
Gönül Sokak
Minare Sokak
Külhan Sokak
Boğazkesen
Anbar Arkası Sokak
Avni Sokak
Şimal Sokak
Jurnal Sokak
Sofyalı Sokak
Kumbaracı
Sümbül Sokak
Tünel
Lobut Sokak
Bedrettin Sokak
Camcı
Ormealtı Sokak
Evliya Çelebi Caddesi
Müeyyit
Caddesi
Şahkulu Bostanı Sokak
Yokuşu
Feyzi Sokak
Karabaş Deresi Sokak
Karabaş Caddesi
Şişhane
Tünel Square
Şişhane Square
Paşa Çıplağı Sokak
Galipdede Caddesi
Belediye
İlk
Yolcuzade İskender Caddesi
Şişhane Sokak
Büyük Hendek Sokak
Serdar-ı Ekrem Sokak
Dibek Sokak
Hoca Sokak
Tulumbacı
Sıtkı
Mimi Külhan Sokak
Nazlı Hanım Sokak
MAP 4
Okçu Musa Caddesi
Küçük Hendek Sokak
Tutsuk Sokak
Dik Sokak
Boronat Sokak
56
57
58
59
60
61
62
63
64
65
66
67
68
69
70
71
72
73
74
75
76
77
78
79
80
81
82
83
84
85
86
87
88
89
90
91
92
93
94
95
96
97
98
99
100
101

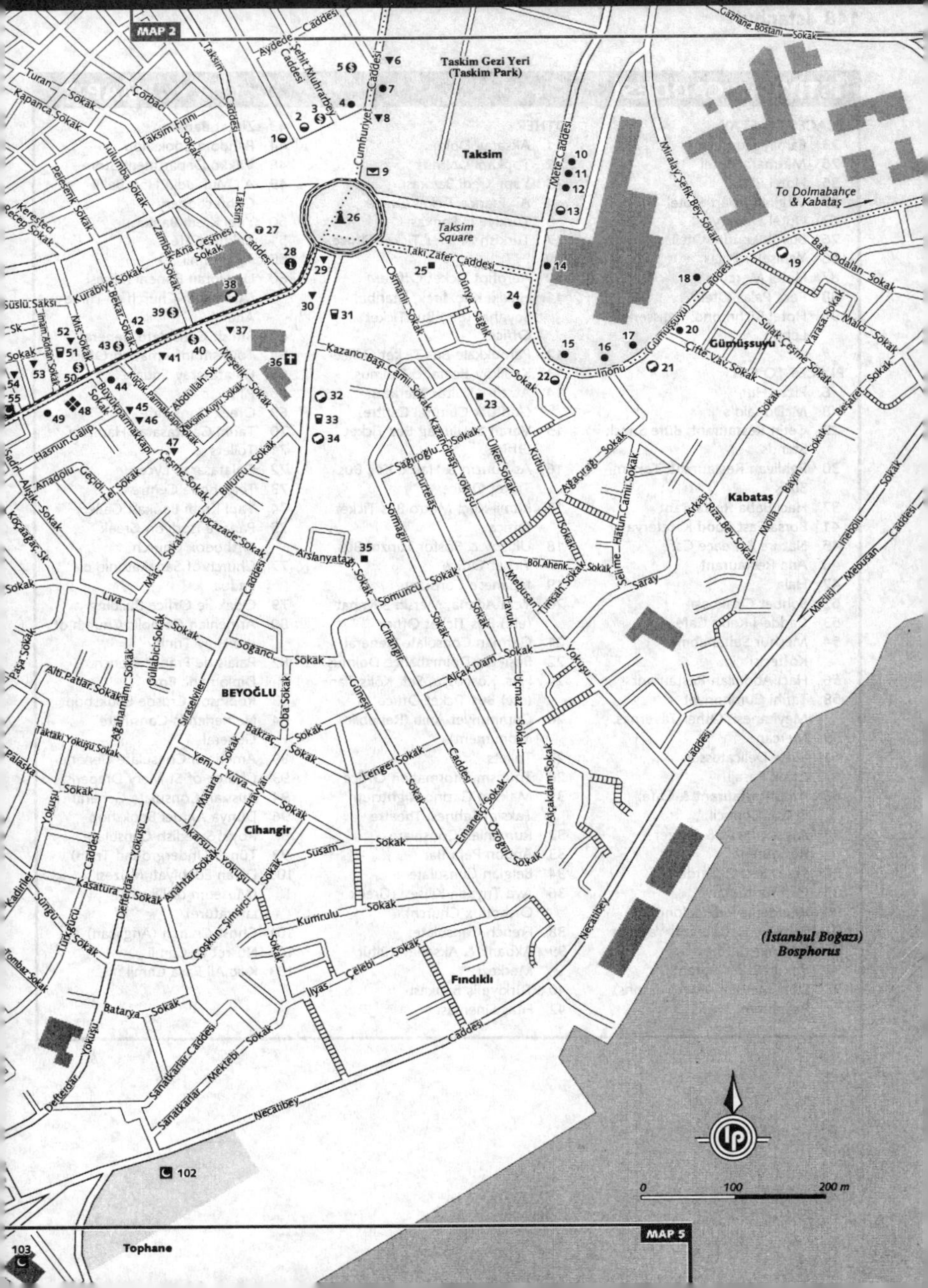
MAP 2
Taskim Gezi Yeri
(Taskim Park)
Taksim
Taksim Square
To Dolmabahçe & Kabataş
Gümüşsuyu
Kabataş
BEYOĞLU
Cihangir
Fındıklı
(İstanbul Boğazı)
Bosphorus
Tophane
MAP 5
Cumhuriyet Caddesi
Aydede Caddesi
Şehit Muhtarbey Caddesi
Taksim Caddesi
Gazhane Bostanı Sokak
Mete Caddesi
Miralay Şefik Bey Sokak
Bağ Odaları Sokak
Taki Zafer Caddesi
İnönü (Gümüşsuyu) Caddesi
Osmanlı Sokak
Dünya Sağlık Sokak
Kazancı Başı Camii Sokak
Kazancıbaşı Yokuşu
Sağıroğlu Sokak
Ülker Sokak
Kutlu Sokak
Ağaçrağı Sokak
Hatun Camii Sokak
Selime
Nolla Bayın Sokak
Arkası Rıza Bey Sokak
İnebolu Sokak
Meclis-i Mebusan Caddesi
Çifte Vav Sokak
Sulak Çeşme Sokak
Yarasa Sokak
Malcı Sokak
Beşaret Sokak
Bol Ahenk Sokak
İmsah Sokak
Mebusan Yokuşu
Saray
Tavuk Sokak
Alçak Dam Sokak
Uçmaz Sokak
Alçakdam Sokak
Emanetçi Sokak
Öğdül Sokak
Necatibey Caddesi
Somuncu Sokak
Arslanyatağı Sokak
Purtelaş Sokak
Somağır
Cihangir Caddesi
Güneşli Sokak
Lenger Sokak
Susam Sokak
Kumrulu Sokak
İlyas Çelebi Sokak
Turan Sokak
Kapanca Sokak
Çorbacı
Taksim Fırını Sokak
Tulumba Sokak
Pelesenk Sokak
Kereşteci Recep Sokak
Zambak Sokak
Ana Çeşmesi Sokak
Kurabiye Sokak
Bekar Sokak
Süslü Saksı Sk
İnam Adnan Sokak
Mis Sokak
Meşelik Sokak
Abdullah Sk
Küçük Parmakkapı Sokak
Büyükparmakkapı Sokak
Taksim Kuyu Sokak
Hasnun Galip
Anadolu Geçidi
Tel Sokak
Çeşme Sokak
Billurcu Sokak
Hocazade Sokak
Sadri Alışık Sokak
Koçaağaç Sk
Maç Sokak
Liva
Soğancı Sokak
Gullabici Sokak
Sıraselviler Caddesi
Ağahamamı Sokak
Altı Patlar Sokak
Paşa Sokak
Taktaki Yokuşu Sokak
Palaska Sokak
Bakraç Sokak
Oba Sokak
Yeni Yuva Sokak
Matara Sokak
Akarsu Yokuşu
Hayyar
Kasatura Sokak
Anahtar Sokak
Defterdar
Coşkun Şimşirci
Kadirler Yokuşu
Süngü Sokak
Türkgücü Caddesi
Tombaz Sokak
Batarya Sokak
Sanatkarlar Caddesi
Sanatkarlar Mektebi Sokak
Defterdar Yokuşu
Necatibey
0 100 200 m
102
103

İSTİKLAL CADDESİ — MAP 3

PLACES TO STAY
23 Family House
25 Marmara Hotel
35 Hotel Plaza
57 Virginie Apart-Hotel
63 Hotel Emperyal
76 Büyük Londra Oteli
86 Yenişehir Palas
87 Hotel Mercure
88 Pera Palas Oteli
95 Hotel Richmond; Patisserie Lebon

PLACES TO EAT
6 Pizza Hut
8 McDonald's
29 Çetin Restaurant; Büfe Snack Stands
30 Pehlivan Restaurant; Taksim Sütiş
37 Hacı Baba Restaurant
41 Borsa Fast Food Kafeteryası
45 Nature & Peace Café
46 Ada Restaurant
47 Hala
52 Sohbet Ocakbaşı
53 Cadde-i Kebir Café
54 Meşhur Sultanahmet Köftecisi
56 Hacı Abdullah Restaurant
58 Tarihi Cumhuriyet Meyhanesi; Other Tavernas
59 Mercan
61 Şütte Delicatessen
67 Çiçek Pasajı
68 Atlas Restaurant & Café; British Council
78 Afacan Pizza & Burger Restaurant
81 Teras Secret Garden
85 Çatı Restaurant
90 Karadeniz Pide Salonu
91 Şemsiye Restaurant; Yağmur Internet Café
92 Yakup 2 Restaurant
98 Dört Mevsim (Four Seasons) Restaurant

OTHER
1 Aksaray Dolmuş
2 Topkapı Dolmuş
3 Yapı Kredi Bankası
4 Air France Ticket Office
5 Türkiye İş Bankası
7 Turkish Airlines Ticket Office
9 PTT
10 Aeroflot Ticket Office
11 Hakiki Koç, İpek, İstanbul Seyahat (etc) Bus Ticket Office
12 Pamukkale Bus Ticket Office
13 Kadıköy-Bostancı Dolmuş
14 Atatürk Kültür Merkezi (Atatürk Cultural Centre)
15 Varan & Uludağ Bus Ticket Office
16 As Turizm & Hakiki Koç Bus Ticket Office
17 Kamil Koç; Metro Bus Ticket Office
18 Ulusoy & Bosfor Turizm Bus Ticket Office
19 Japanese Consulate
20 Yeni Adana, Mersin Seyahat (etc) Bus Ticket Office
21 German Consulate General
22 Beşiktaş-Dolmabahçe Dolmuş
24 Has, Köseoğlu, Set, Köksallar (etc) Bus Ticket Office
26 Cumhuriyet Anıtı (Republic Monument)
27 Toilets
28 Tourism Information Office
31 Maksim Gazino Nightclub; Taksim Sahnesi Theatre
32 Rumanian Consulate
33 Andon Pera Bar
34 Belgian Consulate
36 Aya Triyada Kilisesi (Greek Orthodox Church)
38 French Consulate
39 Akbank & Aksanat Kültür Merkezi
40 Türkiye İş Bankası
42 Fitaş Sineması
43 Ziraat Bankası
44 Pandora Bookshop
48 Vakko Department Store
49 Ali Muhiddin Hacı Bekir Confectionery
50 Yapı Kredi Bankası
51 Kaktüs Café
55 Ağa Camii
60 Üç Horan Ermeni Kilisesi (Armenian Church of Three Altars)
62 British Consulate General
64 Tourism Information Office
65 Galatasaray Square
66 PTT
69 Greek Consulate
70 Tarihi Galatasaray Hamamı
71 Toilets
72 Galatasaray Lycée
73 Telephone Centre
74 Yapı Kredi Bankası Gallery
75 Panaya İsodyon Greek Orthodox Church
77 Church of San Antonio di Padua
79 Odakule Office Building
80 Armenian Catholic Church of the Holy Trinity
82 Palais de France French Diplomatic Post
83 Robinson Crusoe Bookshop
84 Netherlands Consulate General
89 American Consulate General
93 Church of St Mary Draperis
94 Russian Consulate General
96 Dünya Aktüel Bookshop
97 Royal Swedish Consulate
99 Tünel (Underground Train)
100 Divan Edebiyatı Müzesi (Museum of Divan Literature)
101 Christ Church (Anglican)
102 Nusretiye Camii
103 Kılıç Ali Paşa Camii

Old meets new at the Bozdoğan Kemeri.

Galata Kulesi, built by Genoese colonists.

The majestic Dolmabahçe Sarayı, part of a vain attempt to arrest the decline of the Ottoman Empire.

0
100
200 m
Atatürk Bridge
Golden Horn (Haliç)
Küçükpazar
Sarıdemir
Demirtaç
Zeyrek Camii (Pantocrator)
Vefa
Church of St Theodore
Gazanfer Ağa Medresesi (Cartoon & Humour Museum)
Fatih Anıtı Parkı
Aqueduct of Valens
Saraçhane Parkı
Kalenderhane
Molla Hüsrev
Süleymaniye Camii
Beydağı & Kanaat Lokantası
Şehzade Camii
Süleymaniye
İstanbul Üniversitesi
MAP 6
Müstantik Sokak
Kanısıcak Sokak
Şule Sokak
Aydın Bey Sokak
Sivrikoz Sokak
Hisar
Paşa
Nalıncı Cemal Sokak
Anaç Sokak
Cibali Caddesi
Mescidi Sokak
Üsküplü Caddesi
Altı Sokak
Caddesi
Bostan Hamamı Sokak
Salih Paşa Caddesi
Mürşit Sokak
Kerpiç Sokak
Yeni Konak Sokak
Ali Tekin Sokak
Kani Paşa Sokak
Haydar Hamamı Sokak
Haydar Caddesi
Bıçakçı Alaaddin Sokak
Tepedelen Sokak
Şerefli Sokak
Bıçakçı Çeşmesi
Fil Yokuşu Sokak
Zeyrek Mehmet Paşa Sokak
İbadethane Sokak
Zeyrek Caddesi
Ragıp Gümüşpala Caddesi
Çakşırcı Sokak
Leblebici Sokak
Hayat Sokak
Azap Çeşmesi Sokak
Arap Çeşme Sokak
Altamataşı Caddesi
Yeni
Kazancılar Caddesi
Küçükpazar Caddesi
Bodrum Sokak
Kıble Sokak
Kıble Çeşme Caddesi
Hayriye Hanım Sokak
İpçiler
Kepenekçi Sokak
Kepenekçi Sabunhanesi Sokak
Hızır Bey Camii Sokak
Hızır Külhanı Sokak
Hacı Kadın Caddesi
Şükrü Baba Sokak
Tavanlı Çeşme Sokak
Mehmet Paşa Yokuşu
Kasnakçılar Caddesi
Namahrem Sokak
Şemsettin Sokak
Melekşah Sokak
Sabunhane Sokak
İmaret Sokak
Sarı Beyazıt Caddesi
İtfaiye Kendir Sokak
Azep Askeri Sokak
Muabbir Sokak
Darülhadis Sokak
Vefa Türbesi Sokak
Fetvayokuşu Sokak
Şifahane Sokak
Yüksek Oluk Sokak
Süleymaniyelmareti
Mimar Sinan
Dökmeciler Hamamı Sokak
Atatürk Bulvarı
Kahve Sokak
Himmet Sokak
Revani Çelebi Sokak
Kovacılar
Akifpaşa
Katip Çelebi Sokak
Vefa
Müşküle Sokak
Molla Şemsettin Sokak
Yoğurtçuoğlu Sokak
Kanuni Medresesi Sokak
Prof Sıddık Sami Onar Caddesi
Kadın Hamamı Sokak
Avni Paşa Sokak
Ayşe Kadın Hamamı Sokak
İmaret Sokak
Süleymaniye Caddesi
Kirazlı Mescit Sokak
Taş Tekneler Sokak
Cemal Yener Tosyalı Caddesi
Şehzadebaşı
Fuat Paşa Caddesi
Havand
Nargile
Siyavuşpaşa Sokak
Dökmeciler

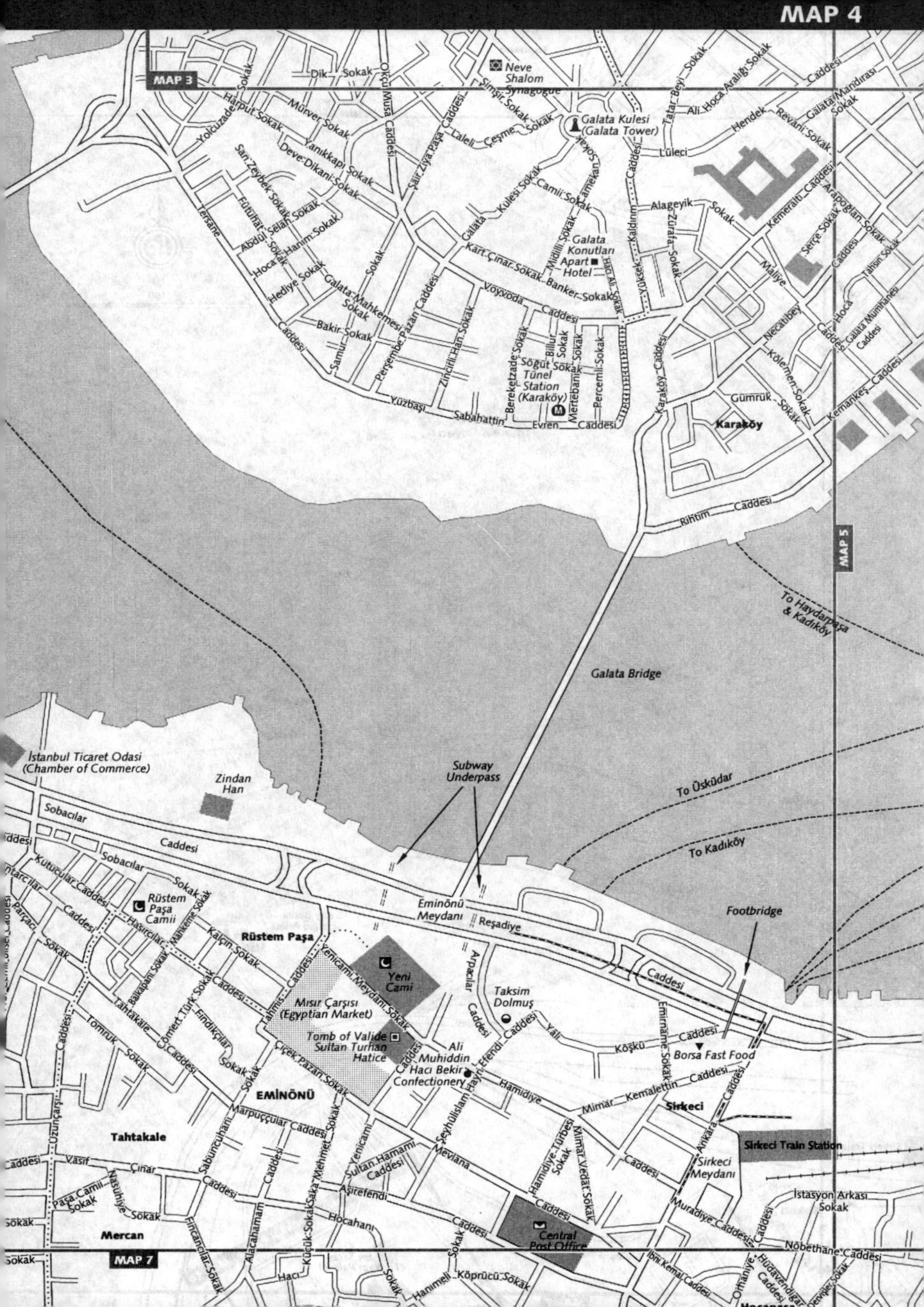
MAP 3
MAP 5
MAP 7
Neve Shalom Synagogue
Galata Kulesi (Galata Tower)
Galata Konutları Apart Hotel
Şöğüt Tünel Station (Karaköy)
Karaköy
Galata Bridge
To Haydarpaşa & Kadıköy
To Üsküdar
To Kadıköy
İstanbul Ticaret Odasi (Chamber of Commerce)
Zindan Han
Subway Underpass
Rüstem Paşa Camii
Rüstem Paşa
Eminönü Meydanı
Yeni Cami
Mısır Çarşısı (Egyptian Market)
Tomb of Valide Sultan Turhan Hatice
Taksim Dolmuş
Ali Muhiddin Hacı Bekir Confectionery
Borsa Fast Food
Footbridge
EMİNÖNÜ
Sirkeci
Sirkeci Train Station
Sirkeci Meydanı
Tahtakale
Mercan
Central Post Office
Dik Sokak
Okçu Musa Caddesi
Harput Sokak
Yolcuzade Sokak
Mürver Sokak
Şimşir Sokak
Laleli Çeşme Sokak
Şair Ziya Paşa Caddesi
Yanıkkapı Sokak
Deve Dikanı Sokak
San Zeybek Sokak
Futuhat Sokak
Abdül Selah Sokak
Hoca Hanım Sokak
Tersane Caddesi
Hediye Sokak
Galata Mahkemesi Sokak
Bakır Sokak
Samur Sokak
Perşembe Pazarı Caddesi
Zincirli Han Sokak
Yüzbaşı Sabahattin Evren Caddesi
Galata Kulesi Sokak
Camii Sokak
Kart Çınar Sokak
Banker Sokak
Voyvoda Caddesi
Midilli Sokak
Hacı Ali Sokak
Bereketzade Sokak
Billur Sokak
Mertebani Sokak
Percemli Sokak
Yüksek Kaldırım Caddesi
Alageyik Sokak
Zürafa Sokak
Tatar Beyi Sokak
Ali Hoca Aralığı Sokak
Lüleci Hendek Caddesi
Revani Sokak
Galata Mandırası Sokak
Kemeraltı Caddesi
Arapoğlan Sokak
Serçe Sokak
Maliye Caddesi
Necatibey Caddesi
Hoca Tahsin Sokak
Galata Mumhanesi Caddesi
Kölemen Sokak
Gümrük Sokak
Kemankeş Caddesi
Karaköy Caddesi
Rıhtım Caddesi
Sobacılar Caddesi
Sobacılar Sokak
Kutucular Caddesi
Hasırcılar Caddesi
Mahkeme Sokak
Kalçın Sokak
Balkapanı Sokak
Tahmis Caddesi
Yenicami Meydanı Sokak
Reşadiye Caddesi
Arpacılar Caddesi
Yalı Köşkü Caddesi
Hayri Efendi Caddesi
Emirname Sokak
Hamidiye Caddesi
Mimar Kemalettin Caddesi
Ankara Caddesi
Tahtakale Caddesi
Cömert Türk Sokak
Fındıkçılar Sokak
Tomruk Sokak
Çiçek Pazarı Sokak
Marpuççular Caddesi
Sabuncuhanı Caddesi
Şeyhülislam Sokak
Saka Mehmet Sokak
Yenicami Caddesi
Sultan Hamamı Caddesi
Mevlana Caddesi
Hamidiye Türbesi Sokak
Mimar Vedat Sokak
Uzunçarşı Caddesi
Vasıf Çınar Caddesi
Paşa Camii Sokak
Nasuhiye Sokak
Aşirefendi Caddesi
Hocahanı Sokak
Alacahamam Caddesi
Fincancılar Sokak
Küçük Sokak
Muradiye Caddesi
İstasyon Arkası Sokak
Nöbethane Caddesi
Hanımeli Köprücü Sokak
İbni Kemal Caddesi
Orhaniye Caddesi
Hüdavendigar Caddesi
Hacı
Parçacı

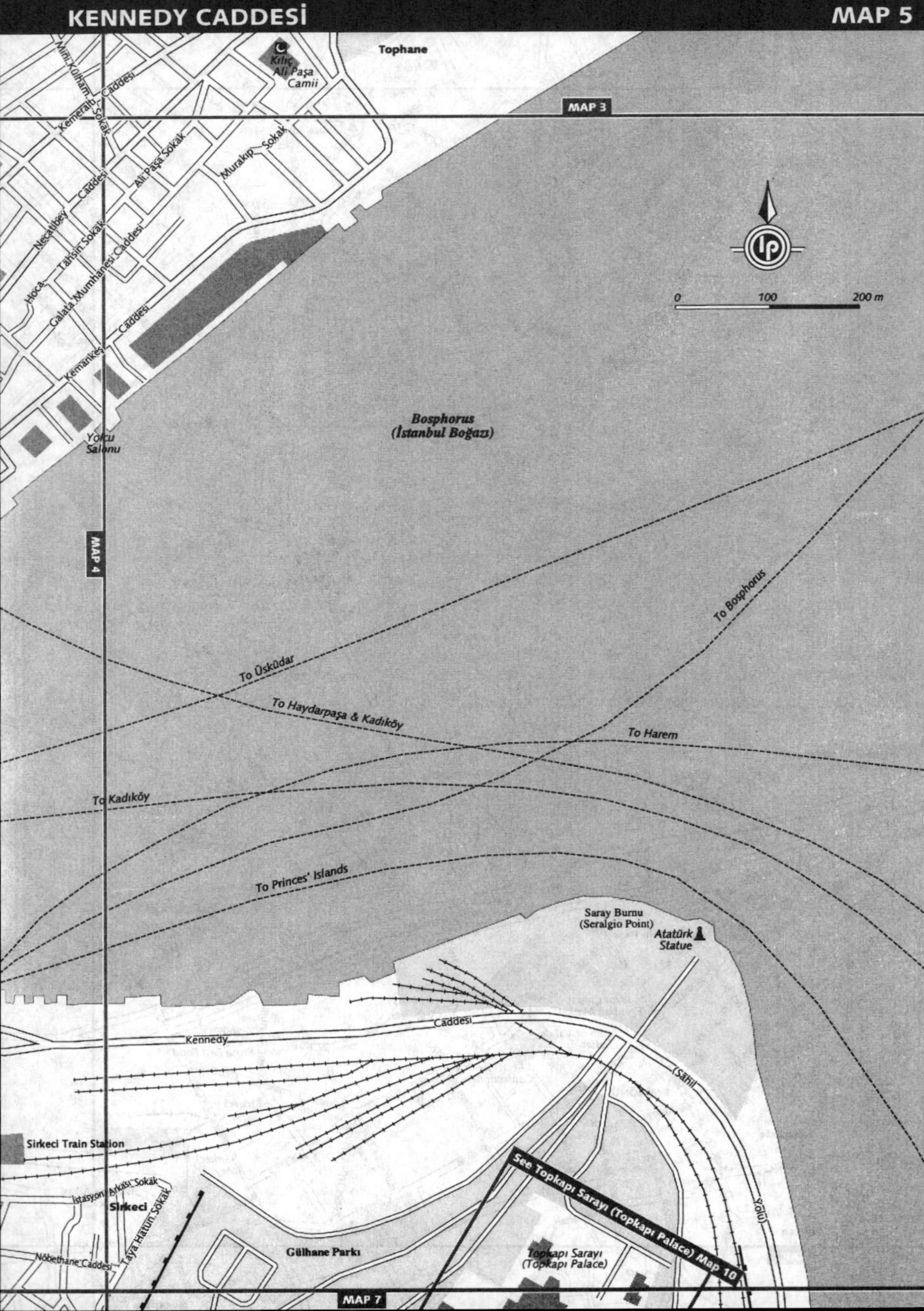
Tophane
Kılıç Ali Paşa Camii
MAP 3
Milli Kulhanı Caddesi
Kemeraltı Caddesi
Sokak
Ali Paşa Sokak
Murakıp Sokak
Necatibey Caddesi
Tahsin Sokak
Mumhanesi Caddesi
Hoca
Galata
Kemankeş Caddesi
Yolcu Salonu
0
100
200 m
Bosphorus
(İstanbul Boğazı)
MAP 4
To Bosphorus
To Üsküdar
To Haydarpaşa & Kadıköy
To Harem
To Kadıköy
To Princes' Islands
Saray Burnu
(Seralgio Point)
Atatürk Statue
Kennedy
Caddesi
Sahil
Yolu
Sirkeci Train Station
İstasyon Arkası Sokak
Sirkeci
Taya Hatun Sokak
Nöbethane Caddesi
Gülhane Parkı
See Topkapı Sarayı (Topkapı Palace) Map 10
Topkapı Sarayı
(Topkapı Palace)
MAP 7

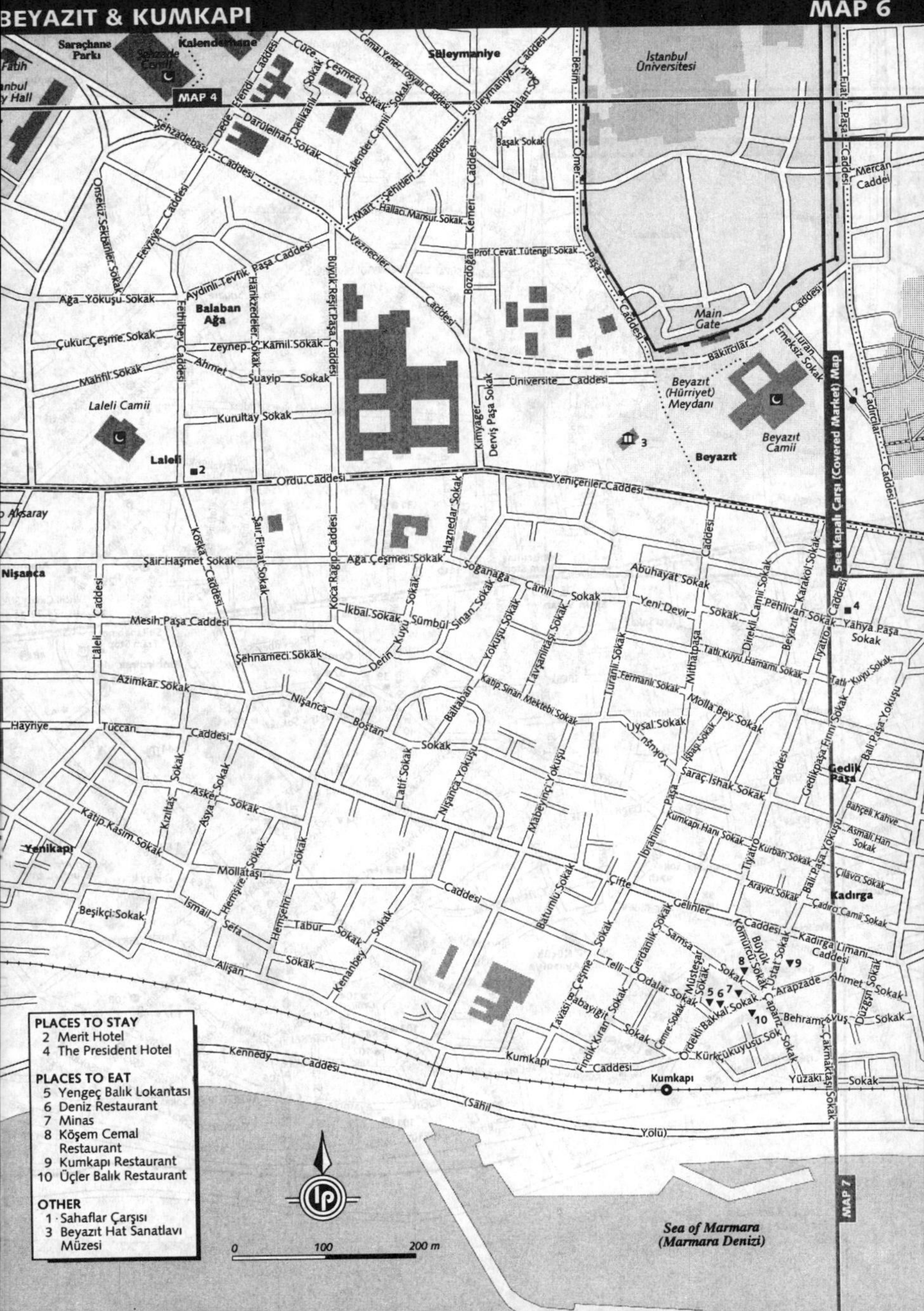
PLACES TO STAY
2 Merit Hotel
4 The President Hotel
PLACES TO EAT
5 Yengeç Balık Lokantası
6 Deniz Restaurant
7 Minas
8 Köşem Cemal Restaurant
9 Kumkapı Restaurant
10 Üçler Balık Restaurant
OTHER
1 Sahaflar Çarşısı
3 Beyazıt Hat Sanatlavı Müzesi
0
100
200 m
Sea of Marmara
(Marmara Denizi)
MAP 4
MAP 7
See Kapalı Çarşı (Covered Market) Map
Saraçhane Parkı
Şehzade Camii
Kalenderhane
Süleymaniye
İstanbul Üniversitesi
Main Gate
Beyazıt (Hürriyet) Meydanı
Beyazıt Camii
Beyazıt
Laleli Camii
Laleli
Balaban Ağa
Aksaray
Nişanca
Yenikapı
Gedik Paşa
Kadırga
Kumkapı
Ordu Caddesi
Yeniçeriler Caddesi
Üniversite Caddesi
Vezneciler Caddesi
Şehzadebaşı Caddesi
Fevziye Caddesi
Aydınlı Tevfik Paşa Caddesi
Büyük Reşit Paşa Caddesi
Koca Ragıp Caddesi
Kennedy Caddesi
(Sahil Yolu)
Kumkapı Caddesi
Mesih Paşa Caddesi
Tüccarı Caddesi
Mercan Caddesi
Fuat Paşa Caddesi
Çadırcılar Caddesi
Besim Ömer Paşa Caddesi
Ağa Yokuşu Sokak
Çukur Çeşme Sokak
Mahfil Sokak
Zeynep Kâmil Sokak
Kurultay Sokak
Ağa Çeşmesi Sokak
Şair Haşmet Sokak
Abuhayat Sokak
Pehlivan Sokak
Yahya Paşa Sokak
Azimkâr Sokak
Şehnameci Sokak
Mollataşı Caddesi
Beşikçi Sokak
Katip Kasım Sokak
Gelinler Caddesi
Kadırga Limanı Caddesi
Çakmaktaşı Sokak
Yüzakı Sokak
Behram Çavuş Sokak
Arapzade Ahmet Sokak
Ördekli Bakkal Sokak
Kürkçükuyusu Sokak
Telli Odalar Sokak
Samsa Sokak

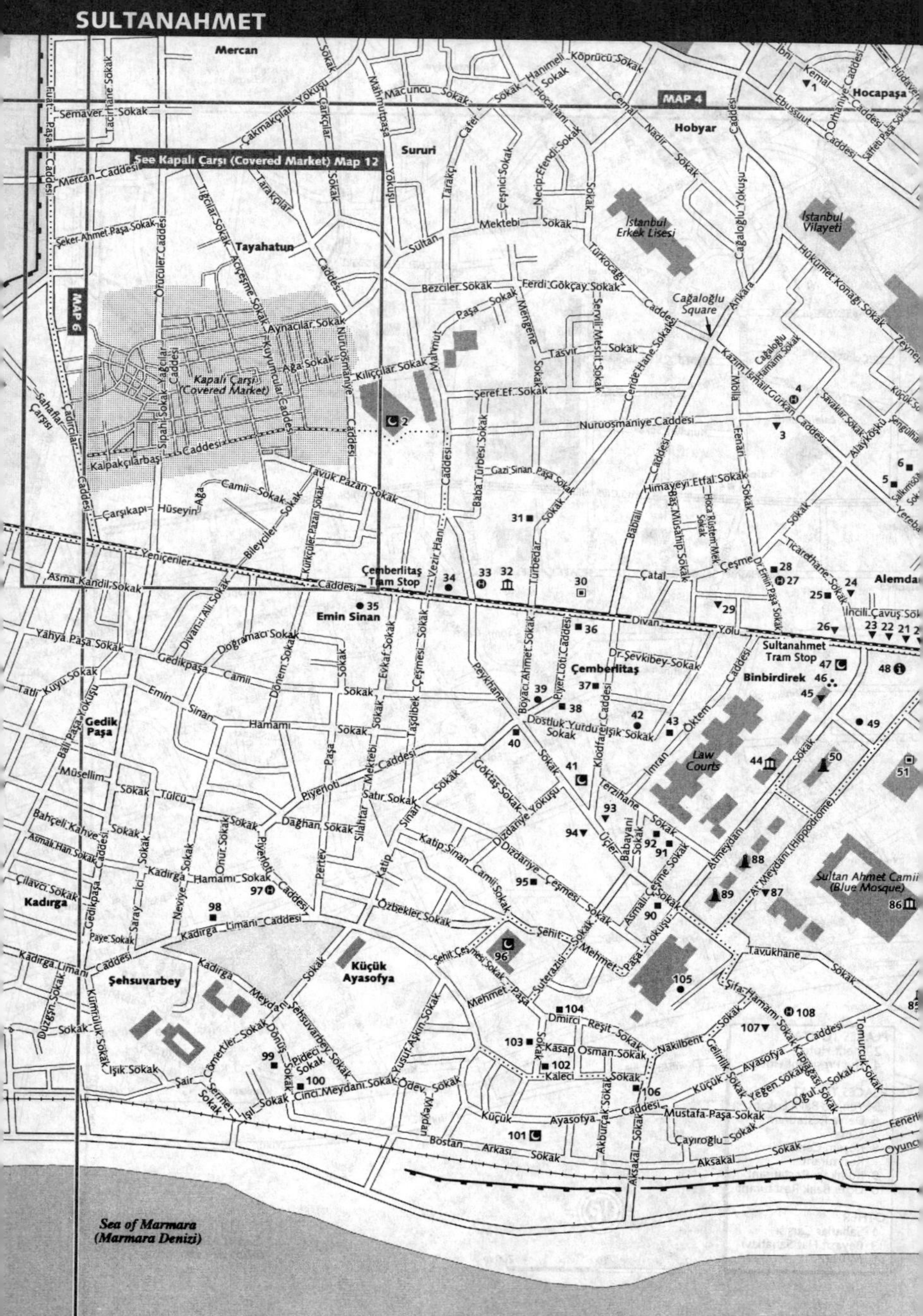
Mercan
Hocapaşa
Hobyar
Sururi
MAP 4
See Kapalı Çarşı (Covered Market) Map 12
MAP 6
Tayahatun
İstanbul Erkek Lisesi
İstanbul Vilayeti
Cağaloğlu Square
Kapalı Çarşı (Covered Market)
Sahaflar Çarşısı
Çemberlitaş Tram Stop
Emin Sinan
Alemdar
Sultanahmet Tram Stop
Binbirdirek
Çemberlitaş
Gedik Paşa
Law Courts
Sultan Ahmet Camii (Blue Mosque)
Kadırga
Şehsuvarbey
Küçük Ayasofya
Sea of Marmara (Marmara Denizi)
Mercan Caddesi
Semaver Sokak
Fuat Paşa Caddesi
Şeker Ahmet Paşa Sokak
Çadırcılar Caddesi
Kalpakçılarbaşı Caddesi
Nuruosmaniye Caddesi
Yeniçeriler Caddesi
Divan Yolu
Asma Kandil Sokak
Yahya Paşa Sokak
Tatlı Kuyu Sokak
Piyerloti Caddesi
Kadırga Limanı Caddesi
Kazım İsmail Gürkan Caddesi
Ankara Caddesi
Babıali Caddesi
Hükümet Konağı Sokak
Ticarethane Sokak
At Meydanı (Hippodrome)
Küçük Ayasofya Caddesi
Mustafa Paşa Sokak
Aksakal Sokak
Bostan Arkası Sokak
Tavukhane Sokak
Şifa Hamamı Sokak
Nakilbent Sokak
Dizdariye Çeşmesi Sokak
Şehit Mehmet Paşa Yokuşu
Mehmet Paşa Sokak
Dostluk Yurdu Sokak
Klodfarer Caddesi
Peykhane Sokak
Dr Şevkibey Sokak
İncili Çavuş Sokak

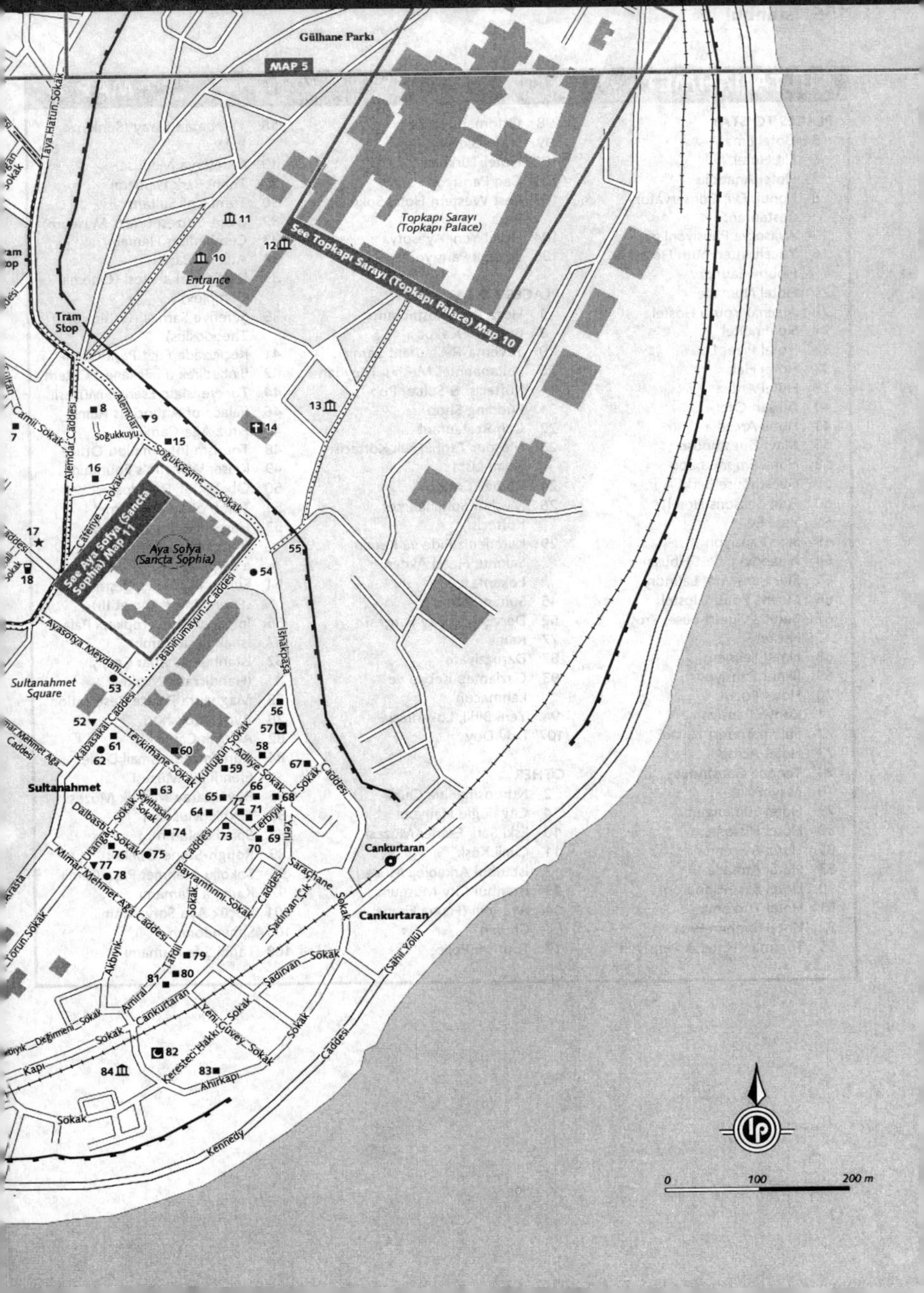

Gülhane Parkı
MAP 5
Topkapı Sarayı
(Topkapı Palace)
See Topkapı Sarayı (Topkapı Palace) Map 10
Entrance
Tram Stop
Aya Sofya
(Sancta Sophia)
See Aya Sofya (Sancta Sophia) Map 11
Sultanahmet Square
Sultanahmet
Cankurtaran
Taya Hatun Sokak
Alemdar Caddesi
Soğukkuyu
Soğukçeşme Sokak
Caferiye Sokak
Camii Sokak
Ayasofya Meydanı
Babıhümayun Caddesi
Ishakpaşa Caddesi
Kabasakal Caddesi
Tevkifhane Sokak
Kutlugün Sokak
Adliye Sokak
Seyithasan Sokak
Dalbastı Sokak
Utangaç Sokak
Terbıyık Sokak
Yeni Sokak
Mimar Mehmet Ağa Caddesi
Bayramfırını Sokak
Şadırvan Çık
Saraçhane Sokak
Akbıyık Caddesi
Tardil
Amiral Tafdil
Şadırvan Sokak
Cankurtaran
Yeni Güvey Sokak
Keresteci Hakkı Sokak
Akbıyık Değirmeni Sokak
Kapı Sokak
Ahırkapı Sokak
Kennedy Caddesi
(Sahil Yolu)
Torun Sokak
Arasta
0
100
200 m

SULTANAHMET — MAP 7

PLACES TO STAY

5 Hotel Ema
6 Elit Hotel
7 Hotel Anadolu
8 Konuk Evi; Conservatory Restaurant
15 Ayasofya Pansiyonları
16 Yücelt Interyouth Hostel & Hobby Laundry
25 Hotel Nomade
28 Arsenal Youth Hostel
31 Sipahi Otel
36 Hotel Piyer Loti
37 Hotel Halı
38 Hotel Antea
40 Gülşah Otel
43 Hotel Arcadia
56 Mavi Guesthouse
58 Hotel Empress Zoe
59 Guesthouse Berk
60 Four Seasons Hotel
61 Yeşil Ev
63 Side Pansiyon
64 Alaaddin Guest House
65 Star Pansiyon; Laundry
66 Orient Youth Hostel
67 Barut's Guesthouse; Troy Hostel
68 Hotel Şebnem
69 İlknur Pansiyon
70 Hotel Poem
71 Konya Pansiyon
72 Sultan Tourist Hostel
73 Hotel Acropol
74 Terrace Guesthouse
76 Mavi Ev
79 Hotel Sümengen
80 Hotel Historia
81 Hotel Avicenna
83 Hotel Armada
90 Hotel Best Hipodrom
91 Hotel Turkoman
92 Hotel İbrahim Paşa
95 Türkmen Hotel & Pansiyon
98 Ottoman House
99 Hotel Sidera
100 Hotel Turkuaz
102 Can Pansiyon
103 Best Western Hotel Sokullu Paşa
104 Hotel Yeni Ayasofya
106 Seagull Pansiyon

PLACES TO EAT

1 Hoca Paşa Restaurants
3 Buhara Ocakbaşı
9 Taverna-Restaurant Sarnıç
20 Sultanahmet Meşhur Meydan Köftecisi & Sultan Pub
21 Pudding Shop
22 Can Restaurant
23 Meşhur Tarihi Halk Köftecisi Selim Usta
24 Rumeli Cafe
26 Meşhur Sultanahmet Köftecisi
29 Karadeniz Pide ve Kebap Salonu; Hotel Akdeniz Lokantası
45 Sultan Sofrası
52 Derviş Aile Çay Bahçesi
77 Rami
87 Daruzziyafe
93 Gaziantep Kebap ve Lahmacun
94 Yeni Birlik Lokantası
107 Doy Doy

OTHER

2 Nuruosmaniye Camii
4 Cağaloğlu Hamamı
10 Eski Şark Eserler Müzesi
11 Çinili Köşk
12 İstanbul Arkeoloji Müzesi
13 İstanbul City Museum
14 Aya İrini (Hagia Eirene Church)
17 Tourism Police
18 Yerebatan Saray (Sunken Palace)
19 Cafeterya Medusa
27 Tarihi Park Hamamı
30 Tombs of Sultans
32 Basın Müzesi (Press Museum)
33 Çemberlitaş Hamamı
34 Atik Ali Paşa
35 Darüşşafaka Sitesi (Cinema Complex)
39 Şerefiye Sarnıçı (Cistern of Theodosius)
41 Keçicizade Fuat Paşa Camii
42 Binbirdirek (Philoxenes) Cistern
44 Türkve İslam Eserleri Müzesi
46 Palace of Antiochus Ruins
47 Firuz Ağa Camii
48 Tourism Information Office
49 Kaiser Wilhelm's Fountain
50 Obelisk of Theodosius
51 Tomb of Sultan Ahmet I
53 Haseki Hürrem Hamamı (Baths of Lady Hürrem, now a carpet shop)
54 Sultan III Ahmet Çeşmesi (Fountain of Ahmet III)
55 Imperial Gate, Topkapı Palace
57 İshak Paşa Camii
62 İstanbul Sanatlar Çarşışı (Handicrafts Market)
75 Magnaura Palace Restoration
78 Aypa Bookshop
82 Akbıyık Camii
84 Hamamzade İsmail Dede Efendi Evi Müzesi
85 Büyüksaray Mozaik Müzesi
86 Textile Museum
88 Spiral Column
89 Rough-Stone Obelisk
96 Sokollu Mehmet Paşa Camii
97 Kadırga Hamamı
101 Küçük Aya Sofya Camii
105 Sphendoneh
108 Tarihi Şifa Hamamı

EDDIE GERALD

Washing feet under the watchful eye of an old man in a hat, within Fatih Camii.

EDDIE GERALD

Locals enjoy watching the tourist watching the locals watching the tourist ...

EDDIE GERALD

Early morning fishing on Galata Bridge.

0 100 200 m
Kınmi Çeşme Sokak
Cebecibaşı
Meşatlık Sokak
Otakçıbaşı Sokak
Edirnekapı
Savaklar Caddesi
Hocaçakır Caddesi
Tekfur Sarayı
Avcı Bey Caddesi
Şişehane
Eğrikapı Mumhanesi
Ebe Sokak
Demirci Hasan Sokak
Molla Şakir Sokak
Kırkambar Sokak
Demirhisar Caddesi
Yatağan Sokak
Şahbudak Sokak
Çinçinli Çeşme Sokak
Kahkaha Sokak
Mahkeme Altı Caddesi
Sunullah Ef. Sokak
Kasim Gösim
Balat Camii
Kaşar Sokak
Püskülcü
İsa Mehkeme Sokak
Düriye Sokak
Vodina Caddesi
Sakianbay Sokak
Yanbolu Sokak
Caddesi
Ulubatlı Hasan Sokak
Karagözcü Sokak
Türkeli Sokak
Gevgili Sokak
Çilingir Sokak
Çakırağa Yokuşu
Kariye İmareti Sokak
Paşa Hamamı Sokak
Kürkçü Çeşmesi Sokak
Hacı Rıza Sokak
Dükkan Sokak
Ayam Sokak
Hızır Ça
Koca Mustafa
Draman
Kantarcı Ali Sokak
Sultan Çeşmesi Caddesi
Kariye Türbesi Sokak
Kariye Müsezi (Chora Church)
Kariye Oteli
Kariye-i Atik
Yatağan Camii
Kesmekaya Caddesi
Kalpakçı Çeşme
Yazıcı Camii
Miraç Sokak
Valiz Sokak
Kariye Bostanı Sokak
Eyüp Sokak
Neşler Sokak
Şeyh Sokak
Evlatlık Sokak
Saldırma Sokak
Tatlıcı Sokak
Katip Muslihittin
Draman Caddesi
Hacı İbrahim
Zülüflü Sokak
Fethiye Kapısı
Fethiye Camii
Kariye Yağhanesi Sokak
Fevzi
Kalfa Efendi Sokak
Avare Sokak
Kasap Sokak
Draman Çeşmesi Sokak
Fethiye Caddesi
Kariye Yağh Sokak
Ali Kuşçu Sokak
Mihrimah Sultan Camii
Yeşilce Direk Sokak
Tetik Sokak
Faizci Sokak
Salma Tomruk Caddesi
Müftü Sokak
Arı Sokak
Sena Sokak
Alişah Sokak
Draman Camii
Eroğlu Sokak
Kasım Odalar Sokak
Karagümrük
Kasım Ağa Camii Sokak
Viranodolar Sokak
Derviş Ali
Kurt Ağa Çeşmesi Caddesi
Kefevi Sokak
Dilmaç Sokak
Yahyazade Sokak
Koltukçu Sokak
Manyasizade
Hatice Sultan
Paşa
Draman Çukuru Sokak
Tercüman Yunus Sokak
Dolaplı Bostan Sokak
Saray Ağası Caddesi
Dede Mehmet Sokak
Prof Naci Şensoy Caddesi
Korucu Sokak
Vefa Stadyumu
Kurt Ağa Çeşmesi Caddesi
Beyceğiz
Niyazi Mısrı Sokak
Kelebek Sokak
Feda Camii
Sarmaşık Sokak
Nurettin Tekkesi Sokak
Beyceğiz Caddesi
Türkistan Sokak
Uzun Yol Sokak
Hasan Fehmi Paşa Caddesi
Lodos Sokak
Beyceğiz Fırını Sokak
Sofalı Çeşme Sokak
Külahlı Sokak
Cemali Sokak
Caddesi
Fatih Nişanca Caddesi

1 Şemsi Paşa Camii
2 Mihrimah Sultan Camii
3 Şeyh Camii
4 Ağa Camii
5 Yeni Valide Camii
6 Mimar Sinan Çarşısı
7 Rumi Mehmet Paşa Camii
8 Ayazma Camii
9 İmrahor Camii
10 Kaptan Paşa Camii
11 Niyazibey İskender Kebapçı
12 Karakadı Alaatin Camii
13 Kara Davut Camii
14 Doğancılar Camii
15 Şehit Süleyman Camii
16 Ahmediye Camii
17 Nasuhi Camii
18 Atik Valide Camii
19 Çinili Cami
Bosphorus
(İstanbul Boğazı)
To Eminönü
To Kabataş
To Beşiktaş
To Beylerbeyi
To Büyük Çamlıca
To Harem & Haydarpaşa
Kız Kulesi
ÜSKÜDAR
Fethi Paşa Korusu
Selman Ağa
Solak Sinan
Selami Ali
T Hacı Mehmet
Toygar Hamza
Tabaklar
Hayrettin Çavuş
İnkilâp
Kefçe Dede
Doğancılar Parkı
Gülfem Hatun
Ahmet Çelebi
İhsaniye
Rumi Mehmet Paşa
Ayazma
Salacak
Demokrasi Meydanı
Hakimiyet-i Milliye Caddesi
Paşa Limanı Caddesi
Cumhuriyet Caddesi
Doğancılar Caddesi
Üsküdar Harem Caddesi
Gündoğumu Caddesi
Toptaşı Caddesi
Büyük Selim Paşa Caddesi
Tabaklar Meydanı Sokak
Selmanı Pak Caddesi
Uncular Caddesi
Çavuşdere Caddesi
Tunus Bağı Caddesi
Halk Caddesi
Selami Ali Efendi Caddesi
Şemsi Paşa Cad
Sahil Yolu
0 125 250 m

continued from page 141

Topkapı Sarayı (Map 10)
Topkapı Sarayı (TOHP-kahp-uh, Topkapı Palace) was the residence of the sultans for almost three centuries. Mehmet the Conqueror built the first palace shortly after the Conquest in 1453, and lived here until his death in 1481. Many sultans lived the drama of the Ottoman monarchy here until the 19th century. Mahmut II (1808-39), the last emperor to occupy the palace, was succeeded by sultans who preferred living in new European-style palaces – Dolmabahçe, Yıldız – which they built on the Bosphorus.

The *Seraglio*, as it was known in Europe, was romantically portrayed by Mozart in his opera *The Abduction from the Seraglio*, which is performed in the palace every summer from late June to early July during the International İstanbul Music Festival (see Entertainment later in this chapter).

Topkapı Sarayı (☎ 512 0480) is open from 9 am to 4.30 pm (later in summer); closed on Tuesday. Admission to the palace costs US$5, US$4 for students; entry to the Harem costs an additional US$1.50. You may also choose to pay US$0.25 as a donation to the İstanbul Kültür ve Sanat Vakfı (İstanbul Culture and Arts Foundation).

Seeing Topkapı requires at least half a day, and preferably more. Be at the door when it opens during the busy summer months. Though it's tempting to nip into Aya Sofya for a look as you go by on your way to Topkapı, I strongly recommend that you resist the urge. Aya Sofya has been there for 1500 years, and it will be there when you come out of Topkapı.

Head straight for the Harem when you enter; tours are every 30 minutes. In summer the crowds are so thick and the tour groups so numerous that individual travellers sometimes are out of luck as the groups book all of the Harem tours in advance.

Court of the Janissaries Topkapı grew and changed with the centuries, but its basic four-courtyard plan remained the same. As you pass through the great gate behind Aya Sofya, you enter the Birinci Avlu (First Court), the Court of the Janissaries. On your left is the former **Aya İrini Kilisesi**, or Church of Divine Peace (☎ 520 6952), Sarayiçi 35, now a concert hall where recitals are given during the International İstanbul Music Festival.

Life in the Cage

Imperial princes were brought up in the Harem as children, taught and cared for by its women and servants.

In the early centuries of the empire, Ottoman princes were schooled as youths in combat and statecraft by direct experience: they practised soldiering, fought in battles and were given provinces to administer. But as the Ottoman dynasty did not observe primogeniture (succession of the first-born), the death of the sultan often resulted in a fratricidal bloodbath as his sons battled it out among themselves for the throne. In the case of Beyazıt II, his sons began the battles even before the sultan's death, realising that to lose the battle for succession meant death for themselves. The victorious son, Selim, even forced Beyazıt to abdicate, and may even have had him murdered as he went into retirement.

Fratricide was not practised by Ahmet I, who could not bring himself to murder his mad brother Mustafa. Instead, he kept him imprisoned in the Harem, beginning the tradition of *kafes hayatı* (cage life). This house arrest, adopted in place of fratricide by later sultans, meant that princes were prey to the intrigues of the women and eunuchs, corrupted by the pleasures of the Harem, ignorant of war and statecraft, and thus usually unfit to rule if and when the occasion arose. Luckily for the empire in this latter period, there were able grand viziers to carry on.

In later centuries the dynasty abandoned kafes hayatı and adopted the practice of having the eldest male in the direct line assume the throne.

PETER PTSCHELINZEW

PETER PTSCHELINZEW

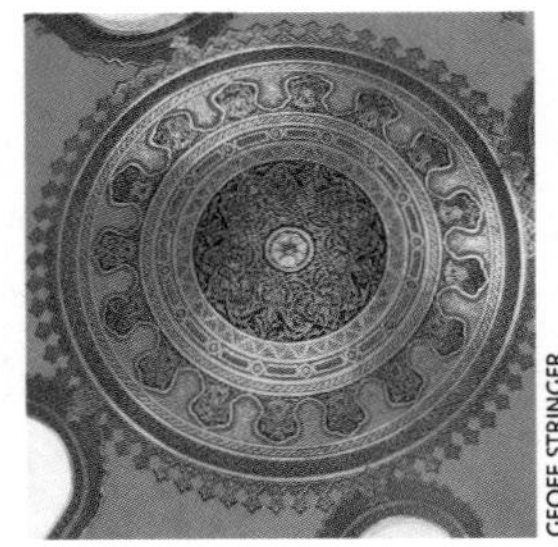

GEOFF STRINGER

EDDIE GERALD

İstanbul will keep you intrigued for days whether it's the mosaics in Aya Sofya depicting Christ the Pantocrator (top), Aya Sofya itself (bottom left), the ceiling of the famous Topkapı Sarayı (middle right) or the view toward the Old City (bottom right).

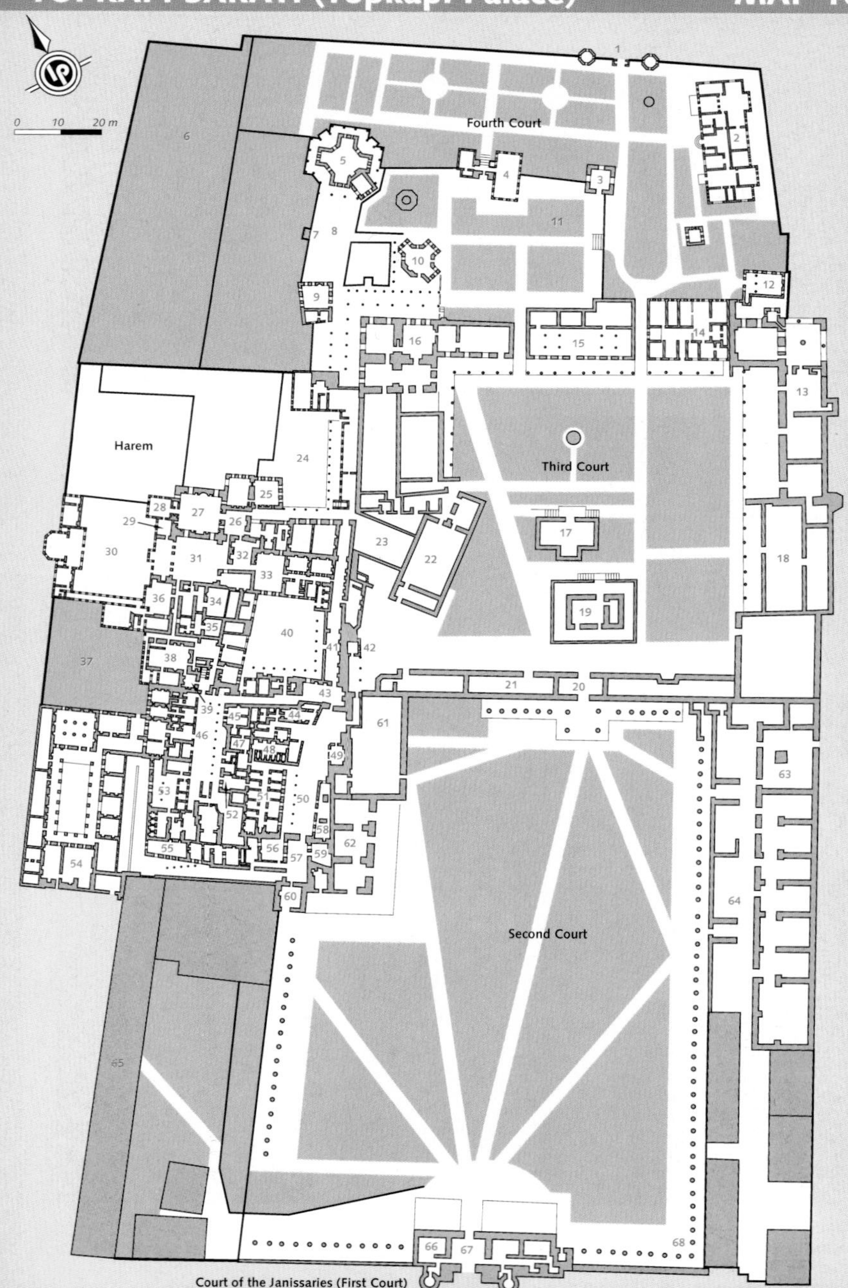

0 10 20 m
Fourth Court
Harem
Third Court
Second Court
Court of the Janissaries (First Court)

TOPKAPI SARAYI (Topkapı Palace) — MAP 10

SECOND COURT

61 Inner Treasury (Enderun Hazinesi; Arms & Armour)
62 Divan Salonu
63 Restored Confectionery (Helvahane)
64 Palace Kitchens (Porcelain & Glass Exhibits)
65 Imperial Stables (Has Ahırları)
66 Bookshop
67 Middle Gate (Ortakapı; Bab-üs Selâm)
68 Imperial Carriages

THIRD COURT

13 Imperial Treasury (Hazine)
14 Museum Directorate
15 Treasury Barracks (Hazine Koğuşu; Calligraphy, Illumination & Miniatures)
16 Sacred Safe Keeping Rooms (Mukaddes Emanetler Dairesi; Prophet's Relics)
17 Library of Ahmet III
18 Dormitory of the Expeditionary Force (Seferli Koğuşu); Imperial Caftans
19 Audience Chamber (Arz Odası)
20 Gate of Felicity (Bab-üs Saade)
21 White Eunuchs Quarters (Akağalar)
22 Mosque/Library (Ağalar Camii)

FOURTH COURT

1 Gate of the Privy Gardens (Has Bahçe Kapısı)
2 Mecidiye Köşkü; Konyalı Restaurant
3 Doctor's Room (Hekimbaşı Odası)
4 Mustafa Paşa (Sofa) Köşkü
5 Baghdad Kiosk (Bağdat Köşkü)
6 Lower Gardens of the Imperial Terrace; Fig Garden; Elephant Garden (Sofa-i Hümayun Alt Bahçeleri; İncir Bahçesi; Fil Bahçesi)
7 Canopy for Breaking the Fast (İftariye Kameriyesi ve Mehtaplık)
8 Marble Terrace & Pool (Mermer Teras ve Havuz)
9 Circumcision Room (Sünnet Odası)
10 Erivan Kiosk (Revan Köşkü)
11 Tulip Garden
12 Sofa or Terrace Mosque (Sofa Camii)

HAREM

23 Harem Mosque
24 Favourites Courtyard & Apartments (Gözdeler Mabeyn Taşlığı ve Daireleri)
25 Double Kiosk with Stained Glass
26 Beautifully Tiled Antechamber
27 Privy Chamber of Murat III
28 Library of Ahmet I; Dining Room of Ahmet III (Fruit Paintings)
29 Ahmet III Dining Room
30 Terrace of Osman III
31 Emperor's Chamber (Hünker Sofası)
32 Room with Hearth (Ocaklı Oda); Room with Fountain (Çeşmeli Oda)
33 Consultation Place of the Genies
34 Valide Sultan's Hamam
35 Sultan's Hamam
36 Chamber of Abdül Hamit I
37 Harem Garden
38 Valide Sultan's Quarters (Valide Sultan Taşlığı)
39 Sultan Ahmet Köşkü
40 Courtyard of the Valide Sultan
41 Golden Road (Altınyol)
42 Birdcage Gate (Kuşhane Kapısı)
43 Main Gate (Cümle Kapısı) with Gilded Mirrors & Sentry Post; Second Guard Room
44 Chief Black Eunuch's Room (Kızlarağası)
45 Concubines' Corridor (Cariyeler Koridoru)
46 Concubines' & Consorts' Courtyard (Cariye & Kadinefendi Taşlığı)
47 Harem Kitchen
48 Imperial Princes' School
49 Harem Chamberlain's Room
50 Black Eunuchs' Courtyard (Ağalar Taşlığı)
51 Black Eunuchs' Dormitories (Ağalar Koğuş)
52 Women's Hamam
53 Women's Dormitory
54 Harem Hospital
55 Laundry Room
56 Black Eunuchs' Mosque
57 Guard Room/Hall with Şadırvan
58 Harem Eunuchs' Mosque
59 Tower of Justice (Adalet Kulesi)
60 Carriage Gate & Dome with Cupboards (Dolaplı Kubbe)

TOM BROSNAHAN

Rehearsal for Mozart's ***Abduction from the Seraglio.***

The Janissaries

The word 'janissary' comes from the Turkish *yeni çeri*, 'new levies'. These soldiers were personal servants of the sultan, 'owned' by him, fed and paid regularly by him, and subject to his will. They were full-time soldiers, an innovation in an age when most soldiers – and all soldiers in Europe – were farmers in spring and autumn, homebodies in winter, and warriors only in summer.

In a process termed *devşirme*, government agents went out from İstanbul into the towns and villages of the Balkans to round up 10-year-old boys from Christian families for the sultan's personal service. Having one's son taken by the devşirme was undoubtedly a blow to the family, which would lose his company and labour forever. The boy would be instructed in Turkish, converted to Islam, and enrolled in the sultan's service.

The imperial service was a meritocracy. Those of normal intelligence and capabilities went into the Janissary corps, the sultan's imperial guard. The brightest and most capable boys went into the palace service, and many eventually rose to the highest offices, including that of grand vizier. This ensured that the top government posts were always held by personal servants of the sultan. These top government and military officers would often remember their families and birthplaces, and would lavish benefits such as public works projects (mosques, bridges, schools etc) upon them.

Topkapı's large **Court of the Janissaries**, stretching from the church to the Ortakapı, is now a shady park, but in the old days this was where the sultan's elite corps of guards gathered to eat the hearty *pilav* provided by him. When they were dissatisfied with the sultan's rule (which meant his treatment of them), they would overturn the great cauldrons of pilav as a symbol of revolt, after which the sultan's hours were numbered.

By the early 19th century, the once-admirable Janissary corps had become unbearably corrupt and self-serving, and a constant threat to the throne. The reforming sultan Mahmut II, risking his life, his throne and his dynasty, readied a new, loyal European-style army; then provoked a revolt of the Janissaries in the Hippodrome and brought in his new army to wipe them out, ending their 350-year history in 1826.

There was a Christian church here from earliest times, and before that, a pagan temple. The early church was replaced by the present one during the reign of the Byzantine emperor Justinian in the 540s, so the church you see is as old as Aya Sofya. When Mehmet the Conqueror began building his palace, the church was within the grounds and thus could not be used for worship. Ironically, it was used as an arsenal for centuries, then as an artillery museum.

In June 1998, archaeologists discovered painted walls and other structures from the Great Palace of the Byzantine emperors in this court. Excavations and preservation efforts were underway at the time of writing.

Janissaries, merchants and tradespeople could circulate as they wished in the Court of the Janissaries, but the Second Court was different. In a way, the same is true today, because you must buy your tickets before entering the Second Court. The ticket booths are on your right as you approach the entrance. Just past them is a little fountain where the imperial executioner used to wash the tools of his trade after decapitating a noble or rebel who had displeased the sultan. The head of the unfortunate was put on a pike and exhibited above the gate you're about to enter.

Ortakapı & Second Court The Ortakapı (Middle Gate, Gate of Greeting or Bab-üs Selâm) led to the palace's Second Court, used for the business of running the empire. Only the sultan and the *valide sultan* (queen mother) were allowed through the Ortakapı on horseback. Everyone else, including the grand vizier, had to dismount. The gate you see was constructed by Süleyman the Magnificent in 1524, utilising architects and workers he had brought back from his conquest of Hungary.

To the right after you enter are models and a map of the palace, and beyond them an exhibit of imperial carriages made for the sultan and his family in Paris, Torino and Vienna.

Within the second courtyard is a beautiful, park-like setting. Topkapı is not a palace on the European plan – one large building with outlying gardens – but rather a series of pavilions, kitchens, barracks, audience chambers, kiosks and sleeping quarters built around a central enclosure, much like a fortified camp.

The great **palace kitchens**, on the right-hand side, hold a small portion of Topkapı Sarayı's vast collection of Chinese celadon porcelain. Beyond the celadon are the collections of fine European and Ottoman porcelain and glassware. The last of the kitchens, the Helvahane in which all the palace sweets were made, is now set up as a kitchen, and you can easily imagine what went on in these rooms as the staff prepared food for the 5000 inhabitants of the palace.

On the left (western) side of the Second Court is the ornate **Kubbealtı** ('beneath the cupola') or Imperial Council Chamber, also called the Divan Salonu, beneath the squarish Adalet Kulesi tower which is among the palace's most distinctive architectural features. The Imperial Divan (council) met in the Divan Salonu to discuss matters of state while the sultan eavesdropped through a grill high on the wall.

North of the Kubbealtı is the *silahlar* (armoury) exhibit of fearsome Ottoman and European weaponry.

Harem The entrance to the Harem, open by guided tour only from 9.30 am to 4.30 pm (3.30 pm in winter), is beneath the Adalet Kulesi (Tower of Justice), the palace's highest point.

Legend vs Reality Fraught with legend and romance, the Harem is usually imagined as a place where the sultan could engage in debauchery at will. In fact, these were the imperial family quarters, and every detail of Harem life was governed by tradition, obligation and ceremony.

Every traditional Muslim household had two distinct parts: the *selamlık* (greeting room) where the master greeted friends, business associates and tradespeople; and the *harem* (private apartments), reserved for himself and his family. The Harem, then, was something akin to the private apartments in Buckingham Palace or the White House.

The women of the Harem had to be foreigners, as Islam forbade enslaving Muslims, Christians or Jews (Christians and Jews could be enslaved in the Balkans – as with the janissaries' devşirme: see 'The Janissaries' boxed text – due to a loophole in Islamic law, or if taken as prisoners of war, or if bought as slaves in a legitimate slave market). Besides prisoners of war, girls were bought as slaves (often sold by their parents at a good price), or received as gifts from nobles and potentates. A favourite source of girls was Circassia, north of the Caucasus Mountains in Russia, as Circassian women were noted for their beauty, and parents were often glad to give up their 10-year-old girls in exchange for hard cash.

Upon entering the Harem, the girls would be schooled in Islam and Turkish culture and language, the arts of make-up, dress, comportment, music, reading and writing, embroidery and dancing. They then entered a meritocracy, first as ladies-in-waiting to the sultan's concubines and children, then to the sultan's mother and finally, if they were the best, to the sultan himself.

Ruling the Harem was the valide sultan, the mother of the reigning sultan. She often owned large estates in her own name and controlled them through black eunuch servants. She was allowed to give orders directly to the grand vizier. Her influence on the sultan, on the selection of his wives and concubines, and on matters of state, was often profound.

The sultan was allowed by Islamic law to have four legitimate wives, who received the title of *kadın* (wife). If a wife bore him a child, she was called *haseki sultan* if it was a son; *haseki kadın* if it was a daughter. The Ottoman dynasty did not observe primogeniture, so in principle the throne was available to any imperial son. Each lady of the Harem contrived mightily to have her son proclaimed heir to the throne, thus assuring her own role and power as the new valide sultan.

As for concubines, Islam permits as many as a man can support in proper style. The Ottoman sultans had the means to support many, sometimes up to 300, though they were not all in the Harem at the same time. The domestic thrills of the sultans were usually less spectacular, however. Mehmet the Conqueror, builder of Topkapı, was the last sultan to have four official wives. After him, sultans did not officially marry, but instead kept four chosen concubines without the legal encumbrances, thereby saving themselves the embarrassments and inconveniences suffered by another famous Renaissance monarch, King Henry VIII of England.

The Harem was much like a village with all the necessary services. About 400 or 500 people lived in this section of the palace at any one time. Not many of the ladies stayed in the Harem all their lives: the sultan might grant them their freedom, after which they would often marry powerful men who wanted the company of these supremely graceful and intelligent women, not to mention their connections with the palace.

The *kızlarağası* (kuhz-LAHR-ah-ah-suh, chief black eunuch), the sultan's personal representative in administration of the Harem and other important affairs of state, was the third most powerful official in the empire, after the grand vizier and the Şeyh-ul İslâm (supreme Islamic judge).

Many of the 300-odd rooms in the Harem were constructed during the reign of Süleyman the Magnificent (1520-66), but much more was added or reconstructed over the years. In 1665 a disastrous fire destroyed much of the complex, which was rebuilt by Mehmet IV and later sultans.

Touring the Harem Although the Harem is built into a hillside and has six levels, the standard tour takes you through or past only a few dozen rooms on one level, but these are among the most splendid. The tour route may vary from time to time as various rooms are closed for restoration, and others are finished and opened to view.

Most Harem tours are given in Turkish and English, with other languages in summer. Plaques in Turkish and English have been placed here and there in the Harem. They're more informative than the guide's brief commentary.

Here is a description of the tour at the time of writing:

You enter the Harem through the Carriage Gate, from which Harem ladies would enter their carriages. Inside the gate is the Dolaplı Kubbe, or **Dome with Cupboards**, decorated with fine İznik faïence (tin-glazed earthenware tiles); the green and yellow colours are unusual in İznik tiles. Beyond it is the **Hall with Şadırvan** (ablutions fountain), a guardroom with more fine coloured tiles. To the left is a doorway to the **black eunuchs' mosque**, on the right the doorway to the Adalet Kulesi, or **Tower of Justice** which rises above the Imperial Divan, or council chamber.

In principle, groups of no more than 20 are allowed to climb to the top of the Adalet Kulesi at 11 am and 2 pm in conjunction with the harem tour, but in practice you will be whisked right by the door. When you reach the door, mention to your guide that you'd like to go up in the tower; the guide will insist that it be done at the end of the tour, but at the end of the tour will ignore you, so after the tour is over insist that the door be opened. A guard will be assigned to escort you up to the top, past the gilded grill through which the sultan eavesdropped on the meetings of his ministers of state. The view from the top is splendid.

Beyond the Hall with Şadırvan is the narrow **Ağalar Taşlığı** (Black Eunuchs' Courtyard), decorated in Kütahya tiles from the 17th century. Behind the marble colonnade on the left are the **Ağalar Koğuşu** (Black Eunuchs' Dormitories). In the early days white eunuchs were used, but black eunuchs sent as presents by the Ottoman governor of Egypt, later took control. As many as 200 lived here, guarding the doors and waiting on the women.

Near the far end of the courtyard on the left, a staircase leads up to the rooms in which imperial princes were given their primary schooling. On the right is the Kızlarağası (Chief Black Eunuch's Room). Neither of these was open to the public at the time of research.

At the far end of the courtyard, safely protected by the eunuchs, is the **Cümle Kapısı** (Main Gate) into the Harem proper, and another **guard room** with two gigantic gilded mirrors. From this, the **Cariyeler Koridoru** (Concubines' Corridor) on the left leads to the **Cariye ve Kadınefendi Taşlığı** (Concubines' and Consorts' Courtyard). A *cariye* (concubine) came by gift or purchase; the more talented and intelligent rose in the palace service to hold offices in the administration of the *kadınefendi*; the less talented waited on the more talented.

The **Valide Sultan's Quarters and Courtyard**, the very centre of power in the Harem, include a large salon, a small bedroom, a room for prayer, and other small chambers. Mannikins dressed in period costumes help you to visualize the scene as the valide sultan oversaw and controlled her huge 'family'. After his accession to the throne, a new sultan came here to receive the allegiance and congratulations of the people of the Harem.

The sultan, as he walked these corridors, wore slippers with silver soles. As no woman was allowed to show herself to the sultan without specific orders, the clatter of the silver soles warned residents of his approach so they could disappear from sight. This rule no doubt solidified the valide sultan's control, as *she* got to choose which girls would be presented to the sultan. She chose the most beautiful, talented and intelligent of the Harem girls to be her personal servants, and thus introduced them to her son the sultan.

From the valide sultan's quarters the tour passes the chamber of Abdül Hamit I on the left, then the private hamams and toilets of the valide sultan and the sultan on the right, to the **Hünkar Sofası** (Emperor's Chamber), decorated in Delft tiles. This grand room was where the sultan and his ladies gathered for entertainment, often with musicians in the balcony. Designed perhaps by Sinan during the reign of Murat III (1574-95), it was redecorated in baroque style by Osman III (1754-7). The smaller part of the room remains baroque; the larger part has been restored to its 16th-century decor.

The tour enters a small, oddly shaped room lavishly decorated with 16th-century İznik tiles. In fact this is the remaining half of a small room which was sacrificed to build the adjoining **Privy Chamber of Murat III** (1578), one of the most sumptuous rooms in the palace. Virtually all of the decoration is original, and is probably the work of Sinan. Besides the gorgeous İznik tiles and a fireplace, there is a three-tiered fountain to give the sound of cascading water and, perhaps not coincidentally, to make it difficult to eavesdrop on the sultan's conversations.

Adjoining the Privy Chamber to the west is the **Library of Ahmet I** (1609), with small fountains by each window to cool the summer breezes as they enter the room. Perhaps Ahmet I retired here to inspect plans of his great building project, the Sultan Ahmet Camii. The adjoining **Dining Room of Ahmet III** (1706), with wonderful painted panels of flowers and fruit, was built by Ahmet I's successor.

East of the Privy Chamber of Murat III is the **Double Kiosk**, two rooms dating from around 1600. Note the painted canvas dome in the first room, and the fine tile panels above the fireplace in the second. Fireplaces and braziers – which give off toxic carbon monoxide – were the palace's winter heating system.

North and east of the Double Kiosk is the **Favourites' Courtyard and Apartments**. The Turkish word for 'favourite', *gözde*, literally means 'in the eye (of the sultan)'.

A long, plain corridor leads east to the **Altınyol** (Golden Road), a passage leading south. A servant of the sultan's would toss gold coins to the women of the Harem here, hence the name.

The tour re-enters the guardroom with the huge gilded mirrors, then exits through the **Kuşhane Kapısı** (Birdcage Gate) into the palace's third courtyard. If you want to ascend the Tower of Justice, this is where you corner the guide and insist.

Third Court If you enter the Third Court through the Harem, and thus by the back door, you should head for the main gate into the court. Get the full effect of entering this holy of holies by going out through the gate, and back in again.

This gate, the **Bab-üs Saade**, or Gate of Felicity, also sometimes called the Akağalar Kapısı (Gate of the White Eunuchs), was the entrance into the sultan's private domain. As is common with oriental potentates, the sultan preserved the imperial mystique by appearing in public very seldom.

The Third Court was staffed and guarded by white eunuchs, who allowed only very few, very important people in. As you enter the Third Court, imagine it alive with the movements of imperial pages and white eunuchs scurrying here and there in their palace costumes. Every now and then the chief white eunuch or the chief black eunuch would appear, and all would bow deferentially. If the sultan walked across the courtyard, all activity stopped until the event was over.

An exception to the imperial seclusion was the ceremony celebrating a new sultan's accession to the throne. After girding on the sword of Osman, which symbolised imperial power, the new monarch would sit enthroned before the Bab-üs Saade and receive the obeisance, allegiance and congratulations of the empire's high and mighty.

Before the annual military campaigns in summertime, the sultan would also appear before this gate bearing the standard of the Prophet Muhammed to inspire his generals to go out and win one for Islam.

During the great days of the empire, foreign ambassadors were received on days when the Janissaries were to get their pay. Huge sacks of silver coins were brought to the Kubbealtı. High court officers would dispense the coins to long lines of the tough, impeccably costumed and faultlessly disciplined troops as the ambassadors looked on in admiration.

Today the Bab-üs Saade is the backdrop for the annual performance of Mozart's *Abduction from the Seraglio* during the International İstanbul Music Festival in late June and early July.

Arz Odası Just inside the Bab-üs Saade is the **Arz Odası**, or Audience Chamber, constructed in the 16th century but refurnished in the 18th century. Important officials and foreign ambassadors were brought to this little kiosk to conduct the high business of state. An ambassador, frisked for weapons and held on each arm by a white eunuch, would approach the sultan. At the proper moment, he knelt and kowtowed; if he didn't, the eunuchs would urge him ever so forcefully to do so.

The sultan, seated on the divans whose cushions are embroidered with more than 15,000 seed pearls, inspected the ambassador's gifts and *pişkeş* (offerings) as they were passed through the small doorway on the left. Even if the sultan and the ambassador could converse in the same language (sultans in the later years knew French, and ambassadors often learned Turkish), all conversation was with the grand vizier. The sultan would not deign to speak to a foreigner, and only the very highest Ottoman officers were allowed to address the monarch directly.

Imperial Robes Right behind the Arz Odası is the pretty little **Library of Ahmet III** (1718). Walk to the right as you leave the Arz Odası, and enter the rooms of the Seferli Koğuşu (Dormitory of the Expeditionary Force), which now house the rich collections of imperial robes, kaftans and uniforms (Padişah Elbiseleri) worked in thread of silver and gold. Textile design reached its highest point during the reign of Süleyman the Magnificent, when the imperial workshops produced cloths of exquisite design and work.

Hazine Next along on the same side are the chambers of the **Hazine** (Imperial Treasury), packed with an incredible number and variety of objects made from or decorated with gold, silver, rubies, emeralds, jade, pearls and diamonds. Look for the tiny figurine of a sultan sitting under a canopy, his body one enormous pearl. Next to him, a black eunuch's pantaloons are also one pearl.

The Kaşıkçının Elması, or Spoonmaker's Diamond, is an 86-carat rock surrounded by several dozen smaller stones. First worn by Mehmet IV at his accession to the throne in 1648, it is the world's fifth-largest diamond. There's also an uncut emerald weighing 3.26kg, and the golden dagger set with three large emeralds which was the object of Peter Ustinov's criminal quest in the movie *Topkapi*.

Also be sure to see the gold throne given by Nadir Shah of Persia to Mahmud I (1730-54). Other thrones are almost as breathtaking.

Next door to the Treasury is the **Hayat Balkonu**, or the Balcony of Life. From here the breeze is cool and there's a marvellous view of the Bosphorus and the Sea of Marmara.

Mukaddes Emanetler Dairesi Opposite the Treasury is another set of wonders, the holy relics in the **Hırka-i Saadet**, or Suite of the Felicitous Cloak, nowadays called the Mukaddes Emanetler Dairesi (Sacred Safe-keeping Rooms). These rooms, sumptuously decorated with İznik faïence, constitute a holy of holies within the palace. Only the chosen could enter the Third Court, but entry into the Hırka-i Saadet rooms was for the chosen of the chosen, and only on ceremonial occasions.

Notice, in the entry room, the carved door from the Kaaba in Mecca and, hanging from the ceiling, gilded rain gutters from the same place. Don't miss the harmonious dome above.

To the right (north) a room contains the cloak of the Prophet Muhammed and other relics. Sometimes an imam is seated here, chanting passages from the Koran. The 'felicitous cloak' itself resides in a golden casket in a special alcove along with the battle standard. During the empire, this suite of rooms was opened only once a year so that the imperial family could pay homage to the memory of the Prophet on the 15th day of the holy month of Ramazan. Even though anyone, prince or commoner, faithful or infidel, can enter the rooms now, you should respect the sacred atmosphere by observing decorous behaviour.

On the opposite side (south) of the entry room are more relics: a letter from Muhammed to the governor of El Aksa mosque in Jerusalem, a hair of the Prophet's beard and a print in clay of his foot; Caliph Omar's sword; the Koran being read by Caliph Osman when he was murdered; Joseph's turban, and even Moses' walking stick!

Other Exhibits Between the Treasury and the Hırka-i Saadet is the Hazine Koğuşu, or Treasury Dormitory, with exhibits of Turkish and Islamic bibliographic arts, including calligraphy and illumination; and portraits of the sultans (Padişah Portreleri).

Other exhibits in the Third Court include the **Ağalar Camii**, or Mosque of the Eunuchs, another little **library**, Turkish miniature paintings, imperial monograms, seals and arms, calligraphy, and portraits of the sultans. In the room with the seals, notice the graceful, elaborate *tuğra* (TOO-rah, monogram) of the sultans. The tuğra, placed at the top of any imperial proclamation, contains elaborate calligraphic rendering of the names of the sultan and his father, eg 'Abdül Hamit Khan, son of Abdül Mecit Khan, Ever Victorious'.

Fourth Court Four imperial pleasure domes occupy the north-easternmost part of the palace, sometimes called the gardens, or Fourth Court. The **Mecidiye Köşkü**, built by Abdül Mecit (1839-61), was designed according to 19th-century European models. Beneath it is the Konyalı Restaurant, which fills up by noon. If you want to dine here, arrive by 11.30 am, or after 2 pm.

In the other direction (north-west) is the **Mustafa Paşa Köşkü**, or Kiosk of Mustafa Pasha, sometimes called the Sofa Köşkü. Also here is the room of the *hekimbaşı*, or chief physician to the sultan, who was always one of the sultan's Jewish subjects.

During the reign of Sultan Ahmet III (1703-30), known as the Tulip Period because of the rage for these flowers which spread through the upper classes, the gardens around the Sofa Köşkü were filled with tulips. Little lamps would be set out among the hundreds of varieties at night. A new variety of the flower earned its creator fame, money and social recognition. Tulips had been grown in Turkey from very early times, having come originally from Persia. Some bulbs were brought to Holland during the Renaissance. The Dutch, fascinated by the possibilities in the flower, developed and created many varieties, some of which made their way back to Turkey and began the tulip craze in Holland.

Up the stairs at the end of the tulip garden are two of the most enchanting kiosks. Sultan Murat IV (1623-40) built the **Revan Köşkü**, or Erivan Kiosk, in 1635 after reclaiming the city of Yerevan (now in Armenia) from Persia. He also constructed the **Bağdat Köşkü**, or Baghdad Kiosk, in 1638 to commemorate his victory over that city. Notice the İznik tiles, the inlay and woodwork, and the views all around.

Just off the open terrace with the wishing well is the **Sünnet Odası**, or Circumcision Room, used for the ritual which admits Muslim boys to manhood. (Circumcision is usually performed when the boy is nine or 10.) The outer walls of the chamber are graced by particularly beautiful tile panels.

Has Ahırları Though closed for renovation, the Has Ahırları (Imperial Stables) are entered from the Second Court, just to the north-west of the main entrance (Ortakapı). Go down the cobbled slope.

Leaving the Palace As you leave the palace proper through the Ortakapı, you can walk to your right and down the slope along Osman Hamdi Bey Yokuşu to the archaeological museums, or straight to Aya Sofya. I'll assume that you're heading for Aya Sofya, only a few steps away.

Soğukçeşme Sokak

Just after you leave the tall gate of the Court of the Janissaries, take a look at the ornate little structure on your left. It's the **Fountain of Ahmet III** (Map 7), built in 1728 by the sultan who so favoured tulips, and restored in 1996. It replaced a Byzantine fountain at the same spring.

The ornate gate across the road from the fountain was the one by which the Sultan would enter Aya Sofya for prayers. It led to the Hünkar Mahfili, or Imperial Loge, which you'll see inside.

The gate is at the beginning of Soğukçeşme Sokak (Street of the Cold Fountain), to the right, a street entirely restored by the Turkish Touring & Automobile Association (Turing). The houses clinging to the palace walls are the Ayasofya Pansiyonlar, or Sancta Sophia Pensions. At the far (western) end of the street is the entrance to the Taverna-Restaurant Sarnıç, or Cistern Restaurant, in a restored Byzantine cistern, and across the street from it the Konuk Evi, a hotel and garden restaurant built in the old İstanbul manner. (For details, see Places to Eat – Top End and Places to Stay – Top End.)

Aya Sofya (Sancta Sophia) (Map 11)

The Church of the Divine Wisdom (Sancta Sophia in Latin, Hagia Sofia in Greek, Aya Sofya in Turkish) was not named after a saint, but after Holy (sancta, hagia) Wisdom (sophia). Aya Sofya (☎ 522 1750) is open daily except Monday from 9 am to 4 pm

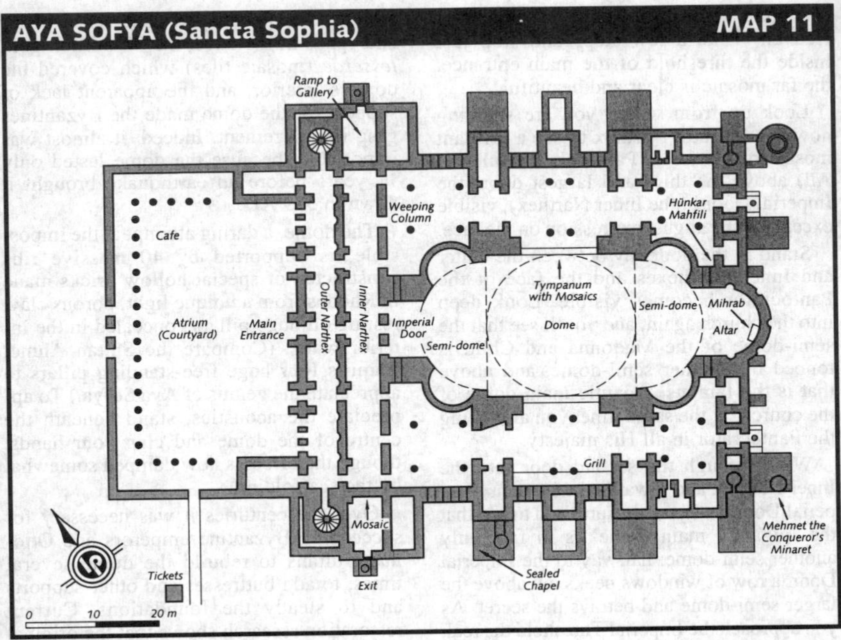

(later in summer); the galleries with their mosaics are open from 9 am to 3.30 pm and to 4.30 pm in summer. Admission costs US$5, half price for students.

Emperor Justinian (527-65 AD) had the church built as yet another effort to restore the greatness of the Roman Empire. It was constructed on the site of Byzantium's acropolis, which had also been the site of an earlier Sancta Sophia destroyed in the Nika riots of 532 AD. Justinian's church was completed in 537 AD and reigned as the greatest church in Christendom until the conquest of Constantinople in 1453.

A lot can happen to a building in 14 centuries, especially in an earthquake zone, and a lot has certainly happened to Aya Sofya. Ignore, if you can, the clutter of buttresses and supports, kiosks, tombs and outbuildings which hug its massive walls, and the renovations which are filling the interior with scaffolding.

In Justinian's time, a street led uphill from the west directly to the main door. Today the ticket kiosk is at the south-western side. To experience the church as its architects, Anthemius of Tralles and Isidorus of Miletus, intended, walk to the Atrium (courtyard) before the main entrance. Here are the sunken ruins of a Theodosian church (404-15 AD), and the low original steps. Enter through the main entrance slowly, one step at a time, looking ahead: at first there is only darkness broken by the brilliant colours of stained-glass windows. As your eyes adjust to the dark, two massive doorways appear within, in the Outer Narthex and Inner Narthex, and far beyond them in the dim light, a semi-dome blazing with gold mosaics (presently obscured by scaffolding) portraying the

Madonna and Child – she as Queen of Heaven. Take a few steps and stop just inside the threshold of the main entrance: the far mosaic is clear and beautiful.

Look up from where you are standing now in the Outer Narthex to see a brilliant mosaic of Christ as Pantocrator (Ruler of All) above the third and largest door (the Imperial Door in the Inner Narthex), visible except for the august expression on the face.

Stand in the doorway between the Outer and Inner Narthexes and the face of the Pantocrator becomes visible. Look deep into the church again, and you'll see that the semi-dome of the Madonna and Child is topped by another semi-dome, and above that is the famous, gigantic main dome of the church; at the same time, you are facing the Pantocrator in all His majesty.

Walk through the second door into the Inner Narthex and towards the immense Imperial Door, and you are surprised to see that the 'gigantic main dome' is in fact only another semi-dome: halfway to the Imperial Door, a row of windows peeks out above the larger semi-dome and betrays the secret. As you approach the Imperial Threshold the real, magnificent main dome soars above you and seems to be held up by nothing. Justinian, on entering his great creation for the first time almost 1500 years ago, exclaimed, 'Glory to God that I have been judged worthy of such a work. Oh Solomon! I have outdone you!'.

During its years as a church (almost 1000), only imperial processions were permitted to enter through the central, Imperial Door. You can still notice the depressions in the stone by each door just inside the threshold where imperial guards stood. It was through the Imperial Door that Mehmet the Conqueror came in 1453 to take possession for Islam of the greatest religious edifice in the world. Before he entered, historians tell us, he sprinkled earth on his head in a gesture of humility. Aya Sofya remained a mosque until 1935, when Atatürk proclaimed it a museum.

There are bigger buildings, and bigger domes, but not without modern construction materials such as reinforced concrete and steel girders. The achievement of the architects is unequalled. The sense of air and space in the nave, the 30 million gold *tesserae* (mosaic tiles) which covered the dome's interior, and the apparent lack of support for the dome made the Byzantines gasp in amazement. Indeed, it almost was impossible, because the dome lasted only 11 years before an earthquake brought it down in 559 AD.

The dome, a daring attempt at the impossible, is supported by 40 massive ribs constructed of special hollow bricks made in Rhodes from a unique light, porous clay, resting on huge pillars concealed in the interior walls. (Compare the Sultan Ahmet Camii's four huge free-standing pillars to appreciate the genius of Aya Sofya.) To appreciate the acoustics, stand beneath the centre of the dome and clap your hands, though the effect is now damped somewhat by the scaffolding.

Over the centuries it was necessary for succeeding Byzantine emperors and Ottoman sultans to rebuild the dome several times, to add buttresses and other supports and to steady the foundations. Current restoration research shows that the original 6th-century mosaic work was extremely fine, but that later 14th-century repairs were done quickly and poorly.

The Ottoman chandeliers, hanging low above the floor, combined their light with the rows of glass oil lamps which lined the balustrades of the gallery and even the walkway at the base of the dome. Imagine them all lit to celebrate some great state occasion, with the smell of incense and the chants of the Orthodox liturgy reverberating through the huge interior space!

Justinian ordered the most precious materials for his church. Note the matched marble panels in the walls, and the breccia columns. The Byzantine emperor was crowned while seated in a throne placed within the Omphalion, the square of inlaid marble in the main floor. The nearby raised platform is an Ottoman addition, as is the *mihrab* (prayer niche), which shows the faithful the direction in which Mecca lies. The large alabaster urns were added by

Sultan Murat III (1574-95) so that worshippers could perform their ritual ablutions here before prayer.

The large 19th-century medallions inscribed with gilt Arabic letters, the work of master calligrapher Mustafa İzzet Efendi, give the names of God (Allah), Muhammed and the early caliphs Ali and Abu Bakr.

The curious, elevated kiosk, screened from public view, is the **Hünkar Mahfili** or Sultan's Loge. Ahmet III (1703-30) had it built so he could come, pray, and go unseen, preserving the imperial mystique.

In the side aisle to the left of the Imperial Door is the 'weeping column', with a copper facing pierced by a hole. Legend has it that those who put their finger in the hole and make a wish will see it come true if the finger emerges moist.

Mosaics Justinian filled his church with fine mosaics. The Byzantine church and state later endured a fierce civil war (726-87 AD) over the question of whether images were biblically correct or not. The debated passage was Exodus 20:4:

> Thou shalt not make unto thee any graven image, or any likeness of anything that is in heaven above, or that is in the earth beneath, or that is in the water under the earth: Thou shalt not bow down thyself to them, nor serve them.

Though the Bible seems clear, images (icons, mosaics, statues) were very popular, and the iconoclasts ('image-breakers') were ultimately defeated. It's interesting to speculate whether iconoclastic Islam, militant and triumphant at this time, had any influence on Byzantine theology.

When the Turks took Constantinople there was no controversy. The Koran repeatedly rails against idolatry, as in Sura 16:

> We sent a Messenger into every nation saying, Serve God and give up idols.

Islamic art is supposed to have no saints' portraits, no pictures of animals, fish or fowl, nor anything else with an immortal soul, and the mosaics had to go. Luckily they were covered with plaster rather than destroyed, and some have been uncovered successfully.

From the floor of Aya Sofya, 9th-century mosaic portraits of St Ignatius the Younger (800s), St John Chrysostom (around 400) and St Ignatius Theodorus of Antioch are visible high up at the base of the northern tympanum (semicircle) beneath the dome. Even better mosaics are in the galleries, reached by a switchback ramp at the northern end of the narthex, and reserved for female worshippers in Byzantine times.

The striking Deesis, in the southern gallery (where the best mosaics are found), dates from the early 14th century. Christ is at the centre, with the Virgin Mary on the left, and John the Baptist on the right.

At the eastern (apse) end of the southern gallery is the famous mosaic portrait of the Empress Zoe (1028-50). When her portrait was done she was 50 years old and newly married (by her dying father's command) to the aged Romanus III Argyrus. Upon Romanus' 'mysterious' death in his bath in 1034, she had his face excised and that of her youthful, virile new husband, Michael IV, put in its place. Eight years later, with Michael dead from an illness contracted on campaign, Zoe and her sister Theodora ruled as empresses in their own right, but did it so badly that it was clear she had to marry again. At the age of 64, Zoe wed an eminent senator who became the third Mr Zoe, Constantine IX Monomachus, whose portrait remains only because he outlived the empress. The inscription reads, 'Constantine, by the Divine Christ, Faithful King of the Romans'.

As you leave the narthex and enter the passage to the outside, turn and look up to see the Madonna and Child, one of the church's finest late 10th-century mosaics, above the door. Constantine the Great, on the left, offers Mary the city of Constantinople; Emperor Justinian, on the right, offers her Sancta Sophia.

Upon exiting the museum, the şadırvan fountain to the right was for Muslim ablutions. Immediately to your left is the church's baptistery, converted after the Conquest to a tomb for sultans Mustafa and Ibrahim. Other tombs are clustered behind it: those of Murat III, Selim II, Mehmet III and various princes. The minarets were added by Mehmet the Conqueror (1451-81), Beyazıt II (1481-1512) and Selim II (1566-74).

Baths of Lady Hürrem (Map 7) Every mosque had a Turkish steam bath nearby. Aya Sofya's is across the road to the left (east) of the park with the fountain. It's the Haseki Hürrem Hamamı, or Turkish baths of Lady Hürrem, built by the great Sinan in 1556 on the site of earlier Byzantine baths, and now fixed up as a government-run carpet gallery and shop, the Turkish Hand-woven Carpets Sale Centre (☎ 511 8192). It's open daily from 9.30 am to 5 pm except Tuesday; admission is free.

Designed as a 'double hamam' with identical baths for men and women, the centre wall dividing the two has now been breached by a small doorway. Both sides have the three traditional rooms: first the square frigidarium for disrobing (on the men's side, this has a pretty marble fountain and stained-glass windows); then the long tepidarium for washing, and finally the octagonal caldarium for sweating and massage. In the caldarium, note the four *eyvan* niches and the four semi-private washing rooms. The *göbektaşı* (hot platform) in the men's bath is inlaid with coloured marble.

The carpet shop, by the way, offers guaranteed quality and fixed prices, but some readers of this book have found its prices quite high.

Sultan Ahmet Camii (Map 7)

There used to be palaces where the Sultan Ahmet Camii (Mosque of Sultan Ahmet or Blue Mosque) now stands. The Byzantine emperors built several of them, stretching from near Aya Sofya all the way to the site of the mosque. You can see a mosaic from one of these palaces, still in place, in the Mosaic Museum (described later).

Sultan Ahmet I (1603-17) set out to build a mosque that would rival and even surpass the achievement of Justinian. He came close to his goal. The Sultan Ahmet Camii is a triumph of harmony, proportion and elegance, and its architect, Mehmet Ağa, achieves the sort of visual experience on the exterior which Aya Sofya has been blessed with on the interior.

As at Aya Sofya, you must approach the Sultan Ahmet Camii properly in order to appreciate its architectural mastery. Don't walk straight from Aya Sofya to the Sultan Ahmet Camii through the crowd of touts. Rather, go out to the middle of the Hippodrome and approach the mosque from its front.

Walk towards the mosque and through the gate in the peripheral wall. Note the small dome atop the gate: this is the motif Mehmet Ağa uses to lift your eyes to heaven. As you walk through the gate, your eyes follow a flight of stairs up to another gate topped by another dome; through this gate is yet another dome, that of the *şadırvan* (ablutions fountain) in the centre of the mosque courtyard. As you ascend the stairs, semi-domes come into view, one after another: first the one over the mosque's main door, then the one above it, and another, and another. Finally the main dome crowns the whole, and your attention is drawn to the sides, where forests of smaller domes reinforce the effect, completed by the minarets, which lift your eyes to the heavens.

The layout of the Sultan Ahmet Camii is classic Ottoman design. The forecourt has an ablutions fountain in its centre. The portico around three sides could be used for prayer, meditation or study during warm weather.

The Sultan Ahmet Camii is such a popular tourist sight that admission is controlled so as to preserve its sacred atmosphere. Only worshippers are admitted through the main door; tourists must use the northern door, and are not admitted at prayer times. At the northern door an attendant will take your shoes; if your clothing is immodest by local standards, you'll be lent a robe. There's no charge for this, but you may be asked to make a donation for the mosque, to which the money will actually go.

Though the stained-glass windows are replacements, they still create the luminous effects of the originals. The semi-domes and the dome are painted in graceful arabesques. The 'blue' of the mosque's name comes from the İznik tiles which line the walls, particularly in the gallery (which is not open to the public).

You can see immediately why the Sultan Ahmet Camii, constructed between 1606 and 1616, more than 1000 years after Aya Sofya, is not as daring as Aya Sofya. Four massive pillars hold up the dome, a less elegant but sturdier solution to the problem.

Note also the imperial loge, covered with marble latticework, to the left; the piece of the sacred Black Stone from the Kaaba in Mecca, embedded in the mihrab; the grandfather clock, useful as prayers must be made at exact times; and the high, elaborate *mahfil* (chair) from which the *imam*, or teacher, gives the sermon on Friday. The *mimber*, or pulpit, is the structure with a curtained doorway at floor level, a flight of steps and a small kiosk topped by a spire. From this mimber of skilfully carved, fine marble, the destruction of the Janissary corps was proclaimed in 1826 (see 'The Janissaries' boxed text earlier).

Mosques built by the great and powerful usually included numerous public-service institutions. Clustered around the Sultan Ahmet Camii were a *medrese* (theological school); an *imaret* (soup kitchen) serving the poor; a hamam so that the faithful could wash on Friday, the holy day; and shops, the rent from which supported the upkeep of the mosque. The *türbe* (tomb) of the mosque's great patron, Sultan Ahmet I, is on the northern side facing the fountain park (open for visits daily except Monday and Tuesday from 9.30 am to 4.30 pm). Buried with Ahmet are his brothers, Sultan Osman II and Sultan Murat IV.

Halı ve Kilim Müzesi (Map 7) Up the stone ramp on the Sultan Ahmet Camii's northern side is the Halı ve Kilim Müzesi (Carpet and Kilim Museum) (☎ 528 5332), with displays of some of the country's finest. It's open from 9 am to 4 pm, closed Sunday and Monday; admission costs US$1.

Büyüksaray Mozaik Müzesi (Map 7) When archaeologists from the University of Ankara and the University of St Andrew's (Scotland) dug at the back (east) of the Sultan Ahmet Camii in the mid-1950s, they uncovered a mosaic pavement dating from early Byzantine times, circa 500 AD. The pavement, filled with wonderful hunting and mythological scenes and emperors' portraits, was a triumphal way which led from the Byzantine emperor's Great Palace, which stood where the Sultan Ahmet Camii now stands, down to the harbour of Boucoleon. The dust and rubble of 1500 years have sunk the pavement considerably below ground level.

Other 5th-century mosaics were saved providentially when Sultan Ahmet had shops built on top of them. The row of shops, called the **Arasta**, was intended to provide rent revenues for the upkeep of the mosque. Now they house numerous souvenir vendors, a little teahouse, and the exit from the Büyüksaray Mozaik Müzesi (Great Palace Mosaic Museum). The museum is open daily except Tuesday from 9 am to 5 pm, for US$1. For the entrance, go halfway along the Arasta and turn east through a passage, then right (south).

After you've paid your admission fee, descend to the walkways around the sunken mosaics. The intricate work is impressive, with hunters, beasts, maidens and swains. Note the ribbon border with heart-shaped leaves which surrounds the mosaic. In the westernmost room is the most colourful and dramatic picture, that of two men in leggings carrying spears and holding off a raging tiger. If you can convince the custodian to wipe the mosaics with a wet cloth, the colours will become much more vivid.

The Hippodrome (Map 7)

The Hippodrome was the centre of Byzantium's life for 1000 years and of Ottoman life for another 400. It was the scene of countless political and military dramas during the long life of this city.

History In Byzantine times, the rival chariot teams of 'Greens' and 'Blues' were politically connected. Support for a team was the same as membership in a political party, and a team victory had important effects on policy. A Byzantine emperor might lose his throne as the result of a post-match riot.

Ottoman sultans kept an eye on activities in the Hippodrome. If things were going badly in the empire, a surly crowd gathering here could signal the start of a disturbance, then a riot, then a revolution. In 1826, the slaughter of the debased and unruly Janissary corps was carried out by the reformer sultan, Mahmut II. Almost a century later, in 1909, there were riots here which caused the downfall of Abdül Hamit II and the repromulgation of the Ottoman constitution.

Though the Hippodrome might be the scene of their downfall, Byzantine emperors and Ottoman sultans outdid one another in beautifying it. Many of the priceless statues carved by ancient masters have disappeared. The soldiers of the Fourth Crusade sacked Constantinople, a Christian ally city, in 1204, tearing all the bronze plates from the stone obelisk at the Hippodrome's southern end in the mistaken belief that they were gold. The crusaders also stole the famous 'quadriga', or team of four horses cast in bronze, which now sits atop the main door to St Mark's Church in Venice.

Monuments Near the northern end of the Hippodrome, the little gazebo in beautiful stonework is actually **Kaiser Wilhelm's fountain**. The German emperor paid a state visit to Abdül Hamit II in 1901, and presented this fountain to the sultan and his people as a token of friendship. According to the Ottoman inscription, the fountain was built in the Hijri (Muslim lunar calendar) year of 1316 (1898-99 AD). The monograms in the stonework are those of Abdül Hamit II and Wilhelm II.

The impressive granite obelisk with hieroglyphs is called the **Obelisk of Theodosius**, carved in Egypt around 1500 BC. According to the hieroglyphs, it was erected in Heliopolis (now a suburb of Cairo) to commemorate the victories of Thutmose III (1504-1450 BC). The Byzantine emperor, Theodosius, had it brought from Egypt to Constantinople in 390 AD. He then had it erected on a marble pedestal engraved with scenes of himself in the midst of various imperial pastimes. Theodosius' marble billboards have weathered badly over the centuries. The magnificent obelisk, spaced above the pedestal by four bronze blocks, is as crisply cut and shiny as when it was carved from the living rock in Upper Egypt 3500 years ago.

South of the obelisk is a strange **spiral column** coming up out of a hole in the ground. It was once much taller and was topped by three serpents' heads. Originally cast to commemorate a victory of the Hellenic confederation over the Persians, it stood in front of the temple of Apollo at Delphi from 478 BC until Constantine the Great had it brought to his new capital city around 330 AD. Though badly bashed up in the Byzantine struggle over the place of images in the church (called the Iconoclastic Controversy), the serpents' heads survived until the early 18th century. Now all that remains of them is one upper jaw in the Archaeological Museum.

The level of the Hippodrome rose over the centuries, as civilisation piled up its dust and refuse here. The obelisk and serpentine column were cleaned out and tidied up by the English troops who occupied the city after the Ottoman defeat in WWI.

No one is quite sure who built the large **rough-stone obelisk** at the southern end of the Hippodrome. All we know is that it was repaired by Constantine VII Porphyrogenetus (913-59 AD), and that the bronze plates were ripped off during the Fourth Crusade.

Türk ve İslam Eserleri Müzesi (Map 7)

The Palace of İbrahim Paşa (1524) is on the western side of the Hippodrome. Now housing the Türk ve İslam Eserleri Müzesi, or Turkish & Islamic Arts Museum (☎ 522 1888), it gives you a good glimpse into the opulent life of the Ottoman upper class in the time of Süleyman the Magnificent. İbrahim Paşa was Süleyman's close friend, son-in-law and grand vizier. His enormous wealth, power and influence on the monarch became so great that others wishing to influence the sultan became envious. After a rival accused İbrahim of disloyalty, Süleyman's favourite, Hürrem Sultan (Roxelana), convinced her husband that İbrahim was a threat. Süleyman had him strangled.

The museum is open from 9 am to 4.30 pm daily; closed on Monday. Admission costs US$2.50. Labels are in Turkish and English. A video show on the 1st floor gives you a quick summary of Turkish history, and explains the sultan's *tuğra* (monogram) and *ferman* (imperial edict). The coffee shop in the museum is a welcome refuge from the press of crowds and touts in the Hippodrome.

Highlights among the exhibits, which date from the 8th and 9th centuries up to the 19th century, are the decorated wooden Koran cases from the high Ottoman period; the calligraphy exhibits, including fermans with tuğras, Turkish miniatures, and illuminated manuscripts. You'll also want to have a look at the *rahles*, or Koran stands, and the many carpets from all periods.

The lower floor of the museum houses ethnographic exhibits including a *kara çadır* (black tent) like those used by nomads in eastern Turkey. Inside the tent is an explanation of nomadic customs, in English. Also here are village looms on which carpets and kilims are woven, and an exhibit of the plants and materials used to make natural textile dyes for the carpets. Perhaps most fascinating are the domestic interiors, including those of a *yurt* (Central Asian felt hut), a village house from Yuntdağ, and a late 19th-century house from Bursa. One display shows women shopping for cloth; another, a scene of daily life in an İstanbul home of the early 20th century.

The buildings behind and beside İbrahim Paşa's palace are İstanbul's law courts and legal administration buildings.

South of the Hippodrome (Map 7)

Take a detour into the district's back streets for a look at a feat of Byzantine engineering and two exquisite small mosques.

Facing south, with the Sultan Ahmet Camii on your left, go to the end of the Hippodrome and turn left, then right, onto Aksakal Sokak. Soon you'll be able to recognise the filled-in arches of the **Sphendoneh**, a feat of Byzantine engineering, on your right. The Sphendoneh supported the southern end of the Hippodrome.

Follow the curve of the street around to the right and onto Kaleci Sokak. The next intersecting street is Şehit Mehmet Paşa Sokak; turn left to the **Küçük Aya Sofya Camii**, or 'Little' Aya Sofya. If the mosque is not open, look around or signal to a boy on the street and the guardian will come with the key.

Justinian and Theodora built this little church sometime between 527 and 536 AD. Inside, the layout and decor are typical of an early Byzantine church, though the building was repaired and expanded several times during its life as a mosque after the Conquest. Repairs and enlargements to convert the church to a mosque were added by the chief white eunuch Hüseyin Ağa around 1500. His tomb is to the left as you enter. The medrese cells are arranged around the mosque's forecourt (compare it to the Sokollu Mehmet Paşa Camii), which is now a park with a teahouse.

Go north on Şehit Mehmet Paşa Sokak, back up the hill to the neighbouring **Sokollu Mehmet Paşa Camii**. This was built during the height of Ottoman architectural development in 1571 by the empire's greatest architect, Sinan. Though named for the grand vizier of the time, it was really sponsored by his wife Esmahan, daughter of Sultan Selim II. Besides its architectural harmony, typical of Sinan's great works, the mosque is unusual because the medrese is not a separate building but actually part of the mosque structure, built around the forecourt (compare the similar plan of the Mihrimah Camii near Edirnekapı, described later in the Western Districts section).

If the mosque is not open, wait for the guardian to appear. When you enter, notice the harmonious architecture, the coloured marble, and the spectacular İznik tiles, some of the best ever made. The mosque contains four fragments from the sacred Black Stone in the Kaaba at Mecca: one above the entrance framed in gold, two in the mimber, and one in the mihrab. The marble pillars by the mihrab revolve if the foundations have been disturbed by earthquake – an ingenious signalling device.

Surrounding the mosque are several ruinous religious buildings, including a ruined Halveti dervish tekke, and an Uzbek tekke for Nakşibendi dervishes.

Walk back up the hill on Suterazisi Sokak to return to the Hippodrome.

South-east of the Sultan Ahmet Camii near the shore is the **Hamamîzade İsmail Dede Efendi Evi Müzesi** (☎ 516 4314), Akbıyık, Ahırkapı Sokak 17, the restored house of Dede Efendi (1778-1846) a famous Ottoman musical composer of the Mevlevi whirling dervish order. The well-restored house gives you a good idea of living conditions among the Ottoman intelligentsia of the 18th and 19th centuries.

Across the street, the modest **Akbıyık Camii** dates from 1453, and is thus one of the oldest mosques in the city.

The Sublime Porte

In Islamic societies, and in other societies with strong clan roots, it was customary for the chief or ruler to adjudicate disputes and grant favours. Petitioners wishing justice or favours would appear at the door of the chief's tent, house, or palace, and await the chance to protest their claims.

When a western ambassador arrived at the sultan's door, or 'porte', he was looked on as just another petitioner asking favours. In response to an embassy, the sultan would often issue a proclamation which began with the words, 'The ambassador of (country) having come to my sublime porte ...' Thus the term 'Sublime Porte' was adopted by European embassies to mean the Ottoman state as personified by the sultan in his palace.

In later centuries, when the grand vizier was the active head of government, ambassadors reported not to the palace but to the grand vizierate, and the term Sublime Porte (or simply 'the Porte') came to mean not the sultan's door but the grand vizierate as functioning head of the Ottoman government.

Yerebatan Saray (Map 7)

On the northern side of Divan Yolu is a little park with a stone pillar rising from it. The pillar is part of an ancient aqueduct. Beneath the park, entered by a doorway on its northern side (on Yerebatan Caddesi) is the Yerebatan Saray (Sunken Palace), or Cistern Basilica (☎ 522 1259). See the 'Yerebatan Saray' colour aside opposite page 192 for more information.

Gülhane Parkı & Sublime Porte (Map 7)

Walk downhill from Yerebatan Saray along Alemdar Caddesi with Aya Sofya on your right. Just past a big tree in the middle of the road, the street turns left, but just in front of you is the arched gateway to Gülhane Parkı.

Before entering the park, look to the left. That bulbous little kiosk built into the park walls at the next street corner is the **Alay Köşkü**, or Parade Kiosk, from which the sultan would watch the periodic parades of troops and trade guilds which commemorated great holidays and military victories.

Across the street from the Alay Köşkü (not quite visible right from the Gülhane gate) is a gate leading into the precincts of what was once the grand vizierate, or Ottoman prime ministry, known in the west as the Sublime Porte. Today the buildings beyond the gate hold various offices of the İstanbul provincial government.

Gülhane Parkı was once the palace park of Topkapı. The over-urbanised crowds pack it at weekends to enjoy its green shade, its small zoo (the camels and Angora goats are the most interesting exhibits), live music, street food and the musty **Tanzimat Müzesi** (Map 7, ☎ 512 6384), open daily from 9 am to 5 pm. 'Tanzimat' (Reorganisation) was the name given to the political and societal reforms planned by Sultan Abdül Mecit in 1839 and carried out through the middle of the 19th century.

At the far (northern) end of the park, up the hill, is a flight of steps used as seats, and a small tea garden – a secret corner good for a few quiet moments.

Archaeological Museums

İstanbul's Arkeoloji Müzeleri (archaeological museum complex), between Gülhane Parkı and Topkapı Sarayı, can be reached by walking up from Gülhane or down from Topkapı's Court of the Janissaries. Admission to the complex (closed Monday) costs US$2.50.

The complex is divided into nine separate exhibit areas which are never all open at the same time due to insufficient staff. The schedule changes from time to time, but presently the İstanbul Arkeoloji Müzesi (Archaeological Museum) (Map 7, ☎ 520 7740) is open most days from 9 am to 4.30 pm (last ticket sold at 4 pm), but the Museum of the Ancient Orient is open only Tuesday to Friday, and the Tiled Kiosk only on Tuesday afternoon.

These museums were the palace collections, formed during the 19th century and added to greatly during the republic. While not immediately as dazzling as Topkapı, they contain a wealth of artefacts from the 50 centuries of Anatolia's history.

The **Eski Şark Eserler Müzesi** (Museum of the Ancient Orient, Map 7) holds the gates of ancient Babylon in the time of Nebuchadnezzar II (604-562 BC), clay tablets bearing Hammurabi's famous law code (in cuneiform, of course), ancient Egyptian scarabs, and artefacts from the Assyrian and Hittite empires. It is a rich collection.

The Ottoman Turkish inscription over the door of the **Arkeoloji Müzesi** reads 'Eser-i Atika Müzesi', or Museum of Ancient Works. The neoclassical building houses an extensive collection of Hellenic, Hellenistic and Roman statuary and sarcophagi. The signs are in Turkish and English.

A Roman statue in archaic style of the daemonic god Bes greets you as you enter. Turn left to see the ancient monolithic basalt sarcophagus of King Tabnit of Egypt, its former occupant having been transferred to a neighbouring glass case. Nearby, the famous marble Alexander sarcophagus, exquisitely carved in high relief, is now known not to have been Alexander's, but is nonetheless impressive as a work of art.

In a long room behind the entrance hall is a mock-up of the facade of the Temple of Athena at Assos (Behramkale). Erected in 525 BC, it was the first and only temple of the Archaic Period designed in the Doric order. The frieze depicted hunting and banquet scenes, and battles of the centaurs. Some parts of the original frieze have been incorporated here; other bits are in the Louvre and in Boston.

On the mezzanine level above the Temple of Athena is an exhibition called 'İstanbul Through the Ages', tracing the city's entire history, concentrating on its most famous buildings and public spaces: Archaic, Hellenistic, Roman, Byzantine and Ottoman.

To the right of the entrance hall are the statuary galleries. In Greek and Roman architecture, sculpture was an important element in the decoration of building facades and public spaces. Artisans at Anatolia's three main sculpture centres – Aphrodisias, Ephesus and Miletus – turned out thousands of beautiful works, the best of which have been collected here and arranged by period: Archaic, Persian, Hellenistic and Roman.

The museum's 2nd and 3rd floors were closed at the time of research for renovation.

The **Çinili Köşk** (Tiled Kiosk, Map 7) of Sultan Mehmet the Conqueror is the oldest surviving nonreligious Turkish building in İstanbul, constructed in 1472 not long after the Conquest. Though once completely covered in fine tile work, only the tile work on the facade remains. The kiosk, once an imperial residence, now houses an excellent collection of Turkish faïence including many good examples of İznik tiles from the period in the 17th and 18th centuries when that city produced the finest coloured tiles in the world.

Divan Yolu (Map 7)

Divan Yolu, the Road to the Imperial Council, is the main thoroughfare of the Old City. Starting from the Hippodrome and Yerebatan Saray on the city's first of seven hills, it heads due west, up another hill, past the Kapalı Çarşı, through Beyazıt Square and past İstanbul University to Aksaray Square. Turning north a bit, it continues to the Topkapı (Cannon Gate) in the ancient city walls. In its progress through the city, its name changes from Divan Yolu to become Yeniçeriler Caddesi, Ordu Caddesi and Turgut Özal (formerly Millet) Caddesi.

This thoroughfare, dating from the early times of Constantinople, was laid out by Roman engineers to connect the city with the Roman roads heading west. The Milion, the great marble milestone from which all distances in Byzantium were measured, is on the southern side of the tall shaft of stones which rises above Yerebatan Saray. The street held its importance in Ottoman times, as Mehmet the Conqueror's first palace was in Beyazıt Square, and his new one, Topkapı, was under construction.

Start from Aya Sofya and the Hippodrome and go up the slope on Divan Yolu. The little **Firuz Ağa Camii** on the left, built in 1491, was commissioned by the chief treasurer to Beyazıt II (1481-1512). The style is the simple one of the early Ottomans: a dome on a square base with a plain porch in front.

Just behind Firuz Ağa Camii are the ruins of the **Palace of Antiochus** (5th century), now mere ruined foundations.

The first major intersection on the right is that with Babıali Caddesi. Turn right onto this street until you reach Nuruosmaniye Caddesi; a block to the right is **Cağaloğlu Square**, once the centre of İstanbul's newspaper and book publishing industry. Most of the newspaper publishers have moved to large, modern buildings outside the city walls, though some of the smaller book publishers survive here. The **Cağaloğlu Hamamı** is just off the square, on the right (see the Entertainment section for details).

If instead you turn left (south) from Divan Yolu, you'll be on Klodfarer Caddesi, named after the Turcophile French novelist Claude Farrère. It leads to a small park beneath which lies the 4th-century Byzantine Philoxenes cistern now called **Binbirdirek**, or 'A Thousand-and-One Columns'. A door in the only building on the park grounds opens onto stairs leading down to the cistern, which, regrettably, has been ruined: ugly, intrusive concrete floors have been built to hold shops, but shopkeepers have refused to rent them because of the dampness. It's a total tragedy. The echoing, gloomy space has been violated and spoiled and lots of money wasted at the same time.

Back on Divan Yolu, the impressive enclosure on the corner of Babıali Caddesi is filled with **tombs** of the Ottoman high and mighty, including several sultans. The first to be built was for Sultan Mahmut II (1808-39), the reforming emperor who wiped out the Janissaries and revamped the Ottoman army. Several of Mahmut's successors, including sultans Abdül Aziz (1861-76) and Abdül Hamit II (1876-1909), are here as well. The tombs are usually open for visits from 10 am to 5 pm (donation requested).

Directly across Divan Yolu from the tombs is a small stone **library** built by the Köprülü family in 1659. The Köprülüs rose to prominence in the mid-17th century and furnished the empire with a succession of grand viziers, generals and grand admirals for centuries. They administered the empire during a time when the scions of the Ottoman dynasty fell well below the standards of Mehmet the Conqueror and Süleyman the Magnificent.

Running south downhill near the library is Piyerloti Caddesi, named after another French Turcophile author. Follow this street for a short distance and look for the large Eminönü Belediye Başkanlığı (Eminönü Municipal Presidency) building on the right. To the right of the main entrance is a doorway with Şerefiye Sarnıçı carved into its lintel which leads to the **Cistern of Theodosius**. Wander in, have the guard turn on the lights, and you can see what Binbirdirek and Yerebatan Saray looked like before being tarted up for tourism.

Back on Divan Yolu, on the corner of Türbedar Sokak is the **Basın Müzesi** (Press Museum), Divan Yolu 84, open from 10 am to 5.30 pm (closed Sunday). Admission is free. The old printing presses will interest some, the lively ***Müze Café*** will interest more as it serves cappuccino (US$1.75), tea (US$0.50), Turkish coffee, sahlep (US$1.25), pastries and light meals of soups, salads and sandwiches.

Stroll a bit further along Divan Yolu. On the left, the curious tomb with wrought-iron grillework on top is that of Köprülü Mehmet Paşa (1575-1661). Across the street, that strange building with a row of streetfront shops is actually an ancient Turkish bath, the **Çemberlitaş Hamamı** (1580). (See Entertainment later in this chapter.)

The derelict, time-worn column rising from a little plaza is one of İstanbul's most ancient and revered monuments. Called **Çemberlitaş** (The Banded Stone or Burnt Column), it was erected by Constantine the Great (324-37 AD) to celebrate the dedication of Constantinople as capital of the Roman Empire in 330. This area was the grand Forum of Constantine, and the column was topped by a statue of the great emperor himself. In an earthquake zone erecting columns can be a risky business. This one has survived, though it needed iron bands for support within a century after it was built. The statue crashed to the ground in a quake almost 1000 years ago.

The little **mosque** nearby is that of Atik Ali Paşa, a eunuch and grand vizier of Beyazıt II.

Beyond Çemberlitaş along Divan Yolu, on the right (northern) side is the cemetery of the Atik Ali Paşa Medresesi. Past the impressive tomb of Grand Vezir Koca Sinan Paşa and to the right is the ***İlesam Lokalı*** (Map 11), a club formed by the enigmatically named Professional Union of Owners of the Works of Science and Literature. Touted as a 'traditional mystic water pipe and tea garden', it almost lives up to its billing. Tables and chairs are set out in the shady cemetery, and low benches covered with kilims in the medrese courtyard. Try a *nargile* (water pipe, US$1) or a glass of tea or cup of coffee. Some of the other patrons may speak some English.

Just on the other side of Bileyciler Sokak from İlesam Lokalı is a similar place, ***Erenler Nargile Salonu***, in the courtyard of the Çorlulu Ali Paşa Medresesi and to the right. Most of the other people in this lofty türbe-like structure will either be absorbed in studying the racing formguide or watching a horse race on television. If a race is running, better leave them to it or you risk becoming *persona non grata*.

Kapalı Çarşı & Nuruosmaniye Camii (Map 12)

İstanbul's Kapalı Çarşı (Covered Market or Grand Bazaar) is 4000 shops, mosques, banks, police stations, restaurants and workshops lining kilometres of streets, open daily except Sunday from 8.30 am to 6.30 pm. Today the main streets are touristy, with touts badgering bus tour groups, but many of the back streets and *hans* (warehouse and workshop courtyards) still serve a local clientele as they have for centuries. Guard your bag and wallet here as purse-snatchers and bag and pocket-slashers are not unknown, especially in the midst of crowds.

Starting from a small *bedesten* (warehouse) built in the time of Mehmet the Conqueror, the bazaar grew to cover a vast area as roofs and walls were extended so that commerce could be conducted comfortably in all weather. Great people built hans, or caravanserais, at the edges of the bazaar so that caravans could bring wealth from all parts of the empire, unload and trade right in the bazaar's precincts. A system of locked gates and doors was provided so that the entire mini-city could be closed up tight at the end of the business day.

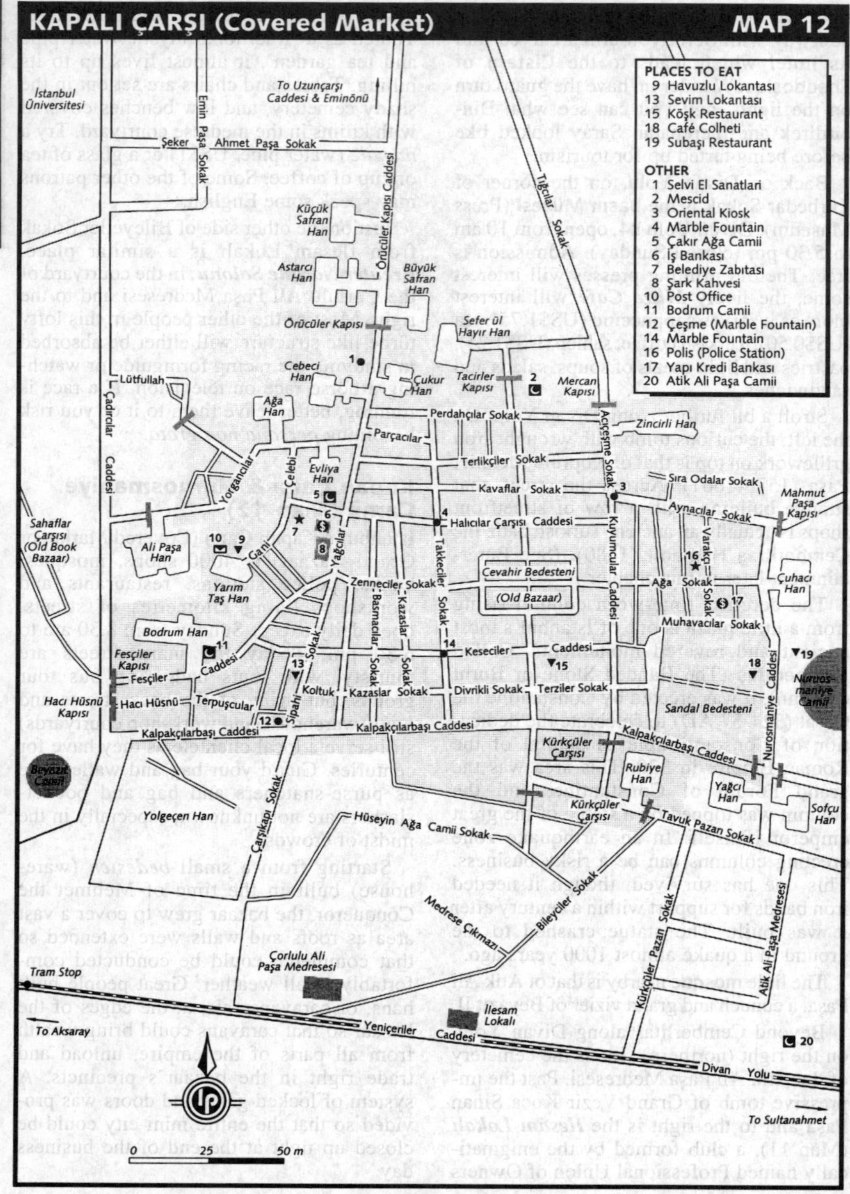
KAPALI ÇARŞI (Covered Market)
MAP 12
PLACES TO EAT
9 Havuzlu Lokantası
13 Sevim Lokantası
15 Köşk Restaurant
18 Café Colheti
19 Subaşı Restaurant
OTHER
1 Selvi El Sanatlari
2 Mescid
3 Oriental Kiosk
4 Marble Fountain
5 Çakır Ağa Camii
6 İş Bankası
7 Belediye Zabıtası
8 Şark Kahvesi
10 Post Office
11 Bodrum Camii
12 Çeşme (Marble Fountain)
14 Marble Fountain
16 Polis (Police Station)
17 Yapı Kredi Bankası
20 Atik Ali Paşa Camii
İstanbul Üniversitesi
To Uzunçarşı Caddesi & Eminönü
Şeker
Ahmet Paşa Sokak
Emin Paşa Sokak
Örücüler Kapısı Caddesi
Tığcılar Sokak
Küçük Safran Han
Astarcı Han
Büyük Safran Han
Örücüler Kapısı
Sefer ül Hayır Han
Cebeci Han
Çukur Han
Tacirler Kapısı
Mercan Kapısı
Lütfullah
Ağa Han
Perdahçılar Sokak
Zincirli Han
Çadırcılar Caddesi
Parçacılar
Terlikçiler Sokak
Yorgancılar
Çelebi
Evliya Han
Kavaflar Sokak
Sıra Odalar Sokak
Aynacılar Sokak
Mahmut Paşa Kapısı
Sahaflar Çarşısı (Old Book Bazaar)
Halıcılar Çarşısı Caddesi
Ali Paşa Han
Gani
Yağcılar
Takkeciler Sokak
Kuyumcular Caddesi
Acıçeşme Sokak
Varakçı Sokak
Cevahir Bedesteni
(Old Bazaar)
Ağa Sokak
Zenneciler Sokak
Yarım Taş Han
Basmacılar Sokak
Kazaslar Sokak
Çuhacı Han
Muhavacılar Sokak
Bodrum Han
Keseciler Caddesi
Fesçiler Kapısı
Fesçiler
Caddesi
Sokak
Nuruosmaniye Camii
Koltuk
Kazaslar Sokak
Divrikli Sokak
Terziler Sokak
Hacı Hüsnü Kapısı
Hacı Hüsnü
Terpuşçular
Sipahi
Sandal Bedesteni
Nurosmaniye Caddesi
Kalpakçılarbaşı Caddesi
Kalpakçılarbaşı Caddesi
Kürkçüler Çarşısı
Kalpakçılarbaşı Caddesi
Rubiye Han
Beyazıt Camii
Yağcı Han
Sofçu Han
Çarşıkapı Sokak
Kürkçüler Çarşısı
Tavuk Pazarı Sokak
Yolgeçen Han
Hüseyin Ağa Camii Sokak
Bileyciler Sokak
Medrese Çıkmazı
Kürkçüler Pazarı Sokak
Atik Ali Paşa Medresesi
Çorlulu Ali Paşa Medresesi
Tram Stop
İlesam Lokalı
To Aksaray
Yeniçeriler Caddesi
Divan Yolu
To Sultanahmet
0
25
50 m

Though tourist shops now crowd the bazaar, it is also still a place where an İstanbullu (citizen of İstanbul) may come to buy a few metres of printed cloth, a gold bangle for a daughter's birthday gift, an antique carpet or a fluffy sheepskin. Whether you want to buy or not, you should see the bazaar.

Turn right off Yeniçeriler Caddesi (the continuation of Divan Yolu) at the Çemberlitaş and walk down Vezir Hanı Caddesi to the big **Nuruosmaniye Camii** built in Ottoman Baroque style between 1748 and 1755 by Mahmut I and his successor Osman III. Though meant to exhibit the sultans' 'modern' taste, the Nuruosmaniye (Light of Osman Mosque) has surprisingly strong echoes of Aya Sofya: the broad, lofty dome, colonnaded mezzanine galleries, Roman-arch-topped windows, and the broad band of calligraphy around the interior. About 1200 years after it was built, Aya Sofya was still 'the one to beat'.

Turn left through the mosque gate to the peaceful, green courtyard with its constant flow of pedestrian traffic heading to and from the bazaar.

Out the other side of the courtyard, you're standing in Çarşıkapı Sokak before the Çarşıkapı (Bazaar Gate), its gold-toned Ottoman armorial emblem restored in 1998.

Enter the gate to **Kalpakçılarbaşı Caddesi**, the bazaar's main east-west street. The bazaar was traditionally ordered according to trade or goods, a plan which was reflected in the street names: Mirror-makers' Street St, Pearl Merchants St, Fez-makers' St. The plan has long since been abandoned, with a few exceptions. **Kuyumcular Caddesi**, the second street on the right as you walk along Kalpakçılarbaşı Caddesi, is still Jewellers St, aglitter with tonnes of gold and gems.

The Sandal Bedesteni, once the city's auction place for used and antique goods, is now filled with shops and a decent cafe.

The Furriers Bazaar (Kürkçüler Çarşısı) now houses shops selling mostly leather garments.

At the centre of the bazaar is the Cevahir Bedesteni (Jewellery Warehouse; signs read 'Old Bazaar'), the original core of the bazaar dating from the 15th century, which can be closed off with its own set of doors. Shops here hold the best of the bazaar's antiques, old coins and jewellery, and silver new and old. The atmospheric **Zincirli Han** at the far (northern) end of Jewellers St, on the right, holds workshops where custom jewellery is made.

Sahaflar Çarşısı (Map 12) Exit the bazaar by walking to the western end of Kalpakçılarbaşı Caddesi. Once outside, turn right onto Çadırcılar Caddesi, then left through a doorway and you'll enter the Sahaflar Çarşısı, or Old Book Bazaar. Go up the steps and along to the shady little courtyard. Actually, the wares in the shops are both new and old; mostly new, though, and mostly in Turkish.

The book bazaar dates from Byzantine times, but today many of its booksellers are members of the Halveti dervish order founded by Hazreti Mehmet Nureddin-i Cerrahi-i Halveti. Their *sema* (religious ceremony) includes chanting from the Koran, praying, and rhythmic dancing and breathing to the accompaniment of classical Turkish liturgical music. As with all dervish orders, the sema is an attempt at close knowledge of and communion with God. The Mevlevi dervishes attempt it by their whirling dance, the Halveti through their circular dance and hyperventilation. Dervishes, unlike Christian monks, live and work in the 'secular' world, and confine their overt dervish activities to periodic meetings for the sema.

Out the northern gate of the Sahaflar Çarşısı is a small daily flea market. On Sunday the flea market has traditionally expanded to fill neighbouring Beyazıt Square. Signs erected by the city forbid street selling, but they are cheerfully ignored by one and all.

Uzunçarşı Caddesi (Map 4) The Kapalı Çarşı is the southern anchor of a vast market district which spills northward downhill to the Golden Horn, ending at Eminönü's Mısır Çarşısı (Egyptian, or

Spice, Bazaar). Mahmutpaşa Yokuşu curves downhill on the district's eastern side, featuring hundreds of clothing shops, but aptly named Uzunçarşı Caddesi (Longmarket Street) goes right through the heart of the market. This makes for an interesting walk, as much as an introduction to Turkish society and traditional commerce as for shopping possibilities. At its northern end you're rewarded with views of the splendid Rüstem Paşa Camii, and the Spice Market.

From the Şark Kahvesi (cafe) in the middle of the bazaar, walk north along Yağcılar and Örücüler Kapısı (Gate of the Darners) Sokak, across Mercan Caddesi (to the left) and Çakmakçılar Yokuşu (to the right), and continue on Uzunçarşı Caddesi.

'Longmarket St' lives up to its name: one long market of woodturners' shops, bakeries for simits, stores selling luggage, guns and hunting equipment, second-hand clothing and hundreds of other products. This is the market district of Tahtakale, where almost anything, legal or illegal, can be purchased.

Uzunçarşı Caddesi ends at the exquisite Rüstem Paşa Camii, perhaps the most beautiful small mosque in the city, which is described in the Eminönü section.

Beyazıt & İstanbul University (Map 6)

The Sahaflar Çarşısı is right next to **Beyazıt Camii** (Map 6), or Mosque of Sultan Beyazıt II (1481-1512). Beyazıt used an exceptional amount of fine stone in his mosque – marble, porphyry, verd antique and rare granite – which he built in 1501-6. The mihrab is simple except for the rich stone columns framing it.

This was the second imperial mosque to be built in the city after Mehmet the Conqueror's Fatih Camii (described later in the Western Districts section), and was the prototype for the great imperial mosques which would come after it. In effect, it is the link between Aya Sofya, which obviously inspired its design, and the great mosques such as the Süleymaniye which are realisations of Aya Sofya's design as fully adapted to Muslim worship.

The main street here, which started out as Divan Yolu, is now called Yeniçeriler Caddesi. It runs past Beyazıt Square, officially called Hürriyet Meydanı (Freedom Square, Map 6), though everyone knows it simply as Beyazıt. Under the Byzantines, this was the largest of the city's many forums, the **Forum of Theodosius**, built by that emperor in 393 AD.

The plaza is backed by the impressive portal of İstanbul University. The grand gates, main building and tall tower of the university were originally built as the Ottoman War Ministry, which explains their grandiose and martial aspect. After the Conquest, Mehmet the Conqueror built his first palace here, a wooden structure which burnt down centuries ago. After Mehmet built Topkapı, he used the Old Palace as a home for ageing harem women.

The small building at the western side of the square, once the medrese of the Beyazıt Camii, is now the **Beyazıt Hat Sanatları Müzesi**, or Beyazıt Calligraphy Museum, open from 9 am to 4 pm (closed Sunday and Monday), for US$0.50 admission. Though you may not be fascinated by Ottoman calligraphy, the building, once a theological college, is certainly worth a look.

Laleli (Map 6) & Aksaray

As you continue west along the main street, which is now named Ordu Caddesi (Army or 'Horde' Ave), notice the huge broken marble columns decorated with stylised oak knot designs on the left-hand side of the road. These were part of the decoration in the Forum of Theodosius. There was a monumental arch near this spot.

A bit further along, on the right, are more university buildings, and beyond them the hotel district of Laleli. Stay on Ordu Caddesi and, just past the big Merit Hotel, you'll come to the **Laleli Camii** (Map 6), an Ottoman Baroque mosque built in 1759-63 by Sultan Mustafa III. The ornate baroque architecture houses a sumptuous interior. Underneath the mosque are shops and a plaza with a fountain, the former producing rent for the upkeep of the mosque.

Continue down the hill on Ordu Caddesi and you will enter the confused clamour of Aksaray Square, once and open grassy plaza, but now a chaos of traffic. **Valide Camii** on the square's north-western side is an ornate late Ottoman work built in 1871 by Valide Sultan Pertevniyal, mother of Sultan Abdül Aziz. When it's clean it looks like a white wedding cake among the drab structures of Aksaray, but exhaust fumes have sullied it and traffic flyovers block a full view.

Süleymaniye Camii (Map 4)

The Süleymaniye Camii, or Mosque of Sultan Süleyman the Magnificent, directly north of (behind) the university, is İstanbul's largest mosque. Facing the university portal in Beyazıt, go to the left along Takvimhane Caddesi to reach the mosque and its tombs, which are open every day.

The Süleymaniye Camii crowns one of İstanbul's hills, dominating the Golden Horn and providing a magnificent landmark for the entire city. This, the grandest of all Turkish mosques, was built between 1550 and 1557 by the greatest, richest, and most powerful of Ottoman sultans, Süleyman I (1520-66), 'The Magnificent'.

Süleyman, the patron of Mimar Sinan, Turkey's greatest architect, was a great builder who restored the mighty walls of Jerusalem (an Ottoman city from 1516) and built countless other monuments throughout his empire. Though the smaller Selimiye Camii in Edirne is generally counted as Sinan's masterpiece, the Süleymaniye is without doubt his grandest work.

Most visitors enter the mosque precincts by a side door. Though this is the most convenient entrance coming from Beyazıt, the effect of entering from the north-western side and through the courtyard, seeing the four towering minarets and the enormous billowing domes, is far better.

Inside, the mosque is breathtaking in its size and pleasing in its simplicity. There is little decoration except for some very fine İznik tiles in the mihrab, gorgeous stained-glass windows done by one İbrahim the Drunkard, and four massive columns, one from Baalbek, one from Alexandria and two from Byzantine palaces in İstanbul. The painted arabesques on the dome are 19th-century additions, recently renewed. Sinan, ever challenged by the technical accomplishments of Aya Sofya, took the floorplan of that church, and here adapted to the requirements of Muslim worship.

The *külliye* (mosque complex) of the Süleymaniye is particularly elaborate, with the full complement of public services: soup kitchen, hostel, hospital, theological college etc. Near the south-eastern wall of the mosque is the cemetery, with the *türbeler* (tombs) of Süleyman and his wife Haseki Hürrem Sultan (known in the West as Roxelana). The tilework in both is superb. In Süleyman's tomb, little jewel-like lights in the dome are surrogate stars. In Hürrem's tomb, the many tile panels of flowers and the delicate stained glass produce a serene, feminine effect.

Places to Eat Several little eateries are in the row of souvenir shops outside the mosque enclosure to the south-west, including the ***Beydağı*** and ***Kanaat Lokantası*** restaurants (Map 4).

For upscale meals, try ***Darüzziyafe*** *(Map 4, ☎ 511 8414, Şifahane Caddesi 6)*, in the *imaret* (soup kitchen) opposite the mosque's main portal. Constructed as part of the külliye, the building has a courtyard surrounded by porches and centred on a fountain. The court is used for dining in fine weather, and several rooms opening onto it have changing art exhibits. The menu is Ottoman with mid-range prices, such as soup for US$2.50, meze plates for US$3, main courses for US$5 to US$8, and full meals for US$10 to US$18.

Şehzadebaşı Caddesi (Map 4)

Bozdoğan Kemeri Walk along Süleymaniye Caddesi, which goes south-west from the mosque, and turn right onto Şehzadebaşı Caddesi. You can see remnants of the high Bozdoğan Kemeri, or Aqueduct of Valens, on the left side of the street. It's not really certain that the aqueduct was constructed by the Emperor Valens (364-78 AD), though we do know it was repaired in 1019, and in later times by several sultans. After the reign of Süleyman the Magnificent, parts of it collapsed, but restoration work was begun in the late 1980s.

Şehzade Camii (Map 6) On the southern side of the aqueduct, beyond the Saraçhane Parkı, is the Şehzade Camii, the Mosque of the Prince. Süleyman had it built between 1544 and 1548 as a memorial to his son Mehmet, who died in 1543. It was the first important mosque to be designed by Mimar Sinan, who spent the first part of his long career as a military architect. Among the many important people buried in tile-encrusted tombs here are Prince Mehmet, his brothers and sisters, and Süleyman's grand viziers, Rüstem Paşa and İbrahim Paşa. The mosque is currently under restoration, which may last for years.

Fatih Anıtı Parkı (Map 1) Across Atatürk Bulvarı from the Şehzade Camii and Saraçhane Parkı is Fatih Anıtı Parkı, the Conqueror Monument Park, so named for the obvious monument to the mounted Mehmet II.

South of the park across Macar Kardeşler Caddesi are a few bits of marble ruin and foundation, all that remains of the gigantic Byzantine church of St Polyeuchtos. The church, built during the reign of Justinian by one of the immensely powerful noble families which the emperor sought to control, is thought to have been a physical symbol of the nobles' challenge to Justinian's authority. Larger and grander than Sancta Sophia, it was the nobles' way of one-upping the head of state. Earthquakes ruined it utterly, however, while Justinian's great church still exists to this day.

Gazanfer Ağa Medresesi (Map 4) If you have a few minutes to spare, have a look at the former medrese of Gazanfer Ağa (1599), now the **İstanbul Karikatür ve Mizah Müzesi** (Cartoon & Humour Museum). It's on the northern side of the Aqueduct of Valens, on the western side of Atatürk Bulvarı. Turkish cartoon artistry has been lively and politically important since Ottoman times, as the changing exhibits show. The pleasant sunny courtyard, with its fountain, grapevines, cafe and toilets, is an excellent place for a rest-stop in warm weather. Hours are from 10 am to 6 pm daily; admission is free.

THE GOLDEN HORN

The Golden Horn, or Haliç, is İstanbul's historic harbour, shipyard and city-centre waterway. Bordered by forests, fields and palaces in the 18th century, by the mid-20th century it had become a poisonous sewer of industrial waste, lined with dilapidated warehouses and workshops.

An ambitious programme of beautification was carried out during the 1980s under Mayor Bedreddin Dalan. The shores were stripped of ugly buildings and landscaped as parks, and the dumping of wastes into the water was curtailed, though as any sentient being with a nose can tell, it was not stopped. The waterway still puts out a powerful stench.

Many of the districts along the Golden Horn are heavy with history. Eminönü, with its Mısır Çarşısı, New Mosque and Galata Bridge, was the main customs entry point and market throughout Byzantine and Ottoman times. Fener (Phanar), to the north-west, is the seat of the Ecumenical Orthodox Patriarchate, and was once home to many wealthy and powerful Ottoman Greeks. Balat and Hasköy were once populated heavily by Jews. Between Balat and Fener stands one of the city's most intriguing architectural curiosities: the Bulgarian Church of St Stephen, constructed completely of cast iron.

A limited ferry service (US$0.50) still operates on the Haliç between Eminönü and Eyüp stopping at Balat, Fener and Kasımpaşa, and boaters still ferry passengers from one side to the other as they have done for centuries, but bus and taxi transport has taken much of the trade from these more leisurely forms of transport.

Eminönü (Map 4)

No doubt you've already seen Eminönü. The view of the Galata Bridge, crowded with ferries and dominated by the Yeni Cami (New Mosque), also called the Pigeon Mosque because of the ever present flocks of these birds, is a favourite for advertisements and magazine articles about İstanbul. The Yeni Cami sits comfortably and serenely in the midst of the bustling Eminönü district as the traffic, both vehicular and pedestrian, swirls around it. Visitors to İstanbul find themselves passing through Eminönü frequently.

Eminönü is the inner city's transportation hub. Bosphorus and Marmara ferries dock here, Galata Bridge traffic passes through, and Sirkeci Station is nearby.

Galata Bridge In Byzantine times the Golden Horn provided a perfect natural harbour for the city's commerce. Suppliers of fresh vegetables and fruits, grain and staple goods set up shop in the harbour. Until a decade ago, their successors in İstanbul's wholesale vegetable, fruit and fish markets performed the same services, in the same area to the west of the Galata Bridge in Eminönü. With the drive to clean up and beautify the Golden Horn, the wholesale markets have been moved to the outskirts of the city.

Until June 1992 the Galata Bridge, which crosses the mouth of the Golden Horn, was a 19th-century structure which floated on pontoons. Ramshackle fish restaurants, teahouses and hookah joints filled the dark recesses beneath the roadway, while an intense stream of pedestrian and vehicular traffic passed above.

The pontoon bridge blocked the natural flow of water and kept the Golden Horn from flushing itself of pollution, so it was replaced by a new bridge which allowed the water to flow.

Still picturesque and interesting is the retail market district which surrounds the Mısır Çarşısı. But before wandering into this maze of market streets, take a look inside the Yeni Cami.

Yeni Cami Only in İstanbul would a 400-year-old mosque be called 'New'. The Yeni Cami (New Mosque) was begun in 1597, commissioned by Valide Sultan Safiye, mother of Sultan Mehmet III (1595-1603). The site was earlier occupied by a community of Karaite Jews, radical dissenters from orthodox Judaism. When the valide sultan decided to build her grand mosque here, the Karaites were moved to Hasköy, a district further up the Golden Horn which still bears traces of their presence.

The valide sultan lost her august position when her son the sultan died, and the mosque was completed six sultans later in 1663 by Valide Sultan Turhan Hatice, mother of Sultan Mehmet IV (1648-87).

In plan, the Yeni Cami is much like the Sultan Ahmet Camii and the Süleymaniye Camii, with a large forecourt and a square sanctuary surmounted by a series of semi-domes crowned by a grand dome. The interior is richly decorated with gold, coloured tiles and carved marble. The mosque and its tiles are 'late', past the period when Ottoman architecture was at its peak. The tilemakers of İznik were turning out slightly inferior products by the late 17th century. Compare these tiles to the ones in the Rüstem Paşa Camii, which are from the high period of İznik tile work.

Mısır Çarşısı The Mısır Çarşısı (MUH-suhr chahr-shuh-shuh, Egyptian Market) is also called the Spice Bazaar because of its many spice shops. A century or two ago, its merchants sold such things as cinnamon, gunpowder, rabbit fat, pine gum, peach-pit powder, sesame seeds, sarsaparilla root, aloe, saffron, liquorice root, donkey's milk and parsley seeds, all to be used as folk remedies.

Gunpowder, for instance, was prescribed as a remedy for haemorrhoids: you'd boil a little gunpowder with the juice of a whole lemon, strain off the liquid, dry the powder and swallow it the next morning with a little water on an empty stomach. It was also supposed to be a good cure for pimples when mixed with crushed garlic. Whatever its values as a pharmaceutical, it was finally banned from the market because the shops in which it was sold kept blowing up.

The market was constructed in the 1660s as part of the Yeni Cami complex, the rents from the shops going to support the mosque's upkeep and charitable activities. These included a school, baths, hospital and fountains.

Enter the market (open Monday to Saturday from 8.30 am to 6.30 pm, closed Sunday) through the big armoured doors which open onto Eminönü Square. Just inside the doors, to the left, is the little stairway which leads up to the Pandeli restaurant, set in delightful tiled rooms, but now quite overpriced.

Strolling through the market, the number of shops selling tourist trinkets is increasing annually, though there are still some shops which sell *baharat* (bah-hah-RAHT, spices) and even a few which specialise in the old-time remedies. Some of the hottest items are bee pollen and royal jelly, used to restore virility (in pre-Viagra days). You'll also see shops selling nuts, candied fruits, chocolate and other snacks. Try some *incir* (een-JEER, figs) or *lokum* (low-KOOM, Turkish delight). Fruit pressed into sheets and dried (looks like leather) is a country snack called *pestil*. It's often made from apricots or mulberries, and is relatively cheap.

When you come to the crossroads within the market, turn left, see the rest of the market, then return to the crossroads and take the street to the right.

Walking east in the market, turn left again at the first opportunity, and you'll leave the bazaar and enter its busy courtyard, backed by the Yeni Cami. This is the city's major market for flowers, plants, seeds and songbirds. There's a toilet to your left, down the stairs, subject to a small fee. To the right, across the courtyard, is the **tomb of Valide Sultan Turhan Hatice**, founder of the Yeni Cami. Buried with her are no less than six other sultans, including her son Mehmet IV, plus dozens of imperial princes and princesses.

Now, back at that crossroads within the bazaar, take the right turn and exit through another set of armoured doors. Just outside the doors is another crossroads of bustling market streets. You can always smell coffee here, because directly across the intersection is the shop of Kurukahveci Mehmet Efendi. To the right, down towards the Golden Horn, is a small fish market and a few butchers' shops. Up to the left, the shops and street pedlars sell mostly household and kitchen items.

Head out the bazaar doors and straight across the intersection to **Hasırcılar Caddesi**, Mat Makers St. Shops along it sell fresh fruits, spices, nuts, condiments, cutlery, coffee, tea, cocoa, hardware and similar retail necessities. The colours, smells, sights and sounds make this one of the liveliest and most interesting streets in the city.

Rüstem Paşa Camii Walk a few short blocks along Hasırcılar Caddesi from the Mısır Çarşısı to the Rüstem Paşa Camii. It's easy to miss as it is not at street level: look for a stone doorway and a flight of steps leading up; there is also a small marble fountain and plaque.

At the top of the steps is a terrace and the mosque's colonnaded porch. You'll notice at once the panels of İznik faïence set into the mosque's facade. The interior is covered in similarly gorgeous tiles, so take off your shoes (women should also cover their head and shoulders) and venture inside. This beautiful mosque was built by Sinan for Rüstem Paşa, son-in-law and grand vizier of Süleyman the Magnificent. Ottoman power, glory, architecture and tilework were all at their zenith when the mosque was built in 1561.

Tahtakale After your visit to the mosque, you might want to spend some more time wandering the streets of this fascinating market quarter. Tahtakale, as it's called, is synonymous with buying and selling anything and everything, including the bizarre and the illegal. Informal money changers here will give you the best rate for your foreign currency, but be careful of conmen and petty thieves if you do change money here.

If you need a goal during your walk, head up the hill (south) on Uzunçarşı Caddesi, which begins near the Rüstem Paşa Camii and ends at the Kapalı Çarşı. (See the earlier Kapalı Çarşı section for a description of Uzunçarşı Caddesi.)

Fener (Map 1)

Fener (fehn-EHR; Greek: *Phanar*, lantern or lighthouse) was the centre of Greek life in Ottoman İstanbul, and is still the seat of the Ecumenical Orthodox patriarchate.

Ecumenical Orthodox Patriarchate

The Ecumenical patriarch is a ceremonial head of the Orthodox churches, though most of the churches – in Greece, Cyprus, Russia and other countries – have their own patriarchs or archbishops who are independent of İstanbul. Nevertheless, the 'sentimental' importance of the patriarchate, here in the city which saw the great era of Byzantine and Orthodox influence, is considerable.

In the eyes of the Turkish government, the patriarch is a Turkish citizen of Greek descent nominated by the church and appointed by the government as an official in the Directorate of Religious Affairs. In this capacity he is the religious leader of the country's Orthodox citizens, known officially as the Greek Patriarch of Fener (Fener Rum Patriği).

The *patrikhane* (patriarchate, or Fener Köşkü) (☎ 527 0323), has been in this district since 1601. To find it, go inland from the Fener ferry dock on the Golden Horn, and ask the way. It's a good idea to phone in advance if you want to enter the compound.

The **Church of St George**, within the patriarchate compound, is a modest place, built in 1720, but the ornate patriarchal throne may date from the last years of Byzantium. In 1941 a disastrous fire destroyed many of the buildings but spared the church.

St Stephen Church The St Stephen Church of the Bulgars, between Balat and Fener on the Golden Horn, is made completely of cast iron, as is most of its interior decoration. The building is unusual, and its history even more so.

The church is not normally open for visits, but well-dressed visitors arriving during or after services on Sunday morning may well be invited in for a look around.

During the 19th century the spirit of ethnic nationalism swept through the Ottoman Empire. Each of the many ethnic groups in the empire wanted to rule its own affairs. Groups identified themselves on the bases of language, religion and racial heritage. This sometimes led to problems, as with the Bulgars.

The Bulgars, originally a Turkic-speaking people, came from the Volga in about 680 AD and overwhelmed the Slavic peoples living in what is today Bulgaria. They adopted the Slavic language and customs, and founded an empire which threatened the power of Byzantium. In the 9th century they were converted to Christianity.

The Orthodox Patriarch, head of the Eastern church in the Ottoman Empire, was an ethnic Greek; in order to retain as much power as possible, the patriarch was opposed to any ethnic divisions within the Orthodox church. He put pressure on the sultan not to allow the Bulgarians, Macedonians and Romanians to establish their own religious groups.

The pressures of nationalism became too great, however, and the sultan was finally forced to recognise some sort of autonomy for the Bulgars. He established not a Bulgarian patriarchate, but an 'exarchate', with a leader supposedly of lesser rank, yet independent of the Greek Orthodox patriarch. In this way the Bulgarians would get their desired ethnic recognition and would get out from under the dominance of the Greeks, but the Greek Patriarch would allegedly suffer no diminution of his glory or power.

St Stephen is the Bulgarian exarch's church. The Gothic structure was cast in Vienna, shipped down the Danube on 100 barges, and assembled in İstanbul in 1871. A duplicate church erected in Vienna, the only other copy, was destroyed by aerial bombing during WWII.

Balat (Map 1)

The quarter on the Golden Horn called Balat used to house a large portion of the city's Jewish population. Spanish Jews driven from their country by the judges of the Spanish Inquisition found refuge in the Ottoman Empire in the late 15th and early 16th centuries. The quincentenary (500th anniversary) of their migration to Ottoman lands was celebrated in 1992. As the sultan recognised, they were a boon to his empire: they brought news of the latest western advances in medicine, clockmaking, ballistics and other sciences and arts of war. The refugees from the Inquisition set up the first printing presses in Turkey. Like all other religious 'nations' within the empire, the Jewish people were governed by a supreme religious leader, the Chief Rabbi, who oversaw their adherence to biblical law and who was responsible to the sultan for their good conduct.

Balat used to have dozens of synagogues, of which two remain for worship: the recently restored Ahrida and the nearby Yanbol. Admission is by reservation only. Contact the Chief Rabbinate (☎ 243 5166 or 293 8794), Yemenici Sokak 23, Tünel, Beyoğlu, for information.

Many of the city's Jewish residents have long since moved to more attractive quarters or emigrated to Europe or Israel, leaving a community of some 12,000 here. There is still one İstanbul newspaper published in Ladino Spanish, the language brought by the immigrants in Renaissance times and still remembered, if not actively spoken, in this city today.

Eyüp (Map 1)

The district of Eyüp, once a village outside the walls, is named for the standard-bearer of the Prophet Muhammed. Many buses and dolmuşes travel along the southern shore of the Golden Horn from Eminönü to Eyüp.

History Eyüp Ensari (Ayoub in Arabic, Job in English) fell in battle here while carrying the banner of Islam during the Arab assault and siege of the city in 674-8 AD. Eyüp had been a friend of the Prophet and a revered member of Islam's early leadership. His tomb and the Eyüp Sultan Camii are very sacred places for most Muslims, ranking after Mecca, Medina and Jerusalem.

Ironically, Eyüp's tomb was first venerated by the Byzantines after the Arab armies withdrew, long before the coming of the Turks.

When Mehmet the Conqueror besieged the city in 1453, the tomb was no doubt known to him, and he undertook to build a grander and more fitting structure to commemorate it. A legend persists, though, that the tomb had been lost and was miraculously rediscovered by Mehmet's Şeyh-ül İslam (Supreme Islamic Judge). Perhaps both are true. If the tomb was known to Mehmet Fatih and his leadership, but not to the common soldiers, it could be used for inspiration – have it miraculously 'rediscovered', and the army would take it as a good omen for the holy war in which they were engaged.

Whatever the truth, the tomb has been a holy place ever since the Conquest. Mehmet had a mosque built here within five years of his victory, and succeeding sultans came to it to be girded with the Sword of Osman, the Ottoman equivalent of coronation, signifying their power and title as *padişah* (king of kings) or sultan. Mehmet's mosque was levelled by an earthquake in 1766, and a new mosque was built on the site by Sultan Selim III in 1800.

Visiting the Tomb & Eyüp Sultan Camii From the open space next to the complex, enter the great doorway to a large courtyard, then to a smaller court shaded by a huge, ancient plane tree. Note the wealth of brilliant İznik tilework on the walls here. To the left, behind the tilework and the gilded grillework, is Eyüp's tomb; to the right is the mosque. Be careful to observe the Islamic proprieties when visiting: decent clothing (no shorts for men), and modest dresses for women, who should also have their head, shoulders and arms covered. Take your shoes off before entering the small tomb enclosure, rich with silver, gold, crystal chandeliers and coloured tiles. Try not to stand in front of those at prayer; act respectfully; don't use a camera.

Across the court from the tomb is the Eyüp Sultan Camii (Mosque of the Great Eyüp). The baroque style of the mosque – gilding, marble, windows, calligraphy and other decoration lavished on it – is elegant and even simple, if baroque can ever be described as simple. The mosque is open long hours every day, free; avoid visiting on Friday and on Muslim holy days, when the mosque and tomb will be even busier than usual with worshippers. For a snack or lunch, there are little pastry shops and snack stands on Kalenderhane Caddesi across from the mosque.

Maşallah

In İstanbul's Egyptian Bazaar you may see a shop which specialises in the white outfits boys wear on the day (usually Sunday) of their *sünnet* (circumcision). The white satin suit is supplemented with a spangled hat and red satin sash emblazoned with the word *Maşallah* (MAH-shah-lah, 'What wonders God has willed!').

Circumcision, or the surgical removal of the foreskin on the penis, is performed on a Turkish Muslim boy when he is between eight and 10 years old, and marks his formal admission into the faith, as does confirmation in Christianity and bar mitzvah in Judaism.

On the day of the operation the boy is dressed in the special suit, visits relatives and friends, and leads a parade – formerly on horseback, now in cars – around his neighbourhood or city attended by musicians and merrymakers. You may come across these lads while visiting the **Eyüp Sultan Camii**, one of Islam's holiest places, where they often stop on the way to their circumcision.

The simple operation, performed in a hospital or clinic in the afternoon, is followed by a celebration with music and feasting. The newly circumcised lad attends, resting in a bed, as his friends and relatives bring him gifts and congratulate him on having entered manhood.

As the Eyüp Sultan Camii is such a sacred place, many important people including lots of grand viziers wanted to be buried in its precincts. Between the mosque-tomb complex and the Golden Horn you will see a virtual 'village' of octagonal tombs. Even those who were not to be buried here left their mark. The Valide Sultan Mihrişah, Queen Mother of Selim III, built important charitable institutions such as schools, baths and soup kitchens. Sokollu Mehmet Paşa, among the greatest of Ottoman grand viziers, donated a hospital which still functions as a medical clinic to this day.

Pierre Loti Café Up the hill to the north of the mosque is a cafe where 'Pierre Loti' (Louis Marie Julien Viaud, 1850-1923) used to sit and admire the city. Loti pursued a distinguished career in the French navy, and at the same time became his country's most celebrated novelist. Though a hard-headed mariner, he was also an inspired and incurable romantic who fell in love with the graceful and mysterious way of life he discovered in Ottoman İstanbul.

Loti set up house in Eyüp for several years and had a love affair, fraught with peril, with a married Turkish woman whom he called Aziyadé (the title of his most romantic and successful novel). He was transferred back to France and forced to leave his mistress and his beloved İstanbul, but he decorated his French home in Ottoman style and begged Aziyadé to flee and join him. Instead, her infidelity was discovered and she 'disappeared'.

Pierre Loti's romantic novels about the daily life of İstanbul under the last sultans introduced millions of European readers to Turkish customs and habits, and helped to counteract the politically inspired Turkophobia then spreading through Europe.

Loti loved the city, the decadent grandeur of the empire, and the fascinating late-medieval customs of a society in decline. When he sat in this cafe, under a shady grapevine, sipping *çay* (tea), he saw a Golden Horn busy with caiques, schooners and a few steam vessels. The water in the Golden Horn was still clean enough to swim in, and the vicinity of the cafe was all pastureland.

The cafe which today bears his name may not have any actual connection to Loti, but it occupies a spot and enjoys a view which he must have enjoyed. It's in a warren of little streets on a promontory surrounded by the Eyüp Sultan Mezarlığı (Cemetery of the Great Eyüp), just north of the Eyüp Sultan Camii. The surest way to find it is to ask the way to the cafe via Karyağdı Sokak. Walk out of the mosque enclosure, turn right, and walk around the mosque complex, keeping it on your right, to the northern side of the mosque until you see the street going uphill into the cemetery marked by a marble sign, 'Maraşal Fevzi Çakmak'. Hike up the steep hill on Karyağdı Sokak for 15 minutes to reach the cafe. If you take a taxi, it will follow a completely different route because of one-way streets. A few snacks and sandwiches are served as well as drinks, and all are relatively expensive.

Hasköy (Map 1)

The northern bank of the Golden Horn is of less historical interest, except for the imperial lodge at Aynalıkavak in the district of Hasköy.

Aynalıkavak Kasrı İstanbul's *kasrs* (imperial lodges) are less impressive but more charming than its many palaces. Designed to a more human scale, kasrs were built not to impress visitors but to please the monarchs themselves. Among the least frequently visited is Aynalıkavak Kasrı, an early 19th-century hunting lodge in the district called Hasköy, on the northern shore of the Golden Horn, about 6km from Karaköy.

Several centuries ago an imperial naval arsenal was established at Kasımpaşa, south-east of Hasköy, and near it a *tersane* (shipyard). The collection of imperial hunting lodges and pleasure kiosks at Hasköy became known as the Tersane Palace, after the shipyard. A wooden palace was built on this site by Sultan Ahmet III (1703-30), and restored by Selim III (1789-1807). What you see today is mostly the work of Sultan Mahmut II (1808-39).

With its Lale Devri (Tulip Period, early 18th century) decoration and Ottoman furnishings, the pavilion is a splendid if dusty place giving a vivid impression of the lifestyle of the Ottoman ruling class at the turn of the 19th century, when Hasköy was a thriving Jewish neighbourhood. Some rooms are furnished in Eastern style, others in the less commodious European style which was then penetrating the sultan's domains.

Selim III composed poetry and music in one of its eastern rooms; futon-like beds were tucked away into cabinets during the day. The Bekleme Salonu (Waiting Room) has the only existing Tulip Period ceiling. Of the European-style rooms, one is filled with sumptuous mother-of-pearl furniture. There's a small museum of Turkish musical instruments on the lower level.

The only practical way to reach it is by taxi (US$3 from Beyoğlu). Tell the driver to take you to the Hasköy Polis Karakolu (police station) or the Şükrü Urcan Spor Tesisleri (athletic facilities), which are well known. A one-minute walk south-east of the Hasköy police station along Kasımpaşa-Hasköy Yolu brings you to Aynalıkavak Kasrı (☎ 250 4094), open from 9.30 am to 4 pm (closed Monday and Thursday); admission costs US$1, with reductions for students. The pavilion's gardens and grounds provide a welcome respite from the city's concrete landscape.

Rahmi M Koç Müzesi The Koç Museum (☎ 256 7153), Hasköy Caddesi 27, Sütlüce, was founded by the current head of the Koç ('coach') industrial group, one of Turkey's most prominent conglomerates, to exhibit artefacts from İstanbul's industrial past. The museum is open from 10 am to 5 pm and is closed on Monday. Admission costs US$2.50.

Exhibits include engines and anything having to do with them: Bosphorus ferryboat parts and machinery, Hotchkiss guns, ship and train models, cars (how about that 1936 Austin roadster!), jet engines, soda machines and even much of the fuselage of 'Hadley's Harem', a US B-24D Liberator bomber which crashed off Antalya in August, 1943.

Café du Levant (☎ *250 8938*), on the museum's grounds, is a surprisingly elegant French bistro serving lunch and dinner at moderate prices daily except Monday.

The museum is located near the northern end of the old Galata Bridge on Kumbarahane Caddesi about 1km north-west of Aynalıkavak Kasrı.

WESTERN DISTRICTS

From early times the heart of this ancient city has been near the tip of Seraglio Point. As the city grew over the centuries, its boundaries moved westward. That process continues.

There are several points of interest further west, and if you have at least four days to tour İstanbul you should be able to see all the centre's essential sights and still have time for these outlying ones. They include the Fatih Camii, the Church of the Holy Saviour in Chora (Kariye Müzesi), famous for its Byzantine mosaics, the Palace of Constantine Porphyrogenetus (Tekfur Saray), several other mosques, the mammoth city walls, and Yedikule, the Fortress of the Seven Towers. You can combine a tour of these sites with some of those in the Golden Horn section easily.

Fatih Camii (Map 1)

The Mosque of the Conqueror is 750m north-west of the Bozdoğan Kemeri, on Fevzi Paşa Caddesi. Catch a dolmuş from Aksaray or Taksim to the city hall (ask for the Belediye Sarayı, behl-eh-DEE-yeh sar-rah-yuh) near the Aqueduct and walk five blocks; or you can catch any bus or dolmuş that has 'Fatih' or 'Edirnekapı' listed on its itinerary board.

The Fatih Camii was the first great imperial mosque to be built in İstanbul following the Conquest. For its location, Sultan Mehmet the Conqueror chose the hilltop site of the ruined Church of the Apostles. The mosque complex, finished in 1470, was enormous, set in extensive grounds, and included in its külliye 15 charitable establishments – religious schools, a hospice for travellers, a caravanserai etc. The mosque you see, however, is not the one he built. The original stood for nearly 300 years before toppling in an earthquake in 1766. It was rebuilt, but destroyed by fire in 1782. The present mosque dates from the reign of Abdül Hamit I, and is on a completely different plan. The exterior of the mosque still bears some of the original decoration; the great doors have been beautifully restored; the interior is of less interest, though there is a simple but beautiful mihrab and plenty of fine stained glass.

Directly behind (south-east) the mosque are the tombs of Mehmet the Conqueror and of his wife Gülbahar, who is rumoured to have been a French princess.

Places to Eat If you need refreshment, cross Fevzi Paşa Caddesi and walk south-east one block to ***Dilek Pastanesi***. The glass cases are a pastry-lover's sweet dream come true. There are other eateries here as well.

Mihrimah Camii (Map 8)

When you're finished at the Fatih Camii, go back to Fevzi Paşa Caddesi and catch a bus or dolmuş headed north-west towards Edirnekapı. Get out just before the city walls at the Mihrimah Camii, a mosque built by Süleyman the Magnificent's favourite daughter, Mihrimah, in the 1560s. Mihrimah married Rüstem Paşa, Süleyman's brilliant and powerful grand vizier (his little tile-covered mosque is down by the Mısır Çarşısı).

The architect of the Mihrimah Camii was Sinan, and the mosque, a departure from his usual style, is among his best works. Visit in the morning to get the full effect of the light streaming through the delicate stained glass windows on the eastern side. The interior space is very light, with 19 windows in each arched tympanum. Virtually every other surface is painted in arabesques, creating a delicate feminine effect. The inevitable earthquakes worked their destruction in 1766 and 1894, and the building is again under restoration, though at the time of research visits were still allowed.

Cross the road from the Mihrimah Camii and, still inside the walls, head north towards the Golden Horn. You'll see signs, and children pointing the way, to the Chora Church.

Chora Church (Map 8)

If we translate the original name *(Chora)* of this building, it would be called 'Church of the Holy Saviour Outside the Walls' or 'in the Country', because the first church on this site was indeed outside the walls built by Constantine the Great. But just as London's church of St Martin-in-the-Fields is hardly surrounded by bucolic scenery these days, the Church of the Holy Saviour was soon engulfed by Byzantine urban sprawl. It was enclosed within the walls built by the Emperor Theodosius II in 413 AD, less than 100 years after Constantine. So the Holy Saviour in the Country was 'in the country' for about 80 years, and has been 'in the city' for 1550 years.

It was not only the environs of the church which changed: for four centuries it served as a mosque (Kariye Camii), and is now a museum, the **Kariye Müzesi** (☎ 523 3009). It is open daily from 9 am to 4 pm, closed Wednesday; admission costs US$3. You reach it by taking any Edirnekapı bus along Fevzi Paşa Caddesi.

The building you see is not the original church-outside-the-walls. Rather, this one was built in the late 11th century, with repairs and restructuring in the following centuries. Virtually all of the interior decoration – the famous mosaics and the less renowned, but equally striking, mural paintings – dates from about 1320. Between 1948 and 1959 the decoration was carefully restored under the auspices of the Byzantine Society of America.

The **mosaics** are breathtaking, and follow the standard Byzantine order. The first ones are those of the dedication, to Christ and to the Virgin Mary. Then come the offertory ones: Theodore Metochites, builder of the church, offering it to Christ. The two small domes of the inner narthex have portraits of all Christ's ancestors back to Adam. A series outlines the Virgin Mary's life, and another, Christ's early years. Yet another series concentrates on Christ's ministry. Various saints and martyrs fill the interstices.

In the nave are three mosaics: of Christ, of the Virgin as Teacher, and of the Dormition (Assumption) of the Blessed Virgin – turn around to see this one, it's over the main door you just entered. The 'infant' in the painting is actually Mary's soul, being held by Jesus, while her body lies 'asleep' on its bier.

South of the nave is the parecclesion, a side chapel built to hold the tombs of the church's founder and his relatives, close friends and associates. The frescoes appropriately deal with the theme of death and resurrection. The striking painting in the apse shows Christ breaking down the gates of Hell and raising Adam and Eve, with saints and kings in attendance.

Places to Eat *Café Kariye* in the plaza in front of the museum serves drinks and snacks. For a full meal, try ***Asitane Restaurant*** in the adjoining Kariye Oteli, where a three-course meal might cost US$10 to US$15.

Tekfur Saray (Map 8)

From Kariye, head west to the city walls, then north again, and you'll soon come to the Palace of Constantine Porphyrogenetus, the Tekfur Saray. It's nominally open on Wednesday, Thursday and Sunday from 9 am to 5 pm, but you can usually just wander in on any day. The caretaker may appear and sell you a ticket for US$0.25.

Though the building is only a shell these days, it is remarkably preserved for a Byzantine palace built in the 14th century. Sacred buildings often survive the ravages of time because they continue to be used even though they may be converted for use in another religion. Secular buildings, however, are often torn down and used as quarries for building materials once their owners die. The

YEREBATAN SARAY

GEOFF STRINGER

Built in 532 AD the Yerebatan Saray, or Basilica Cistern, is the largest surviving Byzantine cistern in İstanbul.

In fact it's not a basilica at all, but an enormous water storage tank constructed by Emperor Justinian the Great (527-65), who was incapable of thinking in small terms. Columns, capitals and plinths from ruined buildings were among those used in its construction.

The cistern, also known as the Sunken Palace, is 70m wide and 140m long and its roof is supported by 336 columns. Two columns in the north-western corner are supported by two blocks carved into Medusa heads. The cistern was used to support part of the city during lengthy sieges. The water was pumped and delivered through nearly 20km of aqueducts from a reservoir near the Black Sea.

The cistern once held 80,000 cubic metres of water but it became a dumping ground for all sorts of junk, as well as corpses. Since it was built the cistern has undergone a number of facelifts most notably in the 18th century and then between 1955 and 1960. The cistern was then cleaned and renovated between 1985 and 1988 by the İstanbul Municipality.

Today, water still drips through the ceiling and you can see coloured lights, listen to recorded western classical music, wander a maze of walkways and spot carp in the water.

Located diagonally across the street from the Aya Sofya, Yerebatan Saray is open from 9 am to 4.30 pm (5.30 pm in summer) and admission costs US$3.50, US$3 for students. The exit from Yerebatan Saray is through a gift shop onto Alemdar Caddesi.

EDDIE GERALD

EDDIE GERALD

A total of 336 columns support the roof of the eerie Yerebatan Saray, a huge water storage tank in Sultanahmet, İstanbul.

ALL PHOTOGRAPHS BY EDDIE GERALD

The best memories of Turkey are often of the generosity and hospitality of the people. From curious children eager to practise their English to the wise old street vendor, Turkey is a friendly country.

Byzantine palaces which once crowded Sultanahmet Square are all gone; so is the great Palace of Blachernae, which adjoined the Tekfur Saray. Only this one remains.

The caretaker may put a ladder against the wall for you, so you can climb up onto the walls for a view of the palace, the city walls, the Golden Horn, and much of the city.

The City Walls (Map 8)

Since being built in the 5th century, the city walls have been breached by hostile forces only twice. The first time was in the 13th century, when Byzantium's 'allies', the armies of the Fourth Crusade, broke through and pillaged the town, deposing the emperor and setting up a king of their own. The second time occured in 1453 under Mehmet the Conqueror. Even though Mehmet was ultimately successful, he was continually frustrated during the siege as the walls withstood admirably even the heaviest bombardments by the largest cannon in existence at the time.

The walls were kept defensible and in good repair until about a century ago, when the development of mighty naval guns made such expense pointless: if İstanbul was going to fall, it would fall to ships firing from the Bosphorus, not to soldiers advancing on the land walls.

During the late 1980s, the city undertook to rebuild the major gates for the delight of tourists. Debates raged in the Turkish newspapers over the style of the reconstruction. Some said the restorations were too theatrical, while others said that if the walls never actually did look like that, perhaps they *should* have. Anyway, the work allows you to imagine what it must have looked like in the Middle Ages. The gates which have been completed include the Topkapı, Mevlanakapı and Belgrat Kapısı.

For a look at the most spectacular of the defences in the walls see Yedikule (later in this section).

Heading north, you can make your way on foot to the Golden Horn at Balat or Ayvansaray and then take a bus, dolmuş or ferry to Eyüp. Otherwise, return to the Kariye Müzesi and make your way through the maze of streets to the Fethiye Camii, built as a Byzantine church.

To walk to the Fethiye Camii from the Kariye Müzesi (eight to 10 minutes), walk back toward Fevzi Paşa Caddesi, but just past the Kariye Oteli turn left downhill on Neşler Sokak, then left at the bottom of the hill around a little mosque, then straight on along a level street and uphill on Fethiye Caddesi. At the top of the slope most traffic goes right, but you go left toward the church, which is visible from this point.

Fethiye Camii (Map 8)

Fethiye Camii (Mosque of the Conquest) was built in the 12th century as the Church of the Theotokos Pammakaristos or the Church of the Joyous Mother of God.

The original monastery church was added to several times over the centuries, then converted to a mosque in 1591 to commemorate Sultan Murat III's victories in Georgia and Azerbaijan. Before its conversion it served as the headquarters of the Ecumenical Orthodox Patriarch (1456-1568); Mehmet the Conqueror visited to discuss theological questions here with Patriarch Gennadios not long after the conquest of the city. They talked things over in the side chapel known as the parecclesion, which has been restored to its former Byzantine splendour; the rest of the building remains a mosque. Unfortunately, the parecclesion is not currently open to visitors, and the church itself is something of a disappointment inside, though the exterior still bears some inscriptions in Greek on the southern side.

From the Fethiye Camii you can continue your explorations by walking south-east to the Selimiye Camii, or north-east to the seat of the Ecumenical Orthodox Patriarchate (see the earlier Golden Horn section). For the Selimiye Camii, continue uphill on Fethiye Caddesi for five minutes, then turn sharp left around the Çarşamba Polis Karakolu (police station), onto Sultan Selim Caddesi, with the mosque visible ahead.

Selimiye Camii (Map 1)

Looming above the central stretch of the Golden Horn is the mosque of Yavuz Selim (Selim I, 1512-20). Sultan Selim 'the Grim' laid the foundations of Ottoman greatness for his son Süleyman the Magnificent.

Approaching the mosque along Sultan Selim Caddesi, you pass the huge Roman **Cistern of Aspar** (Çukur Bostan in Turkish), built by a Gothic general in the Roman army in the 400s AD. After it ceased being used as a cistern, a Turkish village grew up sheltered in its depths. That was recently swept away to make room for spacious sports-grounds and parkland.

Renovations were being carried out at the Selimiye at the time of writing, though it's still possible to visit the mosque.

Though his reign was relatively short, Selim greatly expanded the empire's territory, solidified its institutions and filled its treasury. He came to power by deposing his father, Beyazıt II (1481-1512), who died 'mysteriously' soon thereafter. To avoid any threat to his power, and thus the sort of disastrous civil war which had torn the empire apart in the days before Mehmet the Conqueror, he went about earning his epithet of 'The Grim' by having all his brothers put to death, and in the eight years of his reign he had eight grand viziers beheaded.

But his violence was in the interests of empire-building, at which he was a master. He doubled the empire's extent during his short reign, conquering part of Persia and all of Syria and Egypt. He took from Egypt's decadent, defeated rulers the title Caliph of Islam, which was borne by his successors until 1924. In his spare time he wrote poetry in Persian, the literary language of the time.

The architect of Selim's imperial mosque, finished in 1522 during the reign of his son Süleyman, is unknown. It is especially pretty, with lots of fine, very early İznik tiles (the yellow colour is a clue to their 'earliness'), brilliant stained glass windows, and a shallow dome similar to that of Aya Sofya. Selim's tomb behind the mosque is also very fine, if simple. Among the others buried nearby are Sultan Abdül Mecit (1839-61) and several children of Süleyman the Magnificent. All but one of the buildings in the mosque's külliye have been destroyed, the sole survivor being the small domed primary school.

From the Selimiye you can descend easily to the Fener district on the Golden Horn (see the earlier Golden Horn section) by going down the steps on the northern side of the mosque gardens by the toilets.

Yedikule

If you arrived in İstanbul by train from Europe, or if you rode in from the airport along the seashore, you've already had a glance at Yedikule, the Fortress of the Seven Towers, looming over the southern approaches to the city.

The fortress is open every day from 9.30 am to 5 pm; admission costs US$1.

History Theodosius I built a triumphal arch here in the late 4th century. When the next Theodosius (408-50 AD) built his great land walls, he incorporated the arch. Four of the fortress' seven towers were built as part of Theodosius II's walls; the other three, inside the walls, were added by Mehmet the Conqueror. Under the Byzantines, the great arch became known as the **Golden Gate**, and was used for triumphal state processions into and out of the city. For a time, its gates were indeed plated with gold. The doorway was sealed in the late Byzantine period.

In Ottoman times the fortress was used for defence, as a repository for the imperial treasury, a prison and a place of execution. Diplomatic practice in Renaissance times included throwing into loathsome prisons the ambassadors of countries with which yours didn't get along. For foreign ambassadors to the Sublime Porte, Yedikule was that prison. Latin and German inscriptions still visible in the Ambassadors' Tower bring its history to light. It was also here that Sultan Osman II, a 17-year-old youth, was executed in 1622 during a revolt of the Janissary corps. The kaftan he was wearing when he was murdered is now on display in Topkapı Sarayı's costumes collection.

Visiting Yedikule & the Walls The best view of the city walls and of the fortress is from the **Tower of Sultan Ahmet III**, near the gate in the city wall. It is possible to walk along the land walls from the Sea of Marmara past Yedikule, even making some of the walk atop the walls. The district is not the safest, however, and I know of at least one robbery attempt, so it's best to go in a group and to take the normal precautions.

Down at the shoreline, where the land walls meet the Sea of Marmara, is the **Marble Tower**, once part of a small Byzantine imperial seaside villa.

Getting There & Away Yedikule is a long way from most other sights of interest in İstanbul and involves a special trip. Situated where the great city walls meet the Sea of Marmara, it's accessible by cheap train from Sirkeci. Take any *banliyö* (commuter) train and hop off at Yedikule, then walk around to the entrance in the north-east. You can take bus No 80 ('Yedikule') from Eminönü (on the western side of the Yeni Cami), but the ride may take more than an hour if there's any sort of traffic.

BEYOĞLU (MAP 3)

Beyoğlu (BEY-oh-loo) is fascinating because it holds the architectural evidence of the Ottoman Empire's frantic attempts to modernise and reform itself, and the evidence of the European powers' attempts to undermine and subvert it. The Ottomans were struggling for their very existence as a state; the Europeans were struggling for domination of the entire Middle East so as to control its holy places, its sea lanes through the Suez Canal to India, and especially its oil, already important at that time.

New ideas walked into Ottoman daily life down the streets of Pera which, with Galata, makes up Beyoğlu. The Europeans, who lived in Pera, brought new fashions, machines, arts and manners, and rules for the diplomatic game. The Old City across the Golden Horn was content to sit tight and continue living in the Middle Ages with its oriental bazaars, great mosques and palaces, narrow streets and traditional values. But Pera was to have telephones, underground trains, tramways, electric light and modern municipal government. The sultans followed Pera's lead. From the reign of Abdül Mecit (1839-61) onwards, no sultan lived in Mehmet the Conqueror's palace at Topkapı. Rather, they built opulent European-style palaces along the shores of the Bosphorus to the north.

The easiest way to tour Beyoğlu is to start from its busy nerve-centre: Taksim Square. You can get a dolmuş directly to Taksim from Aksaray or Sirkeci; there are buses as well.

History

Sometimes called the New City, Beyoğlu is 'new' only in a relative sense. There was a settlement on the northern shore of the Golden Horn, near Karaköy Square, before the birth of Jesus. By the time of Theodosius II (408-50 AD), it was large enough to become an official suburb of Constantinople. Theodosius built a fortress here, no doubt to complete the defence system of his great land walls, and called it Galata (gah-LAH-tah), as the suburb was then the home of many Galatians.

During the height of the Byzantine Empire, Galata became a favourite place for foreign trading companies to set up business, and stayed that way until the late 20th century.

The word 'new' actually applies more to Pera, the quarter above Galata, running along the crest of the hill from the Galata Tower to Taksim Square. This was built up only in later Ottoman times.

In the 19th century, the European powers were waiting eagerly for the 'Sick Man of Europe' (the decadent Ottoman Empire) to collapse so that they could grab territory and spheres of influence. All the great colonial powers – the British, Russian, Austro-Hungarian and German empires, France and the kingdom of Italy – maintained lavish embassies and tried to cajole and pressure the Sublime Porte into concessions of territory, trade and influence.

The embassy buildings, as lavish as ever, still stand in Pera. Ironically, most of the great empires which built them collapsed along with that of the Ottomans. Only the British and French survived to grab any of the spoils. Their occupation of Middle Eastern countries under League of Nations 'mandates' has given us the Middle East we have today.

Taksim Square

'Taksim' could mean 'my taxi' in Turkish, but it doesn't; after a look at the square, you may wonder why not. Rather, it is named after the *taksim* (tahk-SEEM, distribution point) in the city's water-conduit system. The main water line from the Belgrade Forest, north of the city, was laid to this point in 1732 by Sultan Mahmut I (1730-54), and the branch lines led from the taksim to all parts of the city.

The first thing you'll notice in the elongated 'square' is the **Atatürk Kültür Merkezi**, or Atatürk Cultural Centre, the large building at the eastern end. In the summertime, during the International İstanbul Music Festival, tickets for the various concerts are on sale in the ticket kiosks here, and numerous performances are staged in its various halls.

At the opposite end of the square, at the centre of the İstiklal Caddesi tram's turnaround, is the **Cumhuriyet Anıtı** (Republic Monument), the work of the Italian sculptor Canonica, finished in 1928. Atatürk, his assistant and successor İsmet İnönü and other revolutionary leaders appear prominently. The monument's purpose was not only to commemorate revolutionary heroes, but also to break down the Ottoman-Islamic prohibition against the making of 'graven images' (there is no figurative painting or sculpture of living beings in traditional Islamic art).

To the south of the square is the luxury Marmara Hotel. To the north is the **Taksim Gezi Yeri**, Taksim Park or Promenade, with the Ceylan Inter-Continental Hotel (Map 2) at its northern end.

North of Taksim (Map 2)

From the roundabout, Cumhuriyet Caddesi (Republic Ave) leads north past streetside cafes and restaurants, banks, travel agencies, airline offices, nightclubs and the Divan and İstanbul Hilton hotels to the districts of Harbiye, Nişantaşı and Şişli.

Askeri Müze About 1km north of Taksim, in Harbiye, is the Askeri Müze (Military Museum) (☎ 248 7115), open from 9 am to noon and 1 to 5 pm, closed Tuesday; admission costs US$1.50. Concerts by the Mehter, the medieval Ottoman Military Band, are at 3 and 4 pm (none on Monday or Tuesday). To reach the museum, walk north out of Taksim Square along the eastern side of Cumhuriyet Caddesi (by Taksim Park) and up past the İstanbul Hilton Hotel. When you come to Harbiye, the point where Valikonağı Caddesi bears right off Cumhuriyet Caddesi, you'll see the gate to the Military Museum on your right.

The museum, within a military complex, has two parts. Entering from Cumhuriyet Caddesi, you'll come first to the new section. On the ground floor are displays of weapons, a *şehit galerisi* (heroes' gallery) with artefacts from fallen Turkish soldiers of many wars, displays of Turkish military uniforms through the ages, and many glass cases holding battle standards, both Turkish and captured. The captured ones include Byzantine, Greek, British, Italian, Austro-Hungarian and Imperial Russian. Perhaps the most interesting of the exhibits are the *sayebanlar*, or imperial pavilions. These luxurious cloth shelters, heavily worked with thread of silver and gold, jewels, precious silks and elegant tracery, were the battle headquarters for sultans during the summer campaign season.

The upper floor of the new section has fascinating displays of Ottoman tents, more imperial pavilions, and a room devoted to Atatürk who was, of course, a famous Ottoman general before he became founder and commander-in-chief of the Turkish republican army, and first president of the Turkish Republic.

To reach the old section of the Military Museum, walk out of the new section, turn right, and walk down the hill past displays of old cannons, then turn right again and climb the steps into the museum. Signs along the way read 'To the Other Departments'. The cannons, by the way, include Gatling guns bearing the sultan's monogram, cast in Vienna.

The old section is where you really feel the spirit of the Ottoman Empire. It has exhibits of armour (including cavalry), uniforms, field furniture made out of weapons (such as chairs with rifles for legs), and a Türk-Alman Dostluk Köşesi (Turco-German Friendship Corner) with mementoes of Turkish and German military collaboration before and during WWI. Some of the exhibits here are truly amazing. My favourites are the great chain that the Byzantines spread across the mouth of the Golden Horn to keep Mehmet the Conqueror's ships out during the battle for Constantinople in 1453; and a tapestry woven by Ottoman sailors (who must have had lots of time on their hands) showing the flags of all of the world's important maritime nations.

Perhaps the best reason to visit the Military Museum is for a little concert by the Mehter. The Mehter, according to historians, was the first true military band in the world. Its purpose was not to make music for dancing, but to precede the conquering Ottoman paşas into vanquished towns, impressing upon the defeated populace that everything was going to be different now. They would march in with a steady, measured pace, turning all together to face the left side of the line of march, then the right side. With tall Janissary headdresses, fierce moustaches, brilliant instruments and even kettledrums, they did their job admirably.

Around Taksim Square (Map 3)

To the south-west, two streets meet before entering the square. Sıraselviler Caddesi goes south and İstiklal Caddesi goes south-west. The famous **taksim**, a small octagonal stone building, is to the south-west of the Republic Monument, just to the right of İstiklal Caddesi.

Nestled in the small triangle formed by the two mentioned streets, rising above the shops and restaurants which hide its foundations, is the **Aya Triada Kilisesi**, or Greek Orthodox Church of the Holy Trinity. If it's open, as it is daily for services, you can visit. Walk along İstiklal Caddesi and turn left.

Now head down İstiklal Caddesi for a look at the vestiges of 19th-century Ottoman life. The restored turn-of-the-century tram runs from Taksim via Galatasaray to Tünel for US$0.35. It's fun, but it runs too seldom to be very useful, and is always crowded.

İstiklal Caddesi (Map 3)

Stretching between Taksim Square and Tünel Square, İstiklal Caddesi (ees-teek-LAHL, Independence Ave) was formerly the Grande Rue de Péra. It was the street with all the smart shops, several large embassies and churches, many impressive residential buildings and a scattering of tea shops and restaurants. Renovation efforts in the past decade have restored much of the street's appeal. It's now a pedestrian way, which in Turkey means that there are fewer cars, not no cars.

As you stroll along İstiklal Caddesi, try to imagine it during its heyday a century ago, peopled by frock-coated merchants and Ottoman officials, European officers in uniform, lightly veiled Turkish women and European women in the latest fashions.

Just out of Taksim Square, the first building on the right is the former French plague hospital (1719), for years used as the **French consulate general** in İstanbul. There's a French library here as well.

İstiklal Caddesi is packed with little restaurants and snack shops, bank branches, clothing stores, itinerant pedlars, shoppers and strollers. If you have the time, take a few detours down the narrow side streets. Any one will reveal glimpses of Beyoğlu life. The street names alone are intriguing: Büyükparmakkapı Sokak, 'Gate of the Thumb St'; Sakızağacı Sokak, 'Pine-Gum Tree St'; Kuloğlu Sokak, 'Slave's Son St'.

The **Tarihi Galatasaray Hamamı** (Historic Galatasaray Turkish Bath) is at Turnacıbaşı Sokak 24, off İstiklal Caddesi just north of Galatasaray Square (see Hamams in the Entertainment section later in this chapter).

Galatasaray Square Halfway along the length of İstiklal Caddesi is Galatasaray (gah-LAH-tah-sah-rah-yee) Square, really an intersection, named after the imperial lycée you can see behind the huge gates on your left. This building once housed the country's most prestigious school, established in its present form by Sultan Abdül Aziz in 1868, who wanted a place where Ottoman youth could hear lectures in both Turkish and French. Across İstiklal Caddesi from the school is the Galatasaray PTT.

Çiçek Pasajı Before coming into Galatasaray square, turn right into the Çiçek Pasajı (chee-CHEHK pah-sah-zhuh, or Flower Passage). This is the inner court of the 19th-century 'Cité de Péra' building which symbolised Pera's growth as a 'modern' European-style city. For years the courtyard held a dozen cheap little restaurant-taverns. In good weather beer barrels were rolled out onto the pavement, marble slabs were balanced on top, wooden stools were put around, and enthusiastic revellers filled the stools as soon as they hit the ground.

In the late 1980s parts of the Cité de Péra building collapsed. In rebuilding, the venerable Çiçek Pasajı was 'beautified', its makeshift barrelhead slabs and stools replaced by comfortable, solid wooden tables and benches, the broken pavement with smooth tiles, all topped by a glass canopy to keep out foul weather. The clientele is better behaved now, and its smattering of adventurous tourists has become a significant proportion. It's a favourite destination for local guys who have picked up foreign women and want to show them some tame İstanbul nightlife. The Çiçek Pasajı is still OK for an evening of beer drinking, food and conversation, but prices are relatively high.

Pick a good place, pull up a stool and order a mug of beer, *beyaz* (pale) or *siyah* (dark). For something stronger, ask for *Bir kadeh rakı* (BEER kah-deh rah-KUH), 'a shot of rakı'. As for food, printed menus, even if you can find them, mean little here. If you already know a few Turkish dishes you like, order them, but ask prices first. Otherwise, the waiter will lead you to the kitchen so you can see what's cooking. As you eat and drink, at least three nearby revellers will want to know where you are from; when you tell them, the response is always *Çok iyi*, 'Very good!'

Many regulars have now abandoned the Çiçek Pasajı to the tourists and their attendant carpet and leather-apparel touts, opting instead to dine at little *meyhanes* (tavernas) deeper in the market.

Balık Pazar Walk out of the courtyard to neighbouring Sahne Sokak, turn right, then look for a little passage off to the left. This is the Avrupa Pasajı, the 'European Passage', a small gallery with marble paving and shops selling upscale goods.

Sahne Sokak is the heart of Beyoğlu's Balık Pazar (fish market), actually a general-purpose market with a good number of fish merchants. Small stands sell *midye* (skewered mussels) fried in hot oil and other stands sell grilled *kokoreç* (lamb intestines packed with more lamb intestines). I recommend the mussels, but get a skewer that's been freshly cooked.

Further up Sahne Sokak, Duduodaları Sokak leads off to the left and down to the British consulate general (more of that in a moment). Continuing along Sahne Sokak, near this junction on your right is the entrance to the Üç Horan Ermeni Kilisesi, the Armenian Church of Three Altars. You can visit if the doors are open.

Past the Armenian church, Sahne Sokak changes names to become Balık Sokak. Leading off to the right from Sahne Sokak is Nevizade Sokak, lined with meyhanes where the old-time life of the Çiçek Pasajı continues, untrammelled by the glossy overlays of tourist İstanbul. Feel free to wander in and have a meal and a drink. (See Galata Saray in Places to Eat – Mid-Range for suggestions.)

Unless you want to continue down the slope among the fishmongers on Balık Sokak, turn back and then right into Duduodaları Sokak, and stroll down this little street past fancy food shops, butchers', bakers', and greengrocers' shops to the British consulate general.

Meşrutiyet Caddesi At the end of the market street you emerge into the light. Right in front of you is Meşrutiyet Caddesi, and on the corner are the huge gates to the **British consulate general**, an Italian palazzo built in 1845 to plans by Sir Charles Barry, architect of London's Houses of Parliament.

Walk past the British consulate general along Meşrutiyet Caddesi, which makes its way down to the Pera Palas Oteli and the American consulate general. Watch for an iron gate and a small passage on the left, leading into a little courtyard with a derelict lamp post in the centre. Enter the courtyard, turn right up the stairs, and you'll discover the Greek Orthodox church **Panaya İsodyon**. It's quiet and very tidy, hidden away in the midst of other buildings. The doors are open to visitors most of the day.

When you've seen the church, go down the stairs *behind* it (not the stairs you came up). Turn right, and just past the church property on the right-hand side you will see the entrance to the ***Yeni Rejans Lokantası***, or New Regency Restaurant. Founded, as legend would have it, by three Russian dancing girls who fled the Russian Revolution, the restaurant is still operated by their Russian-speaking descendants.

This area of Beyoğlu was a favourite with Russian *émigrés* after the revolution. The Yeni Rejans, by the look of it, was a cabaret complete with orchestra loft and grand piano. Lunch and dinner are still served except on Sunday.

When you go out the restaurant door and down the steps, turn right, then left along the narrow alley called Olivia Han Pasajı, and this will bring you back to İstiklal Caddesi.

Back on İstiklal Caddesi Across İstiklal Caddesi notice the large Italian Gothic church behind a fence. The Franciscan **Church of San Antonio di Padua** was founded here in 1725; the red brick building dates from 1913.

Cross over to the church, turn right, and head down İstiklal Caddesi once more. After the church you will pass Eskiçiçekçi Sokak on the left, then Nuriziya Sokak. The third street, a little cul-de-sac, ends at the gates of the **Palais de France**, once the French embassy to the Ottoman sultan. The grounds are extensive and include the chapel of St Louis of the French, founded here in 1581, though the present chapel building dates from the 1830s. You can get a better look at the palace and grounds another way: read on.

A few steps along İstiklal Caddesi brings you to the pretty **Netherlands consulate general**, built as the Dutch embassy in 1855 by the Fossati brothers, formerly architects to the Russian tsar. The first embassy building here dated from 1612. Past the consulate, turn left down the hill on Postacılar Sokak. The **Dutch Chapel**, on the left, is now the home of the Union Church of İstanbul, a multinational English-speaking Protestant congregation.

The narrow street turns right, bringing you face to face with the former Spanish embassy. The little chapel, founded in 1670, is still in use though the embassy is not.

The street then bends left and changes names to become Tomtom Kaptan Sokak. At the foot of the slope, on the right, is the **Palazzo di Venezia**, once the embassy for Venice, now the Italian consulate. Venice was one of the great Mediterranean maritime powers during Renaissance times, and when Venetian and Ottoman fleets were not madly trading with one another, they were locked in ferocious combat.

To the left across the open space is a side gate to the Palais de France. Peek through the gates for another, better view of the old French embassy grounds, then slog back uphill to İstiklal Caddesi.

Continuing along İstiklal Caddesi, the **Church of St Mary Draperis**, built in 1678 and extensively reconstructed in 1789, is behind an iron fence and down a flight of steps.

Past the church, still on the left-hand side, is the grand **Russian consulate general**, once the embassy of the tsars, built in 1837 to designs by the Fossati brothers. After designing several embassies, the Fossatis were employed by the sultan to do extensive restorations on Aya Sofya.

Now take a detour: turn right (north-west) off İstiklal Caddesi along Asmalımescit Caddesi, a narrow, typical Beyoğlu street with some antique shops, food shops, suspect hotels and little eateries. After about 100m the street intersects Meşrutiyet Caddesi. To the left of the intersection is the American Library & Cultural Center (once the Constantinople Club), and just beyond it the Palazzo Corpi (1880), a pretty marble palace built by an Italian shipping magnate and later rented, then sold (1907), to the United States for use as the American embassy to the Sublime Porte. It is now the American consulate general, and heavily fortified.

Pera Palas Oteli The Pera Palas, opposite the American consulate, was built in the 1890s by Georges Nagelmackers, the Belgian entrepreneur who founded the Compagnie Internationale des Wagons-Lits et Grands Express Européens, in 1868. Nagelmackers, who had succeeded in linking Paris and Constantinople by luxury train, found that once he got his esteemed passengers to the Ottoman imperial capital there was no suitable place for them to stay. So he built the hotel here in the section today called Tepebaşı. It opened in the 1890s, advertised as having 'a thoroughly healthy situation, being high up and isolated on all four sides', and 'overlooking the Golden Horn and the whole panorama of Stamboul'.

The Pera Palas Oteli is a grand place, with huge public rooms, a pleasant bar, a good but very pricey pastry shop, and a birdcage lift. Atatürk stayed here; his luxurious suite on the 2nd floor (room No 101) is now a museum, preserved as it was when he used it (ask at the reception desk for a visit). Once you've taken a turn through the hotel, and perhaps had a drink in the Orient Express bar (water: US$1.75) or tea in the salon (not for the budget-minded), walk back up Asmalımescit Caddesi toward İstiklal Caddesi.

Just before reaching İstiklal Caddesi, turn right onto Sofyalı Sokak, a typical Beyoğlu back street with backgammon and bridge parlours, small eateries, and shops selling a range of goods from antiques to electrical equipment.

Near Tünel Square Back on İstiklal Caddesi, you will notice, on your left, the **Swedish consulate**, once the Swedish em-

The Pera Palas

Pera Palas Oteli (*☎ 212-251 4560; fax 251 4089, Meşrutiyet Caddesi 98-100*), fills up regularly with individual tourists and groups looking to relive the great age of Constantinople. The public salons and the bar amply fulfill the need for nostalgia, though the indifferent service and rather mediocre restaurant are strong reminders that things were much better here a century ago.

The Pera's 145 rooms are varied, from the high-ceilinged guest chambers with period furnishings and bathrooms to match, to the cramped upper-floor servants' quarters and uninspiring annexe rooms. Rooms with bath and breakfast are priced at US$120/180 a single/double in the hotel, US$70/100 in the annexe. You're paying a substantial premium for nostalgia here, much of which you can enjoy at huge savings just by having a coffee in the grand salon or a drink at the bar.

The Pera Palas' ingenious promoters claim that Agatha Christie stayed in room 411 when she visited İstanbul, though reliable sources affirm that she stayed at the once prime but now long-gone Tokatlıyan Hotel on İstiklal Caddesi. There's no disputing that the great Atatürk preferred room 101, which, kept just as he used it, is now a museum (ask at reception for admission).

bassy. Across İstiklal Caddesi, the large pillared building was the Russian embassy before the larger building on İstiklal was built.

Beside the Swedish consulate, turn left downhill on Şahkulu Bostanı Sokak. At the base of the slope turn left, then right onto Serdari Ekrem Sokak to find the Anglican sanctuary of **Christ Church** (☎ 244 4828) at No 82. Designed by CE Street (who did London's Law Courts), its cornerstone was laid in 1858 by Lord Stratford de Redcliffe, known as 'The Great Elchi' *(elçi*: ambassador) because of his paramount influence in mid-19th-century Ottoman affairs. The church, dedicated in 1868 as the Crimean Memorial Church, is the largest of the city's Protestant churches. It had fallen into disrepair, but was restored and renamed in the mid-1990s. Ring the bell and with luck the caretaker will admit you for a look around.

Back up on İstiklal Caddesi, the road curves to the right into Tünel Square.

Tünel (Map 3)

İstanbul's short underground railway, the Tünel, was built by French engineers in 1875. It allowed European merchants to get from their offices in Galata to their homes in Pera without hiking up the steep hillside. Until the 1970s, the carriages were of dark wood with numerous coats of bright lacquer, and the Turkish signs within read 'It is Requested that Cigarettes not be Smoked in the Cars'. A modernisation programme replaced them with rubber-tyred Paris metro-type steel trains in which the signs read 'No Smoking'.

The fare is US$0.40. Trains run on the 80-second trip as frequently as necessary during rush hours, about every five or 10 minutes at other times.

In Tünel Square, stop for a rest at *Café Gramofon (☎ 293 0786)*, which echoes the style of the restored trams with its turn-of-the-century decor. Sandwiches, pastries, light meals and drinks are served all day.

Galata Mevlevihanesi Though the main road (İstiklal Caddesi) bears right as you come into Tünel Square, you should continue walking straight along Galip Dede Caddesi. On the left is **Divan Edebiyatı Müzesi** (Museum of Divan Literature) (☎ 245 4141), originally a meeting-place for Mevlevi (Whirling) Dervishes, and preserved as such.

The museum is open from 9.30 am to 5 pm, closed on Tuesday. Admission costs US$0.75. The dervishes still occasionally whirl here, usually on the last Sunday of each month. Ask for current times and dates.

Dervish orders were banned in the early days of the republic because of their ultra-conservative religious politics, and this hall, once the Galata Whirling Dervish Monastery (Galata Mevlevi Tekkesi), now holds exhibits of *hattat* (Arabic calligraphy) and *Divan* (Ottoman) poetry.

The Whirling Dervishes took their name from the great sufi mystic and poet, Celaleddin Rumi (1207-73), called *Mevlana* (Our Leader) by his disciples. Sufis seek mystical communion with God through various means. For Mevlana, it was through a *sema* (ceremony) involving chants, prayers, music and a whirling dance. The whirling induced a trancelike state which made it easier for the mystic to seek spiritual union with God.

The Mevlevi *tarikat* (order), founded in Konya during the 13th century, flourished throughout the Ottoman Empire and survives in Konya even today. Like several other orders, the Mevlevis stressed the unity of humankind before God regardless of creed.

In Ottoman times, the Galata Mevlevihanesi (Whirling Dervish Hall) was open to all who wished to witness the sema, including foreign, non-Muslim visitors.

This modest frame *tekke* (a place where dervishes hold religious meetings and ceremonies) was restored between 1967 and 1972, but the first building here was erected by a high officer in the court of Sultan Beyazıt II in 1491. Its first *şeyh* (sheik, or leader) was Muhammed Şemai Sultan Divani, a grandson of the great Mevlana. The building burned in 1766, but was repaired that same year by Sultan Mustafa III.

In the midst of the city, this former monastery is an oasis of flowers and shady nooks. As you approach the building, notice the little graveyard on the left and its stones with graceful Ottoman inscriptions. The shapes atop the stones reflect the headgear of the deceased, each hat denoting a different religious rank. Note also the tomb of the sheik by the entrance passage, and the şadırvan.

Inside the tekke, the central area was for the whirling sema. Several times a year Mevlevi groups from Konya (now supposedly organised as 'social clubs') come to perform the sema here. In the galleries above, visitors sit and watch. Separate areas were set aside for the orchestra and for female visitors (behind the lattices).

Don't neglect the exhibits of calligraphy, writing instruments and other paraphernalia associated with this highly developed Ottoman art.

Back on Galipdede Caddesi Leaving the mevlevihane, turn left down Galipdede Caddesi, lined with shops selling books, Turkish and European musical instruments, plumbing supplies and cabinetmakers' necessities such as wood veneers. The hillside is covered with winding streets, passageways, alleys of stairs and European-style houses built mostly in the 19th century. There are also older 'Frankish' houses giving a glimpse of what life was like for the European émigrés who came to make their fortunes centuries ago.

A few minutes' walk along Galipdede Caddesi will bring you to Beyoğlu's oldest landmark, the Galata Tower.

Galata Kulesi (Map 4)

The cylindrical Galata Kulesi (Galata Tower) (☎ 245 1160) was the highpoint in the Genoese fortifications of Galata, and has been rebuilt many times. Today it holds a forgettable restaurant/nightclub as well as a memorable **panorama balcony** open to visitors from 9 am to 9 pm every day, for US$1.75 (US$1 on Monday).

In the shadow of the tower are woodworking shops, turners' lathes, workshops making veneer and other materials for interior decoration, and a few dusty antique stores. During the 19th century, Galata had a large Sephardic Jewish population, but most of this community has now moved to more desirable residential areas. **Neve Shalom Synagogue**, a block north-east of the Galata Tower towards Şişhane Square on Büyük Hendek Sokak, was the site of a brutal massacre by Arab gunmen during the summer of 1986. Now restored, it is used by İstanbul's Jewish community for weddings, funerals and other ceremonies.

From the Galata Tower, continue downhill on the street called Yüksek Kaldırım Caddesi to reach Karaköy.

Karaköy (Map 4)

In order to avoid 'contamination' of their way of life, both the later Byzantine emperors and the Ottoman sultans relegated European traders to offices and residences in Galata, now called Karaköy. Under the later Byzantines, Genoese traders took over the town. Today Karaköy still harbours many shipping and commercial offices and banks, as well as small traders.

As you approach the Galata Bridge from Karaköy, the busy ferry docks and also the docks for Mediterranean cruise ships are to your left. To your right is a warren of little streets filled with hardware stores and plumbing-supply houses. Scattered throughout this neighbourhood are Greek and Armenian churches and schools and a large Ashkenazi synagogue, reminders of the time when virtually all of the empire's businesspeople were non-Muslims.

At the far end of the square from the Galata Bridge, at the lower end of Yüksek Kaldırım Caddesi, Voyvoda Caddesi (also called Bankalar Caddesi) leads up a slope to the right towards Şişhane Square. This street was the banking centre during the days of the empire, and many merchant banks still have their headquarters or branches here. The biggest building was that of the Ottoman Bank, now a branch of the Turkish Republic's Central Bank. On 26 August 1896, Armenian revolutionaries seized the Ottoman Bank building and threatened to blow it up if their demands were not met. They were not, and the terrorists surrendered, but anti-Armenian riots following the incident caused many Armenian casualties.

Karaköy has busy bus stops, dolmuş queues and the lower station of the Tünel. To find the Tünel station descend into the hubbub of the square from Yüksek Kaldırım, and turn into the next major street on the right, Yüzbaşı Sabahattin Evren Caddesi. The Tünel station is a few steps along this street, on the right-hand side, in a concrete bunker.

THE BOSPHORUS

The strait which connects the Black Sea and Sea of Marmara, 32km long, from 500m to 3km wide and 50m to 120m (average 60m) deep, has determined the history not only of İstanbul, but of the empires governed from this city.

In Turkish, the strait is the İstanbul Boğazı, from *boğaz*, throat or strait, or Boğaziçi (*iç*, inside or interior: 'within the strait').

The Bosphorus provides a convenient boundary for geographers. As it was a military bottleneck, armies marching from the east tended to stop on the eastern side, and those from the west on the western. So the western side was always more like Europe, the eastern more like Asia. Though the modern Turks think of themselves as Europeans, it is still common to say that Europe ends and Asia begins at the Bosphorus.

Except for the few occasions when the Bosphorus froze solid, crossing it always meant going by boat – until 1973. Late in that year, the Bosphorus Bridge, the fourth-longest in the world, was opened to travellers. For the first time in history there was a firm physical link across the straits from Europe to Asia. (Plans had been drawn up for a bridge during the late years of the Ottoman Empire, but it was never built.)

Traffic was so heavy over the new bridge that it paid for itself in less than a decade. Now there is a second bridge, the Fatih Köprüsü (named after Mehmet the Conqueror, Mehmet Fatih), just north of Rumeli Hisarı. A third bridge, even further north, is planned.

History

Greek legend recounts that Zeus, unfaithful to his wife Hera in an affair with Io, tried to make up for it by turning his former lover into a cow. Hera, for good measure, provided a horsefly to sting Io on the rump and drive her across the strait. In ancient Greek, *bous* is cow, and *poros* is crossing place, giving us Bosphorus: the place where the cow crossed.

From earliest times the Bosphorus has been a maritime road to adventure. It is thought that Ulysses' travels brought him through the Bosphorus. Byzas, founder of Byzantium, explored these waters before the time of Jesus. Mehmet the Conqueror built two mighty fortresses at the strait's narrowest point so as to close it off to allies of the Byzantines. Each spring, enormous Ottoman armies would take several days to cross the Bosphorus on their way to campaigns in Asia. At the end of WWI, the defeated Ottoman capital cowered under the guns of Allied frigates anchored in the strait. When the republic was proclaimed, the last sultan of the Ottoman Empire snuck quietly down to the Bosphorus shore, boarded a launch, and sailed away to exile in a British man-of-war. And when Kemal Atatürk died, his body was taken aboard a man-of-war at Seraglio Point for the first part of its journey to Ankara.

Touring the Bosphorus

You could spend several days exploring the sights of the Bosphorus: five Ottoman palaces, four castles, Üsküdar and other Asian suburbs, and several interesting small towns, but one day will do at a pinch.

The essential feature of any Bosphorus tour is a cruise along the strait, though visits to particular buildings are best done by land, so a trip combining travel by both land and sea is best. Begin your explorations with a ferry cruise for a general view, then visit selected sites by bus and taxi.

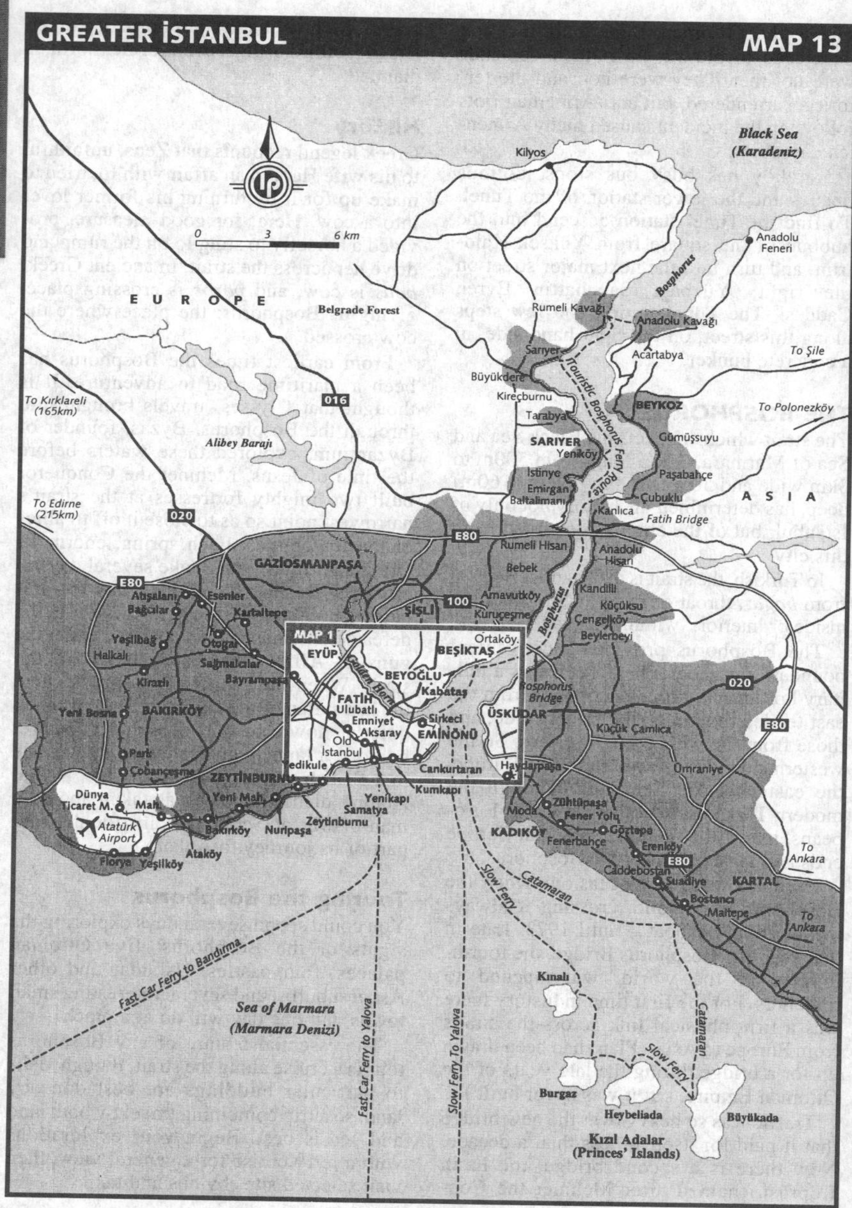

GREATER İSTANBUL
MAP 13
Black Sea
(Karadeniz)
Kilyos
Anadolu Feneri
Bosphorus
0
3
6 km
E U R O P E
Belgrade Forest
Rumeli Kavağı
Anadolu Kavağı
Sarıyer
Acartabya
To Şile
Büyükdere
Kireçburnu
Touristic Bosphorus Ferry Route
BEYKOZ
To Polonezköy
To Kırklareli (165km)
016
Tarabya
SARIYER
Gümüşsuyu
Alibey Barajı
Yeniköy
İstinye
Paşabahçe
Emirgan
Baltalimanı
Çubuklu
A S I A
To Edirne (215km)
020
Kanlıca
Fatih Bridge
E80
Rumeli Hisarı
Anadolu Hisarı
GAZİOSMANPAŞA
Bebek
E80
Kandilli
Atışalanı
Esenler
ŞİŞLİ
100
Arnavutköy
Bağcılar
Kartaltepe
Kuruçeşme
Küçüksu
Çengelköy
Yeşilbağ
Otogar
MAP 1
Ortaköy
Beylerbeyi
Halkalı
Sağmalcılar
EYÜP
BEŞİKTAŞ
Golden Horn
BEYOĞLU
020
Kirazlı
Bayrampaşa
Kabataş
Bosphorus Bridge
FATİH
Yeni Bosna
BAKIRKÖY
Ulubatlı
Sirkeci
ÜSKÜDAR
Emniyet
EMİNÖNÜ
Küçük Çamlıca
E80
Aksaray
Old İstanbul
Park
Çobançeşme
Yedikule
Cankurtaran
Haydarpaşa
Ümraniye
ZEYTİNBURNU
Kumkapı
Dünya Ticaret M.
Mah.
Yeni Mah.
Yenikapı
Samatya
Zühtüpaşa
Moda
Fener Yolu
Zeytinburnu
Atatürk Airport
Bakırköy
Nuripaşa
KADIKÖY
Göztepe
Fenerbahçe
Erenköy
To Ankara
Ataköy
Florya
Yeşilköy
E80
Caddebostan
Suadiye
KARTAL
Catamaran
Slow Ferry
Bostancı
Maltepe
To Ankara
Fast Car Ferry to Bandırma
Kınalı
Sea of Marmara
(Marmara Denizi)
Fast Car Ferry to Yalova
Slow Ferry To Yalova
Catamaran
Slow Ferry
Burgaz
Heybeliada
Büyükada
Kızıl Adalar
(Princes' Islands)

Bosphorus Excursion Ferries Though tour agencies and luxury hotels have private boats for cruises on the Bosphorus, it's considerably cheaper to go on one of the Bosphorus excursion ferries. See Getting Around at the end of this chapter for details on the Bosphorus excursion ferries, and on cross-Bosphorus ferries.

Sights on the European Shore

Coming from Sultanahmet or Eminönü to visit the sights along the Bosphorus, your best bet is to take a bus or dolmuş to reach Dolmabahçe, 1km down the hill from Taksim Square. Bus No 210 from Sultanahmet (near the tourist office) goes up the European shore of the Bosphorus to Emirgan about every two hours; it's a 'luxury' service costing twice the normal fare, but no standees are allowed. Get out at Kabataş.

From Eminönü, bus No 25-E 'Eminönü-Sarıyer' goes all the way up the Bosphorus along the European shore, but shore road traffic is slow (particularly on weekends) so allow several hours for the trip. The bus leaves from 2 Nolu Peron (the 2nd bus rank) in the lot just west of the Yeni Cami.

From Taksim, the downhill walk along İnönü Caddesi to Dolmabahçe is short (about 10 minutes) and pleasant with views of the Bosphorus and the palace. On the right-hand side of İnönü Caddesi just out of Taksim are dolmuşes going to Beşiktaş, which will drop you at Dolmabahçe if you want to ride. There are also dolmuş minibuses to Sarıyer from Mete Caddesi west of the Hotel Gezi, east of the Ceylan Inter-Continental Hotel.

Coming from other parts of the city, catch a bus that goes via Eminönü and/or Karaköy to Beşiktaş. Get off at Kabataş, which is just south of the Dolmabahçe Palace and Mosque.

Dolmabahçe Palace (Map 1) For centuries the padişah, the Ottoman sultan, had been the envy of other monarchs. Cultured, urbane, sensitive, courageous; controller of vast territories, great wealth and invincible armies and navies, he was the Grand Turk. The principalities, city-states and kingdoms of Europe, Africa and the Near East stood in fear of a Turkish conquest. Indeed, the Turks conquered all of North Africa, parts of southern Italy, and eastern Europe to the gates of Vienna. The opulent Dolmabahçe Palace might be seen as an apt expression of this Ottoman glory – but it's not.

History Dolmabahçe was built between 1843 and 1856, when the homeland of the once-mighty padişah had become the 'Sick Man of Europe'. His many peoples, aroused by a wave of European-inspired ethnic nationalism, were in revolt; his wealth was mostly mortgaged to, or under the control of, European bankers; his armies, while still considerable, were obsolescent and disorganised. The western, European, Christian way of life was everywhere ascendant over the eastern, Asian, Muslim one. Attempting to turn the tide, 19th-century sultans turned to European models, modernising the army and civil service, granting autonomy to subject peoples, and adopting – sometimes wholesale – European ways.

The name Dolmabahçe, 'filled-in garden', dates from the reign of Sultan Ahmet I (1607-17), when a little cove here was filled in and an imperial pleasure kiosk built on it. Other wooden buildings followed, but all burned to the ground in 1814. Sultan Abdül Mecit, whose favourite architects were scions of an Armenian family named Balyan, wanted a 'European-style' marble palace. What he got is partly European, partly oriental, and certainly sumptuous and overdecorated.

Admission & Tours The palace is divided into two *bölüm* (sections), the **Selamlık** (ceremonial suites) and the **Harem-Cariyeler** (Harem & Concubines' Quarters). You must take a guided tour, which lasts about an hour, to see either section. Only 1500 people are allowed into each section each day, so it's not a bad idea to reserve your space on a tour in advance. The palace (☎ 227 3441) is open from 9 am to 4 pm, closed Monday and Thursday. Entrance to the Selamlık (ceremonial suites) costs

US$8, to the Harem and Cariyeler (Concubines' Quarters) the same; a ticket good for both sections costs US$14. The charge for a camera is US$8 and US$16 for a video camera. Thus, for a couple with a camera and video to see the entire palace costs a cool US$52. Save the camera fee and check your camera at the door as the palace interior is too dark to photograph (even with fast film) and flash and tripod are not allowed. Rather, take your photos from the small garden near the clock tower, or the park on the southern side of the mosque.

The tourist entrance to the palace is near the ornate clock tower, north of the mosque.

Touring the Palace The tours pass through opulent public and private rooms, into a harem with steel doors, past numerous Sèvres vases and Bohemian chandeliers, and up a staircase with a crystal balustrade. One room was used by the fat Sultan Abdül Aziz (1861-76) who needed an enormously large bed. The magnificent throne room, used in 1877 for the first meeting of the Ottoman Chamber of Deputies, has a chandelier that weighs more than 4000kg.

Don't set your watch by any of the palace clocks, all of which are stopped at 9.05 am, the moment at which Kemal Atatürk died in Dolmabahçe on 10 November 1938. You will be shown the small bedroom which he used during his last days. Each year on 10 November, at 9.05 am, the entire country observes a moment of silence in commemoration of the republic's founder.

Dolmabahçe's **Kuşluk ve Sanat Galerisi** (Aviary & Art Gallery) is on the inland side of the palace, entered from Dolmabahçe Caddesi from 9.30 am to 4 pm (closed Monday and Thursday). This section of the palace, of less interest, was the aviary, with its birdhouse and cages now restored, and a pretty garden restaurant added. The art gallery is a single corridor more than 100m long lined with paintings by 19th and 20th-century Ottoman artists (many of them from the nobility).

When you've finished at the aviary and gallery, turn right (north) and walk for five minutes to the suburb of **Beşiktaş**, sometimes called Barbaros Hayrettin Paşa, to visit the Deniz Müzesi.

Deniz Müzesi (Map 1) The Deniz Müzesi, or Maritime Museum, is on the Bosphorus shore just south of the flyover in Beşiktaş, open from 9 am to 12.30 pm and 1.30 to 5 pm, closed Wednesday and Thursday, for US$1.

History Though the Ottoman Empire is most remembered for its conquests on land, its maritime power was equally impressive. During the reign of Süleyman the Magnificent, the eastern Mediterranean was virtually an Ottoman lake. The sultan's navies cut a swath in the Indian Ocean as well. Sea power was instrumental in the conquests of the Aegean coasts and islands, Egypt and North Africa. Discipline, well-organised supply and good ship design contributed to Ottoman victories.

However the navy, like the army and the government, lagged behind the west in modernisation during the later centuries. The great battle which broke the spell of Ottoman naval invincibility was fought in 1571 at Lepanto, in the Gulf of Patras off the Greek coast. (Cervantes fought on the Christian side and was badly wounded.) Though the Turkish fleet was destroyed, the sultan quickly produced another, partly with the help of rich Greek shipowners who were his subjects.

Exhibits Be sure to see the swift imperial barges in which the sultan, avoiding the primitive roads, would speed up and down the Bosphorus from palace to palace. More than 30m in length but only 2m wide, propelled by 13 banks of oars, the barges were obviously the rocket boats of their day. The ones with latticework screens were for the imperial ladies. There's also a war galley with 24 pairs of oars.

You may also be curious to see a replica of the *Map of Piri Reis*, an early Ottoman map (1513) which purports to show the coasts and continents of the New World. It's assumed that Piri Reis (Captain Piri) got hold of the work of Columbus for his map. The original map is in Topkapı Sarayı; this one is on the wall above the door as you enter the Bosphorus section. Copies are on sale.

Several of the museum's most interesting exhibits are in the garden outside, open to view all the time. Among them is a display of cannons (including Selim the Grim's 21-tonne monster) and a statue of Barbaros Hayrettin Paşa (1483-1546), the famous Turkish admiral known also as Barbarossa who conquered North Africa for Süleyman the Magnificent. The admiral's tomb, designed by Sinan, is close by. Also look for the Allied submarine which was blown up in the Bosphorus and sunk during WWI.

Ihlamur Kasrı Sheltered in a narrow valley inland to the north of Dolmabahçe Palace and the Deniz Müzesi is the Ihlamur Kasrı (UHH-lah-moor kahss-ruh), or Kiosk of the Linden Tree (☎ 261 2991), surrounded by a maze of twisting streets.

The park and its two small, ornate imperial pavilions are open from 9.30 am to 4 pm every day except Monday and Thursday. Admission to the park and kiosks costs US$0.75, or US$0.25 if you just want to stroll through the park. The fee for using a camera is US$6. The easiest way to find this place in its maze of streets is to take a taxi which, from Dolmabahçe or Beşiktaş, should cost only US$1 or so. Bus No 26 (from Dikilitaş to Eminönü) departs from Eminönü, stops at Karaköy, Dolmabahçe and Beşiktaş, before heading inland to the Ihlamur stop and continuing to Dikilitaş (DEE-kee-LEE-tahsh), which is not far past Ihlamur. Other buses are Nos 26A, 26B or 26C.

Once a quiet, sheltered valley neighbouring the imperial palaces of Yıldız and Dolmabahçe, the site now hums with the noise of traffic and is surrounded by modern apartment blocks. It's not difficult to imagine, however, what it must have been like when these two miniature palaces stood here alone, in the midst of a forest. Near the entry gate the park is open and formal, with grassy lawns, ornamental trees and a quiet pool. To the right behind the Maiyet Köşkü the gardens are more rustic, shady and cool, with naturalistic spring-like fountains.

As you enter, look across the pool to find the **Merasim Köşkü**, or Ceremonial Kiosk, built on the orders of Sultan Abdül Mecit between 1849 and 1855 by Nikogos Balyan, of the family of imperial architects. As you enter, a guide will approach to offer you a free guided tour. Up the marble stairway and through the ornate door is the Hall of Mirrors, with crystal from Bohemia and vases from France. The baroque decor includes patterns of shells, flowers, vines, fruits and lots of gold leaf.

The music room which is to the right of the entrance has precious Hereke fabrics on the chairs and an enamelled coal-grate fireplace painted with flowers. Similarly beautiful fireplaces ornament the other rooms; the music room's walls are faux-marble.

The main appliance in the Imperial Water Closet is of the traditional flat Turkish type, demonstrating that in here even the sultan was dethroned.

The room to the left of the entrance was a reception salon with a sofa-throne and faux-marble decoration of plaster with gold flecks. The tour ends downstairs, where displays of photographs show details of the restoration work carried out in the 1980s.

The **Maiyet Köşkü**, or Retinue Kiosk, was for the sultan's suite of attendants, guests or harem. It's now a teahouse serving tea, coffee and snacks (for around US$2). Downstairs are toilets and a shop selling books and other publications.

Çirağan Palace (Map 1) Unsatisfied with the architectural exertions of his predecessor at Dolmabahçe, Sultan Abdül Aziz built his own grand residence at Çirağan on the Bosphorus shore in 1874, only 1km north of Dolmabahçe, replacing an earlier wooden palace. The architect was the self-same Balyan as for Dolmabahçe.

The sultan was deposed, however, and later died in Çirağan under mysterious circumstances. His mentally unstable nephew Murat came to the throne, but was deposed within a year by his brother Abdül Hamit II, who kept Murat a virtual prisoner in Çirağan. Much later (1909) it was the seat of the Ottoman Chamber of Deputies and Senate, but in 1910 it was destroyed by fire, again under suspicious circumstances.

From the Deniz Müzesi and the flyover in Beşiktaş, you can walk north for 10 minutes, or catch a bus or dolmuş heading north along the shore (get out at the Yahya Efendi stop), to reach the entrance to the Çirağan complex. The palace has been restored as part of the luxury Çirağan Palace Hotel Kempinski İstanbul, and is now used for meetings and functions. If you're decently dressed, feel free to enter the grounds, wander around, admire the view and perhaps have refreshments, although prices are breathtaking, even for five-star places.

Just a minute's walk north of Çirağan is the entrance, on the left, to Yıldız Park.

Yıldız Palace & Park (Map 1) Sultan Abdül Hamit II (1876-1909), who succeeded Murat V, also had to build his own palace. He added considerably to the structures built by earlier sultans in Yıldız Park, on the hillside above Çirağan.

The park is open from 9 am to 6 pm every day; admission costs US$1.75 for cars (including taxis); it's free to pedestrians. If you come to the park by taxi, have it take you up the steep slope to the Şale Köşkü. You can visit the other kiosks on the walk down. A taxi from Taksim Square to the top of the hill might cost US$6.

The park, with its kiosks, became derelict, but was beautifully restored by Turing in the 1980s, under lease from the city government. In 1994 the newly elected city government declined to renew the lease, and took over operation of the park.

The park began life as the imperial reserve for Çirağan Palace, but when Abdül Hamit built the **Şale Köşkü**, largest of the park's surviving structures, the park served that palace. Under Abdül Hamit, the park was planted with rare and exotic trees, shrubs and flowers, and was provided with carefully tended paths and a superior electric lighting and drainage system.

Pavilion & Malta Kiosks As you toil up the hill along the road, near the top of the slope to the left you'll see the Çadır Köşkü (Pavilion Kiosk) (☎ 258 9020), an ornate kiosk built between 1865 and 1870 as a place for the sultan to enjoy the view, rest from a walk, and have a cup of tea or coffee. It still serves coffee, tea, soft drinks and snacks, and is the prettiest place in the park for refreshments.

To the right (north) as you hike up the road from the gate are two greenhouses, the **Kış Bahçesi** (Winter Garden) and the **Yeşil Sera** (Green Nursery), and the Malta Köşkü. The Malta Köşkü (☎ 258 9453), restored in 1979, is now a cafe serving refreshments and light meals, but no alcoholic beverages. The view from here is the best in the park, much better than that at the Çadır Köşkü. If you sit down to a plate of grilled lamb and then finish up with something sweet, your bill will come to something like US$8 to US$12.

Also to the right is the **Yıldız Porselen Fabrikası**, or Yıldız Porcelain Factory, constructed to manufacture dinner services for the palace. It still operates and is open to visitors.

Yıldız Şale At the very top of the hill, enclosed by a lofty wall, is the Yıldız Şale (☎ 258 3080), a 'guesthouse/chalet' built in 1882 and expanded in 1898 by Abdül Hamit for use by Kaiser Wilhelm II of Germany during a state visit. You must pay a separate admission fee of US$4 (plus US$8 for a camera or US$16 for a video camera) to see the chalet which is open from 9.30 am to 5 pm, closed Monday and Thursday.

I expect the Kaiser had enough space to move in, as the 'chalet' has 64 rooms. After his imperial guest departed, the sultan became quite attached to his 'rustic' creation, and decided to live here himself, forsaking the more lavish but less well-protected palaces on the Bosphorus shore. Abdül Hamit was paranoid, and for good reason. Fate determined that his fears would come true. He was deposed, left the wooden palace in April 1909 and boarded a special train which took him to house arrest in Ottoman Salonika (today Thessaloniki, Greece). He was later allowed by the Young Turks' government to return to İstanbul and live out his years in Beylerbeyi Palace, on the Asian shore of the Bosphorus.

This place was to be associated with more dolorous history. The last sultan of the Ottoman Empire, Mehmet V (Vahideddin), lived here until, at 6 am on 11 November 1922, he and his first chamberlain, bandmaster, doctor, two secretaries, valet, barber and two eunuchs accompanied by trunks of jewels, gold and antiques, boarded two British Red Cross ambulances for the secret journey to the dockyard at Tophane. There they boarded the British battleship HMS *Malaya* for a trip into exile, ending the Ottoman Empire. On the way to the quay, one of the tyres on the sultan's ambulance went flat; while it was being changed, the 'Shadow of God on Earth' quaked, fearing that he might be discovered.

In the republican era, the Yıldız Şale has served as a guesthouse for visiting heads of state, including Charles de Gaulle, Pope Paul VI and the Empress Soraya of Iran. As you enter the palace, a guide will approach you to give you the tour, which is required.

The first section you visit was the original chalet, built in 1882. The first room on the tour was used by Abdül Hamit's mother for her religious devotions, the second was her guest reception room, with a very fine mosaic tabletop. Then comes a women's resting room, and afterwards a tearoom with furniture marked with a gold star on a blue background, which reminds one that this is the 'star' *(yıldız)* palace.

In 1898 the chalet was expanded, and the older section became the harem (with steel doors), while the new section was the selamlık. In the selamlık are a bathroom with tiles from the Yıldız Porcelain Factory, and several reception rooms, one of which has furniture made by Abdül Hamit himself, an accomplished woodworker. The grand hall of the selamlık is vast, its floor covered by a 7½-tonne Hereke carpet woven just for this room. So huge is the rug that it had to be brought in through the far (northern) wall before the building was finished and the wall was closed.

Merasim Köşkü (Map 1) Other buildings at Yıldız include the Merasim Köşkü, or Ceremonial Kiosk and barracks. Part of the kiosk was restored in 1988 and opened as the **İstanbul Şehir Müzesi** (İstanbul City Museum), open daily except Thursday from 9 am to 4.30 pm; admission costs US$1. It's reached from Barbaros Bulvarı, the road along the southern side of the park, not from within the park itself.

Yıldız Palace Museum The *marangozhane* (carpentry shop) at Yıldız, where Sultan Abdül Hamit II liked to lay down the burdens of rank and office, pick up chisel and malet and make furniture, is now a museum (☎ 258 3080, ext 280); closed Monday and Tuesday. It houses rare porcelain vases and urns, and some of the sultan's joinery projects.

Onward Transport After seeing Yıldız, you can take a bus or dolmuş north to Bebek and Rumeli Hisarı, or return to Beşiktaş to catch a shuttle ferry over to Üsküdar, on the Asian side, in order to continue your sightseeing. The ferries operate every 15 or 20 minutes in each direction, from 6 am to midnight. There are also boats between Üsküdar and Eminönü. Ferries going to Eminönü may bear the sign 'Köprü' (Bridge) meaning the Galata Bridge.

Ortaköy Literally 'middle village', this Bosphorus suburb has an interesting ethnic history in which church, synagogue and mosque coexist peacefully in its narrow streets. Today it is a trendy gathering-place for the young and hip, with art galleries, chic cafe-bars, and boutiques selling antiques, carpets and jewellery. On warm Sundays artisans display their wares in the narrow streets in an impromptu arts-and-crafts show.

The Etz Ahayim Synagogue has been here since 1660, though the current building dates from 1941, when the old one was destroyed by a disastrous fire. The Church of Hagios Phocas (1856) is a short distance north of it.

At the water's edge by the ornate mosque called the **Ortaköy Camii** are terrace cafes (the ***Çadır*** is most popular), their open-air tables enjoying views of the Bosphorus and the mosque. Officially named the Büyük Mecidiye Camii, the eclectic-baroque mosque is the work of Nikogos Balyan, architect of Dolmabahçe Palace, who designed it for Sultan Abdül Mecit in 1854. Within the mosque hang several masterful examples of Arabic calligraphy executed by the sultan, who was an accomplished calligrapher.

Get out of the bus or dolmuş at Osmanzade Sokak, near the doorway to the Etz Ahayim Synagogue, and walk eastward. ***The Wall***, against the wall of the synagogue, is a cafe-bar with dancing and beer for US$1.50, local drinks for US$3. ***İlhami'nin Yeri*** (İlhami's Place) is a full-service restaurant specialising in seafood. Meat, fish and *kalamar* (squid) dishes are usually available for about US$4 to US$8 each. Osmanzade Sokak has other cafe-bar-restaurants as well, including ***Vito Internet Café*** *(☎ 227 6598)*, Osmanzade Sokak 13.

The streets near Osmanzade Sokak have more browsing, eating and drinking possibilities. On Yelkovan Sokak, look for ***Çardak Café***, which sometimes has live music, and ***Café-bar Maria***, which serves cappuccino at outdoor tables in summer, *sıcak şarap* (mulled wine) in winter.

At Hazine Sokak 8, ***Alaturka*** *(☎ 258 7924)* is Ortaköy's most popular cafe-restaurant, serving light meals for about US$4 to US$6 and full meals for around US$8 to US$10.

Fast food follows the crowd, and it has come to Ortaköy in the form of ***Burger King***, in a garish yellow building, and ***McDonald's***. Next to the McDonald's on Mecidiye Köprüsü Sokak is a row of snack stands selling *kumpir*, big baked potatoes topped with various sauces and condiments; *gözleme*, Turkish crêpes; and *midye tavası*, stuffed mussels which can be the equivalent of gastroenteritic hand grenades.

Bebek & Rumeli Hisarı Bebek is a prosperous suburb of İstanbul with a surprising foreign and academic presence because of Boğaziçi Üniversitesi (Bosphorus University). A ring ferry service here joins Bebek with Kanlıca and Anadolu Hisarı on the Asian shore.

About 1.5km north of Bebek centre is Rumeli Hisarı, the Fortress of Europe. The fortress is open from 9.30 am to 5 pm daily; closed on Monday. Admission costs US$2.50, half price on Sundays and holidays. Within the walls are park-like grounds, an open-air theatre and the minaret of a ruined mosque. Stairs lead up to the ramparts and towers.

Here at the narrowest part of the Bosphorus, Mehmet the Conqueror had this fortress built in a mere four months during 1452, in preparation for his planned siege of Byzantine Constantinople. To speed its completion in line with his impatience to conquer Constantinople, Mehmet the Conqueror ordered each of his three viziers to take responsibility for one of the three main towers. If the tower's construction was not completed on schedule, the vizier would pay with his life, or so legend has it. Not surprisingly, the work was completed on time, with Mehmet's three generals competing fiercely with one another to finish.

Once completed, Rumeli Hisarı, in concert with Anadolu Hisarı on the Asian shore just opposite, controlled all traffic on the Bosphorus, and cut the city off from resupply by sea from the north.

The mighty fortress's useful military life lasted less than one year. After the conquest of Constantinople, it was used as a glorified Bosphorus toll booth for a while, then as a barracks, later as a prison, and finally as an open-air theatre, but never again as a fortress.

Above the town you'll notice the New England 19th-century-style architecture of **Boğaziçi Üniversitesi** (Bosphorus University) on a hilltop above the town of Bebek. Founded as Robert College in the mid-19th century by the American Board of Foreign Missions, the college had an important influence on the modernisation of political, social, economic and scientific thought in Turkey. Though donated by the board to the Turkish Republic in the early 1970s, instruction is still in English and Turkish.

Places to Eat Just north of Rumeli Hisarı on the shore is ***Karaca Fish Restaurant*** *(☎ 265 2968, Yahya Kemal Caddesi 10)*, with fine Bosphorus views, excellent fish and squid, and a plethora of mezes; avoid shrimp which are, as everywhere in Turkey, very expensive for what you get. Expect to pay US$12 to US$24 per person with rakı. Cheaper alternatives – snack stands and pastry shops – are nearby.

Getting There & Away From Eminönü, go to the bus lot on the western side of the Yeni Cami, to the 2 Nolu Peron (2nd bus rank) and take bus Nos 22 ('Emirgan'), 22-C ('Bebek') or 25-E ('Sarıyer'). The 22-C goes only as far as Bebek, leaving a 1.5km walk to Rumeli Hisarı, if that's where you're headed.

Emirgan & Yeniköy Each spring a **tulip festival** takes place in Emirgan, a wealthy suburb north of the Fatih Bridge. North of Emirgan, at İstinye, is a cove with a dry dock. A ring ferry service runs from İstinye to Beykoz and Paşabahçe on the Asian shore and may be replaced in the future by a third Bosphorus bridge. Bus No 22 runs from Eminönü to Emirgan and back.

On a point jutting out from the European shore is Yeniköy, first settled in classical times. This place later became a favourite summer resort, indicated by the lavish 19th-century Ottoman *yalı*, or seaside villa, of the one-time grand vizier, Sait Halim Paşa. Fire destroyed many of these luxurious wooden villas. Economics and desire for modern conveniences caused many others to be torn down before preservation laws were promulgated. Today it is against the law to remove a yalı from the Bosphorus – it must either be repaired or rebuilt.

İstinye Continue northward from Bebek, under the Fatih Bridge, to the village of İstinye and the famous restaurant called ***Süreyya*** *(☎ 263 8385, İstinye Caddesi 26)*. The cuisine is superb and varied, with Russian, Turkish and continental dishes to choose from. Chicken Kiev is a favourite here, but there's also good borsch and French-inspired dishes. Hours are from noon to 3 pm and from 8 pm to midnight, reservations are essential, and dinner for two can hit US$100 if you're not careful.

Tarabya Originally called Therapeia for its wonderful climate, the little cove of Tarabya has been a favourite summer watering place for İstanbul's well-to-do for centuries. North of the village are some of the old summer embassies of foreign powers. When the heat and fear of disease increased in the warm months, foreign ambassadors and their staff would retire to palatial residences, complete with lush gardens, on this shore. The region for such embassy residences extended north to the village of Büyükdere.

Places to Eat More than a dozen seafood restaurants ring the cove. Stroll around the cove looking at the various restaurants, their menus and prices. Choose a restaurant that's busy with local people, ask prices, do not accept delivery at your table of dishes that you did not order, check your bill carefully, and you'll have a good meal here.

Possibilities include ***Garaj Restaurant*** *(☎ 262 0032, Yeniköy Caddesi 30)*, on the southern side of the cove, where the fish is fresh and in vast array. A seafood lunch or dinner here costs from US$18 to US$30 and up per person, wine, tax and tip included.

Going north around the cove you can inspect the ***Aquarius 2, Aka Golden Fish, The Grill, La Mer, Palet 1, Hristo, Moni, Filiz, Arif Susam, Köşem Bistro, Yıldızlar*** and ***Sevillanas*** restaurants, all at similar prices.

Büyükdere North of Tarabya is its societal continuation, Büyükdere, notable for a number of churches, summer embassies, and the **Sadberk Hanım Müzesi** (☎ 242 3813), Piyasa Caddesi 27-29, on the shore road just north of the Surp Boğos Armenian Catholic Church (1885).

Named after the wife of the late Mr Vehbi Koç, founder of Turkey's foremost commercial empire, the museum is her private collection of Anatolian antiquities and Ottoman heirlooms. It's open from April to September from 10.30 am to 6 pm and in winter from 10 am to 5 pm; closed on Wednesday all year. Admission costs US$2.50. Plaques are in English and Turkish.

The original museum building, a 12 to 15-minute walk south of the ferry docks in Sarıyer, is the graceful old Bosphorus yalı which was once the summer residence of Manuk Azaryan Efendi, an Ottoman Armenian who was speaker of the upper house of the Ottoman parliament. It houses the most interesting of the museum's collections, which are artefacts and exhibits from Turkey's Islamic past, such as worry beads of solid gold; golden, bejewelled tobacco boxes and watches (one bears the sultan's monogram in diamonds); beautiful Kütahya pottery; even a table that once belonged to Napoleon (he's pictured on it, surrounded by his generals). A number of rooms in the great old house have been arranged and decorated in Ottoman style – the style of the ruling class, obviously. There's a sumptuous maternity room with embroidered cloth and lots of lace, a salon with all the paraphernalia of the Ottoman coffee ceremony, and a third set up as a circumcision room. A display case holds a fine collection of Ottoman spoons (the prime dining utensil) made from tortoiseshell, ebony, ivory and other precious materials.

The collections in the new building include choice artefacts dating from as early as the 6th century BC, and continuing through Roman and Byzantine times. There is also a well-chosen collection of Chinese celadon ware from the 14th to 16th centuries, later Chinese blue-and-white porcelain, and some 18th-century Chinese porcelain made specifically for the Ottoman market.

Sarıyer The villagers of Sarıyer have occupied themselves for most of their history by fishing in the currents of the Bosphorus. Fishing is still a pastime and a livelihood here, and Sarıyer is justly noted for its several good fish restaurants. Turn right as you leave the ferry dock, stay as close to the shore as possible, and you will pass the seabus terminal and then the village's historic fish market, the Balıkçılar Çarşısı, and come to several fish restaurants.

Places to Eat Just north of the Balıkçılar Çarşısı on Cami Arkası Sokak are several small fish restaurants, including ***Deniz Kızı*** (Mermaid), serving seasonal fish for US$6 to US$8 per plate; and also ***Captain's Terrace*** at similar prices. ***Dolphin Class*** has an upstairs dining room with Bosphorus views.

For cheaper meals, try the kebapçıs just inland from these fish restaurants, such as ***A & H Kebapçı***, Yeni Mahalle Caddesi 20, serving *kebap*, *pide* (flat bread) and *lahmacun* (Arabic-style pizza). For afters, ***Hünkar Muhallebicisi***, Mesar Burnu Caddesi 117, has two sweets shops across the street from one another just inland from the seabus terminal. Both have upstairs dining rooms for consumption of your baklava and çay.

North of these places and just south of the town fish market, ***Sirene*** *(☎ 242 2621, Mesar Burnu Caddesi 2)* is upscale with fresh fish laid out on beds of crushed ice, baskets of crabs and lobsters, buckets of shellfish and shrimp. Try to get a table next to the windows overlooking the Bosphorus, choose a fish, determine the price, then order wine, soup or mezes and salads. Expect to pay from US$25 to US$50 per person, all in, for dinners based on fish in season. Lobster and fish out of season can be breathtakingly expensive.

Getting There & Away The Bosphorus excursion ferries from Eminönü (see under Cross-Bosphorus Ferries in the Getting Around section at the end of this chapter) stop at Sarıyer on both the outbound and return voyages. There is a seabus service to the city centre as well.

From 7.15 am to 11 pm, 17 ferries a day cross the Bosphorus (US$0.50) from Sarıyer to Anadolu Kavağı on the Asian side, some stopping at Rumeli Kavağı as well.

Most of Sarıyer's dolmuş and bus stops are near or 500m inland from the small mosque by the fish restaurants. Dolmuş minibuses link Taksim Square via Dolmabahçe, Beşiktaş, Levent, Mecidiyeköy and Maslak to Sarıyer (US$1). The stop (Map 2) in Taksim is on Mete Caddesi, east of the Ceylan Inter-Continental hotel.

Heading north, city buses to Kilyos (US$0.40) depart from beside the mosque; dolmuşes to Kilyos (US$0.50) depart from a stop 600m inland along Sular Caddesi. The trip takes less than half an hour.

Heading south, it's easy enough to get back to Taksim Square by dolmuş (the stop is on Sular Caddesi 500m inland from the mosque); other dolmuş services also head south along the shore for a few kilometres before turning inland, like the Taksim service, at Büyükdere, Tarabya or İstinye to reach their destinations. Thus they are of little use if you want to stop at Rumeli Hisarı, Bebek, Ortaköy, Yıldız Parkı or Çirağan Palace on your trip south.

Bus Nos 25-A, 'Rumelikavağı-Beşiktaş', and 25-E, 'Sarıyer-Eminönü', are the exceptions, driving along the shore road via Bebek and Rumeli Hisarı back to the Golden Horn in a few hours. But this shore service is infrequent compared to the inland services, as the narrow shore road, busy with traffic, takes much longer than the inland route.

If you're in doubt as to whether a vehicle follows the shore all the way south, say 'Sahilden mi gidiyor?' (sah-heel-DEHN mee gee-dee-yohr, 'Does it go along the shore?') to the driver. If he says 'Yukarıdan' (yoo-kah-ruh-DAHN, 'Via the heights') you'll know it goes inland, not along the shore.

Rumeli Kavağı The sleepy little town north of Sarıyer gets most of its excitement from the arrival and departure of ferries. There are a few fish restaurants, and a little public beach named **Altınkum**. North of Rumeli Kavağı is a military zone, off limits to casual visitors.

Dolmuşes for Rumeli Kavağı leave from Sular Caddesi in Sarıyer, 500m inland from the mosque.

Kilyos İstanbul's coastal resort of Kilyos is a favourite place for a swim in the chilly waters of the Black Sea, or a leisurely meal at any time of year. You can even stay overnight if you like.

Dolmuşes and buses from Sarıyer make the trip over the hills to Kilyos in less than a half hour, passing little impromptu open-air roadside restaurants featuring *kuzu çevirme* (spit-roasted lamb).

Kilyos' best beach is the fenced one in front of the Turban Kilyos Moteli, open daily in warm weather from 8 am to 6 pm for US$3.50 per person. It's very crowded on summer weekends, but not bad during the week. Parking costs US$2, so if you drive, park elsewhere in the village and walk to the beach.

Note that there can be a deadly undertow on Black Sea beaches. Swim only in protected areas or where there is an attentive lifeguard, don't swim alone, and be on guard against undertow and riptide.

Places to Stay & Eat On summer weekends all accommodation in Kilyos is likely to be filled from advance reservations. You will have a better chance of finding a room if you plan your visit for the middle of the week, reserve ahead, or visit outside the high season (which lasts from mid-July to the end of August). Many of these hotels are adjuncts to their more popular restaurants; all offer two-star comforts, and charge around US$35 for a double room with private bath and breakfast in summer. The restaurants are all genteel, offering good food and drink for US$10 to US$20 per person.

Walk uphill from the bus and dolmuş stops to find ***Yuva Motel & Restaurant*** *(☎ 201 1043, Kale Caddesi 28)*. All rooms have little porches, but the rooms on the sea side are preferable.

Though its name means 'abundance' in Turkish, the two-star, 42 room ***Gurup Hotel*** *(☎ 201 1194, fax 201 1266, Kale Caddesi 21/1)*, is also often filled by British holiday groups (its other Turkish meaning) who like its swimming pool and jacuzzi.

Erzurumlu Otel Restaurant *(☎ 201 1003, fax 201 1108, Kale Caddesi 77)* is next up the hill and also has rooms with splendid views.

The modernised 35 room ***Kilyos Kale Hotel*** *(☎ 201 1818, fax 201 1823, Kale Caddesi 78)* has a swimming pool as well as comfortable rooms with sea views.

Yonca Hotel *(☎ 201 1018, Kale Caddesi 32)* has old fashioned but tidy rooms to rent, but its main business is its seafood restaurant.

For cheaper food, look down in the village. ***Mustafa'nın Yeri Karadeniz Pide***, on the left as you walk from the bus stop to the beach, serves fresh pide; ***Çimen Lokantası*** a bit further along has a variety of dishes, and ***Hünkar Börek*** right by the beach entrance serves the flaky pastry which makes a good, filling, cheap snack.

Getting There & Away Kilyos is 35km north of the Galata Bridge, and can take several hours to reach in moderately heavy traffic. All public transport comes through Sarıyer; see Getting There & Away in that section (earlier) for details.

Sights on the Asian Shore

The Asian shore of the Bosphorus has a number of possibilities for excursions, with the advantage that you will meet far fewer tourists than in European İstanbul.

Crossing the Bosphorus To reach the Asian shore, hop on the Üsküdar ferry from Eminönü, which runs every 15 or 20 minutes between 6 am and midnight, even more frequently during rush hours, for US$0.50. A similarly frequent ferry service operates between Beşiktaş and Üsküdar. From Kabataş, just south of Dolmabahçe Palace, ferries run to Üsküdar every 30 minutes on the hour and half hour from 7 am to 8 pm. There are also city buses and dolmuşes departing from Taksim Square for Üsküdar, but the ferries are faster and more enjoyable.

If you take the ferry to Üsküdar, you'll notice **Leander's Tower**, called the Kız Kulesi (Maiden's Tower) in Turkish, to the south just off the Asian mainland. The tower was a toll booth and defence point in ancient times; the Bosphorus could be closed off by means of a chain stretching from here to Seraglio Point. The tower has really nothing to do with Leander, who was no maiden, and who swam not the Bosphorus but the Hellespont (Dardanelles), 340km from here.

The tower is subject to the usual legend: oracle says maiden will die by snakebite; concerned father puts maiden in snake-proof tower; fruit vendor comes by boat, sells basket of fruit (complete with snake) to maiden, who gets hers. The legend seems to crop up wherever there are offshore towers and maidens, and then we've got to repeat them in guidebooks.

Another landmark is the tall spear of a television tower on Büyük Çamlıca hilltop, a lookout you can visit from Üsküdar.

A landmark especially for travellers is the German-style **Haydarpaşa Station**, south of Üsküdar, the city's terminus for Asian trains. During the late 19th century, when Kaiser Wilhelm was trying to charm the sultan into economic and military cooperation, he gave him the station as a little gift.

You will also notice the large **Selimiye Kışlası** (Selimiye Barracks), a square building with towers at the corners. It dates from the early 19th century, when Selim III and Mahmut II reorganised the Ottoman armed forces along European lines. Not far away is the **Selimiye Camii** (1805) and the storybook Ottoman rest home for ageing palace ladies which is now used by Marmara University.

Üsküdar (Map 9) Üsküdar (ER-sker-dahr) is Turkish for Scutari. Legend has it that the first ancient colonists established themselves at Chalcedon, the modern Kadıköy, south of Üsküdar. Byzas, bearing the oracle's message to found a colony 'opposite the blind', thought the Chalcedonites blind to the advantages of Seraglio Point as a town site, and founded his town on the European shore. Still, people have lived on this, the Asian shore, longer than they've lived on the other.

Florence Nightingale

During the Crimean War (1853-56), when Britain and France fought on the Ottoman side against the Russian Empire, Üsküdar's Selimiye Barracks (Map 1) served as a military hospital. It was here that the English nurse Florence Nightingale, horrified at the conditions suffered by the wounded, established with the assistance of 38 companion nurses, the first model military hospital with modern standards of discipline, order, sanitation and care. In effect, her work at the Selimiye Barracks laid down the norms of modern nursing, and turned nursing into a skilled, respected profession.

A small **museum** (☎ 216-343 7310) in the barracks is dedicated to her work, but it's presently 'closed for renovation' and shows no sign of opening soon.

Today Üsküdar is a busy dormitory suburb for İstanbul, and you may enjoy several hours of browsing through its streets, markets and mosques.

Üsküdar Mosques As you leave the ferry dock in Üsküdar, the **main square**, Demokrasi Meydanı, is right before you. North-east of the square behind the dolmuş ranks and near the ferry landing is the **Mihrimah Sultan Camii** (1547), sometimes called the İskele Camii (Dock Mosque), designed by Sinan for Süleyman the Magnificent's daughter. To the south of the square is the **Yeni Valide Camii**, or New Queen Mother's Mosque (1710), built by Sultan Ahmet III for his mother Gülnuş Emetullah. It resembles the Rüstem Paşa Camii near the Mısır Çarşısı in Eminönü. Built late in the period of classical Ottoman architecture, it is not as fine as earlier works.

West of the square, overlooking the harbour, is the delightful **Şemsi Paşa Camii** (1580), also designed by Sinan and built in a fine location. After you have explored downtown Üsküdar a bit, head up to the Çamlıca hilltops.

Büyük Çamlıca The hilltop park, highest point in İstanbul at 261m, has long been enjoyed by İstanbul's nobility, poets and common folk.

Once favoured by Sultan Mahmut II (1808-39), by the late 1970s it was a dusty (or muddy), unkempt car park threatened by illegal and unplanned construction. In 1980 the municipal government leased the land to the Turing, which landscaped the hilltop and built a coffee-house restaurant such as Mahmut might have enjoyed. The municipal government took over management of the park in 1994.

To reach the hilltop from Üsküdar's main square, you can take a taxi (US$3) all the way to the summit, or a dolmuş most of the way. For the latter, walk to the dolmuş ranks in front of the Mihrimah Sultan Camii, take a dolmuş headed for Ümraniye, and ask for Büyük Çamlıca. The dolmuş will pass the entrance to Küçük Çamlıca and drop you off shortly thereafter in a district called Kısıklı. The walk uphill following the signs to the summit takes from 20 to 30 minutes, depending on your speed and stamina.

At the car park you'll find the **Aydınlatma ve Isıtma Araçları Müzesi** (Museum of Illuminating & Heating Appliances), which might well escape your interest, even though it has its own cafe and gift shop.

Once at the top you can rest and marvel at the view (and the crowds, if it's a weekend). From Büyük Çamlıca the Bosphorus is laid out like a map, with its twists and turns, and the minaretted skyline of Old İstanbul looks just like the picture postcards. Ottoman-style refreshments and snacks are sold in the park during warm weather.

Neighbouring **Küçük Çamlıca** hilltop, with its tea garden, is not quite as fancy as its loftier sibling, but equally pleasant.

Çinili Cami (Map 9) The Çinili Cami (CHEE-nee-lee jah-mee, Tiled Mosque) is Üsküdar's jewel, a small and unassuming building harbouring a wealth of brilliant İznik faïence on its interior walls.

It's a neighbourhood mosque in the quarter called Tabaklar, up the hillside a way from Üsküdar's main square. It can be tricky to find on your own (a 30-minute walk); a taxi costs less than US$2, and is well worth it. If you're descending from Büyük Çamlıca, a taxi is the way to go.

To get there on foot from Üsküdar's main square, walk out of the square along the main street south, Hakimiyet-i Milliye Caddesi. You'll pass the **Mimar Sinan Çarşısı**, thought to have been the first hamam designed by Sinan. Built by Nurbanu Sultan, mother of Sultan Murat III in 1574-83, it was a double hamam. Having fallen into ruins, part of it was torn down to accommodate construction of the avenue; the remaining half was restored in 1966 and now holds shops.

A bit further along, ***Niyazibey İskender Kebapçı***, on the corner of Tavukçu Bakkal Sokak near the Akbank, is a good place for lunch.

Walk for several more minutes and turn left onto Eski Toptaşı Caddesi, with the Vacı Bedel Mustafa Efendi Camii on the right. Then bear left onto Sansar Sokak at the fork with Bahçelievler Sokak, walk for six or seven minutes uphill, bear right and walk uphill another 10 or 12 minutes. Along this route you'll pass close to the prominent **Atik Valide Camii**, the grandest of Sinan's İstanbul mosques except for his Süleymaniye. It was built for Valide Sultan Nurbanu, wife of Selim II and mother of Ahmet III in 1583.

Approaching the Çinili Cami, you first come to the **Çinili Hamam**, the mosque's Turkish bath, which, because it gets virtually no foreign visitors, is cheap (US$4) and friendly.

The **Çinili Cami** uphill from the bath is unprepossessing from the outside: just a shady little neighbourhood mosque with the usual collection of bearded old men sitting around. Take a moment to greet them pleasantly and they will respond with fulsome welcomes, gratified that someone has come so far to see their historic mosque.

Inside, the mosque is brilliant with İznik faïence, the bequest of Mahpeyker Kösem (1640), wife of Sultan Ahmet I (1603-17) and mother of sultans Murat IV (1623-40) and İbrahim (1640-8). As it is used heavily by local people for prayer, be properly dressed and on your best behaviour when you visit, and avoid visiting on Friday.

Beylerbeyi Palace Both shores of the Bosphorus have their Ottoman palaces. The grandest on the Asian side is Beylerbeyi, a few kilometres north of Üsküdar. Catch a bus or dolmuş north along the shore road from Üsküdar's main square, and get out at the Çayırbaşı stop, just north of Beylerbeyi and the Asian pylons of the Bosphorus Bridge.

Beylerbeyi Palace (☎ 216-321 9320) is open from 9.30 am to 5 pm, closed on Monday and Thursday; admission for the obligatory guided tour costs US$4; a camera permit (no flash or tripod) costs US$8, a video permit is US$16, and is a waste of money.

The entrance to the palace is down a long, vaulted stone passage which used to be a vehicular tunnel on the coast road; traffic was rerouted when the Bosphorus Bridge was built. The tunnel is now a gallery for small exhibits. At its southern end is a beautiful small garden with a bamboo grove, and the entrance to the palace.

Today the palace, for all its grandeur, is musty but impressive, particularly on a sunny afternoon when golden light floods the rooms. The tour goes too fast. Soon you are overwhelmed by Bohemian crystal chandeliers, Sèvres and Ming vases and sumptuous carpets.

Every emperor needs some little place to get away to, and 30 room Beylerbeyi Palace was the place for Abdül Aziz (1861-76). Mahmut II had built a wooden palace here, but like so many other wooden palaces it burned down. Abdül Aziz wanted stone and marble, so he ordered Serkis Balyan to get to work on Beylerbeyi Palace. The architect came up with an Ottoman gem, with fountain in the entrance hall, and two little tent-like kiosks in the sea wall. The sultan provided much of the woodwork himself.

Abdül Aziz spent a lot of time here, as did other monarchs and royal guests, for this was, in effect, the sultan's guest quarters. Empress Eugénie of France stayed here on a long visit in 1869. Other royal guests included Nasruddin, Shah of Persia; Nicholas, grand duke of Russia; and Nicholas, king of Montenegro. The palace's last imperial 'guest' was none other than the former sultan, Abdül Hamit II, who was brought here to spend the remainder of his life (from 1913 to 1918) under house arrest, having spent the four years immediately following his deposition in 1909 in Ottoman Salonika. He had the dubious pleasure of gazing across the Bosphorus at Yıldız and watching the great empire which he had ruled with an iron hand for more than 30 years crumble before his very eyes.

Çengelköy (Map 13) The village of Çengelköy, to the north of Beylerbeyi, is a good place for a break. At its centre, ***Tarihi Çengelköy Çınaraltı Çay Bahçesi*** (Historic Anchor-Village Tea Garden Beneath the Plane Tree) lives up to its name, clustered around the trunk of a gigantic and ancient plane behind a little mosque at the edge of the Bosphorus. Light meals and beverages are served as well as tea.

Küçüksu Kasrı (Lodge) The Büyük Göksu Deresi (Great Heavenly Stream) and Küçük Göksu Deresi (Small Heavenly Stream) were two brooks which descended from the Asian hills into the Bosphorus. Between them was a flat, fertile delta, grassy and shady, just perfect for picnics, which the Ottoman upper classes enjoyed here frequently. Foreign residents, referring to the place as 'The Sweet Waters of Asia', would often join them.

If it was good, the sultan was there, and in style. Sultan Abdül Mecit's answer to a simple picnic blanket was the Küçüksu Kasrı (☎ 216-332 0237), an ornate lodge, actually a tiny palace, built in 1856. Earlier sultans had wooden kiosks here, but architect Nikogos Balyan, son of the designer of Dolmabahçe, produced a rococo gem in marble for his monarch.

Take a bus or dolmuş along the shore road north from Beylerbeyi to reach Küçüksu Kasrı, open from 9.30 am to 5 pm, closed on Monday and Thursday; admission is US$3.

Anadolu Hisarı (Map 13) North of Küçüksu, in the shadow of the Fatih Bridge is the castle and village of Anadolu Hisarı. This small castle, built by Sultan Beyazıt I in 1391, was repaired and strengthened as the Asian strongpoint in Mehmet the Conqueror's stranglehold on Byzantine Constantinople. Anadolu Hisarı is a fraction the size of its great European counterpart, Rumeli Hisarı. You are free to wander about the ruined walls at your leisure.

Kanlıca (Map 13) The Fatih Bridge soars across the Bosphorus just north of Rumeli Hisarı and Anadolu Hisarı. North of the bridge are more small Asian Bosphorus towns, including Kanlıca, famous for its yoghurt. The **mosque** in the town square dates from 1560.

Hıdiv Kasrı High on a promontory above the town, overlooking the Bosphorus, is the Art-Nouveau villa called the Hıdiv Kasrı (Khedive's Villa) (☎ 216-413 9644) built by the khedive of Egypt to be his summer cottage during visits to İstanbul. Here's a bit of its history:

Having ruled Egypt for centuries, the Ottomans lost control to an adventurer named Muhammed

Ali, who took over the government of Egypt and defied the sultan in İstanbul to dislodge him. The sultan, unable to do so, gave him quasi-independence and had to be satisfied with reigning over Egypt rather than ruling. The ruling was left to Muhammed Ali and his line, and the ruler of Egypt was styled *hıdiv*, 'khedive' (not 'king', as that would be unbearably independent). The khedives of Egypt kept up the pretence of Ottoman suzerainty by paying tribute to İstanbul. The Egyptian royal family, which looked upon themselves as Turkish and spoke Turkish rather than Arabic as the court language, often spent their summers in a traditional yalı on the Bosphorus shore. In 1906, Khedive Abbas Hilmi built himself a palatial villa on the most dramatic promontory on the Bosphorus, a place commanding a magnificent view. The Egyptian royal family occupied it into the 1930s, after which it became the property of the municipality.

Restored by Turing after decades of neglect, the Hıdiv Kasrı served as a hotel, restaurant and tea garden much to the delight of İstanbullus and tourists alike. It's now run by an organ of the city government, and serves tea, pastries and meals, but no alcohol. The villa is a gem and the views from its gardens are superb.

The villa is a few minutes by taxi (US$2) uphill from Kanlıca or Çubuklu. To walk, go north from Kanlıca's main square and mosque and turn right at the first street (Kafadar Sokak) which winds up to the villa car park in 15 or 20 minutes.

A much nicer walk is the one up from Çubuklu through the villa's grounds. Take a bus or dolmuş north to the stop marked 'Çubuklu Dalgıç Okulu' (a naval installation). Just north of the stop is a fire station (look for signs saying 'Dikkat İtfaiye' and 'İstanbul Büyükşehir Belediye Başkanlığı İtfaiye Müdürlüğü Çubuklu Müfrezesi'). Walk in the gate and to the right of the fire station, then up the winding forest road to the villa, a 20 to 30-minute walk.

Paşabahçe & Beykoz (Map 13) North of Çubuklu, Paşabahçe has a large glassware factory with products you've no doubt already used, perhaps unwittingly.

In Beykoz, legend says that Pollux, son of Leda (she of the swan) and one of Jason's Argonauts, won a boxing match with the local king, Amicus, son of Poseidon.

At Hünkar İskelesi (Emperor's Landing), further north, is a former imperial palace designed by Sarkis Balyan for Sultan Abdül Mecit. There had been imperial kiosks here for centuries. In 1833, the Ottoman and Russian empires signed a historic peace treaty here which took its name, the Treaty of Unkiar Skelessi, from the place. The peace lasted 20 years.

From Beykoz, a road heads eastward towards the Polish village of Polonezköy and the Black Sea beach resort of Şile (see Şile later in this section). Much of the land along the Bosphorus shore north of Beykoz is in a military zone, and you may be denied entry. You can, however, reach the village of Anadolu Kavağı by ferry, either on the Bosphorus touristic cruise from Eminönü or from Sarıyer and Rumeli Kavağı on the European shore.

Anadolu Kavağı (Map 13) Perched above the village are the ruins of Anadolu Kavağı, a medieval castle with seven massive towers in its walls. First built by the Byzantines, it was restored and reinforced by the Genoese in 1350, and later by the Ottomans. As the straits are narrow here, it was a good choice for a defensive site to control traffic. Two more fortresses, put up by Sultan Murat IV, are north of here.

Anadolu Kavağı is the final stop on the special cruise-ferry route, and the land to the north is in a military zone. If you have a picnic lunch, climb up to the fortress, which provides a comfortable picnic location with spectacular views.

Polonezköy What's a Polish village doing in İstanbul? Polonezköy is a quaint and dying anachronism, a relic of 19th-century politics and the Crimean War.

Founded in 1842 as Adampol, it was named after Prince Adam Jerzy Czartoryski (1770-1861), once the Imperial Russian foreign minister and later head of a short-lived Polish revolutionary government (1830-1). When the revolution failed, he bought land in the Ottoman Empire for some of his former soldiers. In 1853 Russia provoked war with the Ottoman Empire; England, France and Sardinia joined the Ottomans in battling the Russians in the Crimea. The men of Adampol formed a regiment of Ottoman Cossacks and fought with such bravery that Sultan Abdül Mecit exempted them and their heirs from taxation.

A generation ago, Polish was still the lingua franca in the village, but with modern media, the language and customs of old Poland are dying out. Once Poles in a time warp, the people of Polonezköy are now Turkish citizens of Polish ancestry. Even so, the 'Polish Pope' John Paul II visited the village in 1979.

For more than a century, city people would come here for authentic Polish farm food: wild mushrooms, wild boar, omelettes with eggs from free-range chickens and excellent fruit. Farmhouses provided simple lodgings as well as meals, and this attracted another, nonculinary clientele: lovers who, unable to show a marriage licence, could not shack up in İstanbul's hotels.

Alas, Polonezköy has lost much of its charm. Simple meals and lodgings are still available, but at relatively high prices; lovers still make up a hefty segment of the trade. Transport is a problem also; it's only easily reachable if you have your own vehicle. If you do, stop and take a turn through the village, have a look at the tiny church, and ponder the vicissitudes of history.

Şile Seaside getaways from İstanbul tend to be disappointing. Ataköy and Florya, on the Sea of Marmara, are crowded and citified. Kilyos is small and crowded. But Şile, 72km north-east of Üsküdar on the Black Sea coast, has long sand beaches and a fairly laid-back atmosphere – at least on weekdays.

Buses (US$2.50) depart from the western side of Üsküdar's main square on the hour from 9 am to 4 pm for the two-hour journey.

Known as Kalpe in classical times, Şile was a port of call for ships sailing east from the Bosphorus. As an important port, it was visited by Xenophon and his Ten Thousand on their way back to Greece from their disastrous campaign against Artaxerxes II of Persia in the 4th century BC. Unable to find ships to sail them to Greece, Xenophon and his men marched to Chrysopolis (Üsküdar) along the route now followed by the modern road.

Şile's other claim to fame is *Şile bezi*, an open-weave cotton cloth with hand embroidery, usually made up into shirts and blouses which are wonderfully cool in the summer heat.

Numerous hotels provide accommodation, with highest prices on weekends. ***Kumbaba Hotel*** *(☎ 216-711 1038)*, 2km south of town, is among the oldest yet still the most congenial, with 40 rooms for US$50 to US$70 a double. They have a camping ground as well. The similarly priced two-star ***Değirmen Hotel*** *(☎ 216-711 5048, fax 711 5248, Plaj Yolu 24)*, has 76 rooms, restaurants and bars, and overlooks the beach. The aptly named ***Resort Hotel*** *(☎ 216-711 3627, fax 711 4003)*, Uzunkum, Ağlayan Kaya Mevkii, is a four-star lodging.

As İstanbul expands, so do the getaway spots on its outskirts. If Şile is too busy for you, hop on the bus to the village of **Ağva**, less than an hour eastward on the coast. Accommodation is limited, but there are good possibilities for camping – and peace and quiet.

THE PRINCES' ISLANDS

The Turks call the Princes' Islands, which lie about 20km south-east of the city in the Sea of Marmara, the Kızıl Adalar, 'Red Islands'. Most İstanbullus get along with 'Adalar' (The Islands), however.

In Byzantine times, refractory princes, deposed monarchs and others whose bodies had outlived their roles were interned here. A Greek Orthodox monastery and seminary on Heybeliada turned out Orthodox priests until the 1970s.

In the 19th century the Ottoman business community of Greeks, Jews and Armenians favoured the islands as summer resorts.

Many of the fine Victorian villas built by these wealthy Ottomans survive, and make the larger islands, Büyükada and Heybeliada, charming places.

When you visit the islands, bear in mind that there is no naturally occurring fresh water here. Use water sparingly as all fresh water must be brought from the mainland.

Touring the Islands

At least 10 ferries (US$1.30) run to the islands each day from 7 am to 11.30 pm, departing from Sirkeci's 'Adalar İskelesi' dock, east of the dock for car ferries to Harem. On weekdays there are additional boats for commuters. On summer weekends, board the vessel and seize a seat at least half an hour before departure time unless you want to stand the whole way.

You can also take a fast catamaran from Eminönü or Kabataş to Bostancı, then another from Bostancı to Büyükada, but you save little time, and the cost is much higher.

The ferry leaves from Sirkeci, out of the Golden Horn and around Seraglio Point, offering fine views of Topkapı Sarayı, Aya Sofya and the Sultan Ahmet Camii on the right; Üsküdar, Haydarpaşa and Kadıköy to the left. After about 45 minutes, the ferry reaches Kınalı, the first small island; another 30 minutes brings you to Heybeliada, the second-largest island, and another 15 minutes to Büyükada, the largest. Some express ferries go directly to Büyükada, from which there are occasional ferries to Heybeli, and catamarans to Bostancı on the Asian shore.

Büyükada

The 'Great Island's' splendid Victoriana greets you as you approach by sea, its gingerbread villas climbing up the slopes of the hill and the bulbous twin domes of the Splendid Otel providing an unmistakable landmark.

Only a few minutes after landing, you'll realize Büyükada's surprise: there are no cars! Except for the necessary police, fire and sanitation vehicles, transportation is by bicycle, horse-drawn carriage and foot, as in centuries past.

Walk from the ferry to the clock tower in İskele Meydanı (Dock Square). The market district is to the left along Recep Koç Caddesi. For a stroll up the hill and through the lovely old houses, bear right onto 23 Nisan Caddesi. If you need a goal for your wanderings, head for the Greek Monastery of St George, in the 'saddle' between Büyükada's two highest hills. Bicycles are available for *kiralık bisiklet* (rent) in several shops, and shops on the market street can provide the wherewithal for picnics, though food is obviously cheaper on the mainland.

Just to the left off the square by the clock tower is the waiting area for horse-drawn *fayton* (carriages). Hire one for a *büyük tur* (long tour) of about an hour for US$16, or a *küçük tur* (short tour) which gives you a look mostly at the town, not the shores or hills, for US$12. Prices are set by the city government, and prominently posted, though you may be able to haggle out of season.

Places to Stay & Eat Next to the clock tower, ***Hotel Princess*** *(☎ 216-382 1628, fax 382 1949)*, charges US$60/80 a single/double in summer, breakfast with swimming pool fee included. An extra bed costs US$20.

Splendid Otel *(☎ 216-382 6950, fax 382 6775)*, to the right, 200m up the hill from the clock tower at 23 Nisan Caddesi, No 71 is a perfect if faded Ottoman Victorian period piece, complete with grand dames taking tea on the terrace each afternoon. A room with Victorian-era comforts (the baths have been upgraded, though) costs US$80 per couple, breakfast included.

İskele Meydanı is surrounded with restaurants. To the left as you come up from the dock are several small places featuring *kokoreç* (lamb intestines), but ***Altın Fıçı*** has a much longer menu, and beer from its namesake Golden Barrel as well. ***Taş Fırını*** (Stone Oven) further into the market along Recep Koç Caddesi serves cheap lahmacun (US$0.50) and pide (US$2) as well as more substantial plates. Up to the right of the clock tower are even cheaper *büfes* (snack stands). For fancier meals, ***Birtat Restaurant*** on the waterfront to the east of the ferry docks is a favourite, with meals for US$6 to US$18 and more.

Heybeliada

Called Heybeli for short, this island is home to the Turkish Naval Academy (located to the left of the ferry dock). Within the academy grounds is the grave of Sir Edward Barton (died 1598), ambassador of Queen Elizabeth I to the Sublime Porte. Much less touristed than Büyükada, it's a delightful place for walking in the pine groves and swimming from the tiny, crowded beaches. There's not much accommodation if you don't have your own villa (or an invitation to a friend's), but there are several restaurants with good food and decent prices.

A 50-minute carriage büyük tur of the island costs US$12, the shorter küçük tur US$8. Battered bicycles are for rent at several shops. For picnic supplies, turn left from the ferry docks onto the street behind the waterfront restaurants. ***Mehtap Pasta ve Unlu Mamülleri*** is a bakery selling pastries and French-style bread. Other shops, such as ***Gül Market***, can provide other picnic supplies such as preserved meats, cheese, olives, pickles and drinks.

Prime lodging here is ***Merit Halki Palace*** *(☎ 216-351 8890, fax 351 8483, Refah Şehitleri Caddesi 88)*, a restored Ottoman Victorian gingerbread villa with 45 rooms, all comforts, and premium prices at US$100 a double per night.

For dining, walk to the right off the ferry dock. ***Ada Kebap ve Lahmacun Salonu*** has these cheap dishes, and stews as well: seaside dining at bargain prices.

Burgaz & Kınalı

These two smaller islands are also accessible by ferry, but offer less reward for the trouble. They're mostly for the well-to-do İstanbullus who have summer villas here.

Burgaz has a church, a synagogue, and the home of the late writer Sait Faik, now a museum.

Kınalı, flat and fairly featureless except for a forest of cell phone antennas, is even more a collection of summer villas, favoured by Armenian families. If you stop here to eat (there are no hotels), you'll probably be the only foreigner in sight.

PLACES TO STAY

İstanbul is well provided with hotels in all categories, particularly in the mid-range price, but Turkish tourism is booming, and by late afternoon in August, the place you want to stay at may be full.

As everywhere in Turkey, the appearance of the lobby tells you little about the rooms. Look at several if possible, and choose the best. If the first one you see won't do, ask *Başka var mı* (BAHSH-kah VAHR-muh, Are there others?).

Sultanahmet is the best place to look for a budget or mid-range hotel room, especially if you favour a restored Ottoman-mansion hotel. Camping areas are in the beach sections named Ataköy and Florya. Taksim Square has many modern upper mid-range hotels as well as most of the top-end places; Beşiktaş, to Taksim's north, has the rest of the luxury hotels.

Places to Stay – Budget

Student Hostels In summer (July and August), several university dormitories open their doors to foreign students. These dorms tend to be extremely basic and cheap. They're not for all tastes, but if you want to look into one, ask for the latest information from the Tourism Information Office in Sultanahmet, at the northern end of the Hippodrome.

Some cheap hotels use the word 'hostel' in their names, but they are not official hostels.

Hotels Budget hotels may provide dormitory beds for as little as US$6 or US$8 per person, and others offer double rooms with private toilet, sink and hot-water shower for as much as US$50. Mostly though, these places have simple but adequate double rooms with a sink or private shower for US$25 to US$40.

Hotels – Sultanahmet & Cankurtaran (Map 7) The Sultan Ahmet Camii gives its name to the quarter surrounding it. This is İstanbul's premier sightseeing area, so the hotels here, and in the adjoining neighbourhoods to the south and east named Cankurtaran and Çatladıkapı, are supremely convenient. Unless otherwise noted, the Sultanahmet postal code is 34400.

Many Sultanahmet hotels, hostels and pensions are run by carpet merchants, who may be tedious in their efforts to get you to buy a rug. See the special section on Turkish Carpets in the Facts for the Visitor chapter.

Cankurtaran This quiet residential district east of Aya Sofya and the Sultan Ahmet Camii is accessible on foot from Sultanahmet (ask for the Four Seasons Hotel on Tevkifhane Sokak), or by *banliyö train* (suburban train) from Sirkeci to the Cankurtaran station.

Side Pansiyon *(☎/fax 517 6590, Utangaç Sokak 20)* has two buildings, an older one (the Side Pension) with rooms for US$20/25/35 a single/double/triple with sink, US$30/35/45 with private shower; and the new Side Hotel with quite nice rooms for US$40/50/60 with bath and balcony – as good as rooms costing much more.

Continue down Tevkifhane Sokak to Kutlugün Sokak and turn left.

Mavi Guesthouse *(☎ 516 5878, fax 517 7287, Kutlugün Sokak 3)*, not to be confused with the expensive Mavi Ev nearby, charges US$20 for a waterless double room, with breakfast – right next door to the US$350-a-night Four Seasons Hotel. Other identically priced options only two blocks away include ***Troy Hostel*** *(☎ 516 8757, fax 638 6450, Yeni Saraçhane Sokak 6)*; and ***Konya Pansiyon*** *(☎ 638 3638, Terbıyık Sokak 15)* where a few rooms also have private bath for US$35. If the Konya is full, try ***İlknur*** across the street.

Just around the corner, is the ***Orient Youth Hostel*** *(☎ 517 9493, fax 518 3894, orienthostel@superonline.com, www.hostels.com/orienthostel, Akbıyık Caddesi 13)*. It's been renovated and staff improved, and beds cost US$7 per person in waterless quad rooms, a bit more in a double room. Services include a travel agency, bar and pool table, email and Internet service, roof bar with good views, sun deck and currency exchange. There's a street market on Akbıyık Caddesi on Wednesday.

Across the street, ***Star Pansiyon*** *(☎ 638 2302, fax 516 1827, Akbıyık Caddesi 18)* has tidy doubles with shower and breakfast for US$35, and a public laundry as well. The nearby ***Alaaddin Guest House*** *(☎ 516 2330, fax 638 6059, Akbıyık Caddesi 32)* is similar, if a bit more expensive. The ***Sultan Tourist Hostel*** *(☎ 516 9260 or 517 1626, Terbıyık Sokak 3)* is cheaper, with waterless rooms going for US$25.

Terrace Guesthouse *(☎ 638 9733, fax 638 9734, terrace@escortnet.com, Kutlugün Sokak 39)*, has only a few rooms, but they're cheerful, with tiny baths, balconies, and sea views, for US$40 to US$45 a double with breakfast served in the rooftop dining room.

Around the corner, ***Hotel Şebnem*** *(☎ 517 6623, fax 638 1056, Adliye Sokak 1)* is clean and fairly quiet with double rooms priced at US$40 to US$50 in summer, private shower and breakfast included.

Off Yerebatan Caddesi ***Yücelt Interyouth Hostel*** *(☎ 513 6150, fax 512 7628, yucelt hostel@escortnet.com, www.travelturkey.com/yucelt.html, Caferiye Sokak 6/1)* is literally across the street from the front (western) door of Aya Sofya. Though called a hostel, it's a cheap hotel with restaurant, bulletin board, TV room, terrace, email, travel service, coin-operated laundry and hamam. Doubles with sink cost US$18, rooms with three or four beds go for US$8 per person, and dormitory beds (eight to a room) cost US$6 each. Some readers enjoy this place, others complain.

Another few cheap hotels are a short walk north-west from Aya Sofya along Yerebatan Caddesi to Salkımsöğüt Sokak, on the right. This area is not as quiet or desirable as Cankurtaran, but still serviceable.

Hotel Ema *(☎ 511 7166, fax 512 4878, Salkımsöğüt Sokak 18)*, is friendly, simple and not too noisy for US$20 a waterless double, or US$30 with private shower. The neighbouring ***Elit Hotel*** *(☎ 526 2549, fax 512 4878, Salkımsöğüt Sokak 14)* has 12 clean, slightly fancier rooms with private facilities above a carpet shop. Prices can go as high as US$30/50 a single/double in summer, but they're ready to bargain.

Down Salkımsöğüt Sokak a few more steps on the right is ***Hotel Anadolu*** *(☎ 512 1035, Salkımsöğüt Sokak 3)*, perhaps the oldest hotel in the quarter, but also the cheapest and quietest. By the front door are a few little tables overlooking a car park, a good place to sip tea or write a letter. The rooms are tiny, and in summer prices can go as high as US$20 a double for a room with a sink, or US$30 a double with shower, but hot showers are free, and there's no carpet shop.

Binbirdirek Just uphill west of the Hippodrome is the district of Binbirdirek, named after the Byzantine cistern of that name.

Türkmen Hotel & Pansiyon *(☎ 517 1355, fax 638 5546, Dizdariye Çeşmesi Sokak 27)* is a modern nondescript but friendly place on a quiet back street a bit out of the way. Double rooms in the pension have private showers, but no toilets, and are priced at US$18; in the hotel, nicer rooms with toilet, sink and shower are US$35 in high summer.

Küçük Ayasofya Downhill from the southwestern end of the Hippodrome is this neighbourhood.

Just off the Hippodrome is ***Hotel Best Hipodrom*** *(☎/fax 516 0902, Üçler Sokak 9)*, offering excellent value: decent rooms with shower, TV and breakfast for US$35 a double.

Can Pansiyon *(☎ 638 6608, Şehit Mehmet Paşa Yokuşu, Liman Caddesi, Kaleci Sokak 2)*, just downhill from the Hotel Sokullu Paşa, is very simple and basic, but very cheap at US$5 per person in waterless rooms. More expensive but also more comfortable is ***Seagull Pension*** *(☎ 517 1142, fax 516 0972, Küçük Ayasofya Caddesi, Aksakal Sokak 22)*, charging US$18 for a double with private bath.

Divan Yolu Arsenal Youth Hostel *(☎ 513 6407, Dr Emin Paşa Sokak 12)*, by the Tarihi Park Hamamı, is cramped and rundown but centrally located. Dorm rooms with four beds each cost US$8 per bed, with showers down the hall.

Hotels – Taksim & Tepebaşı A few inexpensive hostelries exist amidst the banks, airline offices, nightclubs and towering luxury hotels of Taksim Square. The postal code for Taksim is 80090.

One such place is ***Otel Avrupa*** *(Map 2, ☎ 250 9420, fax 250 7399, Topçu Caddesi 32)*. It's a converted apartment house with an entrance at street level, a cheerful breakfast room one flight up, and guest rooms of varying sizes priced at US$36/45 a single/double with private bath and breakfast.

Also take a look at the old-fashioned ***Hotel Plaza*** *(Map 3, ☎ 245 3273, fax 293 7040, Aslanyatağı Sokak 19-21)*, off Sıraselviler Caddesi. A bit difficult to find, but quiet and with some fine Bosphorus views, it charges US$40 a double for its aged rooms with bath and breakfast.

Camping İstanbul's camping areas are situated along the Sea of Marmara in Florya, Yeşilköy and Ataköy near the airport, about 20km from Sultanahmet. They have good sea-view locations and average prices of US$10 for two people in a tent. All are served by the frequent commuter trains which run between Sirkeci Station and the western suburb of Halkalı for less than US$1.

Ataköy Mokamp *(☎ 559 6000, fax 559 6007)*, in the Ataköy Tatil Köyü (holiday village) complex with bar, restaurant, swimming pools and other services, charges US$10 for two in a tent (try to get a *sahile yakın* – sah-heel-EH yah-kuhn, site – near the shore) and away from the highway. Ataköy is accessible by banliyö tren from Sirkeci and by Eminönü-Ataköy and Taksim-Ataköy buses. Coming from the airport, the Havaş bus does not stop here; the closest stop is several kilometres further east at Bakırköy, so it's best to take a 10-minute taxi ride for US$3.

***Florya Turistik Tesisleri** (☎ 574 0000)*, on the shore road south of the airport and west of Yeşilköy, is more than 20km from the city centre, but more pleasant because of it. Two-person tent sites cost US$9. Transport is by banliyö tren (the station is 500m away), or by Taksim-Florya bus.

***Londra Kamping** (☎ 560 4200)* is on the southern side of the Londra Asfaltı highway between the airport and Topkapı gate across from the Süt Sanayi (milk factory). On the highway is a truck fuel and service station, but behind it, further off the road, are grassy plots with small trees. You won't escape the noise and pollution completely here, but it's not an impossible location. To reach it you must be going eastward from the airport towards Topkapı gate and turn into the *servis yolu* (service road); watch carefully for the sign. About 300m after the turn, the camping ground is on the right-hand side.

Places to Stay – Mid-Range

Mid-range hotels, usually newer buildings constructed during the past two decades, vary in size from 30 to 80 rooms and charge from US$40 to US$100 for a double with private shower and/or bath; most include breakfast in the price. Most rooms, though, fall in the range of US$50 to US$75. Except for a few hotels in Sultanahmet and Taksim, virtually all of these mid-range places are rated at two or three stars by the Ministry of Tourism, which means they can be depended upon to have lifts, restaurants and bars (though often empty), and staff who speak foreign languages. Many rooms come with TV and some with minibar.

Sultanahmet (Map 7) Mid-range hotels are either historic buildings with character – even Ottoman-style mansions – or comfortable but characterless modern buildings.

Ottoman-Style Hotels The lobby of the small ***Hotel Empress Zoe** (☎ 518 2504 or 518 4360, fax 518 5699, emzoe@ibm.net, Akbıyık Caddesi, Adliye Sokak 10)* is in a Byzantine cistern next to an old Ottoman hamam. The small rooms above, reached by a narrow staircase, are simply decorated with taste and character. The rooftop bar-lounge-terrace gives fine views of the sea and the Sultan Ahmet Camii, the pleasant 'secret garden' is a flower-bordered haven. Prices are US$50/70/85 a single/double/triple (US$5 discount for cash), a good breakfast included. Run by American expatriate Ann Nevens, it's a fine choice for single women.

A block away, ***Hotel Poem** (☎/fax 517 6836, Terbıyık Sokak 12)*, is two buildings with a small glass-covered restaurant in between, and rooms (some with sea views) for US$50/75 a single/double, breakfast included. There's a poem in each room; this is among the quietest of locations. ***Hotel Acropol** (☎ 638 9021, fax 518 3031, Akbıyık Caddesi 25)* is among the newer and most comfortable hotels in this quarter, with 26 fully equipped rooms going for US$70/90, and fine views from the penthouse restaurant.

For maximum Ottoman ambience, the award goes to ***Hotel Turkuaz** (☎ 518 1897, fax 517 3380, Cinci Meydanı Sokak 36, Kadırga)*, at the bottom of the hill from the south-western corner of the Hippodrome, somewhat out of the way. The rooms, furnishings, hamam, and Turkish folk-art lounge in this period house are the real thing, not posh modern imitations. When you stay in the 'Sultan's Room', you feel the part. The 14 rooms, all with private shower, cost between US$40 and US$80 double, breakfast included.

Just around the corner, ***Hotel Sidera** (☎ 638 3460, fax 518 7262, Dönüş Sokak 14)* is the modern version of an Ottoman mansion, quiet and suitable, charging US$55/85 for its bath-equipped rooms in summer, less off season.

Go east (downhill) from the Hippodrome along Mehmet Paşa Yokuşu and Suterazisi Sokak to find the ***Hotel Yeni Ayasofya** (☎ 516 9446, fax 518 0700, Küçük Ayasofya Caddesi, Demirci Reşit Sokak 28)*. Another nicely renovated house in a quiet residential area charging US$70/95 for its rooms with shower, and likewise the staff are ready to haggle with you for lower rates.

PETER PTSCHELINZEW

Many treasures can be found at İstanbul's Kapalı Çarşı (Covered Market).

EDDIE GERALD

View from Karaköy harbour toward the old city.

PETER PTSCHELINZEW

Looking toward Beyoğlu from Galata Tower.

Every İstanbullu has a thousand fascinating stories about life in this great city.

Government building in Fatih.

Anyone for smoked fish in a fresh bun?

Restored 19th century tram on İstiklal Caddesi.

ALL PHOTOGRAPHS BY EDDIE GERALD

Ottoman House *(☎ 517 4203, fax 517 3512, Kadırga Limanı Caddesi 85)*, on the northern side of the park, posts an outrageous price of US$90 double, but charges barely half that for so-so modern rooms.

Up the hill a few steps off the Hippodrome, ***Hotel Turkoman*** *(☎ 516 2956, fax 516 2957, Asmalı Çeşme Sokak, Adliye Yanı 2)*, is a recently renovated 19th-century building with the feeling of a private club. The 12 bath-equipped rooms have names, not numbers, are simply but tastefully decorated, and cost US$70/85/100 a single/double/triple. Take your breakfast (included in the rates) on the roof terrace with fine views of the Hippodrome, Sultan Ahmet Camii, and Museum of Turkish and Islamic Arts, which is right next door.

Behind the Turkoman the small, simple, mostly modern ***Hotel İbrahim Paşa*** *(☎ 518 0349, fax 518 4457, pasha@ibm.net, www.all-hotels.com/a/tkpasha/tkpasha.htm)* has a lift and 18 small shower-equipped rooms, a bit too pricey at US$80/95 a single/double, breakfast included, but the location is quietish and convenient, the management friendly and accommodating.

Hotel Sokullu Paşa *(☎ 518 1790, fax 518 1793, Sokullu@superonline.com, Şehit Mehmet Paşa Sokak 5/7)*, Küçük Ayasofya, is a restored Ottoman house with its own small terrace and hamam. Get one of the light, airy, high-ceilinged rooms such as Nos 306 or 308 for US$65/90, breakfast included; some other rooms are not as good. Note that they'll cut their price quickly if they're not full.

Hotel Sümengen *(☎ 517 6869, fax 516 8282, Amiral Tafdil Sokak 21)* is an Ottoman town house with its own marble-covered hamam (US$10 extra) and an airy, light dining room and open-air rooftop terrace with views of the Sea of Marmara. The 30 guest rooms are small with tiny showers and twin or double beds. A few of the rooms have views of the sea but many rooms open only onto corridors, giving their inhabitants very little privacy. Rates are a bit too high at US$90/120/110 a single/double/triple with breakfast included.

Hotel Historia *(☎ 517 7472, fax 516 8169, Amiral Tafdil Sokak 23)*, to the right of the Sümengen, is Ottoman on the outside, more modern on the inside, though there is a marble-clad hamam. Some of the 27 rooms have short bathtubs as well as showers, and all rent for US$70/90/110, lower if they're not full. Corner rooms such as Nos 401 and 501 are choice.

Hotel Avicenna *(☎ 517 0550, fax 516 6555, avicenna@superonline.com, www.avicenna.com.tr, Amiral Tafdil Sokak 31-33)*, to the right of the Historia, is also Ottoman on the outside but modern on the inside, with satellite TV, a roof-terrace cafe-bar, and 49 small though pleasant rooms for US$90/110 (bargainable), breakfast included.

Pensions ***Guesthouse Berk*** *(☎ 516 9671, fax 517 7715, Kutlugün Sokak 27)* is family run and a good choice for single women, though comparatively expensive. The six rooms all have private bath and cost US$40 to US$70 a single and US$50 to US$90 a double.

Barut's Guesthouse *(☎ 516 5256, fax 516 2944, İshakpaşa Caddesi 8)* is a 23 room pension run by artists Hikmet and Füsun Barut (Hikmet Bey specialises in the old Turkish craft of paper marbling – look at the fine examples in the lobby). Guest rooms are quite basic and simple, but the family atmosphere makes up for them. Rates are $40/50/60/70 a single/double/triple/quad.

Modern Hotels ***Hotel Halı*** *(☎ 516 2170, fax 516 2172, Klodfarer Caddesi 20)*, in Çemberlitaş, uphill to the north-west of the Hippodrome, is another good modern choice at a lower price: US$48/65 a single/double, breakfast included. There's a bit more street noise here. The simpler but acceptable ***Gülşah Otel*** *(☎ 516 2760, fax 516 9476)*, around the corner at Piyerloti Caddesi 6, is a cheaper choice at US$42/45 a single/double, but without the Halı's views.

Hotel Piyer Loti *(☎ 518 5700, fax 516 1886, Piyerloti Caddesi 5)*, Çemberlitaş, is a modern building with a popular glass-covered sidewalk cafe-restaurant on Divan Yolu two blocks west of the Hippodrome.

The simple modern rooms cost US$60/75 a single/double, a great price for such a convenient location. Half a block south, the three-star ***Hotel Antea*** *(☎ 638 1121, fax 517 7949, Piyerloti Caddesi 21)* is fancier and more expensive at US$70/100/130.

The friendly ***Hotel Nomade*** *(☎ 511 1296, fax 513 2404, Divan Yolu, Ticarethane Sokak 15)* is just a few steps off busy Divan Yolu. French is spoken here, and the price is a comparatively expensive US$45/60 a single/double with private shower and breakfast. It's a good place for single women.

Aksaray-Laleli (Maps 1 & 6) The districts of Aksaray and Laleli, 2.5km west of Sultanahmet, are packed with one to three-star hotels at decent prices. Most of the patrons are Eastern European small merchants shopping for Turkish-made apparel, especially blue jeans and leather goods. If you're not in the garment trade, you may find the constant bustle of shopping and the huge bundles of goods stacked in hotel lobbies, hallways and lifts a bit tedious. If hoteliers here speak a foreign language, it's most probably Polish, Serbo-Croat, Romanian or Russian. Other hotels in this area are filled by foreign groups on incredibly cheap tours who are expected to shop early and often in shops attached to the hotel in order to swell the hotel's coffers.

Taksim (Map 3) Airline offices, foreign banks and luxury hotels are mostly near Taksim Square.

Family House *(☎ 249 7351, fax 249 9667, Kutlu Sokak 53)*, has five small four-room apartments for rent in a quiet building. The owner-manager, Mr Atıl Erman, is available to answer any question or solve any problem. He can even arrange your transport from the airport for US$25. Apartments have two single beds and one double bed, telephone, colour TV, kitchen with fridge, two-burner gas cooker and utensils. In summer it's US$96 per day and US$600 per week for up to four people. To find Family House, go down İnönü Caddesi from Taksim, turn right, walk beneath the large red Chinese gate and down the steps, down another flight, following the Family House signs. Ask him about his guest house in rural Göynük.

Virginie Apart-Hotel *(☎ 251 7856, fax 251 0184, İstiklal Caddesi 100)* has five little apartments overlooking the trendy street for US$75/100/120 a single/double/triple.

The area also has nearly a dozen modern four-star hotels charging US$90 to US$150 for comfortable double rooms with private bath, TV, minibar and air-con, breakfast included. All are fairly quiet and have lifts, bars and restaurants, 24-hour room service (of sorts) and English-speaking personnel. You should be granted a discount if you stay for several days off season; be sure to ask about it. Most customers are here on business or organised tours. The following hotels can all be found on Map 2:

Eresin Taksim Hotel *(☎ 256 0803, fax 253 2247, Topçu Caddesi 34)* is older but well maintained, with rooms for US$90/110/130 a single/double/triple.

Feronya Hotel *(☎ 238 0901, fax 238 0866, Abdülhak Hamit Caddesi 70-72)* is among the newer hotels, nominally charging US$100/140, but I was quoted US$100 a double during off season.

Hotel İstanbul Kervansaray *(☎ 235 5000, fax 253 4378, Şehit Muhtar Bey Caddesi 61)* just around the corner from the Eresin, has a quiet location and charges US$90/110 a single/double.

Hotel Lamartine *(☎ 254 6270, fax 256 2776, Lamartin Caddesi 25)* has 58 rooms for US$90/110 a single/double.

Nippon Hotel *(☎ 254 9900, fax 250 4553, Topçu Caddesi 10)* has 94 rooms, is a bit more expensive and is often filled by tour groups at US$90/110.

Riva Otel *(☎ 256 4420, fax 256 2033, Aydede Caddesi 8)* charges US$80/100 a single/double and has its own currency exchange office.

The Madison Hotel *(☎ 238 5460, fax 238 5151, Recep Paşa Caddesi 23)* is among the newest ones, with rates for its 108 rooms of US$85/110 a single/double. There's a hamam, sauna and small indoor swimming pool.

Tepebaşı (Map 3) Between Galatasaray Square and Tünel Square, west of İstiklal Caddesi, the district of Tepebaşı (TEH-peh-bah-shuh) was the first luxury hotel district in the city. The main street through Tepebaşı is Meşrutiyet Caddesi.

The four-star ***Yenişehir Palas*** *(☎ 252 7160, fax 249 7507, newcity@comnet.com.tr, Meşrutiyet Caddesi, Oteller Sokak 1-3)* is a hotel of eight floors with few views but in a convenient location. Its 138 comfortable rooms with bath, TV and minibar go for US$75 to US$100 a single and US$100 to US$130 a double, breakfast included.

Büyük Londra Oteli *(☎ 245 0670, fax 245 0671, Meşrutiyet Caddesi 117)* dates from the same era as Pera Palas Oteli (see the 'Pera Palas Oteli' boxed text), but has much smaller rooms and bathrooms, and is a bit the worse for wear. But it does preserve some of the Victorian-era glory (in the public rooms at least) at a price which includes a significant nostalgia mark-up, but is nonetheless lower than the Pera's. A room with shower costs US$60 with one double bed, US$80 with two beds, breakfast included, but they'll come down in price if business is slow.

Next to the British consulate general is the new, modern, four-star ***Hotel Emperyal*** *(☎ 293 3955, fax 252 4370, Meşrutiyet Caddesi 38)*, offering good value for money at US$80/100/130 a single/double/triple.

Places to Stay – Top End

The centre of the posh hotel district is certainly Taksim Square, but there are numerous luxury hotels in other parts of the city. Prices range from US$125 to US$300 and higher for a double, but most rooms cost from US$140 to US$200. At the big international hotels, try not to pay the 'normal' published rates ('rack rates'), which are quite high. Often these hotels offer special packages; ask when you make reservations. The big international chains usually allow children (of any age) to share a double room with their parents at no extra charge or, if two rooms are needed, they charge only the single rate.

Sultanahmet (Map 7) Turing has restored historic buildings throughout the city, including several Ottoman mansions next door to Aya Sofya and the Sultan Ahmet Camii.

Yeşil Ev *(☎ 517 6785, fax 517 6780, Kabasakal Caddesi 5)* is an Ottoman house rebuilt by Turing with 22 rooms furnished with period pieces and antiques in fine taste; it's the classiest of the restored Ottoman mansion hotels. Behind the hotel is a lovely shaded garden-terrace restaurant. It costs US$115/150/195 a single/double/triple or US$240, breakfast included, for the Pasha's Room, with its own private Turkish bath.

Mavi Ev (Blue House) *(☎ 638 9010, fax 638 9017, bluehouse@istanbulhotels.com, www.istanbulhotels.com/bluehouse.htm, Dalbastı Sokak 14)* opened in 1997 and has comfortable rooms, a supremely convenient location, and excellent morning views of the Sultan Ahmet Camii from its rooftop restaurant for US$110/130 a single/double, breakfast included.

Hotel Arcadia *(☎ 516 9696, fax 516 6118, Dr İmren Öktem Caddesi 1)*, on the north-western side of the modern Adliye Sarayı (law courts), is a modern mid-rise hotel with comfortable rooms for a somewhat high US$120/140, breakfast included. The location is excellent – quiet and convenient – and the afternoon views of the Sultan Ahmet Camii, Aya Sofya, Topkapı Sarayı and the Sea of Marmara from the upper-floor rooms and rooftop restaurant are nothing short of spectacular.

On the northern side of Aya Sofya against the walls of Topkapı Sarayı is a row of Ottoman houses, the ***Ayasofya Pansiyonları*** *(☎ 513 3660, fax 513 3669, ayapans@escortnet.com.tr)*, Soğukçeşme Sokak, which have also been rebuilt and refitted by Turing. The 58 rooms with private baths are in 19th-century Ottoman style with brass or antique wooden beds, glass lamps, Turkish carpets and period wall hangings. Prices are from US$80 to US$90 a single, US$100 to US$120 a double, US$160 a triple with breakfast included. The cheaper rooms, at the back, get less light; front rooms look directly onto Aya Sofya.

Across the street, ***Konuk Evi***, was rebuilt by Turing in 1992 to duplicate a historic mansion which stood on this site during the reign of Sultan Abdül Hamit. It now has a garden, conservatory restaurant and 20 guest rooms with all mod cons with prices the same as Yeşil Ev (described earlier).

The Four Seasons Hotel İstanbul (☎ 638 8200, fax 638 8210, Huluer@fshr.com, www.fshr.com, Tevkifhane Sokak 1), is İstanbul's top hotel in every respect: location, accommodation, design, furnishings and service. With only 65 rooms and a staff of around 200, this perfectly restored Ottoman building literally in the shadow of the Sultan Ahmet Camii and Aya Sofya has only one problem: there aren't enough rooms for everyone who wants one, even at the lofty price of US$220 to US$350 a single, US$250 to US$380 a double, plus 15% tax (breakfast extra).

Taksim (Map 2) *Divan Oteli (☎ 231 4100, fax 248 8527, Cumhuriyet Caddesi 2)*, Elmadağ, is a small European-style hotel with excellent cuisine and personal service by well-trained multilingual staff. Rooms cost US$170/205 a single/double, tax included. Breakfast is an alarming US$18 extra.

Two blocks north is ***İstanbul Hilton Hotel*** *(☎ 231 4650, fax 240 4165)*, set in a 14-acre park overlooking the Bosphorus with tennis courts, swimming pool, and rooms from US$200 to US$275 a single, US$235 to US$295 a double.

The 360 room ***Hyatt Regency Istanbul*** *(☎ 225 7000, fax 225 7007)*, Taşkışla Caddesi, has the feel of a vast Ottoman mansion – but with a popular jazz bar, Italian restaurant and swimming pool. Rooms cost US$210 to US$270 a single, and US$240 to US$300 a double.

The 390 room ***Ceylan Inter-Continental Istanbul*** *(☎ 231 2121, fax 231 2180, www.interconti.com)*, towers above Taksim Parkı, with fine views from its upper floors, and even some from the outdoor swimming pool. Rates rise along with the rooms, costing US$282/317 on the lower floors, US$317/351 on upper floors.

Marmara Hotel *(Map 3, ☎ 251 4696, fax 244 0509)*, towers over busy Taksim Square, affording splendid views of the Old City, Beyoğlu and the Bosphorus from its upper floors. The 432 guest rooms are priced from US$175 to US$200 a single, US$200 to US$250 a double with a buffet breakfast included.

Tepebaşı (Map 3) *Hotel Richmond (☎ 252 5460, fax 252 9707, İstiklal Caddesi 445)*, next to the palatial Russian consulate, is one of the few hotels on İstiklal Caddesi. Behind and around its 19th-century facade, the Richmond is modern, quite comfortable and well-run, with 101 full-service rooms priced at US$135/165 a single/double, breakfast included. Most guests are American.

Hotel Mercure *(☎ 251 4646, fax 249 8033)*, Meşrutiyet Caddesi, is a modern 22-storey tower across the street from the Pera Palas. All 200 simple rooms have satellite TV and minibar; some have great views of the Golden Horn, the Old City and the Bosphorus, for US$150/190, breakfast included.

Bosphorus Several other luxury hotels are up the Bosphorus in Beşiktaş. Unfortunately, these require you to take a taxi everywhere:

Çirağan Palace Hotel Kempinski Istanbul *(☎ 258 3377, fax 259 6687, Çirağan Caddesi 84)*, 80700 Beşiktaş

Conrad International Istanbul *(Map 1, ☎ 227 3000, fax 259 6667)*, Yıldız Caddesi, 80700 Beşiktaş

Swissôtel İstanbul The Bosphorus *(☎ 259 0101, fax 259 0105, Bayıldım Caddesi 2)*, Maçka, 80680 Beşiktaş

PLACES TO EAT

Good food has been a Turkish passion for centuries. The fearsome Janissary corps, the sultan's shock troops, were organised along the lines of a kitchen staff. Their habit of signalling revolt was to overturn the cauldrons which held their dinner of pilav, the message to the sovereign being, 'If you call this food, we have confidence in neither your taste buds nor your leadership'.

Small *hazır yemek* (ready food) restaurants, kebapçıs and pidecis, described in the following budget section, charge from US$2 to US$3 for a simple main-course lunch to perhaps US$5 or US$6 for a several-course tuck-in. They don't normally serve alcohol.

Mid-range restaurants with white tablecloths, waiters and alcoholic beverages charge from US$8 to US$20 for a three-course meal with wine, beer or rakı.

Though meals costing more than US$20 per person used to be rare in Turkey, this is changing. Chic cafe-restaurants with designer decor and innovative menus are attracting a well-heeled local and foreign clientele willing to pay US$25 to US$35 and higher per person, and the growing scarcity of seafood has also driven up the cost of meals at luxury seafood restaurants.

Places to Eat – Budget

Sultanahmet (Map 7) The most obvious restaurants in Sultanahmet, on Divan Yolu, offer decent food in pleasant surroundings, but prices are high by Turkish standards.

Köftecis Divan Yolu's köftecis were traditionally where the district's workers ate cheap, filling, tasty lunches. Now *meşhur* (famous), their prices have risen a bit, but the *köfte* and *şiş kebap* are still good, and the clientele a mix of locals and foreigners. Order by the *porsyon* (portion): *bir porsyon* (BEER porss-yohn, one portion) if you're not overly hungry, *bir buçuk porsyon* (BEER boo-CHOOK, one and a half) if you are, and *duble porsyon* (DOOB-leh, double) if you're ravenous. An order of köfte, a plate of salad, bread and a glass of *ayran* (a yoghurt drink) should cost around US$4.

Meşhur Sultanahmet Köftecisi, on Divan Yolu opposite the Firuz Ağa Camii and the tram stop, is about the cheapest. As if the length of its name determined its prices, ***Meşhur Tarihi Halk Köftecisi Selim Usta*** (Chef Selim, Famous Historic Popular Köfte-maker), Divan Yolu 12/A, is somewhat more expensive. ***Sultanahmet Meşhur Meydan Köftecisi***, just to the left (west) of the Sultan Pub, is in the middle as far as price is concerned.

Hazır Yemek Restaurants Divan Yolu has many ready food restaurants and grills, priced higher than equivalent restaurants outside the tourist zone. Most don't serve alcohol.

The cheap favourite is ***Doy-Doy*** ('Fill up! Fill up!'). At the south-eastern end of the Hippodrome, walk downhill to Şifa Hamamı Sokak 13. This is a simple, cheap restaurant busy with locals and backpackers. *Kuru fasulye* (broad beans in tomato sauce), *pilav* (rice), bread and a soft drink costs about US$2 and other meals are not much more.

The famous ***Pudding Shop***, where the drop-out generation of the 1960s kept alive and happy on inexpensive puddings, is still in operation, though it has become self-conscious and gone upscale in price. A meal taken for nostalgia's sake might cost US$5 to US$8, a sandwich and soft drink less. Breakfast is also expensive.

A few doors down Divan Yolu, overlooking the small park atop Yerebatan Saray, is ***Sultan Pub*** *(☎ 526 6347, Divan Yolu 2)*. The upper floor holds a mid-range restaurant, but the ground-floor cafe serves sandwiches and drinks for US$5 or so. It's a favourite place to meet and talk.

Up the street from the Pudding Shop is ***Can Restaurant***, a cafeteria-style place with better food and lower prices than the Pudding Shop. It's also generally preferred to the nearby ***Vitamin*** *(☎ 526 5086, Divan Yolu 16)*, at which you must check your bill carefully. ***Baran 2 Lokantası***, at Divan Yolu 54, is another decent choice.

Going off the beaten track even a block gets you more value for money.

At the western end of the Hippodrome, walk up Üçler Sokak to ***Yeni Birlik Lokantası*** *(☎ 517 6465)* at No 46, a large, light ready-food restaurant favoured by lawyers from the nearby law courts. Meals are available for US$2.50 to US$4; no alcohol.

Across the street from Yeni Birlik Lokantası, ***Gaziantep Kebap ve Lahmacun*** will serve you a full meal of roast meat, salad and soft drink for US$5 or US$6, or a snack of lahmacun for half that.

Karadeniz Pide ve Kebap Salonu, a cheap, simple place on Hacı Tahsin Bey Sokak half a block north of Divan Yolu, does a good business sending out meals to local shopkeepers. Have stuffed cabbage leaves, rice pilav, bread and a drink for less than US$3. The upstairs dining room is nicer than downstairs, and both are open on Sunday. A few steps away, ***Hotel Akdeniz Lokantası*** is similar.

Cafes Sultan Sofrası, a cafe-restaurant facing the Hippodrome on its north-western side, is good for a snack or sandwich and soft drink (US$2.50), and people-watching.

If you prefer shade to sun, seek out ***Derviş Aile Çay Bahçesi*** (Dervish Family Tea Garden), Kabasakal Caddesi 2/1, west of the Yeşil Ev Hotel. Stimulants and small sandwiches (US$1) are served in the cool, dark shadows cast by great plane trees. Try *peynirli tost*, a cheese sandwich mashed in a vice-like cooker.

Sirkeci & Hocapaşa (Map 4) Only three short blocks south of Sirkeci train station are good small restaurants in the neighbourhood called Hocapaşa (HO-ja pah-shah). Exit the train station by the western door (to the tram line), turn left and walk up the slope on Ankara Caddesi, turning into the third little street on the left, İbni Kemal Caddesi, to find the Hoca Paşa Camii and a dozen small restaurants. In good weather, tables are set out in the narrow, shady pedestrian-only street for pleasant dining.

There's variety: ***Ali Bey Köfte Piyaz*** features grilled lamb meatballs and *piyaz* (white beans vinaigrette), as does ***Et-İş Köfte ve Hazır Yemek***. ***Meşhur Tarihi Hocapaşa Pidecisi*** serves Turkish pizza, fresh, good and cheap for as little as US$1.50. ***İskender Et ve Kebap*** sells meat cooked or uncooked, and several steam-table places, including ***Anadolu Lokantası***, ***Özgüven*** and ***Kardeşler*** feature lots of stews and vegetable dishes as well as some grills priced at US$1 to US$1.75 per plate. Fresh fruit for afters is available from sidewalk vendors.

Eminönü (Map 4) About the cheapest way to enjoy fresh fish is to buy a ***fish sandwich*** from a boatman. Go to the Eminönü

Turkish Delight

For a traditional Ottoman treat, walk through the archway to the left of the Yeni Cami in Eminönü, and turn left onto Hamidiye Caddesi. One short block along, on the right-hand (south) side of the street near the corner with Şeyhülislam Hayri Efendi Caddesi, is the original shop of ***Ali Muhiddin Hacı Bekir*** (☎ 212-522 0666), inventor of Turkish delight.

History notes that Ali Muhiddin came to İstanbul from the Black Sea mountain town of Kastamonu and established himself as a confectioner in the Ottoman capital in the late 18th century. Dissatisfaction with hard candies and traditional sweets led the impetuous Ali Muhiddin to invent a new confection that would be easy to chew and swallow. He called his soft, gummy creation *rahat lokum*, the 'comfortable morsel'. 'Lokum', as it soon came to be called, was an immediate hit with the denizens of the imperial palace, and anything that goes well with the palace goes well with the populace.

Ali Muhiddin elaborated on his original confection, as did his offspring (the shop is still owned by his descendants), and now you can buy lokum made with various fillings: *cevizli* (JEH-veez-LEE, with walnuts), *şam fıstıklı* (SHAHM fuhss-tuhk-LUH, with pistachios), *portakkallı* (POHR-tah-kahl-LUH, orange-flavoured), or *bademli* (BAH-dehm-LEE, with almonds). You can also get a *çeşitli* (CHEH-sheet-LEE, assortment). Price is according to weight; 1kg costs US$3 to US$9, depending upon variety. Ask for a free sample by indicating your choice and saying *Deneyelim!* (DEH-neh-yeh-LEEM, 'Let's try it').

During the winter, a cool-weather speciality is added to the list of treats for sale. *Helvah*, a crumbly sweet block of sesame mash, is flavoured with chocolate or pistachio nuts or sold plain. Ali Muhiddin Hacı Bekir has another, more modern shop on İstiklal Caddesi between Taksim Square and Galatasaray next to Vakko.

end of the old Galata Bridge, and on both sides of the bridge, tied to the quay railing between the ferry docks, are boats bobbing in the water. In each boat, two men cook fish on a grill or griddle. The fried fish, slid into a slit quarter-loaf of bread, costs US$1. I've never been disappointed, nor made sick, by one of these.

For more upscale fare, try ***Borsa Fast Food,*** on Yalı Köşkü Caddesi inland from the ferry docks. Turkish classics such as stuffed vine leaves, and imports such as hamburgers, are served up quickly in modern surrounds. Meals cost US$2.50 to US$4.

Kapalı Çarşı (Map 12) Within the Kapalı Çarşı, ***Sevim Lokantası***, on Koltuk Kazaslar and Kahvehane sokaks, was founded (a sign states proudly) in 1945. Take a seat in the little dining room or sit at a table set out in one of the little streets and order one or two plates of food. The bill shouldn't exceed US$4 or US$5.

You will no doubt pass ***Şark Kahvesi*** (SHARK kahh-veh-see, Oriental Cafe), at the end of Fesçiler Caddesi, always filled with locals and tourists. The arched ceilings betray its former existence as part of a bazaar street; some enterprising *kahveci* (coffee-house owner) walled up several sides and turned it into a cafe. On the grimy walls hang paintings of Ottoman scenes and framed portraits of sultans and champion Turkish freestyle wrestlers. A cup of Turkish coffee, a soft drink or a glass of tea costs less than US$1; Nescafé is overpriced.

Taksim (Map 3) The cheapest eats in Taksim are at the *büfes* between Sıraselviler and İstiklal caddesis. Look for the prominent ***Çetin Restaurant*** at İstiklal Caddesi 1, and the büfes are just to the left. They serve fresh-squeezed fruit juices, döner sandwiches (both lamb and chicken) etc for about US$1 each. The Çetin, by the way, specialises in rotisserie chicken, ranks and rows of spitted birds revolving slowly. The upstairs terrace is the place to dine in fair weather.

A few steps down İstiklal Caddesi from the Çetin is ***Pehlivan Restaurant***. This bright, plain place has the standard cafeteria line, steam tables and low prices. Don't take too much; three dishes is plenty. Fill up at lunch or dinner for US$4. ***Taksim Sütiş***, to the right, specialises in sweets, but serves light meals as well.

Elsewhere around Taksim, the local ***McDonald's*** burger restaurant, always packed, is on the eastern side of Cumhuriyet Caddesi near the Turkish Airlines office, along with ***Pizza Hut*** and several streetside cafes.

İstiklal Caddesi (Map 3) ***Borsa Fast Food Kefeteryası***, İstiklal Caddesi 89, is modern, bright and popular with Turkish youth – especially the *dondurma* (ice cream) kiosk. Grills (US$2 to US$3) are the speciality, and beer is served.

Continuing along İstiklal Caddesi, Büyükparmakkapı Sokak holds many eating and drinking possibilities, including the cheap ***Ada Restaurant***, at No 25, where you can fill up for US$3 to US$5. ***Nature & Peace***, at No 21, serves vegetarian soups (US$1.50), salads (US$2 to US$3) and main courses (US$3), plus a few chicken dishes, at lunch and dinner (closed Sunday). Around the corner on Çukurlu Çeşmesi Sokak, ***Hala*** serves *mantı* (Turkish ravioli) and other home-cooking favourites. Look for the traditionally clad woman rolling out flats of dough in the window.

For meat-eaters, ***Sohbet Ocakbaşı***, Mis Sokak 9, specialises in Kozan kebap, a spicy Arab-influenced shish from south-eastern Turkey, with full meals for less than US$10, and sidewalk dining in fine weather. Behind (north of) the Ağa Camii on Mahyacı Sokak, the ***Meşhur Sultanahmet Köftecisi*** serves grilled lamb meatballs, lahmacun and pide at prices below those on İstiklal Caddesi.

Galatasaray (Map 3) ***Atlas Restaurant & Cafe***, İstiklal Caddesi 251, in the Örs İş Merkezi directly across from the Çiçek Pasajı, was built by an Armenian architect in 1815. Once the residence of Mr Fethi Okyar, first prime minister in the Turkish Republic (1930s), it's now a favourite lunch place for students at the British Council (in the same building) who come for the good daily three-course set-price lunch for US$3.

Just north of Galatasaray is the ***Balık Pazar*** (Fish Market), actually a full food market spread out in two little streets, Sahne Sokak and Duduodaları Sokak, next to the touristy Çiçek Pasajı. The cheapest and simplest is ***Mercan***, specialising in midye tavası for about US$0.30, a bit more *sandviçli* (in bread); the favoured beverage is draught beer. The more expensive restaurants nearby are described in Places to Eat – Mid-Range.

This is a prime area for picnic assembly, with greengrocers, *şarküteri* (charcuterie, delicatessen) shops and bakeries offering cheeses, dried meats such as pastırma, pickled fish, olives, jams and preserves, and several varieties of bread including wholegrain. ***Şütte*** *(☎ 244 9292, Duduodaları Sokak 21)*, is regarded by many as the best of the delis.

Afacan Pizza & Burger Restaurant, İstiklal Caddesi 331, south of the red brick Church of San Antonio di Padua, is popular for its namesake dishes and low prices.

Tepebaşı & Tünel (Map 3) ***Teras Secret Garden***, in the Beyoğlu İş Merkezi building at İstiklal Caddesi 365/19, lives up to its intriguing name by providing a peaceful terrace dining area overlooking the historic Palais de France. Drinks, snacks, light and more substantial meals are served in good weather at moderate prices. To find it, walk down Nuruziya Sokak half a block, enter on the right and walk straight until you must turn, then turn left.

Near Pera Palas Oteli and the American consulate general, ***Şemsiye*** *(☎ 292 2046, Şeyhbender Sokak 18)*, serves vegetarian meals (US$5 to US$9) at lunch and dinner, with at least one or two meat, fowl or fish dishes as well. It's popular with diplomats and young professionals, who also come for ***Yağmur*** ('rain'), the cybercafe upstairs (see Internet Resources at the beginning of this chapter).

For a light lunch or snack near the Pera Palas Oteli, go to ***Karadeniz Pide Salonu*** behind and to the left of the Hotel Mercure, where you can get a fresh pide with butter and cheese for little more than US$1. No alcohol is served.

Places to Eat – Mid-Range

Sultanahmet (Map 7) The obvious ***Sultan Pub*** *(☎ 526 6347, Divan Yolu 2)*, between the Pudding Shop and the small park atop Yerebatan Saray, has a cafe-bar on the ground floor and a nicer restaurant one flight up. A full meal upstairs, with wine or beer, costs between US$12 and US$18.

Buhara Ocakbaşı *(☎ 513 7424, Nuruosmaniye Caddesi 7)*, off Yerebatan Caddesi near the Cağaloğlu Hamamı, is a neighbourhood grill with good *mezes* (Turkish hors-d'oeuvres), lamb grills and alcoholic beverages. A big, full dinner with drinks usually costs around US$10 or US$12 per person.

Yeşil Ev hotel's garden restaurant has a very pleasant setting and decent food, with light meals for US$10 to US$15.

Topkapı Sarayı (Map 10) ***Konyalı Restaurant*** *(☎ 513 9696)*, beneath the Mecidiye Köşkü in Topkapı Sarayı, serves decent food at moderate prices (US$12 to US$18 per person for lunch), with views of the Bosphorus, but is impossibly crowded at noon. Go early or late, or snack instead on the cafe terrace beneath the Konyalı.

Kapalı Çarşı (Map 12) Though most Kapalı Çarşı eateries are low budget, ***Havuzlu Lokantası's*** *(☎ 527 3346, Gani Çelebi Sokak 3)*, prices are in the moderate range of US$8 to US$14 for a meal. The food is about the same as at the budget places in this area, but you get a lofty dining room made of several bazaar streets walled off for the purpose long ago, and a few tables set out in front of the entrance by a little stone pool (*havuzlu* means 'with pool'), which I suspect was a deep well centuries ago. Waiter service here is more polite and unhurried, though slow when there are tour groups. To find the Havuzlu, follow the yellow-and-black signs and ask for the PTT, which is next door.

Taksim (Map 3) ***Hacı Baba Restaurant*** *(☎ 244 1886, İstiklal Caddesi 49)*, has a pleasant terrace with tables overlooking the courtyard of the Aya Triada Kilisesi next door. The menu is long and varied, food good, and service usually competent; some English is spoken. Have a look in the kitchen to help you choose your meal. You'll pay from US$10 to US$20 per person for a full lunch or dinner with wine or beer.

İstiklal Caddesi (Map 3) ***Hacı Abdullah*** *(☎ 293 8561, Sakızağacı Caddesi 17)*, beside the Ağa Camii (İstiklal Caddesi's only mosque), is a Beyoğlu institution, having been in business for a century. Its dining rooms are simple but tasteful, its Turkish and Ottoman cuisine outstanding, with a varied menu of traditional dishes otherwise rarely found in restaurants. Service is friendly, single women are welcomed, and a full meal with soft drink (no alcohol is served) costs US$9 to US$15.

Galatasaray (Map 3) At İstiklal Caddesi 172 is an entrance to the Çicek Pasajı, the 'Flower Passage', a collection of taverna-restaurants open long hours every day in the courtyard of a historic building.

This used to be a jolly place where locals gathered for drinking, singing and good, cheap food. It has now been tarted up for tourists, and while the food can still be good, prices and the hassle factor have increased dramatically. Prices are twice as high as elsewhere, overcharging and bringing unordered items are commonplace. If you must eat here (and it *can* be enjoyable) ask prices, don't accept unordered items, and be cautious with locals who chat you up and propose outings or nightclubs, which may turn into rip-offs or even, occasionally, robberies.

The locals who used to patronise the Çiçek Pasajı have moved on to the meyhanes deeper in the market. Walk along Sahne Sokak into the market to the first street on the right, Nevizade Sokak. There are at least eight restaurants here with streetside tables in fine weather charging about US$1.50 to US$2.25 for plates of meze, about twice that for kebaps; ask prices of fish before you order. Alcohol is served enthusiastically. ***Tarihi Cumhuriyet Meyhanesi*** is among the nicest ones. ***Cağlar Restaurant*** *(☎ 249 7665)* is at No 6 and ***Kadri'nin Yeri*** *(☎ 243 6130)* nearby. My favourite, however, is ***İmroz Restaurant*** *(☎ 249 9073, Nevizade Sokak 24)*, down at the end of the row on the right. Run by a Turk and a Greek from the island of İmroz (Gökçeada, Imbros), it specialises in fish and other island dishes.

Tünel (Map 3) Popular with the diplomatic set at lunch time is ***Dört Mevsim*** (Four Seasons) *(☎ 293 3941, İstiklal Caddesi 509)*, almost in Tünel Square. Under Turkish-English management, it is well located to draw diners from the US, UK, Dutch, Russian and Swedish consulates. The food is continental with concessions to Turkish cuisine; preparation and service are first-rate, and there's a guitar and violin duo most evenings. Lunch is served from noon to 3 pm, dinner from 6 pm to midnight; closed Sunday. If you order the fixed menu at lunch, you might pay US$10, drink and tip included. Ordering from the regular menu at dinner may bring your bill to US$20 or US$25 per person.

Çatı Restaurant *(☎ 251 0000, İstiklal Caddesi, Orhan Adli Apaydın Sokak 20/7)*, is on the 7th (top) floor of a building on a small side street which runs between İstiklal and Meşrutiyet caddesis. Though the view is vestigial at best, the greenhouse-style dining room is pleasant, the food quite good and not expensive. Try the *çatı böreği* for an appetiser; it's halfway between a Turkish *börek* (flaky pastry) and a turnover, made with cheese. Main courses are mostly Turkish, with a few European specialities. Expect to spend from US$12 to US$18 per person. If you don't like syrupy organ music, come early for dinner. It's open for lunch and dinner every day.

Yakup 2 Restaurant *(☎ 249 2925, Asmalımescit Caddesi 35-37)*, is popular with local artists, musicians, actors and professors. It hasn't been fancied up for tourists, so the decor is minimal but the food is quite good and moderately priced. Strike up a conversation with those at a neighbouring table; they may well speak a foreign language. Full meals with wine, beer or rakı cost about US$8 to US$15. It's open every day for dinner, and for lunch daily except Sunday.

Places to Eat – Top End

Sultanahmet (Map 7) For ambience, food and service, ***Rumeli Cafe*** *(☎ 512 0008, Ticarethane Sokak 8)*, half a block north off Divan Yolu, gets top marks. Haydar Sarıgül, the congenial owner, had his friend Nikos from Athens design the cafe with cool stone walls for hot days and three fireplaces in the four tiny dining rooms for chilly evenings. Classical music or cool jazz plays quietly; there's similar live music at weekends. The menu lists updated Ottoman classics, and a three-course meal with drinks might cost US$15 to US$30 per person.

Daruzziyafe *(☎ 518 1351)*, at Meydanı 27, on the Hippodrome to the right (south) of the Sultan Ahmet Camii, serves good Ottoman cuisine. A full lunch might cost US$10 to US$15. Though hardly as fancy as its namesake by the Süleymaniye Camii (see the section in Old İstanbul, earlier), it is much more conveniently located.

Rami Restaurant *(☎ 517 6593, Utangaç Sokak 6)*, in a restored house behind the Sultan Ahmet Camii, is named after Turkish painter Rami Uluer (1913-88), whose work decorates the dining rooms. Interesting Ottoman specialities such as *hünkar beğendi* (grilled lamb and rich aubergine purée) or *kağıt kebap* (lamb and vegetables cooked in a paper pouch) fill the menu; food and service are of varying quality. With drinks, a meal costs about US$20 to US$30 per person. The rooftop terrace has fine views of the Sultan Ahmet Camii.

Two hotel restaurants have good views of the Sultan Ahmet Camii as well. Try the one at the Mavi Ev, near Rami. The restaurant of the Hotel Arcadia has a truly breathtaking view of the Sultan Ahmet Camii late in the afternoon, and full meals for US$12 to US$25. See Places to Stay – Top-End, earlier.

Taverna-Restaurant Sarnıç *(☎ 512 4291)*, on the corner of Caferiye and Soğukçeşme sokaks, is a Turkish Touring and Automobile Association restaurant which gives you the experience of dining on continental dishes in a Byzantine cistern (*sarnıç*) by an incongruous baronial fireplace for US$20 to US$30 per person. Across the street from the Sarnıç, Turing's ***Conservatory Restaurant*** has the opposite ambience, being a glass greenhouse with an open-air terrace serving light meals and snacks.

Eminönü (Map 4) ***Pandeli*** *(☎ 527 3909)*, over the main entrance (facing the Galata Bridge) of the Mısır Çarşısı, was founded decades ago by a Greek chef, now long gone to that great kitchen in the sky. Its small dining rooms panelled in faïence are beautiful, and its specialty in seafood alluring, but readers have complained of high prices and a charge even for hanging up your coat.

Taksim (Map 2) The posh ***Boğaziçi Borsa Restaurant*** *(☎ 232 4201)*, just north of the İstanbul Hilton in the Lütfi Kırdar Kongre ve Sergi Salonu (Convention Centre), serves creatively updated Ottoman specialities and new-wave Turkish cuisine in deluxe surroundings at reasonable prices. A three or four-course meal with wine need cost only US$15 to US$30 per person.

The dining room at ***Divan Oteli*** *(☎ 231 4100)*, serves continental and Turkish cuisine in posh surroundings at decent prices, about US$35 to US$50 per person for a fine meal, all in. ***Divan Pub***, adjoining, is still fairly fancy but significantly cheaper. The speciality here is excellent Turkish döner kebap.

ENTERTAINMENT

For many first-time visitors, the name 'İstanbul' conjures up Hollywood-baroque images of mysterious intrigues in dusky streets, sultry belly dancers undulating in smoky dens, and dangerous liaisons from the sublime to the bestial. As with most aged stereotypes, the reality is entirely different.

There are symphony, opera and ballet seasons, and tour performances by world renowned virtuosi. Many but not all of these performances are given in the Atatürk Cultural Centre. News of performances and concerts is carried in the *Weekend* supplement to the *Turkish Daily News'* Friday edition, and its *Arts & Culture* on Sunday.

İstanbul's major venues for concerts and performances of dance and opera are the Atatürk Cultural Centre (Map 3, ☎ 251 5600, fax 245 3916) in Taksim Square; the Cemal Reşit Rey Konser Salonu (Map 3, ☎ 240 5012), on Gümüş Sokak just north of the İstanbul Hilton and east of the Military Museum; and the former Aya İrini church in the First Court of Topkapı Sarayı.

Outdoor venues for summer performances include the Açık Hava Tiyatrosu (Open-Air Theatre, Map 2) just north of the İstanbul Hilton, and Rumeli Hisarı, north of Bebek on the Bosphorus.

Traditional Turkish belly dancing is high among the list of must-sees for travellers.

International İstanbul Music Festival

This, the most prominent entertainment event in İstanbul, begins in late June and continues to mid-July. World-class performers – soloists and virtuosos, orchestras, dance companies, rock and jazz groups – perform in many concert halls, historic buildings and palaces. The highlight is Mozart's *Abduction from the Seraglio* performed in Topkapı Sarayı, with the Gate of Felicity as the backdrop. Check at the box offices in the Atatürk Cultural Centre for schedules, ticket prices and availability, or contact the festival office (☎ 260 4533 or 293 3133, fax 261 8823), İstanbul Kültür ve Sanat Vakfı, Yıldız Kültür ve Sanat Merkezi, 80700 Beşiktaş, İstanbul.

Theatre

The Turks are enthusiastic theatre-goers, and as a people they seem to have a special genius for dramatic art, though the language barrier makes their performances relatively inaccessible to foreign visitors. Theatre buffs might well enjoy a performance of a familiar classic.

Theatres are concentrated in Beyoğlu along İstiklal Caddesi and near Taksim Square. The International İstanbul Theatre Festival, with performances by Turkish and foreign casts, takes place in mid-May. Contact the İstanbul Kültür ve Sanat Vakfı.

Cinema

The İstanbul International Film Festival is held annually from mid-April to early May. Tickets are sold at the Atatürk Cultural Centre.

İstiklal Caddesi between Taksim and Galatasaray is the centre of İstanbul's *sinema* (cinema) district, with many foreign films being shown. The advent of television has put many cinemas out of business, and some of the survivors screen the racier movies, plus the much-beloved Turkish melodramas. For current listings, refer to the *Turkish Daily News'* Friday edition.

Look on the cinema posters or ask at the box office to see if the film is in the original language, *Orijinal* (ohr-zhee-NAHL), or dubbed in Turkish. Most are dubbed.

When possible, buy your tickets a few hours in advance. Tickets cost from US$3 to US$5. Also, the usher will expect a small tip for showing you to your seat.

Beyoğlu (Map 3) Along İstiklal Caddesi, look for these:

Aksanat Kültür Merkezi (Aksanat Cultural Centre)
(☎ 252 3500) İstiklal Caddesi 16-18, in the Akbank building on İstiklal just out of Taksim; movies and films of musical and theatrical performances

Alkazar Sinema Merkezi
(☎ 293 2466) İstiklal Caddesi 179

Atlas
(☎ 252 8576) İstiklal Caddesi 209, Kuyumcular Pasajı

Emek
(☎ 293 8439) İstiklal Caddesi, Yeşilçam Sokak 5

Fitaş & Fitaş Cep
(☎ 249 0166) İstiklal Caddesi 24-26, Fitaş Pasajı; four cinemas in one

Sinepop
(☎ 251 1176) İstiklal Caddesi, Yeşilçam Sokak 22

Cafe-Bars

Many of Sultanahmet's cafe-restaurants such as ***Rumeli Cafe*** on Ticarethane Sokak, ***Sultan Pub*** on Divan Yolu, ***Cafeterya Medusa*** (all Map 7), Yerebatan Caddesi, and the numerous small places along Hoca Rüstem Sokak (between Divan Yolu and Yerebatan Caddesi) have cool music and outdoor tables that are very pleasant in good weather. Make sure you check prices before you order.

Real cafe-bars are in Beyoğlu (Map 3). Two of the best are ***Kaktüs Café*** (☎ 249 5979), half a block south off İstiklal Caddesi at İmam Adnan Sokak 4, and ***Cadde-i Kebir***, directly across the street. Kaktüs is lighter, noisier, more active, with a longer menu. Cadde-i Kebir is quieter; *çerez* (snacks) and light meals are served. At either place, beer is US$1.75, rakı US$2.50. There are sidewalk tables at both.

Urban, Kartal Sokak 6/A, just out of Galatasaray Square, is among Beyoğlu's coolest cafes. Classical music or cool jazz greets you as you enter past a rack of periodicals in six languages. Many and varied caffeine and alcoholic stimulants are served along with a cafe menu of sandwiches and omelets (US$3), salads (US$4) and a few meat dishes (US$6). The stonewalled rear room was once a Byzantine cistern.

Two-thirds of the way along İstiklal Caddesi toward Tünel, next to the Odakule office tower, is ***Garibaldi*** (☎ 249 6895), a restaurant-bar with live music (jazz, smooth or Turkish pop) many nights starting around 8.30 pm. The specialities here are steaks and the extensive salad bar.

Just north of the İstanbul Hilton Hotel at Cumhuriyet Caddesi 239 is ***Pub Avni*** (☎ 246 1136), a neighbourhood bar with a nightly crowd of middle-aged regulars, American and European recorded music, and snacks and full meals. It's closed on Sundays.

Discos & Rock Clubs

Several music-and-dance clubs are located along Sıraselviler Caddesi, south out of Taksim. For rock, try ***Kemancı*** in the Taksim Sitesi building at Siraselviler Caddesi 69, a block south of Taksim on the left-hand (eastern) side. ***Andon Dancing***, open from 9.30 pm to 2 am, is part of the popular ***Andon Pera*** (Map 3, ☎ 251 0222) cafe-bar at Sıraselviler Caddesi 89/2, just a short walk further along the street.

Cadde-i Kebir Kültür ve Eğlence Merkezi, on İmam Adnan Sokak just down from the Cadde-i Kebir (see Cafe-Bars, earlier) often has bands and special events.

Jazz Bars

Kehribar (Map 2, ☎ 231 4100) in the Divan Oteli is smooth and luxurious, with excellent music and expensive drinks. Next door in the Hyatt Regency Istanbul, it's ***Harry's Jazz Bar*** (Map 2, ☎ 225 7000), with a similar reputation. Also try ***Tepe Lounge Bar*** (Map 3, ☎ 251 4696) at the Marmara Hotel in Taksim, where there's jazz from 10.30 pm to 1 am.

For Turkish music, try the friendly ***Jasmine*** cafe-bar (☎ 252 7266), Akarsu Sokak 10, off İstiklal Caddesi between Taksim and Galatasaray, open from 3 pm to 2 am.

Nightclubs

Nightclubs with entertainment are mostly in Beyoğlu and along the Bosphorus shores. In the Old City there are several Ottoman theme restaurants which offer dinner and an 'Ottoman' show including belly dancers and folk troupes. The larger, more expensive clubs are tame – and hardly authentic – but safe, as are the clubs in the big hotels. You may get ripped off in smaller clubs.

Kervansaray (☎ 247 1630), Cumhuriyet Caddesi 30, Harbiye, on the northern side of the İstanbul Hilton Hotel arcade, is a good club of long standing with decent food and drinks and a good show at top prices of around US$35 to US$60 per person. It's popular with tour groups.

A similar club is ***Maksim Gazino Nightclub*** (Map 3, ☎ 293 4110), Sıraselviler Caddesi 37, just out of Taksim to the right of the Hotel Savoy. Maksim has a set menu (US$50) which includes dinner and a show (8.30 or 11.30 pm).

Casinos

Many luxury hotels used to have profitable gambling casinos, but when the Islamist Refah Partisi came to power in the mid-1990s laws were passed to close them, throwing hundreds of casino staffers out of work. Refah is gone, but at the time of writing the law remained the same and it is still illegal to gamble in Turkey.

A traditional Turkish *gazino*, by the way, is not a gambling place, but an open-air nightclub popular in the summertime. A few still survive along the European shore of the Bosphorus, serving up Turkish popular singers, dinner and drinks.

Night Cruises

About the cheapest yet most enjoyable night-time activity in İstanbul is to take a ferryboat from Eminönü to Üsküdar or from Karaköy to Haydarpaşa/Kadıköy. The great, historic buildings are illuminated, and the twinkling city lights, the boats bobbing in the waves, the powerful searchlights of the ferries sweeping the sea lanes, make a lasting impression. The round trip takes only about an hour, and costs only US$1.

Hamams

A visit to the hamam, or Turkish bath, can be wonderful: cleansing, refreshing, relaxing, and sociable.

The tradition of the steam bath was passed from the Romans to the Byzantines, and from them to the Turks, who have fostered it ever since. Islam's emphasis on personal cleanliness resulted in the construction of hundreds of hamams throughout İstanbul. Though modern bath and shower facilities in the home have now cut public bath usage to a fraction of what it was, the tradition of a leisurely steam bath in grand public facilities is alive and well in Turkey.

Traditionally, men and women bathed separately, and bath attendants had to be of the same gender as their clients. Baths were taken frequently – especially on a Friday, the Muslim Sabbath – and prices were low.

Tourism has changed the tradition radically. Some of the finest old baths have raised prices dramatically, meaning that only tourists can afford them. Service has fallen as prices have risen, so you must shop carefully for your Turkish bath experience. For a description of taking a Turkish bath, see the boxed text 'The Hamam Experience' in the South of the Sea of Marmara chapter.

In İstanbul, the price for the entire experience can be US$3 to US$6 in a local bath if you bring your own soap, shampoo and towel, and bathe yourself; from US$8 to US$10 for an assisted bath; from US$16 to US$25 and more at an 'historic' bath, with a perfunctory massage. Tips will be expected.

After you're all done, you'll be utterly refreshed, hyper-clean, and almost unable to walk due to the wonderful relaxation of muscles, mind and spirit.

Fancy Tourist Baths Cağaloğlu Hamamı (jaa-AHL-oh-loo) (Map 7, ☎ 522 2424, www.cagalogluhamami.com.tr), on Yerebatan Caddesi at Babıali Caddesi, 200m north-west of Aya Sofya, was built more than three centuries ago. It boasts (without evidence) that King Edward VIII, Kaiser Wilhelm II, Franz Liszt and Florence Nightingale have all enjoyed its pleasures, no doubt at the same time. Hours are from 7 am to 10 pm (men) or 8 am to 8 pm (women). A self-service bath (wash yourself) costs US$10, the full treatment US$20, the deluxe treatment US$30, plus tips.

Çemberlitaş Hamamı (Map 7, ☎ 522 7974), Vezirhan Caddesi 8, off Divan Yolu near the Kapalı Çarşı, is a double hamam (twin baths for men and women) designed by Sinan for Nurbanu Sultan, wife of Sultan Selim II, in 1584. Hours are 6 am to midnight, and prices are similar to those at the Cağaloğlu Hamamı.

Tarihi Galatasaray Hamamı (Map 3, ☎ 251 8653), or Historic Galatasaray Turkish Bath, Turnacıbaşı Sokak 24, is off İstiklal Caddesi just north of Galatasaray Square. The men's side, rich in marble decoration, pretty fountains and tip-hungry staff, is open from 5 am to midnight, and charges an un-Turkish US$30 for the full treatment – bath, scrub, massage and rest-cubicle use, plus at least 20% more for the many sweaty, outstretched palms. The women's side, open from 8 am to 8 pm, is not as nice, and charges a few dollars more.

Local Baths If it's just a bath you're interested in, ask at your hotel for directions to a *mahalli hamam* (neighbourhood bath) where locals go. Neighbourhood baths will treat you much better for much less money than the touristy baths, though as more foreigners patronise these local baths they may suffer the same fate. Here are some suggestions near Sultanahmet (Map 7):

Kadırga Hamamı – on Kadırga Hamamı Sokak, just off Piyerloti Caddesi opposite the park (the women's section, or Kadınlar Kısmı, is on the opposite side up the hill on Kadırga Hamamı Sokak). A one-hour bath costs just US$4 or less, a few dollars more with a massage.

Tarihi Hocapaşa Hamamı – at İbni Kemal Caddesi 23 near the Hocapaşa mosque near Sirkeci train station; the area is described in Places to Eat.

Tarihi Park Hamamı – a small and unpretentious place at Doktor Emin Paşa Sokak 10; turn off Divan Yolu opposite the Hippodrome.

SHOPPING

İstanbul has it all, and prices for craft items are not necessarily higher than at the village source. Leather apparel offers good value, but you must shop around, get to know the market, and inspect your prospective purchase carefully for flaws and bad craftwork.

Carpets

There must be as many carpet shops as there are taxis. The carpet shop touts become exceedingly tedious very early in your visit, but a Turkish carpet – a good one at a fair price – is a beautiful, durable and useful souvenir.

The carpet shops of longstanding are in and around Kapalı Çarşı. Their proprietors and sales personnel are more knowledgeable and less pushy than those at the newly opened shops in Cankurtaran and other hotel areas.

The government-run carpet shop in the Haseki Hürrem Hamamı between Aya Sofya and the Sultan Ahmet Camii, described previously, is a safe choice, with guaranteed quality and fixed prices.

If you haggle for a carpet, at least shop around and get to know price levels a bit. Beware of this scam:

You make friends with a charming Turk, or perhaps a Turkish-American or Turkish-European couple. They recommend a friend's shop, so you go and have a look. There's no pressure to buy. Indeed, your new friends wine and dine you (always in a jolly group with others), paying for everything. Before you leave İstanbul you decide to buy a carpet. You go to the shop, choose one you like, and ask the price. So far so good; if you can buy that carpet at a good price, everything's fine. But if the owner strongly urges you to buy a 'better' carpet, more expensive because it's 'old' or 'Persian' or 'rare', or 'makes a good investment', beware. You may return home with it to find you've paid many times more than the carpet is worth. If the shopkeeper ships the carpet for you, the cheap carpet which arrives may not be the expensive carpet you bought.

Make sure that *you* choose the carpet, inspect it carefully, compare prices for similar work at other shops, then buy and, preferably, take it with you or ship it yourself.

For fine antique carpets and textiles readers have reported being satisfied with Su-De (☎/fax 516 5488, capas@escortnet.com), İletişim Han 7/2, facing the entrance to the Binbirdirek Cistern a block west of the Hippodrome.

Leather Apparel

The traditional leather apparel centre is the Kürkçüler Çarşısı section of the Kapalı Çarşı, but today the leather shops fill street after street in the Beyazıt, Laleli and Aksaray districts.

The best way to be assured of quality is to shop around, trying on garments in several shops. Look especially for quality stitching and lining, sufficient fullness of sleeve and leg, and the amount of care taken in the small things such as attaching buttons and zippers.

Fashions & Silk

İstiklal Caddesi in Beyoğlu, once known as the Grand Rue de Péra, has reclaimed some of its Ottoman chicness, and is now lined with shops selling upscale clothing, fashions, leather apparel, furs and silks. For silk scarves, try İpek (☎ 249 8207), İstiklal Caddesi 230/7-8, just south of Galatasaray.

Handicrafts

Although the Kapalı Çarşı has a great deal of general tourist ware, a few shops specialise in high-quality handicrafts. One such is Selvi El Sanatları (☎ 527 0997, fax 527 0226), Yağlıkçılar Caddesi 54, Kapalı Çarşı. The speciality here is Kütahya faïence, and not just the *turist işi* (tourist-ware) sold in most shops. Many of the tile panels, vases, plates and other items here are fine, artistic Kütahya ware.

İstanbul Sanatlar Çarşısı (Handicrafts Market) is in the 18th-century Cedid Mehmed Efendi Medresesi, restored by Turing on the southern side of the Yeşil Ev hotel on Kabasakal Caddesi, between Aya Sofya and the Sultan Ahmet Camii. Local artisans ply their traditional Turkish arts and crafts here, and sell their products.

Old Books, Maps & Prints

Librairie de Péra (☎ 245 4998), Galip Dede Caddesi 22, Tünel, just south of the Galata Mevlevihanesi (whirling dervish lodge), is a good antiquarian shop with old books in Turkish, Greek, Armenian, Arabic, French, German, English and more.

Eren (☎ 251 2858), Sofyalı Sokak 34, Tünel, has old and new history and art books and maps.

Sahaflar Çarşısı (Map 6), the used-book bazaar just west of the Kapalı Çarşı across Çadırcılar Caddesi, in the shadow of the Beyazıt Camii, is best for browsing and not bad for buying. The Üniversiteli Kitabevi (☎ 511 3987, fax 216-345 9387), at No 5, is among the best shops, with a modern outlook and the most current books published in Turkey. The Zorlu Kitabevi (☎ 511 2660, fax 526 0495), at No 22, specialises in books about İstanbul, old documents and maps. Dilmen Kitabevi (☎ 527 9934), at No 20, has a good selection of titles on Turkey and Turkish history in English.

Beyoğlu Anabala Han Sahafları is a passage lined with dusty shops selling whatever old printed materials fall into their hands: books in all languages, magazines Turkish and foreign, movie posters, stock and bond certificates, even some 45rpm vinyl records. From Galatasaray, follow Turnacıbaşı Sokak to No 23, just past the İlyada art and crafts shop.

Follow Turnacıbaşı Sokak further, turn right onto Faik Paşa Sokak and among the antiques shops here and along Çukurcuma Caddesi to the east are some which stock old prints and maps, and a few picture books. The finest is perhaps Galeri Alfa (☎ 251 1672, fax 243 2429), Faikpaşa Sokak 47.

Shopping Centres

Grandest of them all is, of course, the Kapalı Çarşı, or Grand Bazaar, described earlier. Almost as popular and enjoyable is pedestrianised İstiklal Caddesi from Taksim Square to Tünel Square, lined with boutiques and places to eat.

Several modern American-style malls have opened as well. Many of the shops in the new malls are branches of the same retailers you're used to at home, at similar prices, so they offer little acquisitive thrill to foreign visitors.

İstanbul's first mall was the Galleria (gah-LEHR-ree-yah) (☎ 559 9560), on the Marmara shore road at Ataköy, west of the city walls. The bonus here is the small indoor ice-skating rink in winter.

The Akmerkez (☎ 282 0170) in Etiler, well north of Taksim, west of Bebek, is poshest. When you get tired of shopping at Ralph Lauren and Benetton, take sustenance from the supermarket, or relax in one of the cinemas.

GETTING THERE & AWAY

All roads lead to İstanbul. As the country's foremost transportation hub, the question is not how to get there (see the Getting There & Away chapter at the front of this book), but how to negotiate the sprawling urban mass when you arrive. Here is the information you may need on arrival.

Air

Atatürk (Yeşilköy) airport's international terminal is insufficient to handle the volume of air traffic. A new international terminal is under construction. The airport has two other terminals, the İç Hatlar Terminali (domestic routes terminal) and 'Terminal C' for charter flights from abroad.

The Ministry of Tourism maintains an information office in the international arrivals terminal (lower floor). There is also a hotel-reservation desk in the arrivals terminal, but some readers of this guide have written to say that they always recommend the same expensive, inconvenient hotel to everyone, regardless of their preference. This may change, so check anyway.

Also in the arrivals terminal are ATMs paying out Turkish liras, and various currency exchange offices operated by Turkish banks. If you change money here, count your money carefully and make sure it agrees with the total on the exchange slip. These guys will often short-change you by several percent, relying upon your confusion as a new arrival to get away with it. Also, don't accept an excuse that they 'have no small change'. It's their business to have the proper change.

Before you pass through customs, you might want to take the opportunity to buy duty-free goods at the shops in the baggage claim area.

For examples of airfares from İstanbul to other Turkish cities, see the earlier Getting Around chapter. For details on transport to and from İstanbul's Atatürk Airport, see the Getting Around section later in this chapter.

Airline Offices Most of the offices are on Cumhuriyet Caddesi between Taksim Square and Harbiye, in the Elmadağ district, but Turkish Airlines has offices around the city. Travel agencies can also sell tickets and make reservations. Some addresses follow:

Aeroflot
(☎ 243 4725, fax 252 3998) Mete Caddesi 30, Taksim

Air France
(☎ 254 4356 or 254 3196, fax 254 4334) corner of Cumhuriyet & Tarlabaşı Caddesis, Taksim
(☎ 663 0600) Atatürk airport

Alitalia
(☎ 231 3391 or 232 7065, fax 230 6304) Cumhuriyet Caddesi 12/4, Elmadağ
(☎ 663 0577) Atatürk airport

American Airlines
(☎ 237 2003, fax 237 2005) Cumhuriyet Caddesi 47/2, Elmadağ

British Airways
(☎ 234 1300, fax 234 1308) Cumhuriyet Caddesi 10, Elmadağ
(☎ 663 0574) Atatürk airport

Delta Airlines
(☎ 231 2339, fax 231 2346) in the İstanbul Hilton Hotel arcade
(☎ 663 0752) Atatürk airport

El Al
(☎ 246 5303, fax 230 3705) Rumeli Caddesi 4/1, Nişantaşı
(☎ 663 0810) Atatürk airport

Iberia
(☎ 237 3104, fax 250 5478) Topçu Caddesi 2/2, Elmadağ
(☎ 663 0826) Atatürk airport

İstanbul Airlines
(☎ 231 7526, fax 246 4967) Harbiye Ticket Office, Cumhuriyet Caddesi 289

(☎ 663 0664, fax 663 2712) Atatürk airport, international routes; (☎ 574 4271, fax 663 2713) domestic routes

Japan Air Lines
(☎ 241 7366, fax 234 2209) Cumhuriyet Caddesi 141/6, Elmadağ

KLM
(☎ 230 0311, fax 232 8749) Abdi İpekçi Caddesi 8, Nişantaşı, north-east of Harbiye
(☎ 663 0603) Atatürk airport

Lot
(☎ 240 7927, fax 246 7626) Cumhuriyet Caddesi 91/2, Elmadağ

Lufthansa
(☎ 288 1050, fax 275 6961) Maya Akar Center, Büyükdere Caddesi 100-102, Esentepe
(☎ 663 0594) Atatürk airport

Malev
(☎ 248 8153, fax 230 2034) Cumhuriyet Caddesi 141, Elmadağ
(☎ 663 6400) Atatürk airport

Olympic Airways
(☎ 246 5081, fax 232 2173) Cumhuriyet Caddesi 203, Elmadağ
(☎ 663 0820) Atatürk airport

Qantas Airways
(☎ 240 5032, fax 241 5552) Cumhuriyet Caddesi 155/1, Elmadağ

Sabena
(☎ 254 7254, fax 240 1513) Topçu Caddesi 2/1, Taksim
(☎ 663 0824) Atatürk airport

SAS
(☎ 246 6075, fax 233 8803) Cumhuriyet Caddesi 26/A, Elmadağ
(☎ 663 0818) Atatürk airport

Singapore Airlines
(☎ 232 3706, fax 248 8620) Halaskargazi Caddesi 113, Harbiye
(☎ 663 0710) Atatürk airport

Swissair
(☎ 231 2850, fax 240 1513) Cumhuriyet Caddesi 6, Elmadağ
(☎ 663 6778) Atatürk airport

Turkish Airlines
(☎ 663 6363, fax 240 2984) reservations
(☎ 252 1106) Taksim Square Ticket Office, Cumhuriyet Caddesi, in the Taksim Gezi Yeri shops

Bus

The Uluslararası İstanbul Otogarı (International Istanbul Bus Terminal) (☎ 658 0505, fax 658 2858), called simply the otogar, is in the western district of Esenler, just south of the expressway and about 10km west of Sultanahmet or Taksim. With 168 ticket offices, restaurants, mosques and shops, it is a town in itself, and one of the world's largest bus terminals. For Turkish travellers, this is the domestic equivalent of London-Heathrow or New York-JFK.

Buses depart the otogar for virtually all cities and towns in Turkey and to neighbouring countries including Azerbaijan, Bulgaria, Greece, Iran, Romania, Saudi Arabia, Syria, and other destinations in Eastern Europe and the Middle East. The top national lines, giving premium service at somewhat higher prices, are As Turizm (office 117), Bosfor Turizm (127), Pamukkale (43), Ulusoy (128) and Varan (15). Other lines are smaller regional or local lines which may have more frequent service and less polished service at lower prices.

Except in busy holiday periods, you can usually just come to the otogar, spend 30 minutes shopping for tickets, and be on your way to your destination at a good price within the hour. There is no easy way to find the best bus company and the best fare; you've got to go from one office to another asking for information and looking at the buses parked at the *perons* (gates) at the back.

Metro, municipal buses and taxis connect the otogar with the city centre and the airport. See Getting Around, following, for details.

There is another bus terminal on the Asian shore of the Bosphorus at Harem (☎ 216-333 3763), 2km north-west of Haydarpaşa train station. If you're arriving from the east, by all means get out at Harem and take the car ferry to Sirkeci; it'll save you two hours' crawl through traffic to the main otogar, then the Metro ride back to the centre. If you're heading east you can save some time and hassle by taking the Harem car ferry from Sirkeci and getting the bus there. But the selection of buses, seats, routes and companies is nowhere near as big at Harem as at the main otogar in Esenler.

Bus Ticket Offices Travel agencies on Divan Yolu by the Hippodrome and in Cankurtaran will sell you bus tickets, often at inflated prices.

Some bus companies have city ticket offices near Taksim Square on Mete and İnönü Caddesis (all on Map 3). Pamukkale (☎ 249 2791) is at Mete Caddesi 16; Nev Tur (☎ 249 7961), with buses to Cappadocia, is nearby. Down the hill along İnönü Caddesi are Varan (☎ 249 1903, fax 251 7481), at İnönü Caddesi 29/B, a premium line with routes to major Turkish cities and to several points in Europe (including Athens); Kamil Koç (☎ 257 7223), İnönü Caddesi 31; As Turizm and Hakiki Koç lines (☎ 245 4244); and Ulusoy (☎ 249 4373), İnönü Caddesi 59.

Fares & Travel Times Here are some examples of bus fares and travel times from İstanbul to other cities in Turkey. Fares vary among companies, and sometimes can be reduced by haggling or by showing a student card. Departures to major cities and resorts are very frequent.

Alanya – 840km, 17 hours, US$23
Ankara – 450km, six hours, US$15 to US$24
Antakya – 1115km, 20 hours, US$23 to US$31
Antalya – 725km, 12 hours, US$16 to US$20
Artvin – 1352km, 24 hours, US$34 to US$40
Ayvalık – 570km, nine hours, US$16 to US$21
Bodrum – 830km, 14 hours, US$24
Bursa – 230km, four hours, US$9
Çanakkale – 340km, six hours, US$9 to US$12
Denizli (for Pamukkale) – 665km, 13 hours, US$13 to US$20
Edirne – 235km, 1/2 hour, US$6
Erzurum – 1275km, 18 hours, US$18 to US$30
Fethiye – 980km, 12 to 14 hours, US$18 to US$23
Gazinatep – 1136km, 14 hours, US$21
Göreme (Cappadocia) – 725km, 11 hours, US$12 to US$18
İzmir – 610km, eight hours, US$12
Kaş – 1090km, 14 hours, US$20
Konya – 6660km, 10 hours, US$16
Kuşadası – 700km, 10 hours, US$15
Marmaris – 900km, 14 hours, US$18 to US$24
Side – 790km, 12 hours, US$19 to US$24
Trabzon – 1110km, 18 hours, US$20 to US$30

Train

Sirkeci Garı (Map 4) All trains from Europe terminate at Sirkeci Garı (SEER-keh-jee) (☎ 527 0051), next to Eminönü in the shadow of Topkapı Sarayı. The station has a small post office and currency exchange booth, as well as a restaurant and cafe, and a tourism office (☎ 511 5888).

The northern facade of the building was where passengers entered to board the fabled *Orient Express* to Paris. The new main (western) door is a boring modern structure.

Outside the station's western door is the tram up the hill to Sultanahmet, Beyazıt, Laleli, Aksaray and eventually the otogar. On the shore north of the station are car ferries for the Asian otogar at Harem.

If you're going to Taksim, go out the station door and turn right. Walk towards the sea and you'll see the Eminönü bus ranks to your left, with departures to many parts of the city. For a dolmuş to Taksim, go to the Yeni Cami at the southern end of the Galata Bridge and look for the Kentbank building on the mosque's south-eastern side. The dolmuş rank is behind the Kentbank.

Departures Trains depart Sirkeci for the following destinations:

train	destination	departs
Balkan Ekspresi	Budapest	10.20 pm
Bükreş Ekspresi	Bucharest	8.05 pm
Ekspresi	Edirne	7.00 am
Ekspresi	Edirne	3.25 pm
Uzunköprü Ekspresi	Uzunköprü	8.25 am

Haydarpaşa Garı Haydarpaşa Garı (☎ 216-336 0475 or 348 8020), on the Asian shore of the Bosphorus, is the terminus for trains to and from Anatolia and points east and south. For train information, see the Getting Around chapter at the beginning of this book.

Ferries (US$0.50, 20 minutes) run every 15 to 30 minutes between Karaköy (northern end of Galata Bridge) and Haydarpaşa.

Ignore anyone who suggests that you take a taxi to Haydarpaşa. The ferry is cheap, convenient, pleasant and speedy. Taxis across the Bosphorus are expensive and slow.

Haydarpaşa has an *emniyet* (left luggage room), a restaurant serving alcohol, snack shops, bank ATMs and a small PTT.

Car

The E80 Trans-European Motorway from Europe passes north of Atatürk airport, then crosses the Bosphorus on the Fatih Bridge. Exit signs direct you to various districts of the city.

For a scenic entrance to the city, leave the expressway at the airport and follow signs for Yeşilköy or Ataköy, which will take you to the shore of the Sea of Marmara so you can drive into the city along the water's edge. You'll pass the city walls near Yedikule, the Fortress of the Seven Towers and the Marble Tower, as well as the city's southern wall, which will be on your left as you drive. Across the Bosphorus are Üsküdar, Haydarpaşa and Kadıköy, with the large four-square Selimiye Barracks acting as a landmark. For Cankurtaran and the hotels near Sultanahmet, follow signs to the Hotel Armada, turning left and passing through the ancient walls, but turn right after you pass under the railroad bridge. If you stay on the shore road it will take you to Sirkeci, Eminönü and the Galata Bridge.

Car Rental Getting into and out of İstanbul is frustrating. Traffic is chaotic, signs inadequate, and no other driver will give you a break. It's best to rent your car at the airport, where you can get directly on the motorway, or even in a smaller city.

The well-known international car-rental firms have desks at Atatürk airport and downtown, mostly near Taksim Square and the Elmadağ district, a few blocks north of it.

Avis
- (☎ 663 0858) Atatürk airport international arrivals hall (☎ 663 6400, fax 663 0724) Atatürk airport domestic arrivals hall
- (☎ 257 7670, fax 263 3918) Reservations centre
- (☎ 516 6109, fax 516 6108) Beyazıt office, Ordu Caddesi, Haznedar Sokak 1

Budget
- (☎ 663 0858, fax 663 0724) Atatürk airport international arrivals hall
- (☎ 296 3196, fax 296 3188) Reservations Centre, Cumhuriyet Caddesi 12, Seyhan Apartmanı, 4th floor, office 10, just north of Taksim Square
- (☎ 253 9200, fax 237 2919, www.budgettr.com, budget@escortnet.com) Office, Cumhuriyet Caddesi 19/A, Gezi Apartımanı

Europcar/Inter-rent
- (☎ 663 0746, fax 663 6830) Atatürk airport international arrivals hall
- (☎ 254 7788, emergency 663 0746, fax 237 3158) Esin Turizm, Topçu Caddesi, Uygun İş Merkezi 2, 80090 Talimhane, a few short blocks north of Taksim Square and only steps west of Cumhuriyet Caddesi

Hertz
- (☎ 234 4300, fax 232 9260) Ekin Turizm, Cumhuriyet Caddesi 295, Harbiye

Sun Rent a Car
- (☎ 216-318 9040, fax 321 4014), Kısıklı Caddesi, Nurbaba Sokak 1, 81190 Üsküdar; Auto Europe's representative, a local firm with a good reputation and offices in major cities and resorts

Boat

See the following Getting Around section for details on ferryboat routes within greater İstanbul.

Karaköy (Map 4) Cruise liners dock at Karaköy, near the Yolcu Salonu (YOHL-joo sahl-oh-noo), or International Maritime Passenger Terminal on Rıhtım Caddesi. The Ministry of Tourism has an information office (☎ 249 5776) in the Yolcu Salonu, near the front (street) doors.

This international dock is next to the Karaköy ferry dock and only 100m east of the Galata Bridge. Bus and dolmuş routes to Taksim pass along Kemeraltı Caddesi, a few short blocks north-west of the Yolcu Salonu. For destinations in the Old City such as Sultanahmet, go to the western side of Karaköy Square itself, at the end of the Galata Bridge, via the pedestrian underpass; or you can walk across the bridge and get on the tram at Eminönü.

Sarayburnu (Map 5) Seraglio Point (Sarayburnu), east of Sirkeci, is the dock for the weekly car ferries to İzmir. (See the Getting Around chapter earlier in this book for details.)

Yenikapı (Map 6) Yenikapı, south of Aksaray Square, is the dock for intracity catamarans and for fast *hızlı feribot* (car ferries) on routes across the Sea of Marmara. To **Yalova**, ferries leave about every two hours and get you to Yalova (for **Bursa**) in less than an hour for US$35 (car and driver) or US$6 (pedestrian/passenger).

To **Bandırma**, the voyage is made in less than two hours for US$70 (car and driver), or US$12 (pedestrian/passenger).

Kabataş (Map 3) Ferries run from Kabataş (KAH-bah-tahsh), 3km north of Karaköy on the Bosphorus shore, just south of the Dolmabahçe Palace and Mosque, to Üsküdar. Catamarans run from here to Bostancı on the Asian shore, with a few to other destinations as well.

GETTING AROUND

Even though several wide boulevards have been cut through the city's medieval street pattern, they are insufficient to move the glut of traffic quickly. Transport by road often creeps. Transport by sea is far more pleasant and speedy, although it serves only a handful of routes.

To/From the Airport

Airport Terminal Shuttle In principle, free shuttle buses leave the Atatürk airport international terminal arrivals level for the İç Hatlar Terminali (domestic terminal) every 20 minutes or so throughout the day. In fact the taxi drivers lurking at international arrivals run a racket whereby the shuttle bus doesn't arrive, and you end up taking a taxi over to the domestic terminal, only a 1½-minute drive for an outrageous US$3. You can walk it in five minutes if you can carry your stuff that long.

Airport to City The fastest way to get into town from the airport is by taxi (from 20 to 30 minutes, US$10 to US$20); the fare depends upon what part of the city you're headed for and whether it's night or day.

A far cheaper but less speedy alternative is the Havaş airport bus (from 35 to 60 minutes, US$3.50), which departs from the international terminal, stops at the domestic terminal, then goes to Taksim Square. Buses leave every 30 minutes from 5.30 to 10 am, every hour from 10 am to 2 pm, every 30 minutes from 2 to 8 pm, and every hour from 9 to 11 pm; there are no buses between 11 pm and 5.30 am.

For even less, find two or three other thrifty travellers and share a taxi (US$5 total; make sure the driver runs the meter) from the airport to the Yeşilköy *banliyö tren istasyonu*, the suburban railway station in the neighbouring town of Yeşilköy. From here, battered trains (US$0.50) run every 30 minutes or less to Sirkeci station. Get off at Yenikapı for Aksaray and Laleli, at Cankurtaran for Sultanahmet hotels, or at Eminönü (end of the line) for Beyoğlu.

City to Airport You must check in *at least* 30 minutes before departure time for domestic flights, and it's not a bad idea to check in 45 minutes to an hour before. For international flights, you should be in line at the check-in counter at least an hour before take-off, and as it can take 30 minutes just to get through the first security check and into the terminal building, you should plan to arrive at the airport 1½ or two hours before departure time. After check-in, you must go through passport control, customs, and another security check before boarding. If the aircraft is large, the officials will have to process about 400 passengers at once.

If you're staying in Old İstanbul and you have plenty of time (60 to 90 minutes) for the return trip to the airport, catch bus No 96 (US$0.50) on the eastern side of Mustafa Kemal Paşa Bulvarı south of Aksaray, across the street from McDonald's. Departures are at 7, 8.40, 10.15 and 11.45 am, and 1.35, 2.45, 4.05, 5.55 and 7.40 pm. Otherwise, get on a suburban train ('Halkalı', US$0.50) at Sirkeci, Cankurtaran or Yenikapı, and get out at Yeşilköy, then take a taxi (US$5) to the airport.

There are also frequent minibus dolmuşes from the corner of Şehit Muhtarbey and Ayede caddesis just north of Taksim Square (US$1.50).

Several private services run minibuses to the airport, advertising their services at budget hotels in and around Sultanahmet. Fares range from US$4 to US$6 per person. Reserve your seat in advance for pick-up from your hotel. Allow lots of time for the trip: the minibus may spend an hour circulating through the city collecting all the passengers before heading out to the airport (30 to 45 minutes).

If you're staying in Beyoğlu, the cheapest and most convenient way to the airport is the Havaş bus (US$3.50) which departs from in front of the DHL office on Cumhuriyet Caddesi just north of McDonald's in Taksim Square. The trip takes 45 minutes to an hour. There are also dolmuşes to the airport from the Yeşilköy-Ataköy-Florya-Hava Limanı (Map 2) dolmuş stand on Şehit Muhtar Bey Caddesi two blocks north of Taksim.

A taxi to the airport costs US$10 to US$20.

Bus

Otogars If you arrive at the main otogar in Esenler, take the Metro east toward Aksaray or Yenikapı. In Aksaray, board the other tram (Eminönü) to Sultanahmet. City bus No 91 goes from the Esenler otogar to the western side of the Yeni Cami in Eminönü, but takes much longer than the Metro.

To get to the Harem bus terminal, take the Harem car ferry from Sirkeci. An alternative is to take a ferry from Karaköy to Haydarpaşa or Kadıköy, then catch one of the frequent dolmuşes northward along the shore to Harem. You can also take a ferry from Eminönü, Kabataş or Beşiktaş to Üsküdar, then a dolmuş or bus south 2.5km to Harem.

City Buses There are two classes of buses. Red-and-beige İETT city buses, owned and operated by the city, require you to have a ticket before boarding. Blue-and-silver 'peoples' buses' *(Özel Halk Otobüsü)* are privately owned and operated, and allow you to pay by either city bus ticket or cash. Both kinds of buses are useful, but slow and often packed solid.

Fares are US$0.50 per ride, around half price for students, but you may need a Turkish student ID card to get the discount. Fares are paid on a ticket system (see the Getting Around chapter at the front of this book). Hawkers near the major bus stops usually sell tickets for a markup of 20% for your convenience. On the kerb side of each bus is a list of stops along the route.

Most buses require one ticket for passage (look for *Tek* or *Bir Bilet Geçerlidir* in the windscreen), others on longer routes or for 'luxury' services require two tickets *(Çift* or *İki Bilet Geçerlidir)*.

Some buses fill to capacity at the departure point, leaving no room for passengers en route. If you're jammed in the middle of the bus when your stop comes, shout *İnecek var!* (een-neh-JEK vahr, 'Someone needs to get out!').

Dolmuş

İstanbul dolmuşes are minibuses running on defined routes at a set price. Useful routes are mentioned in the text.

Metro

İstanbul's Metro system will be under construction for a decade more, but several useful lines are already in service. The fare is US$0.50.

The main *hızlı tramvay* (fast-tram) line goes from Aksaray north-westward along Adnan Menderes Bulvarı (formerly Vatan Caddesi) through the Bayrampaşa and Sağmalcılar districts to the otogar in Esenler, then turns south-westward to pass the airport, terminating at Ataköy on the Sea of Marmara, where it meets the suburban train line.

The Sirkeci-Halkalı suburban train line follows the Sea of Marmara shore south-westward from Seraglio Point to the south-western suburbs. At Ataköy it links to the main Metro line. The suburban trains are decrepit but serviceable and cheap.

A shorter, slower tram line goes from Eminönü past Sirkeci and uphill to Sultanahmet; then along Divan Yolu/Yeniçeriler Caddesi/Ordu Caddesi past Beyazıt and the Kapalı Çarşı to Laleli and Aksaray; it continues out Turgut Özal Caddesi to the Topkapı (Cannon Gate) and on to the Marmara shore district of Zeytinburnu.

In Beyoğlu, a restored early 20th-century tram runs along İstiklal Caddesi between Taksim and Tünel squares, but is too small and infrequent to be of great use.

The 7.8km-long Taksim to 4. Levent underground line is nearing completion, and may be in service by the time you arrive.

Tünel

İstanbul's little underground train, the Tünel, runs between Karaköy and the southern end of İstiklal Caddesi called Tünel Meydanı (Tünel Square) every five to 10 minutes from early morning until 10 pm. The 80-second trip costs US$0.40. With only two stations, the upper (Tünel) and lower (Karaköy), there's no getting lost.

Car

It makes no sense to drive in İstanbul. If you have a car, park it in a spot recommended by your hotel and use public transport, except perhaps for excursions up the Bosphorus. If you plan to rent a car, do so when you're ready to leave İstanbul or, better yet, use public transport to get to your next destination, and rent the car in that smaller place. (For addresses of car rental agencies in İstanbul see the Getting There & Away section earlier in this chapter.)

Taxi

Taxis are plentiful, as are honest drivers, though the many dishonest ones seem to congregate in tourist areas. Most taxis run on nonpolluting natural gas. The fact that some drivers have their blood types painted on the taxi bumper bar should tell you something about their expectations of surviving İstanbul traffic.

All taxis have digital meters, and it is an offence punishable by a large fine to take a passenger but to refuse to run the meter, or to demand a flat fare in place of the metered fare. Still, such practices are common on trips originating from touristic areas (see the warning under Taxi in the Getting Around chapter). Some drivers also take advantage of the many zeros on Turkish currency to charge you 10 times what the meter reads.

The base rate (drop rate, flag fall) is about US$1.25 during the *gündüz* (daytime); the *gece* (night-time) rate is 50% higher. A daytime trip between Aksaray and Sultanahmet costs about US$1.75; between Taksim and Karaköy about US$3; between Taksim and Sultanahmet about US$5, between Sultanahmet and the airport about US$12 to US$15.

Older meters have tiny red lights marked with 'gündüz' and 'gece' to show which rate is being used. Newer meters with LCD displays flash 'gündüz' or 'gece' when they are started. Even this will not stop creative cheaters:

> One driver I used had discovered that if he whacked a certain spot on the instrument panel of his car with his fist, the meter would skip from 'gündüz' to 'gece', thereby increasing his profit by 50%. One can hardly fail to notice a driver beating violently on the interior of his vehicle, however, and when I looked at the meter the fare seemed unusually high. I noticed that his fit of vehicular abuse had resulted in the 'gece' light coming on, so I deducted 33% from the final fare.

Ferryboats

Without doubt, the nicest and cheapest way to travel any considerable distance in İstanbul is by ferry. The familiar white İstanbul ferries have been replaced on many routes by fast, modern catamarans called *deniz otobüsü* (seabus) which cost several times as much (see Catamaran (Seabus) following).

The major ferry docks are at the mouth of the Golden Horn (Eminönü, Sirkeci and Karaköy) and at Kabataş, 3km north-east of the Galata Bridge, just south of Dolmabahçe Palace. Short ferry rides (less than 30 minutes) cost US$0.50, most longer ones (up to an hour) are US$1.30.

Buy your token or ticket from the agent in the booth; if you buy them from the men who stand around outside the ferry docks hawking them, you may pay four times the fare.

Ferries to Üsküdar Ferries depart from Eminönü every 15 minutes between 6 am and midnight for Üsküdar, even more frequently during rush hour. From Kabataş, just south of Dolmabahçe Palace, ferries run to Üsküdar every 30 minutes on the hour and half hour from 7 am to 8 pm. A similarly frequent ferry service operates between Beşiktaş and Üsküdar.

Karaköy to Haydarpaşa/Kadıköy To get to the Asia train station at Haydarpaşa, or for a cruise around Seraglio Point and across the Bosphorus (good for photos of Topkapı Sarayı, Aya Sofya and the Sultan Ahmet Camii), catch a ferry from Karaköy; they depart every 15 minutes (20 minutes on weekends). Some go only to Kadıköy, 1km south of Haydarpaşa, so check your boat's itinerary. The round-trip to Haydarpaşa and/or Kadıköy (US$1) takes about an hour.

Bosphorus Excursion Ferries The ferry most tourists use is the Eminönü-Kavaklar Boğaziçi Özel Gezi Seferleri (Eminönü-Kavaklar Bosphorus Special Touristic Excursions) up the Bosphorus. These ferries depart from Eminönü daily at 10.35 am and 12.35 and 2.10 pm each weekday, stop at Beşiktaş on the European shore, Kanlıca on the Asian shore, Yeniköy, Sarıyer and Rumeli Kavağı on the European shore, and Anadolu Kavağı on the Asian shore (the turn-around point). Times are subject to change.

The ferries go all the way to Rumeli Kavağı and Anadolu Kavağı (1¾ hours), but you may want to go only as far as Sarıyer, then take a dolmuş or bus back down, stopping at various sights along the way. Arrival at Sarıyer, on the European shore about three quarters of the way up the Bosphorus, is at 11.50 am and 1.50 and 3.30 pm respectively. Departures from Sarıyer for the trip back down the Bosphorus are at 2.20, 3.10 and 5.50 pm on weekdays.

Trips are added on Sunday and holidays, with boats departing from Eminönü at 10 and 11 am, noon, 1.30 and 3 pm.

The weekday round-trip fare is US$5, half price on Saturday and Sunday. Prices are printed on all tickets. Hold onto your ticket; you need to show it to re-board the boat for the return trip. The boats fill up early in summer – on weekends particularly – so buy your ticket and walk aboard at least 30 or 45 minutes prior to departure to get a seat.

Cross-Bosphorus Ferries At several points along the Bosphorus, passenger ferries run between the European and Asian shores, allowing you to cross from one side to the other. You can also hire a boatman to motor you across the Bosphorus for a few dollars.

Southernmost are the routes from Eminönü, Kabataş and Beşiktaş in Europe to Üsküdar in Asia. See Sights on the Asian Shore section earlier for details.

Another ring route is from Kanlıca to Anadolu Hisarı on the Asian shore, thence across the Bosphorus to Bebek on the European shore. Departures from Kanlıca are at 8.30, 9.30, 10.30 and 11.30 am, and 12.30, 2.30, 4, 5.15 and 6.15 pm. The voyage to Bebek takes 25 minutes and costs US$0.50.

Other ring ferries run from İstinye on the European side to Beykoz and Paşabahçe on the Asian side. Yet another ring ferry operates from Sarıyer and Rumeli Kavağı in Europe to Anadolu Kavağı in Asia, with 17 ferries a day (at least one every hour) from 7.15 am to 11 pm.

Catamaran (Seabus)

Called deniz otobüsü, fast catamarans run on commuter routes between the European and Asian shores of İstanbul, and up the Bosphorus. Major docks on the European side are at Yenikapı and Kabataş, with less frequently served docks at Eminönü, Karaköy and several Bosphorus docks such as İstinye and Sarıyer. On the Asian side, major docks are at Bostancı and Kartal, and minor docks at Büyükada and Heybeliada.

Fares for the catamarans are several times higher than those for ferries. Except for the route up the Bosphorus, you may find that you rarely use the intracity catamarans on touristic excursions.

On Foot

With an overburdened public transport system, walking in İstanbul can often be faster and more rewarding. Watch out for broken pavement, bits of pipe sticking a few centimetres out of the pavement, ankle-breaking holes and an assortment of other health hazards.

Don't expect car drivers to stop for you, a pedestrian, in any situation. Cars seize the right of way everywhere, and drivers become furious with pedestrians who assert ridiculous claims to right of way. The halt, the lame, the infant and the aged flee before the onslaught of the automobile. Swallow your pride – step lively to avoid being maimed.

Thrace

The Roman province of Thrace, to the north of the Aegean and Marmara seas, today is divided among Turkey, Bulgaria and Greece, with Turkey holding the eastern-most part. Turkish Thrace (Trakya) is famous for its vast, rolling fields of sunflowers, grown for their seeds and cooking oil, and for Edirne, second capital of the Ottoman Empire.

HIGHLIGHTS

- Exploring Selimiye Camii in Edirne – the elegant masterpiece that is Mimar Sinan's 'finest work'
- Touring the Gallipoli battlefields, with echoes of battles fought nearly a century ago
- Swimming in the refreshing coastal waters

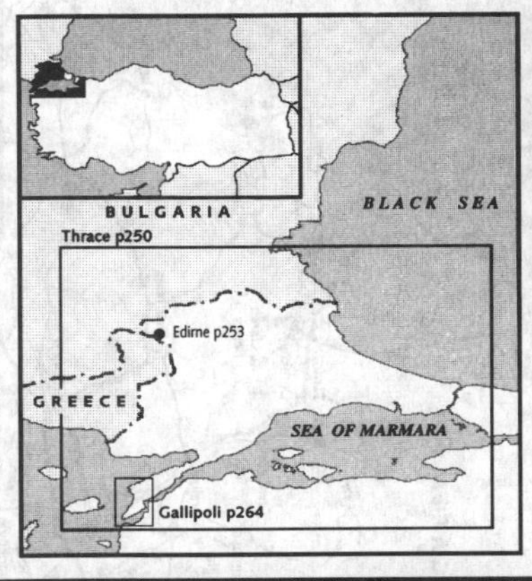

EDİRNE

For most of history, Edirne (eh-DEER-neh, altitude 40m, population 115,000), once called Adrianople, has been a stopping point on the road to İstanbul. The Trans European Motorway (TEM) has reduced the time needed to travel the 250km from a journey of several days on a camel to a 2½-hour ride by bus or car.

Edirne was the second capital city (after Bursa) of the Ottoman Empire, and an important staging-point for the sultan's annual military campaigns in Europe. As such it was graced with fine mosques, baths and caravanserais, including the serene Selimiye Camii, masterwork of the great Sienna.

Today Adrienne is among the most pleasant of Turkish cities: a farming and trading centre of manageable size, with an impressive number of great public buildings, some fine old houses, shady parks along two rivers, and a good attitude toward travellers.

History

The Roman emperor Hadrian founded Adrienne in the 2nd century AD as Hadrianopolis. It was soon to become a forward defence post for Constantinople. The town's name was later shortened by Europeans to Adrianople, and later changed by the Turks to Edirne.

The Ottoman state, an emirate founded around 1288 in north-western Anatolia, used Bursa as its capital. By the mid-14th century, the Ottoman state had grown substantially in power and size, and was looking for new conquests. The mighty walls of Constantinople were beyond its powers, but not the fertile, rolling country of Thrace. Bent on further conquest, the Ottoman armies crossed the Dardanelles, skirting the great capital. Capturing Adrianople in 1363, they made it their new capital and base of operations for military campaigns in Europe.

For almost 100 years, this was the city from which the Ottoman sultan set out on his campaigns to Europe and Asia. When at last the time was ripe for the final conquest of the Byzantine Empire, Mehmet the Conqueror rode out from Edirne on the Via Ignatia (the ancient road from Rome) to Constantinople.

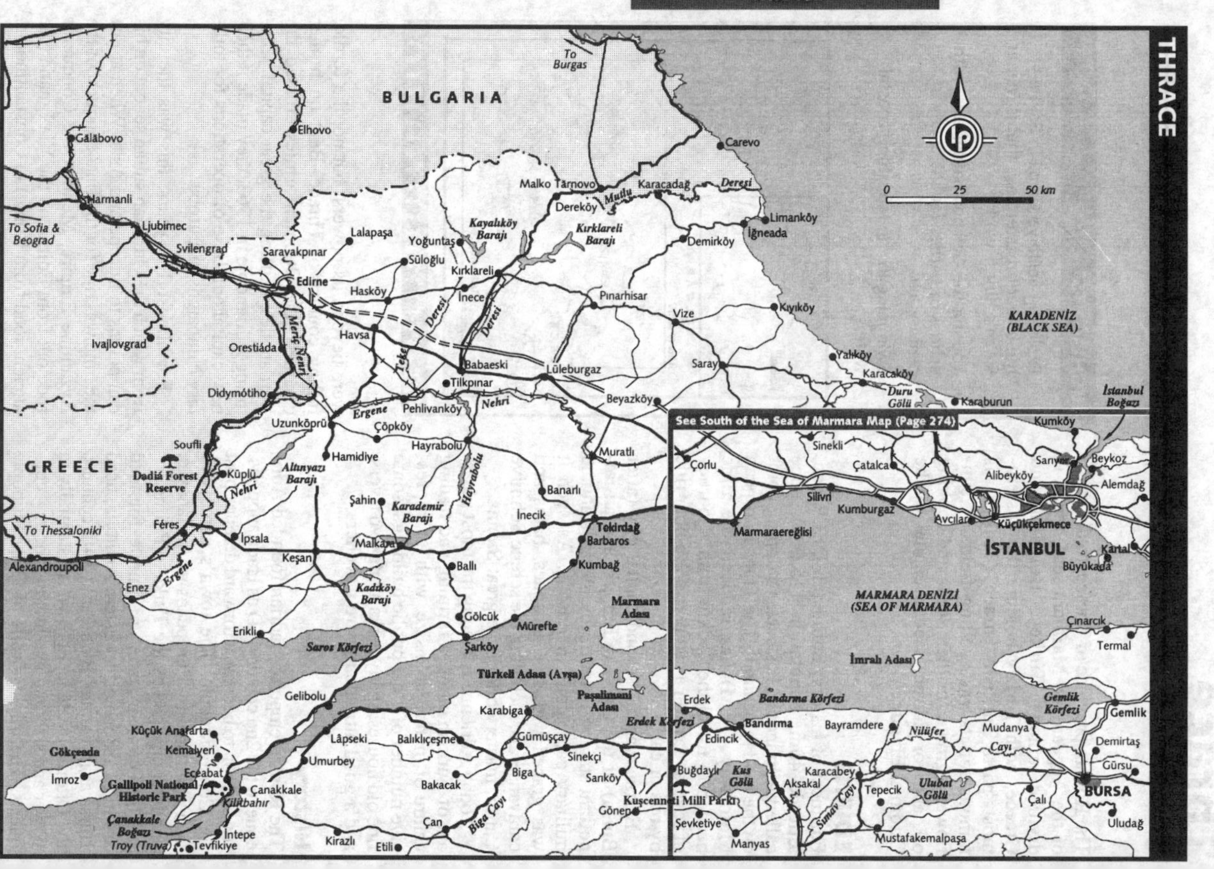
THRACE
BULGARIA
GREECE
KARADENİZ
(BLACK SEA)
MARMARA DENİZİ
(SEA OF MARMARA)
0
25
50 km
See South of the Sea of Marmara Map (Page 274)
To Burgas
To Sofia & Beograd
To Thessaloniki
Gălăbovo
Elhovo
Harmanli
Ljubimec
Svilengrad
Saravakpınar
Edirne
Lalapaşa
Yoğuntaş
Kayalıköy Barajı
Süloğlu
Kırklareli
Kırklareli Barajı
Malko Tărnovo
Dereköy
Mutlu
Karacadağ
Deresi
Carevo
Limanköy
İğneada
Demirköy
Hasköy
İnece
Pınarhisar
Vize
Kıyıköy
Havsa
Babaeski
Tilkpınar
Lüleburgaz
Saray
Yalıköy
Karacaköy
Duru Gölü
Karaburun
İstanbul Boğazı
Ivajlovgrad
Orestiáda
Meriç Nehri
Teke
Didymótiho
Uzunköprü
Ergene
Pehlivanköy
Nehri
Çöpköy
Hayrabolu
Beyazköy
Muratlı
Soufli
Dadiá Forest Reserve
Küplü
Hamidiye
Altınyazı Barajı
Şahin
Karademir Barajı
Banarlı
İnecik
Tekirdağ
Barbaros
Féres
İpsala
Keşan
Malkara
Ballı
Kumbağ
Alexandroupoli
Enez
Kadıköy Barajı
Marmara Adası
Erikli
Gölcük
Mürefte
Saros Körfezi
Şarköy
Türkeli Adası (Avşa)
Paşalimanı Adası
Gelibolu
Karabiga
Erdek Körfezi
Küçük Anafarta
Kemalyeri
Gökçeada
Lâpseki
Balıklıçeşme
Gümüşçay
Sinekçi
Eceabat
Umurbey
İmroz
Gallipoli National Historic Park
Çanakkale
Kilitbahir
Bakacak
Biga
Sarıköy
Kuşcenneti Milli Parkı
Gönen
Çanakkale Boğazı
İntepe
Troy (Truva)
Tevfikiye
Kirazlı
Etili
Çan
Biga Çayı
Kumköy
Sinekli
Çorlu
Çatalca
Sarıyer
Beykoz
Alibeyköy
Alemdağ
Silivri
Kumburgaz
Avcılar
Küçükçekmece
Marmaraereğlisi
İSTANBUL
Kartal
Büyükada
Çınarcık
Termal
İmralı Adası
Erdek
Bandırma Körfezi
Gemlik Körfezi
Gemlik
Bandırma
Bayramdere
Nilüfer
Mudanya
Çayı
Edincik
Demirtaş
Buğdaylı
Kuş Gölü
Karacabey
Aksakal
Tepecik
Ulubat Gölü
Gürsu
BURSA
Çalı
Simav Çayı
Şevketiye
Manyas
Mustafakemalpaşa
Uludağ

When the Ottoman Empire disintegrated after WWI, the Allies granted all of Thrace to the Greek kingdom. Constantinople (now İstanbul) was to become an independent, international city. In the summer of 1920, Greek armies occupied Edirne, but several years later Atatürk's republican armies drove them out, and the Treaty of Lausanne left Edirne and eastern Thrace to the Turks.

Edirne is largely disregarded by tourists, which has helped preserve its Turkish character and appeal. While the towns along the Aegean and Mediterranean coasts are clogged with foreigners and with vast new European-style building projects, Edirne attracts the discerning few who come to enjoy the harmony and history of its mosques, covered bazaars, bridges and caravanserais, and the easy pace of life. If you've just arrived overland from Europe, it's the perfect introduction to Turkey and the Turks.

Orientation

The centre of town is Hürriyet Meydanı (Freedom Square), at the intersection of the two main streets, Saraçlar/Hükümet Caddesi and Talat Paşa Caddesi. Just north-east of the square is Üçşerefeli Cami. Going east along Talat Paşa Caddesi and north-east along Mimar Sinan Caddesi will bring you to Edirne's masterpiece, the Selimiye Camii. On the way to the Selimiye, you'll pass the Eski Cami. South of Hürriyet Meydanı is the Ali Paşa Çarşısı, Edirne's largest covered bazaar.

The *otogar* (bus station) is 2km south-east of the Eski Cami on the old highway (D100) to İstanbul. The main *dolmuş* (minibus or sedan) station downtown, with services to the Greek and Bulgarian border posts, is behind (east of) the Hotel Kervansaray.

Edirne's postal code is 22100.

Information

Tourist Offices The Ministry of Tourism's Office (☎ 284-225 1518, 213 9208, fax 225 2518), Hürriyet Meydanı 17, is just off the main square, half a block south-west of the Üçşerefeli Cami. They can help with accommodation, transport and also answer money changing questions.

The provincial tourism information office (Edirne İl Turizm Müdürlüğü) (☎ 284-225 5260) is further west at Talat Paşa Caddesi 76/A. There are also offices at the Kapıkule (☎ 284-238 2019, fax 238 2009) and İpsala (☎ 284-616 1577) border posts.

Money Araz Döviz, to the right of the central tourism office on Hürriyet Meydanı, changes money, as do other *döviz* offices nearby and around the corner on Saraçlar Caddesi. Most ATMs are in the same locations. The well-wired Yapı Kredi Bankası ATM is next to the post, telephone and telegraph office (PTT) on Saraçlar Caddesi.

Consulates & Visas The Bulgarian consulate (☎ 284-225 1069) at Talat Paşa Asfaltı 31, east of Hürriyet Meydanı on the way to the otogar, is open Monday to Friday from 9 am to 12.30 pm. A transit visa for 30 hours costs US$12 for many nationalities; if you buy it at the border it will cost US$16. Visas for longer stays are more expensive.

To find the low-profile Greek consulate (☎ 284-225 1074; open Monday to Friday from 9 am to 12.30 pm), follow Maarif Caddesi for about 500m to Cumhuriyet Caddesi, turn left and look for the police kiosk across the street from the consulate.

Üçşerefeli Cami

The Üçşerefeli (EWCH-sheh-reh-feh-LEE) Cami, with its four strikingly different minarets built at different times, dominates Hürriyet Meydanı. The name means 'mosque with three galleries (balconies)', though the three galleries – an innovation at the time – are on the tallest of the minarets.

Construction was begun in 1440 and finished by 1447. Its design shows the transition from the Seljuk Turkish-style mosques of Konya and Bursa to a truly Ottoman style, which would be perfected later in İstanbul. In the Seljuk style, smaller domes are mounted on square rooms. At the Üçşerefeli, the wide (24m) dome is mounted on a hexagonal drum and supported by two walls and two pillars. Keep this transitional style in mind as you visit Edirne's other mosques which reflect either earlier or later styles.

THRACE

The courtyard, with its central *şadırvan* (ablutions fountain), was an innovation in mosque architecture which came to be standard in the great Ottoman mosques. The architect's genius is best appreciated if you enter the mosque across the courtyard from the west, but the courtyard is presently closed for restoration, and the mosque itself will continue to be filled with scaffolding for years to come.

Across the street from the mosque is the **Sokollu Mehmet Paşa Hamamı**, or Turkish baths, built in the late 16th century and still in use. Designed by the great Mimar Sinan for Grand Vizier Sokollu Mehmet Paşa, it is a *çifte hamam* (twin baths) with identical but separate sections for men *(erkekler kısmı)*, and women *(kadınlar kısmı)*. The opening hours of this hamam are from 6 am to 10 pm. Simple admission costs US$2; washing by an attendant US$3; and a massage US$4.

Ruined fireplaces clinging to the baths' exterior wall facing the street are evidence that a *medrese* (theological seminary) was once attached to the baths.

Eski Cami

From Hürriyet Meydanı, walk east on Talat Paşa Asfaltı to the Eski Cami, or Old Mosque. On your way you will pass the *bedesten* (covered market) across the park on your right. Dating from 1418, it is now known as the **Bedesten Çarşısı** or Bedesten Bazaar, and is still filled with shops. Behind it to the east is the Rüstem Paşa Hanı, a grand caravanserai built 100 years after the bedesten.

The Eski Cami (1414) exemplifies one of two principal mosque styles used by the Ottomans in their earlier capital, Bursa. Like Bursa's great Ulu Cami, the Eski Cami has rows of arches and pillars supporting a series of small domes. Inside, there is a marvellous *mihrab* (niche indicating the direction of Mecca) and huge calligraphic inscriptions on the walls. The columns at the front of the mosque were lifted from a Roman building, a common practice over the centuries.

Selimiye Camii

Up the hill to the north-east past the Eski Cami stands the Selimiye mosque (1569-75), the finest work of the great Ottoman architect Mimar Sinan – or so the architect himself believed. Constructed for Sultan Selim II (1566-74) and finished just after the sultan's death, it is smaller than Sinan's earlier (1557), tremendous Süleymaniye mosque in İstanbul, but more elegant and harmonious. Crowning its small hill, it was meant to dominate the town and be easily visible from all approaches across the rolling Thracian landscape.

To fully appreciate its excellence you should enter it from the west as the architect intended. Walk up the street and through the courtyard rather than through the park and the *arasta* (row of shops), a financially necessary but obtrusive later addition built during the reign of Murat III.

The harmony and serenity of this most symmetrical of mosques surrounds you as you enter. The broad, lofty dome – at 31.5m, wider than that of İstanbul's Aya Sofya by a few centimetres – is supported unobtrusively by eight pillars, arches and external buttresses. This was done so well that the interior is surprisingly spacious and the walls, because they bear only a portion of the dome's weight, can be filled with windows, thus admitting plentiful light to the wide, airy central space.

Centred beneath the main dome is the *kürsü*, or prayer-reader's platform, and centred beneath that is a small fountain which gives the soothing sound of running water to the quiet interior.

As you might expect, the interior furnishings of the Selimiye are exquisite, from the delicately carved marble *mimber* (pulpit) to the outstanding İznik faïence in and around the mihrab.

In contrast to its many 'twinnings' (pairs of windows, columns etc), the northern side of the mosque (near the Türk-İslam Eserleri Müzesi) has playful groupings of threes – arches, domes, niches etc; and even triads of pairs (windows).

Part of the Selimiye's excellent effect comes from its four slender, very tall (71m)

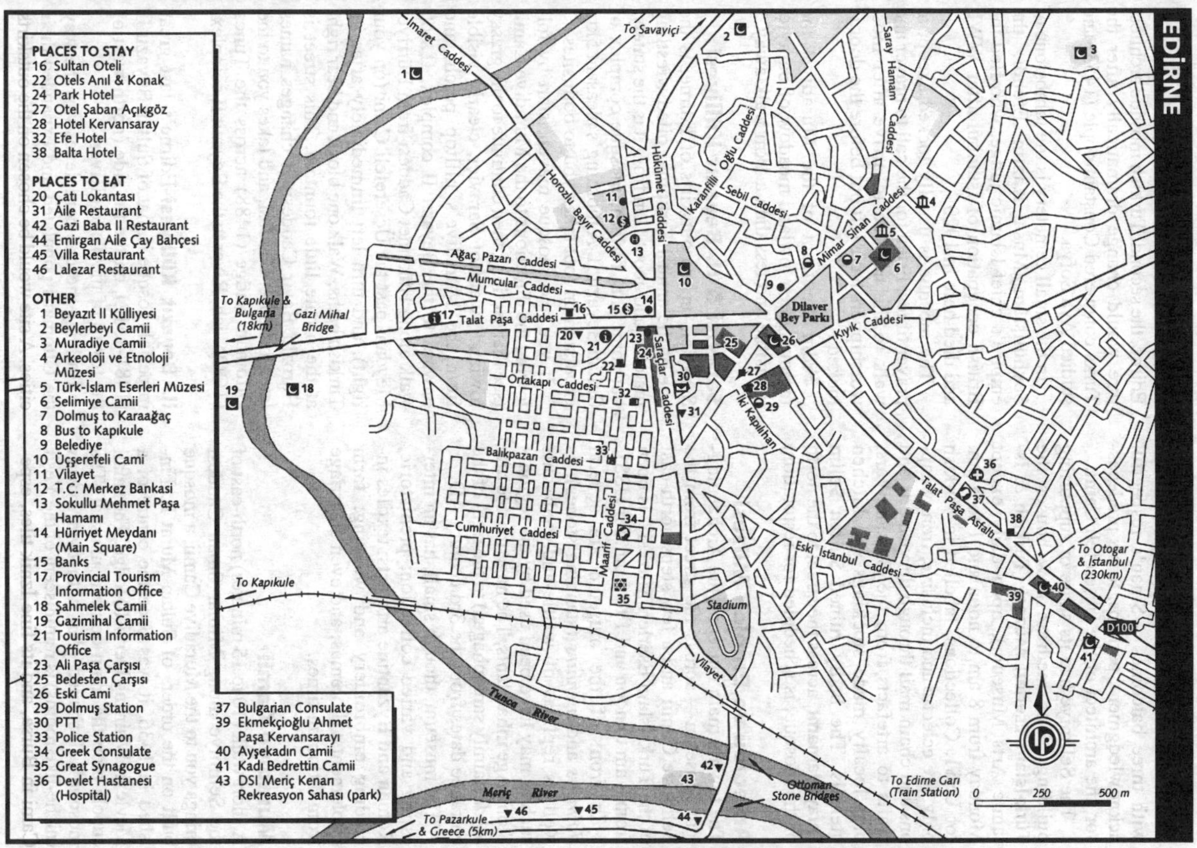
EDİRNE
Saray Hamam Caddesi
Mimar Sinan Caddesi
Kıyık Caddesi
Dilaver Bey Parkı
Talat Paşa Asfaltı
Eski İstanbul Caddesi
İki Kapılıhan
Sebil Caddesi
Karanfiloğlu Caddesi
Hükümet Caddesi
Saraçlar Caddesi
Horozlu Bayır Caddesi
İmaret Caddesi
Ağaç Pazarı Caddesi
Mumcular Caddesi
Talat Paşa Caddesi
Ortakapı Caddesi
Balıkpazarı Caddesi
Cumhuriyet Caddesi
Maarif Caddesi
Vilayet
Stadium
Tunca River
Meriç River
Ottoman Stone Bridges
Gazi Mihal Bridge
To Savayiçi
To Otogar & İstanbul (230km)
D100
To Edirne Garı (Train Station)
To Kapıkule
To Kapıkule & Bulgaria (18km)
To Pazarkule & Greece (5km)
0 250 500 m
THRACE
PLACES TO STAY
16 Sultan Oteli
22 Otels Anıl & Konak
24 Park Hotel
27 Otel Şaban Açıkgöz
28 Hotel Kervansaray
32 Efe Hotel
38 Balta Hotel
PLACES TO EAT
20 Çatı Lokantası
31 Aile Restaurant
42 Gazi Baba II Restaurant
44 Emirgan Aile Çay Bahçesi
45 Villa Restaurant
46 Lalezar Restaurant
OTHER
1 Beyazıt II Külliyesi
2 Beylerbeyi Camii
3 Muradiye Camii
4 Arkeoloji ve Etnoloji Müzesi
5 Türk-İslam Eserleri Müzesi
6 Selimiye Camii
7 Dolmuş to Karaağaç
8 Bus to Kapıkule
9 Belediye
10 Üçşerefeli Cami
11 Vilayet
12 T.C. Merkez Bankasi
13 Sokullu Mehmet Paşa Hamamı
14 Hürriyet Meydanı (Main Square)
15 Banks
17 Provincial Tourism Information Office
18 Şahmelek Camii
19 Gazimihal Camii
21 Tourism Information Office
23 Ali Paşa Çarşısı
25 Bedesten Çarşısı
26 Eski Cami
29 Dolmuş Station
30 PTT
33 Police Station
34 Greek Consulate
35 Great Synagogue
36 Devlet Hastanesi (Hospital)
37 Bulgarian Consulate
39 Ekmekçioğlu Ahmet Paşa Kervansarayı
40 Ayşekadın Camii
41 Kadı Bedrettin Camii
43 DSI Meriç Kenarı Rekreasyon Sahası (park)

minarets, fluted to emphasize their height. You'll notice that each is *üçşerefeli*, or built with three balconies – Sinan's respectful acknowledgment, perhaps, to his predecessor, the architect of the Üçşerefeli Cami.

The Selimiye had its share of supporting buildings. The medrese now houses the **Türk-İslam Eserleri Müzesi** (Turkish & Islamic Arts Museum), open daily except Monday from 8 am to noon and 1 to 5 pm, for US$1. Collections, labelled in Turkish only, are eclectic and inclusive, from weapons and chain mail through dervish arts and crafts to artefacts from the Balkan Wars, plus locally made stockings and kitchen utensils. The badly ruined **Sultan Selim Saray Hamamı**, across the street to the north of the mosque, is scheduled for restoration.

Arkeoloji ve Etnoloji Müzesi

The town's main museum, the Archaeological Museum – across the street from the Selimiye Camii and a few steps north-east of the Türk-İslam Eserleri Müzesi – is open from 8 am to noon and 1 to 5 pm, for US$1.

In front of the museum are several *dolmens* and *menhirs* (standing stones), as well as replicas of wattle-and-daub huts such as may have been used by the region's Stone Age inhabitants. The huge marble *aile lâhdi* (family sarcophagus) to the right of the entrance dates from the 3rd century AD.

The museum, though small, has an interesting and varied collection: prehistoric, Roman and Byzantine artefacts; textiles including embroidery and weaving; farm implements; dioramas; and even a carriage from Ottoman times.

Muradiye Camii

A short walk (10 to 15 minutes) north-east of the Selimiye along Mimar Sinan Caddesi brings you to the Muradiye Camii, a mosque built on the orders of Sultan Murat II. Finished in 1436, it was once the centre of a Mevlevi (Whirling Dervish) lodge. The small cupola atop the main dome is unusual. The mosque's T-shaped plan with twin *eyvans* (niche-like rooms) is reminiscent of the Yeşil Cami in Bursa, and its fine İznik tiles, especially in the mihrab, remind one that Bursa (near İznik) was the first Ottoman capital and Edirne, the second. Turkish mosque architecture would change dramatically after the Turks conquered Constantinople (1453) and studied Aya Sofya.

In the small cemetery is the tombstone of Şeyhülislâm Musa Kâzım Efendi, the empire's chief Islamic judge, who fled the British occupation of İstanbul after WWI, and died here in 1920.

The mosque is usually locked except at prayer times; listen for the call to prayer and walk to the mosque to arrive after most worshippers have left but before the door is locked.

From the front of the Muradiye, the famous green lowland meadow of Sarayiçi is visible and less than a 1km walk away.

Sarayiçi & II. Beyazıt Külliyesi

Sarayiçi, on the outskirts of Edirne, is the site of the annual Kırkpınar oiled wrestling matches and about 1km from it is the stately, but somewhat forlorn, mosque complex of Sultan Beyazıt II. A morning's pleasant 5km excursion on foot takes you to both sites.

If you're a mosque maven, start by following the directions to the Muradiye Camii (see that section), then continue to the grassy lowland swath of Sarayiçi, clearly visible from the Muradiye's hilltop perch, and onward to the Beyazıt II complex. If not, walk along Hükümet Caddesi from Hürriyet Meydanı past the Üçşerefeli Cami (on your right), and turn left immediately after its Turkish baths. Walk one block and bear right at the ornate little fountain. This street is Horozlu Bayır Caddesi; it changes names later to İmaret Caddesi, and takes you to the Ottoman bridge (1488) across the Tunca (TOON-jah) River to the Beyazıt II complex.

II. Beyazıt Külliyesi Edirne's last great imperial mosque is that of Sultan Beyazıt II (1481-1512), on the far side (north-west of the town) of the Tunca River.

Building mosque complexes was the way the Ottomans populated and expanded their cities. A site would be chosen on the outskirts of a populated area and workers employed for construction. Many of the workers and their families would settle near the mosque construction, thereby attracting necessary services (grocers, cookshops, tailors etc) on which they would spend their pay. The scheme seems not to have worked for the Beyazıt complex (the İkinci Beyazıt Külliyesi), built from 1484 to 1488, as it remains on Edirne's outskirts, unpopulated and little used, after 500 years.

The architect of the complex, one Hayrettin, did a creditable job, though he was obviously no Sinan. The mosque's style is between that of the Üçşerefeli and the Selimiye, moving back a bit rather than advancing: its large prayer hall has one large dome, more like in Bursa's mosques, but it has a courtyard and şadırvan like the Üçşerefeli Cami's. Though of a high standard, Hayrettin's work can't compare with the Selimiye, built less than a century later.

The mosque's külliye is extensive and includes a *tabhane* (hostel for travellers), medrese, bakery, *imaret* (soup kitchen), *tımarhane* (insane asylum) and *darüşşifa* (hospital). These buildings were fully restored in the late 1970s, though time has obviously been at work since then.

Eski Saray A pleasant 1km walk upriver (east) from the II. Beyazıt Külliyesi are the ruins of the Eski Saray (Old Palace). The shortest and most scenic route is to walk along the raised flood-control levee; cars can follow a curving (and longer) paved road.

Begun by Sultan Beyazıt II in 1450, this palace once rivalled İstanbul's Topkapı in luxury and size. Today, little is left but a few ruins: a kitchen, a hamam etc, some of which are off limits in a military zone.

Sarayiçi East of Eski Saray, across a branch of the Tunca, is Sarayiçi (Within the Palace). This scrub-covered island was once the sultans' private hunting preserve, and today is the site of the famous annual Kırkpınar oiled wrestling matches or Tarihi Kırkpınar Yağlı Güreş Festivali (yah-LUH gew-RESH, oiled wrestling).

Next to the rather drab modern stadium is a stone tower with a pointed roof, the **Kasr-i Adalet** (Justice Hall, 1561), dating from the time of Süleyman the Magnificent, with two stones in front of it. On one stone, the Seng-i Hürmet (Stone of Respect), petitioners would put their petitions to the sultan to be collected by his staff. On the other, the Seng-i İbret (Stone of Warning), would be displayed the heads of high court officers who had lost the sultan's confidence in a major way.

If you've made it all the way to Sarayiçi, look for the bridge Kanuni Köprüsü to get back to the south bank of the Tunca. Bear right coming off the bridge; the road leads to Hükümet Caddesi, and eventually to Hürriyet Meydanı.

Kaleiçi

The Old Town, called Kaleiçi (Within the Fortress), was the original medieval town with streets laid out on a grid plan. Saraçlar Caddesi is its eastern boundary, with Talat Paşa Caddesi on the north and the railway line on the south.

Walk south along Maarif Caddesi past the Anıl, Park and Efe hotels to pass some fine, if fragile, old Ottoman wooden houses designed in an ornate style known as *Edirnekâri*; as well as abandoned churches; and at the southern end of Maarif Caddesi, Edirne's **great synagogue**. Though presently a sad ruin of vanished grandeur, this synagogue is scheduled for restoration by Thracian University. Some other fine old houses are along Cumhuriyet Caddesi, which crosses Maarif Caddesi north of the synagogue.

The covered market called the **Ali Paşa Çarşısı**, located east of Maarif Caddesi near Saraçlar Caddesi, was designed by Mimar Sinan, built in 1569, restored in 1805, 1867 and 1947, destroyed by fire in 1992 and again restored in 1994-97. There is an entrance off Hürriyet Meydanı to the left of the tourism office.

Some fragments of Byzantine city walls are still visible at the edges of Kaleiçi, down by the Tunca River.

Oiled Wrestling

The origins of *Yağlı güreş* (oiled wrestling) are lost in legend, but it's thought that matches have been held near Edirne for at least six centuries.

According to the best-known version of the tale, Süleyman Paşa, son of Orhan Gazi, the second Ottoman sultan, crossed the Dardanelles in the mid-14th century bent on conquest. His vanguard consisted of 40 enthusiastic warriors who wrestled at rest stops to break the monotony of the march through Thrace. At a meadow in Ahırköy, near Edirne, they wrestled until only two remained standing. These two, unwilling to yield, wrestled long into the night and finally died of exhaustion. They were buried where they fell. The next day a spring of clear, cold water sprang up at the spot and was named *Kırkpınar*, or Forty Springs, for the 40 warriors.

A Wrestlers' Lodge was soon thriving in Edirne. Matches were held indoors in winter, and outdoors in summer in the Kırkpınar meadow, which today is just across the border in Greece. The highpoint of the year was the three-day series of matches held during the traditional spring festival of Hıdrellez.

These days hundreds of amateur wrestlers from all over Turkey gather in early June at Sarayiçi. Clad only in knickers of goat or calf leather, they slather themselves with olive oil, then chant:

Allah Allah illallah
May we prosper
Our patron is Hamza the wrestler
Our ancestors were wrestlers
Two valiant men take the field
One is blonde, one dark
Both are keen to win the prize
Do not despair when down
Do not boast when up
When above, do not loosen your grip
Meet leg trip with leg trip
Offer a prayer to Muhammad
I hastened to the spring
May Allah be with you both

After this the *cazgır*, or master of ceremonies, offers a prayer, and introduces the matches. Then the *davul* (folk bass drum) and *zurna* (Turkish double-reed instrument) begin the frenetic music which will play throughout the festival. The wrestlers go through *peşrev* (the traditional warm-up routine) consisting of a series of exaggerated arm-swinging steps and gestures.

Wrestlers are organised into 11 classes, from *teşvik* (encouragement) to *baş güreşler* (head wrestlers), with the winner in each class being designated a *başpehlivan*, or master wrestler. On the last day of the festival, the başpehlivans wrestle for the supreme honour. Finally only two are left, and these compete for the top prize, the coveted gold belt, and a small cash prize. With victory comes fame, honour, and the opportunity to earn money endorsing commercial products.

Folk-dancing exhibitions, musical performances and crafts displays are organised as part of the festivities, and these begin on Tuesday. The wrestling begins on Friday, with the winning başpehlivan chosen on Sunday. For exact dates and ticket information, contact the tourism offices in Edirne.

BOTH PHOTOGRAPHS BY TOM BROSNAHAN

Thrace Top: The Ottoman-era Meriç Köprüsü (Maritsa River Bridge) at sunset in Edirne. **Bottom:** The Selimiye Camii of Edirne is considered to be the masterpiece of the Ottoman architect Mimar Sinan.

BOTH PHOTOGRAPHS BY TOM BROSNAHAN

South of the Sea of Marmara **Top:** The Yeşil Cami (1492) in İznik features a minaret of green-glazed bricks. **Bottom:** Inscriptions from the Koran above a window in Yeşil Türbe, Bursa.

River Walks

Follow Saraçlar Caddesi south and out of town, under the railway line and across the Tunca Köprüsü, an Ottoman stone humpback bridge spanning the Tunca River. The Meriç Köprüsü, a longer Ottoman bridge, crosses the Meriç to the south. In between the two bridges are several restaurants, tea gardens and bars good for an outdoor drink or a meal in warm weather (see Places to Eat).

The DSI Meriç Kenarı Rekreasyon Sahası (Meriç Riverbank Recreation Area) is on the northern bank of the Meriç. It lies upriver from the army club which occupies the prime riverbank spot at the northern footing of the Meriç Köprüsü. The Recreation Area is a shady park with a children's playground, riverview benches, and paths for strolling.

On the southern side of the Meriç bridge are even better, more scenic restaurants and tea gardens such as the ***Emirgan***, opposite the restored Ottoman *çeşme* (fountain) of Hacı Adil Bey, with welcome shade and fine sunset views of the river and bridge.

Places to Stay – Budget

Otel Anıl *(☎ 284-212 1782, Maarif Caddesi 8)* is a grand old Edirne townhouse which, although central and cheap, is now cracked, threadbare, rickety, musty and stained. Clean beds cost US$4 per person in waterless rooms.

Next door to the Anıl another grand old house, the ***Konak*** *(☎ 284-212 1348)*, is under restoration and may re-open as a good but more expensive boutique hotel.

Camping ***Fifi Mocamp*** *(☎ 284-225 1554)*, on Demirkapı Mevkii, is 9km east of Edirne on the old İstanbul road (D100; the eastward continuation of Talat Paşa Asfaltı). It has motel rooms open all year, as well as hook-ups and services for tents and caravans open from April to October.

Places to Stay – Mid-Range

Otel Şaban Açıkgöz *(☎ 284-213 1404, fax 213 4516, Tahmis Meydanı Çilingirler Caddesi 9)* is near the park next to the Eski Cami. Relatively new and – for Edirne – upscale, they charge US$16/23 for fairly quiet rooms with shower, TV and breakfast.

A block south of Hürriyet Meydanı, the ***Park Hotel*** *(☎ 284-225 4610, fax 225 4635, Maarif Caddesi 7)* is clean, comfortable and convenient. Rooms cost US$22/30 for a single/double with bath, TV and breakfast. Avoid rooms opening onto Maarif Caddesi, which has some loud traffic.

A few metres south, the cheaper ***Efe Hotel*** *(☎ 284-213 6166, fax 212 9446, Maarif Caddesi 13)* has an air-conditioned lobby, lobby bar, and newish rooms with shower and TV (but without air-con) for US$18/26. There's a noisy 'English Pub' in the basement.

The top hotel, right in the centre of town, is the two-star, 83 room ***Sultan Oteli*** *(☎ 284-225 1372, fax 225 5763, Talat Paşa Caddesi 170)*, half a block west of the tourism information office. Rooms with shower, TV, good reading lamps and a good breakfast cost US$30/45. There's plentiful parking in the hotel's rear lot.

The two-star, 80 room ***Balta Hotel*** *(☎ 284-225 5210, fax 225 3529, Talat Paşa Asfaltı 97)*, halfway from the otogar to Hürriyet Meydanı, has the disadvantages of being 1km south-east of the Eski Cami, facing a noisy street, and having rooms which catch the heat of the afternoon sun. Posted prices are a ridiculous US$60/100, breakfast included, but with a bit of banter they'll knock at least 50% off.

The 100 room ***Hotel Kervansaray*** *(☎ 284-225 2195, fax 212 0462, İki Kapılıhan Caddesi 57)*, facing the park next to the Eski Cami, is in fact an Ottoman caravanserai built by order of Rüstem Paşa, a grand vizier of Süleyman the Magnificent, in about 1550. The camel caravans on the road between Europe, İstanbul and points further east rested here for the night, their valuable freight safe within the building's massive stone walls and great armoured doors. Despite its romantic history, the hotel now depends more on its billiards room and nightclub for profits. Its guest rooms are mostly occupied for purposes other than rest after travel.

Places to Eat

Edirne has many small eateries, especially *köftecis* (serving grilled lamb meatballs) and *ciğercis* (serving fried liver). Among the brightest and best is ***Serhad Köftecisi*** on Saraçlar Caddesi just off Hürriyet Meydanı, where köfte with yoghurt, salad, bread and a drink costs US$3.

Gaziantep Kebapçısı, to the right (west) of the main tourism office, near Hürriyet Maydanı, is as good a place as any for grilled kebaps and salads (it doesn't serve alcohol) for around US$3 or US$4 per meal. Even nicer, and not much more expensive, is the ***Modern Park Restaurant*** on the ground floor of the Park Hotel at Maarif Caddesi 7.

There's a row of small restaurants facing a tiny park west of the Rüstem Paşa Kervansarayı by the Hotel Şaban Açıkgöz. ***Serhad 1 Köftecisi*** is the nicest of the four köftecis here; ***Polat Lokantası*** is best for stews, but serves grilled meats as well. Facing these eateries, with a name that looks like a menu, is ***Edirne Lahmacun Döner Pide***, a more modern place.

For fancier meals with alcoholic drinks, try ***Çatı Lokantası*** across from the Sultan Oteli on Talat Paşa Caddesi, or ***Aile Restaurant***, Saraçlar Caddesi, on the upper floor in the Belediye İş Hanı, just south of the PTT. The entrance is on the side street by the post office. Kebaps, stews and other traditional Turkish dishes are served for US$5 or US$7 per meal.

More atmospheric, and only slightly more expensive, are the restaurants a five-minute walk south of the centre by the rivers. ***Gazi Baba II Restaurant***, between the two Ottoman stone bridges on the road to the Greek border, has white tablecloth formality at moderate prices. ***Emirgan Aile Çay Bahçesi***, at the southern end of the Meriç bridge, serves snacks and light meals as well as soft drinks and the ubiquitous *çay* (tea).

Restaurants located upriver from the bridge – the ***Villa*** and ***Lalezar*** – serve more substantial meat and fish dishes outdoors in warm weather, for US$10 or US$12 per person.

Getting There & Away

Bulgarian Border Crossing The highway from Svilengrad, Bulgaria, leads to the busy Turkish border post of Kapıkule 18km west of Edirne, open 24 hours. After the formalities, you enter Edirne by crossing the Tunca River at the Gazi Mihal Bridge and passing some fragments of Byzantine city walls. City bus C-1 runs along the route from Kapıkule to behind the Belediye, just uphill from the Eski Cami in the centre of Edirne. There are dolmuşes (US$0.65) every 20 minutes or so from Kapıkule to the dolmuş station behind the Rüstem Paşa Kervansarayı, but both buses and dolmuşes are infrequent in the early morning and late at night. By the way, you may be required to hitch a ride or rent a taxi (ie not walk) on the Bulgarian side.

Greek Border Crossing Saraçlar Caddesi continues south from the centre of Edirne across the Tunca and Meriç rivers for 5km to the suburb of Karaağaç; then another 2km to Pazarkule, a border post originally meant to serve the railway line. The frontier, as determined by the Treaty of Lausanne (1923), left the Turkish railway line passing through Greece on its way to Edirne; a bypass line was built in the 1970s.

The Greek border post of Kastanies is midway in the 1km-wide no-man's-land which separates the two border posts. On the Turkish side, you can usually walk to and from Pazarkule, but the Greeks have declared the border area a military zone and do not permit anyone to walk through it without a military escort. You will probably have to take a Greek taxi (US$6, two minutes) to cross the no-man's-land.

These small border posts are usually open during daylight hours, but if relations between the two countries are not good (which is common) they may be open only in the morning. Ask at the tourism office, or plan to arrive at the border after 9 but before 11 am.

City buses run between Karaağaç and Edirne's Belediye about every half hour during the day; dolmuşes (US$0.25) make the same run, departing from the street between the Belediye and Selimiye Camii. If you can lug your gear the 2km to Karaağaç, you can make it into Edirne easily. The alternative is a Turkish taxi (US$5, 15 minutes) into town as there is not much traffic and hitching is not easy, though you may be lucky. From Edirne, connections are frequent, fast and easy to İstanbul; less frequent to points south (see later in this chapter).

If you're crossing from Turkey into Greece, do so as soon after 9 am as possible in order to catch one of the few trains or buses from Kastanies south to Alexandroùpolis, where there are better connections. Or consider crossing further south at İpsala/Kipi on the E84/110 highway.

Road The highway between Europe and Edirne follows closely the Via Ignatia, the ancient road which connected Rome and Constantinople. It travels along the river valleys past Niš and Sofia, on between the mountain ranges of the Stara and Rhodope to Plovdiv, and along the Maritsa (Meriç) riverbank into Edirne. The city stands alone on the gently undulating plain, snuggled into a bend of the Tunca River.

After Edirne, the old Edirne-İstanbul highway (D100) heads east into the rolling, steppe-like terrain of eastern Thrace towards İstanbul, still following the Via Ignatia. The E80 Avrupa Otoyol/Trans European Motorway is far preferable in terms of condition, speed and safety. The toll of about US$3.50 to İstanbul is a small price to pay.

Bus Buses to İstanbul depart Edirne's Otobüs Garajı, also called the Terminal (TEHR-mee-NAHL), 2km south-east of the Eski Cami every 20 minutes or so throughout the day. The 235km journey takes under three hours and tickets cost US$6. Take a city bus from the Belediye or along Talat Paşa Asfaltı and look for 'Terminal' on the signboard. Dolmuşes (US$0.25) run to the Terminal quite frequently from the lot on the south-eastern side of the Rüstem Paşa Kervansarayı.

The terminus in İstanbul is the main bus station, the Uluslararası İstanbul Otogar (İstanbul International Bus Station) in Esenler, from which you can take the Metro to Aksaray and change to the tram for Sultanahmet, or a city bus to Taksim Square.

Heading south from Edirne, there are at least five buses daily to Çanakkale, though some require a transfer at Keşan; Truva Turizm has a direct bus (four hours, US$7).

Train The train service between Edirne and İstanbul is slow, infrequent and inconvenient. The *Edirne Ekspresi* (US$3, students US$2.25) connects Edirne and İstanbul, departing Edirne at 8 am, and İstanbul at 3.25 pm, taking six hours (over twice as long as the bus) to make the run. The *Bükreş* (Bucharest) *Ekspresi* comes through Edirne in the middle of the night, as does the *Balkan Ekspresi*.

Edirne has two train stations: the city station (Edirne Garı), 3.5km south-east of the Eski Cami; and the one 18km away at Kapıkule on the Bulgarian border. Dolmuşes and city buses running south-east along Talat Paşa Asfaltı can drop you within 350m of the Edirne Garı.

AROUND EDIRNE

East of Edirne

The ride to İstanbul is largely uneventful, even though this part of the country has had a tumultuous history. Enemy armies from the west intent on seizing Constantinople/İstanbul passed easily over this rolling countryside.

In 1877 the Russians held all of Turkish Thrace, and came within a few kilometres of İstanbul's city walls. During WWI, Allied armies marched this way; in WWII Thrace was heavily militarised by the Turks to fend off the Germans and to protect Turkey's fragile neutrality. A Turkish friend tells the story of his time on the line in Thrace:

> It was late in a bitter winter. The wolves found little to eat in the countryside, and began coming dangerously close to our outpost. Ammunition was very scarce, but we asked permission to use a few rounds to defend ourselves against the wolves. Our commander said, 'You are Turkish soldiers. Use your bayonets'.

THRACE

Havsa The first town along the İstanbul road is Havsa (population 10,000), a town of some importance during Ottoman times. Its **Sokollu Kasım Paşa Külliyesi** is a mosque complex which was designed by Sinan and was built in 1576-7 from orders of the son of Sokollu Mehmet Paşa, a grand vizier under Sultan Süleyman the Magnificent.

Midnight Express

It's interesting to note that the original *Midnight Express* ran between İstanbul and Edirne through Greece. When the Ottoman Empire collapsed, the new Turkish-Greek border was drawn so that the old railway line was partly in Greece. Greek border police would board when the train entered Greek territory and get off when it re-entered Turkish territory.

During the 1960s and 70s there was a slow, late-night train on this run. Foreigners convicted of drug-related offences in Turkey would be released by the Turkish government while their convictions were being appealed. They'd be given all of their possessions except their passports, and told in a whisper about the *Midnight Express*.

They'd climb aboard in İstanbul and jump off the train in Greece, where Greek border police would pick them up and jail them. They'd call their consulate, arrange for a new passport, be let out of jail and sent on their way. This system allowed the Turkish government to meet the US government's demands that it be strict with drug smugglers, but it avoided the expense and bother of actually incarcerating the convicted smugglers. In the late 1970s, the Turkish State Railways built a bypass line and the Greek corridor route was abandoned.

The truth of the *Midnight Express* is quite different from that portrayed in the politically inspired anti-Turkish movie of the same name, in which a convicted drug-smuggler is magically transmuted into a suffering hero.

Lüleburgaz About 75km east of Edirne is the market town of Lüleburgaz (population 56,000), the ancient Arcadiopolis. Unremarkable in itself, Lüleburgaz holds the fine **Sokollu Mehmet Paşa Camii**, a mosque built from the orders (1549) of Sokollu Mehmet Paşa, the *beylerbey* of Rumeli (governor of European Turkey) and later grand vizier to Sultan Süleyman the Magnificent. The mosque was part of a larger complex which was finally completed in 1569. Incorporated into the mosque's design is a medrese. Across the street, the hamam is ruined and now used for storage, but the arasta which surround it are still in use.

Lüleburgaz is not a tourist town, so anyone and everyone stands ready to help you if you need help, or to ignore you if you don't. Useful services such as bus ticket offices, restaurants, pastry shops and cheap hotels are all within a few minutes walk of the Sokollu Mehmet Paşa Camii.

Hotel Sürücü *(☎ 288-417 1451, İstanbul Caddesi 6)*, close to the mosque, charges US$13 for a double with private shower. ***Hotel Şentürk*** *(☎ 288-417 2112, fax 412 5541, İstanbul Caddesi 12)*, a block further east across from the park, is a bit newer and better. Up two flights of stairs are rooms with shower and TV costing US$7/12/16 for a single/double/triple. On the eastern outskirts of the town on the D100, you'll find ***Hotel Yaman*** *(☎ 288-414 1613, fax 414 1523)* offering four-star comforts at a three-star price of US$28 a double, breakfast included.

Çorlu Though wonderfully ancient, having been founded by the Phrygians around 1000 BC, Çorlu (population 75,000) has little to show for its long history. A farmers' market town at best, it was a way-station on the İstanbul-Edirne road and thus received its share of mosque-building, and also a caravanserai and hamam. The **Sultan Süleyman Camii** (1521) is its most noteworthy old building. A few small hotels and restaurants provide for travellers.

Tekirdağ Once known for its luxuriant vineyards and excellent wines, Tekirdağ (population 85,000), formerly Rodosto, today is a bustling modern place with little to hold your interest. Traces of Early Bronze Age life have been found in the vicinity.

The tourism office (☎/fax 282-261 2083) is at Atatürk Bulvarı 65, on the waterfront street next to the Eski İskele (Old Dock).

The Ottomans – particularly Süleyman the Magnificent's grand vizier Rüstem Paşa – left Tekirdağ a legacy of great buildings, including the mosque, bedesten and medrese named after Rüstem.

Also here is the **Rakoczy Museum** (☎ 282-261 2082) on Barbaros Caddesi just in from the waterfront near the centre of the town. Prince Francis II Rakoczy (1676-1735) led rebellious Hungarians in their struggle against Hapsburg repression in the early 1700s. Forced to flee in 1711, he went into exile in Poland, then France, and finally in Turkey, where he died. Rakoczy's remains were returned to Hungary in 1906, and his Tekirdağ home (1720-35) became a museum in 1932.

East & West of Tekirdağ Most maps show the road east of Tekirdağ, leading to Silivri and İstanbul, as a major highway. In fact, it's very narrow for the volume of traffic that passes through, so you should expect some slow going.

West of Tekirdağ the coast road is easily passable as far as Kumbağ, but then becomes a rough, unpaved track, that may be impassable after heavy rains or in snow. If you're an experienced driver and don't mind heights and unprotected drop-offs, you might enjoy the spectacular views from the ridges of 924m-high Işıklar Dağı. Go from east to west – not west to east – so as to be on the inside of the road, away from the precipitous cliffs.

The better road heads due west from Kumbağ to İnecik and Keşan. About 48km west of Tekirdağ a rough road heads south over the mountains to Ballı, Gölcük and Şarköy (32km). The latter is a seaside resort for holidaymakers from İstanbul and a handful of enterprising Europeans, with a decent beach and several typically noisy Turkish nightclubs.

South of Edirne

The fertile Thracian landscape rolls on south from Edirne, ending in the seaside resorts of İbrice and Erikli on the Gulf of Saros.

Uzunköprü About 36km south of Havsa along E87/D550 is the farming town of Uzunköprü (population 36,000). Named 'Long Bridge' for its Ottoman viaduct, 1270m long with 173 arches, Uzunköprü has the nearest train station to the border on the line connecting İstanbul and Athens. A daily train (5½ hours, US$3) connects İstanbul and Uzunköprü, but buses, as usual, are faster, if a bit more expensive.

The Long Bridge itself, begun in 1427 and finished in 1443, is still in use as the town's main access road from the north, a monument to the durability of Ottoman construction. Its southern end is in the town centre, where there are simple, cheap hotels including ***Hotel Ergene***, and basic eateries. The town's otogar is 2km south-east of the centre on the road to Keşan, 46km further along.

İpsala & Keşan İpsala is the main border-crossing point between Turkey and Greece, on the E84/D110 highway; the Greek station is named Kipi. Both stations – with currency exchange facilities – are open 24 hours a day.

The actual Turkish border station is 5km west of the town of İpsala, reachable by taxi (US$5). There is a tourism office (☎/fax 284-616 1577) at the border station. If you're coming from Greece, go straight through İpsala to Keşan (US$2 by dolmuş, US$15 by taxi), from which bus connections to Edirne (102km), İstanbul (220km), Gelibolu (77km) and Çanakkale (120km) are available.

Keşan's otogar (Belediye Terminalı) is on the E87/D550 south of the E84/D110, but most minibuses terminate at a lot just off the main square, 2.5km south-east and uphill from the intersection of these two highways, and 2.5km east of the otogar. Keşan's main square has several small köftecis, restaurants and pastanes. ***Hotel Ayhan*** *(☎ 284-714 5467)*, just south of the main square, can put you up cheaply, though the best lodgings are at the three-star, 67 room ***Hotel Yener*** *(☎ 284-714 3660)* on Demirciler Caddesi.

South of Keşan on the Bay of Saros is the village of **Saros**, with numerous little cheap beachfront pensions and hotels.

GALLIPOLI PENINSULA

The slender peninsula which forms the north-western side of the Çanakkale Boğazı (Dardanelles), across the water from Çanakkale, is called Gelibolu in Turkish. For a millennium it has been the key to İstanbul: the navy that could force the straits had a good chance of capturing the capital of the Eastern European world. Many fleets have tried to force the straits. Most, including the mighty Allied fleet mustered in WWI, have failed.

Today the Gallipoli battlefields are peaceful places covered in scrubby brush, pine forests, and farmers' fields. But the momentous battles fought here nearly a century ago are still alive in the memories of many people, both Turkish and foreign.

On the hillside by Kilitbahir, clearly visible from Çanakkale on the far shore, are gigantic letters spelling out the first few words of a poem by Necmettin Halil Onan commemorating the momentous 1915 struggle for Gallipoli:

Dur yolcu! Bilmeden gelip bastığın
bu toprak bir devrin battığı yerdir.
Eğil de kulak ver, bu sessiz yığın
bir vatan kalbinin attığı yerdir.

Traveller, halt! The soil you
heedlessly tread
once witnessed the end of an era.
Listen! In this quiet mound
there once beat the heart of a nation.

History

Since Byzantine times the straits have been well defended. The Ottomans maintained numerous fortresses: Seddülbahir and Kumkale at the southern end of the straits; Çamburun and Karaburun, and Bigalı and Nara within the straits; Bozcaada on the island at the southern mouth; Çimenlik in the town of Çanakkale, and Kilitbahir, the 'Lock on the Sea', on the Gallipoli side across from Çanakkale.

With the intention of capturing the Ottoman capital and the road to Eastern Europe during WWI, Winston Churchill, British First Lord of the Admiralty, organised a naval assault on the straits. A strong Franco-British fleet tried first to force them in March 1915 but failed. Then, in April, British, Australian, New Zealand and Indian troops were landed on Gallipoli, and French troops near Çanakkale. Both Turkish and Allied troops fought desperately and fearlessly, and devastated one another. After nine months of ferocious combat but little progress, the Allied forces were withdrawn.

The Turkish success at Gallipoli was partly due to bad luck and bad leadership on the Allied side, and partly due to the timely provision of reinforcements coming to the aid of the Turkish side under the command of General Liman von Sanders. But a crucial element in the defeat was that the Allied troops happened to land in a sector where they faced Lieutenant-Colonel Mustafa Kemal (Atatürk).

He was a relatively minor officer, but he had General von Sanders' confidence. He guessed the Allied battle plan correctly when his commanders did not, and stalled the invasion by bitter fighting which wiped out his division. Though suffering from malaria, he commanded in full view of his troops and of the enemy, and miraculously escaped death several times. At one point a piece of shrapnel tore through the breast pocket of his uniform, but was stopped by his pocket watch (now in the Çanakkale Military & Naval Museum). His brilliant performance made him a folk hero and paved the way for his promotion to pasha (general).

The Gallipoli campaign lasted for nine months, until January 1916, and resulted in a total of more than half a million casualties. The British Empire suffered over 200,000 casualties, with the loss of some 36,000 lives.

French casualties of 47,000 were over half of the entire French contingent. Half of the

A Proud Day

A young Australian soldier runs into the heat of battle. His feet dig deep with each step into the golden sand. His life rests on each step, death waits impatiently. Gun shots echo in the night; screams pierce the tranquility of Turkey's Aegean coast. Soldiers fall like rain and lives are lost as though nobody cares.

A sharp stabbing pain grips the young soldier. He clutches his chest, he can't keep his feet any longer. The war continues but the young man has lost his own personal battle, and now lies in peace at Gallipoli ...

April 25 is Anzac Day. It is a public holiday in Australia and New Zealand but I had been guilty of shrugging off Anzac Day as just another holiday. But that all changed in September 1994 when I travelled around Turkey. Undoubtedly the highlight was a trip to the battlefields of Gallipoli.

I stood on the beach at Kabatepe where the Anzacs were supposed to have landed. The sea was calm and the land was flat, a perfect place for an amphibious landing. Then I went to the beach where the Anzacs actually landed, at Anzac Cove several kilometres to the north-east. Steep cliffs confronted the Anzacs here, with Turkish soldiers at the top. Our men didn't stand a chance.

It was an eerie feeling standing at the site where the Anzac soldiers sacrificed their lives for our countries. We visited the trenches, the tunnels and the beautiful memorials built in tribute to our hero soldiers. I was very proud to be an Australian that day.

Turkey's national hero, Atatürk, had a memorial built at Anzac Cove to honour our fallen soldiers. His words left a lump in my throat:

'Those heroes that shed their blood and lost their lives ... you are now lying in the soil of a friendly country. Therefore rest in peace. There is no difference between the Johnnies (Anzacs) and the Mehmets (Turks) to us where they lie side by side here in this country of ours ... you the mothers who sent their sons from far away countries, wipe away your tears; your sons are now lying in our bosom and are in peace. After having lost their lives on this land, they have become our sons as well.'

I was not embarrassed by my tears, nor were my tour companions. It is impossible to describe how much I learned that day, how proud I was, and how lucky I feel. April 25 isn't just another day. April 25 is Anzac Day.

Justin Flynn

500,000 Ottoman troops who participated in the battle became a casualty, with more than 55,000 dead. There are now 31 war cemeteries on the peninsula, as well as several important monuments.

Orientation

Gallipoli is a fairly large area to tour, especially without your own transport. It's more than 35km as the crow flies from the northernmost battlefield to the southern tip of the

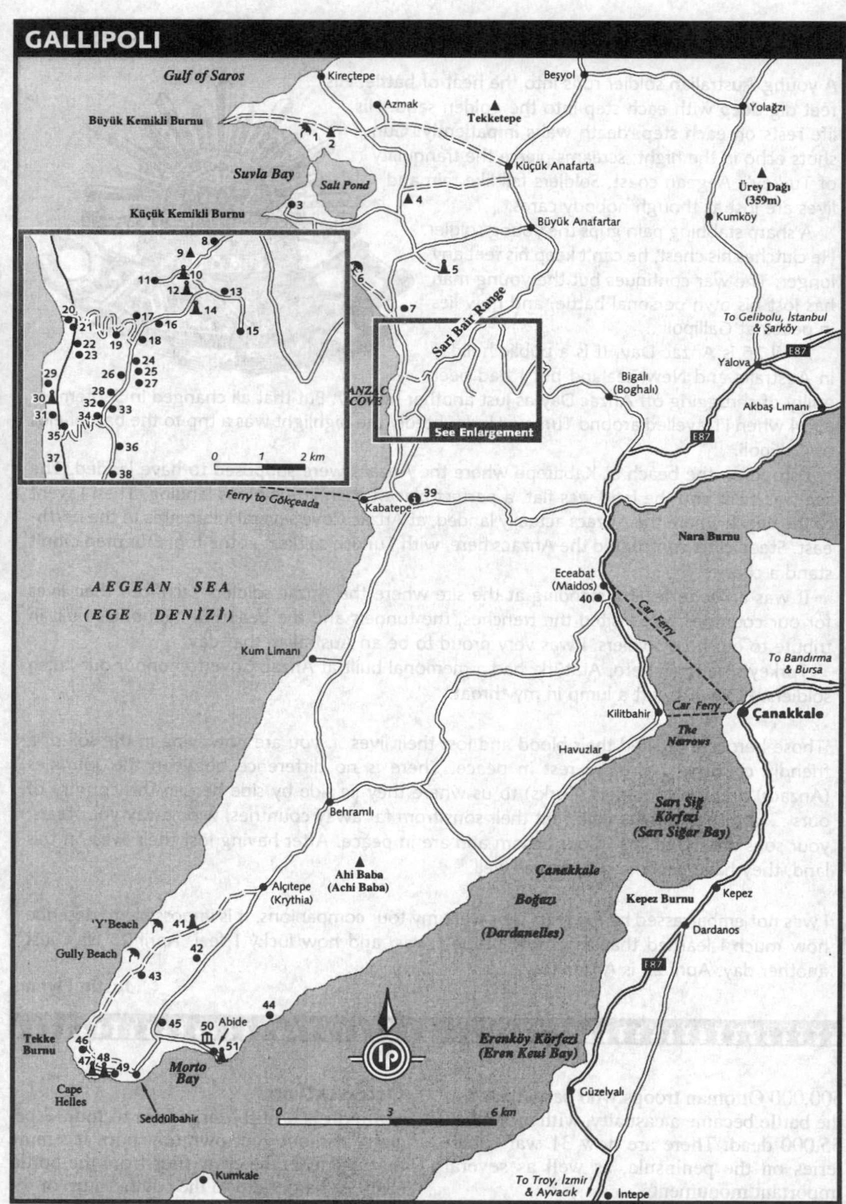
GALLIPOLI
Gulf of Saros
Kireçtepe
Beşyol
Azmak
Tekketepe
Yolağzı
Büyük Kemikli Burnu
Suvla Bay
Salt Pond
Küçük Anafarta
Ürey Dağı
(359m)
Küçük Kemikli Burnu
Kumköy
Büyük Anafartar
Sarı Bair Range
To Gelibolu, İstanbul
& Şarköy
E87
Yalova
ANZAC
COVE
Bigalı
(Boghalı)
Akbaş Limanı
See Enlargement
0
1
2 km
Ferry to Gökçeada
Kabatepe
Nara Burnu
AEGEAN SEA
(EGE DENİZİ)
Eceabat
(Maidos)
Car Ferry
Kum Limanı
To Bandırma
& Bursa
Kilitbahir
Çanakkale
The
Narrows
Havuzlar
Behramlı
Sarı Siğ
Körfezi
(Sarı Siğar Bay)
Ahi Baba
(Achi Baba)
Çanakkale
Boğazı
(Dardanelles)
Alçıtepe
(Krythia)
Kepez Burnu
Kepez
'Y' Beach
Dardanos
Gully Beach
Abide
Tekke
Burnu
Erenköy Körfezi
(Eren Keui Bay)
Morto
Bay
Cape
Helles
Güzelyalı
Seddülbahir
0
3
6 km
Kumkale
To Troy, İzmir
& Ayvacık
İntepe

GALLIPOLI

1	Büyük Kemikli Picnic Area & Beach	18	Baby 700 Cemetery & Mesudiye Topu	36	Kanlı Sırt Kitabesi (Bloody Ridge Inscription)
2	Hill 10	19	The Nek	37	Beach (Hell Spit) Cemetery
3	Lala Baba	20	Lala Baba Cemetery	38	Mehmetçiğe Saygı Anıtı (Memorial to Mehmetçik)
4	Green Hill	21	Embarkation Pier Cemetery	39	Kabatepe Information Centre & Museum
5	Hill 60 New Zealand Memorial	22	New Zealand No 2 Outpost Cemetery	40	Gelibolu Tarihi Milli Park (Gallipoli National Historic Park); Ziyaretçi Merkezi (Park Visitors Centre) & Picnic Area
6	'B' Beach	23	No 2 Outpost Cemetery	41	Twelve Tree Copse Cemetery & NZ Memorial
7	7th Field Ambulance Cemetery	24	57th Regiment (57 Alay) Cemetery	42	Redoubt Cemetery
8	Kocaçimentepe	25	Bomba Sırt (Bomb Ridge)	43	Pink Farm Cemetery
9	Hill Q	26	Quinn's Post	44	Kerevizdere Picnic Area
10	Chunuk Bair New Zealand Memorial	27	Yüzbaşı Metrmet Şehıtlığı	45	Skew Bridge Cemetery
11	The Farm	28	Courtney Steele's Post	46	Lancashire Landing Cemetery
12	Conkbayırı Mehmetçik Memorials	29	Canterbury Cemetery	47	Cape Helles British Memorial
13	Place where Atatürk Spent the Night of 9-10 August 1915	30	Anzac Memorial & Arıburnu	48	İlk Şehitler & Yahya Çavuş Memorials
14	Talat Göktepe Monument	31	Anzac Cove	49	'V' Beach Cemetery
15	Kemalyeri (Scrubby Knoll, Turkish HQ)	32	Kırmızı Sırt (125. Alay Cephesi)	50	French Memorial & Museum
16	Düztepe (10. Alay Cephesi)	33	Johnston's Jolly	51	Çanakkale Şehitleri Abidesi Memorial
17	Mehmet Çavuş Cemetery	34	Lone Pine (Kanlı Sırt) Cemetery		
		35	Shrapnel Valley (Korkudere) & Plugge's Plateau Cemeteries		

THRACE

peninsula. The two best bases for a visit are Çanakkale on the eastern shore, and Gelibolu on the western. Eceabat, 45km south-west of Gelibolu, though closer to the battlefields, has mostly emergency accommodation.

Ferries run from Kilitbahir and Eceabat across the Dardanelles to Çanakkale (for details, see Getting There & Away in the Çanakkale section of the North Aegean Turkey chapter).

The principal battles took place on the western shore of the peninsula near Anzac Cove and Arıburnu, and in the hills just to the east. Anzac Cove is about 12km from Eceabat, 19km from Kilitbahir, and 57km from Gelibolu. If your time is limited or if you're touring by public transport, head for these places first.

Transport & Tours

With your own transport you can tour the battlefields easily in a day or less. Touring by public transport is possible, but dolmuşes serve only certain sites or nearby villages, and you must expect to do some waiting and walking. In summer, hitching greatly facilitates getting around on your own, but in other seasons traffic may not be sufficient. The most important group of monuments and cemeteries, from Lone Pine uphill to Chunuk Bair, can be toured on foot, an excellent idea in fine weather.

Joining an organised tour is a good idea as you save time and trouble, and get the benefit of a guide who can relate the history and explain the battles. Some readers have complained that tours go too fast and allow too little time at the beach, so you'd be well advised to talk with other travellers who have just taken a tour and find out what they recommend. Most tours include a picnic and some time at a Gallipoli beach for swimming. Tours are organised by several agencies in Çanakkale, and in the town of Gelibolu on the Gallipoli Peninsula. (See the sections on those towns for details.)

Gelibolu

Coming from Edirne or Keşan, or from İstanbul along the northern shore of the Sea of Marmara, the little town of Gelibolu (population 17,000) can provide transport connections, a meal or a bed.

Orientation The centre of Gelibolu is by the docks for the car ferry to Lapseki, and everything you may need is within 100m of here. The stone tower which looms above the ancient harbour is a remnant of the Byzantine town of Kallipolis, which gave the present town and peninsula their name. The tower is now the Gelibolu Promotion Centre and Piri Reis Museum, named after the famous Turkish cartographer, with changing exhibits and free admission. The otogar is 500m south-west of the stone tower on the Eceabat road.

Information Go to the Gelibolu Promotion Centre in the stone tower. The PTT has a yellow-and-black kiosk right at the docks where you can convert currency and buy stamps. Across the road is a Yapı Kredi ATM. Other banks are along Yukarı Çarşı Sokak, the town's main shopping street, which starts opposite the Hotel Yılmaz (by the Emlak Bankası) and goes uphill.

Gallipoli Tours Several companies run tours of the Gallipoli battlefields. From the Hotel Yılmaz, for instance, tours depart at 8.30 am, returning at 3.30 pm, for US$20 per person.

Places to Stay Best in town is the two-star ***Hotel Oya*** *(☎ 286-566 0392)* on Miralay Şefik Aker Caddesi, 100m from the ferry docks, with TV and shower-equipped rooms for US$15/24/28 a single/double/triple. A block away is the older ***Hotel Yılmaz*** *(☎ 286-566 1256, Liman Meydanı 6)*, priced identically, though you get less. A better, quieter, cheaper choice is the nearby ***Otel Yelkenci*** *(☎ 286-566 7060)* on Liman Meydanı, above the restaurant of that name, charging US$15 for a double, but there's no heating.

Otel Hakan *(☎ 286-566 2424, Liman Meydanı Belediye Caddesi 8)*, facing the stone tower on the main square, is simple but clean; doubles with sink go for US$5.

Otel Dilmaç *(☎ 286-566 1242, Yukarı Çarşı Caddesi 3)*, one short block uphill from the Yılmaz, has double rooms with private bath, TV and breakfast for US$20, a good deal.

Camping Obidi, 1.5km from the stone tower and off the road south-west to Eceabat and Kilitbahir (follow the signs), is on the shore, has some shade, and can be pleasant for a night or two.

About 12km south of Gelibolu on the road to Eceabat is the two-star, 48 room ***Hotel Boncuk*** *(☎ 286-576 8292, fax 576 8158)*, on the shore, charging US$28 a double. ***Cennet Camping & Motel***, 19km south of Gelibolu, is better for camping than motel accommdation, with some shady sites. ***Derya Camping***, across the road, is not as good.

Places to Eat Amid the hotels at the centre are many small restaurants, kebapçıs and büfes serving everything from stand-up snacks to sit-down dinners with white tablecloths and wine.

The best view and breeze are at ***Café Nezih*** next to the Denizyolları ferryboat ticket office by the docks, but they serve only drinks and snacks. For full meals, the ***İmren***, ***Boğaz***, ***Liman*** and ***Yelken*** restaurants near the Otel Yelkenci are best in the evening, with nice views, tables on the pavement, and fish menus (*sardalya* or fresh sardines are the local speciality), but no alcohol. Expect to spend from US$5 to US$12 here, the latter for fish.

Yarımada Lokantası advertises 'Ottoman cuisine' and has a nice garden dining area, and full meals for US$4 to US$8. For fine water views, try ***İlhan*** and also ***Belediye Kafeterya Restaurant***, which serves alcoholic beverages.

As usual, the further you go from the sea, the lower the prices. Just east of the Hotel Yılmaz is ***İpek Urfa Kebap Salonu*** for cheap kebaps.

Entertainment Dining near the water is the prime evening entertainment here, but if you just want to sit, drink and nibble at lower prices, walk inland from the ferry docks past the cafes on the left, then turn left. This street, which heads south toward Eceabat, has two small *birahanes* (beer halls), called the ***Albatros*** and the ***Dostlar***, as well as the coffee house ***İkinci Adres***.

Getting There & Away Gelibolu's otogar is 500m south-west of the stone tower on the road to Eceabat. Dolmuşes or buses run hourly via Eceabat to Kilitbahir; there are ferries from both these towns to Çanakkale. To get to the Gallipoli battlefields, go to Eceabat, then look for a dolmuş (or hitch a ride) to Kabatepe. Details of services follow:

Balıkesir – change at Çanakkale
Bursa – change at Çanakkale
Çanakkale – 49km plus ferry ride, less than two hours, US$2; take the Gelibolu-Lapseki ferry and catch a bus or minibus going to Çanakkale; or take the minibus to Eceabat or Kilitbahir and then the ferry to Çanakkale
Eceabat – 45km, 50 minutes, US$1.75; hourly buses or minibuses
Edirne – three hours, US$6; three direct buses daily; or take one of the frequent buses to Keşan and change
İstanbul – 288km, 4½ hours, US$8 to US$10; hourly buses from 7 am to 7 pm, plus some later buses
İzmir – 384km, 6½ hours, US$9 to US$11; frequent buses
Keşan – 100km, two hours, US$4; frequent buses
Kilitbahir – 52km, one hour, US$2; hourly minibuses

The Gelibolu-Lapseki car ferry departs from Gelibolu at 6.30, 7.30, 8.15, 9 and 11 am, and 1, 3, 5, 6, 7, 8, 9, 10, 11 pm and midnight. Departures from Lapseki are at 6.30, 7.30, 8.15 and 10 am, noon, 2, 4, 5, 6, 7, 8, 9, 10, 11 pm and midnight. The fare is US$0.60 per person, US$1.50 for a bicycle or moped, US$4.50 for a car.

If you miss this ferry, you can go south-west to Eceabat (45km, one hour) and catch the similar car ferry, or to Kilitbahir 7km beyond Eceabat and catch the small private ferry, which can take a few cars as well, and charges less than the other ferries. See the Çanakkale section for details.

Eceabat

The small town of Eceabat (formerly Maidos; population 4500) exists for the car ferries to Çanakkale and for the Gallipoli National Park headquarters and visitors centre, 2km south of the town. For details on the car ferries to Çanakkale, see that section.

Also facing the ferry dock on İskele Meydanı (Dock Square) are ***Hotel Ece, Hotel Eceabat*** and ***Hotel Boss***, noisy and nothing special but useful in emergencies, with doubles for around US$12; and ***Cafe-Restaurant Gül*** for food and drink.

Buses or minibuses run hourly north-east to Gelibolu (45km, one hour, US$1.75). In summer there are several dolmuşes daily to the ferry dock at Kabatepe (10km, 15 minutes) on the western shore of the peninsula, and these can drop you at the national park's Kabatepe information centre and museum, or at the base of the road up to Lone Pine and Chunuk Bair. Dolmuşes also run down the coast to Kilitbahir, from where dolmuşes travel south to Abide at the southern tip of the peninsula.

Kilitbahir

The small hamlet of Kilitbahir, at the foot of the Kilitbahir castle, hosts the small private ferry from Çanakkale, which arrives at a dock just north-east of the castle walls. There are a few small teahouses and restaurants, and the fortress is well worth a look, but these days Kilitbahir is a pass-through place. Dolmuşes and taxis await the ferry to shuttle you north-west to Eceabat (7km), or south-west via Alçıtepe (Krythia, 19.5km) to Çanakkale Şehitleri Abidesi (28km), the Turkish war memorial on Morto Bay, in Abide.

Gallipoli National Historic Park

Gallipoli National Historic Park (Gelibolu Tarihi Milli Parkı) covers much of the peninsula and all of the significant battle sites. Park headquarters is 2km south-west of Eceabat (5km north-east of Kilitbahir) at the Ziyaretçi Merkezi (Visitors Centre); there's a picnic ground here as well.

In the national park there are several different signage systems: the normal Turkish highway signs, the national park administration signs, and those posted by the Commonwealth War Graves Commission. This leads to confusion because the foreign troops had a completely different nomenclature for battlefield sites from the Turks, and the Turkish battlefield markings do not necessarily agree with the ones erected by the highway department. I've put both English and Turkish names in the text and on the Gallipoli map.

There are camping grounds at Kabatepe, Kum Limanı and Seddülbahir, and simple accommodation at Kum Limanı, Seddülbahir and Abide.

Tours of the battlefields are arranged by companies and individuals in Gelibolu and Çanakkale. See those sections for details.

About 3km north of Eceabat a road marked for Kabatepe and Kemalyeri heads west.

Kabatepe Information Centre & Museum
The Kabatepe Tanıtma Merkezi, 9km from Eceabat and 1km or so east of the village of Kabatepe, holds a small museum (US$0.50) with period uniforms, soldiers' letters, rusty weapons and other battlefield finds such as the skull of a luckless Turkish soldier with a ball lodged right in the forehead.

The road uphill to Lone Pine (Kanlı Sırt) and Chunuk Bair (Conkbayırı) begins 750m west of the information centre. Anzac Cove is situated about 3.5km from the information centre.

Kabatepe Village The small harbour here was the object of the Allied landing on 25 April 1915, but in the pitch dark of early morning the landing craft were swept northwards by currents to the steep cliffs of Arıburnu – a bit of bad luck which was crucial to the course of the campaign. Today there is little here but a camping ground and the dock for ferries to the Turkish Aegean island of Gökçeada.

Anzac Cove & Beaches Going west from the information centre, it's 3km to the **Beach Cemetery**, and another 90m to where a road goes inland to the Shrapnel Valley & Plugge's Plateau cemeteries.

Another 400m along is **Anzac Cove** (Anzac Koyu). The ill-fated Allied landing was made here on 25 April 1915, beneath and just south of the Arıburnu cliffs. The Allied forces were ordered to advance inland, but met with fierce resistance from the Ottoman forces under Mustafa Kemal (Atatürk), who had foreseen the landing here and, disobeyed a direct order from his commanders to send his troops south to Cape Helles. After this first failed effort, the Anzacs concentrated on consolidating and expanding the beachhead, which they did until June while awaiting reinforcements.

In August a major offensive was staged in an attempt to advance beyond the beachhead and up to the ridges of Chunuk Bair and Sarı Bair, and resulted in the bloodiest battles of the campaign, but little progress was made.

Anzac Cove is marked by a Turkish monument, another 300m along, which repeats Atatürk's famous words uttered in 1934 for the Anzac troops (see boxed text 'A Proud Day' earlier in this chapter). As a memorial reserve, the beach here is off-limits to swimmers and picnickers.

Beyond Anzac Cove a few hundred metres is the **Arıburnu Cemetery** and, 750m further along, the **Canterbury Cemetery**. Less than 1km further along the seaside road are the cemeteries at the **No 2 Outpost**, set back inland from the road, and the **New Zealand No 2 Outpost**, right next to the road. The **Embarkation Pier Cemetery** is 200m beyond the New Zealand No 2 Outpost.

Lone Pine to Chunuk Bair Retrace your steps to the Kabatepe information centre and follow the signs up the hill for Lone Pine (Kanlı Sırt), perhaps the most poignant and affecting of all the Anzac cemeteries. It's just under 3km to Lone Pine from the junction with the beach road, and another 3km uphill to the New Zealand Memorial at Chunuk Bair (Conkbayırı).

This area, which saw the most bitter fighting of the campaign, was later cloaked in pines, but a disastrous forest fire in 1994 denuded the hills. Reforestation efforts are under way.

Anzac Day

The great WWI battles of Gallipoli are commemorated each year during March and April.

Turkish 'Victory Day' (*Çanakkale Deniz Zaferi*), when Ottoman cannons and mines succeeded in keeping the Allied fleet from passing through the Dardanelles, is celebrated on 18 March, with festivities from 12 to 19 March.

Most Australians and New Zealanders choose to visit on Anzac Day (*Anzac Günü*; 25 April), the anniversary of the Allied landings on the peninsula in 1915. A dawn service at Bee Point begins a day of commemorative events.

Alan Moorehead, the author of *Gallipoli*, wrote in the 1950s, 'Except for occasional organized tours not more than half a dozen visitors arrive from one year's end to the other.'

In recent years, however, the memory of Gallipoli has come to life in surprising and sometimes alarming ways. The battlefields are now among the most-visited places in Turkey, particularly on Anzac Day, when thousands of visitors crowd the cemeteries and monument sites. Long rows of buses block the narrow roads, and dignitaries as well as visitors are often unable to reach the site of an event. The traffic snarl lasts most of the day.

In Çanakkale, all lodgings are booked solid at high prices months before 25 April, and other tourist services increase their prices. Drunken Australian, New Zealand, British and other foreign visitors careen about the streets, and reactionary Turkish youth gangs pick fights with them in an absurd revival of WWI antipathies.

Some tour operators convince visitors that it's possible to drive from İstanbul to Çanakkale in time for the Anzac Day dawn service, when in fact many people coming from Çanakkale can't even make it to the site in time.

All in all, a day which in the past was a solemn commemoration of heroic courage and sacrifice has recently turned into a logistical nightmare best avoided. To experience the poignant beauty of Gallipoli, you'd do well to visit at some other time.

Mehmetçiğe Saygı Anıtı The first monument, on the right-hand side of the road 1200m up from the junction, is to 'Mehmetçik' (Little Mehmet), the Turkish 'Johnnie' or 'G I Joe' for his contribution to national defence. Another 1200m brings you to the **Kanlı Sırt Kitabesi**, the inscription monument (in Turkish) detailing the battle of Lone Pine from the Turkish viewpoint.

Lone Pine At Lone Pine, 400m uphill from the Kanlı Sırt Kitabesi, Australian forces captured the Turkish positions on the evening of 6 August. In the few days of the August assault 4000 men died here. The trees which shaded the cemetery were swept away by the fire in 1994, leaving only one: a lone pine planted years ago as a memorial from the seed of the original tree which had stood here during the battle. The small tombstones carry touching epitaphs: 'Only son', 'He died for his country' and 'If I could hold your hand once more just to say well done'.

Johnston's Jolly to Quinn's Post As you progress up the hill, you quickly come to understand the ferocity of the battles here. At some points the trenches were only a few metres apart. The order to attack meant certain death to all who followed it, and virtually all – on both the Ottoman and Allied sides – did as they were ordered.

At Johnston's Jolly (Kırmızı Sırt/125 Alay Cephesi), 200m beyond Lone Pine, at Courtney's & Steele's Post, another 300m along, and especially at Quinn's Post (Bomba Sırt, Yüzbaşı Mehmet Şehitliği), another 400m uphill, the trenches were separated only by the width of the modern road.

THRACE

On the eastern side at **Johnston's Jolly** is the Turkish monument to the soldiers of the 125th Regiment who died here on 'Red Ridge'. At **Quinn's Post** is the memorial to Sergeant Mehmet, who fought with rocks and his fists after he ran out of ammunition; and the Captain Mehmet Cemetery.

57. Alay (57th Regiment) Just over 1km uphill from Lone Pine is another monument to Mehmetçik on the western side of the road and, on the eastern side, the cemetery and monument for officers and soldiers of the Ottoman 57th Regiment, which was sacrificed to the first Anzac assaults. The cemetery, built only a few years ago, has a surprising amount of religious symbolism for a Turkish army site, as the republican army has historically been steadfastly secular. The statue of an old man showing his granddaughter the battle sites portrays veteran Hüseyin Kaçmaz, who fought in the Balkan Wars, the Gallipoli campaign and the War of Independence at the fateful Battle of Dumlupınar. He died in 1994 at the age of 110.

Mehmet Çavuş & The Nek About 100m uphill past the 57th Regiment Cemetery, a road goes west to the monument for Mehmet Çavuş (another Sergeant Mehmet) and The Nek. It was at The Nek on 7 August 1915 that the eighth (Victorian) and 10th (Western Australian) regiments of the third Light Horse Brigade vaulted out of their trenches into withering fire and certain death – doomed but utterly courageous.

Baby 700/Mesudiye Topu About 300m uphill from the road to The Nek is the Baby 700 Cemetery and the Ottoman cannon called the Mesudiye Topu.

Düztepe 10. Alay Cephesi Another 1.5km uphill brings you to this monument, which marks the spot where the Ottoman 10th Regiment held the line. The views of the strait and the surrounding countryside are very fine.

Talat Göktepe Monument About 1km further along from Düztepe is the monument to Talat Göktepe, Chief Director of the Çanakkale Forestry District, the 'martyred forester' who died at the age of 50 fighting the forest fire which ravaged these hills on 25 July 1994.

Chunuk Bair At the top of the hill, 600m past the Talat Göktepe Monument, is a T-intersection. A right turn takes you east to the spot where, having stayed awake for four days straight, Atatürk spent the night of 9 to 10 August, and also to **Kemalyeri** (Scrubby Knoll), his command post. A left turn leads after 100m to **Chunuk Bair** (Conkbayırı), the first objective of the Allied landing in April 1915, and now the site of the New Zealand memorial.

As the Anzac troops made their way up the scrub-covered slopes on 25 April, the divisional commander Mustafa Kemal (Atatürk) brought up the 57th Infantry Regiment and gave them his famous order: 'I order you not just to attack, but to die. In the time it takes us to die, other troops and commanders will arrive to take our places.' The 57th was wiped out, but held the line and inflicted equally heavy casualties on the Anzacs below.

Chunuk Bair was also at the heart of the struggle from 6 to 9 August 1915, when 28,000 men died on this ridge. The peaceful pine grove of today makes it difficult to imagine the blasted wasteland of almost a century ago, when bullets, bombs and shrapnel mowed down men as the fighting went on day and night with huge numbers of casualties. The Anzac attack on 6-7 August, which included the New Zealand Mounted Rifle Brigade and a Maori contingent, was deadly, but the attack on the following day was of a ferocity which, according to Atatürk, 'could scarcely be described'.

On the western side of the road is the **New Zealand memorial** and some **reconstructed Turkish trenches** *(Türk Siperleri)*. A sign indicates the spots at which Mustafa Kemal (Atatürk) stood on 8 August 1915, known to every Turkish schoolchild: where he gave the order for the crucial attack at 4.30 am (Atatürk'ün taarruz emrini verdiği yer); where he watched the progress of the battle (Savaş gözetleme yeri); and the spot where shrapnel would have hit his heart, but was stopped by his pocket watch (Atatürk'ün saatinin parçaladığı yeri).

To the east a side road leads up to the **Turkish Conkbayırı Memorial**, five gigantic tablets with inscriptions (in Turkish) describing the progress of the battle.

Beyond Chunuk Bair the road leads to Kocaçimentepe, less than 2km along.

Kabatepe to Seddülbahir A road goes south from near the Kabatepe information centre past the side road to **Kum Limanı**, where there's a good swimming beach and the ***Hotel Kum and Kum Camping*** (*☎ 286-814 1466, fax 814 1917*), just over 6km south-west of the information centre. It has comfortable shower-equipped rooms for US$40 in summer, and camping places with some shade for US$6. This is the place to stop for a swim; if you're on a guided tour, you will probably swim here.

From Kabatepe (Gaba Tepe) it's about 12km to the village of **Alçıtepe**, formerly known as Krythia or Kirte. In the village, signs point out the road south-west to the **Twelve Tree Copse** and **Pink Farm** cemeteries, and north to the Turkish **Sargı Yeri Cemetery** and **Nuri Yamut monument**.

Heading south, the road passes the **Redoubt Cemetery**. About 5.5km south of Alçıtepe, south of the **Skew Bridge Cemetery**, the road divides, the right fork for the village of Seddülbahir and several Allied memorials. **Seddülbahir** (Sedd el Bahr), 1.5km from the intersection, is a sleepy farming village with a few small pensions, including the ***Helles Panorama***, ***Evim***, ***Kale*** and ***Fulda***; a PTT; a ruined Ottoman/Byzantine fortress; an army post; and a small harbour.

Follow the signs for Yahya Çavuş Şehitliği to reach the **Helles Memorial**, 1km beyond the Seddülbahir village square. There are fine views of the straits, with ships cruising placidly up and down. Half a million men were killed, wounded or lost in the dispute over which ships should (or should not) go through.

The initial Allied attack was two-pronged, with the southern landing being here at the tip of the peninsula on 'V' Beach. Yahya Çavuş (Sergeant Yahya) was the Turkish officer who led the first resistance to the Allied landing on 25 April 1915, causing heavy casualties. The cemetery named after him, known as **Yahya Çavuş Şehitliği**, is between the Helles Memorial and 'V' Beach.

Lancashire Landing cemetery is off to the north along a road marked by a sign; another sign points south to **'V' Beach**, 550m downhill. Right next to the beach is ***Mocamp Seddülbahir***, with tent and caravan sites and a few pension-like rooms.

Retrace your steps from the Helles Memorial back to the road division and then head east following signs for Abide and/or Çanakkale Şehitleri Abidesi (Çanakkale Martyrs' Memorial) at Morto Bay. Along the way you will pass the **French Memorial & Museum**. French troops, including a regiment of Africans, attacked Kumkale on the Asian shore in March 1915 with complete success, then re-embarked and landed in support of their British comrades-in-arms at Cape Helles.

At the foot of the Turkish monument hill is a fine pine-shaded picnic area. The monument, known as the **Çanakkale Şehitleri Abidesi**, commemorates all of the Turkish soldiers who fought and died at Gallipoli. It's a gigantic four-legged stone table almost 42m high and surrounded by landscaped grounds, which stands above a war museum (admission US$0.50). Exhibits include interesting bits of metal turned up by farmers' ploughs, including English forks and spoons; soldiers' seals and medals; scimitars; French bayonets; and machine guns. The poem on the side of the memorial translates:

Soldiers who have fallen on this land defending this land!
Would that your ancestors might descend from the skies to kiss your pure brows.
Who could dig the grave that was not too small for you?
All of history itself is too small a place for you.

THRACE

The most touching exhibit at the museum is a letter (written in Ottoman Turkish) from a young officer who had left law school in Constantinople to volunteer in the Gallipoli campaign. He wrote to his mother in poetic terms about the beauty of the landscape and of his love for life. Two days later he died in battle.

South of the Sea of Marmara

The southern shore of the Sea of Marmara is a land of small villages surrounded by olive groves, orchards, sunflower fields, rolling hills and rich valleys. During the time of the Ottoman Empire, the choice olives for the sultan's table came from here, and snow from the slopes of Bursa's Uludağ (the Bithynian Mt Olympus) cooled his drinks. The region's few cities are of moderate size and significant interest.

You can enjoy this region and its sights in only two days: catch an early boat from İstanbul to Yalova, make a quick tour of İznik (ancient Nicaea) and spend the night in Bursa. After seeing the sights of Bursa, the next morning catch a bus westward to Çanakkale. You'll reach that town on the Dardanelles in time for a late supper.

Spending from three to five days is more realistic if you want to do justice to all this, and also to enjoy the mineral baths at Termal and Çekirge.

Plan to spend some of your extra time in Bursa, where the mosques and museums are particularly fine as this was the Ottoman Empire's first capital city, before Edirne and İstanbul. You can also take a ride on a cablecar to the top of Uludağ, which is snowcapped for most of the year, and offers skiing in winter.

HIGHLIGHTS

- Relaxing in the mineral baths at Çekirge (Bursa) or Termal (Yalova)
- Walking the city walls and gates in İznik
- Riding the cablecar up the slopes of Uludağ
- Touring Bursa's Ulu Cami (Great Mosque) and Yeşil Cami (Green Mosque)
- Eating the best İskender kebap in the country

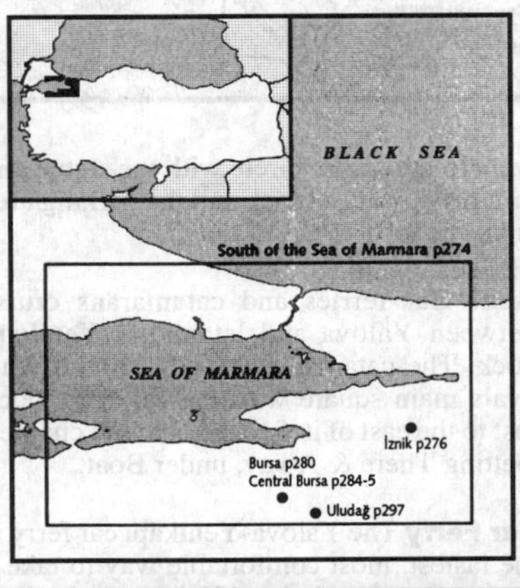

YALOVA

Yalova (population 60,000) is a farming and transportation centre. The highway between the industrial cities of Bursa and Kocaeli (İzmit) passes near here, as does the car ferry/bus link between Bursa and İstanbul. It's a pleasant enough town, with a few modest hotels and restaurants, most within two blocks of the ferry dock. Everything else you'd need is here as well, including banks, chemists etc.

There's nothing to detain you in Yalova. Head for the spa at Termal, the ancient city of Bursa or İznik without delay.

Getting There & Away

Bus On arrival in Yalova, as you walk from the wharf you will see a traffic circle centred on an enormous statue of Atatürk. Just off the dock to the left are rows of buses and minibuses. Buses to İznik and Bursa leave about every 30 minutes or less. The fare is US$2 to İznik, US$3 to Bursa.

Yalova city bus No 4 (Taşköprü-Termal) takes you to Termal for US$0.50, a dolmuş charges US$0.65. Coming off the ferry,

SOUTH OF MARMARA SEA

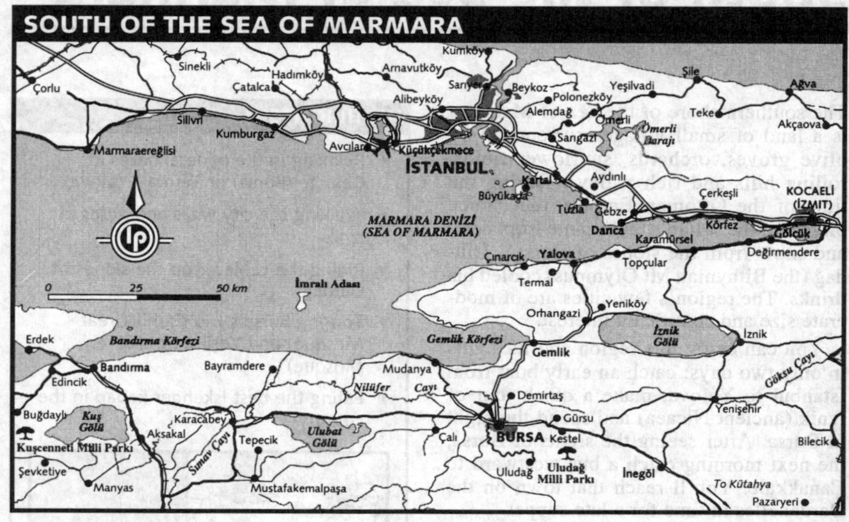

walk to the traffic circle with the statue and turn right, walk a block and the parking area is on the left.

Boat Car ferries and catamarans cruise between Yalova and İstanbul's Yenikapı dock. The catamaran dock is just off Yalova's main square with the car ferry dock just to the east of it. See the İstanbul chapter, Getting There & Away, under Boat.

Car Ferry The Yalova-Yenikapı car ferry is the fastest, most comfortable way to take a car between İstanbul and Yalova. A cheaper, slower alternative is the traditional car ferry between Eskihisar (near Darıca, south-west of Gebze) across the Bay of İzmit to Topçular, on the southern shore east of Yalova. By catching a ferry, you'll save yourself a 100km drive along chaotic roads through an industrial wasteland. Ferries run every 30 minutes around the clock on the 25-minute voyage; the fare for car and driver is US$10.

A bridge to cross the Bay of İzmit from Gebze to a point between Karaburun and Dilburnu is under construction, to be completed by 2001.

TERMAL

About 12km south-west of Yalova, off the road to Çınarcık, is the spa town of Termal. The baths here take advantage of hot, mineral-rich waters that gush from the earth, and were first exploited in Roman times. The Ottomans used the baths from the 1500s and Abdül Hamit II repaired and refurbished them in 1900 in a gaudy Ottoman baroque style to celebrate the 25th anniversary of his accession to the throne.

Atatürk added a simple but comfortable spa hotel. In the midst of the tourism boom, the simple hotels here were upgraded to deluxe comforts and prices.

You can come just to stroll through the gardens and have a look at the facilities, or you can come to bathe or stay the night.

Things to See & Do

The **gardens** and greenery at Termal are worth the trip, and Atatürk had a small house here, which is now a **museum**. There are also some excellent baths. At the **Valide Banyo** you get a locker for your clothes, then take a shower and enter a pool. An admission charge of around US$1 gets you 1½ hours of bathing. Soap and shampoo cost extra, so bring your own. The **Sultan Banyo** is even grander and much pricier at US$3/4 a single/double; you can rent a swimsuit here. The **Kurşunlu Banyo** features an open-air pool for US$2, an enclosed pool and sauna for US$2.50, and small private cubicles for US$2/2.50 a single/double.

Places to Stay

The villages several kilometres from the centre of Termal have numerous modest little pensions charging from US$7 to US$10 per person for rooms with or without running water. You may find yourself hitching in, or waiting for the infrequent buses and dolmuşes.

The ***Turban Yalova Termal Hotel*** *(☎ 216-835 7400, fax 835 7413)* is in the process of being privatised, which may raise prices above the normal US$60 to US$85 a single, US$75 to US$100 a double, breakfast included. The front rooms are the more expensive.

Places to Eat

Termal has several restaurants and cafes, but all are fairly pricey: a mere cup of Nescafé costs over US$1.

İZNİK

The road from Yalova to İznik (population 18,000) runs along fertile green hills punctuated by tall, spiky cypress trees, passing peach orchards, cornfields and vineyards. The journey of 60km takes about one hour.

As you approach İznik you may notice fruit-packing plants among the orchards. You will certainly have admired the vast İznik Gölü (İznik Lake). Watch for the great Byzantine city walls: one entrance to the city is through the old İstanbul Kapısı (İstanbul Gate) on Atatürk Caddesi, which leads directly to the centre and the ruined church Aya Sofya (Hagia Sophia), now a museum.

History

This ancient city may have been founded around 1000 BC. We know that it was revitalised by one of Alexander the Great's generals in 316 BC. Another of the generals, Lysimachus, soon got hold of it and named it after his wife Nikaea. It became the capital city of the province of Bithynia.

Nicaea lost some of its prominence with the founding of Nicomedia (today's Kocaeli) in 264 BC, and by 74 BC the entire area had been incorporated into the Roman Empire.

Nicaea flourished under Rome, but invasions by the Goths and the Persians brought ruin by 300 AD.

Ecumenical Councils With the rise of Constantinople, Nicaea took on a new importance. In 325 AD, the first Ecumenical Council was held here to condemn the heresy of Arianism. During the reign of Justinian I, Nicaea was grandly refurbished with new buildings and defences, which served the city well a few centuries later when the Arabs invaded. Like Constantinople, Nicaea never fell to its Arab besiegers.

In 787 AD another Ecumenical Council, the seventh, was held in Nicaea's Hagia Sofia church. The deliberations solved the problem of iconoclasm: henceforth it would be church policy not to destroy icons. Theologians who saw icons as 'images' prohibited by the Bible, were dismayed, but Byzantine artists were delighted, and went to work on their art with even more vigour.

Nicaea and Constantinople did, however, fall to the crusaders. From 1204 to 1261, when a Latin king sat on the throne of Byzantium, the true Byzantine emperor Theodore I (called Lascaris) reigned over the 'Empire of Nicaea'. When the crusaders left, the imperial capital returned to Constantinople.

The Turks The Seljuk Turks had a flourishing empire in Central Anatolia before 1250, and various tribes of nomadic warriors had circulated near the walls of Nicaea during those times. In fact, Turkish soldiers had served as mercenaries in the interminable battles which raged among rival claimants to the Byzantine throne. At one point, a Byzantine battle over Nicaea ended with a Turkish emir as its ruler.

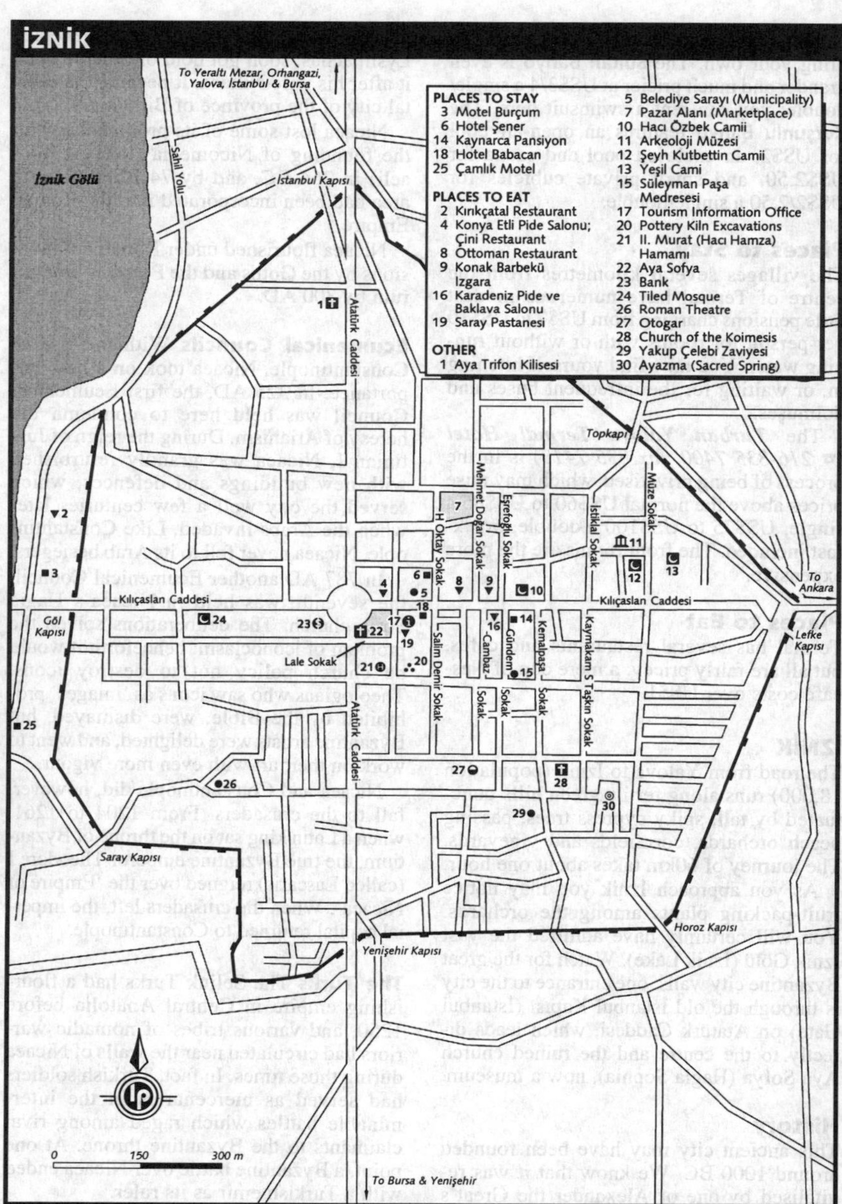
İZNİK
PLACES TO STAY
3 Motel Burçum
6 Hotel Şener
14 Kaynarca Pansiyon
18 Hotel Babacan
25 Çamlık Motel
PLACES TO EAT
2 Kırkçatal Restaurant
4 Konya Etli Pide Salonu; Çini Restaurant
8 Ottoman Restaurant
9 Konak Barbekü Izgara
16 Karadeniz Pide ve Baklava Salonu
19 Saray Pastanesi
OTHER
1 Aya Trifon Kilisesi
5 Belediye Sarayı (Municipality)
7 Pazar Alanı (Marketplace)
10 Hacı Özbek Camii
11 Arkeoloji Müzesi
12 Şeyh Kutbettin Camii
13 Yeşil Cami
15 Süleyman Paşa Medresesi
17 Tourism Information Office
20 Pottery Kiln Excavations
21 II. Murat (Hacı Hamza) Hamamı
22 Aya Sofya
23 Bank
24 Tiled Mosque
26 Roman Theatre
27 Otogar
28 Church of the Koimesis
29 Yakup Çelebi Zaviyesi
30 Ayazma (Sacred Spring)
To Yeraltı Mezar, Orhangazi, Yalova, İstanbul & Bursa
İznik Gölü
Sahil Yolu
İstanbul Kapısı
Atatürk Caddesi
Topkapı
Mehmet Doğan Sokak
Eşrefoğlu Sokak
İstiklal Sokak
Müze Sokak
To Ankara
Kılıçaslan Caddesi
Göl Kapısı
H Oktay Sokak
Lale Sokak
Salim Demir Sokak
Cambaz Sokak
Gündem Sokak
Kemalpaşa Sokak
Kaymakam S Taşkın Sokak
Lefke Kapısı
Saray Kapısı
Horoz Kapısı
Yenişehir Kapısı
0
150
300 m
To Bursa & Yenişehir

It was Orhan, son of Osman and second sultan (1326-61) of the Ottoman Empire, who conquered İznik on 2 March 1331. The city soon had the honour of harbouring the first Ottoman theological school. Prusa (Bursa) had fallen to the Ottomans on 6 April 1326, and became their first capital city. In 1337 they took Nicomedia and effectively blocked the Byzantines from entering Anatolia.

Sultan Selim I (1512-20), a mighty conqueror nicknamed 'The Grim', rolled his armies over Azerbaijan in 1514 and took the Persian city of Tabriz. Packing up all of the region's artisans, he sent them westward to İznik. They brought with them a high level of expertise in the making of coloured tiles. Soon İznik's kilns were turning out faïence, unequalled even today. The great period of İznik faïence continued almost to 1700. At one point, artisans were sent to Tunisia, then an Ottoman possession, to begin a high-quality faïence industry.

The art of coloured tile-making is being revived in İznik today, but nowhere near the scale of the trade in Kütahya. Though new tiles make good purchases, 17th and 18th century İznik tiles are considered antiquities, and cannot legally be exported from Turkey.

Orientation

Aya Sofya (known for centuries as Hagia Sophia), is a good vantage point from which to consider the town's Roman layout: two straight boulevards, north-south (Atatürk Caddesi) and east-west (Kılıçaslan Caddesi), leading to the four principal gates in the city walls. To the north is the İstanbul Kapısı, to the south the Yenişehir Kapısı, to the east Lefke Kapısı and to the west, the Göl Kapısı.

The *otogar* (bus station) is a few blocks south-east of the church.

Information

The Tourism Information Office (☎/fax 224-757 1933), Kılıçaslan Caddesi 130, is a block north-east of Aya Sofya, just to the west of the Hotel Babacan, on the 2nd floor. It's open from 9 am to noon and from 1 to 5.30 pm every day in the warm months, with shorter hours (closed on weekends) off season.

Aya Sofya

Aya Sofya, the Church of the Divine Wisdom, is hardly striking in its grandeur, but it has a fascinating past.

What you see is the ruin of three different buildings. Inside is a mosaic floor and a mural of Jesus with Mary and John the Baptist which dates from the time of Justinian. That original church was destroyed by an earthquake in 1065 and was later rebuilt. Mosaics were set into the walls at that time. With the Ottoman conquest, the church became a mosque. A fire in the 16th century ruined everything, but reconstruction was carried out under the expert eye of Mimar Sinan, who added İznik tiles to the decoration.

Aya Sofya is open from 9 am to noon and from 2 to 5 pm daily, closed on Monday. If there's no one about when you visit, continue with your tour. The key is probably at the museum. After visiting there, ask to be let into the church.

South-east of Aya Sofya is the **II. Murat Hamamı**, also called the Hacı Hamza Hamamı, a Turkish bath constructed during the reign of Sultan Murat II, in the first half of the 15th century, and still in operation.

Kılıçaslan Caddesi

İznik's main street, Kılıçaslan Caddesi, leads eventually to the Lefke Kapısı (Lefke Gate). Walking from Aya Sofya, on the left is the Belediye Sarayı or Municipality building, with a sign out the front that reads (in Turkish) 'Our motto is, Clean City, Green City'. The motto is carried out in the small but agreeable park with its big poplars shading the commercial district from the hot summer sun.

A bit further along on the left is the **Hacı Özbek Camii**, one of the town's oldest mosques, dating from 1332.

Walk one block south along Gündem Sokak, opposite the Hacı Özbek Camii, to reach the **Süleyman Paşa Medresesi**. Founded by Sultan Orhan shortly after he captured Nicaea, it has the distinction of being the very first college (actually a theological seminary) founded by a member of the Ottoman dynasty.

SOUTH OF MARMARA SEA

Back on the main street, continue eastward and soon, to the left, you can see the tile-covered minaret of the Yeşil Cami.

Yeşil Cami

Built in 1492, the year of Columbus' first voyage to America, the Yeşil Cami, or Green Mosque, has Seljuk Turkish proportions influenced more by Persia (the Seljuk homeland) than by İstanbul. The green-glazed bricks of the minaret foreshadowed the tile industry that arose a few decades after the mosque was built.

Arkeoloji Müzesi

Opposite the Yeşil Cami is the Nilüfer Hatun İmareti (Soup Kitchen of Lady Nilüfer), now the town's museum. It's open from 8.30 am to noon and 1 to 5 pm, closed on Monday (usually). Admission costs US$1.25.

Begun in 1388, it was built by Sultan Murat I for his mother, Nilüfer Hatun, who was born a Byzantine princess but was married off to Orhan, second sultan of the Ottoman state, to form a diplomatic alliance.

Though intended as a place where the poor could come for free food, it now dispenses culture to the masses. The front court is filled with marble statuary, bits of cornice and column, and similar archaeological flotsam and jetsam. In the lofty, cool halls are exhibits of İznik faïence; Ottoman weaponry, embroidery and calligraphy; and several items from the city's Roman past. Many of the little signs are in French and English, but you'll need to know the word *yüzyıl* (century), as in XVI Yüzyıl (16th century).

While at the museum, enquire about a visit to the **Yeraltı Mezar** (underground tomb), a Byzantine tomb on the outskirts of town. You must have a museum official accompany you with the key; there is a small charge for admission, and the official should receive a small tip. Also, you will have to haggle with a taxi driver for a return-trip price.

The little tomb, discovered by accident in the 1960s, has delightful Byzantine murals covering its walls and ceiling. There is another tomb nearby, but it's not really worth the bother or expense to see.

Across the road to the south of the museum is the **Şeyh Kutbettin Camii** (1492), in ruins.

City Walls

Return to Kılıçaslan Caddesi and continue east toward the **Lefke Kapısı**. Lefke, now a small town called Osmaneli, was a city of considerable size in Byzantine times. This charming old monument is actually three gates in a row, dating from Byzantine times. The middle one has an inscription which tells us it was built by Proconsul Plancius Varus in 123 AD. It's possible to climb to the top of the gate and the walls here, a good vantage point for inspecting the ancient walls.

Outside the gate is an **aqueduct**, and the **tomb of Çandarlı Halil Hayrettin Paşa** (late 14th century), with the graves of many lesser mortals nearby.

Re-enter the city through the Lefke Kapısı, and turn left. Follow the walls south and west to the **Yenişehir Kapısı**. On the way you will pass near the ruined **Church of the Koimesis**, on the western side of Kaymakam S Taşkın Sokak, which dates from about 800 AD. Only some of the foundations remain, but it is famous as the burial place of the Byzantine emperor Theodore I (Lascaris). When the crusaders took Constantinople in 1204, Lascaris fled to Nicaea and established his court here.

Lascaris built Nicaea's outer ring of walls, supported by over 100 towers and protected by a wide moat. No doubt he didn't trust the crusaders, having lost one city to them. The emperor died and was buried here, and when the court finally returned to Constantinople in 1261, it was under the leadership of Michael VIII Palaeologus. Lascaris never made it back to his beloved capital.

Half a block east of the church is an *ayazma* or **sacred fountain**, also called a *yeraltı çeşme* (underground spring).

After admiring the Yenişehir Kapısı, start towards the centre along Atatürk Caddesi. Halfway to Aya Sofya, a road on the left leads to the ruins of a Roman theatre. To the south-west is the **Saray Kapısı**, or Palace Gate. Sultan Orhan had a palace near here in the 14th century.

İznik Gölü
Make your way to the lakeshore where there's a park and bathing beach. The water tends to be weedy and chilly except in high summer.

Places to Stay
The few hotels in İznik may fill up with Turks from nearby cities on summer weekends, and you may need to reserve a room in advance.

İznik has a few modest hotels good for an overnight stay. ***Kaynarca Pansiyon*** *(☎ 224-757 1753, fax 757 1723, Gündem Sokak 1)*, run by the irrepressible Ali Bulmuş, is clean and central, charging US$10/14/19 a single/double/triple with bath, TV and breakfast.

In the centre, just across the street from the Belediye, is the plain, drab ***Hotel Babacan*** *(☎ 224-757 1211, Kılıçaslan Caddesi 104)*. There are also 30 rooms with sinks for US$8/10 a single/double. With private shower, the prices are US$12/14, without breakfast.

Hotel Şener *(☎ 224-757 1338, fax 757 2280, Belediye Arkası, H Oktay Sokak 7)*, prides itself on being the fanciest hotel in the centre, with a lift, lounge, restaurant, and comfortable rooms going for US$15/24/32 a single/double/triple with shower. You can sometimes haggle for a lower rate.

Motel Burcum *(☎ 224-757 1011)* on Sahil Yolu has verdant grounds and tidy rooms, some with views of the lake, for US$22 a double, breakfast included. Get a room on the 2nd or 3rd floor if you want that view. You can also camp in the garden for a few dollars per night.

Çamlık Motel *(☎ 224-757 1631)*, at the southern end of Sahil Yolu, has good rooms and a restaurant, with prices identical to those at the Burcum. There's camping here as well.

Places to Eat
On Kılıçaslan Caddesi, look for ***Konya Etli Pide Salonu***, which serves good, cheap, freshly made Turkish-style pizzas for US$1.50 to US$3, depending upon toppings. Arab-style *lahmacun* (soft pizza) costs less than US$1 per portion. ***Konak Barbekü Izgara***, further east along Kılıçaslan Caddesi, is the fancy version of a Turkish grill, with a greater variety of lamb and chicken grills but only slightly higher prices.

For *hazır yemek* (ready food), try the ***Çini Restaurant*** next to the Konya Etli Pide Salonu, or the ***Ottoman Restaurant*** further east. ***Kırıkçatal*** (Broken Fork), north of the Motel Burcum by the lake, has a long-standing reputation.

There are also several *pastanes* (pastry shops) here, including ***Saray Pastanesi*** east of Aya Sofya, good for breakfast, dinner or a snack.

Getting There & Away
Bursa has a much better selection of hotels and restaurants than İznik, so unless you're unusually interested in İznik, take one of the hourly buses from the city's otogar to Bursa or Yalova. Don't wait until too late in the day, however, as the last bus heads out at 6 or 7 pm on the 1½-hour trip. A ticket costs from US$2 to US$2.75, depending upon the bus company.

BURSA
Bursa, with a population of one million, has a special place in the hearts of the Turks. It was the first capital city of the Ottoman Empire and, in a real sense, the birthplace of modern Turkish culture. The city, at an altitude of 155m, has its pretty parts despite its industrial base.

History
Called Prusa by the Byzantines, Bursa is a very old and important city. It was founded – according to legend, by Prusias, the King of Bithynia – before 200 BC; there may have been an even older settlement on the site. It soon came under the sway of Eumenes II of Pergamum, and thereafter under direct Roman control.

Bursa grew to importance in the early centuries of Christianity, when the thermal baths at Çekirge were first developed on a large scale and when a silk trade was founded here. The importation of silkworms and the establishment of looms began an industry

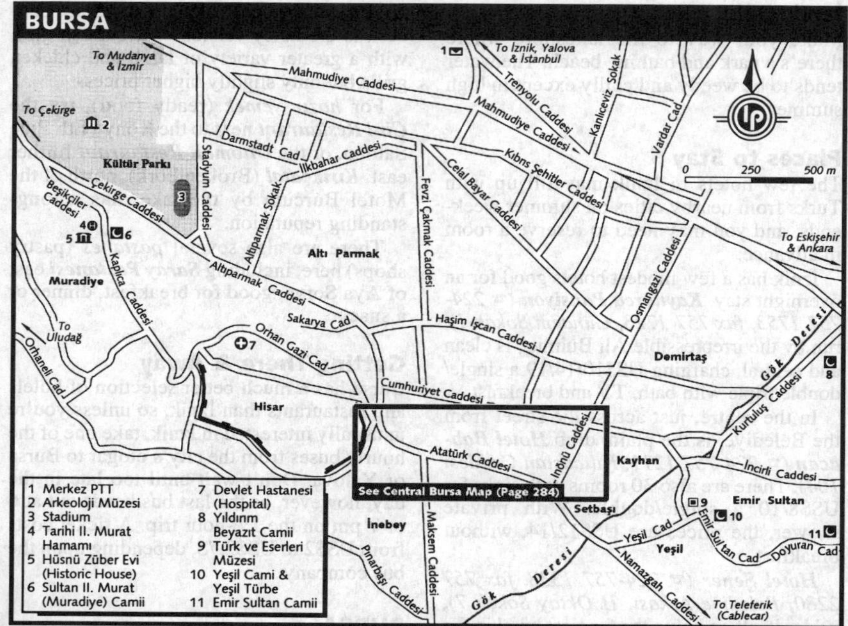

which survives to this day. However, it was Justinian I (527-65) who really put Bursa on the map. Besides favouring the silk trade, he built a palace for himself and bathhouses in Çekirge.

With the decline of the Byzantine Empire, Bursa's location near Constantinople drew the interest of would-be conquerors, including the Arab armies (circa 700 AD) and the Seljuk Turks. The Seljuks, having conquered much of Anatolia by 1075, took Bursa with ease that same year, and planted the seeds of the great Ottoman Empire to come.

With the arrival of the First Crusade in 1097, Bursa reverted to Christian hands, though it was to be conquered and reconquered by both sides for the next 100 years. When the rapacious armies of the Fourth Crusade sacked Constantinople in 1204, the Byzantine emperor fled to İznik and set up his capital there. He succeeded in controlling the hinterland of İznik, including Bursa, until the capital was moved back to Constantinople in 1261.

Ever since the Turkish migration into Anatolia during the 11th and 12th centuries, small principalities had risen here and there around Turkish military leaders. A *gazi* (warrior chieftain or 'Hero of the Faith') would rally a group of followers, gain control of a territory, govern it and seek to expand its borders. One such prince was Ertuğrul Gazi (died 1281), who formed a small state near Bursa. Under the rule of his son Osman Gazi (1281-1326) the small state grew to a nascent empire and took Osman's name *(Osmanlı*, 'Ottoman'). Bursa was besieged by Osman's forces in 1317 and was finally starved into submission on 6 April 1326 when it immediately became the Ottoman capital.

After Osman had expanded and enriched his principality, he was succeeded by Orhan Gazi (1326-61) who, from his base at

Bursa, expanded the empire to include everything from what is now Ankara in Central Anatolia to Thrace in Europe. The Byzantine capital at Constantinople was thus surrounded, and the Byzantine Empire had only about a century to survive. Orhan took the title of *sultan* (lord), struck the first Ottoman coinage and near the end of his reign was able to dictate to the Byzantine emperors. One of them, John VI Cantacuzene, was Orhan's close ally and later even his father-in-law (Orhan married the Princess Theodora).

Even though the Ottoman capital moved to Adrianople (Edirne) in 1402, Bursa remained an important, even revered, Ottoman city throughout the long history of the empire. Both Osman and Orhan were buried there; their tombs are still important monuments in Turkish history.

With the founding of the Turkish Republic (1923), Bursa's industrial development began in earnest. What really brought the boom was the automobile assembly plants, set up in the 1960s and 1970s. Large factories still assemble Renaults, Fiats and other motor vehicles.

Karagöz

Bursa is traditionally regarded as the 'birthplace' of the Turkish Karagöz shadow puppet theatre. The puppets – cut from camel hide, treated with oil to promote translucency, and brought to life with coloured paint – are manipulated behind a white cloth onto which their images are cast by a light behind them.

Legend has it that one of the construction foremen working on Bursa's Ulu Cami was a hunchback called Karagöz (Black-eye). He and his straight man Hacivat indulged in such humorous antics that the other workers abandoned their tasks to watch. This infuriated the sultan, who had the two miscreants put to death. Their comic routines (many of them bawdy) live on in the Karagöz shadow puppet theatre, a Central Asian tradition brought to Bursa from where it spread throughout the Ottoman lands.

Once commonly performed in tea and coffee houses, salons and parks throughout the empire, the traditional Karagöz show has long since succumbed to the ravages of cinema, video and television.

In the Eski Aynalı Çarşı of Bursa's bedesten is a shop called Karagöz (☎ 224-221 8727), open daily except Sunday, and run by a man named Şinasi Çelikkol. He sells Turkish antiques and handicrafts, including the Karagöz shadow puppets. Şinasi Bey has led efforts to revive and perpetuate the Karagöz show, including the establishment of the Karagöz Sanat Evi (Karagöz Art House) and organisation of the annual Karagöz Festival.

The **Karagöz Sanat Evi**, on the south side of Altıparmak Caddesi opposite the Karagöz monument, hosts exhibits of local and regional arts and crafts, and organises Karagöz shows.

The **Karagöz Festival**, held in mid-November, brings Karagöz *hayali* (shadow puppeteers), Western puppeteers and marionette performers from Turkey and neighbouring countries to Bursa for five days of festivities and performances.

Also, as Bursa has always been noted for its fruit, it is logical that a large fruit juice and soft drink industry should be centred here. Tourism is also important.

Orientation

Bursa clings to the slopes of Uludağ and spills down into the fertile valley. The major boulevards are Kıbrıs Şehitler Caddesi and Atatürk Caddesi, which is the main axis in the commercial district. Both run across the slope, not up and down it.

Bursa's main square is Cumhuriyet Alanı (Republic Square), with its equestrian statue of Atatürk. Most people refer to the square as Heykel (statue), and this is what you will see on the illuminated signs atop dolmuşes which wait near the bus station to take you to the city centre.

Bursa's main street, Atatürk Caddesi, runs west from Heykel to the Ulu Cami (Great Mosque), a distance of about 700m. This is the business section, the centre of Bursa. Heavy traffic makes it almost impossible to cross the street, so use the *altgeçidi* (pedestrian subways), each of which bears a name.

To the north-west, Atatürk Caddesi becomes Cemal Nadir Caddesi, then Altıparmak Caddesi, then Çekirge Caddesi. It leads to the spa suburb of Çekirge, about a 10 minute bus ride away.

South-east of Heykel, Namazgah Caddesi crosses the Gök Deresi trickling along the bottom of a dramatic gorge. Just after the stream, Yeşil Caddesi branches off to the left to the Yeşil Cami and Yeşil Türbe, after which it changes names to become Emir Sultan Caddesi.

From Heykel and Atatürk Caddesi you can get dolmuşes and buses to all other parts of the city.

Information

Tourist Office The Tourism Information Office (☎ 224-251 1834, fax 220 1848) is beneath Atatürk Caddesi at the northern entrance to the Orhan Gazi Altgeçidi, facing the Koza Han and Orhan Gazi Camii across the park. Staff are well-informed and helpful, particularly to readers of this guidebook.

Bookshops TAŞ Kitapçılık & Yayıncılık (☎ 224-222 9453), Adliye Karşısı, Kültür Sokak 8/A, just a few steps uphill from Heykel, has Penguin books and a number of other English titles, as well as some English-language newspapers and periodicals.

Emir Sultan Camii

You can see most of Bursa's sights in one full day, though a leisurely tour will take a little more time. Start with the city's most famous architectural monuments, east of the city centre.

The Emir Sultan Camii is a favourite of Bursa's pious Muslims. Rebuilt by Selim III in 1805 and restored in the early 1990s, it echoes the romantic decadence of Ottoman rococo style. The setting, next to a large hillside cemetery surrounded by huge trees and overlooking the city and valley, is as pleasant as the mosque itself.

To reach the mosque, take an 'Emirsultan' dolmuş or any bus with 'Emirsultan' in its name, such as Nos 1, 1A, 2A, 6 or 18, and head east. You'll pass by the Yeşil Cami and Yeşil Türbe before coming to the Emir Sultan Camii, but this way you can walk downhill, not up.

Yıldırım Beyazıt Camii

Gazing across the valley from the Emir Sultan Camii, you'll see the two domes of the Yıldırım Beyazıt Camii, the Mosque of Beyazıt the Thunderbolt. It was built earlier (in 1391) than Bursa's famous Yeşil Cami, and forms part of the same architectural evolution. You can walk through the city to this mosque if you like, but go and see the Yeşil Cami first.

Next to the Yıldırım Beyazıt Camii is its *medrese*, once a Muslim theological seminary, now a public health centre. Here also are the tombs of the mosque's founder, Sultan Beyazıt I, and his son İsa. This peaceful spot gives one no sense of the turbulent times which brought Beyazıt to his death.

Yıldırım Beyazıt (Sultan Beyazıt I, 1389-1402) led his Ottoman armies into Yugoslavia and Hungary, and captured even more of Anatolia for the Ottomans.

But he was brought down by Tamerlane, who defeated him and took him prisoner at the Battle of Ankara in 1402. Beyazıt died a year later in captivity, and Tamerlane marched all the way to İzmir and Bursa. With this blow, the Ottoman Empire all but collapsed.

Dolmuşes ('Heykel-Beyazıt Yıldırım' or 'Heykel-Fakülte') depart from Heykel and pass near the mosque.

Yeşil Cami

After the disastrous victories of Tamerlane, Beyazıt's sons argued over the succession to the weakened Ottoman throne. The civil war between them lasted for 10 years until 1413, when one son, Mehmet Çelebi, was able to gain supreme power. Six years after becoming sultan, Mehmet I (1413-21) ordered his architect Hacı İvaz to begin construction on Bursa's greatest monument, the Yeşil Cami or Green Mosque. It was finished in 1424.

The mosque is a supremely beautiful building in a fine setting and represents a turning point in Turkish architectural style. Before this, Turkish mosques echoed the style of the great Seljuks which was basically Persian, but in the Yeşil Cami a purely Turkish style emerges. Notice the harmonious facade and the beautiful carved marble work around the central doorway. As you enter, you will pass beneath the sultan's private apartments into a domed central hall. The rooms to the left and right, if not being used for prayer, were used by high court officials for transacting government business. The room straight ahead, with the 15m-high *mihrab* (niche indicating the direction of Mecca), is the main prayer room. Greenish-blue tiles on the interior walls gave the mosque its name.

Much of Bursa, including the Yeşil Cami, was destroyed in an earthquake in 1855 but the mosque was restored, authentically, by 1864.

Just inside the mosque's main entrance, a narrow stairway leads up to the **hünkar mahfili**, or sultan's loge, above the main door. The loge is sumptuously tiled and decorated. This is where the sultan actually lived (or at least it was one of his residences), with his harem and household staff in less plush quarters on either side. The caretaker used to choose single travellers or couples, give them a conspiratorial wink, and lead them up for a peek, after which he would receive a tip. Somebody higher up must have caught on, as he no longer seems to be doing it.

Yeşil Türbe

Sharing the small park surrounding the Yeşil Cami is the Yeşil Türbe, or Green Tomb. It's not green, of course. The blue exterior tiles were put on during restoration work in the 19th century; the lavish use of tiles inside is original work, however. The tomb is open from 8.30 am to noon and 1 to 5.30 pm. There is no charge and no need to remove your shoes.

The most prominent tomb is that of the Yeşil Cami's founder, Mehmet I (Çelebi). Other tombs include those of his children. Take a walk around the outside of the tomb to look at the tiled calligraphy above several windows. The huge tiled mihrab here is very impressive.

After seeing the mosque and the tomb, you might want to take a rest and have something to drink at one of the cafes on the eastern side of the mosque, which have wonderful views of the valley, though you pay a premium for them.

Türk ve İslam Eserleri Müzesi

Down the road a few steps from the Yeşil Cami is its medrese which is now the Turkish & Islamic Arts Museum. The building is in the Seljuk style of religious schools, and is open from 8.30 am to noon and 1 to 5 pm, closed on Monday; admission costs US$1.25, half-price for students.

Start to the right to see a re-creation of an Ottoman *sünnet odası* (circumcision room), then, in the *eyvan* or niche-like hall, an exhibit of ceramics from the Seljuk period (12th and 13th centuries), İznik ware from the 14th to 18th centuries, and more modern Kütahya ware (18th to 20th centuries).

Next comes an exhibit of Karagöz shadow puppets. It's thought that these painted

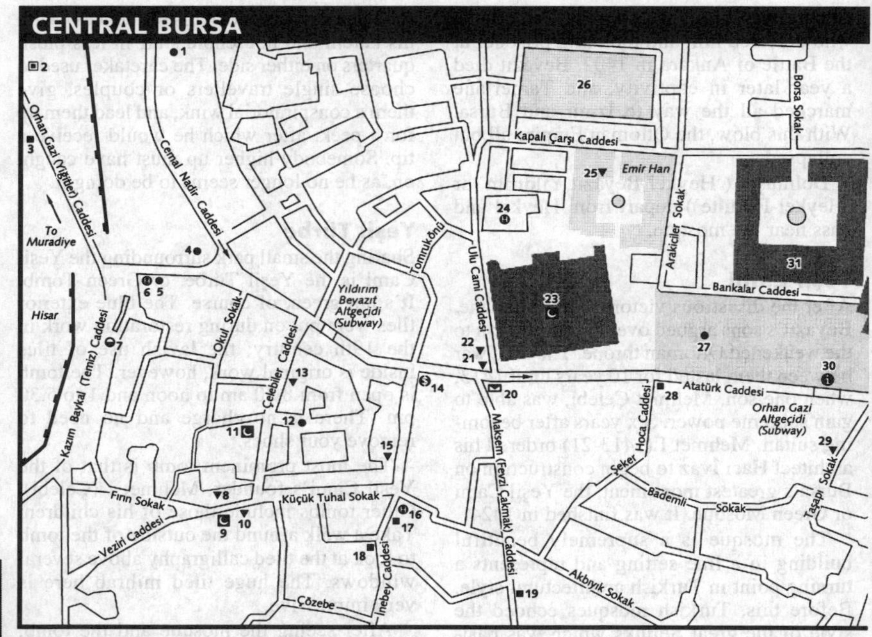

CENTRAL BURSA

PLACES TO STAY

3 Safran Otel & Restaurant
17 Otel Güneş
18 Otel Çamlıbel
19 Hotel Dikmen
28 Kent Hotel
41 Hotel Çeşmeli
51 Hotel İpekçi

PLACES TO EAT

8 Yeşil İnci Lokantası
10 Öz Anadolu Kebap ve Lahmacun Salonu
13 Alış Izgara; Ali Baba Baklavacısı
15 Şehir Lokantası; Ümit
21 Çınaraltı Çay ve Nargile Salonu
22 Ömür Köftecisi
25 Emirhan Çay Evi
29 Hacıbey Kebapçısı
33 Çiçek Izgara
35 Kebapçı İskenderoğlu Nurettin
36 İnegöl Köftecisi & Kamil Koç Co Bus Tickets
39 Sazende Restaurant & Bar
42 Okyanus Fırın Salonu
49 Adanur Hacıbey
50 Kebapçı İskender

OTHER

1 Ottomantur (Turkish Airlines)
2 Osman Gazi ve Orhan Gazi Türbeleri
4 Timurtaş Paşa Parkı
5 Uludağ Co Bus Tickets
6 Çakır Ağa Hamamı
7 Muradiye Dolmuş
9 Hacı Sevinç Camii
11 Mecnundede Camii
12 Tahtakale Çarşısı (Market)
14 Türkiye Emlak Bankası
16 Tarihi İnebey Hamamı
20 PTT
23 Ulu Cami
24 Ulu Cami Hamamı
26 Bedesten
27 Orhan Gazi Camii Parki (Koza Parki)
30 Tourism Information Office
31 Koza Han
32 Belediye Sarayı (Town Hall)
34 Çiçek Pazarı (Flower Market)
37 Katlı Otopark
38 Karaşeyh Camii
40 Kocaahmet Katlı Otopark
43 TAŞ Kitapçılık & Yayıncılık Bookshop
44 Vilayet (Government Building)
45 Heykel
46 Ahmet Vefik Paşa Tiyatrosu (Theatre)
47 Dolmuşes to Muradiye, Santral Garaj & Çekirge
48 TC Ziraat Bankası
52 Karakedi Camii
53 Bat Pazarı

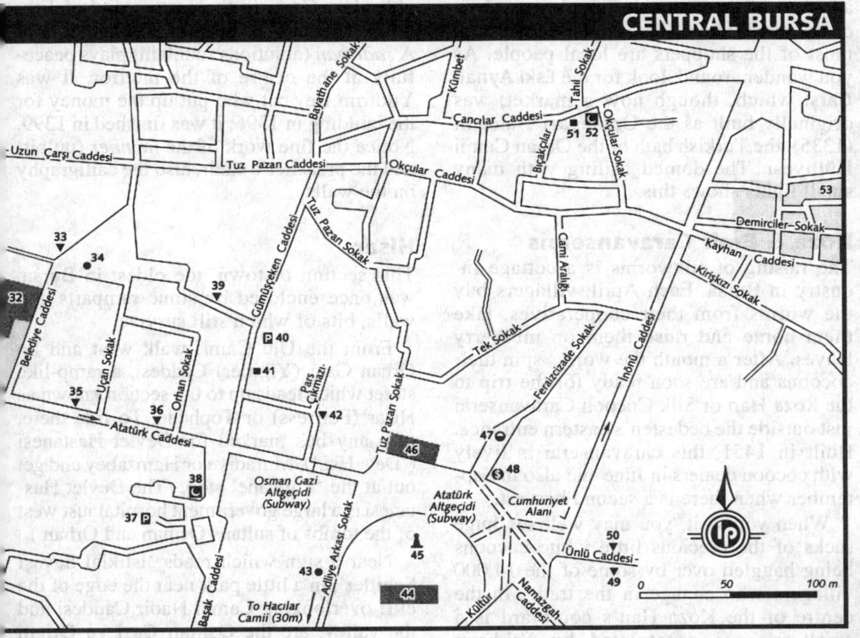

camel-hide puppets originated in China and Mongolia, and were brought to the Middle East by the Turks.

After Karagöz, museum displays include costumes, carpets, jewellery, metalwork and arms; *dergah* (dervish hall) musical instruments, turbans and other paraphernalia; illuminated Korans, carpet weaving and embroidery.

Bat Pazarı

From the plaza at Heykel, walk down the hill on the eastern (right) side of İnönü Caddesi one very long block. Cross Kirişkızı Sokak and turn right onto the next street, Kayhan Caddesi, to enter a warren of little streets called the Bat Pazarı (Goose Market), or, more appropriately, the Demirciler Çarşısı (Ironmongers' Market). The one thing you won't find here today are geese, but you will find ironmongers' shops and pedlars of old clothes, carpets, rope, utensils, potions and just about everything else. This market area is lively and colourful, perfect for photographing. When you snap a shot of the blacksmith at his forge, chances are he will ask you to send him a copy. It's only fair; you should try to do so.

Bedesten

After a half-hour stroll through the Bat Pazarı, head back to İnönü Caddesi and ask someone to point the way to the *Bedesten* or Covered Bazaar. Cross İnönü Caddesi and head into the side streets, following the directions given. The actual covered market is surrounded by a network of small shopping streets.

The Bedesten was originally built in the late 14th century by Yıldırım Beyazıt, but the earthquake of 1855 brought it down. The reconstructed Bedesten retains the look and feel of the original, though it is obviously much tidier. This is not a tourist trap; most of the shoppers are local people. As you wander around, look for the **Eski Aynalı Çarşı** which, though now a market, was originally built as the Orhangazi Hamamı (1335), the Turkish bath of the Orhan Camii Külliyesi. The domed ceiling with many small lights shows this.

Koza & Emir Caravanserais

The raising of silkworms is a cottage industry in Bursa. Each April, villagers buy the worms from their cooperatives, take them home and raise them on mulberry leaves. After a month the worms spin their cocoons and are soon ready for the trip to the **Koza Han** or Silk Cocoon Caravanserai just outside the bedesten's eastern entrance. Built in 1451, this caravanserai is lively with cocoon dealers in June and also in September when there is a second harvest.

When you visit, you may well see huge sacks of the precious little white cocoons being haggled over by some of the 14,000 villagers who engage in the trade. In the centre of the Koza Han's courtyard is a small mosque constructed by Yıldırım Beyazıt in 1393, restored by the guild of silk traders in 1948, and again in 1985 by the Aga Khan. The product of all this industry, *ipek* (silk cloth), is for sale in the Bedesten.

Adjoining the north-eastern corner of the Ulu Cami is the **Emir Han**, a caravanserai used by many of Bursa's silk brokers today, as it has been for centuries. There's a lovely fountain in the centre of the courtyard, and a tea garden for refreshments. Camels from the silk caravans used to be corralled in the courtyard, while goods were stored in the ground-floor rooms and drovers and merchants slept and did business in the rooms above.

Ulu Cami

Next to the bedesten and Emir Han is Bursa's Ulu Cami. This one is completely Seljuk in style, a big rectangular building with immense portals and a forest of supporting columns inside, similar to the much older Ulu Cami in the eastern city of Erzurum. The roof is a mass of 20 small domes. A *şadırvan* (ablutions fountain) plays peacefully at the centre of the interior. It was Yıldırım Beyazıt who put up the money for the building in 1396; it was finished in 1399. Notice the fine work of the *mimber* (pulpit) and the preacher's chair, also the calligraphy on the walls.

Hisar

This section of town, the oldest in Bursa, was once enclosed by stone ramparts and walls, bits of which still survive.

From the Ulu Cami, walk west and up Orhan Gazi (Yiğitler) Caddesi, a ramp-like street which leads up to the section known as Hisar (Fortress) or Tophane. To ride there, take any bus marked for Devlet Hastanesi ('Dev. Hst.'), Muradiye or Hamzabey and get out at the 'Tophane' stop. (The Devlet Hastanesi is a large government hospital just west of the tombs of sultans Osman and Orhan.)

Near a sign which reads 'İstiklal Savaşı Şehitler', in a little park near the edge of the cliff overlooking Cemal Nadir Caddesi and the valley, are the **Osman Gazi ve Orhan Gazi Türbeleri** (tombs of sultans Osman and Orhan), founders of the Ottoman Empire. The original structures were destroyed in the earthquake of 1855 and rebuilt in Ottoman baroque style by Sultan Abdül Aziz in 1868.

Osman Gazi's tomb is the more richly decorated of the two. A small donation is requested; remove your shoes before entering.

The tomb of Orhan Gazi was built on the foundations of a small Byzantine church, and you can see some remnants of the church's floor.

The park here is attractive, as is the view of the city. Büfes and snack stands across Osmangazi Caddesi provide sustinence. Try ***Merkez Pastanesi*** for pastries and puddings.

Hop in a bus or dolmuş marked 'Muradiye' to continue along Hasta Yurdu Caddesi to Muradiye, about 2.5km to the west. You'll dip down into the valley of the Cılımboz Deresi before arriving in the verdant residential quarter of Muradiye.

Muradiye Complex

With a shady park in front and a quiet cemetery behind, the **Sultan II. Murat (Muradiye) Camii**, also called the Hüdavendigar Camii, is pretty and peaceful. The mosque proper dates from 1426 and follows the style of the Yeşil Cami. A vegetable and fruit market fills the neighbouring street on Tuesday.

Dolmuşes ('Muradiye') and buses ('Muradiye' or 'Hamzabey') take you here from Heykel and Atatürk Caddesi.

Beside the mosque are 12 tombs dating from the 15th and 16th centuries, including that of Sultan Murat II (1404-51) himself. The Ottoman dynasty, like other Islamic and Asiatic dynasties, did not practise primogeniture, or succession of the first-born. Any son of a sultan could claim the throne upon his father's death, so the designated heir (or the strongest son) would have his brothers put to death rather than see civil war rend the empire. Many of the occupants of tombs here, including all the *şehzades* (imperial sons), were killed by close relatives.

Tomb-visiting may not be high on your list of priorities but you should see the beautiful decoration in some of the tombs. The superb decoration on the woodwork porch of the **II. Murat Türbesi** contrasts with the rest of the tomb's austerity. The sultan's tomb has an opening to the sky so that his

Nasreddin Hodja ... Storyteller Supreme

You won't be long in Turkey before you spot a picture of a bearded man in an outsize turban riding backwards on a donkey. This is Nasreddin Hodja, a medieval joker whose witty moralising stories are as familiar to Turkish children as Aesop's fables are to Europeans.

Strangely enough, almost nothing is known about the man to whom almost 500 stories are attributed. There are even some who claim that there was no such living man.

Assuming Hodja is a real character, it seems likely that he was born the son of an imam around 1208 in the village of Hortu in Sivrihisar. As an adult he may have served time as a judge, as an imam, as a university professor and as a dervish. He probably died in 1284 in Akşehir, near Konya. His stories first turned up in a book called *Saltukname*, produced in 1480 and incorporating other folk tales and legends as well.

A typical Nasreddin Hodja story is written in a clipped prose style and concludes with an epigram intended to make people think. Themes are taken from daily life: cooking, riding a donkey, visiting a Turkish bath. Some so-called Nasreddin Hodja stories were clearly written by other people, and new 'Nasreddin Hodja' stories are still produced today.

The following tale is typical:

Hodja went to Bursa market to buy a pair of trousers. Having selected a pair, he was just about to pay when he spotted a robe and decided to take that instead.

As he walked towards the door, the shopkeeper called out that he hadn't paid for the robe. Hodja pointed out that he had returned the pair of trousers.

'But you hadn't paid for those either,' he was reminded.

'What a strange man you are,' Hodja exclaimed. 'You expect me to pay for a pair of trousers I didn't buy.'

It's also typical of Hodja humour that his tomb in Akşehir has a padlocked gate on one side, although the other three sides are unfenced. What's more, the date inside is written backwards.

Every 5 to 10 July, an **International Nasreddin Hodja Festival** is held in Akşehir. The Association of Turkish Caricaturists also runs an annual international Nasreddin Hodja competition.

grave could be washed by the rain, and his unadorned sarcophagus has no lid, following common Muslim custom rather than imperial tradition. The tomb's architect did add a bit of Byzantine grandeur by borrowing some old Corinthian columns, but he used capitals as both capitals and plinths.

The beautiful coloured İznik tilework in the gaudy **Cem Türbesi** celebrates Cem Sultan (1459-95), the youngest son of Sultan Mehmet the Conqueror. Cem reigned for 18 days, but was chased from the throne by Beyazıt II and fled to Europe, where he became a hostage of the pope and a pawn in Ottoman-European diplomacy.

The İznik tiles in the **Şehzade Mustafa Türbesi** are as fine as those in the Rüstem Paşa Camii in İstanbul. Mustafa (1515-53), son of Süleyman the Magnificent, was governor of Amasya when Süleyman's wife Roxelana intrigued against him, causing the sultan to order his execution – which he soon regretted bitterly.

The **Şehzade Ahmet Türbesi** is elegant in its simplicity of light and dark blue tiles framed by a vine-patterned blue-and-white border. The stained glass window is restrained as well. Ahmet's mother Bülbül Hatun is buried beside him.

Facing the park before the mosque is ***Darüzziyafe*** *(☎ 224-224 6439)*, a restaurant serving classic Turkish cuisine. Order the plate of assorted Turkish specialities and your lunch bill might be US$7 or US$8. Even cheaper meals are available up the street at the ***Yalçın Pide Salonu***, at No 24.

Across the park from the mosque and tombs is an old Ottoman house (the sign says **'17 Y. Y. Osmanlı Evi Müzesi'**, or '17th century Ottoman House Museum'). Visit for a fascinating glimpse into the daily life of the Ottoman nobility. Carpets and furnishings are all authentic. It used to be open Tuesday to Sunday from 8.30 am to noon, and 1 to 5 pm, but the house has been closed for restoration for some time.

On the western side of the tombs is the 15th century **Muradiye Medresesi**, a theological seminary restored in 1951 as a tuberculosis clinic. A block further west on Kaplıca Caddesi near the bus stop, the **Tarihi II. Murat Hamamı**, or Historic Turkish Bath of Sultan Murat II, is still in use (see Mineral Baths, later in this section).

A minute's walk uphill behind the Tarihi II. Murat Hamamı brings you to the **Hüsnü Züber Evi** at Uzunyol Sokak 3 (follow the signs). It's a 'living museum' because the owner still lives in this restored Ottoman dwelling. Hüsnü Bey did much of the restoration himself, and made many of the woodworking exhibits in the house. It's supposedly open from 10 am to noon and 1 to 5 pm (closed Monday), but you may find no one at home. Admission costs US$1.

Kültür Parkı

Bursa's Kültür Parkı or Cultural Park, is laid out to the north of the Muradiye complex, down the hill some distance. You can reach it from Heykel by any bus or dolmuş going to Altıparmak, Sigorta or Çekirge. Besides offering a pleasant stroll, the Kültür Parkı has a fun park with children's rides, a small zoo, an open-air theatre, a rose garden, many tea gardens, and shady outdoor restaurants (see Places to Eat later in this section).

The park also houses the **Arkeoloji Müzesi**. Bursa's history goes back to the time of Hannibal (200 BC), and Roman artefacts are preserved here. The collection is nice, but not at all exceptional. If you've seen another good Turkish collection, this is more of the same. Find the bus stop named 'Arkeoloji Müzesı', and enter the park by the gate nearby. The museum (US$0.50) is open from 8.30 am to noon and 1 to 5 pm (closed Monday).

I. Murat (Hüdavendigâr) Camii

In this city of early Ottoman mosques, the I. Murat (Hüdavendigâr) Camii in Çekirge is among the more unusual. Its basic design is the early Ottoman inverted 'T' plan which first appeared in the *imaret* (soup kitchen for the poor) built in 1388 by Murat's mother Nilüfer Hatun in İznik. Here, however, the 'T' wings are barrel-vaulted rather than dome-topped. On the ground floor at the front are the rooms of a *zaviye*, or dervish

SOUTH OF MARMARA SEA

TURKISH TILES

Tiles are one of the most striking features of Turkish architecture. Tile-making played a major role in Ottoman art and architecture between the 14th and 17th centuries and was most prominent in İznik and Kütahya.

Most of the designs were inspired by flowers with turquoise, green, yellow, dark blue and red as the dominant colours; geometric shapes and calligraphy were also popular. Tiles were mainly used in mosques, hamams, palaces, mansions, fountains and churches; and were intended to enhance the architectural effect of buildings, not just to cover up surfaces. The unique styles and designs inspired enormous pride among the Turkish people, particularly the master artisans.

Some of the oldest Ottoman tiles can be seen today in the minaret of Bursa's Yeşil Cami (1424). The architecture of this impressive construction heralded the emergence of a distinctly Turkish style, and features yellow and green encaustic tiles made by architect Hacı İvaz. But perhaps the most well-known tiles can be found on İznik's Yeşil Cami (built 1492), about 150km from İstanbul.

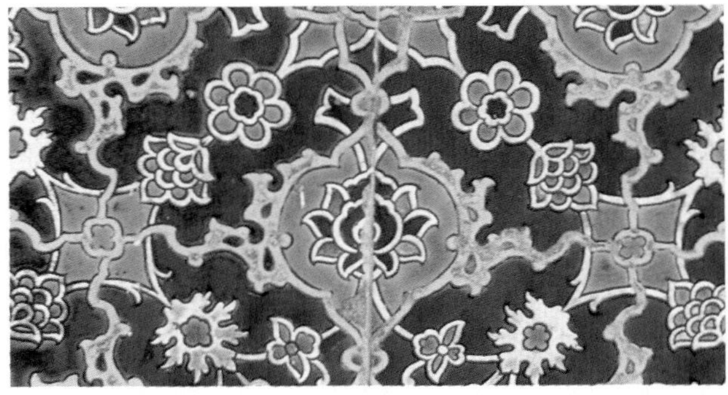

Each tile design is unique, distinctive and obviously a labour of love for a proud master craftsman.

ALL PHOTOGRAPHS BY OLIVIER CIRENDINI

By the mid-16th century Turkey's tiles were becoming more multi-coloured. Instead of mosaic and gilded tiles of one distinct colour, a new glazing technique was adopted for the rectangular-shaped tiles which introduced a burst of different colours to the designs. It was around this time that 'Iznik red' – brilliant red tiles made from an Anatolian clay rich in iron oxide – became popular; one of the finest examples being İstanbul's Süleymaniye Camii.

During the second half of the 16th century, tiles were being made using another new glazing technique. İstanbul's Süleymaniye Camii houses some exquisite examples as does the Topkapı Palace, the Piyale Paşa Camii in Kasımpasa, Yeni Valide Camii in Üsküdar and the Selimiye Camii in Edirne.

Tile-making became less popular at the start of the 17th century only to be rejuvenated when factories producing hard-glaze delftware and porcelain were opened in İstanbul's Beykoz and Yıldız districts. Today Kütahya has become the centre of tile producing with walls, floors and facades decorated in this uniquely Turkish way.

OLIVIER CIRENDINI

GEOFF STRINGER

The exquisitely designed coloured tiles in İstanbul's Topkapı Sarayı are representative of a traditional Ottoman art form.

hostel. The 2nd floor gallery on the facade, built as a medrese, is not evident from within except for the sultan's loge in the middle at the back of the mosque.

Sultan Murat I (1359-89), who died after a victorious battle against his rebellious Albanian, Bosnian, Bulgarian, Hungarian and Serbian subjects at Kosovo, is buried in the tomb across the street. On the eastern side of the Tuğra Termal Oteli, the rather grand mosque toilet is all that is left of the mosque's imaret.

Mineral Baths

The warm, mineral-rich waters which spring from the slopes of Uludağ have been famous for their curative powers since ancient times. Today the ailing and the infirm come here for several weeks at a time, take a daily soak or two in the tub, and spend the rest of the time chatting, reading and dining. Most people stay in hotels which have their own mineral bath facilities. There are independent *kaplıca* (baths) as well, some of historical importance.

Baths will be crowded on Friday, the Muslim holy day, as local people clean up for it.

The **Yeni Kaplıca** (☎ 224-236 6955), Mudanya Caddesi 10, on the north-western side of the Kültür Parkı, is a bath renovated in 1522 by Sultan Süleyman the Magnificent's grand vizier, Rüstem Paşa, on the site of a much older one built by Justinian. Besides the Yeni (New) baths, you'll find the Kaynarca (Boiling), limited to women; and the Karamustafa, which has facilities for family bathing. All baths in the complex are open from 6 am to 11 pm (last admission at 10 pm).

Perhaps the most attractive place is the **Eski Kaplıca** (☎ 224-233 9300) next door to the Kervansaray Termal Hotel on Çekirge's eastern outskirts. Beautifully restored, the baths now cater to an upmarket clientele of business travellers, tourists and local notables who stay at or socialise in the hotel.

The bathing rooms are covered in creamy marble; in the hot room are plunging pools; use of the nice swimming pool downstairs is subject to a hefty additional charge. The cool room has lounge chairs for relaxing, and a bar with waiter service.

Prices are higher here than at unrestored local baths, but the building is beautiful, though service is fairly inattentive. Hours are daily from 7 am to 11 pm for men, from 7.30 am to 11 pm for women. There's an entry fee of US$6, and US$4 for a massage or to have an attendant wash you; the cost of soap is additional, so figure on spending US$20 for the works, including massage and tips. You can bring your own soap and wash yourself for little more than the basic entry fee.

To get to the Eski Kaplıca, take a bus or dolmuş marked 'SSK Hast(anesi)' or 'Sigorta'.

For a simpler, less expensive bath near the hotels in the centre of Bursa, try **Çakır Ağa Hamamı**, on the corner of Atatürk Caddesi and Kazım Baykal (Temiz) Caddesi, just west of the Tahtakale/İnebey district. Posted prices are US$3 for a wash, another US$1.50 for soap and scrub, US$1 for a massage, US$3 for use of a resting cubicle, or the works for US$10 or so. The hamam is open daily from 7 am to 11 pm.

The Tarihi İnebey Hamamı on İnebey Caddesi is even closer to several recommended hotels.

Next to the Muradiye mosque is the Tarihi II. Murat Hamamı (that's İkinci Murat), open to men on Friday and Sunday, to women all other days, from 10 am to 6 pm. The Tarihi Çekirge Hamamı opposite the Otel Hüsnügüzel on Kanal Caddesi is for women only.

Places to Stay

Because of its industrial and touristic prosperity, hotels in Bursa tend to be somewhat expensive.

Places to Stay – Budget

Central Bursa The Tahtakale/İnebey district just south of the Ulu Cami is an interesting area with many narrow streets and historic houses. Some of the houses are being restored, and will no doubt soon be turned into expensive shops and moderately priced 'boutique' hotels. There's a good produce market here as well.

The Hamam Experience

The history of steam baths goes back thousands of years and many of Turkey's natural spas were enjoyed by the ancient Greeks and Romans. Turks built beautiful, elaborate *hamams* (baths) to serve their communities, partly because Islam demands high standards of personal hygiene, and partly because bathing is such a pleasure.

Public baths used to be required because private homes didn't have bathing facilities. Everybody, rich and poor alike, went to the baths. For a workman, it was simply to get clean. For a high-born woman, it was a ritual of attendants and polite courtesies, and many museums display the gorgeous gold-embroidered towels, mother-of-pearl pattens and lovely accessories she would have taken with her.

Most Turkish towns still have hamams of varying degrees of fanciness, although they are becoming scarcer in the west as homes acquire plumbed-in bathrooms. The custom of going to the hamam continues because the public facilities are so much grander than what is available at home, and because, for Turks, it is still a social occasion. To steam clean, have a massage, relax, watch television, sip tea and chat with friends is looked upon as wonderful, affordable luxury.

What happens in a hamam? Well, you will be shown to a *camekan* (cubicle) where you can undress, store your clothes, lock up your valuables and wrap the cloth that's provided (the *pestemal*) around you. A *tellak* (attendant) will lead you through to the hot room where you sit and sweat for a while.

Then you have to make a choice. It's cheapest to wash yourself with the *sabun* (soap), *sampuan* (shampoo) and *havlu* (towel) you brought with you. The hot room will be ringed with individual basins which you fill from the taps above before sluicing the water over yourself with a plastic scoop. You should try not to get soap into the water in the basin, and avoid splashing your neighbours, especially on a Friday when someone who has completed their ritual wash would have to start all over again if soaked by an infidel.

But it's far more enjoyable to let an attendant wash you. In the hot room you'll be doused with warm water and then scrubbed with a coarse cloth *kese* (mitten), loosening dirt you never suspected you had. Afterwards you'll be lathered with a sudsy swab, rinsed off and shampooed.

When all this is done you'll be offered the chance of a massage, an experience worth having at least once during your trip. Some massages are carried out on the floor or a table but often you'll be spread out on the great marble bench (or *göbektasi*) beneath the dome. In touristy areas (other than İstanbul) the massage is likely to be pretty cursory and unless you're prepared to pay the extra for an 'oil massage' you may be disappointed. Elsewhere, however, a Turkish massage can be an unforgettable, if occasionally rough, experience.

The cheapest rooms in Tahtakale are at ***Otel Güneş*** *(☎ 224-222 1404, İnebey Caddesi 75)*, where you can stay in a waterless room for US$8/12 a single/double.

Though somewhat overpriced, the nearby ***Otel Çamlıbel*** *(☎ 224-221 2565, İnebey Caddesi 71)*, is a renovated hotel with these advantages: a quiet location, rooms with constant hot water and good cross-ventilation, a lift and even a few parking places in front of the hotel. Rates are US$20/30/40 a single/double/triple with private shower; breakfast costs extra.

Hotel İpekçi *(☎ 224-221 1935, Çancılar Caddesi 38)*, about four blocks north of Heykel near the Karakedi Camii, has quiet rooms for US$12/20 a single/double with shower, even less with just a sink.

Çekirge Most Çekirge hotels have their own facilities for 'taking the waters'. You may find that the bathtub or shower at your hotel

The Hamam Experience

The massage over, you'll be led back to the cold room, there to be swathed in towels and taken to your cubicle for a rest. Tea, coffee, soft drinks and beer are usually available.

Traditional hamams have separate sections for men and women or admit men and women at separate times. As the number of baths declines, it's usually the ones for women that go first as there is some ambivalence about how desirable it is for women to be out of the home. Opening hours for women are almost invariably more restricted than for men.

Bath etiquette dictates that men should keep the pestemal on at all times, washing their own private parts without ever removing this modesty wrap. In the women's section, the amount of modesty expected varies considerably: in some baths total nudity is fine, in others it would be a blunder to remove your knickers. Play it safe by keeping your underwear on under your pestemal until inside the hot room when you can remove what looks appropriate. Women also wash their own private parts. If you want to shave your legs or armpits, you should do this in the outer warm room rather than in the bath.

In the touristy areas, most hamams are more than happy for foreign men and women to bathe together, usually for a premium price. In traditional hamams, women are washed and massaged by other women. No Turkish woman would let a male masseur anywhere near her, however, and while Turkish men continue to frequent baths used by tourists, the Turkish women vanish, and with them go the female masseuses.

Sexual activity has no place in the traditional bath ritual. Women who accept a masseur should have their massage within view of their male companions or friends. At the first sign of impropriety, they should protest loudly.

runs only mineral water, or there may be private or public bathing rooms in the basement of the hotel. A day's dip in the mineral waters is no great thrill; the therapeutic benefits are supposedly acquired over weeks. All the same, a soak in the bath may be included in the price of the room so take advantage of it.

Çekirge's main street is I. Murat Caddesi (Birinci Murat Caddesi). For all of the Çekirge hotels, get a bus or dolmuş from Heykel or along Atatürk Caddesi to 'Çekirge' or 'SSK Hastanesi'. Most Çekirge hotels suffer from street noise. Here are the ones that don't:

Öz Yeşil Yayla Oteli *(☎/fax 224-236 8026, Çekirge Caddesi, Selvi Sokak 6)*, between the Boyugüzel and Yıldız II hotels at the upper end of the village, is simple and old-fashioned – a living piece of 1950s Çekirge – charging US$22 a double for rooms with sink, but free use of the mineral baths.

Next door, the ***Boyugüzel Termal Otel*** *(☎ 224-233 3850, fax 233 9999)* on Selvi Sokak, charges US$22 for a double room with sink and toilet, with a half-hour mineral bath downstairs included each day.

Hotel Gold 2 *(☎/fax 224-236 8099 I. Murat Caddesi, Cami Aralığı 2)*, is behind the more visible Ada Palas. It has usable, quiet rooms with showers, and a terrace in front, and charges US$20/30 a single/double for a room with private shower.

Places to Stay – Mid-Range

Central Bursa In central Bursa noise is a big problem, but the best hotels are off the main streets in any case.

Hotel Çeşmeli *(☎ 224-224 1511, Gümüşçeken Caddesi 6)*, just a few steps north of Atatürk Caddesi near Heykel, is friendly, simple, fairly quiet, very clean, run by God-fearing Muslims and conveniently located. Rooms cost US$28/42/55 a single/double/triple for a room with shower and breakfast. Though expensive, this is a good choice for women travellers.

Hotel Dikmen *(☎ 224-224 1840, fax 224 1844, Maksem (Fevzi Çakmak) Caddesi 78)*, is further west, then south. This 50 room, three-star hotel's lobby is pleasant, with a small enclosed garden terrace, complete with fountain, at the back; a lift takes you up to your room. Rooms with little luxuries such as bathtubs, TVs and minibars rent for US$30/40 a single/double, slightly cheaper without the frills. Remember to ask for *sakin bir oda* (a quiet room). The hotel is about 50m uphill on the street which begins beside the PTT.

Places to Stay – Top End

Central Bursa In the centre of Bursa there's the nominally three-star ***Kent Hotel*** *(☎ 224-223 5420, fax 224 4015, Atatürk Caddesi 69)*. All 64 rooms have air-con, private showers, minibars and satellite TVs. Although posted prices may be as high as US$75/100 a single/double, I was quoted US$55 a double when I asked, so rates are negotiable.

Opposite the Osman and Orhan tombs, ***Safran Oteli & Restaurant*** *(☎ 224-224 7216, fax 224 7219)* on Kale Sokak, is a restored Ottoman house in a historic neighbourhood. Rooms with private bathroom and TV cost US$55/80 a single/double, breakfast included. The adjoining restaurant and Mavi Bar are good, too.

Çekirge The three-star ***Termal Hotel Gönlü Ferah*** *(☎ 224-233 9210, fax 233 9218)*, on I. Murat Caddesi 24, is in the very centre of the village. Some of the 62 rooms have fine views over the valley. The ambience here is 'European spa', the service experienced. Rates are US$70/90 a single/double with breakfast.

Next door, the four-star ***Hotel Dilmen*** *(☎ 224-233 9500, fax 235 2568)* on I. Murat Caddesi, boasts a garden terrace restaurant/bar, an exercise room with sauna and mineral water baths, and 100 posh rooms with TVs and minibars for US$80/100 a single/double on the panoramic side, breakfast included.

Places to Eat

Bursa's culinary specialities include fresh fruit (especially *şeftali* – peaches – in season), *kestane şekeri* (candied chestnuts) and two types of roast meat.

Bursa kebap, or *İskender kebap*, is döner kebap laid on a bed of fresh pide bread and topped with savoury tomato sauce and browned butter. *İnegöl köftesi*, is a rich grilled meatball in the style of the nearby town of İnegöl.

The following places to eat are arranged according to the type of food, location and style.

Bursa Kebapçıs Cost differences among restaurants of the same class are small due to fixed municipal prices. A *bir porsyon* (one-serving) plate of kebap with yoghurt costs US$5 or US$6, soft drink included (alcohol is not normally served at kebapçıs). Add US$2 if you order *bir buçuk porsyon* (1½ portions). All these places are open seven days a week from 11 am until 9 or 10 pm.

The owners of ***Kebapçı İskender*** *(☎ 224-221 4615, Ünlü Caddesi 7)*, half a block south-east of Heykel, claim to be descendants of the eponymous İskender Usta himself. The elaborate Ottomanesque facade and semi-formal waiters belie moderate prices (US$6 to US$8 for Bursa kebap with yoghurt, plus a soft drink). İskender kebap and a few salads and sweets are all that is served.

İskender Kebap

Roast lamb and mutton have been staples of the Turkish diet for millennia, and it does not take an overly fertile imagination to picture nomadic Turkish warriors skewering chunks of mutton on their swords and roasting it over a campfire 1500 years ago. Melted fat would drip into the fire causing flare-ups, smoking and burning of the meat.

Along comes İskender Usta (Chef Alexander), a cook in Bursa. In 1867 he had the idea to build a vertical grill, fill it with hot coals, and put the meat-packed sword on its point next to the grill. This way the fat would baste the meat rather than char it. He sliced the meat off in thin strips as it was cooked.

Like *lokum* (Turkish delight) and the sandwich, this simple innovation was an instant success. Why any of these culinary inventions took centuries to appear is a mystery.

Today *döner kebap* (revolving roast) is Turkey's national dish, served everywhere from street corners to posh dining rooms. Many of the specially made döner grills even continue the symbolism of the sword, with a miniature hilt at the top.

İskender used lamb and mutton from sheep fed on the wild spices (especially thyme) of Uludağ. To compound his fame, he laid the slices of lamb on a bed of flat pide bread, and topped the whole with savoury tomato sauce and browned butter.

The dish's popularity has spread throughout the country and indeed the world, but it's still best in Bursa. The city's most prominent İskender kebapçıs claim direct descent – in both blood and method – from the original İskender Usta.

Directly across Ünlü Caddesi is ***Adanur Hacıbey*** *(☎ 224-221 6440)*, a simpler place where the Bursa kebap comes with a dab of smoky aubergine purée on the side. Don't begin eating your kebap until the waiter brings the tomato sauce and browned butter.

The original ***Hacıbey Kebapçısı*** *(☎ 224-222 6604, Taşkapı Sokak 4/11)*, is just south of the Koza Parkı. Two floors of narrow rooms have marble floors, beautiful tiled walls and dark polished woodwork. Waiters in waistcoats serve politely and efficiently, and the kebap is very good.

Bursa kebap was invented in a small restaurant now called ***Kebapçı İskenderoğlu Nurettin*** (İskender's Son) at Atatürk Caddesi 60, between Heykel and the Ulu Cami. The surroundings are basic and simple, the kebap good but unremarkable.

İnegöl Köfteci For İnegöl köftesi, try ***İnegöl Köftecisi***, Atatürk Caddesi 48, on the corner of a little side street. Variations of the basic grilled lamb meatball include those stuffed with onions or cheese. A full lunch costs US$5.

Other Grills ***Çiçek Izgara*** *(☎ 221 6526, Belediye Caddesi 15)*, one block from the Koza Parkı behind the half-timbered Belediye, doesn't specialise in Bursa kebap, but serves excellent grills in a white-tablecloth setting that's especially comfortable for single women. Prices range from US$2.50 for köfte to US$7 for the big mixed grill; a *bonfile* (small beef filet steak) costs US$5.

Okyanus Fırın Salonu, on Pars Çıkmazı, the side street between the Vakıfbank and Atatürk Caddesi 44, is shiny and modern, specialising in *Konya fırın kebap* – rich joints of roasted mutton. A filling meal costs US$6.

Ömür Köftecisi, on the western side of the Ulu Cami, is in the historic *arasta* (the complex of shops attached to a mosque). The grills range from köfte with *kaşarlı köfte* (yellow cheese) for US$2 to a *karışık ızgara* (mixed grill) for US$3.50.

Sazende Restaurant & Bar, a 'white-tablecloth and goblet' dining place off a small pedestrian alley in the bazaar, serves a variety of Turkish and European dishes and alcoholic beverages in formal surroundings. Outside in the alley, local lace and embroidery is for sale in small booths and shops.

Hazır Yemek Ready-food restaurants have steam tables and pre-cooked soups, stews, *pilavs* (rice) and stuffed vegetables. Many close by 7 pm. The Tahtakale/İnebey district is a particularly good place to look for a good, cheap meal. ***Şehir Lokantası,*** İnebey Caddesi 85, half a block up the hill from Atatürk Caddesi, serves hazır yemek meals for around US$3 or US$4, as does the neighbouring ***Ümit***.

Further up the street from the Şehir, turn right (west) and walk to the market area known as the Tahtakale Çarşısı. To the north-west, at Çelebiler Caddesi 18, is the ***Alış Izgara*** and the adjoining ***Ali Baba Baklavacısı***. But my favourite is a bit further south. Walk uphill two blocks on Çelebiler Caddesi to a T-intersection, turn right and walk half a block to the ***Yeşil İnci Lokantası*** (Green Pearl), which has a separate 10 table *aile salonu* (family dining room). This restaurant, facing the Hacı Sevinç Camii, stays open later than many other local eateries and serves delicious ready food accompanied by its own freshly baked pide bread. You need spend no more than US$4 to fill up. ***Öz Anadolu Kebap ve Lahmacun Salonu*** across the street is also good.

Kültür Parkı Strolling around the Cultural Park is pleasant, and having a meal here is more so. The ***Seljuk Restaurant*** *(☎ 224-220 9695)* near the mosque is good, quiet, shady, serves alcoholic beverages, and is not overly expensive, with three-course meals for US$8 to US$15.

Çekirge The more expensive hotels in Çekirge have their own dining rooms. Besides these, there's the ***Sezen Restaurant*** *(☎ 224-236 9156)*, on Çekirge Caddesi to the right of the Ada Palas Hotel. The food is fine and the prices fairly low, at US$5 or US$6 for a full meal.

Markets The Tahtakale Çarşısı is the nicest and most convenient market area in central Bursa. Walk west from the Ulu Cami along Atatürk Caddesi to the subway (pedestrian underpass) named Yıldırım Beyazıt Altgeçidi. From the southern end of the subway, go left or right a few steps, then south along a narrow street to the market area.

Another market lies downhill (north) of the Çiçek Pazarı (Flower Market) behind Koza Parkı and the Belediye.

Cafes ***Café Koza***, above Koza Parkı on Atatürk Caddesi near the Ulu Cami is Bursa's central people-watching place, but it's not cheap. A simple tea costs US$0.60, coffee twice as much.

Want to try a Turkish water pipe? ***Çınaraltı Çay ve Nargile Salonu*** next to the Ulu Cami will rent you one for US$1. Ask for a *nargile*. Coffee and soft drinks are served.

Entertainment

Bursa's equivalent of İstanbul's Kumkapı district is Sakarya Caddesi, a small street lined with *meyhanes* (taverns), some of them serving fish. The street is on the northern side of the Hisar district, just south of Altıparmak Caddesi. To find it, take a bus or dolmuş from Heykel bound for Çekirge and get out at the Çatal Fırın bus stop across from the Sabahettin Paşa Camii. Cross to the southern side of Altıparmak Caddesi and walk west into Sakarya Caddesi. If you're walking, go downhill from the Ulu Cami along Atatürk/Altıparmak on the Hisar side of the road; it's less than 10 minutes.

Sakarya Caddesi was once the main street of Bursa's **Jewish quarter**, which thrived from 1492 until recent times. There are still several operating synagogues on the street, most notably the 500-year-old Geruş Havrası (visits by special arrangement only).

Sakarya Caddesi's fame was made by one Arap Şükrü who opened a restaurant here decades ago. It was so popular and successful that, as with İskender and his kebap, Arap Şükrü's descendants have gone into the business. The street, now generally known as Arap Şükrü Sokak, has no less than five restaurants with that name, all run by relatives or descendants. Among them, perhaps the favourite is ***Arap Şükrü Yılmaz*** *(☎ 224-221 9239, Sakarya Caddesi 4)*. Fish is the speciality, but grills are always served, and a full meal with rakı, beer or wine need cost no more than US$10 or US$15 per person.

Most of the clientele of these restaurants are male, but women usually feel comfortable at ***Hanzade Bar-Restaurant*** *(☎ 224-221 0052, Sakarya Caddesi 43)* which is among the nicest places. ***Barantico*** *(☎ 224-222 4049, Sakarya Caddesi 55)*, has a long menu of drinks, grills, light meals and sweets, and offers a popular dance floor.

Another place for drinks in is the ***Mavi Bar*** at the Safran Oteli & Restaurant.

Shopping

Bursa's specialities are silk cloth (especially scarves), handknitted woollen mittens, gloves and socks, Karagöz shadow puppets and candied chestnuts. Other good items are thick Bursa Turkish towels (some say they were invented here, for those taking the Çekirge waters). If you have lots of room in your luggage, buy a *bornoz*, a huge, thick, heavy terry-cloth bathrobe.

Getting There & Away

The fastest and cheapest way to reach Bursa from İstanbul is by fast catamaran and bus. A new airport is being readied at Yenişehir, 40km east of Bursa. The train line bypasses Bursa inconveniently to the east, running between Adapazarı, Bozüyük and Eskişehir.

Air When the new airport opens there may be more flights, but at the time of writing Sönmez Holding Hava Yolları – at Bursa's airport (☎ 224-246 5445); in İstanbul (☎ 212-573 9323, 573 7240 ext 712) – runs flights from Bursa to İstanbul at 8.30 am and 3 pm from Monday to Friday, and 9 am Saturday, for US$55 each way. Return flights from İstanbul to Bursa run at 9.30 am and 4 pm on weekdays, 10.30 am on Saturday; no flights on Sunday. A bus departs from the Ottomantur office 45 minutes prior to flight time.

In Bursa, tickets can be bought at Ottomantur (☎ 224-210 099, 222 097, fax 218 948), Cemal Nadir Caddesi, Kızılay Pasajı, Çakırhamam, a few minutes walk downhill from the Ulu Cami.

Bus For information on reaching Bursa from İstanbul or Yalova, see the previous Yalova section.

Bursa's bus station, the Bursa Şehirlerarası Otobüs Terminalı, is located 10km north of the centre on the Yalova road. Special 'Terminal' buses (grey with a blue stripe) shuttle between the bus station and the city centre.

The Doğ Garaj (Eastern Garage) and Batı Garaj (Western Garage) – separate, small minibus terminals to the east and west of the city centre – serve regional routes.

The fastest way to İstanbul is a bus to Yalova, then a catamaran or fast car ferry to İstanbul's Yenikapı docks. Get a bus that departs at least 90 minutes before the scheduled boat departure.

Buses going all the way to İstanbul are designated either *karayolu ile* (by road), or *feribot ile* (by car ferry). Karayolu ile buses take four hours and drag you all around the Bay of İzmit. Those designated feribot ile take you to Topçular, east of Yalova, and drive aboard the car ferry to Eskihisar, a much quicker and more pleasant way to go. You must also determine whether your chosen bus terminates its journey at İstanbul's Harem bus station on the Asian shore, or at the Yeni Otogar in Esenler; some buses stop at both.

For other destinations, buy your ticket in advance to ensure a good seat and departure time. Here are some routes from Bursa:

Afyon – 290km, 4½ hours, US$10; eight buses daily
Ankara – 400km, 5½ hours, US$12; hourly buses
Bandırma – 115km, two hours, US$4; 12 buses daily
Çanakkale (for Troy and Gallipoli) – 310km, five hours, US$6; a dozen buses daily
Erdek – 135km, 2¼ hours, US$4; three buses daily
Eskişehir – 155km, 2½ hours, US$6; hourly buses

İstanbul – 230km, four to five hours karayolu ile (by road) or 2½ hours by feribot ile (by car ferry: 135km by road plus 25 minutes by sea), US$6 to US$10; hourly buses
İzmir – 375km, six hours, US$6; hourly buses
İznik – 82km, 1½ hours, US$2 to US$2.75; hourly buses until 6 or 7 pm
Kütahya – 190km, three hours, US$5; several buses daily
Yalova – 60km, 70 minutes, US$3; minibuses every 30 minutes (see the Yalova section)

Getting Around

To/From the Otogar Take the special 'Terminal' bus (grey with a blue stripe; US$0.75) to travel the 10km between the otogar and the city centre. A taxi costs US$6.

City Bus Bursa's city buses ('BOİ'; US$0.40) have destinations and stops marked on the front and kerb side. A major set of stops is by Koza Parkı on Atatürk Caddesi. Catch a bus from Peron (stop) 1 for Emir Sultan and Teleferuç (Uludağ cable-car); from Peron 2 for Muradiye; from Peron 4 for Altıparmak and the Kültür Parki; from the BOİ Ekspres Peron for the Osman Gazi and Orhan Gazi tombs and Muradiye.

Dolmuş In Bursa, sedans operate as dolmuşes along with the minibuses. The destination is indicated by the illuminated sign on the roof. The minimum fare is US$0.50.

A major dolmuş starting-point is just north of Heykel. Among other destinations, cars go to Çekirge via the Kültür Parkı, Eski Kaplıca and I. Murat Camii.

Taxi A ride from Heykel to Muradiye costs about US$2; about US$6 to the otogar.

AROUND BURSA

Typical villages in the region of Bursa are worth a visit if you have time and an interest in Turkish ethnography. You can go on your own or by tour. Mr Uğur Çelikkol at Karagöz Turizm-Seyahat Acentası (travel agency; ☎ 224-221 8727, fax 220 5350) reachable through the Karagöz Antique Shop in the Eski Aynalı Çarşı, organises guided trips to most of these villages at reasonable prices.

Cumalı Kızık

It is said that Osman Gazi, founder of the Ottoman Empire, founded seven villages for his seven sons and their brides about 700 years ago on lands just east of Bursa. Five of the villages, built before the Ottoman conquest of Bursa, survive to this day and retain many features of Ottoman domestic architecture.

The village of Cumalı Kızık, set on the slopes of Uludağ amid fruit and nut orchards, is registered as a national monument and protected from development. Transportation is difficult without your own vehicle. Go 12km eastward from Bursa along the main road to İnegöl and Ankara, then 3.5km south to Cumalı Kızık. Facilities are limited, so you might want to bring a picnic.

The other four old villages, all south of the Bursa-Ankara highway, are Hamamlı Kızık, not far from Cumalı Kızık; Dere Kızık, further east; and Fidye Kızık and Değirmenlı Kızık, closer to Bursa.

Güneybudaklar

With your own vehicle, go west from Bursa, and on the outskirts turn south on the road marked for Keles. The road winds around Uludağ and climbs its southern slopes, passing through the wine-making village of Misi before reaching a road, 45km from Bursa, marked for Güneybudaklar. The village, 3km north of the main road, was founded some 500 years ago by Turcoman nomads on the site of a Roman-Byzantine settlement. The land around is planted with strawberries and other fruits, beans, potatoes, wheat and barley. Flocks graze on the rich mountain grasses while the women of the village weave colourful cloths at their looms. There are few tourists and no services, but you can stop, enjoy the views and the air, and have a satisfying glass of tea before retracing your way to Bursa.

ULUDAĞ

In the ancient world, a number of mountains bore the name Olympus. Uludağ (Great Mountain, 2543m) was on the outskirts of the ancient city of Bithynia (now Bursa), so this was the Bithynian Olympus.

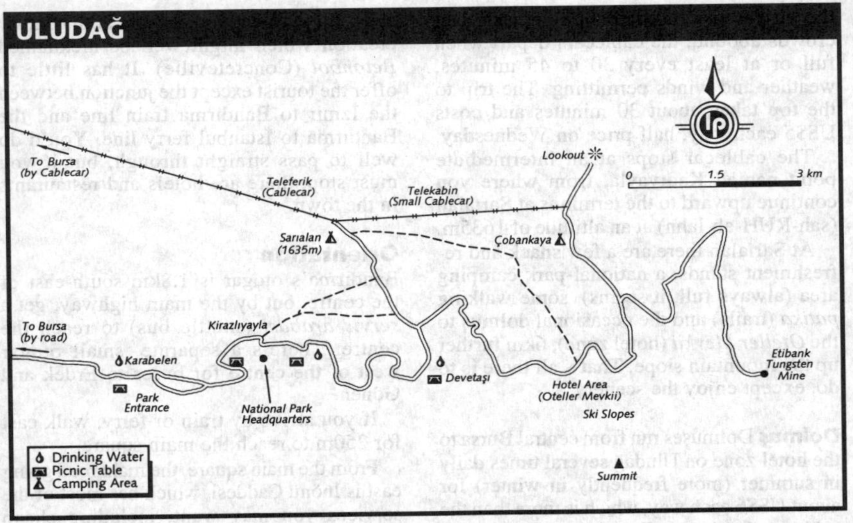

The gods no longer live on top of Uludağ, but there is a *teleferik* (cablecar), a selection of hotels, a national park, cool forests and often snow. Even if you don't plan to hike to the summit (three hours each way from the hotel area) or to go skiing (in winter only), you might want to take the cablecar or a dolmuş up for the view and a draught of cool air. If you take a picnic, beware of groups of boy thieves, aged seven to 13, who circulate in the summer. Report any such groups to the *jandarmas* (paramilitary police).

Skiing

Though a fairly sleepy place in summer, the hotel and ski area on Uludağ comes to life during the skiing season from December to early April.

Places to Stay

More than a dozen inns and hotels are scattered about the mountainside in the area called Oteller Mevkii (2000m). All are meant for skiers, so they close for much of the year. A few places stay open all the time, though they have little business in summer unless they can schedule a commercial meeting.

Among the better places to stay is the 80 room, three-star ***Beceren Hotel*** (*☎ 224-285 2111, fax 285 2119*). For US$40 a double you get a room with bath and satellite TV. For US$60 two people can have a room and all three meals in summer. Prices almost double in winter, but all three meals are included.

The small, 20 room ***Ergün Hotel*** (*☎ 224-285 2100, fax 285 2101*), offers good value during the ski season, as does the 32 room ***Ulukardeşler*** (*☎ 224-285 2136, fax 285 2139*).

The four-star status address on the mountain is the 127 room ***Kervansaray Uludağ Hotel*** (*☎ 224-285 2187, fax 285 2193*), where comfortable, though not really luxurious, rooms cost US$75/100 a single/double. Services include a swimming pool, sauna, casino and disco.

Getting There & Away

Cablecar For a summer visit to Uludağ, getting there is most of the fun. Take a Bursa city bus from Koza Parkı (Peron 1), or a dolmuş, marked for 'Teleferik' (☎ 224-221 3635), to the lower terminus of the cablecar – a 15-minute ride from Heykel at

SOUTH OF MARMARA SEA

the city's eastern edge. In summer when crowds abound, the cablecars depart when full or at least every 30 to 45 minutes, weather and winds permitting. The trip to the top takes about 30 minutes and costs US$5 each way, half price on Wednesday.

The cablecar stops at an intermediate point named Kadıyayla, from where you continue upward to the terminus at Sarıalan (sah-RUH-ah-lahn) at an altitude of 1635m.

At Sarıalan there are a few snack and refreshment stands, a national-park camping area (always full, it seems), some walking *patika* (trails) and the occasional dolmuş to the *Oteller Mevkii* (hotel zone), 6km further up the mountain slope. That's all there is to do, except enjoy the scenery.

Dolmuş Dolmuşes run from central Bursa to the hotel zone on Uludağ several times daily in summer (more frequently in winter) for about US$6 each way, which is more than the cablecar. On the winding, 32km trip you pass the İnkaya Çınarı, a gigantic ancient plane tree about 3km beyond Çekirge (watch for the sign reading 'Tarihi Ağaç'). The tree, set in a little park, is said to have been alive when the Ottomans conquered Bursa in 1326.

At the 11km marker you must stop and pay an entry fee for the national park of US$0.50 per person, US$1.50 for a car and driver. The hotel zone is 11km further up from the national park entrance. Almost half of the entire drive from Bursa is on rough granite-block pavement.

The return ride can be difficult in summer as there are few dolmuşes or taxis in evidence. In winter there are usually plenty, and they are eager to get at least some fare before they head back down, so you may be able to get back to Bursa for less – haggle.

Car If you're driving, have tyre chains in winter (December to early April) as they are required (*Zincir takmak mecburidir*) when the road is icy or snowy.

BANDIRMA

The port town of Bandırma with 80,000 residents has an ancient history, but nothing to show for it. What you see is a 20th century creation which might well be nicknamed *Betonbol* (Concreteville). It has little to offer the tourist except the junction between the İzmir to Bandırma train line and the Bandırma to İstanbul ferry line. You'd do well to pass straight through, but if you must stop, there are hotels and restaurants in the town.

Orientation

Bandırma's otogar is 1.8km south-east of the centre, out by the main highway; get a *servis arabası* (shuttle bus) to reach the centre. There's a separate, small otogar west of the centre for buses to Erdek and Gönen.

If you arrive by train or ferry, walk east for 250m to reach the main square.

From the main square, the main road going east is İnönü Caddesi, which has most of the services you may want, including cheap hotels and restaurants and bus ticket offices.

Places to Stay

There are several cheap hotels on and east of the main square on İnönü Caddesi. Facing the noisy square is ***Sahil Hotel*** *(☎ 266-718 4485, İnönü Caddesi 10)*, a simple and convenient place favoured by Turkish businessmen. It offers rooms for US$8/11 a single/double with sink, US$14/16 with private shower. The Sahil's nearby sister hotel, ***Çetin Otel*** *(☎ 266-718 8750, Haydarçavuş Sokak 5-B)*, up the street opposite the Kamil Koç bus office, is quieter, charges the same, and has rooms with TV.

Özdil Hotel *(☎ 266-718 2200, Saatçiler Caddesi 16)*, east of the square near the water facing the Haydar Çavuş Camii, charges a bit less.

Türe Otel *(☎ 266-714 5550, fax 713 4594, General Halit Caddesi 15)*, inland a block from the main traffic circle, posts prices of US$32/45, but will quickly drop them if not full.

The older ***Hotel Eken*** *(☎ 266-714 7800, fax 712 5355, Uğur Mumcu Caddesi 9)*, half a block west of the main square up the hill, charges US$38 for a double with private shower, TV and breakfast. It's overshadowed by the newer, fancier four-star ***Hotel Eken Prestige*** (☎ *266-714 7600, Mehmet Akif Ersoy Caddesi 7*), which thinks it's the Hilton: US$100 single, US$180 double.

Places to Eat

İnönü Caddesi, the main shopping street, has many little restaurants. Try the ***Moby Dick Restaurant*** off the main traffic circle, or ***Kapıdağ*** off İnönü toward the water.

Getting There & Away

Very fast *hızlı feribot* (car-ferries) connect Bandırma with İstanbul's Yenikapı docks, making the run in under two hours. See the Getting Around chapter at the front of this book for details on the Marmara Ekspresi train between Bandırma and İzmir.

Bandırma is midway on the run between Bursa (115km, two hours, US$5; 12 buses daily) and Çanakkale (195km, three hours, US$7; 12 buses daily). There are also buses southward to Balıkesir and points beyond. For route, schedule and fare information, ask at the otogar, or at the bus-company ticket offices on İnönü Caddesi.

For information on the cities located south of Bursa and Bandırma, see the North Aegean Turkey chapter under North Aegean Hinterland.

KUŞCENNETİ MİLLİ PARKI

Though Bandırma will not hold your interest for very long, bird fanciers will want to make a detour (18.5km) to Kuşcenneti Milli Parkı (Bird Paradise National Park). This 64 hectare reserve on the shores of Kuş Gölü (Bird Lake, the ancient Manias), due south of Bandırma, boasts from two to three million feathered visitors, of 255 different varieties, each year.

The best times to visit are in spring (from April to June) and autumn (from September to November) when the birds are making their annual migration. In high summer and mid-winter there is little to see. Avoid weekends, when it's very crowded and noisy – the birds do. Bring binoculars if you have them.

From the Bandırma-Bursa highway, turn south 13km east of Bandırma centre. After 3km, turn west following signs for the park, which is 2.5km further along. Admission costs US$1 (half price for students).

The Visitors Centre has exhibits – reminiscent of 19th century natural history museums – of stuffed birds in simulated habitats. From the centre, walk along the patika to the observation tower for the view over the lake. No camping or picnicking is permitted, and there's only the sleepy ***Cennet Restaurant*** for food, so your visit may be cut short by hunger.

North Aegean Turkey

Turkey's Aegean coast, among the country's richest agricultural areas, was one of the first regions to be developed for tourism.

Unfortunately, a coastline which was once a procession of beautiful, historic ruins, ancient fishing villages, golden wheat fields and fig and olive orchards has fallen victim to rash development in places. But if you're prepared to venture beyond the teeming coastal highway and the honeypot resorts, you can still find reminders of what existed before the tourism boom. Many small to medium-sized inland cities support light manufacturing and commerce.

Most people start exploring the region at Çanakkale, visiting the famous Gallipoli battlefields and the ruins of Troy (for more information on Gallipoli see the earlier Thrace chapter). Ayvalık, to the south, is a booming resort town with beaches, seafood restaurants and panoramas of Lesbos. At Bergama (the ancient Pergamum) you can see the impressive ruins of the acropolis where parchment was invented, and the Asclepion, an early medical centre. The small coastal towns of Dikili, Çandarlı and Foça are less well-known and thus more pleasant seaside resorts.

İzmir, Turkey's third largest city, is a pleasant place, although there's little to hold your interest. However, Adnan Menderes airport, south of İzmir proper, is a useful arrival or departure point. If you come to Çeşme from Chios you'll probably have to transit İzmir on your way to other parts of the Aegean.

Several hours inland, the cities of the northern Aegean hinterland are rarely visited by tourists, which makes them all the more appealing for travellers looking to experience the essence of Turkey. Eskişehir, Balıkesir, Kütahya and Afyon all have their good points. Whether you stop for the night or just for some tea, each is likely to yield interesting experiences and lasting memories.

HIGHLIGHTS

- Picnicking amid the ruins of ancient Pergamum (Bergama)
- Being scrubbed clean in a Turkish Bath at Çanakkale
- Having a fish lunch on Alibey Adası, off Ayvalık
- Enjoying the nightlife of Alsancak in İzmir
- Shopping for Turkish faïence in Kütahya
- Sampling clotted cream and Turkish Delight in Afyon

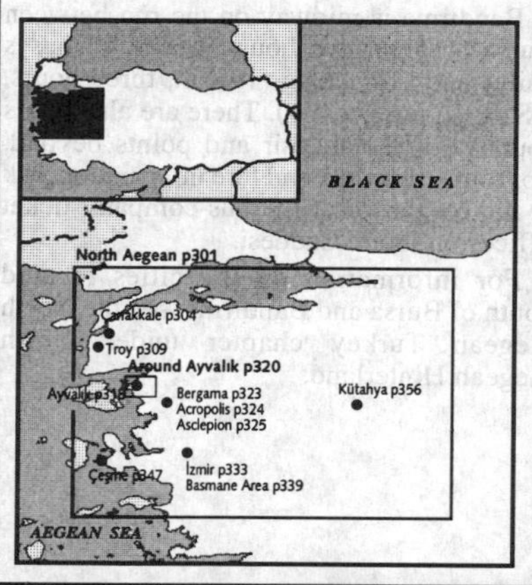

Getting There & Away

Air Most people fly to İstanbul and then travel west and south by bus, via Tekirdağ or Yalova/Bursa, to the northern Aegean (see Getting There & Away under İstanbul for details), although İzmir is also a gateway (see Getting There & Away under İzmir).

Boat It's perfectly possible – if more expensive than you might hope – to reach the

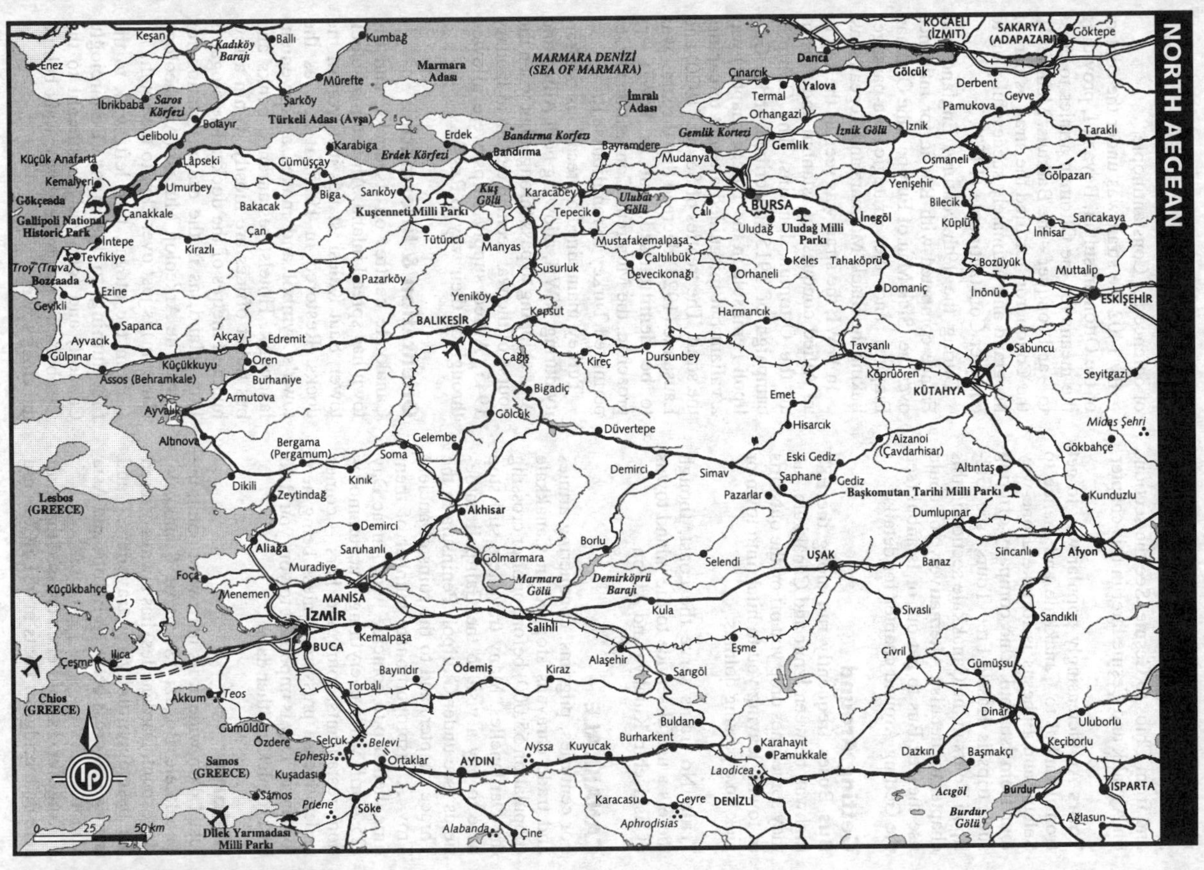
NORTH AEGEAN
MARMARA DENİZİ
(SEA OF MARMARA)
Marmara Adası
İmralı Adası
Türkeli Adası (Avşa)
Gökçeada
Lesbos
(GREECE)
Chios
(GREECE)
Samos
(GREECE)
Saros Körfezi
Erdek Körfezi
Bandırma Korfezı
Gemlik Korfezi
İznik Gölü
Ulubat Gölü
Kuş Gölü
Marmara Gölü
Demirköprü Barajı
Kadıköy Barajı
Acıgöl
Burdur Gölü
Gallipoli National Historic Park
Kuşcenneti Milli Parkı
Uludağ Milli Parkı
Başkomutan Tarihi Milli Parkı
Dilek Yarımadası Milli Parkı
Troy (Truva)
Bergama (Pergamum)
Ephesus
Priene
Laodicea
Aphrodisias
Nyssa
Alabanda
Teos
Midas Şehri
SAKARYA (ADAPAZARI)
KOCAELİ (İZMİT)
ESKİŞEHİR
BURSA
KÜTAHYA
BALIKESİR
MANİSA
İZMİR
BUCA
AYDIN
DENİZLİ
UŞAK
ISPARTA
Afyon
Göktepe
Taraklı
Sarıcakaya
Seyitgazi
Gökbahçe
Kunduzlu
Derbent
Geyve
Pamukova
Gölpazarı
Osmaneli
Bilecik
Küplü
Bozüyük
İnönü
Sabuncu
İnhisar
Muttalip
Gölcük
İznik
Yenişehir
İnegöl
Domaniç
Köprüören
Tavşanlı
Tahaköprü
Keles
Yalova
Darıca
Termal
Çınarcık
Orhangazi
Gemlik
Mudanya
Uludağ
Orhaneli
Harmancık
Emet
Hisarcık
Çalı
Çaltılıbük
Devecikonağı
Mustafakemalpaşa
Dursunbey
Kireç
Düvertepe
Bayramdere
Tepecik
Karacabey
Susurluk
Kepsut
Bigadiç
Çağış
Gölcük
Bandırma
Erdek
Manyas
Tütüncü
Yeniköy
Kumbağ
Mürefte
Şarköy
Karabiga
Sarıköy
Biga
Pazarköy
Gümüşçay
Bakacak
Çan
Ballı
Bolayır
Gelibolu
Lâpseki
Umurbey
Kirazlı
Çanakkale
Keşan
İbrikbaba
İntepe
Tevfikiye
Kemalyeri
Küçük Anafarta
Enez
Bozcaada
Geyikli
Gülpınar
Ayvacık
Ezine
Sapanca
Assos (Behramkale)
Küçükkuyu
Ayvalık
Altınova
Akçay
Edremit
Ören
Burhaniye
Armutova
Dikili
Zeytindağ
Kınık
Soma
Gelembe
Akhisar
Gölmarmara
Demirci
Saruhanlı
Muradiye
Aliağa
Menemen
Foça
Kemalpaşa
Salihli
Borlu
Kula
Ödemiş
Kiraz
Alaşehir
Bayındır
Torbalı
Belevi
Selçuk
Kuşadası
Samos
Özdere
Gümüldür
Akkum
Ilıca
Çeşme
Küçükbahçe
Ortaklar
Söke
Çine
Kuyucak
Karacasu
Burharkent
Buldan
Geyre
Sarıgöl
Eşme
Selendi
Simav
Pazarlar
Şaphane
Eski Gediz
Gediz
Altıntaş
Aizanoi (Çavdarhisar)
Dumlupınar
Banaz
Sivaslı
Sincanlı
Sandıklı
Çivril
Gümüşsu
Dinar
Dazkırı
Başmakçı
Karahayıt
Pamukkale
Keçiborlu
Uluborlu
Burdur
Ağlasun
0
25
50 km

north Aegean from the Greek islands. There are regular boats from Lesbos to Ayvalık and from Chios to Çeşme. See the sections on Ayvalık and Çeşme later in this chapter.

Tours An increasingly popular way to get from İstanbul to Çanakkale and thence to Selçuk and Ephesus is to take a one-way tour from İstanbul. One company offering such trips is Hassle-Free Tours (see Gallipoli Tours in the Çanakkale section in this chapter for details). Alternatively you could use the Fez Bus to get out of İstanbul (see the Getting Around chapter for details).

Getting Around

Bus Buses frequently run along the E87 highway between İzmir and Çanakkale, but they sometimes drop you off on the outskirts of towns, leaving you to hitch into town or pick up a passing dolmuş.

Train No trains serve the coast, though there's a useful service to the inland towns of Eskişehir, Kütahya and Afyon.

ÇANAKKALE

For centuries, pilgrims, conquering armies and trade caravans stopped in Çanakkale (population 55,000) before or after crossing the Dardanelles. Many travellers still stop here to pay a visit to the Gallipoli battlefields (see under Gallipoli Peninsula in the Thrace chapter) and to the ruins of ancient Troy. A disproportionate number of them time their trip to coincide with Anzac Day (25 April) when everything – accommodation, restaurants, tours and bars – comes under intense pressure. Unless being here for Anzac Day is important to you, you'd do best to pick another date.

History

Just 1.4km wide at its narrowest point, the Çanakkale Boğazı (Strait of Çanakkale, Hellespont, Dardanelles) has always offered the best opportunity for travellers – and armies – to cross between Europe and Asia Minor.

King Xerxes I of Persia crossed the strait here on a bridge of boats in 481 BC, as did Alexander the Great a century-and-a-half later. In Byzantine times it was the first line of defence for Constantinople.

By 1402 the strait was under the control of the Ottoman sultan, Beyazıt I, providing the means for the Ottoman armies to cross to – and conquer – the Balkans. Mehmet II, the Conqueror, fortified the strait as part of his grand and ultimately successful plan to conquer Constantinople (1453).

During the 19th century, England and France competed with Russia for influence over the 'Sick Man of Europe' (the Ottoman Empire) and the strategic sea-passages linking the Black, Marmara and Aegean seas.

In WWI, the strait was seen as the key to an Allied conquest of İstanbul and thus of all the Ottoman domains. The Gallipoli campaign of 1915 (described under Gallipoli Peninsula in the Thrace chapter) was a valiant but misguided attempt to capture the strait. The treaties of Sévres (1920) and Lausanne (1923) decreed that the strait was to be demilitarised, but as WWII approached, the Montreux Convention (1936) permitted Turkey to remilitarise it.

Turkey maintained a precarious neutrality during WWII, allowing both Allied and Axis shipping to pass through, but when the course of the war seemed certain in January 1945, Allied supply ships were allowed through on their way to Russia.

Orientation & Information

Çanakkale centres on its docks, and the town has spread inland. An Ottoman clock tower, Saat Kulesi, stands just west of the docks. Restored in 1995, it acts as the town's symbol and makes a convenient landmark. Hotels, restaurants, banks and bus ticket offices are mostly within a few hundred metres of the docks. The otogar is 1km inland, as is the dolmuş station for Troy. The Arkeoloji Müzesi (Archaeology Museum) is just over 2km to the south.

From the otogar, turn left, walk to the first turning to the right (Demircioğlu Caddesi) and follow signs straight to the 'Feribot'. To reach the shops, walk behind the clock tower.

The Hellespont

Hellespont, the ancient name of the Çanakkale Boğazı (Dardanelles), is the product of a classical myth.

Athamas, a king of Thessaly, tired of his wife, Nephele, and set her aside in favour of Princess Ino of Thebes. Ino, who had a son by Athamas, set to work to eliminate Nephele's son Phryxus, and daughter Helle, so that her own son might inherit Athamas' crown. She secretly parched all of the kingdom's seed corn before the spring sowing, resulting in a disastrous harvest.

The king sent a messenger to the nearest oracle asking what he should do to relieve the terrible distress. As the messenger returned, Ino intercepted, bribed and threatened him to forget what the oracle had said in favour of her own pronouncement. The messenger told Athamas that Phryxus must die in sacrifice to the gods before the corn would grow again.

With the boy on the altar about to go under the knife, Hermes, in answer to Nephele's prayer, sent a golden-fleeced flying ram to save him. Phryxus and Helle leapt on the ram's back and were whisked into the sky and across the strait which separates Europe from Asia. During the flight, Helle fell off and drowned in the strait, which was named Hellespont (Helle's Sea) in her memory.

Phryxus continued his flight, finally landing in Colchis at the eastern end of the Unfriendly (Black) Sea, where he sacrificed the ram in honour of Zeus, giving its priceless golden fleece to King Aeetes, who permitted Phryxus to marry one of his daughters. The golden fleece was placed in a sacred grove under the watchful eye of a sleepless dragon, obviously a set-up so that Jason would later have a quest worthy of his heroism.

The strait's other name, Dardanelles, comes from the ancient town of Dardanus, the ruins of which were discovered between Çanakkale and Güzelyalı on its Asian shore. The town was named for Dardanus, son of Zeus and the Pleiad Electra, who founded Troy and the Trojan race, or Dardani.

The Hellespont was also the setting for the legend of Hero and Leander. Leander, a youth from Abydos (Çanakkale), fell in love with Hero, a priestess in the Temple of Venus at Sestos (Kilitbahir). Each night Leander would plunge into the chill waters of the Hellespont and swim to the European shore, guided by a torch which Hero held up in the temple tower. One stormy night the torch was blown out by the wind and Leander, without guidance, was exhausted trying to find the shore, and drowned. Hero, in despair at finding his body on the shore, threw herself from her tower.

The myth was thought to be an impossible exaggeration until Lord Byron, ever the romantic, arrived in 1807 to prove it possible. Born lame, he had no trouble swimming and completed the crossing to incredulous acclaim. He later used Abydos as the setting for his verse tale *The Bride of Abydos* (1813). Since Byron, many others have come to swim the Hellespont, including the American ambassador to Turkey, William Macomber, in 1975.

The Tarihi Yalı Hamamı (Turkish bath) is a few short blocks south of the clock tower.

The town's Tourism Information Office (☎/fax 286-217 1187) is between the clock tower and the ferry docks.

Çanakkale's postal code is 17100.

Arkeoloji Müzesi

Çanakkale's Archaeological Museum is on the southern outskirts of town, just over 2km south-east of the clock tower, on the road to Troy. It's open daily from 10 am to 5 pm except Monday. Admission costs

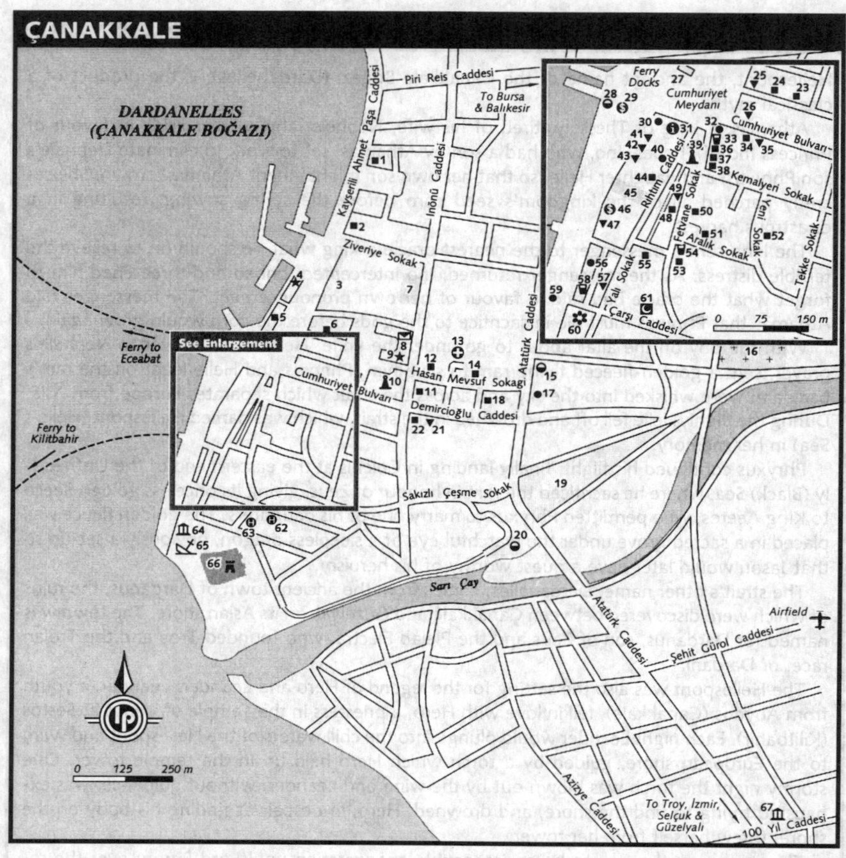

US$2. From the town centre, city buses and dolmuşes to İntepe or Güzelyalı run past the museum.

The museum's exhibits are arranged chronologically, starting with prehistoric fossils and continuing with Bronze Age and later artefacts. Probably the most interesting exhibits are those from Troy, labelled, in Turkish and English, by 'city': that is Troy I, Troy II etc (see History in the Troy section later in this chapter). The exhibits from Dardanos, an ancient town near Çanakkale, are also interesting. Don't miss the glass case of bone pins and small implements near the exit.

Other Things to See

In the military zone at the southern end of the quay are the **Askeri Müzesi** (Military Museum) and **Deniz Müzesi** (Naval Museum), set in a park surrounding the Çimenlik Kalesi. The park is open daily from 9 am to 10 pm; the museums are open daily except Monday and Thursday from 9 to 11 am and

ÇANAKKALE

PLACES TO STAY	25 Trakya Restaurant	29 PTT Exchange Office
1 Büyük Truva Otelı	26 Trakya Restaurant	30 Bus Ticket Office
2 Hotel Akol	27 Takeaways	31 Tourism Information Office
5 Otel Anafartalar	35 Trakya	32 Bus Ticket Offices
6 Yaldız 2	41 Çekiç	33 TNT Café (bar)
11 Hotel Fatih 2	42 Rıhtım	39 Saat Kulesi (Clock Tower)
12 Hotel Kestanbol	43 Entellektüel	40 Troy-Anzac Tours
14 Otel Aşkın	47 Şehir Restaurant	45 Park
18 Aşkın Pansiyon	49 Gaziantep Aile Kebap ve Pide Salonu	46 Etibank
22 Hotel Temizay	57 Aussie & Kiwi Restaurant	54 Bars
23 Koç Pansiyon		56 Gümrük (Customs) Office
24 Otel Yaldız	**OTHER**	58 Belediye Halk Gazinosu (Nightclub)
34 Anzac House	3 Cafés; gazinos (bars)	59 Teahouses
36 Umut Otel	4 Police	60 Tea Garden
37 Hotel Anzac	7 Park	61 Yalı Camii
38 Erdem Oteli	8 PTT	62 Tarihi Yalı Hamamı (Men's Entrance)
44 Hotel Bakır	9 Police	63 Tarihi Yalı Hamamı (Women's Entrance)
48 Hotel Konak	10 Cannon Monument	64 Askeri Müzesi (Military Museum)
50 Hotel Kervansaray	13 Hospital	65 Nusrat Minelayer
51 Hotel Efes	15 Otogar	66 Çimenlik Kalesi (Fortress)
52 Yellow Rose Pension	16 British Cemetery	67 Arkeoloji Müzesi
53 Konak Oteli	17 Town Hall	
55 Avrupa Pansiyon	19 Market Place	
PLACES TO EAT	20 Dolmuş Station	
21 Doğum Pide ve Kebap Salonu	28 Ferry Ticket Office	

from 2.30 to 7.30 pm. Admission is free to the park, US$0.50 to the museums (half-price for students).

Beside the Naval Museum is a mock-up of the minelayer *Nusrat*, which had a heroic role in the Gallipoli campaign. The day before the Allied fleet tried to force the straits, Allied minesweepers proclaimed the water cleared. At night the *Nusrat* went out, picked up loose mines and relaid them. Three Allied ships struck the Nusrat's mines and were sunk or crippled.

Another small **museum** houses reminders of Atatürk and the battles of Gallipoli.

Mehmet the Conqueror built the impressive **Çimenlik Kalesi** in the mid-15th century. The cannons surrounding the stone walls are leftovers from assorted battles; many were made in French, English and German foundries.

In Demircioğlu Caddesi, the broad main street, stands a **monument** constructed of old WWI cannons. The inscription reads: 'Turkish soldiers used these cannons on 18 March 1915 to ensure the impassability of the Çanakkale strait'.

Gallipoli Tours

Organising tours of the Gallipoli battlefields (see the Gallipoli Peninsula section in the Thrace chapter) is a lucrative business for people in Çanakkale, and any hotel can reserve a place for you. To whet your appetite for the atmosphere of the battlefields, Peter Weir's film *Gallipoli* is screened most nights at Anzac House (see Places to Stay – Budget).

The tours vary by company and individual guide and from day to day. Ask other travellers if their tours were good value. If you have a whole day and enjoy hiking, you can visit the most important sites on foot and by dolmuş. You'll miss the guide's often interesting commentary but will be able to linger as long as you like, wherever you like. What's more the Gallipoli Peninsula is beautiful in its own right and more enjoyable when you're not part of a gaggle of 20 to 40 other people.

The typical four-hour (morning or afternoon) battlefield tour includes transport by car or minibus, driver and guide, lunch and a swim from a beach on the western shore. It costs from US$14 to US$20 per person, depending upon the company and the number of people signed up. Most people complain that tours don't allow enough time at each site.

Troy-Anzac Tours (☎ 286-217 5849, fax 217 0196), Saat Kulesi Meydanı 6, Çanakkale, facing the clock tower, has been in business longest and seems the most reliable but Down Under Travel Agency (☎ 286-814 2431, fax 814 2430, d.under@mailexcite.com) tours, in Ecebat, also gets good reports.

A lot of people use Hassle-Free Tours which provides transport out of İstanbul to Gallipoli, staying one night at Anzac House before visiting the ruins at Troy and either travelling onto Selçuk or back to İstanbul. These tours cost UK£45 per person, including lunch. Unless you're a military specialist or an archaeologist you should find the site tours adequate and enjoyable. However, driving round in circles picking up other travellers at the crack of dawn, or hanging around waiting for the bus back, is less fun. Some of the guides on tours from İstanbul are not very communicative. Travel agencies in İstanbul and Selçuk can book you a ticket.

Special Events

For one week in mid-August, the Çanakkale Trova Festivali brings dance and musical troupes to town. Art and craft exhibits, sports and chess tournaments and an underwater rubbish-pickup contest fill the days.

Places to Stay

Except for on Anzac Day, Çanakkale has a selection of hotels in all price ranges. Many of them are less well-kept, less well-run and less friendly than those in other Turkish towns.

Places to Stay – Budget

The hotels in the centre of town are near the clock tower. Check the sheets for signs of previous occupancy before you take a room.

Anzac House *(☎ 286-217 1392, fax 217 2906)*, Cumhuriyet Bulvarı, provides clean, simple budget accommodation, with a choice of dorm beds for US$4, singles for US$6 or doubles for US$10. Be warned that some of the doubles are claustrophobic, windowless boxes. Some people reckon breakfasts are a tad pricey but the ground-floor sitting area/bar is great for meeting other travellers.

It may not look much on the outside but ***Hotel Efes*** *(☎ 286-217 3256, Aralık Sokak 5)*, behind the clock tower, is bright and cheerful and charges US$6/8 a single/double without running water, a little more with a shower. What's more, it's run by a Turkish woman which might make it particularly appealing to female visitors.

Judging by its architecture alone, the quaint old ***Hotel Kervansaray*** *(☎ 286-217 8192, Fetvane Sokak 13)*, the 200-year-old former home of a Turkish paşa, is another promising choice. Very basic rooms cost US$6/8 a single/double without running water and there's an attractive courtyard and garden. But if you stay here, make sure breakfast is included in the price before tucking in – some readers have come to blows over this.

Yellow Rose Pension *(☎ 286-217 3343, Yeni Sokak 5)* is 50m south-east of the clock tower in an attractive 50-year-old house along a quiet side street. Guests have access to a garden, washing machine and kitchen. Rooms, at US$5 per person, are very basic. Once again, some travellers have reported arguments, mainly over double-bookings and grumpy management.

Other cheapies, with little to distinguish them, include ***Hotel Akgün*** *(☎ 286-217 3049)*, across the street from the Efes; and ***Erdem Oteli*** *(☎ 286-217 4986)* and ***Ümüt Otel*** *(☎ 286-213 4246)* nearer to the clock tower. ***Koç Pansiyon*** *(☎ 286-217 0121)*, Kızılay Sokak, south-east of the Otel Yaldız, has a TV on the hall landing which could lead to some sleepless nights.

Konak Oteli *(☎ 286-217 1150, Fetvane Sokak 14),* boasts central heating and constant hot water. Prices for waterless rooms are US$6/10 a single/double; and US$8/12 a single/double with shower.

Close to the bars, ***Avrupa Pansiyon*** *(☎ 286-217 4084, Matbaa Sokak 8),* also falls into the US$8/12 a single/double with shower price bracket. The wallpaper is a little alarming but the place is comfortable enough.

The family run ***Otel Fatih 2*** *(☎ 286-217 7884, İnönü Caddesi 149),* opposite the PTT, charges US$12 for a double with shower.

Otel Aşkın *(☎/fax 286-217 4956, Hasan Mevsuf Sokak 53),* only one short block from the otogar, charges US$16 for a double room with shower, breakfast included. Its sister establishment, the nearby ***Aşkın Pansiyon*** (same phone), offers cheerless service and waterless doubles for US$8.

Camping ***Mocamp Trova*** *(☎ 286-232 8025),* open in summer only, is 16km from Çanakkale off the Troy road at Güzelyalı, reachable by Güzelyalı dolmuş from Çanakkale.

Places to Stay – Mid-Range

You can't miss the two-star, 70 room ***Otel Anafartalar*** *(☎ 286-217 4454, fax 217 2622),* İskele Meydanı, a seven-storey high-rise on the northern side of the ferry docks. The hall carpet could do with replacement but the front rooms are good value with harbour views, bath and breakfast for US$31/42 a single/double. There's also a pleasant seaside restaurant (see Places to Eat, later in this section).

Anzac Hotel *(☎ 286-217 7777, fax 217 2018, Saat Kulesi Meydanı 8),* more or less facing the clock tower, is a newish, two-star lodging with 27 rooms, all with showers (some with tubs) going for US$30/40 a single/double without breakfast (US$5). The housekeeping has come in for some criticism but it's a friendly, accommodating place nonetheless.

A good choice because it's clean and new is ***Hotel Temizay*** *(☎ 286-212 8760, fax 217 5885, Cumhuriyet Meydanı 15),* with singles/doubles/triples for US$20/30/45. If you like to read in bed you might find the lights too dim here.

The three-star ***Büyük Truva Oteli*** *(☎ 286-217 1024, fax 217 0903, Mehmet Akif Ersoy Caddesi 2),* on the waterfront 200m north of the docks, has 66 clean, serviceable rooms, many with lovely sea views. Rates are US$40/50/65 a single/double/triple, for a room with TV, minibar, and private shower or tub/shower combination, breakfast included.

The 35 room ***Hotel Bakır*** (bah-KUHR) *(☎ 286-217 2908, fax 217 4090, Yalı Sokak 12),* is very near the clock tower. A clean room with shower and view of the straits costs US$40/50/60 a single/double/triple, breakfast included.

One block east of the ferry docks is the one-star, 33 room ***Otel Yaldız*** *(☎ 286-217 1793, fax 212 6704, Kızılay Sokak 20),* on a side street. It's clean, simple and offers singles/doubles/triples with shower for US$14/22/30. There are more rooms across the road in ***Yaldız 2***.

The one-star ***Hotel Kestanbol*** *(☎ 286-217 0857, fax 217 9173, Hasan Mevsuf Sokak 5),* inland a few blocks and across the street from the Emniyet Sarayı (police station), has 26 rooms, all with bath, costing US$20/30 a single/double including breakfast. It's quiet and proper, with a pleasant rooftop bar.

Tour groups stay at the high-rise, four-star ***Hotel Akol*** *(☎ 286-217 9456, fax 217 2897),* Kordonboyu, on the waterfront north of the docks. The 136 rooms with bath cost US$60/90 a single/double. Services include an outdoor pool, several restaurants and bars, a disco, and satellite TV in guest rooms. A few rooms at the back miss out on the sea views but cost the same.

There are a few more three-star hotels in the seaside suburb of Güzelyalı, 16km southwest of Çanakkale off the road to Troy, of which the best are the older ***Tusan Hotel*** *(☎ 286-232 8746, fax 232 8226),* charging US$23 per person in an air-con room, with breakfast; and the similarly-priced ***İris Otel*** *(☎ 286-232 8628, fax 232 8028).*

Places to Eat – Budget

Çanakkale has cheap places to eat throughout town. Look along the main street or past the clock tower for köfteci and pideci shops. Typical places include ***Gaziantep Aile Kebap ve Pide Salonu***, a few steps behind the clock tower where a meal of soup, pide or köfte, bread and a soft drink costs US$4; or ***Doğum Pide ve Kebap Salonu*** along Demiricioğlu Caddesi which is very popular with the locals.

There are several branches of ***Trakya Restaurant*** *(☎ 286-217 7257)*. The branch opposite Anzac House is bright and cheerful, always with a selection of ready-food in the steam tables and supposedly open 24 hours a day. The branch beside Anzac House dishes up all sorts of tasty meat dishes for a US$4 to US$5 price tag.

Aussie & Kiwi Restaurant in Yalı Sokak does its best to oblige antipodeans, serving up vegemite toast for US$2 alongside cheap kebaps and köfte.

Look out for shops serving *peynirli helva* (a local pudding of soft, marzipan-like helva, faintly flavoured with cheese).

Places to Eat – Mid-Range

The best places face the quay to the north and south of the ferry docks. ***Rıhtım***, ***Entellektüel*** (Intellectuals' Restaurant, but goatee beards are optional) and ***Çekiç*** are all places of long standing. An appetiser, fried or grilled fish, salad and a bottle of beer at any one of them might cost from US$10 to US$14. Be sure to ask prices, as bill-fiddling is not unknown, especially at busy times.

On the northern side, the seaside restaurant at ***Otel Anafartalar*** is popular, with prices posted prominently.

Entertainment

Playing to its popularity with young Aussies and Kiwis, Çanakkale now has half a dozen bars, mostly clustered in Fetvane Sokak. One of the most comfortable, with live music and a snooker table, is the ***TNT Bar***, round the corner from Anzac House, facing the clock tower. Watch out for happy hours with cheap grog from 7 to 9 pm.

A cluster of ***tea gardens*** at the southern end of the quay make good places to sit and observe the comings and goings across the straits. Alternatively, in Yalı Sokak, there's a pleasant tea courtyard in what was once the Yalı Han.

Getting There & Away

Bus Çanakkale's otogar is 1km east of the ferry docks but you may never need to use it as many buses pick up and drop off at the bus company offices near the clock tower. Walk straight inland from the docks to Atatürk Caddesi and turn left; the otogar is 100m along on the right. For transport to Troy (30km), see that section, following.

You can buy bus tickets at the otogar or at the bus company offices on the main street, in the centre of Çanakkale near the ferry docks.

For information on buses to, from and around Gallipoli, see the Gallipoli Peninsula section in the Thrace chapter. Details of some daily bus services from Çanakkale are:

Ankara – 700km, 10 hours, US$12; several
Ayvalık – 200km, 3½ hours, US$5; many
Bandırma – 195km, three hours, US$6.50; 12 buses
Behramkale (Assos) – 100km, two hours or more, US$6; many – change to dolmuş at Ayvacık
Bursa – 310km, five hours, US$6; 12 buses
Edirne – 230km, 3½ hours, US$7; five direct, or change at Keşan
Gelibolu – 49km plus ferry ride, less than two hours, US$2; take a bus or minibus north-east to the Lapseki-Gelibolu ferry or take the ferry to Eceabat or Kilitbahir and then the minibus to Gelibolu
İstanbul – 340km, six hours, US$9 to US$12; hourly
İzmir – 340km, five hours, US$7 to US$10; hourly
Lapseki – 33km, 45 minutes, US$1.50; take a bus bound for Gönen, Bandırma or Bursa, but make sure you'll be allowed to get off at Lapseki
Truva (Troy) – 30km, 35 minutes, US$1.50; frequent dolmuşes in summer

Boat Two ferries connect Çanakkale with the Gallipoli peninsula, one going to Kilitbahir, the other to Eceabat; both carry cars as well as passengers. For information on the Gelibolu-Lapseki car ferry, see Gelibolu in the Gallipoli Peninsula section of the Thrace chapter.

The Çanakkale-Eceabat car ferries take approximately 25 minutes to cross in good weather. From 6 am to 11 pm boats run in each direction every hour on the hour. There are also boats at midnight and at 2 and 4 am from Eceabat and at 1, 3 and 5 am from Çanakkale. Fares are US$0.50 per person, US$1.50 per bicycle, and US$4 per car.

The Çanakkale-Kilitbahir ferry, *SS Alınteri* ('Sweat-of-the-brow') is a smaller boat which takes mostly passengers and a few cars. There is only one boat which departs from near the Hotel Bakır, which is located to the south-west of the main docks. It takes just 15 minutes to cross but the schedule is irregular. It costs US$0.40 per passenger, US$3 per car.

TROY

The approach to Troy (Truva), 30km from Çanakkale, is across low, rolling grain fields, dotted with villages. This is the ancient Troad, all but lost to legend until German-born Californian treasure-seeker and amateur archaeologist Heinrich Schliemann (1822-90) excavated it in 1871. At that time the poetry of Homer was assumed to be based on legend, not history. Schliemann got permission from the Ottoman government to dig here at his own expense and uncovered four ancient towns, more or less destroying three others in the process (for another view on the affair, see the 'Frank Calvert, Discoverer of Troy' boxed text in this section).

Schliemann had been particularly keen to uncover the treasure of King Priam and on the last day of excavations he quite literally hit gold. However, what he thought dated

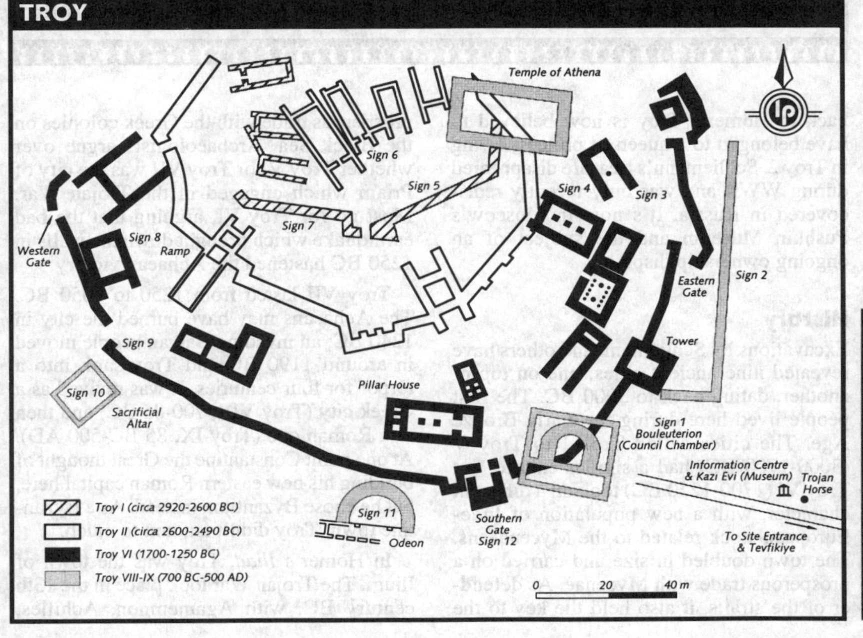

Frank Calvert, Discoverer of Troy

While Heinrich Schliemann is traditionally credited with rediscovering Troy, others claim that it was Frank Calvert (1828-1908), a Malta-born British expatriate and sometime American consul at the Dardanelles, who was the actual discoverer.

In 1859 Calvert, an amateur archaeologist, who owned much of the land around the site, published a pioneering excavation report on his work at Hanay Tepe, a prehistoric site near Troy. He later moved on to Pınarbaşı, believing it to be the site of Troy. By 1863, however, he was convinced that the hill on his land called Hisarlık, identified in 1812 as the site of the Roman city of Ilium Novum, was the site of Troy. He began to excavate by digging a trench, in which he found numerous artefacts from several periods.

Calvert applied to the British Museum for support in his excavations but was turned down. He continued his excavations on a small scale, but was hampered by financial difficulties and family responsibilities.

In 1868 Calvert was visited by Heinrich Schliemann, who had been excavating, in vain, for Troy at Pınarbaşı. Convinced by the artefacts which Calvert had uncovered that this was Troy, Schliemann began to excavate on Calvert's land at Hisarlık. The two men later had a falling out, but Calvert continued to support Schliemann's work for the sake of science, and Schliemann continued to fund Calvert's own explorations elsewhere in exchange for the benefit of Calvert's knowledge.

Schliemann, a peerless self-promoter, saw to it that his name was inscribed in the history books as the discoverer of Troy, but it was Frank Calvert who made Schliemann's success possible. In the 20th century, Calvert's priceless collection of artefacts from Troy and nearby sites was dispersed to museums in Çanakkale, London, and Boston and Worcester, Massachusetts.

back to Homeric Troy is now believed to have belonged to a queen or princess living in Troy 2. Schliemann's treasure disappeared during WWII and was only recently rediscovered in Russia. It's now in Moscow's Pushkin Museum and the subject of an ongoing ownership dispute.

History

Excavations by Schliemann and others have revealed nine ancient cities, one on top of another, dating back to 3000 BC. The first people lived here during the Early Bronze Age. The cities called Troy I to Troy V (3000-1700 BC) had a similar culture, but Troy VI (1700-1250 BC) took on a different character, with a new population of Indo-European stock related to the Mycenaeans. The town doubled in size and carried on a prosperous trade with Mycenae. As defender of the straits, it also held the key to the prosperous trade with the Greek colonies on the Black Sea. Archaeologists argue over whether Troy VI or Troy VII was the city of Priam which engaged in the Trojan War. Most go for Troy VI, arguing that the bad earthquake which brought down the walls in 1250 BC hastened the Achaean victory.

Troy VII lasted from 1250 to 1050 BC. The Achaeans may have burned the city in 1240 BC; an invading Balkan people moved in around 1190 BC and Troy sank into a torpor for four centuries. It was revived as a Greek city (Troy VIII, 700-85 BC) and then as a Roman one (Troy IX, 85 BC-500 AD). At one point Constantine the Great thought of building his new eastern Roman capital here, but he chose Byzantium instead. As a Byzantine town, Troy didn't amount to much.

In Homer's *Iliad*, Troy was the town of Ilium. The Trojan War took place in the 13th century BC, with Agamemnon, Achilles,

Odysseus (Ulysses), Patroclus and Nestor on the Achaean (Greek) side, and Priam with his sons Hector and Paris on the Trojan side. Rather than suggesting commercial rivalries as a cause for the war, Homer claimed that Paris had kidnapped the beautiful Helen from her husband Menelaus, King of Sparta (his reward for giving the golden apple for most beautiful woman to Aphrodite, goddess of love), and the king asked the Achaeans to help him get her back.

During the decade-long war, Hector killed Patroclus and Achilles killed Hector. Paris knew that Achilles' mother had dipped her son in the River Styx to make him invincible. However, to do so she held him by his heel, the one part of his body that remained unprotected. Hence Paris shot Achilles in the heel and bequeathed a phrase to the English language.

When 10 years of carnage couldn't end the war, Odysseus came up with the idea of the wooden horse filled with soldiers, against which Cassandra warned the Trojans in vain. It was left outside the west gate for the Trojans to wheel inside the walls.

One theory has it that the earthquake of 1250 BC gave the Achaeans the break they needed, bringing down Troy's formidable walls and allowing them to battle their way into the city. In gratitude to Poseidon, the Earth-Shaker, they built a monumental wooden statue of his horse. So there may well have been a real Trojan horse, even though Homer's account is less than fully historical.

The last people to live here were Turkish soldiers and their families, subjects of the emir of Karası, in the 14th century. After them, the town disappeared.

Ruins of Troy

The *gişe* (booth) where you buy your admission ticket (US$2, plus US$1 per car) is 500m before the site. The ruins are open from 8 am to 5 pm daily.

A huge replica of the wooden Trojan horse catches your eye as you approach Troy – it should, as it was put here so you'd have something distinctive to photograph. Before that, visitors used to complain that Troy lacked anything eye-catching.

The **Kazı Evi** (Excavation House) to the right of the path was used by earlier archaeological teams. Today it holds exhibits on work in progress. The models and superimposed pictures should help you understand what Troy looked like at different points in its history. There's a small bookshop on the other side of the path.

The identifiable structures at Troy are marked by explanatory signs: the walls from various periods, including one of the five oldest still standing in the world are especially interesting; the **bouleuterion** (council chamber) built at about Homer's time (circa 800 BC); the **stone ramp** from Troy II; and the **Temple of Athena** from Troy VIII, rebuilt by the Romans.

The replica wooden horse, made famous in Homer's *Iliad*, greets tourists at the entrance of the ruins of Troy.

Don't miss the beautiful views of the Troad, particularly over towards the straits. On a clear day you can see the **Çanakkale Martyrs' Memorial** on the far shore, and ships passing through the Dardanelles. You can almost imagine the Achaean fleet beached on the Troad's shores, ready to begin a battle that would be remembered over 3000 years later.

Tevfikiye

Facing the gates to the archaeological site are a hotel, drinks stand, restaurants, souvenir shops, and replicas of Schliemann's cabin and the Trojan treasure. The relics of two old restaurants opposite the Hotel Hisarlık are slated to become a museum.

Most visitors stay in Çanakkale and visit Troy in passing, leaving their gear at the ticket office or at a restaurant. However, the atmosphere of Tevfikiye village, spreading out 500m to the north of the gates is a pleasant change from the hassle of Çanakkale. If you decide to stay, ***Deniz Pansiyon***, in a quiet street at the heart of the village (follow the signs), is tidy and relatively cheap at US$12 for two in a waterless room; you may have to ask around for the key. ***Varol Pansiyon***, above a teashop next to the mosque, would be a very poor second choice.

Hotel Hisarlık *(☎ 286-283 1126)*, opposite the site gates, has straightforward rooms with showers named after characters from Greek myths but is a bit overpriced at US$20/30 a single/double. The ***restaurant*** below is a bus tour favourite. If you come alone you might prefer to eat at the ***Priamos Restaurant*** next door. You are also permitted to camp in the grounds for US$2 per person.

Getting There & Away

For minibuses to Tevfikiye and Troy from Çanakkale, walk straight inland from the ferry docks and turn right onto Atatürk Caddesi, the Troy road; the dolmuş station is several hundred metres along by a small bridge, about 1km from the docks. Dolmuşes go to Troy (30km, 35 minutes, US$1.50) every 30 to 60 minutes in high summer.

Consider taking a tour because a good guide can bring the ruins of Troy to life in a way that's difficult for the casual visitor. Contact Troy-Anzac Tours (☎ 286-217 5847, 217 5049, fax 217 0196), Saat Kulesi Meydanı 6, in Çanakkale.

If you plan to visit Troy and then head south, buy a ticket on a southbound bus a day in advance. Let the ticket seller know you want to be picked up at Troy, do your sightseeing, then be out on the main highway in plenty of time to catch the bus. Without a ticket, you can hitch out to the highway from Troy and hope a bus with vacant seats comes by. This often works, though it entails some waiting and uncertainty.

If you're coming from the south, ask to be let out on the highway at the access road to Troy, which is 4.5km north of the big Geyikli/Çimento Fabrikası crossroads. From the highway it's 5km west to Troy. Hitch, or wait for a dolmuş (infrequent except in high summer).

ÇANAKKALE TO ASSOS (BEHRAMKALE)

Heading south from Çanakkale and Troy on the main highway (as the buses do), there's little reason to stop until you reach the town of **Ayvacık** (population 6000), from where dolmuşes run 19km west to Behramkale. If you have your own transport, consider taking a much more interesting side road through the western part of the Biga Peninsula, which takes you to little-visited minor ruins and beaches which are good for camping.

Some 4.5km south of the Troy road is a narrow, paved road heading west and marked for Alexandria Troas and Apollo Smintheon. After passing the cement factory the road proceeds south-west to the small towns of Geyikli and Oduniskelesi, 24km along, has a few simple restaurants and basic hotels.

Bozcaada

Bozcaada, formerly known as Tenedos, has always been known to Anatolian oenophiles for its wines (Dimitrakopulo, Doruk, Talay) and to soldiers for its defences. A big medieval fortress towers over the north-eastern tip of the island, and vineyards blanket its sunny slopes. The island has the advantage of being small (about 5-6km across) and easy to explore, and the disadvantage of being too small to host much accommodation. Rooms and beds are usually filled by İstanbullus in summer, so advance bookings are essential unless you're only staying for the day.

Ferries depart from the mainland village of Yükyeri İskelesi, 5km west of Geyikli, south of Troy; look for the access road (and a sign) in Geyikli. Boats depart in the morning and afternoon for US$0.75 per passenger, US$10 per car. There may be additional boat services in high summer.

There's actually not much to do on the island, so you may want to make it a day trip. Poke around the enormous fortress, then hike across the island to the beaches for a dip.

Alexandria Troas

About 5km south of Oduniskelesi the road passes through the widely scattered ruins of Alexandria Troas near the village of Dalyan. (Some signs read 'Alexandria (Truva)', but this is not Troy.)

Antigonus, one of Alexander the Great's generals, took control of this land after the collapse of the Alexandrian empire and founded the city of Antigoneia in 310 BC in his own honour. He was later defeated in battle by Lysimachus, another of Alexander's generals, who took the city and renamed it in honour of his late commander. An earthquake later destroyed much of the city.

Archaeologists have identified bits of the city's theatre, palace, temple, agora, baths, necropolis, harbour and city walls amid the farmers' fields. But for most visitors Alexandria Troas is more about atmosphere, a place which, like so in Turkey, conjures up that feeling of great antiquity slowly disappearing beneath the grinding wheels of time.

Dolmuşes run infrequently between Ezine, on the main highway, and Dalyan. Don't make a special trip, but if you pass by, it's worth pausing to climb a ruined wall for the view.

Neandria When Antigonus founded the city of Antigoneia, he forced the inhabitants of nearby Neandria, settled around 700 BC, to populate his new city. The ruins of Neandria, 1.5km north-east of the village of Kayacık and 500m inland from the sea, offer nothing to the casual visitor today, but archaeologists have discovered the oldest Aeolian temple with a clearly distinguishable plan.

Gülpınar

Just 3km south of Alexandria Troas are the **hot springs of Kestanbol Kaplıcaları** (13km south of Geyikli), with a small bathhouse. Continue south 32km to Gülpınar, a small farming town with no services beyond a fuel station. This was once the ancient city of Khrysa, famous for its Ionic temple to Apollo and mice. Cretan colonists who came to this area had been told by an oracle that they should settle where they were attacked by 'the sons of the earth'. They awoke to find mice chewing their equipment, so they settled here and built a temple to the 'Lord of the Mice' (Smintheion). The **Apollo Smintheion**, 400m down a steep hill from the centre of the town, has some bits of marble column on top of a short flight of steps. The cult statue of the god, now disappeared, once had marble mice carved at its feet. Reliefs on the temple's walls illustrated scenes from the *Iliad*.

Gülpınar Belediyesi buses connect Gülpınar with Çanakkale and Ayvacık.

Babakale & Akliman

In Gülpınar a road heading west is signed for Babakale (Lekton), 9km away. The road to Akliman, a coastal settlement with a nice long beach backed by olive groves, and several good, cheap camping places and motels is 3km along. About 6km further on is Babakale, with a small village clustered at the base of a ruined fortress overlooking a long sweep of sea. A new yacht and fishing harbour is being completed, and the first tourist hotels – the Karayel and Ser-Tur – have been opened, with undoubtedly many more to follow. Some İstanbullus have already fixed up stone village houses (and one windmill) as villas.

From Gülpınar the road east to Behramkale (25km) passes through several small villages. From some of these, unpaved roads head down to the shore where there's sure to be a beach shack with a primitive toilet and perhaps fresh water for the ever-increasing number of camper-van owners who have discovered this road.

ASSOS (BEHRAMKALE)

Called Assos in ancient times, the ruins and village of Behramkale share a gorgeous setting, overlooking the Aegean and the nearby island of Lesbos (Mytileni or Midilli; MEE-dee-lee in Turkish).

It's 73km from Çanakkale along the main highway (E87/D550) to Ayvacık (not to be confused with nearby Ayvalık), a bus ride of under two hours. From Ayvacık, sporadic dolmuşes run the 19km to Behramkale, and hitching is often possible.

Assos makes a brave sight as you approach, its craggy summit surrounded by huge remnants of a mighty wall. The main part of the village and the acropolis ruins are perched at the top, but down the far (sea) side of the hill at the *iskele* (wharf), a tiny cluster of stone buildings clings to the cliff in a romantic and unlikely setting. There's a short, narrow pebble beach. For many kilometres of wider beach head on to **Kadırga**, 4km to the east.

History

In its long history, Assos has flourished as a port, agricultural town and centre for Platonic learning.

The Mysian city of Assos was founded in the 8th century BC by colonists from Lesbos, who later built its great temple to Athena in 530 BC. The city enjoyed its greatest prosperity and renown under the rule of Hermeias, a one-time student of Plato who also ruled the Troad and Lesbos. Hermeias encouraged philosophers and savants to live in Assos; Aristotle lived here from 348 to 345 BC and ended up marrying Hermeias' niece, Pythia. Assos' glory days came to an end with the advent of the Persians, who tortured Hermeias to death.

Alexander the Great drove the Persians out, but Assos' importance was challenged by the ascendancy of Alexandria Troas to the north. From 241 to 133 BC, the city was ruled by the kings of Pergamum.

St Paul visited Assos briefly during his third missionary journey through Asia Minor (53-57 AD), walking here from Alexandria Troas to meet St Luke and others before taking a boat to Lesbos.

In Byzantine times the city dwindled to a village, which it has remained ever since. Excavations of the ruins continue. Tourists, both Turkish and foreign, crowd the iskele, and the local people plough their fields and tend their olive trees, awaiting the day when a developer will buy their land at a fat price and make them rich.

Things to See

As you approach the village there's a fine **Ottoman hump-back bridge**, built in the 14th century, to the left of the road. Shortly afterwards, you'll come to a crossroads; the road left leads to the beach at Kadırga, the road right to the modern village of Behramkale and on to Gülpınar. Continue until you reach a fork in the road. Go left (uphill) for the old village, or right (downhill) to see the massive city walls, necropolis and iskele.

Taking the village road, you wind up to a small square with a few shops and restaurants. Continue upwards, and you'll come to a small square with a teahouse and a bust of Atatürk. At the very top of the hill there's a spectacular view, which you can enjoy after fending off villagers eager to sell you embroidery and woollen socks.

The **Murad Hüdavendigar Camii**, the 14th century mosque beside the entrance to the ruins, is a simple pre-Ottoman work – a dome on squinches set on top of a square room – accomplished before Turks and Turkish architects had conquered Constantinople and assimilated the lessons of Sancta Sophia. The lintel above the entrance bears Greek inscriptions, a reminder that the Byzantine emperor was still on his throne when this mosque was built with parts permanently borrowed from a 6th century church.

The principal sight on top of the hill (altitude 228m) is the **Temple of Athena**, built in Doric style, and now partly reconstructed. Its short, tapered columns with plain capitals are hardly elegant, and the concrete reconstruction (and rusting scaffolding) hurts more than helps. But the site and the view out to Lesbos are, as with so many ancient cities, spectacular and well worth the admission fee.

Ringing the hill are stretches of the **city walls**, among the most impressive classical fortifications in Turkey. Scramble down the hillside to find the **necropolis**, or cemetery. Assos' sarcophagi ('flesh-eaters') were famous: according to Pliny the stone itself was caustic and 'ate' the flesh off the deceased in 40 days. There are also remains of a **theatre** and **basilica**. An exit gate emerges on the block-paved road which winds down the cliff side to the iskele, the most picturesque spot in Behramkale.

Entrance to the site costs US$1.50. It's open from 8 am to 5 pm (7 pm in summer).

Places to Stay

In high summer, virtually all accommodation is *yarım pansiyon* (half-pension, ie breakfast and dinner). Room prices are 35% lower in the off season (April, May and October), when you may be able to wriggle out of the half-pension requirement; the double room which costs US$60 (with two meals) in August may be priced as low as US$25 in early October. The hotels in the iskele are all atmospheric old stone buildings right next to the sea.

Places to Stay – Budget

Most of the cheaper accommodation is in the picturesque old village where the pensions include the very simple ***Athena Pansiyon***, ***Sidar Pansiyon*** *(☎ 286-721 7047)* and, near the top of the hill, ***Halıcı Han Pansiyon***. All charge what the traffic will bear; usually about US$12 for a waterless double in summer. At other times you may find them closed.

The newer ***Dolunay Pension*** *(☎ 286-721 7172)* has a few simple rooms set round a stone courtyard, with a restaurant attached. It charges US$20 for a double room with bath but no breakfast.

In the iskele, cheaper rooms can be found at ***Plaj Pansiyon*** *(☎ 286-721 7593)* and ***Hotel Mehtap*** *(☎ 286-321 7221)*, at the far end of the quay behind the Hotel Assos.

Camping The cheapest option here is to camp in the olive groves just inland where the few primitive ***camping grounds*** charge about US$2 per person.

Dost Camping *(☎ 286-721 7096)* has inviting pitches among the fig and olive trees for US$5.50 (two persons in a tent) and a vine-shaded restaurant. ***Şen Camping*** below it is second-best.

There are many more ***camping grounds*** among beachfront olive groves at Kadırga, 4km to the east, and beyond it along the road which ultimately rejoins the coastal highway at Küçükkuyu.

Places to Stay – Mid-Range

Assos Harbour In summer expect to pay around US$40/60 a single/double with half-board at any of the following hotels.

Hotel Yıldız Saray *(☎ 286-721 7025, fax 721 7169)*, on the left as you enter the harbour, is set back from the quay but has cosy rooms with partial sea views. Some rooms have stone chimneys and bathtubs.

First of the places on the quay as you turn left is ***Behram Hotel*** *(☎ 286-721 7016, fax 721 7044)* which has comfortable, simple rooms with old bathrooms. Next along on a corner of the harbour is ***Hotel Assos*** *(☎ 286-721 7017, fax 721 7249)*, which has comfy air-con rooms, a few with balconies, and some with sea views on two sides.

Immediately behind the Hotel Assos is ***Hotel Assos Kervansaray*** *(☎ 286-721 7093, fax 721 7200)*, perhaps the most popular place and beautifully kept, with a swimming pool, sauna and courtyard restaurant.

Up an alarming wooden ladder, ***Assos Şen Pansiyon*** *(☎ 286-721 7076)*, behind the Ikun Ev, has a roof restaurant with marvellous views and interesting architectural information on the Assos ruins. The rooms are only pansiyon quality in terms of their furnishings, but that doesn't mean prices fall much below the US$50 price tag for half-board in high summer.

Turn right instead of left along the harbour and you'll come to ***Hotel Nazlıhan*** *(☎ 286-721 7064, fax 721 7387)*, beyond the *jandarma* (police) post and encompassing two restored stone houses. The rooms are quite small but imaginatively decorated, with İznik-style tiles in the bathrooms. Rates are US$45/60 a single/double with sea view, slightly less without.

Kadırga There are many more hotels on the beach at Kadırga, 4km east, though reaching them is difficult without your own wheels.

Troy Otel *(☎ 286-721 7154, fax 721 7241)* has four-star comforts for US$70 a double, breakfast and dinner included. ***Yeni Yıldız Saray*** *(☎ 286-721 7204)* offers air-con and an American Bar for the same US$50 it charges for a double at Behramkale Harboure.

Several kilometres further east, perched on a terrace overlooking the sea, ***Assos Terrace Motel*** *(☎ 286-762 9885, fax 762 9884)* has comfortable rooms with excellent views for US$40 a double with two meals.

Places to Eat

If you can get out of paying for half-board it's fun to pop around the hotels, trying their different restaurants. If you're not paying half-board, be sure to check prices carefully, especially for fish and bottles of wine. Most of the hotels serve excellent evening meals, although breakfasts are pretty mundane, especially for the high summer prices.

Otherwise, Dost Camping's ***restaurant*** is one of the cheapest options, and quite pleasant. The ***Assos Antik Restaurant***, just inland from Hotel Assos, serves *gözleme* (thin pastry folded over a filling) and *mantı* (ravioli). The fancy ***Fenerli Han Restaurant***, beside the Nazlıhan Hotel, has a beautiful harbourside setting and a set-price dinner for about US$10, plus drinks and tip.

Ikun Ev is a cool place to wind up the evening with a drink.

If you're on a budget, you'll need to walk up to the old village where the ***Cengiz Lokantası*** will serve you dinner for a more reasonable US$7.

Getting There & Away

Dolmuşes depart from Ayvacık for Behramkale hourly in high summer although some only run as far as the old village, leaving you to trek down to the harbour with your baggage or barter for an unofficial, and costly, 'taxi'.

In the off season, dolmuşes run much less frequently and you can have trouble getting away from the village. If you visit during the off season, which is highly advisable, get to Ayvacık as early in the day as you can to catch a dolmuş (US$0.75). If you miss the last one, Ayvacık has a couple of hotels, or a taxi driver may be talked into running you down to the harbour for around US$12.

ASSOS TO AYVALIK

The road east from Behramkale and Kadırga follows the coast to rejoin the main coastal highway at Küçükkuyu, then continues round the Bay of Edremit. Along the way at **Altınoluk** the highway passes a motley collection of hotels, motels and beachfront eateries which, though right on the water, are subject to road noise. Seaside accommodation is somewhat better at **Akçay** and **Ören**, off the highway. At Akçay there's a fine 5km-long beach featuring sulphur springs. The beach at Ören stretches for 9km.

Inland is the farming centre of **Edremit** (population 37,000), called Adramyttium in classical times. There's nothing to draw you today except that it's an important transport hub; coming from Ayvacık to Ayvalık you may well have to change in Edremit which is also served by frequent buses to Balıkesir. Ayvalık, your most likely destination, is 130km (over two hours) south-east of Behramkale and 110km (two hours) south-east of Ayvacık, by road.

AYVALIK

Across a narrow strait from the island of Lesbos, Ayvalık ('quince-orchard'; population 30,000) is a seaside resort, fishing town, olive oil and soap-making centre, and a terminus for boats to and from Greece. The coast here is cloaked in pine forests and olive orchards, the offshore waters sprinkled with 23 islands.

Now about 350 years old, Ayvalık was inhabited by Ottoman Greeks until after WWI. During the exchange of minority populations between Greece and Turkey in the 1920s, Ayvalık's Turkish-speaking Greeks went to Greece, and Greek-speaking Turks came here from Lesbos, the Balkans and Crete. A few locals still speak some Greek, and most of the local mosques are converted Orthodox churches. The **Saatli Camii**, or Mosque with a Clock, was once the church of Agios Yannis (St John); the **Çınarlı Camii** used to be the Agios Yorgos (St George) church.

Orientation & Information

Ayvalık is small and manageable but with a few inconveniences: the otogar is 1.5km north of the town centre and the Tourism Information Office (☎/fax 266-312 2122) is 1km south of the main square around the curve of the bay, across from the yacht harbour. In summer a small kiosk on the waterfront at the southern side of the main square is staffed by Ayvalık Tourism Association personnel.

A few kilometres further to the south are Çamlık and Orta Çamlık, with a scattering of pensions and camping areas popular with holidaying Turks. Sarımsaklı Plaj (Garlic Beach), also known as Küçükköy or Plajlar (The Beaches) is 8km south of the centre. Packed with hotels, motels and pensions, Sarımsaklı is very much package-holiday territory. Alibey Adası (Alibey Island) is about 8km north-west of Ayvalık centre by road although it's more pleasant going by boat.

The White Knight Tourist Bazaar behind the statue of Atatürk on the waterfront sells the *Turkish Daily News* and some foreign newspapers.

Ayvalık's postal code is 10400.

Alibey Adası

Alibey Adası, called Cunda (JOON-dah) by locals, is the island visible across the bay which boasts abandoned, ruinous Greek churches, seaside restaurants in old stone houses, and hundreds of condominiums. Two causeways link the island to tiny Lale Adası and the mainland; you can get there by city bus (US$0.30) or taxi (US$8) at any time of the year, although this isn't as much fun as taking the boats which depart in summer from the centre of town near the Ayvalık Tourism Society kiosk (15 minutes, US$0.50).

The northern part of the island forms the **Patrica Nature Reserve**, with ruins of an ancient Greek temple and a Genoese watch tower.

Things to See & Do

The quay is crowded with day-cruisers eager to take you on a daytime or evening sail around the dozens of islands in the bay. Competition is fierce in high summer, with most cruises priced at US$6 to US$8 including a meal.

As you walk along the quayside you'll also find people advertising six-hour excursions to **local villages** for US$12 per person.

Another goal for excursions is **Şeytan Sofrası** (Devil's Dinner table), a hilltop south of the town, offering magnificent views and a snack stand. The only regular dolmuş goes up there just before sunset. Otherwise you'll have to walk, hitch (unlikely) or take a taxi.

Places to Stay

There are plenty of cheap, convenient hotels in the town centre. Pensions, camping areas and hotels also line the road 8km south to Sarımsaklı Plaj, where there are numerous beach resort hotels. Prices are highest in July and August; at other times, look around for discounts.

Places to Stay – Budget

The most interesting is ***Taksiyarhis Pansiyon*** *(☎ 266-312 1494, İsmetpaşa Mahallesi, Mareşal Çakmak Caddesi 71)*, a renovated Ottoman house, five-minutes walk east of the

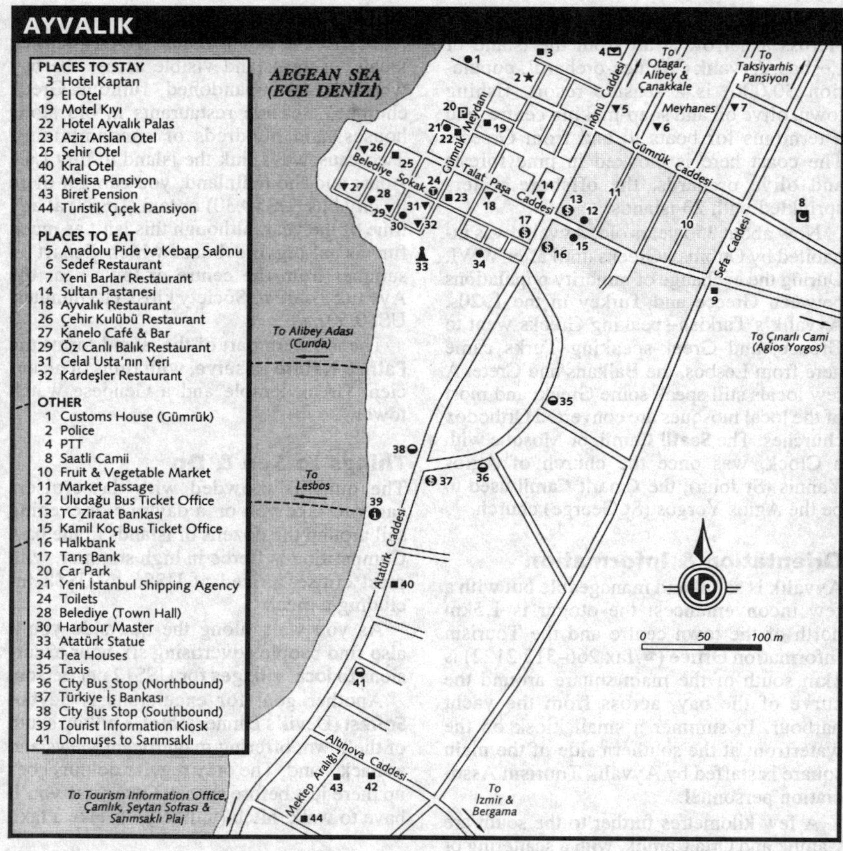

PTT behind the former Taxiarkhis church. The hand-painted signs are difficult to spot – if you get stuck, phone from the PTT. The owners (he's Austrian, she's Turkish) lovingly restored the priest's house, with five guest rooms, two shared bathrooms, two terraces, wonderful views and a kitchen for guests' use. At just US$5 per person plus US$2 for breakfast, it's often full in summer, so reserve in advance if possible. By the time you read this, another 10 rooms should be available in the adjacent house.

The extremely faded ***Turistik Çiçek Pansiyon*** *(☎ 266-312 1201)*, on Mektep Aralığı, is about 200m south of the main square, just off the main road. Very basic rooms with showers cost US$4 per person without breakfast. ***Biret Pansiyon*** *(☎ 266-312 2175)*, at the other end of Mektep Aralığı, and ***Melisa Pansiyon*** *(☎ 266-312 6584)* around the corner take the overflow.

A few small, cheap, old-style hotels lurk in the warren of streets just north of the main square. The cheapest of them is the noisy ***Şehir Oteli***, again charging around US$4 per person.

El Otel *(☎ 266-312 2217, Vehbibey Mahallesi, Sefa Caddesi 3)* is one long block east of the main street near the main square, in the midst of the market. It's a clean, no-frills place, run by God-fearing types who will rent you a room with shower for US$5 per person.

The renovated ***Motel Kıyı*** *(☎ 266-312 6677, Gümrük Meydanı 18)*, charges US$8 per person for small rooms with shower but without breakfast. Front rooms have water views.

Camping The best camping is on Alibey Adası, with the pitches located inconveniently – but quietly – outside the village. The ubiquitously advertised ***Ada Camp*** *(☎ 266-312 1211)* is 3km to the west, as are ***Ortunü Hidden Paradise*** and ***Cunda Motel-Camping***.

At the southern end of Çamlık, on the way to Sarımsaklı Plaj, there's a pleasant national forest camping ground ***(Orman Kampı)*** and several private camping grounds.

Places to Stay – Mid-Range

For more comfort at higher prices, try the defiantly modern ***Hotel Ayvalık Palas*** *(☎ 266-312 1064, fax 312 1046)*, Gümrük Meydanı, which charges US$16 per person with shower, TV and breakfast. A diving centre operates out of the hotel. The nearby 20-room ***Aziz Arslan Otel*** *(☎ 266-312 5331, fax 312 6888)* is a good choice, offering spacious doubles with TV, balcony and clean bathroom for US$24, including breakfast.

The new ***Hotel Kaptan*** *(☎ 266-312 8834)*, Balıkhane Sokak, charges US$25 for doubles whose wallpaper looks more suited to England than Turkey. Despite its harbourside position, only three rooms have sea views.

As you head south from the main square you'll come to ***Kral Otel*** *(☎ 266-312 2102, fax 312 1671)*, above some shops at Sahil Boyu 26. this place is pleasantly new, with smallish rooms for US$16 per person. The breakfast room has enticing views of the harbour.

Alibey Adası ***Günay Motel*** *(☎ 266-327 1048)*, set back from the waterfront, is quiet, simple and reasonably priced at US$12/18 for a single/double with shower but no breakfast. ***Artur*** *(☎ 266-327 1014)* restaurant also has a few rooms but they're likely to be noisy.

Sarımsaklı These days it's hard to recommend staying at Sarımsaklı Plaj, where buildings are being thrown up willy-nilly inland from an unexceptional beach without the infrastructure to go with them. If you do want to stay, the more long-standing hotels include the 102 room ***Otel Ankara*** *(☎ 266-324 1048, fax 324 0022)*, the modern 112-room ***Büyük Berk Oteli*** *(☎ 266-324 1045, fax 324 1194)*, and the fancier ***Hotel Club Berk*** and ***Hotel Zeytinci*** (both sharing the same phone as Büyük Berk).

Beside the Ankara, the new ***Kalif Hotel*** *(☎ 266-324 1494)* is highly recommended for its very comfortable rooms with bath.

Places to Stay – Top End

Alibey Adası Tiny Lale Adası on the road to Alibey Adası is dominated by the four-star ***Hotel Florium*** *(☎ 266-312 9628, fax 312 9631)* where comfortable double rooms cost US$75 with breakfast.

Sarımsaklı At the western end of the beach, not far from the north-south highway, the five-star, 164 room ***Grand Temizel*** *(☎ 266-324 2000, fax 324 1274)* is the class act; its rooms equipped with satellite TV, minibars, air-con, balconies and even hair dryers. Water sports, six bars and a disco, a health club and casino – all the services are yours for US$90/110 a single/double, breakfast included. One reader complained it was noisy though.

Places to Eat

Ayvalık Most restaurants put out signboards listing prices, at least in the busy summer months, but it's still wise to be careful when ordering fish.

The narrow streets north of the harbour have lots of small, simple restaurants with

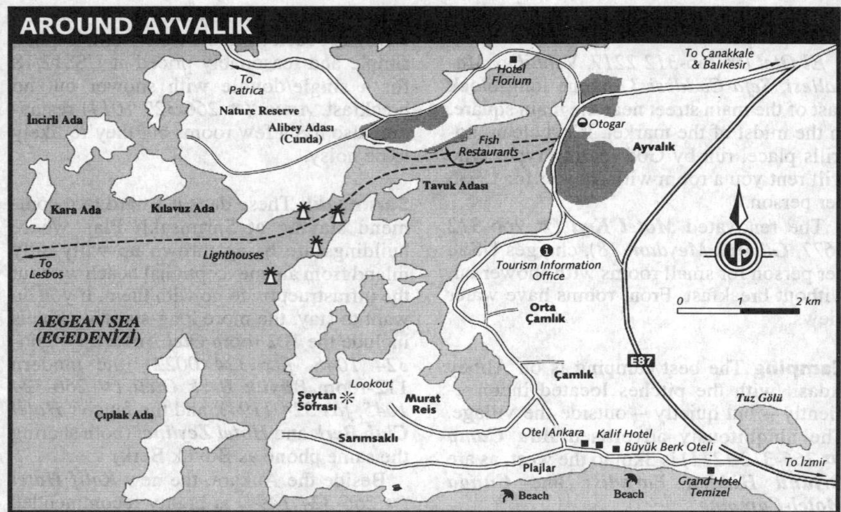

good food and low prices. ***Ayvalık Restaurant*** has good soups and stews which, with bread, make a filling meal for US$3 or so; kebaps cost around US$1.50. ***Celal Usta'nın Yeri*** is similar. ***Osmanlı Mutfağı*** at Eminzade İşhanı 21 next to the Hotel Ayvalık Palas serves meat dishes for US$2, with vegetable stews for slightly less. ***Anadolu Pide ve Kebap Salonu*** at İnönü Caddesi 33 serves Turkish pizza for about US$2. ***Sultan Pastanesi*** is good for biscuits or pastries.

In the market to the east of İnönü Caddesi the ***Yeni Barlar*** and ***Sedef*** restaurants are popular with locals who can be found tucking into kebaps and good cheap bain-marie fare 24 hours a day. Nearby, the narrow market streets harbour various ***meyhanes***, the Turkish equivalent of tavernas, patronised by local men. They have good food and lots of drinks at non-tourist prices.

Pricier fish restaurants ring the waterfront. Here you'll find the ***Öz Canlı Balık*** and ***Kardeşler*** restaurants, with spacious, airy dining rooms and nicely lit terraces with sea views. A full dinner will cost you between US$10 and US$12 per person for meat, and more for fish, drinks included. At the far end of the quay is ***Kanelo Café & Bar***, a good place for a drink while you watch the sun set.

Alibey Adası Taking the boat to Alibey Adası for lunch or dinner is a favoured pastime. Expect to spend around US$12 to US$18 per person for a full seafood dinner with wine.

The promenade is all restaurants, with indoor tables in old stone houses and outdoor tables lining the quay. In general, those further east are a bit cheaper, but it's easy to check as they all have signboards with prices. In the off season, it's best to patronise the busiest one because it will have the freshest food. Even though it's fun to come across on the boats, coming by bus means you avoid arriving en masse with others and might get better service.

Pizza Veranda offers an alternative to seafood and ***Taşkahve*** is a pleasant waterside place for a cuppa.

Getting There & Away

Bus Ayvalık is served by the frequent bus services running up and down the Aegean

TOM BROSNAHAN

North Aegean All the grandeur and elegance of restored Ottoman-era houses in Alsancak, İzmir.

PETER PTSCHELINZEW

JON DAVISON

South Aegean **Top:** The crystal clear waters at Kumbahce Bay, Bodrum. **Bottom:** The necropolis of ancient Hierapolis near Pamukkale stretches for several kilometres and contains striking tombs.

coast between Çanakkale and İzmir. If you're on a main intercity service you'll probably be dropped off and have to hitch in from the highway. See Getting Around in this section.

When leaving Ayvalık, it's often easiest to buy a ticket from the otogar to Edremit and transfer there to services for Çanakkale rather than have to make your way back out to the highway to pick up one of the long-distance services. You can buy a ticket at the bus company offices in the main square. Check departure times and availability early in the day as few buses depart in the evening. Here are details of services from Ayvalık to:

Balıkesir – 104km, 2½ hours, US$3.50; frequent
Behramkale (Assos, via Ayvacık) – 130km, over two hours, US$6; a few buses to Ayvacık, or change at Edremit
Bergama – 50km, 45 minutes, US$3; many buses to highway junction, a few into town
Bursa – 300km, 4½ hours, US$7; a dozen daily, continuing to İstanbul or Ankara
Çanakkale – 200km, 3½ hours, US$8; many to highway, or change at Edremit
Edremit – 56km, 30 minutes, US$1.50; frequent minibuses
İzmir – 240km, 3½ hours, US$3; many to highway, or change at Edremit

Boat The passage by sea between Ayvalık and Lesbos is now so expensive (US$50 one-way, US$65 same-day round trip) that few people use it. If you're coming from Greece (ie not returning to Turkey after a day trip), you must also pay an outrageous 5000-drachma Greek port tax. Turkish boats make the two-hour voyage to Lesbos on Tuesday, Thursday and Saturday at 9 am in summer (sporadic services at other times). Usually you must buy your ticket and hand over your passport for paperwork a day in advance of the voyage, whether you're departing from Turkey or from Greece.

For information and tickets, contact one of the shipping agencies in the warren of streets north and west of the main square, including the Yeni İstanbul Shipping Agency (☎ 266-312 6123) and the Jale Ayvalık Tur Shipping Agency (☎ 266-312 2740, fax 312 2470).

Getting Around

Buses along the highway will drop you at the northern turn-off for Ayvalık, exactly 5km from the centre, unless the company specifically designates Ayvalık otogar as a stop. From the highway you must hitch into town; drivers readily understand your situation and stop to give you a lift.

If you're dropped in town, it will be at the Şehirlerarası Otobüs Garajı (Intercity Bus Garage), which is 1.5km (15 or 20 minutes' walk) north of the main square. City buses marked 'Ayvalık Belediyesi' run all the way through the town and will carry you from the bus station to the main square, south to the Tourism Information Office, and further south to Çamlık, Orta Çamlık and Sarımsaklı, for US$0.30. A taxi from the otogar to the town centre costs US$2.

Minibuses (US$0.35) depart for the beaches from the fifth side street south of the main square.

DİKİLİ

Travelling 41km south from Ayvalık along the coast road, a road on the right leads to Dikili (population 20,000), 4km west of the coastal highway, and 30km west of Bergama. A wharf capable of serving ocean liners brings the occasional Aegean cruise ship to Dikili to see the ruins at Bergama but mostly Dikili is a summer resort for families from İstanbul and İzmir.

The town's main beach (of dark, coarse sand) starts about 600m north of the main square and goes west for about 1km. The PTT is a few steps north of the main square, towards the beach. The otogar is 400m north of the main square.

Places to Stay

Özdemir Pansiyon** (☎ 232-671 1295),* 100m north of the main square along the main street, is good if you expect to spend only a night or two and want to do it cheaply; likewise ***Güneş Pansiyon** (☎ 232-671 1847),* a bit further north then east (inland) 100m (follow the signs). Both charge about US$6 per person. ***Dikili Pansiyon, further north and a bit inland (there

NORTH AEGEAN TURKEY

are no street names in this new section yet) is much newer, and costs just a bit more.

For three-star comforts, try ***Ümmetoğlu Dikili Hotel*** *(☎ 232-671 9030)* right beside the otogar.

Getting There & Away

Although there are direct buses between İzmir and Dikili via Çandarlı, most long-distance bus traffic goes via Bergama. Take one of the frequent minibuses to Bergama (35 minutes, US$1.25) for connections with more distant points.

BERGAMA (PERGAMUM)

Modern Bergama (BEHR-gah-mah; population 50,000), in the province of İzmir, is a sleepy agricultural market town in the midst of a well-watered plain. There has been a town here since Trojan times, but Pergamum's heyday was during the period between Alexander the Great and the Roman domination of all Asia Minor. At that time, Pergamum was one of the Middle East's richest and most powerful small kingdoms.

History

Pergamum owes its prosperity to Lysimachus, one of Alexander the Great's generals, and his downfall. Lysimachus controlled much of the Aegean region when Alexander's far-flung empire fell apart after his death in 323 BC. In the battles over the spoils Lysimachus captured a great treasure, which he secured in Pergamum before going off to fight Seleucus for control of Asia Minor. But Lysimachus lost and was killed in 281 BC, whereupon Philetarus, the commander he had posted at Pergamum to protect the treasure, set himself up nicely as governor.

Philetarus was a eunuch, but he was succeeded by his nephew Eumenes I (263-241 BC), and Eumenes was followed by his adopted son Attalus I (241-197 BC). Attalus took the title of king, expanded his power and made an alliance with Rome. He was succeeded by his son Eumenes II (197-159 BC), and that's when the fun began.

Eumenes II was the man who really built Pergamum. Rich and powerful, he added the library and the Altar of Zeus to the hilltop city, and built the 'middle city' on terraces halfway down the hill. He also expanded and beautified the already famous medical centre of the Asclepion.

The Pergamum of Eumenes II is remembered most of all for its library. Said to have held more than 200,000 volumes, it was a symbol of Pergamum's social and cultural climb. Eumenes was a passionate book collector; and his library came to challenge the world's greatest in Alexandria (700,000 books). The Egyptians were afraid Pergamum and its library would attract famous scholars away from Alexandria, so they cut off the supply of papyrus from the Nile. Eumenes set his scientists to work, and they came up with *pergamen* (Latin for 'parchment'), a writing surface made from animal hides rather than pressed papyrus reeds.

The Egyptians were to have their revenge, however. When Eumenes died, he was succeeded by his brother Attalus II (159-138 BC). Things went pretty well for a while, but under Attalus II's son Attalus III (138-133 BC) the kingdom began falling to pieces. With no heir he willed his kingdom to Rome and the Kingdom of Pergamum became the Roman province of Asia in 129 BC.

In the early years of the Christian era the great library at Alexandria was damaged by fire. Marc Antony pillaged the library at Pergamum for books to give Cleopatra.

Orientation

Almost everything you'll need in Bergama is between the otogar to the south and the market to the north, including cheap hotels, restaurants, banks and the Arkeoloji Müzesi (Archaeology Museum). All but the cheapest hotels are located west of the otogar away from the centre towards the coastal highway.

The centre of town, for our purposes, is the Arkeoloji Müzesi on the main street, İzmir Caddesi, İzmir Yolu, Cumhuriyet Caddesi, Hükümet Caddesi, Bankalar Caddesi, or Uzun Çarşı Caddesi, depending upon whom and where you ask.

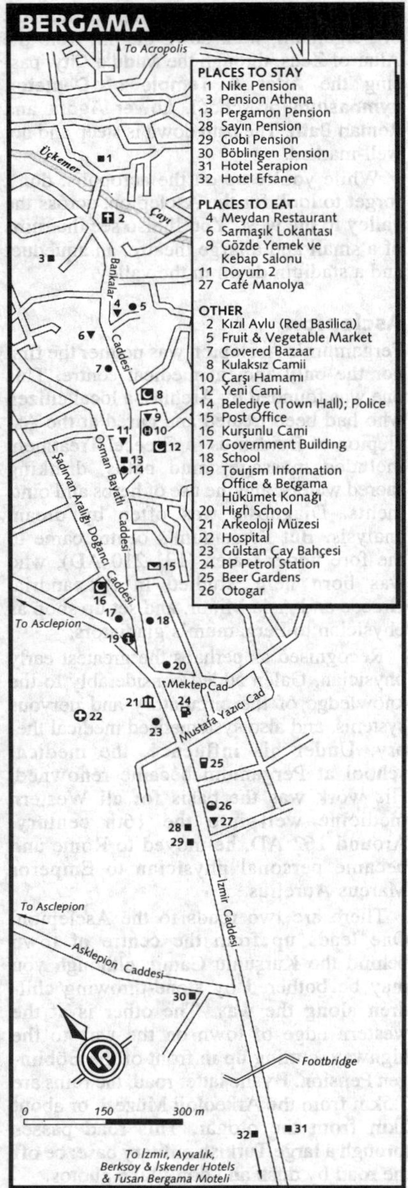

Of Bergama's four main sites, only the museum is in the centre of town. The two principal archaeological sites are several kilometres out of town in different directions and require some healthy hiking or the hire of a taxi.

Information

Bergama's Tourism Information Office (☎/fax 232-633 1862) is at İzmir Caddesi 54, midway between the bus station and the market.

The sites at the Acropolis and Asclepion both have soft drinks for sale, but no food. If you're walking, take plenty of water as you won't be able to stock up on the way.

Bergama's postal code is 35700.

Acropolis

Much of what was built by the ambitious kings of Pergamum didn't survive, but what did is impressive, dramatically sited and often beautifully restored.

The road up to the acropolis winds 6km from the museum (over 4km from the Red Basilica), around the northern and eastern sides of the hill, to a car park at the top. Next to the car park are some souvenir and refreshment stands, and a ticket seller (US$2, parking US$0.70). You can visit the acropolis any day from 9 am to 5 pm (till 7 pm in summer) but note that the road is only open from 8.30 am to 5.30 pm (till 7.30 pm in summer).

Blue dots mark a suggested route around the main structures and multilingual signboards detail what you'll see. The main structures include the **library** as well as the marble-columned **Temple of Trajan**, rebuilt by the German Archaeological Institute. This temple was built during the reigns of the emperors Trajan and Hadrian and was used to worship them as well as Zeus. It's the only Roman structure surviving on the acropolis. The foundations underneath were used as cisterns during the Middle Ages.

The vertigo-inducing, 10,000-seat **theatre** is impressive and unusual. Pergamum borrowed from Hellenistic architecture, but in the case of the theatre made major modifications.

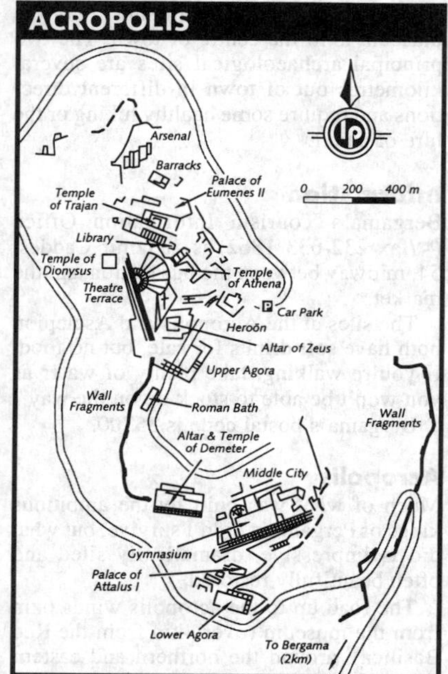

To take advantage of the spectacular view and conserve precious building space on top of the hill, the theatre was built into the hillside. Hellenistic theatres are usually wider and rounder, but because of this one's location, rounding proved impossible and it was increased in height instead.

Below the stage is the ruined **Temple of Dionysus**. The **Altar of Zeus**, south of the theatre and shaded by evergreen trees, is in an idyllic setting. Originally it was covered with magnificent friezes depicting the battle between the Olympian gods and their subterranean foes but most of this famous building was removed to Berlin by the 19th century German excavators of Pergamum (with the sultan's permission). Only the base remains.

Several piles of rubble on top of the acropolis are marked as the **Palaces of Attalus I and Eumenes II**, and there's an **agora** as well as stretches of magnificent defensive **walls**.

If you want to see everything that remains of Pergamum, walk down the hill from the Altar of Zeus, through the **Middle City**, passing the **Altar & Temple of Demeter**, **gymnasium** or school, **Lower Agora** and **Roman Bath**. The path down is steep and not well-marked.

While you're up on the acropolis, don't forget to look for the Asclepion, across the valley to the west. You'll also see the ruins of a small and a large theatre, an aqueduct and a stadium down in the valley.

Asclepion

Pergamum's Asclepion was neither the first nor the only ancient medical centre. This one was founded by Archias, a local citizen who had been treated and cured at the Asclepion of Epidaurus in Greece. Treatment included massage, mud baths, drinking sacred waters, and the use of herbs and ointments. Diagnosis was often by dream analysis. But Pergamum's centre came to the fore under Galen (131-210 AD), who was born here, studied in Alexandria, Greece and Asia Minor, and set up shop as physician to Pergamum's gladiators.

Recognised as perhaps the greatest early physician, Galen added considerably to the knowledge of the circulatory and nervous systems, and also systematised medical theory. Under his influence, the medical school at Pergamum became renowned. His work was the basis for all Western medicine well into the 16th century. Around 162 AD, he moved to Rome and became personal physician to Emperor Marcus Aurelius.

There are two roads to the Asclepion. One leads up from the centre of town behind the Kurşunlu Camii, although you may be bothered by stone-throwing children along the way. The other is at the western edge of town on the way to the highway, cutting up in front of the Böblingen Pension. By the latter road, the ruins are 3.5km from the Arkeoloji Müzesi, or about 2km from the otogar. This road passes through a large Turkish military base; be off the road by dusk and don't take photos.

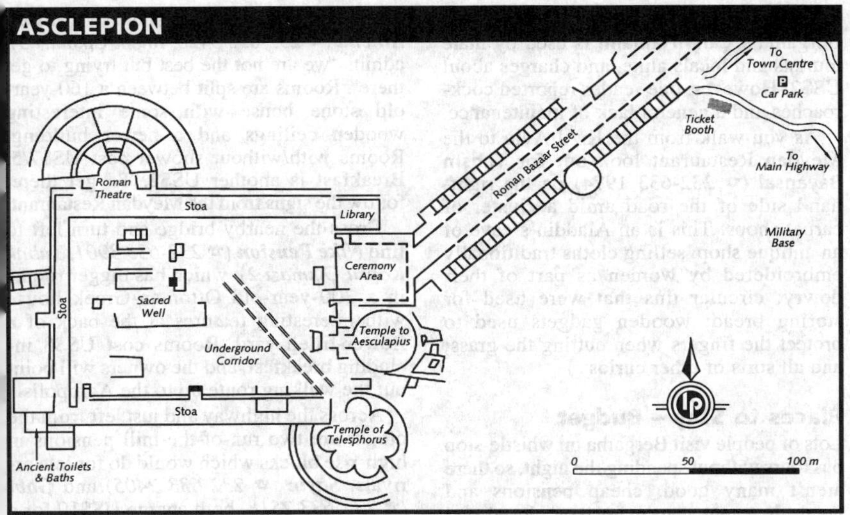

A **Roman bazaar street**, once lined with shops, leads from the car park to the centre where you'll see the base of a column carved with snakes, the symbol of Aesculapius (Asclepios), god of medicine. Just as the snake sheds its skin and gains a 'new life', so the patients at the Asclepion were supposed to 'shed' their illnesses. Signs mark a **Temple to Aesculapius**, a **library** and a **Roman Theatre**.

Take a drink of cool water from the **Sacred Well**, then pass along the vaulted underground corridor to the **Temple of Telesphorus**. Patients slept in the temple hoping that Telesphorus, another god of medicine, would send a cure, or at least a diagnosis, in a dream. Telesphorus had two daughters named Hygeia and Panacea, whose names have passed into modern medical technology.

The Asclepion's opening hours and fees are the same as for the acropolis.

Arkeoloji Müzesi

In the town centre next to Gülstan Çay Bahçesi is the Arkeoloji Müzesi, which has a substantial collection of artefacts for so small a town, and an excellent ethnology section. At the time of writing it was closed for restoration. The old opening hours were from 8.30 am to 5 pm daily; admission was US$1.

Kızıl Avlu (Red Basilica)

The cathedral-sized **Kızıl Avlu** (KUH-zuhl ahv-loo; Red Basilica or Red Courtyard), 150m north-east of the Meydan Restaurant, was originally a temple, built in the 2nd century AD, to Serapis, an Egyptian god. Look out for a hole in the podium in the centre which allowed someone to hide and appear to speak through the cult statue. It was converted into a Christian basilica by the Byzantines and now houses the small Kurtuluş Camii, proving the theory that sacred ground tends to remain sacred even though the religion may change. The curious red flat-brick walls of the large, roofless structure are visible from midway down the road to the acropolis. You can easily walk to the Kızıl Avlu, or stop your taxi there on your way to or from the acropolis.

Admission costs US$1.75; opening hours are from 8.30 am to 7 pm in summer.

Other Things to See & Do

Bergama's **Çarşı Hamamı** is used by male tourists and locals alike, and charges about US$2. However, one reader reported cockroaches and a general lack of maintenance.

As you walk from the Kızıl Avlu to the Meydan Restaurant look out for **Tahsin Bayansal** (☎ 232-633 1974) on the right-hand side of the road amid a cluster of carpet shops. This is an Aladdin's cave of an antique shop, selling cloths traditionally embroidered by women as part of their dowry; circular tins that were used for storing bread; wooden gadgets used to protect the fingers when cutting the grass; and all sorts of other curios.

Places to Stay – Budget

Lots of people visit Bergama on whistle-stop bus tours without spending the night, so there aren't many good, cheap pensions and hotels. In recent years many have closed, and others are some way from the main sights.

Böblingen Pension *(☎ 232-633 2153, Asklepion Caddesi 2),* is run by the welcoming Altın family who spent many years in Germany. It's quiet, friendly, and charges US$12 for a double with shower and breakfast. The roof terrace lacks views but is a good place for meeting other travellers. Ideally placed for visiting the Asclepion, the pension is remote from the Acropolis. To find it, come out of the otogar and turn left along the highway until you see a sign to the Asclepion on the right. The pension is just up on the hill beside the road junction.

Pergamon Pension *(☎ 232-632 3492, Bankalar Caddesi 3, Polis Karakolu Yanı),* an old stone house right next to the city's police station, looks more promising than it is. Three simple upstairs rooms to one side of the courtyard restaurant share a bathroom across the other side of the courtyard. Only one room has its own facilities. The filthy stair carpet says a lot about the housekeeping. For US$12 per person you can do better than this.

If you're after a place with old-fashioned character, two places near the Kızıl Avlu fit the bill better, provided you don't mind their simplicity. With a touching honesty ***Pension Athena*** *(☎ 232-633 3420, İmam Çikmazı 5),* admits 'we are not the best but trying to get there'. Rooms are split between a 160-year-old stone house with some interesting wooden ceilings and a newer building. Rooms with/without shower cost US$7/5. Breakfast is another US$2. To get there, follow the signs from the Meydan Restaurant.

Cross the nearby bridge and turn left to find ***Nike Pension*** *(☎ 232-633 3901, Tabak Köprü Çıkmazı 2),* which has bigger rooms in a 300-year-old Ottoman-Greek house with interesting features at the back of a flower-filled yard. Rooms cost US$8 including breakfast, and the owners will point out the walking route up to the Acropolis.

Across the highway and just left from the otogar are two run-of-the-mill pensions in high-rise blocks which would do for late arrivals. ***Sayın*** *(☎ 232-633 2405)* and ***Gobi*** *(☎ 232-633 2518)* both charge US$10 for a double with bathroom.

As a last resort, ***Manolya Pension*** *(☎ 232-633 4488, 633 2583, Tanpınar Sokak 5),* is managed by the people who run Café Manolya on the corner of the main street just outside the otogar. Ask at the cafe for price and availability (the pension isn't open all year).

Camping ***Hotel Berksoy*** (see following) and, just west of it, ***Karavan Camping*** have sites for tents, caravans and camper vans. Sometimes cheaper places pop up for a brief life nearer to the coastal highway.

Places to Stay – Mid-Range

Bergama's smartest place to stay is the three-star, 57 room ***Hotel Berksoy*** *(☎ 232-633 2595, fax 633 5346),* PK (PO Box) 19, 2km west of the centre on the main highway. Just back from the road in flower-filled grounds, it boasts a restaurant, bar, tennis court and swimming pool for US$45/65 a modern single/double in season, breakfast included. Expect some traffic noise though. Just west of the Berksoy, ***Hotel İskender*** *(☎ 232-633 2123, fax 632 9710)* is a cuboid three-star high-rise, newer

NORTH AEGEAN TURKEY

than the Berksoy but charging the same. Both these hotels are popular with tour groups.

There are several more hotels between the Berksoy and the otogar, including the three-star ***Asude Hotel*** *(☎ 232-663 1669, fax 663 3143, İzmir Caddesi 93)*, with slightly cheaper rates. Its 52 rooms have satellite TV and minibar, but some are noisier than at the Berksoy.

The pleasant two-star, 23 room ***Hotel Serapion*** *(☎ 232-633 3434, İzmir Caddesi 75)*, posts prices of US$22/40 a single/double, discountable if they're not busy. Spacious rooms with shower and TV are fitted with thicker glass to deaden traffic noise from the main road outside. The pink and purple, two-star ***Efsane Hotel*** *(☎ 232-632 6350, fax 632 6353, İzmir Caddesi 86)*, across the road, charges US$23/35 a single/double for its 24 bath-equipped but rather faded rooms.

The 42 room ***Tusan Bergama Moteli*** *(☎ 232-667 2236)*, Çatı Mevkii, near the junction of the highway and the road into town, is Bergama's oldest tourist hotel, with a restaurant and a quiet, isolated location. Rooms with bath cost US$24/35 a single/double, breakfast another US$4.

Places to Eat

About 150m before you reach the Kızıl Avlu (Red Basilica) you'll come to a small plaza (meydan) dominated by the Meydan Restaurant with a pleasant front terrace. It serves shish kebap for US$2, half a roasted chicken for US$2.75 or pide for US$1.50. Club 2000 next door is similar.

Across the plaza from the Meydan is the ***Sarmaşık Lokantası***, a villagers' place without streetside tables, but with good hearty stews and lower prices. Walk south-west along the main street to find simpler places such as ***Şen Kardeşler*** and ***Çiçeksever Kebap Salonu***, where full meals cost US$3 or US$4.

Readers have recommended the ***Sağlam Restaurant***. There are two branches of this kebapçı, one on the left as you head into town from the otogar, the other down at the meydan, near the Meydan Restaurant and specialising in Urfa-style cuisine.

The Pergamon Pension may disappoint but the restaurant, set round a tinkling fountain, is inviting. Expect to pay more like US$8 for a full meal here.

West of the otogar the road is lined with pleasant outdoor restaurants, cafes and bars. Stroll along and see which one is the current 'in' place (often where the sports channel is on the TV). Heading west towards the turn-off for the Asclepion you'll pass the popular ***Özen Pide ve Kebap Salonu*** and the simpler ***Urfa Kebap ve Lahmacun Salonu***. Fill up at either and you should get change from US$4.

The two branches of ***Café Manolya*** – one near the otogar, the other opposite the Kurşunlu Cami – are good for coffee and baklava for around US$1.50.

Getting There & Away

Whether you approach Bergama from the north or south, check to see if your bus actually stops *in* Bergama at the otogar. Most buses will drop you along the highway at the turn-off to Bergama, leaving you to hitch 7km into town. Hitching is pretty easy, except in the evening.

Ask the driver, *Bergama otogarına gidiyor musunuz?* (BEHR-gah-mah oh-toh-GAHR-uh-NAH gee-dee-YOHR moo-soonooz; 'Do you go to Bergama's bus terminal?') Even then many drivers will nod *Evet!* (Yes!), and then blithely drop you on the highway.

At the time of writing the grungy otogar was on the main street at the western end of the centre. A new site 1km north out along the road to the main highway was expected to open in 1999.

Following are the major routes. Note that bus traffic dies down dramatically in late afternoon and evening, so if you're heading onward, check schedules and reserve your seat earlier in the day. Several bus companies have ticket offices on the main street not far from the Tourism Information Office.

Ayvalık – 50km, 45 minutes, US$2; many from the highway junction, limited but timetabled service from the otogar

Dikili – 30km, 35 minutes, US$1.50; frequent minibuses

İstanbul – A few direct night buses, but it's far cheaper and, surprisingly, quicker to travel via İzmir.
İzmir – 100km, 1¾ hours, US$4; Pamukkale runs buses almost every 30 minutes; Bergama municipal buses ('Bergama Belediyesi') run eight times daily

Buses to other destinations are not all that frequent. In winter, you may find yourself changing buses in İzmir or Balıkesir to get to Ankara, Bursa or İstanbul.

Getting Around

On Foot Bergama's sights are so spread out that you'll find the effort taxing if you're not in good shape. The Kızıl Avlu is over a kilometre from the otogar, the Asclepion is 2km, and the Acropolis is over 6km.

If you enjoy walking but have limited time, find others to share a taxi to the top of the acropolis, then walk down the hill to the Kızıl Avlu, either following the tarmac road or cutting down the slope beneath the theatre. From the Kızıl Avlu, walk through the market district into town, have lunch and take a taxi, or hitch, or walk to the Asclepion, depending upon your budget, your level of fatigue and your schedule.

Taxi Tours The standard taxi-tour rates (per car) from town are:

Acropolis – one way: US$4.50
Acropolis – one hour wait (barely enough), then return to town: US$10
Acropolis – one hour wait, then to Kızıl Avlu (short stop), to museum (15 minute wait), to Asclepion (30 minute wait), then return to town: US$20

Taxis for hire cluster near the Kurşunlu Cami and near the market by the Meydan Restaurant.

ÇANDARLI

The comely little resort town of Çandarlı, dominated by a small but stately restored Genoese castle *(Pıtane)*, is 11km west of the main highway, and over 18km south of Dikili. The castle and village are on a peninsula jutting southward into the Aegean. Although it's a pleasant place to while away a few days, the condominiums across the bay are steadily closing in on the views. Local tourism fills most of the small pensions and hotels in high summer, while the village shops cater to the owners of the villas on the outskirts. Most lodgings close between late October and April/May.

The main square, the Friday market and the shops, are to the east of the castle. The PTT is in the market square, just south of the main square.

Places to Stay

Most of the hotels and pensions are west of the castle, facing the thin strip of coarse-sand beach. To find them walk towards the castle and then skirt round the back; the Samyeli and Senger are to the right, the Martı and Philippi to the left.

One of the most prominent places is ***Otel Samyeli*** *(☎ 232-673 3428)*, with bright, clean but somewhat spartan rooms, some with a sea view, for US$24 a double with mediocre breakfast.

A few buildings along is ***Senger Pansiyon*** *(☎/fax 232-673 3117)*, run by a family who winter in Germany. Attractive, well-kept rooms cost US$16 a double.

Inland a block from the Samyeli are several cheaper places, among them the very basic ***Gül Pansiyon*** *(☎ 232-673 33347)* in an ordinary apartment block. Follow the signs along İncirli Çeşme Sokak to ***Bağış Pansiyon*** *(☎ 232-673 2459)*, with no sea views but a nice courtyard and a low price of US$12 a double, breakfast included.

Near the Senger, ***Oral Pansiyon*** *(☎/fax 232-673 3122)* is older, friendly and on the seafront but not always open.

Heading in the other direction along the beach towards the tip of the peninsula, ***Martı Motel*** *(☎ 232-673 3441)* is simple, with a rosy terrace restaurant and views of the sea. ***Philippi Pansiyon*** *(☎ 232-673 3053)*, 200m south of the Martı, is a better choice: a modern house with a little terrace cafe and obliging owners. The rate for either place is

US$20 a double, breakfast included. The ***Tuna*** next door is similar.

Near the main square where the buses stop is the prominent ***Kaya Pension*** *(☎ 232-673 3058)*. This was closed at the time of writing but check if it has since re-opened because it's handy if you need to make an early departure.

Places to Eat

Locals prefer the restaurants around the main square which, though not as pleasant as the touristy places to the west, are cheaper. ***Temizocak Pide Salonu*** ('Tidy Hearth'), between the Kaya Pansiyon and the market, serves pides for less than US$2 at a few streetside tables. ***Çarşı Lokantası,*** facing the market square, serves good cheap grilled meats.

The Senger and Samyeli hotels both have fish restaurants on their ground floors, but just as good (and pretty friendly) is the independent ***Kalender Restaurant*** in between the two of them. A fish main course with two *mezes* (appetisers) and a cold drink is likely to cost about US$8.

Getting There & Away

Buses run frequently between Çandarlı and İzmir and Dikili (1½ hours, US$2). There are also four daily minibuses to and from Bergama.

FOÇA

Old Ottoman-Greek stone houses line a sinuous shore crowded with fishing boats. A Genoese fortress (1275) continues its slow centuries of crumbling on a hill in the town. Turkish sailors in nautical whites crowd the cheaper cafes, while the more expensive ones are a babble of European languages. This is Foça (FOH-chah; population 12,000), sometimes called Eski Foça, a pleasant resort town resembling Kuşadası before it exploded into hyper-tourism.

Eski Foça, the ancient Phocaea, was founded before 600 BC and flourished during the 5th century BC. During their golden age, the Phocaeans were famous mariners, sending swift vessels powered by 50 oars into the Aegean, Mediterranean and Black seas. They were also great colonists, founding Samsun on the Black Sea as well as towns in southern Italy, Corsica, France and Spain.

Little remains of the ancient city: a ruined theatre, some bits of wall, and a monumental tomb *(anıt mezarı)* 7km east of the town (west of the town of Bağarası) on the way to the İzmir highway. There are also traces of two shrines to the Mother Goddess Cybele: the first hovers between the two bays of Foça, while the second is on the hillside as you come into town from İzmir, beside the remains of two 19th century stone windmills.

More recently this was an Ottoman-Greek fishing and trading town. It's now a prosperous, middle-class Turkish resort with yachts bobbing in the harbour and holiday villas marshalling on the outskirts. Rare Mediterranean monk seals lurk on the offshore islands, providing the inspiration for hundreds of souvenir mugs and T-shirts. Several fountains in the main square are renowned for the sweetness of their water, and you'll see people queuing to fill plastic bottles at them.

Orientation & Information

Foça's circular bay is partially divided by a peninsula cutting in from the south-east, dividing the eastern part of the bay into the Küçük Deniz (Small Sea) to the north and the Büyük Deniz (Big Sea) to the south. The Küçük Deniz, ringed with restaurants, is the more picturesque part, while bigger fishing vessels pull into the Büyük Deniz.

The otogar, on the eastern edge of the Büyük Deniz, is just south of the main square. Walk north through the square, passing the Tourism Information Office (☎/fax 232-812 1222), PTT and shady park. After 350m you'll arrive at the bay and the restaurants; continue along the left-hand (eastern) side to find the pensions, about 600m from the otogar.

Foça's postal code is 35680.

Foça's Castles

West of the Küçük Deniz, Aşıklar Caddesi passes before some modern apartment blocks as it rounds the peninsula holding the fortress called **Beşkapılar** (Five Gates). This was built by the Genoese, repaired by the Ottomans, and partially restored in 1993.

Another fortress, the **Dışkale** (External Fortress) guards the approaches to the town from its perch at the end of the peninsula which shapes the south-western arc of the bay.

Boat Trips

In summer boats leave the Küçük Deniz every day at 10.30 am for trips around the outlying islands. Lunch and drinks are included in the US$17 price, and you'll have ample time for swimming and relaxation. Don't hold out too much hope of seeing the seals though; there are very few of them and they keep a pretty low profile.

North to Yeni Foça

The road north from Eski Foça to Yeni Foça passes several camping grounds, resort hotels and holiday villa clusters, offering dramatic sea views, small coves and beaches, and numerous opportunities for rough or organised camping and/or swimming and water sports.

Yeni Foça, 25km north of Foça and 12km west of the Çanakkale-İzmir highway, has a few old stone houses, many more new houses, hotels, condos and holiday villages, and a sand-and-pebble beach, all ranged around a picture-perfect bay which must have been created by nature expressly for water sports.

Places to Stay

Most of Foça's lodgings are little pensions charging between US$8 and US$12 for double rooms with breakfast, and small hotels charging up to US$25 for double rooms with bath. Rooms can book up especially quickly at weekends when parents like to visit sons based at Foça's commando and marine commando bases.

The friendly 22-room ***Hotel Karaçam*** *(☎ 232-812 1416, fax 812 2042, Sahil Caddesi 70)* is an Ottoman house (1881) with something of the air of a British seaside hotel. In addition to its location, its advantages include a roof-terrace bar, streetside cafe, fancy furniture in the lobby and plentiful plants. The few rooms with water views go quickly at weekends. Rates are US$28/38 a single/double in season, breakfast included. The adjoining ***Villa Dedem*** *(☎ 232-812 2838, fax 812 1700)* looks perkier on the outside than on the inside. Prices are the same as at the Karaçam.

Walk inland one block from the Celep Restaurant to find ***Pansiyon Bir*** *(☎ 232-812 1108, 187 Sokak 6)*, a quiet, family-run place charging US$14 a double when business is slow. It's right next to the ***Dembay Restaurant***, a popular kebapçı.

Visitors speak well of ***Ensar Aile Pansiyonu*** *(☎ 232-812 1777, fax 812 1401, İsmetpaşa Mahallesi, 161 Sokak 15)* a modern building one block inland from the water, charging US$8 per person for its 18 rooms with private showers. The adjoining 13-room ***Siren Pansiyon*** *(☎ 232-812 2660, fax 812 6620)* is similar. ***Hotel Melaike*** *(☎ 232-812 2414, fax 812 3117, 32 Sokak 4)*, at the end of the street, is clean, quiet, and charges US$24 a double with shower. There are no water views here.

The 16 room ***Sempatik Hotel Güneş*** *(☎ 232-812 2195, 206 Sokak No 11)*, is nice, new and comfy. Rates for the rooms, some with sofas, are US$24 a double.

Even further along, the spartan ***Hotel Celep*** *(☎ 232-812 1395)* has plain rooms with bath for US$20 a double, and its own very popular restaurant with water views. There are several other pensions near the Celep, including ***İyigün Café-Pension*** *(☎ 232-812 1445)* up the road, which charges US$6 per person for very basic rooms set around a small pleasant courtyard. It also has its own restaurant.

At the northern end of the street is ***Fokai Pansiyon*** *(☎ 232-812 1765)*, right on the water and a little pricey at US$20 for a simple twin room with shower. There's a kitchen for guests' use on the roof terrace. The nearby ***Huzur*** *(☎ 232-872 7203)* is similar.

Camping The coast north of Foça is sculpted into small coves with sandy beaches, mostly backed by holiday condominiums, but a few have camping places. The closest is ***Belediye Halk Plajı*** (Municipal Beach), 3km north of Eski Foça.

Further up the coast are smaller, less well-organised private camping grounds, the nicest of which is ***Yeni Pınar Camping***, 6km north of Foça, with electrical and water hook-ups in an olive grove on the beach, and no condos nearby. Less than 4km further north (10km from Foça), ***Acar Camping*** is set on a beautiful beach. Another 3.5km brings you to the unfortunately-named Club Pollen, a hill-side full of holiday flats. There's a small cove with some fishing industry 1km beyond it. Finally, 17km north of Foça and 4km before reaching Yeni Foça, ***Azak Restaurant***, set on its own cove, has places for campers.

Places to Eat

As you walk up from the main square to the Küçük Deniz you'll pass several simple Turkish restaurants where meals will cost a fraction of the bill by the waterside. These include ***Zümrüt***, with meat stews for US$2 or so, and ***Julianna's Restaurant***, a few doors along, which is especially popular with foreigners. ***İmren Restaurant***, two short blocks to the north, is cheaper still, with good *sulu yemekler* (stews), making a two-course meal possible for US$3. For grills, try the neighbouring ***Rumeli Köftecisi***, which also has a few outside tables. The popular ***Sedef Restaurant*** is the last of the kebap houses before you move into the harbour and the fish restaurants.

Be sure to ask prices first at any of the restaurants along the water, particularly when ordering fish. All waterfront restaurants – ***Celep, Gemici*** and ***Foça*** along one side; ***Sempatik, Sahil, Bedesten*** and ***İkizler*** on the other – charge from US$12 to US$20 for a full fish dinner, half that for meat. The Celep does good food although passing cars can be an irritant. The Bedesten has set menus for US$7, including fish and rakı. All these places are good for sunset dining, though the smell of the water can be a bit much at times. There are similar fish restaurants (***Dede, Ayos Balık, Fokai***) as you round the peninsula heading for the Büyük Deniz.

Ali Baba Restaurant near the otogar is popular on Saturday nights when it has live music. A chicken kebap costs US$3.

Entertainment

There's a lively market on Saturdays which is when people from İzmir pop up to Foça for the day. Foça has many fashionable cafes, including ***Balıkçı*** by the harbour, and several of the bars and restaurants have live music.

On the south-western side of the Beşkapılar is ***Amfi Tiyatro Café***, a tea garden set up in a reconstructed odeon.

The **Belediye Şehir Hamamı**, 115 Sokak, opens for men and women from 8 am to midnight. It's popular with off-duty soldiers.

Getting There & Away

Foça is 83km south of Bergama, 73km south of Çandarlı, 70km north-west of İzmir, and 25km west of the İzmir-Çanakkale highway. Virtually all bus traffic is to and from İzmir (hourly buses in summer, 1½ hours, US$1.75), with a stop midway in Menemen (37km, 35 minutes, US$1.25). If you're bound for somewhere other than İzmir (Manisa in particular), you'll be dropped off on the highway opposite Menemen otogar where it's usually easy to pick up onward transportation.

Hanedan-Plajlar dolmuşes (US$0.50) run through town periodically in the summer, ferrying passengers between the town centre and the northern beach (Belediye Halk Plajı).

MANİSA

A road goes east 30km to the modern town of Manisa (mah-NEES-ah; population 160,000), the ancient town of Magnesia ad Sipylus, backed by craggy mountains. An early king was Tantalus, whose name gave us the word 'tantalise'.

As punishment for offending the gods he was left in a lake but the water receded every time he tried to take a drink. White apples hung 'tantalisingly' out of reach above his head.

The early, great Ottoman sultans favoured it as a residence, and for a while the province of Manisa was the training ground for promising Ottoman princes.

During the War of Independence, retreating Greek soldiers wreaked terrible destruction on the town, leaving only 500 of its 18,000 historic buildings still standing. The main reason to visit today is to see its historic mosques and some of the finds from Sardis in the local museum.

Orientation & Information

Doğu Caddesi is the main street in the commercial district. The historic mosques are only a few hundred metres to the south along İbrahim Gökçen Caddesi. The train station is less than 1km north-east of the centre; the otogar, 600m north-west.

Manisa's Tourism Information Office (☎ 236-231 2541, fax 232 7423) is in the Özel İdare İşhanı building, Yarhasanlar Mahallesi, Doğu Caddesi 14/3.

Things to See

Of Manisa's many old mosques, the **Muradiye Camii** (1585) has the most impressive tilework. The adjoining building, constructed originally as a soup kitchen, is now the **Manisa Müzesi** (open from 9 am to noon and 1 to 5 pm, closed Monday), with the standard collections, including some fine mosaics from the ruins of Sardis. At the time of writing the archaeological collections were closed for no obvious reason, making it hardly worth the US$1 entry fee.

More or less across the road from the Muradiye, the **Sultan Camii** (1522) has some gaudy painting, but an agreeable hamam next door with separate entrances for men and women. Perched on the steep hillside above the town centre is the **Ulu Cami** (1366), ravished by the ages and not as impressive as the view from the teahouse next to it. Other historic mosques in town are the **Hatuniye** (1490) and the **İlyas Bey** (1363).

Special Events

For four days around the spring equinox (21 March) each year, Manisa rejoices in the **Mesir Şenlikleri**, a festival celebrating *Mesir macunu* (power gum). Legend says that over 450 years ago, a local pharmacist named Merkez Müslihiddin Efendi concocted a potion to cure a mysterious ailment of Hafza Sultan, mother of Sultan Süleyman the Magnificent. Delighted with her swift recovery, the queen mother ordered that the amazing elixir be distributed to the local people at her expense. In fact, the Ottomans had a long-standing custom of eating spiced sweets at *Nevruz*, the Persian new year (spring equinox).

Hafza Sultan's bank account is long closed, and these days the municipal authorities pick up the tab for the 10 tonnes of mesir, mixed from sugar and 40 spices and ingredients. Townsfolk in period costumes re-enact the mixing of the potion, then throw it from the dome of the Sultan Camii. Locals credit mesir with improving the circulation, calming the nerves, stimulating hormones, increasing appetite, immunising against poisonous stings and bites, and doubling tourist revenue.

Places to Stay

Since almost everyone stays in İzmir and drives to Manisa for the day, there are unfortunately few decent places to stay. Amid the shops of Doğu Caddesi the 42 room, two-star ***Hotel Arma*** *(☎ 236-231 1980, fax 232 4501)*, has reasonable rooms with rather faded wallpaper for US$40/55 a single/double. Another option is the four-star ***Büyük Saruhan*** *(☎ 236-233 0272. fax 233 2648, Nusret Köklü Caddesi 1)* as you head out of town bound for İzmir, and that's about it.

İZMİR

İzmir (EEZ-meer; population two million) is Turkey's third-largest city and its major port on the Aegean. It has a dramatic setting, sprawling around a great bay and backed by mountains to the east and south. Most of the city is modern, the traffic is nightmarish, and for most people this is somewhere to get through as quickly as possible.

If you do take the time to explore you will find broad modern boulevards lined with glass-fronted apartment and office blocks, and dotted with shady streetside cafes. Especially in the bazaar area, the odd red-tile roof and bull's-eye window of a 19th-century warehouse pops up to remind you

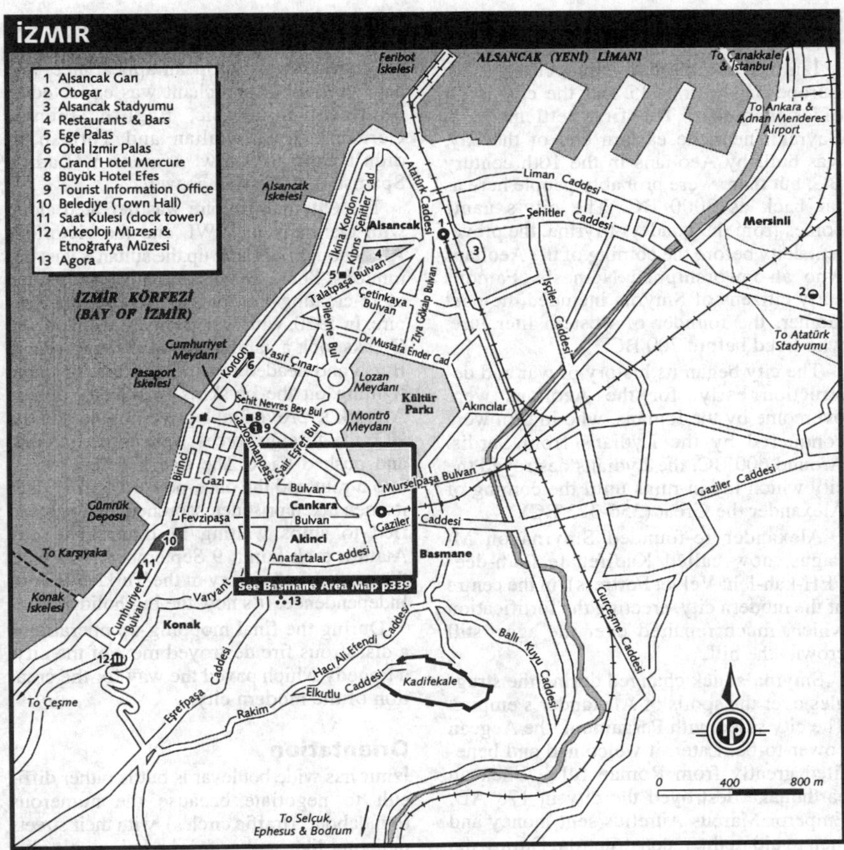

that there was an older İzmir too. But when you come upon an old mosque – so common in other Turkish cities – it hardly seems to belong here.

Most other traces of İzmir's past have been swept away by war, fire and earthquake. With just a day to spare, you can take in the few antiquities and museums, explore the labyrinthine bazaar, loiter in the cafes along the waterfront, and enjoy the wonderful, sweeping views from the 2000-year-old castle.

History

İzmir owes its special atmosphere, indeed its entire appearance, to its turbulent history. What you see today has risen from the ashes of Ottoman İzmir since 1923, when a Greek invasion and a disastrous fire razed most of the city. Before that, İzmir was Smyrna, the most westernised and cosmopolitan of Turkish cities, where more citizens were Christian and Jewish than Muslim, and there were thousands of foreign diplomats, traders, merchants and sailors. Its connections with

Greece and Europe were close. To the Turks it was *gavur İzmir* ('infidel Smyrna').

İzmir's commercial connections with Europe began in 1535, but the city is far older than that. The first settlement, at Bayraklı near the eastern end of the bay, was built by Aeolians in the 10th century BC, but there were probably people here as far back as 3000 BC. The city's name comes from the goddess Myrina, the prevalent deity before the coming of the Aeolians who also worshipped Nemesis. Famous early citizens of Smyrna included the poet Homer, the founder of western literature, who lived before 700 BC.

The city began its history of war and destruction early, for the Aeolians were overcome by the Ionians, who in turn were conquered by the Lydians from Sardis. Around 600 BC, the Lydians destroyed the city which lay in ruins until the coming of Alexander the Great (356-323 BC).

Alexander re-founded Smyrna on Mt Pagus, now called Kadifekale (kah-dee-FEH-kah-leh; Velvet Fortress), in the centre of the modern city, erecting the fortification which, much repaired over the ages, still crowns the hill.

Smyrna's luck changed during the struggles over the spoils of Alexander's empire. The city sided with Pergamum, the Aegean power-to-be. Later, it welcomed and benefited greatly from Roman rule. When an earthquake destroyed the city in 178 AD, Emperor Marcus Aurelius sent money and men to aid in the reconstruction. During the Byzantine period, it became one of the busiest ports along the coast.

As Byzantium's power declined, the armies of the Arabs, Seljuk Turks, Genoese and crusaders marched in, and often out again. Tamerlane arrived in 1402 and, true to form, destroyed the city. After he left, the Ottomans took over in 1415 and things began to look up.

In 1535, Süleyman the Magnificent signed the Ottomans' first-ever commercial treaty with François I of France, which permitted foreign merchants to reside in the sultan's dominions. After that humble start, İzmir became Turkey's most sophisticated commercial city. Its streets and buildings took on a quasi-European appearance, and any worthwhile merchant was expected to be fluent in Arabic, English, French, German, Greek, Italian and Turkish. It didn't hurt to know Armenian, Ladino Spanish and Russian as well.

The Ottoman Empire was defeated along with Germany in WWI, and the victorious Allies sought to carve up the sultan's vast dominions. Some Greeks had always dreamed of re-creating the long-lost Byzantine Empire. In 1920, with Allied encouragement, the Greeks took a gamble, invaded İzmir, seized Bursa and headed towards Ankara. In fierce fighting on the outskirts of Ankara, where Atatürk's provisional government had its HQ, the foreign forces were turned around and pushed back. The Greek defeat turned into a rout and the once-powerful army, half its men taken prisoner, scorched the earth and fled to ships waiting in İzmir. The day Atatürk took İzmir, 9 September 1922, was the moment of victory in the Turkish War of Independence. It's now the big holiday.

During the final mopping-up operations, a disastrous fire destroyed most of the city, a tragedy which paved the way for the creation of the modern city.

Orientation

İzmir has wide boulevards but is rather difficult to negotiate because the numerous roundabouts (traffic circles), with their streets radiating like spokes from a hub, don't give you the sense of direction a grid plan does. Nor are there many obvious landmarks.

The two main avenues run parallel to the waterfront. The waterfront street is officially Atatürk Caddesi, but locals call it the Birinci Kordon (beer-EEN-jee kohr-DOHN; First Cordon). Just inland from it is Cumhuriyet Bulvarı, the İkinci Kordon (ee-KEEN-jee; Second Cordon).

The city's two main squares are along these two parallel avenues. The very centre is Konak Meydanı (Government House Square) where you'll find the municipality buildings, the Ottoman clock tower (İzmir's symbol), the little Konak Camii mosque decorated with coloured Kütahya tiles, and a dock for ferries to Karşıyaka, the suburb across the bay.

The central district of Konak is the heart of İzmir, and opens onto the bazaar. Anafartalar Caddesi, the bazaar's main street, winds through İzmir's most picturesque quarter all the way to the Basmane Garı train station. The Basmane (BAHS-mah-NEH) area is home to dozens of small and medium-priced hotels and restaurants, and many intercity bus ticket offices.

The other main square, Cumhuriyet Meydanı, is about a kilometre north of Konak along the two main streets and holds an equestrian statue of Atatürk. The PTT, Tourism Information Office, Turkish Airlines office, car rental offices and expensive hotels are all near here.

The area called Çankaya (CHAN-kah-yah) is two long blocks inland, south-east of Cumhuriyet Meydanı.

Another İzmir landmark is the Kültür Parkı (kewl-TEWR pahr-kuh; Culture Park), site of the annual İzmir International Fair. The hill directly behind the main part of town is crowned by Kadifekale, the Velvet Fortress.

If you arrive in İzmir from Manisa, the road passes through the suburb of **Bornova**, once the summer residence of wealthy Levantine traders. Some of their mansions still stand; most now converted for public use as municipal offices, schools and the like. Ege Üniversitesi (Aegean University) is here as well. İzmir city buses run from Bornova to the centre of İzmir but progress is slow as the motorway is being extended in this direction.

Information

The Tourism Information Office (☎ 232-484 2147, fax 489 9278), Gaziosmanpaşa Bulvarı 1/D, is next to Turkish Airlines in the Büyük Hotel Efes building. Opening hours are from 8.30 am to 7 pm daily from June to October, till 5.30 pm and closed Sunday in the off season. There's also an office at Adnan Menderes airport (☎ 232-274 2110, fax 274 2214) and in the Belediye in Konak.

The Tourism Police can be reached on ☎ 232-421 8652.

İzmir's postal code is 35000.

Consulates For addresses of consulates, see Embassies in the Facts for the Visitor chapter.

Money Many banks have offices in Konak; Akbank and Türkiye İş Bankası have ATMs here, and there's an İş Bankası ATM in Basmane Garı. You can exchange currency at the PTT on Cumhuriyet Meydanı as well. The Bamka Döviz currency exchange office on the corner of 1369 and 1364 Sokaks, 1½ blocks west of the hotels on 1369 Sokak, changes money quickly and efficiently.

Bookshops Try Dünya Aktüel Kitabevi (☎ 232-463 6877) for foreign periodicals and a few books.

English-language periodicals can be read at the Türk-Amerikan Derneği (Turkish-American Association, ☎ 421 5206), Şehit Nevres Bey Bulvarı 23-A, at 1379 Sokak, just north-east of the Büyük Hotel Efes. It's open Monday to Friday from 1.30 to 6.30 pm.

Konak & the Bazaar

Konak was named for the Ottoman government mansion (Hükümet Konağı) which still stands here at the back of a park-like plaza. In the plaza is the late-Ottoman **saat kulesi** (clock tower) given to the city in 1901 by Sultan Abdül Hamit II. Its ornate orientalist style may have been meant to compensate for 'infidel Smyrna's' European ambience.

İzmir's large bazaar, entered by walking along the right wall of the konak, is fascinating. An hour or two of exploration along **Anafartalar Caddesi**, the main street, is a must, and it's worth trying to find the **Kızlarağası Hanı**, a covered market built in 1744, restored in 1995 and full of shops aimed at the tourist trade. You can also enter the bazaar from Basmane, or from Eşrefpaşa Caddesi near Çankaya after your visit to the Agora. Get well and truly lost, and when you're ready to leave, ask the way to Basmane, Çankaya or Konak. Virtually all the shops close on Sunday, a bad day to visit.

Agora

The marketplace built on the orders of Alexander was ruined in an earthquake in 178 AD, but much remains of the Agora as it was rebuilt by Marcus Aurelius. Corinthian colonnades, vaulted chambers and a reconstructed arch fill this conspicuously open spot in the midst of the crowded city, and give you a good idea of what a Roman 'bazaar' looked like.

To reach the agora, walk up Eşrefpaşa Caddesi from Fevzipaşa Bulvarı, one short and one long block, to 816 Sokak on the left. This street of bakeries and radio-repair shops leads to the Agora, one short block away. You can also reach the Agora via 943 Sokak, off Anafartalar Caddesi near the Hatuniye Camii in the bazaar. Follow the signs.

It's open from 8.30 am to 5.30 pm daily for US$1. If you're only moderately interested in agoras or pinched for cash, you can see most of what there is to see from the street without paying the admission fee.

Museums

These two museums are in Bahri Baba Park, a short, unsigned walk up the hill from Konak along the road to Kadifekale called the Varyant. The entrance is positioned on the one-way road which brings traffic down the hillside so, to reach the museums, walk up that way. If you walk up the road for uphill traffic, you'll walk all the way around the museums but you won't be able to enter.

The **Arkeoloji Müzesi** is in a modern building. You enter on a floor with fine exhibits of Greek and Roman statuary, then move to an upper level (closed at the time of writing) dedicated to terracotta objects, tools and vessels, glassware, metalwork and jewellery of silver and gold. The lower level has tomb statuary and sarcophagi, and also the head of a gigantic statue of Domitian which once stood at Ephesus. Be sure to see the beautiful frieze depicting the funeral games from the mausoleum at Belevi (250 BC), south of İzmir, and also the high relief of Poseidon and Demeter dating from 200 AD.

Even more interesting is the **Etnoğrafya Müzesi** next door. Once İzmir's Department of Public Health, this fine old stone building now houses colourful displays demonstrating local folk arts, crafts and customs. You'll learn about camel wrestling, the potter's craft, the important task of tinplating which renders toxic copper vessels safe for kitchen use, felt-making, embroidery, and wood-block printing for scarves and cloth. You can even see how those curious little blue-and-white 'evil eye' beads are made, a craft going back hundreds, perhaps even thousands, of years.

Other exhibits include an Ottoman chemist's shop, a fully decorated salon from a 19th-century Ottoman residence, an Ottoman bridal chamber, a circumcision celebration room from the same period and a kitchen. There are also displays of armour, weapons, carpets and local costumes.

The Archaeological Museum is open from 8.30 to 5 pm (US$2), the Ethnography Museum from 9 am to noon and from 1 to 5 pm (US$1). Both are closed on Monday.

Kadifekale

The time to ride up the mountain is an hour before sunset. Catch a city bus south of Konak (it may say only 'K Kale' on the sign), allowing 20 minutes for the ride. The view on all sides is spectacular. At sunset, as the muezzins give the call to prayer from İzmir's minarets the wave of sound rolls across the city as the lights twinkle on.

Near the gate are a few terrace teahouses for tea, soft drinks or beer.

Other Sights

As you make your way around town, you'll certainly see the **equestrian statue of Atatürk** in Cumhuriyet Meydanı. It symbolises Atatürk's leadership as he began the counteroffensive from Ankara during the War of Independence. His battle order to the troops on the first day (26 August 1922) read 'Soldiers, your goal is the Aegean'.

The **Kültür Parkı**, or Culture Park, is a pleasant place for a quiet walk or picnic away from the city bustle. In late August and early September, the fairgrounds hold centre stage during the İzmir International Fair.

Had it with the crowded, noisy city? Head down to the dock on the Konak waterfront and board a ferry for **Karşıyaka**, on the far side of the bay. The view is beautiful, the air fresh and cool. The return trip takes up to 75 minutes, and costs less than US$1.

Special Events

From mid-June to mid-July, the International İzmir Festival offers performances of music and dance in Çeşme and Ephesus as well as İzmir. Check with the İzmir Kültür Vakfı (İzmir Culture Foundation), Mahmut Esat Bozkurt Caddesi 4-6, Alsancak, or the Tourism Information Office for what's on where.

The annual İzmir International Fair is an amusement and industry show which takes place from late August to mid-September, at which time hotel space may be tight.

Places to Stay

Although İzmir has dozens of hotels, the choice isn't wonderful. Because so few tourists stay here, there are few of those cheap, pleasant pensions you find in İstanbul or even Kuşadası. Instead, İzmir's cheapies tend to be grungy places with little to recommend them except low prices.

The better hotels are certainly more comfortable but remain pretty mundane and overpriced in comparison to elsewhere. Some hotels post prices so high it hardly seems worth trying to argue them down.

Luckily there are lots of small, cheap hotels, and a good selection of mid-priced places just a few steps from Basmane Garı, so you can look around before deciding. The top-end hotels are mostly grouped around Cumhuriyet Meydanı, with the odd straggler in Alsancak.

Places to Stay – Budget

The quarter named Akıncı (also called Yenigün) is bounded by Fevzipaşa Bulvarı, Basmane Meydanı, Anafartalar Caddesi and Eşrefpaşa Caddesi. Right next to Basmane Garı, İzmir's main train station, is a low-budget traveller's dream. Several entire streets are lined with cheap places to stay and equally cheap places to eat. The Basmane Hamamı, adjoining the Basmane mosque facing the station, is a convenient Turkish bath (men only). Bus ticket offices for your onward journey are only 50m away in Dokuz Eylül Meydanı. The better bus companies have shuttle buses to take you between Dokuz Eylül Meydanı and the otogar.

Note that there are also a lot of bars and nightclubs and, with them, a lot of 'Natashas' (See 'The Natasha Syndrome' boxed text in the Black Sea Coast chapter) activity in this area. Watch the comings and goings around the various hotels carefully if this would bother you.

1296 Sokak For the cheapest places to stay, walk out of the front of Basmane station, turn left, cross the large street and walk up shady Anafartalar Caddesi. Take the first small street on your right, which is 1296 Sokak, lined with small hotels – some in new buildings, others in once-grand old İzmir houses with coloured glass, fancy woodwork and mosaic floors, now somewhat dilapidated. The cheapest of these hotels charge about US$8 for a waterless double room. Prices go as high as US$15 for a room with private shower. The hotels seem to improve in quality and fall in price the further you walk. Look at several rooms before making your choice.

In the Bazaar Several other hotels are located near the bazaar. Walk along Anafartalar Caddesi through the bazaar to the Hatuniye Camii (also called the Kuşlu Cami). Just past it, on the right, is ***Otel Saray*** *(☎ 232-483 6946, Anafartalar Caddesi 635, Tilkilik)*, a backpackers' favourite, charging US$12 for a clean double with sink, opening onto a small enclosed central courtyard. Get a room on the upper floor if you can.

Much better is the ***Otel Hikmet*** *(☎ 232-484 2672, 945 Sokak 26, Tilkilik/Dönertaş)*, up the side street opposite the Hatuniye Camii. It's a step up in quality, but still has singles/doubles without bath for US$3/6 or with bath for US$7.50/14. The lobby is an inviting place to relax.

1368 Sokak For a slightly better class of hotel, from Basmane Gari, head straight down the right-hand side of Fevzipaşa Bulvarı to the three-star Hotel Hisar. Turn right onto 1368 Sokak, which is lined with a dozen small hotels (***Çiçek Palas, Divan, Kamioğlu, Ova, Gönen Palas, Akgün***) charging about US$12 to US$18 for a double room with a private shower. Most give you a choice of rooms with or without private shower, and most are relatively quiet. Prices tend to rise and fall with room availability. Look at several places before you make a decision. Readers have recommended ***Güzel İzmir Oteli*** *(☎ 232-483 5069, 1368 Sokak 8)* but unfortunately the leaky plumbing won't be to everyone's liking. Expect to pay US$8/15 a single/double.

Places to Stay – Mid-Range

Basmane Try the two-star, 33 room ***Hotel Baylan*** *(☎ 232-483 1426, fax 483 3844, 1299 Sokak 8),* with accommodating staff, clean, modern (if small) air-con rooms with shower and TV, and private car park. Hefty posted prices of US$55/70 are subject to negotiation. Walk up 1296 Sokak and enter through the car park, or turn left onto 1299 Sokak by the Otel Gümüş Palas.

Another good choice is the new ***Otel Antik Han*** *(☎ 232-489 2750, fax 483 5925, Anafartalar Caddesi 600),* in a restored house right in the bazaar. Singles/doubles currently cost US$20/30 with baths, TVs, ceiling fans and plenty of character, but these prices are unlikely to last once word gets about.

The 36-room, two-star ***Tanık Otel*** *(☎ 232-441 2007, fax 483 1119, 1364 Sokak 13, Çankaya)* is grander but a little further from the station. Walk two blocks down Gazi Bulvarı to find it. Rooms with bathroom, TV and sound insulation cost US$35/50 a single/double, including breakfast. Avoid rooms on busy, noisy Gazi Bulvarı to be on the safe side.

Down Fevzipaşa Bulvarı, a block from the station, is the three-star ***Hotel Hisar*** *(☎ 232-484 5400, fax 425 8830, Fevzipaşa Bulvarı 153, or 1368 Sokak 2),* older but serviceable, with 63 rooms with bath, TV, minibar and air-con for US$42/64 a single/double, breakfast included.

Just around the corner, on 1368 Sokak, is the two-star, 36 room ***Hotel Zeybek*** *(☎ 232-489 6694, fax 483 5020, 1368 Sokak 5),* and ***Grand Hotel Zeybek*** *(☎ 232-441 9590, fax 484 6791),* facing it across the narrow street. In the Hotel Zeybek, the tiny guest rooms have TVs, fans and bathrooms (some with small tubs), but cost a ridiculous US$80/100 a single/double. The Grand Hotel Zeybek charges US$96/120 a single/double for a grander room, breakfast included. These prices have more than doubled since the last edition of this guide for no apparent reason.

Cumhuriyet Meydanı Although this area is undeniably central and convenient, prices are extremely high. It would be wise to book through a travel agent or be prepared for some hard bargaining.

The three-star, 73 room ***Otel Karaca*** *(☎ 232-489 1940, fax 483 1498, Necati Bey Bulvarı, 1379 Sokak 55, 35210 Alsancak,)* is between the Hilton and the Büyük Efes. The quiet location, comfortable, modern rooms with TVs and minibars, and English-speaking staff make this a long-time favourite of NATO military and diplomatic families. Rooms cost US$74/103 a single/double, breakfast included. There's a restaurant and cinema attached.

The three-star, 78 room ***Hotel İsmira*** *(☎ 232-445 6060, fax 445 6071, Gaziosmanpaşa Bulvarı 28),* across from the Hilton, charges US$84/112 a single/double for similar comforts.

The three-star ***Otel İzmir Palas*** *(☎ 232-421 5583, fax 422 6870, Vasıf Çınar Bulvarı 2),* just off Atatürk Bulvarı, is a short walk north of Cumhuriyet Meydanı. It's a comfortable place, with sea views from many rooms but posted prices are a whopping US$95/110/145 a single/double/triple. The good Deniz Restaurant adjoins.

Otel Marla *(☎ 232-441 4000, fax 441 1150, Kazım Dirik Caddesi 7, 35210 Pasaport),* advertises 'five-star comforts at three-star-prices'. Its 68 rooms almost meet this claim, with marble bathroom, trendy

BASMANE AREA

PLACES TO STAY

1 Hotel Karaca
2 Ismir Hilton
3 Hotel Ismira
4 Tanık Otel
6 Otel Ova
7 Hotel Divan
8 Kamiloğlu Oteli
10 Otel Çiçek Palas
11 Gönen Palas Oteli
12 Otel Akgün
15 Ömür Oteli
18 Hotel Zeybek & Restaurant
19 Güzel İzmir Hotel & Restaurant
20 Grand Hotel Zeybek
21 Hotel Hisar
25 Hotel Akpınar
26 Hotel Kafkas
27 Otel Kahraman
31 Güzel Konya Oteli
34 Yıldız Palas Oteli
35 Otel Gümüş Palas
36 Hotel Baylan
41 Otel Saray
45 Otel Antik Han
47 Otel Aksu
50 Otel Hikmet

PLACES TO EAT

5 Dört Mevsim Et Lokantası
9 Marmara Börekçisi
13 Kömürde Piliç ve Izgara Çeşitleri
14 İnci Kebap, Pide ve Lahmacun Salonu
17 Lidaki Balıkevi
23 Budget Restaurants
30 Güneydoğu Kebap Salonu
39 Meşhur Trakya Mandırası
46 Konya Etli Pide Salonu

OTHER

16 Bamka Döviz Currency Exchange
22 PTT
24 Taxi Stand
28 Basmane Camii
29 Basmane Hamamı
32 Şifa Hastanesi (Hospital)
33 Cami
37 Police
38 Fettah Camii
40 Hatuniye (Kuşlu) Camii
42 Hamam
43 Hasan Hoca Camii
44 Big Car Park
48 Mum Yakmaz Camii
49 Hamam

NORTH AEGEAN TURKEY

decor, satellite TV, minibar and air-con. The location is quiet, yet only a block from Cumhuriyet Meydanı. Rates are US$60/80 for a single/double.

Places to Stay – Top End

As you enter İzmir, you can't help noticing the 381 room ***İzmir Hilton*** *(☎ 232-441 6060, fax 441 2277, Gaziosmanpaşa Bulvarı 7)*, which soars 40 storeys above the centre, the tallest building – and the best hotel – by far. There are two tennis courts, two squash courts and an indoor pool. The complex includes a shopping centre and car park. Posted room rates are as high as the building: US$230/265/300 a single/double/triple.

The five-star, 127 room ***Grand Hotel Mercure*** *(☎ 232-489 4090, fax 489 40 89, Cumhuriyet Bulvarı 138)* faces Cumhuriyet Meydanı. Its air-con, minibar and TV-equipped rooms cost US$150/200/240 in summer. The sister hotel, the four-star, 76 room ***Mercure Konak*** *(☎ 232-489 1500, fax 489 1709, Mithatpaşa Caddesi 128)*, is just south-west of Konak on the way to the museums. It's marginally cheaper and many rooms have fine sea views.

İzmir's newest four-star is ***Ege Palas*** *(☎ 232-463 9090, fax 463 8100, Cumhuriyet Bulvarı 210)*, rising 20 storeys above northern Alsancak. Close to Alsancak's cafe and nightlife, its 109 rooms cost US$130/190 a single/double for a sea view, about US$10 less for a land view.

The 446 room ***Büyük Efes Oteli*** *(☎ 232-484 4300, fax 441 5695, Gaziosmanpaşa Bulvarı 1)* faces out to sea across Cumhuriyet Meydanı. For decades it was İzmir's best, but now seems to concentrate on revenues from weddings and receptions. Double rooms cost US$150 to US$170.

Places to Eat – Budget

The cheapest meals are found in the same areas as the cheapest hotels.

Basmane If you're in a hurry, there are three noisy restaurants right across from Basmane station at the beginning of Anafartalar Caddesi. Though hardly atmospheric, they're good for a quick, cheap meal before boarding a train. ***Aydın-Denizli-Nazilli*** fries up local fish (get a freshly-fried one) for US$2, while ***Ödemiş Azim*** and ***Ankara*** serve good ready-made stews.

There are several cheap kebapçıs on 1296 Sokak, including ***Güneydoğu Kebap Salonu***, with meals for US$4 or less. There are also a few eateries at the beginning of Anafartalar Caddesi opposite the Basmane Hamamı.

1368 & 1369 Sokaks ***Güzel İzmir Restaurant*** *(☎ 232-484 0501, 1368 Sokak 8/B)*, in front of the hotel of the same name, has kebaps and bain-marie dishes, streetside tables and lowish prices. A three-course meal costs about US$5 or US$6.

A few steps away at the junction of 1368 and 1369 Sokaks, ***Marmara Börekçisi*** serves large portions of flaky *börek* (flaky pastry) and freshly baked pide with a soft drink for US$2.50.

On 1369 Sokak, look for the similarly cheap ***İnci Kebap, Pide ve Lahmacun Salonu*** – the restaurant's name is its menu. Almost next door, ***Kömürde Piliç ve Izgara Çesitleri*** offers big portions of spit-roasted chicken for US$2.

Other good choices are further along 1369 Sokak. A block west on the right-hand side is the very popular ***Dört Mevsim Et Lokantası*** at 51/A, specialising in meats and with an *ocakbaşı* grill. Fill up for about US$5.

Anafartalar Caddesi If you're staying at the Otel Hikmet or Otel Saray, try the modern ***Konya Etli Pide Salonu***, on Anafartalar between the two hotels. ***Nazilli Pide Salonu*** at Anafartalar 543, closer to Konak, has cheap fresh pide. For a good breakfast, try ***Meşhur Trakya Mandırası*** *(Anafartalar Caddesi 451)*.

Vegetarian Food İzmir's only ***Vejeteryan Restaurant*** *(1375 Sokak 11)* is a tiny place a block north of Şehit Nevres Bey Bulvarı, near the Turkish-American Association (ask for the Türk-Amerikan Derneği) and the American Hospital.

The Bazaar Enter the bazaar along Anafartalar Caddesi from Konak. At 66, the courtyard of the Meserret building holds the ***Meserret Kafeterya***, İzmir's answer to a food court, with prices posted prominently. Across the street at 61, in the courtyard of the dilapidated 19th-century Yeni Şükran Oteli, is ***Şükran Lokantası***, a bazaar merchants' hang-out which serves booze and food in an atmospheric courtyard. Expect to pay from US$8 to US$10 for a full dinner.

The teeming bazaar has an assortment of other eateries, including several cheap, quick pidecis.

Places to Eat – Mid-Range

Birinci Kordon North of Cumhuriyet Meydanı along the Birinci Kordon, many of the restaurants have streetside tables, views of the bay, lots of meze dishes and fresh fish prepared in various ways. On summer evenings, this is the place to be as the street is closed to traffic and the cafes spill out into the roadway. At other times, the traffic and the sea defence wall detract from the setting.

Café Sisim, the first place north of Cumhuriyet Meydanı, is a posh restaurant offering full meals for under US$10, occasional live music and the best people-watching in the city. Just north of it, the ***British Restaurant*** and ***Café Niray*** serve draught beer (US$2), snacks and light meals at streetside tables. Just a bit further north, ***Pizzeria Z*** *(Atatürk Caddesi 186)* serves hamburgers and pizza at streetside tables for US$1.25 to US$8. There's no alcohol. It's next door to a cinema.

The seafood restaurant of choice for İzmir's business community is ***Deniz Restaurant*** *(☎ 232-422 0601, Atatürk Caddesi 188-B on)*, on the corner of Vasıf Çınar Bulvarı, on the ground floor of the Otel İzmir Palas. Prices are reasonable (about US$10 to US$18 for a full meal), with outdoor tables more or less regardless of the weather.

Across Vasıf Çınar from Deniz is ***La Sera***, which also serves full meals at the tables closest to the building; the ones further out in the street are usually filled with drinkers.

Alsancak North of Cumhuriyet Meydanı, inland from the water, is the wealthy residential district of Alsancak, with many good restaurants. A taxi from Basmane to Alsancak costs less than US$1.

For Italian fare in attractive surroundings, try the very popular ***Pizza Venedik*** *(☎ 232-422 2735, 1382 (Gül) Sokak 10-B)*, half a block inland from the Birinci Kordon. Dining rooms and outdoor tables are open from 11 am to 11 pm daily. The menu lists 20 types of pizzas (US$3 to US$5 for fairly small portions) and several reasonably priced Italian main courses. Alcohol is served.

Even further north, several streets and squares have been closed to traffic (which in Turkey means fewer cars rather than no cars) and ***streetside cafes*** and ***restaurants*** have flourished. Start at Gündoğdu Meydanı at the intersection of İkinci Kordon (Cumhuriyet Bulvarı), Plevne and Ali Çetinkaya Caddesis, walk east on Ali Çetinkaya and bear left on Kıbrıs Şehitleri Caddesi. You'll pass everything from McDonald's and İskender kebap places to cafes and bars accommodating İzmir's elite. The side streets hold some of the city's better restaurants, some in restored 19th century stone houses.

1444 Sokak, a small street running west off Kıbrıs Şehitleri Caddesi, is filled with restaurants, like the large ***Altın Kapı***, specialising in grilled lamb and so popular it has taken over both sides of the street. Placemats bear pictures of the dishes. If you're tired of lamb, have the *piliç şiş* (chicken kebap) for US$4. The adjoining ***Sofra*** is also good.

A bit further north along Kıbrıs Şehitleri brings you to 1453 Sokak, a street of prettily restored houses. Several restaurants put tables out in the evening, including ***Kemal'ın Yeri Deniz Mahsülleri*** *(☎ 232-422 3190)* at No 20/A, noted for its reasonably-priced seafood. As fish are subject to market fluctuations, ask prices before you order.

Entertainment

Dining at the waterfront cafes along the Birinci Kordon, and taking a stroll along Kıbrıs Şehitleri Caddesi, are the prime evening activities.

Alsancak is the centre of the club scene. Some of the waterfront places along the Birinci Kordon have evening entertainment of high amplification and low quality, but the small indoor clubs off Kıbrıs Şehitleri Caddesi tend to be better. 1482 Sokak, full of attractive old houses, is a good place to start looking, but ***Mavi***, beside the Ege Palas Hotel, is also inviting. ***Kalyon***, opposite McDonald's on Cumhuriyet Bulvarı, has the air of an English pub – and you'll be hard-pressed to get a seat on a Saturday night.

For highbrow entertainment, the ***İzmir Devlet Opera ve Balesi*** (İzmir State Opera and Ballet, ☎ 232-484 6445) and the ***İzmir Devlet Senfoni Orkestrası*** (İzmir State Symphony Orchestra, ☎ 232-425 4115) perform from September to May. The *Turkish Daily News* usually carries schedules. You can also try the ***Atatürk Kültür Merkezi*** (Atatürk Cultural Centre, ☎ 232-484 8526) in Konak.

Getting There & Away

Air For information on flights and fares, see the Getting Around chapter. For airport transport, see the Getting Around section. The Adnan Menderes airport information number is ☎ 232-274 2626.

Turkish Airlines (☎ 232-484 1220, for reservations 425 8280, fax 483 6281) is in the row of shops in the Büyük Hotel Efes at Gaziosmanpaşa Bulvarı 1, open seven days.

İstanbul Airlines (☎ 232-489 0541, fax 445 5768; at Menderes airport ☎ 232-274 2076, fax 274 2229), Gaziosmanpaşa Caddesi 2-E, is across the street from the Büyük Hotel Efes and Turkish Airlines.

Details of the offices of foreign airlines, all close to Cumhuriyet Meydanı are:

Air France
(☎ 232-425 9004) Halit Ziya Bulvarı, 1353 Sokak 1, two blocks south of the Tourism Information Office

Austrian Airlines
(☎ 232-425 8020) Şair Eşref Bulvarı 1371 Sokak 5, Çankaya

British Airways
(☎ 232-441 3829, fax 441 6284) Şair Eşref Bulvarı 18/304 Alsancak

KLM
(☎ 232-274 2052) Menderes airport

Lufthansa
(☎ 232-274 2055) Menderes airport

Swissair
(☎ 232-421 4757) Cumhuriyet Meydanı 11/2, on the south side of the square

Bus İzmir's otogar, a mammoth and seemingly chaotic place almost 3km north-east of the city's centre, is long overdue for replacement. Even getting into it can be a problem as the busy main road outside has no bridge or underpass. Inside, buses roar around while throngs of passengers mill about helplessly. There's a small Tourism Information Office and complaints office near the terminal's main gate. If you're at the otogar to buy a ticket to another city, ask for directions to the *bilet gişeleri* (bee-LEHT geesheh-leh-ree; ticket windows) – they're not all that obvious amid the hubbub. There are also several *emanethane* (left-luggage offices); make sure you note the position of the one you've used.

The larger bus companies provide *servis arabası* (shuttle services) between the otogar and Dokuz Eylül Meydanı next to Basmane. For other transport to and from the otogar, see the following Getting Around section.

In the city centre, bus companies with ticket offices around Dokus Eylül Meydanı are Aydın, Dadaş, Hakiki Koç, İzmir Seyahat, Kamil Koç, Karadeveci, Kent, Kontur, Metro, Pamukkale, Uludağ, and Vantur. Premium companies Pamukkale, Ulusoy and Varan have offices on Gaziosmanpaşa Bulvarı opposite the entrance to the Büyük Hotel Efes.

Here are details on travel from İzmir to:

Ankara – 600km, eight hours, US$10; at least every hour

Antalya – 550km, nine hours, US$10; at least every two hours

Bergama – 100km, one hour, US$3; Pammukale company buses every 30 minutes from 6 am to 7.30 pm; also several Bergama municipality ('Bergama Belediyesi') buses

Bodrum – 250km, four hours, US$7; every hour in summer

Bursa – 375km, six hours, US$6; hourly

Çanakkale – 340km, six hours, US$7; at least every two hours

Çeşme (for Chios) – 85km, 1½ hours, US$2; frequent buses (at least hourly) depart from a separate bus station in Üçkuyular, 6.5km south-west of Konak; take a Balçova minibus from Konak to Üçkuyular
Denizli – 250km, four hours, US$6; every hour
İstanbul – 610km, eight hours, from US$12; every hour
Konya – 575km, eight hours, US$12; at least every two hours
Kuşadası – 95km, 1½ hours, US$2.25; at least every 30 minutes from 6.30 am to 7 pm in summer
Marmaris – 320km, six hours, US$7.50; at least every two hours
Sardis – 90km, 1¼ hours, US$2; buses for Salihli (get off at Sart) at least every 30 minutes
Selçuk (for Ephesus) – 80km, 1¼ hours, US$2; every 15 minutes from 6.30 am to 7 pm in summer
Trabzon – 1375km, 22 hours, US$20; several daily
Van – 1600km, 28 hours, US$24; several daily

Train Most intercity trains come into Basmane Garı (☎ 232-484 8638, for reservations 484 5350), from where there are buses to other areas İzmir's other terminus, Alsancak Garı (☎ 232-421 0114), at the northern end of the city near the port, is mostly for commuter and suburban lines but has frequent trains to Adnan Menderes airport.

For information on trains, don't ask at the prominent Anahat (Main Lines) ticket kiosk in Basmane. Rather, consult the agent at Danışma (Information), who has all the schedules in his head.

The following train services depart daily from Basmane Garı unless it says otherwise:

Afyon
Some Ankara-bound trains; check at Danışma. A rail-bus (*ray otobüsü*) departs Basmane for Afyon daily at 11.30 pm.

Ankara
The fastest and most comfortable train is the *Ankara Mavi Tren*, departing at 7.40 pm, arriving in Ankara at 9.45 am. The one-way fare is US$7; sleeping compartments cost US$10 for one person and US$9 per person for two people. Table d'hôte dinner on board costs from US$6 to US$10. The next best train is the *İzmir Ekspresi*, departing at 6 pm, arriving in Ankara at 9.17 am. The one-way fare is US$6/5 in 1st/2nd-class.

Balıkesir
Marmara Ekspresi trains to and from Bandırma (see following) stop in Balıkesir, as do some Ankara-bound trains.

Bandırma
The *Marmara Ekspresi* departs at 8 am for Bandırma (US$3) on the Sea of Marmara, arriving at 2.12 pm. From Bandırma there's a fast car ferry service to İstanbul.

Denizli (Pamukkale)
Express trains depart for Denizli (near Pamukkale) at 8.20 am (arriving at 1.47 pm), 3.15 pm (arriving at 10 pm), and 6.05 pm (arriving at 11.28 pm), stopping at Adnan Menderes airport, Selçuk (for Ephesus and Kuşadası), Aydın, and Nazilli (for Afrodisias). The one-way fare is US$3, US$2.50 for students.

Eskişehir
All Ankara-bound trains stop at Eskişehir, a major railway junction. In addition, the *Ege Ekspresi* (Aegean Express) departs İzmir each morning at 6.40 am for Eskişehir. The fare is US$5.50.

Isparta
One train a day leaves for Isparta at 11 pm, arriving at 8 am. The fare is US$4. The same service also calls at Burdur.

İstanbul
See Bandırma, above.

Kütahya
All Ankara-bound trains stop at Kütahya.

Manisa
All trains bound for Bandırma/İstanbul and Ankara stop at Manisa. In addition, rail-buses depart for Manisa at 2.40 and 6.30 pm daily. The fare is US$1.

Selçuk (Ephesus)
The three Denizli-bound trains and the Söke-bound trains (departing at 6.46 and 10.40 pm) stop at Selçuk. The one-way fare is US$1 (US$0.75 for students).

Besides these trains, there are also daily services to Aliağa (6.40 am, 4.25 pm), Ödemiş (4.10 pm) and Söke (6.46 and 10.40 pm), and *banliyö* trains to Karşıyaka, across the bay.

Boat The İstanbul-İzmir car ferry service operates each weekend throughout the year. See the Getting Around chapter for details. Also, see the Getting There & Away chapter for information on the car-ferry service between İzmir/Çeşme and Venice (Italy).

Should you be lucky enough to arrive by sea, you'll see İzmir at its best as you glide into Alsancak Limanı (Alsancak Harbour) (☎/fax 232-421 1484), also called Yeni Liman (New Harbour), at the northern tip of Alsancak. The harbour is about equidistant (2km) from the otogar and from Konak. For transport, turn left as you leave the dock area and walk the block to Alsancak Gari, from where buses (US$0.40) and taxis (US$3) take you to the centre.

Getting Around

To/From the Airport You can travel between the centre of İzmir and Adnan Menderes airport (25km south of the city near Cumaovası on the road to Ephesus and Kuşadası) by airport bus, city bus, intercity bus, commuter train or express train.

Havaş airport buses (US$2.50) leave for the 30-minute trip from the Turkish Airlines (THY) office about 90 minutes before each Turkish Airlines departure. If you're not flying THY, ask for the schedule and catch a bus that leaves at least 90 minutes before your domestic departure, or two hours before an international departure.

Cheaper city buses trundle fairly slowly between Menderes airport and Montrö Meydanı, at the Kültür Parkı end of Şehit Nevres Bey Bulvarı, every 30 minutes throughout the day, but the trip takes twice as long.

A taxi between İzmir and Menderes airport can cost between US$18 and US$35, depending upon your haggling abilities and whether or not the driver actually runs the meter.

More or less hourly suburban trains (US$0.50) connect Menderes airport with Alsancak Garı. Most travellers prefer to take a dolmuş as this is likely to be faster and more dependable.

The Otogar If you've come on one of the bigger bus lines, there may be a *servis arabası* (shuttle bus) to take you to Dokuz Eylül Meydanı at no extra charge; ask as you descend from your bus, *Servis arabası var mı?* Otherwise, take a city bus *(şehir otobüsü)* No 50, 51 or 52 marked 'Yeni Garaj-Konak', which stops at Alsancak Garı and Çankaya as well. Find the tourism and complaints office, go out the gate nearby, turn right, walk to the bus shelter, and buy a ticket at the kiosk.

Minibus dolmuşes depart from in front of this bus rank. Most convenient is the dolmuş marked 'Çankaya-Mersinli', which will take you to the bus ticket offices at Dokuz Eylül Meydanı, just a few steps from Basmane Garı, then to Çankaya.

If you're arriving in İzmir by bus from the south, ask to be let out at Tepecik (TEH-peh-jeek), which is 700m east of Basmane Gari, and closer to the centre than the otogar. Minibuses and dolmuşes run from Tepecik along Gaziler Caddesi to Basmane.

If you're arriving in İzmir by train from the north, get out at Çınarlı station, the penultimate stop, and walk the 300m to the otogar.

To get to Çeşme, catch any bus or dolmuş bound westward from Konak to Güzelyalı, Altay Meydanı or Balçova, and get out at Güzelyalı/Altay Meydanı to board a Çeşme-bound bus.

Bus & Dolmuş City buses lumber along the major thoroughfares. Two major *terminali*/transfer points are at Montrö Meydanı by the Kültür Parkı, and at Konak in front of the Atatürk Kültür Merkezi. You must buy a ticket (US$0.40) from a white kiosk in advance and place it in the box by the driver.

İzmir Metro Work has finally begun on the İzmir metro and Konak is full of posters boasting how it will soon (well, relatively) be possible to cross the city in just 15 minutes. The first 9.2km-long stretch of the Metro will connect Basmane with Konak, then run west along the shore via Üçyol to Altay Meydanı in Güzelyalı, the beginning of the Çeşme Otoyol (highway). A new otogar is slated to be part of these developments. In the meantime, expect a lot of mud, noise and traffic disruption as work continues.

Car Rental The large international franchises and many small local companies all have offices in İzmir. There's a cluster of offices on Şehit Fethi Bey Caddesi, the street between the Büyük Hotel Efes and the İkinci

Kordon, near the Otel Anba; and on the İkinci Kordon north of Cumhuriyet Meydanı.

Some addresses are:

Avis
(☎ 232-441 4417, fax 441 4420)
Şair Eşref Bulvarı;
(☎ 232-441 6016) 18-D İzmir Hilton;
(☎/fax 232-274 2172) Menderes airport

Budget
(☎ 232-482 0505, fax 441 9375)
Şair Eşref Bulvarı 22/1;
(☎ 232-274 2203, fax 274 2260)
Menderes airport

Dem Car
(☎ 232-446 2829, fax 484 1691)
1395 Sokak 2/A

Europcar/Interrent
(☎ 232-441 5141, fax 483 0031)
Esin Turizm, Şehit Fethi Bey Caddesi 122-F

Hertz
(☎ 232-274 2248) Menderes airport

Yes Rent a Car
(☎ 232-422 7107, fax 422 2499)
1377 Sokak 8-B

Zafer Rent a Car
(☎ 232-484 6096, fax 483 0904)
Akdeniz Caddesi 8/A;
(☎ 232-274 2274) Menderes airport

Taxi To ensure a reliable driver it's best to take a taxi from a *durak* (taxi stand), or to have your hotel call one.

SARDIS (SART) & SALİHLİ

Croesus (560-546 BC) was the King of Lydia, of which Sardis was the capital. It is here that coinage appears to have been invented, and the phrase 'rich as Croesus' was coined. No doubt the Greeks thought Croesus rich because he could store so much wealth in such a small form. Rather than having vast estates and far-ranging herds of livestock, Croesus kept his wealth in his seemingly bottomless pockets.

For all his wealth, Croesus was defeated and captured by Cyrus and his Persians, after which he leapt onto a funeral pyre, proving that not even he could take it with him.

The Lydian Kingdom dominated much of the Aegean before the Persians came. Besides being the kingdom's wealthy capital, Sardis was a great trading centre because its coinage facilitated trade.

After the Persians, Alexander the Great took the city in 334 BC and embellished it even more. The inevitable earthquake brought its fine buildings down in 17 AD, but it was rebuilt by Tiberius and developed into a thriving provincial Roman town. It became part of the Ottoman Empire at the end of the 14th century.

Orientation

About 90km east of İzmir, there are actually two small villages at Sardis, nestled in a valley rich in vineyards (for sultanas, not wine grapes), olive groves, melon fields and tobacco fields. **Sartmustafa** (SART-MOOS-tah-fah; usually just called Sart) is the village on the highway, with a few teahouses and grocery shops. **Sartmahmut** (SART-mah-MOOT) is 1km north of the highway, clustered around the train station.

During the day the farmers come into town, park their tractors in front of the teahouses, sit down for a few glasses and discuss the crops. In early August when the harvest is in progress, children sell huge bunches of luscious, crisp, sweet sultanas to passers-by from roadside stalls. This is one of those areas where whole families careen around on motorcycles with sidecars attached.

A short hop further east, Salihli (population 71,000) is a local farming town with a sizeable otogar, an open-air marketplace, and three hotels to suit all budgets clustered around the otogar.

Archaeological Sites

The ruins of Sardis are scattered throughout the valley which lies beneath the striking ragged mountain range to the south, but two areas are particularly interesting.

At the eastern end of Sart, immediately north of the highway, lies the most extensive area of ruins, open virtually all the time during daylight hours, for US$1.75.

Buy your ticket at the little booth, then enter the ruins along the **Roman Road**, past a well-preserved **Byzantine latrine** and rows of **Byzantine shops**. Many of these once belonged to Jewish merchants and artisans, as they backed onto the wall of the great synagogue. Note the elaborate drainage system, with pipes buried in the stone walls. Some of the shops have been identified from inscriptions. There's a restaurant, Jacob's Paint Shop, an office, a hardware shop, and shops belonging to Sabbatios and Jacob, an elder of the synagogue. At the end of the Roman Road is an inscription on the marble paving stones done in either 17 or 43 AD, honouring Prince Germanicus.

Turn left from the Roman Road and enter the **synagogue** *(havra)*, impressive because of its size and beautiful decoration. It was built over the site of the old baths and gymnasium and has lots of fine geometric mosaic paving, and coloured stone on its walls. A plaque lists donors to the Sardis American Excavation Fund who supported excavation work between 1965 and 1973.

From the synagogue you cross a grassy area to reach the striking, two-storey facade of a building described as the **Marble Court of the Hall of the Imperial Cult**. Whether you like the restoration or not, it's certainly imposing – and provides plentiful nesting sites for local birds. Note especially the finely chiselled inscriptions in Greek, and the serpentine fluting on the columns. Behind it you'll find an ancient swimming pool and rest area.

A yellow sign points south down the road beside the teahouses to the **Temple of Artemis**, just over 1km away. Today only a few columns of a once-magnificent building, which was never completed, still stand but the temple's plan is clearly visible and quite impressive. Next to it is an **altar** used since ancient times, refurbished by Alexander the Great and later by the Romans. Clinging to the south-eastern corner of the temple is a small brick **Byzantine church**. From archaic times until the Hellenistic, Roman and Byzantine periods, this was a sacred spot, no matter what the religion. You may have to pay another admission fee if there's anyone in the booth to collect it.

As you're going back to İzmir, look to the north of the highway and you'll see a series of softly-rounded **tumuli**, the burial mounds of the Lydian kings.

Organised Tours

İzmir travel agencies operate full-day tours to Sardis and Manisa for about US$35, lunch included.

Places to Stay & Eat

Snacks are available at the crossroads in Sart although the noise and dust of the main road discourages lingering. For full meals and hotel rooms, catch any bus going east from Sart along the E96/D300 to Salihli (9km).

Hotel Yener *(☎ 236-712 5003, fax 714 3207, Zafer Mahallesi, Dede Çelik Sokak 7)* is a block south of the otogar across the open-air marketplace. Clean singles/doubles with shower cost US$6/10. A sign just inside the door says 'We accept no drunken customers'. ***Toros Et Lokantası*** shares the ground floor and terrace with the hotel.

Across the road is the smart two-star ***Otel Berrak*** *(☎ 236-713 1452, fax 713 1457, Belediye Caddesi 59)*, much more comfortable but charging US$55/70 for a single/double with shower.

Finally, behind the Belediye and in sight of the otogar is the impersonal ***Otel Akgül*** *(☎/fax 236-713 3787)* which offers pretty ordinary rooms but with panoramic views of Salihli for US$16/28 a single/double with breakfast, shower and TV.

Getting There & Away

Bus Buses depart at least every 30 minutes for the 90km, 1½-hour trip from İzmir's otogar. There's no need to buy a ticket in advance – just go to the otogar and buy a ticket for the next bus to Salihli (US$2). Tell them you want to get out at Sart.

Dolmuş minibuses run between Salihli and Sart, and Manisa, the provincial capital (US$1.75, 1½ hours).

Train Several daily trains from İzmir (Basmane) stop here but they're slower than the buses. Take the bus out to Sardis, but ask in town about return trains to İzmir, as you may find one at a convenient time.

ÇEŞME

Çeşme (CHESH-meh; population 100,000), 85km due west of İzmir, means 'fountain' or 'spring'. From the town, it's only about 10km across the water to the Greek island of Chios and the ferries to Greece are the main reason people come here. However, the fast-growing resort area encircling the town is popular with weekend-trippers from İzmir.

Çeşme itself is a pleasant seaside town, and the land to the east of it is rolling steppe, a foretaste of Anatolia. This barrenness subsides as you approach İzmir, giving way to wheat fields, lush orchards, olive groves and tobacco fields. About 23km east of Çeşme is the pretty **Uzunkuyu Piknik Yeri**, a roadside picnic area in a pine forest. About 50km east of Çeşme you pass the official city limits of İzmir, a full 30km west of Konak Meydanı.

Orientation

Çeşme is right on the coast. **Ilıca**, a seaside resort town 6km to the east, has numerous hotels in all price ranges. There are frequent dolmuşes running between Ilıca and Çeşme (US$1) – and buses from İzmir call in there first – but unless you want to spend all your time at the beach you're better off staying in Çeşme proper.

Çeşme's otogar is less than 1km south of the main square Cumhuriyet Meydanı although you can pick up a bus to İzmir from immediately west of the monument at the western end of İnkilap Caddesi. Everything you need is near the main square on the waterfront, with its inevitable statue of Atatürk. The Tourism Information Office, Customs House (Gümrük), ferry ticket offices, bus ticket offices, restaurants and hotels are all within two blocks.

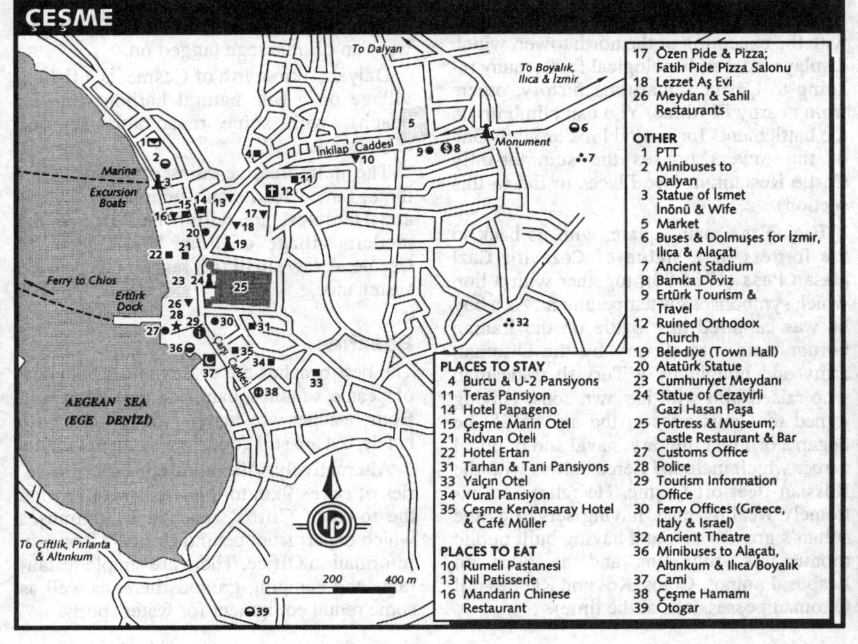

Information

The Tourism Information Office (☎/fax 232-712 6653) is down by the dock at İskele Meydanı 6.

You can change money at Bamka Döviz (☎ 232-712 0853), İnkilap Caddesi 80.

The annual Çeşme Film Festival is held during the third week of August.

The postal code is 35930.

Kalesi ve Müzesi

The huge Genoese fortress dominating the centre of town was repaired by Sultan Beyazıt, son of Sultan Mehmet the Conqueror, to defend the coast from attack by pirates and by the Knights of St John of Jerusalem based on Rhodes. It is now the **Çeşme Kalesi ve Müzesi** (Çeşme Fortress & Museum), which is open every day from 8.30 am to noon and from 1 to 5 pm. Admission costs US$1. The entrance is up the hill by the steps more or less opposite the Tourism Information Office.

Most of the castle's interior is empty, with the exception of the north tower, which displays local archaeological finds, many relating to Çeşme's maritime history, others from nearby Erythrae. You can climb up on the battlements for a good look around. One of the towers houses the summer-only Castle Restaurant (see Places to Eat in this section).

Facing the main square, with its back to the fortress, is a **statue of Cezayirli Gazi Hasan Paşa** (1714-90), together with a lion which symbolises his temperament. As a boy he was captured in a battle on the Iranian border, sold into slavery by the Ottoman army and bought by a Turkish tradesman who raised him with his own sons. Having joined the Janissaries at the age of 25, he began a brilliant military, naval and political career which included fierce battles with the Russian fleet off Çeşme. He retired an extremely wealthy man, having served as the sultan's grand vizier and having built public monuments, fountains and mosques on Lesbos, Lemnos, Chios, Kos and Rhodes (all Ottoman possessions at the time).

Things to See & Do

Çeşme's **caravanserai** was built in 1528, during the reign of Süleyman the Magnificent, but has been restored and converted into the Kervansaray Hotel, with limited success. It's worth taking a look around.

On İnkilap Caddesi is the ruined **orthodox church** of Ayios Haralambos, sometimes used for shows and exhibitions.

In the evening the people of Çeşme still observe the old Mediterranean custom of *piyasa vakti* ('plaza time'): dressing up and coming down to the main square for a stroll, a glass of tea, a bit of conversation and some people-watching. The men, some with their wives, then linger in the seaside restaurants and teahouses.

Vessels moored along Çeşme's waterfront make day excursions up and down the coast, stopping at good swimming spots. Trips cost around US$15 per person, lunch included.

Çeşme has a **hamam**, just past the Kervansaray Hotel. However, it charges a ridiculous US$20 for a wash and massage and an even more exorbitant US$32 if you want an oil massage tagged on.

Dalyan, 4km north of Çeşme, is a fishing village on a fine natural harbour (but no beach), with some reasonable seafood restaurants.

The unimpressive ruins of ancient Erythrae, famed for its cult temples of Cybele and Hercules, are within and around the modern village of **Ildır**, 27km north of Çeşme. A few small fish restaurants provide sustenance.

Beaches

The best beaches are at **Boyalık,** 1.5km east of Çeşme's main square, and **Ilıca,** 6km east. Both beaches are heavily developed with hotels, but are still good for a swim in the sun.

Alternatively, **Altınkum** consists of a series of coves 9km to the south-west beyond the town of Çiftlik, reached by dolmuşes which depart from behind Çeşme's Tourism Information Office. There are simple restaurants and camping grounds here, as well as some rental equipment for water sports.

Alaçatı

If you think Çeşme is becoming too package-tourist orientated like Side, you could move out to **Alaçatı**, 9km to the south-east. A well-preserved village of old stone houses populated by Ottoman Greeks a century ago, Alaçatı is backed by three windmills and equipped with a few small restaurants, pensions and hotels. The nearest beach is 4km away, but, like many other spots along this coast, it's famed for its windsurfing. Alaçatı Sörf Cenneti (Surf Paradise) in the Çark Mevkii district rents sailboards, bicycles, mopeds and camp sites. Dolmuşes run from Ilıca to Alaçatı, a distance less than 4km.

Places to Stay

Although Çeşme has several inexpensive pensions and hotels, several moderately priced hotels, and a restored caravanserai, most charge over the odds; and many lodgings are booked solid in the summer season. Check the package holiday brochures if you're after a longer stay.

Places to Stay – Budget

There are several good pensions in the midst of the action just off İnkilap Caddesi. The unmissable pink and black ***Teras Pansiyon*** *(☎ 232-712 7463),* on Ertürk Sokak near the church, is clean and relatively quiet, with shower-equipped rooms above a restaurant for US$13/17 a single/double. Some signs still call it the Birlik.

On the opposite side of İnkilap in a narrow lane of crumbling old houses, ***Burcu Pansiyon*** *(☎ 232-712 0387)* has a fine terrace and good shower-equipped rooms for slightly less, as does the nearby ***U-2 Pansiyon*** *(☎ 232-712 6381).* Both charge around US$6 per person.

Tarhan Pansiyon *(☎ 232-712 6061),* behind the Çeşme Kervansaray Hotel, charges US$13/17 a single/double for rooms in a pretty house draped with bougainvillea. ***Tani Pansiyon*** next door is similar.

Places to Stay – Mid-Range

Right on the shore, facing the main square, the two-star ***Hotel Ertan*** *(☎ 232-712 6795, fax 712 7852, Cumhuriyet Meydanı 12)* has a lift, open-air terrace bar, air-con restaurant and 60 rather ordinary guest rooms with bath, some facing the sea. Rates are US$40/50 a single/double, breakfast included.

Next door to the Ertan, the newer 36-room ***Rıdvan Oteli*** *(☎ 232-712 6336, fax 712 7627)* charges the same for rooms with similar facilities, but usually with balconies. The lobby is decorated with works by local photographer Çavit Kürnek.

Just north of the Ertan and Rıdvan near the water, ***Çeşme Marin Otel*** *(☎ 232-712 7579, fax 712 6484, Hürriyet Caddesi 10)* offers even better value, with shower-equipped rooms for US$20/24 a single/double with breakfast included, but the staff are in need of cheering up.

Parla Apart Otel *(☎ 232-712 6366, Musalla Mahallesi, Kabadayı Sokak 27),* run by an energetic woman named Çiğdem, rents clean, modern double rooms for US$25, and small apartments (lounge, bedroom, kitchen and bath) for US$32 – great value. The cheaper ***Vural Pansiyon***, just behind the Tarhan Pansiyon, is under the same competent management.

Yalçın Otel *(☎ 232-712 6981, fax 712 0623, Musalla Mahallesi, Kale Sokak 38)* is perched on the hillside overlooking the town. Its 16 pleasant rooms, all with private showers, some with excellent views, cost US$18/25/32 a single/double/triple.

Hotel Papageno *(☎ 232-712 8327, fax 712 0105, 16 Eylül Mahallesi, 1 Yalı Sokak 11)* is clean, modern, comfortable, and decently priced at US$16/20 a single/double with shower, breakfast included. One reader complained of noise from the market outside.

The historic ***Çeşme Kervansaray Hotel*** *(☎ 232-712 7177, fax 712 6491),* just south of the main square, was restored a decade ago and even more work was underway at the time of writing. The posted price of US$80, for a pleasantly furnished double room with tiny bathroom, has been known to halve when it's quiet. Turkish Night shows are held at least twice a week when you should go elsewhere or be kept awake by the racket.

Places to Eat

Çeşme's restaurants are all reasonably cheap, but of varying standards. Virtually all restaurants post their prices prominently. For a local taste treat, try the *sakızlı dondurma* (sah-kuhz-LUH dohn-door-mah), ice cream flavoured with pine resin, the same stuff they put in Greek retsina wine. If you like retsina, you should like this weird reincarnation of the flavour.

Behind the old church are numerous small eateries, including ***Özen Pide & Pizza***, which serves grills and Turkish pizza, also the speciality of ***Fatih Pide Pizza Salonu*** next door. Both places have outdoor tables by the church.

On İnkilap Caddesi, ***Lezzet Aş Evi*** (Flavour Cook-House) is still hanging on as one of the cheapest eateries in town, with vegetable plates for US$1, and *salçalı köfte* (meatballs) for US$1.25.

Nearby, ***Nil Patisserie*** serves excellent *baklava* (pastry with nuts and honey) and *lokum* (Turkish delight) for US$1 to US$2, and has a few streetside cafe tables. ***Rumeli Pastanesi*** on İnkilap specialises in the local *reçel* (jellies and preserves), which include *patlıcan* (aubergine), *turunç* (bitter orange), *incir* (fig), *limon çiçeği* (lemon-flower), *sakız* (pine gum – unusual white jam), *ayva* (quince), *gül* (rose) and *karpuz* (watermelon).

Sevim Café, in front of the Kervansaray, has outdoor tables which suffer a bit from traffic noise, but it's a good place for a sunset drink.

Chinese restaurants have been popping up in Turkish coastal resorts. The cuisine may not be authentic but it makes for a pleasant change. The ***Mandarin Chinese Restaurant***, in front of the Çeşme Marin Otel, has good main courses priced from US$6 to US$12.

The ***Castle Restaurant & Bar*** (☎ *232-712 8339)*, in a tower of the fortress, is a romantic place to watch the sunset, especially on your last Turkish night before catching the ferry bound for Greece. A full dinner will cost you between US$10 to US$15 but it's only open from late May to September.

Down on the waterfront at the main square, the ***Meydan*** and ***Sahil*** restaurants have the best location but higher prices: pizza is US$3.50, şiş kebap and similar simple grills US$4, fish substantially more. Both restaurants have outdoor tables, some facing the sea.

Getting There & Away

Bus The opening of the Çeşme-İzmir *otoyol* (expressway) has made it harder to get to Çeşme without transitting İzmir. If you're coming from Selçuk or Kuşadası, don't think you can avoid İzmir by taking a bus to Urla – there's no longer any onward public transport from Urla to Çeşme.

This is a drag because the bus to Çeşme doesn't leave from İzmir otogar. You'll have to come into the otogar, and then catch a bus across town to the separate terminal for Çeşme in Üçkuyular, a neighbourhood 6km west of Konak. This can add a good hour to the journey time (see Bus under Getting There & Away in the İzmir section).

Once you've got to the Çeşme terminal it's simple. Çeşme Turizm buses and minibuses make the 85-km, 1¼-hour run every 15 minutes or so from 6 am to 6 pm, for US$2, stopping at Ilıca and Alaçatı on the way.

If you buy an onward ticket from Çeşme to Ankara or İstanbul, your bus will still stop in İzmir en route.

Ferry – Chios Most people come to Çeşme on their way to or from Chios.

In high summer (1 July to 10 September) there are daily boats; the Monday boat connects at Chios with a boat for Piraeus, arriving in time to connect with a boat to Israel.

At other times of the year the schedule is:

16 to 30 April and throughout October, boats run Tuesday and Thursday.

1 to 15 May boats run Tuesday, Thursday and Sunday.

16 May to 30 June boats run Tuesday, Thursday, Friday, Saturday and Sunday.

11 to 30 September boats run on Tuesday, Thursday, Friday and Sunday.

1 November to 15 April, boats run Thursday only.

Departure is at 9 am on Tuesday, Thursday and Saturday and at 4 pm on other days. Return journeys are at 6 pm every day.

A one-way fare between Çeşme and Chios is US$30 but a same-day return costs US$40, making for a nice day trip. An open-date round trip costs US$50; a 3000 drachmae (US$10) Greek port tax is levied if you stay overnight. Children aged from four to 12 years get a 50% reduction in fare (but not tax). Motorcycles, cars, even caravans, minibuses and buses can be carried on the ferries. Car fares cost US$70 or US$90, depending upon length.

You should buy tickets at least a day in advance. For details, reservations and tickets, contact Ertürk Travel Agency (☎ 232-712 6768, fax 712 6223), Beyazıt Caddesi 6/7; or Maskot Turizm Seyahat (☎ 232-712 7654, fax 712 8435), İnkilap Caddesi 93/19, or at the harbour (☎ 232-712 0206).

These agencies can also provide information about onward connections by sea and air from Chios to other Aegean islands, Athens, Bari, Brindisi and Venice. From Chios there are usually close connections with ships for Athens (Piraeus), Lesbos, Samos and Thessaloniki, as well as flights to Athens, Samos, Mykonos and Venice.

Çeşme is also served by direct car/passenger ferries to and from Italy. See the Getting There & Away chapter for details.

Getting Around

Ertürk Rent a Car (☎ 232-712 6768, fax 712 6223), Beyazıt Caddesi 6/7, has perhaps been in business the longest – look for it beside the fortress.

SOUTH TO EPHESUS

The route from Çeşme via Seferihisar, Gümüldür and Özdere to Pamucak beach, Ephesus, Selçuk and Kuşadası (about 150km) follows shallow river valleys, passes through farming towns, and then skirts the coast at points. The region has a dozen ancient cities (Colophon, Claros, Notion, Teos) in an advanced state of ruin; most are of no great interest to anyone but archaeologists.

Since the construction of the motorway, the only way to get from Çeşme to Seferihisar is via İzmir; no dolmuşes run along the coast road from Çeşme to Urla any more. Coming from Selçuk, catch a minibus to Seferihisar (72km). From Seferihisar, regular dolmuşes and city buses run west to Sığacık (4.5km) and Akkum (7.2km).

Sığacık

Sığacık is a pretty, yet-to-be-discovered port village backed by a crumbling castle. Judging by the number of *Emlak* (real-estate) offices springing up, it won't be undiscovered for long. For now most people pass through quickly on their way to the white sands of Akkum, just over the hills to the west.

The centre of Sığacık is Atatürk Meydanı, the park bordered by the PTT, teahouses and restaurants. Lined up by the yacht harbour are the ***Burç*** and the fancier ***Liman*** restaurants, where businessmen babble into mobile phones while tucking into fish for around US$6 a portion. For a good view of the village, go around the harbour to ***Deniz Restaurant***, on the road to Akkum. Cut in from the square to find ***Şadırvan Pide Salonu*** and more down-to-earth prices.

The best place to stay is the inviting ***Teos Pension-Bar-Restaurant*** *(☎ 232-745 7463)* behind the castle. Attractive rooms painted in autumnal colours cost US$8 per person, including breakfast. There's cool Turkish music in the bar, and Internet access for those who need it. Alternatively, in the main square, ***Burg Pansiyon*** *(☎ 232-745 7464 Atatürk Meydanı 14)* is in a modern building, charging US$12 for a double with shower. Some rooms have harbour views.

In a far less attractive location on the road to Akkum are ***Liman Pansiyon*** *(☎ 232-745 7680, Akkum Caddesi 19)*, a clean family-run place with a pide salonu downstairs, and ***Deniz Moteli*** *(☎ 232-745 2533)*.

Akkum

Just 2km around the bay and over the hills is the turn-off westward to Akkum, another 700m along. The protected cove draws sailboarders in summer; and two small but smooth sand beaches, Büyük Akkum and Küçük Akkum, backed by olive groves, accommodate non-sailing companions.

For accommodation, there's the gorgeous but rather exclusive 230-room ***Neptun Holiday Village Windsurf Center*** *(☎ 232-745 7455, fax 745 3038)*, the sailboarders' hotel behind Büyük Akkum. When available, rooms cost from US$35 to US$55 per person with full board. Also backing on to the beach is ***Belediye Tesisleri***, a holiday village run by the Seferihisar town government. In comparison the small pensions on the hillside are rather an eyesore. Slightly up the hillside, ***Yakamoz Restaurant*** provides meals with a view of the cove.

Teos

Scattered amid the farmers' fields and olive groves 3km from Akkum are the ruins of ancient Teos. The few fluted column bases and chunks of marble rubble suggest that this was once a major Ionian city. It was home to the poet Anacreon and noted for its devotion to Dionysus and the pleasures of the cup and the table.

From Akkum, go up to the road and turn right to reach the **Teos Orman İçi Dinlenme Yeri**, 1km east of the turn-off, a pine-shaded picnic grove run by the forestry department. Entry costs less than US$1 per person, about US$1 per car.

Another 600m along, the road splits: the left fork goes to the ruins of Teos (800m); the right, to the Teos-Emeksiz Plajı, a ***Çadırlı Kamp-Günnübirlik Plaj*** (beach, day-use and tent-camping ground), 1km over the hill.

Northern Aegean Hinterland

The Aegean coast is Turkey's tourist mecca. The cities further inland have less appeal for holidaymakers, but offer plenty for adventurous travellers. Unlike the coastal towns, the inland cities offer a chance to experience modern Turkish daily life and culture, without the overheated prices of the resorts.

For most travellers, Balikesir is a transit point with just enough interest to fill an hour or so. Eskişehir, 150km south of Bursa, is Turkey's *meerschaum* mining centre. The soft white stone is artistically carved into bracelets, earrings, necklaces, cigarette holders and, of course, meerschaum pipes. A 90km detour south-east of Eskişehir brings you to Kütahya, its neighbourhoods of historic houses sheltering Turkey's *faïence* (coloured tile) ateliers.

Afyon, the centre of government-controlled opium production, is famous for its clotted cream and Turkish delight.

BALIKESİR

The triangular province of Balıkesir includes coastline on both the Marmara and Aegean seas, and a mountainous eastern region bordering on Kütahya. Its namesake capital city (population 200,000) is less interesting than its overt tourist centres: the resort town of Erdek and the railhead town of Bandırma on the Sea of Marmara, and the Aegean coastal resorts at Akçay, Edremit, Ören and Ayvalık. The historic hot springs at Gönen have been used since Roman times.

At Sındırgı, 63km south of Balıkesir, the famous Yağcıbeydir Turkish carpets are woven by descendants of early Turkish nomads who came here from Central Asia.

At least 5000 years old, the city of Balıkesir was known as Palaeokastron to the Romans and Byzantines. Though there are a few old buildings, including the **Zağanos Paşa Camii** (1461), the **Yıldırım Camii** (1388), the **Umur Bey Camii** (1412) and the **Karesi Bey Türbesi** (1336), this is not really a tourist town. You'll probably whip through it on the bus or train.

Information

The Tourism Directorate (☎ 266-241 1820, fax 244 7271) is at Dumlupınar Mahallesi, Anafartalar Caddesi, Sayar İşhanı 42/5.

Places to Stay

There are several cheap hotels near the otogar. The one-star, 22 room ***İnanöz Hotel***

(☎ *266-241 4265, fax 245 2124*), just opposite the Garaj Karşısı, offers rooms with bath for US$8/12 a single/double. The two-star, 36 room ***İmanoğlu Hotel*** (☎ *266-241 1302, fax 243 7137, Örücüler Caddesi 18*), charges US$20/27 for singles/doubles with bath. Best in town is the three-star, 57 room ***Kervansaray Oteli*** (☎ *266-241 1635, fax 241 4861*), İstasyon Caddesi.

ESKİŞEHİR

Despite its name, Eskişehir ('Old City'; population 430,000, altitude 788m) is a thoroughly modern centre. The scant ruins of the earlier Graeco-Roman city of Dorylaeum mostly lie beneath recent buildings.

This has always been an important transit point on the natural routes from north to south and east to west. Railway locomotives manufactured here haul trains throughout Turkey, sometimes laden with the products of Eskişehir's other industries: cement, sugar, textiles and more. The crack and whoosh of fighter jets announce a major air force base on the outskirts. The slightly more sedate Anadolu Universitesi (Anatolia University) is also here.

Dusty in summer and muddy in winter, the unremarkable city centre is brightened by a riverside promenade with streetside cafes, and a bustling market. Make sure you sample the local *nuga helvası* (nougat), on sale at the many confectioners' shops in the otogar.

Coming from İstanbul, the road south from İzmit to Bilecik and Eskişehir is frustratingly jammed with slow-moving trucks, which often reduce traffic to a crawl.

Orientation & Information

Really there are two Eskişehirs: the modern city you whip through on the bus and the older Ottoman city hidden away to the south of Atatürk and İki Eylül caddesis. The modern city centre is easily negotiated on foot. Hotels, restaurants, banks and other services are not far from the train station, which is north-west of the centre, but the new otogar is 3km from the centre by the sugar factory; take bus No 13 (US$0.25).

The most historically interesting part of town can be found by walking south along Seyh Sahabettin Caddesi towards the Kurşunlu Camii complex.

The friendly Tourism Information Office (☎ 222-230 1752, fax 230 3865) is in the Vilayet (provincial government headquarters) at İki Eylül Caddesi 175. There's no sign so you may have trouble locating it but when you do it can supply a basic map and directions to local sights.

Eskişehir's postal code is 26000.

Things to See & Do

At the southern end of İki Eylül Caddesi next to the post office is the Yunus Emre Kültür Sarayı with, on the fourth floor, the **Lületaşı Müzesi**, a fine collection of old and new meerschaum pipes, and photos of the mine at Sepetçi Köyü. You may have to wait for someone to find the key; and having them hover while you look around hardly makes for a relaxing visit. If you don't manage to get in, the modern pipes on sale in Eskişehir are mostly copies of these originals.

All along Şeyh Sahabettin Caddesi a wonderful **fruit and vegetable market** features stalls selling tomatoes the size of a man's fist and stripy aubergines and runner beans. Look out for a baker's cart offering *haşhaşlı*, a flat bread seasoned and stuffed with potato – utterly delicious when hot (US$0.60).

Narrow streets are lined with crumbling, colourful old **Ottoman houses**. The gracious **Osmanlı Evi Müzesi** in Yeşilefendi Sokak, is open to the public (free of charge) from 9 am to noon and 1 to 4 pm – knock if the door is closed. In theory the nearby **Etnografya Müzesi** is open the same hours.

At the heart of this old district the large **Kurşunlu Camii** (1525) is surrounded by pretty, flower-filled gardens and old tombs.

Still south of Atatürk Caddesi but west along H. Polatkan Bulvarı, the **Arkeoloji Müzesi** is open from 8.30 am to noon and from 1.30 to 5 pm (admission US$0.60). Here you'll see the finds from Dorylaeum including several crude mosaic floors, together with Roman statuettes of Cybele, Hecate and Mithras.

Meerschaum Mining Villages

Meerschaum is collected in lumps from open-cast mines up to 100m deep which are scattered for 5km in every direction around the villages of **Sepetçi Köyü** and **Kozlubel**. While there are poultry and grain farmers here, 85% of Sepetçi's wealth comes from meerschaum and the village now prefers to be called Beyaz Altın (White Gold) in honour of its most valuable commodity.

There are no services in either village, but if you ask for Mr Bülent Girgin in Sepetçi, he will take you to his prominent carving workshop at the eastern edge of the village. If you're lucky he may also show you a mining pit *(lületaşı ocağı)* further east.

Getting there can be tricky without your own vehicle. There are a few daily buses to the village of Yakaboyu which continue to Sepetçi and then Kozlubel (US$1) but you either have to go straight back when the driver's had his tea or hang around for several hours. Hitching is likely to be time-consuming as there's hardly any traffic out

Dream Pipes

Most of the travellers who stop in Eskişehir are looking for meerschaum (German for 'sea foam', *lületaşı* in Turkish). This soft, light, porous white stone, a hydrous magnesium silicate called sepiolite by mineralogists, is mined at numerous villages east of Eskişehir, including Başören, Karahöyük (Karatepe), Kemikli, Kozlubel Köyü, Nemli, Sarısıva, Sepetçi Köyü, Söğütçük and Yarmalar. Eskişehir has the world's largest and most easily accessible deposits of the mineral.

Miners are lowered into vertical shafts which penetrate the meerschaum beds to depths from 10m to 150m. The miners fill buckets with heavy mud, which is hauled to the surface, dumped and sluiced, revealing rough chunks of meerschaum. It's dark, dirty, dangerous work. There are no veins where large blocks can be cut. The larger the chunk, the higher its value.

Though once pulverised and made into tooth powder, meerschaum is now used for carving; while the stone is still wet and as soft as soap, carvers in the villages and in Eskişehir work it into fanciful shapes and decorative objects, most of which are exported. Block meerschaum was also exported until 1979, when someone figured out that to export the material was to export the carving jobs as well, and so it became illegal to export it. Prayer beads, necklaces, belts, earrings, baubles and cigarette-holders are commonly made items, but the most popular is the meerschaum pipe.

A good carver can make about four pipes a day, while highly elaborate pieces can take a week. Meerschaum pipes are valued because the strong, light, porous material smokes cool and sweet, drawing off the burning tobacco's heat and some of the tar. Devoted meerschaum pipe smokers wear special gloves while smoking to protect their prized pipes from being tarnished by skin oils. With time, a coddled pipe will take on an even nut-brown patina that is highly valued by devotees.

You can view carvers at work and buy their art in Eskişehir, Monday to Saturday from 9 am to about 7 pm at Işık Pipo (☎ 222-323 8702), Sakarya Caddesi, Konya İşhanı 12/17; and Pipo Burhan Yücel, both in the city centre near the Büyük Otel. Burhan Yücel also has a shop beneath the otogar.

here. With your own wheels, drive north-east from Eskişehir on the road to Alpu as far as Çavlum (18km), then turn left (north) and go via Kızılcaören, Yakakayı and Gündüzler to Sepetçi/Beyaz Altın (40km) and, 6km beyond it, to Kozlubel.

Places to Stay

There's no problem finding somewhere central to stay although the real cheapies are very basic and not very used to travellers. Some of the other hotels are relatively pricey, considering their universally drab decor, but may be open to haggling.

Buses into town run along Sivrihisar Caddesi. Ask to be dropped at the old ('eski') otogar and you'll be put off at the junction with Yunus Emre Caddesi. As you head south along it, the first place you'll pass is the two-star ***Emek Otel*** *(☎ 222-231 2940)*, right beside the old otogar, which is now largely empty. Though well worn with ropey wiring, it's serviceable and friendly. Rooms with bath cost US$21/31 a single/double; breakfast costs another US$3.50.

Across Yunus Emre Caddesi from the old otogar are three more two-star hotels, all with lifts and all perfectly welcoming. The 35 room ***Otel Dural*** *(☎ 222-233 1347)* at No 97, charges US$20 a double with sink, US$45 with private shower. ***Soyiç Hotel*** *(☎ 222-230 7190, fax 230 5120)* at No 101 charges US$18/30/36 for a single/double/triple with bath. ***Hotel Arslan*** *(☎ 222-231 0909, fax 231 5018)*, at No 107 charges US$12/17 a single/double. At No 93 is ***Atışhan Otel*** *(☎ 222-220 1666, fax 232 4547)*, undoubtedly the smartest place in town but charging US$60/ 75/100 for a single/double/triple.

Turn left at the north end of Yunus Emre Caddesi and you'll quickly arrive at the confluence of İnönü, Cengiz Topel, Sakarya, Muttalip and Sivrihisar Caddesis (in the district called Köprübaşı). Here you'll find ***Eskişehir Büyük Otel*** *(☎ 222-230 6800, fax 234 6508, Sivrihisar Caddesi 40)*, an older three-star place charging US$30 for doubles with all mod cons (TV, minibar, radio, shower, hairdryer) but the same drab, brown decor. Get a room at the back to avoid street noise.

The one-star, 45 room ***Otel Şale*** *(☎ 222-231 4743, İsmet İnönü Caddesi 17/1)*, across the street from the prominent Ordu Evi (army building – ask for that to find the hotel), is central but quite noisy. It charges US$15/23 for a single/double room with shower.

There are a couple of cheapies near here too. ***Otel Divan*** (☎ 222-231 1728, *İsmet İnönü Caddesi* 13) costs US$5/9/14 a single/double/triple but its clientele is solidly male and the TV in the hall makes a quiet night unlikely. If you're down to your last liras, ***Çiçek Palas Oteli*** *(☎ 222-234 4056, Sivrihisar Caddesi 29)* charges just US$4 per person but a female guest would be an oddity.

In the heart of the shopping district you'll find a pair of hotels with natural spring water that is said to help rheumatism, lumbago and other health problems. ***Termal Otel Sultan*** *(☎ 222-231 8371, Hamamyolu Caddesi 1)* offers shabby, noisy rooms for US$15/24 a single/double. Better is ***Has Hotel Termal*** *(☎ 222-231 9191, fax 234 6488, Hamamyolu Caddesi* 7*)* which charges exactly the same for cleaner, quieter rooms. It's another US$5 to use the attached hamam (women admitted Tuesday only).

Places to Eat

The stretch of road between the Büyük Otel and the Otel Şale is full of cheap kebap shops. Turn down Köprübaşı Caddesi for the bright, cheerful and busy ***Şahin İşkembe Salonu*** where a bowl of beans and rice with bread and a soft drink will come to about US$2. Across the road ***Nasir*** is truly a family-friendly place whose upstairs *aile salonu* boasts a swing, slide and other child-diverting playthings; İskender kebap with a soft drink will cost US$3.

A few doors away from the Nasir is the ***Altı Kardeşler*** pastry shop which stocks, among other gooey desserts, the two puddings made with chicken: *tavukgögsü* and *kazandibi* (US$1 a bowl).

There's a delightful *çay bahçesi* (tea garden) beside the market off Şeyh Sahabettin Caddesi where men sip their tea around a fountain surrounded by pine and plane trees, closely observed by white ducks.

Getting There & Away

As Eskişehir is an important stop on the İstanbul-Ankara line, there are frequent train services throughout the day and night. (See the Getting Around chapter for information on the major train services.)

The vast new otogar in the outskirts is served by innumerable city buses along Sivrihisar Caddesi (look for signs saying 'Terminal' or 'Yeni Otogar'), or by dolmuş from Yunus Emre Caddesi. Services include:

Ankara – 230km, 3¼ hours, US$9; hourly
Bursa – 155km, 2½ hours, US$6; hourly
İstanbul – 310km, 6 hours, US$10; hourly
Konya – 420km, 6 hours, US$10; several direct buses, or change at Afyon
Kütahya – 91km, 1¼ hours, US$3; hourly

KÜTAHYA

Spread beneath the walls of an imposing hilltop fortress in the midst of hill country, Kütahya (population 150,000, altitude 949m) is a small city famous for the manufacture of coloured tiles and pottery. Faïence (*çini*: coloured tile) is used everywhere – on building facades, in floors and walls, and in unexpected places. Every year scholars flock from around the world to attend the International Faïence & Ceramics Congress. The Dumlupınar Fuarı, held each year in the fairgrounds of the same name not far from the otogar, is Turkey's largest handicrafts fair. Kütahya's factories also turn out more mundane clay products such as water pipes, conduits and other industrial ceramics.

The Temple of Zeus at Aizanoi, one of Anatolia's best-preserved Roman temples, is one hour away.

History

No one is sure when Kütahya was founded; its earliest known inhabitants were Phry-

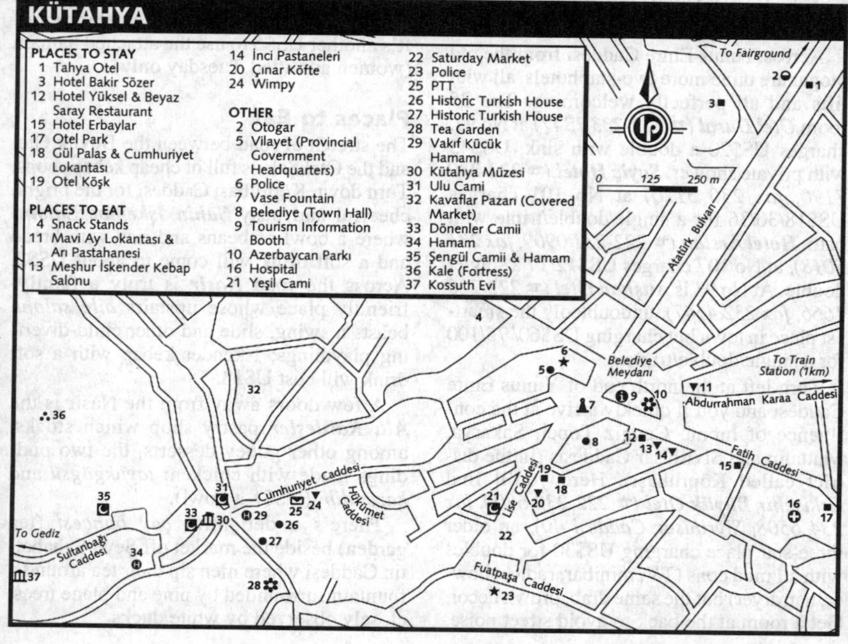

gians. In 546 BC it was captured by the Persians, and then saw the usual succession of rulers, from Alexander the Great to the kings of Bithynia and the emperors of Rome and Byzantium, who called the town Cotiaeum.

The first Turks to arrive were the Seljuks, in 1182. Later they were pushed out by the crusaders but returned to found the Emirate of Germiyan (1302-1428), with Kütahya as its capital. The emirs cooperated with the Ottomans in nearby Bursa, and, upon the death of the last emir, his lands were incorporated in the growing Ottoman Empire. When Tamerlane swept in at the beginning of the 15th century, he upset everyone's applecart, made Kütahya his headquarters for a while and then went back to where he came from.

As an Ottoman province, Kütahya settled down to tile-making. After Selim I took Tabriz in 1514, he brought all of its ceramic artisans to Kütahya and İznik, and set them to work. The two towns rivalled one another in the excellence of their faïence.

After the collapse of the 1848 Hungarian revolution, the great leader Lajos Kossuth fled to the Ottoman Empire, where he was given refuge and settled in Kütahya for a short time. His house is now a museum, Kossuth Evi.

The Battle of Dumlupınar

The decisive battle of the Turkish War of Independence was fought around Kütahya.

During the Turkish War of Independence, Greek armies intent on claiming Ottoman lands for Greece pushed inland from İzmir, occupied Kütahya and threatened the fledgling Turkish republican government at Ankara. Twice the Greek advance was checked by the Turks at the village of İnönü, north-east of Kütahya, but the invading forces finally broke through, took Eskişehir and Afyon, and made them strong points in a defensive line that stretched 500km from the Sea of Marmara to the valley of the Menderes (Meander) River.

Since the beginning of WWI, Turkish soldiers had been fighting defensive battles. In the Battle of the Sakarya, the longest pitched battle in history, the Greek armies had been fought to a standstill, with many casualties on both sides. The republican capital at Ankara had been successfully defended. The time had come for a Turkish offensive.

Plans were carried out with the utmost secrecy. Mustafa Kemal (Atatürk) got all his generals together at a football game, so spies would never suspect that high-level consultations were under way. Troops were moved at night, under cover of darkness, resting by day beneath trees and in houses, away from the prying eyes of Greek reconnaissance flights. Small troops of soldiers were sent out to raise great clouds of dust to simulate larger troop movements. The Greek occupiers were so lulled into complacency that many of the commanders attended a dance in Afyon on the evening of 25 August 1922.

At first light the next morning, the Turkish forces began a bold and risky counterattack, with a thunderous barrage of artillery. The Turkish generals directed their troops from the front lines, not from observation points in the rear. By 9.30 am, the Turkish forces had taken all but two of their hilltop objectives, breaking through the Greek defences along the valley of Dumlupınar, due south of Kütahya, near the highway from İzmir to Afyon. They followed up quickly and relentlessly on this advantage, driving the enemy soldiers just as quickly from their second and third lines of defence.

In the battle for the valley, half of the Greek expeditionary force was annihilated or captured, while the other half beat a hasty retreat towards İzmir. The Dumlupınar victory (30 August 1922) was the turning point in the war.

Orientation & Information

The roundabout centred on a huge tiled fountain in the shape of a vase is Belediye Meydanı, the city's main square. Overlooking it are the Vilayet and the Belediye. The otogar, Kütahya Çinigar (Tile Station), is less than 1km north-east of Belediye Meydanı; leave the otogar's front gateway, turn right and walk straight on. Hotels, restaurants and tile shops cluster within 100m of the square.

The town's main commercial street is Cumhuriyet Caddesi and runs south-west from the Vilayet, past the PTT, and on to the Ulu Cami.

In summer an information kiosk in the Azerbaycan Parkı just east of Belediye Meydanı is sometimes open. The Tourism Ministry Office (☎ 274-223 1962) is on Fuatpaşa Caddesi on the 4th floor of the Kütahya Valiliği Kültür Müdurlüğü building.

Kütahya's postal code is 43000.

Kütahya Tilework

Kütahya tiles are made of kaolin, quartz, chalk, clay and sand. Refined in a time-consuming, laborious process, the base material is covered with an even more refined slip, then painted, glazed and fired again.

Kütahya ware comes in three general grades. *Turist işi* ('tourist work') is the lowest, painted quickly to basic designs and sold to souvenir shops. *Normal* or *fabrika işi* is good quality work painted carefully by apprentices under the direction of a master. *Özel işi* ('special work') is the master's own, often signed. Painting a single özel plate can take four or five days.

Kütahya has about 50 faïence ateliers of greater or lesser size producing plates, vases and other decorative tableware, flat tiles for wall mounting, and many other objects. The designs are mostly floral, geometric, or based on Kuranic inscriptions.

You can find Kütahya pottery in any Turkish souvenir shop, but the shops around Belediye Meydanı have the widest selection of the best work. Each pottery has its authorised shop. Besides the expected tourist stuff, shops have fine mid-range pieces in a surprising variety of designs, plus some masterworks for connoisseurs. Heading out of town towards Eskişehir or Afyon you'll also find vast porcelain warehouses all geared up for the coach party trade.

The sons of Ahmet Şahin (see boxed text 'Kütahya Çini'), Faruk Şahin and Zafer Şahin, are *çinici*s (master craftspeople) as is Zafer Bey's son Ahmet Hürriyet Şahin. But Ahmet Hürriyet Şahin's wife, Nurten Şahin, is an acknowledged çinici of the first rank, even though she had never painted a tile before her marriage. Look for their work from the former Işıl Çini atelier, their present work from Metin Çini, and that of other masters such as Ali Özker and İhsan and İbrahim Erdeyer of Süsler Çini, and Hakkı Ermumcu and Mehmet Gürsoy of İznik Çini.

If you're really into pots, it should be easy to arrange a factory visit if you ask at a shop and give a bit of notice.

Ulu Cami & Bazaar

The Ulu Cami, at the far end of Cumhuriyet Caddesi from Belediye Meydanı, has been restored several times since it was built in 1410. From a distance it still manages to look a bit like Aya Sofya in İstanbul. It's surrounded by a colourful bazaar, in which you might stumble upon the **Kavaflar Pazarı**, a 16th century market building, the **İshak Fakih Camii** (1434) and the **İmaret Mescidi** (1440), a former *medrese* (theological seminary).

Kütahya Müzesi

The Kütahya Müzesi is housed in the Vacidiye Medresesi right next door to the Ulu Cami. The medrese was built by Umur bin Savcı of the princely family of Germiyan in 1314 and has a fine central dome above a marble pool. Apart from the usual medley of artefacts from the Chalcolithic to Ottoman periods, the museum contains finds from the great Temple of Zeus (see Aizanoi later in this chapter), including a magnificent Roman sarcophagus carved with scenes of battling Amazons. Hardly surprisingly, it also has a room devoted to local pottery and tiles.

The museum is open from 8 am to noon and 1.30 to 5.30 pm except Monday. Admission costs US$1.

Kütahya Çini

The Kütahya *çini* (faïence, coloured tile) industry was founded in the late 14th century, and given a boost in the early 16th century when Sultan Selim I brought expert tile-makers here from his newly-conquered city of Tabriz in Persia. It thrived until the cataclysm of WWI, which resulted in the closure of all but two of the city's pottery ateliers. One of these was run by David Ohannessian, an Ottoman Armenian. When he was called to Jerusalem to repair the tiles in the famous Dome of the Rock, he took a team of Kütahya's best artisans. Instead of returning, they established a traditional Turkish faïence industry in Jerusalem, where it thrives today.

That left one working atelier in Kütahya whose master, Hafız Mehmet Emin, died in 1922. Luckily, he had a skilled and inspired apprentice named Ahmet Şahin (born 1907) who, with another young and enthusiastic tile-maker named Hakkı Çinicioğlu, worked to maintain the traditions of Kütahya tile-making. Though still a tenuous industry in 1950, Kütahya faïence has since grown to include some 50 ateliers.

From the beginning, Ahmet Şahin insisted on creating coloured tiles of the highest standards of artisanship and aesthetics. Though he is master of every part of the complicated and laborious process, Şahin is renowned mostly as a designer. His patterns for the designs and calligraphy used on Kütahya faïence fill nine trunks. About 70% of all Kütahya designs are his, or have been derived from his designs.

In traditional Turkish art – as in the art of America's Shaker communities – the artist's role is to affirm the unity and harmony of Allah's creation by producing beautiful objects: each work of art is a prayer, a tribute to God and a gift to one's fellow humans. Each motif, flower, pattern or Koranic inscription is laden with significance and tradition. Though change and innovation are possible, they are attempted only after deep reflection and in a creative spirit. It is an art of continuity, of community, not of iconoclasm or egotism.

Kossuth Evi

Follow the signs behind the Ulu Cami to the Kossuth Evi (Kossuth House), also called the Macar Evi (Hungarian House). It's more or less 250m straight on up the hill; look for the house on the left, marked by plaques in Turkish and Hungarian. On the way you'll pass the 16th century **Şengül Camii** and its thriving hamam.

Lajos Kossuth (1802-94) was a prominent member of the Hungarian parliament. In 1848, chafing at Habsburg rule from Vienna, he and others rose in revolt, declaring Hungary an independent republic in 1849. When Russian troops intervened on the side of the Austrians, he was forced to flee. The Ottomans offered him a refuge and he lived in Kütahya from 1850-51.

His house, with its perfectly preserved kitchen, dining room, bedroom, and office, is open daily except Monday from 8 am to noon and 1.30 to 5.30 pm; admission costs US$1. The first floor verandah offers lovely views over a rose garden complete with statue of Kossuth and of the encircling hills. This is how upper-class Kütahyans lived in the mid-19th century. Unfortunately the rooms are roped off so you can't inspect the Kossuth memorabilia more closely.

Kütahya Fortress

The ruins of the kale are accessed by a steep path from the neighbourhood of the Ulu Cami, or by a road which winds around the hill and approaches the top from the far side (follow black-on-yellow signs reading 'Döner Gazino').

Built in two stages by the Byzantines, the castle was restored and used by their successors, the Seljuks, the emirs of Germiyan, and the Ottomans. The latest building work seems to have taken place in the 15th century. One look at the remains of the dozens of cylindrical towers makes it easy to imagine what a formidable obstacle this would have been to any army.

Tea gardens with splendid views and the Döner Gazino, a cylindrical restaurant/nightclub, reward your climb.

Places to Stay

Most of Kütahya's hotels are clustered around the vase fountain. Although that makes them easy to find it also ensures that traffic noise should be a consideration when you choose your room.

Hotel Yüksel *(☎ 274-212 0111, Belediye Meydanı 1)* is a well-worn hostel charging US$7/11 for a single/double without shower. ***Otel Köşk*** *(☎ 274-216 2024, Lise Caddesi 1)* offers simple double rooms with sinks for US$9 or US$12 with shower; the stair carpet is very threadbare but you'll get a TV, towels, soap and a fair amount of space for your money. ***Otel Park*** *(☎ 274-216 2310, Afyon Caddesi 20)* is for emergencies only.

Kütahya's best hotel, ***Gül Palas*** *(☎ 274-216 1759, fax 216 2135, Belediye Meydanı)*, is tiled in light blue and navy. It was completely renovated in 1995 and readers rate it highly. Pleasant rooms with showers and reasonably up-to-date decor cost US$27/38 a single/double, breakfast included. There's a sauna in the basement.

The three-star, ***Hotel Erbaylar*** *(☎ 274-223 6960, fax 216 1046, Afyon Caddesi 14)* has decent rooms with shower for an outrageous US$40/60 a single/double; haggle like mad. Some rooms have TV and minibar.

The welcoming three-star ***Tahya Otel*** *(☎ 274-224 3071, 224 3074)*, on Atatürk Bulvarı opposite the otogar, has 35 bath-equipped rooms for US$20/35 a single/double, breakfast included. For peace and quiet you might be better off at the 52 room ***Hotel Bakır Sözer*** *(☎ 274-224 8146, fax 224 8149)*, Çinigar Caddesi, on the southern side of the otogar, but away from the main roads. Beds cost US$12 per person in clean rooms with baths as well as showers.

Places to Eat

Çınar Köfte on Lise Caddesi 7, near the Otel Yeni Köşk, serves köfte, soup, salad, bread and beverages for US$4 or less.

Cumhuriyet Lokantası, beside the Gül Palas, is a quiet eatery open from breakfast time and serving three-course meals for under US$8.

Beyaz Saray on Afyon Caddesi 2 is a white-tablecloth place only a few steps from the vase fountain on Belediye Meydanı. It specialises in İskender kebap for US$2.50. The nearby ***Meşhur İskender Kebap Salonu*** on Afyon Caddesi 6 is also popular, though portions are quite small. A few doors further along is the cheerful ***İnci Pastaneleri***, selling coffee and thick chocolate mousse for around US$1.50.

On the north-eastern side of Belediye Meydanı across Abdurrahman Karaa Caddesi and Fatih Caddesi are several other cheap restaurants (try the popular ***Mavi Ay Lokantası***) and a pastry shop, ***Arı Pastahanesi***, where coffee and a dessert will cost US$1.50. For fresh fruit, vegetables and picnic supplies, browse the open-air market one block south up the hill on Lise Caddesi; it's at its liveliest on Saturday and has a pleasant ***çay bahçesi*** attached.

At night a few booths selling köfte, gözleme and other snacks open at the fountain end of Adnan Menderes Bulvarı. Sampling their wares should be fun if you have a sturdy constitution. For those with queasier stomachs Kütahya now has its own ***Wimpy***, serving up standard burgers and fries. It's in Cumhuriyet Caddesi, close to the PTT.

Getting There & Away

Because Kütahya is a provincial capital, its otogar supports fairly busy traffic. Here are details of bus services from Kütahya to:

Afyon – 100km, under two hours, US$3; many buses daily
Aizanoi – see Çavdarhisar
Ankara – 315km, five hours, US$7; a dozen buses daily
Antalya – 375km, eight hours, US$9; a few buses daily in summer, fewer in winter

Bursa – 190km, three hours, US$5; a dozen buses daily
Çavdarhisar – 60km, one hour, US$2; a few buses and minibuses daily
Eskişehir – 91km, 1¼ hours, US$3; very frequent buses daily
İstanbul – 355km, six hours, US$9; a dozen buses daily
İzmir – 385km, six hours, US$9; a dozen buses daily
Konya (via Afyon) – 335km, five hours, US$9; several direct buses, or change at Afyon

AİZANOİ (ÇAVDARHİSAR)

The village of Çavdarhisar (population 4100), 60km south-west of Kütahya, is home to Aizanoi (or Aezani), the site of Anatolia's best-preserved Roman temple. The great **Temple of Zeus** (or Jupiter) dates from the reign of Hadrian (117-38 AD), and was dedicated to the worship of Zeus and to the Anatolian fertility goddess Cybele (Artemis, Diana).

Hours are officially from 9 am to noon and 1 to 5 pm, but there's no fence so the friendly custodian, Mr Nazim Ertaş, will come to find you and sell you a ticket for US$1.50. He'll also unlock the gate and take you down to the crypt-like sanctuary of Cybele beneath the temple.

The temple stands on a broad terrace built to serve as the temple precinct. Like some ancient Hollywood set, the north and west faces of the temple have their double rows of Ionic and Corinthian columns intact, but the south and east rows have fallen in a picturesque jumble. The three columns at the north-eastern corner were toppled by the disastrous Gediz earthquake of 1970, but have since been re-erected. The *cella* (interior) walls are intact enough to give a good impression of the whole. A wire enclosure on the north-western edge of the temple precinct holds some of the best bits of sculpture found here.

The road out of Çavdarhisar is lined with chunks of fallen Roman masonry but turn right along the path into the fields opposite the temple and you'll come first to remains of a 2nd century **palaestra** or gymnasium, and then to more substantial remains of a linked **theatre** and **stadium**. The stones have crumbled badly and now provide a home for innumerable wheatears and the odd woodpecker. Look out on the right for a stretch of wall with the names of Olympic winners inscribed in medallions.

Return to the road and turn left back into the village, crossing a bridge over a small stream; divert down beside it and you'll realise much of the stonework that you'll see dates back to Hadrian's reign. Turn left after the bridge and you'll come to the remains of a **bath complex**. The locked shed contains a fine mosaic pavement, mostly covered with geometric patterns but with a representation of a satyr and maenad too; ask Mr Ertaş to let you in.

Go back to the road by the bridge and take the path right along the stream. Eventually you'll emerge by the remains of the Roman **forum**, or marketplace, with fine standing columns and a marble pavement. Around the corner from the Eski Pazar Camii are the remains of an unusual **circular market building** with a little turret reconstructed beside it. Look closely at the walls and you'll see the fixed prices for market goods inscribed in Roman numerals.

At the Çavdarhisar crossroads there are a few ***eateries*** and shops although the village itself boasts only a basic tearoom. You may be able to get permission to camp somewhere at the edge of the village, but there are no facilities except at the fuel stations and the toilets opposite the temple.

Getting There & Away

Çavdarhisar is on the Kütahya to Uşak road. A few direct buses from Kütahya's otogar take one hour to get to the village (US$3). Alternatively, take a Gediz or Emet minibus and ask to be dropped at Çavdarhisar.

Driving, take the Afyon road for 10km, then turn right (west) on the road marked for Aizanoi and for Çavdarhisar another 50km. At the Çavdarhisar crossroads turn right towards Emet. The Temple of Zeus is 800m along this road on the left.

To make a day of it, start early and bring a picnic. As soon as you arrive in Çavdarhisar, check the times of return buses or minibuses to Kütahya (they run pretty infrequently). Alternatively, there are onward minibuses to Gediz (37km) and Uşak (65km more); from Uşak you can easily catch a bus to Afyon, Ankara, Denizli/Pamukkale, İzmir, Konya or Manisa.

MİDAS ŞEHRİ

The rock-hewn monuments at Midas Şehri, midway between Afyon and Eskişehir, are the most impressive we've inherited from the civilisation of the Phrygians. If you have your own transport, it's worth a half-day detour to see them. It's best done in the early morning, the only time when sunlight bathes the Midas Tomb at Midas Şehri. Without your own wheels, you must have an intense interest in things Phrygian as public transport is slow and uncertain.

What archaeologists call Midas Şehri is in the village of **Yazılıkaya** ('inscribed rock'), 72km north of Afyon or 107km south of Eskişehir, not to be confused with the Yazılıkaya at the Hittite capital of Boğazkale, east of Ankara.

Midas Tomb

Most prominent of the works in Midas Şehri is the so-called Midas Tomb, a 17m-high relief carved into the soft tufa representing the facade of a temple covered in geometric patterns. At the centre near the base of the facade is a niche where an effigy of the Anatolian fertility goddess Cybele would be displayed during festivals. Inscriptions in the Phrygian alphabet, one bearing the name of Midas, decorate the facade. A small **museum**, which you pass on the walk up to the Midas Tomb, holds a few finds from the site, and diagrams. A portion of the ancient road, visible from the wagon-wheel ruts worn into the rock, connects the museum with the Midas Tomb.

Beside the Midas Tomb is a later rock-cut 'monastery', with tombs beneath.

A few hundred metres to the west is **Küçük Yazılıkaya** (Little Inscribed Rock), another 6th century BC rock-hewn cult monument which was never completed.

The Phrygians

The Phrygians emigrated from Thrace to central Anatolia around 1200 BC. They spoke an Indo-European language, used an alphabet similar to the Greek, and established a kingdom with its capital at Gordion, 106km west of Ankara (see the Central Anatolia chapter). Phrygian culture was based on that of their neighbours the Greeks, but with strong Neo-Hittite and Urartian influences.

The Phrygians are credited with having invented the frieze, embroidery, and numerous musical instruments including cymbals (for which Turkey is still famous), *aulos* (double clarinet), flute, lyre, syrinx (panpipes) and triangle.

The Phrygian Empire flourished under its most famous king, Midas (circa 725-675 BC), one of many Phrygian monarchs to have that name, until the empire was overrun by the Cimmerians (676-585 BC).

Phrygian art and culture flourished from around 585 to 550 BC, when the rock-cut monuments at Midas Şehri – the most impressive Phrygian monuments extant – were carved. The area was later ruled by the Lydian kings from Sardis, and still later by the kings of Pergamum.

Phrygian art, executed in ceramics, wood, mosaics, metal and rock, is vigorous, spirited and original, and seems to have influenced later Greek vase painters in the Aegean Cyclades islands.

The Phrygians' most notable exports seem to have been metal objects, textiles, slaves and the names of their kings: Midas and Gordios. Several kings bore these names, and archaeologists have found it difficult to solve the mystery of which Midas was which.

About 150m south of the Midas Tomb on the plateau's eastern side, a rock-hewn stairway decorated with reliefs of figures leads to the acropolis atop the 30m-high plateau. Here there are signs of a rock-hewn throne-altar, defensive walls, and other stairways leading down into the rock to a well. The site guardian will show you around for a tip.

Nearby Phrygian Sites

Another Phrygian cult temple is at **Arezastis**, about 1km away on the Seyitgazi road.

Even more Phrygian rock carvings are to be found east and south of Midas Şehri along the roads to Afyon. Heading west from Midas Şehri along unpaved roads, the village of **Kümbet** (17km) has a Selçuk tomb *(kümbet)* and a Phrygian shrine with a relief of a lion (Aslanlı Mabet).

Just 2km west of Kümbet is the narrow but paved Seyitgazi-Afyon road (03-78). Go south towards Afyon (21km) to an unpaved road on the right (west) marked for the **Göynüş Vadisi**, a valley of tufa outcrops bearing several Phrygian reliefs, including Aslantaş (a lion), Yılantaş (a snake) and Maltaş (a sheep). Continue along the poor unpaved road to İhsaniye (or go back to the Afyon road), and head south to the hot-springs town of **Gazlıgöl** (14km), then north-west to İhsaniye (16km) via road 03-77). From İhsaniye take the unpaved road north towards Döğer (13km) to reach other Phrygian carvings at **Kapıkayalar** and **Arslankaya** (Cybele with a lion at each side).

About 5km south of the Göynüş Vadisi turn on the way to Gazlıgöl and Afyon is a turn on the left (east) at Kayahan for **Ayazinköyü**, the site of an ancient rock-hewn settlement called Metropolis. The village, 5km east of Kayahan, is set amid Cappadocia-like rock formations of soft tufa which have been hollowed out to make dwellings, storerooms and churches. These troglodyte dwellings and the decoration in the churches are not nearly as well preserved as those in the Göreme valley but are worth a look if you won't reach Cappadocia. There are also a few minor Phrygian lion reliefs.

Getting There & Away

Public transport is very limited. You'll almost certainly have to hitch rides at some point – and these roads have little traffic. Plan to spend the whole day on this excursion.

With your own vehicle, transport is easy enough, and you can visit most of these sites in less than a day. The best access road to Midas Şehri is the paved, one-lane road approaching from the east via Çifteler.

From Eskişehir Take a bus or dolmuş south to Seyitgazi, then ask. There may be a dolmuş south from Seyitgazi via Şükranlı and Çukurca to Yazılıkaya along the paved road. If not, take something bound for Gazlıgöl or Afyon along road 03-78, get out at the Kümbet turn, and hope to hitch a ride, or expect a long walk along the unpaved road eastward.

If you're driving, it's faster to take the Ankara highway (E90) east for 37km to the turn-off south for Mahmudiye and Çifteler. At Çifteler, 60km south-east of Eskişehir, turn right (west) on the one-lane macadam road for Gökçeköyü and Yazılıkaya, another 36km along.

From Afyon If you're driving, head due north from Afyon following signs for 'Organize Sanayi Bölgesi', 'Gazlıgöl' and 'Seyitgazi', then follow the guidance given above under 'Nearby Phrygian Sites'.

Dolmuşes from Afyon go as far as Gazlıgöl and perhaps İhsaniye, where you'll probably have to change for onward rides. A few trains can take you to İhsaniye and Döğer; after visiting Arslankaya and Kapıkayalar, you'll probably find it easiest to return to Afyon by dolmuş.

AFYON

Formerly called Afyonkarahisar (The Black Fortress of Opium), this workaday agricultural and carpet-weaving town (population 100,000, altitude 1021m), capital of the province of the same name, hardly lives up to its sinister moniker.

Although still an important region for producing opium for pharmaceutical use, these days the opium poppies are grown by the 'poppy straw' method, which is easier to police and control. The young plants are cut down before the narcotic sap begins to flow, and the 'straw' is processed in special government-operated factories. Afyon produces more than a third of the world's legally grown opium.

An important local by-product of opium cultivation is *kaymak*, or clotted cream. Afyon's dairy cattle, fed opium poppy straw, are *very* contented and give rich milk from which farmers produce the sweet cheese-thick cream. Local *şekerleme* (confectioners) put dollops of it on sweet desserts such as *kadayıf*, and even work it into the local *kaymaklı lokum*. Don't leave Afyon without trying it.

The eponymous fortress stands atop the massive rock in the historic centre of town with crumbling wooden houses at its base. Twentieth century life in the form of parking meters complete with wardens to police them has caught up with Afyon. It's a pleasant enough place to pause, and you're unlikely to bump into many other tourists.

History

As with so many Anatolian towns, Afyon's history starts some 3000 years ago. After occupation by the Hittites, Phrygians, Lydians and Persians, it was settled by the Romans and then the Byzantines, who called the town Akroenos, and later Nikopolis. Following the Selçuk victory at Manzikert (Malazgirt) in 1071, Afyon was governed by the Selçuk Turks. The important Selçuk vizier Sahip Ata took direct control of the town, and it was called Karahisar-i Sahip even through Ottoman times (1428-1923).

During the War of Independence, Greek forces occupied the town on their push towards Ankara. During the Battle of the Sakarya, in late August 1921, the republican armies under Mustafa Kemal (Atatürk) stopped the invading force within earshot of Ankara in one of history's longest pitched battles. The Greek forces retreated and dug in for the winter near Eskişehir and Afyon.

On 26 August 1922 the Turks began their counteroffensive, advancing rapidly on the Greek army. Within days Kemal had set up his headquarters in Afyon's Belediye building and had half the Greek army surrounded at Dumlupınar, 40km to the west. The Battle of the Commander-in-Chief, as it came to be known, destroyed the Greek expeditionary army as a fighting force, and sent its survivors fleeing towards İzmir and the ships waiting in the harbour.

Cream from Contented Cows

The claim to fame among Turks of Afyon in the Aegean Hinterland is not its opium, but its clotted cream *(kaymak)*.

The story is this: Afyon's opium farmers rarely use the drug themselves, but they use every other part of the plant. The poppy seeds are sprinkled on bread and pastries, the tender leaves are good in salads and the leftover opium plants are fed to the cattle. The cattle become very contented and produce rich cream in abundance.

Early each morning, near the Ot Pazarı Camii just a few blocks from Hükümet Meydanı, you can see the dairy farmers carrying their cylindrical kaymak containers. Brokers and restaurant owners meet them in front of the mosque and haggle over prices for the precious cream, carefully protected in flat circular dishes of glass or plastic. Later in the day, the kaymak will end up atop a serving of *kadayıf* (crumpet in syrup), in *kaymaklı baklava*, or even stuffed in *lokum* (Turkish delight).

The popularity of eating kaymak on, in and with sweets may have inspired many locals to open confectioners' shops, *şekerleme*. Afyon has dozens of them, on Millet Caddesi off Hükümet Meydanı, and at the otogar.

Orientation & Information

The main square, called Hükümet Meydanı, lies east of the citadel, at the intersection of Ordu Bulvarı and Milli Egemenlik (usually called Bankalar) Caddesi; you'll recognise it by a fountain in the shape of a revolving ball of marble. About 250m south is another traffic roundabout, the starting point for Ambar Yolu (which goes north-east 2km to the otogar) and other streets.

Almost everything important is on or just off Bankalar Caddesi between the two traffic roundabouts, including the PTT, several hotels, restaurants, and the local hamam.

The train station is 2km from the centre, at the north-eastern end of Ordu Bulvarı. Minibuses (US$0.25) connect both the gar (train station) and the otogar to the centre.

The tourist information booth in Hükümet Meydanı can handle only basic inquiries. The main office (☎ 272-213 5447, fax 213 2623) is in the Hükümet Konağı (provincial government headquarters) on the 2nd floor, office 228, but here, too, there's little more than a town plan available.

Afyon's postal code is 03000.

A Walking Tour

Start at the **İmaret Camii**, Afyon's major mosque, just south of the traffic roundabout at the southern end of Bankalar Caddesi. Built on the orders of Gedik Ahmet Paşa in 1472, its design shows the transition from the Selçuk to the Ottoman style. The spiral-fluted minaret is decorated, Selçuk style, with blue tiles. The entrance on the eastern side is like an *eyvan* (large recess) and leads to a main sanctuary topped by two domes, front and back, a design also to be seen in the early Ottoman capitals of Bursa and Edirne. A shady park with fountain provides a peaceful refuge from bustling Bankalar Caddesi. The mosque's medrese is on the western side; its hamam, still popular with both men and women, is nearer to the busy traffic roundabout.

Walk north along Bankalar Caddesi to Hükümet Meydanı, named for the neighbouring **Hükümet Konağı**, or provincial government headquarters. The Hükümet Konağı used to be the building facing the dramatic black Zafer Anıtı (Victory Monument; 1936). Today the government resides in a modern building beside the old one, and the former headquarters is the **Zafer Müzesi** (Victory Museum), with exhibits relating to the battles of the War of Independence which were fought nearby. It's rarely open though.

From Hükümet Meydanı opposite the Hotel Oruçoğlu, walk south-west up Millet (or Uzunçarşı) Caddesi, lined with *şekerleme* (confectionery shops) several short blocks to the small park in front of the Ot Pazarı Camii, where the makers of *kaymak* (clotted cream) sell their wares to confectioners in the early morning hours. Turn right and follow the main road (Köprübaşı and Camii Kebir Caddesis) uphill until you come to a fork. Take the left route and look for the **Mevlevihane Camii** on your left.

This was the site of the Afyonkarahisar Mevlevihanesi, or dervish meeting place, dating from Selçuk times (13th century). Sultan Veled, son of Celaleddin Rumi, the founder of the Mevlevi (Whirling Dervish) order, established Afyon as the second most important Mevlevi centre in the empire. The present mosque, with twin domes, twin pyramidal roofs above its courtyard and a rather church-like aspect, dates only from 1908, when it was built on the orders of Sultan Abdül Hamit II. It's usually locked except at prayer times.

Continue walking up the main road to the square **Ulu Cami** (1273), about 1100m from Hükümet Meydanı. The Ulu Cami is one of the most important surviving examples of the Selçuk architectural style which called for brick walls and a roof supported by carved wooden columns and beams – here you'll find 40 columns with stalactite capitals and a flat beamed roof. Note the green tiles on the minaret. Unless you come just after prayer time, you may have to ask around for the *bekçi* (custodian) to let you in.

On your way to the Ulu Cami you'll doubtless have noticed the many old **Ottoman houses**. Those in some other cities, including Kütahya, may be in better repair, but Afyon boasts an interesting variety of styles of domestic architecture.

Across the street from the Ulu Cami, a lane marked by a sign ('Kale – City Castle') leads up towards the rock and its fortress. At the end of the lane is the first of some 700 steps to the summit, 226m high.

Despite its eventful history, there's little left to see inside the **citadel**. The Hittite king Mursilis II is thought to have built the first fortress by circa 1350 BC, and every other conqueror elaborated on it afterwards. The views are spectacular and it's well worth coming up here at prayer time to listen to the wraparound calls of the muezzins from Afyon's many mosques.

Arkeoloji Müzesi

Take a dolmuş along Kurtuluş Caddesi, the continuation of Bankalar Caddesi, for almost 2km and you'll see Afyon's museum on the right-hand side, near the intersection with İnönü Caddesi. The museum has been closed for restoration for years, but if you're lucky and find it open again (probably from 9 am to noon and 1.30 to 5.30 pm), the Roman collection is particularly good.

Places to Stay

Central Afyon lacks any really good hotels and in this pious town it'll be difficult to miss the muezzins' wake-up call wherever you are. If you're planning a brief visit you might as well stay in one of the hotels overlooking the otogar.

Otel Mesut *(☎ 272-212 0429, Dumlupınar 2 Caddesi 5)*, on the northern side of the PTT half a block east of Bankalar Caddesi, offers presentable accommodation at the heart of things, although the lift doesn't inspire confidence. Rooms, priced at US$9/15/23 a single/double/triple with shower, are beat-up and a bit depressing, but will do for a night. There are several even cheaper hotels further along this street.

Otel Hocaoğlu *(☎ 272-213 8182, fax 213 0188, Ambaryolu 12)*, is closer to the İmaret Camii. Its reasonably comfortable rooms with shower cost US$10 per person. It doesn't pay to look too hard at its carpets, although they're spotless in comparison with those down the road at ***Otel Sinada*** *(☎ 272-215 6530 Ambaryolu 25)* – a place that charges the same prices for much scruffier facilities.

The two-star, 57 room ***Otel Oruçoğlu*** *(☎ 272-212 0120, fax 213 1313)* on Bankalar Caddesi, facing Hükümet Meydanı on the corner of Ordu Bulvarı, is well-used but serviceable. Rooms with private shower cost US$22/33/50 a single/double/triple. The top floor restaurant offers the best food in town and wonderful views of the town's rocky outcrops. However, some readers wrote to complain that tables are not always reserved for individual guests when groups are in residence. Their response was to take their trade around the corner to the top-floor restaurant at the Hotel Soydan.

Hotel Soydan *(☎ 272-215 6070, fax 212 2111, Turan Emeksiz Caddesi 2)*, is a clean two-star place charging US$18/27/36 a single/double/triple. At the time of writing it was the best place in town, its 36 rooms boasting such luxuries (for Afyon) as frilly bedcovers, TVs and minibars.

For four-star comforts you must head out of Afyon on the Kütahya road 14km to ***Termal Resort Oruçoğlu*** *(☎ 272-251 5050, fax 213 9895)*, where one of the 104 comfy rooms can be had for US$45/65 a single/double.

Places to Eat

The little street named Ziraat Bankası Geçidi, across Bankalar from the Hotel Oruçoğlu, just south of Hükümet Meydanı, has a good assortment of eateries, including the ***Narin***, ***Arzu*** and ***Doyum*** restaurants and ***Zümrüt Etli Pide Salonu***. The first three are good for cheap, simple, filling meals (US$3 to US$4), including, of course, kaymak on your sweet. The pide salonu is cheaper still.

İkbal Lokantası on Millet (Uzunçarşı) Caddesi 21, half a block south-west of Hükümet Meydanı, was founded in 1956, and is an interesting period piece, well worth trying for its old-time atmosphere. Chicken stew with rice, a soft drink and a pudding will cost around US$4.50; they're particularly proud of their overly-sweet cherry-flavoured bread pudding.

A set dinner in the top-floor dining room of ***Hotel Oruçoğlu*** on Bankalar Caddesi costs US$10.

Don't forget to pop into one of the local şekerleme for a taste of Afyon's famous lokum. Free samples are usually on offer (point to something and say *Deneyelim!*, 'Let's try it!'). A 500g portion costs between US$1.50 and US$2, depending upon the type.

Getting There & Away

Afyon is on the inland routes connecting İstanbul with Antalya and Konya, and İzmir with Ankara and the east, so bus traffic is heavy. Trains will take you to Eskişehir, İstanbul, İzmir, Konya and Kütahya (see the introductory Getting Around chapter for details).

Daily bus services include:

Ankara – 260km, four hours, US$5; at least hourly
Antalya – 300km, five hours, US$6; frequent buses passing through
Eskişehir – 191km, three hours, US$5; hourly
Isparta – 165km, three hours, US$4; several
İstanbul – 455km, eight hours, US$17; hourly
İzmir – 340km, 5½ hours, US$5; hourly
Konya – 235km, 3¾ hours, US$6; several
Kütahya – 100km, 1½ hours, US$3; hourly
Pamukkale – 240km, four hours, US$5; several

South Aegean Turkey

South of İzmir the Aegean coast is thickly studded with beaches and ancient ruins, most of them easily accessible by the fast coastal road. The area immediately south of İzmir was ancient Ionia where colonists from Greece arrived around 1000 BC, fleeing an invasion by the Dorians. Not surprisingly the main attractions are the many ruined Ionian cities, most obviously Ephesus, the best-preserved classical city in the Mediterranean, but also Priene, Miletus, Didyma, and several others which are all the more pleasant for being less well known.

If you're coming to visit Ephesus, the most obvious bases are Selçuk or Kuşadası. The pleasant small town of Selçuk is only 3km from Ephesus and is packed with cheap pensions and eateries aimed at backpackers. Just 7km south is Pamucak Beach, a 4km-long wide swath of sand.

Alternatively, Kuşadası is a sprawling resort town and port for Aegean cruise ships doing the Greek Islands route. Although this is solid package holiday territory, Kuşadası also makes a decent base for exploring Ionia while getting in some swimming on the side.

It's easy to spend at least three days seeing the sights of Ionia. Plan one day for Selçuk and Ephesus, another for Priene, Miletus and Didyma, and a third day for Kuşadası and the beaches.

The far south-western corner of the coast is mountainous and somewhat isolated. In ancient times this was the Kingdom of Caria, with its own indigenous customs and people. Nowadays most people come here to stay in Bodrum, which is, like Kuşadası geared primarily to the needs of package holidaymakers. Even so, the wonderful crusader castle and pretty sugarcube houses make Bodrum an enjoyable place to visit if you travel outside peak season.

If you prefer something smaller and quieter you'd do better to head for resorts like Ören, Güllük or Iasos where development is still relatively low key. Some of the smaller resorts of the Bodrum peninsula, especially Gümüşlük and Yalıkavak, are also enjoyable; Gümbet is best avoided by anyone not intent on a full-on nightlife.

You might want to divert inland to visit the magnificent ruins at Afrodisias and the travertines at Pamukkale, near Denizli. Although Pamukkale is undergoing a transformation and the travertines are presently

HIGHLIGHTS

- Touring the marble ruins of Ephesus
- Exploring the less well-known ruins at Priene, Miletus, Hierapolis (Pamukkale) and Afrodisias
- Watching the stork activity on Selçuk's old aqueduct
- Shopping for lace and wine in Şirince
- Touring the crusader Castle of St Peter at Bodrum, now the Museum of Underwater Archaeology
- Eating a sunset supper at Gümüşlük, near Bodrum
- Getting away from it all on Eğirdir Gölü

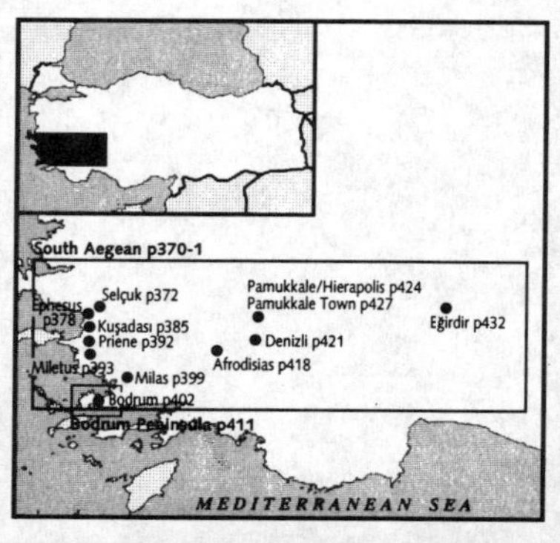

off limits, it's still worth heading this way to visit the ruins of Roman Hierapolis on the ridge above them.

Even further inland (and also accessible from the Mediterranean coast) is Turkey's Lake District. Eğirdir, near Isparta, has its historic corners but most visitors come for its setting at the edge of a vast lake where an island resort catering mainly for backpackers has grown. Nearby Burdur is of little interest but those heading on to Konya and Cappadocia might want to break their journey at the small lakeside town of Beyşehir to see its magnificent mosque.

Getting There & Away

Air Until recently the busiest access point for the southern Aegean was İzmir's Adnan Menderes airport, about half an hour's drive from Selçuk and served by daily flights from İstanbul on Turkish Airlines and İstanbul Airlines. There are also direct flights from many European and Middle Eastern cities.

A new airport has now opened near Bodrum and European charter airlines are increasingly likely to use this to get people to the southern Aegean. See Bodrum later in this section for details.

Boat You can easily travel between the Greek Islands and the southern Aegean. There are regular boats to Samos from Kuşadası and to Kos from Bodrum. See those sections for details.

Getting Around

As usual the easiest way to get around is by bus. Selçuk is a stopping-place for many buses travelling between İzmir and Denizli, Pamukkale, Marmaris, Bodrum, Fethiye, Antalya and other south-western points. Kuşadası has lots of direct bus services to İzmir, some direct bus services to Denizli, Pamukkale and other cities further east, and dolmuş minibus services to beaches and archaeological sites nearby.

Getting to Denizli and the lakes you could try using the trains, bearing in mind that they're often hot, crowded and late (see the Turkish Lake District section later in this chapter for details).

Car Rental It's simple but expensive to rent a car in İzmir, Kuşadası or Bodrum. See the Getting Around chapter for more information.

SELÇUK

Once a modest farming town with a sideline in tourism, Selçuk has been transformed by the tourism boom of the 1990s. Tourism is now the driving force in the local economy, though the lush fields of cotton and tobacco and the orchards of apples and figs surrounding the ever-growing town attest to the continuing efforts of the farmers.

Orientation

Ayasoluk Hill, with its castle, is north-west of the centre. Cengiz Topel Caddesi, the pedestrian way which is the heart of the commercial and tourist district, runs from an elaborate round fountain at the intersection with the main road to the train station. A few hundred metres south of the fountain on the main road is the otogar. On the west side of the main road is a shady park, and west of it is the famous Ephesus Museum. On the southern side of the park is the Tourism Information Office.

Selçuk's postal code is 35920.

Information

Tourist Office Selçuk's Tourism Information Office (☎ 232-892 1328, fax 892 1945) is at Efes Müzesi Karşısı 23, across the main İzmir-Bodrum highway from the otogar.

Money The PTT on Cengiz Topel Caddesi is open 24 hours every day, and will change cash, travellers cheques or Eurocheques. Ziraat Bankası has an office with ATM on Cengiz Topel Caddesi; İş Bankası and Akbank have ATMs on Namık Kemal Caddesi, a block north. There are foreign exchange offices along Cengiz Topel Caddesi as well.

Parking If you park a car near the Tourism Information Office, Ephesus Museum, St John Basilica or a few other touristy places in Selçuk, you may be approached by a man wanting to collect a parking fee of up to

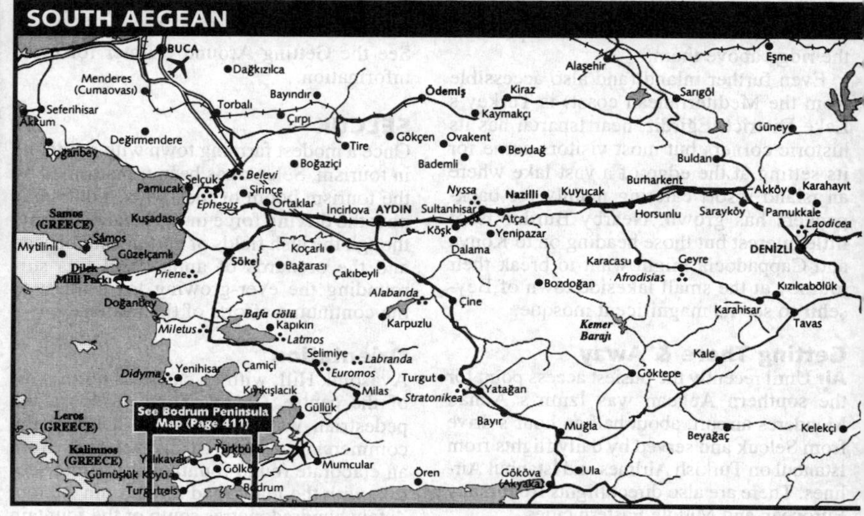

US$1.50. Although the charge is official, ask for a *bilet* (ticket) or *makbuz* (receipt) to make sure the cash is going into the right pockets. Alternatively, move your car and park a few blocks away for free.

Ayasoluk Hill

Before going to Ephesus, take an hour or two to visit the ancient buildings in Selçuk. The best place to start is the **St John Basilica** on top of the hill; look for signs pointing the way to St Jean.

It is said that St John came to Ephesus at the end of his life and wrote his Gospel here. A tomb built in the 4th century was thought to be his, so Justinian erected this magnificent church above it in the 6th century. Earthquakes and scavengers for building materials had left the church a heap of rubble until a century ago when restoration began; virtually all of what you see now is restored. The church site is open every day from 8 am to 5.30 pm (later in summer) for US$2.50. Parking at the entrance costs almost as much, so if you have a car, park a block or two away.

This hill, including the higher peak with the fortress, is called Ayasoluk and it offers an attractive view. Look west: at the foot of the hill is the **İsa Bey Camii**, built in 1375 by the Emir of Aydın in a transitional style which was post-Seljuk and pre-Ottoman. Keep a picture of it in your mind if you plan to venture deep into Anatolia for a look at more Seljuk buildings. There's a bust of İsa Bey more or less opposite.

Beyond the mosque you can see how the Aegean Sea once invaded this plain, allowing Ephesus to prosper from maritime commerce. When the harbour silted up, Ephesus began to lose its famous wealth.

The hilltop **citadel** to the north of St John Basilica was originally constructed by the Byzantines in the 6th century, rebuilt by the Seljuks and restored in modern times. A Seljuk mosque and a ruined church are inside.

Early in the town's existence it earned money from pilgrims paying homage to Cybele or Artemis. The many-breasted Anatolian fertility goddess had a fabulous temple, the **Artemision**, to the south-west of the St John Basilica. A sign on the road to

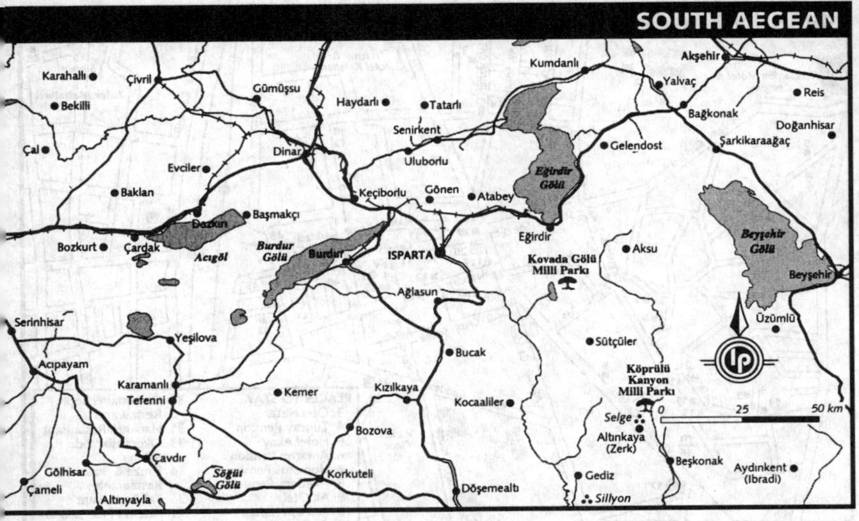

Ephesus marks the spot today, and you can see a re-erected column and the outline of the foundation. When you visit the huge temple at Didyma you get an idea of what this great temple must once have looked like, as Didyma's is thought to have been similar. If you walk to Ephesus you can take in the Artemision on the way.

Ephesus Müzesi

Don't miss Selçuk's beautiful museum, across from the Tourism Information Office. The collection is significant, and its statuary, mosaics and artefacts are attractively displayed. Highlights include the small, bronze figure of the Boy on a Dolphin in the first room; the marble statues of Cybele/Artemis with rows of egg-like breasts representing fertility; several effigies of Priapus, the phallic god; and pieces from a gigantic statue of the emperor Domitian. Beyond the courtyard is the ethnographic section set up in an *arasta* (row of shops) concentrating on traditional Turkish and Ottoman life with tools, costumes and a *topuk ev* (tent-like dwelling) used by Turkic nomads.

It's open from 8.30 am to noon and 1 to 5 pm for US$3.50 (half price for students; free for those over 65). You'll probably appreciate it most if you visit the site at Ephesus first.

Meryemana (Mary's House)

Since at least the Renaissance, some people have believed that the Virgin Mary came to Ephesus with St John at the end of her life (37-45 AD). In the 19th century Catherine Emmerich of Germany had visions of Mary at Ephesus. Using her descriptions, clergy from İzmir discovered the foundations of an old house in the hills near Ephesus, later verified by Pope Paul VI on a visit to the site in 1967. A small traditional service is held in the chapel on the site every 15 August to honour Mary's Assumption into heaven. To Muslims, Mary is Meryemana, Mother Mary, who bore İsa Peygamber, the Prophet Jesus.

The site is 7km from Ephesus' Lower (northern) Gate and 5.5km from the Upper (southern) Gate. It's 9km from Selçuk itself, up a steep hill. There's no dolmuş service so you'll have to hitch, rent a taxi (around US$13 round trip from the otogar) or take a

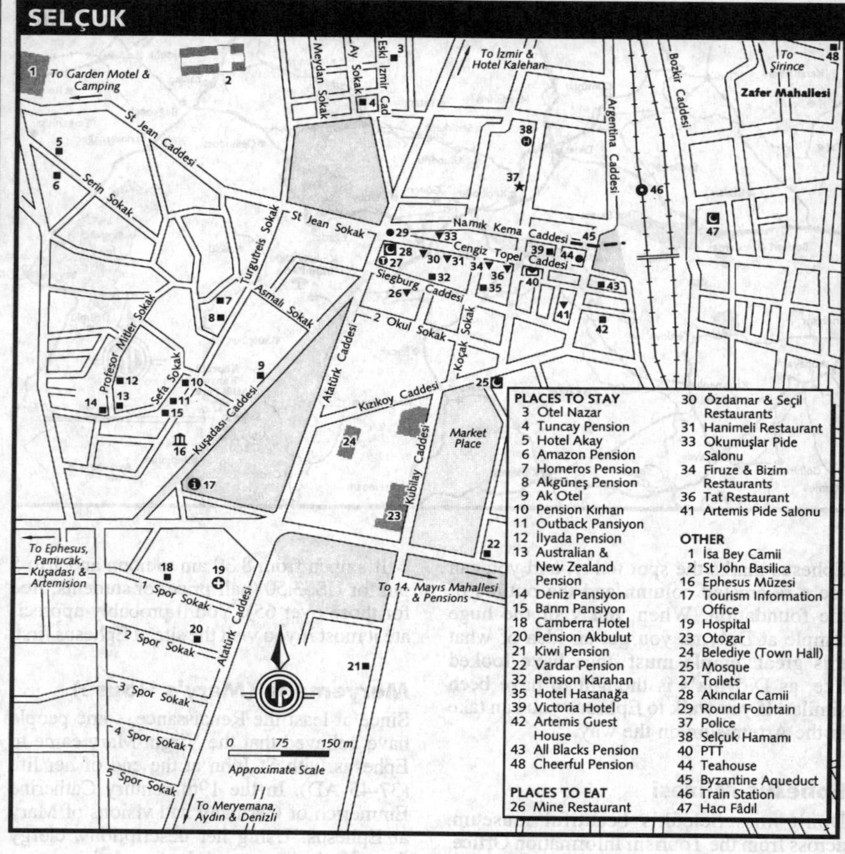

tour. It costs another US$2 to get into the site which is mobbed by coach parties. Unless the house has special meaning for you, you might prefer to save your money for something less commercialised.

Other Sites

Selçuk has some **tombs** and a little **mosque** dating from the Seljuk period just south of the otogar. On Namık Kemal Caddesi are the remains of a **Byzantine aqueduct**, now a favourite nesting place for *leylekler* (storks). Eggs are laid in late April or May, and the storks are there right into September.

Special Events

The Ephesus Festival, held at varying times in the year, brings world-class performers to the Great Theatre at Ephesus and other venues. From mid-June to mid-July, performances of music and dance are organised under the rubric of the International İzmir Festival and there are some performances at Ephesus.

Places to Stay – Budget

Selçuk has almost 100 small pensions so finding a room shouldn't be too difficult except at the busiest times.

For many years, Selçuk's biggest problem has been the pension and carpet-shop touts. It's good to report that the hassle at the otogar is better than it was, although you should still be wary of people approaching you with unlikely stories about the closure of your pension due to fire, family bereavement or other misfortune. Most pension owners dislike the touts who badger them for commissions for bringing travellers to their pensions; you'd do well to seek out a pension on your own with the help of this book or ask the Tourism Information Office to help you find an empty room.

Some of the pensions have their own carpet shops, either on the premises or elsewhere in town. They'll do their best to get you to shop at their particular outlet, which is fine if you want a carpet. If you don't, remember that there's rarely such a thing as a free lunch and one way to soften people up so they'll be ready to shop is to run them to Ephesus or help in similar ways. See the section on Carpets in the Facts for the Visitor chapter for more information.

Most pension and hotel prices are set by the town government, so in high season they compete not on price but on extras like cheap home-made meals, views, and rooms with private facilities. When business is slow, they compete on price as well.

Pensions fall into several groups according to location. The cheapest but most remote are those east of the centre in Zafer Mahallesi, across the train tracks and up the hill, a 10 or 15-minute walk from the centre; and north-east of Ayasoluk Hill, reached by going north along the main road towards İzmir, then left. The most convenient and congenial, but also a bit more expensive, are those in the sections called Atatürk Mahallesi and İsabey Mahallesi, on the hill behind (north and west of) the museum. A few pensions and hotels are in the heart of the shopping and restaurant district; and there are a few smaller pensions south of the centre and the otogar.

Rooms in these modest, friendly places cost from $US6 to US$8 a single, US$8 to US$12 a double without bath; or from US$8 to US$10 a single, US$12 to US$15 a double with private shower. In some cases it's possible to sleep on the roof or camp in the garden for US$2 to US$3 per person. Some places are run by women, making them good choices for female travellers.

Behind the Museum Facing the museum, walk up the street to the right of it to find ***Pension Kırhan*** *(☎ 232-892 2257, Turgutreis Sokak 7)*, which sometimes lets out four rooms in a convenient location.

Further along Turgutreis Sokak, ***Akgüneş Pension*** *(☎ 232-892 3869, Turgutreis Sokak 14)*, has nine simple rooms, all with bath, and a reasonable roof terrace. Follow the signs to find ***Homeros Pension*** *(☎ 232-892 3995, Asmalı Sokak 17)*, with lots of character and a nice terrace and rooftop bar with a panoramic view. Many readers enjoy their stays here although I was disappointed to be offered a bed with no top sheet or blanket at the end of a long journey.

Back down Turgutreis Sokak past the Kırhan, you'll find ***Outback Pansiyon*** *(☎/fax 232-891 4039, Turgutreis Sokak 5)*, formerly the Gedik, with 10 rooms, some with showers, and some singles. There's a roof terrace which should offer Internet access by the time you read this, and kitchen facilities. Owner Mark Mercan lived for many years in Australia. He has a carpet shop, hence the carpets and kilims decorating the rooms.

Further along, ***Barım Pansiyon*** *(☎ 232-892 6923, Turgutreis Sokak 34)*, is thoroughly kitschy on the outside (iron camels slouching along the facade) but inside it's an old stone house with a mixture of rooms with and without bath. The rear courtyard would make an inviting place to sit and read at the end of a long day.

Behind Pension Kırhan, Sefa Sokak winds uphill to the ***Australian & New Zealand Pension*** *(☎ 232-892 1050, Profesör Mitler Sokak 17)*, run by the Toparlak family who spent 12 years Down Under. This has been a favourite with travellers for many years, and offers such pluses as a lovely rooftop terrace, a kitchen, a washing machine and Internet access (US$1 for 15 minutes). Although private facilities are being added to some of the rooms, at the time of writing washing facilities were sadly overstretched. There was also something pretty mysterious about a price structure which offered half-board for US$8 – or about the same if you didn't eat dinner!

If the Australian & New Zealand Pension is full, the five room ***Deniz Pansiyon*** *(☎ 232-892 1741, Sefa Sokak 9)*, is across the street, while ***İlayda*** *(☎ 232-892 3278)* is just up the road.

Provided it's open, the quiet ***Amazon Pension*** *(☎ 232-892 3215, Serin Sokak 8)*, located near the İsa Bey Camii and Hotel Akay, has seven bathless rooms and a pretty garden courtyard where breakfast is served.

East of Ayasoluk Hill East of Ayasoluk Hill and the castle are several other possibilities. ***Tuncay Pension*** *(☎ 232-892 6260, Ay Sokak 3)*, is the best choice here, with cool, quiet, waterless rooms, and a washing machine which guests can use.

Town Centre The most promising newcomer to the Selçuk pension scene is the five-storey ***All Blacks*** *(☎/fax 232-892 3657, 1011 Sokak 1)*, overlooking the aqueduct with the storks' nests and close to the train station. Run by the enthusiastic and knowledgeable Hamdullah Akın ('Jesse') and Mehmet Nazlı ('Jeff'), it has a good rooftop terrace and the advantage of bathrooms for every room, although there's no lift.

Pension Karahan *(☎ 232-892 2575, Siegburg Caddesi 11)*, has received several recommendations from readers. There are 12 simple rooms here, but they're in the heart of the action and could be noisy in summer.

Another newcomer is ***Artemis Guest House*** *(☎ 232-892 6191, 1012 Sokak 2)*, otherwise known as Jimmy's Place. Clean, simple rooms are supplemented by a large lounge with TV-video player and a rear courtyard with murals.

Close to the market, Ms Seval Demirel-Molenaar runs the popular ***Vardar Pension*** *(☎ 232-891 4967, fax 891 4099, Sahabettin Dede Caddesi 9)*, with 16 small, clean rooms, most with bath, and a nice dining terrace where breakfast and dinner are served. Seval Hanım speaks some Dutch, English, French, German and Japanese, and stresses that she does not employ touts at the bus station, though she herself sometimes meets buses.

Readers have also recommended ***Pamukkale Family Pension*** *(☎ 232-892 2388, 14 Mayıs Mahellesi, Sedir Sokak 1)*, run by Mehmet İrdem whose hospitality has been described as 'awe inspiring'. His wife's cooking also comes in for high praise.

South of the Centre South of the centre are quiet neighbourhoods of modern apartment blocks. Some of them have been converted into small pensions. ***Kiwi Pension*** *(☎ 232-891 4892, fax 892 3474, Kubilay Caddesi 8)*, has been recommended by readers. Most rooms share bathrooms but are quite spacious. There's a washing machine and kitchen facilities, plus a pool table in the basement. If that's full, ***Pension Akbulut*** *(☎ 232-892 1139, 2 Spor Sokak 4)*, has five quiet rooms with shared facilities.

East of the Centre The aptly named ***Cheerful Pension*** *(☎ 232-892 2732, Zafer Mahallesi, Çimenlik Sokak 3)*, is well away from the centre, but has eight bathless rooms and gives excellent service.

Camping On the western side of Ayasoluk Hill 200m beyond the İsa Bey Camii, ***Garden Motel & Camping*** *(☎ 232-892 6165, fax 892 2997)* offers grassy pitches in the shade of aspen trees. At US$7 for a two-person tent, it's only a bit cheaper than the cheapest pensions, but the setting is delightful. There are also some pension rooms with a few dorm beds for US$3 per person. Carpets are made here for export to Italy, so you get the chance to see the dying and weaving in progress without pressure to buy.

There's also camping at Pamucak (see the Pamucak section later in this chapter).

Places to Stay – Mid-Range

Selçuk has several one and two-star hotels in quiet locations with private facilities. Breakfast is usually included in the price.

First choice is the atmospheric 52-room ***Otel Kalehan*** *(☎ 232-892 6154, fax 892 2169)*, İzmir Caddesi, on the main road just north of the Shell station. Built to resemble a group of old Turkish houses, it's decorated with antiques, local crafts and textiles. Rooms with double-glazing are set back from the noisy road around a small swimming pool and verdant terrace. There's something to suit most tastes and budgets. The best rooms have showers, mini-fridges and air-con (and possibly bathtubs), and cost US$30/50/60 a single/double/triple, but there are also a few bungalows costing US$20. The air-conditioned restaurant is excellent (see Places to Eat – Mid-Range). The owner, Erol Ergir, comes from an old Ottoman family, and has put many historic momentoes on display.

The welcoming 16-room ***Hotel Akay*** *(☎ 232-892 3172, fax 892 3009, İsa Bey Camii Karşısı, Serin Sokak 3)*, is beside the İsa Bey Camii and thus well away from the noise of the town. Simple guest rooms are built around an interior courtyard and reached by walkways. All have tiled baths with showers, and cost US$17/25 a single/double, breakfast included. The rooftop restaurant has lovely views of the mosque.

North of the centre is the simple ***Otel Nazar*** *(☎ 232-892 2222, fax 891 4016, Eski İzmir Caddesi 14)*. The enthusiastic owner will show you his tidy rooms and castle-view roof terrace, and rent them to you for US$25 a double, breakfast included, with reductions for stays of several days.

There are also several hotels on and off Cengiz Topel Caddesi between the fountain and the train station. The two-star ***Victoria Otel*** *(☎ 232-892 3203, Cengiz Topel Caddesi 4)* has a good restaurant on the ground floor and a lift to take you up to your room. The 24 small rooms cost US$24 a double, breakfast included, in high season. Some rooms have views of the storks' nests on the old aqueduct.

Half a block south of Cengiz Topel Caddesi, ***Hotel Hasanağa*** *(☎ 232-892 6317, Koçak Sokak 5)* has 23 quiet rooms, with private baths, for US$8/16 a single/double.

The two-star ***Ak Otel*** *(☎ 232-892 2161, fax 892 3142, Kuşadası Caddesi 14)* is owned by a Turkish family which spent many years in Belgium. It has 60 rather faded rooms in two buildings, all with showers. Those at the back are quieter. Rates are US$20/35 a single/double, breakfast included, but they'll haggle if not busy.

One block in from Atatürk Caddesi and facing the museum is the new high-rise ***Camberra Hotel*** *(☎/fax 232-892 7668, 1067 Sokak 13)*, offering clean, modern rooms with bath for US$12 per person. There's a pleasant roof terrace, accessible by lift, and a downstairs restaurant.

Places to Eat

In high season Selçuk's restaurant prices can soar towards İzmir or İstanbul levels. Out of season, they drop considerably. On average, soups cost US$1.25, meze from US$1.50 to US$2 and meat dishes from US$2.50 to US$4. The simple pide and köfte places may not serve alcohol.

A speciality of this region is *çöp şiş* (splinter kebap), bits of lamb or beef skewered on a sliver of bamboo and grilled on charcoal.

All the restaurants along Cengiz Topel Caddesi between the highway and the train station have streetside tables in good weather, and most display prices prominently.

Places to Eat – Budget

Many pensions will prepare home-cooked meals for you – great food at low prices, especially when served on a roof terrace. Don't let them coax you into staying put on the one site all the time though, because Selçuk has plenty of nice places to eat.

For cheap pide, try ***Artemis Pide Salonu***, half a block south of the teahouse at the eastern end of Cengiz Topel Caddesi, where Turkish-style pizza costs US$1.50 to US$2.50. Similar is ***Okumuşlar Pide Salonu*** on Namık Kemal Caddesi, across from the Akbank. ***Kodalak Restaurant*** at the otogar serves cheap stews, but ask for prices before you order. There's also a market in the otogar to buy snacks for the journey.

Places to Eat – Mid-Range

On Cengiz Topel Caddesi, ***Özdamar Restaurant*** and ***Seçil***, facing the fountain, are perennially popular. The nearby ***Hanımeli Restaurant*** advertises vegetarian food.

On the next block, ***Firuze*** and ***Bizim*** restaurants are a bit simpler, and may have slightly lower prices. Particularly popular is the ***Tat*** where a full meal with wine will cost around US$7. Try the mushroom börek – it's delicious.

Mine Restaurant at Seigburg Caddesi 4 has lots of inside tables and a few outside for tucking into good cooking. *Peynirli börek* (flaky pastry with cheese) followed by a kebap washed down with wine will come to around US$8.

At the time of writing ***Ephesus Restaurant***, on Namık Kemal Caddesi near the İş Bankası, was being rebuilt. The restaurant in the ***Victoria Hotel*** serves all sorts of food from spaghetti to şiş kebap at value-for-money prices.

Even if you aren't staying at ***Hotel Kalehan***, you can drop in for the excellent table d'hôte dinner, a carefully prepared three-course meal for less than US$8 with a simple main course; US$10 with a fancier one, plus drinks. ***Hotel Akay***, near the İsa Bey Camii, also has a pleasant roof restaurant on a quiet street.

By the train station there are several shaded tea gardens where you can sip tea and watch the stork action on top of the aqueduct.

For a sweet treat, drop into ***Tadım Şekerleme***, near the PTT behind the Emlak Bankası, No 37/C. A 125g package of Turkish delight will cost you less than US$1, and you can make your choice from 40 different varieties.

Entertainment

Sipping drinks and talking are the main evening entertainments in Selçuk. Besides the restaurants on Cengiz Topel Caddesi, you'll find ***Ekselans Bar*** on Siegburg Caddesi with outdoor tables and, next to it, the currently more popular ***Pink Bistro Bar***. ***Cheers*** is also popular but a quick stroll around town should point out this season's place to be.

The Selçuk Hamamı is north of the police station. Traditionally, women bathe on Friday, but, this being a tourist area, they can actually show up at any time and be allowed in. The fee is still US$2 for a simple wash, US$6 for the works and everything is thoroughly clean and respectable. It stays open until midnight.

Getting Around

Bus Selçuk's otogar is across from the Tourism Information Office. Most services are local. Long-distance services usually start somewhere else (İzmir, Kuşadası, Bodrum) and pick up passengers on the way through. There are dolmuş minibus services to Kuşadası, Pamucak, Şirince, Söke and other nearby points.

Details of some of the main bus services are:

Ephesus – 3km, five minutes, US$0.50; frequent minibuses in summer, but it's also pleasant to walk (see the following Ephesus section). Many pensions also offer free lifts to Ephesus

İzmir – 80km, 1¼ hours, US$1.75; buses every 15 minutes from 6.30 am to 7 pm in summer

Kuşadası – 20km, 30 minutes, US$0.90; minibuses run frequently in summer, with the last minibus departing from Selçuk at 8.30 pm, from Kuşadası at 9 pm. After hours, look for taxis lurking near the Tourism Information Office

Pamucak – 7km, 10 minutes, US$0.75; last minibus departs long before sunset; a taxi costs US$8

Söke – 35km, one hour, US$2; frequent minibuses in summer, or change at Kuşadası

Minibus Tours For details of minibus tours to Priene, Miletus, Didyma and Altınkum (Yenihisar), see Minibus Tours under Getting There & Away in the Kuşadasi section later in this chapter. If the tours are not running, or if you'd rather go on your own, catch a bus or minibus to Söke. From there, minibuses run to Priene, Didyma and Altınkum. Going on your own is cheaper but takes much longer.

Taxi Taxi drivers charge about US$4 per car to take you the 3km to the Ephesus ruins, and about US$13 to Meryemana and back. For US$25 per car, they'll take you to the main ruins, wait, take you to Meryemana, and return you to Selçuk. Perhaps the best plan is to take a taxi to Meryemana for a short visit, then have it drop you at Ephesus' southern entrance so you can walk downhill through the ruins rather than up. You'll get as long a visit as you want, after which you can walk the 3km back to Selçuk.

EPHESUS (EFES)

Ephesus is the best-preserved classical city on the eastern Mediterranean, and among the best places in the world to get a feel for what life was like in Roman times. Needless to say, it's a major tourist destination.

Ancient Ephesus was a great trading and religious city, a centre for the cult of Cybele, the Anatolian fertility goddess. Under the influence of the Ionians, Cybele became Artemis, the virgin goddess of the hunt and the moon, and a fabulous temple was built in her honour. When the Romans took over and made this the province of Asia, Artemis became Diana and Ephesus became the Roman provincial capital. Its Temple of Diana was counted among the Seven Wonders of the World.

As a large and busy Roman town with ships and caravans coming from all over, it quickly acquired a sizeable Christian congregation. St Paul visited Ephesus and later wrote the most profound of his epistles to the Ephesians.

Ephesus was renowned for its wealth and beauty even before it was pillaged by Gothic invaders in 262 AD, and it was still an important enough place in 431 AD for a church council to be held there. Much of the city remains for you to see.

In high summer it gets very hot here. It's best to start your tramping early in the morning, then retire to a shady restaurant for lunch at the peak of the heat. Unfortunately this is what the coach parties also do; lunch time is when you're most likely to avoid the bedlam of tour groups.

If your interest in ancient ruins is slight, half a day may suffice, but real ruins buffs will want to continue their explorations in the afternoon. Take a water bottle as drinks at the site are more expensive.

It's 3km from the Tourism Information Office in Selçuk to the admission gate at Ephesus, a pleasant 30 to 45-minute walk along a shady lane at the side of the highway. The lane, actually the old road, is named after Doktor Sabri Yayla, who had the foresight to plant the trees earlier in the century.

Admission to the archaeological site costs US$6 (half price for students and free for those over 65); parking costs US$1.25. The site is open from 8.30 am to 5.30 pm (7 pm in summer) every day.

History

Earliest Times According to a legend related by Athenaeus, Androclus, son of King Codrus of Athens, consulted an oracle about where he should found a settlement in Ionia. The oracle answered, in typically cryptic style, 'choose the site indicated by the fish and the boar'.

Androclus sat down with some fishermen near the mouth of the Cayster River and Panayır Dağı (Mt Pion), the hill into which Ephesus' Great Theatre was later built. As they grilled some fish for lunch, one of the fish leapt out of the brazier, taking with it a hot coal which ignited some shavings, which in turn ignited the nearby brush. A wild boar hiding in the brush ran in alarm from the fire; the spot at which it was killed by the fishermen became the site of Ephesus' temple of Athena.

For many years thereafter the wild boar was a symbol of the city. Until the 1970s it was still common to see wild pigs in scrub thickets near Ephesus.

In ancient times the sea came much further inland, almost as far as present-day Selçuk, even lapping at the feet of Panayır Dağı. The first settlement, of which virtually nothing remains, was built on the hill's northern slope, and was a prosperous city by about 600 BC. The nearby sanctuary of Cybele/Artemis (Anatolian mother

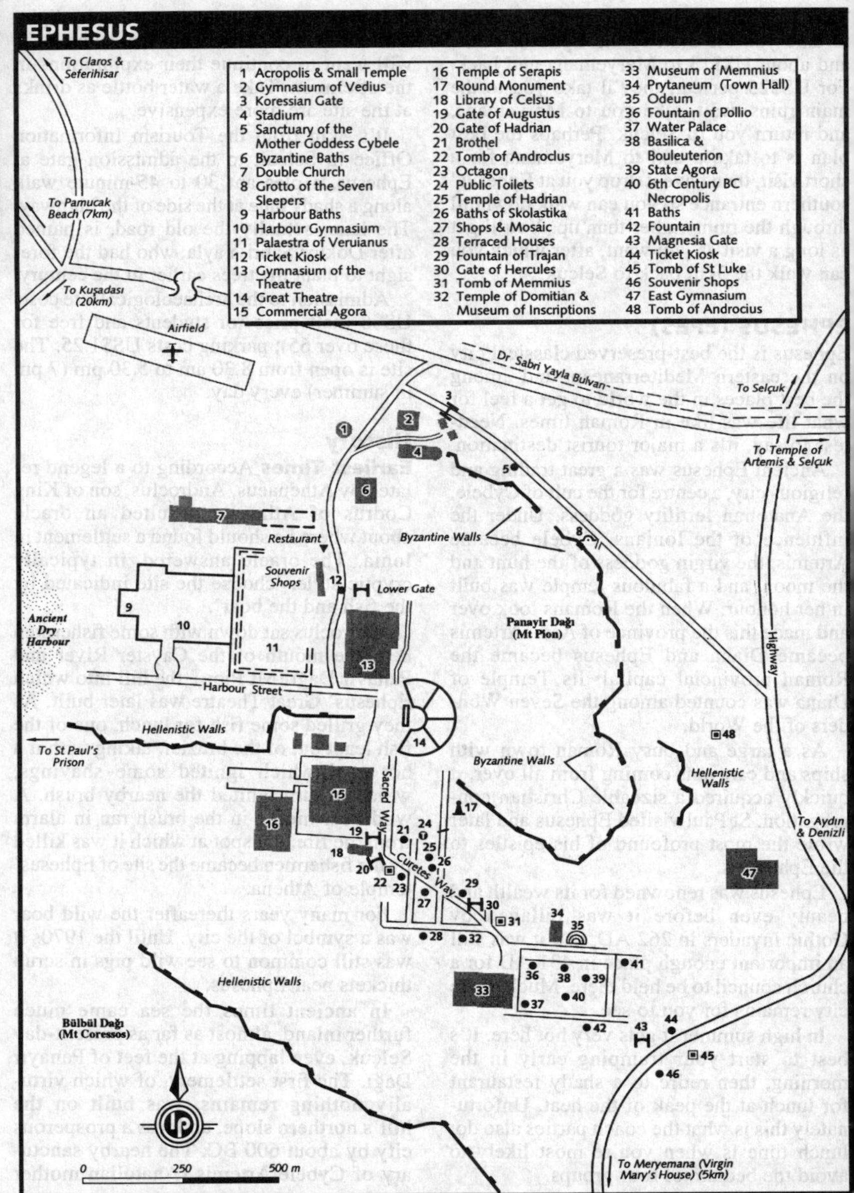
EPHESUS
1 Acropolis & Small Temple
2 Gymnasium of Vedius
3 Koressian Gate
4 Stadium
5 Sanctuary of the Mother Goddess Cybele
6 Byzantine Baths
7 Double Church
8 Grotto of the Seven Sleepers
9 Harbour Baths
10 Harbour Gymnasium
11 Palaestra of Veruianus
12 Ticket Kiosk
13 Gymnasium of the Theatre
14 Great Theatre
15 Commercial Agora
16 Temple of Serapis
17 Round Monument
18 Library of Celsus
19 Gate of Augustus
20 Gate of Hadrian
21 Brothel
22 Tomb of Androclus
23 Octagon
24 Public Toilets
25 Temple of Hadrian
26 Baths of Skolastika
27 Shops & Mosaic
28 Terraced Houses
29 Fountain of Trajan
30 Gate of Hercules
31 Tomb of Memmius
32 Temple of Domitian & Museum of Inscriptions
33 Museum of Memmius
34 Prytaneum (Town Hall)
35 Odeum
36 Fountain of Pollio
37 Water Palace
38 Basilica & Bouleuterion
39 State Agora
40 6th Century BC Necropolis
41 Baths
42 Fountain
43 Magnesia Gate
44 Ticket Kiosk
45 Tomb of St Luke
46 Souvenir Shops
47 East Gymnasium
48 Tomb of Androcius
To Claros & Seferihisar
To Pamucak Beach (7km)
To Kuşadası (20km)
Airfield
Dr Sabri Yayla Bulvarı
To Selçuk
To Temple of Artemis & Selçuk
Restaurant
Byzantine Walls
Souvenir Shops
Lower Gate
Ancient Dry Harbour
Panayır Dağı (Mt Pion)
Harbour Street
Highway
Hellenistic Walls
To St Paul's Prison
Sacred Way
Curetes Way
Byzantine Walls
Hellenistic Walls
To Aydın & Denizli
Hellenistic Walls
Bülbül Dağı (Mt Coressos)
0
250
500 m
To Meryemana (Virgin Mary's House) (5km)

Meryemana

Legend has it that the Virgin Mary, accompanied by St John, came to Ephesus at the end of her life, circa 37-45 AD. Renaissance church historians mentioned the trip, and it is said that local Christians venerated a small house near Ephesus as Mary's.

In the 19th century a German woman named Catherine Emmerich (1774-1824) had visions of Mary and of her surroundings at Ephesus. When Lazarist clergy from İzmir followed Emmerich's detailed descriptions, they discovered the foundations of an old house in the hills near Ephesus; a tomb, also described by Emmerich, was not found.

In 1967 Pope Paul VI visited the site, where a chapel now stands, and confirmed the authenticity of the legend. A small traditional service, celebrated by Orthodox and Muslim clergy on 15 August each year in honour of Mary's Assumption into heaven, is now the major event here. To Muslims, Mary is Meryemana, Mother Mary, who bore İsa Peygamber, the Prophet Jesus.

The site is now a Selçuk municipal park; there is no regular dolmuş service, so you'll have to hitch, rent a taxi (about US$10 per car to Meryemana and back) or take a tour. The park is 7km from Ephesus' Lower (northern) Gate, or 5.5 km from the Upper (southern) Gate, and 9km from Selçuk, up steep grades. The views of Ephesus, Selçuk, Ayasoluk Hill, and the surrounding countryside are wonderful along the way. Entry to the site costs US$2.

Along the approach to the house are signboards explaining its significance in various languages. The house is usually busy with pilgrims, the devout and the curious. A small restaurant and snack stand provide meals at relatively moderate prices. If you are travelling on a tight budget, bring along some picnic supplies and enjoy lunch on your own in the shady park.

goddess) had been a place of pilgrimage since at least 800 BC and may – let's face it – have had more to do with the selection of the site than the fish and the pig.

Croesus & The Persians Ephesus prospered so much that it aroused the envy of King Croesus of Lydia, who attacked it around 600 BC. The Ephesians, who neglected to build defensive walls, stretched a rope from the temple of Artemis to the town, a distance of 1200m, hoping thus to place themselves under the protection of the goddess. Croesus responded to this quaint defensive measure by giving some of his famous wealth for the completion of the temple, which was still under construction. But he destroyed the city of Ephesus and relocated its citizens inland to the southern side of the temple, where they rebuilt and lived through classical times.

Neglecting again (or perhaps forbidden) to build walls, the Ephesians were tributaries of Croesus' Lydia and, later, of the Persians. They then joined the Athenian confederacy, but later fell back under Persian control.

Rebuilding the Temple In 356 BC the temple of Cybele/Artemis was destroyed in a fire set by one Herostratus, who claimed to have done it to get a mention in history, proving that modern society has no monopoly on a perverted sense of celebrity.

The Ephesians planned a new, even grander temple, the construction of which was well under way when Alexander the Great arrived in 334 BC. Much impressed by the plans, Alexander offered to pay the cost of construction if only it would be dedicated to him. The Ephesians declined his generous offer, saying – with monumental tact – that it was not fitting for one god to make a dedication to another. When the temple was finished, it was recognised as one of the Seven Wonders of the World.

Under Lysimachus After Alexander's death, Ionia came under the control of Lysimachus, one of his generals. As the Cayster brought more silt into the harbour, it became clear that the city would have to move westward or die a commercial death. Lysimachus, unable to convince the Ephesians to budge, blocked the sewers of the old city during a downpour causing major flooding of their homes. The Ephesians then reluctantly moved to a site on the western side of Mt Pion, where the Roman city now stands.

Little survives of Lysimachus' city, though it finally got a defensive wall almost 10km long which served it well as it allied itself first with the Seleucid kings of Syria, then with the Ptolemies of Egypt, later with King Antiochus, then Eumenes of Pergamum; and finally with the Romans. Long stretches of the wall survive atop Bülbül Dağı (Mt Coressos), the high ridge on the southern side of Ephesus, as does a prominent square tower, nicknamed 'St Paul's Prison', on a low hill to the west.

Roman Ephesus Roman Ephesus boasted that it was the 'first and greatest metropolis of Asia', with a population nearing 250,000. It became the Roman capital of Asia Minor, honoured and beautified by succeeding emperors. With its brisk sea traffic, rich commerce and right of sanctuary in the Temple of Artemis, it drew many immigrants of various nations and creeds. It's said that St John came here with the Virgin Mary, followed by St Paul, whose Letter to the Ephesians was written to people he had known during his three-year stay.

Its prosperity from commerce and temple pilgrimage was unrivalled, but the Cayster continued to bring silt down into the harbour. Despite great works by Attalus II of Pergamum, who rebuilt the harbour, and Nero's proconsul, who dredged it, the silting continued. Emperor Hadrian had the Cayster diverted, but the harbour continued to silt up, ultimately pushing the sea back to Pamucak, 4km to the west. Cut off from its commerce, Ephesus lost its wealth. By the 6th century AD, when the Emperor Justinian was looking for a site for the St John Basilica, he chose Ayasoluk Hill in Selçuk, which became the new city centre.

Demetrius the Silversmith

St Paul lived at Ephesus for three years, perhaps in the 60s AD. According to the Bible (Acts 19:24-41), his mission was so successful that the trade in religious artefacts for the Artemis cult dropped off precipitously.

Hurt by the slump, a silversmith named Demetrius, who made silver Artemis shrines, gathered a group of other artisans who had lost business. At first they grumbled about the effects of Paul's preaching on their incomes, but they soon sought a higher rationale and blamed Paul's preaching for a loss of respect for the goddess herself.

Rumours spread throughout the city that someone was being disrespectful of Artemis. People flooded into the Great Theatre, sweeping along several of Paul's Christian travelling companions. Paul, set on entering the theatre (perhaps to give the sermon of his life to a packed house), was dissuaded from doing so by his disciples.

Unclear on the cause of the uproar, the mob in the theatre shouted 'Great is Artemis of the Ephesians!' for an hour before the secretary of the city council calmed them down enough to speak. The Christians, having broken no law, were released and the uproar subsided, but Paul left Ephesus shortly thereafter for Macedonia.

Walking Tour

As you walk into the site from Dr Sabri Yayla Bulvarı, a road to the left is marked for the Grotto of the Seven Sleepers, on the northeastern side of Panayır Dağı about 1km away.

Grotto of the Seven Sleepers According to legend, seven persecuted Christian youths fled from Ephesus in the 3rd century AD and took refuge in this cave. Agents of the Emperor Decius, a terror to Christians, found the cave and sealed it. Two centuries later an earthquake broke down the wall, awakening the sleepers, and they ambled back to town for a meal. Finding that all their old friends were long dead, they concluded that they had undergone a sort of resurrection – Ephesus was by this time a Christian city. When they died they were buried in the cave, and a cult following developed.

The grotto is actually a fairly elaborate Byzantine-era **necropolis** with scores of tombs cut into the rock. Many people feel it's hardly worth paying the extra admission charge (at least in season).

Gymnasium of Vedius & Stadium Back on the entry road you pass the Gymnasium of Vedius (2nd century AD), with its exercise fields, baths, toilets, covered exercise rooms, a swimming pool and a ceremonial hall, on your left. Just south of it is the Stadium, dating from about the same period. Most of its finely cut stones were taken by the Byzantines to build the citadel and walls of the castle on Ayasoluk Hill. This 'quarrying' of pre-cut building stone from older, often earthquake-ruined structures continued throughout the history of Ephesus.

Double Church The road comes over a low rise and descends to the car park, where there are teahouses, restaurants, souvenir shops, a PTT and banks. To the right (west) of the road are the ruins of the Church of the Virgin Mary, also called the Double Church. The original building was a museum – a Hall of the Muses – a place for lectures, teaching and educated discussions and debates. Destroyed by fire, it was rebuilt in the 4th century AD as a church, later to become the site of the third Ecumenical Council (431 AD) which condemned the Nestorian heresy. Over the centuries several other churches were built here, somewhat obscuring the original layout.

Harbour St As you walk down a lane bordered by evergreen trees, a few colossal remains of the **Harbour Gymnasium** are off to the right (west) before you reach the marble-paved Harbour St. This, the grandest street in Ephesus, had water and sewer lines beneath the marble flags, 50 streetlights along its colonnades, shops along its sides, and near its western (harbour) end a **Nymphaeum** (fountain and pool) and triumphal columns. It was and is a grand sight – a legacy of the Byzantine emperor Arcadius (395-408).

Great Theatre At the eastern end of Harbour St is the Great Theatre, skilfully reconstructed by the Romans between 41 and 117 AD, which means that the riot of Demetrius the Silversmith (see the boxed text on the previous page) took place in a theatre under reconstruction.

The first theatre here dates from the Hellenistic city of Lysimachus, and many features of the original building were incorporated into the Roman structure. Among these is the ingenious design of the *cavea* (seating area), capable of holding 25,000 people: each successive range of seating up from the stage is pitched more steeply than the one below it, thereby improving the view and acoustics for spectators in the upper seats. Among other modifications, the Romans enlarged the stage, pitched it towards the audience, and built a three-story decorative stage wall behind it, further improving the acoustics.

The Great Theatre is still used for performances, though it was partly closed for restoration at the time of writing.

Behind the Great Theatre is Panayır Dağı, which bears a few traces of the **ruined city walls** of Lysimachus.

Sacred Way From the theatre, walk south along the marble-paved Sacred Way, also called the Marble Way. Note the remains of the city's elaborate water and sewer systems beneath the paving stones, and the ruts made by wheeled vehicles (which were not permitted along Harbour St). The large, open space to the right (west) of the street, once surrounded by a colonnade and shops, was the **commercial agora** (3 BC) or marketplace, heart of Ephesus' business life.

On the left as you approach the end of the street is an elaborate building which some archaeologists call a **brothel** and others describe as a private house. Either way, its main hall contains a rich mosaic of the Four Seasons.

The Sacred Way ends at the **Embolos**, or 'central Ephesus', with the Library of Celsus and the monumental Gate of Augustus to the right (west), and Curetes Way heading east up the slope.

Library of Celsus Tiberius Julius Celsus Polemaeanus was the Roman governor of Asia Minor early in the 2nd century AD. In 114, after the governor's death, his son, Consul Tiberius Julius Aquila, erected this library in his father's honour, according to an inscription in Latin and Greek on the side of the front staircase. Celsus was buried under the western side of the library.

The library held 12,000 scrolls in niches around its walls. A 1m gap between the inner and outer walls protected the valuable books from extremes of temperature and humidity. Though it now stands alone, the library was originally built between other buildings, and architectural trickery was used to make it look bigger than it is: the base of the facade is convex, adding height to the central elements; and the central columns and capitals are larger than those at the ends.

Niches on the facade hold statues (the originals are in Vienna's Ephesus Museum) representing the Virtues: Arete (Goodness), Ennoia (Thought), Episteme (Knowledge) and Sophia (Wisdom). The library was restored with the aid of the Austrian Archaeological Institute.

As you leave the library, on the left is the **Gate of Augustus**, also called the Gate of Mazaeus and Mithridates, which leads into the 110m-square commercial agora where food and craftwork items were sold. The monumental gate, dedicated to the Emperor Augustus and members of his family, was apparently a favourite place for Roman ne'er-do-wells to relieve themselves, as a bit of ancient graffiti curses 'those who piss here'.

Curetes Way As you head up Curetes Way, a passage on the left (north) leads to the **public toilets**. These posh premises were for men only; the women's were elsewhere. The famous figure of Priapus (now in the Ephesus Museum in Selçuk) with the penis of most men's dreams was found in the nearby **well**, right next to the presumed brothel.

You can't miss the impressive Corinthian-style **Temple of Hadrian**, on the left, with beautiful friezes in the porch and a head of Medusa to keep out evil spirits. It was dedicated to Hadrian, Artemis and the people of Ephesus in 118 AD, but greatly reconstructed in the 5th century. Across the street is a row of 10 shops from the same period, fronted by an elaborate 5th century mosaic.

On the right side of Curetes Way across from the Temple of Hadrian, excavation and restoration work is still in progress on the **Yamaç Evleri** (terrace houses). These are usually closed to visitors although some of the finds can be seen in Ephesus Museum. Should you get the opportunity, be sure to see the rare **glass mosaic** in a niche off the atrium of one of the houses.

Further along Curetes Way, on the left, is the **Fountain of Trajan**. A huge statue of the emperor (98-117) used to tower above the pool; only one foot now remains.

Curetes Way ends at the two-storey **Gate of Hercules**, constructed in the 4th century AD, with reliefs of Hercules on both main pillars.

To the right is a side street leading to a colossal temple dedicated to the Emperor Domitian (81-96 AD), part of which serves as a rarely accessible **Museum of Inscriptions**.

Up the hill on the left (east) are the very ruined remains of the **Prytaneum**, a municipal hall; and the **Temple of Hestia Boulaea**, in which the perpetual flame was guarded. Finally you come to the **Odeum**, a small 1400-seat theatre dating from 150 AD and used for lectures, musical performances and meetings of the town council. Its lower seats of marble show something of the magnificence of the original.

To the east of the Odeum are more **baths** and, further east, the **East Gymnasium** and **Magnesia Gate**, of which virtually nothing remains.

PAMUCAK

About 7km west of Selçuk (3km west of the highway junction with the Kuşadası and Seferihisar roads) lies Pamucak (PAH-moo-jahk) beach, a long, wide crescent of soft sand. As you approach from Selçuk or Kuşadası, the signs are not encouraging, with a dirt track cutting down to the sea opposite some half-built villas. Persevere and you may be pleasantly surprised. The beach is crowded with free campers and Turkish families on summer weekends, but mostly deserted at other times except for the weekend litter.

Places to Stay

The shady ***Dereli Motel*** *(☎ 232-893 1204, fax 893 1203)* offers rooms with bath and shady camping facilities. It may be stretching it to compare the Dereli to a Thai beach resort but when you're sitting on your verandah sipping a drink that may be the comparison that most readily comes to mind. Smaller cabins cost US$26 for two people, larger ones will set you back US$35. Some face onto a rose garden instead of the sea. The complex incorporates a restaurant, food shop and camping area – US$9 for a tent, free for caravans or camper vans.

Right beside the Dereli, the ***Selçuk Belediyesi Halk Plajları*** *(☎ 232-852 3836)* is the municipal beach and camping ground but looks thoroughly miserable. You'll pay about US$6 for up to four people in a tent but it's only open from June to September.

If you must stay in a hotel the four-star, 150 room ***Otel Tamsa*** *(☎ 232-892 1190, fax 892 2771)*, Çorak Mevkii in Pamucak, has all the exterior charm of a barracks, although the interior is comfortable enough at US$45/60 a single/double during the high season.

Getting There & Away

There are regular minibuses from Selçuk and Kuşadası in summer and hitching is easier during the hot months as well. Be sure to find out when the last minibus departs from the beach as it may leave well before sunset.

ŞİRİNCE

Up in the hills 9km east of Selçuk, amid grapevines, peach and apple orchards, sits Şirince (population 800). The old-fashioned stone-and-stucco houses have red-tile roofs, and the villagers, who were moved here from Salonica and its vicinity during the exchange of populations in 1924, are ardent fruit farmers who also make interesting grape and apple wines. Locals regale you with the story that in Ottoman times, when it was populated mostly by Greeks, the village was called Çirkince ('ugliness'), but that it was changed to Şirince ('pleasantness') shortly after they arrived. A century ago it was also much larger and more prosperous – the economic focus for seven monasteries in the hills around.

Stroll the winding cobbled streets, peek at the Byzantine churches and monasteries, walk in the hills, and haggle with local women for handmade lace. If someone invites you to inspect her 'antique house', you can be sure she'll have lace for sale. Mostly the invitations are genuine, although one reader complained of being charged an outrageous amount for a 'welcoming' glass of tea.

Places to Stay & Eat

Of the several pensions, the welcoming ***Esra*** *(☎ 232-898 3140)* has five simple, waterless rooms; the best of them upstairs. Beds costs US$5 per person, with another US$2.75 for breakfast. Others are nameless, but similar to Mrs Naciye Çatal's ***Şirin Pansiyon*** *(☎ 232-898 3167)*, offering clean beds in waterless rooms for US$8 a double.

Fancier places in restored village houses include the German-run ***Erdem Pansion*** *(☎ 232-898 3430; in İzmir 481 4928)* and the picturesque ***Hotel Şirince Evleri*** *(☎/fax 232-898 3099 in İzmir)*, with a lovely traditional sitting room and nicely decorated rooms for US$50 a single/double. The Erdem was under renovation at the time of writing.

The minibus from Selçuk drops you at the centre of the village near the restaurants. ***Köy Restaurant*** and ***Sultan Han Café*** have the best shade and views, and specialise in village dishes like *mantı* (Turkish ravioli), *gözleme* (thin pastry folded over a filling), *yayık ayran* (churned yogurt and spring water) and *ev şarabı* (homemade wine).

Getting There & Away

From 8 am to 7 pm hourly minibuses connect Selçuk and Şirince (US$0.70) in summer.

BELEVİ

About 9km out of Selçuk on the İzmir highway is the village of Belevi, and about 2km east of the village, just to the side of the İzmir-Aydın otoyol, stands the **Belevi Mezar Anıtı** (Belevi Mausoleum), an ancient funerary monument resting on a base of about 30 square metres cut from the limestone bedrock. The roof was decorated with lion-griffins (now in Selçuk's Ephesus Museum and in İzmir's Archaeological Museum), and the interior held a large sarcophagus with a carved effigy of its occupant; this, too, is now in Selçuk's Ephesus Museum. Archaeologists are not certain who built this great tomb; possible candidates include the Seleucid ruler Antiochus II Theos (261-246 BC), or Persian invaders a century or more earlier.

Just west of the mausoleum are scant remains of a tumulus, or burial mound, thought to date from the 4th century BC.

KUŞADASI

About 20km from Selçuk is Kuşadası (koo-SHAH-dah-suh), a seaside resort town with a resident population of 50,000. Like Marmaris it's swollen out of all recognition throughout the summer with package holidaymakers from Europe.

Many cruise ships on the Aegean Islands circuit stop at Kuşadası so passengers can tour Ephesus and haggle for trinkets in the bazaar. The town centre is all shops and *işportacılar* (itinerant pedlars and touts ready to sell you anything and everything). The pleasant, easy-going atmosphere which made it popular in the 1970s is long gone, even though a few businesses still hang on to serve the farmers, beekeepers and fishermen who make up an ever-dwindling portion of the population.

Kuşadası gets its name (Bird Island) from a small island now connected to the mainland by a causeway, called Güvercinada, or Güvercin Adası (Pigeon Island). It's recognizable by the small stone fort which is its most prominent feature.

Like Selçuk, Kuşadası makes a good base for excursions to the ancient cities of Ephesus, Priene, Miletus, and Didyma, to Altınkum Beach and Dilek National Park, and even inland to Afrodisias and Pamukkale.

History

The natural port here may have been in use several centuries BC, and was probably known to the Byzantines, but modern Kuşadası's history begins in medieval times when Venetian and Genoese traders came here, calling it Scala Nuova. Two centuries after the Ottoman conquest in 1413, Öküz Mehmet Paşa, vizier and sometime grand vizier to sultans Ahmet I and Osman II, ordered the building of the Kaleiçi mosque and hamam, the city walls, and the caravanserai in order to improve the city's prospects as a trading port with Europe and Africa.

Useful for exporting agricultural goods, Kuşadası was also an important defensive port along the Ottoman Aegean coast. In 1834 the Güvercinada fortress was restored and improved. Kuşadası maintained its modest trade, farming and fishing economy and its quiet character until the tourism boom of the late 1980s turned it into the brash resort you see today.

Orientation

Kuşadası's central landmark is the Öküz Mehmet Paşa Kervansarayı, an Ottoman caravanserai which is now a hotel. It's 100m inland from the cruise-ship docks, at the intersection of the waterfront boulevard, Atatürk Bulvarı, and the town's main street, the pedestrianised Barbaros Hayrettin Caddesi which cuts inland from the caravanserai.

Just beyond the PTT on the northern side of Barbaros Hayrettin Caddesi, a passage leads to the Öküz Mehmet Paşa Camii and the Kaleiçi Hamamı. Further along at the stone tower, Barbaros Hayrettin Caddesi

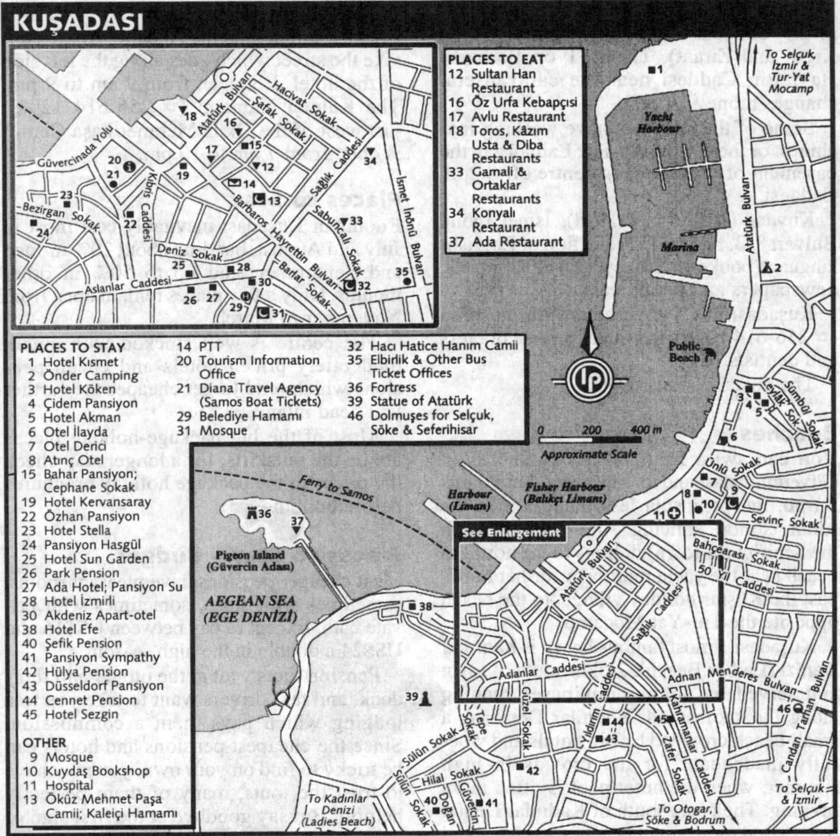

crosses Sağlık Caddesi and becomes Kahramanlar Caddesi, lined with shops and restaurants. Turn left onto Sağlık Caddesi to explore Kuşadası's market and the old Kaleiçi neighbourhood of narrow streets packed with restaurants and bars. Turn right off Barbaros Hayrettin Caddesi to find raucous Barlar Sokak (Bars Street), and the hillside pensions overlooking the harbour.

The Hacı Hatice Hanım Camii (Hanım Camii for short) about 100m along Kahramanlar Caddesi makes a convenient landmark.

The otogar and dolmuş station is more than 1km east of the caravanserai on the bypass road.

Information

The Tourism Information Office (☎ 256-614 1103, fax 614 6295), on İskele Meydanı, is right near the wharf where the cruise ships dock, located about 100m west of the caravanserai. This office is usually open from 8 am to noon and from 1.30 to 5.30 pm but keeps longer hours in summer.

Banks with ATMs are on Barbaros Hayrettin Caddesi (Akbank, Garanti, Yapı Kredi and Ziraat). The PTT on Barbaros Hayrettin Caddesi near the caravanserai changes money as well.

Some of the pensions have washing machines, or there's the Ak-Pak Laundry in the basement of the shopping centre off Sağlık Caddesi.

Kuydaş (☎ 256-614 1828), İsmet İnönü Bulvarı 8/B, has a good selection of English-language books on Turkey, as well as novels, newspapers and periodicals.

Kuşadası has a government-run hospital (☎ 256-614 1026) and many private doctors and dentists.

The postal code is 09400.

Beaches

You can swim from the rocky shores of Güvercin Adası and its causeway, but **Yılancı Burnu**, the peninsula less than 1km to the south, is more enticing. Alternatively, catch the Şehiriçi (in-town) dolmuş to the northern beach near the yacht marina or further north, past the Kuştur holiday village, to the beach opposite the Tur-Yat Mocamp.

Kuşadası's most famous beach is **Kadınlar Denizi** (Ladies Beach), 2.5km south of town and served by dolmuş minibuses running along the shore road. Kadınlar Denizi is a small beach crowded by big hotels and woefully inadequate for the crowds in high summer, when the hotel pool is often more inviting. The coast south of Kadınlar Denizi has several more small beaches, each backed by ranks of big hotels.

There's also **Pamucak** (see the Pamucak section earlier in this chapter), 15km to the north. Most of the year you can get there on a dolmuş running between Kuşadası and Selçuk; at other times you may have to change to a Pamucak dolmuş in Selçuk, or get out at the Pamucak road and walk 3km.

Hamams

Kuşadası's hamams are of the un-Turkish New Age type, allowing men and women to bathe at the same time, and charging an outrageous US$16 for the full works.

The Belediye Hamamı (☎ 256-614 1219) is up the hill behind the Akdeniz Apart-otel; take the street which goes along the left side of the hotel. It's open from 9 am to 9 pm. The Kaleiçi Hamamı (☎ 256-614 1292), just west of the Öküz Mehmet Paşa Camii, is open from 7 am to 10 pm.

Places to Stay

Rooms in Kuşadası inevitably cost most in July and August, but drop about 20% in June and September, and up to 50% in other months. Only a few places remain open from November to March.

The centre is well stocked with small, moderately priced hotels and cheap pensions which tend to get cheaper the further you head inland.

Most of the big package-holiday places are on the outskirts; for a longer stay check the prices in the package holiday brochures before booking.

Places to Stay – Budget

Most cheaper pensions have pleasant rooms, sometimes with sinks, sometimes with private bath. Expect to pay between US$16 and US$24 a double in the high season.

Pension touts wait at the otogar and ferry dock, and taxi drivers want to take you to a lodging which pays them a commission. Since the cheapest pensions and hotels can be tricky to find on your own, you may have to trust the touts, many of them perfectly helpful. But say goodbye at the first sign of improper dealing to avoid being ripped off. Among pension owners in Kuşadası are a small number of sleazy characters, so it's good to size up a pension carefully before choosing to stay there.

There are several clusters of places to stay near the centre. To find them, when coming from the harbour walk up Barbaros Hayrettin Caddesi, turn right towards the Akdeniz Apart-otel, and take Yıldırım Caddesi, the road to the left of the Akdeniz, or Aslanlar Caddesi, the road to the right. These take you into the neighbourhood called Camiatik Mahallesi, which has lots of pensions and inexpensive hotels.

Yıldırım Caddesi First up this steep street is the small *Seçkin Pansiyon* which is a little too close to the minaret's loudspeaker for comfort. Walk a bit further for ***Düsseldorf Pansiyon*** *(☎ 256-613 1272)*, an excellent choice with spotless rooms arrayed in front of a secluded garden. The best rooms have balconies facing the garden for US$6 per person, plus another US$2 for breakfast.

Readers have also recommended ***Cennet Pension*** *(☎ 256-614 4893)*, even further up the street, where bathless rooms cost US$5 per person. The roof terrace allows a good panoramic view of the town.

Aslanlar Caddesi *Hotel İzmirli (☎ 256-614 4861)*, on Aslanlar Caddesi near the Akdeniz Apart-otel, is right in the thick of things but was closed for renovation at the time of writing. Rooms used to cost US$20/24/28 a single/double/triple, breakfast included.

Follow the signs up an extremely steep hill to the family run, 17 room ***Pansiyon Golden Bed*** *(☎ 256-614 8708, Aslanlar Caddesi, Uğurlu 1 Çıkmazı 4)*, on a quiet cul-de-sac not far from the centre. Some rooms have balconies and sea views, and there are splendid views from the roof terrace. Rooms with shower cost US$20 a double with breakfast.

Further uphill on Aslanlar Caddesi past the Hotel Sun Garden, look for the ***Ada Hotel*** *(☎ 256-614 9559)* and, nearby, the very basic but cheap ***Pansiyon Su*** *(☎ 256-614 1453, Aslanlar Caddesi 13)*, with waterless rooms for US$8 per person.

Nicer than these is the 14 room ***Park Pension*** *(☎ 256-614 3917, Aslanlar Caddesi 17)*, with simple rooms in a restored house set around a shady courtyard with orange trees. Beds cost US$6 including breakfast with marmalade from the oranges.

Kıbrıs Caddesi Continue up the slope to a junction, and turn right downhill along Kıbrıs Caddesi for ***Özhan Pansiyon*** *(☎ 256-614 2932)*. It's very central and normally quiet, with a nice roof terrace with bar and pension-sponsored belly dance parties. Rooms with shower cost US$10/16 a single/double and breakfast is US$2.

Bezirgan Sokak Go back to the junction and continue up to the top of Aslanlar Caddesi, then turn right and follow Bezirgan Sokak. Immediately on the left and attached to a hairdresser's is ***Şanlı Pansiyon*** *(☎ 256-612 9851)* with very simple rooms for just US$4 per person. There's a roof terrace which lacks sea views but does at least catch any breeze in summer. Further along on the left at the bottom of Mercan Sokak ***Pansiyon Dinç*** *(☎ 256-614 4249)* offers small, waterless rooms in high summer only. They're cheap at US$16 a double, breakfast included. Continue past the Hotel Stella to find ***Pansiyon Hasgül*** *(☎ 256-614 3641)*, up steep steps in a quiet area but with sea views.

Güzel Sokak At the top of Aslanlar Caddesi, instead of turning right onto Bezirgan Sokak, turn left into Güzel Sokak. At the end of the road, turn right into İleri Sokak for the rambling, 20 room ***Hülya Pension*** *(☎ 256-614 2075)*, which charges US$10 per person in a room, slightly less if you roll out your own sleeping bag on the roof. Some rooms have sinks or private showers. Laundry is done for an additional fee; cheap, good meals are available, or you may use the kitchen yourself.

Continue along İleri Sokak which rises steeply until you come to a modern residential district on the left. Turn left down Güvercin Sokak for the 17 room ***Pansiyon Sympathy*** *(☎ 256-614 4388)*, run by Güngür Gencer, a smiling dynamo of a woman who provides good, cheap meals in a rooftop dining room as well as clean, cheap accommodation. Rates are from US$12/18 a single/double in summer, breakfast included.

One block further up the hill, ***Şefik Pension*** *(☎ 256-614 4222, Doğan Sokak 11)*, has comparable rates, with good food and friendly family proprietors.

Zafer Sokak Instead of walking towards the harbour from Hanım Camii you can cut up a block, past the end of Bar Lane, to find several more small pensions, including the widely advertised ***Hotel Sezgin***

(☎/fax 256-614 6489, Zafer Sokak 15), which has beds in clean, simple rooms with shower for US$10 per person (10% discount for readers of this book). The Sezgin has lots of services for backpackers, including a laundry, movies in several languages and an Internet link-up for US$2 an hour.

Camping North of the centre about 1km, inland from the yacht marina, are three decent camping areas. Best is ***Önder Camping*** *(☎ 256-614 2413, fax 614 2946)*, open all year, with lots of facilities: tennis, swimming pool, laundry and a good restaurant (open from March to October only). If the Önder is full, the adjoining ***Yat Camping*** *(☎ 256-614 1333)* takes the overflow.

The larger ***Tur-Yat Mocamp*** *(☎ 256-614 1087)*, several kilometres north of these on the shore, is open from mid-April or late May until mid to late October. Across the road from a small beach, it charges US$8 for two people in a tent. Motel rooms cost US$36/42/50 a single/double/triple, breakfast and dinner included. There are a few restaurants and a fuel station close by.

Places to Stay – Mid-Range

Mid-range hotels are scattered throughout town, with some inland from the yacht marina, some on the pension streets of Aslanlar Caddesi and Bezirgan Sokak; and many more along Atatürk Bulvarı and İstiklal Sokak.

Cephane (JEHP-hah-neh) Sokak leads off Barbaros Hayrettin Caddesi opposite the caravanserai. ***Bahar Pansiyon*** *(☎ 256-614 1191, fax 614 9359, Cephane Sokak 12)*, used to be an excellent choice but nowadays its rooms look pretty mundane; the fans and roof terrace barely compensating for the leaky plumbing. Singles/doubles cost US$18/26 per person. The Bahar is closed from November to February.

Walk up Aslanlar Caddesi to the right of the Akdeniz Apart-otel to find ***Hotel Sun Garden*** *(☎ 256-614 3806, fax 614 4225, Aslanlar Caddesi 70-A)*, across from the Ada Hotel. Popular with groups, it has a nice swimming pool and bar, and charges from US$30 to US$38 a spotless double, breakfast included. In a previous incarnation this place was called the Hotel Flash – don't let anyone persuade you that the Flash was anywhere else.

Turn right onto Bezirgan Sokak to find the airy, two-star, 22 room ***Hotel Stella*** *(☎ 256-614 1632, Bezirgan Sokak 44)*, with fabulous views of the town and the harbour. At the time of writing it was closed for renovation but bright, modern rooms used to be priced at US$55 a double with shower, breakfast included.

Facing the sea, just less than 1km north of the caravanserai on Atatürk Bulvarı, are several convenient modern hotels offering comfortable rooms for moderate prices. The three-star ***Otel İlayda*** *(☎ 256-614 3807, fax 614 6766)* has 40 rooms with bath (and many with sea-view balconies) for US$25/40 a single/double. ***Otel Derici*** *(☎ 256-614 8222, fax 614 8226)*, nearby at Atatürk Bulvarı 40, also has three stars, and 87 comfortable rooms (some with sea views) at rates of US$50 a double with breakfast. Right next door ***Atınç Otel*** *(☎ 256-614 7608, fax 614 4967)* charges US$80/100 for its rooms.

Continue along the seafront and, about 1km north of the centre, you'll come to another group of moderately priced lodgings on İstiklal Sokak. ***Hotel Köken*** *(☎ 256-614 1460, fax 614 5723, İstikdal Sokak 5)*, is the standard Turkish two-star: rooms with private bath cost US$24, breakfast included. Next door to the Köken is Yunus Pension, and beyond that the 20 room ***Çidem Pansiyon*** (chee-DEHM) *(☎ 256-614 1895, İstiklal Sokak 9)*, a clean, cheerful place with single rooms for US$22 to US$26, doubles for US$28 to US$34. This was being renovated at the time of writing. When it re-opens the cheaper rooms may be gone.

The nearby two-star, ***Hotel Akman*** *(☎ 256-614 1501, İstiklal Sokak 13)*, is tidy if soulless. It's open from mid-March to the end of October and used by tour groups. Rooms, some with bathtubs, cost US$22/32 a single/double, breakfast included.

Facing Güvercin Adası is the new ***Hotel Efe*** *(☎ 256-614 3660, fax 614 3662)*, a waterfront place with balconies lined up to scoop the sunsets. Readers have enjoyed staying in rooms very reasonably priced at US$33 a double with breakfast but basically it's a tour group place and independent travellers will be lucky to get a bed.

Places to Stay – Top End

The 107 room ***Hotel Kısmet*** *(☎ 256-614 2005, fax 614 4914)*, Akyar Mevkii, just north of the yacht marina perched on a little peninsula, is the best place for a splurge. It's well run and has the feel of a private club. Indeed, there are no signs displaying its name – it gets enough custom by word of mouth. Rates are US$100/135/155 a single/double/triple, breakfast included.

It would be good to be able to recommend ***Hotel Kervansaray*** (or Club Caravansérail) *(☎ 256-614 4115, fax 614 2423)*, near the harbour, but the interior is spoiled by tourist shops, and the 'Turkish Nights' in the courtyard means music until midnight on most summer evenings (see Entertainment). The rate for pleasant small stone rooms is US$50/80 a single/double, breakfast included.

The coast to the north and south of Kuşadası is crowded with huge, gleaming five-star hotels for the package-holiday trade. Rooms cost from US$95 to US$125 a double in summer.

South of the centre on Kadınlar Denizi are comfortable hotels priced from US$50 to US$100 a double. These include the four-star, 319 room ***İmbat Oteli*** *(☎ 256-614 2000, fax 614 4960)*, and the much cheaper three-star ***Martı Oteli*** *(☎ 256-614 3650, fax 614 4700)*, an older, 113 room place that offers a superb location and good value for money.

About 5km south of the centre beyond Kadınlar Denizi at Yavansu Mevkii, the five-star ***Onura Hotel*** *(☎ 256-614 8505, fax 614 3727)* is perched on a cliff right above the sea, offering 330 luxury rooms and full facilities. Next door is the similar ***Fantasia Otel*** *(☎ 256-614 8600, fax 614 2765)*.

Places to Eat

Kuşadası is fish and chips and 'full English breakfast' country. In summer, its restaurant prices are even higher than Selçuk's, which are already higher than İstanbul's but at least most places post prices prominently so you can make comparisons.

Places to Eat – Budget

The cheapest food is in the low-budget pensions mentioned earlier; ask about meals when you book a room. For other cheap eats, you must search well inland and find places patronised mostly by locals.

The restaurants on Sağlık Caddesi between Kahramanlar Caddesi and İsmet İnönü Bulvarı tend to be popular with Turks and so are cheaper than many others. Check prices at the ***Konyalı***, beside the big Kalyon Restaurant, and nearby shopfront places.

Walk along Sabuncalı Sokak off Sağlık Caddesi to the Hotel Karasu and Gündoğdu Restaurant and turn left. The row of grills – ***Gamali***, ***Ortaklar***, ***Ak Gül*** etc specialise in the regional favourite, *çöp şiş* for around US$2.50 per portion.

The grills off Kahramanlar Caddesi next to the Hacı Hatice Hanım Camii mainly serve lamb and chicken grills for US$4 to US$6.

For atmospheric cheap eats you could do worse than pop inside the castle on Güvercin Adası, where several small restaurants sell döner kebap, pide and köfte for prices only US$0.50 or so more than in town.

Places to Eat – Mid-Range

The town's prime dining location is on the waterfront by the harbour, but competition ensures that prices are about the same as those further inland. Meat grills priced at US$4.50 inland may cost US$5 here, but it's worth it for the view. Just be careful to get the price on any seafood you order. A full fish dinner with wine at the ***Toros***, ***Kâzım Usta***, ***Cam*** or ***Diba*** is likely to cost from US$15 to US$25 per person.

One pleasant surprise is the ***Ada Restaurant***, on Güvercin Adası, which offers good food at low prices right on the water. Set meals cost around US$6. Long may it last!

There are many atmospheric places to eat in Kaleiçi, the old section behind the PTT. On Cephane Sokak, the ***Avlu Restaurant*** has outdoor tables and lowish prices for soups and stews. Another favourite is the nearby ***Öz Urfa Kebapçısı***, on Cephane Sokak, which is strong on roast meats, with dishes from US$4 to US$5.

Places to Eat – Top End

Sultan Han Restaurant *(☎ 256-614 6380, Bahar Sokak 8)*, in Kaleiçi, is one of several old caravanserais decorated with carved wood and local crafts. Menus offer fish and Turkish meat choices, a smattering of continental dishes, good mezes and traditional Turkish sweets. Some evenings there's a belly dancer. Lunch and dinner are served daily from 11 am to 11 pm, for US$14 to US$20 per person.

Entertainment

Much of Kuşadası's nightlife is aimed at specific national groups. Barlar Sokak (not to be confused with Barhar Sokak) near the Akdeniz Apart-otel is choked with Olde English and Irish 'pubs', and Deutsches 'bierstuben'. The quieter, classier bars are in Kaleiçi's narrow streets. Wander around to find ***Back Street Bar***, ***Be Bop Café Bar***, ***Orient*** and other places, bearing in mind that names change with surprising rapidity. Most offer dusky courtyards, comfy upholstered seats/benches, drinks, conversation and hip music.

Out on Güvercin Adası, the fort is usually let to disco organisers. Even if the latest incarnation is not to your liking, the walk out to the island and back is pleasant. This is certainly the place to come for a sunset rakı or two.

If you're into organised entertainment, ***Hotel Kervansaray*** plays host to a Turkish night most evenings during summer. To watch the music and dancing without eating costs US$25; with a meal you're looking at US$40.

Things to Buy

Kuşadası's **bazaar** offers the full range of Turkish souvenirs: onyx, meerschaum, leather clothing and accessories, copper, brass, carpets and jewellery. If you're heading on, save your shopping for later as almost anywhere else will be cheaper. If you must shop here, do it before or after the cruise ships are in port, as prices are higher then and dealers are ruder.

Getting There & Away

Bus & Dolmuş In summer frequent *şehiriçi* (intracity) minibuses run from the otogar to the centre, and up and down the coast. Kadınlar Denizi minibuses head along the shore road to the beach. For either, the fare is US$0.40.

Kuşadası's otogar is situated at the southern end of Kahramanlar Caddesi on the bypass highway. Direct buses depart for several far-flung parts of the country, or you can transfer at İzmir.

For Selçuk, Pamucak and Seferihisar you needn't bother going to the otogar; instead you can pick up a minibus on Adnan Menderes Bulvarı.

Several companies have ticket offices on İsmet İnönü Bulvarı. When you purchase a ticket, try to ascertain if it's really a direct service: your 'bus to Priene' may turn out to be a minibus to Söke, where you must change to another for Priene.

Adnan Menderes airport – 80km, 1¼ hours, US$2.75; take an İzmir bus and ask to be dropped off at the airport

Bodrum – 151km, two hours, US$6; frequent buses in summer

Didyma – see Söke

İzmir – 95km, 1½ hours, US$2.50; buses every 30 minutes from 6 to 8 am, then every 20 minutes to 9 pm in summer

Miletus – see Söke

Pamukkale – 220km, three hours, US$7; some direct buses, or change at Denizli

Priene – see Söke

Seferihisar – 65km, 1½ hours, US$2; a few minibuses

Selçuk – 20km, 30 minutes, US$1; minibuses run frequently in summer, with the last minibus departing from Selçuk at 8.30 pm, and from Kuşadası at 9 pm

Söke – 20km, 30 minutes, US$1; frequent minibuses, especially on Wednesday (Söke's market day). From Söke's otogar, transfer to minibuses for Güllübahçe (Priene), Balat (Miletus); or Yenihisar for Didyma (Didim) and Altınkum Beach.

Minibus Tours In summer, minibus drivers organise tours to Priene, Miletus and Didyma for about US$20 per person. The tours may cost a bit more than normal dolmuş and bus fares, but save the time you'd spend waiting for a lift or an onward minibus. When booking the tour, try and persuade the driver to allow an hour at each site – often they'll try to rush you through.

In spring and autumn, tours to Priene, Miletus and Didyma may run on Wednesday, Saturday and/or Sunday, or only when a group can be gathered.

The drivers at the otogar also run tours to Ephesus and Meryemana for about US$15 per person.

Boat – Samos Walk into any travel agency in Kuşadası and purchase a ticket for a boat to Samos. You can go over for the day and return in the evening, or you can stay. Boats depart from Samos and Kuşadası at 8.30 am and 5 pm daily from April to October, with less frequent services in winter. The trip costs US$30 one way, US$35 same-day round trip, or US$55 for a round-trip ticket valid for a year, including taxes. Some agencies discount these tickets, so ask, and flash your student card if you have one. You must be at the harbour 45 minutes before sailing time for immigration formalities.

You can book through Ekol Tourism & Travel Agency (☎ 256-614 5591), Buyral Sokak 9; Diana Travel Agency (☎ 256-614 3859, fax 614 3170), at the harbour end of Kıbrıs Caddesi; or Azim Tour (☎ 256-614 4635, fax 614 5479), Liman Caddesi Yayla Pasajı. These agencies also handle tickets for car ferries to Greece and Italy.

DİLEK MİLLİ PARKI

About 30km south of Kuşadası, the Dilek peninsula juts westward into the Aegean, almost touching the island of Samos. West of the village of Güzelçamlı the land has been set aside as Dilek Milli Parkı (National Park), a nature reserve with some areas for day visitors; no camping is allowed. The mountain slopes here are clad in pines, the wildlife is abundant, the air is clean and the sun is bright.

The park is open daily from 8 am to 6 pm for US$0.50 per person, US$2.50 per car.

Approaching Dilek from Kuşadası or Söke, the road passes through the villages of Davutlar and **Güzelçamlı**. The latter, once a sleepy village, is now backed by thousands of holiday villas. Among the ranks of flats are several small two and three-star hotels.

It's 2km from Güzelçamlı to the national park entrance, then another 1km to **İçmeler Köyü**, a protected cove with a small but cigarette-butt-strewn beach, lounge chairs and umbrellas, a restaurant and picnic area.

About 3km beyond İçmeler Köyü an unpaved road heads 1km downhill on the right, to **Aydınlık Beach**, a quieter pebble-and-sand strand about 800m long with surf, backed by pines, and served by a small cafe.

Less than 1km further along is a jandarma post. Another 1km brings you to **Kavaklı Burun**, another sand-and-pebble surf beach 500m to the right of the road. As at Aydınlık, there's a second entrance to the beach at the far end, another 1km along. West of that is a military zone where entry is forbidden. It's 8.5km back to the park entrance.

Getting There & Away

You can walk the 3km from Güzelçamlı to İçmeler Köyü in about 30 minutes. Otherwise, without your own transport you must rely on dolmuşes from Kuşadası and Söke (45 minutes, US$1.25). They run from 8 am to dusk in summer and usually go all the way to the far end of Kavaklı Burun. Don't leave the park too long after mid-afternoon, as the later dolmuşes fill up quickly.

PRIENE, MILETUS & DIDYMA

Ephesus may be the *crème-de-la-crème* of the Aegean archaeological sites but south of Kuşadası are the ruins of three other very ancient and important settlements well worth a day trip. Priene occupies a dramatic position overlooking the plain of the River Menderes (formerly Meander); Miletus preserves a great theatre; and Didyma's Temple of Apollo is among the world's most impressive religious structures. If you find the coach parties at Ephesus bothersome, you will enjoy exploring these less popular sites all the more.

Beyond Didyma is Altınkum Beach, good for an after-ruins swim off season but usually festooned with cigarette butts.

Priene

Priene was important around 300 BC when the League of Ionian Cities held congresses and festivals here. Otherwise, it was smaller and less important than nearby Miletus, which means that its Hellenistic buildings were not buried by Roman buildings.

Priene was a planned town, with its streets laid out in a grid, a system which originated in Miletus. Of the buildings which remain, the **bouleuterion** (city council meeting place) is in very good condition. The five standing columns of the **Temple of Athena**, designed by Pythius of Halicarnassus and looked upon as the epitome of an Ionian temple, form Priene's most familiar landmark; the view from here is superb. Take a look at the **theatre** with its finely carved front seats for VIPs, the ruins of a **Byzantine church**, the **gymnasium** and **stadium**.

Although the ruins are good there's a strong chance you'll remember Priene's magnificent setting the most, with steep Mt Mykale rising behind it, and the broad flood plain of the River Menderes spread out at its feet.

Priene is open from 8 am to 7.30 pm daily in summer (from 8.30 am to 5.30 pm in winter) and costs US$2.

The well-signed ***Priene Pension*** (☎ *256-547 1725*) offers pleasant pine-ceilinged rooms set around a rose and orange tree garden. A twin room with breakfast costs US$16, or you can camp for US$4.

Near the site entrance is a shady rest spot with water cascading from an old aqueduct next to the ***Şelale Restaurant***, where you can get a cool drink or hot tea, make a telephone call or have a meal. A ***teahouse*** opposite competes fiercely with the Şelale for the drinks traffic. There are several smaller, cheaper restaurants as well.

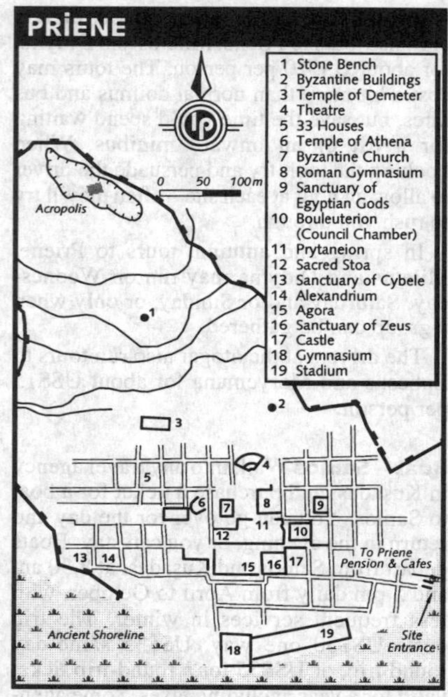

Miletus

Miletus is 22km south of Priene. Its **Great Theatre** rises to greet you as you approach the flood plain's southern boundary and turn left (east), riding through swampy cotton fields to reach the site. It's the most significant reminder of a once-grand city, which was an important commercial and governmental centre from about 700 BC to 700 AD. After that time the harbour filled with silt, and Miletus' commerce dwindled. The 15,000-seat theatre was originally a Hellenistic building, but the Romans reconstructed it extensively during the 1st century. It's still in good condition and exciting to explore.

Climb to the top of the theatre where the ramparts of a later Byzantine castle provide a viewing platform for several groups of ruins scattered around. Look left and you'll see what remains of the **harbour**, called Lion Bay for the stone statues of lions which guarded it. Look right and you'll see the **stadium**; the northern, western and southern **agoras**; the vast **Baths of Faustina**, constructed on the order of Emperor Marcus Aurelius' wife; and a **bouleuterion** between the northern and southern agoras. Some of the site is underwater for much of the year and although that makes it hard to walk around, it also makes it even more picturesque. Note that the northern gateway to the southern agora is now one of the prized exhibits in Berlin's Pergamum Museum.

To the south of the main ruins is the **İlyas Bey Camii** (1404), dating from a period after the Seljuks but before the Ottomans when this region was ruled by the Turkish emirs of Menteşe. The doorway and mihrab are well worth noticing, and you'll probably have this neglected corner of Miletus to yourself.

The site is open from 8 am to 7.30 pm in summer (to 5.30 pm in winter) for US$2. The **Milet Müzesi** (Miletus Museum), about

1km south of the theatre, is open from 8.30 am to 12.30 pm, and 1.30 to 5.30 pm and costs US$1, but it's hardly worth it. Across the road from the Great Theatre are a couple of small ***snack bars*** where you can get sandwiches and drinks.

A **Seljuk caravanserai**, 100m south of the ticket booth, has been restored and converted to shops, although it's been unoccupied for so long one wonders whether any shopkeepers will ever move in now.

Didyma

Called Didim in Turkish, this was the site of a stupendous temple to Apollo, occupied by an oracle as important as the one at Delphi. The ruins you see today belong to a temple started in the late 4th century. This replaced the original temple, which was destroyed in 494 BC by the Persians, and a later construction which was completed under Alexander the Great.

The Temple of Apollo was never finished, though its oracle and priests were hard at work until, after 1400 years of soothsaying, Christianity became the state religion of the Byzantines and brought an end to pagan practices.

Ancient Didyma was never a real town. Only the priests who specialised in oracular temple management lived here. Originally from Delphi, they had a pretty cushy life, sitting on the considerable temple treasure.

When you approach Didyma today, you come into the town of **Yenihisar**, which has grown phenomenally in the last few years to engulf both Altınkum, the beach to the south, and Didim, formerly the Ottoman-Greek town of Yeronda. It's a popular place with tour groups, and carpet shops gush forth touts at the approach of each new bus.

Temple of Apollo The temple porch held 120 huge columns with richly carved bases vaguely reminiscent of Luxor in Egypt. Behind the porch is a great doorway where oracular poems were written and presented to petitioners. Beyond the doorway is the *cella* (court), where the oracle sat and prophesied after drinking from the sacred spring. We can only speculate on what that water contained to make the prophesies possible. The cella is reached today by covered ramps on both sides of the porch.

The temple grounds contain fragments of rich decoration, including a photogenic head of Medusa (she of the snakes for hair). There used to be a road lined with statues which led to a small harbour but after standing unmoved for 23 centuries the statues were taken to the British Museum in 1858.

Admission is from 9 am to 7 pm in summer (8 am to 5.30 pm in winter) and costs US$2.

Places to Stay & Eat There are two good pensions beside the temple. The 10 room ***Oracle Pension*** *(☎ 256-811 0270)* is perched above the temple precinct to the south, with close-up views of the marble pile. If you don't stay here (US$15/30/40 a single/double/triple for rooms with bath), at least come for a drink on the terrace for the view.

Just around the corner from the temple, on the Altınkum road, ***Medusa House*** *(☎ 256-813 4491)* is a pretty restored stone village house with lovely gardens. Inviting rooms cost US$22 a double, breakfast included. Although it's only steps from the temple, it has no temple view and noise from the road could be annoying.

A striking stone statue of Medusa's head of snakes is a feature of the Temple of Apollo at Didyma

The vast ***restaurants*** across the road from the temple entrance are geared up for the tourist trade, with prices to match.

Altınkum Beach

About 4km south of Didyma through the town of Yenihisar is Altınkum (Golden Sand) Beach, a resort visited mostly by Turkish families who patronise a typical assortment of restaurants, pensions and hotels rated from no stars to three stars. Most accommodation – and especially the cheapest – is booked solid in summer, and the sand is so strewn with cigarette butts that you hesitate to walk on it. At a pinch, go west from the access road and look at the pensions a block inland from the beach. A better plan is to forget Altınkum unless you come during the low season.

Getting Around

If you start early in the morning from Kuşadası or Selçuk, you can get to Priene, Miletus and Didyma by dolmuş and return to your base at night. If you have a car, you can see all three sites, have a swim and be back by mid-afternoon.

Minibus Tours Minibus drivers at the Selçuk otogar organise tours to Priene, Miletus, Didyma and Altınkum Beach during summer. The tour should take a whole day, with the minibus departing from the bus station between 8.30 and 9.30 am, spending an hour at Priene, 1½ hours at Miletus, 2½ hours at Didyma and its museum, and about 1½ hours at Altınkum Beach before returning to Selçuk between 5.30 and 6.30 pm. Often the drivers hope to squeeze in two trips, halving these times which is not really enough.

The cost is between US$18 and US$25, depending upon how many people there are. Lunch isn't normally included in this price. It's a good idea to reserve your seat in advance.

If you want to do the trip yourself, begin by catching a dolmuş to Söke from Kuşadası (20km, US$1) or Selçuk (40km, US$2), then another onward to Priene (US$0.75).

When you've finished at Priene, wait for a passing dolmuş (US$1) or hitch across the flat flood plain to Miletus (22km). Take any dolmuş saying 'Balat' (the village next to Miletus), 'Akköy' (a larger village beyond Balat) or 'Yenihisar'.

From Miletus, fairly frequent dolmuşes head south again to Akköy (4.5km, US$1.25) where you can pick up a minibus to Söke or Didyma, 14km beyond Akköy. There's not much traffic about, so it may take some time to hitch to Akköy. South of Akköy there's more traffic, most of it heading on past Didyma to Altınkum Beach.

SÖKE

Söke is a cheerless modern town with some of the worst repaired road surfaces around. Unfortunately, except in high season, you may be forced to come here to change buses as you travel around the coast.

The big otogar is divided into separate bus and dolmuş sections. From the bus side of the station, Söke municipal buses depart for İzmir every hour on the half-hour until 7.30 pm for US$3. Others head east to Denizli and Pamukkale, south to Bodrum and to Muğla (for Marmaris).

The dolmuş side of the station serves vehicles going to the following places:

Altınkum Beach – 61km, US$2
Aydın – 55km, US$1.50 (the provincial capital on the way to Afrodisias, Denizli and Pamukkale)
Balat – 35km, US$1 (the village near Miletus)
Davutlar – 13km, US$1 (on the way to Dilek Milli Parkı)
Didyma – 56km, US$1.50
Güllübahçe – 14km, US$1 (the village next to Priene)
Güzelçamlı – 22km, US$1.50 (near Dilek Milli Parkı)
Kuşadası – 20km, US$1
Milas – 82km, US$2 (on the way to Bodrum)

If you arrive in Söke too late to move on, the modern ***Hotel Akalın*** *(☎ 256-512 7793)*, immediately opposite the otogar, has singles/doubles for US$14/24, including breakfast.

SÖKE TO MİLAS

The 86km ride from Söke, near Selçuk and Kuşadası, to Milas takes only 1¼ hours if you go nonstop, but so many interesting detours are possible that it may take you several days.

About 29km south of Söke there is a road on the right for Akköy (7km), Miletus and Didyma, described above. Soon afterwards, the highway skirts the southern shore of the huge **Bafa Gölü** (Bafa Lake). This was once a gulf of the Aegean Sea, but became a lake as the sea retreated. About 13km beyond the Akköy turn-off are several restaurants, motels and camping areas, most prominently the ***Turgut***.

About 4km further south-east is a small island bearing traces of a ruined Byzantine monastery, and just beyond this is ***Ceri'nin Yeri***, a restaurant serving sea bass, eel, carp and grey mullet which find their way into the lake to spawn. Ceri's has a few ***pension*** and ***motel*** rooms, and a ***camp site*** as well. Sometimes you can arrange a boat trip to Herakleia.

Herakleia/Kapıkırı (Latmos)

At the south-eastern end of the lake is a village called Çamiçi, from which a paved road on the left is marked for **Kapıkırı**, 10km to the north, though it's actually less than 9km; watch carefully for the sign which is easily missed. Minibuses from Söke or Milas will drop you at the road junction but you'll have to hike or hitch along the side road unless you manage to catch one of the very infrequent dolmuşes.

At the end of the wonderful, twisting, rock-dominated road, you'll come to the **ruins of Herakleia ad Latmos** in and around the village of Kapıkırı. Behind the village looms the dramatic, five peaked **Beşparmak Dağı**, the Five-fingered Mountain (1500m). This was the ancient Mt Latmos.

History Latmos is famous because of Endymion, the legendary shepherd boy. The story relates how the handsome Endymion was asleep on Mt Latmos when Selene, the moon goddess, fell in love with him. Myths differ as to what happened next.

It seems that Endymion slept forever, and Selene (also called Diana) got to come down and sleep with him every night. She also saw to the care of his flocks, while he slept on. And that's about it.

Ringed by mountains, this area was one of refuge for Christian hermits during the Arab invasions of the 8th century AD, hence the ruined churches and monasteries. The monks reputedly thought Endymion a Christian saint because they admired his powers of self-denial, though catatonia seems a more appropriate word.

Things to See As you enter the village in summer, you may be asked to pay an admission fee of US$1.50. Bear right at the ticket booth, pass the Pelikan Restaurant, and you'll come to the Agora Restaurant. Park here and explore on foot.

A path behind the car park leads westward up to the **Temple of Athena**, on a promontory overlooking the lake. Also from the car park, paths lead eastward to the **agora**, the **bouleuterion** and then several hundred metres through stone-walled pastures and across a valley to the unrestored **theatre**. The badly ruined theatre is oddly sited, with no spectacular view. Its most interesting feature is the several rows of seats and flights of steps cut into the rock. You will also see many remnants of the **city walls** dating from 300 BC.

Much of the fun of a visit to Latmos is to observe Turkish village life. Beehives dot the fields, and camomile flowers *(papatya)* grow wild by the roadsides in spring and summer. During the day women sit by the road, making lace which they then attempt to sell to passers-by. In the evenings villagers herd their animals along the main street.

When you're finished in the village, follow the road down to the lake, past the **Endymion Temple** built partly into the rock, the ruins of a **Byzantine castle** and the city's **necropolis**.

Down at the lakeside, near the ruins of a Byzantine church, are several small restaurants for fish (if they've caught any that day), including the ***Zeybek***, ***Kaya*** and ***Selene***. All offer camping and boat tours of the lake. There's a small beach of white coarse sand. Just offshore is an 'island' which may be reached from the shore on foot as the level of the lake sometimes falls. Around its base are foundations of ancient buildings.

Places to Stay & Eat Of the several pensions in the village the best is certainly the 14 room *Agora Pansiyon (☎/fax 252-543 5445)*, which charges US$15 for a waterless double (clean shared baths). Included in the price is a village breakfast: fresh eggs, local butter and honey (no packets). Three wooden bungalows are also available for the same price. The pension and its restaurant are surrounded by flowers, and the owners have lots of information available for lovers of ruins or birds.

The 10 room ***Pelikan Pansiyon*** *(☎ 252-543 5158)* has more basic rooms but with lake views and showers for US$12. Its ***restaurant*** also offers panoramic lake views.

A third place, ***Haus Jasemin***, was nearing completion at the time of writing.

When it comes to ***camping***, the less well-kept lakeside sites win out because of their position.

Euromos

About 15km past Bafa Lake and 1km south of the village of **Selimiye**, keep your eyes open for the picturesque **Temple of Zeus**, on the left-hand (eastern) side of the road in the midst of the ancient city of Euromos. Of the town, only the temple and a few scattered ruins now remain. The Corinthian columns set in an olive grove seem too good to be true, like a Hollywood set of a classical scene.

First settled in the 6th century BC, Euromos held a sanctuary to a local deity. With the coming of Greek, then Roman, culture, the local god's place was taken by Zeus. Euromos reached the height of its prosperity between 200 BC and 200 AD. Emperor Hadrian (117-38 AD), who built so many monuments in Anatolia, is thought to have built this one as well. The several unfluted columns which remain suggest that the work was never finished.

If you're interested in ruins, you can clamber up the slopes to find other bits of the town. Look up behind the ticket booth at the big stone fortification wall on the hillside. Climb up through the olive groves, go over the wall, and continue at the same altitude (the path dips a bit, which is OK, but don't climb higher). After 100m you'll cross another stone wall and find yourself on flat ground which was the stage of the ancient **theatre**. It's badly ruined now, with olive trees growing among the few remaining rows of seats. Besides the theatre, the town's **agora** is down by the highway, with only a few toppled column drums to mark it.

The site is open from 8.30 am to 5.30 pm (7 pm in summer) for US$1. There are no services except soft drinks sales in summer only. To get here, take a bus or dolmuş between Söke and Milas and ask to get out at the ruins. Alternatively, take a dolmuş from Milas to Iasos, get out at the road junction for Iasos and walk the short distance north along the highway until you see the Euromos ruins on the right.

Milas is about 12km south of Euromos, but before you arrive there you could divert to visit Iasos and Labranda.

Kıyıkışlacık (Iasos)

About 4km south-east of Euromos (8km north-west of Milas) is a road on the right (west) marked for **Kıyıkışlacık** (Iasos), about 18km along a twisting road. The Turkish name means 'Little Barracks on the Coast', but Iasos was in fact a fine city set on its dramatic perch several centuries before Christ. Earliest settlement may date from the Old Bronze Age, and may have included a civilisation much like the Minoan one on Crete.

Today Iasos is a sleepy Aegean fishing village set amid the tumbled ruins of an ancient city. As you approach it, past a cluster of visually unfortunate, half-built concrete villas, the road forks. The right fork leads to the **Balıkpazarı Iasos Müzesi** holding the village's most interesting ruin, a monumental Roman tomb; the left fork leads to the port, up over the hill and along the coast.

Iasos was built on a hill at the tip of a peninsula framed by two picture-perfect bays. Excavations have revealed the city's bouleuterion and agora, a gymnasium, a basilica, a Roman temple of Artemis Astias (190 AD) and numerous other buildings besides the prominent Byzantine fortress.

Today the hill above the port is covered with ruins, including a walled acropolis-fortress (admission costs US$1 if there's anyone there to collect it). Olive groves surround the town, somehow taking purchase in the rocky soil, and reach nearly to its centre. South-west of the hill on the bay is a small yacht harbour. Fishing boats crowd the quay, and a handful of small pensions and restaurants cater to travellers who want to get away from it all for a few days. Have *çipura* (gilt head bream), if it's in season, at ***Iasos Deniz Restaurant***, right down on the water, or at the less interesting ***Yıldız***, behind it.

Climb the hill behind the restaurants to find the delightful ***Cengiz*** *(☎ 252-537 7181)* and ***Zeytin*** *(☎ 252-537 7008)* pensions, both clean and modern with simple rooms for US$20 a double, including breakfast. Their biggest pluses are the views down over Iasos to the sea. In the unlikely event that both these places are full, others were about to open at the time of writing. There were even rumours that the half-built concrete monstrosities on the outskirts would soon be completed. Don't hold your breath.

In summer boats come to Iasos from Güllük to the south. Otherwise you can get there by infrequent dolmuş from Milas (US$1.50).

Labranda

Labranda was a sanctuary to Zeus Stratius, controlled for a long time by Milas. There may have been an oracle here; it's certainly known that festivals and Olympic games were held at the site. Set into a steep hillside at 600m elevation in an area from which the ancient city of Mylasa and the modern town of Milas took their water supplies, Labranda today is surrounded by fragrant pine forests peopled by beekeepers. Late in the season (October) you can see their tents pitched in cool groves as they go about their business of extracting the honey and rendering the wax from the honeycombs. It's a beautiful site, worth seeing partly because so few people come here.

The junction for the road to Labranda is 12km south of Euromos, just before Milas. It's 14km to the site: the first 6km are paved and easy to travel on, the remaining 8km are along a rough but scenic road deep in dust which winds tortuously up into the mountains. In rainy weather (October to April) the road turns to a slurry of mud that may require a 4WD. The village of Kargıcak is 8km along the way, and though you may be able to get a dolmuş from Milas to Kargıcak, that still leaves 6km to walk. Hitching is possible but not at all reliable, particularly later in the day. A taxi from Milas costs about US$40 for the round trip but drivers are reluctant to subject their cars to the punishment even for such a sizeable sum.

Labranda was a holy place, not a settlement, where worship of a god was going on by the 7th century BC, and perhaps long before. The site seems to have been abandoned circa 1000 AD. Today a caretaker will welcome you, have you sign the guest book and show you around the site; he speaks only Turkish, with a few words of other languages, but the site is well marked.

The great **Temple of Zeus** honours the god's warlike aspect (Stratius, or Labrayndus, 'Axe-bearing'). Two men's religious gathering places, the **First Andron** and the **Second Andron**, are in surprisingly good condition, as is a large 4th century **tomb** of fine construction, and other buildings. The ruins, excavated by a Swedish team in the early part of this century, are interesting, but it's the site itself, with its spectacular view over the valley, which is most impressive.

MİLAS

Milas (MEE-lahs, population 35,000) is a very old town. As Mylasa, it was capital of the Kingdom of Caria, except during the period when Mausolus ruled the kingdom from Halicarnassus (now Bodrum). Today it's a fairly sleepy agricultural town, with many homes where carpets are handwoven.

Since Milas is actually closer to the new Bodrum international airport than Bodrum itself, you could stay the night in Milas if you arrive late in high season when Bodrum is likely to be full.

Orientation

Approaching Milas from Söke, you pass the new otogar on 19 Mayıs Bulvarı 1km before coming to Labranda Bulvarı to the left. To the right İnönü Caddesi is marked for 'Şehir Merkezi' (City Centre). It's another 1km to the centre of town at the Milas Belediye Parkı.

Milas' postal code is 48200.

Things to See

Coming into town from the otogar along İnönü Caddesi, watch for signs pointing to the right for the Belediye and, opposite, turn left for the **Baltalı Kapı**, or 'Gate with an Axe'. Cross a small bridge and look left to see the well-preserved Roman gate, which has marble posts and lintel and Corinthian capitals. The eponymous double-headed axe is carved into the keystone on the northern side.

Return to the road and continue south past the forgettable **museum**, bearing right to the traffic roundabout, in the centre of which is a marble scale model of the Gümüşkesen monumental tomb next to the shady Milas Belediye Parkı.

Continue straight on for three blocks, turn right, then turn again at Gümüşkesen Caddesi to reach the tomb, 1.4km from the roundabout on a hill west of the centre.

The **Gümüşkesen** ('That which cuts silver' or, construed as Gümüşkese, 'silver purse') is a Roman monumental tomb dating from the 1st century, thought to have been modelled on the great Tomb of Mausolus at Halicarnassus. As in the Mausoleum, Corinthian columns here support a pyramidal roof, beneath which is a tomb chamber, which you can enter. A hole in the platform floor allowed devotees to pour libations into the tomb to quench the dead soul's thirst.

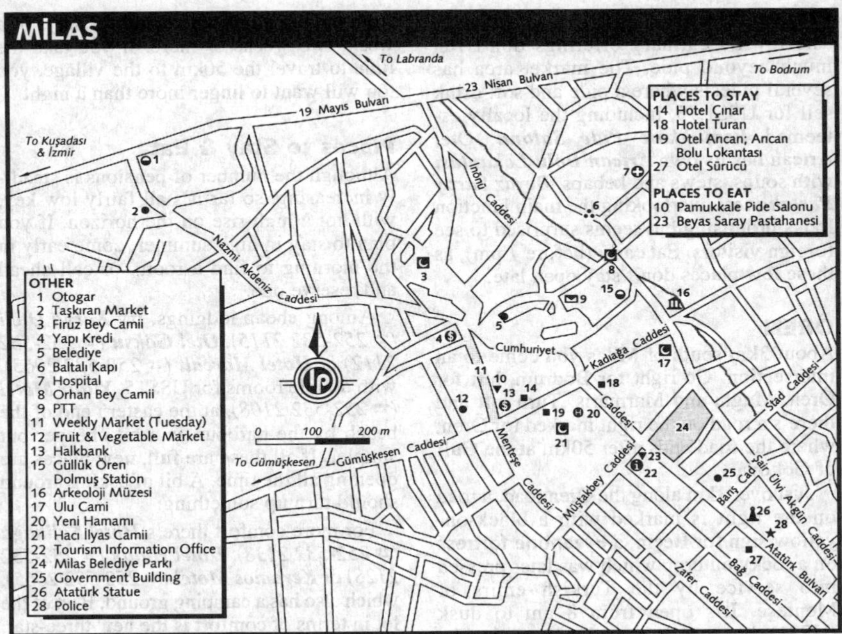

The tomb enclosure, in a little park, is usually open. If he's around, the guardian will charge you the US$1.25 admission fee.

You might also want to see some of Milas' fine mosques, especially the **Ulu Cami** (1378) and **Orhan Bey Camii** (1330), built when Milas was the capital of the Turkish principality of Menteşe. The larger, more impressive **Firuz Bey Camii** (1394) was built shortly after Menteşe became part of the new and growing Ottoman Empire.

Like Muğla, Milas has held on to some of its older houses, and especially along Atatürk Bulvarı is some very impressive architecture dating back to the start of this century.

Places to Stay

Otel Arıcan *(☎ 252-512 1215)*, next to the Hacı İlyas Camii (and, alas, its minaret), has cheap rooms for US$8 a double without bath, or US$12 with private shower. ***Hotel Akdeniz*** *(☎ 252-512 8661)*, across the street, is a distant second choice. The Yeni Hamamı, across Hacı İlyas Sokak from the Otel Arıcan, fills the need for a Turkish bath.

A better option is ***Hotel Çınar*** *(☎/fax 252-512 2102, Kadıağa Caddesi 52)*, which offers much more congenial accommodation, with a lobby one flight up. Take a room at the back to avoid street noise. Rates are US$12/18 for a single/double, with private bath and breakfast. ***Hotel Turan*** *(☎ 252-512 1342, Cumhuriyet Caddesi 26)*, has comparable rooms for about US$4 less per person than the Çınar.

The plastic-looking ***Otel Sürücü*** *(☎ 252-512 4001, fax 512 4000)*, on Atatürk Bulvarı opposite the statue of Atatürk, is slightly more comfortable, with bigger rooms than the Çınar or Turan, for US$12/18 a single/double, with breakfast. The lobby is imposing and some rooms have TV.

Places to Eat

The town's culinary offerings don't run much beyond pide. The market area has several pidecis where a pide and soft drink sell for US$1.75, including the locally esteemed ***Pamukkale Pide Salonu***. Otel Arıcan has its own ***Arıcan Bolu Lokantası*** with soups, stews and kebaps. ***Beyaz Saray Pastahanesi*** overlooking the main junction looks promising but seems surprised to see foreign visitors. Eat early (before 7 pm), as these few places don't stay open late.

ÖREN

About 3km south of Milas you come to an intersection. Go right for Bodrum, left for Ören, Muğla and Marmaris. Turn left and there's a road on the right marked for Ören, where the road ends after 50km at the Gulf of Gökova.

Just over 1km along the Ören road, a road on the right is marked with a black-on-yellow sign for Beçin, a **Byzantine fortress** on a rocky outcrop which was later pressed into service by the Turkish emirs of Menteşe. It's open from 8 am to dusk (US$1), but there's not a lot to see inside. Less than 500m on are remnants of the **14th century Menteşe settlement**, including the Kızıl Han caravanserai, Orhan Bey Camii, and the Ahmet Gazi tomb and *medrese* (theological seminary).

The road to Ören is slow and winding and for the most part picturesque, although there are a couple of unsightly power stations and, closer to the village, some proliferating second-home developments.

On the whole Ören has hung on to the tranquil atmosphere which was once common to villages along the Turkish coasts. The village comes in two parts. About 1.5km inland from the beach is the centre, with its PTT, shops, and old Ottoman houses with geranium-filled gardens set amid the **ruins of the ancient city of Keramos** (or Ceramus), which flourished from the 6th century BC until at least the 3rd century AD.

But the 1km-long sand-and-pebble **beach** ringed with mountains is the centre of visitor interest and draws Turkish holidaymakers from the big cities who come for stays of a week, two weeks or more. If you take the time to travel the 50km to the village, you too will want to linger more than a night.

Places to Stay & Eat

Although the number of pensions is steadily increasing, so far it's all fairly low-key, with not a high-rise on the horizon. If you plan to stay in high summer, come early in the morning to find a room, or call ahead and reserve one.

Among cheap lodgings, try ***Karya Oteli*** *(☎ 252-532 2115)*, ***Otel Göksu*** *(☎ 252-532 2112)* or ***Hotel Marçalı*** *(☎ 252-532 2063)*, with double rooms for US$15. ***Yıltur Motel*** *(☎ 252-532 2108)*, at the eastern end of the beach by the harbour, is a bit cheaper but simpler. If all these are full, new places are opening all the time. A bit of asking around should turn up something.

For more comfort there's ***Hotel Salihağa*** *(☎ 252-532 2138)*, ***Hotel Haluk*** *(☎ 252-532 2128)* or ***Keramos Motel*** *(☎ 252-532 2065)*, which also has a camping ground. Best of the lot in terms of comfort is the new three-star, 50 room ***Hotel Alnata*** *(☎ 252-532 2823)*, at the western end of the beach, where cheerful modern rooms come with marble floors, marble bath tubs and sea views. There's a pool and the hotel can arrange all sorts of watersports for you, but none of this comes cheap; expect to pay US$36/48 a single/double with half-board.

Ören also has a few restaurants, including the waterfront ***Café Palmiye*** which dishes up burgers for US$1 and ***Kerme Restaurant*** with şiş kebap for US$2. There's also a small shop for putting together a picnic. Don't expect any banks or other services though.

Getting There & Away

A timetabled minibus service runs from Milas to Ören and back roughly every hour from 8 am to 6 pm. If you ask, the driver may drop you right at the beach instead of in the village. The journey takes an hour and costs US$1.50.

GÜLLÜK

Turn right at the intersection 3km south of Milas, and another 15km brings you to the road on the right for Güllük, a mining port and minor seaside resort town which retains a semblance of authentic daily life.

About 8km west of the highway through olive groves, Güllük is spread along three bays. The road brings you and a steady stream of bauxite ore trucks to the central bay and the centre of town, where the ore is loaded onto waiting ships. Fishing boats are moored south of the ore dock, and beyond them more fishing craft are built in the traditional way at simple open-air boat yards. Though there's a yacht mooring area, the harbour is mostly for working vessels.

Güllük is a working town with a sideline in tourism which is its main attraction. There's sufficient accommodation and other services but none of the hassle encountered in hyper-resorts like Kuşadası, Marmaris or Bodrum. If you'd like a few days in a traditional Turkish seaside town with swimming and ruins nearby, Güllük should do nicely. Should the port for the bauxite ore be relocated along the coast as planned, then the main drawbacks of dust and noise from the lorries will become a thing of the past.

Orientation & Information

The bay to the left (south) of the central one is monopolised by a Türk Petrol company resort; to the right, the northern bay is lined with posh summer villas. The northern bay is best for swimming although there's no beach here. Day trips by boat to Iasos and nearby beaches can be arranged from the restaurants along the waterfront. To hire a whole boat to get to Iasos is likely to cost about US$28. By the time you read this it's possible that some boatmen will be offering trips to Didim too.

Places to Stay & Eat

Nicest of the small pensions is ***Kemer*** *(☎ 252-522 2143)* on the hillside above the harbour. Clean, simple rooms cost US$12 to US$16. There's a pleasant front garden and good views from the terrace. Follow the signs from the dolmuş terminal to find the simple ***Gökçe Pansiyon*** *(☎ 252-522 2994)*, also charging US$12 a double. ***Kordon Motel*** *(☎ 252-522 2356)*, attached to the harbourside restaurant of the same name, has balconied sea-view rooms for about the same price.

Of the mid-range hotels, the three-star, 36 room ***Kont Hotel*** *(☎ 252-522 2427, fax 522 2426)* is way out on the hillside amid the holiday homes on the southern side of the bay. More central is the 26 room ***Park Otel*** *(☎/fax 252-522 2699)*, inland from the dolmuş terminal and likely to have grown (and possibly acquired a pool) by the time you read this. Beds in rooms with showers cost from US$10 per person; they're clean and adequate if unexceptional.

At the time of writing the 138 room, four-star ***Labranda Corinthia Hotel*** *(☎ 252-522 2911, fax 522 2009)*, dominating the northern side of the bay, was closed. However, a change of owner was anticipated and it may have re-opened by the time you read this, in which case expect rates of about US$45/60 a single/double.

A few Ottoman-era buildings survive in the centre, including the fine house now inhabited by *Tekel* and, north of it, a stone *han* and warehouse, the latter fronted with restaurants including ***Çiçek, Kosova, Yakamoz, Dost*** and ***Eski Depo***, all of which post prices, serve alcohol, have good sunset water views and can arrange boat excursions. Just inland on the market square (the market begins at dawn on Friday) is the cheaper ***Barış Pide Pizza Kebap Salonu***.

Getting There & Away

Dolmuşes run to Güllük from Milas (US$2), and also from the village of Koru, on the highway a few kilometres north of the Güllük turn-off.

BODRUM

Bodrum (population 25,000) owes its fame to a man long dead and a building long disappeared. It is, however, the South Aegean's most picturesque resort, with a yacht harbour and a port for ferries to the Greek island of Kos.

The man long dead is King Mausolus, and the building is his tomb, the Mausoleum, but Bodrum has many other attractions. Most striking is the Castle of St Peter in the middle of town, guarding twin bays now busy with yachts. Palm-lined streets ring the bays, and white sugarcube houses, now joined by ranks of villas, crowd the hillside. Yachting, boating, swimming, snorkelling and scuba diving are prime Bodrum activities. Daytime diversions include boat or minibus trips to nearby secluded beaches and villages, or over to the Greek island of Kos.

At night, Bodrum's famous discos throb, boom and blare, keeping much of the town awake until dawn. Both Turkish and foreign visitors complain about the ear-splitting cacophony, but a former provincial governor was quoted in the newspaper as asking, 'If they want peace and quiet, why do they come to Bodrum?'. The answer seems to be to avoid the peak season; come in spring or autumn and Bodrum reverts to a pleasant, relatively low-key resort.

The local economy is now dedicated to tourism, though winter brings a bounteous

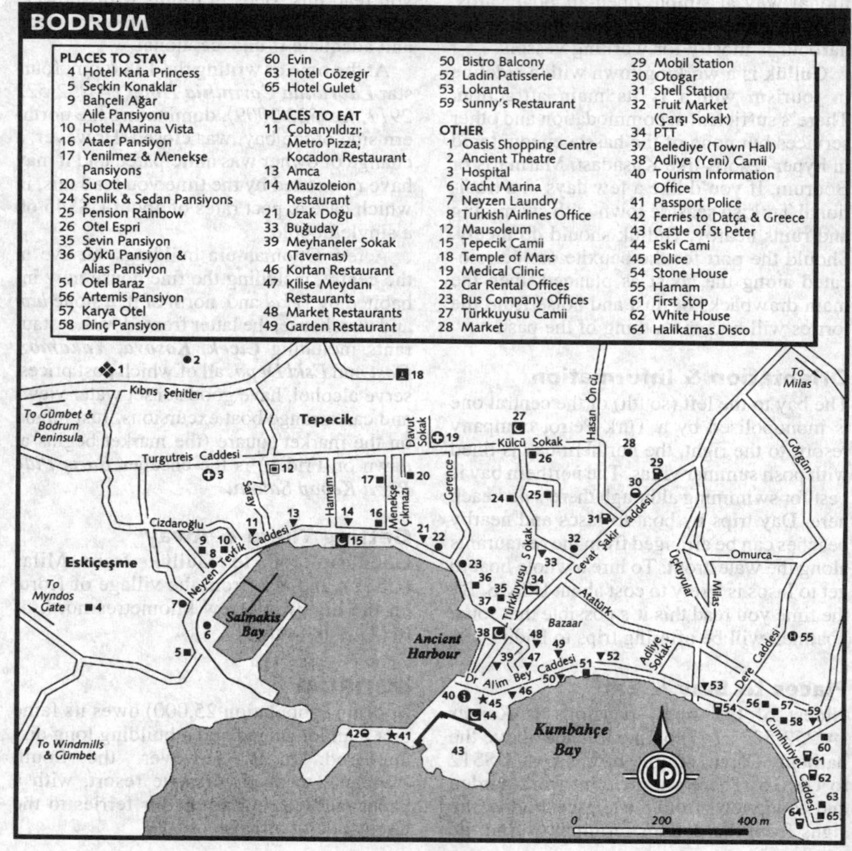

citrus crop (especially tangerines). A few sponge-fishing boats survive as well.

History

Following the Persian invasion, Caria was ruled by a satrap named Mausolus (circa 376-353 BC), who moved the capital here from Mylasa and called this town Halicarnassus. After the satrap's death, his wife undertook construction of the monumental tomb which Mausolus had planned for himself. The Mausoleum, an enormous white-marble tomb topped by a stepped pyramid, came to be considered one of the Seven Wonders of the World. It stood relatively intact for almost 19 centuries, until it was broken up by the crusaders and the pieces used as building material in 1522.

Bodrum's other claim to fame comes from Herodotus (circa 485-circa 425 BC), the 'Father of History', who was born here. Herodotus was the first person to write a comprehensive 'world history'; all later historians of western civilisation are indebted to him.

Orientation

The road to Bodrum winds through pine forests, finally cresting a hill to reveal a panorama of the town with its striking crusader castle.

The otogar is located several hundred metres inland from the sea, on Cevat Şakir Caddesi, the main street into the centre of town. Walk down from the otogar towards the castle, passing the fruit and vegetable market, and you'll come to a small white mosque called the Adliye Camii (AHD-lee-yeh jah-mee, Courthouse Mosque), or Yeni Cami. Turn right, and you'll be heading west on Neyzen Tevfik Caddesi towards the Yat Limanı (Yacht Marina), passing various restaurants and the quieter pensions. Turn left and go through the bazaar, then walk along Doktor Alim Bey Caddesi, which later becomes Cumhuriyet Caddesi, to reach the noisier hotels and pensions. Lodging places continue all the way around the bay, then along the shore of another bay further on.

Go straight on from the Adliye Camii towards the castle and you'll be walking along Kale Caddesi, the tourist axis of Bodrum, lined with boutiques selling clothing, carpets, souvenirs and trinkets. At the end of Kale Caddesi, beneath the castle walls, is Oniki Eylül Meydanı (12 September Square), also called İskele Meydanı (Dock Square), the main plaza. Here you'll find the Tourism Information Office, customs office, teahouses and, along the wharf, day-excursion boats.

Bodrum's postal code is 48400.

Information

Tourist Office The Tourism Information Office (☎ 252-316 1091, fax 316 7694) is on İskele (Oniki Eylül) Meydanı. In summer it opens from Monday to Friday between 8 am and 8 pm and on Saturday from 9 am to noon and 3.30 to 7.30 pm. Several bus and ferry companies have ticket offices nearby.

Laundry The yachters lack hotel staff to do their washing, so there are several laundries near the marina. The Neyzen laundry is on Neyzen Tevfik Caddesi. To wash and dry a full load costs US$4. The Can laundry in Türkkuyusu Sokak, catering to us poor landlubbers, charges just half that.

Internet Access The big new Oasis shopping centre (☎ 252-313 7872) off the Gümbet road, just west of the ancient theatre, will contain a theatre, cinemas and an Internet cafe once it's completed.

Castle of St Peter

When Tamerlane invaded Anatolia in 1402, throwing the nascent Ottoman Empire temporarily off balance, the Knights Hospitaller or Knights of St John of Jerusalem based on Rhodes took the opportunity to capture Bodrum. They built the Castle of St Peter, which defended Bodrum (not always successfully) until the end of WWI.

The castle now holds Bodrum's famous and excellent **Museum of Underwater Archaeology**. Hours are from 8.30 am to 5 pm (closed Monday), with an hour off for lunch between noon and 1 pm. Admission costs US$3.50; students pay half price. The **Glass-Shipwreck Hall** is open from Monday to Friday only, between 10 to 11 am and from 2 to 4 pm, for an additional US$1. The **Carian Princess Exhibit** is open Monday to Friday from 10 am to noon and 2 to 4 pm.

Signs are in Turkish and English. The occasional maps of the castle and the directional signs are not always clear or helpful, and construction work often leads to diversions.

Head up the stone ramp into the castle past crusader **coats of arms** carved in marble and mounted on the stone walls. Keep an eye out for bits of marble taken from the ancient Mausoleum. The ramp leads to the castle's main court, centred on an aged, ivy-covered mulberry tree. To the left are **exhibits of amphorae** and other artefacts dating from the 14th century BC recovered from the waters of south-western Turkey. At a small stall, **artisans** demonstrate techniques used centuries ago. The courtyard cafe, amid displays of Greek and Roman statuary, provides a shady resting place for those who have already climbed the stone towers.

The former chapel contains a full-sized reconstruction of the stern half of a **7th century eastern Roman ship** discovered off Yassıada and excavated by a University of Pennsylvania team between 1961 and 1964. Visitors can walk the decks, stand at the helm, look below decks at the cargo of wine, and peek into the galley where the cook prepared meals for the crew.

Follow the path on the left side of the chapel to ascend to the towers past flocks of pigeons, roosters and peacocks. Up the ramp is the **glass-shipwreck exhibit**. As you enter, look for the castle-like dovecote on the castle wall beyond.

Discovered by a sponge diver in 1973 and excavated from 1977 to 1979 by Professor George Bass of Texas A&M University and his international team of marine archaeologists, the 16m-long, 5m-wide ship sank in 1025 while carrying a cargo of 25 tons of commercial glass between Byzantine and Fatimid ports. It's the oldest shipwreck ever discovered.

Further up in the castle are the **Snake Tower** and the **German Tower**. Both are closed, but you can climb up to the ramparts nearby for fine views of the town.

Descend past the Ottoman toilets to the **Gatineau Tower** and the **dungeons** beneath. Over the inner gate is the inscription '*Inde deus abest*' ('Where god does not exist'). The dungeon was used as a place of confinement and torture by the Knights of St John from 1513 to 1523. A sign warns that the exhibits of torture implements might not be suitable for children but most video-hardened visitors will find it tame stuff.

The **English Tower** was built during the reign of King Henry IV of England, and bears his arms above the entrance to the uppermost hall, now fitted out as a medieval refectory. The standards of the Grand Masters and their Turkish adversaries hang from the walls. Suits of Turkish chain mail and authentic crusader graffiti carved into the stones (especially prominent in the window niches) serve as decoration. The long wooden tables are handy for taking a breather and enjoying a glass of wine (at US$1, it's cheaper than in the town below) while listening to recordings of *Carmina Burana*, lute music, or other pseudo-medieval strains.

The **Uluburun Wreck Exhibit Hall** was due to open in 1999.

Within the **French Tower**, the highest point in the castle, are the remains and sarcophagus of **Queen Ada**, a *Karyalı prenses* (Carian princess) whose intact tomb was discovered by Turkish archaeologists in 1989. The princess, who died sometime between 360 and 325 BC aged about 40, was of the Hecatomnid dynasty, probably the sister of Satrap Mausolus and the wife of Idreus. She was buried with a gold crown, necklace, bracelets, rings, and an exquisite wreath of gold myrtle leaves. Using modern reconstruction techniques, experts at Manchester University modelled what the princess' face might have looked like when she was alive; a video in Turkish explains their work.

Mausoleum

Though most of the Mausoleum is long gone, the site is still worth visiting. It's a few blocks inland from Neyzen Tevfik Caddesi. Turn right near the little white Tepecik Camii on the shore of the western bay, then left onto the road to Turgutreis Caddesi, following the signs.

The site has pleasant gardens, with the excavations to the right and a covered arcade to the left. Here archaeologists have arranged models, drawings and translations of documents to give you a idea of why this tomb was among the Seven Wonders of the World. Exhibits also include bits of sculpted marble found at the site, a model of Halicarnassus at the time of King Mausolus, a model of the Mausoleum and its precincts, plus various diagrams and plans.

A description written in 1581 and supposedly taken from an eyewitness account of 1522 tells the alarming, if barely credible, story: the Knights Hospitaller from Rhodes discovered the Mausoleum, largely buried and preserved by the dust of ages. They uncovered it, admired it for a while, then went back to the castle for the night. During the night, pirates broke in and stole the tomb treasures, which had been safe as long as the Mausoleum was buried. The next day the knights returned and broke the tomb to pieces for use as building stone. Some bits were pulverised to make lime for mortar which was used to repair their castle in anticipation of an attack by Süleyman the Magnificent. They knew they would lose the battle and have to abandon the castle, but saw the effort as a holding action. So the Mausoleum was supposedly sacrificed to the honour of a crusader military order. In reality, earlier earthquakes had probably shattered it long before the Knights set foot in Turkey.

The arcade contains a copy of the famous frieze mainly recovered from the castle walls; the original is now in the British Museum. The four original fragments on display were discovered more recently.

Of the actual remains, there's little to impress: a few pre-Mausolean stairways and tomb chambers, the Mausolean drainage system, the entry to Mausolus' tomb chamber, a few bits of precinct wall and some large, fluted marble column drums.

The site is open daily except Monday from 8 am to noon and 1 to 5 pm. Admission costs US$1.75. Most information is written in English and Turkish; although some is in French.

Ancient Theatre

The theatre is cut into the rock of the hillside behind town on the Gümbet road. The view is splendid but the traffic on the busy road is noisy and smelly. Cross with the greatest of care.

Boat Excursions

Dozens of yachts are moored along Neyzen Tevfik Caddesi on the western bay, and most have sales agents who will try and cajole you into taking a day trip. Most boat excursions depart at 10 or 11 am, return at 4.30 or 5 pm and cost US$12.

Typically, you sail to **Karaada** (Black Island) south of Bodrum, where **hot springs** issue in a strong current from a cave. Swimmers rub the orange mud from the springs on their bodies, hoping for some aesthetic improvement. After a 30-minute stop at Karaada, the boat makes for the coarse sand-and-pebble beach at **Ortakent Yalısı**, west of Bodrum. The lovely cove is backed with beachfront restaurants, small pensions and camping areas, but there are big hotels nearby as well.

After Ortakent, the boat sails to the 'Aquarium', a small cove deserted except for other excursion boats, for its last stop. The water is beautifully clear, and the idea is that you'll see lots of fish, although the boating and swimming activity usually scares them away.

Special Events

The Bodrum Festival is held annually during the first week in September. Accommodation may be especially scarce then.

Places to Stay

In high summer, especially at weekends, Bodrum can fill up with holidaymakers. Try to arrive early in the day to find a room. The Tourism Information Office may be able to help you find a room if space is tight. If you're planning to stay a week or so, especially if you're thinking of a hotel rather than a pension, check the package holiday brochures before leaving home since they may offer a cheaper deal than you'll get in the resort itself.

Places to Stay – Budget

The narrow streets north of the western bay harbour has pleasant family run pensions which tend to be quieter than those on the eastern bay because they're further from the nuclear-powered Halikarnas Disco. Pensions charge from US$18 to US$25 a double for rooms in high summer. Some rooms have private facilities, some include breakfast in the price. Off season, prices drop, and the breakfast which costs extra in season may be included in the price.

Türkkuyusu Sokak This street with a tongue-twister name starts just north of the Adliye Camii and goes north past several good, cheap, convenient pensions, mostly with shady courtyards.

Şenlik Pansiyon *(☎ 252-316 6382, Türkkuyusu Sokak 115)*, is just off the street, with cosy doubles for US$12 including breakfast. There's a kitchen on the roof which offers fine views of Bodrum. Behind it (down the same narrow alley – watch for potholes when coming back in the dark) is the friendly, family run ***Sedan Pansiyon*** *(☎ 252-316 0355, Türkkuyusu 121)*. The Sedan's courtyard, shaded by grapevines heavy with fruit in August, connects two buildings. In the newer one, double rooms with shower cost US$24; in the older, waterless doubles are US$16.

Signs on Türkkuyusu Sokak point to the right to Gencel Çıkmazı, a narrow alley harbouring ***Pension Rainbow*** *(☎ 252-316 5170)*, which is quiet and charges US$20 for waterless doubles; breakfast costs extra.

If you've got a car with you, the nearby ***Dönen Pansiyon*** has a large car park and comfortable rooms for US$24 a double. You can camp in the grounds for around US$4 per person.

Close to the seafront, ***Sevin Pansiyon*** *(☎ 252-316 7682, Türkkuyusu Caddesi, Gencel Çıkmazı 12)*, is the least inviting, its basic rooms overpriced at US$32 a double.

Otel Espri *(☎ 252-316 1129, Türkkuyusu 98)*, on the corner of Külcü Sokak, has a swimming pool, a bougainvillea-shaded terrace and 40 rooms with bath costing US$38 a double, breakfast included.

Menekşe Cıkmazı & Neyzen Tevfik Caddesi Menekşe Çıkmazı is a narrow alley which begins between Neyzen Tevfik Caddesi 84 and 86. At its very end are two nearly identical plain, quiet, modern pensions, ***Yenilmez*** *(☎ 252-316 2520)* at No 30, and ***Menekşe*** *(☎ 252-316 5890)* at No 34. Both have rooms with showers for US$20. During the low season, breakfast is included. They're set around picturesque gardens, and the Menekşe in particular has lots of cats.

Ataer Pansiyon *(☎ 252-316 5357, Neyzen Tevfik 102)*, is just east of the Tepecik Camii, back from the street, with clean, simple doubles for US$24, breakfast included.

Set back from the street at the end of a passage beside the Turkish Airlines Office is ***Bahçeli Ağar Aile Pansiyonu*** *(☎ 252-316 1648)*, with quiet, basic rooms for US$20 a double.

Right on the seafront, the small ***Öykü Pansiyon*** *(☎ 252-316 4604, Neyzen Tevfik Caddesi 200)*, has slightly cramped rooms but lovely views from its rooftop terrace. Beds cost US$10 including breakfast. ***Alias Pansiyon*** *(☎ 252-316 3146)* nearby has small, rather crowded cabins set around a pool and rose garden. In high season expect to pay US$20 per person.

Eastern Bay In general pensions on the eastern bay are priced identically to those on the western bay, but are less friendly and subject to disco noise. If you want to be in the midst of the nightlife, look on Rasathane

Sokak, a narrow alley beginning between Cumhuriyet Caddesi 147 and 149. ***Durak Villa*** *(☎ 252-316 1564)* has rooms with (US$16 a double) or without (US$12); the neighbouring ***Berlin Pansiyon*** *(☎ 252-316 2524)* is similarly priced. The nearby ***Evin*** *(☎ 252-316 1312)* is swathed from top to bottom in bougainvillea, but isn't open all year round. The narrow streets eastward harbour a few more pensions.

Camping Some of the smaller villages on the peninsula such as Bitez Yalısı and Ortakent Yalısı have camp sites. There are more on the peninsula's north shore.

Places to Stay – Mid-Range

Western Bay Best is the charming ***Su Otel*** *(☎ 252-316 6906, fax 316 7391)*, at the end of a cul-de-sac and an oasis of quiet and charm. Decorated with local crafts and an abundance of bougainvillea, rooms overlook a courtyard with a small central swimming pool. Rooms cost US$30/55 a single/double, buffet breakfast included. With only 30 beds, it's often full, so reserve if you can. Follow the street opposite the Tepecik Camii, turn right at the 'T' intersection, and walk several hundred metres following the signs.

The cheerful ***Seçkin Konaklar*** *(☎ 252-316 1351, fax 316 3336, Neyzen Tevfik Caddesi 246)* facing the marina, has multi-bed apartments sleeping up to six people, as well as some normal bedrooms set around a central pool. It's often busy with tour groups, so ring ahead to be on the safe side. Singles/doubles cost from US$30/40.

Eastern Bay The two-star ***Otel Baraz*** *(☎ 252-316 1857, fax 316 6719, Cumhuriyet 70)*, is open all year. Go for the back rooms for the sea views. Its 26 rooms with shower are US$29/41 a single/double, including breakfast which can be served on your balcony.

Further east along Cumhuriyet Caddesi are three comparable places in a row facing the narrow beach (the water's a bit murky, though). ***Artemis Pansiyon*** *(☎ 252-316 2530, fax 316 2907, Cumhuriyet Caddesi 117)* has 22 rooms priced identically to those at the Baraz. There's a cafe right in front.

A few steps east, ***Karya Otel*** *(☎ 252-316 1535, fax 316 4814, Cumhuriyet Caddesi 127)* charges US$40 a double. Its front rooms are double-glazed against the noise, and have ceiling fans and TVs with satellite channels.

The 18 room ***Dinç Pansiyon*** *(☎ 252-316 1141, fax 316 2051, Cumhuriyet Caddesi 129)* is similar to the Artemis, as are the newer ***Hotel Gözegir*** *(☎ 252-316 2541, fax 316 6348)* and ***Hotel Gulet*** *(☎ 252-316 6636, fax 316 1030)*.

Places to Stay – Top End

Bodrum has lots of luxury accommodation on the outskirts. If you prefer to stay closer to the centre, try the five-star ***Hotel Karia Princess*** *(☎ 252-316 8971, fax 316 8979, Canlıdere Sokak 15)*. The 58 rooms have air-con, satellite TV, minibars and king-size French beds. Facilities include a Turkish bath, sauna, fitness room, tennis court and large swimming pool, plus two private hotel yachts. Posted rates are US$120/160 for a single/double with breakfast, but discounts are often available.

The 84 room, four-star ***Hotel Marina Vista*** *(☎ 252-313 0356, fax 316 2347, Neyzen Tevfik Caddesi 226)* faces the marina and boasts lots of marble, two pools and many other services, for US$75/100 a double, breakfast included.

Hotel Arcade *(☎ 252-313 3185, fax 313 4876)*, in the noisier part of town at Cumhuriyet Caddesi 159, has rooms with sea views for US$60/80 a single/double. Rooms at the back lack the views but are likely to be quieter. ***Baç Pansiyon*** *(☎ 252-316 1602, fax 316 7917, Cumhuriyet Caddesi 18)* is even more centrally located, clean, new and comfortable, with doubles for US$60.

Places to Eat

You'll have no trouble finding places to eat, but because many of the restaurants are seasonal, with inexperienced part-time staff, food and service are often mediocre. In July and August, prices are double those of İstanbul, but at least they're usually available for inspection before you sit down. As ever, check the price before ordering fish.

Restaurants open and close all the time in Bodrum. Those described in the following sections are mostly dependable long-established ones.

Places to Eat – Budget

During the low season you should have no problem finding cheap eats. You can buy a *dönerli sandviç* (dur-nehr-LEE sahn-DVEECH, sandwich with roast lamb) for less than US$2 at a streetside büfe.

In July and August, the cheapest food is at simple local eateries well inland, without menus in English and German. Most places don't serve alcohol.

Türkkuyusu Sokak ***Buğuday*** ('Wheat'), at No 72, is a 60s-style vegetarian restaurant serving wholefood, herbal teas and freshly squeezed juices on a shady terrace. Tofu appetisers cost US$1, vegetarian salads US$2, and big plates of stir-fry are less than US$3.

East of Adliye Camii In the grid of small market streets just east of the Adliye Camii are several restaurants which serve reasonable döner kebap and pizza. ***Babadan*** and ***Ziya'nın Yeri*** are patronised by locals as well as foreigners, and serve plates of döner for about US$3, beer for US$1.50. Around the corner from Üsküdarlı by the Garanti Bankası is the ***Sakallı Köfteci*** ('Bearded Meatball-Maker'), serving full meals of grilled lamb meatballs, salad, bread and a drink for US$4, but no booze.

Just east of the bazaar is Hilmi Uran Meydanı, called Kilise Meydanı (Church Square) by locals because it once had an Orthodox church on its eastern side. Here the ***Nazilli*** and ***Karadeniz*** both serve pide (US$3 to US$4), pizzas and kebaps.

For cheap breakfast or lunch, try ***Yunuslar Karadeniz Börekçisi***, just east of Karadeniz Restaurant at the eastern edge of Kilise Meydanı on Taşlık Sokak. *Peynirli börek* costs US$1.50 a serving in the morning. There's a grander branch of this börekçi on Dr Alim Bey Caddesi.

For a sweet, try *lokma*, the traditional Aegean fritters, light balls of deep-fried dough dipped in syrup and sold in a paper cone for less than US$1. ***Ladin Patisserie*** at Cumhuriyet 75-77 serves them as well as böreks, pastries, puddings, fruitcups and other light fare.

Cumhuriyet Caddesi The branch of ***06 Lokanta*** midway along Cumhuriyet Caddesi presents a fine array of Turkish stews, soups and kebaps. A full meal with soft drink shouldn't cost more than US$6.

Cevat Şakir Caddesi Inland along Cevat Şakir Caddesi are several little grill shops where locals eat; some open for lunch only. Food for picnics is available at the fruit market just south of Çarşı Sokak and the Shell station, and in the shops behind the market.

Places to Eat – Mid-Range

Meyhaneler Sokak Walk from the Adliye Camii along Kale Caddesi towards İskele Meydanı and turn left just after the Tütünbank into Meyhaneler Sokak (Taverna St), a narrow alley shaded by foliage, crowded with long rows of wooden tables, and cooled by ceiling fans. On summer evenings the mixed crowd of locals and foreigners is jolly without being raucous. The half-dozen restaurants – ***Hades, Erkal, No 7 Orhan, Ibo, Ayaz, Farketmez*** etc – all serve alcohol and a varied menu of Turkish and continental dishes. Look at a few menus, find a seat, meet your neighbours, and get into the scene. The bill for a long dinner with drinks might be from US$12 to US$18, perhaps more if you have fish. There may well be live music to keep you company.

Western Bay Neyzen Tevfik Caddesi has several good places, all serving alcohol. ***Mauzoleion*** is a modest but long-established place with a simple indoor dining room (used in winter), and a seaside open-air dining area across the street. Meat dishes are priced from US$4 to US$6, and the fish, though more expensive, is usually good.

Amca, at No 78, seems a little unclear about its identity. While calling itself a Chinese restaurant it also serves Mexican, Indian and English meals on a breezy 2nd-floor terrace with good views, and reasonable prices. A main course, sweet and drink cost less than US$10. Similarly uncertain about its identity is ***Uzak Doğu***, again with a weird mix of Chinese, Mexican and Indian cuisine.

Çobanyıldızı *(☎ 252-316 7060, Neyzen Tevfik 164)*, across from the marina, has streetside tables and an interior dining room in an old stone commercial building. Turkish carpets add colour, and bits of seafaring equipment provide visual interest. Start with a plate of mixed mezes for US$4 and go on to grilled meat or fish (US$4 to US$10).

Metro Pizza offers good Italian-style pizzas for around US$4 and cheerful, willing service.

Eastern Bay Adliye Sokak runs inland off Cumhuriyet Caddesi opposite a break in the buildings which allows access to the sea. ***Pierre Loti***, at Adliye Sokak 5, in an old stone house, has a pretty courtyard and set-price French-style table d'hôte three-course meals priced from US$8 to US$35. A la carte, main course steak and chicken dishes cost US$18 to US$22.

Choice *(☎ 252-316 7184)*, behind Cumhuriyet 143, has the requisite steaks and chicken (US$6 to US$10), but also *Kirgiz mantı* (ravioli) as a starter for US$3.50. It only opens in the high season.

Inland on Rasathane Sokak and set around a nice courtyard, ***Sunny's Restaurant*** *(☎ 252-316 0716)* has a Turkish and continental menu on which most main courses (chicken Kiev, Mexican beef) cost US$8; vegetarian plates are US$1 less.

Places to Eat – Top End

The restaurants along Dr Alim Bey Caddesi have pleasant seaside dining areas but can be very pricey. In high summer, a full meal with drinks would cost US$25 to US$30 per person. In May, June, September and October when the restaurants are competing for custom, you can do better on price. Worth looking at are ***Bistro Balcony***, with its wonderful display of fish, ***Kortan Restaurant*** in an old stone house, and the cheaper ***Garden*** which serves Turkish staples like İskender kebap for perhaps US$2 more than you'd normally pay.

Kocadon Restaurant *(☎ 252-316 3705, fax 316 5338, Neyzen Tevfik Caddesi 160)*, is the place for a romantic dinner. Sheltered from the street by atmospheric old stone houses, a quiet courtyard is filled with soft music and lighting. Try the revived Ottoman dishes, such as *hünkar beğendi* (grilled şiş kebap over buttery aubergine purée). Dinner for two with a bottle of wine should cost around US$25 or US$30 per person. It's open daily in summer from 8 pm to midnight.

Entertainment

In summer, bars are everywhere, opening and closing with revolving-door frequency. Most are on the eastern bay along Dr Alim Bey Caddesi/Cumhuriyet Caddesi, or in narrow alleys off it, or in Gümbet. Most are empty until around 10 pm, after which the currently favoured places fill up. Local drinks (beer, rakı, Turkish gin and vodka) are always significantly cheaper than foreign liquor.

İskele Meydanı is a good place to sit, sip a beer and watch the passing parade. ***Kale Café***, just past the western entrance to the castle, has boat and water views, and drinks and food at prices a bit below most. Just inside the castle walls at the western entrance, ***Bodrum West Cafeteria***, run by the Ministry of Culture, offers drinks at lowish prices (US$1 for beer) and an atmospheric setting. It stays open in the evening when the castle is closed.

The roads east of Adliye Camii are dotted with discos, pubs and bars which come thicker and faster the further east you go. At the time of writing popular places included ***Sokak***, ***Foça***, ***The Stone House***, ***The White House*** and ***First Stop***, but names come and go with the seasons.

On the western bay, ***Heaven Bar*** next to the Kocadon restaurant draws a diverse crowd, and is one of the few bars in the area.

The infamous ***Halikarnas Disco***, on the eastern bay at the end of Cumhuriyet Caddesi, is renowned for being the loudest disco on the Aegean, if not the whole Mediterranean. Staff look you up and down for proper trendy dress and take a cover charge of between US$8 to US$12 (the latter on weekends) before admitting you to Turkey's classiest and most presumptuous disco. Inside it's like a Hollywood set, with a laser light show on some evenings.

But these days the throbbing heart of the disco scene is in Gümbet, over the hill to the west. Clubs line the shore, and are packed in summer.

Getting There & Away

Air A new Bodrum International airport has opened between Milas and Bodrum. Turkish Airlines has daily flights from İstanbul and İstanbul Airlines flies there on Monday, Thursday and Friday; expect to pay around US$40 on top of the fare to İstanbul.

An increasing number of European charter airlines are likely to start flying to Bodrum; check the brochures for bargains, especially at the start and end of the season.

Havaş buses leave Bodrum otogar two hours before each flight and the journey takes 45 minutes (US$4). A taxi to the airport would cost around US$30; to Milas just US$14.

The road between Bodrum and the airport was being widened at the time of writing, with consequent traffic hold-ups, dust and general disturbance. Hopefully, the work will be finished by the time you arrive.

Bus As usual, Bodrum's bus service is frequent and far flung. Here are some useful summer services:

Ankara – 785km, 13 hours, US$20; a dozen buses daily
Antalya – 640km, 11 hours, US$12; one bus daily
Dalaman – 220km, four hours, US$4; six buses daily
Fethiye – 265km, 4½ hours, US$6; six buses daily
Gökova – 135km, 2½ hours, US$10; Marmaris bus, then a dolmuş or hitch
İstanbul – 830km, 14 hours, US$24; hourly buses in summer
İzmir – 250km, four hours, US$10; buses at least every hour in summer
Kaş – 400km, six hours, US$12; Fethiye bus, then change
Konya – 750km, 12 hours, US$12; one bus daily
Kuşadası – 151km, 2½ hours, US$5; buses every half-hour in summer
Marmaris – 165km, three hours, US$4; hourly buses in summer
Milas – 66km, one hour, US$1.50; frequent minibuses
Ören – 95km, two hours, US$8; bus to Milas and change
Pamukkale – 310km, five hours, US$6; two direct buses daily
Söke – 171km, two hours, US$1; frequent buses
Trabzon – 1565km, 28 hours, US$24; one bus daily

Boat Ferries leave Bodrum's western bay for Datça, Didyma and Knidos, and for the Greek islands of Kos and Rhodes. For information and tickets contact Bodrum Express Lines (☎ 252-316 1087, fax 313 0077) or the Bodrum Ferryboat Association (☎ 252-316 0882, fax 313 0205), on the docks past the western entrance to the castle.

To Didyma Ferries depart Bodrum on Wednesday and Friday mornings at 7.30 am in summer on the two-hour voyage to Didyma (US$13 return); the return leg departs Didyma at 4 pm.

To Knidos On Sunday mornings in summer, boats (1½ hours, US$22.50 one way, US$29 same-day round trip) and hydrofoils (45 minutes, US$32 round trip, lunch included) leave Bodrum for Knidos at 9 am, returning in the afternoon at about 4.30 pm.

To Datça Hydrofoils (35 minutes) and car-and-passenger ferries (two hours) operate daily from May to September between Bodrum and Datça; the fare is US$14 return. The ferry actually docks at Körmen on the peninsula's northern coast, from which Datça is only a 10 to 15-minute drive south; bus transport to Datça is included in your fare.

To Kos Hydrofoils (20 minutes) and ferries (50 minutes) carry passengers and cars across to Kos daily from May to September. Buy tickets (US$20 one way, US$25 same-day round trip by hydrofoil; US$14 single, US$19 return by ferry) at least a day in advance. Limited ferry services (usually two or three days per week, weather permitting) continue throughout winter.

To Rhodes Hydrofoils (two hours) depart Bodrum for Rhodes at 8.30 am on Monday and Thursday from May to September. The return trip departs Rhodes at 4 pm. Buy tickets (US$45 one way, US$50 same-day return) a day in advance.

BODRUM PENINSULA

The volcanic landscape of the Bodrum Peninsula is one of high hills, dramatic rock outcrops and surprising marine panoramas. It comes as a surprise to see so much traditional life in the midst of booming touristic modernisation, but in a few peninsula villages you may still be able see local women

wearing the traditional *şalvar* (pantaloons) and white headscarves. Donkeys laden with sticks for fuel plod stubbornly to the domed, beehive-shaped earthen ovens still used to bake bread and roast mutton. But many of the distinctive igloo-shaped stone cisterns *(gümbet*, 'dome') are falling to ruin, having been superseded by the ubiquitous tank trucks supplying *kullanma su* ('utility water'), not for drinking. On the hilltops the ruins of old windmills tell a similar story of changing lifestyles.

Several of the beach villages are good for day trips. If you've come to stay for a while, you might even move your base from Bodrum.

Frequent dolmuşes depart from Bodrum's otogar to all of the places described below in high summer. Fares are rarely more than US$1. Off season, be aware of departure times for the last minibus back to Bodrum.

The following description assumes you head west out of Bodrum and travel around the peninsula in a clockwise direction. Note, however, that there's no road from Gümüslük to Yalıkavak and no dolmuş service from Yalıkavak to Gölköy, so you'll have to keep returning to Bodrum to proceed along the northern coast. Wherever you decide to stay (except perhaps at Gümüslük), it's wise to arrive in daylight to be sure you won't wake up and find yourself surrounded by building work.

Gümbet

Just 5km west of Bodrum, Gümbet would be many people's idea of a nightmare. Indeed one reader described it as 'the biggest waste of space in Turkey', an opinion many independent travellers would undoubtedly share. The narrow beach is backed by scores of hotels and pensions aimed fair and square at the package holiday market. If you do want to stay you'd do well to consult the brochures at home before setting out.

Among the myriad identikit hotel and apartment blocks a couple of five-star places are possibly worth noting. The brand-new ***Dedeman Bodrum*** *(☎ 212-274 8800, in İstanbul)* has all the comforts associated with that countrywide chain, while ***Tatlıses Hotel*** *(☎ 252-313 4950, fax 313 3491)* is part of a chain owned by *arabesk* singer-supremo İbrahim Tatlıses.

Gümbet is a 10-minute dolmuş ride from Bodrum otogar (US$0.60) or you can walk there in about 45 minutes over the hills west of the yacht marina. The water is not all that clean, but it's always crowded in summer nevertheless.

West of Gümbet, past the next peninsula, are the bays of **Bitez Yalısı**, **Ortakent Yalısı** and **Yahşi Yalısı**, backed by white hotels, pensions, camping grounds and resort villas and offering small but good beaches and services. At Bitez Yalısı there's a windsurfing school. Dolmuşes run direct from Bodrum to Bitez and to Yahşi Yalısı.

From Ortakent and Yahşi beaches you must travel inland via Gürece to continue your circuit of the peninsula, as there's no coastal road west of Yahşi.

Akyarlar

Akyarlar, 30km from Bodrum, is a pretty, unspoilt harbour village, formerly inhabited by Ottoman Greeks. There's a narrow beach, and a small yacht and fishing port. Holiday villas crowd the hillsides above. If you want to stay, ***Babadan Motel-Restaurant*** *(☎ 252-393 6002)* has clean, simple rooms with shower, some with sea view, for US$12/24 a single/double. There's a big rear car park. You could eat here too, or at ***Küçük Ev*** which does fish and kebap meals. Be sure to check prices before ordering.

The next bay to the east is **Karaincir**, a similar cove with a grey gravel beach, hotels, a few pensions and a holiday village but far less inviting than Akyarlar.

Following the coastal road west and north from Akyarlar brings you to **Akçabük**, with another cove and beach. North of Akçabük all the way to Turgutreis the coast is lined with holiday villages.

Turgutreis

Old Turgutreis (toor-GOOT-reh-yeess) is about 3km inland from the newly developed modern town 20km west of Bodrum. The great Turkish admiral Turgut Reis (died 1560) was born here and a monument to him stands south of the town on the shore.

Dolmuşes (US$0.75) from Bodrum leave you at the main square right on the thin strip of sandy beach. The square is surrounded with places to eat and drink, offering everything from Turkish standards to pizza. The ***34 Mangal Restaurant*** can do you a fish soup for US$3 or octopus stew for US$5.

Turgutreis wouldn't be a bad place to stay. Right on the seafront by the square is ***Otel Monalisa*** *(☎ 252-382 2932, fax 382 3969)* with a pool and fairly ordinary rooms, some with views straight onto the sand. Across the road and in the same ownership is ***Otel Kortan*** where much smarter rooms make up for a more distant view of the sea. In either place you'll pay US$38/50 for half-board in high season. Out of season the requirement to eat dinner at the hotel is waived.

One block in from these hotels is the modern bazaar with lots of small pensions above the shops. Typical is ***Ceylan Pansiyon*** *(☎ 252-382 2376)* with basic rooms with shower for US$10 a double (no discounts for singles). Breakfast is taken on a pleasant roof terrace. Near here is ***Nostaljia Motel*** *(☎ 252-382 4527)*, which was nearing completion at the time of writing and offers comfortable rooms above a restaurant for US$24/32 a single/double, bath and breakfast included. All these places are likely to be noisy.

Kadıkalesi

From Turgutreis, a road travels 1km inland and then 3.5km north to Kadıkalesi, a village with a narrow but partly protected beach, several small ***pension-restaurants***, a disused church in fair condition, and the inevitable holiday villages.

Gümüşlük

To the north of Kadıkalesi 3km by road (2km along the beach and over the hills) is Gümüşlük, little more than a hamlet on the shore of a fine small natural harbour protected by high headlands. New building work is prohibited which should ensure it hangs onto its quiet charm.

On the rocky islet south of the hamlet, the ruins (some underwater) of ancient **Mindos** are amusing to explore during a swim. The beach on the village's southern side is long and generally uncrowded. Though weedy in places, the sea is suitable for swimming; you can jump off wooden platforms extending into the water from the village foreshore.

Gümüşlük is perhaps the best goal for a day trip from Bodrum. Come here to swim or climb on the headlands and to take lunch on the shore; or come for an afternoon swim and stay for a sunset dinner. The waterfront is lined with restaurants, all with excellent sea, island and sunset views; their tables ranged along the water under shady vines. Most post their prices and start to fill up an hour before sunset.

Places to Stay & Eat In the off season, Gümüşlük is a haven of peace and quiet, a sleepy place with enough small pensions and restaurants to provide for the very few visitors who seek it out. Bear in mind, however, that before mid-May many of the pensions will be closed, so it's sensible to phone ahead to check that rooms will be available.

At the quiet southern end of the bay ***Özak Pansiyon*** *(☎ 252-394 3388)* is set around a large garden with a ***restaurant***. A double room with private bath and breakfast costs from US$20. Just a little closer to the centre is ***Arriba Apartotel*** *(☎ 252-365 4699)* where rent of a fully fitted, if somewhat spartan, apartment costs US$250 a week. There's a pleasant front garden where you can sip coffee in the shade.

Right in the centre overlooking the fish restaurants and open all year is ***Gümüşlük Motel*** *(☎ 252-394 3007)* where two people share a simple room, perhaps with balcony and sea view, for US$24.

At the northern end of the beach are a group of pretty stone villas – ***Jasmine Cottage***, ***Villa Leila***, ***Villa Magnolia*** and ***Mindos Cottage*** – right on the beach but contracted to the British tour company Simply Turkey.

As you walk to the beach from the dolmuş stand the first thing you see is a row of fish restaurants – ***Akvaryum, Balık, Yakanos, Siesta*** and ***Gümüşlük*** – all much the same. Be sure to ask the price of fish before ordering; you should be able to find a main course for around US$6 but a full fish meal is likely to cost between US$12 and US$15 per person.

Head north along the beach and you'll come to smaller places – ***Mimoza, Gümüs Café*** – where prices may be marginally lower and the throngs less pressing. Set back a little from the shore right in the centre is ***Dalgiç Restaurant*** which serves kebaps and stuffed vine leaves for those days when fish isn't what you fancy.

Getting There & Away Gümüşlük is accessible by dolmuş from Bodrum (US$1) or from Turgutreis (US$0.50). Vehicles are banned from entering the village. The last dolmuş to Bodrum departs at midnight (10 pm out of season). You may want to leave before then in case it's full.

Yalıkavak

The northern shore of the peninsula is the least developed and the most tricky to get around by public transport.

In the north-western corner, 18km from Bodrum, is Yalıkavak. As you approach you'll see the ruins of three old windmills on the hill; another has been reconstructed on the waterfront. As Datça is to Marmaris, so Yalıkavak is to Bodrum: a smaller, quieter version with the constant threat of similar development looming over it. In the meantime it's surprisingly pleasant, with no high-rise buildings to spoil the harbour and several attractive hotels and restaurants.

Cruise boats will take you out to hidden bays along the peninsula and as far as Gümüşlük to see the ruins of Mindos. A day trip costs about US$16.

Places to Stay & Eat There are a handful of pensions in and around the village where you can expect to get a bed for about US$6 per person. One of the most central is ***Yalıkavak Pansiyon*** but it's likely to be noisy because of the restaurants and bars. Walk east along the promenade and you'll come to ***Yüksel Pension***, with chickens in the backyard. Most of these places only open during the height of the season.

Otherwise, Yalıkavak has several very comfortable, attractive hotels and apartment blocks, all with swimming pools and all east of the restaurants along the promenade (Plaj Yolu Caddesi). These are contracted to European tour operators for most of the season but in April/early May and again at the end of September/early October individual travellers may be able to find a bed.

Most attractive is ***Otel Taşkule*** *(☎ 252-385 4935)* as you head out along the eastern promenade. Pretty, feminine rooms with lovely tiled showers cost US$30/45 with breakfast when you can get them. Also inviting, though one block in from the sea, is ***Yeldeğirmen Konuk Evi*** (Windmill Hotel) *(☎ 252-385 4805)*, with a stream flowing through the grounds.

Altinköy Apart Hotel *(☎ 252-385 2685, fax 385 4909)* is a gorgeous, glistening white pile set around a central pool, with bright, beautifully equipped apartments to sleep four for US$100 a night.

A cluster of seafood restaurants line up beside the harbour. The ***Liman*** and ***Windmill*** are no doubt good but ***Çakıroğlu Çardak*** *(☎ 252-385 4143)* wins first prize both for its presentation and for delicious food such as seafood croquettes for US$2 and shrimp casseroles for US$6.

As usual, to find food at lower prices cut inland a block and look for places like ***Devecıoğlu Lokantası*** offering *ev yemekleri* (home cooking). The ***Margül Restaurant*** does gözleme and pide from US$2.25, while ***Meltem*** does İskender kebap for US$3.

Getting There & Away Frequent dolmuşes ply back and forth between Bodrum and Yalıkavak, taking just over 30 minutes and charging US$0.75. Quite amazingly, although the road's good, there's no onward dolmuş to Gölköy; you'll have to take a taxi costing around US$12, or return to Bodrum and catch another dolmuş from there.

Gölköy

About 17km north of Bodrum, the village of Gölköy is arrayed along a perfect little bay, a 'Gümüşlük without the ruins or fish restaurants' as one traveller described it. In July and August family pensions open to accommodate most arrivals. Otherwise ***Sahil Motel*** *(☎ 252-357 7183)* and ***Sultan Motel*** *(☎ 252-357 7260)* guard the bay. Both have pretty gardens, and simple, furnished rooms with shower for US$16 per person, including breakfast. Wooden docks serve the fishing boats; the boat owners will also take you out for short excursions if you wish.

Close to 1.5km around the point from Gölköy, and served by the same dolmuş from Bodrum, is **Türkbükü**, another village with a few modest pensions and motels, a PTT, the ***Ship Ahoy*** restaurant and shops for the yachters who anchor in its harbour.

Torba

The road from Gölköy sweeps around to another beautiful harbour at Torba before returning to Bodrum. Unfortunately, condominiums and tower-block hotels run right down to the harbourside, leaving little scope for individual travellers.

Afrodisias & Pamukkale Region

Perhaps the most popular detour inland from Selçuk and Kuşadası has traditionally been to Pamukkale (pah-MOO-kah-leh, Cotton Fortress) where hot calcium-laden mineral waters flowed through a ruined Hellenistic city before cascading over a cliff. As the water cooled, the calcium precipitated and clung to the cliffs, forming snowy white travertines, the waterfalls of white stone which gave the spa its name. In recent years, sadly, the flow of water has diminished and the terraces are now a pale shadow of their former selves (see the Pamukkale section later). But the ruins of Hierapolis, scattered along the top of the ridge at Pamukkale are still a remarkable sight, well worth visiting in their own right.

On the way to Pamukkale you can visit several other important archaeological sites, including the hilltop city of Nyssa about 100km east of Kuşadası. About 150km east of Kuşadası is Afrodisias, one of Turkey's most complete and absorbing archaeological sites. Near Pamukkale itself are the ruins of Laodicea, one of the Seven Churches of Asia.

As you start out you'll probably pass the ruins of Magnesia and Meander, which lie on the road between Söke and Ortaklar. This ancient city is not really worth a stop, but the fragments of wall easily visible from the road are certainly impressive. It's 33km from Ortaklar to the provincial capital of Aydın.

AYDIN

Framed by the mountains of Aydın Dağı to the north and Menteşe Dağı to the south, Aydın (population 120,000) is at the centre of the agriculturally rich Menderes river valley. Olives, figs, cotton, grain and fruit grow in abundance. The valley has always been an important natural travel route, which today includes an east-west highway and the railway to Denizli, Burdur and Isparta.

Aydın was formerly Tralles, which flourished during Roman times. Its most famous son was perhaps the architect Anthemius of Tralles who, at the order of the Emperor Justinian and with the help of Isidore of Miletus, designed and built the great church of Sancta Sophia in Constantinople between 532 and 537 AD.

During the War of Independence Aydın was occupied by the invading Greek forces and then burned to the ground when they left. Nor has being at the centre of an earthquake zone helped Aydın's appearance. What you see today is mostly pretty modern and charmless.

Orientation & Information

The otogar is on the main highway a few hundred metres west of a large traffic roundabout which marks the beginning of Adnan Menderes Bulvarı. The centre of town is 1km north along Adnan Menderes

Bulvarı. At the centre, marked by the main square and a park, are various hotels, the PTT and the train station.

The Tourism Information Office (☎ 256-225 4145, fax 212 6226), on the traffic roundabout on the main highway east of the otogar, stocks an excellent map.

Aydın's postal code is 09000.

Things to See

Though Aydın retains a good number of **Ottoman mosques**, they are in somewhat distant neighbourhoods and hardly worth seeking out unless you're doing a close study of Ottoman religious architecture. Make do with inspecting the **Süleyman Bey Camii** (1683), designed by one of Sinan's apprentices. It's between the train station and the park on the main square.

The **Archaeology Museum**, 750m uphill from the main square, houses finds from Afrodisias, Didyma, Miletus, Priene and Tralles, including good statues of Athena and Nike, and a fine bust of Marcus Aurelius. It's open from 9 am to noon and 1.30 to 5 pm daily except Monday; admission is US$1.

Places to Stay & Eat

Chances are you're just passing through Aydın on the way to somewhere else but should you need to stay, there are several hotels just north of the main square that will do nicely for a night. Perhaps the best value for money is ***Hotel Kabaçam*** *(☎ 256-212 2794, Hükümet Bulvarı, 11 Sokak 2)*, where rooms with particularly comfortable beds and private showers cost US$10/16 a single/double, including breakfast. Across the street is ***Hotel Erdem*** *(☎ 256-225 1754)*, marginally cheaper but certainly less comfortable.

To find ***Hotel Baltacı*** *(☎ 256-225 1320, fax 225 1321, Gazi Bulvarı, 3 Sokak)*, continue up the hill from the Kabaçam, turn right at the mosque and then bear right down a side street. This charges about the same as the Kabaçam, but is not as nice. Turn left instead of right at the mosque for the 28 room ***Orhan Hotel*** *(☎ 256-225 1713, fax 225 1781, Gazi Bulvarı 63)*, which charges US$12 per person for two-star comforts.

Back on Adnan Menderes Bulvarı is the 30 room ***Otel Özlü*** *(☎/fax 256-225 3371)*, also offering two-star comforts but for US$16 per person. Bear in mind the noise from the main road and ask for a room at the back.

Aydın's best, the four-star ***Turtay Hotel*** *(☎ 256-213 3003, fax 213 0351)*, is on the road to Muğla and boasts 70 air-con rooms with satellite TV for US$50/70 a single/double. It might be fun to fantasise about using its private helicopter and plane service.

If you're staying at the Karaçam Hotel, return to the main road and cross over to walk through Aydın's downmarket version of İstanbul's Çiçek Pasajı. At the other end of the passage you'll come to a pedestrianised street with lots of little kebapçıs, including ***Lezzet Lokantası*** and ***Merkez Lokantası***, both serving soups, stews and kebaps for around US$3.

Getting There & Away

Bus Frequent buses run to Denizli, Pamukkale, Kuşadası, Selçuk and İzmir, where you may have to change for other destinations.

Train Three daily trains connect Aydın with Denizli, Selçuk, Menderes airport and İzmir. See those sections for details. For once the train station is right in the centre of town.

NYSSA

East of Aydın, you're deep in the fertile farming country of the Büyük Menderes river valley. Cotton fields sweep away from the road, and during the late October harvest, the highways are dangerously jammed with tractors hauling wagons overloaded with the white puffy stuff. Other important crops include pomegranates, pears, citrus fruits, apples, melons, olives and tobacco.

About 31km east of Aydın is the town of Sultanhisar where a 3km uphill walk to the north brings you to ancient Nyssa, set on a hilltop amid olive groves. When you get there you'll find public toilets, a soft-drink stand and a guard who will charge you US$1.50 admission during daylight hours and show you around the site in return for a tip.

NEIL WILSON

South Aegean The library of Celsus (2 AD) of Ephesus is a well-preserved example of Corinthian architecture.

PETER PTSCHELINZEW

JON DAVISON

South Aegean **Top:** The Great Theatre at Ephesus, capable of seating 25,000 people. **Bottom:** Two standing columns remain from the Prytaneum, or Town Hall, at Ephesus.

The major ruins consist of the **theatre**, and a 115m-long **tunnel** beneath the road and the parking area which was once the ancient city's main square. Walk another five minutes up the hill along the road and through a field and you'll come to the **bouleuterion**, which has some nice fragments of sculpture.

But what you're most likely to remember about Nyssa is the site's peaceful beauty, so different from the hubbub at honeypot metropolises like Ephesus. The walk back down to Sultanhisar and the highway is very enjoyable in late afternoon.

Though Sultanhisar has a few simple eateries, there are no real hotels. The İzmir-Denizli trains stop in town, and the highway carries many east-west buses. Dolmuşes run to Sultanhisar from Nazilli every 15 minutes (US$0.75).

NAZİLLİ

The market town of Nazilli (NAH-zee-lee, population 100,000), 14km east of Nyssa and Sultanhisar, is the most obvious transfer point for a trip to Afrodisias. The otogar is just north of the main highway, one block west of the main traffic roundabout. The train station is south of the highway.

Places to Stay & Eat

Unfortunately, Nazilli has no cheap hotels around its otogar, though there are a few small places near the train station. The two-star, 40 room ***Hotel Metya** (☎ 256-312 8888, fax 312 8891, 92 Sokak 10)* in Karaçay Mahallesi, just across from the otogar, facing the Shell fuel station, charges US$16/26 a single/double for a bath-equipped room and breakfast. There's a restaurant with live music too.

Go north 200m from the main traffic roundabout on the highway east of the otogar to reach the comfortable two-star, 55 room ***Nazilli Ticaret Odası Oteli** (☎ 256-313 9678, fax 313 9681)*, Hürriyet Caddesi. Decent rooms with bath and balcony cost US$16/26 a single/double, breakfast included. There's a ***restaurant*** and ***bar***, and a decent ***pastry shop*** adjoins the hotel.

The little eateries around the otogar are more than adequate for snacks if you're passing through.

Getting There & Away

Bus Nazilli is the local transportation hub, with buses to and from İzmir and Selçuk about every 45 minutes or so until early evening.

You're most likely to be transitting in Nazilli on the way to or from Afrodisias, although you can also visit Nyssa from here.

Daily services from Nazilli include:

Ankara – 545km, eight hours, US$10; several buses
Antalya – 360km, six hours, US$10; several buses
Bodrum – 225km, four hours, US$6; several buses
Denizli – 65km, one hour, US$2; very frequent buses and dolmuşes
İstanbul – 600km, 12 hours, US$14; several buses
İzmir – 170km, 2½ to three hours, US$4; very frequent buses
Konya – 505km, eight hours, US$10; several buses
Kuşadası – 150km, 2½ hours, US$4; several buses
Pamukkale – 85km, 1½ hours, US$2; several buses
Selçuk – 130km, 1½ hours, US$3.50; buses at least every hour

Train The three daily trains between Denizli and İzmir stop at Nazilli. See the Denizli, Selçuk and İzmir sections for details.

AFRODİSİAS

The city's name quickly brings to mind 'aphrodisiac'. Both words come from the Greek name for the goddess of love, Aphrodite, called Venus by the Romans. Aphrodite was many things to many people. As Aphrodite Urania she was the goddess of pure, spiritual love; as Aphrodite Pandemos she was the goddess of sensual love, married to Hephaestus but lover also of Ares, Hermes, Dionysus and Adonis. Her children included Harmonia, Eros, Hermaphroditus, Aeneas and Priapus, the phallic god. All in all, she was the complete goddess of fertility, fornication and fun.

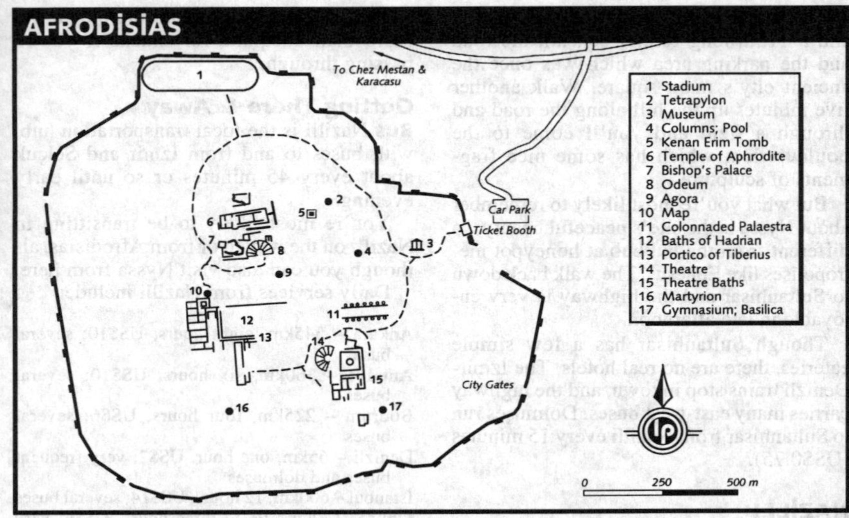

You will probably come to Afrodisias from Nazilli by way of the town of **Karacasu** (KAH-rah-jah-soo) which is surrounded by tobacco fields, fig trees and orchards. Besides farming, Karacasu is famous for its potters, who work with the local reddish-brown clay, firing it in wood-fired kilns. To see the potters at work, ask to be directed to the *çanakçı ocakları*.

History

Excavations have proved that the Afrodisias acropolis isn't a natural hill but a prehistoric mound built up by successive settlements beginning in the Early Bronze Age (2800-2200 BC). From the 8th century BC, its famous temple was a favourite goal of pilgrims, and the city prospered. But under the Byzantines the city changed substantially: the steamy Temple of Aphrodite was transformed into a chaste Christian church, and ancient buildings were pulled down to provide building stones for defensive walls (circa 350 AD).

Diminished from its former glory, the town was attacked by Tamerlane on his Anatolian rampage in 1402 and never recovered. The village of **Geyre** sprang up on the site sometime later. In 1956 an earthquake devastated the village, which was rebuilt to the west at its present location, allowing easier excavation of the site. The pleasant plaza by the big plane tree in front of the museum was the main square of pre-1956 Geyre.

Preliminary explorations of Afrodisias were carried out by French and Italian archaeologists early in the 20th century. After the earthquake of 1956, US and Turkish archaeologists began to resurrect the city. They found a surprisingly well-preserved stadium, odeum and theatre. From 1961 to 1990 work at the site was directed by Professor Kenan T Erim of New York University. His book, *Afrodisias: City of Venus Aphrodite* (1986), tells the story of his work. After his death, Professor Erim was buried at the site which he had done so much to reveal and explain.

Information

The site at Afrodisias is open from 8.30 am to 7 pm in summer and from 9 am to 5 pm in winter. Admission to these ruins costs

US$2.50, with another US$2.50 required for visiting the museum. No photography is permitted in the museum, nor are you allowed to photograph excavations in progress. Signs in the car park prohibit camping; they're afraid of antiquity thieves.

Museum

During Roman times Afrodisias was home to a famous school for sculptors who were attracted by the beds of high-grade white and blue-grey marble 2km away at the foot of Babadağ Mountain. The statuary in the museum reflects the excellence of their work. Note the 'cult statue of Aphrodite, second century' and the 'cuirassed statue of an emperor or high official, second century, signed by Appolonius Aster'. The 'portrait statue of Flavius Palmatus, governor of the province of Asia', looks like a man with big problems. Did they make his head that small on purpose, or as an insult? One of the finest pieces is the tomb of C Julius Zovios, a freedman from Afrodisias who died in the 1st century AD.

The Ruins

Follow the path to the right as you come from the museum. Most of what you see dates back to the 2nd century AD or later. Unfortunately quite a lot of the site is fenced off behind barbed wire and is inaccessible.

The first site you pass, on your left, is an unmarked collection of serpentine **columns** in a murky pool. Further along on the left is the magnificently elaborate **Tetrapylon**, or monumental gateway, which greeted pilgrims as they approached the temple of Aphrodite. The tomb of Professor Erim is just south-west of it.

Follow the footpath until you come to a right turn which leads across the fields (filled with poppies in spring) to the well-preserved **stadium**. Most of its 30,000 seats are overgrown but still in useable condition and you can almost imagine the football-crowd atmosphere when games were in progress.

Return to the main path and continue to the **Temple of Aphrodite**, completely rebuilt when it was converted into a basilica church (circa 500 AD). Its cella was removed, its columns shifted to form a nave, and an apse added at the eastern end, making it difficult to picture the place in which orgies to Aphrodite were held. Near the temple-church is the **Bishop's Palace**, dating from Byzantine times.

Just south of the Bishop's Palace a path leads eastward to the beautiful marble **odeum**, preserved almost undamaged for a thousand years in a bath of mud.

South of the odeum was Afrodisias' main **agora**, once enclosed by Ionic porticoes but now little more than a grassy field. Next the path leads you to the **Baths of Hadrian**, five large **galleries** and a **colonnaded palaestra** or playing field, and the grand **Portico of Tiberius**.

Climb up the earthen mound to find the white marble **theatre**, complete with stage and individually labelled seats, and at least as impressive as the one at Aspendos. South of it stood a large **baths** complex.

Because Afrodisias is so isolated and so much of it still survives, here more than in most places you get a very real sense of the grandeur and extent of the lost classical cities.

Antiocheia

On the road between the main highway and Karacasu you may notice signs pointing the way to Antiocheia; to get there you turn north at the centre of the village of Başaran, which is18km north-west of Karacasu. From Başaran it's 1km to the impressively sited and extensive ruins of another ancient hilltop city but this time totally unexcavated and unrestored so you get an idea of what the archaeologists see on the day they begin their fieldwork.

With your own vehicle, you can return to the Nazilli-Denizli highway, 6km to the north, by continuing past Antiocheia across the intensely fertile flood plain of the Büyük Menderes river and through the farming village of **Azizabat**, with some fine fieldstone walls and houses. You regain the highway at a point 5.6km east of the Karacasu turn-off, 21km east of Nazilli. Turn right (east) for Denizli.

Places to Stay

Nazilli has the nearest two and three-star hotels, but the most promising places, all of which offer the option of camping, are near Geyre.

About 500m before you reach the ruins, on the main road from Karacasu to Tavas, you'll spot ***Chez Mestan*** *(☎ 256-448 8046)*, a restaurant with a shady front porch on the left-hand side of the road. Mestan Bey is Turkish; his wife Nicole, is French. Attached to the restaurant are a few very basic rooms equipped with sinks and hand-held showers (but not toilets) for US$10/12 a single/double, breakfast included.

Walk another 500m back towards Karacasu and you'll see Mestan's other offering, ***Afrodisias Hotel*** *(☎ 256-448 8132, fax 448 8422)*, on the right-hand side of the road. The building itself is uninspiring but it's surrounded by gardens, with a wisteria arbour, and olive trees. Inside smart, clean rooms cost US$20/26 including breakfast. There's a rooftop restaurant (and carpet shop), a good place to wind down and listen to Mestan's stories. If you phone from the booth beside the museum, someone may be able to collect you.

Closer to the ruins is ***Belle Vue Pension***, 200m up from the crossroads, a simple village house which may or may not be receiving visitors when you arrive. Rates are as at Chez Mestan.

Heading back towards Karacasu, the village of Dandalaz has ***Elmas Pension & Restaurant***, possibly useful if you have your own transport, although the Afrodisias dolmuş passes the door. In Karacasu itself, ***Otogar Moteli***, on the upper floor of the otogar, is strictly for emergencies.

Places to Eat

Although there's a cafeteria of sorts at Afrodisias, it often serves only ice creams and cold drinks. Your best bet for a meal is to walk back along the highway to ***Chez Mestan*** where lunch on the shady porch will cost about US$4. The rooftop restaurant at ***Afrodisias Hotel*** is also very inviting but gets busy with tour groups.

If you're hanging about in Karacasu, there's no problem picking up a simple kebap meal, although the surroundings won't be anything special.

Getting There & Away

Bus A few direct buses link Karacasu with İzmir (210km, 3½ hours, US$10) and Selçuk (130km, two hours, US$8.50). Otherwise, take a bus from İzmir, Selçuk, Ortaklar, Aydın or Denizli to Nazilli, and from there pick up a dolmuş to Afrodisias or to Geyre, the village next to the ruins. If you can't find a dolmuş to Geyre or Afrodisias, there are services to Karacasu from Nazilli every 20 minutes during the main part of the day. Then take a dolmuş, hitch a ride or hire a taxi (US$12 return) for the final 13km to the ruins. Hitching should be easy in summer.

If you arrive at the ruins by dolmuş, be sure to check the time of the service back. The dolmuş driver may want to convert himself into a private taxi service at this point. Whether you accept or not is up to you, but bear in mind that if you refuse you may end up having to walk to one of the restaurants on the main road and summon a normal taxi from Karacusu to get back to Nazilli.

Minibus Tours Bearing in mind the difficulties of getting to Afrodisias by public transport it's worth knowing that several bus companies, including Pamukkale and Kamil Koç, operate special minibuses services from Pamukkale. These leave at 10 am and take 1½ hours to get to Afrodisias. They return at 3 pm, thus leaving you ample time to explore the ruins and have a picnic lunch. The cost is US$10 per person. Even at quiet times of the year it's worth asking at your pension in case enough people can be found to justify a special trip.

Car Afrodisias is 55km from Nazilli, 101km from Denizli and 38km off the east-west highway.

DENİZLİ

Denizli, with a population of 250,000 and an altitude of 354m, is a prosperous, busy agricultural city with some light industry. It's noisy and dusty, but has hotels and restaurants in all price ranges, which you might need to patronise if Pamukkale is full. Otherwise, there's not much need to hang about.

Orientation & Information

The train station is on the main highway near the roundabout with the statue of a rooster, one block west of the otogar and a short distance west of the three-point traffic roundabout called Üçgen.

Delikli Çınar Meydanı, the city's main square, is 1km south of the train station and otogar. The main Tourism Information Office (☎ 258-264 3971, fax 264 7621) is inconveniently out of the way at Çaybaşı Caddesi 64/1. Smaller, handier offices in the train station and otogar are rarely open.

At the time of writing the **Atatürk ve Etnografya Müzesi** was closed for restoration. It's diagonally opposite the imposing **Ulu Cami** at the top of İstasyon Caddesi.

Denizli's postal code is 20100.

DENİZLİ

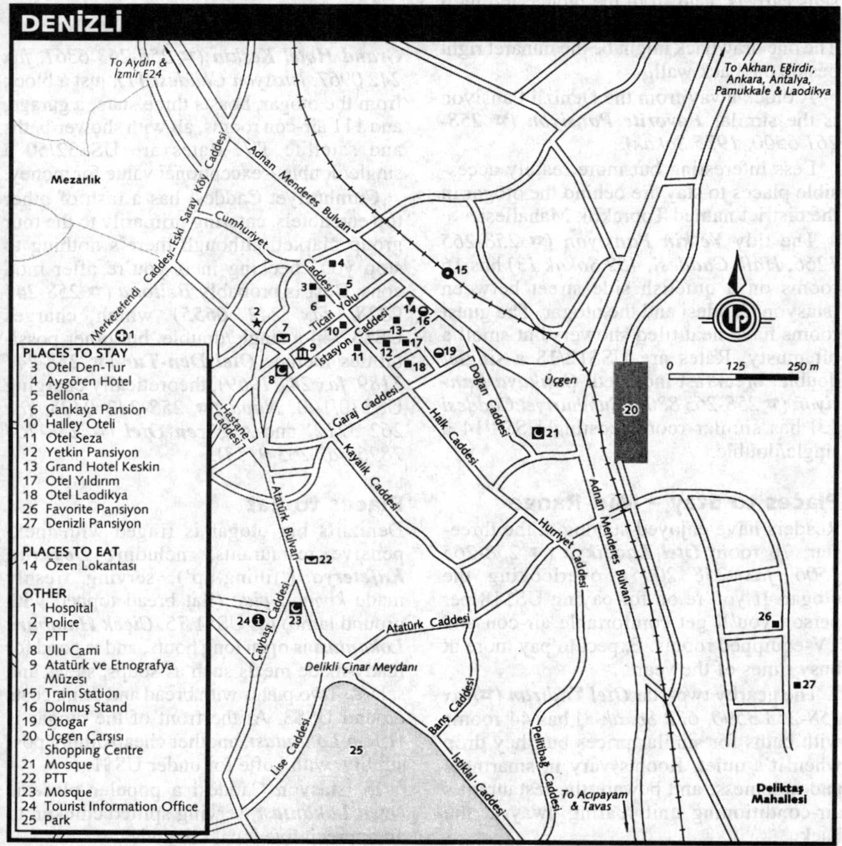

Places to Stay – Budget

Denizli's best pensions are in Deliktaş Mahallesi, about 1km from the otogar on the eastern side of the highway to the south of the Üçgen Çarşısı. First choice should certainly be ***Denizli Pansiyon*** *(☎ 258-261 8738)*, clearly signposted at 1993 Sokak 14. All rooms have private showers and toilets and cost US$15 a double in summer, less during the low season; breakfast costs another US$2 per person, dinner another US$3. The pension has a nice courtyard with a fountain and lots of fruit trees. The owner, Süleyman Can (pronounced 'john'), also sells carpets. Call from the otogar and he'll pick you up to save you the 25-minute walk. The one drawback might be the minaret right beside the back wall.

A block away from the Denizli Pansiyon is the similar ***Favorite Pansiyon*** *(☎ 258-261 6500, 1975 Sokak)*.

Less interesting but more readily accessible places to stay are behind the otogar in the district named Topraklık Mahallesi.

The tidy ***Yetkin Pansiyon*** *(☎ 258-265 1266, Halk Caddesi, 452 Sokak 13)* has 16 rooms on a quietish side street between İstasyon Caddesi and the otogar. The guest rooms have neat tiled showers but smell a bit musty. Rates are US$12/18 a single/double, breakfast included. ***Çankaya Pansiyon*** *(☎ 258-263 8802, Cumhuriyet Caddesi 13)* has similar rooms costing US$8/14 a single/double.

Places to Stay – Mid-Range

Readers have enjoyed staying at the three-star, 76 room ***Otel Laodikya*** *(☎ 258-265 1506, fax 258 2005)*, overlooking the otogar. If you're on for paying US$18 per person you'll get comfortable air-con and TV-equipped rooms. Expect to pay more at busy times of the year.

The nearby two-star ***Otel Yıldırım*** *(☎/fax 258-263 3590, 632 Sokak 3)* has 44 rooms with baths for similar prices but they drop when it's quiet. Rooms vary in smartness and quietness, and beware the restaurant's air-conditioning unit roaring away at the back.

Otel Subaşıoğlu *(☎ 258-264 9207, fax 264 9215)*, right beside the otogar but on the main road, rates three stars and charges US$18/32 for a single/double with bath and breakfast. The older two-star ***Otel Seza*** *(☎ 258-264 6844, fax 262 4630)*, Halk Caddesi, charges the same for its 36 bath-equipped rooms.

Up the hill from the train station along noisy İstasyon Caddesi are more hotels, including the three-star ***Halley Oteli*** (named after the comet) *(☎ 258-261 9544, fax 263 5218)*; and the two-star, 30 room ***Keskinkaya Oteli*** *(☎ 258-264 9938, fax 263 3564, İstasyon Caddesi 83)*, with similar prices.

Places to Stay – Top End

Grand Hotel Keskin *(☎ 258-263 6361, fax 242 0967, İstasyon Caddesi 11)*, just a block from the otogar, boasts three stars, a garage, and 111 air-con rooms, all with shower/baths and satellite TV. Rates are US$32/50 a single/double – exceptional value for money.

Cumhuriyet Caddesi has a rash of other top end hotels, catering primarily to the tour group market, although there's nothing to stop you checking in if you're after mod cons. Best is probably ***Bellona*** *(☎ 258-241 9828, fax 242 0655)* which charges US$32/44 a single/double, but other possibilities include ***Otel Den-Tur*** *(☎ 258-241 7189, fax 241 1969)*, theoretically charging US$70/100, ***Napa*** *(☎ 258-242 0428, fax 262 3712)* and ***Aygören Otel*** *(☎ 258-264 7896, fax 263 9153)*.

Places to Eat

Denizli's big otogar is ringed with inexpensive restaurants, including ***Doyuran Kafeterya*** ('filling-up'), serving freshly made *kıymalı pide* (flat bread topped with ground lamb) for US$1.75. ***Çiçek Hamburg Lokantası*** is open long hours, and is good for ready-made meals such as soups, stews and salads. Two plates with bread and drink costs around US$3. At the front of the otogar is ***Özlem Lokantası***, another cheap dining possibility, with köfte for under US$1.

In İstasyon Caddesi a popular place is ***Özen Lokantası***, serving spitted chicken to an appreciative local clientele.

Getting There & Away

Bus There are frequent buses between İzmir and Denizli otogar via Selçuk, Ortaklar, Aydın and Nazilli. The otogar has an *emanetçi* (left-luggage room) next to the PTT and the toilets.

You can catch a bus in Denizli for virtually any major city in Turkey, including these daily routes:

Ankara – 480km, seven hours, US$8; frequent buses
Antalya – 300km, five hours, US$6; several buses
Bodrum – 290km, five hours, US$6; several buses
Bursa – 532km, nine hours, US$12; several buses
Fethiye – 280km, five hours, US$8; several buses
Isparta – 172km, three hours, US$4; frequent buses
İstanbul – 665km, 13 hours, US$13 to US$20; frequent buses
İzmir – 250km, four hours, US$8; frequent buses
Konya – 440km, seven hours, US$8; several buses
Kuşadası – 215km, 3½ hours, US$5; frequent buses
Marmaris – 185km, three hours, US$6; several buses
Nevşehir – 674km, 11 hours, US$14; at least one night bus
Selçuk – 195km, three hours, US$6; hourly buses

Warning Most people come to Denizli en route to Pamukkale. Some bus companies, particularly in Selçuk, sell tickets for Pamukkale which actually drop you in Denizli where you must change to a city bus or dolmuş for the onward journey. Sometimes the price is included in your ticket, sometimes it isn't. Often you'll be hanging around Denizli waiting for the dolmuş to fill up.

There are two separate services from Denizli to Pamukkale. The local bus service leaves from inside the otogar and runs roughly every 30 minutes with no waiting about for it to fill up. It also passes many of the pensions and hotels. Bus station hustlers will try and get you to take the dolmuş minibuses which wait just beside the otogar. In summer these fill up quickly, but at other times you'll have to wait around. The hustlers use this waiting time to try and divert you to their favoured pensions, often spinning unlikely stories about problems at your chosen accommodation. Stick to your guns and insist on going where you originally planned. If in doubt, head for a *kontürlü telefon* (metered phone) in the otogar and phone to check. The buses and dolmuşes cost exactly the same US$1 to Pamukkale.

Train Three trains a day ply between Denizli and İzmir. Tickets (US$3) go on sale at Denizli station an hour before departure.

The nightly *Pamukkale Ekspresi* between Denizli and İstanbul via Afyon hauls sleeping, couchette and Pullman cars, departing from İstanbul (Haydarpaşa) at 8.10 am and from Denizli at 7.50 pm. The journey takes 14 hours. A 1st/2nd-class seat costs US$7/5; sleeping compartments range from an additional US$10 in a one person compartment to US$8 in a three person compartment.

There's also a daily *mototren* (motor train) between Denizli and Afyon, departing from Denizli at 7.30 am and from Afyon at 11.10 pm for a five-hour journey.

When you arrive at the train station, walk out the front door, cross the busy highway, turn left and walk one block to the otogar, where you can catch a dolmuş or bus to Pamukkale.

PAMUKKALE

One of the most familiar images of Turkey is of the gleaming white calcium formations (travertines) of Pamukkale (pah-MOO-kah-leh), 19km north of Denizli. From a distance these form a white scar on the side of a ridge. As you come closer, they take on a more distinct shape, giving credence to the name, which means 'cotton castle.'

Pamukkale was formed when warm calcium-rich mineral water cascaded over the cliff edge, cooling and depositing its calcium in the process. The calcium built natural shelves, pools and stalactites in which tourists delighted to splash and soak. The Romans built a large spa city, Hierapolis, above the travertines to take advantage of the water's curative powers, and in the 1960s through the 1980s modern hotels were built on the ridge to serve visitors. So

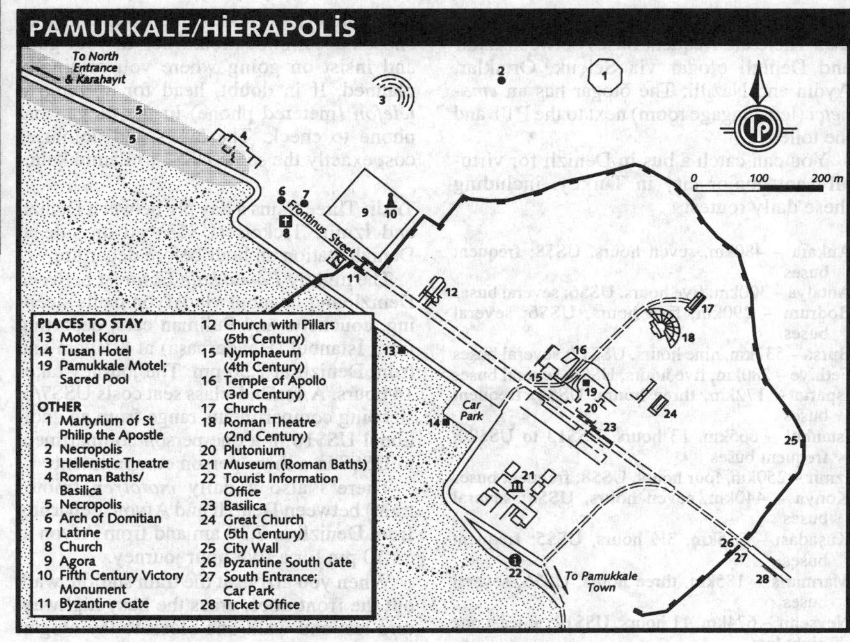

special was Pamukkale that UNESCO declared it a world heritage site.

The tourist boom of the 1990s brought so many tourists to Pamukkale that the travertines and water supply were threatened. A conservation plan is now being carried out: the hotels have been demolished, and the travertine pools have been closed in order to preserve them. It is not yet clear whether or not a few of the pools will be re-opened in the future.

Without the pools, why go to Pamukkale? Well, the travertines are just as beautiful and interesting when seen from a distance, and the ruins of Hierapolis still as impressive. Pamukkale also makes a good base for day trips to Afrodisias and Laodikya. Pension owners organise picnic excursions to Ağlayan Kayalar, a waterfall at Sakızcılar between Denizli and Çal for about US$10 per person. The village is also well stocked with small family run pensions and hotels, most with their own pools and perfect for a few days of gentle relaxation.

Orientation

Pamukkale and Hierapolis now constitute a national park with formal entrances and visitor centres on the northern and southern sides. To the west, at the base of the travertine ridge, is Pamukkale town, once a farming village but now a small town with dozens of lodging and dining places.

About 5km west of the northern entrance is the village of Karahayıt where you'll find most of the luxury hotel development.

Cars can reach the southern entrance of the national park via Pamukkale town (2km), or the northern entrance via Pamukkale town or Karahayıt. It's a short walk from the *güney girişi* (southern entrance) to the centre of the site, but 2.5km from the *kuzey girişi* (northern entrance).

Information

Although Pamukkale has a Tourism Information Office (☎/fax 258-272 2077) on the plateau, it sees its business solely in terms of selling visitors the same books and postcards they could buy outside. There's also a PTT, souvenir shops, a museum and a first aid post.

Pamukkale's postal code is 20210.

Travertines

It costs US$3 to enter the national park, plus US$1 to park a car. The site is reputedly open 24 hours a day which means you can visit for sunrise and sunset.

At the time of writing you can still swim in the beautiful pool at the Pamukkale Motel, with its submerged fragments of fluted marble columns. A two-hour dip costs US$4 (children half price), but they rarely check your pass so you may be able to stretch it out a bit. A safe box for your belongings costs another US$2.

Hierapolis

Hierapolis was a cure centre founded around 190 BC by Eumenes II, King of Pergamum, which prospered under the Romans and even more under the Byzantines. It had a large Jewish community and therefore an early Christian church. Earthquakes brought disaster a few times; after the one in 1334 the locals finally called it a day and moved away.

These days the primary reason for coming to Pamukkale should really be to explore the ruins of Hierapolis where Fiat is sponsoring ongoing excavations and restoration work. The ruins sprawl over a wide area within the national park. To inspect everything carefully could take the best part of a day, although most visitors settle for an hour or two.

The centre of Hierapolis may have been the **sacred pool**, now the swimming pool in the courtyard of the Pamukkale Motel. If the motel is torn down as planned, the pool may again be visible as it was to the ancients, instead of being ringed with overpriced ice cream stands. The city's **Roman baths**, parts of which are now the **Pamukkale Museum**, are in front of the Pamukkale Motel. At the time of writing the museum was closed for restoration but opening hours used to be daily except Monday from 8.30 am to noon and 1.30 to 5 pm. Admission will probably be US$1.50 when it re-opens.

Near the museum stands a ruined **Byzantine church** and the foundations of a **Temple of Apollo**. As at Didyma and Delphi, the temple had an oracle attended by eunuch priests. The source of inspiration was an adjoining spring called the Plutonium, dedicated appropriately to Pluto, god of the underworld. The spring gives off toxic vapours, lethal to all but the priests, who would demonstrate its powers to visitors by throwing small animals and birds in and watching them die.

To find the spring, walk up towards the Roman theatre but enter the first gate in the fence on the right, then follow the path down to the right about 30m. To the left and in front of the big, block-like temple is a small subterranean entry closed by a rusted grate and marked by a sign reading 'Tehlikelidir – Zehirli Gaz' (Dangerous – Poisonous Gas). If you listen, you can hear the gas bubbling up from the waters below. Note that the gas is still deadly poisonous. Before the grate was installed there were several fatalities among those with more curiosity than sense.

The spectacular **Roman theatre**, capable of seating more than 12,000 spectators, was built in two stages by the emperors Hadrian and Septimius Severus. Much of the stage survives, along with some of the decorative panels and the front-row 'box' seats for VIPs. It was carefully restored by Italian stonecutters in the 1970s.

From the theatre take one of the rough tracks heading uphill and eventually you'll come to the extraordinary octagonal **Martyrium of St Philip**, built on the site where it's believed that St Philip was martyred. The arches of the eight individual chapels are all marked with crosses. Views from here are wonderful and you'll probably share them only with the goldfinches and skylarks.

If you hack across the hillside in a westerly direction, eventually you'll come to a completely ruinous **Hellenistic theatre** along unmarked goat tracks.

Standing beside the theatre and looking down you'll see the 2nd century **agora**, one of the largest ever discovered. On three sides it was surrounded by marble porticoes with Ionic columns, while the fourth side was closed off by a basilica.

Walk down the hill and through the agora, and you'll re-emerge on the main road along the top of the ridge. Turn right towards the northern exit and you'll come to the remains of the marvellous colonnaded **Frontinus Street**, still with some of its paving and columns intact. Once the city's main north-south commercial axis, this street was bounded at both ends by monumental archways. The ruins of the **Arch of Domitian**, with its twin towers, are at the northern end, but just before them don't miss the surprisingly large **latrine** building, with two channels cut into its floor, one to carry away sewage, the other for fresh water.

Beyond the Arch of Domitian you come first to the ruins of the **Byzantine baths** and then to the Appian Way of Hierapolis, an extraordinary **necropolis** (cemetery), extending several kilometres to the north, with many striking, even stupendous, tombs in all shapes and sizes. Look out in particular for a cluster of circular tombs, supposedly topped with phallic symbols in antiquity. Hierapolis was a health spa, but obviously the cure didn't work for everyone.

Special Events

In late May or early June, the Pamukkale Festival brings spectators to Hierapolis' restored Roman theatre for musical and folkloric performances.

Places to Stay

With the razing of the motels on top of the ridge, accommodation is now in Pamukkale town or in Karahayıt, the building site of choice for large hotels catering to the tour-group trade (see later in this section). At weekends you may find Pamukkale's pensions and motels full and be forced to seek accommodation in Denizli.

Prices vary greatly according to the season, being highest in mid-summer. To avoid the crush – and find a bargain – come during the week, or very early on Friday or Saturday, and preferably in spring or autumn, not high summer. Many of the village pensions and hotels stay open all year, so a winter visit is also an option, provided you don't mind forgoing the pleasures of the swimming pools.

Places to Stay – Budget

The town at the base of the ridge is filled with little family pensions, some more elaborate and expensive than others. Many have swimming pools, often oddly shaped and filled with the calcium mineral water – cool by the time it gets there – and shady places to sit, read, sip tea or have a meal. If rooms are available, you'll have no problem finding one, as pension owners will crowd around your bus as it arrives and flood you with offers. Those with rooms available after the initial onslaught will intercept you as you walk along the road into the village. If you have your heart set on somewhere specific you may have to be very determined to rid yourself of the touts.

Right at the entrance to town, just off the highway, is Mehmet Semerci's ***Hotel Konak Sade*** *(☎ 258-272 2002, fax 272 2175)*, Pamukkale's first lodging place, opened more than 25 years ago. It's a mixture of newer rooms and some in an old village house decorated with Turkish carpets, kilims and copperware. The shady rear garden holds a small swimming pool surrounded by tables and chairs; the view of the travertines from here is the best around. The 32 simple rooms all have private baths. You pay US$30 a double with breakfast.

Across the road from the Konak Sade is ***Pension Mustafa*** *(☎ 258-272 2240, fax 272 2830)*, with clean simple rooms, all with their own shower, for US$5 per person. Breakfast is another US$2 and a sizeable dinner costs US$5. Just a couple of doors along, and charging the same prices, is Şerif Bakan's ***Arkadaş Pansiyon*** *(☎ 258-272 2183, fax 272 2589)*, with nine cosy rooms set around a shady courtyard. A new upstairs ***restaurant*** with travertine views should have opened by the time you read this.

A cluster of welcoming, family run pensions can be found at the junction of İnönü Caddesi and Menderes Caddesi. The honeysuckle-scented ***Kervansaray Pension*** *(☎ 258-272 2209, fax 272 2143)*, offers cheerful rooms with shower for US$18, a swimming pool, and a friendly family atmosphere. It's been a favourite for years and the new central heating system makes it a year-round possibility.

Very close to the Kervansaray is the friendly ***Aspawa Pansiyon*** *(☎ 258-272 2094, fax 272 2631)*, which has beds for US$4 or US$5, a front pool and an upstairs ***restaurant***. It, too, has central heating and opens all year round. Readers have also heartily recommended the ***Weisse Burg Pension*** *(☎ 258-272 2064)* which has eight ground-floor rooms, a small pool and a rooftop ***restaurant*** where Haçer's cooking is particularly warmly endorsed – she can cater for vegetarians if you ask. Rooms cost US$12, breakfast is US$2 and dinner will set you back US$5.

Hotel Turku *(☎ 258-272 2181)* is tucked away down a side street, near the Commando Disco. Clean rooms with private showers cost US$25 a double and meals in the dining room are said to be tasty. The pool is a little disappointing though.

As you come into town from Denizli there are several other pensions in a very quiet location. Readers have recommended ***Venüs Pension*** *(☎ 258-272 2152)*, with spotless modern bedrooms on three floors for US$8 per person without breakfast. The pool here looks very inviting and you can eat out around it on sunny evenings. The ***Allgâu*** *(☎ 258-272 2767)*, opposite, is owned by the same family but has its own pool.

Camping There are several camping grounds along the road between Denizli and Pamukkale, including ***Çankur Kamping*** *(☎ 258-272 2784)*, attached to the Şafak Restaurant, as you come into Pamukkale from Denizli and ***Ege Camping*** nearby.

Places to Stay – Mid-Range

Pamukkale also has a few extremely inviting motels. One of the nicest is Rifat Durmuş's

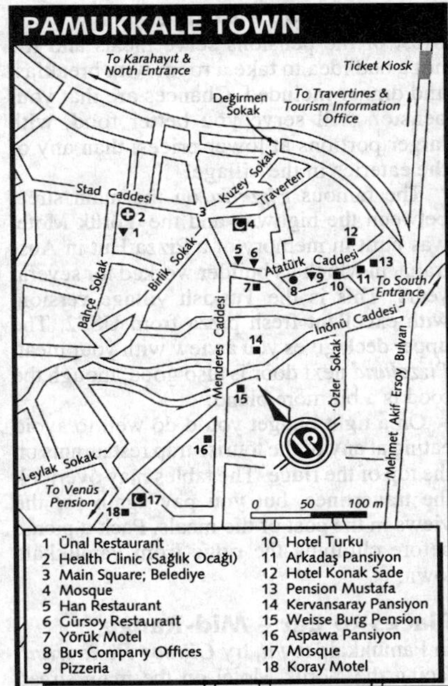

Koray Motel *(☎ 258-272 2300, fax 272 2095)*, an excellent choice with a pool set in a central courtyard surrounded by trees and plants – a romantic setting for evening meals. Well kept and friendly, it offers double rooms with shower and bath for US$18; for US$10 more you get breakfast and dinner as well. A new terrace ***restaurant*** was due to open at the time of writing. If you call from Denizli otogar, a hotel car will pick you up, thereby avoiding the touts.

The 58 room ***Yörük Motel*** *(☎/fax 258-272 2073)*, a short walk down the hill in the village centre, is more inviting than its lobby initially suggests. Guest rooms are on two levels, surrounding a courtyard with swimming pool. The restaurant is often busy with tour groups. Rooms with shower, balcony and breakfast cost US$20/32 a single/double in summer. A couple of four-bedded rooms can be snapped up for US$40.

Places to Eat – Budget

Most of the pensions serve meals and it's not a bad idea to take a room with breakfast and dinner included. Chances are that your pension will serve you better food, with larger portions at lower prices, than any of the eateries in the village.

The famous ***Pizzeria*** on the main street between the highway and the Yörük Motel was built in memory of a Pizza Hut in Australia, in which its builder worked for several years. This is the Turkish village version, with excellent fresh pizza from US$2. The upper deck gives you a view with your meal. ***Pizzaland*** next door is also good, though the food is a bit more bland.

On a tight budget you'd do well to avoid eating at any of the tourist-trap restaurants on the top of the ridge. The tables may overlook the travertines, but you pay again for the views in the cost of the meals. Pack a picnic before climbing the ridge from Pamukkale town.

Places to Eat – Mid-Range

In Pamukkale town, try ***Gürsoy Restaurant***, facing the Yörük Motel on the main street. With its small, shady front terrace, it's great for people-watching. A three-course meal with a drink costs about US$4. Similarly priced is the popular ***Han Restaurant***, facing the main square. The menu has many popular dishes like grills for US$2.75 to US$3.75.

Ünal Restaurant, below the square, has less of a view and simpler decor, but is significantly cheaper, with set-price meals for US$3.50 and US$4.50. ***Mustafa Restaurant***, attached to the pension of the same name at the top of the hill near the main road, advertises vegetarian food.

For a drink, try ***Harem Restaurant & Bar***, on Menderes Caddesi, with a good view of the foot traffic.

Getting There & Away

Bus In summer, Pamukkale has a surprising number of direct buses to and from other cities, many of them continuing to Pamukkale from Denizli. Companies serving the town with direct buses include Kamil Koç, Köseoğlu, Pamukkale and Paklale. For distances and prices, see under Getting There & Away in the earlier Denizli section. At other times of year it's best to assume you'll have to change in Denizli.

Pamukkale has no proper otogar. Ticket offices are near the junction of the highway and the town's main street.

Municipal buses make the half-hour trip between Denizli and Pamukkale every 30 minutes or so, more frequently on Saturday and Sunday, for US$1; the last bus runs at 10 pm in summer, probably around sunset in other seasons. A few of these buses actually go to the top of the ridge for no extra charge. In summer dolmuşes go more frequently but see the warning on delays and pension touts in the earlier Denizli section.

The dolmuş from Denizli to Pamukkale usually continues as far as Karahayıt, or there's a separate Karahayıt municipal bus service.

Car If you're driving from Afrodisias and Nazilli, you might want to note a short cut to Pamukkale. About 600m after you pass the exit sign from Sarayköy ('Sarayköy' with a red diagonal stripe through it), a narrow road on the left leads to Pamukkale via the villages of Sığma (SUH-mah), Akköy and Karahayıt. The road is not well marked, so you should ask directions for Pamukkale in each village. If enough people ask, the locals might erect signs.

Taxi A taxi between Denizli and Pamukkale costs about US$8, but don't take one until you're *sure* the bus and dolmuş services have stopped for the day, which is what you're liable to hear from every taxi driver. Taxis also wait on top of the ridge to run people back to Pamukkale. This journey should cost between US$3 and US$4 but some readers have complained of being told it was a metered taxi and then being landed with a bill twice as high as this. A taxi from Pamukkale to Karahayıt costs about US$8.

KARAHAYIT

About 5km to the north of Pamukkale is the village of Karahayıt (KAH-rah-hah-yuht), which boasts deep red iron-rich mineral waters instead of travertines. You can get cured (and stained red) at any of several small family pensions and camping places here, patronised mostly by ageing locals in search of the fountain of youth.

About 1km south of Karahayıt village on the Pamukkale road are a few pensions, including the ***Selçuklu*** *(☎ 258-271 4189)* and the ***Osmanlı*** *(☎ 258-271 4212)* but most lodgings are in the dozen three, four and five-star hotels aimed at the tour-group market. None of these are high-rise monstrosities, although Karahayıt itself is a rather soulless place of half-finished buildings.

The four-star, 225 room ***Polat Hotel*** *(☎ 258-271 4111, fax 271 4092)* has well-established gardens and good guest rooms in two-storey brown and green blocks. Singles/doubles cost US$80/100, breakfast included, and afterwards you can soak in a mock geyser at the back of the hotel.

Similar comforts are available at the five-star, 230 room ***Club Colossea*** *(☎ 258-271 4156, fax 271 4250)*; the four-star, 210 room ***Ergür Hotel*** *(☎ 258-271 4170, fax 271 4146)*; the three-star, 158 room ***Pam Oteli*** *(☎ 258-271 4140, fax 271 4097)* and ***Denizli Richmond Otel*** *(☎ 258-271 4294, fax 271 4078)*; and the 208 room mock classical ***Club Hierapolis Thermal Resort*** *(☎ 258-271 4108, fax 271 4816)*.

LAODİCEA (LAODİKYA)

Laodicea was a prosperous commercial city at the junction of two major trade routes running north to south and east to west. Famed for its black wool, banking and medicines, it had a large Jewish community and a prominent Christian congregation. It's one of the Seven Churches of Asia mentioned in the New Testament Book of Revelation. Cicero lived here a few years before he was put to death at the request of Marc Antony.

To reach the ruins of Laodicea on your own, you'll need a car, a taxi, a hired minibus, or good strong legs. Head north towards Pamukkale from the Üçgen, the large traffic roundabout near Denizli's otogar. Take the left turn marked for Pamukkale, and then almost immediately (just before the village of Korucuk) another left marked for Laodicea.

From this point it's just more than 3km to the edge of the archaeological site, or just more than 4km from Laodicea's most prominent theatre. There are several possible routes to the ruins, but this one takes you through a little farming village; the road is unmarked, so ask, or when in doubt, bear right. You should soon come to a railway level crossing; on the other side of the tracks, the ruins are visible. (Another route leaves the main road closer to Pamukkale, and brings you to the theatre first.)

At present there's no guard at the site, no fee and no appointed visiting hours, so you can come anytime in daylight.

Though the city was a big one, as proved by the ruins spread over a large area, there's not much of interest left for the casual tourist. The **stadium** is visible, but most of the cut stones were purloined to construct the railway. One of the **two theatres** is in better shape, with many of its upper tiers of seats remaining, though the bottom ones have collapsed.

Without your own transport you might want to sign up for a tour from Pamukkale. The Koray Motel, in Pamukkale, organises trips to Laodicea for around US$10 per person, depending on the number of people. These tours also take in the Ak Han.

Ak Han

En route to Laodicea, you can also visit the Ak Han (White Caravanserai), a marble Seljuk Turkish caravan 'motel' just 1km past the Pamukkale turn-off from the main road. Heading north from the Üçgen in Denizli, don't take the Pamukkale road, but continue in the direction marked for Dinar for another 1km. The caravanserai is set just off the highway on the left as you come down the slope of a hill. It still awaits restoration but is in quite marvellous shape considering that it dates from the early 1250s.

Turkish Lake District

East of Denizli and north of Antalya, Turkey has its own Lake District, with three main lakes – Burdur Gölü, Eğirdir Gölü and Beyşehir Gölü – and several smaller ones, including Acıgöl, Akşehir Gölü and Çavuşcu Gölü. These lakes were formed after depressions caused by the clashing of tectonic plates filled up with water.

The main town in the lakes area is Isparta, but neither it, nor Burdur, is especially interesting to visitors. Eğirdir, on the other hand, lives for tourism. Its beautiful freshwater lake is ringed with mountains and two islands linked to the mainland by a causeway jut into the lake, a beautiful sight as you descend the hill from Isparta. Beyşehir is also well worth a visit for its wonderful 13th century lakeside mosque.

Spring is an especially good time to visit the lakes. The apple trees are in blossom in April while the annual rose harvest begins on 20 May. Isparta's sandy soil has been growing roses for oil since the late 19th century when the first plants were brought from Bulgaria and established here. Most of the *attar* (rose oil) produced here is exported to France.

Some parts of the lake district are good for birdwatching. Burdur Gölü in particular is home to huge flocks of white-headed ducks in winter.

Burdur, Isparta and Eğirdir all have train stations but you will probably get around the area more quickly if you stick with the buses.

ISPARTA

Famous for its kilims, carpets and attar, Isparta (population 125,000, altitude 1035m) is at an important highway junction on the way east to Eğirdir (36km). You could while away the odd hour here but it's not an exciting town. Nor, despite its position, is it the easiest to negotiate in terms of public transport.

Orientation & Information

The main road, Süleyman Demirel Bulvarı, sweeps from the Kaymakkapı Meydanı traffic roundabout near the Otel Bolat all the way up to the inevitable statue of Atatürk in front of the Büyük Isparta Oteli, changing its name to Mimar Sinan Caddesi somewhere along the way. Here you'll find the banks and exchange offices and most of the bus company offices.

The otogar is 1.5km away and the train station is a little further. The main dolmuş terminal is hidden away in the *çarşı* (market) area beyond the Belediye İşhanı.

The Tourism Information Office (☎ 246-218 4438, fax 212 1065) is on the 3rd floor of the Hükümet Konağı (provincial government building).

Isparta's postal code is 32000.

Things to See

Should you need to spend time here, stop in at the **Ulu Cami** (1417) and the **Firdevs Bey Camii** (1561) with its neighbouring **bedesten**, the latter two buildings attributed to Mimar Sinan. Also, wander into the huge **Halı Saray** (Carpet Palace) on Mimar Sinan Caddesi. On four days each week, fine Isparta carpets are auctioned to dealers and anyone else with the money to buy them.

The **Archaeology Museum** on Kenan Evren Caddesi, is open from 8.30 am to 6 pm for US$1, but is way out from the centre.

Places to Stay & Eat

Süleyman Demirel Bulvarı/Mimar Sinan Caddesi has several hotels to choose from.

***Hotel Yeni Gülistan** (☎ 246-218 4085, Mimar Sinan Caddesi 31)*, is new only in name. Basic but serviceable singles/doubles with shower cost US$11/18.

The two-star ***Otel Akkoç** (☎ 246-232 5811, fax 232 5810)*, across the road, has clean, spacious rooms but wants US$20/30 a single/double, probably subject to negotiation.

The three-star, 60 room ***Otel Bolat** (☎ 246-223 9001, fax 218 5506, Süleyman Demirel Bulvarı 71)*, has pretty good, if rather dark, rooms and posts rates of US$30/40 a single/double, breakfast included.

One of the city's newer hotels is the three-star, 41 room ***Hotel Artan*** *(☎ 246-232 5700, fax 218 6629, Cengiz Topel Caddesi 12/B)*, on a quietish pedestrianised street. Singles/doubles with shower and TV cost US$22/34, breakfast included. To find it walk downhill along the pedestrian way from the fountain beside the Firdevs Bey Camii.

Isparta's best is the six-storey, 63 room ***Büyük Ispara Oteli*** *(☎ 246-232 4422, fax 232 4422)*, which faces the Belediye İşhanı with its mock travertines. Singles/doubles officially cost US$80/130, for which you get modern decor and furnishings. There's a lot of street noise though.

Near the Bolat is the popular ***Başkent Döner Kebap ve Pide Salonu***, a moderately priced eatery. Otherwise turn down the pedestrianised street behind the Firdevs Bey Camii and you'll find plenty of lokantas, including ***Karadeniz Pide Salonu*** where pide costs just US$1, and ***Zeyrel Abıdan Sofrası*** where an İskender kebap will set you back US$2. There are also several beer halls down here, good for an evening's thirst-quenching.

Getting There & Away

In theory Isparta's otogar is the main transit point for the lakes. In fact because it's 1.5km from the main traffic roundabout in the centre, some bus services, including the most frequent service to Eğirdir, leave from a minibus terminal in town. Coming north from Antalya you may find yourself dropped on the outskirts of Isparta and ferried to the otogar in a *servis* minibus – only to find you need the minibus terminal anyway!

You can buy a seat on a long-distance bus service to Eğirdir from the otogar, but this is likely to involve more hanging about than catching the half-hourly minibus from the terminal in town. To get from the otogar to the Çarşı terminal, catch a Çarşı local bus from in front of the otogar. This is where you'll need to come, too, for a dolmuş to Ağlasun (for Sagalassos, US$1) or Bucak.

Note that the hourly service to Burdur leaves from the otogar.

Afyon – 175km, 2½ hours, US$4; frequent buses
Antalya – 175km, two hours, US$3; hourly buses
Burdur – 50km, 45 minutes, US$1.50; hourly minibuses
Denizli – 175km, 2½ hours, US$4; several buses
Eğirdir – 36km, 30 minutes, US$1; minibuses every 30 minutes from Çarşı terminal
İzmir – 425km, seven hours, US$8; several buses
Konya – 270km, four hours, US$7; frequent buses

EĞİRDİR

Eğirdir (pronounced eh-YEER-deer; population 18,000, altitude 950m) enjoys a beautiful situation on the road from Konya to the Aegean, near the southern tip of Eğirdir Gölü (Lake Eğirdir). The lake is Turkey's fourth largest, covering 517 sq km, with an average depth of 12m and a maximum depth of 16.5m. On the hillside by the road into town from Isparta is a large Turkish army commando training base, the commando slogan emblazoned in gigantic letters on the slope above: 'We're commandos: strong, brave, and ready' *('Komandoyuz, Güçlüyüz, Cesuruz, Hazırız')*. On their day off, the commandos' blue berets are a common sight about town.

In Lydian times this highway was the Royal Road, the main route between Ephesus and Babylon, and Eğirdir was a beautiful and convenient place to stop, so the town prospered.

Today's town, clinging to the base of the steep slopes of Davras Dağı (2635m), serves something of the same purpose. Travellers on their way to or from Konya stop for a day or two to enjoy views of the lake, dine on fish, and generally relax in one of the pensions on Yeşilada, the small island – now connected to the shore by a causeway – which stands a short distance out into the lake. The town is proud of its carpet and kilim weaving, mostly carried out by descendants of the Yörük nomads, and of its apple orchards and rose gardens, but really what it excels at is helping people to relax. Indeed, once you've crossed the causeway there's little else to do except relax!

History

Founded by the Hittites, Eğirdir was taken by the Phrygians (circa 1200 BC), and was

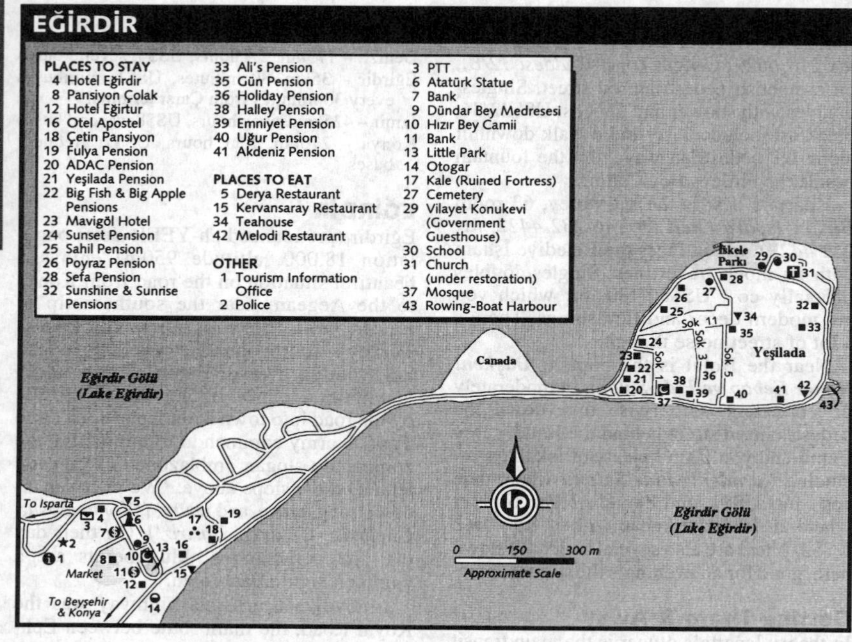

later ruled by the Lydians, captured by the Persians, and conquered by Alexander the Great, followed by the Romans who called it Prostanna. Documents from the period hint that it was large and prosperous, but no excavations have been done at the site, which lies within a large military enclave.

In Byzantine times, as Akrotiri ('steep mountain'), it was the seat of a bishopric. With the coming of the Turks, it became first a Selçuk city (circa 1080-1280), then the capital of a small principality covering the lakes region and ruled by the Hamidoğulları (1280-1381). Most of the historic buildings in town date from the Selçuk and Hamidoğulları periods. The Ottomans took control in 1417.

Under the Turks, Akrotiri was transformed into Eğridir, a word meaning 'crooked' and 'wrong'. In the 1980s, public relations caught up with Eğridir and the town officially changed its name to Eğirdir, which evokes much nicer images, of spinning, sweet flag (a flower) and propolis (a sticky sap used by bees in hive building).

Orientation & Information

Eğirdir stretches along the lakeshore for several kilometres. Its centre is on a point of land jutting into the lake, marked by the statue of Atatürk, the historic Hızır Bey Camii, Dündar Bey Medresesi and the otogar. The Hotel Eğirdir is at the northern side of the town centre. The police station and PTT are in between the Hotel Eğirdir and the Tourism Information Office.

A few hundred metres north-west of the centre, the *kale* (fortress) rises at the beginning of the isthmus and 25-year-old causeway which leads to the Yeşilada peninsula, 1.5km north-west of the otogar. Many of the town's best pensions are on

Yeşilada, or around the kale's crumbling walls. The train station is 3km from the centre of town on the Isparta road.

The Tourism Information Office (☎ 246-311 4388, fax 312 2098) is at 2 Sahilyolu 13, 600m north-west of the otogar on the shore road towards Isparta.

Eğirdir's postal code is 32500.

Things to See

You can walk round Eğirdir's sights in an hour or so, starting from the **Hızır Bey Camii**, a Selçuk construction built as a warehouse in 1237, but restored as a mosque in 1308 by Hızır Bey, a Hamidoğulları emir. Note especially the finely carved wooden doors, and the bits of blue tile still to be seen on the minaret. Otherwise, the mosque is quite simple, with a clerestory above the central hall. The tiles around the mihrab are new.

Facing the mosque is the **Dündar Bey Medresesi**, a theological school built first by the Selçuk sultan Alaeddin Keykubat as a caravanserai in 1218, but converted to a medrese in 1285 at the order of Felekeddin Dündar Bey, a Hamidoğulları emir. It was last restored in 1979, and is now filled with shops. You can enter by the door near the **Atatürk statue**, but the grand main portal is the one facing the mosque. Note the Kufic inscription around the doorway.

A few hundred metres out towards Yeşilada, the massive but crumbling walls of the **kale** rise above the beach. Its foundations may have been laid on the order of Croesus, the 5th century BC King of Lydia, but it was restored by successive rulers, including the Byzantines, Hamidoğulları, Seljuks and Ottomans. On the causeway side of the walls is the **tomb of Devran Dede**, a local Muslim mystic.

Beaches & Boat Tours

Yeşilada has no real beaches to speak of so the best beaches are out of the centre. All of the following beaches have facilities such as changing cabins and food stands or restaurants. **Belediye Plajı** is less than 1km from the centre on the Isparta road in the district called Yazla. **Altınkum Plajı** is several kilometres further north, near the train station, 3km from the centre along the Isparta road. Even further north (about 11km) on the road to Barla is **Bedre Plajı**, perhaps the best of all – 1.5km of sand and water with adequate facilities.

As soon as you arrive in town you'll be besieged with offers of pensions and boat tours. Choosing the first is often choosing the second as well, for each pension owner has a boat or a brother, cousin, or a son with a boat, or a deal with someone who has a boat. Offerings are fairly standard, and how much you enjoy the voyage may depend more on the force of the wind that day than on the boat or owner.

Excursions

When the citizens of Eğirdir take an outing, they usually head 25km south to **Kovada Gölü Milli Parkı** (Lake Kovada National Park), the small (40 sq km) lake filled by the runoff from Eğirdir Gölü. Noted for its flora and fauna, it's a pleasant place for a hike and a picnic. Beyond the lake on the Çandır road are the Çandır canyons.

The easiest way to get to Kovada Gölü is to sign up with a tour from one of the pensions. Out of season taxi tours to Kovada Gölü, including a three-hour wait while you enjoy the scenery, will cost around US$25 per carload. You could also try hitching on a Sunday in summer, when locals make excursions. You may be able to camp on the lakeshore.

Another excursion is to **Zından Mağarası** (Zından Caverns), 30km to the south-west, 1km north of the village of Aksu across a fine Roman bridge. The 1km-long cave has Byzantine ruins at its mouth, lots of stalactites and stalagmites, and a curious room dubbed the Hamam. Bring a torch if you plan to explore more than superficially. Once again the pensions organise tours in summer, or taxis will take you there for about US$25 per carload.

Special Events

Eğirdir celebrates its apples and fish during the first week of September each year with the Golden Apple & Silver Fish Festival.

Places to Stay

Most people want to stay on Yeşilada which essentially consists of about 15 small, family run pensions and restaurants interspersed with second homes for the İstanbul elite who come here for a fortnight every year. Prices are fixed by the municipality; expect to pay around US$8/9 for a double without bath or US$12/13 with private facilities. The island is small enough to walk around in 15 minutes, so you might want to make a quick circuit and weigh up the relative positions and views before deciding.

If you arrive at the start or end of the season, bear in mind that nights can be cold; the pensions with central heating come into their own then. Most places have hot water although you may need to tell your host so they can turn it on for your shower.

If for some reason you prefer to stay on the mainland there are more pensions in the town centre, the most inviting of them clustered near the castle. In the bazaar streets west of the Atatürk statue are some typical small hotels, but they're not as pleasant as the pensions.

In high season you may find Eğirdir pension owners, especially on Yeşilada, biased against single travellers. Even if you offer to pay the double rate for just one person, they may turn you down because they won't be able to sell two meals.

Yeşilada Yeşilada, the 'green island' peninsula, is the best place to stay because of its scenery and ambience. At the time of writing there were no noisy discos or importunate carpet sellers to disturb its tranquillity. Let's hope it stays that way.

As you come onto the island, walk straight ahead with the water on your right. ***Halley Pension*** *(☎ 246-312 3625)* offers airy rooms with showers. Several readers have written to recommend the welcome here and to praise Mehmet and Esna's home-cooked meals.

Uğur Pension *(☎ 246-311 2212)* nearby is of similar quality, if marginally cheaper. Its lakeview rooms have balconies and private showers.

Some of the most pleasant pensions are at the far end of the island. ***Sunrise Pension*** *(☎ 246-311 3032)*, also called the Mustafa, offers excellent lake views and doubles with bath for US$13. Breakfast, taken on the front garden terrace, is included. Adjoining the Sunrise is the very similar ***Sunshine Pension***.

Akdeniz Pension *(☎ 246-311 2432)* has a small restaurant, and friendly family proprietors. ***Sahil Pension*** *(☎ 246-311 2167)* is among the newer ones, and very clean. Top-floor rooms have nice woodwork ceilings. A waterless double costs US$8.

Perhaps the most charming pension if you don't mind forgoing the lake views is Mustafa and Ayşe Gökdal's ***Sefa Pension*** *(☎ 246-311 1877)*, a homey, traditional village house. Though retired, Ayşe Hanım works hard to keep it tidy, and Mustafa provides a warm welcome. Remove your shoes as you enter, in the old-fashioned way. ***Ali's Pension*** *(☎ 246-312 2547)* is another family run place that comes in for lots of praise.

If you turn left at the end of the causeway you'll come to the ***Yeşilada Pansiyon/Big Fish Restaurant*** *(☎ 246-311 4413)* and ***Big Apple Pansiyon Restaurant*** *(☎ 246-311 5808)*. Both these places have biggish restaurants and the Big Apple in particular seems very popular with the locals, always a good sign.

Yeşilada's two hotels – the ***Mavigöl*** and the ***Atabey*** – hardly add to the scenery. You're better off in the pensions.

Mainland As you pass the kale on your way out to Yeşilada, look up to the left to see the ***Fulya Pension*** *(☎ 246-311 2175)*, one of the best in town with its roof terrace, restaurant and panoramic views. Big double rooms with shower and breakfast cost US$7 per person. Down the hill from the Fulya is the five room, friendly and family run ***Çetin Pansiyon*** *(☎ 246-311 2154)*. Rates are US$7/10/15 a single/double/triple for rooms, some with fine lake views. Other places nearby include the ***Mehtap*** *(☎ 246-311 1517)* and the ***Eğirdir*** *(☎ 246-311 2033)*, 'where you live just like one of the family'.

If you prefer to stay in a hotel, the cheapest is the very central ***Pansiyon Çolak*** *(☎ 246-311 4069)*, behind the Hotel Barla across the street from the minaret of the Hızır Bey Camii, where you'll pay US$4/7 a single/double for pretty basic rooms. The lobby is usually full of men gazing avidly at the TV.

Immediately opposite the otogar, ***Hotel Eğirtur*** *(☎ 246-312 3700, fax 311 5598, Güney Sahil Yolu 2)* was another reliable cheapie but was undergoing restoration at the time of writing which probably means higher prices to come.

The three-star, 51 room ***Hotel Eğirdir*** *(☎ 246-311 4992, fax 311 4219)*, facing the water beside the PTT, is the tour-group favourite, with comfortable rooms for US$39/51 a single/double, breakfast included. More reasonably priced is the two-star, 27 room ***Otel Apostel*** *(☎ 246-311 5451, fax 312 3533, Atayolu 7)*, on the left as you head out to Yeşilada. Cheerful rooms, some with lake views, cost US$12/24 a single/double, breakfast included. Check out the view from the rooftop terrace.

Places to Eat

Many Yeşilada pension owners have their own restaurants, usually specialising in fish, but if you don't want to dine 'at home' there's also ***Melodi Restaurant***, next to the Akdeniz Pension at the tip of the island, where every dish except the fish fillet seems to cost US$2. There are good lake views from the dining room.

On the mainland, ***Derya Restaurant***, across the street from the Hotel Eğirdir, is the class act, with outdoor tables set by the water and a sprawling indoor dining room as well. Full meals are likely to cost about US$6. Also grand for this town is ***Kervansaray Restaurant*** *(☎ 248-311 6340)* opposite the Otel Apostel on the lakeshore. Prices aren't bad though; köfte costs just US$2. Both these places are popular with tour groups.

For cheaper kebapçıs, look in the narrow bazaar streets on the opposite side of the Atatürk statue. ***Halil İbrahim Sofrası*** behind Hotel Barla and near Pansiyon Çolak serves *Anadolu ev yemekleri* (Anatolian home cooking), meaning the more traditional Turkish dishes. Dinner will cost you around US$4.

Getting There & Away

Although trains come into Eğirdir from the İzmir-Aydın line via Isparta, you'll probably get here much quicker by bus. If there's no bus leaving straight away for your destination, hop on a minibus to Isparta and catch one there (see Getting There & Away in the earlier Isparta section). Details of some services from Eğirdir follow:

Ankara – 457km, seven hours, US$8
Antalya – 186km, 2½ hours, US$3
Denizli – 203km, three hours, US$5
Isparta – 36km, 30 minutes, US$1; minibuses every 30 minutes
İstanbul – 638km, 11 hours, US$12
İzmir – 418km, seven hours, US$8
Konya – 236km, four hours, US$6
Nevşehir – 443km, eight hours, US$10

BURDUR

Despite its proximity to the saltwater Burdur Gölü, Burdur (population 60,000) is a dreary small town you're only likely to want to visit if you'd like to see the finds from Sagalassos in the museum. Buses from Isparta drop you on the eastern outskirts. Come out of the otogar, turn right and walk along Gazi Caddesi for 15 minutes to the town centre, or catch a Burdur Belediyesi bus from just outside.

To find **Burdur Müzesi**, turn right opposite the Haci Mahmut Bey Camii in Gazi Caddesi. The most impressive exhibits are Hellenistic and Roman objects from Kremna and Sagalassos, although there are also Neolithic bits and pieces from the nearby Hacılar and Kuruçay mounds. One of the finest exhibits is a 2nd century bronze torso of an athlete, but there are also some fine bronze jugs. The museum is open from 8.30 am to noon and from 1.30 to 5.30 pm daily except Monday. Admission costs US$1.

If you need to stay there are several hotels along Gazi Caddesi. One fairly basic place is ***Otel Altın*** *(☎ 248-234 4942, Gazi*

Caddesi 61), where beds cost US$7 per person. Much better value for money is ***Hotel Özeren*** *(☎ 248-233 9607, Gazi Caddesi 51)*. Although not geared up for foreign visitors, this is a smart, clean place, which is a good deal at US$10/16 prices for singles/doubles with showers.

Gazi Caddesi also has plenty of places to eat simple meals. Try ***Özgü Restaurant*** with its frilly chair covers, or the popular ***Ege Lokantası*** which has pictures of beach resorts on its walls. In neither case will a meal cost more than US$4.

BEYŞEHİR

If Burdur disappoints, Beyşehir (population 32,000) is a charming lakeside town with a mixture of traditional and modern houses and one of the best medieval mosques in central Anatolia. From 1071 Beyşehir was a local administrative centre, but its glory days came at the end of the 13th century. Şeyheddin Süleyman Bey was responsible for creating the **Eşrefoğlu Camii**, with its 39 soaring wooden pillars and beautiful blue-tiled mihrab, second only in architectural importance to the Ulu Cami in Afyon. Süleyman is buried beside the mosque. Nearby are a contemporary **medrese** with an impressive portal and the many-domed **Dökumacılar Hanı** (Cloth Hall).

Since the mosque and Beyşehir Gölü are right beside the otogar you could easily visit en route from Eğirdir to Konya or vice versa. If you want to make a longer trip of it, come out of the otogar and bear right onto the main highway. When you reach the bridge, drop down on the left for the town centre with its hotels and restaurants.

At the time of writing the most promising place to stay was ***Beyaz Park Motel*** *(☎ 332-512 3865)*, an old house with a riverside restaurant in Atatürk Caddesi. Singles/doubles with shower cost US$10/16, but if it's still under construction head on down the road to the smaller ***Park Oteli*** *(☎ 332-512 4745)* which overlooks the main square and has simple rooms with bath for US$5/8.

Atatürk Caddesi is also the place to look for food. Popular places include the big ***Kanarya Restaurant***, serving *etli ekmek* (flat bread with minced lamb), and ***Anıt Restaurant***, with spitted chicken.

Beyşehir is two hours by bus from Eğirdir (US$4) and one hour from Konya (US$2).

THE ROAD TO ANTALYA

After exploring the lake district you may want to go south to Antalya. A reasonably good road climbs up and down the mountains, passing through the town of **Ağlasun** after 35km. Here a turn-off on the right leads 7km to dramatically sited **Sagalassos**, an ancient city perched on a plateau backed by the sheer rock of ragged mountains.

If you have your own wheels, it's worth following the narrow but paved road to visit the site. Otherwise you can take a dolmuş to Ağlasun from Isparta and then hitch the last 7km. Since dolmuşes are infrequent, it would be best to make an early start. If you want to stop at Sagalassos on your way to Antalya, it may be possible to arrange for a long-distance bus to pick you up at the road junction afterwards.

Founded by a warlike tribe of the 'People from the Sea', Sagalassos became an important Pisidian city second only to Antioch in Pisidia near Yalvaç. Archaeologists are still excavating the site but the late Hellenistic Fountain House and the Roman library with a fine mosaic floor have recently been rebuilt and opened to the public. There's also a theatre, and a temple with two walls standing.

The next settlement you'll pass through is **Bucak**, 63km south of Isparta. There's nothing here to detain you, but with your own transport you might want to divert 20km east along the Kocaaliler road to the hilltop site of **Kremna** where the historian Zosimus recorded how the Romans besieged a Pisidian bandit who holed up there in 278 AD. If you do get there you'll find scant traces of the walls, of a theatre and of a ceremonial gateway or propylaea.

The road continues to climb and drop until eventually you come to a flatter stretch where, in season, villagers sell bags of olives by the roadside. The last 37km into Antalya is good, solid dual carriageway.

Western Mediterranean Turkey

The southern coast of Turkey is a succession of scenic roads and dramatically sited ancient ruins interspersed with resort towns ranging from charming to maddening. Until the 1970s, parts of this coast could only be explored with a pack animal, boat or sturdy 4WD vehicle. Highway construction during the 1980s changed all that and you can ride easily from Marmaris, where the Aegean and Mediterranean seas meet, to Antakya, near the Syrian border. The advent of convenient transportation has brought on the ruin of some otherwise delightful places as crowds out of all proportion to a town's carrying capacity pour in during the warm months. Other, more remote places are just now coming into their own as enjoyable resorts.

HIGHLIGHTS

- Sailing on a Blue Voyage (boat trip) along the coast
- Walking through the Saklıkent Gorge
- Exploring the ruins at Xanthos or Pınara
- Lazing on Patara beach
- Enjoying a boat ride through the reed beds of Dalyan to İztuzu
- Climbing through the mountainside ruins of Termessos
- Strolling the labyrinthine streets of Kaleiçi (Old Antalya)

Getting There & Away

Air The airport at Dalaman, 120km east of Marmaris and 50km west of Fethiye, receives at least three daily nonstop flights by Turkish Airlines from İstanbul in summer, and one from Ankara. İstanbul Airlines has three flights per week to İstanbul and one to İzmir, as well as six nonstop flights per week to cities in Europe. There are many charter flights as well.

For detailed information on land transport from Dalaman to other points on the Mediterranean coast refer to the Dalaman section.

The other southern coast airports are at Antalya and Adana.

Bus There may be only a few buses a day on the route you want to travel, and service may dwindle and disappear in the late afternoon or early evening, so do your travelling early in the day and relax in the evening. With fewer buses it's especially important to buy your reserved-seat tickets a day or so in advance.

Train There is no rail service south of Söke, Denizli and Isparta; trains do run from Ankara to Adana and (Mersin) İçel, however. See the Getting Around chapter earlier in this book for details.

BODRUM TO MARMARİS

The trip from Bodrum takes you back to Milas, then up into the mountains. The land

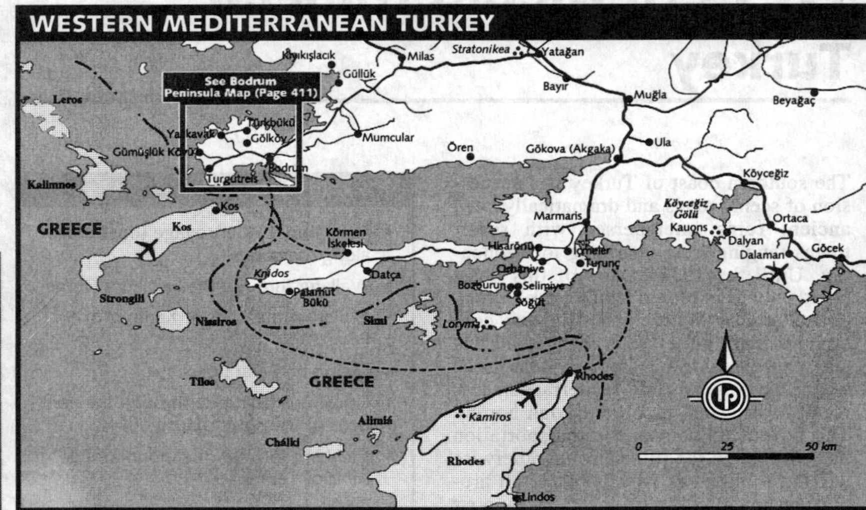

is rich and heavily cultivated, with vast fields of sunflowers and frequent colonies of beehives. In the warm months beekeepers set up stands by the side of the road to sell jars of the translucent, golden, delicately pine-scented honey for which the region is famous.

Stratonikea

Just west of Yatağan at Eskihisar are the ruins of Stratonikea. It was founded under the Seleucids, important under the Romans, and is now threatened by a huge open-cut mine producing soft coal (lignite, *linyit*). Bits of ruin are visible from the road as you pass through, but you must follow the signposted road 1km down to the abandoned former village of Eskihisar to reach the centre of Stratonikea.

It's worth a stop here, especially if you have picnic supplies, as there are two ruined settlements: the Roman city, and the ghost village of Eskihisar, abandoned as the mine tailings crept nearer.

Of Stratonikea, bits of the walls and gates, gymnasium and tomb survive, hidden in the grass and scrub and extending up the slope to the other side of the highway.

The abandoned Turkish village has houses of beautiful stonework and a remarkable absence of modernity: no wires, commercial signs or cars. There is one building, on the shady former village square, maintained and used as a teahouse, which may not be open. At the end of the village road another stone house is the museum/storehouse for archaeological finds from the site. (Admission costs US$1 and is hardly worth it.) Otherwise, Eskihisar is a museum village of Turkish rural life a century ago.

Muğla

If only all of Turkey's provincial capitals were like Muğla (MOO-lah), a compact, attractive city (population 50,000, altitude 625m) with lots of trees set in a rich agricultural valley. An obviously prosperous town, it prides itself on having had Turkey's first female *vali* (governor). Though tourism and farming are important sources of wealth, most people seem to be employed as bureaucrats.

First settled around 1200 BC, Muğla was known as Alinda until Seljuk times. Captured by the Turkish emirs of Menteşe in 1261, it

was seized by the Ottomans in 1390, but was returned to Menteşe control by the victorious Tamerlane in 1402. Mehmet the Conqueror regained control for the Ottomans in 1451. The town seems to have been called Mabolla, Mobella or Mobolia in later Ottoman times, yielding the Muğla of today.

Orientation & Information Muğla's centre is Cumhuriyet Meydanı, the traffic roundabout with the statue of Atatürk. Everything you're likely to need is within walking distance: the otogar a few blocks south-west, the PTT 500m north-west along Recai Güreli Bulvarı, and the bazaar and historic quarter 500m due north along İsmet İnönü Caddesi.

The Tourism Information Office (☎/fax 252-214 3127) is on the north-western side of Cumhuriyet Meydanı, right at the centre.

Muğla's postal code is 48000.

Things to See Go north along İsmet İnönü Caddesi from Cumhuriyet Meydanı to the **Kurşunlu Cami**, built in 1494, repaired in 1853 and with a minaret and courtyard added in 1900. Nearby is the **Ulu Cami** (1344), dating from the time of the Menteşe emirs, though 19th century repairs have rendered its pre-Ottoman design almost unrecognisable.

Continue walking north into the tidy **bazaar**, its narrow lanes jammed with artisans shops and dotted with very basic restaurants. Proceed up the hillside to see Muğla's **Ottoman-era houses**, some still in good condition. Centuries ago there was a small fortress at the top of the hill, but not a stone remains now.

The **Vakıflar Hamamı**, on the corner of Tabakhane and General Mustafa Muğlalı Caddesis, was built in 1258, is still operating and has a separate women's entrance. Near it stands a curiously church-like clocktower.

Advertising itself with imagery shamelessly filched from *Jurassic Park* is Muğla's **Turolian Park Müzesi** which displays finds excavated from fossilbeds at Özlüce in 1993. It's interesting to discover that animals looking much like rhinoceroses once roamed these parts. Admission costs US$0.30 and the museum is open from 9 am to noon and from 1 to 5 pm except on Monday. It's close to the

Belediye and faces the impressive **Konakaltı İskender Alper Kültür Merkezi** which houses small craft shops.

Places to Stay – Budget Follow Tabakhane Caddesi into the bazaar to find the simple ***Doğan Pansiyon*** *(☎ 252-214 3960)*, above a *kiraathane* (coffee house) half a block from the Ulu Cami and with waterless doubles for US$8. Equally basic and cheap is ***Muğla Pansiyon*** *(☎ 252-212 0340, Saatli Kule Caddesi 78)*, entered through a shop front.

Otel Tuncer *(☎ 252-214 8251, Saatli Kule Altı, Kütüphane Sokak 1)*, is a long block north-east of the Kurşunlu Cami (follow the signs). It's relatively clean, fairly quiet, and well priced at US$6/10 a single/double with private shower.

Otel Zeybek *(☎ 252-214 1774, fax 214 3156, Turgutreis Caddesi 5)*, one short block west of the Kurşunlu Cami, is older and a bit noisier, charging US$7 for a bed in a waterless room and US$8 for one with a shower.

Head along Cumhuriyet Caddesi to the large Orgeneral Mustafa Muğlalı İşhanı building and then turn left and cut through the market to find ***Hotel Saray*** *(☎ 252-214 1594, fax 214 3722)*, among the town's newer hotels. Good, clean rooms with shower and views of the market go for US$10/18 a single/double.

Places to Stay – Mid-Range On a quiet street opposite the otogar, the 48 room ***Hotel Yalçın*** *(☎ 252-214 1599, fax 214 1050, Garaj Caddesi 7)*, is Muğla's best value-for-money lodging but is often full. Though three decades old, it's well maintained, charging US$12/24 a single/double for a comfortable room with shower. Breakfast is included.

The three-star ***Hotel Petek*** *(☎/fax 252-214 1897, Marmaris Bulvarı 27)*, 400m east of Cumhuriyet Meydanı, is a good choice for single travellers. Its smaller single rooms, aimed at business travellers, cost only US$16 (although you can land a whole suite for that price when it's quiet), while doubles are US$28, breakfast included.

Muğla's fanciest – and the only place with swimming pool, hamam and sauna – is the three-star ***Hotel Grand Brothers*** *(☎ 252-212 2700, fax 212 2610)*, 1km west of Cumhuriyet Meydanı along the Yatağan-İzmir highway. It's seldom busy and staff are usually willing to discount the posted rates of US$54/70 a single/double.

Places to Eat The bazaar holds numerous köfte grills, pide makers and ready food eateries. Right next to Otel Zeybek, ***Altın Sofra*** is the best kebapçı in the neighbourhood, with full meals for US$5. ***Burhan***, virtually opposite, offers similar food but has a shaded outdoor terrace for dining.

Hotel Yalçın has a terrace restaurant noted for its good food, service and alcoholic beverages. You're likely to spend between US$5 and US$10 here.

Walking along Cumhuriyet Caddesi you'll come to a big office building called the Orgeneral Mustafa Muğlalı İşhanı which is virtually ringed with mid-range eating places. Worth trying are ***Bulvar Ocakbaşı Restaurant*** and ***Köşem Restaurant***, both with indoor and outdoor seating. A good meal should cost no more than US$5 to US$8.

Walk up İsmet İnönü Caddesi to the Kurşunlu Cami and turn right. Hidden away on the right is the aptly named and pleasant ***Saklı Bahçe Restaurant*** ('hidden garden restaurant') where you can tuck into kebaps beneath wisteria and bougainvillea for US$2 to US$4.

Getting There & Away Muğla's busy otogar offers fairly frequent services to all major destinations in the region. For points along the Mediterranean coast east of Marmaris, you may have to take a bus to Marmaris and change there. Details of some services follow:

Aydın – 100km, 1¾ hours, US$3
Bodrum – 110km, two hours, US$3
Dalaman – 86km, 1½ hours, US$2.50
Denizli – 130km, two hours, US$4
Gökova – 28km, 45 minutes, US$0.75
İzmir – 265km, 4½ hours, US$6
İstanbul – 875km, 14 hours, US$14

Köyceğiz – 57km, one hour, US$2
Marmaris – 55km, one hour, US$2
Milas – 57km, one hour, US$2

Gökova (Akyaka)

About 30km north of Marmaris the road comes over the Sakar Geçidi (Sakar Pass, at 670m) to reveal breathtaking views of Gökova Bay from a parachute platform. It then descends by switchbacks into a fertile valley.

At the base of the hill, signs point the way right (west) to the village of Akyaka, often called Gökova after the beautiful bay. Backed by mountains, this fast-growing resort village is built on a hillside which descends to a little grey-sand beach with good bathing beside a river mouth. Instead of the usual high-rises, development here has centred on attractive two-storey houses with wooden balconies. However, as so often, creation of an infrastructure hasn't kept pace with the building work and many roads are still dirt tracks.

Places to Stay & Eat The western side of the waterfront is dominated by ***Otel Yücelen*** *(☎ 252-243 5108, fax 243 5435)*, a beautiful complex largely aimed at tour groups but with attractive rooms set around a pool. It costs US$37/52 a single/double for half-board, although there are also some self-contained bungalows available for US$40.

Inland a bit but with its own pool is the well-signed ***Hotel Engin*** *(☎ 252-243 5727, fax 243 5609)* at the end of Sefa Sokak, offering clean doubles with shower for US$26. Otherwise, there are several small apartment complexes which let rooms as pensions when they're not needed by tour groups. Typical of these are ***Murat*** *(☎ 252-243 5279)* and ***Deniz*** *(☎ 252-243 5553)* in the centre of the village.

A couple of restaurants overlook the beach. ***Kardelen*** serves pizzas while ***Sahil Kafeterya*** has a better choice of dishes. Neither, surprisingly, offers fish. ***Kösem Restaurant***, slightly inland, advertises a few choices for vegetarians.

About 700m beyond the village of Akyaka is an *orman piknik yeri* (forest picnic ground), and another 500m beyond that is the port hamlet of İskele, with a few basic ***restaurants*** serving the tiny beach at the end of the small cove.

Getting There & Away Regular minibuses ply back and forth between Muğla and Akyaka (note that they say 'Gökova' on the front even though the road is signposted to 'Akyaka'). The journey takes 45 minutes and costs US$2.

The Road to Marmaris

From the base of the hill at the Akyaka turnoff, the Marmaris road crosses the floor of the broad river valley beside a magnificent double row – more than 2km long – of great eucalyptus trees. (The old highway went right between the trees; the new one bypasses them on the western side.) At the far end of the trees the road ascends into the hills again before coming down into Marmaris.

MARMARİS

The once-sleepy fishing village of Marmaris (MAHR-mahr-eess, population 18,000) is situated on the marvellous natural harbour where Lord Nelson organised his fleet for the attack on the French at Abukir in 1798. The setting may still be glorious but the picturesque old part of town around the harbour and castle is all but lost now in the sprawl of identikit concrete hotels, pensions and restaurants trailing off to the west. The bazaar is now mostly given over to tourist souvenirs; the streets are thronged with noisy, speeding traffic; and the coastal waters are too redolent to take sitting down if you're at a waterside restaurant and the wind is onshore. If it's an idyllic little resort town you're looking for, take only a brief look at Marmaris, then rush on to Datça or Kaş.

Less cosmopolitan than Kuşadası, and lacking Bodrum's fine castle or Side's impressive ruins, Marmaris still has Turkey's largest and most modern yacht marina and is consequently the country's busiest yacht-charter port.

Once the 'in' place for Turkey's rich and famous, Marmaris has recently taken a dive downmarket in pursuit of the cheap mass

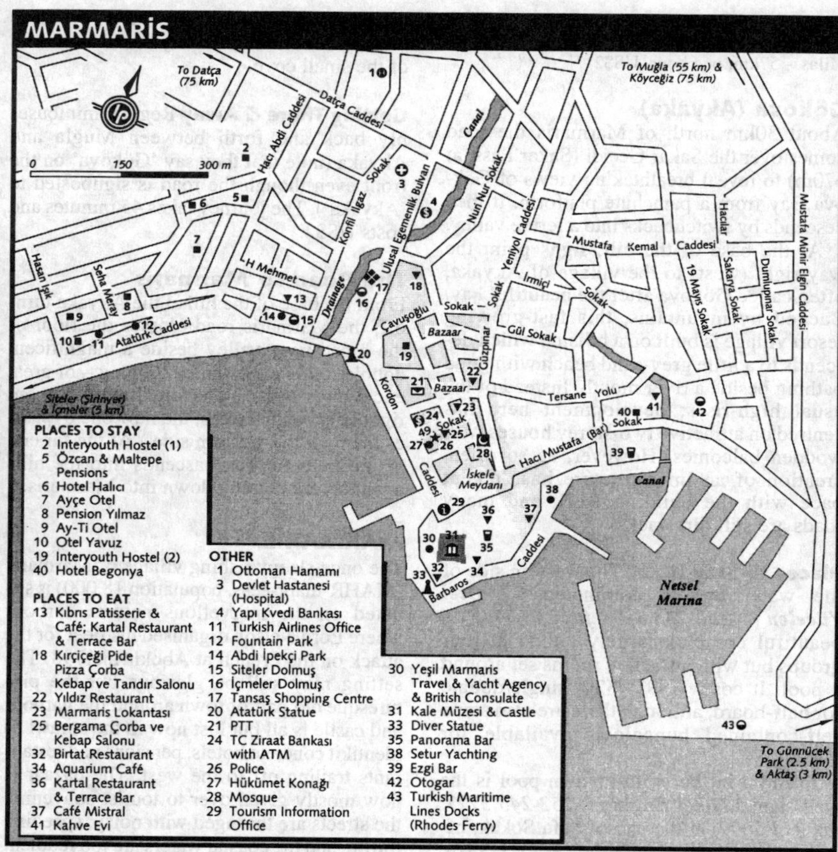

market package holidaymaker. In summer the town's resident population of about 18,000 swells to between 150,000 and 200,000, and that's without the day trippers from Rhodes who – ignoring the dire warnings of Greeks that Turkey is expensive, unfriendly and dangerous – come over to find just the opposite.

Orientation

From the otogar head south through the bazaar for 500m to the İskele Meydanı, the harbourside plaza with the Tourism Information Office. The area behind and above this office is a conservation area with some of Marmaris's few remaining old buildings including its small fortress, now a museum.

Inland from İskele Meydanı stretches the *çarşı*, or shopping district, much of it a pedestrianised covered bazaar.

South and east of İskele Meydanı is the upmarket Netsel Marina and shopping mall. Hacı Mustafa Sokak, otherwise known as Bar Street, runs down from the bridge to the bazaar. Action here keeps going until the early hours.

The waterfront road heading north-west from İskele Meydanı starts out as Kordon Caddesi and then becomes Atatürk Caddesi at the landmark equestrian statue of Atatürk. Heading inland from here is the wide Ulusal Egemenlik (National Sovereignty) Bulvarı, the unofficial dividing line between 'old' Marmaris (to the east) and 'new' Marmaris (to the west).

A few hundred metres west of the Atatürk statue is the small Abdi İpekçi Park, with park benches and children's playground equipment around a dolphin fountain shaded by palms. Yet another few hundred metres south-west is Fountain Park, with its namesake fountain and bits of ancient columns and statues.

Uzunyalı, a beach district full of hotels and tourist restaurants, is 2km to 3km west of İskele Meydanı; Siteler, also called Şirinyer, is about 5km south-west of İskele Meydanı; and İçmeler, another beach resort area, is 8km south-west of the centre. The area immediately inland from Uzunyalı is a badly planned, haphazardly developing wasteland of apartment blocks, small pensions and hotels which extends northwards as far as Armutalan.

About 1km to the south-east is the new harbour for ferries to Rhodes; 3.5km south-east of the centre is Günnücek, a forest park reserve, and just beyond Günnücek is Aktaş, a relatively unspoiled seaside village with several suitable hotels and camping grounds.

Information

The Tourism Information Office (☎ 252-412 1035) is at İskele Meydanı 39. Opening hours are from 8 am to 7.30 pm every day in summer and 8 am to noon and 1 to 5 pm from Monday to Friday in winter.

Marmaris's postal code is 48700.

Money & Postal Services Banks with ATMs are situated along the shore north and west of the Tourism Information Office; others are inland, in the bazaar. The Vakıf Bank on 44 Sokak in the bazaar has an automatic currency exchange machine: you put in cash dollars or deutschmarks and out come Turkish liras. There's a Yapı Kredi Bankası branch 1½ blocks inland along Ulusal Egemenlik Bulvarı, on the right-hand side.

The PTT is open until 6 pm but the phones are accessible 24 hours a day.

British Consulate The consulate (☎ 252-412 6486, in emergencies 262 7661 or 262 5023, fax 412 5077) is in the Yeşil Marmaris Travel Agency & Yacht Management building at Barbaros Caddesi 249, facing the harbour. It's open from Monday to Friday from 9.30 am to noon and also Monday to Thursday from 2.30 to 5 pm in summer.

Beaches

There's a narrow beach along Kordon Caddesi but the water is badly polluted. Better, cleaner ones are out of town near the fancy hotels, although they're all small. Still others can be reached by excursion boat.

Marmaris Kale Müzesi

The small castle on the hill behind the Tourism Information Office was built during the reign of Sultan Süleyman the Magnificent. The sultan massed 200,000 troops here for the attack and seige of Rhodes, defended by the Knights of St John, in 1522. The fortress is now the Marmaris Kale Müzesi (Fortress Museum) open from 8 am to noon and 1 to 5.30 pm daily; admission costs US$1. Exhibits are predictably nautical, historical, ethnographic and unexciting, though the building itself and the views are nice, and the resident free-ranging peacocks and tortoises delight children. To reach it, from the harbour end of the bazaar follow the signs to the Kartal Restaurant and the Panorama Bar up Eski Cami Sokak, then continue uphill to the castle.

Menzilhane

Behind and to the left of the Tourism Information Office is the stone *menzilhane*, an Ottoman 'pony express' way-station also built by Sultan Süleyman the Magnificent in 1545, its appearance now ruined by raucous bars.

Hamams

A new 'Ottoman' bath for tourists has opened off Datça Caddesi across from the Devlet Hastanesi (government hospital). In addition to the usual accoutrements of a Turkish bath, this one boasts a sauna and alarmingly cold 'shock' pool. It's open from 8 am to 11 pm daily and charges a hefty US$16 for a bath, including assisted wash, massage and drink afterwards. If you find the massage too cursory, you can have a 20-minute massage with baby oil for another US$8. The bath is mixed and all the masseurs are male.

The older hamam in the bazaar is still open daily and charges an all-inclusive US$12, still steep by non-Marmaris standards.

Atatürk Statue

The equestrian statue of Atatürk at the foot of Ulusal Egemenlik Bulvarı provides a quick lesson in Turkish civic history. Plaques on the plinth bear the sayings 'Türk Öğün Çalış Güven' ('Turk! Be Proud, Work, Trust') and 'Ne Mutlu Türküm Diyene' ('What joy to him who says, 'I am a Turk''). Both sayings were meant to dispel the feeling of inferiority towards Europeans suffered by Ottoman Turks. Another plaque bears the words 'Egemenlik Ulusundur' ('Sovereignty belongs to the Nation'), Atatürk's assertion that the Turkish people, and not the imperial House of Osman, were in charge of the country's destiny. Yet another reads 'Vatan Sana Minettardır' ('Your Country is Grateful to You'), a tribute to those who fought in the War of Independence – especially Atatürk. The final plaque in this statuary history lesson reads 'İzindeyiz' ('We Follow in Your Footsteps') – the 'footsteps' being the secular, democratic, westernised ones of Atatürk of course.

Boat Tours

Besides the daily boats and hydrofoils to Rhodes, numerous motorsailers along the waterfront offer day tours of the harbour, its beaches and islands. Summer departures are usually at 9 am. Before deciding on your boat talk to the captain about where the excursion goes, what it costs, whether lunch is included and, if so, what's on the menu. A day's outing usually costs around US$16 to US$20 per person, much less in off-season when boats also leave later in the day.

The most popular daily excursions are to Dalyan and Kaunos or to the bays around Marmaris. In the latter case beware an extended lunch stop at Amos Bay where the only eating options available are extremely expensive. Pack a picnic or hang on until you get to Turunç Bay where there's more of a choice.

You can also take longer, more serious boat trips to Datça and Knidos, well out along the hilly peninsula west of Marmaris.

Scuba Diving

There are several places in Marmaris where you can learn to dive on short courses for between US$35 and US$65, depending on the time of year. Look for the Marmaris Diving Centre on a boat moored near the Tourism Information Office. There are several others nearby.

Festivals

The Marmaris Yacht Festival is usually held in the second week in May. Though this is a private convention for yacht owners and brokers, anyone interested in yachts will enjoy seeing all the boats in the harbour and marina. Race Week, at the end of October, provides another chance to see the harbour full of yachts in full sail. For information contact the Marmaris International Yacht Club (☎ 252-412 3835), PO Box 132, 48700 Marmaris.

Places to Stay

Although Marmaris has several hundred hotels and pensions, the cheaper places are being squeezed out by the relentless rise in the number of hotels serving package holidaymakers. The cheapies that remain may be fairly central but often they're noisy. There are several moderately priced hotels a short walk from İskele Meydanı. Most of the really expensive hotels are well around the bay from the town, some as far out as İçmeler.

A Blue Voyage

Between the world wars, writer Cevat Şakir Kabaağaç lived in Bodrum and wrote an account of his idyllic sailing excursions along Turkey's Carian (southern Aegean) and Lycian (western Mediterranean) coasts, an area completely untouched by tourism at the time. Kabaağaç called his book *Mavi Yolculuk* (Blue Voyage), a name now co-opted for any cruise along these shores.

Marmaris is a good place to charter a *gulet* (a Turkish wooden yacht) to explore the coastline. There are several ways to do this. If you don't want to do the crewing yourself and can get a party of up to 16 people together, you can charter a gulet complete with skipper and cook. In May, the cheapest month, chartering the whole boat is likely to cost between US$400 and US$1000 per day, with prices rising to US$800 to US$1750 in August, the most expensive month. Meals might cost an extra US$25 per person per day. Obviously the more people to share the costs, the less each individual will have to pay.

If you're not able to put together a large enough group of people to charter the entire boat, you can still opt for a cabin charter where you just pay for the berths you use, about US$500 to US$600 per person per week, all meals included.

Finally, experienced sailors can opt for a bareboat charter where you do the crewing (and cooking) yourself. To hire a bareboat sleeping six to 11 passengers for one week in spring costs US$1400 to US$3400. In high summer expect to pay US$1900 to US$4900. Extra charges for one-way journeys, employing a skipper, cleaning up at the end of the voyage etc can bump up the price even more.

For more information on yachting and lists of yachts and brokers, contact the Marmaris International Yacht Club (☎ 252-412 3835), PO Box 132, 48700 Marmaris. You can usually book through a yacht broker or travel agency near your home. If not, contact Yeşil Marmaris (☎ 252-412 6486, fax 412 5077, yesilmarmaris@iris.com.tr), Barbaros Caddesi 118 (PO Box 8) 48700 Marmaris. For bareboat charters, contact Setur Bareboat Charter (☎ 252-412 6530, fax 412 4608), Barbaros Caddesi 223, 48700 Marmaris.

Places to Stay – Budget

The Tourism Information Office should be able to help you locate one of the few remaining *ev pansiyonları* (home pensions), where you rent a room in a private home for US$8 to US$12 a double depending on facilities. Some rooms have three and four beds – good for families. At quiet times of the year you may be met at the otogar by people offering rooms in ev pansiyonları. Bear in mind that the families renting these rooms are unlikely to speak anything other than Turkish.

For a look at the cheapest accommodation, go to the district called Kemeraltı Mahallesi. Walk along the waterfront to Abdi İpekçi Park. Turn inland just past the park and left at the first street, then right and past the Ayçe Otel. Cross a footbridge and the ***Maltepe Pension*** *(☎ 252-412 1629)*, with beds for US$10 per person in a room with private shower. The bigger ***Özcan Pension*** *(☎ 252-412 7761, Çam Sokak 3)*, next door charges similar prices.

Marmaris has two Interyouth hostels, neither of which require you to have a hostel card. Keep walking inland from the Maltepe, cross the road and look for the ***Interyouth Hostel (1)*** *(☎/fax 252-412 6432, İyiliktaş Mevkii 14)*, offering beds in dormitory rooms for US$6, a roof-terrace bar, laundry, restaurant, baggage storage room and free hot showers. There are also bathless 'pension' rooms for US$13 a double. Another way to find this place: from the big Tansaş shopping centre on Ulusal Egemenlik Bulvarı, go west on General Mustafa Muğlalı Caddesi 200m past the Türk Telekom building (on the right). Just past Türk Telekom, also on the right, is the hostel.

The other ***Interyouth Hostel (2)*** *(☎ 252-412 3687, fax 412 7823, Tepe Mahallesi, 42 Sokak 45)*, is deep in the bazaar right at the town centre. Prices and services are similar.

Pension Yılmaz *(☎ 252-412 3754)*, is on 107 Sokak just inland from the little park that's just east of the Turkish Airlines office (124 Sokak goes alongside the park). For US$15 a double and being this close to the centre, it's a real find.

For other low-priced lodgings, take a Siteler/Turban minibus from the centre to the district called Siteler or Şirinyer; get out at the Art Marmaris Hotel. Just past this hotel along Barbaros (or Turban) Caddesi are several small hotels patronised mostly by Turkish families, and thus relatively cheap: ***Birol Apart-Motel*** *(☎ 252-412 1054, fax 412 5289)*, at No 24 rents double rooms with private bath and breakfast for US$24; ***Yüzbaşı Otel*** *(☎ 252-412 2762, fax 412 6512)* at No 22 is a step up in comfort and price, with a small swimming pool and sea-view balconies on its front rooms, which cost US$28 to US$32 with breakfast; ***Sembol Motel*** *(☎ 252-412 1356)* and ***Villa Erel*** *(☎ 252-412 1123)*, with prices and comforts similar to the Birol; and ***Tümer Hotel*** *(☎ 252-412 4413, fax 412 1832)* at No 69, where double rooms with bath in a family run hotel cost US$46 with breakfast. There's also a small swimming pool.

If the three-star ***Hotel Nuhoğlu*** *(☎/fax 252-412 9577, Barbaros Caddesi 34)*, has a room free, they'll rent it to you for US$35 a double with breakfast, but they're often booked solid by Austrian tour operators in summer.

Finally, there are several suitable hotels in Aktaş, 4km south-east of İskele Meydanı, including ***Hotel Panorama*** *(☎ 252-412 7036)* and ***Hotel Kartal*** *(☎ 252-412 2164, fax 412 4555)*, although they may be filled by British tour groups.

Camping Camping areas are disappearing as the building boom races on. ***Berk Camping*** *(☎ 252-412 4171)*, on Barbaros Caddesi in Siteler/Şirinyer has tent sites, little cabins and all services for about US$6 per person (more for the cabins). ***Pekuz Camping***, on the shore in Aktaş, 4km south-east of İskele Meydanı, charges a bit less, as does, ***Dimet Camping***, with tent sites in dense shade just inland from Pekuz Camping.

Places to Stay – Mid-Range

If you're in Europe and planning to stay more than a few days in a mid-range Marmaris hotel in summer, check the price of package holidays on sale through travel agencies before booking. The market is so competitive that these may work out cheaper than buying a flight and then booking the room yourself. In July and August most of these hotels are block-booked for groups and it is often difficult to find a room for just one or two nights.

The aptly named ***Hotel Halıcı*** *(☎ 252-412 1683, fax 412 9200, Cem Sokak 1)*, or 'carpet-dealer hotel', is run by a firm which owns three carpet shops in Marmaris' bazaar. Rooms set amid fine gardens in a relatively quiet location cost US$60 a double with breakfast.

Around the corner from Abdi İpekçi Park at 64. Sokak 11, is ***Ayçe Otel*** *(☎ 252-412 3136, fax 412 3705)*. Small, quiet and comfortable, it's usually booked by tour groups. Rooms rent for US$25/35 a single/double.

Otel Yavuz *(☎ 252-412 2937, fax 412 4112)*, further west along Atatürk Caddesi has three-star comforts, 55 rooms and a small swimming pool on top of the building. Your room (with bath) may well have a balcony with a view of the bay. Depending on season the price is US$32 to US$44 a single or US$45 to US$58 a double for B&B.

Around the corner from the Yavuz and inland one block at Hacı Selim Sokak 27, is ***Ay-Ti Otel*** *(☎ 252-412 3056)* offering clean rooms in a convenient location for US$32/40.

Hotel Begonya *(☎ 252-412 4095, fax 412 1518, Hacı Mustafa Sokak 71)*, is a delightful place, with a courtyard filled with plants and birdsong. There are heaps of bars along this street which is good news if you're in for a big night but if you value your sleep, look elsewhere.

Places to Stay – Top End

The first luxury hotel to be built in Marmaris decades ago was ***Otel Lidya*** *(☎ 252-412 2940, fax 412 1478)* in Siteler just past Uzunyalı. Its aging comforts are now superceded by the many luxury palaces nearby. It has the advantage of mature gardens with shady palms in front of the hotel, many luxury hotel services, and sea-view guest rooms priced at only US$60/75 a single/double in summer.

Places to Eat

Marmaris has something in the region of 3000 eating places so you certainly won't starve. There are concentrations of restaurants all along the harbour, along Kordon Caddesi and out along the shore to Uzunyalı, with more places to eat in the bazaar and along Hacı Mustafa Sokak. Small restaurants open, operate and go out of business at an alarming rate. The following suggestions merely scratch the surface.

Places to Eat – Budget

For the very cheapest fare, head for the bazaar and the streets beyond it looking for 'untouristy', local Turkish places selling pide, kebaps and ready food. Find where the farmers eat and you'll save 40% on the price of your meal.

Head for the PTT (post office) on 51 Sokak in the bazaar. Just inland from it are several good, cheap restaurants including ***Sofra***, ***Marmaris Restaurant*** and ***Liman Restaurant*** just off 51 Sokak at 40 Sokak 32. Any of these places will serve you a good lunch or dinner for US$4 to US$7 or so. Even further inland, ***Yıldız Restaurant*** is, if anything, less crowded and a bit cheaper.

Bergama Çorba ve Kebap Salonu, also in the bazaar on 44 Sokak at 49 Sokak, on the north-eastern (inland) side of the police station, is another good choice.

Aquarium Café on Barbaros Caddesi is always full because it's at the centre of the action. Ask prices before ordering, and you'll do alright with a drink here.

Walk inland from the Atatürk statue along Ulusal Egemenlik Bulvarı and turn right opposite the big Tansaş shopping centre to find ***Kırçiçeği Pide Pizza Çorba Kebap ve Tandır Salonu***. Its name reflects the menu and it's always crowded with locals who like the food and the prices. A bowl of soup and a baked pide need cost no more than US$3.

For pastries and drinks near Abdi İpekçi Park, try ***Kıbrıs Patisserie & Café***, which serves ice cream, cappuccino and pastries.

Places to Eat – Top End

Waterfront restaurants to the south and east of the Tourism Information Office have pleasant outdoor dining areas but prices are inevitably higher than those inland and the extra money pays for the setting rather than the quality of the food. Assume you'll spend between US$10 and US$20 per person for a full meal with wine.

Birtat Restaurant *(☎ 252-412 1076, Barbaros Caddesi 19)* has indoor and outdoor seating and full meals based on meat main courses for US$12 to US$16, or fish for US$18 to US$24. Portions of seafood are small and, as at most of the places facing the harbour, drinks are expensive.

Further around the harbour toward the marina, the trendy ***Café Mistral*** has live jazz most nights and a varied, interesting menu which includes six vegetarian dishes. It's a bit quiet here, and a good dinner might cost US$14 to US$20.

If the crowds and stench of the water along the harbour prove unpleasant, follow the signs up to Kartal Restaurant & Terrace Bar. You'll pass a number of small restaurants with fine views of the town, quiet dining rooms and terraces and moderate prices. The owner of ***Kartal Restaurant & Terrace Bar*** *(☎ 252-412 3308)*, on Eski Cami Sokak, has been in the restaurant business for more than three decades. Come early to get a table with a good view. A three-course meal with drinks might cost US$12 to US$18.

Entertainment

Marmaris may not yet have a disco to match Bodrum's Halikarnas, but Hacı Mustafa Sokak (aka Bar Street) nevertheless boasts a good supply of bar-discos which keep the music pumping until the early hours. Places on the eastern side of the street usually have terrace seating areas overlooking the harbour. *Damsız Girilmez* means 'No admittance to men without ladies' but this may apply mostly to local Romeos.

The fashions, inspirations, owners and names change from each year to the next. This year's ***Casablanca, Night Park, Downtown Club, Ambience Bar, Horizon*** and ***Beverly Hills*** may be gone, but if the ***Havana Dance Bar*** is still around, it's the place to go for dance music with a Caribbean beat.

The Back Street has live music in a garden setting most nights and attracts a young crowd, or ***Davy Jones's Locker*** opposite, which is the 'in' place with the sailing fraternity.

Amid all the bars churning out western music you might think there was no room for anything traditionally Turkish, but head down to the yacht harbour and hunt out ***Ezgi Bar*** which has live Turkish music nightly and draws rapturous local audiences.

Kahve Evi, also known as the Marmaris Internet Café *(☎ 252-413 7237, cafe@prizma .net.tr, www.marmariscafe.com.tr)*, Köylü Pazarı Karşısı, near the otogar, provides coffee, tea, drinks and Internet connections.

Finding somewhere for a quiet drink is a tall order but my favourite place for a sundowner is ***Panorama Bar*** with views that more than justify its name. Drinks cost a stiff US$4 for domestic and US$5 for imported stuff. To find it, follow the signs from the kale end of the bazaar uphill on Eski Cami Sokak.

Things to Buy

Marmaris has several shops selling excellent local honey in jars priced from US$2 to US$5, or in larger tins for US$6 to US$12. Well worth visiting is Nur-Bal, 51 Sokak 9-C, one block inland from the PTT on the same side of the street. A few steps further inland, on the opposite side, Hobim (My Hobby), 51 Sokak 8-D, sells honey, alongside Turkish delight and other traditional Turkish sweets.

Because the boats from Rhodes bring hordes of shoppers on day trips, Marmaris merchants stock everything: onyx, leather clothing and accessories, carpets, jewellery, crafts, Turkish delight, meerschaum pipes and baubles, sandals, apple tea powder, copper and beach wear.

Getting There & Away

Air The region's principal airport is at Dalaman, 120km east of Marmaris. A Havaş bus (US$7) runs from the Turkish Airlines office in Marmaris to Dalaman airport, departing about 3½ hours before each Turkish Airlines flight. Alternatively, catch one of the hourly buses to Dalaman from Marmaris' otogar, then take a short but relatively expensive taxi ride to the airport.

A small airport is being built at Ula, 40km north of Marmaris. When finished, it will be able to receive aircraft seating up to 50 passengers.

See the Dalaman section for flight details. Turkish Airlines (☎ 252-412 3751, fax 412 3753), Atatürk Caddesi 26-B, is a short stroll west of İskele Meydanı along the waterfront. İstanbul Airlines (☎ 252-412 1443, fax 412 6747), Kenan Evren Bulvarı 88/A, is in Siteler.

Bus Marmaris' otogar is just north-west of the Netsel Marina, 500m north of İskele Meydanı. There are also convenient bus company ticket offices for Pamukkale, Kamil Koç, Uludağ and Metro on and off Ulusal Egemenlik Bulvarı just inland from the Tansaş shopping centre.

In summer, buses roll in and out of town all day, but in winter services drop to what's required by a small farming town. Destinations include:

Adana – 1025km, 16 hours, US$20; change buses at Antalya

Ankara – 780km, 10 hours, US$15; a dozen buses daily in summer

BOTH PHOTOGRAPHS BY NEIL WILSON

Western Mediterranean Fethiye is a bustling, thriving town with colourful fishing boats dotting the busy harbour by day and a lively nightlife scene.

TOM BROSNAHAN

KIMBERLY GRANT

Western Mediterranean Top: A *gulet* yacht glides along the pine-clad Mediterranean coast.
Bottom: It's simple but it's home ... a typical house in Kaş.

Antalya – 590km, seven hours, US$11; a few buses daily
Bodrum – 165km, three hours, US$7; hourly buses or minibuses in summer
Dalaman – 120km, 1½ to two hours, US$4; hourly buses in summer
Datça – 75km, 1½ hours, US$3.50; hourly buses or minibuses in summer
İstanbul – 900km, 14 hours, from US$21; a dozen buses daily in summer
İzmir – 320km, 4½ hours, US$9; hourly buses in summer
Fethiye – 170km, three hours, US$5; hourly buses or minibuses in summer
Kaş – 305km, four hours, US$8; several buses daily
Köyceğiz – 75km, one hour, US$2; at least nine buses or minibuses daily in summer
Muğla – 55km, one hour, US$2; frequent buses and dolmuşes
Pamukkale – 185km, four hours, US$8.50; via Muğla and Tavas, several buses daily

Boats – to/from Rhodes Hydrofoils operate to Rhodes daily in summer, taking 45 minutes to reach Rhodes Town. Tickets cost US$45 one way or same-day return and US$75 open-date return. Buy your ticket at any travel agency in Marmaris (you'll see them along Kordon Caddesi) at least a day in advance. Entering Turkey from Rhodes on a one-way ticket you'll have to pay a US$10 port tax. When returning from Rhodes to Turkey, you may have to buy a new visa if you've stayed overnight but not if you went on a day trip; it depends on your nationality and the type of visa (single or multiple entry) you were given when you entered the country.

In high summer motorboats also run to and from Rhodes three times a week, taking 2½ hours for the voyage. Turkish boats depart from Marmaris in the morning, returning from Rhodes in the late afternoon; Greek boats depart from Rhodes in the morning, returning from Marmaris in the late afternoon. Some of these ferries are capable of carrying cars as well as passengers. Most places selling hydrofoil tickets also sell boat tickets (US$35 one way, US$40 same-day return, US$50 open-date return) and these too must be booked at least a day in advance.

Getting Around

Dolmuş minibuses run frequently around the bay, beginning from a lot two and a half blocks inland from the Atatürk statue on Ulusal Egemenlik Bulvarı. They go to Uzunyalı (3km, US$0.40), Turban-Siteler (4km, US$0.40) and İçmeler (8km, US$1), as well as to more distant towns on the Reşadiye and Daraçya peninsulas such as Turunç, Hisarönü, Bozburun and Orhaniye. The dolmuş for Datça leaves from in front of the Pamukkale bus office just inland from the Atatürk statue.

'Taxi' boats run from a dock just west of the Tourism Information Office to İçmeler for US$3 per person.

Several places along Kemal Seyfettin Elgin Bulvarı rent out bikes and motorcycles. Aday's bicycle rental costs US$11. The smallest motorcycle costs about US$38 a day, not much less than the cost of renting a five-person car.

İçmeler

Once a separate fishing village, İçmeler, 8km west and south around the bay, is now little more than a beach suburb of Marmaris. However, it feels a much classier place, not least because it has been better planned, with roads laid out to a plan, and a relatively clean beach and sea.

These days İçmeler is nearly as popular with package holidaymakers as Marmaris itself so there's not a lot of cheap accommodation.

REŞADİYE & DARAÇYA PENINSULAS

A narrow, mountainous finger of land stretches westward from Marmaris for about 100km into the Aegean between the Greek islands of Kos and Rhodes. Known in ancient times as the Peraea, it is now called the Reşadiye Peninsula, Datça Peninsula or Hisarönü; its southern branch is known as the Daraçya or Loryma Peninsula, with the ruins of the ancient city of Loryma at its southern tip.

A road twists its way from Marmaris westward to the tip of the peninsula, but a

WESTERN MEDITERRANEAN

voyage by boat is usually preferable. Besides the joy of sailing near the peninsula's pine-clad coasts and anchoring in some of its hundreds of secluded coves, visitors come here to explore Bozburun, a small fishing village 56km south-west of Marmaris; Datça, a fast-growing resort town about 75km west of Marmaris; and the hamlet and ruins of Knidos, the ancient city of the great sculptor Praxiteles, 35km west of Datça.

Leaving Marmaris by road, you immediately climb into the mountains of the peninsula. After about 20km the road divides. Go straight on for Datça and Knidos, turn left (south) for Bozburun.

The Road to Bozburun

At the time of writing, the seaside village of Bozburun was a perfect antidote to the tourist madness of Marmaris. Fishing and farming still employ most villagers, though some work in bars and shops set up to serve the yachters who drop anchor in Sömbeki Körfezi (Bay). Though there's no good beach, there are rocks from which to swim, many interesting walks in the surrounding countryside and boat excursions.

The road into Bozburun is being widened and improved. When it can handle large buses, the village will be utterly altered.

Travelling 2km south from the main road from Marmaris brings you to the village of Hisarönü. **Orhaniye**, set on a beautiful bay, is 8km further along. You might want to stop for a meal here at ***İskele Motel, Café-Bar & Swimming Pool*** *(☎ 252-487 1013)* or ***Palmiye Motel & Restaurant*** *(☎ 252-487 1134, fax 487 1167)*.

About 9km south of Orhaniye is an intersection with roads to Bayır and Bozburun. Follow the Bozburun road to reach the village of **Selimiye**, a traditional boatbuilders' village on its own lovely bay facing an islet topped by bits of ancient ruin. The piles of rough-hewn boards which you see here and there will be turned into shapely sea craft through the artisans' magic.

Though backed by craggy mountains and with no good beach to speak of, Selimiye has a few pleasant cheap restaurants supplying the yachters, including ***Balıkçı Kardeşler***, ***Falcon*** and ***Sardunya*** restaurants and ***Can Pide Salonu***. The inexpensive ***Selim Han Apart Hotel*** *(☎ 252-446 4069)* has a swimming pool and restaurant; ***Motel Begonya*** *(☎ 252-446 4202)* was under construction at the time of writing.

Bozburun

From Selimiye the road twists onward until, after 12km, you reach Bozburun, a yachters' port with 'Yacht Service' and 'Market' shops to serve the boat people, a few small pensions and restaurants, and a PTT. Some of the shops do currency exchange.

Things to Do Bozburun is not known for its beaches, but you can swim from the rocks by the *ilkokul* (primary school) south-east of the bust of Atatürk.

At the moment there are not enough tourists to justify regular excursion boats but you can charter private vessels to explore the surrounding bays.

Places to Stay Bozburun's simple pensions charge from US$5 to US$10 per person, depending upon season and demand.

In town ***Keskin Pension*** *(☎ 252-456 2255)* is on the northern side of the harbour, convenient to the centre. The pensions along the shore from the Atatürk statue are quieter, and have better sea views. First along the shore is the well-kept ***Yılmaz Pension*** *(☎ 252-456 2167)*, and just beyond it the welcoming ***Nail Pension*** *(☎ 252-456 2134)*, similar to the Yılmaz down to the chairs and tables on its porch from where you can enjoy views of the bay.

There are several similar pensions further along this beach such as ***Uslu*** *(☎ 252-456 2006)*, ***Yılmaz Kaptan*** *(☎ 252-456 2112)*, the upscale ***Naturland***, ***Yalçın*** and finally ***Pembe Yunus*** *(☎ 252-456 2154)*, 250m beyond the ilkokul. Pembe Yunus (Pink Dolphin) has a roof terrace for sunning and dining, and the inimitable Ms Fatma Doğanyılmaz as a manager. She will rent you one of her clean but basic, shower-equipped rooms for US$12/20 a single/double, breakfast and dinner included.

Places to Eat Of the restaurants, ***Sahil Pide ve Pastane***, just across the street to the north-east of the Atatürk statue, is among the cheapest, though ***Yaşlı Balıkçı*** and ***Paradise*** on the main promenade are better, though ***Naturland*** gets the prize for 'coolth' and ***Roguish Osman's Place*** for the best name. Full meals are not as cheap as you might imagine because of the need to import most of the raw materials by truck or boat.

Getting There & Away Minibuses leave Bozburun for Marmaris (US$3) at 6.30 and 11 am and 12.30 pm. Return trips from Marmaris are in the afternoon, the last being at 7 pm. Services are most frequent in summer. At other times of year day trips from Marmaris can be tricky.

There are also minibuses to Orhaniye from Marmaris, and to Selimiye from Bozburun.

Datça

About 50km past the Bozburun turn-off is the village of Reşadiye, where a left (south) turn heads for Datça, while the main road continues westward to Knidos.

Orientation Once a small port village, Datça is overflowing onto the surrounding hillsides. The main street, İskele Caddesi, runs downhill from the highway, passing several teahouses, restaurants and the PTT before arriving at the Tourism Information Office and a small roundabout. Immediately before the roundabout, Buxerolles Sokak on the right has several small pensions.

After the roundabout İskele Caddesi forks left and runs to Turgut Özal Meydanı, the main square with a market and otogar. From there it continues to the harbour, with a cluster of small pensions on the left, finally running out at the end of a short peninsula, once an island called Esenada. Just after the main square, Kargı Yolu turns right, skirts Taşlık Plajı and climbs up the hill, past the New Castle disco.

Some buses drop you at the otogar on the highway next to the jandarma post. If that happens, turn right and follow the highway around until you see the signs for Şehir Merkezi. It's about 1km from the otogar to the main square.

Datça has two small beaches: Kumluk Plajı, tucked away behind the shops on İskele Caddesi; and Taşlık Plajı, running west from the end of the harbour.

Information Datça's Tourism Information Office (☎ 252-712 3163) is next to the main square and keeps a list of all the accommodation options. It's open daily from May to October but closes on weekends in winter.

Datça's Devlet Hastanesi (Government Hospital) is 100m north of the Öğretmen Evi hotel on Kumluk Plajı.

Things to See Datça has no specific sights but it's a pretty place to hang around and relax. With its fine yacht-filled harbour, it's a bit like a smaller, quieter, laid-back version of Marmaris.

In the summer there are daily excursion boats to Knidos and to the Greek island of Simi, with less frequent boats to Kos and Rhodes too.

Datça's nightlife certainly can't match Marmaris' but that's not to say it's dead. Apart from the ***New Castle*** disco in Kargı Yolu, there are also three very noisy bars at the town end of the harbour and the rather more restrained ***Eclipse Bar*** at the peninsula end.

Places to Stay – Budget Datça has about 50 small pensions with a total of perhaps 400 or 500 beds costing around US$5 to US$8. Among the quieter pensions are the ***Karaoğlu*** (kah-RAH-oh-loo) *(☎ 252-712 3079)* and ***Huzur*** *(☎ 252-712 3052)*, both on a bluff above Kumluk Plajı. The Karaoğlu has a garden cafe, the Huzur a pleasantly shady breakfast terrace. The nearby ***Kader*** *(☎ 252-712 3553)* is also good, but the ***Kaya*** may suffer from traffic noise in high season.

Quiet places on Buxerolles Sokak include ***Aşkın Pansiyon*** *(☎ 252-712 3406, Buxerolles Sokak 8)* and the adjoining, similar ***Sahil Pansiyon*** and nearby ***Gülhan Pansiyon*** *(☎ 252-712 3634)*.

On İskele Caddesi itself ***Tuna Pansiyon*** *(☎ 252-712 3931)* has comfortable twin rooms with bath and balcony for US$11. Rooms at the back with sea views are particularly good value and quieter than the front rooms. Ask at the Mutlu Market about room availability.

Esenada Oteli (☎ *252-712 3579*), almost at the end of the main street, out on the peninsula, is very run-down, but in a fine location next door to the town's first fancy hotel. The Esenada charges only US$8/12 for a double/triple room without running water. If there is nobody at the reception desk, ask in the Çimen Kardeşler clothing shop next door.

Deniz Motel (☎ *252-712 3038*), facing Turgut Özal Meydanı, charges US$15 for a double room with bath and breakfast.

Camping If you walk along Taşlık Plajı on the eastern bay you'll come to *Camping Ilıca* where a tent site costs US$3 per person in high season (less in low season). There are also a few wooden bungalows with beds for US$6 and a restaurant and picnic area.

Off the main road to Marmaris, *Surf Camping* (☎ *252-712 2355*) is on a stretch of beach good for windsurfing.

Places to Stay – Mid-Range *Hotel Club Dorya* (☎ *252-712 3593, fax 712 3303*), is out on the peninsula at the end of the main street amid lovely gardens. There's a pool at the front and swimming off the rocks at the back. Rooms with bath and perhaps a view cost US$35/$48 a single/double, including breakfast.

At the eastern end of Kumluk Plajı, *Datça Öğretmen Evi* (☎ *252-712 2341*), or Teachers House, is a teachers' social club and hotel and a big tan eyesore. If it's not full of teachers, they'll usually rent you a pleasant modern room with views for US$25 a double with breakfast.

The three-star *Hotel Mare* (☎ *252-712 3211, fax 712 3396*), Yanık Harman Mevkii, is a 50 room hotel further east from the Öğretmen Evi, near Club Datça. It has a pretty, circular swimming pool and comfortable rooms with tiled showers and balconies with sea views for US$50/67 a single/double. The beach is only metres away.

Places to Eat As usual in a harbour town, food prices rise the closer you get to the water. Breakfast, for example, costs less than US$2 in town, rising to nearer US$4 by the harbour.

The harbour is ringed with fish restaurants where you should expect a meal to cost at least US$15. Near the harbour on İskele Caddesi, ***Taraça*** and ***Küçük Ev*** don't look much from the street, but have nice terraces offering lovely harbour views and menus listing meze plates for US$1.50, chicken curry for US$5, and steaks for just a bit more.

On the quayside the aptly named ***Sunrise Café Bar*** is already serving all sorts of breakfasts for US$2 to US$4 when nearby restaurants are just opening up. ***Uğurlu*** and ***Alternatif*** serve light meals and drinks later into the evening.

Looking down on the quayside is the popular and rather cool ***Kristina Bistro*** which serves pizza, lasagne and chicken curry for US$6 to US$12 per meal. Their nonalcoholic fruit cocktails go down a treat too.

Set apart from the other restaurants is ***Yasu Restaurant & Bar*** in an old Greek-style stone house on Kargı Yolu where you can eat chicken in ginger or beef fillet at taverna-style tables overlooking the harbour. A meal here will cost at least US$12, and probably more.

Speaking of views, ***Garden House Restaurant*** on the hillside behind (east of) the Karaoğlu Pansiyon has good sunset views of Kumluk Plajı.

On Kumluk Plajı, ***Dutdibi Pide Salonu*** is run by friendly people and does good, cheap food (pides for US$1) with beach views.

İskele Caddesi also has several restaurants where you can eat without worrying about the bill. ***Kemal Restaurant*** boasts home-cooked dishes including vegetarian options but is closed on Sundays. ***Mandalina Pide Salonu*** in the modern Mandalina Pansiyon on İskele Caddesi is another possibility for a cheap pide supper.

Getting There & Away In summer there are hourly buses and dolmuşes to Marmaris during the day (75km, 1¾ hours, US$3.50), and you can change there for a bus to other destinations. There are also daily buses to İzmir and Muğla and overnight services to Ankara and İstanbul. Kamil Koç, Uludağ and Ulusoy have ticket offices along İskele Caddesi between Buxerolles Sokak and Kargı Yolu.

Boat There are often boat excursions to Datça from Marmaris and sometimes you can buy a one-way ticket.

During the summer months, the Bodrum Ferryboat Association (☎ 252-316 0882) operates scheduled ferry services between Bodrum and Datça. Ferries leave Bodrum on Saturday at 9 am, returning from Datça at 5 pm. Tickets are on sale in the office in Turgut Özul Meydanı (☎ 252-712 2143) opposite the Deniz Motel. The ferry actually departs from Körmen, about a 15-minute ride due north of Datça on the peninsula's northern coast but there are bus connections with the town centre.

Hydrofoils for Bodrum also leave Datça daily except Sunday in summer, at 12.30 and 6 pm; they leave Bodrum at 11.30 am and 5 pm. Tickets are sold all around Datça but for more information phone 252-712 3656. The fare is US$11 one way or US$16 return; a car costs US$22.

For boats to the Greek Islands and Knidos, ask around the harbour.

Knidos

At Knidos, 35km west of Datça at the very tip of the peninsula, are ruins of a prosperous port city dating from about 400 BC. The Dorians who founded it were smart: the winds change as one rounds the peninsula and ships in ancient times often had to wait at Knidos for good winds, giving Knidos a prosperous trade in ship repairs, hospitality and trading. The ship taking St Paul to Rome for trial was one of the many which had to stop for a while in Knidos.

Being rich, Knidos commissioned the great Praxiteles to make a large cult statue of Aphrodite to go in a circular temple within sight of the sea. The statue, said to be the sculptor's masterpiece, has been lost, though copies or derivative versions exist in museums in Munich, New York and Rome.

The ruins aside, Knidos consists of a tiny jandarma post with a telephone for emergencies, a single restaurant unimaginatively called ***Restaurant***, some unpleasant toilets and a repository for artefacts found on the site (no entry). Overnight stays in the village are not allowed, so, unlike in Praxiteles' time, today there are no facilities. You can swim in the bays from wooden piers, but the beaches are several kilometres out of town. The nearest PTT is in Çeşme Köyü, the last village you pass through before coming to Knidos. Excursion boats to Knidos often stop for lunch in the village of Palamutbükü; of the scattering of restaurants here ***Merhaba***, along the beach, is cheaper than ***Liman*** (close to where the boats dock).

The Ruins The ruins of Knidos are scattered along the 3km at the end of a peninsula occupied only by goat herds, their flocks, and the occasional wild boar. The setting is dramatic: steep hillsides terraced and planted with groves of olive, almond and fruit trees rise above two picture-perfect bays in which a handful of yachts rest at anchor.

Few of the ancient buildings are easily recognisable, but you can certainly appreciate the importance of the town by exploring the site. The guardian will show you around for a small tip. Don't miss the ruins of the temple of Aphrodite and the theatre, the 4th century BC sundial and the fine carvings in what was once a Byzantine church.

Getting There & Away Knidos Taxi, opposite the Kaya Pansiyon, near Turgut Özal Meydanı in Datça, will take up to three people from Datça to Knidos and return, with up to two hours waiting time, for US$45.

A ferry departs from Datça in summer at 9 am for a day trip to Knidos, returning at 5 pm and charging US$8 per person. At other times of year, ask in the harbour about excursions to Knidos. They also tend to leave around 9 to 9.30 am and return early evening and cost about US$12 per person.

EASTWARD TO KÖYCEĞİZ

Leaving Marmaris and heading north, the road climbs into mountains with beautiful panoramas and fertile valleys. At the end of that 2km-long double row of eucalyptus trees is a highway junction where you turn right towards Köyceğiz and Fethiye. Along the way are fields of cotton and tobacco, orchards of fruits and nuts and cool pine forests buzzing with honey bees. There are forest picnic areas at Kadırga and Günlük.

KÖYCEĞİZ

Less than 50km east of the turn-off from the Muğla-Marmaris road lies quiet, pretty Köyceğiz (population 6500), a small town at the northern end of the large Köyceğiz Gölü lake which is joined to the Mediterranean Sea via the Dalyan Çayı stream. The main attraction here is the lake itself – broad, beautiful and serene. Except for its small (but growing) tourist trade, Köyceğiz is a farming town producing citrus fruit, olives, honey and cotton. This region is also famous for its liquidambar trees, the sort which produced that precious petrified amber gum ages ago.

Orientation

The otogar and local hospital are near the highway turn-off. To reach the waterfront, head south past a roundabout and then along tree-lined Atatürk Bulvarı for 2km, passing the new precinct with the Belediye, Adliye (court house) and Hükümet Konağı (government house) on the right. You'll come to the main square with the inevitable bust of Atatürk and then to a small mosque right by the waterfront. Kordon Boyu, the road skirting the lake, has several hotels, pensions and restaurants.

Information

The Tourism Information Office (☎ 252-262 4703), opposite the mosque on the square's eastern edge, stocks a simple map.

Things to Do

Stroll along the lakeshore promenade past the pleasant town park, an imaginative children's playground, shady tea gardens and several restaurants. If there's not much activity on the lake, you may see the fish jump.

When you get restless you can take a boat excursion from the promenade to the **Sultaniye Kaplıcaları** or thermal baths, 30km by road or eight nautical miles across the lake on the southern shore. The hot mineral waters are rich in calcium, sulphur, iron, nitrates, potassium and other mineral salts and are said to be good for skin complaints and rheumatism; temperatures sometimes reach 40°C. Admission costs US$1, and you should allow an hour if you plan to bathe in the mud, let it dry, and wash it off.

Other than the hot baths, you can take boat trips to Dalyan and the Kaunos ruins, and to bays along the Mediterranean coast. For details see the following Dalyan section.

Bicycles are for rent by Özay Turizm next to the mosque.

Places to Stay

In general, the better accommodation and camping options are off to the west (right) as you approach the mosque when coming into town. Turn right at the mosque onto Emeksiz Caddesi for the good, newish ***Alila Hotel*** *(☎/fax 252-262 1150)*, an attractive place overlooking the lake with fine bath-equipped rooms for US$28 a double with breakfast. Just beyond it, the aging ***Star Pansiyon*** *(☎ 252-262 1035)* charges US$15 for a double with shower (no breakfast). A bit further on, the two-star, 32 room ***Hotel Özay*** *(☎ 252-262 4300, fax 262 1819, Emeksiz Caddesi 8)*, costs a bit more even though it's older. It's a pleasant place with a small swimming pool in front surrounded by shady vine-covered arbours.

Further along in the same direction (west) is the two-star ***Hotel Kaunos*** *(☎ 252-262 4288, fax 262 4836, Cengiz Topel Caddesi 37)*, even older but well kept, where the 40 double rooms with private showers and balconies overlooking the placid lake are priced at US$34, breakfast included.

Inland across the street from the Kaunos, ***Pansiyon Beyaz Konak*** *(☎ 252-262 4893, fax 262 3378)*, is a simple, modern building with double rooms renting for US$20 a double with shower and breakfast. Inland another block is ***Özbek Pension*** (*☎ 252-262 2840*), set in yet more lovely gardens, with doubles for US$16 in summer. ***Tango Pansiyon*** (*☎ 252-262 2501, fax 262 4345*), Ali İhsan Kalmaz Caddesi, is a newer place at US$24 for a double with shower and breakfast.

Finally, ***Panorama Plaza*** (*☎ 252-262 3773, fax 262 3633, Cengiz Topel Caddesi 69*), almost 1km west of the mosque, is perhaps the best in town, with comfy double rooms for US$60 in summer, breakfast included.

If you turn left (east) when approaching the mosque, you'll find a mixed bag of places to stay.

Cutting inland and following the signs you'll come to the welcoming ***Oba Pansiyon*** (*☎ 252-262 4181, Gülpınar Mahallesi, Gümüşlü Caddesi 10*), a relatively quiet spot (only rooster noise) somewhat overpriced at US$20 for a double with private shower, but no breakfast.

On the waterfront is the brash new ***Kordonboyu Motel*** (*☎ 252-262 3993*), with modern rooms surrounding swimming and trout pools slightly overpriced at US$35 a double (no breakfast).

Just beyond the Panorama Plaza is ***Anatolia Camping*** (*☎ 252-262 4750*), a forest camping ground among liquidambar trees, with a small beach nearby.

Places to Eat

As always, the market area has the cheapest eats. Try ***Meşhur Ali Baba Pide, Kebap ve Yemek Salonu***, on the southern side of the Atatürk statue in the central park, for good cheap Turkish pizza (US$1), kebaps and ready food (US$1.50 to US$2.50). To the north up the same street through the market are ***Güven Restaurant*** for ready food, and ***Penguen Pide Salonu*** for Turkish pizza.

The lakeshore is lined with pricier outdoor fish restaurants and cafes. To the east, try ***Çınaraltı*** while to the west ***Paşa Café Bar Restaurant*** and ***Şamdan*** do good fish and grills.

Getting There & Away

Most buses will drop you at the Köyceğiz otogar on the outskirts of town. Unless you fancy a 2km walk to the lake, you'll need to take a dolmuş from there to the smaller central bus station west of the main street behind the Kamil Koç bus company office.

Kamil Koç runs 14 buses daily to Marmaris (75km, one hour, US$2), and 17 to Fethiye (95km, 1¾ hours, US$3.50). Pamukkale has several buses to Marmaris, even more to Fethiye. It also offers one daily night bus to İstanbul and one to Ankara. Köyceğiz Minibüs Kooperatifi has frequent minibuses to Marmaris, Muğla (57km, one hour, US$2), Ortaca (for Dalyan, 20km, 25 minutes, US$1) and Dalaman (34km, 40 minutes, US$1.75).

DALYAN

Pretty little Dalyan is an increasingly popular holiday destination, especially with Germans. On top of those who choose to stay here, summer afternoons bring a positive armada of motorised excursion boats from Marmaris and Fethiye carving a path through the reedbeds of the Dalyan Çayı on their way to the ruins of ancient Kaunos and the beach at İztuzu. Above the river the weathered facades of Lycian rock tombs gaze silently down on all this activity.

Orientation

It's 13km from the highway at Ortaca to Dalyan's centre by the mosque and the PTT building. Minibuses stop behind the main square where the statue of Atatürk is overshadowed by a statue of a pair of turtles.

To the north along the riverbank are the requisite bars and, inland from them, pensions, hotels and restaurants. To the south most of the town's better hotels and pensions are along Maraş Caddesi, which runs for 1km south and ends at the riverbank.

Information

The Dalyan Tourism Information Office (☎ 252-284 4235) is on Maraş Caddesi in the centre. It's open from Monday to Saturday in summer from 9.30 am to noon and from 2.30 to 6 pm.

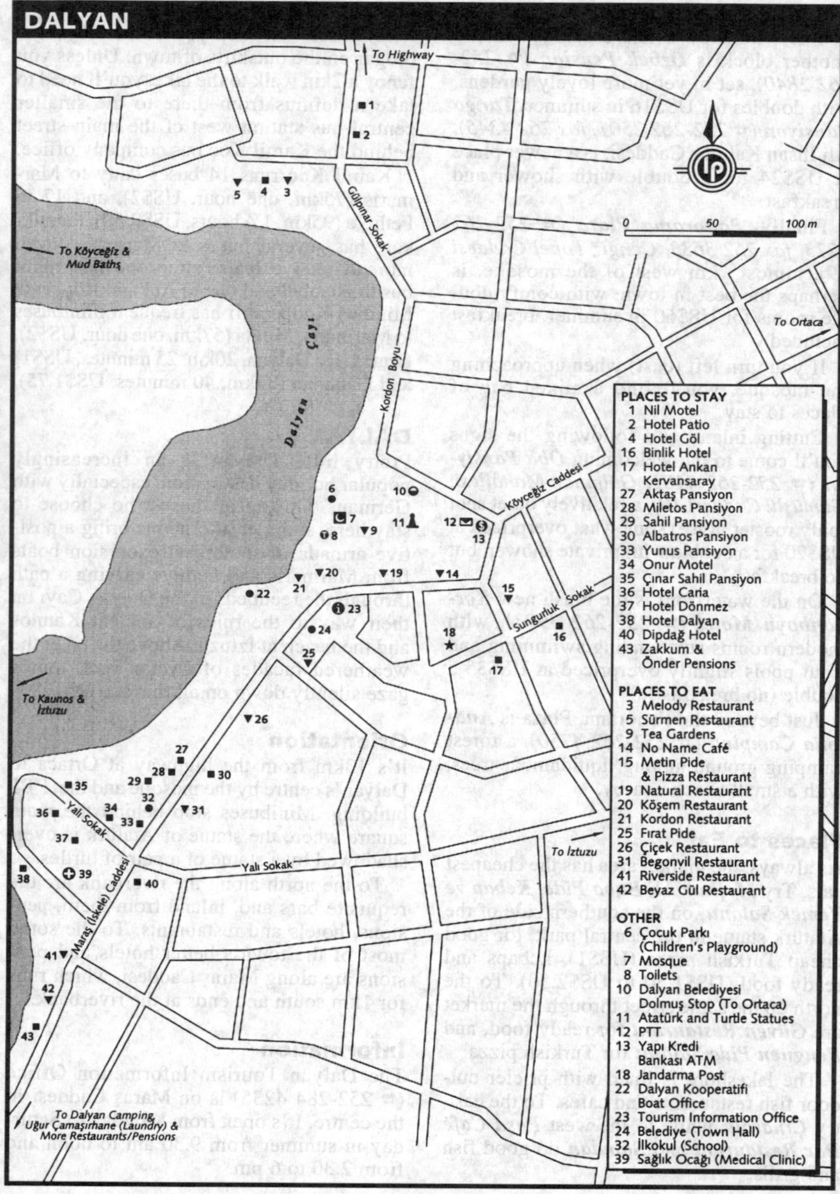
DALYAN
To Highway
To Köyceğiz & Mud Baths
To Kaunos & İztuzu
To Ortaca
To İztuzu
To Dalyan Camping, Uğur Çamaşırhane (Laundry) & More Restaurants/Pensions
Gülpınar Sokak
Kordon Boyu
Dalyan Çayı
Köyceğiz Caddesi
Sungurluk Sokak
Yalı Sokak
Maraş (İskele) Caddesi
0 50 100 m
PLACES TO STAY
1 Nil Motel
2 Hotel Patio
4 Hotel Göl
16 Binlik Hotel
17 Hotel Ankan Kervansaray
27 Aktaş Pansiyon
28 Miletos Pansiyon
29 Sahil Pansiyon
30 Albatros Pansiyon
33 Yunus Pansiyon
34 Onur Motel
35 Çınar Sahil Pansiyon
36 Hotel Caria
37 Hotel Dönmez
38 Hotel Dalyan
40 Dipdağ Hotel
43 Zakkum & Önder Pensions
PLACES TO EAT
3 Melody Restaurant
5 Sürmen Restaurant
9 Tea Gardens
14 No Name Café
15 Metin Pide & Pizza Restaurant
19 Natural Restaurant
20 Köşem Restaurant
21 Kordon Restaurant
25 Fırat Pide
26 Çiçek Restaurant
31 Begonvil Restaurant
41 Riverside Restaurant
42 Beyaz Gül Restaurant
OTHER
6 Çocuk Parkı (Children's Playground)
7 Mosque
8 Toilets
10 Dalyan Belediyesi Dolmuş Stop (To Ortaca)
11 Atatürk and Turtle Statues
12 PTT
13 Yapı Kredi Bankası ATM
18 Jandarma Post
22 Dalyan Kooperatifi Boat Office
23 Tourism Information Office
24 Belediye (Town Hall)
32 İlkokul (School)
39 Sağlık Ocağı (Medical Clinic)

The Yapı Kredi Bankası ATM is on the south-eastern side of the big ugly PTT building in the centre, and the Sağlık Ocağı (medical clinic) is near the Hotel Dalyan, south of the centre off Maraş Caddesi.

Dalyan's postal code is 48840.

Boat Excursions

Every day in summer, excursion boats leave the quayside at 10 am to cruise to Köyceğiz Gölü and the Sultaniye hot springs and mud baths, the ruins of Kaunos and the beach at İztuzu on the Mediterranean coast. Inclusive tickets cost US$5 per person.

If you can organise a small group, it may be more economical to hire an entire passenger boat which holds from eight to 12 people. Haggle to get the best price, particularly if it's early or late in the season and many boats are standing idle. A two-hour tour just to Kaunos costs from US$30 to US$40 for the entire boat; if you want to visit the Sultaniye hot springs as well, figure on three hours and US$50 for the boat.

Boats belonging to the various boat cooperatives operate a 'river dolmuş' service between the town and İztuzu beach, charging US$2 for the return trip. In high summer there may be five or more boats per day, heading out from 9 am to 2 pm and returning between 1 and 6 pm. (In high summer minibuses make the 13km run to İztuzu by land as well.) Take some food as you might not like the kebap stands on the beach.

Boat cooperatives also provide dolmuş boats to Kaunos, three times a day, for US$6 return, and to the mud baths in the early evening for US$2.

Kaunos

Founded around the 9th century BC, Kaunos became an important Carian city by 400 BC. Right on the border with the Kingdom of Lycia, its culture reflected aspects of both kingdoms. The **tombs**, for instance, are in Lycian style (you'll see many more of them at Fethiye, Kaş and other points east). If you don't take a river cruise, walk south from town along Maraş Caddesi to get a good view of the tombs.

When Mausolus of Halicarnassus was ruler of Caria, his Hellenising influence reached the Kaunians, who eagerly adopted that culture. Though of good size, Kaunos suffered from endemic malaria; according to Herodotus, its people were famous for their yellowish skin and eyes. The Kaunians' prosperity was also threatened by the silting of their harbour. The Mediterranean, which once surrounded the hill on which the archaeological site stands, has now retreated 5km to the south, pushed back by silt from the Dalyan Çayı.

Apart from the tombs, the **theatre** is very well preserved; parts of an **acropolis** and other structures (baths, a basilica and defensive walls) are nearby.

Your boat pulls up to the western bank, then it's a five-minute walk to the site. Admission, from 8.30 am to 5.30 pm, costs US$1. The curious wooden structures in the river are *dalyanlar* (fishing weirs). No doubt the ancient Kaunians also benefited from such an industry.

Sultaniye Kaplıcaları & Mud Baths

The Sultaniye Kaplıcaları (thermal baths) lie to the south-west of Köyceğiz Gölü (see Things to Do in the earlier Köyceğiz section). At the smaller mud baths, just before Dalyan Çayı joins the lake, you can give yourself a body pack of mud and then wash it all off again in a sulphur pool with temperatures as hot as in the Sultaniye baths.

İztuzu Beach

About 13km south of the town by road, this 5km sandbar separating the sea from the mouth of the Dalyan Çayı is an excellent swimming beach with some camping possibilities. A parking fee of US$1 is charged.

The beach is important as one of the last nesting sites in the Mediterranean of the loggerhead turtle. Special rules to protect the turtles are strictly enforced and therefore should be respected.

Places to Stay

Once known for its many cheap *ev pansiyonlar* (house pensions), Dalyan is fast

Turtle Alert

A few years ago Dalyan's İztuzu Beach shot to world fame when a serious threat to one of the last Mediterranean nesting sites of *Caretta caretta*, the loggerhead turtle, was identified.

The loggerhead turtle (*deniz kaplumbağa* in Turkish) is a large flat-headed reptile, reddish brown on top and yellow-orange below. An adult can weigh up to 130kg.

Between May and September the female turtles come ashore at night to lay their eggs in the sand. Using their back flippers they scoop out a nest about 40cm deep, lay between 70 and 120 soft-shelled white eggs approximately the size of ping pong balls, and then cover them over again. If disturbed, the females may abandon the nests and return to the sea.

The eggs incubate in the sand for 50 to 65 days and the temperature at which they do so determines the sex of the ensuing young: below 30°C all the young will be male; above 30°C they will be female. At a steady 30°C an even mix of the sexes will hatch out.

As soon as they're born (at night when it's cool and fewer predators are about), the young turtles make their way towards the sea, drawn by the light (the sea reflects more light than land). If hotels and restaurants are built too close to the beach, their lights can confuse the youngsters, leading them to move up the beach towards danger instead of down it to the sea and safety. So when it was discovered that developers wanted to build a hotel right on the beach there was an outcry which eventually lead to the plans being abandoned.

At the same time, rules were introduced to protect the turtles. Although the beach is still open to the public during the day, night-time visits are prohibited from May to September. A line of wooden stakes on the beach indicate the nest sites and visitors are asked to sunbathe behind them to avoid disturbing them. It's particularly important not to leave any litter on the beach which could hamper the turtles' struggle for survival.

The loggerhead turtle also nests on the beaches at Dalaman, Fethiye, Patara, Kale, Kumluca, Tekirova, Belek, Kızılot, Demirtaş, Gazipaşa and Anamur and in the Göksu Delta.

A second larger species of sea turtle, *Chelonia mydas*, the hard-shelled green turtle, also nests in Turkey, at Kazanlı, Akyatan and Samandağ, along the eastern Mediterranean coast. Hunting of these turtles for their flesh (for turtle soup) and eggs has reduced their numbers to danger point.

For more information, contact MEDASSET (30-1-361 3572 or 364 0389, fax 361 3572 or 724 3007, IC Licavitou Street, 106 72, Athens, Greece) which is an association committed to saving Mediterranean turtles.

repositioning itself upmarket. Rooms are being fitted with plumbing, pensions are being razed to make way for hotels and hotels are acquiring swimming pools. At present, however, there are still some good places to stay in all price ranges. Most of the town's accommodation is south of the centre along Maraş Caddesi. The road continues for just more than 1km before ending at the riverbank.

Places to Stay – Budget

There are several pensions in the centre, but the ones along Maraş Caddesi to the south are quieter and some have views of the river and the rock-cut tombs. In general, the further south you walk, the quieter the pensions become. Prices are generally US$7 per person in waterless rooms, US$9 to US$10 with a private shower. Small hotels are usually priced from US$18 to US$22 for a double with shower.

Walking south along Maraş Caddesi, you'll come to ***Albatros Pansiyon*** *(☎ 252-284 3287)* which has no views and a bar pumping out live music in front. ***Aktaş Pansiyon*** *(☎ 252-284 2042, fax 284 4380)* is on the water, with views of the river and tombs; all rooms have showers. ***Miletos Pansiyon*** *(☎ 252-284 2532)* and ***Sahil Pansiyon*** *(☎ 252-284 2187)* are also on the riverbank, but the inland wall of the Sahil is so close to the road that it sounds like the cars are driving between your beds, so get a room on the river side. ***Yunus Pansiyon*** *(☎ 252-284 2102)* inland from the Sahil is quieter.

Dipdağ Hotel *(☎ 252-284 4572, fax 284 2526)* is near the corner of Maraş Caddesi and Yalı Sokak. The spacious rooms have showers, and cost US$24 to US$28 a double. Get a room in the rear wing by the swimming pool to avoid the street noise.

Turn right towards the water at the Dipdağ. Here on Yalı Sokak you'll find the 35 room ***Hotel Dönmez*** *(☎ 252-284 2107, fax 284 2201)*. Hotel rooms with bath and ceiling fans cost US$26 a double with breakfast, and there's a roof terrace with a bar and pool. The neighbouring ***Hotel Caria*** *(☎ 252-284 2075, fax 284 3046, Yalı Sokak 82)* has big, cool rooms for US$16/28 a single/double. Buffet meals can be eaten on a roof terrace with terrific views.

Onur Motel *(☎ 252-284 3074, fax 284 2787)* is a welcoming family run place with clean rooms for US$15/19 a single/double and an attractive roof bar. On Yalı Sokak, on the shore, is the pleasant, similarly priced ***Çınar Sahil Pension*** *(☎ 252-284 2117)*, with a shady terrace from where you can gaze at the river.

Keep heading south along Maraş Caddesi and you'll pass yet more cheap pensions, including ***Zakkum*** *(☎ 252-284 2111)*, a simple, friendly family run place with shower-equipped rooms for US$19; and the similar ***Önder*** next door. Even further south, follow the signs to ***Kilim Pansiyon*** *(☎ 252-284 2253, 284 3464)*, decorated, as you'd expect, with kilims. This is among the nicest pensions in Dalyan, with a clean swimming pool and some of the biggest rooms in Dalyan for U$30 a double with breakfast. There's a ramp for wheelchair access too. Further down this side road are several other, cheaper pensions.

Similar to the Kilim is ***Bur-Al Motel*** *(☎ 252-284 4885)* on Balıkhane Sokak, charging a bit less.

Inland from the Tourism Information Office, ***Hotel Arıkan Kervansaray*** *(☎ 252-284 2487, fax 284 2424, Karakol Sokak 26)*, is a more elaborate hostel with a nice little swimming pool and rooms for US$35 a double, a few dollars less without air-con.

There are more simple places to the north of the centre. ***Hotel Göl*** *(☎ 252-284 2096, fax 284 2555)*, Gülpınar Mahallesi, visible from the tea gardens, is tidy and convenient at US$24 a double with breakfast. A one-minute walk further north is ***Hotel Patio*** *(☎ 252-284 2214, fax 284 3358)*, clean and new, with a swimming pool and double rooms for US$25 with breakfast, and the neighbouring ***Nil Motel*** *(☎ 252-284 2383, fax 284 3359)*, charging slightly less.

Camping

South along Maraş Caddesi is ***Dalyan Camping*** *(☎/fax 252-284 4157)*, which charges US$4 for a single-person tent site in summer and up to US$18 for a small wooden two-person bungalow without running water. There's some shade, the showers and toilets are clean and despite the high prices it fills up early in high summer. Uğur Çamaşırhane across the road will do your laundry for you.

Places to Stay – Mid-Range

In Sungurluk Sokak, down from the Belediye, is the three-star ***Hotel Binlik*** *(☎ 252-284 2148, fax 284 2149)* with comfortable air-con rooms set around two pools for US$40 to US$50. It's usually booked by groups.

Hotel Dalyan (☎ *252-284 2239, fax 284 2240*) is on Yalı Sokak. Set on a point of land at a bend in the river, it has a prime location, which must be what allows it to charge US$100 a double, breakfast included for well-used facilities with solar hot water only available from 11 am to 8 pm.

Places to Stay – Top End

Dalyan now has one four-star hotel, ***Asur Oteli*** (☎ *252-284 3232, fax 284 3244*). Although it's 1km south of the centre at the end of Maraş Caddesi, this is a superb place, designed as a collection of 32 single-storey octagonal units around a big pool by the award-winning architect Nail Çakırhan. The rooms are quite small, but they all have air-con and minibars, TVs and all mod cons. Prices are high at US$77 to US$107 depending on the season, so look to see if any tour operators are offering competitively priced packages before booking.

Places to Eat

Virtually all of the restaurants in Dalyan seem to serve alcohol.

Natural Restaurant is facing the main square. Despite its name there's nothing especially 'natural' about its food, the best of which is döner kebap and toasted sandwiches. Prices are good: US$5 for İskender kebap and a fresh orange juice. ***No Name Café*** nearby looks as if it should be expensive but isn't. Pizzas here cost about US$5. Inland, ***Metin Pide & Pizza Restaurant*** has even cheaper food.

Fırat Pide, in the warren of shops near the Tourism Information Office, is among the cheapest eateries in town.

Facing a terrace leading down to the river at the centre of town are two nice semi-open-air restaurants, ***Köşem*** and ***Kordon***, which are the most popular places in town. The prices are nearly identical, with breakfast costing less than US$3, meat-based meals for US$7 to US$10 and fish for a bit more.

The big open-air ***Çiçek Restaurant***, on Maraş Caddesi, is dependably good and cheap for everything from breakfast (US$2.50) to dinner (US$5 to US$10). Further south, ***Beyaz Gül Restaurant*** serves outdoor grills on the riverbank in the shade of olive and orange trees. Just north of it, ***Riverside Restaurant*** is almost as pleasant. ***Begonvil Restaurant*** a bit further north is more expensive, but atmospheric.

North of the centre, try ***Sürmen*** and ***Melody***, both of which have excellent views of the river and town. A full fish dinner costs from US$10 to US$18 per person.

Entertainment

The town centre usually has at least one seasonal bar or disco, but the reliable action is at the southern end of Maraş Caddesi on the riverbank where currently ***River Club Dance Bar*** and ***Gel Gör Dance Bar*** hold sway.

Getting There & Away

Every day in summer minibuses leave the dolmuş stop in Dalyan at 10 and 11 am for Marmaris, Muğla and Fethiye and at 10 am for Göcek. Otherwise you usually need to take a minibus to Ortaca (US$0.40) and change to another bus there. The minibuses leave Dalyan and Ortaca every 15 minutes during the day in summer, but the last one to Dalyan is at 7 pm, even earlier in winter.

At Ortaca otogar you can connect with buses to Köyceğiz (20km, 25 minutes, US$1) and Dalaman (5km, 15 minutes, US$0.50). You can sometimes catch buses to more distant points at the highway in Ortaca. If not, take a bus or minibus to Dalaman and change there.

Taxis charge US$13 to Ortaca, US$24 to Dalaman, US$23 to İztuzu beach, US$30 to Köyceğiz, US$39 to Sultaniye, US$27 to Sarıgerme beach, and US$57 to Marmaris.

Getting Around

Mountain bikes and motorcycles can be rented from Kaunos Moto opposite the PTT (☎ 252-284 2816), or from Akhan in Maraş Caddesi (☎ 252-284 3802). Expect to pay about US$7 a day for a bike and an outrageous US$50 for a motorcycle.

DALAMAN

This agricultural town (population 16,500) was quite dozy until the regional airport was built on the neighbouring river delta. Now it stirs whenever a jet arrives, before slumping back to sleep again. Most visitors pass straight through and bus connections are good. The only conceivable reason to linger would be to take the turn-off from the airport road to the beach at Sarıgerme.

If you need to stay the night, Dalaman has a reasonable selection of hotels, though at relatively high prices.

Orientation

It's 5.5km from the airport to the town, and another 5.5km from the town to the east-west highway. The road connecting the highway with the town centre is called Kenan Evren Bulvarı, and beyond the town it's called Havaalanı Yolu (Airport Road). A large mosque marks its junction with the town's main street, Atatürk Caddesi; a Yapı Kredi Bankası ATM is here as well. Atatürk Caddesi is about 500m long, running east from Kenan Evren Bulvarı, with banks, shops and simple restaurants. The otogar, served by the Pamukkale, Aydın and Köseoğlu companies, is near the junction of Evren Bulvarı and Atatürk Caddesi. The PTT is a block north on Atatürk Caddesi.

Places to Stay

The well kept ***Otel Hafızoğlu*** *(☎ 252-692 5078)*, on Meltem Sokak, one block south of the otogar across Atatürk Caddesi, charges US$20/30/36 a single/double/triple for its standard one-star rooms with bath.

The cheapest choice is ***Dalaman Pansiyon*** *(☎ 252-692 5543)*, 200m south of the traffic roundabout near the otogar, where a double room costs US$14/18 without/with bath. The town has several other cheap pensions as well.

Most of the other lodgings are spread out along Havaalanı Yolu which doesn't get enough traffic to be very noisy.

The two-star ***Hotel Meltem*** *(☎/fax 252-692 2901)*, further down on the same side of the road as the Dalaman, has 28 rooms with bath, a restaurant and a bar, and charges US$25/35 a single/double with bath and breakfast.

Staying on the same side of the road, the three-star ***Airport Hotel Sevilen*** *(☎ 252-692 2451, fax 692 2452)* is just a bit further south towards the airport. Its 39 rooms with private shower, TV, minibar and air-con cost US$55 a double, breakfast included. There's also a swimming pool.

Across the road is the best place in town, the big ***Hotel Dalaman Park*** *(☎ 252-692 3156, fax 692 3332)* with restaurant, bar, lifts and a huge swimming pool. Impressive though it is, this is hardly the most atmospheric town, so the prices (US$65/85) seem a bit optimistic.

Getting There & Away

In summer, several bus companies pick up passengers from immediately outside the airport. At other times you may need to get a taxi into Dalaman for an expensive US$7 to US$9.

At Dalaman's small otogar you can buy tickets to many destinations. All routes north and east pass through either Muğla or Fethiye. Details of some services follow:

Antalya – 272km, 5½ hours, US$9 (inland – *yayla* – route)
Bodrum – 201km, 3½ hours, US$8
Denizli – 221km, four hours, US$5
Fethiye – 50km, one hour, US$2
Göcek – 23km, 30 minutes, US$1
Gökova – 80km, 1½ hours, US$2
İstanbul – 966km, 15 hours, US$22
İzmir – 356km, five hours, US$10
Kalkan – 131km, 2½ hours, US$5
Kaş – 160km, three hours, US$6
Köyceğiz – 34km, 40 minutes, US$1.50
Marmaris – 120km, 1½ to two hours, US$4
Muğla – 91km, 1½ hours, US$3
Pamukkale – 240km, four hours, US$8 (take the bus to Denizli, which is cheaper, then a city bus or dolmuş to Pamukkale)
Selçuk – 285km, 4½ hours, US$9

DALAMAN TO FETHİYE

The highway east of Dalaman winds through mountains cloaked in fragrant evergreen forests, also with many liquidambar trees, before reaching Fethiye 50km to the southeast. The bends make the road a slow ride but the beauty of the scenery compensates.

Göcek

About 23km east of Dalaman a road on the right (south) leads to Göcek, a delightful small yachting and fishing port on a bay at the foot of the mountains.

Orientation Buses drop you at a petrol station on the main road then it's a 1km walk to the centre. Minibuses drive right down to the main square with the bust of Atatürk and a collection of small restaurants, laundries and a PTT with money-changing facilities. The square aside, Göcek mainly consists of the road running alongside the harbour which is lined with pensions, hotels and restaurants.

Things to Do Göcek is really a place for relaxing. There's only a fairly scrubby beach at the western end of the quayside, although you can take a '12 Island Cruise' to beaches on nearby islands. The Göcek Club Marina boasts a Turkish bath of the modern variety which you can use for US$15.

There are excellent places to shop for souvenirs, including Bazaar Anatolia (☎ 252-645 1768) which sells glorious brightly coloured wall hangings, belts and bedcovers imported from Türkmenistan. These are collector's items and priced accordingly.

Places to Stay At the western end of the harbour ***Başak Pansiyon*** *(☎ 252-645 1024, fax 645 1862)* has a good restaurant and connecting rooms with four beds for US$22, ideal for families. A double with private shower costs US$22 in high summer but only half that during low season.

Also good is ***Sultan Pansiyon*** *(☎ 252-645 1557)*, above the food store of the same name. It's clean and proper; some rooms facing the sea have one double and one single bed, and one room on the street side has four beds. Two people pay US$24 in season, half that in low season. The nearby, similarly priced ***Pınar*** *(☎ 252-645 1369)* has fine views from its terrace, ***Taştepe*** *(☎ 252-645 1372)* is a bit more downscale and cheaper.

Demir Pansiyon *(☎ 252-645 1060)*, is a modest, homey place on the inland side of the street, charging a few dollars less and includes breakfast in the price. ***Ünlü*** *(☎ 252-645 1170)* nearby is similar, as is ***Yıldırım*** *(☎ 252-645 1189)*.

Dim Pansiyon *(☎ 252-645 1294)* is fairly new and clean, with a swimming pool and air-con in some rooms.

Deniz Hotel *(☎ 252-645 1902, fax 645 1903)* facing the marina is posh, pleasant and priced accordingly at US$50/60 a single/double, breakfast included.

Yağmur Apart Otel *(☎/fax 252-645 1080)*, located inland a block on the northwestern side of town, is new and nice, with small apartments for US$40 a double.

In the hills above Göcek, accommodation with a difference is provided at ***Huzur Vadisi***, a settlement of felt *yurts* (nomadic tents). Phone 252-645 2429 for more details.

Places to Eat Göcek has plenty of places to eat along the waterfront but some of them cater to yachters and tend to be on the pricey side. ***Blue Bar & Restaurant*** does fish kebaps for about US$10 (the price changes with the fish and the season). ***Nanai Restaurant-Bar*** offers meat dishes for an expensive US$8 each. You eat them in cool, trendy surroundings. For something cheaper but less atmospheric, head inland to the main square.

Getting There & Away Dolmuşes from Fethiye run to Göcek several times daily and frequently on summer weekends. In summer there is also one minibus a day from Dalyan at 10 am. There are also excursion boats from Marmaris, Dalyan and Fethiye.

Küçük Kargı & Katrancı

At Küçük Kargı, located 33km east of Dalaman, a forest picnic area has a camping place and beach. About 2km further east at Katrancı is another picnic and camping spot with a small restaurant, on a beautiful little cove with a beach. Another 18km brings you to Fethiye.

FETHİYE

Fethiye (population 25,000) is a very old town, with few old buildings. An earthquake in 1958 levelled the town, leaving very little standing. Most of what was left were tombs from the time when Fethiye was called Telmessos (400 BC).

Fethiye's inner bay is an excellent natural harbour, protected from storms by the island called Şövalye Adası. The much larger outer bay has 11 more islands. Beaches are good here, and even better at nearby Ölüdeniz, one of Turkey's seaside hot spots. The Fethiye region has many interesting sites to explore, including the ghost town of Karmylassos, just over the hill (see Kayaköy, later in this chapter).

Orientation

Fethiye's otogar is 2km east of the centre of town, with a separate garage for minibuses 1km east of the centre. Mid-range and top-end hotels are near the centre, but most inexpensive pensions are either east of the centre near the stadium, or west of the centre overlooking the yacht harbour. Dolmuşes run to the centre along Fethiye's main street, Atatürk Caddesi.

The all-important beach at Ölüdeniz is 15km south of Fethiye. For full information see the Ölüdeniz section.

Information

Fethiye's otogar is one where you're likely to be hassled, so it's worth knowing that there's a hotel reservation office right there which can help you better than the touts.

Fethiye's Tourism Information Office (☎ 252-614 1527), open from 8 am to 7 pm daily in summer (from 8 am to 5 pm in winter), is on İskele Meydanı next to Otel Dedeoğlu, near the marina. The staff will help you with accommodation and inexpensive yacht charters. Next door is the office of the Fethiye Turizm Derneğı (Fethiye Tourism Association), a local group which can also provide helpful information.

Fethiye's postal code is 48300.

Money Atatürk Caddesi has banks with ATMs, exchange offices and shops which change money. Double check that the rate advertised is actually the rate used to calculate your transaction; shops that advertise surprisingly good rates of exchange are most suspect of cheating.

Laundry Where there's a yacht marina, there's a laundry. Look for the Güneş Laundry between the Prenses Hotel and the marina.

Ancient Telmessos

Throughout the town you will notice curious Lycian stone **sarcophagi** dating from around 450 BC. There's one sarcophagus near the PTT and others in the middle of streets or in private gardens; the town was built around them. All were broken into by tomb robbers, centuries ago of course.

Carved into the rockface behind the town is the so-called **Tomb of Amyntas** (350 BC), a Doric temple facade carved in the sheer rockface. It's open from 8 am to 7 pm for US$1, and is very crowded at sunset in summer, the most pleasant time to visit. Other smaller tombs are nearby to the left. Follow the signs from the otogar or take a taxi for a look at the tomb and the fine view of the town and bay.

Behind the harbour as you turn up Liman Caddesi to the Yasmin Bar you'll see the recently excavated remains of a **theatre** dating from Roman times.

On the hillside behind the town, just north of the road to Kayaköy, notice the ruined tower of a **crusader fortress** constructed by the Knights of St John on earlier foundations dating back to perhaps 400 BC.

Fethiye Müzesi

Fethiye's museum is open from 8.30 am to 5 pm (closed on Monday) and charges US$1 for admission. The most interesting exhibits are some small statues and votive stones (the 'Stelae of Graves' and 'Stelae of Promise') and the trilingual stele (Lycian-Greek-Aramaic) from Letoön, which helped with deciphering the Lycian language. King Kaunos gave money to do some good work in honour of the gods and the trilingual stele described his benefaction.

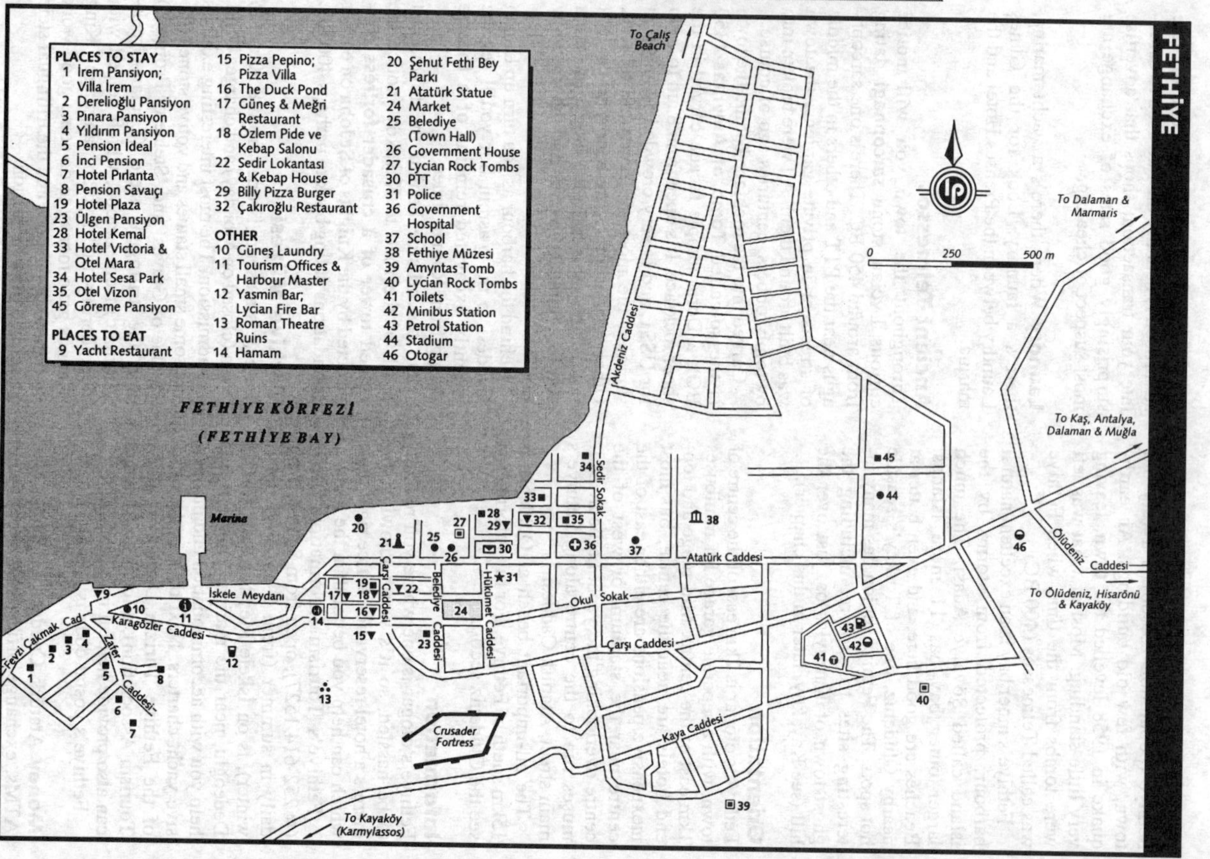
FETHİYE
PLACES TO STAY
1 İrem Pansiyon; Villa İrem
2 Derelioğlu Pansiyon
3 Pınara Pansiyon
4 Yıldırım Pansiyon
5 Pension İdeal
6 İnci Pension
7 Hotel Pırlanta
8 Pension Savaıçı
19 Hotel Plaza
23 Ülgen Pansiyon
28 Hotel Kemal
33 Hotel Victoria & Otel Mara
34 Hotel Sesa Park
35 Otel Vizon
45 Göreme Pansiyon
PLACES TO EAT
9 Yacht Restaurant
15 Pizza Pepino; Pizza Villa
16 The Duck Pond
17 Güneş & Meğri Restaurant
18 Özlem Pide ve Kebap Salonu
22 Sedir Lokantası & Kebap House
29 Billy Pizza Burger
32 Çakıroğlu Restaurant
OTHER
10 Güneş Laundry
11 Tourism Offices & Harbour Master
12 Yasmin Bar; Lycian Fire Bar
13 Roman Theatre Ruins
14 Hamam
20 Şehut Fethi Bey Parkı
21 Atatürk Statue
24 Market
25 Belediye (Town Hall)
26 Government House
27 Lycian Rock Tombs
30 PTT
31 Police
36 Government Hospital
37 School
38 Fethiye Müzesi
39 Amyntas Tomb
40 Lycian Rock Tombs
41 Toilets
42 Minibus Station
43 Petrol Station
44 Stadium
46 Otogar
To Çalış Beach
To Dalaman & Marmaris
0 250 500 m
To Kaş, Antalya, Dalaman & Muğla
Ölüdeniz Caddesi
To Ölüdeniz, Hisarönü & Kayaköy
FETHİYE KÖRFEZİ
(FETHİYE BAY)
Akdeniz Caddesi
Sedir Sokak
Atatürk Caddesi
Okul Sokak
Çarşı Caddesi
Belediye Caddesi
Hükümet Caddesi
Kaya Caddesi
Marina
İskele Meydanı
Karagözler Caddesi
Fevzi Çakmak Cad
Zafer Caddesi
Crusader Fortress
To Kayaköy (Karmylassos)

Archaeological Sites

You can arrange to take a boat or minibus tour to some of the archaeological sites and beaches along the nearby coasts. Standard tours go west to Günlük (Küçük Kargı), Pınarbaşı, Dalyan and Kaunos, and east to Letoön, Kalkan, Kaş, Patara and Xanthos. See those sections for details on the sites and bear in mind that it will often be cheaper just to take a minibus direct to the site.

Beaches

About 5km north-east of the centre is **Çalış**, a wide swath of beach several kilometres long solidly lined with uninspiring hotels and pensions. Once very popular, it's now overshadowed by nearby Ölüdeniz. If you want to stay for more than a day or so, it will almost certainly be cheaper to book through a European tour operator. Dolmuşes depart for Çalış from the minibus garage throughout the day.

12-Island Tour

Be sure to sign up for the 12-Island tour, a boat trip around Fethiye Körfezi which takes most of a day (9 am to 6 or 7 pm) and costs between US$8 and US$11 per person. Any hotel or travel agency can sign you up, or ask around at the harbour.

A normal tour visits **Şövalye Adası**, an island at the mouth of the inner bay, with a beach and restaurant; **Gemile Adası**, with the unrestored ruins of an ancient city; **Katrancık Adası**, offshore from the beach of the same name to the west of Fethiye; **Göcek Adası**, opposite the town 27km west of Fethiye; and the **islands** named Kızılada, Tersane, Domuz, Yassıcalar, Delikli, Şeytanlı and Karacaören.

WESTERN MEDITERRANEAN

The Lycians

Ancient Lycia extended along the Mediterranean coast roughly from Köyceğiz in the west to Antalya in the east. The Lycians first crop up in history when Homer records their presence during an attack on Troy in the *Iliad*. It is thought they may have been descendants of an Anatolian tribe called the Luvians. A matrilineal people with their own language, the Lycians lived in city-states, 23 of which formed the Lycian Federation to make communal decisions about 'foreign affairs'.

By the 6th century BC the Lycians had come under the loose control of Persia. In the 5th century BC the Athenians briefly drove the Persians out of Lycia which became part of the Delian Confederacy. All too soon, however, the Persians were back in charge, followed in turn by Alexander the Great, the Ptolemies, the Romans and the Rhodians. During this period the Lycians abandoned their own language in favour of Greek.

In the 2nd century BC Lycia was governed by the Pergamene kings. When the last of them died without an heir, he bequeathed Lycia to the Romans who incorporated it in their province of Asia. In spite of this nominal loss of independence, the Lycians seem to have continued their own way until, in 42 AD, the resurgent Lycian League made the unwise decision not to support Brutus, leading to the destruction of Xanthos.

In 43 AD the Romans joined Lycia to adjacent Pamphylia as a single province, a union that survived until the 4th century. Lycia never again regained its independence, succumbing in turn to invading Arabs and Turks.

The most obvious reminders of ancient Lycia are the monumental sarcophagi littering the Mediterranean coast and the rock-cut tombs, sometimes resembling temples, high up on the hillsides at Dalyan, Xanthos, Fethiye, Kaş and Myra. At Letoön there are ruins of a huge temple built by the Lycian Federation to commemorate Leto, their supreme deity. Fethiye Müzesi also contains a trilingual stele which was used to decipher the Lycian language.

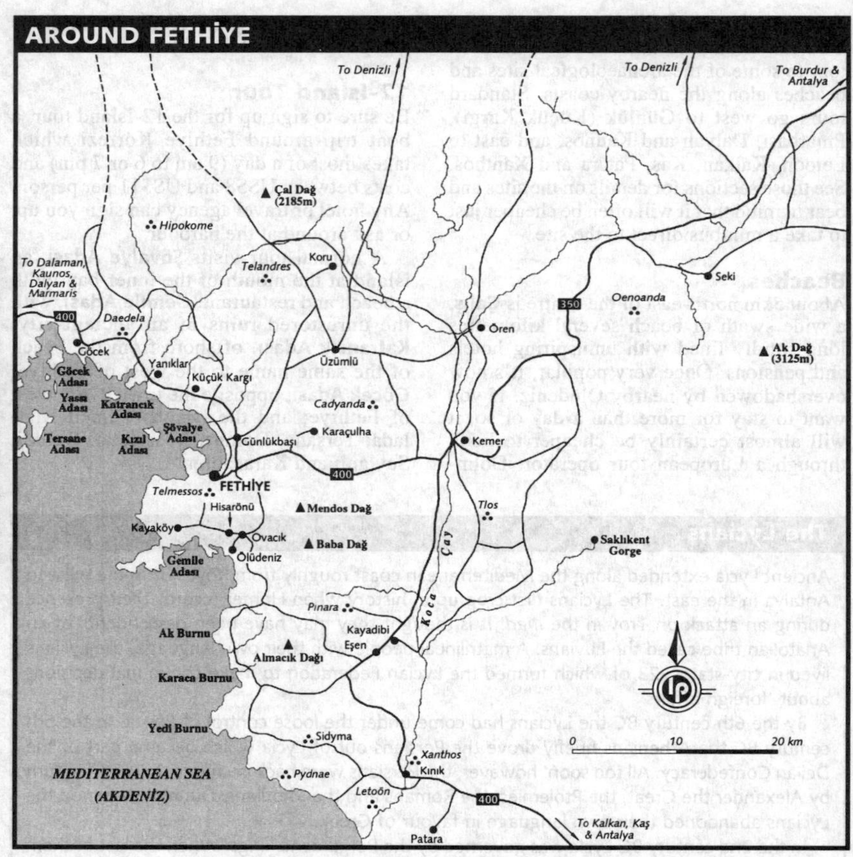

Scuba Diving

The European Diving Centre (☎ 252-614 9771), a scuba diving company located on a boat and founded by two Welshmen, offers day trips for US$55, including two dives and lunch. The diving is well organised and visibility is excellent, though the seabed is somewhat littered, and overfishing (and dynamite fishing) has robbed the area of much of its marine life. If you don't have a diver's certificate, you can take a certification course for US$300. There are other diving companies as well.

Places to Stay

Fethiye has a good selection of budget and mid-range accommodation, but little in the way of luxury. Most of the better places are block-booked by European tour operators in summer.

Places to Stay – Budget

Fethiye has several dozen small, downtown hotels and almost 100 small pensions so you're sure to find something. Pension owners with vacant rooms await your bus at the otogar.

East of the Centre *Göreme Pansiyon (☎/fax 252-614 6944, Dolgu Sahası, Stadyum Yanı 25)*, is run by the friendly, helpful Mrs Duvarcı who once lived in England and speaks English. B&B in spotless rooms congenial to single women costs US$10/16 a single/double. From the minibus station, cross Atatürk Caddesi to the northern side and walk north 450m to the northern side of the stadium.

West of the Centre The main concentration of pensions near the centre is west of the Tourism Information Office, up the hill inland from the yacht marina in the district called 1. Karagözler Mahallesi: look for the 'pansiyon' signs. Many places provide rooms with retro-fitted showers (some crudely), but some rooms are waterless.

Walking along Fevzi Çakmak Caddesi, you'll come to a row of pensions conveniently located but subject to traffic noise. ***Yıldırım Pansiyon*** *(☎ 252-614 3913, Fevzi Çakmak Caddesi 37)* charges US$15 to US$20 for a double with shower, depending upon whether the room is at the back (cheaper) or at the front. ***Pınara Pansiyon*** *(☎ 252-614 2151)* and ***Derelioğlu Pansiyon*** *(☎ 252-614 5983)*, next along in the row, are similar. ***İrem Pansiyon*** *(☎ 252-614 3985, fax 614 5875)* at No 45 is the most elaborate and charges US$24 a double with shower, with breakfast served on the comfy terrace with a sea view. The adjoining ***Villa İrem*** (same phone) is a bit more posh.

Up the steep hill behind these places on Zafer Caddesi (follow signs for Hotel Pırlanta) are several excellent, quieter choices, including the ***Pension İdeal*** *(☎ 252-614 1981, Zafer Caddesi 1)*, with a fine terrace overlooking the bay. All rooms have showers and cost US$16/24 a single/double in high season with breakfast included.

Further uphill on the right is the friendly ***İnci Pension*** *(☎ 252-614 3325)*, with clean, shower-equipped rooms for US$12/18 a single/double. On the left, follow signs to ***Pension Savaşçı*** *(☎ 252-614 6681)* which charges US$15/24 for rooms with spectacular harbour views.

The Centre *Ülgen Pansiyon (☎ 252-614 3491, fax 614 2911)*, up a flight of steps off Çarşı Caddesi, has a warren of assorted, ramshackle rooms administered by the voluble Seyfi Bey. Plumbing arrangements and number of beds differ from room to room, but the standard rate is US$5 per person, with breakfast costing US$2 extra.

Places to Stay – Mid-Range

Hotel Plaza *(☎ 252-614 9030, fax 614 1070, Atatürk Caddesi 2)*, on the corner of Çarşı Caddesi, charges US$18/26 for a double with shower and breakfast, but they'll do a deal if business is slow. Watch out for noise here.

Hotel Kemal *(☎/fax 252-614 5009)*, Kordon Boyu Gezi Yolu, has a quiet, convenient location directly behind the PTT facing the bay. Two-star rooms with private bathroom and breakfast cost US$18/28 a single/double.

An equally quiet area is the one behind the PTT and between the Hükümet Konağı and the museum, where you'll find several good three-star hotels including ***Hotel Sesa Park*** *(☎ 252-614 4656, fax 614 4326, Akdeniz Caddesi 17)*, which overlooks a small park and the sea, with comfortable rooms for US$45 a double with breakfast.

The three-star ***Hotel Victoria*** *(☎ 252-614 4501, fax 614 4596, Hastane Caddesi 7/A)*, is even quieter, at the same price. The adjoining ***Otel Mara*** *(☎ 252-614 6722, fax 614 8039, Kral Caddesi, Yalı Sokak 2)*, is the best of the lot however, charging US$30/48 a single/double, breakfast included.

A block away, ***Otel Vizon*** *(☎ 252-614 4424, fax 614 5173)* is less elaborate, but still good, and well worth the price of US$22/35 a single/double with breakfast.

The three-star ***Hotel Pırlanta*** *(☎ 252-614 4959, fax 614 1686, 1 Karagözler Mevkii)*, is up the hill from the yacht marina. Many of its 72 rooms with bathrooms and balconies have wonderful water views. Rates are posted as US$30/50, but are subject to debate.

Places to Eat

There is no shortage of places to eat in Fethiye but you should always ask prices, at least for the main course, and especially for fish, before you order. If you haven't ordered something don't let waiters put it on your table. If they do, ask *Bedava mı?* (Is it free?) It rarely is. Check your bill carefully for 'errors'.

On Çarşı Caddesi a block off Atatürk Caddesi, ***Özlem Pide ve Kebap Salonu*** will serve you köfte, salad, and soda for less than US$4. A bit further south on Çarşı Caddesi are ***Pizza Pepino*** and ***Pizza Villa*** if you prefer your pide Italian-style. Pepino serves tasty pizzas under a shady vine for reasonable prices; a good vegetarian pizza costs US$6.

Directly across Çarşı Caddesi from the Özlem on Tütün Sokak is ***Sedir Lokantası & Kebap House***, a local favourite serving pizzas for US$2 to US$3.50, meat plates for US$4 to US$5 and a 'vegetarian surprise' for US$3.

Around the corner from the Özlem, the gimmick at ***The Duck Pond*** is just that: as you dine you can watch the ducks who live in the pond and who boast such un-Turkish names as Mike, Lady Diana and Arnold Schwarzenegger.

Behind the PTT, look for ***Billy Pizza Burger*** and the larger, nicer ***Çakıroğlu Restaurant*** across the street, both very popular with local people for all three meals. Lunch or dinner might cost US$5 to US$8.

For serious dining, however, go to the heart of the bazaar and ***Güneş Restaurant***, with indoor dining rooms as well as open-air cafe dining in good weather. There's a good range of meat and fish dishes and cold starters here and prices aren't bad either (chicken kebap for US$5), but service can be slow. The adjoining ***Meğri*** is similar, and locals seem to prefer the nearby ***Han Restaurant***.

For atmosphere, try ***Yacht Restaurant***, facing the yacht marina. The outdoor tables are pleasant, service polite and the food quite good. A fish dinner might cost about US$18, drinks included. Turkish music and dancing are sometimes laid on at no extra charge. ***Daisy Restaurant*** to the right of Yacht Restaurant is a bit cheaper, but otherwise similar.

Entertainment

Up above the harbour, Liman Caddesi boasts several bars. Towards the end of the street up behind the Tourism Information Office an old house has been converted into the ***Yasmin Bar*** with idiosyncratic 'classical' decoration and an odd mix of music (Turkish folk the last time I was there). The adjoining ***Lycian Fire***, also in a restored Ottoman house, will have something different. Locals seem to prefer the ***Yes Bar*** in Cumhuriyet Caddesi in the bazaar.

Getting There & Away

Air The nearest airport is 50km to the west at Dalaman (one hour, US$2). Antalya airport, a four-hour bus ride to the east, has far more flights. The Turkish Airlines agent in Fethiye is Fetur (☎ 252-614 2443, fax 614 3845), Fevzi Çakmak Caddesi, Körfez Apt No 9/1, near the Otel Dedeoğlu and the yacht harbour.

Bus The mountains behind Fethiye force transport to go east or west and for many destinations you must change buses at Antalya or Muğla. There are, however, buses heading eastward along the coast at least every two hours in summer. Bus fares along this stretch of coast tend to be higher than usual as the passengers are mostly tourists. The highways in this region are being improved, with new routes, wider curves and more gentle grades. These improvements shorten highway distances and decrease travel times.

The otogar, situated 2km east of the centre, handles services to main destinations like İstanbul, Ankara, Antalya and Alanya. For intermediate distance destinations such as the ones following, go to the minibus garage off Atatürk Caddesi 1km west of the centre:

Çiftlik, Esenköy, Eşen, Göcek, Günlüklü Plajlar, Hacıosmanlar, Hisarönü, Kadıköy, Karadere, Karamersin, Kargı, Katrancı, Kaya, Kayadibi, Kemer, Kumluova, Otel Tuana, Ovacık, Ölüdeniz (stops at main otogar as well), Saklıkent, Tlos, Yanıklar and Yonca Camping.

Some approximate times and distances for routes from the main otogar include:

Antalya – 295km, 7½ hours, US$8 (*sahil*, 'coastal route'); 222km, four hours, US$6 (*yayla*, 'inland route')
Dalaman – 50km, one hour, US$2
Demre – 155km, three hours, US$5
Denizli – 290km, 4½ hours, US$4
Kalkan – 81km, two hours, US$3.25
Kaş – 110km, 2½ hours, US$3.50
Letoön – 60km, 1¼ hours, US$2
Marmaris – 170km, three hours, US$5; hourly buses in summer
Muğla – 150km, three hours, US$5; frequent buses in summer
Ölüdeniz – 7km, 15 minutes, US$1
Pamukkale – 309km, five hours, US$6; better to take a bus to Denizli, then a dolmuş
Patara – 75km, 1½ hours, US$3.25
Pınara – 52km, one hour, US$2
Tlos – 40km, one hour, US$2
Xanthos (Kınık) – 65km, 1½ hours, US$2.25

Boat In high summer a hydrofoil service operates between Rhodes (Greece) and Fethiye on Tuesday and Thursday. A one-way ticket will cost you US$50; a day return US$75 and an open return US$95. The travel agencies in town can book tickets but will need your passport 24 hours in advance.

Getting Around

Minibuses ply the one-way system along Atatürk Caddesi and up Çarşı Caddesi to the otogar all day. There's a fixed charge of US$0.30 however far you go. A taxi from the otogar to the pensions east of the centre will cost about US$5.

ÖLÜDENİZ

Ölüdeniz (eur-LUR-deh-neez, Dead or Calm Sea), 8.5km south-east of Fethiye, is not devoid of life like its biblical namesake. Rather, it's a sheltered lagoon hidden from the open sea. The scene as you come down from the pine-forested hills is absolutely beautiful: in the distance open sea; in the foreground a peaceful lagoon bordered by forest; in the middle a long spit of perfect sandy beach.

Nowadays Ölüdeniz has a reputation for its party atmosphere. Don't come here in August expecting tranquillity.

As most accommodation at the beach fills early in the day in high summer, you may want to plan your first night's stay in Fethiye. Then come out to Ölüdeniz the same day and find something for the next few nights.

Orientation

As you approach Ölüdeniz, the road passes through the characterless towns of Ovacık and Hisarönü, dormitory towns for the package-tour hordes. The main road descends steeply from Hisarönü another 3km to the beautiful swath of beach. Haphazard development begins a few kilometres inland from the shore, and terminates with a jumble of makeshift camping areas and rentable shacks shaded by pine and olive trees and overlooking the free, public, Belcekız Plajı (beach).

The beach is very much the centre of things. To your right, on the road from Fethiye, you pass a jandarma post, a PTT and the entrance to the Ölüdeniz Tabiat Parkı, with a pay beach (US$0.50) winding around the lagoon. This stretch has been laid out with paths, showers, toilets and makeshift cafes. The road continues behind the park to several camping grounds and the expensive Hotel Meri high above the lagoon.

To your left as you arrive the beach promenade is closed to traffic and backed with restaurants and 'camps' with small cabins, usually full in high season. Behind these cabin camps sprawl an ever-growing number of small and not so small hotels.

At the eastern end of the beach, the road climbs up a slope and clings to the mountainside for 2km before descending to Kıdrak Orman Parkı (Kıdrak Forest Park), with the most beautiful camping grounds of all.

Information

The Ölüdeniz Tourism Development Co-operative (Ölüdeniz Turizm Geliştirme Vakfı) (☎ 252-617 0438, fax 617 0135) maintains an information booth on the access road just inland from the beach. They can help you find a room.

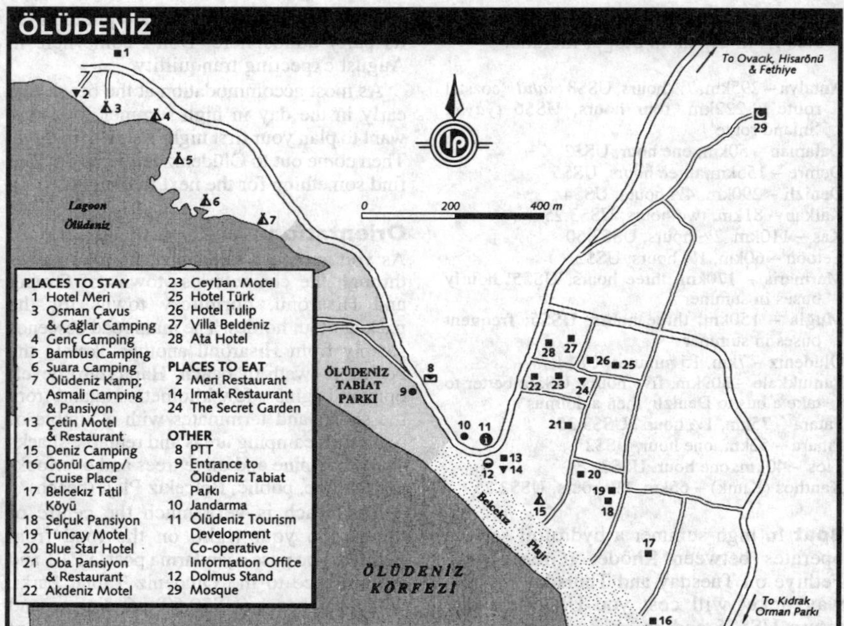

Things to See & Do

Explorations of the coast and Butterfly Valley, as well as water sports and paragliding are among the things to see and do.

Excursions Throughout summer, excursion boats set out to explore the coast, charging roughly US$14 for a day trip including lunch. A typical excursion might take in Gemile Beach, the Blue Cave, Butterfly Valley and St Nicholas Island, with time for swimming as well. Some readers have not thought this trip good value for money. If you want to snorkel, ask how much equipment will be available before booking.

Butterfly Valley Although you can get to Butterfly Valley, home of the unique Jersey Tiger butterfly, on a tour, you might prefer to spend the night there, in which case boats leave Ölüdeniz daily at 11 am and 2 and 6 pm, charging US$12 return. Once there, you can spend the night in a treehouse platform, where beds cost US$4 per person, and eat at the beach cafe; this is not recommended for single women. Alternatively a relatively dangerous path winds up a cliff to a house where better food is available.

Sports You can rent water-sports equipment on the main beach. Several agencies offer tandem paragliding flights from a 1900m cliff for US$100 a thrill. Parasailing comes much cheaper at a mere US$35.

Places to Stay – Budget

These days Ölüdeniz is so much package-holiday territory that those on a tight budget will be scrabbling around to find somewhere suitable. Fortunately there are plenty of camp sites, most of them offering fixed tents and cabins with or without running water for those who don't want the trouble of carting the equipment around with them.

Camping & Cabins The camp sites around the lagoon on the way to Hotel Meri are quieter but less convenient than the ones inland from Belcekız Plajı. Tents sites usually cost about US$6 or US$7 for two people. Most camping grounds have little restaurants or snack shops.

The road heading to Hotel Meri winds past five camping grounds. ***Ölüdeniz Kamp*** *(☎ 252-617 0048, fax 617 0181)* offers a variety of options, including tent sites and waterless cabins for US$12 a double or cabins with shower for US$19. Adjoining it, ***Asmalı Camping & Pansiyon*** *(☎ 252-617 0137)* has tents and a few bungalows for rent, but mostly sites for tents and caravans. About 100m further on, ***Suara Camping*** *(☎ 252-617 0123)* is about the best place to stay if you have your own tent.

Osman Çavuş Camping *(☎ 252-616 6002)* and ***Çağlar Camping*** *(☎ 252-617 0017)*, across from Hotel Meri, have waterless bungalows for US$15 as well as tent sites.

Inland from Belcekız Plajı one of the most popular camping areas is ***Deniz Camping*** *(☎ 252-617 0045, fax 617 0054, cemgurk@hotmail.com)* which has a big restaurant, a book exchange and the popular Buzz Bar, as well as tidy waterless wooden cabins for US$15 a double. Reserve in advance if possible.

Oba Pansiyon *(☎ 252-617 0470, fax 617 0158)* has a grassy lawn and cabins with showers for US$22 to US$26 in high summer. It costs less during low season and for waterless cabins. There's also a good restaurant.

Near the quieter south-eastern end of Belcekız Plajı, ***Gönül Camp*** *(☎ 252-617 0406)*, also called Cruise Place and Gönül Motel, has waterless A-frame shelters for US$15 and rooms with showers for US$20 to US$24.

Finally, ***Kıdrak Orman Parkı***, 2km to the south-east, has cheap tent sites in a pine grove, simple facilities and a good beach, but the huge Club Likya World resort just south of it encroaches on its serenity.

Hotels Most of Ölüdeniz's hotels have their sights firmly fixed on package holidaymakers but if they're not full they'll gladly take individual travellers. There are one or two smaller places as well. The ***Çetin Motel*** *(☎ 252-617 0014, 617 0051)*, behind the Çetin Restaurant on the beach, has an unbeatable location and double rooms with shower and breakfast for US$25 in high summer. ***Blue Lagoon Motel*** *(☎ 252-617 0046, fax 617 0169)*, 300m inland from the beach, is under the same management.

If there's nothing in your price range near the beach, head back 2km up the access road to the junction with Hisarönü. On the right-hand side of the road is a cluster of more affordable, traditional, family-run pensions – ***Mutlu***, ***Demet*** and ***Üstün***. The Üstün is the newest and a good distance from the road so it's likely to be the quietest.

Places to Stay – Mid-Range

Inland from the beach, the 24 room ***Tuncay Motel*** *(☎ 252-617 0034)* is tidy and quiet, charging US$45 a double in high season.

Villa Beldeniz *(☎ 252-617 0103, fax 617 0109)* is older than most Ölüdeniz hotels and therefore not quite up to the group-tour standards, so it charges less (US$36 for a double with bath and breakfast) and may have rooms when you want them. There's a small swimming pool.

The two-star ***Blue Star Hotel*** *(☎ 252-617 0069, fax 617 0128)* is new, with a good swimming pool, a kids pool and a price of US$42 a double with breakfast. ***Hotel Tulip*** *(☎ 252-617 0074, fax 617 0221)* is similar, if a bit more expensive, as is ***Hotel Türk*** *(☎ 252-617 0444)*.

At the far end of Belcekız Plajı there's an even flashier place, ***Belcekız Tatil Köyü*** *(☎ 252-617 0077, fax 617 0372)*, formerly the Club Bekcekız Beach. Rooms here have tiled floors, modern decor and fabrics, pleasant bathrooms and small terraces. There's a huge pool, a Turkish bath and several dining areas. Rooms here don't come cheap, at US$80 a double (virtually the same for single occupancy), but you might get a better deal through a tour operator.

Places to Stay – Top End

At the end of the road winding around the lagoon stands the two-star ***Hotel Meri*** *(☎ 252-617 0001, fax 617 0010)* with 75 rooms tumbling down the hillside amid picturesque gardens. The views from many of the rooms, especially those at the top, are magnificent. The oldest hotel at Ölüdeniz, it has been refurbished and is comfortable but even its position hardly justifies prices of US$110/160 a single/double with full board. The hotel has its own beach and a seaside eatery called ***Meri Restaurant***.

Places to Eat

As staff changes frequently at beachside restaurants, the best approach is to do the beachfront stroll, looking at menus and prices, seeing which restaurants are full or empty and even asking the opinion of other diners (particularly those who, having paid their bill, are just leaving). For lower prices, as always, go inland away from the beach.

The ***Çetin*** and ***Irmak*** restaurants, facing Belcekız beach, seem to be the most popular places. ***The Secret Garden***, inland, is a pleasant restaurant hidden away in dense foliage. Meals may not be particularly cheap here but they will be enjoyable.

Getting There & Away

In summer minibuses leave Fethiye for Ölüdeniz roughly every 15 minutes (8.5km, 20 minutes, US$1). Some of them also drop off in Hisarönü.

KAYAKÖY (KARMYLASSOS)

Called Levissi for much of its history, this town of 2000 stone houses, just more than 5km west of Hisarönü, was deserted by its mostly Ottoman Greek inhabitants after WWI and the Turkish War of Independence. The League of Nations supervised an exchange of populations between Turkey and Greece, with most Greek Muslims coming from Greece to Turkey and most Ottoman Christians moving to Greece. The people of Levissi, most of whom were Orthodox Christians, moved to the outskirts of Athens and founded Nea Levissi there.

As there were far more Ottoman Greeks than Greek Muslims, many of the towns vacated by the Ottoman Greeks were left unoccupied after the exchange of populations. Kayaköy, as it is called now, has only a handful of Turkish inhabitants.

With the tourism boom of the 1980s, a development company wanted to restore Kayaköy's stone houses and turn the town into a holiday village. Scenting money, the local inhabitants were delighted, but Turkish artists and architects were alarmed, and saw to it that the Ministry of Culture declared Kayaköy, or Kaya as it's called locally, a historical monument, safe from unregulated development.

There are now plans for careful restoration of the town, and its use as a venue for cultural presentations.

Two churches are still prominent: the Kataponagia in the lower part of the town and the Taxiarkis further up the slope. Both retain some of their painted decoration and black and white pebble mosaic floors.

In summer there are hourly minibuses from Fethiye to Kaya (30 minutes, US$1). Alternatively it's about a one-hour walk downhill through pine forest from Hisarönü. There's also a marked trail to Ölüdeniz which should take two to 2½ hours (8km) – although some readers have taken much longer!

If you want to stay at Kaya (a pleasant and certainly quieter alternative to staying in Hisarönü or Ölüdeniz) there's ***Çavuşoğlu Motel*** *(☎ 252-616 6749)* with a big swimming pool about 100m west of the Kayaköy entrance. Simple rooms here cost US$22 a double with bath and breakfast. The rather isolated ***Selçuk Pension*** *(☎ 252-616 6757)* is a bit further along.

FETHİYE TO KAŞ

This portion of the Lycian coast, sometimes called the Lycian Peninsula because it extends well south into the Mediterranean, is littered with the remains of ancient cities. With your own transport you can visit as many of these as you like by making a few short detours. Without a car you can still make your way to many of them by dolmuş or bus, with perhaps a bit of a hike here and there.

The highways in the Lycian Peninsula are rapidly being improved which sometimes means changes in their routes. Keep this in mind as you travel to the sites described.

Tlos

Tlos was one of the oldest and most important cities in ancient Lycia. Its prominence is matched by its promontory, as the city has a dramatic setting high on a rocky outcrop. As you climb the winding road to Tlos, look for the fortress-topped **acropolis** on the right. What you see is Ottoman-era work, but the Lycians had a fort in the same place. Beneath it, reached by narrow paths, are the familiar **rock-cut tombs**, including that of Bellerophon, a pseudo-temple facade carved into the rockface which has a fine bas-relief of the hero riding Pegasus, the winged horse. You can reach the tomb by walking along a stream bed, then turning left and climbing a crude ladder.

The **theatre** is 100m further up the road from the ticket kiosk, and is in excellent condition, with most of its marble seating intact, though the stage wall is gone. There's a fine view of the **acropolis** from here. Off to the right of the theatre (as you sit in the centre rows) is an ancient **Lycian sarcophagus** in a farmer's field. The **necropolis** on the path up to the fortress has many stone sarcophagi.

The site is open daily from 8 am to 5 pm for US$1. One of the men at the ticket kiosk will offer to be your guide (for a tip), which is a good idea if you want to see all the rock-cut tombs.

Places to Stay & Eat A meal of trout in garlic sauce, salad, bread and a cold drink will cost you US$10 at ***Café Tlawa Restaurant*** opposite the site. Simple rooms are available here in an emergency, or you could try ***Mountain Lodge*** or ***Çağrı Pension*** back down the road to the highway. With your own transport you could press on for another 2km to the lovely ***Yaka Park Restaurant*** (*☎ 252-638 2011*), where tables cascade down the hillside, shaded with plane trees and cooled with running water. The bar counter here has a channel cut into it along which trout swim so visitors can tickle them. How much the trout enjoy this experience is open to question of course.

Getting There & Away The easiest way to get to Tlos is to take a dolmuş from Fethiye to Saklıkent. This passes within 4km of the site. It would be a tough walk because the road climbs steadily uphill but you might be able to get a lift or negotiate with the driver to drop you off. Driving, follow the signs to Saklıkent from Kayadibi and watch for the yellow ancient monument sign on the left.

Saklıkent Gorge

Another 12km after the turn-off to Tlos you will come to the spectacular Saklıkent Gorge cut into the Akdağlar. The gorge is 18km long and so steep and narrow that the sun doesn't penetrate so the water is icy-cold, even in summer. You approach the gorge along a wooden boardwalk above the river which opens out into a series of wooden platforms suspended above the water where you can buy and eat trout. From there you wade across the river, hanging onto a rope and then continue into the gorge proper, sometimes walking in mud, sometimes in the water. Plastic shoes can be hired for US$0.50, a worthwhile investment if you're going to get the most out of the walk.

The gorge is open daily from 8 am to 5 pm for US$2. Get there in summer by taking a dolmuş from Fethiye. It takes about 45 minutes, past lovely fields of cotton, and costs US$2. If there's no direct minibus, take one to Kayadibi and change. Alternatively you can sign up for an excursion from Fethiye, Kaş or Kalkan.

Back on the highway heading south towards Kaş, the road takes you up into fragrant evergreen forests and down into fertile valleys. You'll see herds of sheep and goats (and a few cattle) along the road near the villages. The road is curvy and the journey somewhat slow.

Pınara

Some 46km south-east of Fethiye, near the village of Esen, is a turn-off (to the right) for Pınara, which lies another 6km up in the mountains. Infrequent minibuses from Fethiye (one hour, US$1.75) drop you at the start of the Pınara road and you can walk to the site, or bargain with the driver to take you all the way.

The road winds through tobacco and cornfields and across irrigation channels for more than 3km to the village of Minare, then takes a sharp left turn to climb the slope. The last 2km or so are extremely steep. If you decide to walk make sure you stock up on water first. There's a cafe at the foot of the slope and nothing after that.

At the top of the slope is an open parking area and near it a cool, shady spring with refreshing water. The guardian will probably appear and offer to show you around the ruins and it would pay to take up the offer as the path around the site (which is always open) is not easy to follow. You should probably tip the guardian if you have a tour.

Pınara was among the most important cities in ancient Lycia but, although the site is vast, the actual ruins are not Turkey's most impressive. Instead it's the sheer splendour of the isolated setting which makes the journey so worthwhile, the new toilet block providing the one jarring note.

The sheer column of rock behind the site, and the rock walls to its left, are honeycombed with **rock-cut tombs**. To reach any of them would take several hours. Other **tombs** are within the ruined city itself. The one called the Royal (or King's) Tomb has particularly fine reliefs, including several showing walled cities. Pınara's **theatre** is in good condition, its **odeum** and **temples** of Apollo, Aphrodite and Athena (with heart-shaped columns) badly ruined.

The village at **Esen**, 3km south-east of the Pınara turn-off, has a few basic restaurants.

Sidyma

About 4km from Esen, a rough dirt road to the left goes 12km to Sidyma. The ruins are not spectacular. If you've seen all the other Lycian cities and are simply aching for more, then take the time to visit Sidyma. Otherwise, press onward.

Letoön

About 17km south of the Pınara turn-off is the road to Letoön. The turn-off is on the right-hand (south-west) side near the village of Kumluova. (Dolmuşes run from Fethiye via Esen to Kumluova. Get out at the Letoön turn-off.) Turn right off the highway, go 3.2km to a T-junction, turn left, then right after 100m (this turn-off is easy to miss) and proceed 1km to the site through fertile fields and orchards and past greenhouses full of tomato plants. If you miss the second turn you'll end up on the main square of the village. There are no services as this is still a farming village largely unaffected by tourism.

When you get to the ruins (open daily from 8.30 am to 5 pm), a person selling soft drinks and admission tickets (US$1) will greet you.

Letoön takes its name and importance from a large shrine to Leto, who according to legend was loved by Zeus. Unimpressed, Zeus' wife Hera commanded that Leto spend an eternity wandering from country to country. According to local folklore she spent much of this enforced holiday time in Lycia, becoming the Lycian national deity. The federation of Lycian cities then built this very impressive religious sanctuary to worship her.

The site consists of three **temples** side by side: Apollo (on the left), Artemis (in the middle) and Leto (on the right). The Temple of Apollo has a nice mosaic showing a lyre and a bow and arrow. The **nymphaeum** is permanently flooded (and inhabited by frogs), which is appropriate as worship of Leto was somehow associated with water. Nearby is a large Hellenistic **theatre** in excellent condition.

Xanthos

At Kınık, 63km from Fethiye, the road crosses a river. Up to the left on a rock outcrop is the ruined city of Xanthos, once the capital and grandest city of Lycia, with a fine **Roman theatre** and **Lycian pillar tombs** with Lycian inscriptions. Dolmuşes run here from Fethiye and Kaş and some long-distance buses will stop if you ask.

It's a short walk up the hill to the site which can be visited from 8.30 am to 5.30 pm for US$2. For all its importance and grandeur, Xanthos had a chequered history of wars and destruction. Several times, when besieged by clearly superior enemy forces, the city was destroyed by its own inhabitants. You'll see the **theatre** at once, with the **agora** opposite. Despite Xanthos's importance, the **acropolis** is now badly ruined. As many of the finest sculptures and inscriptions were carted off to the British Museum in 1842, many of the inscriptions and decorations you see today are copies of the originals. However, French excavations in the 1950s have made Xanthos well worth seeing.

Patara

Heading east again, after 7km you'll reach the turn-off on the right for Patara where the ruins come with a bonus in the form of a wonderful white sand beach some 50m wide and 20km long.

Patara was the birthplace of St Nicholas, the 4th-century Byzantine bishop who later passed into legend as Santa Claus. Before that, Patara was famous for its temple and oracle of Apollo, of which little remains.

These days Patara attracts a party crowd, so don't be fooled by its size into thinking you're going to a particularly quiet resort.

Orientation Look for the Patara turn-off just east of the village of Ovaköy; from here it's 3.5km to the village of Gelemiş, commonly called Patara, and another 1.5km to the Patara ruins. The beach is another 1km past the ruins and some dolmuşes will take you there.

As you come into Gelemiş, on your left is a hillside holding various hotels and pensions. A turn to the right at Golden Pension takes you to the village centre, across the valley and up the other side to more pensions and the three-star Hotel Beyhan Patara.

The Ruins Admission to the ruins and beach costs US$3, payable only once even if you go to the beach on subsequent days (save your ticket). Patara's ruins include a triple-arched **triumphal gate** at the entrance to the site with a **necropolis** with several **Lycian tombs** nearby. Next are the **baths** and much later, a **basilica**.

The good sized **theatre** is striking because it is half-covered by wind-driven sand, which seems intent on making a dune out of it. Climb to the top for a good view of the whole site.

There are also several other **baths**, two **temples** and a **Corinthian temple** by the lake, although the swampy ground may make them difficult to approach. Across the lake is a **granary**. What is now a swamp was once the city's harbour. When it silted up in the Middle Ages, the city declined.

Patara Beach The beach is simply splendid. You can get there by following the road past the ruins, or by turning right at Golden Pension and following the track which heads for the sand dunes on the other (western) side of the archaeological zone. It's about a 30-minute walk. Sometimes you can hitch a ride with vehicles passing along the main road.

Be sure to bring footwear for crossing the 50m of scorching sand to the water's edge, and also something for shelter as there are few places to escape the sun. If you don't have your own shelter, rent an umbrella on the beach for US$2.

Behind the beach ***Patara Restaurant*** provides shade and sustenance, and there's a wooden shack on the sand selling kebaps. Or you might prefer to bring a picnic. The beach closes at dusk as it is a nesting ground for sea turtles. Note that camping is prohibited.

Çayağzı Beach On the western side of the stream by the access road from the highway to Gelemiş (Patara), a sign points the way to Çayağzı Beach (5km), the Patara alternative, with basic beach services and camping facilities.

Places to Stay – Budget Patara has grown quickly and chaotically in recent years and now has accommodation in all price ranges. The ones at higher elevation have fewer mosquitoes, which are a pest here in summer. Bilal's Shop in the village advertises 'We have everything you need to be bite-free'.

The best known of the cheap pensions is ***Golden Pension & Restaurant*** *(☎ 242-843 5162, fax 843 5008)*, right in the village centre, with 15 rooms – six with private shower, nine without – and a restaurant on the roof. The charge for a double room with shower is US$20 in season and slightly less in the low season. The owner, Muzaffer Otlu, speaks some English and French and is very friendly. He also owns ***Hotel Patara Viewpoint*** *(☎ 242-843 5184)*, high up on the hill above the road leading to the ruins. Rooms there are newer and classier and cost a bit more.

On the road into Gelemiş are several pensions charging lower rates: ***Flower***, ***Rose*** and ***Akay***. Longer-established pensions here include ***St Nicholas*** *(☎ 242-843 5024)*, ***Hotel Sisyphos*** *(☎ 242-843 5043)*, and ***Ali Baba*** *(☎ 242-843 5262)* charging about the same as the Golden.

Turn right into the village and continue up the hill by ***Eucalyptus Pension*** *(☎ 242-843 5076)* to ***Topaloğlu*** *(☎ 242-843 5030)* for rooms at US$14 a double.

Turn right past the PTT for ***Patara Motel***, a newer building with double rooms with shower for US$18 to US$20 in season and almost half price in the low season.

On the opposite side of the valley on the road to Hotel Beyhan Patara, ***Zeybek 1*** and ***Apollon*** offer good value for money; ***Zeybek 2*** and ***Ferah*** are almost as good; and ***Sülo*** is suitable.

Camping In the village, there are several camping grounds which are relocated frequently as construction pushes them from one lot to the next.

Places to Stay – Mid-Range Up on the hillside to the left as you enter the village are several hotels and lots of holiday villas. ***Hotel Delfin*** *(☎ 242-843 5215)* has standard Turkish hotel rooms with shower and balcony for US$32 a double, a terrace restaurant and pool. ***Hotel Xanthos*** *(☎ 242-844 2124)*, higher on the hill above the Delfin, also has a swimming pool and tennis court.

Patara's best hotel is the three-star ***Hotel Beyhan Patara*** *(☎ 242-843 5098, fax 843 5097)*, high up on the hill to the west of town. The building itself may be a standard ugly block but it's set in pretty gardens and facilities include a tennis court, hamam, sauna, sun decks, two restaurants, an exercise room and 132 air-con rooms priced at US$45 for a double, breakfast and dinner included. Although this looks a peaceful situation, the hotel has five bars and is popular with tour groups so be sure to specify that you want a quiet room.

Places to Eat Most of the hotels and some of the pensions (including the Golden and the Patara Viewpoint) have restaurants. The most pleasant are the ones highest on the hill. Others open and close by the month, it seems. ***Florya Restaurant***, near the Golden Pension, has good food and reasonable prices at about US$5 for a full meal. About 50m north of the Golden Pension on the road into the village, ***Tlos Terrace – Bolu'lu Osman'ın Yeri*** has a chef-owner from Bolu, where most of Turkey's great chefs come from. Some village shops sell stale packaged food. ***Patara Market*** seems to have the edge on freshness.

Getting There & Away If you come to Patara by bus, be warned that it may drop you on the highway 3.5km from the village.

Patara Tur Minibüs Kooperatifi runs 10 to 15 minibuses daily to Fethiye in summer (at least three per day at other times) for US$3.25. At least five per day run to Kalkan (15km, 25 minutes, US$1.75) and Kaş (42km, one hour, US$2.50). In summer there are some direct long-distance buses, but in general you must take a minibus to Fethiye or Antalya (at least five daily) to catch one. Reserve your seat in the minibus in advance as seats can be scarce.

KALKAN & KAŞ

Just past Patara are Kalkan and Kaş, two very popular, small, if steadily growing, holiday resorts.

Of the two, Kalkan has the more upmarket reputation. There you can often stay in attractively designed and decorated buildings, but dining and nightlife options are relatively limited.

In Kaş you'll find yourself staying in a modern building of little architectural distinction but there are plenty of good places to eat. Nightlife, especially on the eastern side of town, can be pretty lively in summer. Kaş also boasts some excellent shops where you can buy handicrafts and fabrics from all over Turkey.

Kalkan

About 11km east of the Patara turn-off (81km east of Fethiye and 27km west of Kaş) the highway skirts Kalkan, a fishing village formerly occupied by Ottoman Greeks and called Kalamaki, but now completely devoted to tourism. Discovered a decade ago by intrepid travellers in search

of the simple, cheap, quiet life, this perfect Mediterranean village soon boasted a yacht marina, then some modern hotels and now a vast holiday village complex (Hotel Patara Prince and Club Patara) covering an entire hillside to the south.

Orientation Kalkan is built on a hillside sloping down to the bay and you'll find yourself trekking up and down it all day. Coming in from the highway the road zigzags down to a central parking lot with a taxi rank, bus offices, the PTT and banks. It then enters the main commercial area and descends the hill as Hasan Altan Caddesi or 6 Sokak.

The town's *sağlık ocağı* (health clinic) is out to the west past the Diva and Dionysia hotels.

More hotels and pensions can be found around the east of the bay.

Kalkan doesn't have a tourism information office but it has a Web site at www.kalkan.org.tr.

Kalkan's postal code is 07960.

Places to Stay – Budget Although cheap pensions are vanishing in favour of hotels suitable for the package-holiday market, there are still quite a few relatively cheap places to stay right in the centre of Kalkan and in prime positions on the waterfront.

Kalamaki Pension *(☎ 242-844 3649, fax 844 3654)*, run by Christine and Durmuş Uşaklı, is an excellent choice, charging US$19 for a double with bath and breakfast. They have a rooftop restaurant as well.

On the main shopping street, Mehmet Özalp, proprietor of ***Özalp Pansiyon*** *(☎ 242-844 3486)*, charges US$12/18 for good, modern rooms with shower and balcony. Some are tiny, others larger. There's a popular restaurant on the ground floor. The nearby ***Kervan Han Pansiyon*** is similar.

The nearby ***Çelik Pansiyon*** *(☎ 242-844 2126, Yalıboyu 9)*, more or less across from the Kalkan Han, is a standard simple pension charging US$12/18 a single/double with breakfast included. Continue along the road to the end for ***Holiday Pension*** or up the hill across the street for ***Gül Pansiyon*** *(☎ 242-844 3099)*, both more primitive and slightly cheaper.

Further down towards the harbour, ***Akın Pansiyon*** *(☎ 242-844 3025, fax 844 2094)* has some waterless rooms on the top floor priced at US$17 a double; rooms lower down with private showers cost US$22 with breakfast included.

Çetin Pansiyon *(☎ 242-844 3094)*, in the southern part of town, is out of the central bustle, quieter, cheaper and done in traditional style. Rooms cost US$16 a double.

Places to Stay – Mid-Range ***Zinbad Hotel*** *(☎ 242-844 3404, fax 844 3943, Yalıboyu Mahallesi 18)*, is newish, family run, pleasant and well priced at US$31 to US$36 for a double room with breakfast; the higher price buys you a sea view. Good dinners are served in the rooftop restaurant.

Balıkçı Han *(☎ 242-844 3075, fax 844 3640)*, is another house designed to look like an older building, with stone fireplaces, red-tiled floors, and panels of coloured faïence in the walls. Some rooms have brass beds. Rooms with private shower cost US$34 a double with breakfast included.

On the road winding down past the mosque to the harbour is ***Daphne Pansiyon*** *(☎ 242-844 3547)*, Hasan Altan Caddesi, nicely decorated with kilims and carpets, and with good reading lights in the bedrooms. You pay US$16/30 a single/double including breakfast on a pleasant roof terrace.

Almost hidden beneath its veil of bougainvillea is ***Patara Pansiyon*** *(☎ 242-844 3076)*, a lovely old stone house with views from the roof terrace. Rooms cost US$16/24 a single/double with shower and breakfast.

Out towards the west, Aldi Hotels runs four nice small modern hotels, ***Diva, Diana, Dionysia*** and ***Diana Apartments*** *(☎ 242-844 3175, fax 844 3139)* on Cumhuriyet Caddesi. They're all fine places to stay, and prices are reasonable, averaging US$30 to US$40 a double, breakfast included. But all are usually filled with groups; they'll take your reservation within 10 days or a week of the date you intend to stay if they have a vacancy.

The three-star ***Hotel Pirat*** *(☎ 242-844 3178, fax 844 3183)*, Kalkan Marina, has an older 1980s building and a newer complex built to look like a row of village houses. Together these two sections offer 136 comfortable, modern air-con rooms for US$48/66 a single/double, breakfast included.

Places to Eat Kalkan's eateries can be pricey because of their yachting clientele but choose carefully and you can still have a pleasant and not overly expensive meal.

One way to avoid the high prices is to eat where the locals do which would be at ***Ali Baba Lokantası*** and ***Doyum*** just north-west of the PTT. This is not the tourist district, so a full meal can be enjoyed for US$4 or US$5. ***Alternatif Restaurant*** is also well away from the touristy harbour.

Steps Terrace Café-Bar, opposite the bust of Atatürk at the foot of Hasan Altan Caddesi, has a varied cafe menu and takeaway sandwiches. Find ***Kervan Han Pideci*** for a decent pide for US$1.50 to US$3.50.

In the commercial district at the top of the town, ***Köşk Restaurant*** is somewhat expensive, but people come for the views from its terrace seating area. In fact, the rooftop restaurant at ***Zinbad Hotel*** has better views and reasonable prices.

For food in a 'Turkish' setting with tables at floor level and lots of kilims, head for ***Belgin's Kitchen*** where you can sample traditional dishes like *mantı* (Turkish ravioli) and *çiğ börek* (raw ground lamb in a pastry roll). Expect to spend US$10 to US$16 for a meal.

Down on the waterfront by the marina are numerous restaurants which are fun to patronise in the evening, but tend to be more expensive. ***Café Fener*** is beneath the lighthouse and along the quay are ***İstanbul Boğaziçi, Pala'nın Yeri, Yakamoz*** and ***Patara***. In season, you may have to grab a seat where you can find one. Expect to spend from US$15 to US$22 per person for a meal with wine or beer.

Getting There & Away Minibuses connect Kalkan with Fethiye (81km, two hours, US$3.25) and Kaş (29km, 35 minutes, US$1.75) throughout the day in summer. There are also regular minibuses to Patara (15km, 20 minutes, US$1.25) for the beach.

Kalkan to Kaş

It's 27km from Kalkan to Kaş. Kaputaş, just less than 7km east of Kalkan and just more than 20km west of Kaş is a striking mountain gorge crossed by a small highway bridge. The plaques each side of the bridge commemorate four road workers who were killed during the dangerous construction of this part of the highway. Below the bridge is a perfect little sandy cove and beach, accessible by a long flight of stairs. A dolmuş from Kalkan will take you there in summer for US$0.50.

A short distance east of Kaputaş, Mavi Mağara (Blue Cave) lurks beneath the highway, marked by a sign. Look out for boats bringing tourists for a glimpse of this Turkish Capri.

Kaş

Fishing boats and a few yachts in the harbour, a town square with teahouses and restaurants in which one can hear half a dozen languages spoken, inexpensive pensions and hotels, classical ruins scattered about: this is Kaş (KAHSH, population 5000), the quintessential Turkish seaside town.

Kaş is not popular because of its beaches – they are small, pebbly and some are a good way out of town – but because it is pleasant in itself and makes an ideal base for boat excursions to several fascinating spots along the coast.

Life centres on the town square by the harbour, with its teahouses, restaurants, mosque and shops.

A well-preserved ancient theatre is about all that's left of ancient Antiphellus, which was the Lycian town here. Also, on the sheer rock mountain wall above the town are a number of Lycian rock tombs, which are illuminated at night.

Orientation The otogar is a few hundred metres uphill from the town centre. Descend

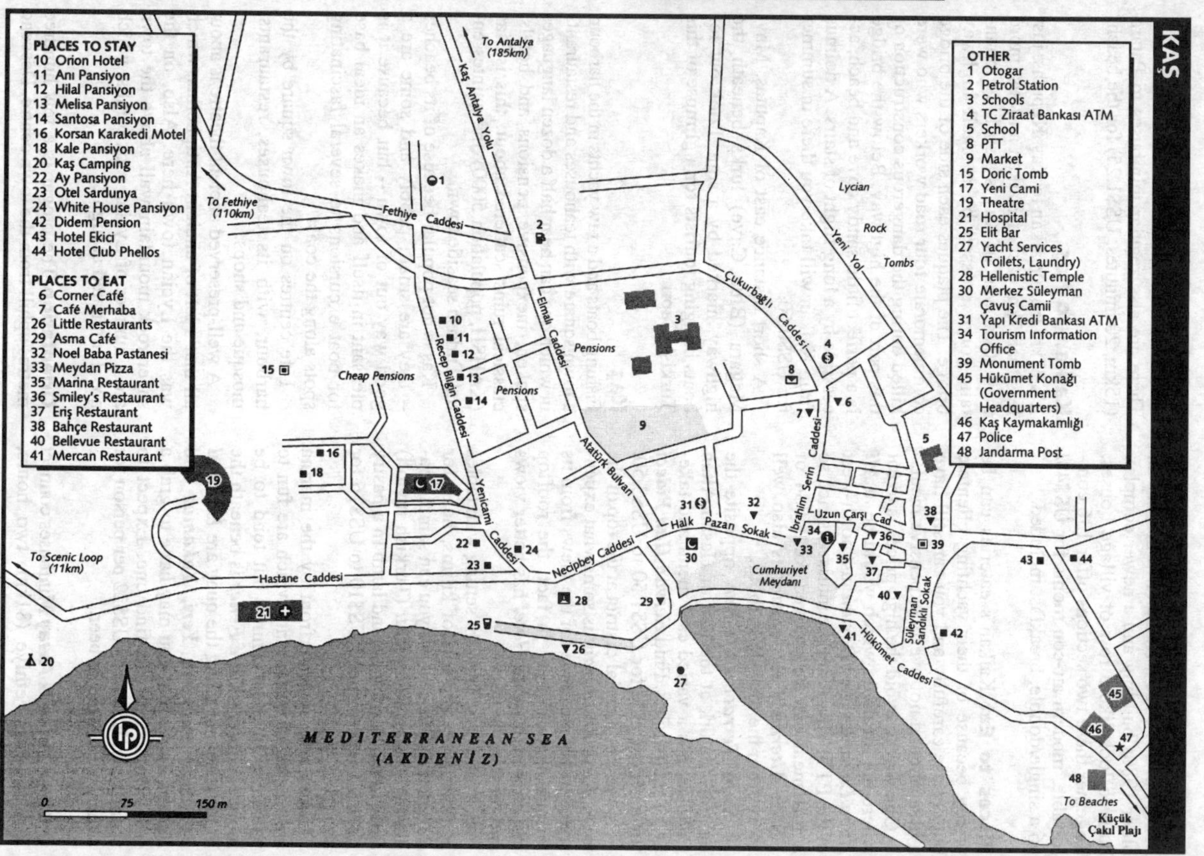
KAŞ
PLACES TO STAY
10 Orion Hotel
11 Anı Pansiyon
12 Hilal Pansiyon
13 Melisa Pansiyon
14 Santosa Pansiyon
16 Korsan Karakedi Motel
18 Kale Pansiyon
20 Kaş Camping
22 Ay Pansiyon
23 Otel Sardunya
24 White House Pansiyon
42 Didem Pension
43 Hotel Ekici
44 Hotel Club Phellos
PLACES TO EAT
6 Corner Café
7 Café Merhaba
26 Little Restaurants
29 Asma Café
32 Noel Baba Pastanesi
33 Meydan Pizza
35 Marina Restaurant
36 Smiley's Restaurant
37 Eriş Restaurant
38 Bahçe Restaurant
40 Bellevue Restaurant
41 Mercan Restaurant
OTHER
1 Otogar
2 Petrol Station
3 Schools
4 TC Ziraat Bankası ATM
5 School
8 PTT
9 Market
15 Doric Tomb
17 Yeni Cami
19 Theatre
21 Hospital
25 Elit Bar
27 Yacht Services (Toilets, Laundry)
28 Hellenistic Temple
30 Merkez Süleyman Çavuş Camii
31 Yapı Kredi Bankası ATM
34 Tourism Information Office
39 Monument Tomb
45 Hükümet Konağı (Government Headquarters)
46 Kaş Kaymakamlığı
47 Police
48 Jandarma Post
To Antalya (185km)
Kaş Antalya Yolu
To Fethiye (110km)
Fethiye Caddesi
Lycian Rock Tombs
Yeni Yol
Çukurbağlı Caddesi
Elmalı Caddesi
Pensions
Recep Bilgin Caddesi
Cheap Pensions
Pensions
Atatürk Bulvarı
İbrahim Serin Caddesi
Uzun Çarşı Cad
Halk Pazarı Sokak
Yenicami Caddesi
Necipbey Caddesi
Cumhuriyet Meydanı
To Scenic Loop (11km)
Hastane Caddesi
Süleyman Sandıklı Sokak
Hükümet Caddesi
MEDITERRANEAN SEA
(AKDENİZ)
0
75
150 m
To Beaches
Küçük Çakıl Plajı

the hill along Atatürk Bulvarı to get into the town centre. Cheap pensions are mostly to your right (west), the more expensive hotels to the left (east). At the Merkez Süleyman Çavuş Camii, turn left to reach the main square, Cumhuriyet Meydanı, and the Tourism Information Office. İbrahim Serin Caddesi strikes north to the PTT and a bank with an ATM dispensing foreign currency, while Uzun Çarşı Caddesi cuts north-east past lovely shops in restored wooden houses to a Lycian sarcophagus. Beyond the main square over the hill are more hotels and a small pebble beach.

Turning right at the mosque onto Necip Bey Caddesi and Hastane Caddesi takes you to the hospital, theatre and camping ground.

Information The Tourism Information Office (☎/fax 242-836 1238) is on the main square. The staff speak English and have numerous hand-outs on local lodgings and sights.

Kaş's postal code is 07580.

Antiphellus Ruins Walk up the hill on the street to the left of the Tourism Information Office to reach the **Monument Tomb**, a Lycian sarcophagus mounted on a high base. It is said that Kaş was once littered with such sarcophagi but that over the years most were broken apart to provide building materials.

The **theatre**, 500m west of the main square, is in very good condition and was restored some time ago. Over the hill behind the theatre is the **Doric Tomb**, cut into the hillside rock in the 3rd century BC. You can also walk to the rock tombs in the cliffs above the town, but as the walk is strenuous go at a cool time of day.

Excursions Several standard excursions will take you along the coast for cruising and swimming. No matter which you take, check to see whether lunch is included in the price. If you're watching your budget you may prefer to pack a picnic or to pick your own place to eat when you reach the lunch stop at around noon.

One popular excursion is to Kekova and Üçağız, about two hours away by boat, where there are several interesting ruins (see Üçağız and Kaleköy below). The cost is from US$10 to US$14 per person.

You can also visit Kastellorizo (Meis Adası in Turkish), the Greek island just off the coast and visible from Kaş, either returning to Kaş in the evening, or perhaps using it as a base to enter Greece and go on to other islands. If you want to do this, the travel agency making the arrangements will need your passport 24 hours in advance. The fare to Kastellorizo is likely to be about US$26.

Other standard excursions go to the Mavi Mağara (Blue Cave), Patara and Kalkan or to Liman Ağzı, Longos and several small nearby islands. There are also overland excursions to Saklıkent Gorge and villages further inland.

Places to Stay As you step off the bus a swarm of hawkers will descend on you, pressing you to patronise their pension. You could ask questions about price and facilities and then follow them home but most of the town's accommodation is within a five or 10-minute walk and some of the best pensions are only a short walk away.

Places to Stay – Budget The cheapest pensions charge US$10/16 a single/double for a room with private bathroom (breakfast included) in high season but prices are more like US$12/20 in places with more comforts.

To start looking, leave the otogar by the back stairs (on the side away from the street). At the bottom of the stairs turn left, cross the road and continue uphill to Recep Bilgin Caddesi and ***Orion Pansiyon*** *(☎/fax 242-836 1286, Recep Bilgin Caddesi 18)*. The top floor is a quiet terrace with a fine view of the town and the sea. Tidy rooms go for US$13/22 a single/double, breakfast included.

Further along Recep Bilgin Caddesi or just off it, are many other simple pensions, including ***Anı Motel*** *(☎ 242-836 1791)*, ***Hilal Pansiyon*** *(☎ 242-836 1207)*, ***Melisa Pansiyon*** *(☎ 242-836 1068)* and ***Santosa*** *(☎ 242-836 1714)*.

Further along on Yenicami Caddesi ***White House Pansiyon*** *(☎ 242-836 1866)* is a bit nicer and more stylish than the rest and worth paying a bit more for. Across the street, ***Ay Pansiyon*** *(☎ 242-836 1562)*, where the front rooms have sea views, has been renovated recently.

Turn right at Ay Pansiyon and follow the signs to the quieter ***Kale Pansiyon*** *(☎ 242-836 1094)*, right by the theatre ruins. Opposite the Çetin is the slightly pricier ***Korsan Karakedi Motel*** *(☎ 242-836 1887)* with a lovely roof terrace and bar. Rooms here cost US$15/23 a single/double but may be full with tour groups in peak season.

Camping The most popular place is ***Kaş Camping*** *(☎ 242-836 1050)*, 1km west of the centre of town along Hastane Caddesi past the theatre. Two people in their own tent pay US$5 but you can rent a waterless cabin for US$12 a double if you don't have your own camping equipment. The site is very pleasant, with a small swimming area and bar.

Places to Stay – Mid-Range Over the hill to the south-east is Küçük Çakıl Plajı (Small Pebble Beach) and behind it, along with the big hotels (Ekici and Club Phellos) are about 40 small one and two-star hotels offering good simple rooms, vine-shaded terraces with sea views and congenial atmosphere. Prices depend upon season and demand, but average US$20 a single, US$40 to US$50 a double with bath and breakfast, with reductions off season. Immediately above the beach try ***Lale*** *(☎ 242-836 1074)*, ***Patara*** *(☎ 242-836 1328)* or ***Nur*** *(☎ 242-836 1203)*. One level higher up are ***Cemil*** *(☎ 242-836 1554)*, ***Antiphellos*** *(☎ 242-836 1136)*, ***Talay*** *(☎ 242-836 1101)* and ***Defne*** *(☎ 242-836 1932)*.

Hotel Kayahan *(☎ 242-836 1313, fax 836 2001, Koza Sokak 9)*, located up the hill from Küçük Çakıl Plajı, is two-star, attractive and family run, with front rooms that have fine sea views. All have baths and cost US$28/34 a single/double with breakfast included. There's a roof terrace as well.

Otel Sardunya *(☎ 242-836 3080, fax 836 3082)*, Hastane Caddesi, on the western 'pension' side of town, charges US$38 a double with breakfast and is very popular.

The three-star ***Hotel Club Phellos*** *(☎ 242-836 1953, fax 836 1890)*, on Doğruyol Sokak, up from Küçük Çakıl beach, was designed to recall the historic houses of Kaş, now mostly swept away. It has a nice airy restaurant and swimming pool, and 81 air-con rooms with bath, going for US$40/60/75 a single/double/triple. As the nicest mid-range hostel in town, it's often full.

Across the street, the three-star ***Hotel Ekici*** *(☎ 242-836 1824, fax 836 1823, Arısan Sokak 1)*, is unsightly and manages to have surprisingly few sea views from its rooms even though it's in a good location for them. Though it posts rates similar to those demanded at Hotel Club Phellos, it usually discounts them to realistic levels.

Places to Eat For breakfast, snacks, pastries and puddings, ***Noel Baba Pastanesi*** on the main square is a favourite and best for people-watching when its outdoor tables are in the shade. Also very popular is ***Corner Café***, at the PTT end of İbrahim Serin Caddesi (a pedestrian way at this point), where you can get juices for US$1, yoghurt with fruit and honey for US$1.75 and a vegetable omelette for US$2. Immediately opposite is ***Café Merhaba***, run by two women, and offering a choice of home-made cakes to eat with coffee or juice. You can buy your foreign-language newspapers here to read while you're tucking in.

Just down at the water's edge from the Tourism Information Office, ***Mercan Restaurant*** is generally regarded as the town's best place to dine because of its longstanding service, waterfront location and seafood. Choose a fish, have it weighed, get the price, then say '*evet*' if you want it, or '*hayır*' if you don't. A fish dinner with mezes and wine can cost from US$12 to US$18 per person.

Just back from the main square is ***Eriş Restaurant***, with shady pseudo-rustic tables in front. Prices are not bad, but the food is good and the atmosphere makes it very popular in the evenings. Full meals run US$5 to US$12. Above the Eriş, ***Marina Restaurant*** has the best views because of its height. The nearby, aptly named ***Bellevue Restaurant*** is also good, with meals for US$7 to US$18.

Beside Eriş in the main square is ***Smiley's Restaurant***, a brasher but popular place serving pizza for around US$3 to US$6. ***Meydan Pizza*** by the Tourism Information Office is even cheaper.

Up behind the Lycian sarcophagus it's also worth looking out for ***Bahçe*** ('garden') ***Restaurant***, set, as its name suggests, in a garden with an excellent selection of cold mezes to choose from and prices similar to those at Eriş.

South of the mosque, the tiny ***Asma Café*** also receives the local seal of approval for its salad lunches and pleasant ambience. Beyond it, out toward the quay and turn right, is a row of little restaurants that are great for breakfast or a sunset drink. ***Elit Bar***, at the western end of the row beneath the Yalı Pansiyon, has a concrete sun deck and unobstructed view of Kastellorizo.

Getting There & Away Most tourists arrive and leave Kaş by bus.

Bus Most buses in and out of Kaş are handled by the Pamukkale, Kaş Turizm and Kamil Koç companies. Some daily services include:

- Antalya – 185km, four hours, US$4; frequent minibuses
- Demre/Kale – 45km, one hour, US$2; frequent minibuses
- Fethiye – 110km, 2½ hours, US$3.50; frequent buses and dolmuşes
- İstanbul – 1088km, 12 hours, US$20 to US$25
- Kalkan – 29km, 35 minutes, US$1.75; frequent minibuses
- Patara – 42km, one hour, US$2.50; regular dolmuşes

For other destinations, connect at Fethiye or Antalya.

ÜÇAĞIZ

About 14km east of Kaş is a road on the right (south) to Üçağız. A 19km ride along a paved road brings you to the village of Kale/Üçağız, the Lycian Teimiussa, in an area of ancient ruined cities, some of them partly submerged in the Mediterranean Sea. This area is regularly visited by day-trippers on boats and yachts from Kaş and Kalkan but you can also stay overnight.

Declared off-limits to development, Üçağız remains a relatively unspoilt Turkish fishing and farming village in an absolutely idyllic setting, on a bay amid islands and peninsulas. The old houses, many white-washed, are of local stone rather than breeze block and the largest building is the modern ilkokul. Cows and chickens wander the streets, villagers lift sacks of carob beans down to the town wharf, and fishermen repair their nets on the quay as yachts glide through the harbour. Village girls sell *yazmalar* (hand-printed scarves) with handmade lace borders, while village women sit outside making lace and doing embroidery.

Here and there are remnants of ancient Lycian tombs. Near the Koç Restaurant in particular, look for two Lycian sarcophagi (one of them in the shape of a house) and a rock-cut tomb.

For the time being, Üçağız slumbers in between boat arrivals. A few carpet shops have opened, however, and the discos can't be far behind.

Orientation

The village you enter is Üçağız (Three Mouths), the ancient Teimiussa. Across the water to the east is **Kale** (Kaleköy), a village on the site of the ancient city of Simena, accessible by boat. South of the villages is a harbour called **Ölüdeniz** (not to be confused with the famous beach spot near Fethiye), and south of that is the channel entrance, shielded from the Mediterranean's occasional fury by a long island named Kekova Adası.

Streets in the village are barely wide enough for one vehicle. If you're driving, park your vehicle well outside the village to avoid time-consuming traffic jams.

WESTERN MEDITERRANEAN

Boat Excursions

Boats from Üçağız will take you on a tour of the area lasting from one to 1½ hours. Chartering an entire boat costs around US$10 to US$16, but haggle as prices are negotiable. Although the water is very clear some readers have thought it worth paying a bit extra to sail past the 'sunken city' ruins in a glass-bottomed boat.

Places to Stay & Eat

Üçağız's small pensions charge around US$7 to US$11 per person.

The tidy ***Ekin Pansiyon*** at the western end of the village is right next to the water, with a pretty garden and insect screens on the windows. ***Flower Pension*** above the restaurant of the same name is ramshackle but cheap; ***Kekova*** is about the same. ***Fisherman's Inn*** is a city-dweller's idea of what a folksy seaside pension should be. ***Koç Pansiyon*** at the eastern end of the village is the fanciest.

You can camp on the western outskirts at ***Kekova Camping*** and there's a small store selling groceries in the village centre, opposite an information booth which is open in high summer.

Though they cater mostly to yachters and boat groups, Üçağız's restaurants are not outrageously priced and a meal for US$4 or US$5 is possible though you can also spend more if you like. A five-minute stroll through the village shows you the restaurant situation, which changes from year to year. This year ***İbrahim Liman Marina***, an Üçağız eatery of longstanding, is the favourite, along with another longtime favourite, ***Hasan***, next door. ***Koç***, on the main square is also good and ***Flower Pansiyon Restaurant*** is worth a try.

Getting There & Away

Occasional minibuses link Kaş to Üçağız in winter, but services in summer are sometimes nonexistent, as most traffic goes by boat. If there's no bus and you don't want to take an excursion you could get a taxi as far as Üçağız and then take a taxi boat to Kaleköy for US$5 each way. In summer there's also a water taxi direct from Kaş; the Kaş Tourism Information Office has details.

Coming from Demre, motorboats can be chartered at the western beach, called Çayağzı, for US$30; sometimes it's possible to buy one place in the boat for a one-way journey for about US$3. You may be able to do this from Kaş as well.

Boat Tours

Given the difficulty of getting to Kekova by public transport most people end up taking a boat tour of the area from Kaş or Kalkan. A standard boat excursion might start by heading for Üçağız, passing **Kekova Adası** (Kekova Island, also called Tersane). Along the shore of the island are Byzantine foundations and ruins, partly submerged in the sea and called the Batık Şehir, the Sunken City. Signs say 'No Skin-Diving Allowed', indicating that this is an archaeological zone and the authorities are afraid of antiquity theft. The boat stops in a cove so you can swim and perhaps explore the ruins on land. Afterwards you head for lunch in Üçağız and then on to Kaleköy, passing **sunken Lycian tombs** just offshore. There's usually about an hour to explore Kaleköy and climb up to the eponymous castle. On the way back to Kaş there should be time for another swim.

Tours generally leave at 10 am and charge around US$8 or US$10 per person.

KALEKÖY

Tours from Kaş normally arrive in Üçağız and then proceed to Kaleköy to see the **ruins of ancient Simena** and the **medieval Byzantine fortress** perched above the picture-perfect hamlet. Within the fortress a little **theatre** is cut into the rock and nearby are **ruins** of several temples and public baths, several sarcophagi and Lycian tombs; the **city walls** are visible on the outskirts. It's a delightfully pretty spot, accessible by motorboat from Üçağız (10 minutes) or on foot (one hour).

Places to Stay & Eat

Kaleköy has a couple of pensions, including the delightfully sited ***Mehtap Pansiyon***

(☎ *242-874 2146)*, high on the hill with spectacular views over the harbour and a sunken Lycian tomb. Beds cost US$8 in waterless rooms. Closer to the harbour there's also ***Kale Pansiyon*** *(☎ 242-874 2111)* with beds for US$7. The harbourside restaurants, ***Simena***, ***Café Ankh*** and ***Kale***, tend to be pricey because of their yachting clientele.

KYANEAİ

From the main highway at the Üçağız turn-off, it's 8km east and south to the turn-off for Kyaneai. About 2km off the highway, Roman and Lycian ruins stand amid the houses and paddocks of the farming hamlet called Yavı. A track starts in the town and leads 3km uphill to the main part of this ancient city, founded in Lycian times, which flourished under the Romans and was the seat of a bishop during the Byzantine era. It was abandoned in the 10th century.

The site has some interesting tombs, a theatre and traces of other buildings, but the rough terrain and undergrowth make exploration difficult. This is one for dedicated antiquities buffs who enjoy having little-visited sites to themselves.

Demre (Kale) is 24km east of the Kyaneai turn-off.

DEMRE

Winding past rocky, scrubby terrain from Kaş, the road descends from the mountains to a fertile river delta, much of it covered in greenhouses. Demre, 46km east of Kaş, was the Roman city of Myra (the name comes from 'myrrh') and by the 4th century was important enough to have its own bishop (one of them St Nicholas, later immortalised as Santa Claus). Several centuries before that, St Paul stopped here on his voyage to Rome.

Though Myra had a long history as a religious, commercial and administrative town, Arab raids in the 7th century and the silting of the harbour led to its decline. Today that same silting is the foundation of the town's wealth. The rich alluvial soil supports the intensive greenhouse production of flowers and vegetables.

Though lots of tourists pass through Demre, few stay for long. Those who do find that the prices of services such as hotels, taxi rides and boat tours are usually negotiable.

Santa Claus

The legend of Father Christmas (Santa Claus; *Noel Baba* in Turkish) is believed to have begun in Demre when a 4th-century Christian bishop, later St Nicholas, gave anonymous gifts to dowryless village girls. He would drop bags of coins down the chimneys of their houses, and this 'gift from heaven' would allow them to marry, which is perhaps why he's the patron saint of virgins. He went on to become the patron saint of sailors, children, pawnbrokers, Holy Russia and others.

St Nicholas' fame grew and in 1087 a raiding party from the Italian city of Bari stole his mortal remains from the church. They missed a few bones which are now in Antalya Museum.

To judge from the carvings on its top, what is touted as St Nicholas' tomb in Demre church is more likely to be that of a Byzantine couple.

Orientation

Demre sprawls over the alluvial plain. At the centre is the main square, near which are several cheap hotels and restaurants. The street going west from the square to the Church of St Nicholas is Müze Caddesi (also called St Nicholas Caddesi). Going north is Alakent Caddesi, which leads 2km to the Lycian rock tombs of Myra. PTT Caddesi (also called Ortaokul Caddesi) heads east to the PTT and the town's best hotel, Grand Hotel Kekova. The street going south from the square passes the otogar (100m) and continues to a cluster of hotels (800m) across from the ilkokul, at the junction with the road to Antalya.

Looming above the town on a hilltop to the north is the huge kale, which looks especially impressive in the late afternoon sun.

Church of St Nicholas

The Church of St Nicholas ('Noel Baba' in Turkish), a block west of the main square, was first built in the 3rd century, held St Nicholas' remains after he died in 343 and became a Byzantine basilica when it was restored in 1043.

Later restorations sponsored by Tsar Nicholas I of Russia in 1862 changed the St Nicholas church even more. More recent work by Turkish archaeologists was designed to protect it from deterioration.

Not vast like Aya Sofya, nor brilliant with mosaics like İstanbul's Chora Church, the Church of St Nicholas at Demre is, at first, a disappointment. What redeems it is the venerable dignity lent it by its age and the stories which surround it.

Admission to the church (open daily 8 am to 5.30 pm and to 7 pm in summer) is overpriced at US$3.

Myra

About 2km inland from Demre's main square lie the ruins of Myra, with a striking honeycomb of rock-hewn **Lycian tombs** and a well-preserved **Roman theatre**. Climb the ladders for a closer look at the tombs, which were thought to have been carved to resemble Lycian houses, wood beams and all. Around to the left as you climb is a tomb topped by a deathbed scene; there are other reliefs to discover as well.

Admission costs US$1; hours are from 7.30 am to 7 pm in summer and 8 am to 5.30 pm the rest of the year.

Taxi drivers in town will offer to take you on a tour, but the walk from the main square only takes about 20 minutes and the site is fairly self-explanatory.

Andriake (Çayağzı)

About 5km west of Demre centre is Çayağzı (Stream Mouth), called Andriake by the Romans. In Roman times this port was an important entrepôt for grain on the sea route between the eastern Mediterranean and Rome.

The ruins of the ancient town cover a wide area around the present settlement, which is little more than a dozen boatyards and a beachfront restaurant with decent food and fine sea views. Some of the land is swampy, so the great granary built by Hadrian (finished in 139 AD), to the south of the beach access road, can be difficult to access in wet weather.

Besides the ruins and the 1km-long beach, it's interesting to watch the boatbuilders at work. You can usually find an excursion boat or a taxi boat to Üçağız departing from Çayağzı as well.

Dolmuşes run out here occasionally from the centre of Demre, but it's more likely that you'll have to take a taxi (US$5).

Beymelek, Kömürlü & Sülüklü

On the eastern outskirts of Demre, about 5km from the centre are more fine beaches, named Kömürlü and Sülüklü, in the district called Beymelek.

Places to Stay & Eat

Despite its several points of interest, Demre doesn't have much accommodation. Most people are passing through.

Hotel Şahin (☎ 242-871 5686, fax 871 5781), Müze Caddesi, just west off the main square on the way to the St Nicholas Church, is convenient and usable, though hardly beautiful. Rooms with private bath and breakfast cost US$14/20 a single/double.

East of the square on PTT Caddesi, ***Hotel Simge*** *(☎ 242-871 4511, fax 871 3677)* is probably OK for US$10/16 a single/double, but further along the street (300m east of the square, across from the PTT), the two-star ***Grand Hotel Kekova*** *(☎ 242-871 3462, fax 871 5366)*, is probably Demre's quietest and best value for money with comfortable modern rooms for US$14/25.

About 300m south of the Myra ruins (and 1.7km north of the main square), ***Kent Aile Pansiyon*** *(☎ 242-871 2042)* has pleasant gardens, new management and low prices of US$6/10 a single/double.

Three more hotels are 800m south of the main square near the junction with the highway to Antalya: ***Otel Kıyak*** *(☎ 242-871 2092, fax 871 2093)*, charging US$12/18 a single/double with bath and breakfast; and the cheaper ***Otel Topçu*** *(☎ 242-871 4506, fax 871 5440)* and ***Kekova Pansiyon*** *(☎ 242-871 2804)*. The Kıyak swears that it will soon have air-con.

Across the highway from this trio, the three-star ***Hotel Andriake*** *(☎ 871 2249, fax 871 5440)*, Finike Caddesi, is the town's best at US$35 a double, breakfast included.

The food from the little restaurants near the main square (***Çınar*** and ***Şehir***) and along Müze Caddesi between the square and the church (***İpek*** in particular and ***İnci Pastanesi*** for sweets) can fill you up. ***Simena*** on Müze Caddesi serves wine and beer with meals; ***Güney Han*** is fancied up, but the food is no better.

ÇAĞILLI & GÖKLİMAN

Heading east from Demre towards Antalya, you'll eventually come to Çağıllı, a small cove with a nice pebble beach overlooked by the highway. At Gökliman, another 4km east (and 4km before Finike), a longer, wider beach is good for a swim stop.

FİNİKE

About 30km further along the twisting mountain road is Finike (FEE-nee-keh, population 7000), the ancient Phoenicus, now a sleepy fishing port and way-station on the tourist route. Most of the tourists are Turks who have built ramshackle dwellings on the long pebble beach to the east of the town. The beach looks inviting but parts of it are polluted and insects can be a problem at certain times of year.

The ruins of ancient Limyra are 11km inland along the Elmalı road in the village of Hasyurt. They're not really worth the effort unless you're out to see every ancient town along the coast. The theatre is fairly well preserved, as are some tombs 200m further north, but beware the bees! Other ruined buildings are scattered among the modern farms and houses.

Arycanda, 35km north along the Elmalı road, is well worth seeing with its dramatic setting and many well-preserved buildings, but requires a special excursion. Finike itself is uninteresting and not worth making a special stop for.

Places to Stay

Paris Pansiyon *(☎ 242-855 1488)*, 200m inland from the highway off the Elmalı road, is up a terrifying flight of steps. Beds here cost just US$7 including breakfast.

In the market district behind the Belediye stand several inexpensive hotels, including the ***Hotel Bahar*** *(☎ 242-855 2020)*, the friendly ***Hotel Bilal*** *(☎ 242-855 2199)* and the older ***Hotel Sedir*** *(☎ 242-855 1183, Cumhuriyet Caddesi 37)*. All three places charge around US$10/18 a single/double with shower and breakfast included. The newer ***Engin Hotel*** *(☎ 242-855 3040)* on the main road through town is similar.

EAST FROM FİNİKE

As you leave Finike the highway skirts a sand-and-pebble beach which runs for about 15km. Once past the long beach, at 19km from Finike, the road transits **Kumluca** (population 17,000), a farming town surrounded by citrus orchards and plastic-roofed greenhouses, particularly worth visiting on Fridays for its lively market. A few small pensions can provide a room in an emergency.

After Kumluca the highway winds back up into the mountains with an especially good panorama about 28km from Finike. About 3km later you enter **Beydağları Sahil Milli Parkı,** the Bey Mountains Coastal National Park.

Just east of Kumluca, a road on the right goes 2km to the small farming towns of Beykonak, and then another 8km to Mavikent. A narrow but scenic road continues from Mavikent through a broad alluvial valley paved in plastic-sheeted greenhouses to Adrasan, another 15km along, and then continues to Olimpos/Çıralı.

OLİMPOS & THE CHIMAERA

Midway between Kumluca and Tekirova two roads lead down from the main highway towards the villages of Çavuşköy and Çıralı, to Adrasan beach, and to the ruins of ancient Olimpos and the site of the Chimaera, all set within the glorious Bey Mountains Coastal National Park. Unless you have your own transport, you should take the road signposted 'Olimpos-Çıralı-Yanartaş/Chimaera 7km' which will bring you straight down to Çıralı village and its numerous pensions, all within walking distance of the Olimpos ruins and the Chimaera; taxis wait at the highway turn-off to take you to Çıralı for a stiff US$7. Coming from Kumluca, this will be the second turn-off signposted to Olimpos; coming from Antalya it will be the first.

If you take the Çavuşköy turn-off it will be 11km to the village.

Olimpos

Though a very ancient city, the early history of Olimpos is shrouded in mystery. We know that it was an important Lycian city by the 2nd century BC, and that the Olympians worshipped Hephaestos (Vulcan), the god of fire. No doubt this veneration sprang from reverence for the mysterious Chimaera, an eternal flame which still springs from the earth not far from the city. Along with the other Lycian coastal cities, Olimpos went into a decline in the 1st century BC. With the coming of the Romans in the 1st century AD, things improved, but in the 3rd century AD pirate attacks brought impoverishment. In the Middle Ages the Venetians, Genoese and Rhodians built fortresses along the coast (bits of which still remain), but by the 15th century Olimpos had been abandoned.

Today the site is fascinating, not just for its ruins (which are fragmentary and widely scattered among the thick verdure of wild grapevines, flowering oleander, bay trees, wild figs and pines), but for its site, just inland from a beautiful beach along the course of a stream which runs through a rocky gorge. The stream dries to a rivulet in high summer and a ramble along its course, listening to the wind in the trees and the songs of innumerable birds, is a rare treat, with never a tour bus in sight.

The site is effectively open all the time but during daylight hours a custodian awaits to relieve those wishing to climb to the acropolis of US$1. There's a car park at the nonbeach end of the site.

The Chimaera

From Çıralı, follow the track marked for the Chimaera (Yanartaş, Burning Rock in Turkish) 3km along a valley to a car park, then climb up a mud track for another 20 to 30 minutes to the site.

The Chimaera, a cluster of spontaneous flames which blaze from crevices on the rocky slopes of Mt Olimpos, is the stuff of legends. It's not difficult to see why ancient peoples attributed these extraordinary flames to the breath of a monster – part lion, part goat and part dragon. Even today, they have not been explained.

In mythology, the Chimaera was the son of Typhon. Typhon was the fierce and monstrous son of Gaia, the earth goddess, who was so frightening that Zeus set him on fire and buried him alive under Mt Aetna, thereby creating the volcano. Typhon's offspring, the Chimaera, was killed by the hero Bellerophon on the orders of King Iobates of Lycia. Bellerophon killed the monster by aerial bombardment – mounting Pegasus, the winged horse, and pouring molten lead into the Chimaera's mouth.

Today gas still seeps from the earth and bursts into flame upon contact with the air. The exact composition of the gas is unknown, though it is thought to contain some methane. Though the flames can be extinguished now by being covered, they will reignite when uncovered. In ancient times they were much more vigorous, being easily recognised at night by mariners sailing along the coast.

Places to Stay & Eat

Çıralı Arriving in Çıralı, you cross a small bridge where a few taxis wait to run people back up to the main road. Continue across the bridge and you'll come to a junction in the road disfigured with innumerable signboards. Go straight on for the pensions nearest to the path up to the Chimaera. Turn right for the pensions closest to the beach and the Olimpos ruins.

The standard price for a pension double room here – actually more like a one-star hotel room, with private bath and breakfast – is US$24.

In Çıralı village, ***Orange Pansiyon*** *(☎ 242-825 7128)* is quite nice, as is ***Aygün Pansiyon*** *(☎ 242-825 7146)* beyond it (not to be confused with the neighbouring Grand Aygün). There are six other decent places here as well.

An even better location is down by the beach. Follow the signs to ***Fehim Pansiyon*** *(☎ 242-825 7250)*, an older place with more spacious, shady grounds and a full ***restaurant***. Adjoining it are ***Sima Peace Pansiyon*** *(☎ 242-825 7245)*, a tidy collection of little honey-coloured pine cabins; and the slightly cheaper, family run ***Emin Pansiyon*** *(☎ 242-825 7155)*, an excellent choice. ***Otel Odile*** *(☎ 242-825 7163, fax 825 7164)* next door is a bit fancier and slightly more expensive. All these places are barely 100m in from the beach, shaded by lofty pines.

The small and friendly ***Rüya Pansiyon*** *(☎ 242-825 7055)*, tucked away behind a school, is another good choice. ***Mini Pansiyon*** *(☎ 242-825 7066)* has good little cabins right on the stream by the Çıralı market just up from Garden Pansiyon.

Walking along the beach towards the Olimpos ruins you'll come to the delightful ***Olympos Lodge*** *(☎ 242-825 7171, fax 825 7173)*, PO Box 38, Çıralı, a beautiful lodge and villas set among citrus orchards and well-tended gardens near the beach. The management is German, everything is well maintained, and the price, at US$63/85/145 a single/double/quad suite, breakfast included, is well worth a splurge.

In summer there are plenty of small beach restaurants serving up simple kebap meals but most close by the end of October.

Along the road leading to the Olimpos ruins are several rustic restaurants which allow camping as well. ***Kadir's Yörük Top Tree House*** *(☎ 242-892 1250, fax 892 1110, treehouse@superonline.com.tr)* is the funkiest and best of several similar establishments (***Olimpos, Olimpos Şerif, Türkmen, Çamlık***) with rustic ramshackle charm and Internet connections. Kadir charges about US$10 per person for a bed in a tree house (communal showers and toilets) with breakfast and dinner included. Kadir's Yörük Top Tree House is 700m inland from the Olimpos ruins.

Adrasan/Çavuşköy South along the coast from Olimpos about 10km is Çavuşköy, more commonly called by its historical name of Adrasan, a tiny little-known coastal resort with a growing collection of beachfront hotels and pensions. Like Çıralı, Adrasan is a farming village, but turn in the main square and follow the sign pointing east 5km to the Adrasan Turistik Tesisleri (Tourism Facilities).

The relatively clean, unpolluted beach is lined with little pensions and hotels, including ***İkizler Pansiyon – Restaurant*** *(☎ 242-883 5227)*, ***Atıcı Motel & Pension***, ***Çizmeci Hotel*** and ***Gelidonya Pension***. The fancier ***Sözen Motel*** *(☎ 242-883 5153)*, ***Koreli Motel*** *(☎ 242-883 5413)* and the adjoining ***Hotel Ford*** *(☎ 242-883 5121, fax 883 5097)* all charge about US$35 for a double room with bath and breakfast and

WESTERN MEDITERRANEAN

perhaps air-con. These three places have swimming pools, and all are only a few steps from the beach.

Getting There & Away

Unless you have your own transport getting to Olimpos is tricky because no dolmuşes run to Çıralı, the most obvious place to base yourself. Buses plying up and down the main road linking Antalya and Fethiye will drop you at either of the road junctions leading to Çıralı or Çavuşköy/Adrasan. Taxis usually wait at the Çıralı junction, charging US$7 for the short run.

In summer boats run from Adrasan beach to Demre and Kaş.

On Friday there are dolmuşes from Çıralı to Kumluca market.

TEKIROVA

About 13km north-east of Olimpos is the turn-off for Tekirova, a resort area with several large luxury hotels (Phaselis Princess, Corinthia Club Hotel Tekirova, etc) and several more under construction. Of the many pensions here, ***Phaselis Pension*** *(☎/fax 242-821 4507)* is off the highway on the old road next to a stream. The benefits are a quiet location, swimming pool and being 750m from the beach. The decent double rooms with bath for US$25, breakfast included are good value. Follow the signs to get there.

PHASELIS

About 3km north of the Tekirova turn-off, 12km before the turn-off to Kemer and about 56km from Antalya, is a road marked for Phaselis, a ruined Lycian city 2km off the highway on the shore.

Phaselis was apparently founded by Greek colonists on the border between Lycia and Pamphylia around 334 BC. Its wealth came from being a port for the shipment of timber, rose oil and perfume.

Shaded by soughing pines, the ruins of Phaselis are arranged around three small perfect bays, each with its own diminutive beach. The ruins are not particularly exciting, and are all from Roman and Byzantine times, but the setting is incomparably romantic.

The site is open from 7.30 am to 7 pm in summer for US$1. About 1km from the highway is the entrance to the site, with a small modern building where you can buy soft drinks, snacks, souvenirs, use the toilet and visit a one-room museum. The ruins and the shore are another 1km further on. The nearest accommodation is in Tekirova.

KEMER

Kemer (population 10,000) is a burgeoning beach holiday resort with its face turned to the rough, rocky beaches of the Mediterranean and its back to the steep, pine-clad Beydağları (Bey Mountains). It was designed as a holding tank for planeloads of sun-seeking charter and group tours, and built to a government master plan. For most nonpackage holidaymakers it has little to offer. Passing through, you can stop for a meal and a look at the Yörük Parkı, an outdoor ethnological exhibit. Accommodation is available in all price ranges, should you want to stay, but most of the bigger places will be block-booked to tour operators throughout the summer.

Orientation

Liman Caddesi, the main street, is a typically narrow Turkish noise-canyon lined with white hotels, palm trees, banks and cafes, where you must run the gauntlet of a string of leather, jewellery and carpet shops. At the end of Liman Caddesi to the north is the large yacht marina and dry-dock; to the south is a peaceful cove with a beautiful crescent of sand-and-pebble beach backed by emerald grass and fragrant pine trees. Stands here rent out equipment for parasailing, water-skiing and windsurfing. Motorboat excursions run from the beach as well.

The otogar is in the north-western part of town.

Information

The Tourism Information Office (☎ 242-814 1537, fax 814 1536) is in the Belediye Binası (municipal building).

Kemer's postal code is 07980.

Yörük Parkı

On a promontory north of the cove beach is Kemer's Yörük Parkı, an ethnographic exhibit meant to introduce you to some of the mysteries of the region. Local *yörüks* (nomads) lived in these black camel-hair tents now furnished with carpets and grass mats. Typical nomad paraphernalia includes distaffs for spinning woollen yarn, looms on which Turkish carpets are being woven, musical instruments and churns for butter and *ayran* (yoghurt drink). Among the tents, in the shade of the pines, are little rustic tables with three-legged stools at which a 'nomad girl' will serve you refreshments and snacks.

Keep walking through the park and you'll emerge above the cove to enjoy the view. At night, Antalya, to the north, is a long string of shore lights in the distance.

Adjoining the Yörük Parkı, the Moonlight Park, between the sea and the Özkaymak Hotel, has a beach and yacht marina.

Places to Stay

Kemer's lodgings mainly cater to the package-holiday trade but a few cheaper places still manage to cling on. One of the longest established and most congenial of them is ***King's Garden Pension*** *(☎ 242-814 1039, fax 814 5546, Yenimahalle, Atatürk Bulvarı 109)*, also called King Pension, located north-east of the otogar. The rooms, set around a garden, are fairly basic but comfortable enough; the location is quiet; and the owners (she's English, he's Turkish) very congenial. The popular ***restaurant*** attached to the pension has now been supplemented by one on the beach itself. In high season, rates for double rooms with shower are US$40, breakfast and dinner included. Off-season you can get B&B for US$20. Camping costs US$6 in a double tent. To find King Pension, find the PTT, then head toward the beach, following the signs.

If the King's prices are too high, cross the channel outside and walk back towards the otogar. You'll come to ***Portakal Pansiyon*** *(☎ 242-814 4701)* where rooms are slightly cheaper.

Other cheap pensions and camping grounds abound in this neighbourhood, and ***Kındılçeşme Kamp Alanı***, operated by the forestry service, is 3.5km north of Kemer centre along the old highway. Set amid fragrant pines at the edge of the sea, it's often fully booked in summer.

Getting There & Away

Frequent dolmuşes run from Antalya to Tekirova and Phaselis along the highway ('Üst yoldan ekspres', which means they stop only on the highway, not at otogars). There are also dolmuşes to Kemer's otogar from Antalya otogar, some of which follow parts of the old highway via Göynük and Beldibi (see below).

Approaching Kemer from Fethiye, Kaş and Kalkan, you're likely to find yourself dropped off on the main highway, 2km from the otogar. A taxi fare, if you don't want to walk or wait for a dolmuş, will be about US$3.

BELDİBİ/GÖYNÜK

North of Kemer, the old Antalya highway follows the shoreline more closely than the new highway, further inland. About 12km north of Kemer is the centre of Beldibi, another planned resort area. The beach here consists of stones, not even pebbles, but the water is clear, the pines cool and the mountain backdrop dramatic. Unfortunately there's also a lot of construction and piles of rubbish here and there.

Among the resorts is ***Göynük Çadırlı Kamp Alanı*** (Tent Camping Ground), about 400m north of Sultansaray Antalya Hotel & Resort on the old road; 23km south-west of Antalya. Take the Göynük exit from the highway, then turn left (north, back toward Antalya) to find it.

ANTALYA

Antalya is the chief city on Turkey's central Mediterranean coast, and though the city itself has a population of less than 400,000, the urban area may have as high as a million. Agriculture, shipping, light industry and tourism have made Antalya boom during the past few decades and this mostly modern Mediterranean city is still growing at a fast pace.

Though always a busy port (trading to Crete, Cyprus and Egypt), Antalya has grown explosively since the 1960s because of the tourism boom. Its new US$75 million airport, the busiest on the Turkish Mediterranean, funnels travellers to the whole coast and beyond.

Rough pebble beaches (several kilometres from the centre to east and west) provide for the seaside crowd and the commercial centre provides necessities. Though Antalya has a historic Roman-Ottoman core, the ancient cities on its outskirts – Perge, Aspendos, Side, Termessos, Phaselis, Olimpos – offer more to see in the way of historic buildings. Antalya is a good base from which to visit them.

History

This area has been inhabited since the earliest times. The oldest artefacts found in the Karain caves, 25km inland from Antalya, have been dated to the Palaeolithic period. Antalya as a city, however, is not as old as many other cities which once lined this coast but it is still prospering while the older cities are dead.

Founded by Attalus II of Pergamum in the 1st century BC, the city was named Attaleia after its founder. When the Pergamene kingdom was willed to Rome, Attaleia became a Roman city. Emperor Hadrian visited here in 130 AD and a triumphal arch (Hadriyanüs Kapısı) was built in his honour.

The Byzantines took over from the Romans. In 1207 the Seljuk Turks based in Konya took the city from the Byzantines and gave Antalya a new version of its name, and also its symbol, the Yivli Minare. After the Mongols broke Seljuk power, Antalya was held for a while by the Turkish Hamidoğulları emirs. It was later taken by the Ottomans in 1391.

During WWI the Allies made plans to divide up the Ottoman Empire and at the end of the war they parcelled it out. Italy got Antalya in 1918, but by 1921 Atatürk's armies had put an end to all such foreign holdings in Anatolia.

Orientation

At the centre of the historic city is the Roman harbour, now the yacht marina. Around it is the historic district called Kaleiçi (Within the Fortress) of Ottoman houses sprinkled with Roman ruins. Many of the graceful old houses have been restored and converted to restaurants, pensions and small hotels – some simple, some quite luxurious.

Around Kaleiçi, outside the Roman walls, is the commercial centre of the city. Antalya's central landmark and symbol is the Yivli Minare (yeev-LEE mee-nah-reh, Grooved Minaret), a monument from the Seljuk period which rises near the main square, called Kale Kapısı (Fortress Gate), marked by an ancient stone *saat kulesi* (clock tower). The broad plaza with the bombastic equestrian statue is Cumhuriyet Meydanı (Republic Square).

From Kale Kapısı, Cumhuriyet Caddesi goes west past the Tourism Information Office and Turkish Airlines office, then becomes Kenan Evren Bulvarı, which continues several kilometres to the Antalya Museum and Konyaaltı Plajı, a pebble beach 10km long, and now partly sullied by industrial development.

North-west from Kale Kapısı, Kazım Özalp Caddesi, formerly Şarampol Caddesi, is a pedestrian way. Antalya's small bazaar, which seems to be mostly jewellery shops, is east of Kazım Özalp Caddesi.

East from Kale Kapısı, Ali Çetinkaya Caddesi goes to the airport (10km), Perge, Aspendos, Side and beyond. Atatürk Caddesi goes south-east from Ali Çetinkaya Caddesi, skirting Kaleiçi through more of the commercial district to the large Karaali Parkı before heading for Lara beach (12km from the centre), lined with hotels and pensions.

A *çevreyolu* (ring road or bypass) named Gazi Bulvarı carries long-distance traffic around the city centre. The big, modern Antalya Otogar (Yeni Garaj) is 4km north of the centre on the D650 highway to Burdur, Ankara and Istanbul.

Information

The Tourism Information Office (☎/fax 242-241 1747) is at Cumhuriyet Caddesi

91. It's 600m west of Kale Kapısı on the right-hand side in the Özel İdare Çarşısı building (the same building as Turkish Airlines and Varan bus company). This building is after the jandarma headquarters but before the pedestrian bridge over the roadway. Look for 'Antalya Devlet Tiyatrosu' emblazoned on it.

Antalya's postal code is 07100.

Money The Yapı Kredi Bankası office at the southern end of Kazım Özalp Caddesi, just off Kale Kapısı, has a cash machine (Tele 24) connected to the major networks, including Visa, MasterCard, Eurocard, Cirrus and Plus Systems. Other banks, including Akbank, are a short distance north along Kazım Özalp Caddesi, as are several currency exchange houses (look for the word 'Döviz' in the name).

Bookshops Try the Owl Bookshop, Barbaros Mahallesi, Akarçeşme Sokak 21, in Kaleiçi. The owner, Kemal Özkurt, stocks old and new books in English, French, German and Turkish.

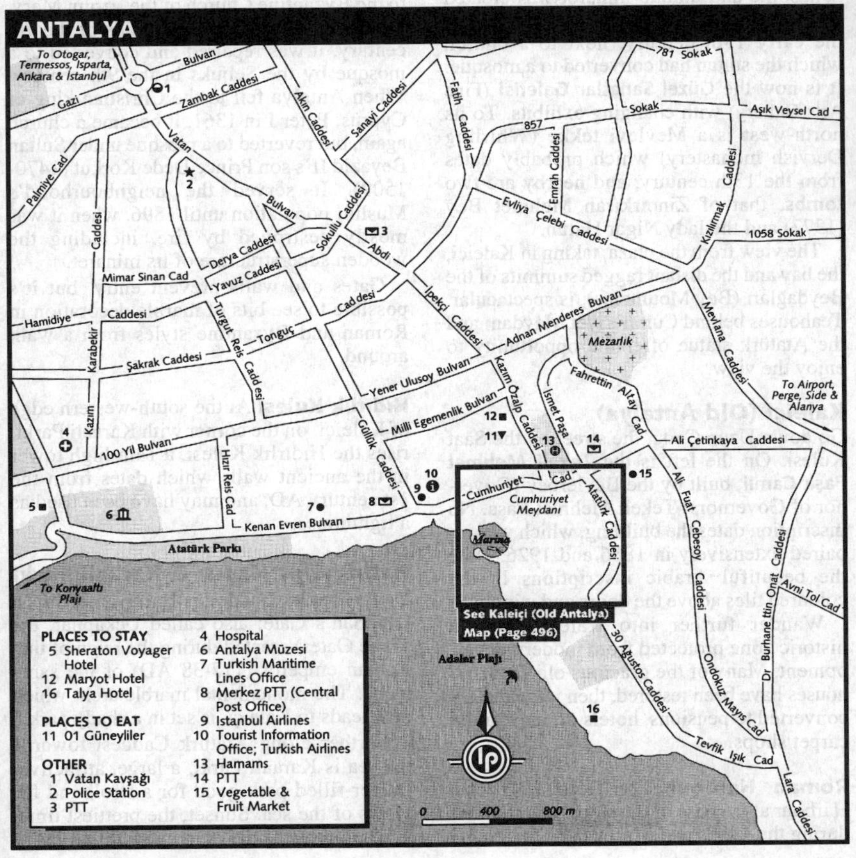

Consulates Britain's honorary consulate (☎ 242-247 7000) is at Kızılsaray Mahallesi, Dolaplıdere Caddesi, Pırıltı Sitesi, 1st floor.

The Swedish consulate (☎ 242-248 9060, fax 241 5222) is at Konyaaltı Bulvarı 78.

Laundry In Kaleiçi, just east of the Kesik Minare in the Ünal Rent-a-Car office is the Ünal Laundry where you can have a 5kg load of washing done for US$3.50.

Yivli Minare & the Bazaar

Start your sightseeing at the Yivli Minare, just downhill from the Saat Kulesi. The handsome and unique minaret was erected by the Seljuk sultan Alaeddin Keykubat I in the early 13th century, next to a church which the sultan had converted to a mosque. It is now the **Güzel Sanatlar Galerisi** (Fine Arts Gallery) with changing exhibits. To its north-west is a Mevlevi tekke (Whirling Dervish monastery) which probably dates from the 13th century, and nearby are two **tombs**, that of Zincirkıran Mehmet Bey (1377) and the lady Nigar Hatun.

The view from the plaza, taking in Kaleiçi, the bay and the distant ragged summits of the Beydağları (Bey Mountains), is spectacular. Teahouses behind Cumhuriyet Meydanı and the Atatürk statue offer the opportunity to enjoy the view.

Kaleiçi (Old Antalya)

Go down Uzun Çarşı, the street by the Saat Kulesi. On the left is the **Tekeli Mehmet Paşa Camii**, built by the Beylerbey (Governor of Governors) Tekeli Mehmet Paşa. No inscription dates the building, which was repaired extensively in 1886 and 1926. Note the beautiful Arabic inscriptions in the coloured tiles above the doors and windows.

Wander further into Kaleiçi, now a historic zone protected from modern development. Many of the gracious old Ottoman houses have been restored, then immediately converted to pensions, hotels or, inevitably, carpet shops.

Roman Harbour The Roman (Yacht) Harbour at the base of the slope was restored during the 1980s and is now used for yachts and excursion boats. It was Antalya's lifeline from the 2nd century BC up until late in this century when a new port was constructed about 12km west of the city, at the far end of Konyaaltı Plajı. Today it's lined with restaurants, tavernas and shops. Day-excursion boats tie up here and tout for passengers.

Kesik Minare & Korkut Camii In the eastern reaches of Kaleiçi is the **Kesik Minare** (Cut Minaret), a stump of a minaret which marks the ruins of a substantial building. Built originally as a 2nd-century Roman temple, it was converted in the 6th century to the Byzantine Church of the Virgin Mary. Destroyed during the Arab raids of the 7th century, it was repaired and converted to a mosque by the Seljuks in the 9th century. When Antalya fell to the Christian king of Cyprus, Peter I in 1361, it became a church again, but reverted to a mosque under Sultan Beyazid II's son Prince Dede Korkut (1470-1509). It served the neighbourhood's Muslim population until 1896, when it was mostly destroyed by fire, including the wooden superstructure of its minaret.

Gates and walls prevent entry, but it's possible to see bits of marble decoration in Roman and Byzantine styles from a walk around.

Hıdırlık Kulesi At the south-western edge of Kaleiçi, on the corner with Karaali Parkı, rises the Hıdırlık Kulesi, a 14m-high tower in the ancient walls which dates from the 1st century AD, and may have been used as a lighthouse.

Hadriyanüs Kapısı & Karaali Parkı

Down Atatürk Caddesi is Hadriyanüs Kapısı (Hadrian's Gate; also called Üçkapılar, the Three Gates) erected during the reign of that Roman emperor (117-38 AD) of the same name. The monumental marble arch, which now leads to Kaleiçı, is set in a shady park.

Further along Atatürk Caddesi towards the sea is Karaali Parkı, a large, attractive, flower-filled park good for a stroll and for views of the sea. Sunset, the prettiest time, is when most Turks come here to stroll.

Antalya Müzesi

Antalya's large and rich museum is west of the centre, just over 2km from the Yivli Minare, reached by bus or dolmuş along Cumhuriyet Caddesi. Ask the driver: *Müzeye gider mi?* (mur-zeh-YEH gee-DEHR mee?), 'Does this go to the museum?'.

The collections include fascinating glimpses into the popular life of the region, with crafts and costume displays as well as a wealth of ancient artefacts. Opening hours are from 9 am to 6 pm (closed Monday). Admission costs US$3.50.

Many exhibits, most of them labelled in English as well as Turkish, are arranged according to provenience (ie, where they were found). They start with fossils, proceed chronologically through the Stone and Bronze ages (in which Turkey is especially rich in artefacts) and continue through the Mycenaean, classical and Hellenistic periods. The Gallery of the Gods has statues of 15 classical gods from Aphrodite to Zeus, some of them very fine. Among the exceptionally good smaller objects are jewellery, vases, glass items and statuettes. Note the surprising sophistication and beauty of the Phrygian (Frig) ornaments, figurines and utensils from the 8th to 7th centuries BC.

The museum has a small collection of Christian art, including a room for icons which also contains pieces of the skull and jaw of St Nicholas, the original Santa Claus. There are also several sections of mosaic pavement.

The collection continues through Seljuk and Ottoman times with costumes, armour, calligraphy, implements, faïence, musical instruments, carpets and saddlebags. The ethnographic exhibits are fascinating and include a fully furnished nomad's tent, a room with a carpet loom from a village home and several rooms from a typical Ottoman household.

A shady patio has tables where you can sit and have a cool drink or hot tea.

Boat Excursions

Excursion yachts tie up in the Roman harbour in Kaleiçi, waiting for customers. They offer a variety of itineraries ranging in length from three to nine hours. Some trips go as far as Kemer, Phaselis, Olimpos, Demre and Kaş. A normal tour of the nearby coast takes 4½ or five hours, visits the Lower Düden Waterfall, gulf islands and some beaches for a swim. It includes lunch and costs US$14 to US$20 person. Ask in detail about lunch when comparing prices; there's a big difference between a sandwich and a three-course hot seafood feast.

Research Institute for Mediterranean Civilisations

The Koç Foundation's Akdeniz Medeniyetleri Araştırma Enstitüsü (☎ 242-243 4274, fax 243 8013), Barbaros Mahallesi, Kocatepe Sokak 25, is dedicated to the study of the archaeology, art, ethnography, history and philology of Turkey's Mediterranean coast. Permanent and changing exhibits highlight the institute's projects.

Festivals

Antalya is famous in Turkey for its Altın Portakkal Filim Festivali (Golden Orange Film Festival), held in late September or early October and the Akdeniz Şarkı Festivali (Mediterranean Song Festival), a performance contest held immediately afterwards. Hotels are heavily booked during the festivities.

Places to Stay

Antalya has hundreds of places to stay in all price ranges. Kaleiçi is the most atmospheric district, with pensions and small hotels in three categories. Cheapest are the run-down old houses and modern concrete buildings with minimal charm and similar plumbing, costing US$12 to US$16 for a double room (about 25% less for a single), probably with a common bathroom, perhaps with breakfast included. Next come the houses renovated or rebuilt in Ottoman style, more or less atmospheric, with private bathrooms, occasionally air-conditioning, and rates of US$16 to US$40 double (25% less for a single). Finally come the 'boutique' hotels, one or more adjoining lavishly furnished Ottoman-style

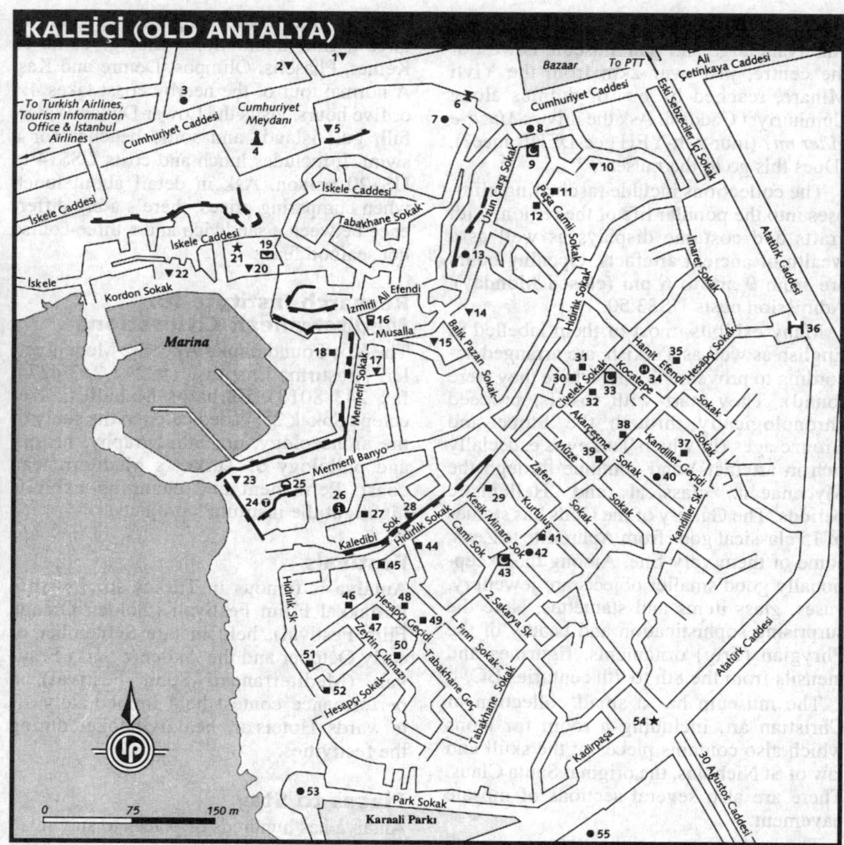

houses, perhaps with a small swimming pool, for US$60 to US$150. Surprisingly, you don't get much more of a guest room for US$100 than you do for US$30.

All prices listed are for B&B in a room with private shower and toilet, unless otherwise stated.

Places to Stay – Budget

Kaleiçi From Kale Kapısı, walk downhill past the Tekeli Ali Paşa mosque along Uzun Çarşı Sokak and turn left onto Balık Pazarı Sokak to reach the pension section. Another route is through Hadriyanüs Kapısı and along Hesapçı Sokak. Once in Kaleiçi, signs at street corners point the way to most pensions.

The tidy, quiet ***Erkal Pansiyon*** (☎ *242-241 0757, fax 244 0159, Kandiller Geçidi 5*), rents fine double rooms with fan or air-con for US$14 to US$22. Room No 304 is a mini-suite with air-con and balcony for the top price.

Excellent value for money and a safe haven for women travellers is the modern ***Senem Family Pension*** (☎ *242-247 1752, fax 247 0615, Kılınçaslan Mahallesi, Zeytin*

KALEİÇİ (OLD ANTALYA)

PLACES TO STAY

- 11 Dedehan Pansiyon
- 12 Antique Pansiyon
- 18 Türk Evi Otelleri
- 27 Hotel Aspen
- 29 Erken Pansiyon
- 30 Pansion Mini Orient
- 31 Adler Pension
- 32 Atelya Pension
- 35 Ninova Pension
- 37 Erkal Pansiyon
- 38 Villa Perla
- 39 Hotel Alp Paşa
- 41 Hodja Pansiyon
- 44 Pansiyon Dedekonak
- 45 Hotel Frankfurt Pansiyon
- 46 Hadriyanüs Pansiyon
- 47 Tamer Pansiyon
- 48 White Garden Pansiyon
- 49 Abadotel Pansiyon
- 50 Sabah Pansiyon
- 51 Keskin Pansiyon
- 52 Senem Family Pansiyon

PLACES TO EAT

- 1 Şehir Ocakbaşı Restaurant
- 2 Parlak Restaurant
- 5 Hisar Restaurant
- 10 Begonvil Restaurant
- 14 Favorit, Sunset & Café Alba Restaurants
- 15 Sırrı Restaurant
- 17 Kırk Merdiven
- 20 Kral Sofrası
- 22 Yat Restaurant
- 23 Mermerli Restaurant
- 28 Sim Restaurant

OTHER

- 3 Government House
- 4 Atatürk Statue
- 6 Kale Kapısı
- 7 Yivli Minare (Grooved Minaret)
- 8 Saat Kulesi (Clock Tower)
- 9 Tekeli Ali Paşa Camii
- 13 Mavi Tour
- 16 Voice Bar
- 19 PTT
- 21 Tourism Police
- 24 Toilets
- 25 Kültür Taxi
- 26 Ministry of Tourism Administrative Offices
- 33 Mosque
- 34 Sefa Hamamı
- 36 Hadriyanüs Kapısı (Hadrian's Gate)
- 40 Owl Bookshop
- 42 Ünal Laundry
- 43 Kesik Minare & Korkut Camii
- 53 Hıdırık Kulesi (Tower)
- 54 Police
- 55 Belediye (Town Hall)

Geçidi Sokak 9), near the Hıdırlık Kulesi. Mrs Seval Ünsal is everyone's Mama, offering clean, simple rooms (most can sleep three) for US$15 to US$18. Home-cooked meals are served on the roof terrace, with one of the best westward views in the neighbourhood.

The neighbouring ***Keskin Pansiyon*** *(☎ 242-241 2865)* is two converted houses (one built to look old) with equally low rates (and some rooms with shared baths) but much lower standards in every regard.

Sabah Pansiyon *(☎ 242-247 5345)*, around the corner at Hesapçı Sokak 60/A, is better, with 16 rooms with shower from US$16 to US$18 a double, or US$10 a double for the rooms with shared bath. Tours, car and motorcycle rental and other useful services are available as well.

The unrestored ***Adler Pension*** *(☎ 242-241 7818), Civelek Sokak 16*, is among the cheapest pensions in the neighbourhood – as it should be – at US$9/15 a single/double, with shared baths and a public hamam half a block away.

Erken Pansiyon *(☎ 242-247 6092, fax 248 9801, Hıdırlık Sokak 5)*, is a well-preserved (not restored) Ottoman house of dark wood and white plaster charging US$18 a double.

Pansiyon Dedekonak *(☎ 242-247 5170, fax 244 0427, Hıdırlık Sokak 13)*, is full of well-preserved character and a good choice at US$15/20 a single/double.

Hadriyanüs Pansiyon *(☎ 242-244 0030, Kılınçarslan Mahallesi, Zeytin Çıkmazı 4/A-B)*, is a series of old, mostly unrestored buildings around a refreshingly large and green walled garden. The friendly owners charge US$14/20 for a single/double room or *sivit* (suite). The neighbouring ***Tamer Pansiyon*** *(☎ 242-248 8147)* is modern and characterless but cheap.

White Garden Pansiyon *(☎ 242-241 9115, fax 241 2062, Hesapçı Geçidi 9)*, has a nice garden and a good price of US$22 a double for more modern, pleasant rooms.

Dedehan Pansiyon *(☎ 242-248 3787, Mescit Sokak 29)*, is another suitable place, priced at US$26 a double with breakfast. Opposite, the similarly priced ***Antique Pansiyon*** *(☎ 242-242 4615, fax 241 5890, Paşa Camii Sokak 28)*, is authentically old-time Ottoman, with congenial management and a largely Dutch clientele.

Camping Camping is expensive (US$8 per tent) and inconvenient. ***Parlar Mocamp***, 14km north on the Burdur highway (D650), is designed for caravans and cars, but there are tent sites as well. Stopping a bus for transport to and from the city can be a problem.

Bambus Motel, Restaurant & Camping (*☎ 242-321 5263, fax 321 3550*), 300m west of Hotel Dedeman Antalya on the coast road, is small and crowded but shady, with room for only eight or 10 caravans at most, but with some tent spaces at similar prices. It's on the road closest to the coast, which at this point is one way heading east.

Places to Stay – Mid-Range

Kaleiçi ***Ninova Pension*** (*☎ 242-248 6114, Hamit Efendi Sokak 9*), is an artistically restored house with a peaceful garden renting double rooms for US$32, breakfast included.

Atelya Pension (*☎ 242-241 6416, fax 241 2848, Civelek Sokak 21*), is a beautifully restored stone house with a vine-shaded garden on a quiet street. Room rates are US$22/30 a single/double, breakfast included – excellent value.

For nice but slightly cheaper rooms, walk a few steps further to ***Pansion Mini Orient*** (*☎/fax 242-244 0015, Civelek Sokak 30*), an old house nicely restored but still simple. The four double and six triple rooms grouped around the small courtyard all have tiny private facilities, and there's a cosy dining room for meals. Prices in summer are US$20/28/36 for a single/double/triple, with reductions in the low season.

Hodja Pansiyon (*☎ 242-248 9486, fax 248 9485, Hesapçı Sokak 37*), is newish and clean, renting double rooms with shower for US$30, breakfast included. The nearby ***Abadotel Pansiyon*** (*☎ 242-247 4466, fax 248 9205, Hesapçı Geçidi 52*), is similar in its comforts and price.

Hotel Frankfurt (*☎/fax 242-247 6224, Hıdırlık Sokak 17*), is a restored house with white plaster walls, bright honey-coloured wood trim on door frames and lattice-covered windows, and German-Turkish management. A little marble fountain burbles in the courtyard. It's pleasant, and excellent value at US$25/35 a single/double in high summer for a room with shower and a good breakfast is included.

The 11 room ***Villa Perla*** (*☎ 242-248 9793, fax 241 2917, Hesapçı Sokak 26*), has lots of character and a tiny swimming pool in the midst of the well-regarded restaurant. Rooms cost US$40/50 with private shower and breakfast.

Hotel Alp Paşa (*☎ 242-247 5676, fax 248 5074, Hesapçı Sokak 30-32*), has been restored into a posh Ottoman dream of comforts, from its hamam and courtyard swimming pool to its suites with whirlpool baths. Rooms with bath and breakfast cost US$36 to US$50 or US$42 to US$95 a single, depending upon the room and season.

The more luxurious places are along Mermerli Sokak, to the east of the yacht harbour.

Türk Evi Otelleri (*☎ 242-248 6591, fax 241 9419, Mermerli Sokak 2*), is three restored Ottoman houses with 20 guest rooms, all done in late Ottoman Baroque decor with lots of gold leaf and Turkish carpets. There's a small octagonal swimming pool, and the sunset-view terrace cafe-bar overlooks the yacht harbour and the mountains beyond. All rooms have private baths and air-con and cost US$55/77 a single/double with breakfast included.

Kazım Özalp Caddesi If you must have a modern hotel, try the three-star, 54 room ***Maryot Hotel*** (*☎ 242-247 4807, fax 248 2196, Elmalı Mahallesi, Kazım Özalp Caddesi 69*), where well-equipped rooms cost US$34/40 a single/double, breakfast included – good value for money.

Places to Stay – Top End

The four-star ***Hotel Aspen*** (*☎ 242-247 0590, fax 241 3364, Mermerli Sokak 16-18*) in Kaleiçi, is a gem of a hotel, beautifully restored with bevelled glass, marble and gilt. The 36 rooms and four suites have air-con, satellite TV, minibars and all the comforts. Indulge yourself in the swimming pool, Turkish restaurant and bar, and sauna. This is the best in Kaleiçi. Rates are US$95/115, breakfast included.

Without doubt, Antalya's most prestigious and luxurious address is the five-star ***Sheraton Voyager Hotel*** *(☎ 242-243 2432, fax 243 2462, 100 Yıl Bulvarı)*, at the western end of Kenan Evren Bulvarı about 2.5km west of Kale Kapısı. All the five-star services are here, in a strikingly modern, appealing building with lavish terraced gardens. Rooms cost from US$120 to US$210 a single, US$180 to US$260 a double, with breakfast. Occasionally, promotional rates are lower.

Closer to the centre, the best local effort is the five-star ***Talya Hotel*** *(☎ 242-248 6800, fax 241 5400, Fevzi Çakmak Caddesi 30)*, a modern 204-room place overlooking the sea. For US$135 a single or from US$155 to US$200 a double, you get a modern air-con room, swimming pool, tennis court, restaurant, bar and other services.

Places to Eat

Town Centre The closer you get to the harbour, the more expensive the food gets.

Go to the intersection of Cumhuriyet and Atatürk caddesis and find the little street (parallel to Atatürk Caddesi) called Eski Sebzeciler İçi Sokak. The name means 'the Old Inner Street of the Greengrocers Market'. The narrow street is now shaded by a huge and unsightly but effective canopy and lined with little restaurants and pastry shops, many of which have outdoor tables. It's now quite touristy, but still enjoyable if you're careful not to let yourself be cheated.

The food is kebaps, mostly the ever-popular döner kebap, but you'll also find Antalya's speciality, *tandır kebap* – mutton baked in an earthenware pot buried in a fire pit; it's rich, tasty and greasy, served on a bed of fresh pide with vegetable garnish. It's sold by weight so you can have as many grams as you like. A normal portion is 150g *(yüz elli gram)*, a small portion 100g *(yüz gram)*. Some or much of the portion may be fat. A full meal costs anywhere from US$5 to US$10; ask prices before you sit down.

A 150g portion of döner kebap, *soslu* (with sauce), and a glass of ayran costs US$5 at ***Azim Döner ve İskender Salonu*** *(☎ 242-241 6610, Eski Sebzeciler İçi Sokak 6)*.

The clientele at ***Şehir Ocakbaşı Restaurant*** *(☎ 242-241 5127)*, not far from Kale Kapısı, is mostly local highrollers who come to talk business and politics. In fine weather streetside tables are set up and many diners make a meal of mezes and drinks (about US$10 or so). From Kale Kapısı cross Cumhuriyet Caddesi to its northern side, climb to the pedestrian walkway, turn left, then right at the second street.

Just around the corner (inland) from the Şehir is the cheaper ***Can İnegöl Köftecisi***, a small grill where you can eat for US$4.

One goes to ***Hisar Restaurant*** *(☎ 242-241 5281)*, more for the view than the food. Diners peer out from old vaulted stone chambers within the retaining wall behind Cumhuriyet Meydanı to the harbour and the sea beyond. The cuisine is Turkish and a three-course meal with wine or beer should cost only US$10 to US$14 per person, unless you have the expensive and disappointing specialty, *kalamar güveç* (shrimp casserole). From the Atatürk statue, walk to the edge of the cliff and find the flight of stairs descending to the harbour.

Kaleiçi Kaleiçi has many small restaurants, mostly catering to foreign tourists with continental-style menus. ***Villa Perla*** (☎ 242-248 9793, fax 241 2917), in the pension of the same name at Hesapçı Sokak 26, is well regarded, with tables out in a verdant courtyard. Have the *Caucasian şaşlık* (skewered meat and vegetables) for US$7, or the chicken şiş kebap for less. Full meals may be had for US$10 to US$16.

Sim Restaurant on Kaledibi Sokak is small and simple and when tables are set out in the street it's pleasant. They serve şiş kebap for US$3.50, 'garlicky beefsteak' for US$4.25, or a four-course set menu for US$8. I love their sign 'We are only a restaurant' (ie, we won't try to sell you a carpet).

Walk along Balık Pazarı Sokak to Uzun Çarşı Sokak to find more restaurants, including ***Favorit***, ***Sunset*** and ***Café Alba***, all on shaded terraces above the street. Prices are posted prominently. ***Sırrı Restaurant*** *(☎ 242-241 7239, Uzun Çarşı Sokak 25)*, has cheap meals like spaghetti for US$2 or steaks for up to US$8. The decor is Ottoman, the atmosphere welcoming.

Deeper into Kaleiçi, ***Kırk Merdiven*** (Forty Steps) across from the Türk Evi Otelleri, has a Euro-Turk menu featuring mushroom soup and various continental-style grills served on a vine-shaded terrace. Your bill might come to US$18 per person for dinner here.

Yacht Harbour For splendid unobstructed sunset views of the bay and Beydağları mountains, the tidy ***Mermerli Restaurant***, perched above the eastern end of the harbour, can't be beat. The bonus is lower prices than at most harbour restaurants: full meals for US$8 to US$12.

If you really want to dine down in the harbour area, try ***Yat Restaurant***, which has been here for years, serving meals for US$12 to US$20. Even cheaper is ***Kral Sofrası*** (*☎ 242-241 2198*), just up from the waterside by the little PTT. It's not quite so fancy, but the food is good and meals cost US$9 to US$15.

Kazım Özalp Caddesi Just a few steps up Kazım Özalp Caddesi from Kale Kapısı on the left-hand side is the entrance to a courtyard which holds ***Parlak Restaurant*** (☎ 242-241 6553), an old Antalya standby for grills. The impressively long grill pit belches smoke generated by its load of skewered chickens and lamb kebaps. Talk and rakı flow freely and the evening passes quickly. If the decor is too basic (there is none), escape to the ***aile salonu*** on the left. A full meal of meze, grills and rakı costs from US$8 to US$16 a person. The neighbouring ***Plaza Fast Food Self Servis*** is the sanitised version of the Parlak.

Antalya's most popular kebapçı, however, is ***01 Güneyliler***, Elmalı Mahallesi, 4 Sokak 12/A, where families and even single women come for the fresh flat bread, authentic kebaps, low prices, alcohol-free atmosphere and full meals for US$3 or US$4. To find it, walk up Kazım Özalp Caddesi, turn left past the big Hotel Kışlahan complex and go 1½ blocks to the restaurant, on your right.

A bit further up the street to the right of Maryot Hotel, ***Has Pide ve Kebap*** is good, simple and cheap, with sidewalk tables.

Entertainment

Long dinners are the rule. Kaleiçi and the yacht harbour have numerous bars and lounges good for drinks and conversation. Many visitors find that their pension owners – particularly in the cheaper places – organise evenings of singing, dancing and storytelling.

Voice Bar, just uphill from the Türk Evi Otelleri, has live entertainment (usually an acoustic guitarist) on most summer evenings.

Getting There & Away

Air The new Antalya airport is 10km east of the city centre on the Alanya highway. Turkish Airlines (☎ 242-243 4383, fax 248 4761), Cumhuriyet Caddesi 91, in the same building as the Tourism Information Office, has at least eight nonstop flights daily in summer to/from İstanbul and at least two from Ankara. There are also nonstop flights to Tel Aviv (Israel) and Zürich (Switzerland) at least weekly.

İstanbul Airlines (☎ 242-243 3890, fax 243 3894), Güllük Caddesi 2, Selekler Çarşısı 82, on the corner with Cumhuriyet Caddesi just west of Turkish Airlines, has nonstop flights at least weekly between Antalya and two dozen European cities, as well as a daily flight to İstanbul.

Bus The new Antalya Otogar (Yeni Garaj), 4km north of the city centre on the highway to Burdur, consists of two large terminals fronted by a park cut by a monumental access road. Approaching the otogar along the access road, the Şehirlerarası Terminalı (Intercity Terminal) is to the right; go here for all long distance buses. The İlçeler Terminalı (Provincial Terminal) to the left handles minibuses and midibuses to nearby points such as Kemer, Side and Alanya.

The otogar has a PTT, left luggage room ('Emanet/Trustee') which is open 24 hours, a PTT which changes foreign currency, a Yapı Kredi ATM and currency exchange office. There's also shops, snack stands and a restaurant.

Minibuses rocket eastward from Antalya to Perge, Aspendos, Side, Manavgat, Alanya and Gazipaşa every 20 minutes throughout the day in summer.

Many bus and dolmuş routes go through the Vatan Kavşağı (vah-TAHN kahv-shah-uh; the intersection of Vatan and Gazi boulevards), so it serves as an informal bus and minibus station for regional traffic. Take an 'Aksu' dolmuş for Perge (US$0.75), or a 'Manavgat' for Side (US$1.75).

Destinations served daily from Antalya are:

Adana – 555km, 11 hours, US$12 to US$15; a few buses
Alanya – 115km, two hours, US$4; every 20 minutes in summer
Ankara – 550km, eight hours, US$12 to US$15; frequent buses
Bodrum – 640km, 11 hours, US$12; one bus
Eğirdir – 186km, 2½ hours, US$5; hourly bus to Isparta, then dolmuş
Fethiye – 295km, 7½ hours, US$8 (*sahil* or coastal route); 222km, four hours, US$6 (*yayla* or inland route); several buses on each route
Göreme/Ürgüp – 485km, 10 hours, US$15; one or two buses
İstanbul – 725km, 12 hours, US$18 to US$22; frequent buses
İzmir – 550km, nine hours, US$10; several buses
Kaş – 185km, four hours, US$4; frequent minibuses in summer
Kemer – 35km, 40 minutes, US$1; minibuses every 10 minutes
Konya – 365km, six hours, US$12 via Isparta; 349km, four hours, US$11 via Akseki; several buses
Marmaris – 590km, seven hours, US$11; a few buses
Olimpos/Çıralı – 79km, 1½ hours, US$2.50; several minibuses and buses
Pamukkale – 300km, four hours, US$7; several buses
Side/Manavgat – 65km, 1½ hours, US$2; every 20 minutes in summer

Getting Around

To/From the Airport The airport is 10km east of the city centre. There's plenty of bus and minibus traffic along the highway, but the terminal is almost 2km south of the highway. If you don't favour walking you can take a taxi (US$7 or US$8 to the city centre). Havaş runs seven to nine airport buses (US$2) a day from the Turkish Airlines office on Cumhuriyet Caddesi.

To/From the Otogar Walk along the otogar access road to the boulevard and catch a dolmuş to the centre; ask for Kale Kapısı (KAH-leh kah-puh-suh). The dolmuş will probably go along Güllük Caddesi to Cumhuriyet Caddesi.

To return to the otogar, catch a dolmuş ('Yeni Garaj', 'Otogar' or 'Terminal', US$0.40) heading north on Güllük Caddesi just north of the Istanbul Airlines office on the corner of Cumhuriyet Caddesi. You can also get a red-and-beige Özel Halk Otobüsü (private bus) for the same fare.

Taxi Tours Kültür Taxi (☎ 242-221 1713) by the Mermerli Restaurant in Kaleiçi will take you on a taxi tour to these sites:

Aspendos	US$42
Düden Şelalesi	US$18
Kemer	US$42
Kurşunlu Şelalesi	US$30
Olimpos	US$88
Phaselis	US$58
Selge/Köprülü Kanyon	US$88
Side	US$58
Termessos	US$47
Tünektepe	US$24

You can combine several of these destinations in the same direction (Aspendos and Side, for example, or Kemer, Phaselis and Olimpos) and pay only the price to the longest destination.

AROUND ANTALYA

You can use Antalya as a base for excursions to Olimpos and Phaselis, Termessos, Perge, Aspendos and Side, but you might find it easier to visit Olimpos and Phaselis on your way to or from Kaş, and Perge and Aspendos on your way to Side or Alanya. With your own car you can stop at Termessos on your way north or west to Ankara, Denizli/Pamukkale, Eğirdir, İstanbul or İzmir.

Travel agencies in Antalya operate tours to all of these sites. For instance, a half-day tour to the Düden Şelalesi (Düden Falls) and Termessos costs US$25 per person and is perhaps a bit rushed – there's a lot to see at Termessos. A full-day tour to Perge, Aspendos and Side costs almost US$50. For taxi tours, which may be a better deal, see Getting Around in the earlier Antalya section.

Beaches

Antalya's reputation as a tourist centre is built not on its own beaches, but on those not far away, like Side's. Antalya's Konyaaltı Plajı to the west is pebbly, shadeless and relatively cheerless. For a real beach holiday, spend your time at Side, Alanya or Patara.

Düden Waterfalls

The Yukarı Düden Şelalesi (Upper Düden Falls), less than 10km north of the city centre, can be reached by dolmuş. Within view of the falls is a nice park and teahouse. This can be a relaxing spot on a hot summer afternoon, but avoid Düden on summer weekends when the park is crowded.

The Aşağı Düden Şelalesi (Lower Düden Falls) are down where the Düden Çayı meets the Mediterranean at Lara Plajı. Excursion boats include a visit to Lower Düden Falls on their rounds of the Gulf of Antalya. See Boat Excursions in the Antalya section for details.

Termessos

High in a rugged mountain valley 34km inland from Antalya lies the ruined city of Termessos. The warlike Termessians, a Pisidian people, lived in their impregnable fortress city and guarded their independence fiercely. Alexander the Great was fought off in 333 BC and the Romans accepted Termessos as an independent ally, not as a subject city in 70 BC.

Start early in the day as you have to walk and climb a good deal to see the ruins. Though it's cooler up in the mountains than on the shore, the sun is still quite hot. Take good shoes, a supply of drinking water and perhaps a picnic lunch. Make this visit in the morning and spend the afternoon at the beach.

The Termessos archaeological site, within the Güllükdağı Milli Parkı (national park) is open daily from 8 am to 6 pm from May to September, until 5 pm in winter; admission costs US$2.50 per person, or US$4 for a car and driver. It's possible to see the site quickly in two hours, but a more leisurely, thorough visit takes more like four or five hours.

At the car park are the remains of a small **Artemis-Hadrian Temple** and **Hadrian Propyleum**, now little more than a doorway. From the trailhead at the car park, it's a steep 20-minute hike via the lower city walls and the city gate to the **lower gymnasium** and **colonnaded street** which leads to the **quarry** and some **sarcophagi**. It's a full hour's walk all the way to the **southern necropolis** with a detour to the **upper agora** and its five large **partitions**, and stops at the **theatre** – the most dramatically sited ever – and the well-preserved **bouleuterion** of finely cut limestone. South of it, the **Temple of Artemis** is badly ruined, but clamber over it to the ruined **Temple of Zeus**, on the south-eastern side of

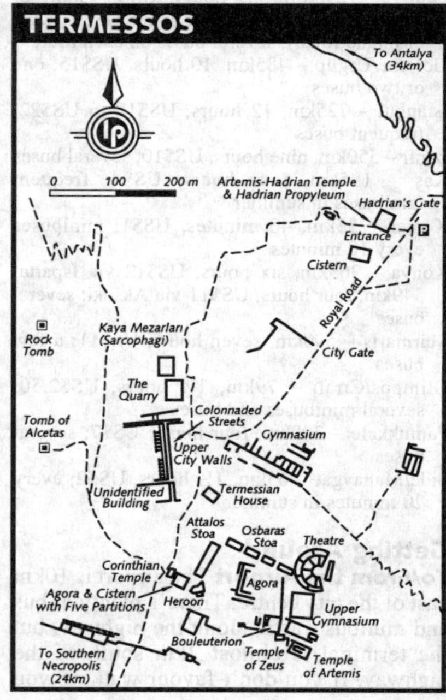

the bouleuterion, to enjoy the **spectacular view** of the mountains and steep valley. Note the narrow ancient road up the ramp just below the small circular foundation.

The **southern necropolis** *(mezarlık)* is at the very top of the valley, 3km up from the car park. It's a vast field of huge stone sarcophagi tumbled about by earthquakes and grave-robbers. The scene is reminiscent of medieval paintings portraying the Judgement Day, when all tombs are to be cast open.

Most famous is the **tomb of Alcetas** (follow the signs), a successor general of Alexander's, with fine reliefs on its facade.

Getting There & Away Kültür Taxi (☎ 242-221 1713) by the Mermerli Restaurant in Kaleiçi will take you on a taxi tour to Termessos for US$47.

If you're driving, leave Antalya by the highway towards Burdur and Isparta, turning left after about 11km onto E87/D350, the road marked for Korkuteli, Denizli and Muğla. Follow this through a stretch of road used for training *sürücü adayı* (student drivers). About 25km from Antalya, look for a road on the right marked for Karain (12km), the cave where important Palaeolithic artefacts were found (see Karain Cave following).

Just after the Karain road, look on the left for the entrance to **Güllükdağı (Termessos) Milli Parkı**, the national park. Pay the park admission fee and check out the small **museum**, the Flora ve Fauna Müzesi, with photographs and artefacts from the ruins, plus displays touching on the botany and zoology of the park. Near the museum are picnic sites. Continue another 9km up the road to the ruins. The road winds up through several gates in the city walls to the lower agora and car park, the largest flat space in this steep valley. From here you must explore the ruins on foot.

Karain Cave

The antiquity of the Karain Cave borders on the incredible. Archaeological evidence has convinced scientists that this cave was continuously occupied for 25,000 years.

Set in a steep rockface 150m above the floor of a fertile, temperate valley and 650m above sea level, the cave offered tolerable year-round living conditions for primitive humans. The valley below was well-watered and fertile, abundant with wild fruit trees, grains and vegetation, and good hunting.

The little museum at the site (open from 8 am to 6 pm daily for US$1.50) has an exhibit of Pleistocene animal bones and teeth, wild wheat, figs, snails, small game, rhinoceros, hippopotamus and elephant bones found in the cave. The cave was first excavated in 1946; excavation continues today.

The cave proper is a 15 or 20-minute hike up the steep hillside from the museum. It's an eerie place, three large interconnected chambers with a common entrance and many signs of long human habitation, not the least of which is a startling relief mask of a human face carved high up on the main 'pillar' of the main inner room.

Getting There & Away Karain is difficult to access by public transport. With your own car you can visit Termessos and Karain in the same day trip. Descending from Termessos, take the Karain road just outside the national park. After 1.4km the road forks; take either road, they rejoin at 4km. At 8km, turn left (there's a sign) and continue 3km to Karain.

Coming from Antalya on the highway to Burdur and Isparta, pass the road on the left to Korkuteli, Denizli and Muğla, and take the next road on the left marked for Yeşilbayır, Yeniköy and Karain.

Termessos to Denizli

If your itinerary takes you north from Termessos towards Denizli, you pass through Korkuteli and Tefenni, two undistinguished farming towns on the Anatolian Plateau. But onward, near Yeşilova, is Salda Gölü, a beautiful lake with a few simple camp sites and restaurants with signs in German.

Kurşunlu Şelalesi

About 14km north-east of Antalya and 1km north of Aksu is Kurşunlu Şelalesi (Leaded Waterfall), a shady park set in a pine forest with a waterfall and pool. It's a good place to get away from the noise and activity of

Turkish cities, except on weekends, when the city folk move here. Opening hours are from 8 am to 5.30 pm; admission costs US$0.50.

Bring a picnic (there are lots of tables), then follow the *geziyolu* (scenic trail) down the steps to the pool and the falls, actually a number of rivulets cascading down a rock wall festooned with ferns, vines and moss.

Perge

Perge, 15km east of Antalya and 2km north of the town of Aksu, is one of those very ancient towns. Greek colonists came here after the Trojan War and probably displaced even earlier inhabitants. The city prospered under Alexander the Great and the Romans but dwindled under the Byzantines before it was abandoned. The ruins are open from 7.30 am to 7 pm from May to October and from 8 am to 5.30 pm in winter; admission is US$3.

As you walk around, recall the grand **Tomb of Plancia Magna**, the city's great benefactress, which you should have seen in the Antalya Museum. Also, note the fine detailed carving in the marble throughout the city.

The great **theatre** and **stadium** are quite impressive, but Perge is famous for its huge **Roman and Hellenistic gates** and an impressive **colonnaded street**. The Roman gate is oddly off axis, so walk through it to the Hellenistic Triumphal Gate to get the effect of the city's original plan: looking through the Hellenistic Triumphal Gate down the colonnaded street.

The **southern baths** are quite impressive, as is the **agora** with the odd circular structure at its centre. At the **acropolis**, on a rise behind the other ruins, there is nothing much to see. For a fine view of the site climb to the top of the theatre.

Getting There & Away A visit to Perge can be included in the trip eastward to Aspendos and Side, doing it all in a day if you're pressed for time. Leave early in the morning.

Dolmuşes leave for Aksu from the Antalya otogar and Vatan Kavşağı. Ride the 13km east from Antalya to Aksu and the turn-off for Perge, then walk (20 to 25 minutes) or hitch the remaining 2km north to the ruins. You can include Perge in a taxi tour to Aspendos for US$42.

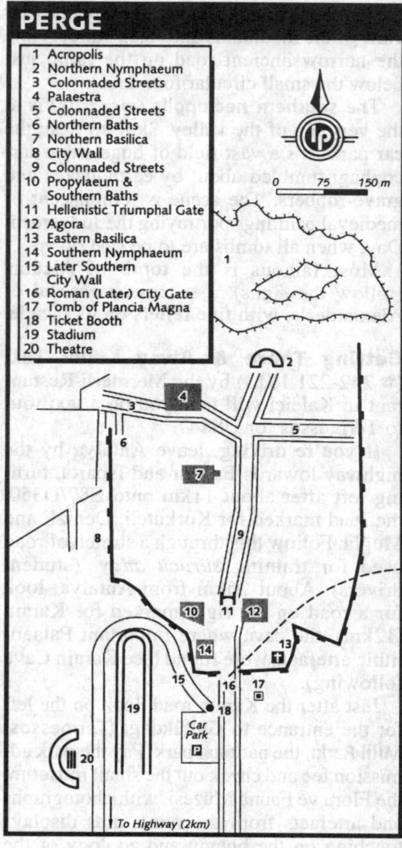

Sillyon

About 7km east of Perge and Aksu, a road on the left (north) is marked for Gebiz and Sillyon. Set on a mesa usually visible from the highway, Sillyon was a thriving city when Alexander the Great came through in the 4th century BC. Unable to take the city, the conqueror passed it by.

Sillyon offers little to the casual visitor. Bits of the ruined theatre, gymnasium and temple remain, but most of the ruins were destroyed by a landslide in 1969. The greatest curiosity here is an inscription in the Pamphylian dialect of ancient Greek, a unique example of this otherwise little-seen language.

Getting There & Away The ruins are difficult to reach without your own vehicle. Despite the sign reading 'Sillyon 8km' on the highway, it is further: 7.2km to a road on the right marked for Sillyon, then 2.2km to another right turn (unmarked). Go 900m and bear left, then another 100m, and turn left at a farm. The ruins are clearly visible 1km further along.

Aspendos

The land east of Antalya was called Pamphylia in ancient times. The Toros Dağları (Taurus Mountains) form a beautiful backdrop to the fertile coast, rich with fields of cotton and vegetables.

Aspendos (Belkis) lies 47km east of Antalya in the Pamphylian plain. Go as far as the Köprü Çayı stream, and notice the old Seljuk humpback bridge. Turn left (north) along the western bank of the stream, following the signs to Aspendos. The four-km ride to the great theatre is now sullied by bus-tour restaurants and all sorts of shops selling leather apparel, jewellery, carpets and the like. Better, simpler, cheaper restaurants serve you in the village just south of the site.

Aspendos is open from 8 am to 7 pm daily in summer and to 5.30 pm in winter; admission is US$3.50.

What you see here remains from Roman times, though the history of the settlement goes back to the Hittite Empire (800 BC). In 468 BC the Greeks and Persians fought a great battle here (the Greeks won, but not for long). Under the Romans, during the reign of Marcus Aurelius (161-80 AD), Aspendos got its theatre.

There are many fine Hellenistic and Roman theatres in Anatolia but the one at Aspendos is the finest of all. Built by the Romans, maintained by the Byzantines and Seljuks, it was restored after a visit by Atatürk. A plaque by the entrance states that when Atatürk saw the theatre he declared that it should be restored and used again for performances and sports.

Purists may question the authenticity of the restorations, but more than any other, the theatre at Aspendos allows the modern visitor to see and feel a true classical theatre: its acoustics, its lighting by day and night, and how the audiences moved in and out. Don't miss it.

Facing the theatre from the car park, a path to the right of the theatre is marked for Theatre Hill, which takes you up above the theatre for the stunning view. Follow the 'Aqueduct' fork in the trail for a good look at the remains of the city's aqueduct and of the modern village to the left of it. You can also follow the unpaved road north for 1km for fine views of the aqueduct.

The ruins of the ancient city are extensive and include a stadium, àgora and basilica, but they offer little to look at. Follow the aqueduct trail along the ridge to reach them.

Getting There & Away Minibuses going to Serik pick up passengers at the Vatan Kavşağı in Antalya (see Getting There & Away in the Antalya section). They'll drop you at the Aspendos turn-off, from which you can walk (45 minutes) or hitch the remaining 4km to the site. Taxis waiting at the highway junction will take you to the theatre for an outrageous US$5, or you can take a taxi tour from Antalya for US$42, perhaps stopping in Perge along the way.

Selge & Köprülü Kanyon

High in the mountains north of the lush Mediterranean littoral, 96km north-east of Antalya, a Roman bridge spans the picturesque canyon of the Köprü Irmağı (Bridge River). Above it, less than 12km away, are the ruins of the Roman city of Selge, scattered amid the stone houses of the Turkish village of Altınkaya in a forest of Mediterranean cypresses. The setting, high in this mountainous country, is spectacular, with

WESTERN MEDITERRANEAN

rock formations reminiscent of southwestern USA. The local people make their living cultivating wheat, corn, barley, apples, plums, chestnuts, walnuts and vetch for fodder.

Roman Selge was thought to have a population of about 20,000 at its peak, though how such a thriving city was sufficiently supplied with water in these arid mountains is something of a mystery. Selge was famous for storax, the balsam of the Asiatic liquidambar tree, which was highly prized for medicinal purposes and for use in perfumes. The city survived into Byzantine times.

Selge Ruins The vine-covered theatre rises dramatically behind the town. Though it is fairly well preserved, with only some rows of seats collapsed, the rest of the city is badly ruined. According to locals, the stage wall of the theatre stood intact until 1948, when it was felled by lightning. As you approach the theatre's left side, traces of the stadium are visible to the left. Climb up past the hamam to the agora. Not much remains, but the situation and views are satisfying. On a hill near the agora is a ruined church and, on a higher hill behind it, a temple of Zeus now completely ruined. Traces of the 2.5km of city walls are still visible.

Mountain Hikes Villagers can guide you on hikes up from Köprülü Kanyon along the original Roman road, about two hours up, or 1½ hours down, for about US$10 each way. They can also arrange mountain treks for groups to Bozburun Dağı (2504m) and other points in the Kuyucuk Dağları (Range), with a guide, *katırcı* (muleteer) and *yemekçi* (cook) for about US$50 per day.

Canoe & Raft Trips Medraft (☎ 242-248 0083, fax 242 7118), Cumhuriyet Caddesi 76/6, Işık Apt, Antalya, operates daily multi-person raft and two-person inflatable 'canoe' trips in summer along the Köprü River in Köprülü Kanyon.

There's also Antalya Rafting (☎ 242-321 8631, fax 321 8233), Ali Çetinkaya Caddesi 107/4.

The company's buses pick you up at your hotel in the morning and drive you to the river. You paddle about 15km downstream, stopping on the way for a picnic lunch. Buses return you to your hotel late in the afternoon. The price per person is US$50 (half price for children aged under 13 years), which includes lunch, insurance, guides and equipment.

Places to Stay You can sleep on the concrete-slab porch of Davut Çevik's house which acts as a drinks stand for US$1 or US$1.50, if you have your own bedding. By the time you visit there may be a few spartan rooms for rent, but Altınkaya will not develop in a hurry because there is a shortage of water; the village's meagre supply is now brought from many kilometres away.

Otherwise, stay at one of the pensions about 15km below on the western bank of the river, ***Selge Pension*** or ***Kanyon Pension***.

Getting There & Away Köprülü Kanyon and Selge are included in some tours run from Antalya, Side and Alanya for about US$25 per person. If you'd rather do it independently, the one daily minibus departs from Altınkaya in the morning for Serik (1½ hours, US$4) on the Antalya-Alanya highway, returning to Altınkaya in the evening. Thus you must plan to spend the night in the mountains, or haggle for a return fare, if you take the minibus.

With your own vehicle, you can make the visit in half a day, though it deserves alot more time. About 5km east of the Aspendos road (48km east of Antalya) along the main highway, a paved road on the left (north) is marked for Beşkonak, Selge and Köprülü Kanyon Milli Parkı (Bridge Canyon National Park).

The road is paved and travelling is fast for the first 33km. Then, about 4km before the town of Beşkonak, the road divides, with the left fork marked for Altınkaya, the right for Beşkonak. If you take the Altınkaya road along the river's western bank, you'll pass ***Medraft Outdoor camp***, ***Öncü Turizm Air Raft camp***, ***Selge Restaurant & Pension***, and ***Kanyon Restaurant & Pension***, both at the river's edge. About 11km from the turn-off is the graceful old arched Oluk bridge, an Ottoman work.

If instead you follow the road through Beşkonak, it's 6.5km from that village to the canyon and the Oluk bridge. Along the way you will pass the camps for various river rafting companies, which include Antalya Rafting, Kaktüs Rafting, Selge Turizm Rafting and Köprü Çay Rafting. Most of these places have small restaurants and camping grounds.

The unpaved road on the western bank of the river marked for Altınkaya (or Zerk), the modern Turkish names for Selge, climbs 11.7km from the bridge to the village through ever more dramatic scenery. When you enter the village, local children will urge you to park next to refreshment stands which charge a parking fee. You can ignore the fee, or have one of them show you around for a tip.

Eastern Mediterranean Turkey

East of Antalya you'll quickly come to several of Turkey's greatest archaeological sites, at Perge, Aspendos and Side, together with some of its most frighteningly built-up stretches of coast, at Alanya and again at Side. Further east development has been restricted by the soaring Taurus Mountains which plough right down to the clifftops squeezing out everything but the road, but wherever the land lies low and flat, there you'll find developments of modern holiday homes, rarely an attractive sight. The resorts at Anamur and Kızkalesi have grown up rapidly around stretches of beach with interesting ruins, but lack the charm of, say, Kaş and Kalkan, further west.

The far eastern end of the coast is heavily industrialised and the cities of Mersin (İçel), Adana and İskenderun offer little to hold your interest; agriculture, commerce and shipping rather than tourism are their *raison d'être*. Cut inland, however, and you can explore relatively little visited Hittite and Roman sites at Karatepe, Anavarza and Hierapolis Castabala.

Things brighten up south of İskenderun, with the Arab influence getting stronger with each kilometre. Antakya, the ancient Antioch, is not a beautiful city but does have a couple of gems (its museum and the cave-church of St Peter) well worth pausing for. The suburb of Harbiye also makes a pleasant place to break a journey south to Syria.

HIGHLIGHTS

- Examining the magnificent mosaics in Antakya Museum
- Visiting the off-the-beaten-track archaeological sites at Seleucia (near Manavgat), Uzuncaburç (near Silifke) and Anavarza (near Kadirli)
- Walking down from the Kale in Alanya
- Wading through wild flowers at Anamurium in spring
- Taking the boat to Northern Cyprus from Taşucu
- Having lunch beside a waterfall at Harbiye (Dafne)

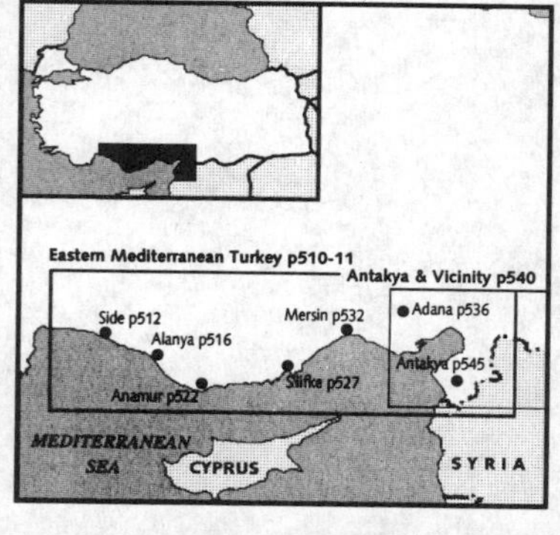

Getting There & Away

Air There are airports serving the eastern Mediterranean at Antalya, to the west, and Adana, to the east. Since European charter companies use Antalya to service their package holidays your best hope of a cheap air ticket is to that airport.

Turkish Airlines has scheduled flights to Adana from Amsterdam, Athens, Basle, Berlin, Brussels, Dusseldorf, Frankfurt, Geneva, London, Munich, Rome and Vienna. There are also daily flights from New York and many Middle Eastern cities. Alternatively, there are several flights a day from İstanbul for which you'll pay around US$75 one way. İstanbul Airlines also operates weekday services from İstanbul to Adana.

Train Trains run from Ankara to Adana and Mersin. See Ankara and Adana Getting There & Away sections for details.

Boat If you want to combine a trip to Turkey with one to Northern Cyprus, there are daily boats and hydrofoils from Taşucu, near Silifke, and Mersin, as well as more sporadic services from Alanya and Anamur in high summer. See those sections for more details.

Getting Around

You will probably get around the coast by bus or hired car. A good road runs all the way along the coast from Antalya to Antakya and then down to the Syrian border, but for much of the way from Alanya to Mersin it's a twisting, winding road that people who suffer from motion sickness will find difficult. Driving yourself, you need to remember that the Taurus Mountains hem the road into the sea, leaving few places to stop or pass other vehicles. Turkey has a terrible road accident record, so drive even more cautiously than you would at home.

SİDE

Once upon a time Side (SEE-deh, population 18,000) was a small Turkish village with 1km of fine sand beach on either side of it and some wonderful Hellenistic ruins. Legend even had it that Cleopatra and Mark Antony had chosen it as the spot for a romantic tryst. Unfortunately the world soon wised up to Side's potential and these days first impressions are not so alluring as you step into a tractor-drawn, advertisement-bedecked *tramvay* to be hauled down to a main street lined with leather, jewellery and carpet shops. As you walk along this street your progress will be punctuated by requests to answer 'just one question' and with stabs at guessing your nationality, usually in German, all in the service of sales.

But first impressions can be deceptive. Come out of season, dive down the side streets to escape the touts and you'll find plenty of the sort of small family run pensions with gardens that Alanya has so completely lost, along with enough ruins to keep you happy for a few days.

That said, if you loathe crowds and don't care for shopping, you'd be best steering clear of Side in high summer.

History

No one knows where Side got its name, though it probably means 'pomegranate' in some ancient Anatolian language. The site was colonised by Aeolians around 600 BC but by the time Alexander the Great swept through, the inhabitants had abandoned much of their Greek culture and language.

Many of Side's great buildings were raised with the profits of piracy and slavery, which flourished under the Greeks, only to be stopped when the city came under Roman control. After that, Side managed to prosper from legitimate commerce; under the Byzantines it was still large enough to rate a bishop. The 7th century Arab raids diminished the town, which was dead within two centuries. During the late 19th century it had another brief flowering under Ottoman rule.

Orientation & Information

Side is set on a promontory 3km south of the east-west highway. The road to the town is littered with trashy signs and dotted with hotels; it then passes the museum, continues under an arch and winds around the theatre. Vehicle access is tightly controlled and you'll almost certainly have to park (for a fee) in the car park outside the village, before the ruins.

The main street, Liman Caddesi, cuts straight through the village to the harbour fronted by a bust of Atatürk with a lion and lioness in front of it. On either side of the promontory are small beaches, although the main beach extends to the west.

The otogar is past the archaeological zone and the way to the village is not clearly indicated. Follow signs for the tramvay and you'll find the main road. Turn left if you want to walk, or board the tramvay for US$0.20.

The Tourism Information Office (☎ 242-753 1265, fax 753 2657) is inconveniently positioned about 1km from the village centre, on the road in from Manavgat.

Side's postal code is 07330.

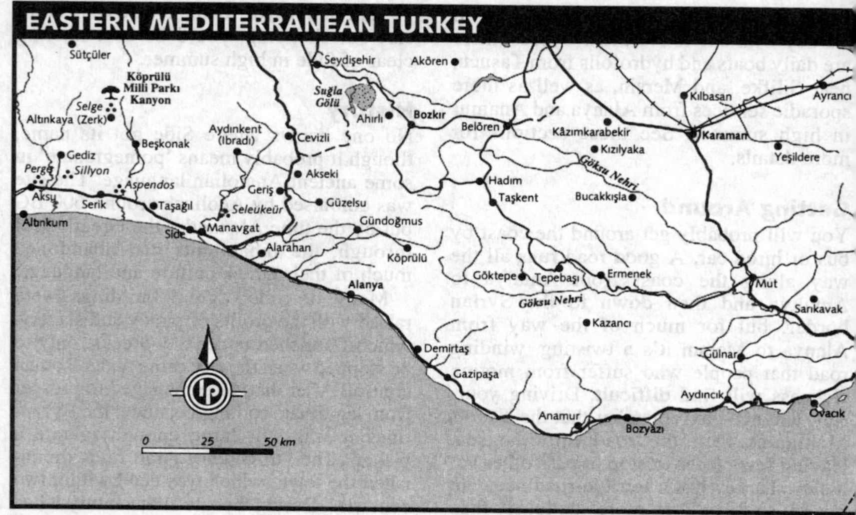

The Ruins

One reason why it makes sense to stay in the village proper is that Side's impressive ruins are just a short walk away. Look first at the **theatre**, one of the largest in Anatolia, with 15,000 seats. Originally constructed during Hellenistic times, it was enlarged under the Romans. At the time of writing it was closed for restoration. Locals will try and persuade you to clamber up the walls which may not be a good idea.

Next to the theatre and across the road from the museum is the **agora**, with many columns still standing. The **museum**, established in the old Roman baths, has an excellent small collection of statuary and reliefs. Opening hours are from 8 am to noon and from 1 to 5 pm daily except Monday; admission costs US$2.50.

To the east, between these buildings and the Hellenistic city walls, is a **Byzantine basilica** and the so-called **colonnaded street**, with some evocative foundations of Byzantine houses with mosaic floors. At the edge of the eastern beach, overlooked by snooty tourist camels, is another **agora**.

At the southern tip of the point of land upon which Side stands are two ruinous buildings, the **Temples of Apollo and Athena**, which date from the 2nd century AD. Some of the columns were re-erected by an American woman who had come here many times with her husband and wanted to commemorate him. They have something of the atmosphere of Cape Sounion, near Athens in Greece, and are especially magical at dusk.

Later, the Byzantines constructed an immense basilica over and around the temple sites and parts of the walls remain. Wandering among these marble remains at dusk is one of the most atmospheric things to do here.

Boat Excursions

As well as the usual sailing and swimming excursions from the waterfront, you can take a cruise from Side to Manavgat to see the Manavgat waterfalls on Monday, Wednesday and Friday, leaving at 10 am and returning at about 5 pm. The cost is US$18 per person, lunch included. The Monday trip allows time to explore Manavgat's market too.

Places to Stay

Side is slow to get going at the start of the tourist season, but although you may find many pensions closed or only half-heartedly open, April is a good time to visit since prices will be roughly half what they are in summer and the crowds won't be so oppressive. October is much the same as April. From June to September you may have trouble finding a room so try and arrive early in the day. Only a few places stay open all year round.

Places to Stay – Budget

In the side streets of the village proper, there are dozens of small family run pensions to choose from, but when making your choice you should take into account the proximity of noisy open-air bars and discos. Prices depend upon season, demand, facilities and even your nationality. In general, you'll pay US$6 to US$10 for a bed out of peak season, and up to twice that in high season. Look for signs reading 'Boş Oda Var' ('Empty Room Available').

As you walk down Liman Caddesi turn left along Gül Caddesi and then left again along Barbaros Caddesi to find some quietly located places to stay. ***Ani Motel*** *(☎ 242-753 3364, fax 753 3363)* is a collection of wooden chalets set around a garden where a room for two people will cost from US$20, including breakfast. Nearby is ***Güven Motel*** *(☎ 242-753 1091)* where clean simple rooms cost around US$24 a double with breakfast. Walk up Lale Caddesi behind the theatre and you'll come to the pretty ***İlhan Motel*** *(☎ 242-753 1099, fax 753 1869)*, with wooden balconies overlooking an attractive garden. Just behind the theatre you'll also find ***Kale Pansiyon***, a pretty basic place in need of some maintenance but often with rooms available.

Readers have recommended the simple ***Morning Star*** and ***Martı*** (mahr-TUH) pensions, both along Ceylan Caddesi, the continuation of Barbaros Caddesi as it heads towards the harbour. Although there are other small pensions at the far end of the promontory they tend to be blighted by noise from the Apollo Dance Bar overlooking the Temple of Apollo.

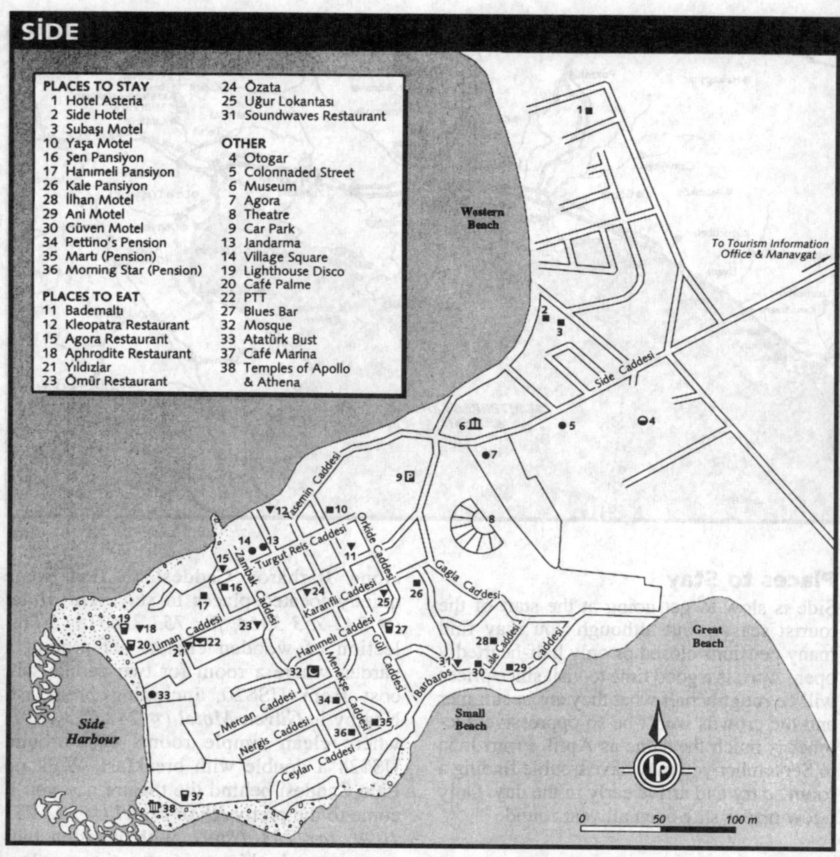

Heading inland along Menekşe Caddesi you'll come to ***Pettino's Pension*** *(☎ 242-753 3608)*, an Australian-Turkish owned enterprise which offers rooms in a cheerfully decorated house for US$10 per person.

More pensions can be found just off Liman Caddesi on the right-hand side as you walk towards the waterfront. One promising one, designed in wood and overlooking a pleasant garden is ***Yaşa Motel*** *(☎ 242-753 4024, fax 753 2299)* in Turgut Reis Caddesi. Beds here can cost as little as US$6 each.

Continue down Turgut Reis Caddesi and you'll come to ***Hanımeli Pansiyon*** *(☎/fax 242-753 1789)*, a beautifully restored stone house, surrounded by gardens scented by jasmine. It's quiet, full of character, and reasonably priced at US$24 a double with shower and breakfast. ***Şen Pansiyon*** opposite, is considerably cheaper.

Camping There are small, simple camping grounds on roads going to motels on the western beach; names and management seem to change from year to year.

Places to Stay – Mid-Range

Near Köseoğlu Hotel is ***Sidemara Motel*** *(☎ 242-753 1083)*, not far from the eastern beach. Double rooms with private shower go for US$36 to US$40, breakfast included.

There are several comfortable motels on the western beach. One of the best is ***Side Hotel*** *(☎ 242-753 3824, fax 753 4671)*. Close to the village, and with a nice patio restaurant and pool, it charges US$24/36 for a single/double room with breakfast and dinner included.

Inland from the Side Hotel is the comfortable, modern ***Subaşı Motel*** (SOO-bah-shuh) *(☎ 242-753 1047, fax 753 1855)*, a 15-minute walk from the village. The rooms have balconies facing east and west to take full advantage of sunrises and sunsets. Two people pay from US$27 for a double with bath and breakfast.

The western beach is lined with three and four-star hotels catering for the package holiday market.

Places to Stay – Top End

There are also scores of four and five-star hotels along the western beach. One of the best is the five-star, 154 room ***Hotel Asteria*** *(☎ 242-753 1830, fax 753 1830)*, set on a rise overlooking the beach about 3km north-east of the village proper. Its extensive grounds have swimming pools, sunning areas, bars and cafes, and lots of equipment for water sports. Each comfortable room has a small terrace; ask for one with an eastern sea view. Rates are from US$74/96 for a single/double, breakfast included.

Places to Eat

Many pensions have cooking facilities which allow you to make substantial savings. At the larger hotels you may be required to buy at least two meals a day, so the food problem is solved whether you like it or not. As for cheap restaurants, you need to duck down the back streets of the village proper and look for the smaller, simple places like ***Uğur Lokantası*** near the Kale Pansiyon, where you can still get a kebap for US$3. Many places also serve pizzas which are rarely too expensive. At the theatre end of Liman Caddesi the ***Bademaltı*** will also do you an aubergine moussaka for US$2.

The waterfront restaurants are more atmospheric but also more expensive. In the past there have been problems with people being charged horrendous sums for fish suppers. Although the situation seems to have improved it still makes sense to inquire carefully what you're getting for your money. A portion of grilled fish should cost between US$6 and US$8.

One pleasant restaurant of long-standing is ***Aphrodite*** *(☎ 242-753 1171)* at the beach end of Liman Caddesi. A large place with lots of garden-terrace dining tables, it usually has a selection of mezes and salads, as well as fish. To eat lightly and cheaply, order three or four meze plates with bread and a drink. Expect to pay around US$12 per person.

Yıldızlar Restaurant, slightly inland from the waterfront, is also popular, if not quite so atmospheric. ***Agora***, on Turgut Reis Caddesi, is another pleasant place to eat fish with sea views, as is ***Kleopatra Restaurant***, attached to a hotel of the same name.

Situated on Barbaros Caddesi, ***Soundwaves Restaurant*** is another long-established restaurant, with Turkish-Australian management, which keeps its menu lively with dishes like garlic prawns and onion steak to top up the Turkish standards. The woody pine interior offers soft lighting and classical music. Full meals cost from US$10 to US$20 per person, drinks included.

If you have a sudden yearning for pork, ***Ömür Restaurant*** in Zambak Caddesi rather bravely touts a menu with all sorts of non-Islamic dishes for around US$5 per person.

Liman Caddesi has several mouth-watering patisseries. Look in particular for ***Özata*** which serves cakes downstairs and fast food on a terrace upstairs.

Entertainment

Side has its fair share of discos, including the large ***Lighthouse*** at the far end of the promontory. Atmospheric places to go for a drink include the ***Blues Bar***, built around the shell of an old village house on the corner of

Gül and Hanimeli caddesis, and ***Café Marina*** with lots of pieces of statuary and a platform overlooking the Temple of Apollo.

Café Palme, opposite the Aphrodite Restaurant, is good for everything from coffees to cocktails. Fruit juices are available throughout the day in the village square off Turgut Reis Caddesi. In Liman Caddesi you should look in at ***Paşabey Restaurant***, a love-it-or-hate-it piece of kitsch with mock travertines where it could be fun to have a drink on a sunny evening.

Getting There & Away

In summer Side has direct buses to Ankara, İzmir and İstanbul. Otherwise, the numerous buses running along the coast between Antalya and Alanya will drop you right in Side or at least in Manavgat, the town on the highway. From Manavgat dolmuşes travel the 4km to the shore every 20 minutes (US$0.30).

Alanya – 63km, 1¼ hours, US$3; frequent buses and dolmuşes in summer
Antalya – 65km, 1¼ hours, US$3; very frequent buses and dolmuşes in summer
Konya – 296km, 5½ hours, US$8; no direct buses from Side, but you can catch one in Manavgat or at the junction with D695, 12km east of Manavgat

AROUND SİDE

Manavgat & Seleukeia in Pamphylia

About 6km to the north and east of Side, Manavgat is a commercial town with a thriving Monday market, worth visiting in the unlikely event that you couldn't find exactly the right leather jacket in Side. The otogar is immediately to the west of the bridge in the main street and except at the height of summer you'll have to come here from Side to connect with bus services to Antalya, Alanya, Konya and the lakes.

River Boat Trips Walk through the otogar to get to the water and you'll find boats waiting to run you upriver to Manavgat's two waterfalls. An 80-minute round trip costs US$5.50 per person, providing there are at least four people.

Manavgat Şelalesi About 4km north of Manavgat is **Manavgat Şelalesi**, a wrap-around waterfall on the Manavgat River, with teahouses, snack shops and restaurants. Although it's a terrible tourist trap, with camels in straw hats, monkeys and donkeys lined up for photographs, it's also a pleasant place to have lunch on a hot summer day. Admission costs US$0.40, and a meal of şiş kebap, salad and a cold drink will cost you US$6. A dolmuş to get there costs US$0.30.

Seleukeia in Pamphylia About 2km north of the waterfall the road crosses a bridge over a stream. To the left is a fine old five-arched Ottoman bridge built next to a bastion which appears to be much older. Another 1km along on the left are the remains of the Roman aqueduct which brought water from Dumanlı to Side.

About 2km past the Ottoman bridge a road on the left is signposted 7km for **Seleukeia**. Follow it through the village of Şıhlar, with many old fieldstone houses, some with bits of columns incorporated into the walls. Take the road to the right opposite the minaret. It's more than 3km uphill to the ruins along an increasingly rough track, which may be impassable for low-slung cars at some times of year. The walk is pleasant provided you bring plenty of water. The last place to buy a drink is in Şıhlar.

The ruins, scattered amid soughing pines in a beautiful and easily defensible hilltop location, include baths, a necropolis, a *bouleuterion* (small theatre), a temple and many unidentified buildings, all badly ruined. Most impressive is the large **market hall** with a ruined **hamam** to one side, but really you could come here as much for the natural beauty of the site where you pick your way over pine cones with only bird-song as an accompaniment.

For years this was believed to be the Seleukeia in Pamphylia which was founded during Hellenistic times, but the recent discovery of an inscription in both Greek and the language of ancient Side (which pre-dated Alexander the Great) makes it more likely that this was the city of Lyrbe. For the time being the signs are sticking with Seleukeia.

If you don't have your own transport, taxi drivers wait both at the otogar and across the bridge in Manavgat to run you up, with a stop at the waterfall thrown in. Expect to pay US$10 to US$12 for the round trip.

NORTH TO KONYA

About 12km east of Manavgat (50km west of Alanya) a highway heads north-west up to the Anatolian plateau and Konya (280km) via Akseki, curving through beautiful mountain scenery. The once-narrow, curvy road has been greatly improved and is now the preferred route to Konya from this part of the coast. The route via Antalya and Isparta takes seven hours from Side.

EAST TO ALANYA

The 63km bus journey from Manavgat to Alanya takes slightly more than an hour, with the highway skirting good **sandy beaches** virtually all the way. Hotels, holiday villages and government rest camps line the coast for much of its length. On the landward side you'll see the occasional stretch of aqueduct or the foundations of an old caravanserai or baths.

About 23km west of Alanya you pass İncekum (Fine Sand) and Avsallar, these days virtual extensions of Alanya with little to recommend them. At İncekum the **İncekum Orman İçi Dinlenme Yeri** (Fine Sand Forest Rest Area) has a ***camping ground*** in a pine grove near the beach. About 13km before Alanya notice the **Şarapsa Hanı**, a Seljuk caravanserai. Another one, the **Alarahan**, is accessible by a side road heading north for 9km.

ALANYA

There's evidence of people living in the Alanya area as far back as the Paleolithic period. It was also settled by the Romans and Byzantines, but present-day Alanya is really the handiwork of the Seljuk Turks who stamped their mark so firmly on the hilltop promontory. The Seljuks built a powerful empire, the Sultanate of Rum (ROOM, Rome), which thrived from 1071 to 1243. Its capital was in Konya, but its primary port was Alanya.

Like Side, Alanya occupies a point of land flanked by two great sweeping beaches. Once a sleepy agricultural, fishing and tourist town, it has grown out of all recognition since the late 1980s. A town with a winter population of around 200,000 now has to cope with three times that number in summer and the infrastructure isn't always up to it; lengthy power cuts are not uncommon. With a wide swath of sandy beach stretching 22km east from the town, Alanya is a mini-Miami Beach, with a similar clutter of high-rise towers and resort hotels, lots of carpet-shop touts and high prices. It's a favourite destination of European package holiday groups, particularly from Scandinavia and Germany.

At first sight those who want more from a holiday than sun and beach might throw up their hands in horror and press straight on. But the Kale district, with its crumbling old houses, magnificent ruins and inviting cafes, is certainly worth a day of anyone's time.

Orientation

The otogar is on the coastal highway (Atatürk Caddesi) 3km west of the centre. It is served by city buses which take you into town every half-hour for US$0.60.

Having gone from a small town to a 20km-long city almost overnight, Alanya has no real main square or civic centre. The centre – such as it is – lies inland (north) from the promontory which bears the roaming walls of the citadel. Scattered in this central area are the PTT, Tourism Information Office and museum. The closest thing to a main square is Hürriyet Meydanı, a nondescript traffic junction at the northern end of İskele Caddesi.

Development inland is limited by the slopes of the Taurus range, so the city sprawls east and west along the coast. The ranks of beach hotels barely thin out until you reach the districts of Mahmutlar and Kargıcak, 15km east of Alanya centre.

Alanya's sandy beaches are perfectly good, although if you're staying out east or

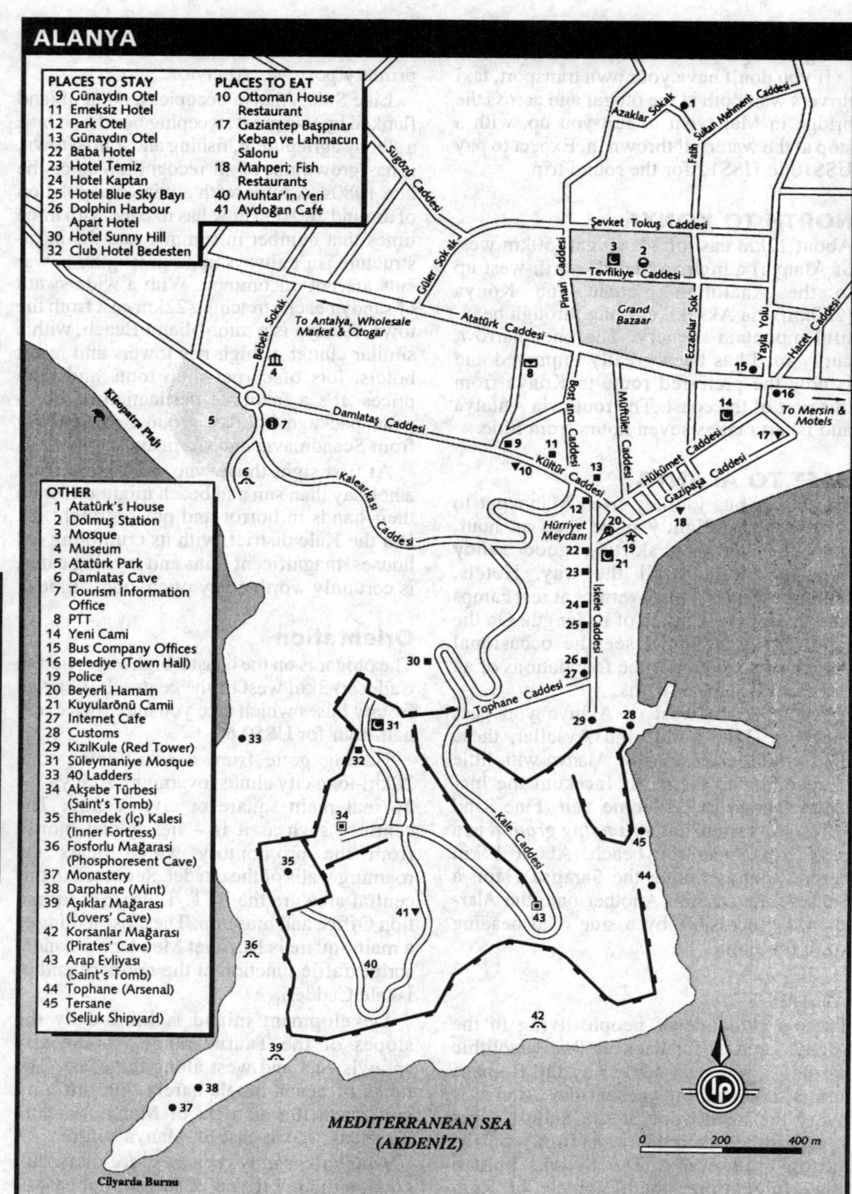

EASTERN MEDITERRANEAN

west of the centre they're fronted by a busy main road. Cleopatra's Beach is accessible on foot from the western side of the promontory, behind the Tourism Information Office. It's sandy and more secluded – at least outside high summer – and has fine views of the Kale up above.

Information

The Tourism Information Office (☎ 242-513 1240, fax 513 5436), Çarşı Mahallesi, Kalearkası Caddesi, is at the north-western foot of the promontory, near the Damlataş Mağarası (Cave).

There's an Internet cafe near the Hotel Kaptan, on İskele Caddesi. You'll be charged U$2 for half an hour on the terminals, with coffee and fast food on offer to keep you going.

The **Beylerli Hamamı** beside the mosque in Hürriyet Meydanı is open every day until midnight. It's for women only on Tuesday from 10 am to 5 pm. A wash with massage costs US$16, or you can wash yourself for US$5.

The area between Atatürk Caddesi and Şevket Tekoş Caddesi is given over to a vast bazaar, some of it undercover. On Friday villagers come here to sell their fruit and vegetables.

Alanya's postal code is 07400.

The Kale

Alanya's most exciting historical site is, of course, the Kale (fortress) on top of the promontory. It's 3km to the top, so it's wise to take transport up and save the walking for coming down when you'll be able to appreciate the splendid views. City buses to the top of the promontory depart from opposite the Tourism Information Office every hour on the hour (US$0.30). Taxis wait at the bottom of all the approach roads (and halfway up in case you think you can't make it); they charge US$6 to run you to the top.

The ancient city was enclosed by a rambling wall (1226) which makes its way all around the peninsula. At the top is the **Ehmedek Kapısı**, the major gateway into the enclosure. From the İç Kalesi (inner fort or keep) you get a panoramic view of the peninsula, walls, town and great expanses of coastline backed by the blue Taurus Mountains. Inside you'll find ruins of a Byzantine church, cisterns and storerooms.

Admission to İç Kalesi, from 8 am to 7 pm daily, costs US$2.50, half price for students. Avoid the toilet inside which, at US$0.50, must rate as the most expensive in Turkey!

Coming down, look for a sign on the right which cuts slightly inland to what was once the Ottoman **bedesten** and is now the Club Hotel Bedesten (see Places to Stay – Top End later in this section). Beside it, the red-brick **Süleymaniye Camii** is another Ottoman work.

Other Selçuk Sites

Overlooking the harbour is the five-storey, octagonal **Kızılkule** (Red Tower), constructed by a Syrian Arab architect in 1226 during the reign of the Seljuk sultan, Alaeddin Keykubad I. Now restored to its former glory, it contains a worthwhile ethnographic museum with lots of old carpets and camel bags and translations of verse by the 13th century Turkish poet Yunus Emre. Climb the 78 steps to the top of the battlements for fine views of the harbour and the town.

The tower is open from 8 am to noon, and 1.30 to 5.30 pm (except Monday) and costs US$1.50.

Afterwards, you can follow the sea walls until you come to the old **Seljuk Tersane** or shipyard (1228). The views are some of Alanya's best.

Atatürk's House

While Atatürk was president of the republic, he spent the night of 18 February 1935 in a house on Azaklar Sokak, off Fatih Sultan Mehmet Caddesi. His stay was of little historical importance, but the owner of the house, Mr Rifat Azakoğlu, left it to be preserved as a museum. The downstairs rooms are filled with so-so photographs illustrating the great man's life. Upstairs, however, the rooms are furnished to show how a well-to-do Alanya family lived during the 1930s.

Opening hours are from 8.30 am to noon and 1.30 to 5.30 pm (closed Saturday and Sunday); admission costs US$1. It'll be surprising if you don't have the house to yourself.

Museum

Alanya has a tidy little museum on the western side of the peninsula, near the Tourism Information Office. Exhibits span the ages from Old Bronze through Greek and Roman to Ottoman. Don't miss the Ethnology Room at the back, with a fine assortment of *kilims* (woven mats), *cicims* (embroidered mats), Turkish carpets, wood and copper-inlay work, gold and silver and beautifully illuminated religious books.

It's open daily except Monday from 8 am to noon and 1.30 to 5.30 pm for US$1.

Damlataş Mağarası

About 100m towards the sea from the Tourism Information Office is the entrance to Damlataş Mağarası (Dripping-stone Cave) noted for its 95% humidity and constant high temperatures. The stalactites do indeed drip, encouraged by the heavy-breathing exhalations of troops of curious tourists. If you have heart problems, the atmosphere may be dangerous for you. Conversely, it's supposed to be good for asthma sufferers. Either way, it's hardly a world-class thrill.

Admission costs US$1.50, from 10 am to 7 or 8 pm daily.

Boat Excursions

Every day at 11 am boats leave from in front of Gazipaşa Caddesi for excursions around the promontory. Tours approach several caves, including those called Aşıklar Mağarası (Lovers' Cave), Korsanlar Mağarası (Pirates' Cave), Fosforlu Mağarası (Phosphorescent Cave), as well as Kleopatra Plajı (Cleopatra's Beach) on the western side of the promontory. The cost per person for a two-hour voyage is US$8, US$5.50 if you opt for a shorter one-hour trip.

Organised Tours

Many local operators organise tours to the ruins along the coast west of Alanya and to Anamur. A typical tour to Aspendos, Side and Manavgat will cost around US$24 per person, while a village-visiting jeep safari into the Taurus Mountains will cost about US$20 per person.

Places to Stay

Alanya has hundreds of hotels and pensions, almost all of them designed for and catering to group visitors and those in search of *apartotels* (self-catering flats). If you want to stay for more than a day or so it's worth checking the package holiday brochures at home first since tours inclusive of flights and transfers may well be cheaper than booking privately. In any case most of these places will be block-booked by tour operators throughout the summer.

On your own, you really need to arrive by early afternoon at the latest to be sure of a bed in one of the few places still catering for individual travellers.

Places to Stay – Budget

In high season your best bet may be to go with a private pension owner who approaches you at the otogar. However, make sure you know how far from the centre you'll be staying before going with them. One recommended private pension is ***Alaiye Pansiyon*** *(☎ 242-247 5731, Elmalı Mahallesi, Milli Egemenlik Caddesi, 4 Sokak 42)*.

There are still a handful of small hotels and pensions around Hürriyet Meydanı which rent rooms for less than US$20 a double. On the whole these are shabby places, too old-fashioned to be snapped up by the tour companies.

As you head down İskele Caddesi the first you'll come to is ***Baba Hotel*** *(☎ 242-513 1032, İskele Caddesi 6)*, where mundane rooms cost US$6/12 a single/double without shower and you must pay cash on arrival. If it's open, ***Alanya Palas*** *(☎ 242-513 1016)* next door is similar.

More expensive but infinitely preferable is the 24 room ***Hotel Temiz*** *(☎ 242-513 1016, İskele Caddesi 12)*, a few steps further along towards the Red Tower. Comfortable singles/doubles with showers cost US$12/18. Rooms at the front have balconies; for a better night's sleep ask for one at the back. This place is used by groups in high season.

A little further along and upstairs on the right is ***Yili Hotel*** *(☎ 242-513 1017)*, which advertises itself as a hostel and does indeed offer the most basic of waterless rooms for US$6 per person. There's a pleasant breakfast terrace but no food is included in the bed price.

At the southern end of Bostancı Caddesi near the Kuyularönü mosque is ***Çınar Otel*** *(☎ 242-512 0063)* where faded rooms rent for US$8/11 a single/double with shower. ***Günaydın Otel*** *(☎ 242-513 1943, Kültür Caddesi 26/B)*, one long block inland towards the Damlataş Mağarası, provides averagely comfortable accommodation for the same price.

Places to Stay – Mid-Range

Snazziest of the centrally placed hotels along İskele Caddesi is the three-star, 45 room ***Hotel Kaptan*** *(☎ 242-513 4900, fax 513 2000)*, which charges US$40/55 for modern singles/doubles with TVs, minibars, air-con and spotless bathrooms. Singles/doubles at the back are cheaper at US$28/38.

A block closer to the Red Tower is ***Hotel Blue Sky Bayırlı*** *(☎ 242-513 6487, fax 513 4320)*, with 60 shower-equipped rooms for US$25/39, many with nice balconies overlooking the town and the bay. If you'd like to rent an apartment, the ***Dolphin Harbour Apart Hotel*** *(☎ 242-513 2996, fax 512 2835, İskele Caddesi 88)*, charges US$32 to US$40 per day, single or double, but is often full.

On Hürriyet Meydanı at the northern end of İskele Caddesi, ***Park Otel*** *(☎ 242-513 1675, fax 513 2589, Eski PTT Caddesi 6)*, charges US$20 a double for rooms with the luxury of a swimming pool. ***Emeksiz Hotel*** *(☎ 242-513 6675)* across the street has posted prices of US$8/12 but tries to ask more for rooms with shower.

The three-star ***Hotel Sunny Hill*** *(☎ 242-511 1211, fax 512 3893, Çarşı Mahallesi, Damlataş Mevkii, Sultan Alaaddin Caddesi 3)*, clings to the hillside above the Tourist Information Office, on the Kale bus route. It boasts a beautiful swimming pool, terrace restaurant and bar and comfortable rooms (some with views) for US$32/48 a single/double, breakfast included.

Better still is ***Club Hotel Bedesten*** *(☎ 242-512 1234, fax 513 7934)*, higher up on the hill and created out of the old Ottoman *bedesten* or covered market. Rooms are smallish and low-lit but this is a thoroughly atmospheric place to stay, with marvellous views from its rooftop restaurant and pool. There's even an echoing 12m-deep cistern underneath. Of course all this clocks up a rate of US$54 a double, including breakfast – worth it to stay in a completely different Alanya from the tacky one below. Any snags? Perhaps the call to prayer from the mosque next door.

Places to Eat

Alanya is one of those towns where the waiters are liable to bring you expensive dishes you didn't order. If you don't want them, be sure they're taken away and check that they don't reappear on your bill.

There's no danger of starving since every other building seems to serve food or drink of some description. The problem is trying to stay within a tight budget. Although they're vanishing fast there are still a few small places to eat in the narrow streets of Alanya's bazaar, in the centre of town on the eastern inland side of the promontory. Look for signs saying 'İnegöl Köftecisi', and snap up grilled meatballs and salad for around US$4. In fine weather, streetside tables are set up.

Many of these places are patronised by tourists, but if you search you may find one which serves mostly Turks. One such place is ***Gaziantep Başpınar Kebap ve Lahmacun Salonu***, inland a bit from the eastern end of the row of water-view restaurants. Head straight inland to the bazaar and you'll find the ***Ravza*** and ***Şölen*** restaurants where something like an İskender kebap and a cold drink will cost US$4. Another area worth exploring for cheap restaurants is behind the Kuyularönü mosque, off Hürriyet Meydanı.

The waterfront promenade has a string of restaurants with attractive terraces looking out towards the sea. ***Mahperi Restaurant*** has been serving meals here for more than 30 years. Seafood is the speciality, of course, but it also does a good chicken şis kebap for US$5. ***Euro, Yönet, Sudsee, Yelken, Alanya, Marina*** and ***Kordon*** are similar, with prices posted prominently.

Along Kültür Caddesi the ***Ottoman House Restaurant*** serves dishes like swordfish for US$6 in the gardens of an attractive old wooden house.

The road up to the kale is lined with small places to eat and drink, often serving *ayran* (a yoghurt drink) and *gözleme* (thin, folded pancakes). The higher you go, the nicer the places, partly because of the views and partly because of the surrounding gardens. Two especially good choices are ***Aydoğan Cafe*** where you can sip a cold drink beneath wisteria, and ***Muhtar'ın Yeri*** which has spectacular views.

At the entrance to the Damlataş Mağarası a ***stall*** serves piping hot gözleme for US$1.75 a portion.

Entertainment

Each district – indeed, each hotel – in this sprawling city has its own collection of bars, tavernas, discos and jazz clubs. The ones in the centre change ownership and approach frequently.

South of Gazipaşa Caddesi there's a cluster of disco bars, including ***Club Manhattan*** and ***Club 13*** which pump out music until the early hours. Out in the western outskirts Alanya's most impressive disco is currently the ***Auditorium*** which has a stream running through the middle. A taxi back afterwards will cost about US$8.

Getting There & Away

Bus Much of Alanya's bus traffic travels via Antalya and you may find yourself switching buses there. Compared to the rest of Turkey, traffic is sparse around the eastward 'bulge' of Anamur. Few buses originate in Alanya so you have to rely on passing buses having empty seats; make your departure arrangements as far in advance as possible. Also keep in mind that the road eastward is mountainous and curvy and takes a good deal longer to traverse than you might think from looking at the map. Nor is it good for anyone suffering from motion sickness.

Some destinations include:

Adana – 440km, 10 hours, US$18; eight buses daily in summer
Anamur – 135km, three hours, US$6; several buses daily in summer
Antalya – 115km, two hours, US$4; hourly buses in summer
İçel – 375km, 8½ hours, US$16; eight buses daily in summer
İstanbul – 840km, 17 hours, US$23; several buses daily, more from Antalya
İzmir – 660km, 12 hours, US$20; via Antalya
Kaş – 300km, seven hours, US$14; via Antalya
Konya – 320km, 6½ hours, US$16 (Akseki-Beyşehir route)
Marmaris – 700km, 11½ hours, US$20; via Antalya
Silifke – 275km, seven hours, US$12; eight buses daily in summer
Ürgüp – 590km, 10 hours, US$22 (Akseki-Beyşehir-Konya route)

Boat – To Cyprus For the last couple of years it has not been possible to sail direct to Northern Cyprus from Alanya. However, in 1998 Fergün Express was hoping to resume twice-weekly services, saving the long haul around to Taşucu.

If you do have to go to Taşucu, you can make a boat reservation and buy a ticket for the very early morning bus to the ferry docks at Alanya's otogar. For more information on these boats, see the Taşucu section later in this chapter.

Getting Around

Frequent dolmuşes shuttle along the coast, transporting passengers from the outlying hotel areas to the centre. Dolmuşes to the otogar can be picked up in the bazaar, north of Atatürk Caddesi (US$0.25).

ALANYA TO SİLİFKE

From Alanya you may want to head north to Konya, Cappadocia and Ankara. Alternatively, a twisting, turning road cut into the cliffs heads east 275km to Silifke. Every now and then it passes through the fertile delta of a stream, planted with bananas (as at Demirtaş) or crowded with glass greenhouses. It's a long drive with few places to stop until you get to Anamur but the sea views and the cool pine forests are extremely beautiful.

This region was the ancient Cilicia, a somewhat forbidding part of the world because of the mountains. Anyone wanting to conquer Cilicia had to have a navy, as the only practicable transport was by sea. Pirates preyed on ships from the hidden coves along this stretch of coast. In the late 1960s the government completed the good paved road from Alanya to Silifke, and since then tourism has grown rapidly.

ANAMUR

At the southernmost point along the Turkish coast, Anamur (population 42,000) is hardly exciting but does make a possible base for exploring the ruined Byzantine city of Anamurium and the wonderfully imposing Mamure Kalesi, impossible to miss as you sweep along the coast road. Due south of Anamur the İskele district has its own beach so unless you have pressing business to transact with the PTT or the banks, you're better off staying either here or near Anamurium or the Mamure Kalesi rather than in Anamur proper.

Orientation

Anamur town centre lies to the north of the highway, 1km from the main square. The otogar is at the junction of the highway and the main street. To reach the beach at İskele, head east from the otogar a short distance and turn right (south) at the signs; the beach is 2km south of the highway and 4km from the main square.

Mamure Kalesi is 7km east of the town centre; the ruins of Anamurium are 8.5km west of the centre.

Anamurium

Approaching Anamur from the west or down from the Cilician mountains, the highway finally reaches some level ground and a straight section. At this point, long before you reach Anamur itself, a road on the right points south towards the ruins. The road bumps 3km past fields and through the ruins to a dead end at the beach.

Founded by the Phoenicians, Anamurium flourished throughout the Roman period. Its Golden Age may have been around 250 AD, after which it lost some importance. When the Arab armies stormed out of Arabia in the 7th century they raided and pillaged this coast, including Anamurium. Despite its mighty walls and remote location, the city fell. It never recovered from the devastation and no one was interested in settling here afterwards.

Had new settlers come, they no doubt would have torn down these old buildings and used the cut stones to build their settlement. Anamurium escaped this destruction and survives as a sprawling Byzantine ghost town, with dozens of buildings perched on the rocky hillside above an unsullied pebble beach. Churches, aqueducts, houses and defensive walls stand silent and empty, their roofs caved in but their walls largely intact. It's surprising that Anatolia's earthquakes did so little damage.

The **public baths** are well-preserved, even to some of the wall decoration and mosaic floor. Many of the tombs in the vast **necropolis** have traces of decoration as well but treasure-hunters have been hard at work, wreaking havoc as they go. You can also visit the ruins of a **theatre** and **stadium**, and make out the remains of shops too.

The site is particularly wonderful in spring when the air is sweet-scented and you can walk ankle-deep in wild flowers.

At US$1, admission to Anamurium is a bargain. Although there are signs forbidding picnicking, they're primarily aimed at stopping Turks lighting stoves and causing fires. It's unlikely anyone will object if you bring out your sandwich box.

Mamure Kalesi

About 7km east of Anamur, the moat-girdled Mamure Kalesi, a maze of crenellated walls and towers with one foot in the Mediterranean, stands right beside the highway.

There has been a fortress here since the Romans built one in the 3rd century AD,

EASTERN MEDITERRANEAN

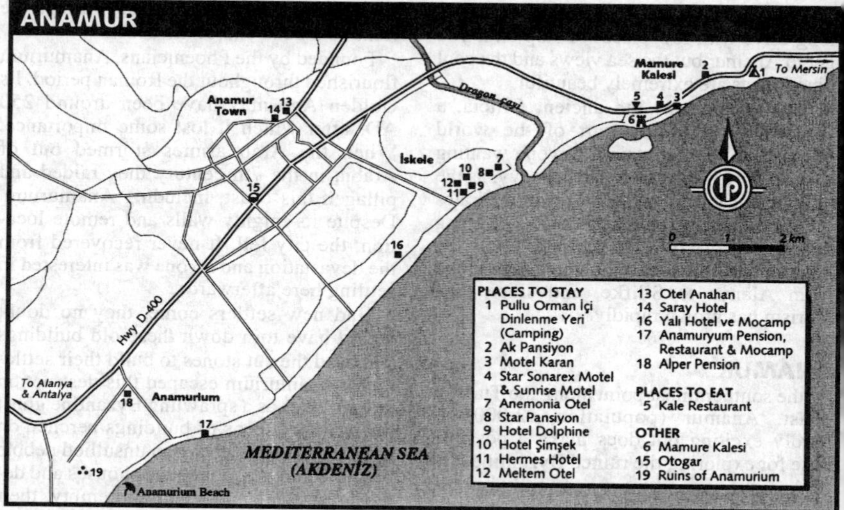

but the present structure dates from the time of the crusades when it was used by the crusader rulers of Cyprus. Later it became a stronghold of the 13th century Karamanoğlu emirs.

The Ottomans took over in the middle of the 14th century and kept the castle in good repair until their empire finally collapsed. Inside there's little to see except a modern **mosque** and grazing sheep but the **fortifications**, with crenellated walls and towers, are as impressive as any in Turkey and you can walk right around them providing you don't mind steep drops.

The castle is open daily from 8 am to 5 or 6 pm; admission costs US$1.

Places to Stay

As well as in the town itself, there are cheap pensions and camping grounds at İskele and near Anamurium and Mamure Kalesi.

Town Centre About 1km east of the main square in the town of Anamur, ***Saray Hotel*** *(☎ 324-814 1191, fax 814 2933)*, Tahsin Soylu Caddesi is simple and cheap, with clean rooms for US$12 a double.

A couple of doors down, the nominally two-star ***Otel Anahan*** *(☎ 324-813 3511, fax 814 1045, Tahsin Soylu Caddesi 109)*, has 30 fairly comfortable rooms with private shower (some with balcony) reached by a marble staircase (no lift). Given the competition from the beach pensions, it's overpriced at US$12/16 – more if you don't haggle. The top-floor breakfast room is pleasant though.

Anamurium On the road to Anamurium you pass the tiny ***Alper Pension***. Bear left and go 650m to the beach where you'll find the ***Anamuryum Pension, Restaurant & Mocamp***, perfectly positioned for walking along the beach to the ruins. Camping costs US$4 per person, which is fair enough, but the US$16 for a room is far too steep, given the dinginess of the building. The restaurant looks fun. Both the Alper and the Anamuryum are open in summer only.

Mamure Kalesi The road east of Mamure Kalesi is dotted with pensions. The one major drawback however is the the busy road in front. Noise is one inevitable snag.

The other, for parents especially, is the danger from traffic.

Two of the first places you'll come to are ***Sunrise Motel*** (☎ *324-827 1352)* and the nicer ***Star Sonarex Motel*** (☎ *324-827 1219)*, both with scenic gardens and charging around US$12 a double with shower. The Sonarex has the plus of a pleasant roof-terrace restaurant.

Even if the site, immediately beside a BP fuel station, is not inspiring, ***Motel Karan*** *(☎ 324-827 1027)* has the great advantage of being on the beach side of the main road. Cheerful rooms with balconies and bathrooms cost US$20 a double, and look straight onto the beach. So, too, does the adjacent restaurant.

Next up are ***Azıtepe Pansiyon*** (☎ *324-827 1100)* and the popular ***Ak Pansiyon*** *(☎ 324-827 1375)* where bed and breakfast is available for just US$4 per person. Then you'll come to the similar ***Girgeç*** and ***Çanlık*** pensions.

Finally 1.5km east of the castle, you'll find ***Pullu Orman İçi Dinlenme Yeri***, a delightful, shady forest camping ground. The cost is US$3 for a tent, US$5 for a caravan, plus US$2 per person. There's a fine sandy beach just below.

İskele (Beach) The İskele (dock) district has numerous pensions and hotels situated along İnönü Caddesi, the main waterfront street and even more lurking in various stages of completion on the road running down from the highway.

Yalı Hotel ve Mocamp (☎ *324-814 3474, fax 814 1435)* has space for tents (US$4) and caravans (US$6) as well as bungalows costing US$20 to US$24 depending on how many they accommodate, all overlooking a private beach.

Star Pansiyon (☎ *324-816 4605)*, on İnönü Caddesi, is covered in morning glories, has a shady front terrace ***restaurant*** and a rooftop terrace with water views and shower-equipped rooms renting for US$12 a double.

Opposite the waterfront tea garden the prominent ***Meltem Otel*** (☎ *324-814 2316, fax 814 4814)* and ***Hotel Şimşek*** (☎ *324-814 3978)* look more expensive than they actually are. Singles/doubles with private bath cost US$10/16. ***Anemonia Otel*** (☎ *324-814 4000, fax 814 1443)*, nearby, is similar, as is ***Hotel Dolphine*** (☎ *324-814 3435, fax 814 1575)* which has a pleasant ***restaurant*** serving alcohol at the front.

The three-star, 70 room ***Hermes Hotel*** (☎ *324-814 3950, fax 814 3995)*, is Anamur's best, charging US$20/40 a single/double, breakfast included. The hotel has a swimming pool and is just across the road from the beach.

A reader wrote to recommend ***Hotel Rolli*** (☎ *324-814 4978)*, in the district of Yalıevleri Mahallesi. The owner is in a wheelchair, ensuring that this hotel, unlike so many in Turkey, is accessible for guests with mobility problems. Unfortunately it's a little way from the beach and surrounded by tall buildings.

Places to Eat

Many pensions provide meals, as do the hotels and motels. Otherwise the best dining is along the waterfront in İskele, where ***Avşaroğlu Restaurant*** near the Hotel Dolphine is popular with the locals and serves up delicious flaps of bread. Classiest of all is the ***Astor***, rather out on a limb to the east, where pleasant fish dinners with trimmings cost US$10.

Across the road from Mamure Kalesi there are several small restaurants which can do you simple meals of kebap and salad. One such spot is ***Kale Restaurant***, almost opposite the gates, where a quick lunch shouldn't cost more than US$4.

Getting Around

Anamur is spread out and tricky to get around without your own transport.

You may be able to persuade a long-distance bus driver to drop you off at the junction for Anamurium, 3km from the ruins. Alternatively, you'll need to take a taxi from Anamur otogar or from İskele. Expect to pay about US$10 to go there and back, with an hour's waiting time – barely enough time to see the site highlights.

There are infrequent dolmuşes between İskele and Anamur centre. Taxis are likely to want about US$4 to run you there.

East of Anamur the transport situation brightens. Frequent dolmuşes to Bozyazı leave the otogar and travel past the town centre hotels and out to Mamure Kalesi and the eastern beach.

EAST TO SİLİFKE

From Anamur it's 160km east to Silifke. About 20km east of Anamur, the first sizeable settlement you'll come to is the town of **Bozyazı**, spread across a fertile alluvial plain backed by rugged mountains. Bozyazı manages several small pensions and some condominiums, as well as the two-star ***Alinko Motel*** *(☎/fax 324-851 3998)*, the four-star ***Vivanco Hotel*** *(☎ 324-851 4200, fax 851 2291)* and the shiny new three-star ***Hotel Mamure*** *(☎ 324-851 5400, fax 851 4604)* on the western outskirts.

Eastward across the plain and clearly visible from miles around, is Softa Kalesi, impossibly perched on the rocks above the little hamlet of **Çubukkoyağı**. This castle, built by the Armenian kings who ruled Cilicia for a short while during the crusades, is now fairly ruined inside but the walls and location are mightily impressive. As you leave Bozyazı, a sign on the left points inland to the castle, but the road doesn't go all the way to the top; take care as you must clamber up the last bit amidst snakes and scorpions.

About 75km from Anamur you come to **Aydıncık**. Although not perhaps the most exciting town, Aydıncık, with its greenhouses and forestry, does at least have the feel of a real town with a life beyond tourism. There's a small harbour with a ***camp site*** and small ***pensions*** and then the highway toils up into the mountains again.

From Aydıncık the road winds up and down and round and round, great for scenery but terrible for anyone who suffers from motion sickness. Every now and then it dips down into a valley with its requisite farming or beach village and semi-tropical crops in greenhouses. But wherever there's a bay, so is the line of holiday homes, seemingly aimed at desecrating every scrap of developable land.

If you'd like to climb into the mountains and see yet another medieval castle, turn left at Sipahili 3km south-west of Aydıncık and head up towards **Gülnar** (25km) for a look at the **Meydancık Kalesi**, which has stood here in one form or another since Hittite times.

East of Aydıncık the highway passes through **Yeşilovacık**, on the sea with a pebble beach and several hotels and government rest camps; **Akdere**, in a valley separated from the sea by a high ridge of mountains; **Boğsak**, with ***Boğsak Motel*** *(☎ 324-741 4450)* and ***Boğsak Camping*** above the beach, and a few small pensions; and **Akçakıl**, just past the small ruined Liman Kalesi which stands in splendid isolation 1km off the road on the sea side.

After interminable curves and switchbacks the highway finally drops down from the mountains to the Cilician Plain, the fertile littoral at the foot of the Taurus Mountains which stretches from Silifke to Adana. Before coming to Silifke proper, you pass the port of Taşucu, where ferries and hydrofoils depart for northern Cyprus.

TAŞUCU

Taşucu (TAHSH-oo-joo), the port of Silifke, lives for the ferries. Hotels put up voyagers, while car ferries and hydrofoils take them to and fro across the sea. For all that, it's a pretty unappealing place where you're unlikely to want to linger.

Orientation & Information

The main square by the ferry dock accommodates a bust of Atatürk, the PTT, a customs house, various banks, assorted shipping offices, restaurants and a small museum of amphoras. It's one block south of the highway. The beach, backed by a waterfront street (Sahil Yolu) and several good pensions, stretches out east of the docks.

Places to Stay

The cheapest place to stay is ***Işık Otel*** *(☎ 324-741 4026)*, an old building facing the

EASTERN MEDITERRANEAN

main square. This place contains a hall that has a wonderful sunsplash wooden ceiling but the rooms, without running water, are pretty basic, even for US$6 per person. It's above the Ali Baba Restaurant and a ferry booking office, so it may be noisy.

Most of the other places to stay are on Atatürk Caddesi, the main highway. ***Yuvam Pansiyon*** *(☎ 324-741 4101)* has clean, simple rooms, some with air-con, for US$6 per person. Right next door the new ***Hotel Konak*** *(☎ 324-741 2999, fax 741 6180)* is both a little smarter and a little more costly (US$8/16 a single/double), with cool tiled floors.

Further along ***Hotel Fatih*** *(☎ 324-741 4125)* has rooms with private showers and balconies for US$9/14/18 a single/double/triple, though you can haggle them down out of season. There's a restaurant as well.

If you don't mind paying a bit more, ***Lades Motel*** *(☎ 324-741 4008, fax 741 4258)* boasts a swimming pool and ***restaurant*** with fine harbour views. At US$20/30 a single/double rooms could be said to be pricey but they do share the views. Halls are decorated with kilims and there's a lot of information about the birdlife of the Göksu Delta.

A few hundred metres west of the Lades and designed to look like a giant ocean-going ship, the five-star ***Taşucu Best Resort Hotel*** *(☎ 324-741 6300, fax 741 3005)*, is Taşucu's best by far, with stylish modern rooms overlooking a huge pool and the harbour. Of course you must expect to pay for the comfort, but not as much as the terrifying posted prices; you'll probably be quoted US$40/80 for half-board if you ask.

A couple of other places are east of the otogar overlooking the harbour. ***Tuğran Pansiyon*** *(☎ 324-741 4493, Sahil Yolu 3)*, has clean, cheerful rooms with private shower for US$13/20 a single/double. If it's open, the nearby ***Holmi Pansiyon*** *(☎ 324-741 2321)* should be similarly priced.

If you fancy a spot of sunbathing before you catch your ferry, a couple of other places face the pebble beach about 500m east of the docks. The family run ***Meltem Pansiyon*** *(☎ 324-741 4391)* charges US$8 per person in rooms which have sea-facing balcony, fridge and sink for washing clothes. Two doors further on, ***Otel Olba*** *(☎ 324-741 4222, fax 741 4227)* has simple but inviting rooms, again with balcony, but for more than twice the price of the Meltem: US$20/30 a single/double with breakfast included. There is a pleasant ***bar-restaurant*** between these two places. Unfortunately the view along the coast is marred by a paper factory jutting out into the sea to the east.

Places to Eat

Denizkızı Restaurant, opposite the bust of Atatürk in the main square, is the locals' favourite for lunch and dinner, and is fairly cheap. Next to the otogar, ***İstanbul Restaurant***, with its sea-view terrace, is popular with travellers waiting for the boat. The ***100. Yıl Restaurant***, on the main square, is a bit more expensive, with full meals costing US$8 to US$12, but it's a pleasant place to come just for a drink. For the cheapest meals, pick up a pide at ***Gaziantep Lahmacun ve Pide Salonu*** for less than US$2.

Getting There & Away

Several companies run *feribotlar* (car ferries) and *ekspresler* (hydrofoils) between Taşucu and Girne (Kyrenia) in northern Cyprus, selling tickets from offices in the main square. Passenger tickets cost less on the car ferry, but the trip is longer. Provided your visa allows for multiple entries within its period of validity you shouldn't have to pay for a new one when you come back into Turkey. If you do need a new visa, expect long queues, so try and be off the boat early.

The best ferry company is Fergün Express (☎ 324-741 2323, fax 741 2802, in Girne 815 2344, fax 815 3866) which has daily express departures at 11 am and 1 and 3 pm, and a car ferry (the MF *Fatih*) leaving at midnight from Monday to Friday. The express services return from Girne runs daily at 9.30 and 1 am and 2 pm, while the car ferry's return is at 11.30 am. A one-way ticket on the express service costs US$27 and a return ticket will set you back US$50. On the car ferry, the passenger fare is US$18/34 a single/return; a car costs US$38 one way.

Turkish Maritime Lines (☎ 324-741 4785) has a car ferry, the MV *Ayvalık*, departing at midnight, Sunday to Thursday, and returning from Girne at noon, Monday through Friday. Başak Denizcilik (☎ 324-741 6296, fax 741 4624) has car ferries departing Taşucu at midnight on Wednesday, Saturday and Sunday and returning at noon the following day. Tickets cost US$17/32 one way/return, plus US$38 for a car.

Ertürk (☎ 324-741 4033, fax 741 4325), with its main office in Çeşme, west of İzmir, operates the MF *Ertürk 1*, departing Taşucu at midnight from Sunday to Thursday and arriving in Girne the next day at 7.30 am. From Girne the ferry departs at noon on Monday to Friday, arriving in Taşucu at 4 pm. Tickets cost US$14 one way for passengers, and US$65 per car. In Girne, call Ertürk on ☎ 081-52308 or 53784 for more details.

Getting Around

Frequent dolmuşes (US$0.30) run between Taşucu and Silifke's otogar. You can pick them up at the fuel station across the road from the Silifke otogar or from the southern side of the bridge near the PTT.

SİLİFKE

Silifke (population 50,000) was the ancient Seleucia, founded by Seleucus I Nicator in the 3rd century BC. Seleucus was one of Alexander the Great's most able generals and founder of the Seleucid dynasty which ruled Syria after Alexander's death.

The town's other claim to fame is that Emperor Frederick I Barbarossa (1125-90) drowned in the river near here while leading his troops on the Third Crusade – an ignominious end for a soldier.

A striking castle dominates the town from a Taurus hillside but to most people Silifke is simply a place to catch the bus to Mersin, Adana or Konya. Reflecting that attitude, Silifike seems to have given up on the struggle to attract visitors. However, there are a few hotels and restaurants for those who do decide to linger.

Orientation & Information

The otogar is near the junction of highways to Alanya, Mersin and Konya, exactly 1km along İnönü Caddesi to the town centre. Halfway along you pass the Temple of Jupiter.

The town is divided by the Göksu River, called the Calycadnus in ancient times. Most of the services, including the otogar, are on the southern bank of the river. Exceptions are the Tourism Information Office, Hotel Çadır and the bus stop for Uzuncaburç, which are on the northern bank.

The Tourism Information Office (☎ 324-714 1151, fax 714 5328), is at Veli Gürten Bozbey Caddesi 6, a few steps north of Atatürk Caddesi and the Hotel Çadır. The staff speak some English, French and German.

Things to See

The **fortress** on the hill dates from medieval times. From it you can gaze down at the **Tekir Ambarı**, an ancient cistern some 46m long, 23m wide and 12m deep, carved from the rock. A circular stone staircase provides access to what was an important feature of the ancient city's water supply. To get to the Tekir Ambarı from the junction of İnönü and Menderes Caddesis, walk up the hill on the street to the left of the Emlak Bankası. A female reader reported being hassled in the fort, so it's probably best make your visit in the middle of the day or preferably with someone else or in a group.

Perhaps the most striking ruin in Silifke is that of the **Temple of Jupiter**, which dates from the 2nd or 3rd century AD. A pair of storks are almost guaranteed to be in residence on the most prominent column throughout the summer months.

The **Archaeological Müzesi**, near the otogar, has the usual mix of archaeological and ethnographical exhibits, including some gold jewellery and a good collection of coins, including some of Alexander the Great. The museum is open daily except Monday from 8 am to 5 pm for US$1.

The town's mosques include the **Ulu Cami**, originally constructed by the Seljuks but

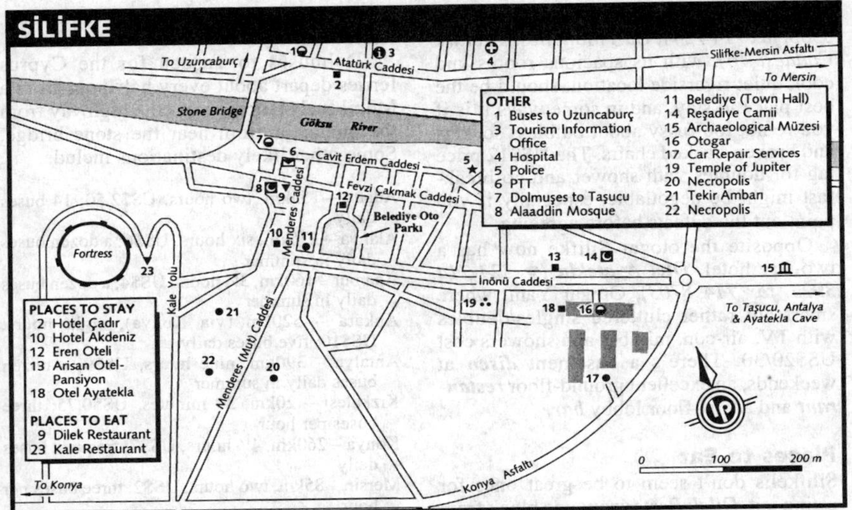

much modified, and the **Reşadiye Camii**, an Ottoman work which re-uses Roman columns in its porches. The **stone bridge**, which you cross to reach the Tourism Information Office, was originally built in Roman times.

Ayatekla (Cave of St Thecla)

Another site of interest for those up on their biblical lore is the cave of St Thecla. The saint (Ayatekla in Turkish) is known as St Paul's first Christian convert. She was also the first woman to be threatened with death for the young faith. An outcast from family and society, she supposedly retreated to a cave outside present-day Silifke, where she pursued good works, particularly healing the sick. The Byzantines built a church over the cave in her honour in 480 AD.

The site is 5km from the Silifke otogar, south past the museum, then to the right up a narrow road. Rubble from the Byzantine settlement is scattered over a large area. Ruins of the basilica and a nearby cistern are evident, but the entrance to the cave is not. With luck when you arrive, a guardian will appear, sell you a ticket (US$1) and unlock the iron gate to the cave. It contains several vaulted chambers, arches and columns, exciting if you're a fan of the saint.

To get there from Silifke take a Taşucu dolmuş and ask to be dropped off at the Ayatekla junction, 1km from the site (the yellow sign is easier to see on the way back to Silifke).

Places to Stay

Most local accommodation is at Taşucu, 11km west of Silifke. Silifke's own hotels tend to be quite modest.

At the cheaper end of the price scale the 27 room ***Hotel Akdeniz*** (AHK-deh-neez) (*☎ 324-714 1285, Menderes Caddesi 96*), at the western end of İnönü Caddesi, is simple but presentable. It charges US$4/6/8 for a waterless single/double/triple, a dollar more per room with shower. The nearby ***Eren Oteli*** (*☎ 324-714 1289*), in a quiet location north of İnönü Caddesi, charges US$9/14 for a single/double room with private shower.

Newer and more cheerful is the 40 room ***Arısan Otel-Pansiyon*** (*☎/fax 324-714 3331, İnönü Caddesi 89*), which charges just US$6/10 for rooms with shower and air-con. These prices are likely to rise.

Across the river, ***Hotel Çadır*** *(☎ 324-714 3535, fax 714 1244, Gazi Mahallesi, Atatürk Caddesi 16)*, with its spacious rooms and cool, quiet riverside location, should be the best place to stay, and in some ways it is if you're not too fussy about bulbless sockets and broken-backed chairs. The US$12 price tag for doubles with shower and no breakfast might be negotiable, especially if you point out the defects before agreeing.

Opposite the otogar Silifke now has a two-star hotel, ***Otel Ayatekla*** *(☎ 324-714 3923, fax 714 8703)*, Otogar Yanı, where smart but rather cluttered singles/doubles with TV, air-con, minibar and showers cost US$20/30. There's a basement ***disco*** at weekends, an excellent ground-floor ***restaurant*** and a first-floor lobby ***bar***.

Places to Eat

Silifkelis don't seem to be great ones for eating out. ***Dilek Restaurant*** one block from the PTT stays open when nearly everything else is closed, serving a standard array of kebaps and stews for around US$2. Near the hilltop fort above the town is the aptly named ***Kale Restaurant*** *(☎ 324-714 1521)*, right at the upper end of the road. It's a great place for lunch or dinner in summer, with meals costing around US$8 per person.

Otherwise there's a restaurant at ***Hotel Çadır*** and a much better one at ***Otel Ayatekla*** where a full dinner of starter, fish and dessert will cost upwards of US$10; wine and beer are available here.

Getting There & Away

Situated at the junction of the coastal highway and the road into the mountains and up to the plateau, Silifke is an important transportation point with good bus services.

The highway east from Silifke to Adana is well travelled by buses. Silifke Koop company buses depart for Adana about every 20 minutes throughout the morning and afternoon and will stop to pick up those who've been visiting one of the many archaeological sites east of town. Heading west can be more problematic since you're dependent on long-distance buses coming from Adana and Mersin which can be full. Reserve ahead if possible.

Dolmuşes to Taşucu for the Cyprus ferries depart about every half-hour from a Mobil fuel station across the highway from the otogar or from near the stone bridge. Some other likely destinations include:

Adana – 155km, two hours, US$2.50; 14 buses daily
Alanya – 275km, six hours, US$6; a dozen buses daily in summer
Anamur – 160km, 3½ hours, US$4; a dozen buses daily in summer
Ankara – 520km (via Konya), eight hours, US$10; five buses daily
Antalya – 390km, nine hours, US$9; a dozen buses daily in summer
Kızkalesi – 20km, 30 minutes, US$0.75; three buses per hour
Konya – 260km, 4½ hours, US$7; frequent buses daily
Mersin – 85km, two hours, US$2; three buses per hour
Narlıkuyu – 23km, 30 minutes, US$0.50; three buses per hour
Ürgüp (via Mersin) – 400km, 6½ hours, US$9; several buses daily (change at Mersin)

UZUNCABURÇ

With time, and preferably with your own transport, it's worth making a detour 28km north of Silifke to the remote village of Uzuncaburç, with its woodpeckers, wild flowers and sense of solitude a world away from the hubbub of the coast.

What is now Uzuncaburç was once the ancient temple-city of Olbia, renamed Diocaesarea in Roman times. It probably began its history as a centre of worship to Zeus Olbius and was ruled by a dynasty of priest-kings, who managed the ceremonies in the large temple.

Because it was a holy place, many people wanted to be buried near it and the priest-kings organised this too. Only 8km up the road from Silifke you encounter the first group of tombs, and then, shortly afterwards, in the village of Demircili, the elegant two-storeyed **Çifte Anıt Mezarları** (Twin Monument Tombs) are plainly visible from the road. Turn right at 23km and proceed through a lovely pine forest to the archaeological site, almost 6km on.

EASTERN MEDITERRANEAN

Entry costs US$1 but opening hours seem pretty flexible.

Just before you get to the car park there are remains of a peaceful Roman **theatre** to the left of the road. From the car park you enter the main site along a colonnaded way, passing the famous **Temple of Zeus Olbius** on your left. The temple offers one of the earliest (circa 300 BC) examples of Corinthian architecture, but was converted to a church by the Byzantines, who removed its central *cella* (portion). Just past the temple, on the right, is a **city gate**, after which you come to the **Temple of Tyche** (circa 100 BC).

Come out of the site and turn left through the village. On your right a road leads to the imposing Hellenistic *burç* (city tower), while, further on, a path to the left winds down 500m to the **necropolis**.

The village has a small restaurant, the ***Burç Kafeterya***, a couple of shops and a ***teahouse***. If you get stuck the ticket office-cum-summer cafe will put you up but only in the simplest style – it's not a real pension.

Getting There & Away Only one bus a day (at 2 pm, one hour, US$1) connects Silifke with Uzuncaburç, so to get there and back in the same day you're dependent on finding someone ready to run you back when you've finished sightseeing. It's safer to round up a few other explorers and hire a taxi (for about US$10 return, waiting time included). This also lets you stop and inspect the tombs along the way.

UZUNCABURÇ TO KONYA

From Uzuncaburç the road continues via Kırobası to Mut and then to Karaman and Konya. Winding up into the forests you may pass huge stacks of logs cut by the Tahtacılar, the mountain woodcutters who live a secluded life in the forest.

About 40km before Mut the road skirts a fantastic limestone **canyon** which extends for several kilometres. High above in the limestone cliffs are **caves** which were probably once inhabited. The land in the valleys is rich and well-watered, exploited by diligent farmers. The air is cool, clean and sweet.

About 20km north of Mut a turn-off on the right leads 5km to the ruins of another **medieval castle** at Alahan.

SİLİFKE TO ADANA

Immediately south of Silifke is the Göksu Delta, a world-renowned wetland area, rich in birdlife. East of Silifke the Cilician Plain opens to an ever-widening swath of arable land which allowed civilisation to flourish.

The Göksu Delta

Accessible from Silifke or Taşucu, the 14,500-hectare Göksu Delta contains several lagoons, most importantly the freshwater Akgöl and the smaller Karadeniz lake. A large area of salt marsh is used for growing rice, while in other parts of the delta strawberries are a popular crop. At the far south of the delta at İncekum a sandspit which changes shape over the years provides the most easterly breeding ground in the Mediterranean for the rare monk seal. Loggerhead and green turtles also nest here.

The Göksu Delta is a paradise for birdwatchers. Of Turkey's 450 species, 332 have been recorded here, while of the 24 globally endangered species found in Turkey, 17 have been seen here. The symbol of the delta is the purple gallinule, but other rare birds found here include marbled teals, black francolins and Audoin's gulls. Whether you visit in summer or winter, something interesting is bound to be on the move.

Unfortunately despite all sorts of legislation to protect the delta (and even the European Union has become involved), its survival is still threatened by projects like the Kayraktepe Dam and the never-ending spread of summer housing blocks. To find out more contact the Society for the Protection of Nature (☎ 212-281 0321, fax 279 5544), Doğal Hayatı Koruma Derneği, PK 18 Bebek, 80810 İstanbul.

The ruins are plentiful until Mersin, where modern commerce and industrialisation begin to take over. There are also several resorts, principally Kızkalesi, where you might want to break your journey.

Atakent (Susanoğlu)

Atakent is a holiday village 16km east of Silifke with a nice little beach backed by a million holiday flats. With all the condos for well-to-do holidaymakers from Mersin and Adana, there's little room for the passing traveller. The four-star, 108 room ***Altınorfoz Banana Hotel** (☎ 324-722 4211, fax 722 4215)*, set around its own private bay, has not too outrageous rates of US$65/86 a single/double with breakfast and dinner included.

Narlıkuyu

About 3km east of Atakent, Narlıkuyu is a pretty village set around a rocky harbour and ringed with fish restaurants. A small museum contains the remains of a 4th century Roman bath with a fine mosaic of the Three Graces – Aglaia, Thalia and Euphrosyne. Admission costs US$1, only worth it if you're a real mosaic freak. Several houses in the village offer *ev pansiyon* (home pension) arrangements for around US$8 per person. There's a small shop for snacks and necessities and that's about it. The restaurants are excellent but your bill is likely to come to at least US$10, depending on the size of your particular fish.

Cennet ve Cehennem Above Narlıkuyu, the road winds 2km up the mountainside to the Cennet ve Cehennem (Caves of Heaven and Hell).

This limestone coast is riddled with caverns but the Cennet (jeh-NEHT) is one of the most impressive. According to legend, this may be the Korykos cave in which the gigantic half-human, half-animal monster Typhon held Zeus captive, though the king of the gods later emerged victorious in this battle between good and evil.

To enter the 250m-long cave, walk through the drinks and souvenir complex and descend the 452 hefty steps to the cavern mouth. Along the way notice strips of cloth and paper tied to twigs and branches by those who have come to this 'mystical' place in search of cures; they're supposed to remind a saint or spirit that a supplicant has asked for help.

At the mouth of the cave are the ruins of a 5th century Byzantine church dedicated to the Virgin. Recently installed lighting lets you penetrate about 100m into the cavern.

Follow the path above the gorge for about 75m and you'll come to Cehennem (jeh-HEHN-nehm), or Hell, a 128m-deep sinkhole where Zeus is supposed to have imprisoned Titan temporarily until he could bury him permanently beneath Mt Etna in Italy. Local legend also holds that this is one of the entrances to the underworld.

As you arrive at the entrance to the complex a custodian will give you a ticket for US$1. He'll be standing beside the remains of a temple to Zeus which was later turned into a church. Turn left here and walk 500m to yet another cave, this one credited with the power to cure asthma.

KIZKALESİ

Boasting one of the finest beaches along this stretch of coast, Kızkalesi, 26km east of Silifke, takes its name from the striking offshore Maiden's Castle (Kızkalesi). Other ruins are scattered around the foreshore and the inland fields. A site as inviting as this couldn't stay secret for long and a resort village of restaurants, pensions, hotels, souvenir shops and camping areas, catering largely to Germans, has grown up all the way around the bay.

Things to See

Though massive, **Maiden's Castle** seems to float on the blue waves, especially when viewed from the mountain road leading to the Caves of Heaven and Hell. Today, strong swimmers can make it out to Maiden's Castle (about 150m) alone. The rest of us need to pay a boatman about US$2 to get there.

Facing it on the shore is the ruinous **Korkyos Castle** which was linked to the sea castle by a causeway in ancient times. Admission costs US$1 although there's no labelling and you'll need to do a bit of scrambling over rocks.

These twin castles crop up in many legends, but historically they were built by the Byzantines and extensively rebuilt in the 1200s by the Armenian kings of Cilicia with the support of the crusaders. The throne of Cilicia passed through two Armenian dynasties in the 1300s before being taken by Peter I of Cyprus while the Mamelukes of Egypt took the rest of Armenian Cilicia to the east.

Immediately across the road from Korkyos Castle is an ancient **necropolis**, with giant sarcophagi scattered among the rocks. Look out for the carving of a soldier with a sword.

Places to Stay & Eat

Virtually every building in Kızkalesi is a pension or hotel, which is not to say you won't have trouble finding a room in high season. Inevitably, the best places are right by the beach and most of them reflect their location in their price. An exception is the small ***Hotel Hantur*** *(☎ 324-523 2367)*, halfway around the bay, where rooms with frilly decor and bathrooms cost US$14/20 a single/double; most have side sea views at least and the owner is extremely welcoming. In the street running down to the beach you'll find many similarly priced pensions (***Star***, ***Holiday***, ***Mavideniz*** and ***Nisam***), often calling themselves motels, and with signs up reading 'Boş Oda Var' indicating they have rooms available.

West of the bay the ***Kilikya*** *(☎ 324-523 2116, fax 523 2084)* and the ***Admiral*** *(☎ 324-523 2213, fax 523 2158)* are similar three-star hotels with pools, geared mainly to tour groups but with singles/doubles for around US$50/75.

Snazziest of all the places on the bay is ***Club Hotel Barbarossa*** *(☎ 324-523 2089, fax 523 2090)*, with pieces of Roman stonework decorating a lawn which sweeps down to the beach. At US$19 per person, it's remarkable value for money.

Many of the pensions have their own restaurants and there are one or two private ***lokantas*** down on the beach, including ***Çağdaş Restaurant*** which is well placed for people-watching over an Adana kebap. But really you're better off paying the US$0.20 bus fare to hop 10 minutes back to Narlıkuyu and eat at one of the fish restaurants there.

Kanlıdivane

East of Kızkalesi the Cilician Plain is littered with ruins, some fairly grand, others little more than fields of cut limestone. About 3km east of Kızkalesi at Ayaş are the extensive but badly ruined remains of ancient Elaiussa-Sebaste, a city with its foundations dating from at least the early Roman period, and perhaps even the Hittite.

About 8.5km east of Kızkalesi at Kumkuyu is the road to Kanlıdivane and a fairly grubby beach with a handful of hotels and plenty of apartment blocks. About 4km north of the highway are the ruins of ancient Kanytelis. This ancient city, founded in Hellenistic times, occupies a vast site around limestone caverns. As you ride into the hills the ruins, mostly dating from Roman and Byzantine times, become more extensive.

Kanytelis thrived through Byzantine times, as indicated by several Greek churches and inscriptions. Its extensive necropolis (cemetery) has many Roman tombs built in the form of miniature temples.

Viranşehir

The suburbs of Mersin now sprawl out as far as Mezikli where a road on the right (south) leads to Viranşehir, the ancient Soles or Pompeiopolis. About 2km down the road a row of Corinthian columns stand in a field, while in the distance is part of an aqueduct, all dating from the 3rd century AD.

MERSİN (İÇEL)

This city (population 1.5 million) was officially renamed İçel although the buses and dolmuşes are sticking with Mersin. It is the capital of the province of İçel and is a sprawling modern city built half a century ago to give Anatolia a port close to Adana and its rich agricultural hinterland. It has

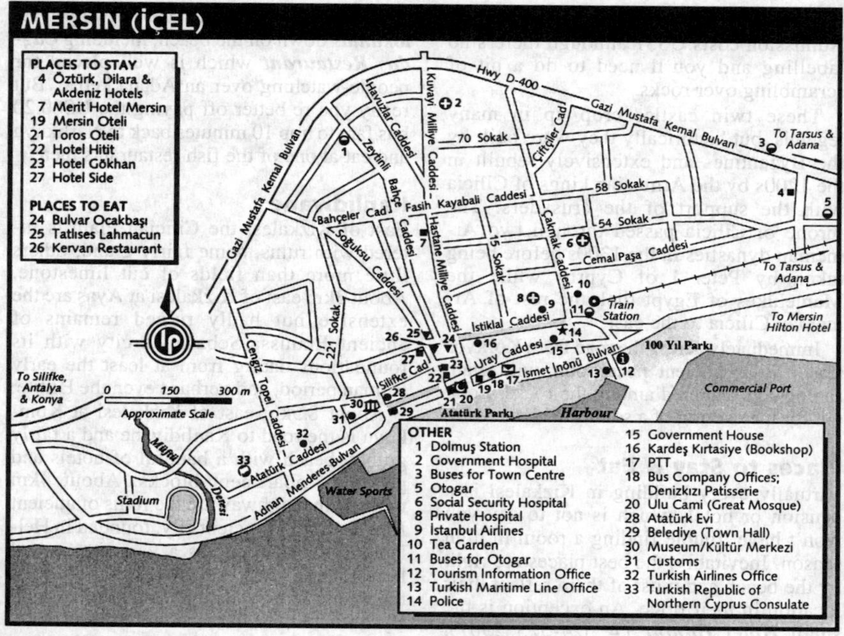

several good hotels in each price range and, since it's traffic is less alarming than Adana's, makes a more manageable stopping point on your way through.

Orientation

The town centre is Gümrük Meydanı, the plaza occupied by the modern Ulu Cami mosque and with the four-star Mersin Oteli on its eastern side. Across the coastal highway from the mosque a large Toyota car dealership makes a more readily recognisable landmark. On the western side is Atatürk Caddesi, a pedestrianised shopping street, while two blocks north is İstiklal Caddesi, the main thoroughfare.

To get to the centre from the otogar, leave by the main exit, turn right and walk up to the main road. Cross to the far side and catch a bus travelling west (US$0.25) which will drop you at the train station.

Information

The Tourism Information Office (☎ 324-238 3271, fax 238 3272) is closed on the weekend and is by the entrance to the docks, east of the park, at Yenimahalle, İsmet İnönü Bulvarı, Liman Giriş Sahası. Next to it is the stop for buses to Mezitli and Viranşehir.

Currency exchange offices and banks are clustered around Gümrük Meydanı and the Ulu Cami. Look for signs for Kanarya Döviz, Kiraz Döviz and many others keen to change dollars and deutschmarks in particular. The Yapı Kredi Bankası, with its well-connected cash machines, is a block north of the Mersin Oteli.

Kardeş Kırtasiye in İstiklal Caddesi, near the junction with Hastane Caddesi, sells the *Turkish Daily News* and foreign newspapers and magazines.

Mersin's postal code is 33000.

Things to See

At the eastern end of Atatürk Caddesi a fine stone house, the **Atatürk Evi**, is open to the public daily except Sunday from 9 am to noon and from 1 to 4.30 pm for US$0.75. It was closed for restoration at the time of writing but looked likely to re-open soon.

A little further west beside the Kültür Merkezi is Mersin's small **museum**, open the same hours as the Atatürk Evi but closed on Monday (US$0.75). This has a reasonably good archaeological collection with many Roman artefacts on the ground floor and the usual ethnographical bits and bobs on the first floor. There's some English labelling.

The **waterfront** makes for a pleasant promenade.

Places to Stay – Budget

Unfortunately, hotels near the otogar tend to be in the middle range. For a good cheapie, you'll have to trek into the centre. Many cheap and medium-priced hotels are in Soğuksu Caddesi, one block west of the Ulu Cami, and just north of it.

Three places on Soğuksu Caddesi charge the same price (US$9/12 a single/double) and are equally likely to be noisy. The clean but simple ***Hotel Hitit*** *(☎ 324-231 6431, Soğuksu Caddesi 12)* is across from the old municipal market, with the ***Hotel Savran*** (☎ 324-232 4473) nearby at No 46 offering similar standards. Further north ***Hotel Side*** *(☎ 324-231 1773, Soğuksu Caddesi 27)* is just as basic.

Much better value is ***Toros Oteli*** *(☎ 324-231 2201, fax 237 8554, Atatürk Caddesi 33)*, 100m west of the Ulu Cami, which rents good singles/doubles with shower and TV for US$17/26. Added bonuses are the small cafe attached and its situation on a relatively quiet pedestrianised street.

Places to Stay – Mid-Range

Soğuksu Caddesi also has a couple of mid-range choices, including the modern two-star, 28 room ***Hotel Gökhan*** *(☎ 324-231 6256, fax 237 4462, Soğuksu Caddesi 20)*. Rates of US$40/50 a single/double are posted, but discounts aren't hard to come by. Rooms boast TV, minibar and air-con and some have balconies.

Lined up outside the otogar gates are 15 hotels, most of them two-star places charging a uniform US$17/25/35 for a single/double/triple room with private bath and breakfast. It's worth shopping around since the same money will buy you something bright and new at ***Hotel Akdeniz*** *(☎ 324-238 0188)* or something more in need of renovation at perhaps ***Hotel Dostlar***. The Akdeniz boasts a decent ***restaurant*** and hamam (men only, of course).

Other reasonable choices include ***Öztürk Hotel*** *(☎ 324-233 9318)* and ***Hotel Dilara*** *(☎ 324-238 6190)*. The cheaper hotels tend to rent rooms by the hour and most of the restaurants double as meeting places for prostitutes and their clients.

Places to Stay – Top End

The four-star ***Mersin Oteli*** *(☎ 324-238 1040, fax 231 2625, Gümrük Meydanı 112)* is on the waterfront a few steps east of the Ulu Cami. Its 103 air-con rooms have comfortable beds, private bath, minibar, telephone and balcony. Rates are posted at US$80/120/150 for a single/double/triple, but 50% reductions are not uncommon.

For luxury, there's the five-star ***Merit Hotel Mersin*** *(☎ 324-336 1010, fax 336 0722, Kuvayi Milliye Caddesi 165)*, with 247 rooms in Mersin's tallest building. If you don't mind braving the airport-style security gates, there's nothing to stop you dropping in for a drink in the 46th floor Panorama Bar. ***Mersin Hilton*** *(☎ 324-326 5000, fax 326 5050)*, Adnan Menderes Bulvarı, right on the waterfront, is another luxury choice. Both of these hotels offer rooms for US$120/130 a single/double without breakfast.

Places to Eat

Soğuksu Caddesi boasts several small fish restaurants, including ***Agora***, in the old municipal market building across from the Hotel Hitit. With outdoor tables in fair weather and full meals for US$5 to US$10, these are very popular places although the portions won't go far if you're really hungry.

North of the Hotel Gökhan, ***Kervan Restaurant***, opposite the Hotel Side, serves a wide variety of dishes, and alcoholic beverages to wash them down.

The western reaches of İstiklal Caddesi have a number of fast food *lahmacun* (Turkish-style pizza) places, including a branch of ***Tatlıses Lahmacun*** where people queue for instant ayran and lahmacun with the same enthusiasm that people at home queue for burgers and chips. Along here ***Bulvar Ocakbaşı***, beside the Etibank at No 85, serves delicious pides and döner kebap for US$3.

For coffee and cakes try ***Denizkızı Patisserie*** on İsmet İnönü Bulvarı by the Toros Pasajı.

If you're just passing through, there are lots of restaurants mixed in with the hotels outside the otogar. There's something to suit most budgets, plus stalls selling fruit and nuts, and several beer halls.

Getting There & Away

Bus From Mersin's otogar, on the eastern outskirts of the city, buses depart for all points, including up to the Anatolian Plateau through the Cilician Gates. Distances, travel times and prices are similar to those from Adana, 70km to the east on a fast four-lane highway. Several of the main companies serving İstanbul, Ankara and İzmir have offices on İsmet İnönü Bulvarı just behind the Toros Oteli.

Train There are frequent services to Tarsus (US$0.50), Adana (US$1) and İskenderun (US$3).

TARSUS

Heading east for 27km you'll come to Tarsus, one of those towns with a name inextricably linked with the memory of one man; St Paul was born here almost 2000 years ago. Unusually, Tarsus has managed to hang on to the same name right through from antiquity despite just as tumultuous a history as anywhere else along the coast.

One reader wrote that Tarsus 'might have done for Saul/Paul but it's come down in the world since then', and at first sight, few people would disagree with his assessment. However, this is one of those towns (population 160,000) that repays perseverance and you could certainly while away three or four hours here quite happily.

Things to See

Buses drop you off beside **Cleopatra's Gate**, a Roman city gate which has nothing to do with Cleopatra, even though the Egyptian queen is thought to have met Mark Antony in Tarsus. In any case, restoration in 1994 has robbed it of any sense of antiquity.

Walk straight ahead and just before the Hükümet Konağı (Government House) you'll see a sign pointing left to the **Senpol Kuyusu** (St Paul's Well). There's little to see except a water-filled hole in the ground but Pauline scholars will probably want to pay the US$0.20 to down a cup of water.

At the same road junction a second sign to the left points to the **Antik Şehir** (Old City). Follow it and you'll come to Cumhuriyet Alanı where ongoing excavations have uncovered a wonderful stretch of Roman road, with heavy basalt paving slabs covering a lengthy drain.

Return to the Hükümet Konağı and continue heading north until you come to the 19th century **Makam Camii** on the right. Turn right beside it and you'll come to the small **Tarsus Müzesi**, housed in the 16th century Mehmet Efendi Medresesi, extensively restored in 1972; admission costs US$1. Continue along the side street and you'll find the 16th century **Ulu Cami,** with a curious 19th century clock tower. Cross the car park beside it and eventually you'll come to the ruins of **St Paul's Church**. The existing church is 19th century and has nothing whatsoever to do with the saint.

Retrace your steps to the Makam Camii and across the road you'll see the more interesting **Eski Cami** (Old Mosque), a medieval structure which may originally have been a church dedicated to St Paul. Located right beside it looms the barely recognisable brickwork of a huge old **Roman bath**.

Beside the Eski Cami you can catch a dolmuş (US$0.20) to Tarsus' other main sight, the **Şelale** (Waterfall) on the Tarsus Çayı (Cydnus River) which cascades over rocks right in the town, providing the perfect setting for tea gardens and restaurants.

Places to Stay & Eat

Tarsus is not brimming over with lovely places to stay. At the time of writing your best hope was ***Hotel Zorbaz*** *(☎ 324-622 2166)*, Eski Belediye Karşısı, right beside the Hükümet Konağı. It has acceptable, basic rooms with shower for US$6/9 a single/double. Ask for a room at the back to escape traffic noise. The nearby ***Cihan Palas Hotel*** was closed for refurbishment at the time of writing and could re-open a step up in quality from the Zorbaz.

If you're prepared to pay more, the externally ugly ***Tarsus Mersin Oteli*** *(☎ 324-614 0600, fax 614 0033)*, Şelale Mevkii, is right beside the waterfall, with all its smart, modern rooms overlooking it. Among other facilities there's a disco and open-air pool. What St Paul would have made of the ***St Paul Bar*** is a question probably better not asked. Singles/doubles/triples cost US$80/120/150.

There are plenty of basic ***lokantas*** on the road up from Kleopatra's Gate, but it makes more sense to come and eat by the waterfall, taking care to check prices before ordering.

Getting There & Away

There are plenty of buses and dolmuşes connecting Tarsus with Adana and Mersin, so you could make it a break point while travelling between the two.

Tarsus to Antakya

About 3km east of Tarsus the E90 highway heads north through the Cilician Gates, a narrow gap in the Taurus Mountains, to Ankara, Nevşehir and Kayseri. The coast road continues around to Adana, becoming ever more built-up along the way.

ADANA

Turkey's fourth largest city, Adana (AH-dah-nah, population 1.6 million), is a big, brash commercial city, the sort of place with branches of Burger King and United Colors of Benetton, where everyone wears denim and newsstands sport copies of *PC World*. Its wealth comes from local industry, the traffic passing through the Cilician Gates, and from the intensely fertile Çukurova, the ancient Cilician Plain deposited as silt by the rivers Seyhan and Ceyhan.

Adana's growth has been rapid and chaotic. Though local people take pride in their modern city, outsiders see it as an unplanned, disorderly, adolescent metropolis, with much noise and confusion but little charm. The constant high temperature and humidity from May to October does little to boost its limited appeal and the barely controlled traffic is positively terrifying.

Most likely you'll only wind up in Adana because it has an airport, a train station, a large otogar and good hotels. Its few sights are just enough to fill the few hours between transport in and transport out.

In 1998 an earthquake devastated parts of Adana, but you may not see much of the damage that mainly affected the suburbs.

Orientation

The Seyhan Nehri (River Seyhan) skirts the city centre to the east.

Adana's airport (Şakirpaşa Havaalanı) is 4km west of the centre on the D400 Highway. The otogar is 2km further west on the northern side of the D400. The train station is at the northern end of Ziyapaşa Bulvarı, 1.5km north of İnönü Caddesi, the main commercial and hotel street.

The E90 expressway skirts the city to the north. If you approach from the north or west, take the Adana Küzey (Adana North) exit to reach the city centre. This brings you south to the D400 Highway which ploughs right through the city centre.

At the western end of İnönü Caddesi is Kuruköprü Meydanı, marked by the high-rise Çetinkaya shopping centre. There are several hotels on Özler Caddesi between Kuruköprü Meydanı and Küçüksaat Meydanı to the south-east, a plaza marked by a statue of Atatürk.

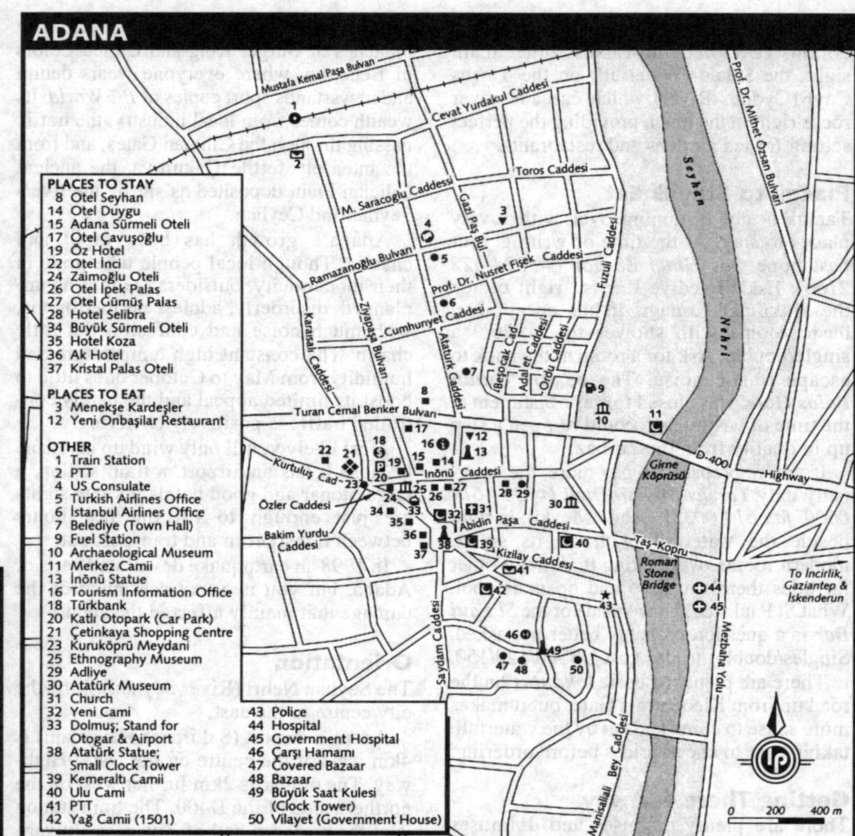

Information

The weekday-only Tourism Information Office (☎ 322-359 1994, fax 352 6790) is at Atatürk Caddesi 13, a block north of İnönü Caddesi, in the centre of town. There's a smaller office at Şakirpaşa Airport (☎/fax 322-436 92314).

Adana's postal code is 01000.

Mosques

The attractive 16th century **Ulu Cami**, off Abidin Paşa Caddesi, is in a style reminiscent of Syria or the Mameluke mosques of Cairo, with black and white banded marble and elaborate surrounds to its windows. The tiles in the mihrab originate from Kütahya and İznik.

The **Yeni Cami** (New Mosque, 1724), follows the general square plan of the Ulu Cami, with 10 domes, while the **Yağ Camii** (1501), with its imposing portal, started life as the church of St James.

More conspicuous than either of these is the brand-new **Merkez Cami**, a six-minaret monster right beside the Girne Köprüsü.

Museums

Adana's two main museums are a cut above most of Turkey's provincial museums. The **Adana Etnoğrafya Müzesi** (Adana Ethnography Museum), on a little side street off İnönü Caddesi, just to the east of the Adana Sürmeli Oteli, is housed in a small, nicely restored Crusader church. It now holds displays of carpets and kilims, weapons, manuscripts, inscriptions and funeral monuments.

The **Adana Bölge Müzesi** (Adana Archaeological Museum) on Fuzuli Caddesi is rich in Roman statuary as the Cilician Gates were an important transit point even in Roman times. Note especially the 2nd century **Achilles sarcophagus**, decorated with scenes from the Iliad; the Roman and Byzantine **mosaics** and the bronze statuary. Hittite and Urartian artefacts are also on display.

Both museums are open from 8.30 am to noon and 1 to 4.30 pm except on Monday; admission to each costs US$1.

Other Sights

Have a look at the 16-arched **Roman stone bridge** (Taş Köprü) over the Seyhan, at the eastern end of Abidin Paşa Caddesi. Built by Hadrian (117-138 AD), repaired by Justinian, and now sullied by modern traffic, it's still an impressive sight.

The **Büyük Saat Kulesi** (Great Clock Tower) dates back to 1881. Around it you'll find Adana's **covered bazaar** and the popular **Çarşı Hamamı** where the full works cost US$6.

Places to Stay

Though Adana has a good selection of lodgings in all price ranges, there are no hotels near the airport, otogar or train station. Most are on İnönü Caddesi, with a few others on nearby Özler Caddesi. All but the cheapest post high prices, then slash them if they're not busy. All suffer from traffic noise, especially when the muggy heat forces you to keep your window open. The top places have half-hearted air-con.

If you fly into Adana and arrive reasonably early, you could take a bus to more manageable Mersin and stay there instead.

Places to Stay – Budget

Öz Hotel *(☎ 322-363 3481, fax 363 3469, İnönü Caddesi 34)*, is a pretty basic cheapy with a large fish tank in its lobby. Singles/doubles cost US$9/16 without bath.

Adjoining Otel İpek Palas in İnönü Caddesi is the rock-bottom ***Otel Gümüş Palas*** *(☎ 322-363 0126)* with rooms for US$5/9 a single/double. It is central with sinks in the rooms but very smelly toilets.

Özler Caddesi, which joins İnönü Caddesi at Kuruköprü Meydanı, has several other bottom-end hotels. ***Ak Hotel*** *(☎ 322-351 4208, fax 352 3878)*, at No 43, just north-west of the roundabout with the statue of Atatürk, is reasonably comfortable, with singles/double for US$5/9 a single/double without private shower. A block closer to the roundabout, ***Kristal Palas Oteli*** *(☎ 322-351 2335)*, at No 19, is marginally cheaper and, arguably, marginally better.

Places to Stay – Mid-Range

Otel Duygu *(☎ 322-363 1510, fax 363 0905, İnönü Caddesi 14/1)*, has a lift, a bar and 27 rooms with private baths and fans with posted rates of US$40/60 a single/double, but I was quoted roughly half that. Opposite the Duygu, the dismal one-star, 840 room ***Otel İpek Palas*** *(☎ 322-363 3512, fax 363 3516, İnönü Caddesi 103)*, charges US$19/29 for singles/doubles with private bath and ceiling fan.

Across from the posh Zaimoğlu Oteli (see Places to Stay – Top End following), the friendly two-star, 60 room ***Hotel Koza*** *(☎ 322-352 5857, fax 359 8571, Özler Caddesi 103)*, posts prices of US$45/60 a single/double, but readily discounts when it's quiet. Breakfasts here are substantial and the best rooms are sizeable and comfortable.

The two-star ***Otel Çavuşoğlu*** *(☎ 322-363 2687, fax 363 3281, Ziyapaşa Bulvarı 115)* is at the southern end of the overpass which spans the D400 Highway. It has a restaurant and bar and 29 passable rooms with bath for US$24/33 a single/double.

The 94 room ***Otel İnci*** *(☎ 322-435 8234, fax 435 8368)*, Kuruköprü Meydanı, Kurtuluş Caddesi, offers perhaps the best value for money: four-star comforts right in the centre for US$60/80/90 a single/double/triple including breakfast.

Another possibility is the two-star ***Otel Selibra*** *(☎ 322-363 3676, fax 363 4283, İnönü Caddesi 40)* where the shabby decor of the corridors means that the fairly modern bedrooms come as a pleasant surprise. Expect to pay US$38/50 a single/double.

Places to Stay – Top End

If you don't mind paying a bit more the smart, modern, four-star, 116 room ***Adana Sürmeli Oteli*** *(☎ 322-363 3437, fax 363 3527, İnönü Caddesi 142)*, has posted prices of US$75/99 a single/double but can usually be persuaded to drop them. Most rooms have baths. Its sister establishment, the five-star, 166 room ***Büyük Sürmeli Oteli*** *(☎ 322-352 3600, fax 352 1945)*, is ridiculously overpriced at US$120/160.

The 77 room ***Zaimoğlu Oteli*** (zah-EEM-oh-loo) *(☎ 322-351 3400, fax 351 6811, Özler Caddesi 72)*, is a smart modern hotel between the two Sürmelis and charges US$130/170 for rooms with air-con, TV, minibar and bath. Hesitate and they'll work with you to discover face-saving reasons for a discount to US$75/85.

Best in town is the unmissable five-star ***Otel Seyhan*** *(☎ 322-457 5810, fax 454 2834, Turhan Cemal Beriker Bulvarı 18)*, not far from the new Merkez Cami. Airport-style security welcomes guests to a hotel which is as luxurious as any outside İstanbul. For the excellent lifts, outdoor pool and all mod cons you'll pay US$115/130 a single/double without breakfast.

Places to Eat

The local speciality is *Adana kebap*, minced lamb mixed with hot pepper, squeezed on a flat skewer then charcoal-grilled. It's served with sliced purple onions dusted with fiery paprika, handfuls of parsley, a lemon wedge and flat bread.

For decades the favoured city-centre restaurant has been ***Yeni Onbaşılar Restaurant*** *(☎ 322-351 4178)*, on Atatürk Caddesi just south of D400 Highway, opposite the Tourism Information Office (enter on the southern side). With little competition, service and food are mediocre, but they do serve alcohol and prices aren't bad. Adana kebap, a salad and a big Efes Pilsen beer comes to less than US$5. Don't tip; they add a presumptuous 20% *garsoniye*.

Otherwise, İnönü Caddesi and its side streets have numerous small kebapçıs and even a few *birahanes* (bars). ***Üç Kardeşler Lokanta ve Kebap Salonu***, to the right of the Adana Sürmeli Oteli, is small and bright, with good kebaps, spectacular hummus, friendly service and low prices, but only soft drinks. ***Menekşe Kardeşler***, a couple of blocks east of the US consulate also gets the local seal of approval.

If the noise and bustle of Adana are too much for you, hop on a dolmuş to nearby İncirlik where there's an American air base. Ask to be dropped off at the ***Mutlu Evi*** (Happy House), a carpet and kilim-covered restaurant which serves excellent bread with cheese baked onto it to go with the house speciality, a variation on *saç kavurma* (wok-fried lamb) with prawns and *börek* (flaky pastry) thrown in. Expect to pay around US$6.

Around town you'll see stands selling beetroot-coloured liquid. This is *şalgam*, a bitter local drink made from turnips, carrots, garlic and lettuce.

Getting There & Away

As an important transfer point, Adana is served by all means of transport.

Air Turkish Airlines (☎ 322-457 0222, fax 454 3088), Stadyum Caddesi 32, operates daily nonstop flights between Adana and Ankara (one hour) and İzmir (1½ hours) and İstanbul (1½ hours). There are also at least weekly flights to and from Amsterdam, Frankfurt, Jeddah, Hanover, Munich and Lefkoşe (Nicosia) in Northern Cyprus. A taxi from the airport into town costs about US$6 and about US$5 to the otogar.

İstanbul Airlines (☎ 322-454 3806, fax 458 3719), Atatürk Caddesi 23/5, has five nonstop flights weekly between Adana and

İstanbul, and at least one weekly to Ankara, Cologne, Düsseldorf, Frankfurt and Munich.

A taxi from the airport into town costs about US$6; to the otogar it's about US$5.

Bus Adana's large, modern otogar offers direct buses or dolmuşes to pretty well anywhere. Some daily services include:

Adıyaman (for Nemrut Dağı) – 370km, six hours, US$9; seven buses per day, two of which go on to Kahta for an extra US$1

Alanya – 440km, 10 hours, US$9; eight buses in summer

Ankara – 490km, 10 hours, US$12; frequent buses

Antalya – 555km, 12 hours, US$13; a few buses

Diyarbakır – 550km, 10 hours, US$13; several buses

Gaziantep – 220km, four hours, US$5; several buses

Haleb (Aleppo, Syria) – 300km, 12 hours, US$25; at least one bus

Kadirli – 75km, one hour, US$1.50; frequent dolmuşes

Kayseri – 335km, 6½ hours, US$9; several buses

Konya – 350km, 6½ hours, US$10; frequent buses

Malatya – 425km, eight hours, US$10; a few buses

Şanlıurfa – 365km, six hours, US$9; several buses

Van – 950km, 18 hours, US$18; at least one bus

Train The facade of the Adana Gar (☎ 322-453 3172), north of İnönü Caddesi at the northern end of Ziyapaşa Bulvarı, is decorated with pretty faïence panels. Trains depart six times daily for Mersin via Tarsus, a 1¼-hour trip.

Adana is served by three express trains which make their way up onto the Anatolian Plateau. The *Erciyes Ekspresi* departs for Kayseri each evening at 5.30 pm, arriving at midnight. Departure from Kayseri is at 4.40 am, arriving in Adana at 10.46 am. One-way tickets cost US$4.

The *Çukurova Ekspresi* departs from Adana each evening at 7.30 pm for Ankara, arriving at 8.20 am. Departure from Ankara is at 8.10 pm, arriving at 8.18 am. One-way tickets cost US$8 for a seat, US$10 for a couchette, US$23/40/58 for a single/double/triple sleeping compartment.

The *Toros Ekspresi* departs from Adana on Tuesday, Thursday and Saturday at 9.45 pm, going via Ankara to İstanbul (Haydarpaşa). Departure from İstanbul is at 9 am, arriving at 6 am. One-way tickets cost US$12/9 in 1st/2nd class; or US$26/46/64 for a single/double/triple sleeping compartment.

ADANA TO ANTAKYA (HATAY)

The far eastern end of the Turkish Mediterranean coast swoops around the Bay of İskenderun to the cities of İskenderun and Antakya, in the province of Hatay. Inland from the bay are ruins of an ancient Hittite city at Karatepe, and of a later Roman one (Anazarbus). Along the road stand assorted medieval fortresses. It's possible to make a loop journey from Adana to Osmaniye via Kadirli, taking in Anazarbus, Karatepe and Hierapolis Castabala on the way. With a car it's an easy day trip and you could even press on from Osmaniye to İskenderun.

Even without your own wheels you can still do the trip provided you're prepared to make use of dolmuşes, buses, taxis and a spot of hitching. Take a Kadirli dolmuş from Adana and ask to be dropped at Ayşehoca, 5km from Anazarbus. With luck a farm tractor will give you a lift to the ruins. Return to the main road and catch a bus or dolmuş on to Kadirli. There you will need to arrange for a taxi to take you to Karatepe and perhaps on to Hierapolis or even Osmaniye. Hierapolis is 6km from the main Osmaniye-Kadirli road, so you could hitch or walk down and then flag a bus or dolmuş.

Yılankale

If you're driving look out for the hilltop Yılankale (Snake Castle), about 45 minutes (35km) east of Adana and 2.5km south of the highway. Built by Armenians and crusaders in the 12th or 13th century, it's said to have taken its name from a serpent which was once entwined in the coat of arms above the main entrance (today you'll see a king and lion, but no snake); other tales claim that this area was once full of snakes.

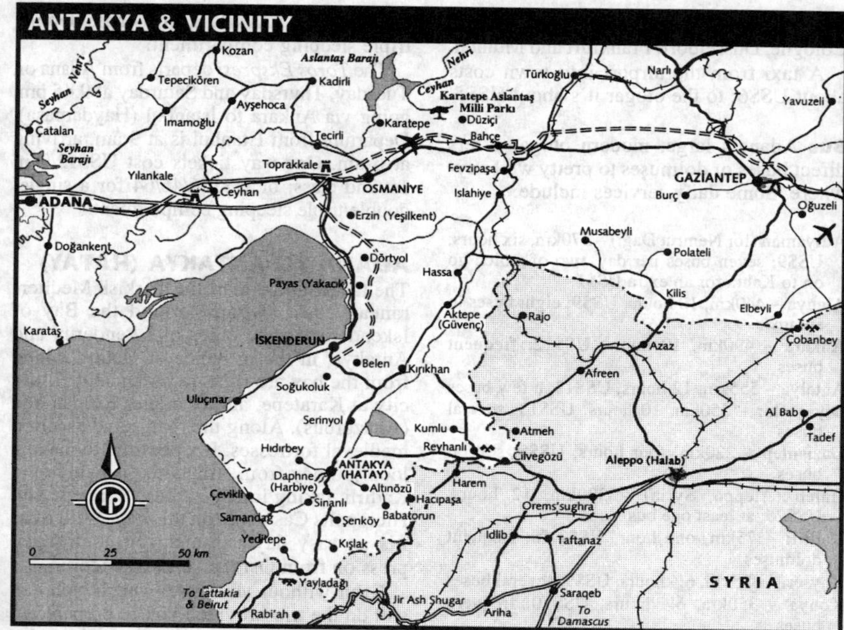

If you have the time, it's about a 20-minute climb over the rocks and up to the fort's highest point. There are no services, no guardian and no admission charge.

To see Anazarbus (Anavarza) and Karatepe, head north and east just after the Yılankale. About 37km east of Adana an intersection is signed on the left (north) for Kozan and Kadirli and on the right (south) for Ceyhan. Take the Kozan/Kadirli road.

Anavarza (Anazarbus)

When the Romans moved into this area around 19 BC they built this fortress city on top of a hill dominating the fertile plain and called it Caesarea ad Anazarbus. Later, when Cilicia was divided in two, Tarsus remained the capital of the west, and Anazarbus became capital of the east. In the 3rd century AD Persian invaders destroyed the city along with lots of others in Anatolia. The Byzantine emperors rebuilt it as they did over and again when later earthquakes destroyed it several times.

The Arab raids of the 8th century gave Anazarbus new rulers and a new Arabicised name, Ain Zarba. The Byzantines reconquered and held it for a brief period, but Anazarbus was an important city at a strategic nexus, and other armies came through and snatched it, including those of the Hamdanid princes of Aleppo, the crusaders, a local Armenian king, the Byzantines again, the Turks and the Mameluks. The last owners didn't care about it much and it fell into decline in the 15th century. Today it's called Anavarza.

From the D400 Highway follow the Kozan/Kadirli road north to the village of Ayşehoca, where a road on the right is marked for Anavarza/Anazarbus, 5km to the east. If you're in a dolmuş or bus you can get out here and usually hitch a ride pretty easily in the morning.

The Site After 5km you reach a road junction and a large **gateway** set in the city walls. Through this gate was the ancient city, now given over to crops and pasture but strewn with ancient stones. Turn left through a village where every other gatepost re-uses a Roman column, and after walking 650m you'll reach the remains of an **aqueduct** with several arches still standing. Sometimes there's a gypsy camp set up around them.

Go back to the junction and turn right and after 200m you'll come to a little private **open-air museum** on the right-hand side of the road. Bits of column and sarcophagi are set in the garden, and an ancient pool has a nice **mosaic** of the goddess Thetis (Nereid), a sea nymph; ask Ayçe and she'll pour water over it so the colours stand out properly. Here you'll be asked to buy a ticket for US$0.50 which seems to cover the castle as well.

A little further on and you'll come to a wonderful **triumphal arch** on the left. Through here you can walk back to the junction if you've had enough. Otherwise to reach the impressive hilltop **fortress** which dominates the old city and the plain, continue past the open-air museum for 2km to a defile cut in the hill. Here a steep path and stone steps lead to the summit and fine views. You'll need a good supply of energy and water to get up on a hot day – not to mention sturdy shoes. An unpaved road leads through the cut to the far side of a hill where a track winds around the base of the rock.

The village of Anavarza has a couple of simple teahouses and a shop with cold drinks but that's it. If you have camping equipment you can probably find a place to set up a tent here.

Heading on to Karatepe, hitch back the 5km to Ayşehoca and take the 817 road north to Naşidiye/Çukurköprü where the road divides. The left fork is marked for Kozan and Feke, the right for Kadirli. Take the right fork.

Kadirli

Kadirli (population 55,000), 20km east of Çukurköprü, is a farming town with a useful bazaar, and a few small restaurants and hotels. ***Aktürk Lokantası***, facing the shady park with the teahouses in the centre, is simple and cheap but there are plenty of other options near the otogar.

It's 21km from Kadirli to Karatepe through lovely hill country given over to farms and evergreen forests, and with a constant backdrop of mountains. The gravel road is easily passable in dry weather, but more uncertain after rain. Hitching is very chancy. It's probably easier to get to Karatepe from Osmaniye, taking a dolmuş towards Tecirli and Kadirli and hitching the last 8.6km to Karatepe.

Karatepe-Aslantaş Milli Parkı

The Karatepe-Aslantaş Milli Parkı incorporates the **Karatepe-Aslantaş Müzesi** (Black Hill-Lion Stone Museum), a site which has been inhabited for almost 4000 years. The ruins date from the 13th century BC when this was a summer retreat for the neo-Hittite kings of Kizzuwatna (Cilicia), the greatest of whom was named Azitawadda.

From its beautiful, forested hilltop, the Karatepe-Aslantaş Milli Parkı (National Park) overlooks the **Ceyhan Gölü** (Lake Ceyhan), an artificial lake used for hydroelectric power and recreation.

The 2km park access road leads to a car park, near picnic tables, charcoal grills and tent camping sites. Entry to the park costs US$1 per person and US$3 for a car.

From here it's a five-minute, 400m walk uphill through the forest to the hilltop archaeological zone. A building above the car park has toilets, and there are soft drinks for sale. Entrance to the Hittite ruins, open from 8 am to noon and from 2 to 5.30 pm (1 to 3.30 pm in winter), costs an extra US$1 per person. Be warned that on top of the difficulty of getting to Karatepe without your own transport, the opening hours are rigorously adhered to, and the custodians will only take you around in a group which can involve hanging about. Nor are you allowed to take photographs at the site.

The Hittite remains here are certainly significant, although you shouldn't come expecting something on a Hattuşaş scale. The city was defended by **walls** 1km long, traces of which are still evident. Before arriving at the southern gate there's a **lookout** giving a fine view of the lake which was dammed and filled during the 1980s.

The city's **southern entrance** is protected by four lions and two sphinxes and lined with fine reliefs showing a coronation or feast complete with sacrificial bull, musicians and chariots. Across the hill at the **northern gate** the lions look scarier and the reliefs sharper as the stones were buried for centuries and thus protected from weathering. The eyes in the volcanic lion statue are of white stone, held in place by lead.

There are several **inscriptions** in Hittite script. A particularly long one with Phoenician translation was deciphered, which is how we know the city's history.

Hierapolis Castabala

About 19km south of Karatepe and 15km north of Osmaniye are the ruins of Hierapolis Castabala, set in the midst of cotton fields. A castle (kale) tops a rocky outcrop above the plain about 1km east of the road. Admission to the site, which is open during daylight hours, costs US$0.75 and the ticket seller will lend you a leaflet in English to take around with you. You can see everything in about an hour.

Hierapolis Castabala flourished during the Hellenistic period and was later the capital of a semi-independent principality paying tribute to Rome. Unfortunately one of its kings, Tarcondimotus I, unwisely sided with Antony in his struggle with Octavian and was defeated at the great sea battle of Actium in 31 BC. Though he was followed by Tarcondimotus II, the dynasty died out in the 1st century AD, as did the city in early Byzantine times.

From the ticket-seller's shed, walk along a **colonnaded street** which once boasted 78 paired columns; some still bear their fine Corinthian capitals. You'll pass a badly ruined **temple** and **baths** on the right. Keeping the kale on your left, walk past the rock outcrop to the **theatre**, also badly ruined. Beyond it to the south in the fields is a ruined Byzantine **basilica**. Further along the same path is a **spring** *(çeşme)* and, in the ridge of rocks further on, some **rock-cut tombs**. As you cross the fields, note the profusion of snails, both spiral and caracol, clinging to plants. The site is especially beautiful in spring when it's covered in wild flowers and skylarks are twittering above the stones.

The kale has a road cut straight through the rock *(kaya kesiği)*, and good views from the summit.

Osmaniye

Osmaniye lies on the E90 linking Adana with Gaziantep. An uninspiring modern town, it nevertheless makes a useful base for getting to Toprakkale, Hierapolis Castabala and the Karatepe National Park, so you might want to spend a night here.

Places to Stay & Eat Unfortunately Osmaniye hasn't cottoned onto the potential of tourism so your choice of places to stay and eat is strictly limited. Virtually everybody ends up at ***Hotel Kervansaray*** *(☎ 322-814 1310)*, Palalı Süleyman Caddesi, a simple place with clean, reasonably comfortable rooms with shower for US$4/7, or US$3/4 without. One reader found it friendly but demands for money upfront seem inappropriate. To find it, come out of the otogar and turn left along the main highway. When you reach the BP garage turn right and the hotel is on the left past the mosque and the MHP office.

This is a town where people eat early. The best place turns out to be on the 7th floor of a building across from the PTT where the ***R & A Restaurant*** is a vast, white-tablecloth place, with friendly service and views of the rooftops as you tuck into your kebap. Hummus, *beldi kebap* and a soft drink will cost US$4. Beer is also available. Otherwise, there are several basic ***lokantas*** near the hotel and around the otogar.

Getting There & Away From the centre of Osmaniye, road 01-08 is signposted north-west for Hierapolis Castabala and the

Karatepe-Aslantaş Müzesi. Follow the road until you come to a sign on the right for Hierapolis-Castabala which is 6km along a bumpy road. About 10km beyond Hierapolis-Castabala, a road on the left is marked for Karatepe (9km).

Without your own transport your best hope of seeing Hierapolis Castabala and Karatepe in one day is to organise a taxi from Osmaniye. There's a handy taxi rank outside the otogar. To go to Hierapolis for one hour, then to Karatepe for two hours and either on to Kadirli or back to Osmaniye should cost about US$28.

Heading south, to get to İskenderun from Osmaniye by dolmuş takes one hour (US$4). There are also frequent connections west to Adana and east to Gaziantep.

Toprakkale

About 9km west of Osmaniye the highway divides, skirting the Toprakkale (Earth Castle), built of dark volcanic stone about the same time as the Snake Castle. Take a bus to İskenderun or a dolmuş to Dörtyol and ask to be dropped off at the kale; it's 400m to the fortress walls, then an easy few minutes walk into the ruins.

Issos

From Toprakkale the E98 expressway runs south to Erzin, bypassing the ruins of the ancient city of Issos. If you follow the older road (817), 8km south of Toprakkale just east of Erzin, you'll notice a long **aqueduct** in the fields to the right, all that remains of the city.

Payas

At Payas, also called Yakacık, 35km south of Toprakkale, look for the inconspicuous signs in the centre of town (north of Payas' big steel factory) pointing right towards the Cinkale Kervansaray, 1km towards the sea.

The huge Ottoman **Sokullu Mehmet Paşa Kervansaray** was built for the grand vizier of Süleyman the Magnificent and Selim II in the 1570s. Opening hours are from 8 am to 4 or 5 pm daily. It's an elaborate complex of courtyards, Turkish baths, mosque, *medrese* (theological seminary) and covered bazaar – a fortified city in what was then recently conquered (1516) and still hostile territory. Parts of it look positively Burgundian, and it was possible that Sokullu Mehmet Paşa's architects, who worked under the guidance of Sinan's school, may have restored and expanded the ruins of a crusader church.

Next to the caravanserai is the **Cin Kalesi** (Fortress of the Genies), a restored bastion protected by a moat. The main gate is a double-bend defensive one which leads to a grassy interior now used as cattle pasture. The ruins of a small mosque are the only other item of interest. If you walk around the outside you can descend and pick figs in the moat by means of a stone subterranean stairway at its westernmost point.

Further along the tarmac road is another little **fortress** with a bent-gate entrance, a keep and gun ports. The ruins of a third fortress are down by the water's edge. You can visit all three forts at any time.

After Payas the road is lined with smoke-belching factories turning out steel, cement and fertiliser, all taking advantage of the port of İskenderun, 22km to the south.

İskenderun

İskenderun (population 155,000), 130km east of Adana, was founded by Alexander the Great in 333 BC – İskenderun is a translation of its original name, Alexandretta. Until Mersin was developed in the 1960s, this was the most important port on this part of the coast. Its continued importance was emphasised during the 1980s with the opening of the oil pipeline from Iraq, and then the shutting of that pipeline during the Gulf War of 1991.

İskenderun was occupied by the English in 1918, turned over to the French in 1919, and incorporated into the French Protectorate of Syria as the Sanjak of Alexandretta. In 1938 Atatürk reclaimed it for the Turkish Republic (with French acquiescence), knowing it would be of great strategic importance in the coming war (WWII).

There's nothing to detain you in modern İskenderun, an unexciting sailors, brokers and shippers town. If you have to stop there are several places to stay near the waterfront, the one attractive part of town.

Orientation & Information Assuming you arrive by bus, come out of the otogar and head due south, passing the minibus station before you reach the main highway. To find the sea you'll need to cross the highway and take a turn on the right, towards Şehit Pamir Caddesi which is lined with hotels, banks and restaurants. Once on this road, head north until you come to Atatürk Bulvarı, the waterfront boulevard, and the sea. The main square at the top of Şehit Pamir Caddesi is marked by a huge *abide* (ah-BEE-deh, monument/statue) on the waterfront, pretentious or imposing depending on your viewpoint. Most hotels are within a few blocks of this abide.

The Tourist Information Office (☎ 326-614 1620, fax 613 2879), is at Atatürk Bulvarı 49/B, 100m west of the abide.

İskenderun's postal code is 31200.

Places to Stay The clean, central ***Hotel Açıkalın*** *(☎ 326-617 3732, Şehit Pamir Caddesi 13)* has singles/doubles with showers and fans for US$14/19.

Nearby, ***Hotel Altındişler*** *(☎/fax 326-617 1011, Şehit Pamir Caddesi 11)*, is similar, if marginally more pricey at US$17/21 a single/double with shower and TV. A step up in comfort is the nearby ***Hotel İmrenay*** *(☎ 326-613 2117, fax 613 5984, Şehit Pamir Caddesi 5)*, charging US$21/31 a single/double with shower and TV.

The best in town – although that's not saying too much – is the shabby 35-room ***Hotel Cabir*** *(☎ 326-612 3391, fax 612 3393, Ulucami Caddesi 16)*, a block east of Şehit Pamir Caddesi, with comfortable singles/doubles with shower for US$25/45, breakfast included.

From İskenderun the coastal road continues south-west to Assos where the few ***hotels*** and the ***camp site*** overlooking a pleasant beach might make alternatives to staying in the city.

Places to Eat The town's best is the big ***Saray Restaurant***, a few blocks west of the Tourist Information Office on Atatürk Bulvarı. For cheaper meals, stroll along the narrow lane which runs between Şehit Pamir Caddesi at Hotel Açıkalın, and Ulucami Caddesi at the Hotel Cabir. The street has half a dozen cheap restaurants serving kebaps, stews etc; ***Yeni Lokanta*** is long established and serves a renowned döner kebap for US$2; also popular is ***Yeşil Dörtyol*** which serves pides as well.

İskenderun to Antakya

Past İskenderun the road winds south through the town of Sarımazı (10km from İskenderun) to Belen, the town at the head of a gorge 15km south of İskenderun. Archaeological excavations nearby have unearthed evidence of settlements dating back to the time of Hammurabi, King of Babylon (1728-1686 BC). Eventually the road passes over the Belen Geçidi (Belen Pass, altitude 740m) and then descends to the vast, flat, fertile Amik Plain, the source of Antakya's prosperity. For much of the way the roadside is littered with half-complete buildings and evidence of industry.

ANTAKYA (HATAY)

Antakya (population 124,000), or Hatay (HAH-tie) was, until 1938, Arabic in culture and language. Many people still speak Arabic as a first language and Turkish as the second. Modern Antakya is hardly a beautiful place but in its museum – one of Turkey's finest – it does boast one gem justifying a lengthy detour. In the cave-church of St Peter, Antakya can also lay claim to possessing 'the world's first cathedral', where the apostle is said to have preached and the term 'Christian' was first used (Acts 11, verse 26).

Throughout Antakya's long history violent earthquakes have shattered the town, most notably in 526 AD when 250,000 people were killed. It explains why so little remains of the old city. One conspicuous exception is the early 20th century French Assembly Rooms, facing the museum on the western bank of the river. Sadly, these days it's reduced to showing soft-porn movies.

EASTERN MEDITERRANEAN

NEIL WILSON

Western Mediterranean Antalya's beautiful old harbour, lined with restaurants, tavernas and shops.

BOTH PHOTOGRAPHS BY TOM BROSNAHAN

Eastern Mediterranean **Top:** The Seljuk-era *kale* (fortress) in Alanya houses an ancient city with sweeping panoramic views. **Bottom:** A building in İskenderun stands as a reminder of the French Protectorate of the Sancak of Hatay (1919-38).

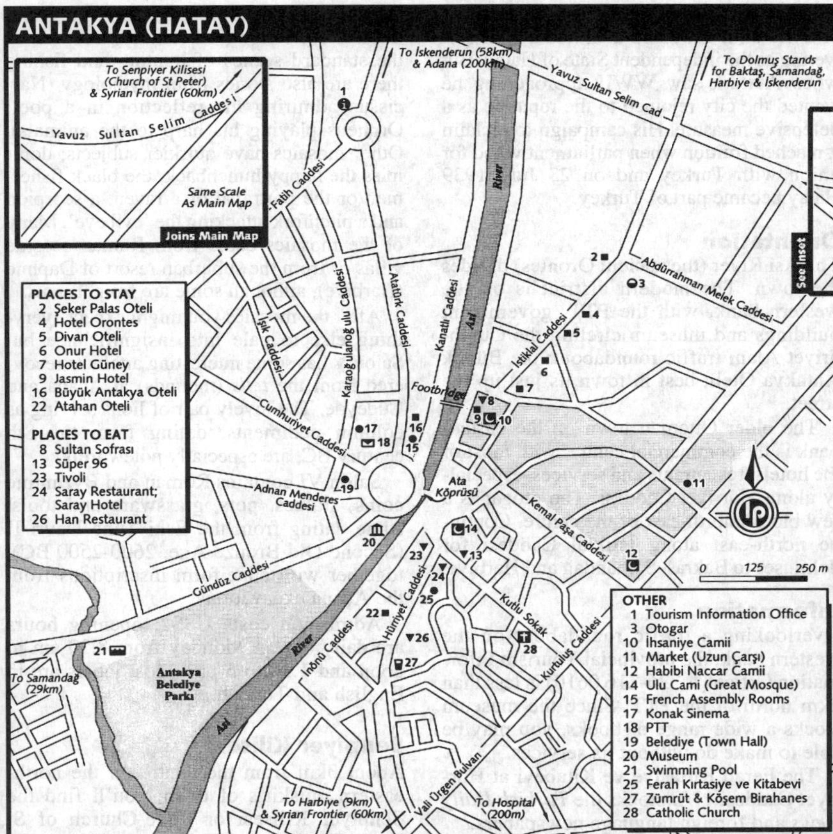

However, the town's relatively small size means that more of the Roman city has been excavated than has been possible in Rome or Alexandria, for example; hence the splendid collection of floor mosaics in the museum.

Antakya is backed by the Altınözü Mountains, with the snow-capped peak of Mt Silpius dominating the surrounding area.

History

Antakya is the ancient Antioch ad Orontes, founded by Seleucus I Nicator in 300 BC and soon became a city of half a million people. Under the Romans an important Christian community developed out of the already large Jewish one. At one time this was headed by St Paul.

Persians, Byzantines, Arabs, Armenians and Seljuks all fought over Antioch, as did the crusaders and Saracens. In 1268 the Mameluks of Egypt took the city and wiped it out. It never regained its former glory.

The Ottomans held the city until Muhammed Ali of Egypt captured it in 1831, but with European help the Ottomans eventually managed to drive their rebellious vassal back.

Antakya was part of the French protectorate of Syria until 1939 and then had a brief flowering as the independent State of Hatay. But when Atatürk saw WWII approaching he wanted the city rejoined to the republic as a defensive measure. His campaign to reclaim it reached fruition when parliament voted for union with Turkey and on 23 July 1939 Hatay became part of Turkey.

Orientation

The Asi River (the ancient Orontes) divides the town. The modern district is on the western bank, with the PTT, government buildings and museum circling the Cumhuriyet Alanı traffic roundabout; the Büyük Antakya Oteli, best in town, is just up the street.

The older Ottoman town on the eastern bank is the commercial centre, with most of the hotels, restaurants and services, especially along Hürriyet Caddesi. The otogar is a few blocks north-east of the centre. Continue north-east along İstiklal Caddesi for dolmuşes to Bakras, Samandağ and Harbiye.

Information

Overlooking a traffic roundabout on the western bank, the provincial Tourism Information Office (☎ 326-216 0610) is less than 2km north of the PTT. Since the museum stocks a wide range of books, you may be able to make do without its services.

The Ferah Kırtasiye ve Kitabevi at Hürriyet Caddesi 17/D stocks the *Turkish Daily News* and foreign language newspapers.

Antakya Arkeoloji Müzesi

The Antakya Arkeoloji Müzesi (Archaeological Museum) is the prime reason for journeying all the way to Antakya. Here you'll see as fine a collection of Roman/Byzantine mosaics that grace any museum in the world, covering a period from the 1st century to the 5th century AD. While some are inevitably fragmentary, others were recovered almost intact.

Salons I to IV are tall, naturally lit rooms, perfect for displaying mosaics so fine that at first glance you could mistake some of them for paintings; check out particularly the Oceanus and Thetis mosaic (2nd century) and the Buffet Mosaic (3rd century). As well as the standard scenes of hunting and fishing there are also stories from mythology (Narcissus admiring his reflection in a pool; Orpheus playing his harp to the animals). Other mosaics have quirkier subjects; don't miss the happy hunchback, the black fisherman or the portrayal of a raven, a scorpion and a pitchfork attacking the 'evil eye'. Many of the mosaics came from Roman seaside villas or from the suburban resort of Daphne (Harbiye), although some are from Tarsus.

After the mosaics you might expect everything else to pale into insignificance but Salon V has some interesting artefacts recovered from the *tells* (mounds) at Açana and Cüdeyde. The lovely pair of lions serving as column pediments, dating from the 8th century BC, are especially noteworthy.

Salon VI contains Roman and Byzantine coins, statues, pots, glassware and tools, some dating from the Eski Tunç Devri II (Second Old Bronze Age, 2600-2500 BC), together with cuneiform inscriptions from the Açana excavations.

Admission costs US$2; opening hours are daily except Monday from 8.30 am to noon and 1.30 to 5 pm. Most labels are in English and Turkish.

Senpiyer Kilisesi

About 3km from the centre on the north-eastern outskirts of town, you'll find the Senpiyer Kilisesi or Cave-Church of St Peter. Tradition has it that this cave was the property of St Luke the Evangelist, who was from Antioch, and that he donated it to the burgeoning Christian congregation as a place of worship. Saints Peter and Paul lived in Antioch for a few years and are thought to have preached here. When the Crusaders marched through in 1098, they constructed the wall at the front, and a narthex.

To the right of the altar faint traces of fresco can still be seen, and some of the simple mosaic floor survives. Mass is still celebrated here each Sunday, at 5 pm in winter and 6 pm in summer. For further information, contact the Capuchins at the

Katolik Kilisesi (Catholic Church) (☎ 326-215 6703), Kurtuluş Caddesi, Kutlu Sokak 6, who have cared for the church since 1846.

The Orthodox liturgy is on Sunday at 8 am in summer and 8.30 am in winter. Avoid visiting on public holidays when, no matter what your religious views, you may be shocked to see local people climbing on the altar to have their picture taken.

The church is open from 8 am to noon and 1.30 to 6 pm (closed Monday). Admission is free. If it's not too hot you can easily walk to the church in about half an hour, heading north-east along Kurtuluş Caddesi. If you're struggling to make it, some of the dolmuşes waiting at the junction of Kurtuluş Caddesi and Yavuz Sultan Selim Caddesi will drop you off for a handful of lira – a sign on the right side of the road marks the turn-off. Taxis charge US$2 one way.

The terrace in front of the church offers a fine view of the city. Note the many vine-shaded roof terraces, where Antakyalı families go in the evening to catch any lingering breeze.

Other Things To See & Do

A sprawling **bazaar** fills the back streets between the otogar and Kurtuluş Caddesi. The Meydan Hamamı is in the bazaar at the southern end. Around **Habibi Naccar Camii** you'll find most of Antakya's remaining **old houses**, with carved stone lintels or wooden overhangs.

If it's hot, a good place to hang out is the riverside **Antakya Belediyesi Parkı** a few blocks south-west of the museum. Here you'll find tea gardens and ice cream booths, as well as shady promenades and a few dried-up ponds.

On the high mountain to the south-east are remnants of the long **city walls** and a badly ruined **acropolis**. It's worth the climb for the view.

The **Konak Sinema**, beside the PTT, shows English-language films subtitled in Turkish.

Harbiye (Daphne)

Frequent dolmuşes (30 minutes, US$0.25) and less frequent city buses run from north of Yavuz Sultan Selim Caddesi to the hill suburb of Harbiye, 9km to the south. This was the ancient Daphne where, according to classical mythology, the virgin Daphne prayed to be rescued from the attentions of the god Apollo and was turned into a laurel tree. There are no laurels to be seen nowadays, although pine trees ring a large pool of water, very popular as a picnic place.

Most visitors will find the litter strewn around the pool very offputting. Instead, get out of the dolmuş opposite the Hotel Çağlayan and walk down into the wooded valley on the left, which is usually full of Antakyalı vacationers enjoying the cool shade, the tea gardens, and the pools and rivulets of cooling water. Some people find the souvenir stalls tacky, but most will enjoy sipping tea or having a fish lunch with curtains of water falling behind them and bottles of beer cooling in the streams around them. Check prices before ordering, though, since it's easy to pay more than what you bargained for.

About another 42km past Harbiye is the **Yayladağı Yazılıtaş Orman Piknik Yeri**, a forest picnic spot near some ancient inscriptions. Along the way the road passes near the village of **Sofular**, next to which is a crusader castle.

Samandağ & Çevlik

Head north-east along İstiklal Caddesi to find dolmuşes waiting to run to Samandağ, a seaside suburb 29km to the south. As they cross over the mountains towards the sea you'll pass endless long plastic greenhouse tunnels used by market gardeners to mature their produce.

Samandağ itself is hardly worth bothering with, but if you continue for 6km north along the beach you'll come to Çevlik and the scant ruins of **Seleucia ad Piera**, the port of Antioch in ancient times. Çevlik itself is pretty dejected, its litter-strewn beach unlikely to seduce you. There are several sea-facing restaurants and a few simple pensions but nothing to write home about. Nor is the water the cleanest if you're hoping to swim.

What you really come here for is the **Titüs ve Vespasiyanüs Tüneli**, an astonishing feat of Roman engineering. During its heyday, Seleucia lived with the constant threat of inundation from a stream which descended the mountains and flowed through the town. To remove this threat, the Roman emperors Titus and Vespasian ordered their engineers to dig a diversion channel around the town.

From the car park in Çevlik, ascend the steps to the gate. If there's anybody in the booth you'll have to pay a US$1 admission fee, after which a guide will accompany you up the hillside, along the channel and through a great gorge. The walk is over rocks and is definitely sturdy-shoe rather than sandal terrain. If you're not up to it, follow the channel until you come to a metal arch on the right; take the path behind the arch (right fork) which follows an irrigation canal past some rock-cut shelters, finally arriving at a humpback Roman bridge across the gorge. Here steps lead down to the tunnel. Bring a torch since the path is still pretty treacherous. At the far end of the channel an inscription provides a date for the work.

The slopes above the Roman bridge provide a perfect picnic spot.

Places to Stay – Budget

Antakya has a reasonable range of accommodation, if nothing wonderful. Since Harbiye is so close, it would be possible to stay in a hotel or pension there to take advantage of the hill air and pleasant views and travel into Antakya to do your sightseeing.

Antakya Closest to the otogar is the simple ***Şeker Palas Oteli*** *(☎ 326-215 1603, İstiklal Caddesi 79)*, which is trying hard with display cabinets in the hall. Basic rooms with sink cost US$4/6 a single/double.

A few blocks south along İstiklal Caddesi, you'll come to ***Jasmin Hotel*** *(☎ 326-212 7171, İstiklal Caddesi 14)*, next door to the Sultan Sofrası restaurant. Rooms cost the same as at Seker Palas Oteli, and although baths are still shared they're clean and new. The lobby-lounge is a good place for meeting and chatting.

The one-star ***Divan Oteli*** (dee-VAHN) *(☎ 326-215 1518, İstiklal Caddesi 62)* offers reasonably good value for money although unnecessary noise can be annoying, and one reader reported a frosty reception. Its 23 serviceable rooms with showers cost US$10/16 a single/double. Some rooms are without windows (let alone fan) which could be stifling in summer, but the large TV lounges on each floor are well ventilated and inviting.

Hotel Güney *(☎ 326-214 9713, fax 215 1778, İstiklal Sokak 28)*, is one narrow street east of İstiklal Caddesi on the edge of the bazaar. Big, bright and bare rooms show signs of suffering but it's friendly enough and has rooms for US$8/12 with shower and US$6/10 without.

At the bridge end of Hürriyet Caddesi is ***Hotel Saray*** *(☎ 326-214 9001, fax 214 9002)*, above the Saray Restaurant. Clean, decently kept rooms with showers go for US$11/16/21 a single/double/triple.

Harbiye ***Hidro Otel*** *(☎ 326-231 4006)*, Çağlayan Mahallesi, was probably once much nicer than it is now. Singles/doubles in simple rooms with shower cost US$12/18. The ***restaurant*** on the terrace overlooking the pool has a lengthy menu and is popular with the locals.

Places to Stay – Mid-Range

Antakya The one-star, 28 room ***Atahan Oteli*** *(☎ 326-214 2140, fax 215 8006, Hürriyet Caddesi 28)* barely scrapes into this category; it may have a restaurant and air-con but there's no lift and the bathrooms are not inviting. At US$26/36 a single/double it's definitely overpriced.

The 35 room ***Hotel Orontes*** *(☎ 326-214 5931, fax 214 5933, İstiklal Caddesi 58)* is comfortably modern, with satellite TVs and sizeable showers. Front rooms get the traffic noise and the ***restaurant*** sometimes has live music but it's a reasonable mid-range choice at US$31/44/55 a single/double/triple. It can get booked full with tour groups though.

Newest in town is the two-star, 36 room ***Onur Hotel*** *(☎ 326-216 2210, fax 216 2214,*

İstiklal Caddesi, İstiklal Sokak 14), on the edge of the bazaar but quiet at night. Comfortable rooms have modern bathrooms, TV and air-con, and cost US$30/44/52 a single/double/triple.

Harbiye *Hotel Çağlayan* (☎ *326-231 4269, fax 231 5489, Ürgen Caddesi 6)* is a bright, cheerful place with balconies positioned to soak up the view over the wooded valley. Singles/doubles/triples with minbar, TV and air-con cost a very reasonable US$15/22/33, and you're right beside the inviting ***Boğaziçi Restaurant***, with a table set around a marble fountain.

Places to Stay – Top End

Officially Antakya's best is the four-star ***Büyük Antakya Oteli*** (☎ *326-213 5860, fax 213 5869, Atatürk Caddesi 8)*, with 72 air-con rooms, some with river views. As you'd expect, rooms have TV and bath, but the US$70/100 a single/double price tag is a bit much for a place which seems to have skimped on the updating. The only credit card they'll accept is Visa.

Places to Eat

The influence of Syria permeates Antakya's cuisine. Handfuls of mint and wedges of lemon accompany many kebaps. Hummus, rare elsewhere in Turkey, is readily available here. Many main courses and salads are dusted with fiery pepper; if this isn't to your taste, ask for yours *acısız* (Ah-juh-SUHZ, without hot pepper). For dessert, try the local specialty, *künefe*, a circular cake of fine shredded wheat laid over a dollop of fresh, mild cheese, floated on a layer of sugar syrup, topped with chopped walnuts and baked. Shops at the northern end of Hürriyet Caddesi sell it. Try and get it hot, straight from the oven.

Many small, cheap eateries line İstiklal Caddesi, near the otogar. Otherwise, try Hürriyet Caddesi, İnönü Caddesi or, across the river, Cumhuriyet Caddesi which has lots of small kebapçıs.

Tivoli (☎ *326-214 7726)*, at the eastern end of the Ata Köprüsü and the beginning of Hürriyet Caddesi, is a convenient landmark. Antakya's gilded youth come here to see and be seen in air-conditioned comfort (mostly in the large dining room upstairs), and to consume fast food, espresso and cappuccino. A döner burger, *pomfrits* (fried potatoes) and drink costs US$3. The pastries look luscious.

Across the square in front of the Tivoli is the tiny ***Süper 96***, a popular place to tuck into lahmacun and other local delicacies for a couple of dollars.

In Hürriyet Caddesi most places have tiny street-level rooms, with larger dining rooms one flight up. First up is the big, two-part ***Saray Restaurant***, friendly, and with a good selection of dishes and a modern salon to eat them in. Full meals can be enjoyed for US$2 to US$3.50. Have your döner served dürüm-style, rolled up in flat village bread.

Perhaps the best all-round choice is ***Han Restaurant*** (☎ *326-215 8538, Hürriyet Caddesi 19/1)*. Go upstairs to either of the two open-air terraces (the rear one with shady trees is nicest) and order döner kebap, served with flat peasant bread, chopped parsley and pepper-dusted sliced red onions. This is also a good place to try künefe; tell them early in the meal that you'll want it for dessert. A full meal of döner, salad, künefe and a beer comes to US$5.

If drink is more important than food, try the ***Zümrüt*** or the ***Köşem***, two birahanes at the southern end of Hürriyet Caddesi, where local men come to sip and talk sports and politics. There are other birahanes on Hürriyet Caddesi as well.

Getting There & Away

Bus Frequent dolmuşes and city buses run from near Antakya otogar to Harbiye (9km, 15 minutes), Samandağ (29km, 35 minutes, US$0.50) and the Turco-Syrian border stations at Reyhanlı (for Aleppo) and Yayladağı (for Lattakia and Beirut).

The otogar also has direct buses to most western and northern points (Ankara, Antalya, İstanbul, İzmir, Kayseri and Konya), usually travelling via Adana and up through the Cilician Gates. There are also direct buses to major cities in neighbouring countries, though you may find it faster to buy a ticket only as far as the border, cross on your own, and catch something on the other side, thus avoiding the tedium of waiting until everyone on the bus has undergone border formalities.

Travel times given here don't include border formalities, which may add several hours to the trip. Have your visas in advance to hasten proceedings.

Daily buses from Antakya serve the following destinations:

Adana – 190km, 2½ hours, US$4; very frequent buses
Amman (Jordan) – 675km, 10 hours, US$14
Çevlik – 32km, one hour, US$1; frequent dolmuşes, changing at Samandağ
Damascus (Syria) – 465km, eight hours, US$8
Gaziantep – 200km, four hours, US$9; frequent buses
Haleb (Aleppo, Syria) – 105km, four hours, US$6; several buses
İskenderun – 58km, one hour, US$1
Şanlıurfa (Urfa) – 345km, seven hours, US$7; several direct buses, or change at Gaziantep, from where buses go east to Urfa every half hour

To/From Syria Syrian visas are not normally issued at the border, but this depends partly upon your nationality and partly upon current regulations. If you plan to travel to Syria and other Middle Eastern countries, plan ahead and obtain the necessary visas, preferably in your home country, but possibly in İstanbul or in Ankara.

To/From Israel It's possble to travel between Jerusalem and İstanbul by bus for around US$100, well below the airfare.

Until there is some direct correspondence between Israeli and Syrian roads and bus companies, you'll need to travel via Jordan. Use the Allenby/King Hussein Bridge to cross to Amman, remembering that you may have to wait two days for a Syrian transit visa. Proceed from Amman to Damascus (Karnack Bus Company). From Damascus, take another Karnack bus to the border at Idlib/Hatay where it will probably take about two hours to cross the border. From Antakya, you can catch a bus to more or less anywhere in Turkey.

Central Anatolia

When nomadic Turkish shepherds moved into Anatolia around the year 1100, they found a land which reminded them of central Asia: semi-arid, rolling steppe covered with grass, perfect for their flocks. Mountains and great lakes (some of them salt) broke up the vast expanse of steppe. By the numerous streams, marked with rows of tall, spindly poplars, the nomads gradually settled down to establish villages.

In spring, Central Anatolia is a sea of wild flowers. Great swaths of vivid colour run across the spare landscape in an annual extravagance born of the April rains. Days are pleasantly warm and nights chilly. In summer the rain disappears and the Anatolian plateau is hotter and drier, never humid like the coasts. As you ride across Anatolia in summer, you will see the dark red of newly ploughed furrows, the straw yellow of wheat and the grey and green bands of sandstone in a rockface. Winter is cold and rainy, with numerous snow falls. The snow is not surprising, for the plateau has an average altitude of 1000m.

The first impression of Central Anatolia as a vast emptiness dotted with oases of civilisation is deceptive. The armies of a dozen empires have moved back and forth across this 'land bridge' between Europe and Asia; a dozen civilisations have risen and fallen here, including the very earliest established human communities, which date from 7500 BC. Crumbling caravanserais scattered along the modern highways testify to rich trade routes which flourished for several millenniums.

Today, Central Anatolia is still flourishing. Wheat and other grains, apples, cabbages, melons, potatoes, sugar beets, tomatoes and many other crops are grown in the dry soil, and flocks of sheep finish off the grass. Ankara, Turkey's capital city, is a sprawling urban mass in the midst of the steppe; Konya and Kayseri, fuelled by the wealth of agriculture and light industry, are growing at a remarkable pace. Modern at first glance, with wide boulevards, apartment blocks and busy traffic, each city has at its heart an old town, perhaps a fortress dating from Roman times, and sometimes even a few foundations dating from the dawn of civilisation.

HIGHLIGHTS

- Staying in a restored Ottoman house in Safranbolu
- Visiting the Mevlâna Müzesi in Konya
- Walking through the Ilhara gorge
- Exploring the Cappadocian valleys, especially Göreme
- Visiting Ankara's Anadolu Medeniyetleri Müzesi
- Hittite-spotting in Hattuşaş
- Staying in a rock-cut room in Cappadocia
- Trying not to get lost in the underground cities of Kaymaklı or Derinkuyu

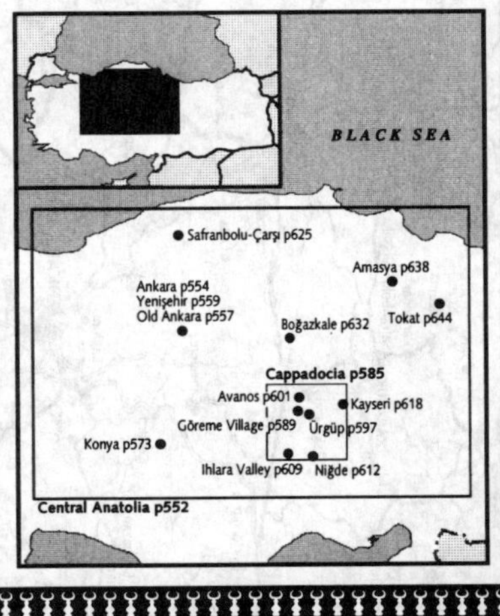

CENTRAL ANATOLIA

Ankara

The capital of the Turkish Republic, Ankara (AHN-kah-rah, population three million, altitude 848m), was once called Angora. The fine, soft *tiftik* (hair) on Angora goats became an industry which still thrives. Today, Ankara's prime concern is government. It is a city of ministries, embassies, universities, medical centres and some light industry. Vast suburbs are scattered on the hillsides which surround the centre, and are mostly filled by country people who have moved here in search of work and a better life.

Ankara has several significant attractions, but you should be able to tour them all in 1½ to two days, or even a day if you're in a hurry.

History

It was the Hittites who named this place Ankuwash before 1200 BC. The town prospered because it was at the intersection of the north-south and east-west trade routes. After the Hittites it was a Phrygian town, then taken by Alexander, claimed by the Seleucids and finally occupied by the Galatians who invaded Anatolia around 250 BC. Augustus Caesar annexed it to Rome in 25 BC as Ankyra.

The Byzantines held the town for centuries, with intermittent raids by the Persians and Arabs. When the Seljuk Turks came to Anatolia after 1071, they made the town (which they called Engüriye) into a Seljuk city but held it with difficulty.

Ottoman possession of Angora did not go well, for it was near here that Sultan Yıldırım Beyazıt was captured by Tamerlane – the sultan later died in captivity. After the Timurid state collapsed and the Ottoman civil war ended, Angora became merely a quiet town where long-haired goats were raised.

Modern Ankara is a planned city. When Atatürk set up his provisional government here in 1920, it was a small, dusty Anatolian town of some 30,000 people, with a strategic position at the heart of the country. After his victory in the War of Independence, Atatürk declared this the new capital of the country (October 1923), and set about developing it. European urban planners were consulted, and the result was a city of long, wide boulevards, a forested park with an artificial lake, and numerous residential and diplomatic neighbourhoods. From 1919 to 1927, Atatürk did not set foot in the old imperial capital of İstanbul, preferring to work at making Ankara the country's capital city in fact as well as in name.

For republican Turks, İstanbul is their glorious historical city, still the centre of business and finance, but Ankara is their true capital, built on the ashes of the empire with blood and sweat.

Orientation

The main boulevard through the city is, of course, Atatürk Bulvarı, which runs from Ulus in the north to the Presidential Mansion in Çankaya, 6km to the south.

The old city of Ankara, dating from Roman times and including the Hisar (citadel), is near Ulus Meydanı, called simply Ulus (oo-LOOSS), the centre of 'old Ankara', marked by a large equestrian statue of Atatürk. The most important museums and sights are near Ulus, as are numerous bottom-end and middle-range hotels and restaurants. The first goal of most visitors is the Hisar, or Kale (KAH-leh), the citadel atop the hill 1000m east of Ulus, and the nearby Anadolu Medeniyetleri Müzesi (Museum of Anatolian Civilisations). The *Gar* (train station), also the terminus for Havaş airport buses, is 1400m south-west of Ulus along Cumhuriyet Bulvarı.

Officially called Hürriyet Meydanı, the intersection of Atatürk Bulvarı and Gazi Mustafa Kemal Bulvarı/Ziya Gökalp Caddesi is known universally as Kızılay (KUH-zuh-'lie').

This is the centre of 'new Ankara', called Yenişehir (yeh-NEE-sheh-heer, New City), with mid-range and top-end hotels, restaurants, airline and bus ticket offices, travel agencies and department stores. Yenişehir's Kocatepe Camii is among the largest in the world.

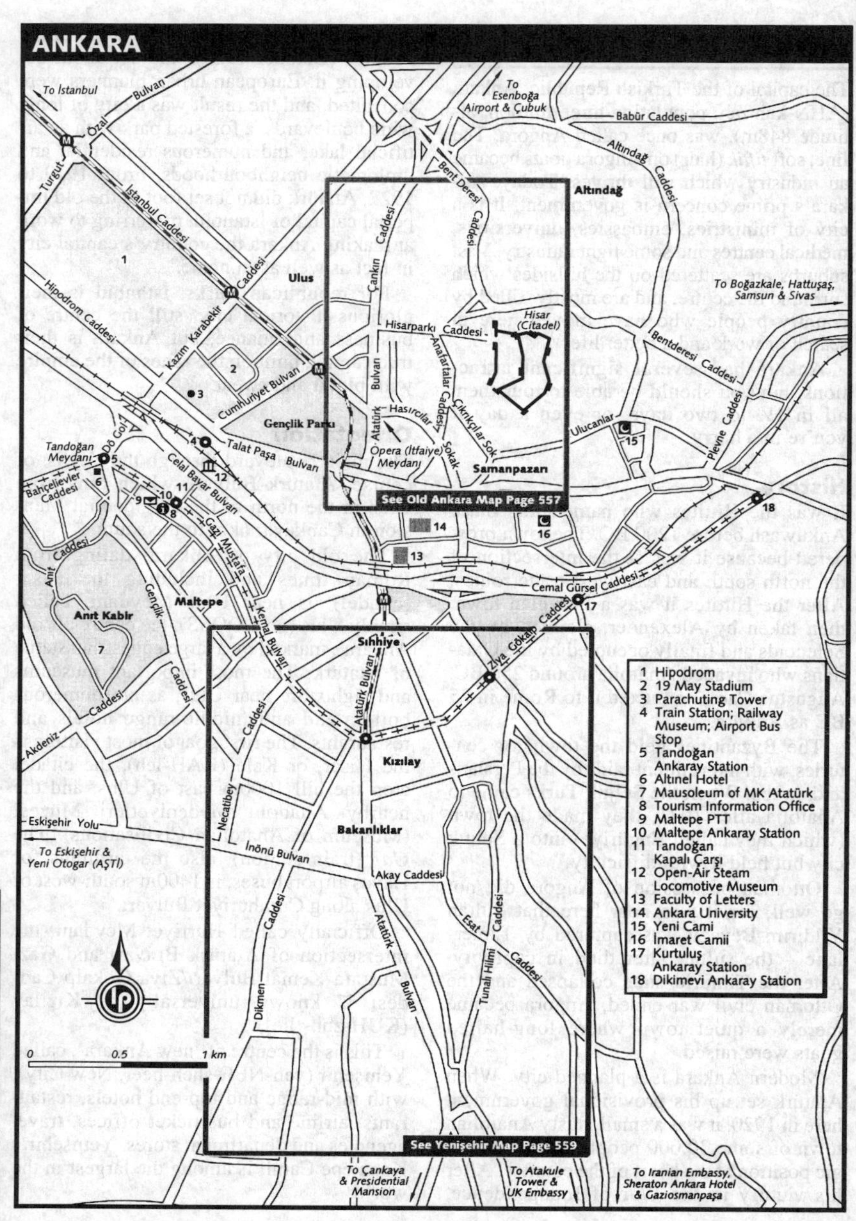
ANKARA
To İstanbul
To Esenboğa Airport & Çubuk
Babür Caddesi
Altındağ Caddesi
Bent Deresi Caddesi
Altındağ
Turgut Özal Bulvarı
İstanbul Caddesi
Çankırı Caddesi
Ulus
Hipodrom Caddesi
Kazım Karabekir Caddesi
To Boğazkale, Hattuşaş, Samsun & Sivas
Hisarparkı Caddesi
Hisar (Citadel)
Anafartalar Caddesi
Bentderesi Caddesi
Cumhuriyet Bulvarı
Atatürk Bulvarı
Gençlik Parkı
Hasırcılar Sokak
Çıkrıkçılar Sok
Ulucanlar
Plevne Caddesi
Opera (İtfaiye) Meydanı
Talat Paşa Bulvarı
Tandoğan Meydanı
Dö Gol
Celal Bayar Bulvarı
Samanpazarı
Bahçelievler Caddesi
See Old Ankara Map Page 557
Gazi Mustafa Kemal Bulvarı
Anıt Caddesi
Cemal Gürsel Caddesi
Maltepe
Gençlik Caddesi
Anıt Kabir
Sıhhiye
Ziya Gökalp Caddesi
Akdeniz Caddesi
Kızılay
Necatibey Caddesi
Eskişehir Yolu
Bakanlıklar
To Eskişehir & Yeni Otogar (AŞTİ)
İnönü Bulvarı
Akay Caddesi
Tunalı Hilmi Caddesi
Esat Caddesi
Dikmen Caddesi
Atatürk Bulvarı
0
0.5
1 km
See Yenişehir Map Page 559
To Çankaya & Presidential Mansion
To Atakule Tower & UK Embassy
To Iranian Embassy, Sheraton Ankara Hotel & Gaziosmanpaşa
1 Hipodrom
2 19 May Stadium
3 Parachuting Tower
4 Train Station; Railway Museum; Airport Bus Stop
5 Tandoğan Ankaray Station
6 Altınel Hotel
7 Mausoleum of MK Atatürk
8 Tourism Information Office
9 Maltepe PTT
10 Maltepe Ankaray Station
11 Tandoğan Kapalı Çarşı
12 Open-Air Steam Locomotive Museum
13 Faculty of Letters
14 Ankara University
15 Yeni Cami
16 İmaret Camii
17 Kurtuluş Ankaray Station
18 Dikimevi Ankaray Station

AŞTİ, Ankara's *otogar* (bus terminal), is 6.5km south-west of Ulus and 6km west of Kızılay.

Kavaklıdere, halfway up the slope south from Kızılay to Çankaya, is the heart of posh Ankara, a fashionable district of embassies, trendy bars, smart shops, and the Hilton and Sheraton hotels.

At the southern end of Atatürk Bulvarı up in the hills is Çankaya, the residential neighbourhood which holds the Presidential Mansion (Cumhurbaşkanlığı Köşkü) and many of the most important ambassadorial residences. The prominent landmark here is the Atakule, a tall office tower and shopping complex with a bulbous top visible throughout the city.

Information

Tourist Offices The Tourism Information Office (☎\fax 312-231 5572) is at Gazi Mustafa Kemal Bulvarı 121, opposite the Maltepe Ankaray station.

Embassies For addresses of diplomatic missions in Ankara, see Embassies & Consulates in the Facts for the Visitor chapter.

Money Bank branches and *döviz* (currency exchange) offices are scattered across the city, with particularly rich concentrations in Ulus, Kızılay and Kavaklıdere. Look near the corner of Sakarya Caddesi and Atatürk Bulvarı for Sakarya Döviz, Sakarya Caddesi 6-A, which has good rates, but is often crowded; also look at Uğurlu Döviz, across Sakarya Caddesi on its northern side. Çankaya Döviz ve Altın (☎ 312-419 3314), Meşrutiyet Caddesi 19-C between Konur and Selanik sokaks, takes no commission and usually has pretty good exchange rates. Near Ulus, Erol Döviz, Alsancak Sokak 2, more or less opposite the Yeni Haller, has good rates as well.

Medical Services Ankara is Turkey's major medical centre. The city's most up-to-date facility is the private Bayındır Medical Centre (☎ 312-287 9000), Eskişehir Yolu, Söğütözü. City Hospital (☎ 312-466 3366, fax 466 2831), Büklüm Sokak 72 east of Tunalı Hilmi Caddesi, is also good and has a beautiful modern Kadın Sağlığı Merkezi (Women's Health Centre) nearby at Büklüm Sokak 53, just west of Tunalı Hilmi. Phone your embassy to find out other health service suggestions.

Anadolu Medeniyetleri Müzesi

Ankara's premier museum is a must-see for anyone with an interest in Turkey's ancient past. The Museum of Anatolian Civilisations (☎ 312-324 3160) is housed in a restored covered market, built by order of Grand Vizier Mahmut Paşa in 1471, and the adjoining Kurşunlu Han, an Ottoman warehouse. Exhibits heavily favour the earlier Anatolian civilisations: Urartu, Hatti, Hittite, Phrygian and Assyrian. Among the more fascinating items are those brought from Çatal Höyük, the earliest known human community. You'll also enjoy the graceful, lively Hittite figures of bulls and stags and the early water vessels.

If you're a walker and the day is not too hot, you can climb the hillside from Ulus to the museum (1km, 12 to 15 minutes); otherwise take a taxi (US$2 from Ulus). Walk east from Ulus on Hisarparkı Caddesi and turn right into Anafartalar Caddesi, then bear left along Çıkrıkçılar Sokak to reach the museum, which is open from 8.30 am to 5.15 pm, 'closed' on Monday in winter unless you pay twice the entry fee of $2.50. Photography is permitted (free) only in the central room of the museum; in other rooms it must be approved by the director and a substantial fee paid.

You may be approached by a guide who will offer to explain the exhibits. Settle on a price in advance, and be sure it is understood the price is for your entire group, not per person.

As you stroll through the museum's exhibits, you should know that MÖ is the Turkish abbreviation for BC.

There are several charming restaurants uphill in the Hisar. See Places to Eat for details.

The Hittites

Before this century little was known about the Hittites, a people who commanded a vast Middle Eastern empire, conquered Babylon, and challenged the Egyptian pharaohs over 3000 years ago. Aside from a few written references to them in the Bible and Egyptian chronicles, there were few clues to their existence until 1834 when the French traveller Charles Texier stumbled on the ruins of the Hittite capital of Hattuşaş next to the Turkish village of Boğazköy (today called Boğazkale).

In 1905 excavations began. The digging produced notable works of art, most of them now preserved in Ankara's Museum of Anatolian Civilisations. Also brought to light were the Hittite state archives, written in cuneiform on thousands of clay tablets.

From these tablets, historians and archaeologists were able to construct a history of the Hittite Empire. Speaking an Indo-European language, the Hittites swept into Anatolia around 2000 BC, conquering the Hatti from whom they borrowed both their culture and name.

They established themselves at Hattuşaş, the Hatti capital, and in the course of a millennium enlarged and beautified the city. From about 1375 to 1200 BC, Hattuşaş was the capital of a Hittite Empire which, at its height, incorporated parts of Syria as well.

The Hittites worshipped over a thousand different deities but among the most important were Teshub, the storm god, and Hepatu, the sun goddess. The cuneiform tablets revealed a well-ordered society with more than 200 laws. The death sentence was prescribed for bestiality while thieves got off more lightly provided they paid their victims compensation. From about 1250 BC the Hittite Empire seems to have gone into a decline, its demise hastened by the arrival of the Phrygians. Only the city-states of Syria survived until they, too, were swallowed by the Assyrians.

Hisar

The imposing fortress just up the hill from the museum took its present form in the 9th century with the construction of the outer walls by the Byzantine emperor Michael II. The earlier inner walls date from the 7th century.

Walk up Gözcü Sokak from the Museum of Anatolian Civilisations past the octagonal tower, then turn left to enter the citadel by the **Parmak Kapısı** (Finger Gate), also called the Saatli Kapı (Clock Gate). Within the citadel is a traditional Turkish village, parts of it under restoration by the Ankara municipality. Not too far inside the Parmak Kapısı, to the left, is the **Old Turkish House Museum**, established and restored by the Ankara government.

As you wander about the citadel, you'll notice that all sorts of rubble, from broken column drums to bits of marble statuary and inscribed lintels, have been incorporated in the mighty walls over the ages. The citadel's small mosque, the **Alaettin Camii**, dates originally from the 12th century, but much has been rebuilt. Wander into the village, following any path that leads higher and you'll soon arrive at a flight of concrete stairs on the right leading to the **Şark Kulesi** (SHARK koo-leh-see, Eastern Tower), with panoramic city views. The tower at the north, **Ak Kale** (White Fort), also offers fine views. See Places to Eat for details of the several good restaurants in the Hisar.

Bazaar

The area around the Hisar's Parmak Kapısı has traditionally been a centre for trading in tiftik (Angora wool). Exiting the Hisar from the Parkmak Kapısı, turn left and walk down through the bazaar area, lined with vegetable stalls, copper and ironmongers and every variety of household item. Soon you will come to the Seljuk-built **Aslanhane Camii** (Lionhouse Mosque), which dates from the 13th century. Continue down the hill on Can Sokak and turn right into Anafartalar Caddesi for Ulus.

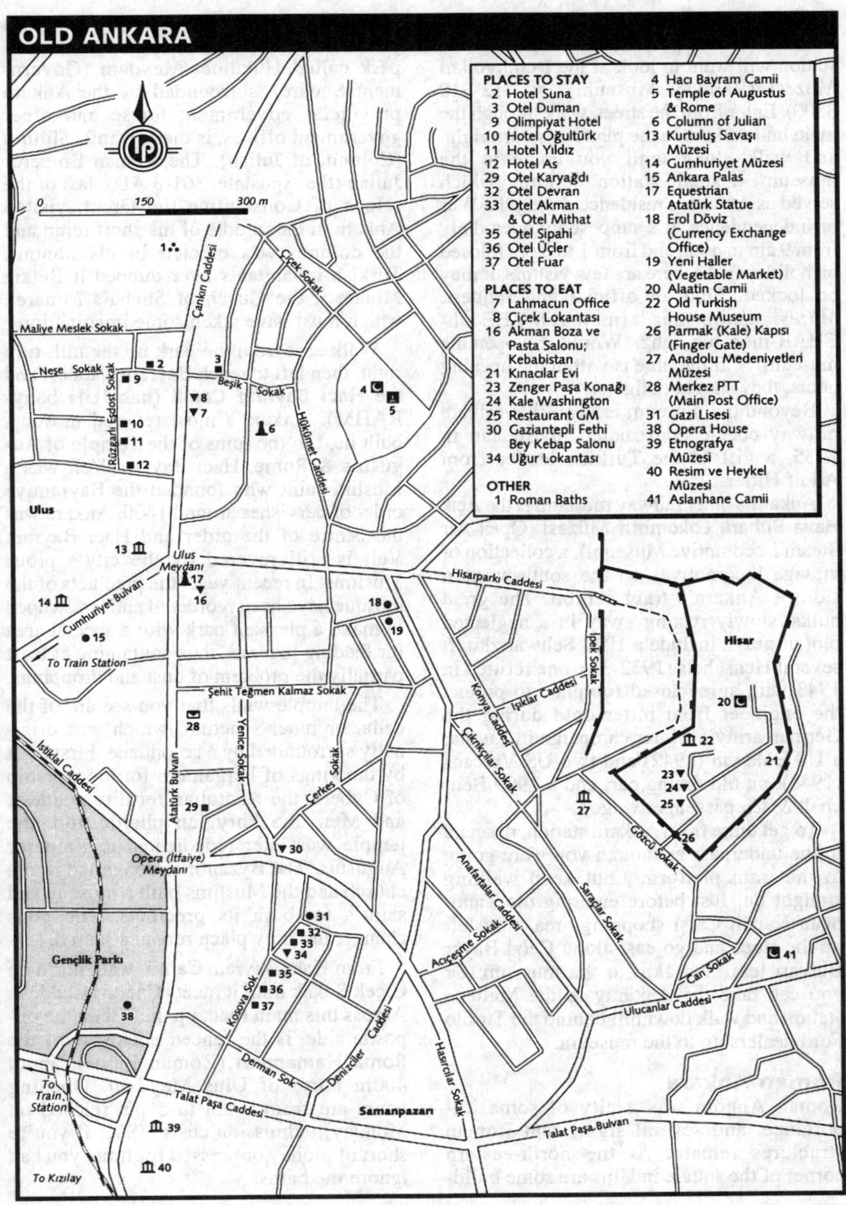
OLD ANKARA
0
150
300 m
PLACES TO STAY
2 Hotel Suna
3 Otel Duman
9 Olimpiyat Hotel
10 Hotel Oğultürk
11 Hotel Yıldız
12 Hotel As
29 Otel Karyağdı
32 Otel Devran
33 Otel Akman & Otel Mithat
35 Otel Sipahi
36 Otel Üçler
37 Otel Fuar
PLACES TO EAT
7 Lahmacun Office
8 Çiçek Lokantası
16 Akman Boza ve Pasta Salonu; Kebabistan
21 Kınacılar Evi
23 Zenger Paşa Konağı
24 Kale Washington
25 Restaurant GM
30 Gaziantepli Fethi Bey Kebap Salonu
34 Uğur Lokantası
OTHER
1 Roman Baths
4 Hacı Bayram Camii
5 Temple of Augustus & Rome
6 Column of Julian
13 Kurtuluş Savaşı Müzesi
14 Gumhuriyet Müzesi
15 Ankara Palas
17 Equestrian Atatürk Statue
18 Erol Döviz (Currency Exchange Office)
19 Yeni Haller (Vegetable Market)
20 Alaatin Camii
22 Old Turkish House Museum
26 Parmak (Kale) Kapısı (Finger Gate)
27 Anadolu Medeniyetleri Müzesi
28 Merkez PTT (Main Post Office)
31 Gazi Lisesi
38 Opera House
39 Etnografya Müzesi
40 Resim ve Heykel Müzesi
41 Aslanhane Camii
Çankırı Caddesi
Çiçek Sokak
Maliye Meslek Sokak
Neşe Sokak
Rüzgarlı Eşdost Sokak
Beşik Sokak
Hükümet Caddesi
Ulus
Ulus Meydanı
Cumhuriyet Bulvarı
Hisarparkı Caddesi
To Train Station
Şehit Teğmen Kalmaz Sokak
İpek Sokak
Konya Caddesi
Işıklar Caddesi
Hisar
Çıkrıkçılar Sokak
İstiklal Caddesi
Yenice Sokak
Atatürk Bulvarı
Çerkes Sokak
Gözcü Sokak
Opera (İtfaiye) Meydanı
Anafartalar Caddesi
Saraçlar Sokak
Gençlik Parkı
Acıçeşme Sokak
Can Sokak
Kosova Sok
Ulucanlar Caddesi
Denizciler Caddesi
Derman Sok
Hasırcılar Sokak
To Train Station
Talat Paşa Caddesi
Samanpazarı
Talat Paşa Bulvarı
To Kızılay

Railway Museums

Rail enthusiasts passing by Ankara's train station will want to look at the **Demiryolları Müzesi** (Railway Museum) (☎ 312-310 3500). Enter from the street, walk through the main hall and out to the platforms, turn right, and walk along until you come to the museum, a small station building which served as Atatürk's residence during the War of Independence. It's supposedly open daily from 9 am to noon and from 1 to 5 pm (closed on holidays). As there are few visitors, it may be locked. Find an official and request, *Müzeyi açarmısınız?* (mew-zeh-YEE ah-CHAR-muh-suh-nuhz, 'Would you open the museum?'). If the time is within the opening hours, they should oblige.

Beyond the museum is Atatürk's private railway coach, constructed in Breslau in 1935, a gift to the Turkish leader from Adolf Hitler.

Ankara's other railway museum is the **Açık Hava Buharlı Lokomotif Müzesi** (Open-Air Steam Locomotive Museum), a collection of vintage locomotives on the south-western side of Ankara's train station. The great hulks, slowly rusting away in a neglected plot of grass, include a 1924 Schwartzkopf; several Henschels (1932-33), one refitted in 1943 with an enclosed footplate to protect the engineer from bitter cold during the German army's winter campaign in Russia; a US Baldwin (1942) and two US Vulcans (1948); an old dining car; and a 1909 Beuchelt & Co passenger wagon.

To get there from Ankara station, descend to the underpass as though you were going to the train platforms, but keep walking straight on. Just before entering the Tandoğan Kapalı Çarşı shopping area, turn left up the steps and go east along Celal Bayar Bulvarı less than 1km to the museum. Or you can take the Ankaray to the Maltepe station and walk downhill behind the Turoto Ford dealership to the museum.

Roman Ankara

Roman Angora was a city of some importance, and several significant Roman structures remain. At the north-eastern corner of the square in Ulus are some buildings and behind them is the first stop on your tour of Roman Ankara. Set in a small park called Hükümet Meydanı (Government Square), surrounded by the Ankara provincial government house and other government offices, is the **Jülyanüs Sütunu** (Column of Julian). The Roman Emperor Julian (the Apostate, 361-3 AD), last of the scions of Constantine the Great, visited Ankara in the middle of his short reign and the column was erected in his honour. Turkish inhabitants later dubbed it Belkız Minaresi, the Queen of Sheba's Minaret, which must have taken some imagination.

Walk east from the park up the hill; turn right, then left to reach Bayram Caddesi and the **Hacı Bayram Camii** (hah-JUH bahy-RAHM), Ankara's most revered mosque, built next to the ruins of the **Temple of Augustus & Rome**. Hacı Bayram Veli was a Muslim saint who founded the Bayramiye order of dervishes around 1400. Ankara was the centre of the order and Hacı Bayram Veli is still revered by the city's pious Muslims. In recent years the precincts of the mosque have been reordered and landscaped to make a pleasant park with a special area for feeding pigeons, thus containing at least partially the problem of dust and droppings.

The temple walls that you see are of the cella, or inner sanctum, which was originally surrounded by a colonnade. First built by the kings of Pergamum for the worship of Cybele, the Anatolian fertility goddess, and Men, the Phrygian phallic god, the temple was later rededicated to Emperor Augustus. The Byzantines converted it to a church and the Muslims built a mosque and saint's tomb in its precincts. The gods change, the holy place remains sacred.

From Hacı Bayram Camii, walk north on Çiçek Sokak until it meets Çankırı Caddesi. Across this main road, up the hill on the opposite side, is the fenced enclosure of the **Roma Hamamları** (Roman Baths), about 400m north of Ulus Meydanı. Opening hours are from 9 am to 5 pm (closed on Monday); admission costs US$1. If you're short of money or pressed for time, you can ignore the baths.

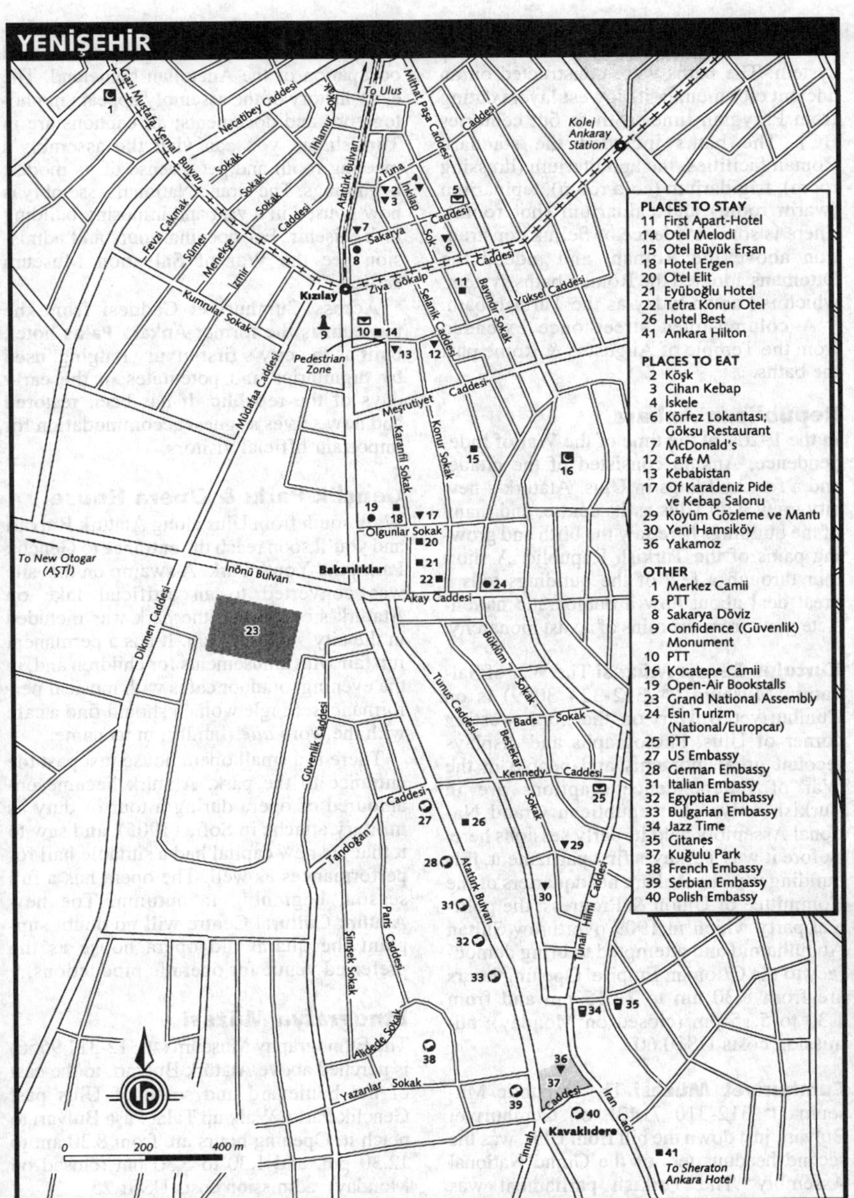
YENİŞEHİR
PLACES TO STAY
11 First Apart-Hotel
14 Otel Melodi
15 Otel Büyük Erşan
18 Hotel Ergen
20 Otel Elit
21 Eyüboğlu Hotel
22 Tetra Konur Otel
26 Hotel Best
41 Ankara Hilton
PLACES TO EAT
2 Köşk
3 Cihan Kebap
4 İskele
6 Körfez Lokantası; Göksu Restaurant
7 McDonald's
12 Café M
13 Kebabistan
17 Of Karadeniz Pide ve Kebap Salonu
29 Köyüm Gözleme ve Mantı
30 Yeni Hamsiköy
36 Yakamoz
OTHER
1 Merkez Camii
5 PTT
8 Sakarya Döviz
9 Confidence (Güvenlik) Monument
10 PTT
16 Kocatepe Camii
19 Open-Air Bookstalls
23 Grand National Assembly
24 Esin Turizm (National/Europcar)
25 PTT
27 US Embassy
28 German Embassy
31 Italian Embassy
32 Egyptian Embassy
33 Bulgarian Embassy
34 Jazz Time
35 Gitanes
37 Kuğulu Park
38 French Embassy
39 Serbian Embassy
40 Polish Embassy
To Ulus
Kolej Ankaray Station
Kızılay
Pedestrian Zone
Bakanlıklar
Kavaklıdere
To New Otogar (AŞTİ)
To Sheraton Ankara Hotel
Gazi Mustafa Kemal Bulvarı
Necatibey Caddesi
Mithat Paşa Caddesi
Atatürk Bulvarı
Ihlamur Sokak
Fevzi Çakmak Sokak
Sümer Sokak
Menekşe Sokak
İzmir Caddesi
Kumrular Sokak
Tuna Caddesi
İnkilap Sok
Sakarya Caddesi
Ziya Gökalp Caddesi
Yüksel Caddesi
Bayındır Sokak
Selanik Caddesi
Meşrutiyet Caddesi
Müdafaa Caddesi
Karanfil Sokak
Konur Sokak
Olgunlar Sokak
İnönü Bulvarı
Akay Caddesi
Dikmen Caddesi
Büklüm Sokak
Tunus Caddesi
Bade Sokak
Bestekar Sokak
Kennedy Caddesi
Güvenlik Caddesi
Tandoğan Caddesi
Paris Caddesi
Şimşek Sokak
Alidede Sokak
Yazanlar Sokak
Tunalı Hilmi Caddesi
Cinnah Caddesi
İran Cad
0 200 400 m

The layout of the 3rd century baths is clearly visible, as is much of the water system. The baths were constructed on an ancient city mound, its lowest layers dating from Phrygian times (8th to 6th centuries BC). The baths included the standard Roman facilities: the apoditerium (dressing room), frigidarium (cold room), tepidarium (warm room) and caldarium (hot room). There is some evidence of Seljuk construction above the Roman, and indeed the Ottomans adopted the Roman baths system, which is known today as the Turkish bath.

A column-lined street once extended from the Temple of Augustus & Rome past the baths.

Republican Ankara

In the 1920s, at the time of the War of Independence, Ankara consisted of the citadel and a few buildings in Ulus. Atatürk's new city grew with Ulus as its centre, and many of the buildings here saw the birth and growing pains of the Turkish Republic. A short tour through a few of the buildings tells a great deal about how a democratic nation-state grew from the ruins of a vast monarchy.

Kurtuluş Savaşı Müzesi The War of Salvation Museum (☎ 312-324 3049) is on Cumhuriyet Bulvarı on the north-western corner of Ulus. Photographs and displays recount great moments and people in the War of Independence; captions are in Turkish only. The republican Grand National Assembly held its early sessions here. Before it was Turkey's first parliament, this building was the Ankara headquarters of the Committee of Union & Progress, the political party which in 1909 overthrew Sultan Abdülhamid and attempted to bring democracy to the Ottoman Empire. Opening hours are from 8.30 am to 12.15 pm and from 1.30 to 5.15 pm (closed on Monday); admission costs US$0.60.

Cumhuriyet Müzesi The Republic Museum (☎ 312-310 7140), on Cumhuriyet Bulvarı, just down the hill from Ulus, was the second headquarters of the Grand National Assembly. The Turkish parliament was founded by Atatürk in his drive for a national consensus to resist foreign invasion and occupation of the Anatolian homeland. The early history of the assembly appears in photographs and documents; all captions are in Turkish but you can visit the assembly's meeting room and get a sense of its modest beginnings. The Grand National Assembly is now housed in a vast and imposing building in Yenişehir. For opening hours and admission see the War of Salvation Museum earlier.

Across Cumhuriyet Caddesi from the museum is the former **Ankara Palas** hotel, built as the city's first luxury lodging, used by dignitaries and potentates in the early days of the republic. It has been restored and now serves as guest accommodation for important official visitors.

Gençlik Parkı & Opera House

Walk south from Ulus along Atatürk Bulvarı and you'll soon reach the entrance to Gençlik Parkı, the Youth Park. A swamp on this site was converted to an artificial lake on Atatürk's orders and the park was included in the city's master plan. It has a permanent fun fair with amusements for children and, in the evening, outdoor cafes with musical performances. Single women should find a cafe with the word *aile* (family) in its name.

There is a small opera house just past the entrance to the park. Atatürk became enamoured of opera during a tour of duty as military attaché in Sofia (1905), and saw to it that his new capital had a suitable hall for performances as well. The opera has a full season, beginning in autumn. The new Atatürk Cultural Centre will no doubt supplant the quaint old opera house as the preferred venue for operatic productions.

Etnografya Müzesi

The Ethnography Museum (☎ 312-311 9556) is perched above Atatürk Bulvarı, to the east of the boulevard and south of Ulus past Gençlik Parkı. Walk up Talat Paşa Bulvarı to reach it. Opening hours are from 8.30 am to 12.30 pm, and 1.30 to 5.30 pm (closed on Monday); admission costs US$1.25.

The building, which once housed Atatürk's offices, is a white marble post-Ottoman structure (1925) with an equestrian statue of the great man in front. Upon entering, you confront a marble slab with an inscription which translates as: 'This is the place where Atatürk, who entered into eternity on 10-xi-1938, lay from 21-xi-1938 until 10-xi-1953', after which his body was transferred to the just completed Anıt Kabir.

The museum's collection is wide-ranging and well chosen, with especially rich exhibits of *hattat* (Islamic calligraphy) and woodwork. The Sünnet Odası (Circumcision Room) is furnished in the sumptuous style of the Ottoman nobility. Weapons, metalwork, costumes, embroidery and musical instruments are represented as well.

Next door to the Ethnography Museum is the **Resim ve Heykel Müzesi** (Painting & Sculpture Museum), in the building which once served as headquarters for Atatürk's nation-building Turkish Hearths organisation. If you have an intense interest in the modern development of Turkish painting – or an hour to really murder – stroll through the galleries picking out the Ottoman-era scenes of Osman Hamdi, the forceful strokework of Hikmet Onat (1882-1977), the pseudo-primitive scenes of village life by Turgut Zaim (1906-74), and the vigorous work in several styles of Bedri Rahmi Eyüboğlu, who was also an accomplished poet. If you've come this far, don't miss the paintings by those who inspired Ottoman painting: hanging on the left side of the main staircase are works by Aivazovsky, Keresagin and Zonaro.

The museum is open from 9 am to noon and 1 to 5 pm (closed on Monday); admission is free.

Ulus Markets

Ulus is the city's shopping epicentre, with huge crowds every day and long lines at the ATMs.

Walk up the hill on Hisarparkı Caddesi, out of Ulus and turn right at the first traffic signal onto Susam Sokak; a Ziraat Bankası will be on your right. Bear left, then turn left and on your right will be Ankara's **Yeni Haller** (vegetable market), a good place for buying supplies or photographing colourful local life.

Behind the vegetable market, on Konya Caddesi, is the **Vakıf Suluhan Çarşısı**, a restored *han* with lots of clothing shops, a cafe, toilets and a free-standing small mosque at the centre of its courtyard.

Anıt Kabir

Atatürk's mausoleum (☎ 312-231 7975), called the Anıt Kabir (ah-NUHT-kah-beer, Monumental Tomb), stands on top of a small hill in a green park about 2km west of Kızılay along Gazi Mustafa Kemal Bulvarı. If you saw Ankara from the Hisar or the terrace of the Ethnography Museum, you've already admired from a distance the rectangular mausoleum, with squared columns around its sides.

A visit to the tomb is essential when you visit Ankara. Opening hours are from 9 am to 5 pm (4 pm in winter) every day; admission is free. The museum within the complex closes from noon to 1.30 pm. The nearest Ankaray station is Tandoğan, which is 1500m north of Anıtkabir. You can walk uphill to the mausoleum (about 20 minutes), or take a taxi (US$2).

Up the steps from the car park you pass between statues and two square kiosks; the right-hand kiosk holds a model of the tomb and photos of its construction. Then you pass down a monumental avenue flanked by Hittite stone lions to the courtyard.

To the right as you enter the courtyard, beneath the western colonnade, is the **sarcophagus of İsmet İnönü** (1884-1973), Atatürk's close friend and chief of staff, a republican general (hero of the Battle of İnönü, from which he took his surname), diplomat, prime minister and second president of the republic.

Across the courtyard, on the eastern side, is a **museum** which holds memorabilia and personal effects of Atatürk. You can also see his official automobiles, several of which are US-made Lincolns. A video of Atatürk's life and times is shown continuously from 10 am to noon and 2 to 4.30 pm.

As you approach the tomb proper, the high-stepping guards will jump to action. Past the colonnade, look left and right at the gilded inscriptions, which are quotations from Atatürk's speech celebrating the 10th anniversary of the republic (in 1932). As you enter the tomb through its huge bronze doors, you must remove your hat (if you don't, a guard will remind you of the correct protocol). The lofty hall is lined in red marble and sparingly decorated with mosaics in timeless Turkish folk designs. At the northern end stands an immense marble **cenotaph**, cut from a single piece of stone. The actual tomb is beneath it.

The Anıt Kabir was begun in 1944 and finished in 1953. Its design seeks to capture the spirit of Anatolia: monumental, spare but beautiful. Echoes of several great Anatolian empires, from the Hittite to the Roman and Seljuk, are included in its design. The final effect is one of Anatolian timelessness.

Cumhurbaşkanlığı Köşkü

At the far southern end of Atatürk Bulvarı in Çankaya is the Presidential Mansion. Within the mansion's beautiful gardens is the **Çankaya Köşkü**, or Çankaya Atatürk Müzesi. This picturesque chalet was Atatürk's country residence, set amid vineyards and evergreens. In the early days of the republic it was a retreat from the town, but now the town spreads beyond it. Visits to the mansion's gardens and grounds and to the museum are permitted on Sunday afternoons from 1.30 to 5.30 pm, and on holidays from 12.30 to 5.30 pm, free of charge. Bring your passport.

Take any Çankaya-bound bus or taxi to the far southern end of Atatürk Bulvarı, where you will find an entrance to the grounds of the Presidential Mansion. Tell the bus or taxi driver you want to go to the Çankaya Köşkü (CHAHN-kah-yah kursh-kur). At the guardhouse, exchange your passport for an identity badge, leave your camera, and a guide will accompany you through the museum.

The house is preserved as Atatürk used it, with decor and furnishings from the 1930s. You enter a vestibule, then turn right into a games room, complete with tables for billiards and cards (the British ambassador was a favourite card partner). The next room is a green (Atatürk's favourite colour) parlour. The large dining room at the back of the house has its own little nook for after-dinner coffee, cigars and brandy.

Upstairs is a formal office, the bedroom and bath, another work room and the library (note the many books in foreign languages).

Downstairs again, to the left of the vestibule is a reception room for dignitaries.

Places to Stay

Ulus has numerous budget and mid-range hotels. Yenişehir has good mid-range hotels. The top-end hotels are in Kavaklıdere.

Places to Stay – Budget

Near Ulus İtfaiye Meydanı (also called Opera Meydanı), on the eastern side of Atatürk Bulvarı across from the opera house, is the centre of the cheap hotel district. To find it, ask anyone to point the way to Gazi Lisesi (GAH-zee lee-seh-see), the renowned high school on the eastern side of the square.

Otel Devran *(☎ 312-311 0485, Tavus Sokak 8)* is an older building, well used, but with nice touches such as marble staircases, brass trim and little chandeliers. Doubles cost US$15 with shower, US$18 with bath.

The two-star, 49 room ***Otel Akman*** *(☎ 312-324 4140, Tavus Sokak 6)*, next to the Devran, is in sore need of renovation. Until then, its rates of US$15/19 a single/double with shower are too high. The much better-kept ***Otel Mithat*** *(☎ 312-311 5410, Tavus Sokak 2)*, adjoining the Akman, is a better choice with shower-equipped doubles for US$17.

Otel Sipahi *(☎ 312-324 0235, Kosova Sokak 1)* is old and dingy but serviceable in a pinch, and certainly cheap at US$10 for a double with shower, even cheaper without. A few steps further down the street, ***Otel Üçler*** *(☎ 312-310 6664, Kosova Sokak 7)* is clean and proper, if very simple and well worn, with waterless rooms for US$9 a double.

Perhaps the best value on the street is at the brightly painted ***Otel Fuar*** *(☎ 312-312 3288, Kosova Sokak 11)*, where US$9 gets you a decent double room and sink, with showers down the hall; but showers cost US$3, so a double room with shower at US$12 is probably a better deal.

On the northern side of Ulus are several other good choices.

Cross to the western side of Çankırı Caddesi and down the slope to Soğukkuyu Sokak to find some quieter hotels. The old ***Hotel Suna*** *(☎ 312-324 3250, Soğukkuyu Sokak 6)* is hardly beautiful, but is at least cheapish at US$14 for a quiet double room with shower.

Also here is ***Olimpiyat Hotel*** *(☎ 312-324 3331, Rüzgarlı Eşdost Sokak 18)*, with more modern, comfortable rooms for just slightly more: US$20 for a double with shower, breakfast included.

Walk south along Rügarlı Eşdost Sokak from the Olimpiyat, past the new Hotel Oğultürk and turn left (east) to find the older but still serviceable one-star ***Hotel As*** *(☎ 312-310 3998, fax 312 7584, Rüzgarlı Sokak 4)*, with double rooms for US$16/20 with sink/shower.

Places to Stay – Mid-Range

Near Ulus Compared to mid-range hotels in Yenişehir, those near Ulus offer similar comfort for less money, with the advantage of being within walking distance of the Hisar and museum.

Otel Duman *(☎ 312-310 0212, fax 310 1034, Çankırı Caddesi, Ortan Sokak 7)* is modern, quiet, convenient, and favoured by Turkish businessmen. Room prices are posted at US$35/60 a single/double, but I was quoted US$19/28 when I asked about the price.

There are nearly a dozen two-and three-star hotels north of Ulus on the western side of Çankırı Caddesi, but most are hopelessly noisy. For the quiet ones, go one street west of Çankırı Caddesi to Rüzgarlı Eşdost Sokak and the new three-star ***Hotel Oğultürk*** *(☎ 312-309 2900, fax 311 8321, Rüzgarlı Eşdost Sokak 6)*. Its boldly modern architecture contrasts sharply with the general workaday look of the modest street. The 54 rooms and five suites, most with TV and minibar, are comfortable at US$26/40, breakfast included.

Hotel Yıldız *(☎ 312-7581, fax 312 7584, Rüzgarlı Eşdost Sokak 4)*, adjoining the Oğultürk to the south, is an equally comfortable and new three-star, 60 room hotel with rooms at even lower prices.

South-east of Ulus, on the way to İtfaiye (Opera) Meydanı, the older two-star ***Otel Karyağdı*** *(☎ 312-310 2440, fax 312 6712, Sanayi Caddesi, Kuruçeşme Sokak 4)* is quiet and still serviceable, though a bit overpriced at US$28/42 a single/double, breakfast included. They're ready to haggle if business is slow.

Near Kızılay Several good hotel choices are on quiet tree-shaded streets south-east of Kızılay in the district called Bakanlıklar. All have rooms with private bath and TV, and many have air-con and minibars as well. Most will drop prices a bit when not busy, especially if you plan to stay for more than one night.

First Apart-Hotel *(☎/fax 312-425 7575, İnkilap Sokak 29)*, a small modern building on a quiet back street three blocks east of Kızılay, has four types of accommodation: standard double rooms with bath and TV for US$55, deluxe for US$75, suites for US$95, and apartments for US$165. These prices are more often than not discounted by at least 20% on the slightest excuse, especially if your stay lasts more than one or two days.

Otel Melodi *(☎ 312-417 6414, fax 418 7858, Karanfil Sokak 10)* is a mere block from Kızılay on a pedestrian-only street, relatively quiet and very convenient, it charges US$50/70 a single/double for room and breakfast.

The three-star, 52 room ***Eyüboğlu Hotel*** *(☎ 312-417 6400, fax 417 8125, Karanfil Sokak 73)* is used by Turkish groups, and offers comfy, quiet rooms for US$50/70.

The two-star, 40 room ***Otel Elit*** *(☎ 312-417 4695, fax 417 4697, Olgunlar Sokak 10)*, at Karanfil Sokak, is shaded by trees, and is steps away from Olgunlar Sokak's used books stalls. Rooms of moderate comfort cost US$65 a double, breakfast included. Across the street, the ***Metropol*** *(☎ 312-417 3060, fax 417 6990, Olgunlar Sokak 5)* is similar in comforts and price.

The simple one-star, 56 room ***Hotel Ergen*** *(☎ 312-417 5906, fax 425 7819, Karanfil Sokak 48)*, near Olgunlar Sokak, has a terrace cafe and charges only US$25/35 for rooms with bath.

The three-star ***Otel Büyük Erşan*** *(☎ 312-417 6045, fax 417 4943, Selanik Caddesi 74)* has 90 standard rooms on a quiet street for a reasonable US$24/40 a double.

Places to Stay – Top End

For dignified, well-located four-star accommodation at decent prices, try ***Hotel Best*** *(☎ 312-467 0880 or 468 1122, fax 467 0885, Atatürk Bulvarı 195)*, across the street from the US embassy. Rates are US$125/150, breakfast included. Advance reservations are usually necessary.

Tetra Konur Otel *(☎ 312-419 2946, fax 417 4915, Konur Sokak 58)* is on a quiet street and has four-star comforts and understated elegance. The posted prices of US$120/140 a single/double with breakfast are usually subject to 30% discounts if they aren't full.

Ankara Hilton *(☎ 312-468 2888, fax 168 0909, Tahran Caddesi 12)*, has 327 plush rooms and suites on 16 floors near Çankaya and the embassies. The hotel's bold, modern architecture uses traditional Anatolian coloured stone, brass, glass and lots of greenery. Rates are from US$150 to US$220 a single, US$160 to US$260 a double.

The 311 room ***Sheraton Ankara Hotel & Towers*** *(☎ 312-468 5454, fax 467 1136)*, Noktalı Sokak, in Gaziosmanpaşa, is a landmark cylindrical high-rise building which towers above this pleasant residential quarter. Views from the upper-floor rooms in the Sheraton Towers section are superb. Rates are from US$160 to US$235 a single, US$180 to US$280 a double.

Places to Eat – Budget

İtfaiye (Opera) Meydanı Facing İtfaiye Meydanı is the ***Gaziantepli Fethi Bey Kebap Salonu***, on the northern side of the Otel Güleryüz, specialising in kebaps from south-eastern Turkey. Expect to spend between US$3.50 and US$5 for a full meal here.

Near Ulus North of Ulus, along Çankırı Caddesi, the left-hand (western) side of the street has several big, bright restaurants featuring rotisserie chicken, and other dishes; many serve beer.

On the eastern side of Çankırı, the brightly coloured, amusingly named ***Lahmacun Office*** specialises in Arab-style pizza, and has Turkish and Italian varieties as well. You can tuck in here for around US$5.

The most refined choice is the long-time favourite ***Çiçek Lokantası*** (chee-CHEK) *(☎ 312-311 5997, Çankırı Caddesi 12/A)*, a half-block north of the square on the right-hand side. Dine next to the little *havuz* (pool, fountain) in the dining room amid the tables with white tablecloths. Soup, kebap, salad and drink comes to US$6 to US$10.

Walk south on the eastern side of Atatürk Bulvarı and turn into the second courtyard to find the ***Akman Boza ve Pasta Salonu***, Atatürk Bulvarı 3. Breakfasts, light lunches (sandwiches, omelettes etc) and pastries are not cheap, but in part you're paying for the pleasant garden setting. Boza, the fermented millet drink, though traditionally a winter favourite, is served all year here. Expect to spend from US$4 or US$5 for a light lunch, less for tea and pastry.

Right above the Akman Boza is ***Kebabistan*** (Kebap-Land) *(☎ 312-310 8080)*, a family oriented kebap and pide parlour serving fresh, cheap pide (US$1.25 to US$2) and kebaps (US$2 to US$3) all day, every day. There's a newer, more modern branch of Kebabistan near Kızılay, but the food's better here in the original location.

You can escape the noise and fumes of the city in Gençlik Parkı and seek out the wistfully named ***Sahil Lokantası*** (Shore

Restaurant), on the northern side of the lake near the open-air theatre called the Muhsin Ertuğrul Açık Hava Tiyatrosu. The Sahil has shaded tables by the lakeside, and inexpensive mezes (US$1.25) and kebaps (US$2.50).

Near Kızılay The streets north of Ziya Gökalp Caddesi and east of Atatürk Bulvarı are closed to motor vehicles and lined with places to eat and drink. Cheap, filling snacks such as *balık-ekmek* (fish-bread, a fried-fish sandwich) and *dönerli sandviç* (döner kebap in bread) sell for about US$1.25. *Kumpir*, a huge baked potato with a sauce or topping, is another favourite. Selanik Sokak north of Ziya Gökalp Caddesi is the best for cheap kebaps, with dozens of places to choose from.

South of Yüksel Caddesi, Selanik Sokak turns into a cafe-pastry shop scene, with a row of streetside cafes drawing the capital's gilded youth. ***Café M*** *(☎ 312-419 3665, Selanik 40-42)*, serves excellent *kazandibi* and decent coffee and tea. Pastry or pudding and a beverage should cost no more than US$2 or US$3, and they do kumpir and pizza as well. Also check out the Selanik incarnation of the ***Akman Boza ve Pasta Salonu*** at No 44, and the neighbouring ***Rest-Out***, yet another cafe.

Sakarya Caddesi is parallel to and one block north of Ziya Gökalp Caddesi. Walk along Sakarya Caddesi to the big Sakarya Süper Marketi, the ground floor of which is devoted to snack stands. Just to the right of the market are more snack stands (try the ***Otlangaç)*** selling İstanbul Çiçek Pasaj-style fried mussels on a stick, *bodrum lokması* (sweet fritters), *kuzu kokoreç* (grilled sheep's intestines) and similar treats.

For good kebap in a sit-down place, find ***Cihan Kebap***, Selanik Caddesi 3/B, between Sakarya and Tuna Caddesis. A full meal with soup, bread and kebap costs from US$4 to US$6.

South of Yüksel Caddesi is the Kızılay branch of ***Kebabistan***, Karanfil Sokak 15/A, across the street from the Hotel Melodi. The outdoor tables are pleasant. Döner kebap with yoghurt, salad and a soft drink costs less than US$4.

Even nicer is the nearby ***Of Karadeniz Pide ve Kebap Salonu***, Karanfil Sokak 63, across the street from the Hotel Elit. The shady vine-covered terrace, complete with tinkling fountain, is a welcome oasis for a meal of soup, kebap and salad for less than US$4.50.

For those who need a Big Mac fix, there's a ***McDonald's*** at Atatürk Bulvarı 89, just north of Kızılay, on the eastern side of the boulevard. A plain burger costs just over US$1, but as usual the combo meals (cheeseburger, drink and fries for US$2.75) provide the best value for money.

Places to Eat – Mid-Range

Citadel (Hisar) Within the citadel walls, several old houses have been converted to atmospheric restaurants. Come here for lunch after a visit to the Museum of Anatolian Civilisations, or for a special dinner. All are open every day from 11 am to midnight, and serve alcoholic beverages.

The historic restaurant trend was begun at the ***Zenger Paşa Konağı*** *(☎ 312-311 7070, Doyran Sokak 13)*, and it is still the best of the lot. A virtual museum of oldtime Ankara with a dining room on top, the Zenger's cuisine is Ottoman and fiercely authentic – even to the extent of having local women knead, roll and bake the wafer-thin village bread before your eyes. Try *gözleme* (folded, fried pastry with cheese, meat or vegetable filling), *mantı* (Turkish ravioli), and köfte or şiş kebap served on a hot tile. Full meals cost US$8 to US$12. The views from the dining room are spectacular, the several museum rooms drenched with atmosphere. Look for the Zenger Paşa downhill beyond the Kale Washington restaurant.

If you go through the Parmak Kapısı and walk straight on for several hundred metres you will come to the ***Kınacılar Evi*** *(☎ 312-311 1010, Kalekapısı Sokak 28)*, on the right. This lofty Ottoman konak (mansion) is popular with tour groups, serving Ottoman and modern Turkish cuisine in gracious old salons decorated in 19th-century style. Try the *çerkez tavuğu* (chicken in walnut sauce), or the chicken and vegetable casserole. Full meals cost from US$8 to US$15 per person, drinks included. There's an open-air cafe at the back.

Restaurant GM *(☎ 312-312 6903 or 310 8041, Doyuran Sokak 3)* features a south-eastern Turkish menu à la Gaziantep, with spicy kebaps and moderate prices of US$7 to US$14 for a meal.

Kale Washington *(☎ 312-311 4344, Doyuran Sokak 5-7)*, has the highest prices and least authentic Ottoman atmosphere of the lot. The menu is Turkish-style continental, which means such things as *şatobriyan* (chateaubriand), böf stroganof, and chicken Kievsky. Meals tend to cost US$10 to US$20 all in, except if you order the outrageous brochette-grilled shrimp for US$35.

Near Kızılay The place to look for good, moderately priced food near Kızılay is along Bayındır Sokak, to the east of Atatürk Bulvarı and south of Ziya Gökalp Caddesi.

Köşk, İnkilap Sokak 2, at Tuna Caddesi, is a veritable kebap palace at unbeatable prices. This huge two-storey eatery blazes with light, shining crystal and burnished brass, with fountains playing. Elaborate kebaps, pides and lahmacuns cost only US$2.50 to US$5.

You can't go wrong at the ***Körfez Lokantası*** (keur-FEHZ, 'gulf'), Bayındır Sokak 24, a half-block north of Ziya Gökalp Caddesi. Dining rooms are starkly plain; the terrace is preferable in good weather. Fish is the speciality for around US$5 to US$9 per plate, but there are many kebaps priced under US$4. Your meal comes with plenteous lavahş, freshly made flat unleavened village bread.

Next door to the Körfez is the ***Göksu Restaurant***, Bayındır Sokak 22/A, a long-standing favourite with much fancier surroundings, diligent service, and Turkish and continental cuisine. Have the filet mignon: good quality at prices similar to those at Körfez.

Another good seafood place with a taverna-style atmosphere is ***İskele***, Sakarya Caddesi, Bayındır Sokak 14/C. Start with fried mussels or a *karides güveçi* (shrimp casserole), and go on to grilled or poached fish, and you'll pay from US$10 to US$14, wine or beer included. İskele is closed on Sunday. Bayındır Sokak is lined with similar places.

Kavaklıdere Kavaklıdere, the posh residential district up the hill towards Çankaya, has a good assortment of restaurants. Take a bus south (uphill) along Atatürk Bulvarı and get out at Kuğulu Park next to the Polonya Büyükelçiliği, (Polish embassy) then walk east one short block to Tunalı Hilmi Caddesi, the district's main commercial street.

Yakamoz *(☎ 312-426 3752, Tunalı Hilmi Caddesi 114/J 2-3)*, right at the edge of Kuğulu Park, is a big, busy place specialising in seafood. The best deal is the set menu with drinks for US$14 per couple. Ordering a la carte, seafood plates cost around US$5 or US$6.

For a look at the district's other restaurants, stroll north (downhill) along Tunalı Hilmi, turning left onto Bestekar Sokak.

Black Sea cookery is the speciality at ***Yeni Hamsiköy*** *(☎ 312-427 7576, Bestekar Sokak 78)*, off Tunalı Hilmi at Bülten Sokak. The garden terrace, open in fine weather, is the place to try *hamsi* (fresh anchovies) served in omelettes, dolmas or corn bread; there's also *kara lahana* (black cabbage) and other Black Sea specialities. The food and service are excellent, and prices are moderate at US$10 to US$16 or so per person, beer, wine or rakı included.

Just up the street on Bülten Sokak (between Bestekar and Tunalı Hilmi), ***Köyüm Gözleme ve Mantı*** *(☎ 312-426 4148)* is decorated in a Turkish village theme. The specialities are *gözleme*, the fried folded pastry filled with cheese, meat or vegetables; and mantı, or Turkish ravioli. A full meal with drinks should cost no more than US$7 or US$8 per person.

For a romantic dinner with low lights and soft music, seek out ***Villa*** *(☎ 312-427 0838, Boğaz Sokak 13)*, on a quiet residential street up the hill behind the Sheraton. The menu is what Ankara diners consider 'exotic', which is to say lots of dishes with mushrooms and cheese. They have pizzas as well. The most expensive main course is bonfile (filet mignon) for US$9. Dinner with drinks won't be much more than US$15 or US$20 per person.

Entertainment

Most visitors don't hang around in Ankara long enough to get deep into the nightlife. However, it's easy enough to find an evening's amusement.

Beer Gardens, Gazinos & Teahouses For drinks and talk Turkish-style, head for Kızılay and Bayındır Sokak between Sakarya Caddesi and Tuna Sokak. The street is lined with Turkish beer gardens, among them ***Forza***, which usually has live Turkish pop music, beers for little more than US$1.25, and food as well.

Another good venue for drinks and conversation is Gençlikı Park, just west of Opera Meydanı. Walk around the lake to the fountain pool on its west. On the southern side of the pool are Turkish-style gazinos with live entertainment, drinks and food at low to moderate prices; on the northern side are mostly teahouses which vie with one another to advertise the lowest-priced beer.

Bars & Discos The posh bar-lounge jazz club scene is in Kavaklıdere, Gaziosmanpaşa and Çankaya. From Kuğulu Park in Kavaklıdere, go north on Tunalı Hilmi Caddesi one block to Bilir Sokak and turn right to find ***Jazz Time***, Bilir Sokak 4/1, which usually has live Turkish pop or folk artists, and, behind it, the quieter ***Gitanes*** bar. Local drinks are the standard US$2.50 for rakı or gin and tonic, and about US$1.50 for beer.

Çengel Café *(☎ 312-426 1851)*, Noktalı Sokak 8/1, directly opposite the entrance to the Sheraton, is a bit more upscale and popular with a young, well-heeled crowd. A shady garden at the back, a menu of Turkish snacks, and live music each evening after 10.30 pm are the draw. It can get very busy on weekends.

Cinema Several cinemas show recently released western films, usually in the original language with Turkish subtitles. Look for these venues: Akün Sineması (☎ 312-427 7656), Atatürk Bulvarı 227 in Kavaklıdere; the Kavaklıdere (☎ 312-426 7379) at Tunalı Hilmi Caddesi 105, and the Metropol (☎ 312-425 7478), at Selanik Caddesi 76 in Kızılay.

Opera, Ballet & Symphony Beginning in the autumn and running through until spring, Ankara has regular seasons of opera, ballet, symphony and chamber music, often with visiting foreign artists. The performances, though not of a standard to win rave reviews in New York, Paris or Rome, are enthusiastically done, and tickets are ridiculously low in price – usually around US$4 to US$6.

Among the most active sponsors of symphony, chamber music and classical recitals is Bilkent University (☎ 312-266 4539), which announces all its upcoming events in the *Turkish Daily News*, as do other sponsors.

Getting There & Away

In Turkey, all roads lead to Ankara.

Air İstanbul's Atatürk airport is the country's major international airport, but Ankara's Esenboğa airport (☎ 312-398 0000), 33km north of the city centre, has good domestic connections.

Turkish Airlines (THY) (☎ 312-419 2825 for information, 419 2800 for reservations, fax 418 9453) has offices at Atatürk Bulvarı 125, Bakanlıklar, and Atatürk Bulvarı 231/3, Kavaklıdere.

İstanbul Airlines (☎ 312-432 2234 or 431 0920, fax 417 2489), Atatürk Bulvarı 64/1, Kızılay, has many nonstop flights.

Most one-way fares from Ankara on THY cost between US$70 and US$100; İstanbul Airlines' fares are somewhat lower. Following is a list of nonstop flights in summer; many more flights are available via connections in İstanbul. All flights are operated by Turkish Airlines unless stated otherwise, and remember that all schedules are subject to change:

Adana – three daily; Friday (İstanbul Airlines)
Ağrı – Tuesday and Friday
Antalya – two daily; Thursday (İstanbul Airlines)
Batman – daily
Bodrum – Friday and Sunday
Dalaman – Friday and Sunday
Diyarbakır – two daily
Elazığ – daily
Erzincan – Tuesday, Thursday and Saturday
Erzurum – twice daily
Gaziantep – daily
İstanbul – more than 15 flights daily; Wednesday and Thursday (İstanbul Airlines)
İzmir – four daily; Saturday (İstanbul Airlines)
Kahramanmaraş – Tuesday and Sunday
Kars – daily
Malatya – daily
Muş – daily
Samsun – Monday and Friday
Şanlıurfa – daily except Tuesday and Thursday
Siirt – daily except Tuesday and Saturday
Sivas – Wednesday and Friday
Tokat – Tuesday
Trabzon – two daily
Van – two daily

Other international airlines sometimes have flights to Ankara, or connections with Turkish Airlines' flights at İstanbul. The addresses of airline offices in Ankara are as follows:

Aeroflot
(☎ 312-440 9874, fax 440 9220)
Cinnah Caddesi 114/2, Çankaya
Air France
(☎ 312-467 4400 or 468 2595)
Atatürk Bulvarı 231/7, Kavaklıdere
Alitalia
(☎ 312-425 3813 or 417 9796)
Emek İşhanı, 11th floor, Kızılay
British Airways
(☎ 312-467 5557 or 427 3313)
Atatürk Bulvarı 237/29, Kavaklıdere
KLM
(☎ 312-417 5617, fax 440 6108)
Atatürk Bulvarı 127, 3rd floor, Bakanlıklar
Sabena World Airlines
(☎ 312-467 2535) Tunalı Hilmi Caddesi 112/1, Kavaklıdere
Singapore Airlines
(☎ 312-468 4670) Tunalı Hilmi Caddesi, Bülten Sokak 17/3, Kavaklıdere
Swissair
(☎ 312-468 1144, fax 468 4845)
Cinnah Caddesi 1/2A, Kavaklıdere

Bus Every city or town of any size – and even the occasional village – has direct buses to Ankara. From İstanbul there is a bus to Ankara at least every 15 minutes throughout the day and even late into the night.

AŞTİ (Ankara Şehirlerarası Terminalı İşletmesi), Ankara's gigantic bus terminal, is also known as the Yeni Terminal, Yeni Otogar and Yeni Garaj. It's at the western end of the Ankaray underground train line, 5km due west of Bakanlıklar and the Grand National Assembly building, on Bahçelerarası Caddesi (Konya Devlet Yolu) just north of İsmet İnönü Bulvarı (Eskişehir Yolu).

The terminal follows the traditional airport plan with departure gates on the upper level and arrivals on the lower. A huge airport-style tote board lists departures and arrivals, but as these are not organised beyond time (ie alphabetically by company or destination), the board is of limited use in determining when the next bus will depart for your desired destination, although it does tell you which *peron* (gate) your bus departs from. The information clerk seated beneath the tote board can advise you on the next bus out.

AŞTİ has a restaurant and tea service, snack shops, a mosque, first aid station, nursery, bank ATMs, telephones and most other services you might want.

The *emanet* (left-luggage room) is on the lower level, with prices based on the value of the item!

On the lower level (Geliş Peronları) are lots of empty benches where you can spread out and have a rest if you have a longish wait.

As Ankara has many buses to all parts of the country, it is often sufficient to arrive at the otogar, with your baggage in hand, buy a ticket, and be on your way within an hour or less.

AŞTİ has 80 *gişe* (ticket counters). The major companies are:

bus company	gişe no
Kamil Koç	17-18
Köseoğlu	48
Metro	41
Pamukkale	58-59
Uludağ	45
Ulusoy	13
Varan	12

If these lines don't go to your destination, officials will give you the number of the gişe with the best company which does go there.

Here are translations of some of the more prominent signs:

Alış Veriş	Shopping
Ankaray	Underground Train
Bekleme Yerleri	Waiting Areas
Gelen Yolcu Katı	Arrivals Level
Giden Yolcu Katı	Departures Level
Gitmedi	Not Yet Departed
Gitti	Departed
İlk Yardım	First-Aid Station
Kayıp Eşya	Lost & Found
Şehiriçi Servis	Local Shuttle Buses

Numerous bus companies maintain city-centre ticket offices near Kızılay on Ziya Gökalp Caddesi, Gazi Mustafa Kemal Bulvarı, İzmir Caddesi and Menekşe Sokak. Several premium bus companies, including Varan and Ulusoy, have their own terminal facilities near the otogar. The Varan ticket office (☎ 312-417 2525) is south of Kızılay on the eastern side of Atatürk Bulvarı.

Here is information on some of the more prominent daily routes from Ankara:

Adana – 490km, 10 hours, US$12; frequent
Amasya – 335km, five hours, US$6; frequent
Antalya – 550km, eight hours, US$12 to US$15; frequent
Bodrum – 785km, 13 hours, US$20; a dozen in summer
Bursa – 400km, 5½ hours, US$12; hourly
Diyarbakır – 945km, 13 hours, US$18; several
Erzurum – 925km, 12 hours, US$18; several
Gaziantep – 705km, 10 hours, US$15; frequent
Göreme – 300km, 4½ hours, US$10; frequent (via Nevşehir)
İstanbul – 450km, six hours, US$10 to US$15; virtual shuttle service
İzmir – 600km, eight hours, US$10; at least hourly
Kayseri – 330km, 4½ hours, US$9; very frequent
Konya – 260km, three hours, US$6; very frequent
Marmaris – 780km, 10 hours, US$15; a dozen in summer
Nevşehir – 285km, four hours, US$8; very frequent
Pamukkale – 480km, seven hours, US$8; frequent
Samsun – 420km, seven hours, US$16; frequent
Sivas – 450km, six hours, US$10; frequent
Sungurlu (for Boğazkale) – 175km, 2½ hours, US$5; hourly
Trabzon – 780km, 12 hours, US$18 to US$20; several

Train The top trains between İstanbul and Ankara – *Anadolu, Ankara, Başkent, Boğaziçi, Fatih* and the *İstanbul-Ankara Mavi Trens* – are quite good, and there's a useful service to Adana, İzmir, Kayseri, Sivas and a few other cities. See the Getting Around chapter at the front of this book for further details.

The Ankara Garı (☎ 312-311 0620 or 310 6515) has a post office, a restaurant and tea room, snack shops, ATMs, telephones and a left-luggage room (emanet), as well as two museums. Havaş buses to Esenboğa airport depart from the forecourt at the train station.

Getting Around

The Airport Esenboğa airport is 33km north of the city. Havaş buses (US$3.50) depart about every 30 minutes from AŞTİ otogar, stopping at Ankara Garı train station. They may leave sooner if they fill up, however, so claim your seat on the bus at least two hours before flight time. The minimum check-in time at the airport for domestic flights is 45 minutes before the flight departs.

When your flight arrives in Ankara, you claim your luggage and then board the Havaş bus as it will depart for the city within a half hour after the flight. Taxis between the airport and the city cost about US$25.

AŞTİ Otogar City bus No 198 leaves from the arrivals level of the bus terminal, headed for the Gar and Ulus; bus No 623 goes via Kızılay to Gaziler.

For a dolmuş to Ulus, go to the avenue in front of AŞTİ, cross to the other side, and catch an 'Ulus-Balgat' dolmuş to Ulus. 'Gölbaşı-Opera Meydanı' dolmuşes take you right to Opera Meydanı and its cheap hotels.

The Ankaray underground train has a station right next to AŞTİ. Take it to Maltepe station for the tourism office or the train station (a 10-minute walk), or to Kızılay for the three and four-star hotels in Kızılay and Bakanlıklar.

A taxi between the otogar and the train station costs about US$2.75, and about US$3.25 to Ulus or Kızılay.

Ankara Garı The train station is about 1.25km south-west of Ulus and 3km north of Kızılay. Any bus or dolmuş headed north-east along Cumhuriyet Bulvarı (straight out the station door) will take you to Ulus (such as No 411 or 281). Many buses (such as No 411) headed east along Talat Paşa Caddesi, which runs past the station, go to Kızılay and/or Kavaklıdere; look on their signboards for your destination.

It's about 1km from the station to Opera Meydanı's hotels; any bus headed east along Talat Paşa Caddesi will drop you within a few hundred metres of them if you ask for Gazi Lisesi, the high school nearby.

To go from the train station to the AŞTİ bus terminal, follow the underpass in the train station through several shopping areas and you'll eventually end up at the Maltepe Ankaray station. Take the Ankaray to AŞTİ.

Bus Ankara is served well and frequently by an extensive bus and minibus network. Signboards on the front and side of the bus are better guides than route numbers. Many buses marked 'Ulus' and 'Çankaya' ply the entire length of Atatürk Bulvarı. Those marked 'Gar' go to the train station; those marked 'AŞTİ' or one of the otogar's other names (see above) will drop you off there.

City bus tickets cost US$0.50 and can be bought from little ticket kiosks at major bus stops or from shops and vendors displaying a sign reading 'EGO Bilet Bayii' or 'EGO Bileti Satılır', or some other phrase with 'EGO Bilet' in it.

Ankaray & Metro The Ankaray is an underground train running between AŞTİ otogar in the west through Kızılay to Dikimevi in the east. A five-ride pass (US$2) is the cheapest ticket sold, making each ride cost US$0.40 if you use all five.

The first line of Ankara's metro system runs from Kızılay north-west via Sıhhiye, Maltepe and Ulus to Batıkent, a distance of 14.6km, connecting to the Ankaray at Kızılay. It may be open by the time you arrive.

Car See the Getting Around chapter for details on hiring cars. Do not rent a car to drive around Ankara, and if you have a car, park it and use public transport. Traffic patterns seem whimsically illogical, signage is woefully insufficient, and local drivers delight in speed, danger and chaos.

If you plan to hire a car and drive beyond Ankara, there are many small local companies, and the major international firms have offices at Esenboğa airport and in the city centre. Details of some of these companies follow:

Avis
  (☎ 312-467 2313, fax 467 5703)
  Tunus Caddesi 68/2, Kavaklıdere
Budget
  (☎ 312-417 5952 or 427 8071, fax 425 9608)
  Tunus Caddesi 39/A, Kavaklıdere
Europcar
  (☎ 312-418 3430 or 418 3877, fax 417 8445)
  (National, Interrent, Kemwel) Küçükesat Caddesi 25/C, Bakanlıklar
Hertz
  (☎ 312-418 8440) Akay Caddesi, Kızılırmak Sokak 1/A, Bakanlıklar
Thrifty
  (☎ 312-436 0505 or 436 0606)
  Köroğlu Caddesi 65/B, Gaziosmanpaşa

Taxi The drop rate is US$0.50 and an average trip costs around US$3 during daylight hours, 50% more at night. The lower fare would be for a trip from the otogar or train station to Ulus; the higher fare, to Kızılay or Kavaklıdere.

GORDİON

Gordion, the capital of ancient Phrygia, lies 106km west of Ankara in the village of Yassıhöyük. Archaeological teams from the University of Pennsylvania have been excavating the 80 mounds at the site since 1950, and have uncovered 18 different levels of civilisation from the Bronze Age to Roman times.

History

The site, formerly a Hittite town, was occupied by the Phrygians as early as the 9th century BC, and soon afterwards became their royal capital. Although destroyed during the Cimmerian invasion, Gordion was later rebuilt, only to be conquered by the Lydians and the Persians in turn. Alexander the Great came through and cut the Gordion Knot in 333 BC, and the Galatian occupation of 278 BC put an end to what was left of the city. (For more on the Phrygians, see Midas Şehri in the North Aegean Turkey chapter.)

Acropolis

Excavations have yielded a wealth of data on these civilisations, but the 8th-century BC acropolis itself, across the road from a fuel station on the near side of the village as you approach, is not particularly exciting for the casual visitor.

The lofty main, or Phrygian Gate, on the city's western side, was approached by a 6m-wide ramp. Within the fortified enclosure were four megara, or large square halls, from which the king and his priests and ministers ruled the empire. Coloured mosaics found in the second megaron are now on display outside the site museum near the royal tomb.

Golden Touch & Gordian Knot

The Phrygians left us two enduring legends. The first is of King Midas, who showed hospitality toward Silenus, chief of the satyrs, and was rewarded by the god with a wish – anything he desired. Midas asked that everything he touch turn to gold.

Granted his wish, at first Midas was delighted to be able to turn common objects into precious ones. But he discovered to his shock that the food he picked up to eat also turned to gold, and that he was in danger of starvation. When he embraced his beloved daughter, she became a lifeless golden statue. He pleaded to the god to relieve him of the golden touch, and was told to bathe in the Pactolus stream, which he did. The sands of the Pactolus supposedly turned to gold, and gold dust continued to be found there in abundance for centuries afterwards.

The second is of the Gordian Knot. Legend says that during a period of civil unrest, a man named Gordius, his wife and his son Midas arrived at the site of Gordion in a wooden peasant's cart. An oracle had declared that the ruler who would save Phrygia from its turmoil would arrive in such a cart, and so Gordius was immediately proclaimed king of Phrygia, with Midas as his successor. Subsequent rulers took the names Gordius and Midas in succession.

The cart which had brought Gordius and his family to glory was enshrined in a temple, and an oracle foretold that whoever could untie the knot of cornel bark which bound the pole to the yoke of the cart would be the ruler of all Asia. Alexander the Great arrived at Gordion in 333 BC, intent on the conquest of Asia, and attempted to untie the knot. Becoming frustrated, the impetuous youth cut it with his sword, and went on to conquer all of Asia anyway.

Midas Tümülüsü

In 1957 the Penn team discovered intact the tomb of a Phrygian king buried here sometime between 750 and 725 BC. The *Midas Tümülüsü* (Royal Tomb) is across the road from the müze, 2km beyond the city mound on the far side of Yassıhöyük village. The undisturbed tomb is actually a gabled 'cottage' of pine surrounded by juniper logs, built then buried beneath a tumulus 60m high and 300m in diameter.

The archaeologists carefully drilled into the tumulus from above to determine the placement and composition of the tomb, then tunnelled in from the side. In the tomb was found the body of a 61 to 65-year-old man, 1.59m tall, surrounded with burial objects, but no weapons or jewellery of silver or gold. Although the occupant's name is unknown, both 'Gordius' and 'Midas' are good bets, as most Phrygian kings seem to have been called one or the other.

The tunnel and tomb entrance are modern; there was no such entrance in ancient times. The tomb, the oldest wooden structure ever found in Anatolia, and perhaps in the world, is open daily from 8 am to 5 pm, as is the nearby museum. Admission to the tomb and museum costs US$1.75.

Museum

The museum across the road from the tomb is built in the form of a megaron. Outside, beneath a sheltering roof, are mosaics moved from the second megaron. Inside the museum are collections from the Bronze Age (3000-2000 BC), Hittite period (2000-1000 BC), and Phrygian and Hellenistic times (1000-330 BC), especially *fibulae* (bone pins), whistles, decorations and arrowheads. The best objects are now in the Anadolu Medeniyetlen Müzesi in Ankara.

Getting There & Away

Gordion is 106km west of Ankara, or 18km west of Polatlı on the E90/D200 Ankara-Eskişehir highway, then north 12km to the village of Yassıhöyük. Though the main railway line passes within 1km of the site, the nearest station is at Polatlı (reachable more easily by bus), from which dolmuşes run occasionally, or you can hire a taxi. For the best chance of getting a dolmuş get to Polatlı early in the morning. Several tour agencies in Ankara run organised tours to Gordion as well.

South Central Anatolia

KONYA

Standing alone in the middle of the vast Anatolian steppe, Konya (population 510,000, altitude 1016m) is like a traditional caravan stopping-place. The wind-swept landscape gives way to patches of greenery in the city, and once in town you forget the loneliness of the plateau. In recent years Konya has been booming. The bare-looking steppe is in fact good for growing grain and Konya is the heart of Turkey's very rich 'bread-basket'. Light industry provides jobs for those who are not farmers.

Much of the city was built within the last two decades but the centre is very old. No-one knows when the hill in the centre of town, the Alaettin Tepesi, was first settled but it contains the bones of Bronze Age men and women.

Plan to spend at least one or two full days in Konya, but avoid Monday as the museums will be closed. If your interest in Seljuk history and art takes wing you could easily spend even longer. As it often takes half a day to reach Konya, and another half day to get away again, you should figure on spending at least two nights in a hotel here.

Konya is conservative, devoutly Muslim, self-satisfied and proud of it. A motto emblazoned on the city's buses proclaims locals' desire for 'All of Turkey to be just like Konya'. Locals will treat you at first with a chilly formality. In most cases this quickly fades into the warm glow of the familiar Turkish hospitality, but in a few cases you may get the distinct feeling that you are being regarded as a *gavur* (infidel).

Take special care not to upset the pious, and look tidy when you enter mosques and

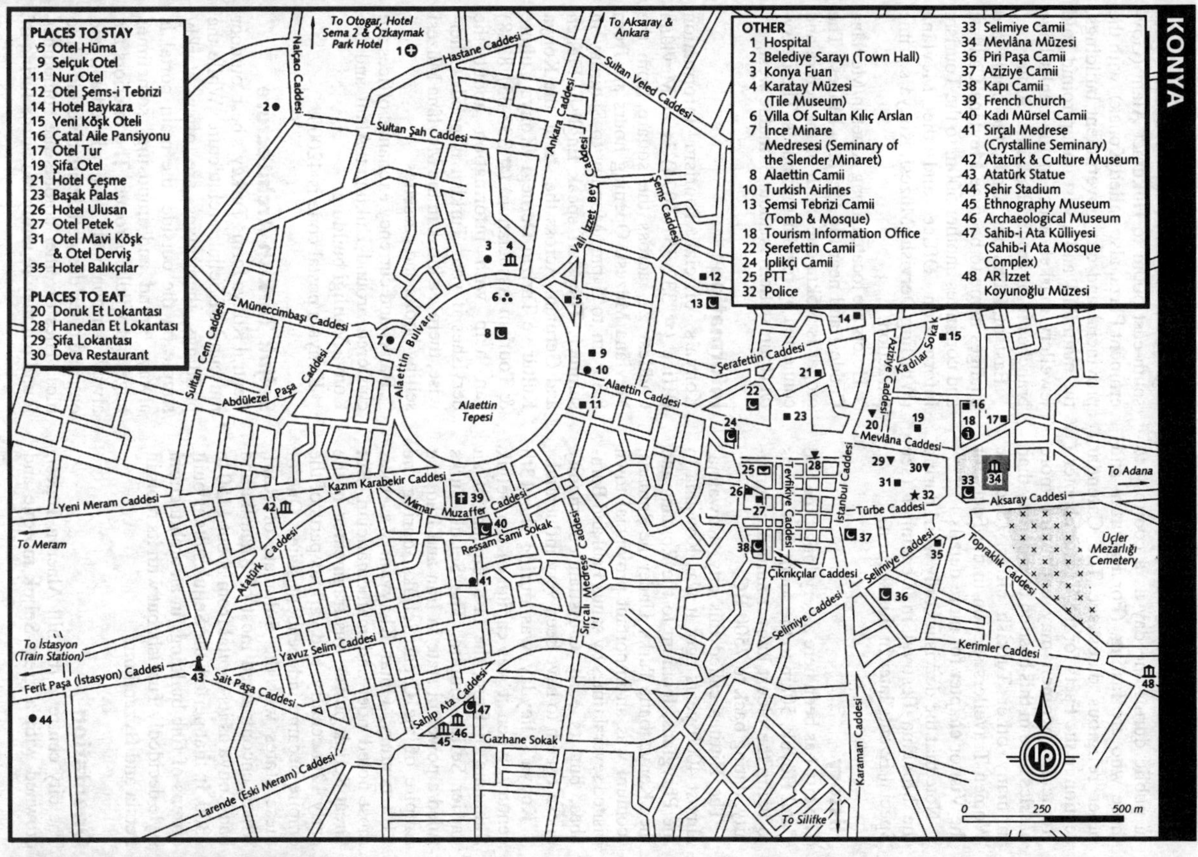

CENTRAL ANATOLIA

the Mevlâna Müzesi. If you visit during the holy month of Ramazan, don't eat or drink in public during the day as a courtesy to those who are fasting. (For Ramazan and other religious dates see The Calendar section in the Facts for the Visitor chapter.) Ironically, women may encounter more hassles here in this bastion of propriety than in many other Turkish cities. (See the Women Travellers section in the Facts for the Visitor chapter for more details.)

Note that the dervishes only whirl during the Mevlâna Festival in December (see Special Events later in this section).

History

The city has been here a very long time and Çatal Höyük, 50km to the south, has claims to being the oldest known human community, dating back to 7500 BC.

The Hittites called this city 'Kuwanna' almost 4000 years ago. It was Kowania to the Phrygians, Iconium to the Romans and then Konya to the Turks. Under the Romans, Iconium was an important provincial town visited several times by saints Paul and Barnabas, but its early Christian community doesn't seem to have been very influential.

Konya's heyday was during the 13th century, when it was capital of the Seljuk Sultanate of Rum, the last remnant of an earlier Seljuk empire. The Seljuk Turks ruled a powerful state in Iran and Iraq, the Empire of the Great Seljuks, during the 11th century. Omar Khayyam was their most noted poet and mathematician. But Great Seljuk power was fragmented in the early 12th century, and various parts of the empire became independent states. One of these states was the Sultanate of Rum, which encompassed most of Anatolia and had Konya as its capital from about 1150 to 1300. In that period, the Seljuk sultans built dozens of fine buildings in an architectural style decidedly Turkish, but with its roots in Persia and Byzantium.

Orientation

The city centre is the hill Alaettin Tepesi, crowned with a great Seljuk mosque and surrounded by the city's best Seljuk buildings. From the hill, Alaettin Caddesi goes south-east 500m to Hükümet Alanı (Government Plaza, also called Konak), with the provincial and city government buildings, the main PTT and a vast underground gold jewellery market. Most of the banks have branches in or around Hükümet Alanı.

East of Hükümet Alanı, the boulevard changes name to become Mevlâna Caddesi and continues another 500m to the Tourism Information Office and the Mevlâna (Whirling Dervish) Müzesi, Konya's prime attraction.

Hotels are located along Alaettin/Mevlâna Caddesi and near the Mevlâna Müzesi. The otogar is 3.5km due north of the centre and connected by regular minibuses. The *istasyon* (train station) is about 3km due west.

Information

Konya's official Tourism Information Office (☎ 332-351 1074) is at Mevlâna Caddesi 21, across the square from the Mevlâna Müzesi. Opening hours are from 8.30 am to 5 pm, Monday to Saturday in summer. The staff speak English, French and German. Across the street, the Konya Kültür ve Turizm Derneği (Konya Culture & Tourism Association) (☎ 332-351 8288) can help with information about the dervishes if your Turkish is good. Otherwise, there's a kiosk in the Mevlâna Müzesi selling books and cassettes.

Banks and currency exchange offices are clustered around Hükümet Alanı and the Konya Valiliği building.

Konya's postal code is 42000.

Seljuk Turkish Architecture

Central Konya forms Turkey's best 'outdoor museum' of Seljuk architecture. While the buildings themselves are often starkly simple on the outside, the main portal is always grand and imposing, sometimes huge and wildly baroque. The interiors are always harmoniously proportioned and laid out, and often decorated with blue and white tiles. Tiles of other colours are sometimes found but they're rarely red as the fusing of vivid reds on faïence was a later Ottoman accomplishment.

You can walk to all of the buildings described here but it would be tiring to do so in one day.

Mevlâna Müzesi

The first place to visit in Konya is the Mevlâna Museum, the former lodge of the Whirling Dervishes, open every day from 9 am to 5 pm (10 am to 5 pm on Monday); admission is US$1. On religious holidays the museum (really a shrine) may be open longer. For Turkish Muslims, this is a very holy place and more than 1.5 million people a year, most of them Turkish, visit it. You will see many people praying and pleading for Mevlâna's intercession. Women should cover their heads and shoulders when they enter.

Look out for the big *Nisan tası,* or April bowl, on the left as you approach Mevlâna's tomb. April rainwater, so important to the farmers of this region, was considered sacred, and was collected in this bowl. The tip of Mevlâna's turban was dipped in the water in the bowl and then offered to those in need of healing.

The lodge is visible from some way away, its fluted dome of turquoise tiles one of the most splendid sights Turkey has to offer. After walking through a pretty courtyard with an ablutions fountain and several tombs, you remove your shoes and pass into the **Mevlâna Türbesi**. Rumi's sarcophagus, the largest one, is flanked by that of his son Sultan Veled (behind Rumi's, closer to the wall) and of Rumi's father. All are covered in velvet shrouds heavy with gold embroidery, and those of Mevlâna and Sultan Veled bear huge symbolic turbans, symbols of spiritual authority.

The Mevlâna Türbesi dates from Seljuk times. The mosque and room for ceremonies were added later by Ottoman sultans (Mehmet the Conqueror was a Mevlevi adherent and Süleyman the Magnificent made large charitable donations to the order). Selim I, conqueror of Egypt, donated the Mameluke crystal lamps.

In the small chapel and *semahane* (dance floor) attached to the sepulchral chamber are exhibits: articles of clothing used by Mevlâna, Sultan Veled and Şemsi Tebrizi, as well as dervish paraphernalia such as musical instruments, vestments, prayer mats, illuminated manuscripts and ethnographic artefacts. In the museum's last room, look on the left near the mihrab for a *seccade* (prayer carpet) bearing a picture of the Kaaba at Mecca. Made in Iran of silk and wool, it is extremely fine, with an estimated three million knots.

The rooms surrounding the courtyard, once offices and quarters for the dervishes, are now furnished as they would have been at the time of Mevlâna (during the 13th century), with mannequins dressed in dervish costumes.

Outside the entrance to the Mevlâna Müzesi is the **Selimiye Camii**, endowed by Sultan Selim II in 1567. Construction on the Ottoman-style mosque started during Selim's term as governor of Konya, before his accession to the throne.

If you walk between the Selimiye Camii and the museum and cross the wide street you'll see a verdant cemetery, the **Üçler Mezarlığı** (urch-LEHR meh-zahr-luh) which offers a shortcut to the Koyunoğlu Museum. Unfortunately, a reader wrote to Lonely Planet to say that she was attacked here (she beat her assailant off with a copy of her *Lonely Planet* guide – but that's another story). If you want to walk through, do so only in daylight when other people are in sight, and women should not walk alone.

Koyunoğlu Müzesi

The AR İzzet Koyunoğlu Museum (☎ 312-351 1857), Kerimler Caddesi 25, 500m from the Mevlâna Müzesi, was donated to the city by a private collector who seemed to collect everything. Opening hours are from 9 am to 5 pm; admission costs US$1. The few labels are in Turkish only.

The modern museum building has three levels. Downstairs are collections of minerals, weapons, fossils, stuffed birds and an atrium filled with plants and live birds. The

Mevlâna & the Whirling Dervishes

In Celaleddin Rumi (Mevlâna, 'Our Guide' to his followers), the Seljuk Sultanate of Rum produced one of the world's great mystic philosophers. His poetic and religious work, mostly in Persian, the literary language of the day, is some of the most beloved and respected in the Islamic world.

Celaleddin was born in 1207 in Balkh, near Mazar-i Sharif in modern Afghanistan. His family fled the impending Mongol invasion by moving to Mecca and then to the Sultanate of Rum, reaching Konya by 1228. His father, Baha'uddin, was a noted preacher and Celaleddin became a brilliant student of Islamic theology. After his father's death in 1231, he studied in Aleppo and Damascus, returning to live in Konya by 1240.

In 1244 he met Mehmet Şemseddin Tebrizi, called Şemsi Tebrizi, one of his father's *Sufi* (Muslim mystic) disciples. Tebrizi had a profound effect on Rumi, who became devoted to him. Jealous of his overwhelming influence on their master, an angry crowd of Rumi's own disciples put Tebrizi to death in 1247. Stunned by the loss, Rumi withdrew from the world to meditate and, in this period, wrote his great poetic work, the *Mathnawi* (called *Mesnevi* in Turkish). He also wrote many *ruba'i* and *ghazal* poems, collected into his 'Great Opus', the *Divan-i Kebir*.

His ecumenical teachings were summed up in this beautiful verse which invited one and all to seek mystical union with God:

Whoever you may be, come
Even though you may be
An infidel, a pagan, or a fire-worshipper, come
Our brotherhood is not one of despair
Even though you have broken
Your vows of repentance a hundred times, come.

Rumi died late in the day on 17 December 1273, the date now known as his 'wedding night' as he was finally united with Allah. His son, Sultan Veled, organised his followers into the brotherhood called the Mevlevi, or Whirling Dervishes.

Though the Mongol invasion put an end to Seljuk sovereignty in Anatolia, the Mevlevi order prospered. In the centuries following Mevlâna's death, over 100 dervish lodges were founded throughout the Ottoman domains in Turkey, Syria and Egypt, and numerous Ottoman sultans were Sufis of the Mevlevi order.

Under the Ottoman Empire, dervish orders exerted considerable influence on the country's political, social and economic life. In most cases their world-view was monarchist, arch-conservative and xenophobic. Committed to democracy and the separation of religion and state, Atatürk saw the dervishes as an obstacle to advancement for the Turkish people, so in 1925 he had the dervish orders proscribed. Many of the monasteries were converted into museums. The shrine of Mevlâna opened as a museum in 1927.

Though outlawed, several of the dervish orders survived as fraternal religious brotherhoods. The dervishes were revived in Konya in 1957 as a 'cultural association' intended to preserve a historical tradition. The annual **festival of Mevlâna** is officially encouraged as a popular rather than a religious event. Groups of dervishes are also sent on cultural exchange tours to other countries, performing the ceremony from Hawaii to Helsinki.

Though called a 'cultural association' by the government, the Mevlevi order is still deeply religious. Young novices are recruited at puberty and devotion to the principles of the order is still lifelong. Konya's dervishes whirl today to celebrate a great tradition and, as they have been doing for over 700 years, to worship and to seek mystical union with God.

CARAVANSERAIS & HANS

Literally 'caravan palace', the grand Seljuk Turkish *kervansaray* was a luxury 'motel' on the 13th-century Silk Road through Anatolia.

The Seljuk sultans of Rum, with their capital at Konya, realised the importance of commerce to the prosperity of their empire, so they built camel caravan way-stations a day's travel (about 15km to 30km) apart to facilitate trade. Expenses for construction and maintenance of the caravanserais were borne by the crown, and paid for by the taxes levied on the rich trade in goods.

The finest examples of Seljuk caravanserais are the Sultan Hanı (the largest in Anatolia) 45km west of Aksaray on the Konya-Aksaray highway; the Sarı Han 6km east of Avanos; and the Karatay Hanı 48km east of Kayseri on the Pınarbaşı-Malatya highway. Dozens of other caravanserais dot the Anatolian landscape, including the Ağzikarahan 13km east of Aksaray on the Nevşehir highway; and the Sultan Hanı 45km north-east of Kayseri off the Sivas highway.

The typical Seljuk caravanserai is a monumental stone building with a huge, highly decorated main portal which provided access through the two-storey-high buttressed walls to a large open court and a slightly smaller but still grand and lofty vaulted hall.

The open court, where the caravans loaded and unloaded, was surrounded by rooms which served as refectory, treasury, repair shop, accounting and exchange office, store rooms, hamams for men and women, and toilets. In the centre of the open court, raised to second storey level on stone piers, there might be a *mescit* (small mosque) to

Known as the 'yellow caravanserai', the Sarı Han is worth a visit when in Avanos.

BOTH PHOTOGRAPHS BY OLIVIER CIRENDINI

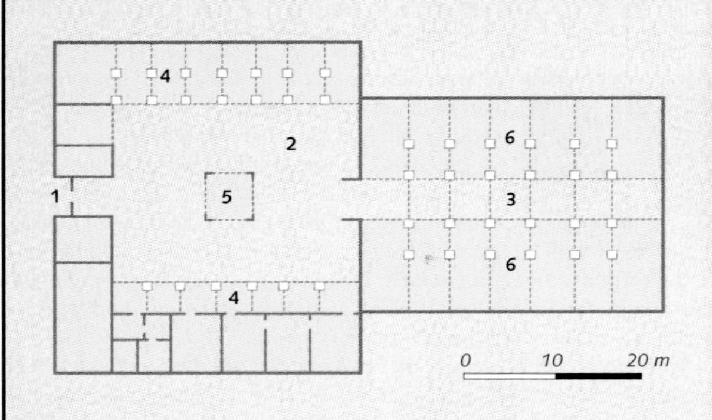

Sultan Hanı

1 Main portal
2 Large open court
3 Vaulted hall
4 Refectory, treasury, repair shop, accounting and exchange office, store rooms, hammam for men and women and toilets
5 Mescit (small mosque
6 Shelter for people and goods in bad weather

serve the travellers. In some caravanserais the mescit is above the grand main portal; in others it is in a room off the court. The vaulted hall was used to shelter people and goods in bad weather.

When the valuable cargoes reached cities and towns, the caravan unloaded in the urban equivalent of the caravanserai, called a han. Here the plan was more simple – a two-storey building, usually square, surrounding an open court with a fountain or raised mescit at its centre. On the upper storey, behind an open arcaded gallery, were offices and rooms for lodging and dining.

The most beautiful hans are the early Ottoman ones in Bursa – the Koza Han and Emir Han – but in fact every Anatolian town has at least a few hans in its market district. İstanbul's vast Kapalı Çarşı is surrounded by dozens of hans still used by traders and artisans.

Though the Ottomans built hundreds of hans in cities, their vast empire, with its command of the sea lanes, had less need for caravanserais, so they did not extend the Seljuk network.

TOM BROSNAHAN

The facade of Karatay Hanı (1219-40), near Kayseri, dates back to the Seljuk era.

main floor has exhibits of ancient coins, sculptures, glass, jewellery, Bronze Age implements and a photo display of old Konya. Upstairs, the ethnographic section displays kilims and carpets (one bears a map of Turkey); illuminated manuscripts and Korans; miniature paintings and clocks; and 19th-century clothing, bath clogs, weapons, household items, coffee sets, musical instruments, embroidery and needlework.

Next door to the museum is the **Koyunoğlu Konya Evi**, a delightful old-fashioned house which shows how a Konyalı family lived a century ago. Leave your shoes at the carved wooden door, put on sandals, as all Turks used to do, and inspect the small ground-floor room with its silk carpet. There is another, smaller salon on the ground floor as well. Upstairs the rooms are traditionally furnished with lots of carpets, kilims, low benches, pillows, a fine tray-table and lots of turned wood. The picture is of the museum's founder.

Alaettin Camii

Except for the Mevlâna Müzesi, many of Konya's principal sights are near the Alaettin Tepesi, or Aladdin's Hill, at the western end of Alaettin Caddesi. The hill's eastern slopes are set with tea gardens and the ancient Alaettin Camii is right on the top.

The mosque of Alaeddin Keykubat I, Seljuk Sultan of Rum from 1219 to 1231, is a great rambling building designed by a Damascene architect in Arab style and finished in 1221. Over the centuries it was embellished, refurbished, ruined and restored. It has only just reopened after decades of restoration.

The main entrance on the northern side is of an odd design, incorporating bits of decoration from earlier Byzantine and Roman buildings. To the right of the portal is the tomb chamber bearing the remains of a dozen Seljuk sultans. The portal led to a door into the mosque which was between two huge Seljuk *türbes* (tombs); today a less imposing entrance on the east is used.

While the exterior is fairly plain, the interior is a forest of old marble columns surmounted with recycled Roman and Byzantine capitals, with a fine, carved wooden *mimber* (pulpit, 1156) and an old marble *mihrab* (prayer niche) framed by modern Seljuk-style blue and black calligraphy of great beauty and harmony.

You can visit the mosque from 8.30 am to 6 pm, but remember that it's still a place of worship: leave your shoes at the door and avoid entering at prayer times.

On the northern side of the Alaettin Tepesi, the scant ruins of the **Villa of Sultan Kılıç Arslan** are protected by a hideous, crumbling concrete shelter.

Karatay Müzesi

The Büyük Karatay Medresesi (Great Karatay Seminary), now called the Karatay Müzesi, is a Seljuk theological seminary just north of the Alaettin Tepesi. It houses Konya's outstanding collection of ceramics and tiles and is open from 9 am to noon and from 1 to 5 pm (closed Monday). Admission costs US$1.

The school was constructed in 1251-52 by the emir Celaleddin Karatay (died 1254), a Seljuk general, vizier and statesman who is buried in the south-western corner room.

Enter from the street through the magnificent marble portal. Inside, the central dome and the *eyvan* contain masterpieces of Seljuk light and dark blue tilework, interspersed with snatches of white and black. The Kufic-style Arabic inscription around the bottom of the dome is the first chapter of the Koran while the triangles below are decorated with the stylised names of the prophets (Muhammed, Jesus, Moses and David) and of the four caliphs who succeeded Muhammed.

Notice the curlicue drain for the central pool: its curved shape made the sound of running water a pleasant background noise in the quiet room where students studied.

The museum's tile collection includes interesting coloured ones from the Seljuk palace on Alaettin Tepesi and from the Palace of Kubadabad near Beyşehir Lake. Compare these with the later Ottoman tiles from İznik.

İnce Minare Medresesi

On the western side of Alaettin Tepesi is the İnce Minare Medresesi (Seminary of the Slender Minaret), now the Museum of Wood & Stone Carving. This religious school was built in 1264 on the order of Sahip Ata, a powerful Seljuk vizier, who may have been trying to outdo the patron of the Karatay Medresesi, built only seven years earlier. Hours and fee are the same as at the Karatay; labels are in Turkish only.

Don't enter the building immediately, for half of what you've come to see is the elaborate doorway with bands of Arabic inscription running up the sides and looping overhead, which is far more impressive than the small building behind it. The minaret beside the door gave the seminary its popular name of 'slender minaret'. Over 600 years old, most of the very tall minaret was knocked off by lightning in 1901. Needless to say the latest restorative efforts included installation of a lightning conductor. One wonders if the opening of a McDonald's right next to this architectural masterpiece is not just as much of a thunderbolt.

Inside, many of the carvings in wood and stone feature motifs similar to those used in the tile and ceramic work. You'll quickly see that the Seljuks didn't let Islam's famous condemnation of images of creatures with souls (humans and animals) stand in the way of their art. There are plenty of images of birds (the Seljuk double-headed eagle, for example), men and women, lions and leopards here. The eyvan in particular contains two delightful carvings of Seljuk angels with distinctly Mongol features. Be sure to visit the *Ahşap Eserler Bölümü* (Carved Wood Section) to see the intricately worked doors.

South of Alaettin Tepesi

Several other Seljuk monuments lurk in a warren of streets to the south of the city. Ask for the Kadı Mürsel Camii, then walk south along Ressam Sami Sokak, the street which begins just east of a small French church and opposite a large white mansion housing offices of the Milli Eğitim Bakanlığı.

A few minutes' walk south along Ressam Sami Sokak is another Seljuk seminary, the **Sırçalı Medrese** (Crystalline Seminary) named after its tiled exterior. Sponsored by Bedreddin Muslih, a Seljuk vizier, construction was completed in 1242. It was originally known as the Muslihiye Medresesi, but is now the Mezar Anıtlar Müzesi. (Museum of Funerary Monuments).

The main portal is grand but formal and restrained compared to the exuberance of those in Konya's other great medreses. In the courtyard, the great eyvan on the western side was used for classes; its arch is decorated with a band of particularly fine calligraphic tilework. The students' cells are on two floors.

The inscriptions on the gravestones on exhibit, done in a variety of Arabic scripts, are often very fine. Symbols of rank – headgear, usually – served to tell the passer-by of the deceased's role in life.

A few blocks further south along Ressam Sami Sokak is the **Sahib-i Ata Külliyesi** (Sahib-i Ata Mosque Complex), founded in 1283. Behind its requisite grand portal – this one with its own minaret (the stairs of which are hidden within the portal) – is the Sahib-i Ata Camii, originally constructed during the reign of Alaettin Keykavus by the Seljuk soldier and statesman Hacı Ebubekirzade Hüseyinoğlu Sahib-i Ata Fahreddin Ali. Destroyed by fire in 1871, it was razed and rebuilt to the same style. The mihrab is original and a fine example of Seljuk light-and-dark blue tilework.

On the south-eastern side of the mosque is another grand portal which once led to the külliye's dervish lodge, now in ruins.

Konya's small but interesting **Archaeological Museum** is to the west of the mosque within the complex, open from 9 am to noon and 1 to 5 pm (closed Monday) for US$1. The forecourt is filled with statuary and sarcophagi from Konya's long history. Some of the small, simple funeral monuments have an appealing primitive directness.

Inside, the museum contains several fine sarcophagi decorated with bold, lively highrelief carvings. The Pamphylian type resembles a small temple; the Roman Sidamara sarcophagus dating from 250-60 AD bears quite striking reliefs of the Labours of Hercules.

About 100m south-west of the Sahib-i Ata Külliyesi is the city's small **Ethnography Museum**, open for the same hours and fee as the Archaeological Museum.

Other Mosques & Tombs

Dotted about town are other buildings of interest. The **Şemsi Tebrizi Camii**, containing the 14th-century tomb of Rumi's spiritual mentor, is just north of Hükümet Alanı, not far from Alaettin Caddesi. The **Aziziye Camii** (1875) in the bazaar was rebuilt in Ottoman late baroque-style after a fire; it's the one with twin minarets bearing little sheltered balconies. The **İplikçi Camii** (1202) on Alaettin Caddesi, perhaps Konya's oldest mosque, was built on orders of the Seljuk vizier Şemseddin Altun-Aba in a plain, unadorned style; a forest of columns, arches and groin vaulting. The **Şerefettin Camii**, off Mevlâna Caddesi near Hükümet Alanı, was first built in the 1200s, but rebuilt in 1636. The **Piri Mehmet Paşa Camii** (1523) and adjoining Siyavüş Sultan Türbesi face the Piri Mehmet Paşa Zaviyesi, or dervish hostel, all restored in 1996.

The Bazaar

Konya's market area is behind the modern PTT building and is divided up in very medieval fashion – here a section for plastic flowers, there one for teapots, here another for coils of rope. Keep walking and you should come to the covered **Melik Hatun Çarşısı**, near the Azizye Camii. Stalls here sell some truly wonderful pungent local cheeses.

Excursions

Çatal Höyük Between 1961 and 1965, British archaeologist James Mellaart excavated two Neolithic mounds at Çatal Höyük, 50km south-east of Konya. He discovered a community from the dawn of civilisation 9000 years ago, and proclaimed it to be the world's oldest known human community.

The 13 layers of remains, dating from 6800 to 5500 BC and thought to be what's left of 150 mud-brick houses, yielded shrines with bulls' horns, painted murals and plaster reliefs, mother-goddess figurines, polished obsidian mirrors, tools and the earliest known pottery. Most of the finds are now in Ankara's Anadolu Medeniyetlen Müzesi, but recently efforts have gotten under way to make the site more visitor-friendly with onsite exhibits, explanations and basic visitors' facilities.

To get there without your own car, take a dolmuş to Çumra and then hire a taxi for the last 10km. To take a virtual tour, surf to http://Catal.arch.cam.uk/catal/catal.html and www.hfg-karlsruhe.de/projects/vam/CATAL-E.html.

Gökyurt Konya may be well south of central Cappadocia but the landscape at Gökyurt (50km south-west of Konya) is reminiscent of what you'll see in Güzelyurt or Ihlara: gorges with medieval churches cut into the rockface. Without a car it's not easy to get there but Mustafa Sarıoğlan at the Yeni Köşk Oteli in Konya may be able to help you arrange transport.

Sille The pretty village of Sille, 9km north-west of Konya, accessible by bus, has an old stone bridge and medieval frescoes rotting away in the barns.

Special Events

The Mevlâna Festival is held in mid-December, culminating on the 17th, the anniversary of Mevlâna's 'wedding night' with God. The festival features numerous performances of the *sema*, or Mevlevi rite. Tickets are sold, and should be bought, well in advance. Contact the Tourism Information Office or the Konya Culture & Tourism Association for information. Reserve your hotel room in advance as well. If you can't make it to the December festival, you may be able to witness the sema in İstanbul at the Galata Mevlevihanesi near Tünel Meydanı on the last Sunday of each month. (See the Tünel section in the İstanbul chapter for details.)

Whirling to Ecstasy

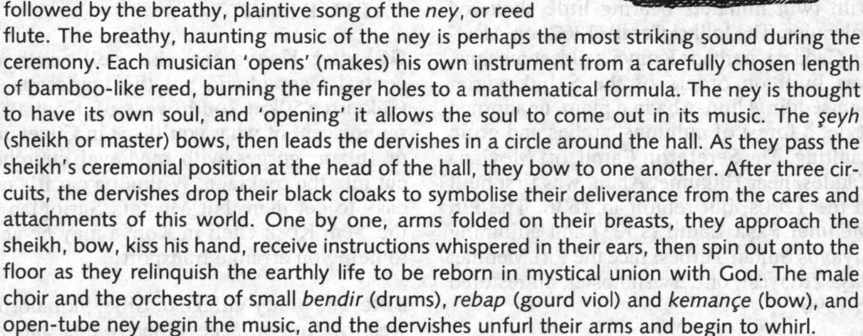

The Mevlevi worship ceremony, which traditionally takes place on a Monday evening ('Tuesday morning' in Islamic thinking), is a ritual dance, or *sema*, representing union with God. The dervishes enter the *semahane*, or whirling hall, dressed in long white robes with full skirts which represent their shrouds. Over them they wear voluminous black cloaks symbolising their worldly tombs; their tall conical red felt hats represent their tombstones.

The ceremony begins with a chant by the *hafız*, a celebrant who has committed the entire Koran to memory. He intones a prayer for Mevlâna and a verse from the Koran. A kettledrum booms out, followed by the breathy, plaintive song of the *ney*, or reed flute. The breathy, haunting music of the ney is perhaps the most striking sound during the ceremony. Each musician 'opens' (makes) his own instrument from a carefully chosen length of bamboo-like reed, burning the finger holes to a mathematical formula. The ney is thought to have its own soul, and 'opening' it allows the soul to come out in its music. The *şeyh* (sheikh or master) bows, then leads the dervishes in a circle around the hall. As they pass the sheikh's ceremonial position at the head of the hall, they bow to one another. After three circuits, the dervishes drop their black cloaks to symbolise their deliverance from the cares and attachments of this world. One by one, arms folded on their breasts, they approach the sheikh, bow, kiss his hand, receive instructions whispered in their ears, then spin out onto the floor as they relinquish the earthly life to be reborn in mystical union with God. The male choir and the orchestra of small *bendir* (drums), *rebap* (gourd viol) and *kemançe* (bow), and open-tube ney begin the music, and the dervishes unfurl their arms and begin to whirl.

By holding their right arms up, palms upwards, they receive the blessings of heaven which are communicated to earth by holding their left arms down, palms downwards. Pivoting on their left heels, the dervishes whirl ever faster, reaching ecstasy with a blissful expression. As they whirl, they form a 'constellation' of revolving bodies which itself slowly rotates. The sheikh walks among them to make sure each dervish is performing the ritual properly. After about 10 minutes, they all stop and kneel down. Then, rising, they begin again. The dance is repeated four times, with the sheikh joining the last circuit. The whirling over, the hafız again chants poetical passages from the holy book, sealing the experience of mystical union with God.

Places to Stay

Given Konya's character as a conservative Muslim city with a healthy pilgrimage trade, it's not surprising that alcohol is banned from most lodgings. Konya's hotels boast mosques, not bars, and with the exception of Hotel Balıkçılar, minibars in the fancier rooms contain soft drinks, not beer or wine.

Places to Stay – Budget

Look for signs off Mevlâna Caddesi to ***Yeni Köşk Oteli*** *(☎ 332-352 0671, fax 352 0901, Yeni Aziziye Caddesi, Kadılar Sokak 28)*, run by Mr Mustafa Sarıoğlan. Clean, tidy and fairly quiet, it features rooms with private showers and TV for US$16/20 a single/double.

Hotel Çeşme *(☎ 332-351 2426, İstanbul Caddesi, Akifpaşa Sokak 35)* is relatively quiet, cheap, clean and well-priced at US$14/16 a single/double for a room with shower, less without. There are many small restaurants nearby. ***Otel Tur*** *(☎ 332-351 9825, fax 352 4299, Mevlâna Caddesi, Eş'arizade Sokak 13)*, priced about the same, is second-best.

In the narrow street beside the tourist office look out for the ***Çatal Aile Pansiyonu*** *(☎ 332-351 4981, Mevlâna Caddesi, Naci Fikret Sokak 14/A)*, where a kilim-decorated lobby leads to more simple rooms for US$14/16.

If this is too expensive for you, the bazaar district behind the PTT has some really cheap places. ***Hotel Ulusan*** *(☎ 332-351 5004, Kurşuncular Sokak 2)*, is immediately behind Türk Telekom. Rooms here are simple but clean and, with sink, cost US$9/12 a single/double. Nearby is the tidy ***Otel Petek*** *(☎ 332-351 2599, Çırıkçılar İçi 40)*, squeezed in between a shop selling helva and another selling nuts and dried fruit. Clean, simple rooms with shower cost US$11/14 without breakfast, a little less without the showers. The top-floor breakfast room offers a panoramic view of the bazaar and all the way up to the Mevlâna Müzesi.

Otel Derviş *(☎ 332-351 1688, Mevlâna Caddesi, Bostançelebi Sokak 11/D)*, is simple but serviceable with shower-equipped double rooms going for US$16, subject to negotiation. The neighbouring ***Otel Mavi Köşk*** *(☎ 332-350 1904, Bostançelebi Sokak 13)* is dingier, but also cheaper.

The first street to the right (south) as you walk along Alaettin Caddesi from Alaettin Tepesi is Karahüyüklü Sokak, and on it is the ***Nur Otel*** *(☎ 332-352 0397)*, run by God-fearing Muslims who charge US$12 for a waterless double room. A bath costs an extra US$1.50.

The one-star ***Başak*** *(☎ 332-351 1338, Hükümet Alanı 3)*, facing the provincial government building midway along Alaettin Caddesi, has been here for decades if not centuries. It's well-used rooms with sinks only (hot and cold water) cost US$16/20, or US$20/30 with private bath.

Near the Otogar ***Hotel Sema 2*** *(☎ 332-233 2557)* is right next to the otogar and looks as tired as a 20-year-old bus. The 33 rooms priced at US$9/12 for a single/double with sink, or US$14/18 with private bath, including breakfast, is bearable if you arrive late or need to make an early start from the otogar.

Places to Stay – Mid-Range

City Centre ***Otel Şems-i Tebrizi*** *(☎ 332-350 5738, fax 351 1771, Şems Caddesi 10)*, across the street from the Şems-i Tebrizi Camii and Türbesi, is modern, comfortable and well located. The posted prices of US$50/70 a single/double with bath and breakfast drop 40% if you haggle a bit. The corner rooms – 202, 302, etc – are larger, with bigger baths and balconies, for the same price.

Proving that even Holy Konya is not immune to irony, ***Hotel Balıkçılar*** *(☎ 332-350 9470, fax 352 3259, Mevlâna Karşısı 1)*, the closest hotel to the Mevlâna Müzesi, is the only place of its class in town to serve alcoholic beverages. Its 51 three-star rooms all have air-con, minibars – with beer, wine and rakı! – and TV sets, and cost US$50/70 a single/double. The quieter rooms are at the back, but some of those at the front have views of the Mevlâna Müzesi.

Near the Büyük Karatay Medresesi, the three-star ***Otel Hüma*** *(☎ 332-350 6618, fax 351 0244, Alaettin Caddesi 8)* is another good choice, its architecture designed to echo that of Konya's Seljuk buildings. Rooms here are bright and modern, with boozeless minibars and TVs, and cost less; US$30/50 with breakfast.

The 82 room ***Selçuk Otel*** *(☎ 332-353 2525, fax 353 2529, Alaaddin Caddesi 4)*, near Alaettin Tepesi, rents 70 air-conditioned rooms with bath, boozeless minibar and TV for US$50/75 a single/double. Front rooms have views of Alaettin Tepesi, and there's a mescit (small mosque) on the premises.

Just east of Hükümet Alanı, the two-star, 31 room ***Şifa Otel*** *(☎ 332-350 4290, fax 351 9251, Mevlâna Caddesi 55)*, provides decent rooms with private shower at US$30/38, breakfast included, but with a strong undercurrent of infidel xenophobia. Street noise is a problem as well.

Sharing the same management, the three-star ***Hotel Baykara*** *(☎ 332-353 6030, fax 353 6035, İstanbul Caddesi 181)*, three short blocks north of Mevlâna Caddesi, is similar.

Near the Otogar The three-star ***Özkaymak Park Otel*** *(☎ 332-233 3770, fax 235 5974)*, across the park from the otogar, has simple rooms with shower for US$23/32.

Places to Eat

Konya's speciality is *fırın kebap*, a rich, fairly greasy oven-roasted joint of mutton. The city bakers also make excellent fresh pide topped with minced lamb, cheese or eggs, but in Konya pide is called *etli ekmek* (bread with meat). *Dürüm* (roll) is thin flat bread topped with a filling, then rolled up.

This being a conservative, religious town, few places other than the restaurant in the Hotel Balıkçılar serve alcohol, and those few places which do serve alcohol are so debased that they make one think the teetotalers may have a point. To buy booze, look for shops marked 'Tekel Bayii'. There's one near the French church on Mimar Muzaffer Caddesi.

The bright, popular ***Şifa Lokantası***, Mevlâna Caddesi 30, is only a short stroll west of the Mevlâna Müzesi. They'll serve you a fırın kebap and cold drink for US$4.

Doruk Et Lokantası on İstanbul Caddesi serves a range of kebaps including fırın for about US$3. It's a clean, cheerful place with an upstairs *aile salonu*.

Hanedan Et Lokantası, Mevlâna Caddesi 2/B, at the south-eastern end of Hükümet Alanı next to the Sümerbank, is famous for its meat dishes. Clean and bright, it's open every day and serves excellent fresh pide, döner kebap, köfte and vegetable dishes. Full meals cost from US$4 to US$6.

On Bostan Çelebi Sokak near the Köşk and Derviş hotels, look for ***Öztemel Konya Fırın Kebap Salonu***, specialising in the local oven kebap.

The bright, airy ***Deva Restaurant***, Mevlâna Caddesi 3, across from the Hotel Dergah, serves an assortment of Turkish dishes including tandır kebap. With salad, bread and soft drink a meal might cost US$4 or so.

Konya Mutfağı (Konya Kitchen) *(☎ 332-352 8547, Akçeşme Mahallesi, Topraklık Caddesi 66)*, across from the Akçeşme İlkokulu school, is in a restored house just a few minutes' walk from the Hotel Balıkçılar, down towards the Koyunoğlu Müzesi. Service is polite, the ambience and menu are traditional and fine, and yet prices are still below US$10 per person.

Getting There & Away

Air Turkish Airlines (☎ 332-351 2000, fax 350 2171) has daily (except Saturday) flights to and from İstanbul. The THY office is at Alaettin Caddesi 9, on the northern side of the street not far from Alaettin Tepesi.

Bus Konya's Otobüs Terminali is 3.5km north of Hükümet Alanı (Konak). To get to the centre take a minibus (US$0.30) from the rank outside the otogar. For the Nur Otel, Hotel Selçuk and Hotel Hüma, get out at İş Bankası/THY; for the Çeşme and Yeni Köşk hotels, the stop is İstanbul Caddesi or Valilik/Konak. Some of the minibuses continue to Mevlâna Meydanı, next to the Tourism Information Office and the Mevlâna Müzesi. A taxi to the centre costs about US$3.50.

Details of some bus services follow:

Adana – 350km, 6½ hours, US$10; frequent buses

Adıyaman (Nemrut Dağı) – 720km, 10 hours, US$16; two daily

Aksaray – 140km, two hours, US$4; frequent buses

Alanya – 320km, 6½hours, US$16; change at Silifke or Antalya

Ankara – 260km, three hours, US$6; very frequent

Antalya – 365km, six hours, US$12 via Isparta; 349km, four hours, US$11 via Akseki; several buses

Bursa – 500km, 8½ hours, US$12; several buses daily
İstanbul – 660km, 10 hours, US$16; frequent buses
İzmir – 575km, eight hours, US$12; buses at least every two hours
Nevşehir (Cappadocia) – 226km, 2½ hours, US$6; several buses daily
Pamukkale – 4505km, eight hours, US$10; several buses daily
Silifke – 260km, 4½ hours, US$7; frequent buses
Side – 296km, 5½ hours, US$8; no direct buses to Side; take one to Manavgat

Train There is no direct rail link across the plateau between Konya and Ankara. The best way to make this journey is by bus. Between İstanbul (Haydarpaşa) and Konya you can ride either the *İç Anadolu Mavi Tren, Meram Ekspresi* or the *Toros Ekspresi*. See the Getting Around chapter for details.

City buses, running at least every half hour, connect the train station with the centre of town. If you take a taxi from the train station to Hükümet Alanı, it will cost about US$4.

Getting Around

As most of the city centre sights are easily reached on foot, you only need public transport to get to the bus and train stations. Konya's efficient system of minibuses does this well; a run from the otogar to the centre costs just US$0.30. The new tram runs from the otogar to Alaettin Tepesi but doesn't continue down Alaettin Caddesi.

To return to the bus station, catch a dolmuş on İstanbul Caddesi near the Yeni Köşk Oteli.

SULTANHANI

The highway between Konya and Aksaray crosses quintessential Anatolian steppe: undulating grassland, sometimes with mountains in the distance. Along the way, 110km from Konya and 42km from Aksaray, is the village of Sultanhanı, which has one of several Seljuk caravanserais bearing that name. This Sultanhanı is 100m from the highway and can be visited on any day in summer from 7 am to 7 pm for US$1.50. You can explore the building thoroughly in about a half hour or less.

It was constructed in 1229, during the reign of the Seljuk sultan Alaettin Keykubat I, restored in 1278 after a fire (when it became the largest caravanserai in Turkey) and restored again and reroofed 20 years ago. Note the wonderful carved portal of yellow and blue marble, the raised central *mescid* and the huge *ahır*, or stable, at the back. Other rooms are marked:

Erkek Hamam – Men's Turkish Bath
Kadın Hamam – Women's Turkish Bath
Muhasebe – Accounting
Oda – Room
Tuvalet – Toilet
Yemekhane – Refectory

Immediately opposite the Sultanhanı, **Sultan Restaurant & Kafeterya** offers a complete touristic service: restaurant, toilets, exchange facilities, shops, stamps, phone cards and somewhere to leave your bag while you look around ... all this and a smile too!

About 150m east of the Sultanhanı is ***Kervansaray Pansiyon & Camping*** *(☎ 382-242 2008)* with beds for US$8 and an adequate camping ground. Its owner has a car and may be willing to organise excursions to the Acı Gölü crater lake and to see the flamingoes on Tuz Gölü.

The nearby ***Sultan Pansiyon*** *(☎ 382-242 2393)*, 150m north-west of the Sultanhanı, is similar.

Walk south-east 850m through the village centre to find ***Kervan Pansiyon, Restaurant & Camping*** *(☎ 382-242 2325)*, which has perhaps the nicest camping ground, a separate space apart from the pension, enclosed by a wall with its own toilets and showers. Though a bit out of the way, this makes it quieter.

To reach the caravanserai, take a Sultanhanı Belediyesi bus from Aksaray otogar (US$1, 45 minutes). Alternatively catch a Konya bus and ask to be dropped off. To be sure of a seat on to Konya afterwards, make a reservation in Aksaray and ask to be picked up on the main road.

UZUN YOL

The drive from Aksaray or Ihlara to Nevşehir takes you along one of the oldest trade routes in the world, the Uzun Yol (Long Road) which linked Konya, the capital of the Seljuk Sultanate of Rum, with its other great cities (Kayseri, Sivas and Erzurum) and ultimately with the birthplace of Seljuk power in Persia.

Following the Long Road today takes you past the remains of several hans, including: the impressive and well-preserved **Ağzıkarahan** (1243) on the southern side of the road, 10km east of Aksaray, open daily from 7 am to 6 pm for a small fee; the 13th-century **Tepesidelik Hanı** (also called the Öresin Hanı) on the southern side, about 13km east of Aksaray; and the 12th-century **Alay Hanı**, badly ruined, on the northern side of the highway, about 33km east of Aksaray. All are marked by signs.

Cappadocia

Cappadocia, the region between Ankara and Malatya, between the Black Sea and the Taurus Mountains, with its centre at Kayseri, was once the heart of the Hittite Empire, later an independent kingdom, then a vast Roman province mentioned several times in the Bible.

Today the name survives to describe one of Turkey's most visited tourist areas, the moonscape around the town of Ürgüp and the Göreme Valley. Since the name doesn't appear on official road maps, you'll need to know that 'Cappadocia' is the area bordered by Kayseri in the east, Aksaray in the west, Hacıbektaş to the north and Niğde to the south.

For all its seeming barrenness, the mineral-laden volcanic soil is very fertile and Cappadocia today is a prime agricultural region with many fruit orchards and vineyards. Little wineries experiment with the excellent grapes, sometimes with pleasant results. Irrigation schemes should greatly increase the productivity of the region.

Another source of wealth is carpet-making, but these days tourism is Cappadocia's industry par excellence. People come from all over the world to visit the Göreme Open-Air Museum, to explore the rock-hewn churches and dwellings in surrounding valleys, to gaze on the fairy chimneys and to plumb the depths of the underground cities at Derinkuyu and Kaymaklı.

History

The history of Cappadocia began with the eruptions of three volcanoes (Erciyes Dağı near Kayseri, Melendiz Dağı near Niğde, and Göllüdağ between them), as much as 10 million years ago. The eruptions spread a thick layer of hot volcanic ash over the region, which hardened into a soft, porous stone called tufa.

Over aeons of geological time, wind, water and sand erosion wore away portions of the tufa, carving it into elaborate and unearthly shapes. Boulders of hard stone, caught in the tufa and then exposed by erosion, protect the tufa directly beneath from further erosion. The result is a column or cone of tufa with a boulder perched on top, whimsically called a *peribaca*, or 'fairy chimney'. Entire valleys are filled with these formations, many of them amusingly phallic in appearance.

The tufa was easily worked with primitive tools and the inhabitants learned early that sturdy dwellings could be cut from it with a minimum of fuss. A cave could be carved out very quickly and, if the family expanded, more easy carving could produce a nursery or storeroom in next to no time.

When invaders flooded across the land bridge between Europe and Asia, Cappadocians went underground, carving elaborate multi-level cave cities beneath the surface of the earth and only coming to the surface to tend their fields.

When Christianity arrived in Cappadocia, its adherents found that cave churches, complete with elaborate decoration, could be carved from the rock as easily as dwellings. Large Christian communities thrived here and their rock-hewn churches became a unique art form. Arab armies swept through in the 7th century but the Christians

retreated into their caves again, rolling stone wheel-doors across the entrances.

Many of the caves and villages were inhabited by the descendants of these early settlers until this century, when the crumbling of the Ottoman Empire forced the reorganisation of the Middle East along ethno-political lines.

Touring Cappadocia

Although you could see something of Cappadocia on a lightning day trip by plane, it's better to stay at least one night in the region. Two or three nights is far better, and indeed you could easily spend a week here and still not see everything.

Most people come to Cappadocia by bus, although there is a train service to Kayseri and Niğde, and a new airport at Gülşehir now serves the region with daily flights.

The most convenient bases for exploration are Göreme (favourite of backpackers and budget travellers), Ürgüp (with a good mix of lodgings, including many group hotels), and Avanos, a pottery-making centre. Göreme village is within walking distance of the Göreme Valley, and Ürgüp and Avanos are a 10-minute ride from the Göreme Valley. Uçhisar, popular with French travellers, is sleepier despite its dramatic volcanic rock **kale**. Ortahisar has a few hotels and pensions, and few tourists. Nevşehir, the provincial capital, has little to offer beyond being a transfer point.

Güzelyurt and the Ihlara Valley make a good day-trip, though they both have accommodation, and more can be found in Niğde and Aksaray if necessary. Separated from Cappadocia by around 70km and a range of hills, Kayseri, the largest city in the region, is not the convenient base for daily excursions you might assume.

In summer, travelling among these places is relatively straightforward, with frequent dolmuş minibuses. In winter, there is less frequent transport, and you may want to consider a tour or a hired car or taxi if your time is short.

Tours organised by local travel agencies allow you to see all the sights cheaply and conveniently, but often dump you in a carpet or souvenir shop in the middle of nowhere for two hours. The tour company gets as much as 30% commission on everything you buy but the tea is free and the 'shopping' can be a rest from walking in the sun. Still, why pay to be fleeced? Find a tour with no shopping stop, shop on your own, and pocket the tour company's 30%.

To hire a taxi or minibus, with driver, for a full-day tour of all Cappadocia, starting at Ürgüp or Göreme, costs from US$50 to US$80. Alternatively, you can rent a bicycle, moped or motorbike to help you get about; see Getting Around in the Göreme section, later. If you have more time than money, plan to walk and hitch through the region, a wonderful way to tour, though it can be tiring in the hot sun.

However you go, wear flat shoes for climbing the metal-rung ladders and stairways to the cave churches, and take a torch (flashlight) if you have one. Refreshments, snacks and light meals are available at all major sites.

NEVŞEHİR

Nevşehir (NEHV-sheh-heer, population 55,000, altitude 1260m), the provincial capital, is a modern town where the Cappadocian moonscape is not much in evidence. Most people pass right through it.

Orientation & Information

Atatürk Bulvarı, the main street, changes its name to become Yeni Kayseri Caddesi along its eastern reaches on the way to Göreme. The main north-south road, Lale Caddesi, intersects with Atatürk Bulvarı at the centre of the town, near the tourist information office. The otogar is 1.5km north of the town's main intersection, on the road towards Gülşehir. As most of the hotels are on the outskirts, you'll probably have to take a taxi to get to them.

The Tourism Information Office (☎ 384-213 3659), on Atatürk Bulvarı just east of the main intersection, is open every day in summer from 8.30 am to noon and from 1 to 5.30 pm. Staff are well informed and helpful.

Nevşehir's postal code is 50000.

Things to See & Do

There is little to see or do in Nevşehir proper except perhaps to visit the Monday **market** or climb up to the **citadel** to enjoy the view and be importuned into buying some of the locally handmade lace.

You might have a look at the **Nevşehirli İbrahim Paşa Külliyesi**. Sultan Ahmet III's grand vizier İbrahim Paşa (1662-1730), sometimes called Damat İbrahim, was a great builder, having supplied his sovereign with many romantic palaces and lodges in İstanbul. He was one of the first great men of the empire to have been influenced by European fashions. He was born in humble conditions in the village of Muşkara, and when he became rich and famous he returned to his village to found a new city (*nev*, new; *şehir*, city). Along with his new city, İbrahim founded this mosque complex (1726), consisting of the mosque, a seminary, a school, a library, a water fountain and a hamam. The mosque and hamam are still in business. Bath hours at the hamam are from 7.30 am to 9 pm. Wednesday is officially for women but female tourists are welcome any time.

The **Nevşehir Müzesi** is 1km out along Yeni Kayseri Caddesi on the road to Göreme and Ürgüp. Opening hours are from 8 am to noon and from 1 to 5 pm, closed Monday; admission is US$1. The arrangement is the familiar one: an archaeological section with Phrygian, Hittite and Bronze Age pots and implements, then Roman, Byzantine and Ottoman articles; and an ethnographic section with costumes, tools, manuscripts and jewellery.

Places to Stay

Nevşehir's hotels cater mostly to local business travellers and bus tour groups.

On Atatürk Bulvarı the 25 room ***Hotel Şems*** (*☎ 384-213 3597, fax 212 4967, Atatürk Bulvarı 29*), above the Aspava Restaurant, is usable but somewhat overpriced at US$14/23. Rooms at the front of the hotel are noisy.

Hotel Seven Brothers (*☎ 384-213 4979, fax 213 0454, Kayseri Caddesi, Tusan Sokak 25*), on the eastern side of town, on the way to Ürgüp, is quieter and charges US$14/23 for a single/double with TV, bath and breakfast. Directly across the street, the three-star ***Hotel Orsan*** (*☎ 384-213 2115, fax 213 4223, Kayseri Caddesi 15*), boasts Nevşehir's only hotel swimming pool and charges US$24/36. Across the avenue, ***Hotel Dilara*** (*☎ 384-212 6052, fax 213 2739*), charges a bit less.

The four-star ***Otel Altınöz*** (*☎ 384-213 5305, fax 213 2817, Ragıp Üner Caddesi 23*) has 120 comfortable guest rooms for US$50/75, breakfast included. Turkish bath, sauna, disco, restaurants and bars are all yours to enjoy, and the location is quiet.

About 3km east of the centre on the Ürgüp road stands the five-star, 350 room group-oriented ***Kapadokya Dedeman Hotel*** (*☎ 384-213 9900, fax 213 2158*). It's hardly a pretty building but the guest rooms have all the comforts, including air-con, TVs and minibars, all yours for US$70/100/140 a single/double/triple.

Places to Eat

For general purposes, the central ***Aspava Restaurant***, on Atatürk Bulvarı 29, is OK for ready-made food, kebaps and pide at low prices. You can figure on spending from US$3 to US$5 for a full meal. The smaller ***Şölen*** further downhill in the same block is a bit better and cheaper.

Özhanedan Restaurant, on Gazhane Caddesi 18/A, specialises in kebaps and does a thriving takeaway business. A plate of lamb kebap, a salad and a glass of ayran costs US$3. It closes in the evening.

Park Restaurant, across Atatürk Bulvarı from the Hotel Epok and up the hill through the park, is where Nevşehir's movers and shakers come in the evening to drink rakı and talk politics, sport and business. A full meal costs from US$7 to US$11. There's a pleasant tea garden at the front.

Getting There & Away

Bus Nevşehir's Adnan Menderes Terminali handles both bus and dolmuş services for the area, although you can usually flag down the dolmuşes outside the tourist office as well.

Many passengers who buy intercity bus tickets to Göreme, Ürgüp or another local destination are often bewildered to find their bus terminating its run at Nevşehir. Get off the bus and then ask for the minibus to your destination and it costs nothing extra.

Details on some daily buses and dolmuşes are:

Adana – 285km, five hours, US$10; several
Aksaray – 65km, 1½ hours, US$2.50; frequent minibuses and buses
Ankara – 285km, four hours, US$8; several
Avanos – 17km, 25 minutes, US$1; frequent dolmuşes
Göreme – 8km, 15 minutes, US$0.75; dolmuşes every half hour in summer
İstanbul – 715km, 11 hours, US$12 to US$16; a few buses nightly
Kayseri – 105km, 1½ hours, US$2; very frequent buses and minibuses
Konya – 226km, three hours, US$7; several
Niğde – 85km, one hour, US$2; frequent dolmuşes every half hour in summer
Pamukkale – 674km, 11 hours, US$14; one

Uçhisar – 12km, 20 minutes, US$0.75; dolmuşes
Ürgüp – 18km, 25 minutes, US$1; minibuses every half hour in summer
Yozgat (via Kayseri) – 300km, four hours, US$6

GÖREME

East of Nevşehir, the panorama of Cappadocia begins to unfold: across the sandy landscape, distant rock formations become visible as the so-called fairy chimneys, and valleys with undulating walls of soft volcanic ash fall away from the road. In the distance, the gigantic snow-capped summit of volcanic **Erciyes Dağı** (Mt Aergius) floats above a layer of cloud.

About 12km east of Nevşehir is Göreme village, a magical place set among towering tufa cones and honeycomb cliffs, surrounded by vineyards, and deservedly popular with backpackers.

Once a sleepy farming village named Avcılar, Göreme grew explosively during the 1980s as Turkey's tourism boom swept over it. Nowadays it's chock-a-block with pensions, camping grounds, restaurants and tour agencies. It's the prime place for budget travellers because the beds and meals are cheap and good, and the sights are within walking distance. The Göreme Open-Air Museum is just 1.5km to the south-east.

Life in Göreme is an odd mixture of the modern and the ultra-conservative, with veiled women in the traditional baggy *şalvar* trousers rubbing shoulders with scantily clad tourists throughout the summer. Not altogether surprisingly, this mixture doesn't always work and in recent years there have been a couple of incidents, one of them serious, in the valleys. Sad though it is to say it, women should probably think carefully about walking in the valleys alone, even in daylight.

Orientation & Information

Buses and minibuses drop you off at an eyesore of an otogar-cum-shopping mall with an office detailing all the local accommodation and several travel agencies where you can change money. Immediately in front of the otogar is the main Nevşehir to Avanos road, with a cluster of eating places. Beside and behind the otogar, dry stream beds cut through the village, with pension options leading off on either side. In the Belediye, a small tourist office is open sporadically.

The ATM in front of the Belediye is always busy. Post Change/Exchange to the left of the SOS restaurant tends to have good rates, and changes a lot of currencies, as well as providing phone and fax services, stamps and postcards.

Göreme's postal code is 50180.

Things to See

The town, set amid cones and pinnacles of volcanic tufa, is its own biggest attraction. At its centre is the so-called **Roma Kalesi**, a tall volcanic column with the remains of a rock-cut Roman temple facade high up. The tops of the columns are intact, but the *bottoms* are missing!

You might also look at the **Konak Türk Evi** (Turkish Mansion House, 1826), hidden in the maze of cobbled streets to the east of the village. Once the home of Mehmet Paşa, the local Ottoman grandee, it has two beautifully decorated rooms, the *Selamlık* (men's room) and *Haremlik* (women's room), open to view as a restaurant. The frescoes on the walls were apparently created by the artist responsible for the paintings in the dining room of İstanbul's Topkapı Sarayı.

At the upper limit of the village, the Göreme Vadisi Yürüyüş Patikası (Göreme Valley Walking Trail) wends its way up the valley for 2km, beginning at the S Ataman Hotel.

Göreme Valley

Of all the Cappadocian valleys, Göreme's is the most famous, and rightly so. The entrance to the **Göreme Açık Hava Müzesi** (Göreme Open-Air Museum) is 1.5km uphill from the centre of the village. Try and get to the valley early in the morning in summer and space yourself between tour groups; when lots of people crowd into one of these little churches they block the doorway, which is often the only source of light. Believe me, the mood in a church is completely different when you're there alone.

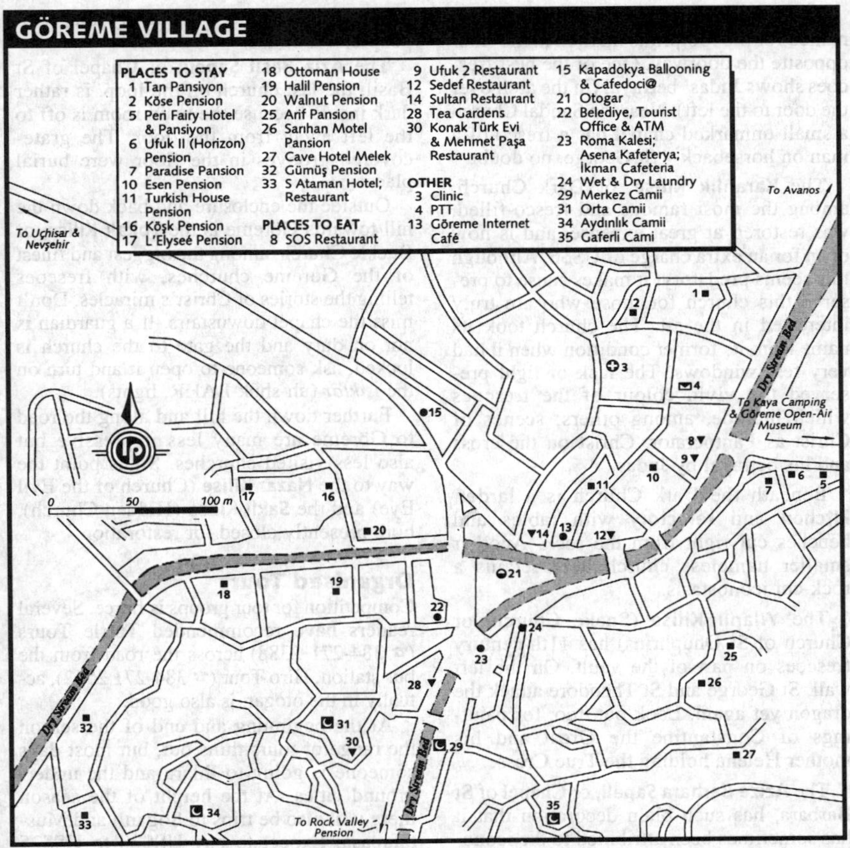

The site is open from 8.30 am to 5.30 pm (4.30 pm in winter) and admission costs US$5 (students US$3). Parking for cars costs US$1.50; for motorcycles and mopeds US$0.60.

It's easy to spend most of the day walking the paths here, climbing stairways or passing through tunnels to reach the various monastery churches with their wonderful, primitive 11th and 12th-century **frescoes**. In between churches, the utter improbability of the landscape floods over you: the lovely, soft textures in the rock, the fairytale cave dwellings, the spare vegetation growing vigorously from the stark but mineral-rich soil.

Walking into the valley from the entrance, you come first to the **Rahibeler Manastırı**, or Nun's Convent, a large plain room with steps up to a smaller domed chapel with frescoes. To the right past the cafe is the similar Monk's Monastery. From this point you can follow a loop path around the valley in either direction. Here are the main sights you come to if you walk clockwise, although the path also winds past various vistas and unmarked churches.

The **Çarıklı Kilise**, or Sandal Church, is named for the footprints marked in the floor opposite the doorway. One of the best frescoes shows Judas' betrayal (in the arch over the door to the left). Near the Sandal Church a small unmarked chapel has a fresco of a man on horseback – St George, no doubt.

The **Karanlık Kilise**, or Dark Church, among the most famous and fresco-filled, was restored at great expense, and is now open for an extra charge of US$6. Although this seems predatory, it makes sense to preserve this church for those who are truly interested in the art. The church took its name from its former condition when it had very few windows. The lack of light preserved the vivid colour of the frescoes which include, among others, scenes of Christ as Pantocrator, Christ on the cross and his betrayal by Judas.

Beneath the Dark Church is a **larder, kitchen** and **refectory** with tables and benches cut right from the rock. Another smaller nameless church here retains a rock-cut iconostasis.

The **Yılanlı Kilise** (Snake Church, or Church of St Onuphrius) has 11th-century frescoes on part of the vault. On the left wall, St George and St Theodore attack the dragon yet again. Look out, too, for paintings of Constantine the Great and his mother Helena holding the True Cross.

The **Azize Barbara Şapeli**, or Chapel of St Barbara, has such plain decoration that it has sometimes been attributed to the iconoclastic period (725-842 AD) when images were outlawed. There are a few fairly worn frescoes of the Virgin Mary and St Barbara as well. On the right three more chapels have carved crosses in the apse and primitive line drawings.

The **Elmalı Kilise**, or Apple Church, has a stunning display of frescoes. There are eight small domes and one large one, and lots of well-preserved paintings. Where's the apple? Some say the Angel Gabriel, above the central nave, is holding it. Underneath the protective plastic covering is some iconoclastic decoration, red ochre painted on the stone, without any images of people or animals.

The **Aziz Basil Şapeli**, or Chapel of St Basil, the last church on the loop, is rather dark inside because the main room is off to the left away from the door. The grate-covered grooves in the floor were burial places.

Outside the enclosure and back down the hill towards Göreme is the **Tokalı Kilise**, or Buckle Church, among the biggest and finest of the Göreme churches, with frescoes telling the stories of Christ's miracles. Don't miss the chapel downstairs. If a guardian is not on duty and the gate to the church is locked, ask someone to open it and turn on the *ışıklar* (uh-shuk-LAHR, lights).

Further down the hill and along the road to Göreme are many less impressive but also less visited churches. Signs point the way to the **Nazar Kilise** (Church of the Evil Eye) and the **Saklı Kilise** (Hidden Church), both presently closed for restoration.

Organised Tours

Competition for tour groups is fierce. Several readers have recommended Turtle Tours (☎ 384-271 2388) across the road from the bus station. Hiro Tour (☎ 384-271 2542), actually in the otogar, is also good.

At the beginning and end of the season the range of tours thins out, but most days someone is going to Ihlara and the underground cities. At the height of the season there will also be trips to Soğanlı and Mustafapaşa. Expect to pay US$20 to US$25 for a day tour by minibus inclusive of lunch. To save arguments later, check whether any visits to carpet shops or onyx factories appear on the itinerary. Most of the pensions either operate their own tours or work with one of the travel agencies.

Rainbow Ranch (☎ 384-271 2413), uphill on the way to the Cave Hotel Melek, rents out horses for US$15 for two hours.

Places to Stay

These days Göreme has 60-plus pensions whose owners have formed a co-operative with an office in Göreme otogar. Head

Floating Above Cappadocia

There's nothing quite like it: you get up before dawn, grab a quick cup of coffee, climb into an all-terrain vehicle and set out for the launch site. As the sky lightens, you watch a pile of fabric the size of a small car become a huge, graceful balloon. Standing in the basket beneath, your pilot turns a valve, flames roar upward into the void, and you lift off into the chill morning air to float across the Cappadocian landscape just as the warming sun makes its way above the horizon.

If you've never taken a flight in a hot-air balloon, Cappadocia is one of the best places in the world to do it. Flight conditions are especially favourable here, with gentle winds most days between April and November. The views are simply unforgettable.

Though the balloon depends upon air currents for lateral movement, a good pilot can control the height with surprising precision. Kaili Kidner and Lars-Eric Möre of Kapadokya Balloons (☎/fax 384-271 2442, fly@kapadokyaballoons.com) boast that they can descend into a Cappadocian valley and 'pick apricots off the trees', which is exactly what they do – if the apricots are ripe and the farmer allows. Because of the winds and the vertical control, every flight is an adventure, and no two flights are the same.

Sturdy Mercedes-Benz all-terrain vehicles follow your flight and assure that wherever the balloon lands it can be recovered.

Flights take place daily at dawn (weather permitting), last for approximately 1¼ hours, and are followed by the traditional champagne toast. Transport from your hotel to the launch site (which is usually near Uçhisar), and return to your hotel after the flight, is included in the price of US$210 per person. The entire adventure takes about four hours, but the memories last a lifetime.

The cost seems high, but life offers few more exhilarating adventures so easily achieved and so thoroughly enjoyable. Reservations are essential. A day in advance is the minimum, but it's even better to book as soon as you arrive in Cappadocia.

From time to time, Kaili and Lars offer promotional fares. You can phone them or, better yet, call in to their office in Göreme uphill on the Uçhisar road to the left of Cafedoci@ for current offerings.

straight there and you'll be guided to the pension of your choice without hassle or deception. The co-operative agrees prices at the start of the season so wherever you go you should get quoted about the same maximum rates for basic accommodation: US$4 to US$5 for a dorm bed, US$6 for a bed in a waterless room and US$7 or US$8 per person in a room with private facilities. Some pensions have areas where you can camp for even less money; others are upgrading some rooms to small-hotel comforts, and raising prices accordingly. Out of season, the discounts may vary.

The lodgings in the central, lower part of the town fill up first. At the height of summer you may have to go up the valley and into the back streets to find the room you want. In general, the further up you go from the centre, the better chance you have of finding a vacant room and getting a discounted price.

Many people want the romance of staying in a tufa cone but few of these have private bathrooms. Rooms cut into the volcanic tufa are also a bit claustrophobic, although they're far cooler than rooms in modern buildings. Some of the pensions are cut into the rockface, so you can get a feel for cave-living in more spacious surroundings.

If you're coming to Göreme from October through May, make sure you pack some warm clothes since it gets very cold at night and most pension owners will delay putting on the heating for as long as possible.

Places to Stay – Budget

Backpackers have always been keen on ***Köse Pension*** *(☎ 384-271 2294, fax 271 2577)*, not far from the PTT. It's run by Mehmet and Dawn Köse and has an 11-bed dorm with mattresses on the floor as well as comfortable bedrooms with balconies and showers. Dinners in the evening cost US$4.50 and there's always one vegetarian and one meat option. Dawn runs a book swap scheme and keeps a visitor's book filled with travel tips rather than adulatory comments.

Close to the Köse, ***Tan Pansiyon*** *(☎ 384-271 2445)*, operated by Göreme's assistant mayor, offers clean doubles with shower in a modern building for US$10 per person, a bit pricey for what you get.

Another place very popular with tight-budget backpackers is Mustafa Yelkalan's ***Rock Valley Pension*** *(☎ 384-271 2153)*, well up the valley from the village centre – follow the bed of the dry canal to find it. As well as the standard double rooms, there's a four-bed dorm in a stone-vaulted room, a laundry service and a restaurant here.

On the road leading to the Göreme Open-Air Museum you'll find the recently upgraded ***Peri (Fairy) Hotel & Pansiyon*** *(☎ 384-271 2136, fax 271 2589)*, where rooms in fairy chimneys stand on one side of a pretty flower-filled courtyard and there's also an inviting bar in a chimney. Meals here are thoroughly enjoyable too. If it's full, the nearby ***Paradise Pansion*** *(☎ 384-271 2248)* and ***Ufuk II (Horizon) Pension*** *(☎ 384-271 2157)* are also good.

For panoramic views of the valley it would be hard to beat ***Arif Pansion*** *(☎ 384-271 2361)*, high up on the south-eastern side of town with several rock-cut rooms. Just below it the similarly quiet and comfortable ***Sarıhan Motel Pansion*** *(☎ 384-271 2216)* also has good views of the town and rock-cut rooms. It boasts central heating as well, useful when the nights grow nippy towards the end of the season.

To the south-west, it's well worth braving the climb up to the flower-bedecked ***Kelebek Pension*** *(☎ 384-271 2531, fax 271 2763)* where you'll be rewarded with panoramic views of Göreme and Uçhisar. A wide choice of accommodation includes a few dorm beds for US$4 and a lovely 'honeymoon' room for US$25. Fairy chimney rooms without bath cost US$12; rooms with stone arches and bath US$18. There's a nice cave bar with rock fireplace and sedir seating. Excellent evening meals are usually available too.

The simple ***Halil Pension*** *(☎ 384-271 2030)*, also has rooms carved right from the rock and slightly lower prices. The similar ***Gümüş*** *(☎ 384-271 2438)*, has a pretty garden and a small rock-cut bar.

On the opposite side of the dry stream bed is the simple ***Köşk Pension*** *(☎ 384-271 2768)* in a quiet position well away from the bars. Some of the bedrooms (US$20) boast spectacular cone views, as does the terrace. Guests can use the cooking facilities.

Nearby, ***L'Elysee Pension*** *(☎ 384-271 2244)*, has French-Turkish management and charges US$14 for a room with shower; breakfast costs US$2 extra, and set-price French-Turkish dinners are sometimes available.

Walnut Pension *(☎ 384-271 2564, fax 271 2235)*, very near the centre and the otogar, has six comfortable rooms designed with traditional vaulted stone ceilings, many comforts, lots of character, and that same low price. There's a cosy, kilim-filled lobby, too.

If all else is full, ***Esen Pension*** *(☎ 384-271 2653)* is serviceable if spartan, and usually quotes prices that are among the lowest in town. ***Turkish House Pension*** nearby is similar.

For a bit more comfort at marginal extra cost, try ***Cave Hotel Melek*** *(☎/fax 384-271 2463)*, 150m uphill from the main street. You enter a small multi-level courtyard, then a village-style lounge with low seats and a fireplace adjoining the dining room.

Guest rooms, in the buildings or carved into the tufa, cost US$18 a waterless double and US$25 a double with private shower, breakfast included.

Camping Best of all is ***Kaya Camping*** *(☎ 384-343 3100, fax 343 3984)*, uphill from the Göreme Open-Air Museum, on the Ortahisar road. Though it's 2km from the centre of Göreme, it's the closest to Göreme Valley and has spectacular views, as well as a swimming pool, solar-heated showers, restaurant, caravan hook-ups, and other services. Camp sites cost US$3.50 per person plus US$1.75 per tent, US$2.25 per caravan. The Aynalıı (Mirror) and Fırkatan churches are reached by paths across the road from the camping ground.

Dilek Camping and ***Berlin Camping***, adjoining camping grounds across from the Peri Hotel & Pension on the Göreme Valley road, are less fancy but convenient to the centre of Göreme village. The price for a tent and two people is US$6.

Places to Stay – Mid-Range

Ottoman House *(☎ 384-271 2616, fax 271 2351, ottoman@indigoturizm.com.tr, Orta Mahalle 21)* boasts near-luxury at affordable prices: US$20/30 a single/double; breakfast costs another US$5 per person; a set menu dinner US$8. Marble steps lead off a comfortable lobby to pleasant modern rooms with pretty quilts and photographs of Cappadocia on the walls. In the basement both the restaurant and the Harem Bar are densely decorated with carpets, kilims, old costumes and other handicrafts.

Places to Stay – Top End

At the end of the road running past the Ottoman House is ***S Ataman Hotel*** *(☎ 384-271 2310, fax 271 2313, info@atamanhotel.com)* created out of a 200-year-old stone building. The 48 rooms are individually decorated with carpets and handicrafts but boast all the mod cons (TV, fridge, hair-drier etc) as well, but at US$100/150 a single/double with breakfast and dinner they are way overpriced. There's a basement disco and bar and a good restaurant.

Places to Eat

Most Göreme pensions provide good, cheap meals. The town's eateries also generally serve wine and beer.

Clustered at the foot of the Roma Kalesi are several popular indoor-outdoor cafe-restaurants, including ***Asena Kafeterya*** and ***İkman Cafeteria***, both serving such things as chicken şiş kebap for around US$3, or pide for less.

The small ***SOS Restaurant*** near the PTT at the intersection of the Göreme Valley and Avanos roads serves good inexpensive pide (US$1.75), as well as a full range of other dishes such as spaghetti for US$1 and meat dishes for US$2. A full Turkish breakfast costs US$1.50.

Göreme's Internet cafe is the drolly named ***Cafedoci@*** *(☎ 384-271 2900 or 271 2901, cafedoci@indigoturizm.com.tr, www.indigoturizm.com.tr/cafedoci@)*, uphill on the Uçhisar road near Kapadokya Balloons and the Motel Yüksel. It features Internet terminals, daily newspapers and magazines, a book exchange, movies on a big-screen TV, as well as light meals, coffee, tea and alcoholic beverages at moderate prices.

Another place for emailers is the Göreme Internet Cafe (nesetour@prizma.net.tr), near Sedef Restaurant which is popular and busy, with TNT magazines available.

One of Göreme's best places to eat is ***Orient Restaurant*** *(☎ 384-271 2346)*, on the left-hand side of the road heading out towards Uçhisar. An excellent, filling four-course meal with soft drink costs $4.50, but you can also pick and choose from the main menu and eat inside or out depending on the weather.

The row of restaurants in the centre along the Uçhisar road are the place for a leisurely, moderately priced meal. The ***Sultan***, for example, does an excellent *güveç kiremitte* (lamb stew with vegetables served on a hot clay tile) for US$3.50. ***Sedef*** and ***Ufuk II*** are similar, each taking its turn as the favourite from one season to the next. A dinner with drinks (which are relatively expensive) might cost US$8 to US$16 in any of them.

Göreme's most historic eatery is ***Mehmet Paşa Restaurant*** *(☎/fax 384-271 2207)* in the Konak Türk Evi, with an open-air terrace, several charming dining rooms and a bar. The menu lists a mixture of Turkish, Ottoman and continental specialities. Expect to spend from US$8 to US$15 for a full meal.

S Ataman Restaurant *(☎ 384-271 2310, fax 271 2313)*, up the valley at the top of the village, is clearly aimed at the bus-tour clientele who arrive frequently and abundantly, but provides good food and service in pleasant surroundings. The rock-hewn dining rooms are decorated with Turkish crafts. A full meal with drinks will probably cost from US$10 to US$20 per person.

Getting There & Away

Minibuses leave Göreme's otogar every half hour in summer for Nevşehir (see that section) where you can connect with services all round the country.

Getting Around

There are several places to hire mountain bikes, mopeds and motor scooters. Bikes cost around US$8, mopeds and scooters go for US$14 for four hours, US$20 for eight hours, or US$30 for 24 hours. For a couple, two scooters will thus cost about the same as a rental car. You must leave your passport as a security deposit.

Some tips on moped and scooter rental: take only a machine that's in good repair, even if it's more expensive. Beware rental places which rent you a bike with dents in it, then charge you for causing the dent when you return the machine. (They'll charge the next renter as well; in effect, one dent can pay for a whole bike.) Zemi Rent-a-Scooter (☎ 384-271 2576, fax 271 2577), in the Zemi Tours office near the SOS Restaurant and the PTT on the main Uçhisar road, is reputable.

Since Göreme doesn't have any fuel stations and the rental companies will hike fuel prices, fill up the tank in Nevşehir, Avanos or Ürgüp before returning the bike.

Warning

A warning is needed about so-called direct bus services to Göreme. Several readers have complained that they bought tickets on buses which, they were told, were going 'directly to Göreme', only to find themselves dumped in Nevşehir in the early hours. It might be best to assume you're going to have to change in Nevşehir to a Göreme-bound minibus to complete your journey. There should be no extra charge. We've also received reports of Göreme tickets costing substantially more than Nevşehir tickets, when in fact there should be only about a US$1 difference.

ÇAVUŞİN

From Göreme, the Avanos road leads north 4km to Çavuşin, with its **Church of John the Baptist** near the top of the cliff which rises behind the village. About 500m north of the village, along the road, is the **Çavuşin Kilisesi** church by the Galeri Kapadokya Onyx Factory (look for the iron stairway).

Çavuşin is the starting point for **scenic hikes** in the volcanic valleys and vineyards to the east of the village, including Güllüdere Vadisi (Rose Valley) and Kızılçukur (Red Gulch Valley). If you're up for a long walk, you can even go as far as the Zindanönü overlook (6.5km), then walk out to the Ürgüp-Ortahisar road and hitch or catch a dolmuş back to your base.

Several small, simple pensions in the village allow you to escape the hustle and-bustle of the larger towns. ***Panorama Pansion*** *(☎ 384-532 7002)* charges US$12 for a waterless double, breakfast included, as does ***Turbel***.

ZELVE

A side road from Çavuşin heads up another valley 5km to Zelve, which is almost as rich in churches and strange panoramas as Göreme, but much less organised. Halfway along the road are groupings of curious 'three-headed' fairy chimneys near a row of souvenir stalls.

Zelve was a monastic retreat. The valleys here don't have as many impressive painted churches, though you should see the few marked by signs.

The **Balıklı Kilise**, or Fish Church, has fish figuring in one of the primitive paintings, and the more impressive **Üzümlü Kilise** (Grape Church) has obvious bunches of grapes. Look also for the **Değirmen** (mill). Unfortunately, erosion continues to destroy the structures in the valley, and some parts may be closed because of the danger of collapse. There are also some sections included in tours which involve walking in pitch dark and scrambling down a frightening ladder. Take a torch/flashlight and be prepared.

Zelve's opening hours are from 8 am to 6 pm (last admission at 5.30 pm) and admission costs US$2.50. There are restaurants and tea gardens just outside.

VALLEY OF THE FAIRY CHIMNEYS

From Zelve, go 400m back down the access road and turn right on a paved road marked for Ürgüp. After 2km you'll come to the village of **Aktepe** (Yeni Zelve). Bear right, follow the Ürgüp road further uphill and, after less than 2km, you'll find yourself in the Valley of the Fairy Chimneys (Peribacalar Vadisi).

Though many Cappadocian valleys boast collections of strange volcanic cones, these are the best-formed and most thickly clustered. Most of the rosy rock cones are topped by flattish, darker stones of harder rock. These dark cap-stones sheltered the cones from the rains which eroded all the surrounding rock, a process known to geologists as differential erosion.

If you continue to the top of the ridge, you will find yourself on the Avanos-Ürgüp road, with Avanos to the left, Ürgüp to the right.

UÇHİSAR

Uçhisar, 8km east of Nevşehir and 4km south-west of Göreme, is dominated by the **Kale**, a tall volcanic rock outcrop riddled with tunnels and windows, and visible for miles around. Now a tourist attraction (open from 8 am to sunset for US$1), it provides panoramic views of the Cappadocian valleys and countryside.

There's less to see and do in Uçhisar than in Göreme or Ürgüp, but that also means there are fewer tourists except in the immediate vicinity of the Kale. There's a pleasant walk to Göreme along the signposted **Dovecote Valley** (Güvercinlik Vadisi) where the rockface is riddled with holes cut to attract nesting pigeons and their valuable fertiliser droppings.

Places to Stay & Eat

Uçhisar has its own collection of pensions, hotels and restaurants, many especially popular with French tourists. Most lodging-places have their own restaurants, and there are several independent restaurants near the central park, called Belediye Meydanı. Lodgings east of the main square are modern places overlooking the Dovecote Valley; those downhill along Göreme Caddesi are older, partly cut into the rock and cones.

Heading east, right by the main square on the edge of Güvercinlik Vadisi, is ***Pension Méditerranée*** *(☎ 384-219 2210, fax 219 2669)*, a hotel-like place with fabulous views, a nice roof restaurant and shower-equipped rooms – some of them surprisingly spartan – for US$13/17/24 a single/double/triple, including breakfast. The nearby ***Villa Pansion*** *(☎ 384-219 2089, fax 219 2680)*, to the left of the PTT, is a pleasant enough building with a terrace restaurant, though it lacks views. So does the adjoining, friendly ***Erciyes Pension*** *(☎ 384-219 2090)* which makes up for it with a lovely garden full of apple and walnut trees. Beds in clean rooms here cost US$7.

Beyond these pensions is the much swisher ***Villa du Club-Kaya Otel*** *(☎ 384-219 2007, fax 219 2363)*, a Club Med hotel carved into the volcanic tufa with fabulous views. Comfortable rooms cost US$40 per person, breakfast and dinner included. Even if you don't stay here you can use the magnificently sited outdoor swimming pool for US$3. The Kaya closes from October to March. Its ***Bindallı Restaurant*** *(☎ 384-219 2690)* is

Uçhisar's best, offering a magnificent lunch buffet for US$10. Beyond Kaya Otel is ***Başaran Pension** (☎ 384-219 2222)* which advertises its 'vue superbe sur la vallée des pigeons'. Clean simple rooms cost US$13 a double including breakfast.

Heading west from the main square, Göreme Caddesi turns downhill through the old village of Uçhisar. Here, 400m along, you'll find ***La Maison du Rêve** (☎ 384-212 2199, fax 219 2775, Tekelli Mahallesi 17)*, with three storeys of simple rock-cut rooms, each with a sweeping terrace, for US$18 a double with shower and breakfast. ***Buket Pansiyon** (☎ 384-219 2490)* has several very nice cave rooms with interesting features and a cave dining room where guests eat together in the evening. Beds cost US$8 per person.

***Le Jardin des 1001 Nuits** (☎ 384-219 2293)* has been created out of a cluster of cones so that each room is different. Beds vary in price, with the cheapest costing US$9 and the most expensive US$22. Nearby is ***Kaya Pension** (☎ 384-219 2441, fax 219 2079)*, with a lovely plant and kilim-filled lobby, a big terrace, fine views, and double rooms with shower and breakfast for US$20.

Uçhisar's finest accommodations are the villas called ***Les Maisons de Cappadoce** (☎ 384-219 2813, fax 219 2782, cappadoce@ilink.fr, www.cappadoce.com, Belediye Meydanı 24)*, rented from an office in the main square. Exquisitely renovated, fully furnished and decorated by French architect Jacques Avizou, the villas sleep between two and eight people and can be rented by the half week, week or longer. Prices range from US$90 (two persons) to US$300 (six persons) per night, with reduced rates for stays of several nights or longer.

Getting There & Away

There are regular Uçhisar Belediyesi buses from Nevşehir, or you can take the half-hourly Nevşehir bus from Göreme and get out at the road junction for Uçhisar.

ORTAHİSAR

The village of Ortahisar, 3km south-east of the Göreme Valley, is near the intersection of the Nevşehir to Ürgüp and Göreme roads. A Cappadocian farming village at heart, Ortahisar's main claim to fame is its **kale**, an 18-metre-high rock used as a fortress in Byzantine times and a great place to come for sunset panoramas. From Ortahisar you can also hike to various lesser churches in the surrounding countryside, especially in the Pancarlık Valley.

Ortahisar's postal code is 50650.

Places to Stay

There are limited accommodation choices in the village centre, 1.5km from the main road intersection. Try the basic ***Hotel Gümüş** (☎ 384-343 3127)*, to the right of the PTT, which charges US$6 per person in a room with shower.

Continue up the hill past the PTT and turn left for the ***Hotel Burcu** (☎ 384-343 3800, fax 343 3500)*, a comfortable, atmospheric hotel which has 49 motel-style rooms around a courtyard. Rooms are comfortable, with immaculate bathrooms, and reasonably priced at US$16/25.

The comfortable ***Hotel Yeni Yükseller** (☎ 384-343 3171, fax 343 3451)*, Kayseri Caddesi, at the junction with the Ürgüp-Nevşehir road, charges a reasonable US$50 for a double with shower and breakfast, and includes use of the swimming pool.

Getting There & Away

There are regular Ortahisar Belediyesi buses from Nevşehir otogar, and plenty of dolmuşes along the Ürgüp-Nevşehir road.

ÜRGÜP

About 23km east of Nevşehir and 7km east of Göreme Valley is the town of Ürgüp (population 11,000, altitude 1060m), at the heart of the Cappadocian wonderland. Because of the volcanic soil, sufficient water and abundant sunshine, the town is surrounded by a rich landscape of grain fields, vineyards and clusters of beehives.

Ürgüp has many large bus tour group hotels on its eastern outskirts, but the centre of town retains many old stone buildings and the businesses necessary to a farming community, which is what Ürgüp is at heart. In its older quarters, houses of tawny volcanic rock still bear many traces of the elaborate decoration with which the town was once graced.

Orientation & Information

Ürgüp is set within a steep valley. The otogar is right in the centre, off the main street, Kayseri Caddesi, which is sprinkled with antique shops, carpet shops and restaurants.

The unusually helpful and well informed Tourism Information Office (☎ 384-341 4059) is at Kayseri Caddesi 37, down the hill from the main square behind a tea garden and open every day from 8 am to 6 pm (8 pm in summer). The town's uninspiring museum, open daily from 8 am to 5 pm, is right next door. Admission costs US$1.

Ürgüp has far too many travel agencies which are competing for too little business. Most are clustered around the otogar and several are staffed by seriously unpleasant young men. Argeus Tours (☎ 384-341 4688, fax 341 5207, info@argeus.com.tr,

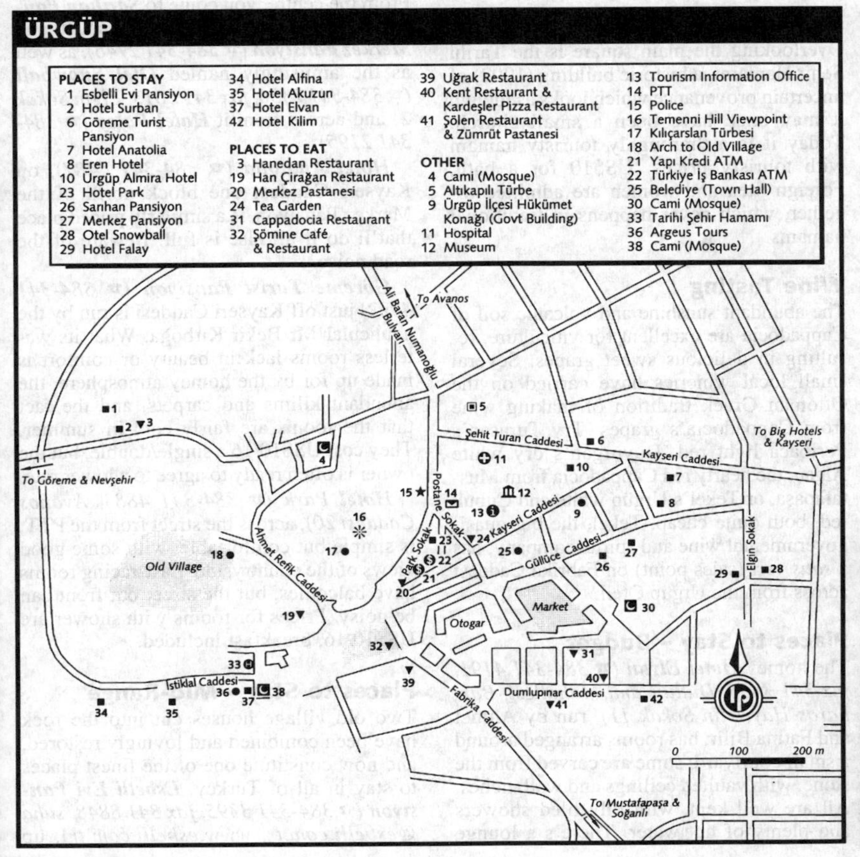

www.argeus.com.tr), İstiklal Caddesi 13, behind the hamam, can help with bicycling, walking and riding holidays as well as with day tours, airport transport and flights.

A Walk Around Town

West of the main square is the oldest part of the town, reached through a stone arch, with many fine old houses. It's worth a stroll, after which you can stroll up Ahmet Refik Caddesi and turn right to reach the Temenni hilltop, with a saint's tomb, a terrace cafe, and fine views of the town. North of the centre is a historic tomb, the Altıkapılı Türbe.

Hamam

Overlooking the main square is the Tarihi Şehir Hamamı, a historic building (1902) of uncertain provenance which looks as though it may once have been a small church. Today it is a thoroughly touristy hamam with touristy prices: US$10 for a bath. Foreign men and women are admitted together, which never happens in traditional hamams.

Wine Tasting

The abundant sunshine and volcanic soil of Cappadocia are excellent for viticulture, resulting in delicious sweet grapes. Several small local wineries have carried on the Ottoman Greek tradition of making wine from Cappadocia's grapes. Try Turasan's Peribaca light red, Duyurgan's dry white Algan, the hearty red Cappadocia from Mustafapaşa, or Tekel's Ürgüp white and Çubuk red, both quite cheap. Tekel, the big quasi-governmental wine and spirits company, has a *satış yeri* (sales point) on Fabrika Caddesi across from the Ürgüp Oteli.

Places to Stay – Budget

The homey ***Hotel Elvan*** *(☎ 384-341 4191, fax 341 3455, Dutlu Cami Mahallesi, Barbaros Hayrettin Sokak 11)*, run by Ahmet and Fatma Bilir, has rooms arranged around a small courtyard; some are carved from the stone, with vaulted ceilings and wall niches. All are well kept, with tidy tiled showers and plenty of hot water. There's a lounge with carpets and sedirs and a roof terrace with a fireplace grill and panoramic views. Older, simpler rooms cost US$20 to US$25 a double; newer, nicer rooms go for US$30, breakfast included.

South of the market ***Hotel Kilim*** *(☎ 384-341 4481, fax 341 3620, Dumlupınar Caddesi 47)* offers good value for money. Clean rooms with insect screens, showers and marvellously kitschy fairy-chimney nightlights go for US$10/16 a single/double.

Güllüce Sokak, the street south of Kayseri Caddesi, has many cheapies, charging US $10/16 for a waterless single/double room. From the centre, you come to ***Sarıhan Pansiyon*** *(☎ 384-341 8813, fax 341 5820)* and ***Merkez Pansiyon*** *(☎ 384-341 2746)*, as well as the amusingly named ***Otel Snowball*** *(☎ 384-341 2356, fax 341 5613, Elgin Sokak 2)* and across from it ***Hotel Falay*** *(☎ 384-341 2195)*.

Hotel Anatolia *(☎ 384-341 4487)*, on Kayseri Caddesi one block north of the Merkez Pansiyon, is a similarly priced place that'll do if all else is full. Beware of the road noise.

Göreme Turist Pansiyon *(☎ 384-341 4022)* just off Kayseri Caddesi is run by the avuncular Mr Bekir Kırboğa. What its waterless rooms lack in beauty or comfort is made up for by the homey atmosphere, the abundant kilims and carpets, and the fact that the rooms are fairly cool in summer. They cost US$10/16 a single/double, but the owner is often ready to agree to a lower rate.

Hotel Park *(☎ 384-341 4883, Avanos Caddesi 20)*, across the street from the PTT, is simple but comfortable, with some good views of the countryside. East-facing rooms have balconies, but the street out front can be noisy. Prices for rooms with shower are US$10/16, breakfast included.

Places to Stay – Mid-Range

Two old village houses cut into the rock have been combined and lovingly restored, and now constitute one of the finest places to stay in all of Turkey. ***Esbelli Evi Pansiyon*** *(☎ 384-341 3395, fax 341 8848, suha @esbelli.com.tr, www.esbelli.com.tr)*, up the long hill from the main square, across the road from the huge, ugly Turban Motel, is the work of Mr Süha Ersöz, for whom it is a labour of love. The pristine rooms, many fashioned from caves, all have modern bathrooms with showers and direct-dial phones. Two sun deck-terraces, two lounges, and a modern kitchen and laundry facilities are at your disposal. Several of the rooms, including the one for honeymooners, have fine iron bedsteads. One room is in what was once a rock-cut kitchen complete with soaring chimney. Another would be ideal for families, with a big double bed, a single and a cot. Rates are US$55/75 a single/double, excellent breakfast included. Advance reservations are essential, and prices are fixed (no discounts).

The new three-storey ***Eren Hotel*** *(☎ 384-341 3115, İmran Mahallesi, Güllüce Sokak 1)* has clean rooms with small balconies and quilts on the beds for US$16/26, breakfast included. Rooms at the back are likely to be quietest.

Hotel Surban *(☎ 384-341 4603, fax 341 3223),* Yunak Mahallesi, is 500m uphill from the centre on the road towards Nevşehir, near the Hanedan Restaurant. Modern and comfortable, it offers value for money: good rooms with bath for US$22/32, breakfast in a rock-cut basement thrown in.

Hotel Alfina *(☎ 384-341 4822, fax 341 2424),* on İstiklal Caddesi, a 10-minute walk back up the hill from the otogar, has 32 comfortable rooms hewn from the volcanic rock. The price, at US$36/53, is hardly prehistoric, but how many times do you get the chance to live in a cave? This place is not for claustrophobes though, and some find the external architecture unsympathetic.

Further down İstiklal Caddesi, a short stroll from the main square, ***Hotel Akuzun*** *(☎ 384-341 3869, fax 341 3785)* has 33 new rooms for US$28/48/66 a single/double/triple; breakfast costs extra.

Places to Stay – Top End

There are numerous four-star hotels on the eastern outskirts catering almost exclusively to groups, but right in town on Kayseri Caddesi just past the museum is the 101 room four-star ***Ürgüp Almira Hotel*** *(☎ 384-341 8990, fax 341 8999, Kayseri Caddesi 43),* with a swimming pool, shop, restaurant and bar. Air-con rooms with TVs and fridges are priced at an unconscionable US$70/100 a single/double, so bargaining may be in order.

Places to Eat – Budget

Cappadocia Restaurant, with a few outdoor tables and many more indoor, fairly attentive service and decent three-course meals for around US$4 or US$5, is in the street beside the market to Dumlupınar Caddesi.

For cheaper meals continue to Dumlupınar Caddesi. ***Kardeşler Pizza Restaurant*** specialises in kebaps and good cheap pide and pizza – including vegetarian – for under US$2. ***Şölen Restaurant & Pide Salonu*** across the street is similar, with sidewalk tables in shade during the afternoon. The drearier ***Kent Restaurant***, more or less across the street from the Hotel Kilim, has *saç kavurma* and *kiremit kebap* for less than US$3. The latter two restaurants serve breakfast.

On Fabrika Caddesi, near the entrance to the otogar, is ***Uğrak Restaurant***, with a few outdoor tables on the busy street corner and full meals for US$4.

Luckily, Ürgüp has many pastry shops near its main square. The longstanding ***Merkez Pastanesi*** is the best in town. A large glass of tea and a portion of cake cost less than US$2. ***Zümrüt*** on Dumlupınar Caddesi is another good one, with outdoor tables.

Places to Eat – Mid-Range

The town's most prominent eatery is ***Şömine Cafe & Restaurant***. Right on the main square, its high terrace provides outdoor tables to supplement those inside. Ürgüp-style kebaps baked on tiles are a speciality; some of the mezes are disappointing so choose carefully. Full meals with drinks cost from US$8 to US$14.

Han Çirağan Restaurant is at the far end of the main square in an old stone house behind a vine-covered garden. In summer you can dine outside in a pleasant small courtyard. During my last visit it had fallen on hard times and had few customers, but it may well revive by the time you arrive.

Grills and good mezes are the specialities at ***Hanedan Restaurant*** *(☎ 384-341 4266)*, uphill from the centre on the road to Nevşehir. Tablecloths and polite service compliment the good food; full meals with drinks cost between US$10 and US$18. This place is popular with groups so it would be wise to ring ahead and reserve a table in advance.

Entertainment

Dining and drinking is Ürgüp's prime evening's entertainment. For a show as well, you can go to the Karakuş Entertainment Center (☎ 384-341 5353, fax 341 5356), on the outskirts of Ürgüp in the Pancarlık district along the Mustafapaşa road. Dinner with unlimited drinks and a Turkish folklore show costs US$15 if you make your reservation directly with Karakuş, or twice as much if you reserve through your hotel or a travel agency.

Getting There & Away

Bus and minibus services are frequent and convenient in high summer with less frequent services in winter.

Arğeus Tours, Ürgüp's Turkish Airlines representative, runs a minibus to transport passengers to and from THY flights. Contact them for details and reserve your place in advance if possible.

Details of some daily services follow:

Adana – 308km, five hours, US$8; one bus
Ankara – 300km, 4½ hours, US$10; at least seven buses in summer
Antalya – 485km, 10 hours, US$15; one or two buses
İstanbul – 725km, 11 hours, US$12 to US$18; at least two buses
Kayseri – 80km, 1½ hours, US$2; hourly minibuses from 7 am to 7 pm
Konya – 250km, three hours, US$7; at least every two hours from 8 am to 8 pm
Nevşehir – 18km, 25 minutes, US$1; minibuses every half-hour
Pamukkale – 690km, 11 hours, US$15; at least one bus in summer

Getting Around

Minibuses run the tourist circuit hourly, each day from June to September, departing from Ürgüp for the Göreme Valley, Göreme village, Zelve, Avanos etc. You can hop on and off anywhere around the loop, but each ride costs US$0.60.

The major international car companies – Avis, Europcar (National), Hertz and Interrent – all have franchisees with offices near Ürgüp's main square, within one block of the otogar. For more details on renting cars, see the Getting Around chapter.

Agencies in town rent bicycles, mopeds and motorcycles at prices similar to those given in the Göreme section.

In summer it's usually fairly easy to hitchhike as well.

AVANOS

North of Göreme, on the banks of the river Kızılırmak, lies Avanos (AH-vah-nohs, population 12,000, altitude 910m), once called Venessa, another potential base for exploring the Cappadocian valleys. Like Ürgüp, Avanos is coy about revealing its charms compared to Göreme, but head up into the old village behind the central square and you'll find lovely old stone houses, some of them decorated with ancient motifs – an almost rural setting inside a small town.

Modern Avanos is famous for its pottery. The town's workshops still turn out pots, ashtrays, lamps, chess sets and other utensils and souvenirs moulded from the red clay of the Kızılırmak, or Red River, as they have been doing for centuries. Most of these workshops welcome visitors who would like to find out about pottery or even try their hand at it.

If you're not staying overnight, Avanos is still a good place for lunch or a çay break. There are banks, a PTT, pensions, hotels, restaurants, pharmacies and other such necessities.

Orientation & Information

Most of the town is on the northern bank of the river, with Atatürk Caddesi providing the main thoroughfare. The otogar is south of the river, although many of the dolmuşes also stop outside the PTT to the north, across from the main square which is marked by a large and amusing monument. There's a Tourism Information Office (☎ 384-511 4360) in the main square.

Avanos' postal code is 50500.

Things to See

In the main square is a marvellous **monument**. Made entirely of red clay pottery, it shows an amazingly lifelike potter at work. Below it is a scene depicting a woman and a girl weaving a Turkish carpet – another traditional Avanos craft. On the left side is a bearded, shorts-clad, camera-toting tourist holding a bunch of grapes and laughing while standing on a huge pair of hands. At the back of the monument a woman sits on a donkey with a child peering out of a saddlebag. On the right side is a self-portrait of the monument's creator, H Ömer Taşkın, who finished the work in 1974.

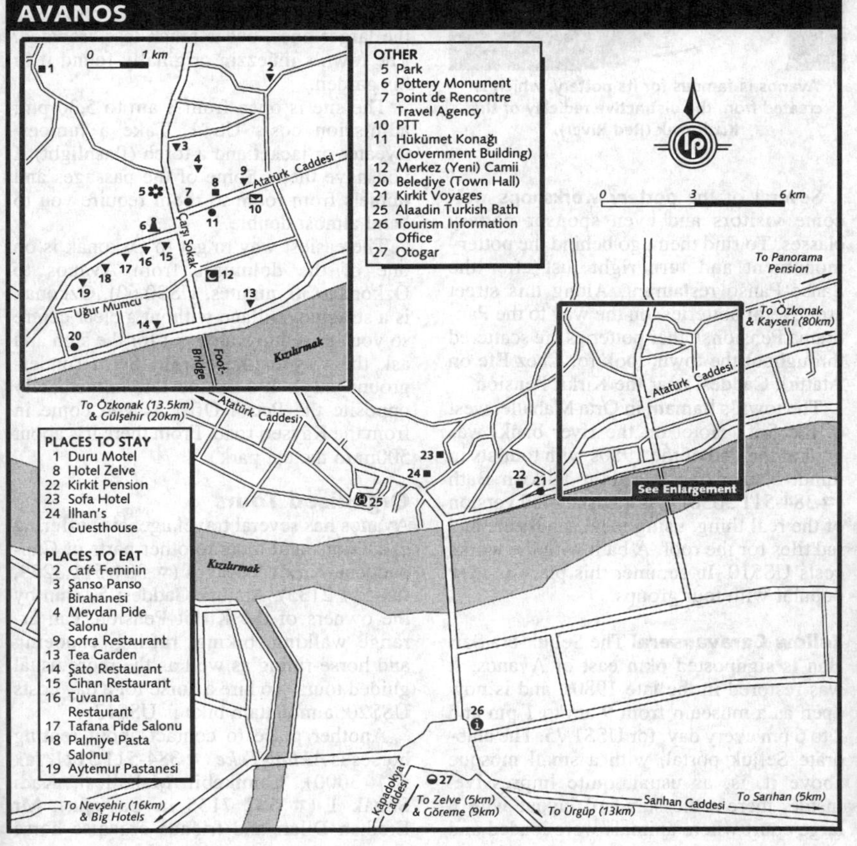

CENTRAL ANATOLIA

Avanos is famous for its pottery, which is created from the distinctive red clay of the Kızılırmak (Red River).

Several of the **pottery workshops** welcome visitors and even sponsor pottery classes. To find them, go behind the pottery monument and turn right just after the Şanso-Panso restaurant. Along this street are several potteries, on the way to the Panorama Pension. Other potteries are scattered throughout the town; look for Chez Efe on Atatürk Caddesi near the Kirkit Pension.

The town's **hamam** in Orta Mahalle, west of the Sofa Hotel on the river bank, was built at the end of the 1980s with tourists in mind. Named the Alaaddin Turkish Bath (☎ 384-511 5036), it is a Disneyfied version of the real thing, using local sandstone and red tiles for the roof. A bath with the works costs US$10. In summer this place is very popular with tour groups.

Yellow Caravanserai The Seljuk-era Sarı Han is signposted 6km east of Avanos. It was restored in the late 1980s, and is now open as a museum from 9 am to 1 pm and 2 to 6 pm every day, for US$1.75. The elaborate Seljuk portal, with a small mosque above it, is, as usual, quite impressive. Inside, there's the standard layout with a large court where animals were loaded and unloaded, and a great hall where people and animals could escape the weather. If you climb to the top of the walls, try to ignore the capstones of concrete in the restoration.

Getting there is difficult without a car, as there are no dolmuşes and few vehicles along the road to hitch a ride with. You may have to haggle with a taxi driver in Avanos.

Özkonak Underground City North of Avanos is the village of Özkonak, beneath which is a small version of the underground cities to be seen at Kaymaklı and Derinkuyu, with the same wine reservoirs, air shafts, rolling stone doors, grindstones etc. It's not nearly so dramatic or impressive as the larger ones, but is much less crowded. The town's müezzin originally found it in his garden.

The site is open from 8 am to 5.30 pm; admission costs US$1. Take a jumper/sweater or jacket and a torch (flashlight) if you have them. Some of the passages and tunnels from room to room require you to bend almost double.

The easiest way to get to Özkonak is on one of the dolmuşes from Avanos to Özkonak (30 minutes, US$0.60). Özkonak is a straggley village without a clear centre so you'll need to watch out for the sign and ask the way to the Yeraltı Şehri (underground city). It's on the left immediately opposite the Petrol Ofisi as you come in from the Kayseri road. From there it's about 500m to the car park.

Organised Tours

Avanos has several travel agencies offering excursions and tours to other parts of Cappadocia. Kirkit Voyages (☎ 384-511 3259, fax 511 2135), Atatürk Caddesi 50, run by the owners of the Kirkit Pension, can arrange walking, biking, rafting, canoeing and horse-riding as well as the more usual guided tours. To hire a horse for a day costs US$20; a mountain bike is US$13.

Another place to contact about renting horses is ***Akhal-Teke*** (☎ 384-511 5171, fax 511 3000), Camikebir Mahallesi, Kadı Sokak 1 (☎ 532 7135 in Çavuşin). Mr Ercihan Dilari and friends organise horse riding trips to the Yellow Caravanserai (Sarı Han), Rose Valley (Güllü Vadisi), and other local sights for about US$46 per day.

Special Events

Avanos is a handicrafts town and its citizens sponsor the annual Avanos Elsanatları Festivalı (Avanos Handicrafts Festival) for three days in late August.

Places to Stay – Budget

Perhaps the best place to stay is ***Kirkit Pension*** (☎ *384-511 3148, fax 511 2135*), run by Tovi and Ahmet Diler who spend the winter months in Paris, but open the pension to guests from April to October. Four old stone houses have been turned into a pension full of nooks and crannies where backpackers can meet and chat. Beds cost US$7 in waterless rooms, US$9 in rooms with shower, breakfast included. There's a restaurant cut into the rockface at the back where good food and wine (as you'd expect in a place popular with the French) are sometimes served up with ad hoc music sessions. Tovi, who is an Australian-Israeli, and Ahmet, who speaks fluent English and French, organise popular walking, bicycle and horseback tours.

Immediately in front of the Sofa Hotel is ***İlhan's Guesthouse*** (☎ *384-511 4828, Orta Mahalle Zafer Sokak 1*), with similar prices. One special room at the back has a fireplace, is furnished in antiques, and costs just a bit more – ask for it. There's a breakfast terrace with river views. İlhan speaks English.

Another low-price favourite is ***Panorama Pension*** (☎ *384-511 1654*), a five-minute walk (250m) uphill through the back streets of the old town, with impressive views from the terrace. There are 18 rooms sleeping from two to four persons; bed and breakfast costs from US$6 to US$11, depending upon the room and whether it has a private shower.

Places to Stay – Mid-Range

Sofa Hotel (☎ *384-511 5186, fax 511 4489, Orta Mahalle 13*) is three old stone houses joined into one, renovated and equipped with mod cons. Several of its shower-equipped rooms are partially built into the rock, and there's a sizeable restaurant, attractively decorated with kilims and cushions and the owner's own paintings. You can live the troglodytic life here for US$20/35 a single/double, breakfast included.

High above the town stands ***Duru Motel*** (☎ *384-511 4005*), a white two-storey block with a grassy terrace and wonderful views over the town, the river and the valley. Rooms have insect screens, tiled bathrooms with showers (hot water all the time) and friendly management. You can have breakfast on the terrace, enjoying the view, then bake your body on the sundeck. Prices are US$15/23, breakfast included; a good home-made four-course dinner goes for US$7. To find it, follow the signs up the winding, narrow street to the top, or ask at the Duru Carpet Shop at the back of the main square.

Hotel Zelve (☎ *384-511 4524, fax 511 4687*), Kenan Evren Caddesi, just off the main square across from the Hükümet Konağuı (Government Building), is pleasant and modern, with kilims in the lobby and functional guest rooms with bath going for US$15/28 a single/double, with breakfast.

Across the bridge on the road to Göreme are a number of three and four-star hotels, intended for the group trade but available to individual travellers as well. These include the four-star, 84 room ***Hotel Altınyazı*** (☎ *384-511 2010*), the four-star, 178 room ***Hotel Yıltok*** (☎ *384-511 2313*), the three-star, 46 room ***Hotel Palansaray*** (☎ *384-511 4044*), and the four-star ***Avrasya Otel*** (☎ *384-511 5181*).

Places to Eat & Drink

For simple meals, ***Cihan Restaurant*** (jee-HAHN) on the main square is a popular ready-food and broiled-chicken place open for all three meals, and usually full. Lunch or dinner might cost US$3 or US$4. ***Sofra Restaurant***, next to the Hotel Zelve and facing the government building, is similar.

Tuvanna is slightly fancier and more expensive, with şiş kebap and small beef steaks priced from US$2.50 to US$5, full meals from US$8 to US$12, but their pizza is only US$2.75.

Şanso-Panso Birahanesi, on the right up the slope of the main square behind the pottery monument, serves Efes Pilsen beer and food and is the closest thing Avanos has to a taverna. Its speciality is *güveç*, beef mixed up with potatoes, tomatoes, garlic, paprika and cumin and baked in a clay pot (US$2.50). Also here is ***Meydan Pide Salonu***, to the left of the Point de Rencontre travel agency, serving cheap pide at outdoor tables. There's another good, cheap pide place, ***Tafana Pide Salonu***, Kenan Evren Caddesi 47.

Along the river, south of the main square, is ***Şato Restaurant***, in a mock castle, which is actually a bar with occasional good live music by local saz players.

For dinner and entertainment, try ***Dragon Restaurant***, 1.5km west of the Sofa Hotel along the Gülşehir road. Popular with tour groups, this cave-club provides food and drink, as well as Turkish folk and belly dancing most summer evenings. Expect to spend a total of about US$20 for the entire evening.

Café Feminin, uphill behind the Şanso-Panso, is an innovative eating, sipping and talking place primarily for women.

For pastries, there's ***Aytemur Pastanesi***, near the Tuvanna, where one of the special banana rolls and a large glass of tea costs under US$1.50, and the nearby ***Palmiye Pasta Salonu***.

Getting There & Away

Avanos Belediyesi buses travel the route from Avanos via Çavuşin, Göreme and Uçhisar to Nevşehir every 30 minutes in summer from 6.45 am to 6.15 pm, for US$1. There are less-frequent services in winter.

MUSTAFAPAŞA

Called Sinasos when it was an Ottoman Greek town before WWI, Mustafapaşa is today the relatively undiscovered gem of Cappadocia, a quiet village with lovely old stone-carved houses, several minor rock-cut churches and a growing selection of places to stay.

On the ride from Ürgüp (5km), you may want to stop at the **Pancarlık Kilisesi**, reached by a road on the right 2km out of Ürgüp. The church is at the end of this unpaved road (2.5km). It's built into a volcanic cone and has quite brilliant frescoes of saints whose visages are relatively undamaged by the stones of shepherds. Admission costs US$0.75, and it's rarely crowded.

Back on the road, you pass turnings for the **Sarıca and Kepez Churches** before entering the town, coming into a large plaza with a dry central fountain. A shop here doubles as a tourist office of sorts and there's a signboard indicating the whereabouts of the **rock-cut churches** in the vicinity. Follow the road downhill and you'll come to Cumhuriyet Meydanı, the centre of the village with the habitual bust of Atatürk and several tea shops.

Things to See

There's a 19th-century **medrese** with a fine carved portal (including stone columns that swivel) to the south-west.

Admission to the churches usually costs US$1. The **Ayios Nikolaos Manastırı** (Monastery of St Nicholas) is less than 500m from the fountain (follow the signs), past the Monastery and Atasoy pensions. Before reaching it, have a look at the **Ayios Stefanos Church** along the way, which is even nicer, with fine carving and painted decoration. The **Sinasos Church**, 150m uphill from Ayios Nikolaos, is also large with fine decoration, though parts of the structure have collapsed.

Other churches in the area include the one in nearby Cemilköy and, just south of it the **Keşlik Manastırı**, 100m south of the road. The **Altıparmak Church** is just north of Şahinefendi.

Places to Stay & Eat

Mustafapaşa has a couple of cheapie pensions on the road leading to St. Nicholas' monastery. The charming ***Atasoy Pension*** *(☎ 384-353 5378)*, has simple shower-equipped rooms with beds for US$6/10 a single/double, including breakfast. ***Monas-***

tery Pension (☎ *384-353 5005)*, next door is similar, but costs a bit more.

The favourite place to stay, however, is Süleyman Öztürk's ***Old Greek House*** (☎ *384-353 5306, fax 353 5141)*, a wonderful old Ottoman Greek house which still bears some of the original 19th-century painting and decoration. Simple double rooms with shower and breakfast cost US$25. Lunch and dinner are excellent as well.

A close runner-up in the local charm contest is ***Hotel Pacha*** (☎ *384-353 5004, fax 353 5331)*, another restored Ottoman Greek house with flower-filled courtyard and top-floor terrace with lovely views. Shower-equipped rooms here can accommodate two to four people and cost US$12 a head, including breakfast.

Another pleasant choice is the modern ***Hotel Cavit*** (☎ *384-353 5186)*, with a nice garden terrace shaded by grapevines (the grapes are ripe in September). For US$9 per person, per day you get a family-style welcome and breakfast of fresh milk from the cow and home-made fruit preserves from the orchard. It's on the southern side of town as you head out to Soğanlı.

Mustafapaşa's fanciest hotel is ***Otel Sinasos*** (☎ *384-353 5009, fax 353 5435)*, to the west as you come into town from Ürgüp. Bedrooms are in a modern extension to an old Greek house and come attractively decorated, with all mod cons. But the real gem is the restaurant in the old house itself, with its wonderful painted wooden ceilings painstakingly restored and a balcony overlooking a lovely garden. Rooms cost US$18/35 a single/double, well worth a splurge if the groups leave a room vacant.

Getting There & Away

Mustafapaşa Belediyesi buses leave Ürgüp for Mustafapaşa every hour. A brief stop in Mustafapaşa is also included in many day trips to Soğanlı.

GÜZELÖZ

Heading south from Mustafapaşa, the Cappadocian village of Güzelöz provides a place to get away from it all. ***Flower Pension & Restaurant*** (☎ *352-657 4565)*, at the top of the village on the road to Ürgüp, can put you up, as can ***Meryemana Pansiyon & Restaurant*** (☎ *352-657 4567)*, 100m from the junction of the Ürgüp road and the Derinkuyu-Yeşilhisar road.

From Güzelöz, it's 11km south to Soğanlı, or 23km west to Derinkuyu.

SOĞANLI

This valley, about 35km south of Ürgüp via Mustafapaşa and Güzelöz, is much less touristy than Göreme or Zelve. Indeed, in recent years the number of visitors to Soğanlı has actually diminished, probably because it's on the road to nowhere. It's a beautiful and interesting place to explore, and unless your visit coincides with one of the day trips from Göreme, you may well have it to yourself.

The valleys of **Aşağı Soğanlı** (Lower Onion Valley) and **Yukarı Soğanlı** (Upper Onion Valley) were, like Göreme and Zelve, largely monastic. Turn off the main road and proceed 5km to the village after passing a barrier and paying the admission fee of US$1 near the Kapadokya Restaurant. The churches are open from 8.30 am to 5.30 pm.

Signs point out the **Tokalı Kilise**, or Buckle Church, on the right, reached by a steep flight of worn steps, and the **Gök Kilise**, or Sky Church, to the left across the stream bed. Follow the signs, walk up the stream bed 50m, then go up on the left to the church. The Gök is a twin-nave church, with the two naves separated by columns, ending in apses. The double frieze of saints is badly worn.

At the point where the valleys divide, the villagers have posted a billboard map indicating the other churches by number. The ticket office is also here. The village square is to the left, backed by ***Cappadocia Restaurant***, toilets, a tea shop and a line of women selling knitted gloves and socks, and the dolls for which Soğanlı is supposedly famous. Just in front of the ticket office is ***Soğanlı Restaurant*** with tables set under shady trees and good food at reasonable prices. At the moment there's nowhere to stay in the village itself.

Of the churches, one of the most interesting is No 4, the **Karabaş** (Black Head), in the right-hand valley and covered in paintings showing the life of Christ, with Gabriel and various saints. A pigeon in the fresco shows local influence. Pigeons were very important to the monks, who wooed them with dovecotes cut in the rock. The dovecote across from the Karabaş Kilise has white paint around its small window entrances to attract the birds; the sides of the entrance are smoothed so the birds cannot alight, but must enter. Inside, a grid of poles provides roosting space for hundreds of birds which dump manure by the kilogram onto the floor below. The monks gathered the manure, put it on the grapevines and got the sweetest grapes and the best wine for miles around. In the yard between the church and the dovecote is a refectory, with tandoor ovens in the ground (note the air-holes for the fires). The monks lived apart but dined communally.

Also in the right-hand valley, across the stream bed and high on the far hillside, are No 5, the **Kubbeli & Saklı** (Cupola & Hidden churches). The Kubbeli is interesting because of its unusual Eastern-style cupola. The Hidden Church is just that: hidden from view until you get close to it.

Farthest up the right-hand valley is No 6, the **Yılanlı** (Snake Church), its frescoes deliberately painted over with black paint, probably to protect them. You can still make out the serpent to the left as you enter.

Getting There & Away

It's not easy to get to Soğanlı by public transport. Buses run from Ürgüp to Mustafapaşa and no further, so you could try to hitch from there, or take a taxi. The easiest way to get there, of course, is to sign up for a day tour costing roughly US$25.

SULTAN MARSHES BIRD PARADISE

Well over 250 species of birds visit the Sultansazlığı Kuş Cenneti, 35km south-east of Soğanlı, beyond Yeşilhisar. Though little developed for tourism, birdwatchers may want to explore the marshes and seek out the observation tower at Ovaçiftlik, on the road to Yahyalı. It offers good views across the marshy lake Eğri Göl, and a little museum with exhibits on the local bird life. Birds you may encounter include cranes, eagles, herons, spoonbills and storks. North of Eğri Göl is Yay Gölü, a lake noted for its populations of flamingos.

UNDERGROUND CITIES

For sheer fascination and mystery, you could hardly beat the underground cities south of Nevşehir along the road to Niğde: Kaymaklı, 20km south of Nevşehir; Mazıköy, 10km east of Kaymaklı; and Derinkuyu, 10km south of Kaymaklı.

Some archaeologists date the earliest portions of these underground cities to Hittite times 4000 years ago. Martin Urban, a German archaeologist, says they were occupied by at least the 8th and 7th centuries BC. The ancient Greek historian Xenophon mentions underground dwellings in Cappadocia in his *Anabasis*.

In times of peace the people of this region lived and farmed above ground, but when invaders threatened they took to their troglodyte dwellings where they could live safely (if not always happily) for up to six months.

Kaymaklı

The countryside around Kaymaklı has no enchanting fairy chimneys or sensuously carved valleys, yet the stone is the same soft volcanic tuff which allowed early residents to develop the real estate cheaply.

At Kaymaklı, an unprepossessing farming village of white houses and many unpaved streets, an unimpressive little cave in a low mound leads down into a maze of tunnels and rooms carved four levels deep into the earth. From the highway, follow the signs which indicate a left (east) turn, or ask for the Yeraltı Şehri (YEHR-ahl-tuh shehh-ree, Underground City). The entrance is one block east of the highway and it's open from 8 am to 5 pm (6.30 pm in summer) every day; admission costs US$2. As this is the most convenient, popular and touristy of the underground cities, you should be here early (7.30 or 7.45 am is not too early) in July and August to enjoy it properly.

Little arrows guide you into the cool depths. (Space yourself to travel in a gap between larger groups.) As you go down, it's like entering a huge and very complex Swiss cheese. Holes here, holes there, 'windows' from room to room, paths going this way and that, more levels of rooms above and below. Without the arrows and the electric wires, it would be fearfully difficult to find the way out again. If you wander off along another passage, separated from the group by only a few metres, you can hear what they say, you can converse with them, but you can't find your way back to them! Suddenly a foot comes into view and you realise that they're on the next level, almost above your head!

Signs of the troglodyte lifestyle are everywhere: storage jars for oil, wine and water, communal kitchens blackened by smoke, stables with mangers, incredibly deep wells. Soon it's easy to believe that tens of thousands of people could have lived here happily year-round, deep within the earth. It's even suspected that there were underground passages which connected Kaymaklı with its sister city of Derinkuyu, 10km away, though the tunnels have yet to be excavated.

Özlüce

Turn left as you enter Kaymaklı from the north and you'll be headed for Özlüce (there's a sign), 6km along. Özlüce also has an **underground city**. More modest than those of Kaymaklı or Derinkuyu, it is also less developed and crowded, and still a good example of troglodytic living. Parts of the walls and ceiling have been shored up with new stonework for safety's sake. In July and August, this is the place to come if there are long lines at the more famous sites. Tip the guardian who will show you around.

Mazıköy

Just north of the turn off for Kaymaklı's Yeraltı Şehri is another turn off east marked for Mazıköy Yeraltı Şehri, 10km away. Nestled in a valley enclosed by the now-familiar sheer rock cliffs is the village of Mazıköy, with its central town square. Buy your ticket here (US$1.50) whenever there's anyone around, then head for the entrance just off the town square.

On top of the valley wall is a **necropolis** with slot-like graves. A guide will probably show you the stone shelter supposedly used for the *güvercin postası* (carrier-pigeon mail service).

At the time of research the village had few services beyond food and drinks shops.

Derinkuyu

The name Derinkuyu (population 8500) means 'deep well', and this underground city, 10km south of Kaymaklı, has larger rooms arrayed on eight levels. Prices and opening times are the same as at Kaymaklı. When you get all the way down, look up the ventilation shaft to see just how deep you are – not for claustrophobics!

Derinkuyu has several restaurants near the main square. There's also the very simple ***Hotel Ali Baba***, though once you've seen the underground city there's little reason to stay. You might have a look at the **mosque**, obviously built as a church, and the large **monastery church** 100m south of the underground city entrance which, according to the guardian, was built in 1358, although the frescoes inside appear to be from the 19th century.

Getting There & Away

Board a Kaymaklı or Derinkuyu Belediyesi bus or minibus at the otogar in Nevşehir; they depart every 30 minutes or so and charge US$1.75 for the ride. Buses to Niğde travel the same road but you may be required to pay the fare all the way to Niğde even if you get out at Kaymaklı or Derinkuyu.

Many of the day trips out of Göreme, Ürgüp and Avanos visit one of the underground cities. This is an easy way to visit them in summer, but means they can become horribly crowded.

GÜZELYURT

About 14km from Ihlara Köyü, on the road east to Derinkuyu, is the village of Güzelyurt (population 3800), an interesting, quiet old Cappadocian farming village of stone houses, orthodox churches converted to mosques, lush fields, valleys, streams and gardens. In Ottoman times this was the town of Karballa (Gelveri), inhabited by 1000 Ottoman-Greek families – many of them wealthy from goldsmithing – and 50 Turkish-Muslim families. In the exchange of populations between Turkey and Greece in 1924, the Greeks of Gelveri went to Nea Karvali near Kavala in Greece, and Turkish families from Kozan and Kastoria in Greece took up residence in Güzelyurt. The orthodox community had some 50 churches here, but most are now abandoned and many badly ruined.

Today Güzelyurt is officially a conservation area so all new building must be of natural stone and no more than two storeys high. You may see other tourists in July or August, but most of the time Güzelyurt is refreshingly Turkish and unvisited.

Things to See

Walk or drive downhill from the main square following the signs to **Manastır Vadisi** (Monastery Valley). About 300m from the square a sign points up on the left to a small **underground city** (yeraltı şehri), actually more of an underground village; other such dwellings are marked as you go along the road, as are churches: the Koç (Ram), Cafarlar (Rivulets) and, most interesting of all, the Aşağı or Büyük Kilise Camii, built as the **Church of St Gregory of Nazianzus** in 385, and restored and modernised in 1896. St Gregory (330-90 AD), grew up in Güzelyurt and went on to become a theologian, patriarch, and one of the Four Fathers of the Greek Church. Plans call for the church to become a museum, and the whitewash to be removed from its frescoes. In the garden, a subterranean stairway leads to an ayasma, or sacred spring. The bell is gone from the bell tower (though the imam proudly guards the clapper), which is now the mosque's minaret. Inside the ancient building, the iconostasis has been moved from the front wall to the side to serve as a frame for the mihrab. A guardian may charge you US$1 to see the church and nearby buildings.

Across the valley and up the hill from the Kilise Camii is the **Sıvışlı Kilise** (Anargyros Church), a much later rock-hewn church with clean lines, square pillars, and some badly ruined frescoes.

The **Kalburlu** (Sieve) and **Kömürlü** (Charcoal) churches are 1.7km from the main square at the end of the road in Monastery Valley.

Off the access road to the town, across the Güzelyurt Göleti lake, is the **Kızıl Kilise** (Red Church), named for the colour of its stone, with three naves and deteriorating frescoes.

Places to Stay & Eat

Tovi and Ahmed Diler of Kirkit Voyages in Avanos have taken a lease on a 19th-century Greek Karballa Monastery which has been converted into ***Otel Karballa*** *(☎ 382-451 2103, fax 451 2107)*. B&B costs US$16 per person and half board US$22; you eat your meals in what was once the monks' refectory. This is a quiet, rather special place to stay and if you're interested in riding or mountain biking they can arrange it for you.

Getting There & Away

Several dolmuşes a day run between Güzelyurt and Aksaray.

IHLARA (PERİSTREMA)

About 45km south-east of Aksaray is Ihlara, at the head of the Peristrema gorge, a remote valley which was once a favourite retreat of Byzantine monks. Dozens of painted churches, carved from the rock or built from the local stone, have survived, but this wildly beautiful place is still less touristy than Göreme.

The hike along the 16km gorge, following the course of the Melendiz Suyu stream all the way from Selime to Ihlara Köyü village, is wilder and more exciting than touring the well-trodden paths amid the rock-hewn churches at Göreme. Start early

BOTH PHOTOGRAPHS BY TOM BROSNAHAN

Central Anatolia **Top:** The 'moonscape' troglodyte dwellings of Göreme valley. **Bottom:** The Anıt Kabir (Atatürk's mausoleum) stands at the centre of modern Ankara both physically and spiritually.

BOTH PHOTOGRAPHS BY PETER PTSCHELINZEW

Central Anatolia **Top:** Pontic tombs and Ottoman houses built into a hillside in Amasya. **Bottom:** Living area in the underground city of Kaymaklı with a maze of rooms carved deep into the earth.

in the day and you'll enjoy the trip more, particularly in the height of summer.

Things to See

The scenery on this trip, especially on the descent into the gorge, is as wonderful as the ancient churches themselves. Allow a full day for seeing Ihlara. If you're coming out from Aksaray, the drive will also take some time.

On the rim of the gorge 2km from Ihlara village, the Ihlara Vadisi Turistik Tesisleri is a restaurant, souvenir shop and ticket booth. Parking costs US$1, admission to the gorge (8.30 am to 5.30 pm) costs US$2.50.

A very long flight of stairs leads down to the floor of the gorge and it will take several hours to find and visit the various churches. Although there are a few simple eateries in the gorge itself, you might want to pack a picnic or at least take snacks and drinks.

Signs mark the **churches** along the way. The most interesting, with the best paintings, are the Yılanlı Kilise, Sümbüllü Kilise, Kokar Kilise and Eğritaş Kilisesi. Further down the valley are the Kırk Dam Altı Kilise, Bahattin Samanlığı Kilise, Direkli Kilise and Ala Kilise. Several of the churches, notably the Çarıklı, Elmalı and Karanlık, are closed because of the risk of structural damage.

IHLARA VALLEY

1 Selime Cathedral & Tomb
2 Ziga Hamamı
3 Church
4 Direkli (Columned) Church
5 Bahattin Samanlığı (Granary) Church
6 Kırk Dam Altı (St George) Church
7 Karagedik (Black Collar) Church
8 Eski Baca (Old Chimney) Church
9 Yılanlı (Serpent) Church
10 Sümbüllü (Hyacinth) Church
11 Ihlara Vadisi Turistik Tesisleri (Entrance; Restaurant)
12 Ağaç Altı (Beneath-a-Tree) Church
13 Karanlık Kale (Dark Castle) Church
14 Kokar (Fragrant) Church
15 Eğritaş (Crooked Stone) Church
16 Pürenli Seki (Platform) Church
17 Historic Bridge

Places to Stay

Ihlara Most lodgings are on the south-western side of the gorge. ***Pansion Anatolia*** *(☎ 382-453 7440, fax 453 7439, Us İşhanı 3/68)* is a small hotel on the road running between the village and the entry to the gorge. Rooms with bathroom cost US$18 a double, or you can camp in the grounds for US$3 per person. This place is often full with Dutch, Belgian or American groups.

Several more small pensions line the road from Ihlara village to Aksaray. ***Akar Pansiyon*** *(☎ 382-453 7018, fax 453 7511)*, is in a pleasant modern building and has clean rooms with bath for US$16 a double. The shop downstairs sells picnic ingredients and there's a restaurant behind. ***Bişginler Ihlara Pansiyon*** *(☎ 382-453 7077)* next door costs about the same. ***Pansiyon Famille*** *(☎ 382-453 7098)*, also called the Pansiyon Family, across the road is a good deal more basic and yet charges the same.

You can camp at the entry to the gorge: US$3 for a tent, plus US$1.50 per person.

Belisırma In Belisırma Köyü, midway along the gorge, you'll find ***Aslan Camping & Pansiyon*** *(☎ 451-213 3780)*, 2km off the main road and about 4km from Ihlara village, with six beds in pre-erected tents which are US$8 a double. There's also a small ***ev pansiyon*** *(☎ 451-213 2429)* in the village, with tiny, waterless rooms for US$8 including a breakfast. The house itself is not particularly pretty but staying there would give you a glimpse of rural life.

Selime At the northern end of the gorge, *Anıl, Selime* and *Çatlak* restaurants by the bridge in Selime have simple camping grounds. ***Piri Pansiyon & Camping*** and ***Piri Motel*** *(☎ 451-454 5114)* are a bit further north near the octagonal-roofed Ali Paşa Türbesi (1317).

Places to Eat

The restaurant at the rim entry to the gorge has a spectacular view, but a limited, not especially good menu. A full meal still costs around US$6 or US$8. Simple eateries operate in the village ***(Ihlara Restaurant)*** and the valley (two along the trail, one in Belisırma Köyü) during the summer months.

Getting There & Away

Bus The rim entry to the gorge is 2km from the village of Ihlara Köyü, 14km from Güzelyurt, 45km from Aksaray and 95km from Nevşehir. Ihlara Belediyesi buses run several times daily from Aksaray's otogar, charging US$0.75 one way. Tour companies in Göreme are often happy to agree on a one-way fare to leave you in the valley, usually after a visit to Derinkuyu underground city.

Car From the Aksaray-Nevşehir highway, turn south (right, if you're coming from Aksaray) at a point 11km east of the intersection of Ankara-Adana and Aksaray-Nevşehir highways. After making this turn, go about 23km to another right turn marked for Ihlara Vadisi. The road passes through Selime village, with numerous rock-hewn buildings, and then 3km further it runs through Yaprakhisar; both villages are dramatically surrounded by rock and marked by Göreme-style fairy chimneys. After another 13km you come to Ihlara Köyü, where you turn left to reach the entrance at the rim of the gorge.

Roads lead to Ihlara from Derinkuyu (53km), and from the village of Gölcük (60km) between Derinkyuy and Niğde. Drive through fertile potato and grain-farming land and up into the mountains through dramatic and beautiful scenery to Güzelyurt.

Tours Several agencies in Göreme and Ürgüp offer tours to Ihlara. Göreme's Zemi Tours (☎ 384-271 2576, fax 271 2577) runs a two-day camping tour that takes in the Derinkuyu underground city, Narlıgöl crater lake, Güzelyurt, hiking through Ihlara gorge, camping overnight at Belisırma, the Ağzıkarahan caravanserai, and Uçhisar costing US$50, including meals, camping equipment and admission fees. Contact Zemi Tours or Dawn Köse at Göreme's Köse Pension.

AKSARAY

Aksaray (population 92,000, altitude 980m) is another of those farming towns with little to offer tourists beyond a bed and a meal, although you can amuse yourself well enough if you have an hour to spare. Aksaray may also be used as a base for visits to Ihlara and Güzelyurt.

It's 500m from Aksaray's otogar to the main square, with its Ulu Cami (Great Mosque) and nicely restored government buildings (behind the equestrian statue of Atatürk); to get there, leave the otogar and take a sharp left.

Aksaray's postal code is 51400.

Things to See

The **Ulu Cami** at the town centre, with decoration characteristic of the post-Seljuk Beylik period, dates from 1408-1409, though repaired extensively in 1483 and later years. The original minaret is gone, replaced by the Ottoman structure you see now. Little of the original yellow stone is left in the grand portal. Inside the mosque is a finely worked wooden minber brought here from the older, ruined Kılıçarslan II mosque.

The **Zinciriye Medresesi** was built by the local Karamanoğulları emir Yahşi Bey in 1336 following the canons of Seljuk architecture. Since then it has been restored several times. Although it's now a repository and museum for Egyptian, Greek, Roman, Seljuk and Ottoman inscriptions arranged around the courtyard and in the rooms, it's the building itself which is interesting since it served as a theological college and a han as well. To find it, walk from the Ulu Cami across the main street and down Vehbibey Caddesi toward the river.

The medrese's adjoining **Tarihi Paşa Hamamı**, an Ottoman work, has been restored and now serves both men and women in separate sections.

The older part of town along Çerdiğin Caddesi (also called Nevşehir Caddesi) has some **old stone houses** and the curious **Kızıl or Eğri Minare** (Leaning, or Red, Minaret), next to the Kızıl Minare Camii, built in 1236 and leaning at an angle of 27 degrees. Inevitably it's known locally as the 'Turkish Tower of Pisa'.

Places to Stay

Cross the road outside the otogar and take the first left to find ***Hitit Pansion*** *(☎ 382-213 1996)*, an apartment house turned into a pension 'alla turka'. You remove your shoes and put on clean slippers when entering. The lobby is decorated with carpets, kilims, low *sedir* (couches) and pillows. The guest rooms upstairs are bare and waterless but the front ones are large and have balconies. Bathrooms down the hall are small but tiled and clean. Rooms cost US$9 per person. The nearby ***Aksaray Pansion*** *(☎ 382-212 4133)* is plainer but clean, with identical prices.

Otel Yoğuran *(☎ 382-213 5490, Nolu Hükümet Caddesi 3)* is in the midst of the bazaar on a street crowded with jewellery shops (turn off the main street opposite the Merkez Lokantası/Beko and follow the signs). Rooms with private shower cost US$13/22/30, breakfast included. It's quiet at night.

Two other reasonable places face each other in Kızılay Caddesi. The two-star ***Otel Tezcanlar*** *(☎ 382-213 8482, fax 215 1234, Kızılay Sokak 5)* has pleasant rooms brightened up with artificial plants and with spacious bathrooms for US$12/20 a single/double with breakfast. Immediately opposite, the one-star ***Çakır İpek Oteli*** *(☎ 382-213 7053)* is drabber but slightly cheaper.

Right on the main square next to the modern Hacıbektaş Kurşunlu Camii is the new ***Otel Yuvam*** *(☎ 382-212 0024, fax 213 2875)*, across the intersection from the Vilayet. Minaret and traffic noise might make the US$14/22 prices seem a bit steep but they're certainly negotiable out of season.

The top place in town is ***Ağaçlı Turistik Tesisleri*** (Ağaçlı Touristic Establishments) *(☎ 382-215 2400, fax 215 2410)*, Ankara-Adana Asfaltı, Nevşehir Kavşağı, at the main highway intersection with the roads to Nevşehir and Niğde. ***Melendiz Motel*** within the complex is the more expensive, charging US$32/45 for a single/double with bath, breakfast included. ***Ihlara Motel*** charges a bit less, US$24/35. There's also a cafeteria, a restaurant, gift shops, swimming and wading pools, a fuel station, and a luxury camping ground where you can pitch your tent or park your camper van for US$3, plus the same amount again for each person in your party.

Places to Eat

Just off the main square to the right of the Hacıbektaş Kurşunlu Camii, ***Kent Lokantası*** is clean and has a good selection of meat dishes at low prices. There are other small restaurants in the centre and in the bazaar, none special. For a beer with your dinner, head for the Ağaçlı Turistik Tesisleri on the outskirts.

Getting There & Away

There are direct buses from Aksaray to Ankara (230km, 4½ hours), Nevşehir (65km, 1½ hours), Niğde (115km, two hours) and Konya (140km, 2½ hours). There are also sporadic dolmuşes and some buses in summer to Ihlara Köyü (45km, one hour, US$0.75), to Güzelyurt and to Sultanhanı.

NİĞDE

Niğde (NEE-deh, population 55,000, altitude 1216m), 85km south of Nevşehir, was built by the Seljuks. Backed by snowcapped mountains, it's a farming centre with a small but fine selection of historic buildings, including a mosque built by the

Mongols. East of the town is the ancient rock-hewn monastery of Eski Gümüşler, with the best-preserved paintings in Cappadocia.

Orientation & Information

İstasyon Caddesi is the main axis of the commercial district, bounded by Atatürk Meydanı (sometimes called Hükümet Meydanı), the main traffic roundabout at its western end, and a hill bearing the lofty *saat kulesi* (clock tower), kale (fortress) and Alaeddin Camii (largest mosque) near its eastern end. The marketplace is beneath the clock tower; Thursday is market day.

The otogar is 1km north-east of İstasyon Caddesi, the train station 1km south-east. Look on and near Atatürk Meydanı for hotels, restaurants and shops and, on aptly named Bankalar Caddesi, for banks.

The Tourism Information Office (☎ 388-232 3393, fax 232 2326), İstiklal Caddesi, Vakıf İş Hanı 1/D, just off the main square, is open daily except Sunday from 8.30 am to noon and from 1.30 to 5.30 pm.

Mosques & Museum

The **Alaeddin Camii** (1223), a Seljuk work on the hill with the fortress and clock tower, is the town's grandest mosque. But the **Süngür Bey Camii** at the foot of the hill by the marketplace is, for me, the city's most interesting building.

Built by the Seljuks but restored by the Mongols in 1335, the Süngür Bey Camii is a curious and affecting blend of architectures. The embellished windows at ground level differ in style from one another. On the upper storey, blind lancet arches take the place of windows. The rose window above the northern window bears a six-pointed 'Star of David', a motif used elsewhere in the building. The big, solid, square doors are finely carved.

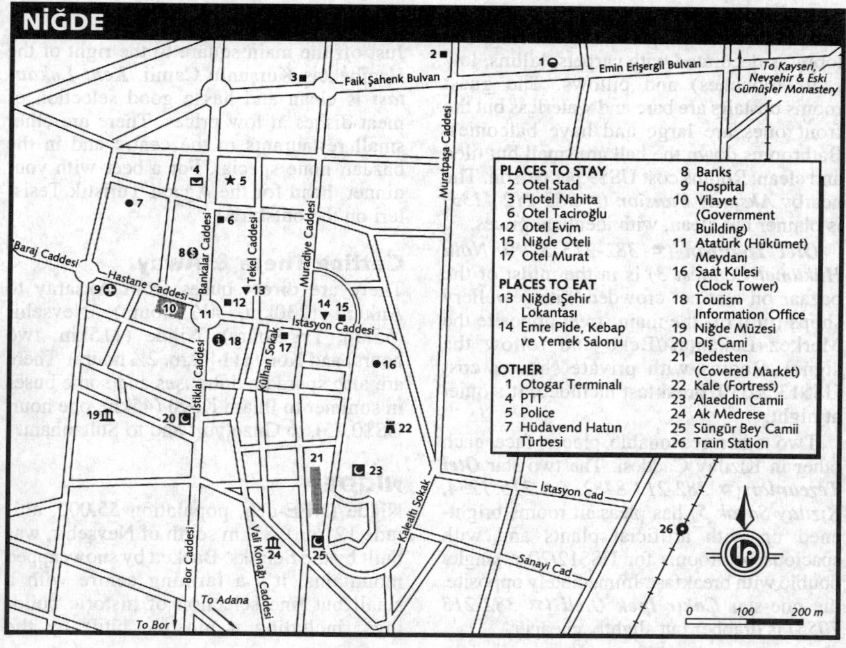

Recent restorations have done wonders for the exterior stonework but have filled the interior with ugly reinforced concrete which breaks the spell cast by this ancient work. Even so, look at the northern galleries, a conglomeration of architectural styles, and the mihrab, wonderfully carved and almost Chinese in appearance.

The attractive, unusual **Ak Medrese** (1409) in the midst of the market district is in a transitional style: post-Seljuk, Mongol, Beylik, with an ogee arch above the main portal. It's presently closed for repairs, but you can admire much of its design from the outside.

In the **Niğde Müzesi**, west of the Dış Cami (follow the signs), pride of place is given to the 10th-century mummy of a blonde nun discovered in the 1960s in the Yılanlı church in the Ihlara Valley. Less sensational exhibits include Assyrian artifacts found in the excavations at Acem Höyük and Köşk (Bahçeli) Höyük; Hellenistic and Ottoman gold and silver coins; late Hittite and Phrygian bronzes, pottery and inscriptions; Roman and Byzantine glass, pottery and marble sculpture; and local woven goods, carpets, kilims and dresses. The museum is open from 8 am to noon and 1.30 to 5 pm (closed Monday) for US$1.

Also take a look at the **Hüdavend Hatun Türbesi** (1312), a fine example of a Seljuk tomb; and the **Dış Cami**, an Ottoman mosque with a carved mimber inlaid with mother-of-pearl.

Eski Gümüşler Monastery

It's 10km east from the clock tower in Niğde to the rock-hewn monastery of Eski Gümüşler.

On Hwy 805, east of the town centre, a Mobil station marks the intersection of roads west (to Niğde) and east to Eski Gümüşler (ess-KEE gur-mursh-LEHR), 4.75km away (follow the signs). Gümüşler Belediyesi minibuses run between the village and Niğde's otogar. You can also hitch to the site.

The village of Gümüşler is in the midst of rich apple orchards which in October yield mountains of fruit. Bagged and boxed, the mountains of apples change the town landscape until the trucks come.

The monastery of Eski Gümüşler, discovered in 1963, is open daily in summer from 9 am to noon and from 1.30 to 6.30 pm; from October to May from 8 am to noon and 1 to 5 pm. The gates are normally locked, but the guardian will have seen you coming and will follow with the key. Admission costs US$1.

Through a rock-cut passage is a large courtyard surrounded by rock-hewn dwellings, crypts, a kitchen and refectory with deep reservoirs for wine and oil. A small hole in the ground is actually the vent for a mysterious 9m-deep shaft beneath. The crypt to the right of the entry passage has several skeletons still in place. Across the courtyard another crypt, beneath protective covers of wood and glass, holds a well-preserved and apparently undisturbed skeleton.

The lofty main church, to the right off the courtyard, has the best-preserved Byzantine coloured frescoes in Cappadocia, painted from the 7th to 11th centuries. The Virgin and Child to the right of the altar-space is particularly affecting, with Mary given a Mona Lisa smile. The church's great columns are of course completely unnecessary, but were left when the rock was cut away to mimic the appearance of a traditional temple. The cross-hatch motif was favoured during the Iconoclastic period (725-842 AD) when sacred images were prohibited and artists resorted to geometrics, a preference soon picked up by Islam.

Places to Stay

Otel Stad *(☎ 388-213 7866, Terminal Caddesi 6)*, one short block west of the otogar, charges US$11/14/24 for a single/double/triple with shower.

The other hotels are in the centre. ***Otel Taciroğlu*** *(☎ 388-213 3047, Bankalar Caddesi 16)*, across from the Ziraat Bankası, is serviceable at US$14/20/24 for a room with shower. ***Otel Murat*** *(☎ 388-213 3978, İstasyon Caddesi 46, Eski Belediye Yanı 5)* has a facade on the main street but its entrance is at the back. The much-abused rooms will do in an emergency, priced as at the

Taciroğlu. The nearby ***Niğde Oteli*** *(☎ 388-213 2940, İstasyon Caddesi 83)* is in the same class, but may quote a slightly lower price.

The three-star ***Otel Evim*** *(☎/fax 388-232 3536, fax 232 1526)*, Atatürk Meydanı, at the beginning of İstasyon Caddesi, has a lift, and simple but comfortable rooms with private baths (showers and short tubs) and balconies for US$18/26, breakfast included – a good choice.

Newest and swellest is the two-star, 60 room ***Hotel Nahita*** *(☎/fax 388-232 5366)*, on Terminal Caddesi one long block west of the otogar, with a restaurant, lift, disco-bar, and rooms priced at US$20/30 a single/double, breakfast included.

Places to Eat

Fancy dining is not Niğde's strong suit. Try one of the small eateries on İstasyon Caddesi, such as ***Emre Pide, Kebap ve Yemek Salonu***, the name of which is its menu. They have stews most days at lunch, kebaps in the evening, and pide anytime. The bill for a quick meal rarely tops US$3. ***Birtad***, on the other side of İstasyon, adjoining the Otel Murat, is stronger on kebaps.

Niğde Şehir Lokantası, hidden away north of İstasyon, is an alternative in which a stew, rice pilav and soda may cost as little as US$2; there are similar places in the narrow side streets. For *pastanes* (pastry-shops), look along Bankalar Caddesi, where they vie with the banks to take your money.

Getting There & Away

Niğde's otogar has buses to most nearby destinations, but perhaps only one or two per day. There is frequent service to Adana (205km, three hours, US$6), Aksaray (115km, 1½ hours, US$3.50), Kayseri (130km, 1½ hours, US$3.50) and Konya (250km, 3½ hours, US$7).

Service to Nevşehir (85km, one hour, US$3) is fast and frequent, with minibuses departing from the otogar every hour on the hour, from 5 am to 6 pm.

GÜLŞEHİR

Gülşehir (population 8500), 23km west of Avanos, has several rocky attractions: **Karşı Kilise**, or St John Church, recently restored and quite impressive, with some of the best frescoes in the region; an unexcavated underground city; and **Açık Saray**, rock formations with a few churches. In the centre of the town stands the **Karavezir Mehmet Paşa Camii & Medrese** (1778), an Ottoman mosque and its college (now a library). With the new airport nearby, Gülşehir may soon wake up from its sleepy life to enjoy an economic boom.

Places to Stay

Kepez Hotel *(☎ 384-411 3163, fax 411 3639)*, the crenellated building on the flat-top hill in the centre of town, was begun years ago in anticipation of a tourist rush which never materialised. The complex was never finished, but the three-star hotel is open and is comfortable enough with rooms for US$25 per person, breakfast and dinner included.

Hotel Gülşehir *(☎ 384-411 3028, fax 411 3906)*, on the northern outskirts by the river, is a three-storey building where airy, decently furnished rooms with bath are officially overpriced at US$53/70 a single/double, breakfast included (though I was offered a price of US$25 for a double). There's a swimming pool and a restaurant.

Getting There & Away

The new airport at Tuzköy, 12km north-west of Gülşehir, is good news for Cappadocia; no longer will the small, inadequte military airport at Kayseri have to serve the needs of this large and popular region.

Buses from Nevşehir to Ankara pass through Gülşehir, but are often already full when they arrive in Nevşehir. If that is the case, go out of Nevşehir otogar and wait on the main road for the hourly Gülşehir Belediyesi minibus (30 minutes, US$1).

HACIBEKTAŞ

Hacıbektaş (population 8000) is on the north-western outskirts of the Cappadocian region, 27.5km west of Gülşehir. It's famous not for its churches or troglodyte dwellings, but as the home of Hacı Bektaş Veli, founder and spiritual leader of the Bektaşi order of dervishes.

Hacı Bektaş Veli & the Bektaşi Sect

Born in Nishapur in Iran at some time in the 13th century, Hacı Bektaş Veli inspired a religious and political following that blended aspects of Islam (both Sunni and Shiite) with Orthodox Christianity. During his life he is known to have travelled around Anatolia and to have lived in Kayseri, Sivas and Kırşehir, but eventually he settled in the hamlet which grew after his death into the small town of Hacıbektaş.

Although not much is known about Hacı Bektaş himself, the book he wrote, the *Makalât*, describes a mystical philosophy which was less austere than mainstream Islam. In it he laid out a four-stage path to enlightenment (the 'Four Doors'). During the first stage dervishes came to know the difference between right and wrong. In the second they prayed constantly. In the third they came to understand God's love. During the fourth and final stage they arrived at an understanding of reality through constant awareness of God and through self-effacement.

Though often scorned by mainstream Islamic clerics, Bektaşi dervishes attained considerable political and religious influence in Ottoman times. Along with all the other dervishes, they were outlawed in 1925.

The Bektaşi spiritual philosophy developed in the borderlands between the Turkish and Byzantine empires, where guerrilla fighters from both sides had more in common with one another than they had with their sovereigns in Konya or Constantinople. Their liberal beliefs caught on with the common people, and Bektaşi ideas are still important in Turkish religious life today.

Every August, in what has been described as a 'mini haj', up to 500,000 believers descend on the saint's tomb in Hacıbektaş. So complete has been his rehabilitation that these days politicians try to muscle in alongside the singing and dancing with speeches claiming the great man for their own beliefs.

Things to See

There's only one thing to see really, the **Hacı Bektaş Monastery**, officially called the Hacıbektaş Müzesi, open from 8.30 am to 12.30 pm and 1.30 to 5 pm, closed on Monday. Admission costs US$1. Plaques are in Turkish, with some in English. Though it's called a museum, you should remember that it is a sacred place.

Several rooms are arranged as they might have been when the dervishes lived here, including the **Aş Evi**, or kitchen, with its implements, and the **Meydan Evi**, where novice dervishes were inducted into the order. Other rooms display musical instruments, costumes, embroidery, turbans and other artefacts of the order, as well as relevant old photographs.

Remove your shoes before stepping inside the **saint's tomb** in the garden at the far end of the building, as this is a place of prayer.

Needless to say, the area immediately in front of the monastery is awash with stalls selling Lourdes-style religious paraphernalia.

Places to Stay & Eat

If you're planning a visit in August around the time of the annual pilgrimage, you'll need to plan well ahead as accommodation is very limited.

Across the street from the monastery is a market and shopping complex, and the simple ***Hotel Hünkar*** *(☎ 384-411 3344)*, with clean rooms and telephone-style showers for US$8/12 a single/double. It's right next door to ***Sila Restaurant***.

Out on the Ankara road, 1km from the monastery, is ***Hotel Cem*** *(☎ 384-411 2414)*, a pleasant three-storey hotel with 26 modern rooms priced at US$15/20 a single/double, breakfast included.

Getting There & Away

Buses from Nevşehir to Ankara pass through Hacıbektaş. Alternatively, you can pick up a Kırşehir Belediyesi minibus from Gülşehir (one hour, US$1) which also passes through. The last bus back to Nevşehir leaves at 5 pm.

KIRŞEHİR

Midway along the road from Ankara to Cappadocia lies Kırşehir (population 75,000, altitude 978m), an ancient city, now a provincial capital with a few old buildings and several cheap, basic hotels. Kırşehir was famous in Ottoman times as the centre of the mystical Ahi (Akhi) brotherhoods, the Muslim equivalent of the Masonic lodges. The Ahi brotherhoods were founded in the 14th century as secret religious societies among members of the crafts guilds, particularly the tanners' guild. Their political power grew to a point where sultans had to reckon with them. The founding father and inspiration for the Akhi brotherhoods was Ahi Evran (1236-1329), a tanner whose family came from Horasan. He lived and died in Kırşehir and his tomb is a Muslim place of pilgrimage.

Orientation & Information

The city centre is Cumhuriyet Meydanı, the main traffic roundabout with an ugly modern clock tower. Almost everything you'll need is within a five-minute walk of here. The main commercial street running out of the square is Ankara Caddesi, with the PTT a few steps along it. Hotels, restaurants and the Ahi Evran Türbesi are a short walk further along Ankara Caddesi. The Cacabey Camii is on the opposite side of Cumhuriyet Meydanı from Ankara Caddesi.

The otogar is 1.5km south of the centre. Local buses stop rather more conveniently within 100m of Cumhuriyet Meydanı.

The Tourism Information Office, (☎ 386-213 1416, fax 213 6808), Cumhuriyet Meydanı, Aşık Paşa Bulvarı, is right in the city centre but the chances of finding it open are minimal. Kırşehir is not a tourist hotbed.

Kırşehir's postal code is 40000.

Things to See

The **Ahi Evran Camii ve Türbesi**, or Ahi Evran Mosque and Tomb, also called the Ahi Evran Zaviyesi (Dervish Lodge), are simple stone structures, obviously very old. Pilgrims in their 'Friday best' are usually crowded into the small rooms in prayer.

Just off the traffic roundabout is the **Cacabey Camii** (JAH-jah-bey), built by the Seljuk Turks in 1272 as a meteorological observatory and theological college and now used as a mosque. The brown and white stonework draws the eye and there's a wonderful portal, too.

The **Alaettin Camii** dates from Seljuk times as well. You may also see a number of tombs dating from the 14th century.

Places to Stay & Eat

Otel Anadolu *(☎ 386-213 1826, Ankara Caddesi 20)*, across the main street from the Ahi Evran Camii, has well-worn rooms with bath for US$8/12 a single/double. The neighbouring ***Otel Banana*** *(☎ 386-213 1879)* is virtually identical.

Going upmarket, the new three-star ***Terme Hotel*** *(☎ 386-212 2404)*, Terme Parkı, on the outskirts of town near the Terme Kaplıcaları hot springs, provides Kırşehir with 132 bath-equipped rooms at US$30/42 for a single/double, a Turkish bath, and a swimming pool. Follow the signs to find it. There's also the ***Otel Kervansary***, conveniently positioned on the highway as you turn into town.

As for meals, places on Ankara Caddesi can fill this need as well. ***Meşhur Kebap 49***, with doner kebaps for US$2.50, is more or less opposite the Otel Banana, while the ***Sofra Lokantası*** is down an alley beside the Banana. In the street behind the Banana look out also for the cheaper ***Yeniler Pide Salonu***.

KAYSERİ

Once the capital of Cappadocia, Kayseri (KAHY-seh-ree, population 425,000, altitude 1054m) is now a booming farm and textile centre. In the shadow of Erciyes Dağı (Mt Aergius, 3916m), the sleepy, conservative town surrounding the ancient black citadel became a bustling city of modern, apartment-lined boulevards during the 1980s. These two aspects of Kayseri aren't completely comfortable together, and something remains of old Kayseri's conservative soul. After 9 pm, for example, you'll be hard pressed to find a restaurant open.

In Turkish folklore, the Kayserili is the sharp dealer, and the stereotype is brought to life daily by the carpet shop touts who hang around any place likely to be visited by a foreign traveller, especially the Hunat Hatun Camii or the tourism office. Tenacious as bulldogs, they refuse to take 'no' for an answer, and may follow you for miles before deciding you must be truly confused because you come to Kayseri as a tourist and then spend all of your time trying to get rid of them. Why don't you just forget about seeing the sights and buy an overpriced carpet?

If you're passing through en route to Cappadocia, take a few hours to tour Kayseri, meet some of the hospitable Kayserilis (ie, those who have nothing to sell you), and visit the many wonderful Seljuk buildings and the bazaar. If it's Sunday, enjoy the open-air market behind the Hunat Hatun Camii. Those heading east might want to see the sights, spend the night, and get an early start the next morning. There are also two superb Seljuk caravanserais north-east of the city, off the Sivas and Malatya roads.

History

This was Hittite country, so its history goes way back. The first Hittite capital, Kanesh, had also been the chief city of the Hatti people. It's at Kültepe, 20km north-east of Kayseri, off the Sivas road. There was probably an early settlement on the site of Kayseri as well, though the earliest traces which have come to light are from Hellenistic times.

Under the Roman emperor Tiberius (14-37 AD), the town received its name, Caesarea, and later became famous as the birthplace of St Basil the Great, one of the early Church Fathers. Its early Christian history was interrupted by the Arab invasions of the 7th century and later.

The Seljuks took over in 1084 and held the city until the Mongols' arrival in 1243, except for a brief period when the crusaders captured it on their way to the Holy Land.

After Kayseri had been part of the Mongol Empire for almost 100 years, its Mongol governor set up his own emirate (1335) which lasted a mere 45 years. It was succeeded by another emirate (that of Kadı Burhaneddin), then captured by the Ottomans (seized during the Ottoman interregnum by the Karamanid emirs), later taken by the Mamelukes of Egypt, and finally conquered by the Ottomans again in 1515, all in just over 100 years.

Orientation & Information

The black-walled citadel at the centre of the old town just south of Cumhuriyet Meydanı, the huge main square, is a good landmark. Another convenient point of reference is Düvenönü Meydanı, 350m west of the citadel along Park Caddesi. Mimar Sinan Parkı, a vast expanse north of Park Caddesi, has some of the city's outstanding Seljuk buildings.

The train station is at the northern end of Atatürk Bulvarı, over half a kilometre north of Düvenönü Meydanı. Kayseri's otogar is just under 2km north-west of the citadel (1.2km north-west of Düvenönü Meydanı) along Osman Kavuncu Caddesi.

The helpful Tourism Information Office (☎ 352-222 3903, fax 222 0879) is right beside the Hunat Camii Medresesi, and is open from 8.30 am to 5.30 pm daily in summer (closed on weekends in winter).

Kayseri's postal code is 38000.

Citadel

The citadel (hisar or İç Kale), which has been restored and turned into a shopping bazaar, was built by Emperor Justinian in the 6th century, and extensively repaired by the Seljuk sultan Keykavus I around 1224. In 1486, the Ottoman sultan, Mehmet the Conqueror, made further repairs. With Erciyes Dağı looming over the town, it's not surprising that the hisar should be made of black volcanic stone.

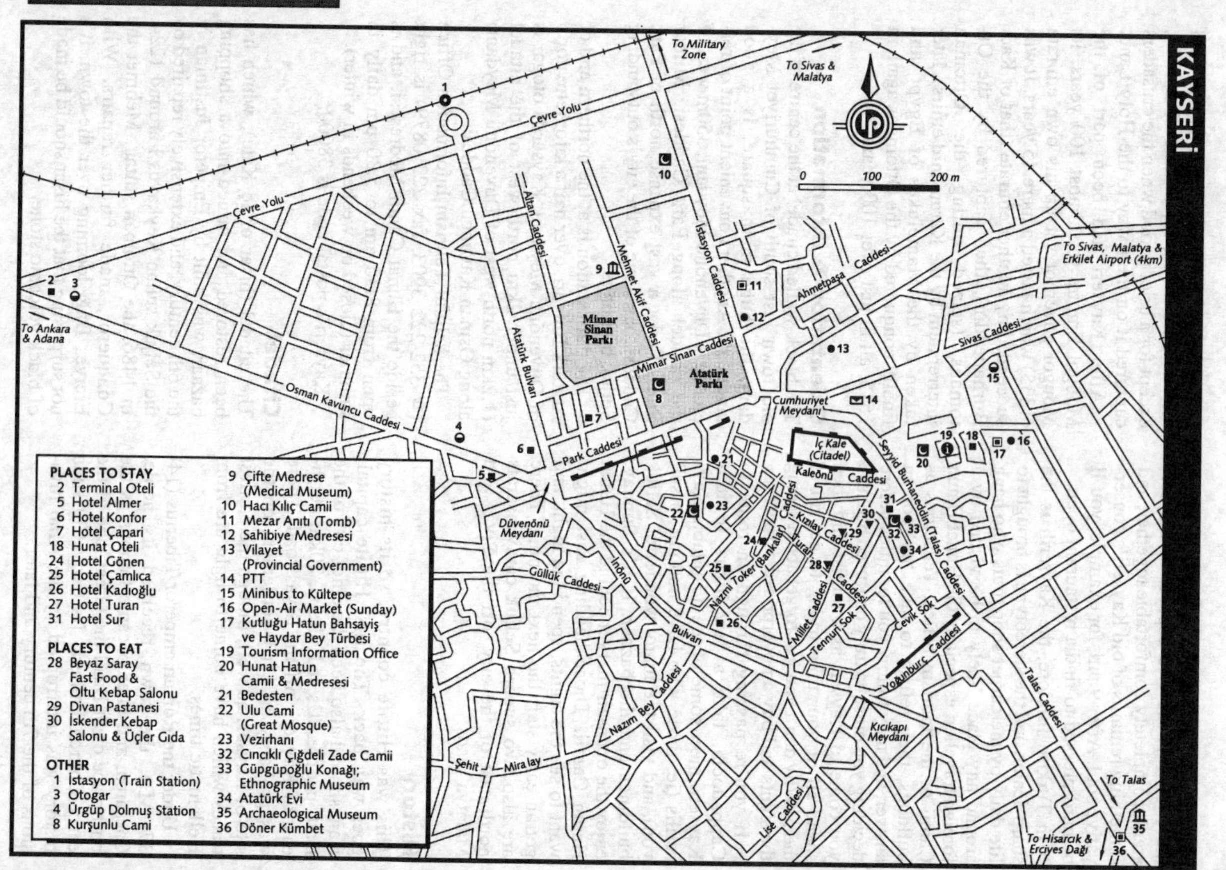
KAYSERİ
To Talas
To Hisarcık & Erciyes Dağı
Talas Caddesi
To Sivas, Malatya & Erkilet Airport (4km)
Sivas Caddesi
To Sivas & Malatya
To Military Zone
Ahmetpaşa Caddesi
Cumhuriyet Meydanı
İstasyon Caddesi
Mehmet Akif Caddesi
Mimar Sinan Caddesi
Atatürk Parkı
Mimar Sinan Parkı
Altan Caddesi
Atatürk Bulvarı
Çevre Yolu
Osman Kavuncu Caddesi
To Ankara & Adana
Park Caddesi
Düvenönü Meydanı
Güllük Caddesi
İnönü Bulvarı
Nazım Bey Caddesi
Şehit Miralay
İç Kale (Citadel)
Kaleönü Caddesi
Seyyid Burhaneddin (Talas) Caddesi
Kızılay Caddesi
Turan Caddesi
Nazmi Toker (Bankalar) Caddesi
Millet Caddesi
Tennuri Sok
Tekin Sok
Kıcıkapı Meydanı
Yoğunburç Caddesi
Lise Caddesi
0
100
200 m
PLACES TO STAY
2 Terminal Oteli
5 Hotel Almer
6 Hotel Konfor
7 Hotel Çapari
18 Hunat Oteli
24 Hotel Gönen
25 Hotel Çamlıca
26 Hotel Kadıoğlu
27 Hotel Turan
31 Hotel Sur
PLACES TO EAT
28 Beyaz Saray Fast Food & Oltu Kebap Salonu
29 Divan Pastanesi
30 İskender Kebap Salonu & Üçler Gıda
OTHER
1 İstasyon (Train Station)
3 Otogar
4 Ürgüp Dolmuş Station
8 Kurşunlu Cami
9 Çifte Medrese (Medical Museum)
10 Hacı Kılıç Camii
11 Mezar Anıtı (Tomb)
12 Sahibiye Medresesi
13 Vilayet (Provincial Government)
14 PTT
15 Minibus to Kültepe
16 Open-Air Market (Sunday)
17 Kutluğu Hatun Bahsayiş ve Haydar Bey Türbesi
19 Tourism Information Office
20 Hunat Hatun Camii & Medresesi
21 Bedesten
22 Ulu Cami (Great Mosque)
23 Vezirhanı
32 Cincikli Çiğdeli Zade Camii
33 Güpgüpoğlu Konağı; Ethnographic Museum
34 Atatürk Evi
35 Archaeological Museum
36 Döner Kümbet

Mahperi Hunat Hatun Camii & Medresesi

Kayseri has several important building complexes which were founded by Seljuk queens and princesses. East of the hisar is a complex which includes the Mahperi Hunat Hatun Camii (1228), built by the wife of the Seljuk sultan Alaettin Keykubat.

Next to the mosque is the Hunat Hatun Medresesi (1237), which was closed to the public at the time of research. Within the medrese is Lady Mahperi Hunat's tomb, an octagonal room with a high-domed ceiling. The tomb also contains the remains of her grandchild and of an unknown other. The complex's Turkish bath is still in use, with separate sections for men and women.

Sahibiye Medresesi

The Sahibiye Medresesi (Seminary), on the northern side of Cumhuriyet Meydanı, dates from 1267 and has an especially beautiful Seljuk portal. It's now used as a book bazaar, with booksellers' shops stocked mostly with Turkish titles.

Kurşunlu Cami

You can spot the Ottoman-style Lead-Domed Mosque by its lead-covered dome, unusual in old Kayseri, north of Park Caddesi and west of Cumhuriyet Meydanı and Atatürk Parkı. Also called the Ahmet Paşa Camii after its founder, it was completed in 1585 following plans possibly drawn by the great Sinan, but certainly influenced by him.

Çifte Medrese

Two adjoining religious schools, the Gıyasiye ve Şifaiye Medreseleri, are sometimes called the Twin Seminaries. Set in the midst of Mimar Sinan Parkı north of Park Caddesi, they were founded at the bequest of the Seljuk sultan Giyasettin I Keyhüsrev and his sister Gevher Nesibe Sultan (1165-1204), who was the daughter of the great sultan Kılıçaslan. Today the twin medreses have been restored, and serve as a **museum of medical history** for Erciyes University.

Princess Gevher Nesibe Sultan is entombed in a chamber on the right side of the courtyard as you enter; a mescit (prayer-room) is above. Topping the mescit outside is a Seljuk-style dome surrounded by an inscription in Arabic which instructs the medrese's administration to accept medical students and patients into the seminary without regard to religion: Muslim, Jew and Christian were to study and be healed side by side.

A doorway on the left side of the courtyard leads to the medical section, which gives fascinating insights into the medical practices of the 13th-century Seljuks. Look out for a replica of an original stone carving of snakes (symbols of medicine and healing since ancient times) and the Seljuk *çark-ı felek* (wheel of fortune), which determined someone's fate in life and presumably their chances of recovering from disease.

The **Ameliyathane** (Operating Room) has a hole in the ceiling which acted as a 'spotlight' on the patient during operations (presumably Seljuk doctors only operated on sunny days). In the **Akıl Hastanesi** (Mental Hospital) is a suite of tiny cells for mental patients, who were kept one to a cell if violent, an unbelievable four to a cell otherwise.

The central heating system for the hamam, combined with an insulating layer of earth on top of the roof, kept the entire medical side of the building warm during Kayseri's sometimes frigid winters. The rooftop earth was used to grow vegetables and fruits to feed the patients. After it was removed during restoration, water penetrated the ceilings below, and caused the plaster to flake. The Seljuks knew more about preservation than we do.

The **Sertabib Başhekim Odası** (Head Doctor's Room) has been furnished in Ottoman style with wood panelling, sedirs and Turkish carpets. As often as not it's kept locked.

The museum is open from 8 am to noon and 1 to 5 pm, closed on Monday and Tuesday; admission costs US$1. Most of the signs explaining Seljuk medical practices are in Turkish which is rather disappointing, as is the state of many of the exhibits.

Hacı Kılıç Camii

North of the Çifte Medrese on İstasyon Caddesi is the mosque (1249) of the Seljuk vizier Abdülgazi, the Hacı Kılıç Camii, with some very fine Seljuk architectural detail, especially in the doorways.

Ulu Cami

Kayseri's Great Mosque is near Düvenönü Meydanı. It was begun in 1142 by the Danışmend Turkish emirs and finished by the Seljuks in 1205. Despite all the repair and 'restoration' over the centuries, it's still a good example of early Seljuk style.

Bazaar

West of the hisar, east of Düvenönü Meydanı and south of Park Caddesi is Kayseri's energetic bazaar, which is definitely worth exploring. Set at the intersection of age-old trade routes, Kayseri has been an important commercial centre for millennia. Its several Ottoman covered markets have recently been beautifully restored.

The **Bedesten**, built in 1497 on orders from Mustafa Bey, was first dedicated to the sale of textiles, but now sells all sorts of things. The **Vezirhanı** was constructed in 1727 on the orders of Damat İbrahim Paşa, and now houses shops selling wool and cotton on the ground floor and carpets on the upper. The **Kapalı Çarşı** (Covered Bazaar) was built in 1859, restored in 1988, and now has 500 shops selling necessities (including huge quantities of gold jewellery) to local people. Look out also for the Pamuk Han or cotton bazaar.

Seljuk Tombs

Among Kayseri's other Seljuk archaeological treasures are several distinctive tombs. The **Döner Kümbet** (deur-NEHR kewmbeht), or Revolving Tomb, is about 1km south-east of the hisar along Talas Caddesi. Though it doesn't (and never did) revolve, its cylindrical shape suggests turning, and as you view its marvellous and elaborate Seljuk decoration (1276), you will at least revolve around it. Nearby is another, the 14th-century **Sırçalı Kümbet**, which used to be covered in coloured tiles and topped by a pyramidal roof.

The **Kutluğu Hatun Bahsayiş ve Haydar Bey Türbesi** behind the tourism office, dating from 1350, is a Seljuk-influenced Mongol structure with worn but still impressive decoration.

Archaeological Museum

The city's Archaeological Museum is near the Döner Kümbet. It houses the finds from Kültepe, site of ancient Kanesh, including the cuneiform tablets which told historians much about the Hittite Empire. Hittite, Hellenistic and Roman statuary, plus exhibits of local ethnography, help to make it worth a visit. Opening hours are from 8 am to noon and from 1 to 5 pm daily except Monday; admission costs US$1.

Historic Houses

Just south-east of the citadel is the wonderful **Güpgüpoğlu Konağı**, a fine stone mansion dating from the 18th century, now opened as the city's **Ethnographic Museum**. The Sofa (main hall), bride's room, kitchen and guest room have been decorated in period style, and the fine woodwork on the ceilings and walls has been beautifully restored. It's open from 8 am to 5 pm (closed Monday) for US$1.

The house was the ancestral home of Ahmet Mithat Güpgüpoğlu, a poet, musical composer and officer in the Ottoman government. His son Arif Güpgüpoğlu founded the first maternity and pediatric hospital in Anatolia in 1921.

Near the Güpgüpoğlu Konağı is the **Atatürk Evi**, the house where Atatürk stayed when he visited Kayseri. Two rooms are sporadically open as a museum.

Kültepe (Kanesh-Karum)

Appropriately named 'Hill of Ashes' in Turkish, this archaeological site 20km north-east of Kayseri was originally settled around 4000 BC. The town of Kanesh came to prominence during Old Bronze times (around 2500-2000 BC) when Zipani, King of Kanesh, joined an alliance of Anatolian kings against the powerful king of Akkadia (Mesopotamia), Naram Sin.

By around 1850 BC, Kanesh was the most powerful kingdom in Anatolia. The neighbouring Assyrian commercial centre of Karum, specialising in metals, was among the oldest and richest bazaars in the world. Then a great fire destroyed Kanesh-Karum. It was rebuilt and by around 1720 BC was the Hittite city of Nisa, capital of King Anitta who conquered the pre-Hittite rulers of Hattuşaş (Boğazkale) and made that a Hittite city.

The size and height of the mound is the most impressive thing about the site, showing that ancient Kanesh-Karum was indeed an important city, but signs warn you not to go near the excavation trenches, so there is little to see. The custodian is also liable to dog your every footstep. The best finds are in the Archaeological Museum in Kayseri. It's only really worth coming out here if you're very interested in the Hittites, although on a clear day there are stunning uncluttered views of Mt Erciyes from the top of the mound.

About 600m beyond Karum is the farming village of **Karahöyük**, a cluster of old stone houses near a graveyard of rough-cut tombstones, providing a glimpse of real country life.

To get to Kültepe take a Bünyan bus or minibus from Sivas Caddesi (30 minutes, US$0.50). About 18km along, just before a BP fuel station (cafe, toilets), a road to the left is marked for 'Kültepe Kaniş Karum'. Just over 2km from the main road is the site marked 'Kültepe Kaniş' and, 200m further along, 'Karum'.

Caravanserais

North and east of Kayseri are several beautiful restored Seljuk caravanserais which anyone interested in Seljuk architecture will want to see.

Sultan Han The Sultan Han is on the old Kayseri-Sivas highway, 45km north-east of Kayseri and 1km off the new highway. Besides being a fine example of the Seljuk royal caravan lodging and the second-largest in Anatolia (after the Sultan Hanı near Aksaray), it has been beautifully restored so it's easy to appreciate the architectural fine points. The han was built from 1232 to 1236, and was restored only a few decades ago.

Don't let the locked gate worry you. Shortly after your car draws up, a boy will come running with the key and a booklet of tickets; admission costs US$0.50. Opening hours are supposedly from 9 am to 1 pm and from 2 to 6 pm, closed Monday, but in fact the han is open whenever the guardian can be found.

Tour the inside, noticing particularly the elegant snake motif on the little mosque's arches. Climb up to the roof, but don't neglect a walk around the exterior as well. Note the lion-faced water spouts on the walls, and the plain towers of varying design.

To get here, take any bus or dolmuş going out the Sivas road and get out at the Sultan Han turn-off.

Karatay Han The covered portion of the Karatay Han was built from 1219 to 1236 at the end of Sultan Alaettin Keykubat's reign for the Seljuk vizier Emir Celaleddin Karatay. The open court dates from 1240, during the reign of Gıyaseddin Keyhüsrev, was restored in the 1960s, and is yet another fine example of high Seljuk art.

The han is open whenever a visitor arrives, for US$0.50.

Inside the grand portal to the left is the unmarked tomb of a prominent person (look for the small but exquisite animal figures along the very top of the decoration). Inside the tomb, above the cenotaph, is a ceiling star pattern painted blue to mimic the heavens.

The new Kayseri-Pınarbaşı-Malatya highway passes right through the village of Karadayı, with the Karatay Han easily visible. Take any bus or dolmuş following the Malatya road and get out at Karadayı.

Erciyes Dağı

Erciyes Dağı, or Mt Aergius (3916m), as it was known in Roman times, is an extinct volcano 26km south of Kayseri. It is one of Turkey's few **ski centres**, with a chairlift, beginners' lift, and a ski lodge, ***Kayak Evi*** (Ski House) *(☎ 352-342 2031)* with 100 beds.

Frequent minibuses go as far as Hisarcık (14km) but you must hitch or take a taxi (US$10) for the last dozen or so kilometres to Tekir Yaylası (2150m) and the ski lodge where equipment can be rented.

Though fairly good for skiing (for Turkey), Erciyes is rather inhospitable to hikers. Short walks can be made from the ski lodge, but longer treks require planning, good equipment and a guide.

Places to Stay – Budget

You won't get much cheaper than ***Hunat Oteli*** *(☎ 352-232 4319, Zengin Sokak 5)*, behind the Hunat Mosque and near the Tourism Information Office. It's a convenient, quiet but basic place with waterless rooms priced at US$7 per person. The proprietor, Ömer Bey, is thoroughly avuncular but some single women would find this a daunting pitstop.

Hotel Gönen *(☎ 352-222 2778, fax 231 6584, Nazmi Toker Caddesi 15)*, convenient to the sights, posts prices of US$20/30 for a single/double, but I was quoted rates several dollars lower for a room with shower and breakfast.

Hotel Sur (SOOR) *(☎ 352-222 4367, fax 231 3992, Talas Caddesi 12)* is conveniently positioned and offers rooms with more furnishing than usual. Those on the street side have windows but are liable to be noisy; those on the inside have no windows but will be quieter. Singles/doubles are pretty expensive at US$26/32 with private shower. To find it, walk south-east along Talas Caddesi from the citadel, with a remnant of the city walls and the Sivas Kapısı (Sivas Gate) on your right. Turn right through a gap in the wall, then right again, and you'll see the hotel.

The two-star ***Hotel Turan*** (too-RAHN) *(☎ 352-222 5537, fax 231 1153, Turan Caddesi 8)* is an old faithful which has served travellers for many decades. Some of the spacious rooms – the largest in Kayseri – have bathtubs instead of showers. They usually cost US$18/28 but the staff are ready to haggle if business is slack. There's a terrace on the roof and a carpet shop off the pleasant lobby.

In the bazaar is the tidy and fairly quiet ***Hotel Çamlıca*** (CHAHM-luh-jah) *(☎ 352-231 4344, Bankalar Caddesi, Gürcü Sokak 14)*, with serviceable rooms priced at US$14 a double with sink, US$16 with shower. From the Divan Pastanesi (see Places to Eat), turn right off Millet Caddesi and take the third street on the left, Nazmi Toker Caddesi, known to the locals as Bankalar Caddesi (Banks St), for obvious reasons. After you come to an intersection, walk one more block along the curving street to the hotel.

Next to the otogar is the faded but nominally one-star, 21 room ***Terminal Oteli*** (TEHR-mee-NAHL) *(☎ 352-330 1120, Osman Kavuncu Caddesi 176)*, which charges US$24 a double with private shower and TV, US$1 a double with just a sink, for room and breakfast.

Places to Stay – Mid-Range

Kayseri has several serviceable hotels around Düvenönü Meydanı. The two-star, 44 room ***Hotel Çapari*** *(☎ 352-222 5278, fax 222 5282, Donanma Caddesi 12)* is hidden away on a quiet back street just one block north-east of Düvenönü Meydanı. All rooms have private bath and TV, and cost US$30/40/55 a single/double/triple, breakfast included.

The two-star ***Hotel Konfor*** *(☎ 352-320 0184, fax 336 5100, Atatürk Bulvarı 5)* is a few dozen metres north of Düvenönü Meydanı on the left. Attractively modern, its rooms are comfy and well located, and cost slightly less than those at the Çapari.

Facing Düvenönü Meydanı on its south-western corner is the three-star, 77 room ***Hotel Almer*** *(☎ 352-320 7970, fax 320 7974, Osman Kavuncu Caddesi 15)*. Comfortable rooms equipped with TV, minibar and air-con cost US$45/60 a single/double, breakfast included. Unfortunately, the staff are tip-hungry and you must check your bills carefully for errors.

Hotel Kadıoğlu *(☎ 352-231 6320, fax 222 8296, Kiçikapı Serdar Caddesi 45)*, more or less across the street from the Merkez Bankası and Kayseri Lisesi, offers views of Mount Erciyes from its noisy front rooms, and quieter rooms at the back, all for US$28 a double with shower and breakfast.

Places to Eat

Kayseri boasts a few special dishes, among them *pastırma* – salted, sun-dried veal coated with *çemen* – a spicy concoction of garlic, red peppers, parsley and water. It takes about a month to prepare, has a very strong flavour, tends to stick in your teeth and rules your breath despotically for hours afterwards, but once you acquire the taste you look forward to returning to Kayseri. The darker the pastırma, the longer it has been allowed to age. Many shops in the centre sell it, among them ***Üçler Gıda***, at street level in the same building as the İskender Kebap Salonu (see later in this section).

Other Kayseri specialities include *sucuk* (soo-JOOK), a spicy sausage; *salam* (sah-LAHM), Turkish salami; *tulum peynir* (tooLOOM pehy-neer), hard cheese cured in a goatskin; and *bal* (BAHL), honey. Apart from pastırma, few of these things appear on restaurant menus, so you must buy them for a picnic.

İskender Kebap Salonu, Millet Caddesi 5, by the citadel one floor above street level, has been serving good Bursa-style döner kebap for several decades. It has a pleasing view of the busy street, and low prices of about US$3 to US$4 for a meal of kebap, ayran and salad. The general dining room is one flight up, the aile salonu up another one.

Divan Pastanesi is a good, fancy pastry shop on Millet Caddesi a block south of the citadel, on the corner of Mevlevi Caddesi. Have their *şam fıstıklı baklava* (many-layered flaky pastry sweet with pistachio nuts) and a large glass of tea for about US$2. There's a second branch in Sivas Caddesi.

Further along Millet Caddesi, near the Hotel Turan, is ***Beyaz Saray Fast Food & Oltu Kebap Salonu***. Normally the words 'fast food' are enough to dampen any appetite, but in this case there's no need to worry. The Beyaz Saray does a wide range of dishes, from soups to pizzas and kebaps, but its speciality is *oltu kebap* which is lamb roasted on a horizontal spit and then served up on a skewer; it's fatty but makes a change and costs US$3.50. Another plus is the on-site pastahane, so you can round the meal off nicely with a cake.

The original Beyaz Saray has done so well that there's now a second branch with a more formal upstairs restaurant down the road at Millet Caddesi 8. The İskender kebap here is in the award-winning category, beautifully presented and absolutely delicious for just US$3.50.

Getting There & Away

Air Turkish Airlines connects Kayseri's Erkilet airport with İstanbul by two daily nonstop flights. Buy your tickets at the THY office (☎ 352-222 3858, fax 222 4748) at Sahibiye Mahallesi, Yıldırım Caddesi 1. At the time of writing, there was no air service to Ankara. An airport bus (US$2.50) connects the city with Erkilet airport. Catch the bus 1¼ hours before flight departure time, or be at the airport at least 30 minutes before the scheduled departure time. Local bus No 2 also runs to the airport from Atatürk Caddesi.

Bus Being at an important north-south and east-west crossroads, Kayseri has lots of bus services. To get to the citadel from the otogar, walk out of the front of the otogar, cross the avenue and board any bus marked 'Merkez' (Centre), or take a dolmuş marked 'Şehir'. A taxi to the citadel should cost less than US$3.

The otogar has a PTT, shops and cafes. Details of some daily services follow:

Adana – 335km, five hours, US$8; several
Ankara – 330km, 4½ hours, US$9; frequent
Gaziantep – 371km, six hours, US$8; several
Kahramanmaraş – 291km, 5½ hours, US$6; several
Malatya – 354km, six hours, US$8; several
Nevşehir – 105km, 1½ hours by bus US$1.75; very frequent buses and minibuses
Sivas – 200km, 3½ hours, US$5; frequent
Ürgüp – 80km, 1½ hours, US$2; at least every two hours from 8 am to 8 pm

Train The *Vangölü/Güney Ekspresi* and the *Doğu Ekspresi* and *Yeni Doğu Ekspresi* stop at Kayseri, as does the *Çukurova Ekspresi*. See the Getting Around chapter for details.

To reach the centre from the train station, walk out of the station, cross the big avenue and board any bus heading down Atatürk Bulvarı to Düvenönü Meydanı.

North Central Anatolia

The region north-east of Ankara and north-west of Sivas has a little of everything: ancient Hittite ruins, gritty industrial cities, graceful old Ottoman towns, mountain scenery and plains. Most travellers stop in this region on their way to somewhere else. Heading for the Black Sea coast, it's worth seeing Tokat, and Çorum can provide lodgings if your itinerary demands it. But a few destinations are worth excursions in themselves: the well-preserved Ottoman town of Safranbolu, the Hittite ruins at Boğazkale, near Sungurlu; and the historic city of Amasya, situated in a dramatic river gorge.

SAFRANBOLU

For many years Safranbolu (population 25,000, altitude 350m) was a closely guarded secret: a small town of well-preserved Ottoman houses hidden in the hill country 225km (four hours' ride) north of Ankara. Turkish architects, painters and photographers knew about it and exploited its artistic potential but only the most adventurous travellers wandered through it, often by accident, on their way to the Black Sea coastal town of Amasra. Safranbolu's charms have now been discovered, but not yet over-exploited. The town, 10km north of the grim steel-manufacturing city of Karabük (population 110,000), is not on the most heavily travelled tour bus routes and you must still make a special effort to get here. Once you do, however, you'll enjoy walking along the narrow, twisting cobbled lanes and seeing traditional trades and crafts practised just as they were in Ottoman times.

History

The settlement founded here between 2000 and 1500 BC was subject to the usual conquest, rule, exploitation and enjoyment by Hittites, Paphlagonians, Persians, Lydians, Romans and Byzantines. Under the Turks, the rulers were the Danışmends, Seljuks, Çobanoğlus, Çandaroğlus and Ottomans. During the 17th century, the main Ottoman trade route between Gerede and the Black Sea coast passed through Safranbolu, bringing commerce, prominence and wealth to the town. Wealthy patrons established caravanserais, mosques and Turkish baths. Safranbolu produced many men and women who were successful in commerce and government, and who shared their success with their birthplace by endowing charitable foundations.

During the 18th and 19th centuries Safranbolu's wealthy families built spacious mansions of sun-dried mud bricks, wood and stucco. The families of the surprisingly large population of prosperous artisans built less impressive but similarly sturdy, harmonious homes, and a surprising number of these buildings survive today. During the 19th century about 20% to 25% of Safranbolu's population were Ottoman Greeks, most of whom moved to Greece during the great exchange of populations following WWI. Their principal church, dedicated to St Stephen, has been restored as Kıranköy's Ulu Cami (Great Mosque).

Orientation

Coming via Karabük, you arrive in Kıranköy, the modern part of Safranbolu, arrayed along the ridge of a hill and formerly called Misaki Milli by its Ottoman Greek inhabitants. If you continue uphill from the traffic roundabout you will reach the section called Bağlar (baa-LAHR), with its centre at Köyiçi, which has many interesting old houses.

Turn right (south-east) at the roundabout and go 1.7km, down the hill, up the other side and down again to reach the centre of Old Safranbolu (Eski Safranbolu), the section called Çarşı (Market). On Saturday

CENTRAL ANATOLIA

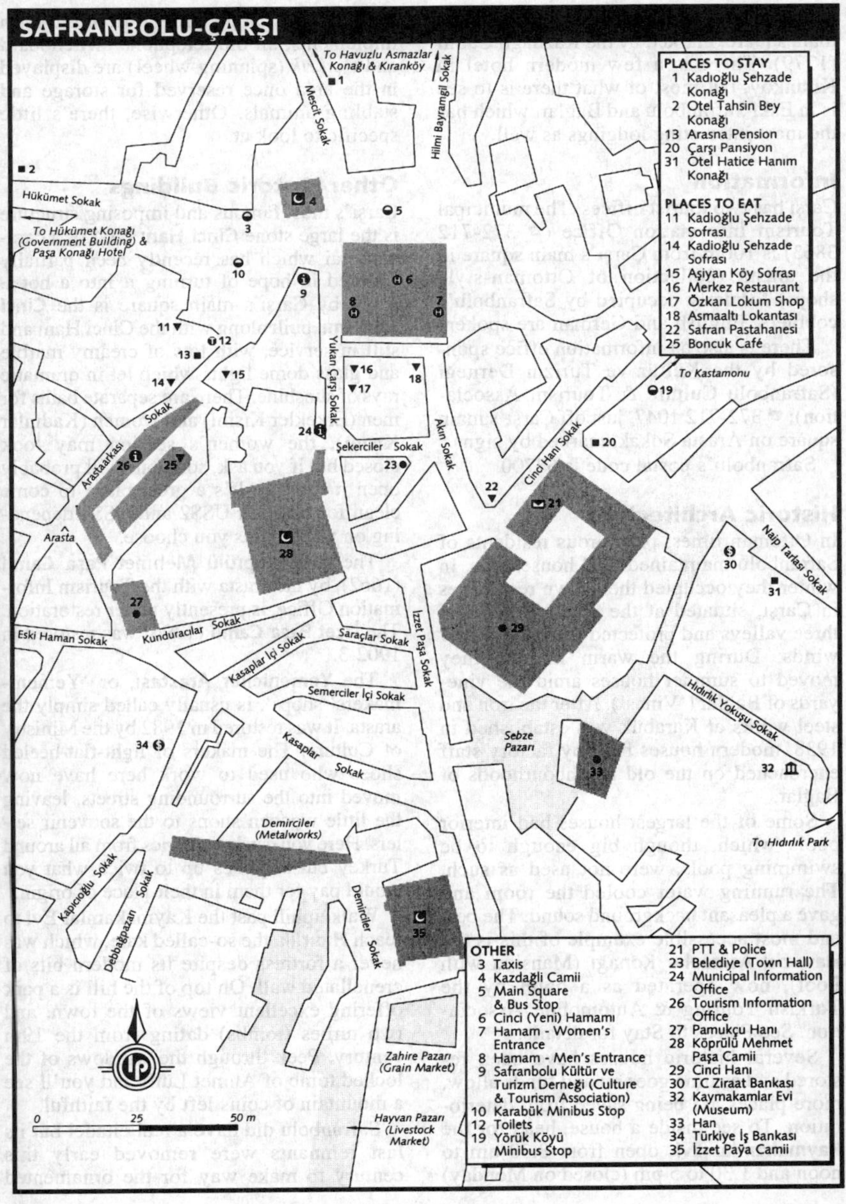

CENTRAL ANATOLIA

a busy market does in fact take place in the main square, marked by the Kazdağlı Camii (1779). There is a few modern hotel in Kıranköy, but most of what there is to see is in Eski Safranbolu and Bağlar, which has the most interesting lodgings as well.

Information

Çarşı has two tourist offices. The municipal Tourism Information Office (☎ 372-712 3863) is 100m from Çarşı's main square in the arasta (collection of Ottoman-style shops) formerly occupied by Safranbolu's cobblers. English and German are spoken.

There is also an information office sponsored by the Kültür ve Turizm Derneği (Safranbolu Culture & Tourism Association); ☎ 372-712 1047, just off Çarşı's main square on Arasta Sokak, marked by signs.

Safranbolu's postal code is 67700.

Historic Architecture

In Ottoman times, prosperous residents of Safranbolu maintained dual households. In winter they occupied their town residences in Çarşı, situated at the meeting point of three valleys and protected from the winter winds. During the warm months they moved to summer houses amid the vineyards of Bağlar ('Vines'). After the iron and steel works at Karabük was established in 1938, modern houses built by factory staff encroached on the old neighbourhoods of Bağlar.

Some of the largest houses had interior pools which, though big enough to be swimming pools, were not used as such. The running water cooled the room and gave a pleasant background sound. The best and most accessible example of this is the **Havuzlu Asmazlar Konağı** (Mansion with Pool), now operated as a hotel by the Turkish Touring & Automobile Association. See Places to Stay for details.

Several historic houses have been restored and as time goes on and funds allow, more places are being saved from deterioration. To see inside a house, head for the **Kaymakamlar Evi**, open from 8.30 am to noon and 1.30 to 5 pm (closed on Monday) for US$0.60. On the ground floor old farm implements, an old telephone switchboard and a *çıkrık* (spinning wheel) are displayed in the area once reserved for storage and stabling animals. Otherwise, there's little specific to look at.

Other Historic Buildings

Çarşı's most famous and imposing structure is the large stone **Cinci Hanı** (1645), a caravanserai which has recently been partially restored in hope of turning it into a hotel. Right by Çarşı's main square is the **Cinci Hamamı**, built along with the Cinci Hanı and still in service, with lots of creamy marble and glass dome lights which let in dramatic rays of sunshine. There are separate baths for men (Erkekler Kısmı) and women (Kadınlar Kısmı); the women's section may look closed but if you ask, someone will probably open it for you. It's a great place to come clean for between US$2 and US$4 depending on what extras you choose.

The large **Köprülü Mehmet Paşa Camii** (1662), by the arasta with the Tourism Information Office, is presently under restoration. The **İzzet Paşa Camii** (1796) was restored in 1902-3.

The **Yemeniciler Arastası**, or 'Yemeni-makers' shops', is usually called simply the arasta. It was restored in 1982 by the Ministry of Culture. The makers of light-flat-heeled shoes who used to work here have now moved into the surrounding streets, leaving the little wooden shops to the souvenir sellers. Here you can buy fabrics from all around Turkey but at prices up to twice what you would pay for them in their place of origin.

Walk uphill past the Kaymakamlar Evi to reach **Hıdırlık**, the so-called kale, which was never a fortress despite its modern bits of crenellated wall. On top of the hill is a park offering excellent views of the town, and two türbes (tombs) dating from the 19th century. Peek through the windows of the locked tomb of Ahmet Lütfi and you'll see a mountain of coins left by the faithful.

Safranbolu did have a real citadel but its last remnants were removed early this century to make way for the ornamented

Hükümet Konağı (government building) on the hilltop across the valley.

Safranbolu's traditional character is now protected by regulation. UNESCO has dubbed the old town a World Heritage Site, on a par with Florence in Italy and Bath in England. Efforts are also being made to preserve the artisans' shops and trades. Most of the active shops and workshops line the streets south of the Cinci Hamamı and the Köprülü Camii.

Bağlar has many wonderful old houses, but they are much more spread out. The best way to visit them is to stay in one (see Places to Stay – Mid-Range).

Excursion to Yörük Köyü

Another, smaller, less renowned village of old houses is Yörük Köyü (which translates oxymoronically as 'Nomad Village'), 11km east of Safranbolu along the Kastamonu road. The people of the village grew rich, somewhat surprisingly, on making bread and some of the houses are truly enormous. Ask around and someone may take you to see the old village *çamaşırlık*, or laundry, with arched hearths where the water was heated in cauldrons and a huge stone table, rather like the *göbektaşı* in a hamam which was used for the actual scrubbing.

Yörük Köyü has a traditional tea-house and a weekends-only cafe selling ayran, baklava and gözleme. Otherwise tourism has hardly touched the village. Dolmuşes depart from a stop on Celal Bayar Caddesi near the Çarşı Pansiyon. Go early in order to get a return dolmuş before nightfall. Failing that, you'll need to haggle with a Safranbolu taxi driver to take you there, wait for an hour or so while you explore the village, then return. This will cost between US$12 and US$15 depending on your bargaining skills.

If you have your own car, there's an excellent restaurant, ***Çevrik Köprü*** *(☎ 372-737 2119)*, on the right side of the road just before the turn off for Yörük Köyü. Here you can tuck into juicy kuyu kebap in shady gardens with fountains and pools.

Places to Stay

Safranbolu is a very popular destination with Turkish tourists at weekends and over public holidays. If you must visit at those times, try and make reservations in advance.

Places to Stay – Budget

Çarşı Pansiyon (☎ 372-725 1079, Babasultan Mahallesi, Bozkurt Sokak 1) is a small, friendly place not far from the Cinci Hanı. Rooms with private baths come with low-level beds, sedirs, carpets and pretty curtains for US$10/15 a single/double (breakfast included). If you want hot water, just ask the proprietor in advance. There's also a small cafe.

A block from the Cinci Hanı, ***Otel Hatice Hanım Konağı*** *(☎ 372-712 7545, Babasultan Mahallesi, Naip Tarlası Sokak 6)*, charges US$18/30 for rooms decorated in Ottoman style with bath and breakfast; rooms without bath cost a bit less. The public rooms are nicely decorated and atmospheric as well.

Arasna Pension *(☎ 372-712 4170)* has a restaurant and live music on Friday and Saturday nights in summer, when an early night might be out of the question. Rooms go for US$12 per person in a room with shower and breakfast.

In Kıranköy, at İnönü Mahallesi, as you head down towards Çarşı from the roundabout, you'll find the ***Konak Pansiyon*** *(☎ 372-725 2485)*, among the quietest and cleanest places to stay, at US$10 per person, breakfast included.

Places to Stay – Mid-Range

Ev Pansiyonculuğu Geliştirme Merkezi (Home Pension Development Centre) *(☎ 372-712 7236 or 712 3863, Yemeniciler Arastası 2)*, beside the Tourism Information Office in the arasta, makes reservations for overnight stays in restored houses in Safranbolu. Rates are US$19 to US$26 a single, US$29 to US$38 a double, breakfast included. Some rooms have private baths, others share a bath with the family. The selection of houses is extensive; have a look at the photos in their scrapbook to help you choose.

Perhaps the most atmospheric of the old houses which now provide lodging is ***Havuzlu Asmazlar Konağı*** *(☎ 372-725 2883, fax 712 3824)*, Mescit Sokak, restored and opearted by the Turkish Touring and Automobile Association. Enclosed behind high walls 400m uphill from Çarşı's main square, opposite the turn off for the Bartın-Zonguldak road, you enter the building to see the fine pool which gives the house its name (havuzlu, with pool), right in the centre of the main room, surrounded by low sofas and small brass-tray tables at which guests take breakfast and afternoon tea.

The 11 guest rooms are beautifully furnished with brass beds, sedirs, brass tables and kilims; rooms 14, 15, 20 and 21 upstairs are the nicest. Bathrooms are minuscule and sound-proofing is at a minimum but these are minor inconveniences. Overflow rooms in a house across the road are cheaper but much less atmospheric.

Bearing in mind the prices you pay for 'Ottoman' comfort in İstanbul, the Havuzlu represents an excellent opportunity to enjoy it without breaking the bank: it charges US$30/40 a single/double.

Kadıoğlu Şehzade Konağı *(☎ 372-725 2762, fax 712 2624, Karaali Mahallesi, Mescit Sokak 24)* is a less grand Ottoman house now converted to an inn. Charming, if small, old rooms with tiny bathrooms go for US$20/35, breakfast included.

Otel Tahsin Bey Konağı *(☎ 372-712 6062, fax 712 5596, Hükümet Sokak 50)* and ***Paşa Konağı*** (same phone and fax) just 50m further up the road and to the left, offer light, airy rooms with built-in cupboards, plastered fireplaces and period decoration. The Tahsin Bey has good views from some rooms, the Paşa Konağı a secluded garden and rather eerie bar. In both cases some of the bathrooms are inside cupboards with high doorsteps which might trouble some guests. Check before agreeing to take your room. Posted rates are US$32/58 a single/double, but I was quoted prices only half as much when I asked.

If you need to stay in Kıranköy, the two-star, 30 room ***Uz Otel*** *(☎ 372-712 1086, fax 712 2215, İnönü Mahallesi, Araphacı Caddesi 3)*, built to resemble (vaguely) an old Safranbolu house, but now faded in a modern way. Shower-equipped guest rooms are pretty expensive at US$30/46 a single/double, breakfast included. A few family rooms have one double bed, one single, and two bunk beds.

Places to Eat

Among the older places favoured by the locals are ***Merkez Restaurant***, plain, clean and typical, with three-course meals for US$3.50. Next door is ***Özkan Lokum Shop***, a beautiful old sweets shop. In the arasta, ***Boncuk Café*** is one of the town's most congenial places, a modern Safranbolulu's conception of what an 'antique' cafe should be. Here you can watch gözleme being made. To sample it will cost you about US$1.50. Opposite the Cinci Hanı the friendly ***Safran Pastahanesi*** makes a very congenial place to stop for breakfast or a cake.

Near the arasta, the newer ***Kadıoğlu Şehzade Sofrası*** has two entrances, a courtyard around a fountain and lots of attractive indoor dining rooms. You can get pide here but the house speciality is kuyu kebap, made by enclosing lamb in an underground firepit where it is self-basted. Kebap, salad and a drink (no alcohol) will set you back about US$5 or US$6.

Aşiyan Köy Sofrası across the street specialises in traditional local village dishes.

The vast basement restaurant of ***Havuzlu Asmazlar Konağı*** has marble floors and an arched fireplace. The menu lists such Ottoman delights as mıklama (fried eggs, tomatoes, spinach, ground lamb, onions and pastırma) and gözleme but they may only be available when the hotel is busy. Otherwise it's şiş kebap. Portions are large and prices moderate: less than US$8 for soup, salad, main course and beer.

Getting There & Away

There are a few direct buses to Safranbolu but most drop you at Karabük's grimy otogar. Minibuses (US$0.50) ply up and down the road outside to run you the last 10km to Safranbolu's Kıranköy district. Ulusoy has regular daily services to Ankara (225km, four hours), and İstanbul (390km, five hours), and picks up passengers from Çarşı as well as Kıranköy. There's also service from Karabük to Kastamonu (100km, two hours, US$3) and Bartın (for Amasra, 92km, 1½ hours). You can get to Amasya (450km, nine hours, US$16) via minibus to Karabük, then to Gerede, then a minibus to Amasya, but it may be more comfortable going via Ankara.

If you're driving, exit from the Ankara-İstanbul highway at Gerede and head north, following signs for Karabük.

You could also reach Safranbolu by taking the Ankara-Zonguldak train (*Karaelmas*) and getting out at Karabük.

Getting Around

Every 30 minutes or so throughout the day local buses (US$0.40) roll along the route from Çarşı's main square over the hills to Kıranköy and up to the Köyiçi stop in Bağlar.

KASTAMONU

Heading on from Safranbolu to Ankara or the Black Sea you may need to stop in Kastamonu, a small town of 50,000 people which is nonetheless an important transport connection point. There's not much specifically to linger for, although you might be interested in the small museum, the castle and the assorted ancient market buildings. There's a reasonable range of places to stay and the chance to sample cheeses and puddings you may not have encountered elsewhere. You can also make a side trip to see one of Turkey's finest surviving wooden mosques in the village of Kasaba.

History

As a result of its position, Kastamonu has had as chequered a history as many central Turkish towns. Archaeological evidence suggests there was a settlement here as far back as 2000 BC, but the Hittites, Persians, Macedonians and Pontic kings all left their mark. In the 11th century the Seljuks descended, followed by the Danışmends. In the late 13th century the Byzantine emperor John Comnenus tried to hold out here but the Mongols and the Ottomans soon swept in and by 1459 Kastamonu was secured as an Ottoman town.

More recently, Kastamonu played an unexpected role as the town Atatürk chose to launch his hat reforms in 1925 (see the boxed text 'The Hat Law' in the Facts about Turkey chapter).

Orientation

Kastamonu's small otogar is on the western side of the city centre, as you come in from Samsun or Sinop. It's about 1km from the centre, reachable by dolmuş or taxi (US$1.50).

A stream runs through the centre of the town. The road along its northern bank is Yalçın Caddesi, which becomes Plevne Caddesi as it reaches the centre and then Atatürk Caddesi. The road along the southern bank is Kışla Caddesi, which becomes Cumhuriyet Caddesi towards the centre.

The centre of town is Cumhuriyet Meydanı, with an imposing Valilik building and statue of Atatürk. This is where you'll find the PTT, the tourism information kiosk and local bus stops.

Just to the west of Cumhuriyet Meydanı the stream passes under a truncated stone bridge. To the southern side a road leads to Nasrullah Meydanı and the bazaar.

Information

A tourist information office-cum-souvenir shop (☎ 366-212 0162, fax 214 6159) is conveniently positioned right in front of Cumhuriyet Meydanı. In theory, it's open daily from 9 am to 10 pm and some English and German are spoken. It sells a town plan for US$2.

Kastamonu's postal code is 37200.

Kastamonu Arkeoloji ve Etnoğrafya Müzesi

About 100m east of Cumhuriyet Meydanı along Cumhuriyet Caddesi is the Kastamonu Museum, open daily except Monday from 8.30 am to 4.30 pm for US$1. It's housed in the attractive building where Atatürk announced his planned headgear reforms on 30 August 1925.

CENTRAL ANATOLIA

There's the usual mildly depressing collection of dusty Roman and Byzantine relics, including a gruesome sarcophagus opened to reveal the skeleton inside still with a full head of hair. Upstairs, look out for some of the wood blocks used to make the printed cloths on sale around here and for some fine carved wood and horn spoons. Among the costumes on display, a couple of fezzes are more interesting when you know the history of the building.

If the custodian doesn't immediately offer, ask him to unlock the **Atatürk Salonu** on the ground floor so you can see the photos of the 1925 visit. Some were taken in İnebolu and show his entourage looking silly in hats with turned-up brims. Two days later they are marching into Kastamonu looking much more confident in their Panamas. There are also assorted quotations from Atatürk's speech, but in Turkish only which is a great shame.

Historic Buildings

Kastamonu is dominated by its **kale**, built on a rock above the town. Parts of it date back to Byzantine times, but most of what you see belongs to the later Seljuk and Ottoman reconstructions. A family still lives inside the castle so you should be able to get in at most reasonable times. It's a steep 1km climb up through the streets of the old town and you'll be rewarded with fine views of the town's roofs. Otherwise, you can appreciate the outline of the walls better from down below.

Nasrullah Meydanı is dominated by the Ottoman **Nasrullah Camii** and the fine double fountain in front of it. The area immediately south of Nasrullah Meydanı is filled with old market buildings, several of them still in use. The modern-day bazaar takes place in and around the **Karanlık Bedesten**, the **Balkapanı Hanı** and the **İsmail Bey Hanı** (1466) which was restored in 1972 to provide workshops. Wander down any of the side streets in this area and you'll come across old hamams, fountains and other buildings.

Excursion to Kasaba Köyü

The tiny village of Kasaba, 17km from Kastamonu as the crow flies, is an unlikely place to find one of the finest wooden mosques still surviving in Turkey. The **Mahmudbey Camii** was built in 1366. Externally there is nothing other than the unusually lovely wooden doors to suggest there is anything special about this mosque. Get the hoca to unlock it, however, and you'll find a stunning, recently restored interior with four painted wooden columns, a wooden gallery and fine painted ceiling rafters.

To get to Kasaba, take a minibus to Daday from Kastamonu otogar and ask to be let off at Subaşı (US$0.75). From there it's another 3km to Kasaba. If there's no sign of a lift, walk through Subaşı and out the other side, bearing right when the road forks and walking through the village of Göçen. After Göçen the road is signposted 'Mahmudbey Camii' on the right. In the village you'll see a bridge on the right. The mosque is the second alongside the stream.

Places to Stay

Kastamonu's hotels are clustered around Belediye and Cumhuriyet Caddesis, right in the centre of town.

One of the cheapest is ***Ilgaz Oteli*** *(☎ 366-212 4217)*, on Belediye Caddesi, which has very basic waterless rooms for US$5/8 a single/double. A couple of doors along ***Otel Hâdi*** *(☎ 366-214 1696)* is twice as expensive and has rooms with private showers. It's a cheerful enough place, although the bedroom decor is rather odd and the bathrooms only so-so.

Nearby on Cumhuriyet Caddesi ***Otel İdrisoğlu*** *(☎ 366-214 1757)* has serviceable rooms with private bath for US$7 per person. Street-facing rooms are noisy. A few doors away is the altogether cheerier ***Ruganci Otel*** *(☎ 366-214 9500, fax 212 4343)* which has pretensions to stylish decor in the bedrooms. For US$15/20 you get TV and breakfast also. Watch for noise here too.

Just off Nasrullah Meydanı is ***Otel Selvi*** *(☎ 366-214 1763, Banka Sokak 10)*. Rooms here are averagely comfortable although in need of modernisation, but some on the top floor have good views of the castle. Beware of doors with glass panels that let hallway light in. Prices are supposedly US$9/15 but bartering can bring reductions.

Kastamonu's best hotel is undoubtedly the two-star ***Otel Mütevelli*** *(☎ 366-212 2020, fax 212 2017, Cumhuriyet Caddesi 10)*, across the road from Cumhuriyet Meydanı. The good, clean rooms manage to escape the standard Turkish blanket bed covering, and although the price might seem a bit high (US$20/30/38 a single/double/triple) there are lots of extras like a decent restaurant and bar.

Places to Eat

Across the road from the Otel Hâdi is an alleyway with several small restaurants. The ***Ender*** does saç kavurma, while ***Uludağ Pide ve Kebap Salonu*** on the corner serves more standard fare, and a meal at either can be had for US$3 or so. ***Merkez Lokantası***, south of the Otel Selvi, stays open later than most other places, although you're liable to be served tepid food after 7 pm.

In Cumhuriyet Caddesi, near Otel Mütevelli, is the cheerful ***Ömür Pastanesi*** where you can sample *tavuk göğsü*, a dessert made from milk, rice and pounded chicken breast (which you won't be able to find or taste in it).

Across the other side of the stream, Plevne Caddesi has several beerhouses, including ***Kervan Saray Bira Salonu*** and ***Agora Birahanesi***, the closest thing in appearance to an English pub that you'll find in central Turkey.

Given Kastamonu's lack of exciting eateries, you might want to make up a picnic, in which case it's worth dropping into ***Kaptan Şarküteri***, as you turn from Cumhuriyet Caddesi into Nasrullah Meydanı. Here you'll find a wide range of Turkish cheeses from Kars, Şanlıurfa, Van and Erzincan, as well as honey from Erzurum and plentiful olives.

Getting There & Away

Kastamonu's small otogar offers regular departures for Ankara (245km, four hours, US$9), İstanbul (507km, 10 hours, US$15) and Samsun (312km, six hours, US$11). To get to Sinop you usually have to travel via Boyabat. There are hourly departures for Karabük (100km, two hours, US$3), with some buses continuing to Safranbolu. Minibuses for İnebolu and Cide also leave from the otogar.

BOYABAT

Heading for the Black Sea from Kastamonu you may need to transit in Boyabat (1½ hours, US$2), a small town with a large brick-making industry. Boyabat's otogar is just off Adnan Menderes Bulvarı, the main road through town. Chances are you'll be passing through, but with an hour or so to spare, go out of the otogar and turn right along the highway toward a road bridge. Just to the left of the bridge you'll find a pleasant pine-tree-shaded tea garden to while away the time. From the bridge itself there's a fine view of Boyabat's **castle**, built to guard a prominent gorge. Beneath the bridge are some unexpectedly clean toilets.

Alternatively, leave the otogar, cross the highway and cut through any of the breaks in the shops to find the **bazaar** behind. Interspersed amid the shops are some fine old timber buildings. You'll also see women wearing a white, black and red headscarf that looks like an Indian bedspread, called a *pita*.

If you need to spend the night here, come out of the otogar, turn right towards the bridge, cross the highway and turn left following the sign marked 'Şehir'. Just past the PTT on the right you'll find ***Merkez Oteli*** (☎ 368-315 1119) with very basic rooms at US$5 per person. There are several places to eat opposite the otogar but none are going to win any prizes for their cuisine.

The road north from Boyabat passes through some stunning forested scenery, zigzagging up to 1370m, so that it takes 2½ hours to reach Sinop (see the Black Sea chapter).

BOĞAZKALE & THE HITTITE CITIES

The farming village of Boğazkale (formerly Boğazköy, population 2510), 200km east of Ankara, 86km south of Çorum and 30km east of Sungurlu, is well worth visiting as the site of Hattuşaş, the Hittite capital. Nearby is Yazılıkaya, an open-air Hittite religious sanctuary with fine rock carvings. Boğazkale also makes a possible base for a visit to Alacahöyük, site of yet more Hittite ruins, 36km to the north-west. (See the boxed text 'The Hitties' earlier in this chapter.)

The modern village of Boğazkale has adequate, though hardly fancy, travellers' services. Sungurlu, a commercial and farming town 175km (three hours) east of Ankara and 30km west of Boğazkale, has a decent motel but not much else. Çorum, the nearby provincial capital, is the nearest city with a full range of hotels and a big otogar.

Orientation

Coming from Sungurlu or Çorum, you enter the village opposite the Aşikoğlu Turistik Moteli. From there it's just 100m south to the museum.

Coming from Yozgat, you follow a road which sweeps over the mountains from the

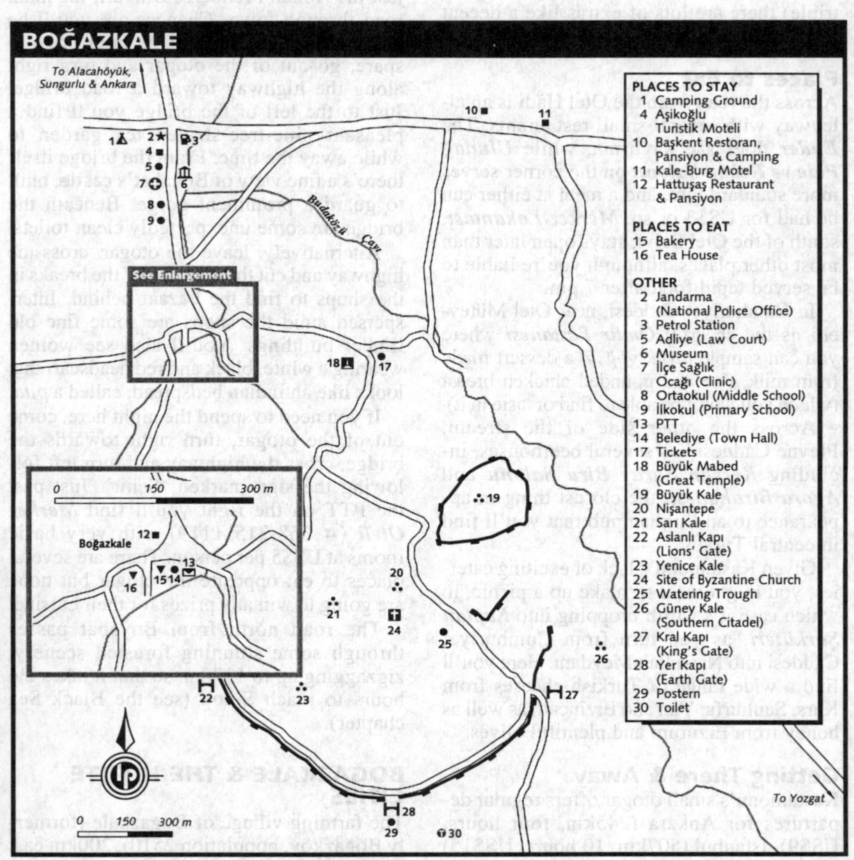

south-east and skirts the eastern part of the archaeological zone. There's a fine view of the ruined city from this road.

South of the village, on the hillside, sprawl the extensive ruins of Hattuşaş. It's exactly 1km from the Aşikoğlu Turistik Moteli to the ticket kiosk, and another 2.5km up the hillside to the farthest point, the Yerkapı (Earth Gate), along the road which loops through the ruins. The separate site of Yazılıkaya is about 3km uphill from the ticket kiosk along another road. If you're a hiker and the day is not too hot, you can trek around these extensive ruins, but most visitors will want to ride at least some of the way.

Boğazkale Müzesi

The little museum in the town (open from 8 am to 5.30 pm, US$1) has a large topographical map of the site, and some Hittite artefacts worth seeing: fascinating cuneiform tablets, signature seals, arrows and axeheads, a saw, and whimsically shaped pots and vessels. High on the walls around the museum are large photographs of the site and Hittite objects found during excavation. The few Byzantine crosses come from a later church on the site. There's some German labelling.

Hattuşaş

Hattuşaş was once a great and impressive city, well defended by stone walls over 6km in length. Today the ruins consist mostly of reconstructed foundations, walls and a few rock carvings, but there are several more interesting features, including a tunnel and some fine hieroglyphic inscriptions preserved in situ. The site itself is strange, almost eerie, exciting for its ruggedness and high antiquity rather than for its buildings or reliefs. Chances are that you'll share it with the birds for much of the day.

The road looping around the entire site of Hattuşaş (not including Yazılıkaya) is 5km long, from the ticket kiosk all the way around and back. The walk itself takes at least an hour, plus time spent exploring the ruins, so figure on spending a good three hours here. Take drinking water and start early in the day before the sun is too hot as there's little shade. Local taxis will take you all the way around for about US$10. You may want to haggle for an all-day tour including Hattuşaş, Yazılıkaya and Alacahöyük.

Hattuşaş is open from 8 am to 5 pm, with a theoretical break for lunch from noon to 1.30 pm; in practice you enter when you like and the ticket-seller catches up with you at some point. Admission costs US$2 and the ticket is valid for Yazılıkaya as well.

The following description assumes you do the loop in an anticlockwise direction.

Exploring Hattuşaş The first site you come to, 300m up (south-west) from the ticket kiosk, is the **Büyük Mabed**, or the Great Temple of the storm god, a vast complex that's almost a town in itself, with its own water and drainage systems, storerooms and ritual altars. It dates from the 14th century BC and seems to have been destroyed in around 1200 BC.

About 350m south past the Great Temple, the road forks; take the right (west) fork and follow the winding road up the hillside. On your left in the midst of the old city you can see several ruined structures fenced off from the road, including the **Sarı Kale** which may be a Phrygian fort on Hittite foundations.

From the fork in the road it's about 1km uphill to the **Aslanlı Kapı**, or Lion Gate, which has two stone lions defending the city. The city's defensive walls have been restored along the ridge, which allows you to appreciate the scope of the construction effort that took place almost 4000 years ago.

Continue another 700m to the top of the hill and you'll find the **Yer Kapı** or **Sfenksli Kapı** (Earth or Sphinx Gate), once defended by two great sphinxes, who are now domesticated in the museums of İstanbul and Berlin. The most interesting feature here is the long, 70m **tunnel** running beneath the walls to a **postern** on the southern side of the hill. As the true arch was not discovered until much later, the Hittites used a corbelled arch, two flat faces of stones leaning towards one another. Primitive or not, the arch has done its job for millennia, and you can still pass down the tunnel as Hittite soldiers did, emerging from the postern. Your reward is a toilet, off to the left at the base of the slope. Climb back up to the Yer Kapı by either of the **monumental stairways** placed on either side of the wide stone glacis beneath the walls. Once back on the top, enjoy the wonderful view from this highest point, sweeping down over Hattuşaş, Boğazkale and beyond. Below you'll see the **Yenice Kale**, where Hittite engineers transformed the very uneven site into a plain on which to build their structures.

Another 600m eastward down the slope brings you to the **Kral Kapı**, or King's Gate, named after the regal-looking figure in the relief carving. The one you see is an obvious copy, as the original was removed for safekeeping to the Ankara museum. Actually, the figure is not a king at all, but the Hittite war god.

Heading downhill again you'll come to the **Nişantaş**, a rock with a long Hittite inscription cut into it, in sore need of conservation. Immediately opposite a path leads up to the recently excavated **Güney Kale**, or Southern Citadel, and to what may have been a royal tomb with fine hieroglyphics and human figures carved into another tunnel-shaped structure.

The ruins of the **Büyük Kale**, or Great Fortress, are 800m downhill from the Kral Kapı. This elaborate fortress also held the royal palace and the Hittite state archives. The archives, discovered in 1906, contained a treaty between Hittite monarch Hattusili III and Egyptian pharaoh Ramses II written in cuneiform on a clay tablet. From the fortress it's just over 1km back to the ticket kiosk.

Yazılıkaya

The Turkish name (yah-zuh-LUH kah-yah) means 'inscribed rock', and that's what you find at this site just under 3km from Boğazkale. Follow the signs from the ticket kiosk. The road circles a hillock called Ambarlı Kaya, on top of which there were more Hittite buildings, before crossing a stream and climbing the hill past the Başkent Motel.

Yazılıkaya was always a naturalistic religious sanctuary open to the sky, but in later Hittite times (13th century BC) monumental gateways and temple structures were built in front of the **natural rock galleries**. It is the foundations of these late structures that you see as you approach from the car park.

There are two natural rock galleries, the larger one to the left, which was the empire's sacred place, and a narrower one to the right, which was the burial place of the royal family. In the large gallery, the low reliefs of numerous conehead gods and goddesses marching in procession indicate this was the Hittites' holiest religious sanctuary. Of the Hittites' 1000 gods, fewer than 100 are represented here.

Alacahöyük

There's less to see at Alacahöyük, a very old site settled from about 4000 BC, 36km north of Boğazkale and 52km south of Çorum. As at the other Hittite sites, movable monuments have been taken to the museum in Ankara, though there is a small site museum, and a few worn sphinxes and good bas-reliefs have been left in place.

To get there, leave Boğazkale heading north-west on the Sungurlu road, and after 13.5km turn right at the road marked for Alaca and Alacahöyük. (Coming from Sungurlu, turn left about 11km after turning onto the Boğazkale road.) Go another 11.5km and turn left for Alacahöyük, another 9km along.

At the time of research there was no dolmuş service. The villagers apparently prefer to get rides with trucks which charge less than the minibus drivers. If you don't fancy copying them, reckon on about US$22 to US$25 to get a taxi or minibus to take you to the ruins and back to Boğazkale.

Alacahöyük is now a farming hamlet with a humble main square on which stands a fountain, a PTT, a souvenir shop, a bakery, a modest grocery shop and ***Hitit Café***, good for tea or a cool drink. The museum is right by the ruins, and both are open from 8 am to noon, and from 1.30 to 5.30 pm, closed on Monday. The admission fee for everything is US$1. In the small **museum** you can inspect tools used in the excavations, and finds from the Chalcolithic and Old Bronze ages. A handy ant-farm-style glass case shows the stratigraphy of Alacahöyük's 15 layers of history. Note also the Hitit Çağı Banyo Teknesi, a Hittite-Age bathtub. Upstairs there's an ethnographic section, which many people find more absorbing than the ancient potsherds.

At the ruins, signs are in Turkish and English. The **monumental gate**, with its lions guarding the door and its very fine reliefs down in front, is what you've come to see. The reliefs show storm-god-worshipping ceremonies and festivals with musicians, acrobats, priests and the Hittite king and queen. Off to the left across the fields is a **secret escape tunnel** leading to a postern as at Hattuşaş.

Leaving Alacahöyük, signs for Sungurlu lead you 7km out to the Sungurlu-Çorum highway. Turn left (south-west) for Sungurlu (27km), right for Çorum (42km) and Samsun (210km). There are frequent buses and dolmuşes along the Sungurlu-Çorum highway.

Places to Stay & Eat

Boğazkale is a pleasant place to spend the odd night or so, with such noise as there is coming from honking geese, crowing cockerels and braying donkeys.

If you want to be at the heart of Boğazkale's limited action, a good first choice is the 23-bed ***Hattuşaş Restaurant & Pansiyon*** (*☎ 364-452 2013, fax 452 2957*), on the main square in the village, renting simple but spacious rooms above a carpet shop (of course) for US$6 per person. It's well located so you can easily walk to the museum and to Hattuşaş, and Ahmed, the friendly proprietor, speaks good English. The restaurant, popular with the locals, is pleasingly decorated with old kilims and other artefacts. The pansiyon is open all year round.

The 25 room ***Aşikoğulu Turistik Moteli*** (ah-SHEEK-oh-loo) (*☎ 364-452 2004, fax 452 2171*), at the entrance to the town, also within easy walking distance of the museum and shops, is open from mid-March to November. Simple double rooms with sink and shower (no toilet) in the old building cost US$25; better rooms in the new three-star hotel go for US$30, breakfast included. The hotel also has a capacious restaurant with acceptable food for around US$5 or US$6 per person. At the back a pretty basic ***camping ground*** charges US$3 for a tent or US$5 for a caravan.

Up the hill, 1km from the museum on the road to Yazılıkaya and Yozgat, is ***Başkent Restoran, Pansiyon & Camping*** (*☎ 364-452 2037 or 452 2567*), Yazılıkaya Yolu Üzeri, with 18 motel-style rooms with twin beds and showers for US$20, breakfast included. To camp here costs US$4. The restaurant, with its white laminate tables, dark wood trim and red tile roof is pleasant, and has good views of the ruins.

Just 400m further up the hill along the Yazılıkaya road is ***Kale-Burg Motel*** (*☎ 364-452 2189*), which looks fancier than it actually is. Very simple double rooms with showers cost US$10/15. The camping ground is primitive, but there's a ***restaurant*** here as well.

Atilla Turistik Tesisleri (*☎ 364-452 2101*), just over 1km west of the Aşikoğlu Motel on the Sungurlu road, charges less in its simple motel, restaurant and primitive camping ground with little shade.

In Sungurlu, 30km to the west, ***Hitit Motel*** (*☎ 364-311 8042, fax 311 3873*), is 1km east of the centre on the Ankara-Samsun road. Its position is rather off-putting and the sign can be hard to spot, squeezed in as it is between the Petrol Ofisi fuel station and the Renault garage. With 23 shower-equipped rooms on two floors with balconies overlooking the pretty gardens and swimming pool (usually empty), it costs US$23/37/48 a single/double/triple, breakfast included. In the restaurant, expect to spend from US$5 to US$7 per person for lunch or dinner, drinks included. Believe it or not, Prince Charles stayed here in May 1992 while on a private birdwatching trip to Turkey.

Getting There & Away

Minibuses connect Boğazkale with Sungurlu (30km, US$1) and Çorum (86km, US$2) several times daily. In a pinch, you can hire a taxi in Sungurlu to run you to Boğazkale for about US$30.

Boğazkale makes an easy day's excursion from Ankara and several tour operators offer tours for US$75 per person. Look out for their advertisements in the *Turkish Daily News*.

YOZGAT

About 35km south-east of Boğazkale and on the Ankara-Sivas highway is Yozgat (population 50,000, altitude 1301m), with a few very basic, rundown hotels, restaurants and an otogar. It's an unprepossessing provincial capital founded by the Ottomans in the 18th century. The main highway is lined with modern Turkish waffle-front apartment buildings. In contrast is the **Nizamoğlu Konağı**, a 19th century Ottoman house converted to hold ethnographic exhibits.

About 5km south of Yozgat is **Çamlık Milli Parkı** (Pine-Grove National Park).

ÇORUM

Set on an alluvial plain on a branch of the Çorum River, this is an agricultural town and provincial capital (population 120,000, altitude 801m). As with so many settlements in Turkey, its origins extend back into the mists of history. People have been living here for at least 4000 years.

You may have thought a chickpea was just a chickpea but that was before you came to Çorum, the chickpea capital of Turkey. The town's main street is lined with *leblebiciler* (chickpea roasters) and sacks upon sacks of the chalky little pulses, all sorted according to fine distinctions obvious to a chickpea dealer but not, perhaps, to anyone else. Turks love to munch leblebi (dry roasted chickpeas) while sipping rakı. They're served plain, sugared, salted, peppered, or flavoured with clove. Shops in the otogar sell them freshly roasted.

If you're travelling north or east by bus you may have to stop in Çorum. Given the lack of transport to Boğazkale from Yozgat and the shortage of accommodation in Sungurlu, it also makes a handy base for getting to the Hittite sites. Çorum has a small **Byzantine kale** on a hilltop, and a Seljuk mosque, the 13th-century **Ulu Cami**. Most of its other old buildings are Ottoman, and there are some fine, if crumbling, old houses near the clock tower.

Orientation & Information

The clock tower marks the centre of Çorum, with the PTT, Belediye and tourist office all within 100m. Nearby is Eğridere Sokak, a small street lined with shops selling gold jewellery and changing money. The otogar is 1km south-west of the clock tower along İnönü Caddesi where there's a fair sprinkling of banks waiting to change your money. Most hotels are within a five or 10-minute walk of the otogar.

Çorum Müzesi

About 400m from the otogar toward the centre is the Çorum Museum (open from 8 am to 5.30 pm every day for US$1), with a small, mildly interesting collection of Hittite, Byzantine-Roman and Ottoman exhibits. Ethnographic exhibits cover Turkish life during the last century. If you're stuck for an hour or two in between buses, go out of the main entrance of the otogar, turn left, then left again at the traffic roundabout. The museum is in the copse of pines on the right-hand side at the next roundabout, across the street from the Çorum Oteli.

Places to Stay

Most hotels are along the İnönü Caddesi (the main street) near the otogar.

Otel Aygün *(☎ 364-213 364, İnönü Caddesi 115)*, opposite the Çorum Oteli, is well past its prime but the rooms are reasonably clean and cheap at just US$7/10 a single/double with private shower.

Hotel Merih *(☎ 364-213 8379)*, facing the clock tower on İnönü Caddesi, is oldish but serviceable, with waterless singles/doubles for US$9/16, or US$11/18 with private facilities.

The two-star ***Hotel Kolağası*** *(☎ 364-213 1971, fax 224 1556, İnönü Caddesi 97)* charges US$14/23 for rooms with shower. It's clean and has a lift.

The tired facade of ***Çorum Oteli*** *(☎ 364-213 8515, fax 212 0613, İnönü Caddesi 80)*, looming above the otogar from its perch on İnönü Caddesi, belies its comfortable, friendly, clean interior with a decent restaurant, hairdresser and shop. Rooms with TV and private bath cost US$20/28.

The best in town is the three-star ***Çorum Büyük Otel*** *(☎ 364-224 6092, fax 224 6094, İnönü Caddesi 90)* opposite the otogar. Spacious modern rooms with pleasant bathrooms cost US$30/40/50 a single/double/triple, and there are plenty of extras: two restaurants, an American bar (with alcohol), a billiards room, a TV lounge and a sauna.

Unfortunately, the three-star ***Hotel Sarıgül*** *(☎ 364-224 2012, fax 224 0396, Azap Ahmet Sokak 18)*, hidden away off Gazi Caddesi near the Kültür Sitesi, is 1.5km from the otogar but otherwise pretty central. It's Çorum's most modern, with restaurant, bar and Turkish bath. Comfortable rooms are overpriced at US$43/55 a single/double, breakfast included.

Places to Eat

İnönü Caddesi offers plenty of restaurant choices. The small ***Karadeniz Lokantası*** offers tandır kebap (pit-roasted lamb), and ***Özler Lokantası***, further up towards the clock tower, does good roast chicken. Across the street, ***Kılıçlar Kebap ve Pide Salonu*** has a popular family room upstairs.

For more upmarket dining, head straight for ***Çorum Büyük Oteli***. The ***restaurant*** on the top floor of the Kültür Sitesi in Gazi Caddesi is another good choice in the evenings.

Getting There & Away

Çorum, on the main Ankara-Samsun highway, has good bus connections. Details of some services follow:

Alaca – 60km, one hour, US$1; several minibuses
Amasya – 95km, 1½ hours, US$2.50; several
Ankara – 242km, 3½ hours, US$6; every 1½ hours
Boğazkale – 86km, 1½ hours, US$2; several minibuses
Kayseri – 274km, four hours, US$7.50; several
Samsun – 176km, three hours, US$5.50; frequent
Sungurlu – 70km, 45 minutes, US$1.50; very frequent

AMASYA

Amasya (ah-MAHSS-yah, population 60,000, altitude 392m), capital of the province of the same name, was once the capital of a great Pontic Kingdom. On the banks of the Yeşilırmak (Green River), surrounded by high cliffs, Amasya's dramatic setting adds interest to its numerous historic buildings: the rock-hewn tombs of the kings of Pontus, some fine old mosques, picturesque Ottoman half-timbered houses and a good little museum. Set away from the rest of Anatolia in its tight mountain valley, Amasya has a feeling of independence, self-sufficiency and civic pride. It's one of Turkey's most pleasant towns.

History

Despite seeming rather sleepy, Amasya has seen exciting times. It was a Hittite town, and was conquered by Alexander the Great. When his empire broke up, Amasya became the capital of a successor-kingdom ruled by a family of Persian satraps. By the time of King Mithridates II (281 BC), the Kingdom of Pontus was entering its golden age and dominated a large part of Anatolia.

During the latter part of Pontus' flowering, Amasya was the birthplace of Strabo (circa 63 BC to 25 AD), the world's first historian. Perhaps he felt constrained by Amasya's surrounding mountains, because he left home and travelled through Europe, west Asia and north Africa, and wrote 47 history and 17 geography books. Though most of Strabo's history books have been lost, we know something of their content because he was quoted by many other classical writers.

Amasya's golden age ended when the Romans decided it was time to take all of Anatolia (47 BC) and call it Asia Minor. After them came the Byzantines, who left

AMASYA

PLACES TO STAY
3 Hotel Saray
4 Büyük Amasya Oteli
9 İlk Pansiyon
17 Zümrüt Pansiyon
21 Emin Efendi Pansiyon
26 Melis Hotel
31 Yuvam Pension 2
32 Apaydın Oteli
33 Konfor Palas & Ocakbaşı Aile Pide ve Kebap Salonu
37 Yuvam Pension
38 Hotel Maden

PLACES TO EAT
12 Çiçek Lokantası
13 Amasya Şehir Derneği
34 Elmas Kebap ve Pide Salonu

OTHER
1 Büyük Ağa Medresesi
2 Beyazıt Paşa Camii
5 Mehmet Paşa Camii
6 Mustafa Bey Hamamı
7 Bimarhane Medresesi
8 Tourism Information Office
10 Gümüşlü Cami
11 Atatürk Monument
14 Vilayet
15 Police
16 Kral Kaya Mezarları (Pontic Tombs)
18 Hazeranlar Konağı
19 Hatuniye Camii
20 Yıldız Hamam (Men)
22 Children's Playground
23 Altınaş Hamamı (Women)
24 Gar (Train Station)
25 Gök Medrese Camii
27 Amasya Müzesi
28 Sultan Beyazıt II Camii
29 Belediye Sarayı (Town Hall)
30 Bus Ticket Offices
35 PTT
36 Vakıf Bedesten Kapalı Çarşı
39 Taş Han
40 Burmalı Minare Camii
41 Hospital
42 Fethiye Camii

little mark on the town, and the Seljuks (1075) and Mongols (early 14th century), who built numerous fine buildings which still stand. In Ottoman times, Amasya was an important base when the sultans led military campaigns into Persia. A tradition developed that the Ottoman crown prince should be taught statecraft in Amasya, and test his knowledge and skill as governor of the province. The town was also noted as a centre of Islamic theological study, with as many as 18 medreses and 2000 theological students in the 19th century.

After WWI, Mustafa Kemal (Atatürk) escaped from the confines of occupied İstanbul and came to Amasya via Samsun. Here he secretly met with several friends on 12 June 1919 and hammered out some basic principles for the Turkish struggle for independence. The monument in the main square commemorates the meeting; other scenes depict the unhappy state of Turks in Anatolia before the War of Independence. Each year, Amasyalıs commemorate the meeting with a week-long art and culture festival beginning on 12 June.

Orientation

The otogar is at the north-eastern edge of town and the train station at the western edge. It's 2km from either to the main square, marked by the statue of Atatürk and a bridge across the river. Most of the town (including the main square, the bazaar and the museum) is on the southern bank of the river. On the northern bank are various government and military offices, the tombs of the Pontic kings, and the kale. You may want to take a bus, minibus, or taxi to and from the otogar and the train station, but everything else is within walking distance, even the Gök Medrese, though it's 1200m from the main square.

Information

The Tourism Information Office (☎ 358-218 7428) is at Mustafa Kemal Bulvarı 27, in a kiosk on the river bank just north of the main square. The staff speak English, French and German. It's open Monday to Friday from 10 am to noon and 3 to 7 pm, and on Saturday and Sunday from 2 to 7 pm.

Amasya's postal code is 05000.

Historic Houses

Start your sightseeing with a walk around the town, admiring the old Ottoman houses along the river. On the northern bank in Hatuniye Mahallesi, the **Hazeranlar Konağı** was constructed in 1865. It was restored in 1979 and opened as an ethnology museum and gallery for travelling exhibits in 1984. It's usually open from 9 to 11.45 am and 1.15 to 4.45 pm for US$1.

Restoration of the old houses is highly valued by some Amasyalıs. However, other local residents would like to replace old buildings they own (which are expensive to renovate) with what they see as more efficient modern structures. The government has now pledged financial help for their restoration which could weigh in favour of conservation.

You can stay the night in a couple of historic houses which have been opened as pensions (see Places to Stay, later).

Also on the northern bank of the river are the police station and Vilayet (government building); beside the latter is the shady **Belediye Parkı** with a tea and soft drink service, and entertainment some evenings. Many of the old houses here are still occupied. Walk beneath the railway line directly behind the huge military building on the river (near the Büyük Amasya Oteli), and you will enter a neighbourhood of such houses.

Pontic Tombs

Looming above the northern bank of the river is a sheer rockface with the easily observed rock-cut Kral Kaya Mezarları, or Tombs of the Pontic Kings, carved into it. Cross the river, climb the well-marked path towards them and you'll come to the **Kızlar Sarayı**, or Palace of the Maidens, now a cafe. Though there were indeed harems full of maidens here, the palace which stood on this rock terrace was not theirs but that of the kings of Pontus and later of the Ottoman governors.

As you follow the path upward you may find yourself accompanied by a youthful unappointed guide repeating a few words of German and hoping for a tip. If you don't want a guide, say *İstemez* (eess-teh-MEHZ). In a few minutes you will reach the royal tombs of Pontus, cut deep into the rock as early as the 4th century BC, and used for cult worship of the deified rulers. There are 14 tombs in this area but there's nothing actually inside any of them. Opening hours are from 8.30 am to 7 pm in summer. Admission costs US$0.50.

One of the best of the Pontic tombs, the **Aynalı Mağara** (Mirror Cave) is apart from the others, signposted to the left on the road in from Samsun, a pleasant 1km walk away. Although you can't hope to get inside the lofty entrance, you can walk right around it to see how the tomb was cut clean away from the rockface. There's also a Greek inscription high above the commonplace graffiti below. If you're feeling lazy, a taxi will run you there and back from the centre for about US$6, waiting time (not much needed) included.

Citadel

Above the tombs and perched precariously on the cliffs is the kale, offering magnificent views. The remnants of the walls date from Pontic times, perhaps from those of King Mithridates. The fortress was repaired by the Ottomans, and again in the late 1980s in the interests of tourism. Somewhat below the citadel on a ledge is an old Russian cannon which is fired during the holy month of Ramazan to mark the ending of the fast.

To reach the kale, cross the northern bridge near the Büyük Ağa Medresesi and follow the Samsun road for 850m to a street on the left marked 'Kale'. It's 1.7km up the mountainside to a small car park, then another 15-minute steep climb to the summit, marked by a flagpole.

Amasya Müzesi

The small Amasya Museum on Atatürk Caddesi is open from 8.30 to 11.45 am and from 1.15 to 5 pm (closed on Monday) for US$1. The collection includes artefacts from Pontic, Roman, Byzantine, Seljuk and Ottoman times, and the usual collection of kilims, costumes and weaponry.

Perhaps the most interesting exhibits are the wooden doors of the ancient Gök Medrese Camii, the carpets, and the strange baked-clay coffins. Upstairs, look out for the bronze figure of Teshub, the Hittite storm god, with pointed cap and huge almond-shaped eyes. In the museum garden is a Seljuk tomb, the **Sultan Mesut Türbesi**, containing some gruesome mummies dating from the Seljuk period which were discovered beneath the Burmalı Cami – an exhibit not for the squeamish.

Sights West of the Main Square

Across Atatürk Caddesi from the museum is the graceful **Sultan Beyazıt II Camii** (1486), Amasya's principal mosque, with a medrese, *kütüphane* (library) and sweet-scented garden.

West of the museum about half a kilometre (1200m from the main square) is the **Gök Medrese Camii** (GEURK meh-dreh-seh), or Mosque of the Blue Seminary, built in 1266-7 on the orders of Seyfettin Torumtay, the Seljuk governor of Amasya. The eyvan serving as its main portal is a unique feature not found elsewhere in Anatolia. The adjoining **kümbet** was once covered in blue (gök) tiles, hence its name. The unfinished **Torumtay Türbesi** (1278), in front of the mosque, is the final resting-place of Seyfettin Bey, the man who founded the Gök Medrese Camii. The neighbouring Ottoman **Yörgüç Paşa Camii** dates from 1428.

East of the museum, across Atatürk Caddesi from the Vakıf Bedesten Kapalı Çarşı (Covered Market, 1483), is the **Taş Han** (1758), an Ottoman caravanserai still used by local traders and artisans. It was originally larger, but much of it has fallen into ruin. Behind it to the south is the **Burmalı Minare Camii**, or Spiral Minaret Mosque, a Seljuk construction (1237-47) with elegant spiral carving on the minaret, true to its name.

TURKEY'S WOODEN HOUSES

These days most Turkish towns are vanishing beneath a blanket of brick and concrete. It wasn't always like this, of course, and in the 19th century most towns and villages boasted fine wooden houses. Enthusiasts for such houses will find many in Afyon, Amasya or Tokat, but the best are in Safranbolu, declared a UNESCO World Heritage Site due to its domestic architecture.

Ottoman wooden houses were generally two or three-storied – the upper storeys jutting out over the lower ones on carved corbel brackets. Their timber frames were filled with adobe and then plastered with a mixture of mud and straw. Sometimes the houses were left unsealed but in towns they were usually given a finish of plaster or whitewash, with

The large Ottoman houses of Yörük Köyü, east of Safranbolu, reflect the historic wealth of this small town.

BOTH PHOTOGRAPHS BY PAT YALE

decorative flourishes in plaster or wood. The wealthier the owner, the fancier the decoration.

Lower storey windows often had ornamental grilles on them, while the upper ones were decorated with fretwork. The houses of the wealthy sometimes had a stained-glass skylight above the door. Many houses had double doors allowing carts through into a courtyard.

Inside, the larger houses had 10 to 12 rooms, divided into *selamlık* (men's quarters) and *haremlik* (women's quarters). Rooms were often decorated with built-in niches and cupboards, and had fine plaster fireplaces with *yaşmaks* (conical hoods). Sometimes the ceilings were very elaborate; that of the Paşa Odası of Tokat's Latifoğlu Konağı, for example, is thought to be emulating a chandelier in wood.

The houses rarely had much furniture beyond the low bench *(sedir)* around the walls. Families dined at a table board which was brought out and placed on a stand at mealtimes and covered with a cloth which also covered the diners' laps and doubled as a napkin. Bedding was spread out at night and stored in cupboards during the day. Washing facilities were usually concealed inside closets.

Many Turks now see these old houses as draughty firetraps, lacking in modern conveniences and expensive to maintain. Cheaper, sturdier, more convenient apartment blocks are preferred. But a conservation movement has taken hold, and government aid is often available to help people maintain these charming, historic houses.

OLIVIER CIRENDINI

İstanbul is home to many Ottoman wooden houses.

Sights North of the Main Square

Perched on a rise to the north-eastern side of the main square is the **Gümüşlü Cami** (Silvery Mosque) which was built in 1326. It was rebuilt in 1491 after an earthquake, in 1612 after a fire, and again in 1688, then added to in 1903, and restored yet again in 1988.

North of the main square along the river are Amasya's other historic buildings. The **Bimarhane Medresesi** (Insane Asylum Seminary) was built on orders of Amber bin Abdullah in the name of Ilduş Hatun, the wife of the Ilkhanid Sultan Oljaytu in 1309. The İlkhans were the successors to the great Mongol Empire of Ghengis Khan, which had conquered the Seljuks of Anatolia. Their architecture reflects styles and motifs borrowed from many conquered peoples. Today only the outer walls of the building are original, the rest having been restored so it could serve the town's **Fine Arts Gallery** (Güzel Sanatlar Galerisi). Changing exhibits are mounted, and the court is used as a tea garden.

On the northern side of the Bimarhane is the **Mustafa Bey Hamamı** (1436).

Next along the river is the pretty **Mehmet Paşa Camii**, an early Ottoman mosque built in 1486 by Lala Mehmet Paşa, the tutor of Şehzade Ahmet, the son of Sultan Beyazıt II. The mosque's külliye originally included the builder's tomb, a *imarethane* (soup kitchen), *tabhane* (hospital), *handan* (hamam and inn).

The **Beyazıt Paşa Camii**, a few hundred metres north and just past the bridge, was finished in 1419 and bears many similarities to the famous early Ottoman Yeşil Cami in Bursa. Note especially the porch with marble arches in two colours of stone, the entranceway with gold and blue and the carved doors.

Across the river from the Beyazıt Paşa Camii is the **Büyük Ağa Medresesi** (Seminary of the Chief White Eunuch), built to an octagonal plan in 1488 by Sultan Beyazıt II's chief white eunuch, Hüseyin Ağa. Nicely restored, it still serves as a seminary for boys who are training to be *hafız* (theologians who have memorised the entire Koran). The medrese is not open to the public, but if the door is open you may peep in to see local boys at their Koranic studies.

On the southern bank of the river, Ziya Paşa Bulvarı is shady and cool with huge old plane trees. There's an early Ottoman **covered bazaar** (1483) or bedesten in the narrow streets of the market south of here.

Nearby Villages

Occasional buses run to villages in the surrounding hills, where villagers still make lovely striped kilims from sheep and goat's hair. At **Yassıçal** there's a pleasant ***restaurant*** *(☎ 358-241 6003)* set around an artificial pool full of fish near the new hotel; you dine in wooden kiosks amid flowers. You can get here easily at any time with your own transport but the last bus back to Amasya goes at 5 pm.

Further along the road, but without reliable bus links, are **Saraycık Köyü** and **Kaleköy**. Of the two, Kaleköy has the most interesting buildings (the eponymous castle, an old wooden mosque, and a crumbling hamam and stone laundry), but the villagers are moving away, so Saraycık is livelier.

You may be able to arrange a taxi excursion to some of these villages. Mr Ali Kamil Yalçın, proprietor of the İlk Pansiyon (see Places to Stay – Budget), may be able to advise on the possibilities.

Yedi Kuğular Gölü

About 15km west of town is the recently made artificial Yedi Kuğular Gölü (Seven Swans Lake), a favourite stopping-place for birds on their spring and autumn migrations. Trees have been planted and when they mature, this *kuş cenneti* (bird paradise) may be as welcoming to humans as to birds.

Places to Stay – Budget

Amasya has one particularly inviting place to stay, the six room ***İlk Pansiyon*** *(☎ 358-218 1689, fax 218 6277, Gümüşlü Mahallesi, Hitit Sokak 1),* by the river east of the Atatürk statue (follow the signs). Ali Kamil Yalçın is an architect who discovered the once grand but then dilapidated mansion of a one-time Armenian priest, rented it and restored it beautifully to its former grace and charm. The five light, airy, spacious salons are now fitted with beds and bathrooms, and offered to travellers for US$12 to US$25 a single, US$16 to US$35 a double, depending upon the room. Some rooms have three beds. There's one smaller, cheaper room with bath off a courtyard which provides a convivial setting (complete with cat and dog) for breakfast and dinner.

If the İlk Pansiyon is full (as it often is), try ***Yuvam Pension*** *(☎ 358-218 1324, fax 218 3409, Atatürk Caddesi 24/5)* on the main thoroughfare, 2½ blocks south-west of the Atatürk statue. Ask about rooms at the *eczane* (pharmacy) at street level, which is where the owners, the Yener family, are during the day. Clean rooms with private shower in a family atmosphere up several flights of stairs cost US$15/20 a single/double.

If the Yuvam is full, the friendly owners may take you to ***Yuvam Pension 2***, their Amasya-style house from the 1930s, about 300m further to the south-west (follow the signs uphill marked 'Hastane' and then turn right at the top). The house, with its quiet garden, is preferable to the apartment rooms on Atatürk Caddesi, though baths are shared.

The cheap, quiet ***Zümrüt Pansiyon*** *(☎ 358-218 2675, Hatuniye Mahallesi, Hazeranlar Sokak 28)*, just across the road from the Yıldız Hamam (men only), has rooms with phone, TV and add-on showers (but no toilet or sink) for US$7 per person. The real advantage is the roof terrace with uninterrupted views of the Pontic Tombs, especially impressive when floodlit at night.

Nearby, ***Emin Efendi Pansiyon*** *(☎ 358-212 0852, Hazeranlar Sokak 73)* is furnished with nice old carpets and crafts. The rooms, all without bath and thus overpriced at US$26 a double, have river views, and are charming and quiet.

Amasya's other cheap lodgings are far less atmospheric. The mundane 31 room ***Apaydın Oteli*** *(☎ 358-218 1184, Atatürk Caddesi 58)* is perhaps the most presentable, charging US$8/12 for a room with sink (cold water only). The common bathrooms have showers with electric-heater shower-heads but there's a Turkish-style splash bath as well.

The inaptly named ***Konfor Palas*** (kohn-FOHR, Comfort Palace) *(☎ 358-218 1260, Ziya Paşa Bulvarı, Irmak Caddesi 2/B)*, by the river, has 36 rooms with sinks, for slightly less.

The 30 room ***Hotel Saray*** *(☎ 358-212 6565, fax 212 6761, Mehmet Varinli Caddesi 10)*, 800m east of the main square and 1km west of the otogar, is used by local business travellers who pay US$13/23/34 a single/double/triple for rooms with private shower, TV and breakfast.

Places to Stay – Mid-Range

About 60m east of the Gök Medrese Camii, the ***Melis Hotel*** *(☎ 358-212 3650, fax 218 2082, Torumtay Sokak 135)*, is a veritable museum of Ottoman artefacts, utensils and knick-knacks. Bright, clean rooms with bath cost US$25/35 a single/double with breakfast.

The two-star ***Büyük Amasya Oteli*** *(☎ 358-218 4054, fax 218 4056, Herkiz Mahallesi, Elmasiye Caddesi 20)*, north of the centre near the Büyük Ağa Medresesi, is a small, fairly quiet 50 room hotel on the river bank. It has a restaurant and bar with fine views of the river, and rooms with shower overpriced at US$39/57, breakfast included. It's often filled by tour groups.

The two-star ***Hotel Maden*** *(☎ 358-218 6050, fax 218 6017, Atatürk Caddesi 5)*, above the Ford-Tofaş car showroom across from the Yuvam Pension, is surprisingly reasonable at US$15/26 a single/double with breakfast.

Places to Eat

Amasya is famed for its apples; don't miss them if you visit during the autumn harvest.

Look for small restaurants in the narrow market streets off the main square (the one with the statue of Atatürk), such as ***Çiçek Lokantası***, which is cheap and serviceable, with decent roast chicken and ready meals for little more than US$3.

Elmas Kebap ve Pide Salonu, on the same street more or less behind the Hotel

Apaydın, is similar, and stays open late in the evening.

There are many small kebapçıs north of the Yuvam Pension in the bazaar streets around the covered market. ***Beslen Kebap ve Pide Salonu***, Kocacık Çarşısı 18, has good food and friendly staff.

Ocakbaşı Aile Pide ve Kebap Salonu, in front of the Konfor Palas, is friendly enough and has outdoor tables where you can enjoy your freshly baked pide (US$2) while gazing across the river.

For nicer dining at a higher price (from US$5 to US$8 for a full meal with drinks), go to the restaurant in ***Büyük Amasya Oteli*** where the speciality is kebaps from south-eastern Turkey.

Foreign tourists are also welcome at ***Amasya Şehir Derneği***, in the dismal Öğretmen Evi building overlooking the river at the northern end of the bridge, opposite the main square. This is a quasi-private club with stark decor but good service and moderately priced food and drink. Amasya's prominent citizens come here to eat, drink, talk business and while away the evening. You can too.

Getting There & Away

Amasya is not far off the busy route between Ankara and Samsun, so buses are frequent. It is also on the railway line between Samsun and Sivas, but the daily trains are quite slow. Some bus companies (Amasyatur, Azimkar) maintain ticket offices on Atatürk Caddesi across from the Belediye building, just east of the Sultan Beyazıt II Camii. There are direct buses from Amasya to many cities, including these:

Adıyaman (for Nemrut Dağı) – 650km, 10 hours, US$12; one bus
Ankara – 335km, five hours, US$5; very frequent buses
Çorum – 95km, 1½ hours, US$3; at least eight buses
İstanbul – 685km, 10 hours, US$12; a dozen buses
Kayseri – 405km, eight hours, US$10; three buses
Malatya – 460km, eight hours, US$15; five buses
Safranbolu – 450km, nine hours, US$16; take a minibus to Gerede, then a minibus to Karabük and another minibus to Safranbolu (a long day!)
Samsun – 130km, two hours, US$3; 10 buses
Sivas – 225km, 3½ hours, US$6; five buses
Tokat – 115km, two hours, US$3; nine buses

TOKAT

Tokat (TOH-kaht, population 90,000, altitude 623m) is on the southern edge of the Black Sea region and shares in its fertility.

The town doesn't get many tourists, and those who do come usually have a quick look at the famous Gök Medrese and then leave, which is a shame since they miss the wonderful Latifoğlu Konağı, as excellent an example of a restored Ottoman house as you'll find in Turkey.

Tokat is a fine place to spend a day or two. Half Ottoman and half modern, it's liberally sprinkled with crumbling ruins, many of them now below ground level. Between the 13th and 20th centuries Tokat's ground is thought to have risen by up to 5m as silt from the hills was carried down into the valley by rain and floods, and debris from earthquakes added to the accumulation.

History

Tokat's history is very long and involved, starting in 3000 BC and proceeding through the sovereignty of 14 states, including the Hittites and Phrygians, the Medes and the Persians, the empire of Alexander the Great, the Kingdom of Pontus, the Romans, the Byzantines, the Turkish principality of Danışmend, the Seljuks and the Mongol İlkhanids.

By the time of the Seljuk Sultanate of Rum, Tokat was the sixth largest city in Anatolia and on important trade routes. The roads approaching the city are littered with great Seljuk bridges and caravanserais testifying to its earlier importance.

After the Mongols rushed in and upset everyone in the mid-13th century, their Ilkhanid successors took over, followed by a succession of petty warlords who did little for Tokat.

Under the Ottomans, who took the town in 1402, it resumed its role as an important trading entrepôt, agricultural town (the grapes are especially good) and copper-mining

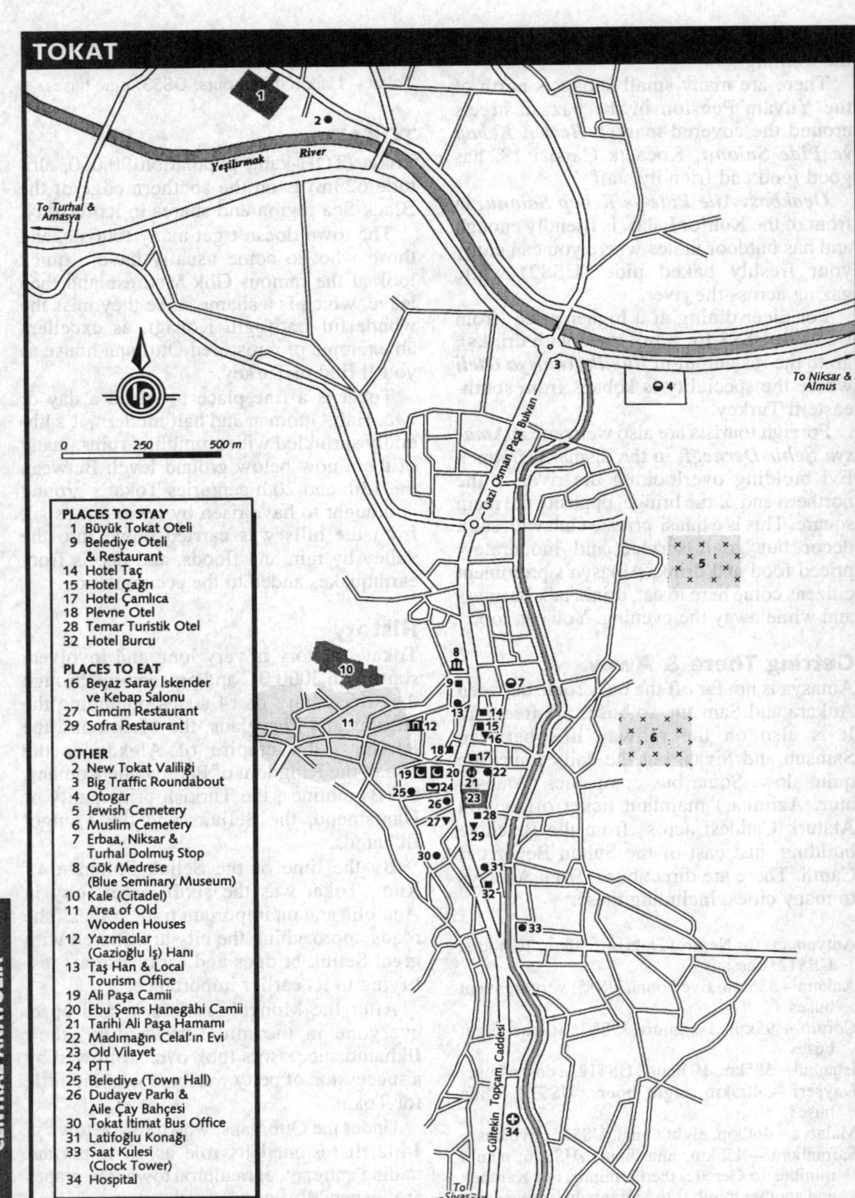
TOKAT
Yeşilırmak River
To Turhal & Amasya
To Niksar & Almus
To Sivas
Gazi Osman Paşa Bulvarı
Gültekin Topçam Caddesi
0 250 500 m
PLACES TO STAY
1 Büyük Tokat Oteli
9 Belediye Oteli & Restaurant
14 Hotel Taç
15 Hotel Çağrı
17 Hotel Çamlıca
18 Plevne Otel
28 Temar Turistik Otel
32 Hotel Burcu
PLACES TO EAT
16 Beyaz Saray İskender ve Kebap Salonu
27 Cimcim Restaurant
29 Sofra Restaurant
OTHER
2 New Tokat Valiliği
3 Big Traffic Roundabout
4 Otogar
5 Jewish Cemetery
6 Muslim Cemetery
7 Erbaa, Niksar & Turhal Dolmuş Stop
8 Gök Medrese (Blue Seminary Museum)
10 Kale (Citadel)
11 Area of Old Wooden Houses
12 Yazmacılar (Gazioğlu İş) Hanı
13 Taş Han & Local Tourism Office
19 Ali Paşa Camii
20 Ebu Şems Hanegâhi Camii
21 Tarihi Ali Paşa Hamamı
22 Madımağın Celal'ın Evi
23 Old Vilayet
24 PTT
25 Belediye (Town Hall)
26 Dudayev Parkı & Aile Çay Bahçesi
30 Tokat İtimat Bus Office
31 Latifoğlu Konağı
33 Saat Kulesi (Clock Tower)
34 Hospital

centre (the copper artisans have been famous for centuries). Significant non-Muslim populations (Greek, Armenian, Jewish) were in charge of the town's commerce until the cataclysm of WWI. There is still a small but active Jewish congregation here.

Orientation & Information

The town centre is the big open square named Cumhuriyet Alanı, where you will find the old Vilayet, the Belediye and the PTT. A subterranean shopping centre has added lots of retail space without ruining the spaciousness of the square. Across the main street from the shopping centre is the Tarihi Ali Paşa Hamamı, an old Turkish bath studded with bulbous glass to let in sunlight.

Looming above the town is a rocky promontory crowned by the obligatory ancient fortress. Beneath it cluster the bazaar and the town's old Ottoman-style houses.

The main street, Gazi Osman Paşa Bulvarı, runs downhill from the main square past the Gök Medrese to a traffic roundabout. The otogar is nearby, 2km from the main square. Many bus companies have offices on Gazi Osman Paşa Bulvarı south of the main square near the Sofra and Cimcim restaurants, mixed in with the currency exchange offices.

There's a helpful local tourist office (☎ 356-211 8252) in the historic Taş Han but its opening hours are erratic.

Tokat's postal code is 60000.

Gök Medrese

The Blue Seminary, next to the Taş Han and the Belediye Oteli several hundred metres down the hill from Cumhuriyet Alanı, is the first thing to see. It was constructed in 1277 by Pervane Muhineddin Süleyman, a local potentate, after the fall of the Seljuks and the coming of the Mongols. Used as a hospital until 1811, it's now the town museum and is open from 8.30 am to 12.30 pm and 1.30 to 5 pm (closed on Monday); admission is US$1. There's some labelling in English.

Gök (sky) is also a word for blue, and it is the building's blue tiles which occasioned the name. Very few of these are left on the façade, which is now well below street level, but there are enough tiles on the interior walls to give an idea of what it must have looked like in its glory days. Museum exhibits include Stone Age and Bronze Age artefacts from excavations at Maşat Höyük, relics from Tokat's churches (most curious is a wax effigy of the Christian Christina, martyred during the reign of Diocletian), tools and weapons, Korans and Islamic calligraphy and an excellent costume display. An ethnographic section also displays local kilims and explains Tokat's famous art of wood-block printing on *yazmalar*, or gauze scarves.

The seminary contains the **Kırkkızlar Türbesi** (Tomb of 40 Maidens), actually an assembly of 20 tombs, probably of the seminary's founders, though popular belief would have it that they are the tombs of 40 girls.

Taş Han & Vicinity

A few steps from the Gök Medrese, on the other side of the Belediye Hotel, is the Taş Han (1631), an Ottoman caravanserai and workshop building. Artisans' and craft shops have been set up in the old work spaces, and there's the inevitable courtyard tea garden.

Behind the Taş Han are bazaar streets lined with old half-timbered Ottoman houses. The bazaar's shops have lots of copperware, yazmalar and local kilims and carpets, some of which have Afghani designs because of the many Afghani refugees who settled here during the Soviet invasion of their country during the 1980s.

For a look at the craft of making yazmalar, walk west up the street opposite the Hotel Taç to find the **Yazmacılar Hanı** (officially the Gazioğulu İş Hanı), opposite the Kabe-i Mescit Camii. Inside the ancient han are equally ancient dying vats and rank upon rank of freshly printed yazmas hanging up to dry. The process hasn't changed in centuries. Locals say the han has caught fire 12 times over the centuries but its thick walls are made with a wood that has a very high flamepoint.

Across Gazi Osman Paşa Bulvarı from the Taş Han, in the fruit and vegetable market, stands the **Hatuniye Camii** and its medrese, dating from 1485 during the reign of Sultan Beyazıt II.

Several hundred metres north down the hill from the Gök Medrese, on the same side of the street, look out for the portal of the **Sümbül Baba Zaviyesi** (dervish lodge), probably built in 1292 and now incorporated into a house. Another block further north is the octagonal **Sefer Paşa Türbesi**, a Seljuk-style tomb dating from 1251. Beside it a road leads up to the kale, of which little remains but the fine view.

Tarihi Ali Paşa Hamamı

Go into any hamam in Turkey and ask the masseur where he came from and chances are he'll answer Tokat. So while in Tokat you should certainly not miss the chance to bathe in the wonderful Tarihi Ali Paşa Hamamı. These baths, with their breast-like glass bulbs to let in light, were built in 1572 for Ali Paşa, and have separate bathing areas for men and women.

A simple bath costs US$2. Near the bath is the Ali Paşa Camii, built from 1566 to 1572.

Historic Houses

On the main street south of Cumhuriyet Alanı stands the **Latifoğlu Konağı**, one of the most splendid 19th-century houses on view in Turkey. The house's large, gracious rooms are surrounded with low sedir sofas. In the bedrooms, bedding was taken up and stored in cabinets during the day, Asian-style. The most spectacular rooms are upstairs: the Paşa Odası (Pasha's Room) for the men of the house, and the Havuzbaşı room for the women. The light, airy upstairs hall would have been used in summer only as it was not heated.

It's open from 8 am to noon and 1.30 to 5 pm (closed on Monday) for US$1. Enter through the garden on the northern side.

Madımağın Celal'ın Evi, Tokat's other well-preserved old house, is one block down on the street to the east of the Tarihi Ali Paşa Hamamı. It contains wonderfully elaborate gold and green plasterwork and painted scenes of Topkapı Sarayı and Sultan Ahmet Camii but is not open to visitors at the moment.

Sulu Sokak

The houses to the east of Gazi Osman Paşa were mainly owned by Tokat's wealthier citizens, but to the west you can find many streets of simpler but elegant houses. Take the street running west beside the Ali Paşa Camii in Cumhuriyet Alanı (it's signposted to the Bedesten) and you'll arrive in Sulu Sokak, which used to be Tokat's main thoroughfare before the Samsun-Sivas road was improved in the 1960s. The further along you go, the more interesting it gets, with the crumbling remains of a bedesten and several medreses, türbes and mosques. At the western end of the road, smaller cobblestoned streets fan out in all directions. Here you can lose yourself amid wonderful old wooden houses, their upper storeys jutting out at all angles to suit the geography of the street.

Excursions

About 70km west of Tokat, **Zile** is near where Caesar battled Pharnaces and afterwards sent his famous one-liner – *Veni, Vidi, Vici* – back to Rome. The actual battle site was along the Amasya-Zile road. The town of Zile has a very old citadel, and mosques and hamams dating from the Danışmend, Seljuk and Ottoman periods.

Formerly Neocaesarea, **Niksar**, 54km north-east of Tokat, was a city of the Pontic kings, then of the Romans. For 40 years after its conquest in 1077 by the Seljuk general Melik Ahmet Danışmend Gazi, it was the capital of the Danışmend Turkish Emirate, and today preserves several rare examples of Danışmendid architecture, as well as many Ottoman works.

About 48km to the west of Tokat and an easy break of journey between Amasya and Tokat, **Turhal** has an impressive citadel with a network of subterranean tunnels. It, too, was a Danışmendid town, and has several mosques, baths and other buildings to show for it, as well as a neighbourhood of fine old Ottoman houses.

The Roman city of Sebastopolis (today **Sulusaray**) lay 67km south-west of Tokat, on the banks of the Çekerek river. Excavations here have produced extensive remains

He Came, He Saw, He Conquered

It may come as quite a surprise to learn that Julius Caesar was at Zile, near Tokat, when he delivered his immortal message back to the Roman Senate, *Veni, Vidi, Vici* (I came, I saw, I conquered). During the first century BC, Tokat lay within the kingdom of Pontus, which had held out against the Romans, indeed declared war against them, even after the rest of Anatolia had submitted. In 47 BC, while Julius Caesar was distracted in Egypt, King Pharnaces II launched an attack on the Roman provinces of Galatia, Armenia and Cappadocia with the intention of recreating the earlier Pontic kingdom of his ancestors. Caesar was forced to retaliate and marched on Pharnaces with his army. At a site between the modern villages of Yünlü and Bacul on the Zile to Amasya road, the two armies clashed. During a fierce five-hour battle, Pharnaces's army drove chariots with scythes fitted to their wheels against the Romans, but despite heavy losses Caesar's troops eventually triumphed. Though a brilliant and fearless military commander, Caesar's talent at composing memorable one-liners was obviously equally formidable.

and there is now a museum with some fine mosaics. Getting to it without your own transport is difficult because it's 49km off the Tokat to Sivas road.

Places to Stay – Budget

Among the cheapest places to stay in Tokat is the old, drab ***Belediye Oteli*** (or 'Boteli') (*☎ 356-212 8983),* Gazi Osman Paşa Bulvarı, which charges US$6/8 a single/double for a noisy, waterless single/double at the front of the hotel, or US$8/10 for a quieter room with shower at the back.

The situation improves as you move towards the centre. ***Hotel Taç*** *(☎ 356-214 1331)*, in the İnci Vakıf İş Hanı building on Gazi Osman Paşa Bulvarı, opposite the Taş Han, charges US$9/15 for waterless rooms with peeling wallpaper, or US$12/20 with private shower. Those on the kale side have fine views.

Hotel Çağrı *(☎ 356-212 1028, Gazi Osman Paşa Bulvarı 92)* is newish; all rooms have private showers and go for US$14 – a good value option.

At ***Plevne Otel*** *(☎ 356-214 2207, Gazi Osman Paşa Bulvarı 83)*, named for the great general's most famous battle, the best rooms are the big, quiet ones at the back, with spacious bathrooms. Posted prices are US$8/15 with sink, US$10/20 with shower, though lower rates are usually offered. Across the street, the 26 room ***Hotel Çamlıca*** *(☎ 356-214 1269, Gazi Osman Paşa Bulvarı 86)*, badly needs renovating but prices are only US$7/12 with cold-water sink or US$12/16 with hot water and private shower. Get a back room if you need peace and quiet.

Next to the Ziraat Bankası, facing the old Vilayet building, is the 20 room ***Temar Turistik Otel*** *(☎ 356-212 7755, Cumhuriyet Meydanı 10)*. The rooms with private showers are old but clean, serviceable and relatively quiet. The cosy lobby is decorated with bits of Roman, Byzantine and Seljuk stonework and local woven and embroidered crafts. Rooms cost US$12/16 with shower.

Camping Tokat has no organised camping grounds, but you can camp at several recreation areas nearby, including Gümenek (the ancient town of Comana, 9km east); Almus, on the shores of the lake, 35km east; Niksar Ayvaz hot springs; and Çamiçi forest, 53km north-east.

Places to Stay – Mid-Range

A block south of the Latifoğlu Konağı on the same side of Gazi Osman Paşa Bulvarı is the two-star ***Hotel Burcu*** *(☎ 356-212 8494, fax 212 7891)*, at No 48, just north of the clock tower. The posted rate for a nice, comfortable double room with bath and breakfast is US$35, but that drops quick and far if they're not busy.

The most comfortable hotel in town is the four-star ***Büyük Tokat Oteli*** (*☎ 356-228 1661, fax 228 1660*), Demirköprü Mevkii, on the north-western outskirts. This is where the local potentates gather to schmooze and party, so the public rooms are well kept. The 60 guest rooms, all with TVs and bathtubs, suffer a bit, but are still comfortable, and not badly priced at US$35/52/76 for a single/double/suite, breakfast included. Enjoy the big swimming pool, Turkish bath, barber's shop and pastry shop at low rates.

Places to Eat

For alcoholic beverages with your meal, you may have to trek out to the Büyük Tokat Oteli, 3km from the centre (see Places to Stay earlier).

Beyaz Saray İskender ve Kebap Salonu, across the street from the Taş Han and the Belediye Hotel, is a simple split-level place with good Bursa-style döner kebap and a selection of grilled meats and salads. Meals for US$3 are easy to get, though you can spend a bit more.

Behind the Beyaz Saray, in the sebze halı (fruit and vegetable market) near the Hatuniye Camii, are little köfte and kebap shops with even lower prices. Try ***Cihan Lokantası*** on the corner: you can find it easily if you walk straight out of the Taş Han, across Gazi Osman Paşa Bulvarı, down the alley and into the market. It's a bit fly-blown but very friendly.

Between the Taş Han and the Gök Medrese, ***Belediye Lokantası***, on the ground floor of the Belediye Oteli, is fancier than the hotel and has a vine-draped central courtyard. Expect to spend around US$3 or US$4.

Just south of Cumhuriyet Alanı on the main street, on the way to the Latifoğlu Museum House, is the light, airy ***Sofra Restaurant*** with good meals for US$4 to US$7. ***Cimcim Restaurant*** on the western side of the main street has gloomier decor but serves good fresh pide. This is also the best place for Tokat kebap: skewers of lamb, sliced potato and aubergine (eggplant) hung vertically and baked in a wood-fired oven. Tomatoes and pimentos (peppers), which take less time to cook, are baked on separate skewers. As the lamb cooks, it releases juices which baste the potato and aubergine.

Getting There & Away

Bus Tokat's small otogar is not as busy as some, but buses still manage to get you where you want to go pretty easily. The better bus companies provide buses to ferry you into town. Otherwise, if you don't want to wait for the infrequent ordinary bus service, a taxi will cost about US$2 to the main square. To walk, go 400m west to the traffic roundabout, turn left (south) and it's just over 1km to the cluster of hotels, 1.5km to the main square. Several bus companies have ticket offices on the southern side of the main square, saving you a trip to the otogar to buy onward tickets. Daily services from Tokat include:

Amasya – 115km, two hours, US$3; about nine buses
Ankara – 440km, 6½ hours, US$8; frequent
Erzurum – 493km, 8½ hours, US$12; a few direct, or change at Sivas
İstanbul – 800km, 12 hours, US$15; several
Samsun – 245km, four hours, US$6; frequent
Sivas – 105km, 1½ hours, US$3; frequent

To/From Sivas From Tokat you can go east up to Kızıliniş Geçidi (Kızıliniş Pass, 1150m) then south into the Çamlıbel Dağları mountain range, up over Çamlıbel Geçidi (Çamlıbel Pass, 2038m), down again to Yıldızeli, then into Sivas. Along the way, you leave the lush Black Sea littoral and enter the Anatolian Plateau with its dry red soil. For information on Sivas, see the Eastern Anatolia chapter.

Black Sea Coast

Turkey's Black Sea coast is a unique part of the country, lush and green throughout the year with plenty of rain, even in summer. Dairy farming, fishing and tea production are big industries, and there are bumper crops of *tütün* (tobacco), *kiraz* (cherries) and *findik* (hazelnuts); during the summer roadsides are lined with hazelnuts laid out to dry in the sun.

You'll catch the occasional glimpse of crumbling old Ottoman houses of wood and plaster, but for the most part the towns of the Black Sea coast, especially those to the east, are conspicuous for their ugly brick and concrete construction.

The Black Sea coast is more popular with Turkish holidaymakers and those from the former Soviet republics than with westerners. Its waters are certainly chillier than those of the Aegean or the Mediterranean but can be refreshing nonetheless.

HIGHLIGHTS

- Eating hazelnuts grown here
- Dining in one of Amasra's fish restaurants
- Climbing up to Sumela Manastırı
- Sipping tea where it's grown in Rize
- Hiking in the Kaçkar Dağları from Ayder
- Making an excursion into Georgia

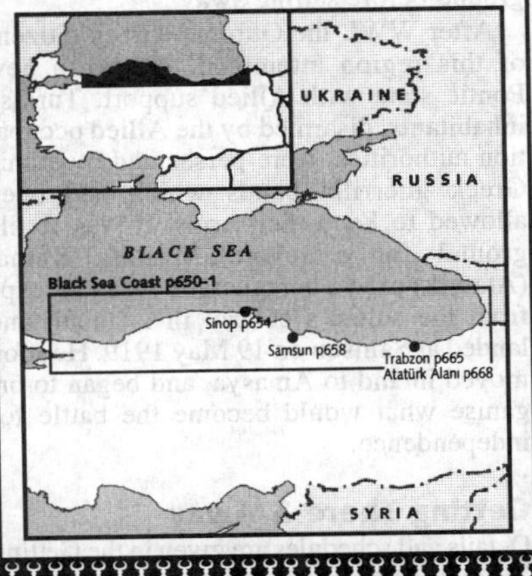

History

The coast was colonised in the 8th century BC by Milesians and Arcadians, who founded towns at Sinop, Samsun and Trabzon. Later it became the Kingdom of Pontus. Most of Pontus' kings were named Mithridates, but it was King Mithridates VI Eupator who gave the Romans a run for their money in 88-84 BC. He conquered Cappadocia and other Anatolian kingdoms, finally reaching Nicomedia (Kocaeli/İzmit), which was allied with Rome. When the latter came to its defence, Mithridates pushed onward to the Aegean. The Roman response was hampered by civil war at home, but Rome's legions finally drove into Cappadocia and Pontus (83-81 BC), and Mithridates was forced to agree to a peace based on pre-war borders.

From 74-64 BC Mithridates was at it again, encouraging his son-in-law Tigranes I of Armenia to seize Cappadocia from the Romans. He tried, but the Romans conquered Pontus in response, and forced Mithridates to flee and later to commit suicide. The Romans left a small client-Kingdom of Pontus at the far eastern end of the coast, based in Trebizond (Trabzon).

The coast was ruled by Byzantium, and Alexius Comnenus, son of Emperor Manuel I, proclaimed himself emperor of Pontus when the crusaders sacked Constantinople and drove him out in 1204. His descendants ruled this small empire until 1461, when it was captured by Mehmet the Conqueror.

While Alexius was in Trabzon, Samsun was under Seljuk rule and the Genoese had trading privileges. But when the Ottomans

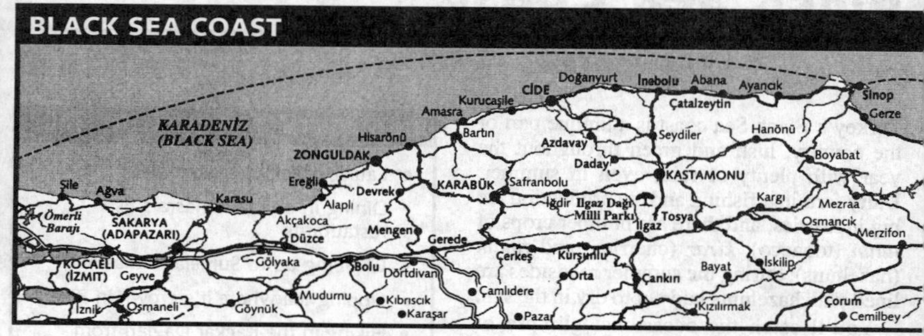

came, the Genoese burned Samsun to the ground before sailing away.

After WWI, the Ottoman Greek citizens of this region attempted to form a new Pontic state with Allied support. Turkish inhabitants, disarmed by the Allied occupation authorities, were persecuted by ethnic Greek guerrilla bands which had been allowed to keep their arms. It was fertile ground for a revolt. Mustafa Kemal (Atatürk) used a bureaucratic ruse to escape from the sultan's control in İstanbul, and landed at Samsun on 19 May 1919. He soon moved inland to Amasya, and began to organise what would become the battle for independence.

Getting There & Away

Details and schedules are given in the Getting There & Away sections for individual towns but this summary should help with planning your travels along the Black Sea coast.

Air Turkish Airlines (THY) has at least two daily nonstop flights from Ankara to Trabzon, three from İstanbul, and several weekly nonstops from Germany. İstanbul Airlines also flies nonstop between İstanbul and Trabzon daily.

Bus Buses to and along the coast are fast, frequent and cheap. Ulusoy, the most prominent company, has normal and luxury services between Trabzon and many other cities. It's quite easy to take the bus to Samsun from Bartın (130km), Ankara (420km), Kayseri (450km) or Sivas (340km).

Train The only passenger rail service to the Black Sea coast is the *Karaelmas* express which departs from Ankara daily at 7.55 am, arriving in Zonguldak at 7.10 pm. Departure from Zonguldak is at 9.20 am, with arrival in Ankara at 8.08 pm. The one-way fare is US$5.

Boat Turkish Maritime Lines runs a weekly car ferry service from İstanbul to Trabzon and Rize, and return. See the Getting Around chapter for details.

Getting Around

With the exception of Amasra, the Black Sea coast west of Sinop is difficult to get to and has little to offer at present. Its chief city, Zonguldak, is a gritty industrial centre and port town.

East of Amasra the road is slow and twisty, but the countryside and sea views range from beautiful to spectacular. It's an all-day ride from Amasra to Sinop.

The coastal road between Sinop and Bafra also passes beautiful, unspoilt scenery, with fields of sunflowers and racks of drying tobacco to catch the eye in summer.

East of Sinop, and especially east of Samsun as far as Trabzon, things pick up considerably. Although some upgrading is taking place near Samsun, the coast road is mainly single carriageway and has trouble

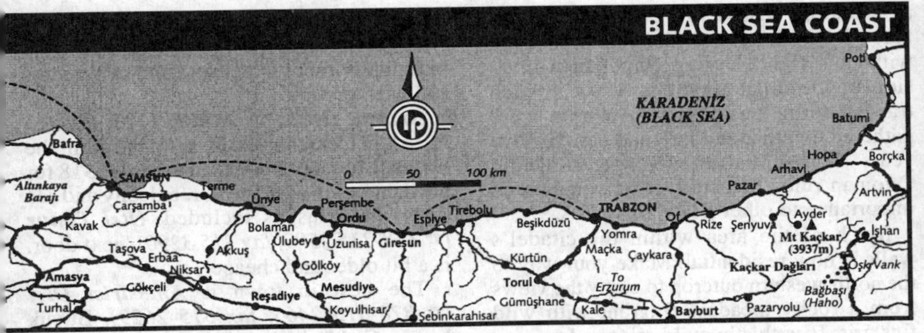

coping with the volume of traffic, especially in summer. Expect some slowdowns.

The 360km ride from Samsun to Trabzon can be done in a day if you wish but the most attractive stretch of coast is between Ordu and Ünye where development has been kept to a minimum and there are several attractive small ports; coming from the west, it would be worth pausing at Bolaman, Yalıköy, Mersin or Perşembe. You'll find camp sites, tea gardens and fish restaurants at regular intervals along the way.

Beyond Trabzon, the scenery deteriorates into a sequence of ugly modern towns.

After taking in Trabzon's sights you can head up onto the plateau to Erzurum, or eastward along the coast through the tea plantations to Rize, Hopa and the Georgian border.

From Hopa you can climb into the mountains to Artvin in Anatolia's north-eastern corner, a region of exceptionally beautiful scenery described in detail in the Eastern Anatolia chapter.

AMASRA

Amasra (population 7000) is a pleasant coastal town in the shadow of a fortified promontory which juts out assertively towards the coastal sea lanes. This small fishing port is little visited by tourists, which adds to its charm. It's on the western Black Sea coast (ancient Paphlagonia), 90km north of Safranbolu (see the earlier Central Anatolia chapter) and 100km east of Zonguldak, and should not be confused with the similarly named inland city of Amasya 130km south of Samsun.

If you're planning to visit out of season, be warned that many of the restaurants and hotels close at the end of October.

Orientation & Information

As you come into Amasra, you pass the museum on the left in an old stone building. Head straight on and you'll reach the eastern beach, which is mostly residential. Turn left at the park and follow Küçük Liman Caddesi around to Atatürk Meydanı (the main square), where most of the buses stop. Continue past the Çınar Pansiyon & Restaurant to find half a dozen small pensions and restaurants, plus the entrance to the citadel. On Tuesdays and Fridays a market is held next to the *Belediye* (municipality/town hall) across the street from the Çınar. There's a small office here for the local Kültür ve Turizm Derneği (Culture & Tourism Association).

Amasra's postal code is 67570.

Kale (Citadel)

Follow Küçük Liman Caddesi through several massive stone portals to reach the kale, the promontory fortified by the Byzantines when this small commercial port was known as Sesamos Amastris. The greater fortress seems to have replaced a smaller one erected against Russian adventurers around 861. Rented by the Genoese as a trading station in 1270, Amasra was taken by Mehmet the Conqueror in 1460 without a fight. During Napoleon's invasion of Ottoman Egypt in 1798, French traders doing business in Anatolia were gathered together and interned here for five years as potential enemy agents. Under Ottoman rule, Amasra lost its commercial importance to other Black Sea ports.

Much of the area within the citadel's walls is now residential. Make your way to the north-western outcrop to enjoy the views from a rocky meadow fragrant with wild figs, iris, bay, thistle, wild mint and sage.

Amasra Müzesi

The museum, north of the park, contains a fairly standard collection of Roman, Byzantine and Hellenistic odds and ends, along with some fine costumes and gold-embroidered bed linen. It's open daily except Monday from 9 am to 5.30 pm and admission costs US$0.75.

Handicrafts

Around town you'll see shops stuffed with turned-wood trinkets known as *ağaç biblo* (wooden bibelots). Amasra's woodworkers traditionally carved utilitarian objects like spoons, forks and spatulas, and these no-nonsense items are still easy to spot. But as cheap stainless steel and aluminium utensils have invaded their markets, carvers have switched to producing things like statuettes, lampshades and key rings.

Places to Stay

Two cheap hotels are on Küçük Liman Caddesi between the Belediye and the citadel gate. ***Otel Pansiyon Belvü Palas*** *(☎ 378-315 1237, Küçük Liman Caddesi 20)* has two floors of clean, bare, musty, waterless rooms for US$6 per person. Sunset views are best from room Nos 6, 7 and 8. ***Çınar Pansiyon*** *(☎ 378-315 1018, Küçük Liman Caddesi 1)* charges the same for fairly basic rooms.

In Çamlık Sokak, between the museum and the park, two small hotels offer harbour views. ***Paşakaptan Oteli*** *(☎ 378-315 1011)* has passable rooms for US$13 a double with shower. Next door at No 5, ***Nur Turistik Pansiyon*** *(☎ 378-315 1015)* is marginally more expensive and sometimes full with groups.

Amasra Oteli *(☎ 378-315 1722, fax 315 3025)*, in Çekiciler Caddesi inland from the Büyük Liman (harbour), charges US$18 for newish rooms with shower, balcony and sea view; breakfast is included. ***Otel Timur*** *(☎ 378-315 2589, fax 315 3290)*, next door, is a bit older and cheaper.

The best in town is ***Amastrist Otel*** *(☎ 378-315 2465, fax 315 2629)*, Büyük Liman Caddesi, at the southern end of the bay near the naval base, about 250m from the centre (go straight through the town centre to the beach and turn right). Decent rooms with water views and breakfast cost US$22 a double.

Places to Eat

Cheap, good food is served at ***Köşem Pide Kebap Salonu***, Amiral Celal Eyüceoğlu Caddesi 23, between the park and the Büyük Liman. A cheese pide and soft drink costs less than US$2; döner kebap and stews cost up to US$5 for a full meal.

Amasra has several pleasant seafront fish restaurants at which you should reckon on paying US$6 to US$8 for a meal. Overlooking the main harbour at Büyük Liman Caddesi 26 is the upstairs ***Çesm-i Cihan*** fish restaurant and, just down from it, ***Bedenaltı Restaurant*** and ***Liman Restaurant***.

Çınar Restaurant, across Küçük Liman Caddesi from the Belediye, has an outdoor terrace where you can dine beneath shady plane trees. The fish here is good, as is the *börek* (flaky pastry), especially when it's piping hot. ***Mustafa Amca'nın Yeri***, next door, advertises *canlı balık* (live fish), and has a nice seaside dining room.

The nearby ***Kupa Birahanesi*** is a favourite local drinking place, but food is served as well. The neighbouring ***Bahçeli Fıçi Bira Salonu*** and ***Şeker Garden*** are similar.

The shady park is the place to enjoy a cool drink or bracing glass of çay in either ***Café Kumsal*** or ***Sefa Park Almina Aile Çay Bahçesi***. ***Kumsal*** serves pide and lahmacun too.

Getting There & Away

If you plan to travel east along the coast from Amasra, start early in the morning. Minibuses become increasingly difficult to find as the day wears on.

Amasra Seyahat, on the eastern side of the park, has minibuses going 16km south to Bartın, where buses depart for Safranbolu (92km, two hours, US$3), Ankara (280km, five hours, US$6), and İstanbul (340km, six hours, US$10). The town of Bartın is interesting only for its expertise in making carved wooden walking sticks so you're unlikely to want to stay.

AMASRA TO SİNOP

Travelling the narrow and twisty but scenic coastal road from Amasra eastward to Sinop (312km) is slow going (average 40km/h to 50km/h), with a broken surface and the occasional *heyelan* (landslide). Public transport is mostly local point-to-point minibus services – start early in the morning!.

If you have your own transport it's enjoyable to explore this relatively untouristy part of the coast, stopping for a swim at Bozköy beach west of **Çakraz**, or to see the boat-wrights at work in the town of **Kurucaşile** (population 2100), 45km east of Amasra which has several modest hotels and pensions. The picturesque village of **Kapısuyu** is another good spot to break your journey.

About 63km east of Amasra the road descends to a broad sand-and-pebble beach which stretches for several kilometres to the aptly named village of Kumluca ('sandy'). The beach continues 8km eastward to **Cide** (JEE-deh, population 5500), with several small summer pensions and restaurants, and ***Motel Yeni Ece*** *(☎ 366-866 1020)*.

İnebolu (population 9000) resembles Amasra in its splendid isolation, but has several hotels, pensions and restaurants to serve travellers. ***Otel Altınöz*** *(☎ 366-811 4502, Cumhuriyet Caddesi 47)*, inland from the PTT opposite the Ziraat Bankası, offers the usual drab, threadbare rooms for US$10 double with shower, as does ***Otel Özlü*** *(☎ 366-811 4198)* half a block up the street. There are small ***restaurants*** and ***pastry shops*** on this street as well. The best lodgings in town are at ***İnebolu Belediyesi Moteli*** *(☎ 366-811 4305, fax 811 3232)*, on İsmet Paşa Caddesi (the shore road) 500m west of the centre, right on the beach. Spare, worn but clean rooms with shower cost US$15/24 a single/double.

West of İnebolu the road improves, and 22km along is **Abana**, a fast-growing resort with a decent beach. About 41km east of İnebolu near Çatalzeytin is a long pebble beach surrounded by beautiful scenery. At Ayancık the road divides, with the left (northern) fork being the more scenic route to Sinop, about a 2½-hour ride from İnebolu.

SİNOP

Sinop (SEE-nohp, population 26,000), on a promontory jutting into the Black Sea, is a natural site for a port, and has been one for a thousand years.

The town takes its name from the legend of Sinope, daughter of the river god Asopus. Zeus fell in love with her and, in order to win her heart, promised to grant her any wish. Sinope, who didn't fancy marrying him, asked for eternal virginity. Outwitted, Zeus allowed Sinope to live out her days in happy solitude at the tip of the peninsula.

History

There is evidence of port life in and around Sinop since the first Chalcolithic settlements of around 4500 BC. Colonised from Miletus in the 8th century BC, its trade slowly grew and successive rulers – Cimmerians, Phrygians, Persians, the Pontic kings (who made it their capital), Romans and Byzantines – turned it into a busy trading centre. The Cynic philosopher Diogenes (circa 412-323 BC) was born here, then lived in Athens.

The Seljuks used Sinop as a port after taking it in 1214; but the Ottomans preferred to develop Samsun, which had better land communications.

On 30 November 1853, Sinop was attacked without any warning by a Russian

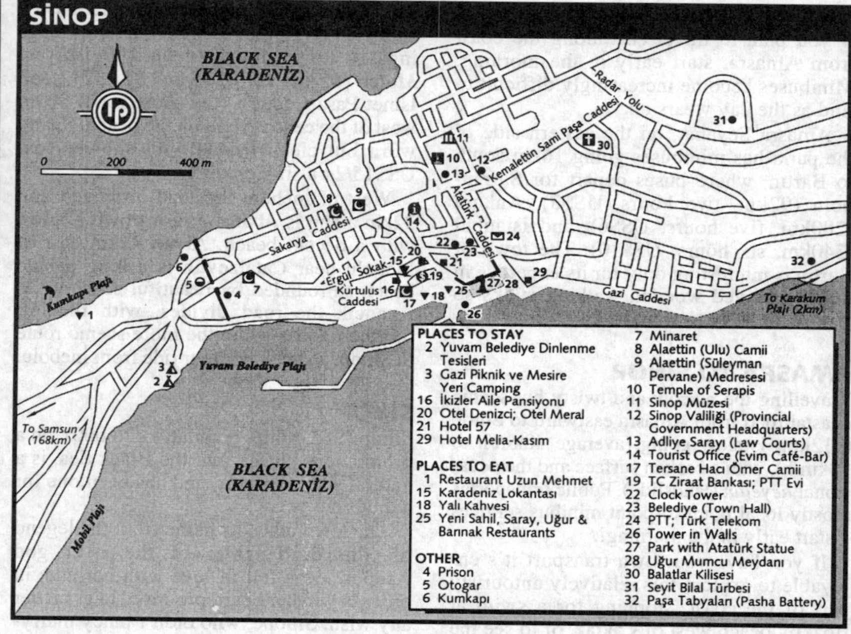

armada and the local garrison was overwhelmed with great loss of life. The battle of Sinop hastened the beginning of the Crimean War in which the Ottomans allied with the British and French to fight Russian ambitions in the Near East.

Orientation

Sinop is at the narrow point of the peninsula, with the road continuing eastward beyond the town to beaches and land's end. The otogar is at the western entrance to the town by the fortified walls. From here the main street, Sakarya Caddesi, goes eastward through the centre 800m directly to the Sinop Valiliği (the provincial government headquarters), just north of which are the museum and the Temple of Serapis.

To reach Kurtuluş Caddesi and the cheap hotels (800m from the otogar), walk from the otogar north along Sakarya Caddesi (the main road), through the city walls, bear right just past the minaret and go straight on downhill.

From the Valiliği, Atatürk Caddesi turns right (south) and descends the hill 250m past the clock tower and Belediye to the PTT, the prominent Hotel Melia-Kasım and the harbour. East of here the road leads along the shore 3km to Karakum Plajı, a municipal beach.

Information

You can try to find information at an office on the fourth floor of the Sinop Valiliği (☎ 368-261 5207, fax 260 0310), but you'll be lucky to find anyone speaking English. Unofficial tourist and tour information is offered by the Evim Café-Bar, a block south of Sakarya Caddesi at Kıbrıs Caddesi 7/A (☎ 368-261 7900). To find it from Kurtuluş Caddesi, take Denizciler Yolu, the road heading inland from opposite the PTT Evi. This becomes Kıbrıs Caddesi as it nears Sakarya Caddesi.

Sinop's postal code is 57000.

Fortifications

Open to easy attack from the sea, Sinop seems to have been fortified since earliest times but the existing walls are developments of those originally erected in 72 BC by Mithridates IV, king of Pontus. At one time the walls, some 3m thick, were more than 2km long.

Across Sakarya Caddesi, south of the otogar, is a Seljuk building converted into a prison by the Ottomans in 1877 and still in use. On the northern side of the otogar down near the shore is an ancient bastion called the Kumkapı (Sand Gate). Another square tower looms above the harbour on the southern side of town.

East of the centre almost at Karakum beach is the Paşa Tabyaları (Pasha Battery), a gun emplacement built to defend the town during the Crimean War.

Religious Buildings

In the town centre on Sakarya Caddesi stands the **Alaettin Camii** (1267), also called the Ulu Cami. It was constructed on the orders of Muinettin Süleyman Pervane, a powerful Seljuk grand vizier. The mosque has been repaired many times; its marble mihrab and mimber were added in 1429 by the local Candaroğlu emir.

Next to the Alaettin Camii is the **Alaettin Medresesi**, also called the Süleyman Pervane or Alaiye Medresesi, built in the late 13th century by the self-same Süleyman Pervane to commemorate the Seljuk conquest of Sinop.

Go eastward uphill from the Sinop Valiliği along Kemalettin Sami Paşa Caddesi to reach the **Balatlar Kilisesi**, a Roman temple converted to a Byzantine church in the 7th century. A few traces of frescoes are visible.

Further uphill, 1km from the Valiliği, is the **Cezayirli Ali Paşa Camii** (Mosque of Ali Pasha the Algerian). Inside is the **Seyit Bilal Türbesi**, or tomb of St Bilal, built for Emir Tayboğa in 1297. Seyit Bilal, grandson of Hüseyin (who was a grandson of the Prophet Muhammed), was blown ashore here in the 7th century and put to death by the Byzantines.

Down near the harbour in the market area on Kurtuluş Caddesi is the **Tersane Hacı Ömer Camii** (1903). Next to it is a touching monument, the Şehitler Çeşmesi ('Heroes' Fountain'), built in memory of the many Turkish soldiers who died in the surprise Russian attack of 1853. The fountain was built using the money recovered from the soldiers' pockets.

Temple & Sinop Müzesi

Just north of the Valiliği is the Sinop Museum, open from 8 am to 5.30 pm (noon to 5.30 pm on Monday, 9 am to 5 pm on weekends) for US$1. The collection spans Sinop's history from the Bronze Age to the Turkish War of Independence. A collection of 19th-century Greek Orthodox icons are reminders that the Black Sea coast was heavily populated by Ottoman Greeks until the War of Independence and the subsequent exchange of populations with Greece.

In the museum's garden are mosaics, tombstones and a few remains of an ancient **Temple of Serapis** (the Egyptian embodiment of Apollo) excavated in 1951.

Beaches

As you approach Sinop, turn right (south) a few hundred metres west of the otogar and prison and descend to the shore to find the Yuvam Belediye Plajı (municipal beach), a forest camping area, and the Yuvam Motel. On the northern side of the peninsula near the Kumkapı is another small beach where the water is cooler.

About 3km east of the harbour on the southern shore is Karakum beach, officially styled the Özel İdare Karakum Yüzgeç Tatil Köyü, with a pay beach of black sand, a restaurant, a nightclub and a nice camping ground with shady tent sites and electrical hook-ups.

Across the peninsula on the northern shore is Akliman, a long beach backed by forest and adjoined by the Hamsaroz fiord.

Places to Stay

Camping South-west of the otogar near the Yuvam Belediye Plajı are two camping grounds. At ***Gazi Piknik ve Mesire Yeri***, 300m south-west of the main road (750m from the otogar), you camp in full shade with fine views of the sea and there are tables and benches, even a playground for the children. There's easy transport to the town centre along the main road. The charge of US$3 per site is rarely levied at slow times of the year.

Further along the same road, 700m off the main road (2km west of the Valiliği), ***Yuvam Belediye Dinlenme Tesisleri*** camping ground is fairly dismal, with shadeless sites with hook-ups, but has a reasonable restaurant with a shady terrace.

The ***camp sites*** *(☎ 368-261 5117)* at Karakum, 3.5km west of the Valiliği along the southern shore, are pleasantly shady, with hook-ups, and cost US$3 per site.

Hotels Start looking by the harbour in Kurtuluş Caddesi, with the PTT Evi (postal workers' club), Ziraat Bankası and Tersane Hacı Ömer Camii as landmarks.

Otel Denizci *(☎ 368-261 0904)* and ***Otel Meral*** (☎ 368-261 3100) are right across the street from the Ziraat Bankası. Of these similarly priced places, the Meral, with small, clean rooms, is probably the better choice at US$6/10/15 a single/double/triple, although the glass-panelled doors let in corridor light infuriatingly. Around the corner from the Denizci, the rock-bottom ***Karahan Oteli*** *(☎ 368-261 0688)* is in a courtyard which should cut down some of the street noise.

Yılmaz Aile Pansiyonu *(☎ 368-261 5752, Tersane Caddesi 11)* just east of the PTT Evi, charges less (US$4.50/6/10 a single/double/triple and US$1.25 for hot showers) for its waterless rooms, but is friendly and lives up to its family reputation. Try also ***İkizler Aile Pansiyonu*** *(☎ 368-260 1544, Derinboğaz Ağzı Sokak 22)*, the continuation of Kurtuluş Caddesi, across from the Tersane Hacı Ömer Camii.

The new ***Hotel 57*** *(☎ 368-261 5462, Kurtuluş Caddesi 29)*, charges US$13/19 for single/double rooms with private bath, TV and phone. The name of the hotel in Turkish is pronounced ho-TEHL ehl-LEE yeh-DEE.

In İskele Caddesi right beside the waterfront cafes, is ***Uğur Oteli*** *(☎ 368-261 3742)* which, on my last visit, was busy with Russian prostitutes.

The best place in town is the rather dingy two-star ***Hotel Melia-Kasım*** *(☎ 368-261 4210, fax 261 1625, Gazi Caddesi 49)*. It's 250m south of the Valiliği, just east of the harbour on the waterfront. The location is good, with sea views from many rooms, but the nuclear-powered nightclub may keep you awake until all hours of the night. Rooms cost US$25/32 a double for land/sea views, breakfast included.

Places to Eat

Most restaurants along Kurtuluş Caddesi charge identical prices: stews for US$1.50, full meals for US$3 to US$4.

Karadeniz Lokantası is in a handy position and serves breakfast, lunch and dinner, but without alcohol. ***Baba Sultan Aile Kebap Salonu*** opposite Hotel 57 is good and clean.

East of the PTT Evi along the waterfront are several open-air restaurants (***Yeni Sahil***, ***Saray*** and ***Uğur***) which serve beer, wine and food on shady terraces. ***Barınak***, for example, can rustle up hamburgers, pizza, spaghetti or steak and eggs. Breakfast goes for less than US$2. Lunch or dinner will cost from US$4 to US$8, slightly more for fish.

The tea-and-beer garden of choice – and a pleasant one it is – is ***Yalı Kahvesi***, behind the Şehitler Çeşmesi and Tersane Hacı Ömer Camii, on the waterfront.

Getting There & Away

Most of the services leaving Sinop's small otogar are heading for Ankara or Samsun, with some buses continuing to Trabzon. For other destinations, you'll probably have to change buses en route.

Amasra – 312km, eight hours; no direct service, point-to-point minibus only
Amasya – 240km, 4½ hours, US$7; via Samsun
Ankara – 443km, nine hours, US$13; frequent buses

İnebolu – 156km, three hours, US$5; one bus at 8 am
İstanbul – 700km, 10½ hours, US$18 to US$23; several buses
Kastamonu – 235km, 2½ hours, US$9; change at Boyabat
Safranbolu – 340km, six hours, US$8; change at Karabük
Samsun – 168km, three hours, US$3.50; frequent minibuses
Trabzon – 365km, six hours, US$13; frequent buses via Samsun

Getting Around

Dolmuşes (US$0.35) run through the town from the otogar in the west to Karakum Plajı on the south-eastern shore. A taxi to the otogar from Kurtuluş Caddesi costs about US$2.

SİNOP TO SAMSUN

On the Samsun road, **Yakakent**, 80km east of Sinop, has a long pebble beach and numerous small family pensions. **Bafra**, 116km east of Sinop, is the centre of Black Sea tobacco growing. Samsun is another 52km eastward.

SAMSUN

Burnt to the ground by the Genoese in the 15th century, Samsun (sahm-SOON, population 310,000) has little to show for its long history. A major port and commercial centre, it's the largest city on the coast, a grim and often dusty place. There's little reason to stop here except to change buses, have a meal or find a bed.

Orientation

The city centre is Cumhuriyet Meydanı (Republic Square), just north-west of a large park with an equestrian statue of Atatürk. Just south-east of the statue stands the old Vilayet (provincial government headquarters). A handy landmark is the Hotel Yafeya on the north-western side of Cumhuriyet Meydanı. The new Vilayet complex is across the coastal highway to the north.

The large building like a celestial ski jump on the waterfront is the new Kültür Sarayı, or Cultural Centre, the venue for ballet, concerts and theatre.

The train station is 1km south-east of the Kültür Sarayı and the otogar just over 2km south-east of Cumhuriyet Meydanı along the shore road, Atatürk Bulvarı. Any city bus or dolmuş heading north-west through Samsun will drop you at Cumhuriyet Meydanı (US$0.35).

Information

The Tourism Information Office (☎ 362-431 1228) is a white fiberglass booth in the Atatürk park and is rarely open. The administrative office (☎ 362-431 2988, fax 435 2887) is at Talimhane Caddesi 6.

The main business street with banks, PTT and restaurants is Kazım Paşa Caddesi (sometimes called Bankalar Caddesi), one block inland from Atatürk Bulvarı, cutting north-west from Cumhuriyet Meydanı. The Turkish Central Bank will change money.

Samsun's postal code is 55000.

Museums

There's not much to detain you in Samsun, but with an hour or so to spare it's worth visiting the **Arkeoloji ve Etnoğrafya Müzesi** (Archaeological Museum), just off Atatürk Bulvarı, west of the big new Vilayet government building. The most striking exhibit is a huge Romano-Byzantine mosaic depicting Thetis and Achilles and the four seasons, found nearby at Karasamsun.

Other exhibits include Bronze Age, Chalcolithic and Hittite finds from the twin mounds at İkiztepe, a bronze statue of an athlete dating from the 2nd century BC and some wonderful embroidery.

Right next door is the **Atatürk Müzesi**. On 19 May 1919 Atatürk arrived in Samsun from İstanbul, preparing the way for the War of Independence. A statue near the Büyük Samsun Oteli commemorates this event, as does this museum, mainly full of photographs and items of Atatürk's apparel. One look at his portable shaving kit and you'll realise this was not a man who believed in travelling light!

Both museums are open from 8 am to noon and from 1.30 to 5.30 pm. You should get into both for US$1.

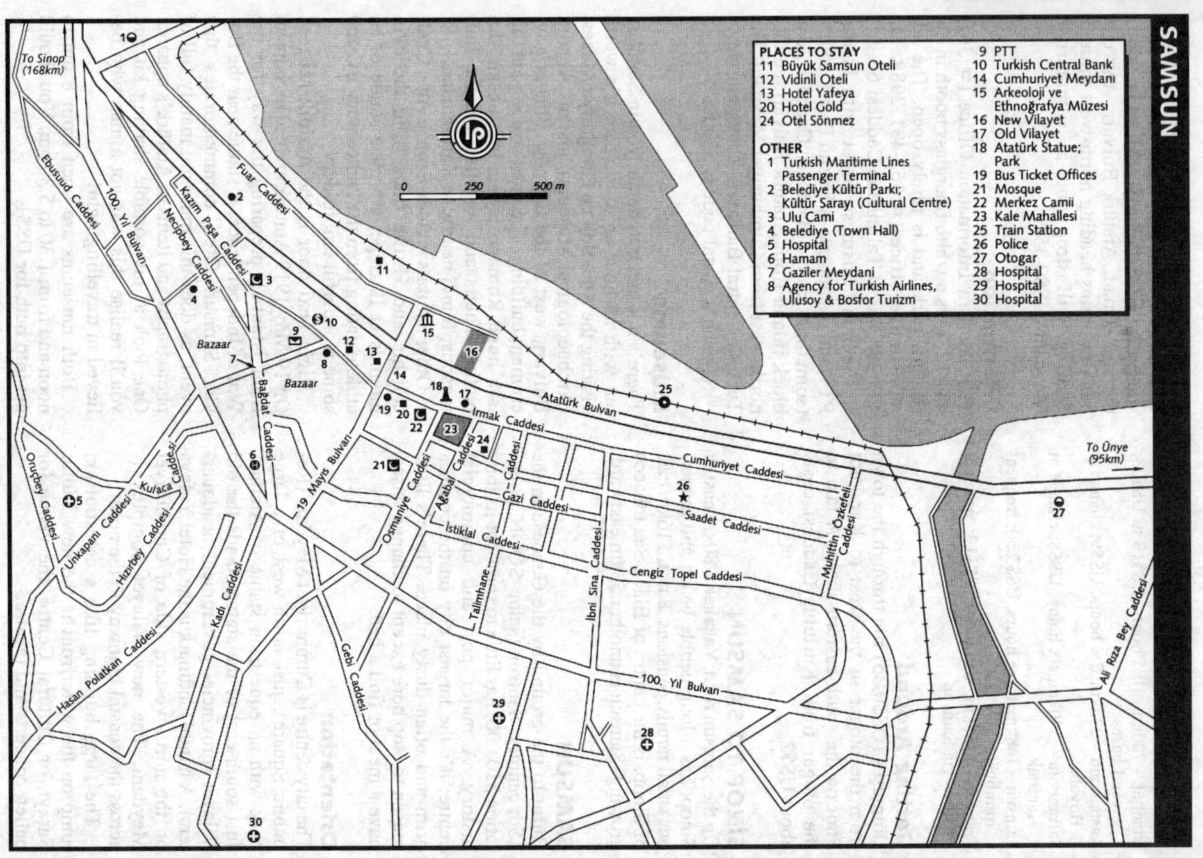
SAMSUN
PLACES TO STAY
11 Büyük Samsun Oteli
12 Vidinli Oteli
13 Hotel Yafeya
20 Hotel Gold
24 Otel Sönmez
OTHER
1 Turkish Maritime Lines Passenger Terminal
2 Belediye Kültür Parkı; Kültür Sarayı (Cultural Centre)
3 Ulu Cami
4 Belediye (Town Hall)
5 Hospital
6 Hamam
7 Gaziler Meydani
8 Agency for Turkish Airlines, Ulusoy & Bosfor Turizm
9 PTT
10 Turkish Central Bank
14 Cumhuriyet Meydanı
15 Arkeoloji ve Ethnoğrafya Müzesi
16 New Vilayet
17 Old Vilayet
18 Atatürk Statue; Park
19 Bus Ticket Offices
21 Mosque
22 Merkez Camii
23 Kale Mahallesi
25 Train Station
26 Police
27 Otogar
28 Hospital
29 Hospital
30 Hospital
0 250 500 m
To Sinop (168km)
To Ünye (95km)
Ebusuud Caddesi
100. Yıl Bulvarı
Necipbey Caddesi
Kazım Paşa Caddesi
Fuar Caddesi
Bazaar
Bağdat Caddesi
19 Mayıs Bulvarı
Atatürk Bulvarı
Irmak Caddesi
Cumhuriyet Caddesi
Gazi Caddesi
Saadet Caddesi
Ağabal Caddesi
Osmaniye Caddesi
İstiklal Caddesi
Talimhane Caddesi
İbni Sina Caddesi
Cengiz Topel Caddesi
Muhittin Özkefeli Caddesi
Ali Rıza Bey Caddesi
Oruçbey Caddesi
Kulaca Caddesi
Unkapanı Caddesi
Hızırbey Caddesi
Kadı Caddesi
Hasan Polatkan Caddesi
Gebi Caddesi

Places to Stay – Budget

Samsun has lots of good cheap hotels in the central district called Kale Mahallesi. Make your way to the Atatürk statue and old (*eski*) Vilayet building just one block south-east of Cumhuriyet Meydanı. Stand midway between these two landmarks and walk inland along Meşrutiyet Sokak towards the futuristic Merkez Camii. The streets here are crowded with cheap hotels like ***Otel Altay*** *(☎ 362-431 6877, fax 230 5215)*, at No 5, a clean, friendly place charging US$12/16 a single/double with private shower.

Nearby are several other choices, including the passable ***Otel Sönmez*** *(☎ 362-431 2669, Hürriyet Sokak 20)*, with similar prices; the borderline ***Otel Menekşe*** *(☎ 362-431 9835)*, and the emergencies-only ***Otel Bahar***.

The best choice in this area is ***Hotel Gold*** *(☎ 362-431 1959, Orhaniye Geçidi 4)*, a good, quiet, clean place renting rooms with shower and TV for US$18/25 a single/double, breakfast included.

If everything is full, there are more cheap hotels around Gaziler Meydanı in the bazaar. Walk north-west along Kazım Paşa Caddesi, turn left after the Turkish Central Bank and walk a few short blocks to get there.

Places to Stay – Mid-Range

The three-star, 96 room ***Hotel Yafeya*** *(☎ 362-435 1131, fax 435 1135)*, Cumhuriyet Meydanı, has comfortable rooms which suffer from the constant traffic noise. Rooms with bath, TV and minibar cost US$40/52 a single/double, breakfast included.

Just around the corner, on Kazım Paşa Caddesi, is the three-star, 46 room ***Vidinli Oteli*** *(☎ 362-431 6050, fax 431 2136)* where some rooms are more like suites, with separate sitting areas and views over Cumhuriyet Meydanı, and prices slightly lower than the Yafeya. The roof restaurant has fine views and works of art on the walls.

Places to Stay – Top End

The completely rebuilt ***Büyük Samsun Oteli*** *(☎ 362-435 4999, fax 431 0740, Sahil Caddesi 629)*, on the shore just north-west of Cumhuriyet Meydanı, is Samsun's status address.

Places to Eat

The hotel areas also have lots of small, good restaurants. Look for the ***Sila Restaurant*** on the corner of Irmak Caddesi and Hürriyet Sokak, directly opposite the old Vilayet. This is the most pleasant place near the park and offers meals for about US$4. A few steps back along Irmak Caddesi (towards the Hotel Yafeya), facing the park, are the ***Ravza Restaurant***, which serves good meals and cheap lahmacun (US$1), and the adjoining ***Zirve Pide ve Kebap Salonu***, another kebap, pide and lahmacun place. Next in this row, ***Birtat Pastanesi*** satisfies desires for sweets and puddings. ***Divan Pastanesi***, closer to Cumhuriyet Meydanı, serves cakes and coffee outdoors.

On the corner of Irmak and Osmaniye Caddesi is the popular ***Oba Restaurant***. Turn down Osmaniye Caddesi for ***Ovalı Restaurant***, where you can have wine or beer with your meal. There are lots more small places to eat around the Merkez Camii.

Ezgi Akçaabat Köfte Salonu at Kazım Paşa Caddesi 31 serves good cheap köfte and other dishes, and tends to be open on holidays and at breakfast time when other places are closed.

The big ***Terminal Café*** at the otogar offers good food, friendly service and clean toilets.

Getting There & Away

Air Turkish Airlines has nonstop daily flights between Samsun and İstanbul for about US$80. Make your reservations at the Turkish Airlines office in the Büyük Samsun Oteli or at Kar-Tur Turizm (☎ 362-431 5065 or 431 3455), at Kazım Paşa Caddesi 11/A.

Bus Samsun seems to offer at least one bus service per day to every important destination in Turkey, and very frequent buses to logical next destinations. There are bus ticket offices around Cumhuriyet Meydanı, and an Ulusoy ticket office in the Büyük Samsun Oteli.

Though there are daily trains between Samsun and Sivas, the train trip takes more than 12 daylight hours, and is hardly worth it when the bus makes the same trip in half the time.

Amasya – 130km, 2½ hours, US$4; 10 buses
Ankara – 420km, seven hours, US$16; frequent buses
Artvin – 615km, 10 hours, US$10; several buses
Giresun – 220km, 3½ hours, US$6; frequent buses
İstanbul – 750km, 11 hours, US$18 to US$23; several buses
Kayseri – 530km, nine hours, US$10; a few buses
Sinop – 168km, three hours, US$3.50; frequent minibuses
Sivas – 345km, 6½ hours, US$10; a few buses
Trabzon – 365km, six hours, US$10; frequent buses
Yozgat – 275km, 7½ hours, US$9; a few buses

Getting Around

Dolmuşes to the otogar ply Atatürk Bulvarı (look for signs saying 'Garaj').

EAST TO TRABZON

Two of Anatolia's great rivers, the Kızılırmak and the Yeşilırmak, empty into the sea on either side of Samsun. The rivers have built up fertile deltas which are now planted with corn and tobacco crops amid scenes of bucolic contentment. Each house has a lush lawn from its door to the roadway, and each lawn has its own fat cow.

The road east of Samsun is being widened to four lanes, with construction virtually completed to **Çarşamba**, 37km east of Samsun, where you might want to stop and examine the town's unusual wooden-framed and tile-roofed mosque.

If you plan to break your journey and spend a night before reaching Trabzon, Giresun is certainly the most pleasant place to do it.

Ünye

Ünye (EURN-yeh, population 46,000), a small port town amid hazelnut groves, is 95km east of Samsun. Its biggest claim to fame is that the great Turkish mystical poet Yunus Emre, who wrote during the early 14th century, is thought to have been born here.

About 7km inland from the town along the Niksar road stands **Ünye Kalesi**, a fortress built by the Byzantines to protect this pass to the interior.

In the centre of Ünye, you might note that the Eski Hamam was once a church. It's open to men in the morning and women in the afternoon (US$2). You can't miss the huge new Merkez Büyük Camii east of the main square.

Ünye's new otogar is almost 3km south-east of the Atatürk statue in the centre.

Information The Tourism Information Office (☎/fax 452-323 4952) is on the northern (sea) side of the Belediye (municipality/town hall).

Places to Stay As you approach Ünye from Samsun, the road skirts the beaches and passes a number of camping grounds, pensions and seaside motels, including the two-star ***Kumsal Hotel*** *(☎ 452-323 1602, fax 323 4490)*, 5km west of Ünye town centre. This is among Ünye's most comfortable lodgings, at US$48 a double with private bath and breakfast.

Çamlık Motel *(☎ 452-312 1333)*, in a pine forest on the shore 2km west of Ünye, is well used but pleasantly situated. A double room with bath and sea view costs US$16, or US$20 for a two-room suite with small kitchen.

There are other small hotels in the town itself. Facing the Belediye is the new ***Otel Burak*** *(☎ 452-312 0186)* which has clean, simple rooms with shower and TV for US$8/13 a single/double. A few doors along is the equally new ***Güney Otel*** *(☎ 452-323 8406)* where even some of the singles are a fair size, and there's a roof terrace with good views. Prices are US$6/9 per person without/with private shower.

Otel Kılıç *(☎ 452-323 1224, Cumhuriyet Meydanı, Hükümet Yanı 4)*, is on the main square next to the Ünye İlçesi Hükümet Konağı (government headquarters). It provides good, clean rooms with showers for US$10/15/20 a single/double/triple. Some front rooms have balconies. Beware the minaret noise from the neighbouring Saray Camii, however.

Florya Camping is 3km west of the centre.

Places to Eat Unusually, Ünye seems to have more jewellers and pharmacies than good eating places. ***Adana Mutfağı Kebap House*** next to Otel Burak, directly opposite the Belediye's front door, is new and nice, with meals for US$4 to US$6. ***Güney Kafeteryası***, adjoining the Güney Oteli, is an alternative. For fancier restaurants serving alcohol, walk east along the shore road for a few hundred metres.

Ordu

About 4km east of Ünye, the road passes a huge cement factory, and, 14km further along, the town of Fatsa (population 40,000). **Bolaman**, a bit further east, has many fine though dilapidated Ottoman wooden houses.

About 78km east of Ünye is Ordu (population 103,000), another fishing port with some nice old houses. When approaching the town from the west, you pass several comfortable moderately priced seaside motels – the ***Turistik Motel Denizcan*** and the ***Balıktası*** – as well as a small forest picnic spot (*orman piknik yeri*).

Orientation & Information The centre of town, at the Atatürk bust by the Aziziye (Yalı) Camii, has cheap hotels and restaurants, and a town plan on a signboard. The bazaar is just inland.

The otogar is 1.5km east of the main square, but the dolmuş station for local routes is just east of the main square. You can buy bus tickets at offices a few steps inland from the mosque by the main square.

The Tourism Information Office (☎ 452-223 1608) is conveniently situated on the ground floor of the Belediye, just east of the mosque on the main road. Rather unexpectedly, good English is spoken here. There's also an office in the Valilik Binası (☎ 452-223 1607, fax 223 2922).

Ordu's postal code is 52100.

Museum The **Paşaoğlu Konağı ve Etnoğrafya Müzesi** (Pasha's Palace & Ethnographic Museum) is 500m uphill from Ordu's main square past the Aziziye Camii. Follow signs reading 'Müze – Museum'.

This late 19th-century house, a pale yellow box decorated with wedding-cake trim, has a fairly tame ethnographic exhibit downstairs. The bedrooms, guest rooms and salon on the 1st floor, however, are fully furnished with period pieces, costumes and embroidery, and bring to life the Ottoman lifestyle of the 19th century. In the garden at the back, don't miss the old stone *ocakbaşı* (grill) for Ottoman banquets.

This is a gem of a place and it's a shame that it doesn't get more visitors. It's open from 8 am to 5 pm daily for US$0.50.

After visiting, follow the signs saying 'Boztepe' for fine views over the town.

Places to Stay & Eat Giresun is a much more pleasant place than Ordu to spend the night, so if you can make it that far, go on.

Ordu's ***Otel Kervansaray*** (*☎ 452-214 1330, Kazım Karabekir Caddesi 1*), just east of the Aziziye Camii and inland from the dolmuş station, is old fashioned, with lackadaisical staff, charging US$13 for a double room with shower. There's a clean restaurant on the ground floor.

Across the street from the Kervansaray, and a big step down in standard, is ***Otel Başar Palas*** (*☎ 452-214 4165*), charging from US$4 per person. Others are in the bazaar nearby.

The two-star, 39 room ***Turist Otel*** (*☎ 452-214 9115, fax 214 1950, Atatürk Bulvarı 134*), 350m east of the Aziziye Camii on the highway, is a bit noisy but moderately priced at US$18/24 a single/double with breakfast.

Fancier and newer is the three-star ***Belde Hotel*** (*☎ 452-214 3987, fax 214 9398*), several kilometres west of Ordu on a promontory at Kirazlılimanı, charging US$30/45 a single/double for rooms with private bath, TV and minibar. There's a swimming pool as well.

Foodwise, ***Merkez Lokantası*** on the eastern side of the Aziziye Camii, right by the dolmuş station, fits the bill fairly cheaply.

Ordu also has many small, clean eateries in the bazaar; the ***Nur Café*** near the PTT is very popular with women. For sea views, try ***Midi Restaurant*** right on the seafront beside the car park.

Giresun

The town of Giresun (GEE-reh-soon, population 68,000), 46km east of Ordu, was founded some 3000 years ago. Legend has it that Jason and the Argonauts passed by on their voyage to the fabled Kingdom of Colchis (Georgia), on the eastern shores of the Black Sea, in search of the Golden Fleece. The Argonauts supposedly stopped at a nearby island (Büyük Ada) where Amazon queens had erected a shrine to Ares, god of war.

After the Romans conquered the Kingdom of Pontus, they discovered that the locals had orchards full of trees bearing delicious little red fruits. One theory holds that the ancient name for the town, Cerasus, is the root for many of the names for the fruit – *cherry* in English, *cerise* in French, *kiraz* in Turkish – as well as for the town's modern name. Cherries are still important here after 2000 years.

You can see the ruins of a medieval castle, Giresun Kalesi, above the town. On the eastern side of the city, a disused Greek Orthodox church has been turned into the Şehir Müzesi (City Museum).

Orientation & Information The centre of Giresun is the Atapark on the main road. The Belediye is just inland from the park. The main commercial street is Gazi Caddesi, climbing steeply uphill from the Belediye. The bus station is 4km west of the centre; if you're coming from the east and heading west, have the bus drop you at the Atapark. Bus companies have ticket offices near the Belediye.

Dolmuşes eastward to the towns of Görele, Espiye and Tirebolu use a more convenient lot, one long block east of the Atapark on the main road. Those to Ordu stop on the main highway opposite the Atapark. The PTT is 500m uphill from the Belediye.

Seed of a Myth?

In ancient times what is now Georgia was known as Colchis. Greek myth relates how Jason and the Argonauts sailed there in search of a Golden Fleece, supposedly owned by the Colchian king Aeëtes. After many adventures along the coast of the Pontus Euxinus (the Black Sea), Jason was helped to acquire the Fleece by the king's sorceress daughter, Medea, whom he married.

Complete fantasy, you might think. However, it's likely that the myth grew out of folk memory of a 13th century BC trading voyage during which sailors saw the Colchians laying fleeces in the river beds to gather alluvial gold.

The Tourism Information Office (☎ 454-212 3190, fax 216 0095) is at Gazi Caddesi 72, but there's a more convenient kiosk in the Atapark. It's open from 9 am to 6 pm daily and has a city plan.

The Turkish Maritime Lines office (☎ 454-216 2382) is at Giresun Liman İşletmesi, Atatürk Bulvarı, Akgül Apartımanı 542/3.

Giresun's postal code is 28000.

Kalepark With time to kill in Giresun, the things to do are to eat hazelnuts and chocolate bars containing hazelnuts, and walk 1.5km uphill to the Kalepark (Castle Park) which is perched on the steep hillside above the town. The beautiful shady park offers panoramic views of the town and the sea, tables for picnickers and tea-sippers, bosky groves for lovers, and barbecues for grillers. It's busy on weekends.

No public transport serves the park, so you must hike there. Walk inland uphill from the Atapark on Gazi Caddesi and turn left one block past the Otel Kit-Tur; this is a shortcut, not passable for cars. If in doubt, ask directions for the vilayet or the Kale. The prominent mansion on the hillside above the minibus lot is the vilayet, near a mosque which was obviously once a church.

Şehir Müzesi The City Museum, with its run-of-the-mill collection, is housed in the disused 18th-century Gogora church, 1.5km around the promontory east of the Atapark on the main road. Perhaps the most interesting exhibits are old French photographs of turn-of-the-century Giresun.

The museum administration is housed in a lovely restored Ottoman building next door and there's a terrace in between where cold drinks are sometimes available.

Festivals The grandly named International Black Sea Giresun Aksu Festival, held annually on 20 May, is a delightful legacy from pagan times. Traditionally celebrated by Ottoman Greeks on 7 May according to the Julian calendar (Gregorian, 20 May), the festival hails rebirth, fecundity and the coming of the new growing season. Locals say it dates back to the days of the Hittite fertility gods: Priapus, the phallic god; Cybele, the Anatolian earth-mother goddess; and other such worthies.

Festivities begin at the mouth of the Aksu creek, where participants pass through a trivet, then through seven double pieces and one single piece of stone to boats waiting at the shore. The boats sail around Büyük Ada while the voyagers cast pebbles representing the last year's troubles into the water. Returning to the town, everyone eats and drinks, and drinks some more.

Places to Stay – Budget ***Hotel Bozbağ*** *(☎ 454-216 1249, Eski Yağcılar Sokak 8)* is in a quiet location one block up the street from the Belediye. The rooms are decently maintained and priced at US$8/13 a single/double with shower. Hot water is on in the evenings only. You pay the same but get less at ***Otel Kent*** *(☎ 454-216 0457, Gazi Caddesi 6)*, next to the Bulut Döviz, uphill behind the Belediye on the main street.

Places to Stay – Mid-Range The two-star, 20 room ***Otel Çarıkçı*** *(☎ 454-216 1026, fax 216 4578, Osmanağa Caddesi 6)*, half a block east of the Belediye, is a good choice. A building almost a century old has been carefully restored, and now provides perhaps the most comfortable rooms with private bath for US$19/32 a single/double, breakfast included. Attentive service is a plus and strong windows keep out most of the street noise.

Around the corner at Çapulacılar Arastası 8 is the quietish, one-star ***Er-Tur Otel*** *(☎ 454-216 1757, fax 216 7762)*, another good choice at US$12/20 a single/double, breakfast included.

The three-star ***Otel Kit-Tur*** *(☎ 454-212 0255, fax 212 3034, Arifbey Caddesi 27)*, two short blocks uphill from the Belediye along Gazi Caddesi. Modern rooms have TV, private bath and insect screens, and prices are good at US$26/34 a single/double. A ludicrously small lift has space for just two people!

Half a block further uphill is ***Otel Ormancılar*** *(☎ 454-212 4391, fax 212 7105, Gazi Caddesi 37)*, at similar prices. Beware of the noisy front rooms.

Once the town's best hotel, the two-star ***Giresun Oteli*** *(☎ 454-216 3017, fax 216 6038)*, on the Black Sea side of the highway to the east of the Atapark, suffers from road and top-floor nightclub noise, so get a mid-level seaside room for US$17/25. Breakfast is served in the 6th floor restaurant with wonderful sea views.

Places to Eat ***Deniz Lokantası***, next to the Belediye and the Ulusoy bus ticket office, is simple, cheap and open from early in the morning to late at night.

In warm weather, a narrow street directly behind Hotel Bozbağ (on the other side of the block) is crowded with dining tables served by several small restaurants including the good, cheap ***Halil Usta Pide ve Kebap***, ***Kahramanmaraş Pide ve Kebap*** and ***Garipoğlu 2 Restaurant***. The restaurants remain open all year, though the tables come in during winter.

Heading up Gazi Caddesi you'll find several bright, cheerful *pastahaneler* (pastry shops) serving cakes, coffee and ice cream. Surrounding shops specialise in hazelnuts.

On Osmanağa Caddesi near Hotel Çarıkçı several ***beer halls*** serve light meals and snacks.

The best dining in town is at ***Tibor Sosyal Tesisleri*** *(☎ 454-212 2878)*, a private club which accepts tourists. Walk up the street to the right of the Belediye for 30m to No 4 (on the right); take the lift to the 4th floor in cool weather, 5th floor (roof) in summer. Local worthies (mostly men) chatting about business and football fill the other tables. Service is attentive, alcohol is served, and a full meal of meat, salad and a drink costs only about US$4 or US$5.

Getting There & Away Frequent buses and minibuses shuttle between Trabzon and Giresun (2½ hours, US$4). Buses and minibuses between Girseun and Ordu are similarly regular (one hour, US$1).

Giresun to Trabzon

From Giresun it's another 150km to Trabzon. Along the way, the road passes through several small towns, including **Espiye**, with the Andoz Kalesi castle, and the attractive town of **Tirebolu**, with a tree-lined shore drive (the highway) and two castles (the St Jean Kalesi and Bedrama Kalesi). Tirebolu has a Çaykur tea-processing plant, which signals your arrival in Turkey's tea country.

Just east of Tirebolu is a stretch of pebble beach. Take a Görele dolmuş to reach it.

Görele is the next town eastward, and after it is **Akçakale**, where you'll see the ruins of a 13th-century Byzantine castle on a little peninsula, marked by a prominent sign.

TRABZON

Immortalised in Rose Macauley's classic novel *The Towers of Trebizond*, the modern town of Trabzon is the largest port along Eastern Turkey's Black Sea coast. Goods arrive here by sea and continue overland by road to Georgia, Armenia, Azerbaijan and Iran, a 20th-century commerce which has given Trabzon new life and a burgeoning population of 150,000 plus.

Modern Trabzon is thoroughly cosmopolitan. With the collapse of the Soviet Union and the opening of formerly closed borders, citizens of the Soviet Union's successor republics, particularly Georgia and Armenia, flooded into Turkey in search of a quick buck. They came to sell whatever they could bring from home, and to buy Turkish consumer goods unavailable in their own countries. With them came an influx of prostitutes, dubbed 'Natashas' by the Turks. The traders and prostitutes are still very much in evidence, but fortunately for Trabzon they have been followed by a new wave of Russian tourists, and several agencies catering to their needs have now opened up. You'll hear Russian spoken about town and see shop signs advertising in Cyrillic script. One or two restaurants have even added a Russian twist to their menus.

Nowadays the main reasons for visiting Trabzon are to see the medieval church of Aya Sofya; to poke around in the old town; to visit Atatürk's lovely villa on the outskirts; and to make an excursion through the alpine scenery to Sumela, a dramatic Byzantine monastery carved out of a sheer rock cliff. The modern town is bright, bustling and very pleased with itself although the traffic fumes and crowds of people, added to the humid air and overcast skies, can make it feel mildly oppressive in summer.

History

Trabzon's recorded history begins around 746 BC, when colonists originally from Miletus (south of Kuşadası) came from Sinop and founded a settlement (Trapezus) with its acropolis on the *trápeza*, or 'table' of land above the harbour.

The town did reasonably well for 2000 years, occupying itself with port activities, until 1204 when the soldiers of the Fourth Crusade seized and sacked Constantinople, driving its noble families to seek refuge in Anatolia. The imperial family of the Comneni established an empire along the Black Sea coast in 1204, with Alexius Comnenus I reigning as the emperor of Trebizond.

The Trapezuntine rulers became skilful at balancing their alliances with the Seljuks, the Mongols, the Genoese and others; it didn't hurt to be cut off from the rest by a

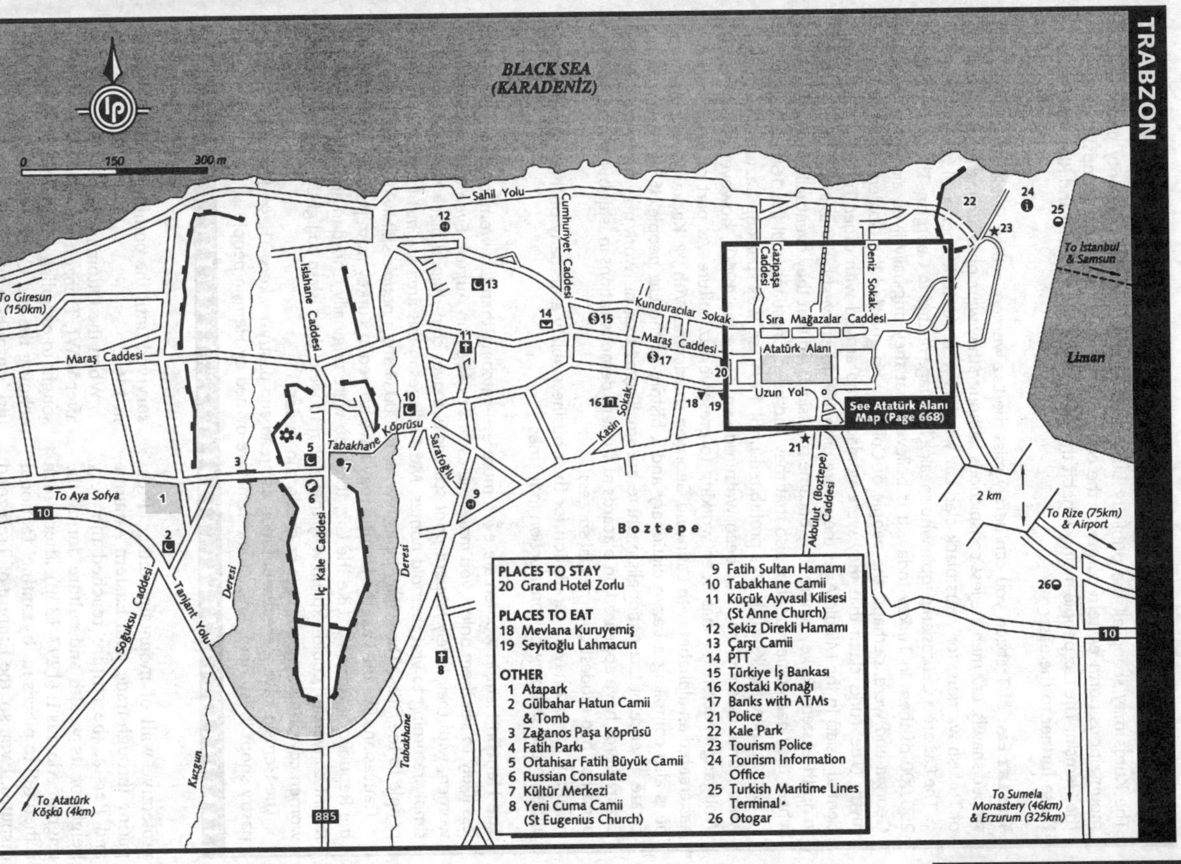
TRABZON
BLACK SEA
(KARADENİZ)
0
150
300 m
Sahil Yolu
Cumhuriyet Caddesi
Gazipaşa Caddesi
Deniz Sokak
Kunduracılar Sokak
Sıra Mağazalar Caddesi
Maraş Caddesi
Atatürk Alanı
Uzun Yol
See Atatürk Alanı Map (Page 668)
Islahane Caddesi
Tabakhane Köprüsü
Sarafoğlu
Kasin Sokak
Akbulut (Boztepe) Caddesi
Boztepe
İç Kale Caddesi
Deresi
Tabakhane
Kuzgun
Tanjant Yolu
Soğuksu Caddesi
Liman
To Giresun (150km)
To Aya Sofya
To Atatürk Köşkü (4km)
To İstanbul & Samsun
To Rize (75km) & Airport
To Sumela Monastery (46km) & Erzurum (325km)
2 km
10
885
PLACES TO STAY
20 Grand Hotel Zorlu
PLACES TO EAT
18 Mevlana Kuruyemiş
19 Seyitoğlu Lahmacun
OTHER
1 Atapark
2 Gülbahar Hatun Camii & Tomb
3 Zağanos Paşa Köprüsü
4 Fatih Parkı
5 Ortahisar Fatih Büyük Camii
6 Russian Consulate
7 Kültür Merkezi
8 Yeni Cuma Camii (St Eugenius Church)
9 Fatih Sultan Hamamı
10 Tabakhane Camii
11 Küçük Ayvasıl Kilisesi (St Anne Church)
12 Sekiz Direkli Hamamı
13 Çarşı Camii
14 PTT
15 Türkiye İş Bankası
16 Kostaki Konağı
17 Banks with ATMs
21 Police
22 Kale Park
23 Tourism Police
24 Tourism Information Office
25 Turkish Maritime Lines Terminal
26 Otogar

The Laz & Hemşin Peoples

The Kurds may scoop all the publicity but Turkey does have other minority peoples. The mountainous north-eastern corner of the country is home to two such groups: the Laz and the Hemşin. The Laz people mainly inhabit the valleys between Trabzon and Rize, the Hemşin those further to the east.

The Laz East of Trabzon you can hardly miss the Laz women in their vivid red and maroon striped shawls. Laz men are less conspicuous, although they were once among the most feared of Turkish warriors; for years black-clad Laz warriors were Atatürk's personal bodyguards.

The Laz are a Caucasian people who speak a language related to Georgian. There are perhaps 250,000 of them in Turkey today. It is believed that they originally lived along the coast of Georgia and were, perhaps, the people of Colchis who guarded the Golden Fleece of Greek myth. (The Turks claim that they were nomads who arrived with other Turkic groups from Central Asia.) In the Middle Ages they were probably driven west by Arab invaders and settled in north-eastern Turkey where they became so assimilated that they eventually forgot not only where they had come from but also that they had been Christians until the 16th century.

Just as speaking Kurdish was prohibited until 1991, so was speaking Lazuri, a language which, until recently, had not been written down. Since the 1960s, however, a German – Wolfgang Feuerstein – has been working to preserve Laz culture. As part of that effort he has created an alphabet with Latin and Georgian characters. With the Kaçkar Working Group he is also compiling a Lazuri dictionary and a history of the Laz people. If his hope was to create a sense of Laz nationalism, there are small signs that his work may be bearing fruit: Lazuri words have appeared on placards at student demonstrations in İstanbul and a Laz pop band has had modest commercial success.

Today the Laz have a reputation for their business ability and many of them are involved either in the shipping or construction industries.

The Hemşin Hemşin women are even more eye-catching than Laz women although you're less likely to see them unless you make the ascent to Ayder in August. Even then many of the women, with their lovely leopard-print scarves tied over coin-draped black head-dresses, are simply returning to visit their old homes. Most villages in this area are fast losing their young people to the cities. There may be as few as 15,000 Hemşin people still living in the area.

Caucasians like the Laz, the Hemşin may have arrived in Turkey from parts of what is now the Republic of Armenia. Like the Laz, they too were originally Christian and their relatively recent conversion could explain why they seem to wear their Islam so lightly. You won't see women cowering beneath veils or chadors in Ayder.

The Hemşin have a great reputation as bread and pastry-makers. These days many of the pastry shops in İstanbul, Ankara and İzmir are owned by Hemşin people.

protective wall of mountains either. Prospering through trade with Eastern Anatolia and Persia, the empire reached the very height of its wealth and culture during the reign of Alexius II (1297-1330), after which it then fell to pieces in 'byzantine' factional disputes. Even so, the Empire of Trebizond survived until the coming of the Ottomans in 1461.

When the Ottoman Empire was defeated after WWI, Trabzon's many Greek residents sought to establish a Republic of Trebizond echoing the old Comneni Empire, but Atatürk's armies were ultimately victorious.

Orientation

Trabzon is built on a mountainside. The port is at the centre of town, with the ancient acropolis on the 'table' now occupied by the main square called Atatürk Alanı (or Meydan Park), rising to the west of it. Most government offices, airline offices, hotels and restaurants are in and around Atatürk Alanı. The Meydan Oto Parkı, just east of the İskender Paşa Camii, charges US$2 to US$3 per day for parking.

Trabzon has few street signs and numbers, making it difficult to find a specific address.

Many of Trabzon's most interesting sights are west of the square along Uzun Yol (oo-ZOON yohl, Long Road), also called Uzun Sokak.

Trabzon's otogar is 3km east of the port on the landward side of the shore road. The airport is 8km east of the town. Buses bearing the legend 'Park' or 'Meydan' go to Atatürk Alanı.

Information

Tourist Office The Tourism Information Office (☎/fax 462-321 4659), is temporarily at the harbour, but may have moved by the time you arrive.

The Tourism Police office (☎ 462-326 0086) is downhill at the end of İskele Caddesi just outside the port enclosure.

Consulates There's a Georgian Consulate (Gürcistan Konsolosluğu) (☎ 462-326 2226, fax 326 2296) at Gazipaşa Caddesi 20 (look for the flag on the facade), open 9 am to noon and 2 to 6 pm, although you can often do business during the lunch break. Mr Tsate Batshshi speaks English, and will sell you a visa: US$30 for 15 days, US$40 for 30 days, or US$10 for a transit visa, but for this you must have a visa for the country to which you're transiting. See the end of this chapter for details on getting to Georgia.

Trabzon also has a Russian Consulate (☎ 462-326 2600) in Ortahisar Mahallesi, opposite the Ortahisar Faith Büyük Camii. At the time of writing, however, visas were not being granted to most foreign nationals; you should apply from your home country instead. But this may change.

Money Most banks and exchange offices are along Maraş Caddesi. The Türkiye İş Bankası is a state-of-the-art place where cashing a travellers cheque is almost a pleasure! Esas Döviz accepts sterling, francs and several other currencies. Other exchange offices are on the northern side of Atatürk Alanı and in the bazaar. Türkiye İş Bankası, Kobank and Faisal Finans have offices facing the Belediye.

Post Office The post office (PTT) (☎ 462-322 4970) is on Maraş Caddesi, which extends west from Atatürk Alanı. For letters and cards there's also a handy booth in Atatürk Alanı.

Trabzon's postal code is 61000.

Newspapers The Büfe Güzel (kiosk) in Güzelhisar Caddesi often stocks the *Turkish Daily News*. If you don't see it, ask.

Atatürk Alanı

The heart of Trabzon's social life is Atatürk Alanı which has a fountain, a statue of Atatürk, tea gardens and lots of trees. In daylight it's a pleasant place to while away a few hours, with men and women, boys and girls going about their business or taking their leisure. At night, of course, it reverts to male-only territory.

Walking Tour

A pleasant way to get to grips with Trabzon's sometimes confusing topography is to go on a walking tour. The one described here starts at Atatürk Alanı and takes you right across the city to the Gülbahar Hatun Camii.

Set off from the İstanbul Airlines office at the north-western corner of Atatürk Alanı. Walk north along Gazipaşa Caddesi and turn left at the first street, Kunduracılar Sokak which cuts through the **bazaar**. Keep going until you reach the **Çarşı Camii** (Market Mosque) which was restored recently.

Enter the mosque by the northern door. On either side above the inner door, note the little 'dove temples', a fairly common feature of Ottoman architecture. The mosque's interior, adorned with crystal chandeliers, is rich in

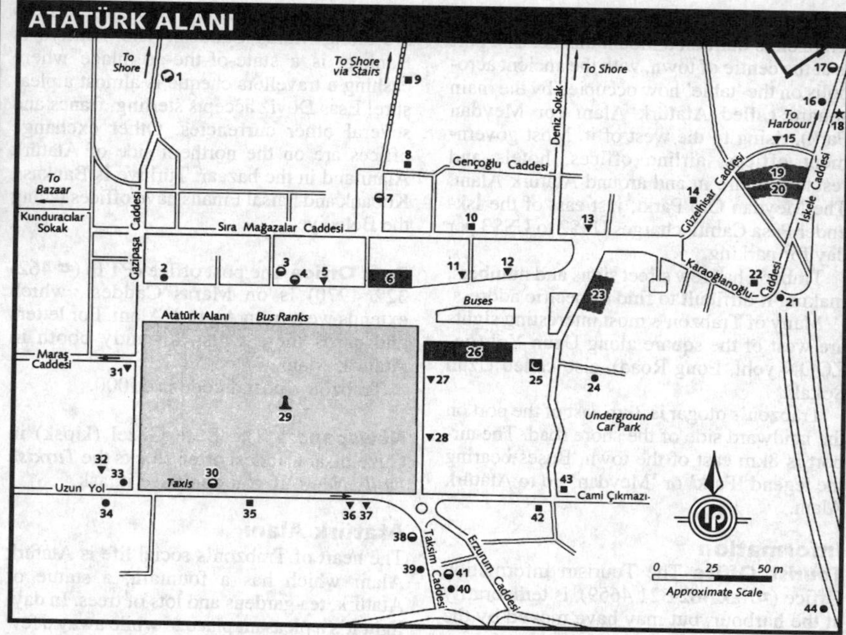

arabesques painted on domes and pillars, and trompe l'oeil 'stonework' painted on pillars and walls.

Just south-east of the Çarşı Camii is the **Taş Han** (or Vakıf Han), a collection of traders and artisans shops set around a courtyard entered by a portal from the street and reminiscent of the hans around İstanbul's covered bazaar.

A block south-west of the Çarşı Camii on Paşahamam Sokak is the **İskender Paşa Hamamı**, an ancient Turkish bath still in use by local men.

Walk west past the İskender Paşa Hamamı and turn left at the second street, Kazazoğlu Sokak, to reach busy Maraş Caddesi at the 19th-century Müftü İsmail Efendi Camii. Follow Maraş Caddesi uphill for one block and then turn right. The crumbling **Küçük Ayvasıl Kilisesi** (Church of St Anne) is among the city's oldest buildings, having been built during the reign of Byzantine emperor Basil I in 884-5, with later renovations. Unfortunately, it's closed to visitors.

To reach the 13th-century **church of St Eugenius**, walk south to Uzun Yol, then right (west) to the Tabakhane Köprüsü, the bridge across the steep-sided Tabakhane ravine with the big Tabakhane Camii beside it. At the east end of the bridge, take Sarafoğlu Sokak uphill following the signs to the Fatih Sultan Hamamı. Cami Sokak is the first right, before the hamam, and halfway up you'll see the old stones of the church-mosque on the right.

Tradition holds that Eugenius, an early Christian living here, raged against the priests of Mithra and was martyred. His skull was miraculously discovered here soon after the arrival of the Comneni imperial family, driven from Constantinople by

ATATÜRK ALANI

PLACES TO STAY
- 8 Hotel Toros
- 9 Sankta Maria Hostel
- 10 Otel Horon
- 14 Gözde Aile Oteli
- 19 Hotel Anıl
- 20 Otel Kalepark
- 22 Otel Konak
- 23 Hotel Usta
- 35 Hotel Özgür
- 42 Hotel Nur
- 43 Hotel Benli

PLACES TO EAT
- 5 Ak Piliç Tavuk Bar
- 6 Meydan Kebap ve Lokantası
- 11 Volkan 2 Lokantası
- 12 Tad Pizza ve Hamburger
- 13 Derya Restaurant
- 15 Hisar Kafeterya (Russian Restaurant)
- 27 Kıbrıs Restaurant
- 28 Palmiye Pasta Salonu
- 31 Nil Restaurant
- 32 Çardak Pide Salonu
- 36 İnan Kebap Salonu
- 37 Çınar Lokantası

OTHER
- 1 Georgian Consulate
- 2 İstanbul Airlines Office
- 3 Boztepe Dolmuş
- 4 Hat C (Aya Sofya) Dolmuş
- 7 Havaalanı (Airport) Dolmuş
- 16 Shipping Companies Offices
- 17 Maritime Passenger Terminal
- 18 Tourism Police Office
- 21 Afacan Tur
- 24 Entrance to Car Park
- 25 İskender Paşa Camii
- 26 Belediye (Town Hall)
- 29 Atatürk Statue
- 30 Dolmuş to Sumela
- 33 Turkish Airlines Office
- 34 Papillon Tur
- 38 Sumela (Ulusoy) Otogar
- 39 Metro Bus Ticket Office
- 40 Fatih Parkı
- 41 Garajlar Dolmuş to Otogar
- 44 Avrasya Pazarı (Eurasian Market); Çömlekçi

the Fourth Crusade. St Eugenius thus became the patron saint of Trabzon.

The church was built in the 13th century, but badly damaged in a fire in 1340, and modified during repairs. After Mehmet the Conqueror took the city in 1461, he performed his Friday ablutions in the nearby baths, proclaimed the church a mosque, prayed there, and ordered the construction of the minaret.

The mosque's northern door is often locked, but the east door, reached by the courtyard to the left, may be open if the *bekçi* (guardian) is about. The building is elegantly simple, lofty and light, with three parallel naves and a transversal topped by a cupola; its design is more easily visible as a mosque than it would have been with the elaborate interior decoration of a Byzantine church.

Cross the Tabakhane bridge westward on Uzun Yol and you're in Ortahisar (Middle Castle), so called from its position within the old city walls and halfway up the slope. Just up the slope is the **Ortahisar Fatih Büyük Camii**, formerly the Panaghia Chrysokephalos (Gold-Topped Church of the Virgin). The building you see dates mostly from the 13th century, the time of the Comneni Empire of Trebizond, though there was probably an earlier church here. It took its name, meaning 'Gold-Topped', from gold-plated copper cladding on the cupola, an affordable Comneni extravagance as this was the principal church for imperial ceremonies. The Byzantine splendour of its decoration, however, has long since been replaced by Islamic austerity therefore aiding appreciation of the church's architecture, though not of its interior furnishings.

As you enter, turn right and walk to the western end, which was the original entrance. Then walk slowly eastward, watching as the succession of seven arches and pseudo-arches open above you, culminating in the dome which, in Byzantine times, would have been ablaze in gold mosaics.

Follow the little street opposite the mosque's present main door for half a block to the **Fatih Parkı**, a rare quiet unpolluted garden oasis amid Trabzon's ceaseless hubbub.

Continue westward along Uzun Yol for several hundred metres, cross the Zağnos Paşa Köprüsü (bridge) and go up the slope on the southern side of the Atapark to find the **Gülbahar Hatun Camii**, built by Selim the Grim, the great Ottoman conqueror of Syria and Egypt, in honour of his mother Gülbahar Hatun in 1514. Gülbahar Hatun, a princess of the Comneni imperial family, was much loved for her charitable works, which she performed for the benefit of Christians and Muslims alike. Her tomb is the little building to the east of the mosque.

The **Atapark** has tea gardens for refreshments after your walk. Afterwards, dolmuşes (US$0.35) run from the north-western corner of the park by the Gülbahar Hatun Camii eastward along Uzun Yol to Atatürk Alanı.

If you walk back, pause to look at the wonderful **Kostaki Konağı**, a typical 19th-century Trabzon town mansion half a block south of Uzun Yol at Zeytinlik Caddesi 10. Sadly, work on turning it into a museum seems to have ground to a halt.

Organised Tours

Afacan Tur (☎ 462-321 5804, fax 321 7001), İskele Caddesi 40/C, does reasonably priced trips to Sumela (daily, 10 am, US$3), Uzungöl (Saturdays, 9 am, US$10) and Ayder (Sundays, 8.30 am, US$8). If you're pushed for time these could be worth taking.

Boztepe

On the hillside 2km south-east of Atatürk Alanı is a lookout and the Boztepe Piknik Alanı with fine views of the city and the sea. In ancient times Boztepe harboured temples to the Persian sun god Mithra and to Apollo. Later the Byzantines built several churches and monasteries here, of which the ruins of the Convent of Panaya Theoskepastos, or Kızlar Manastırı, are the most prominent.

To get there from Atatürk Alanı, take a bus labelled 'Park-Boztepe Bld Dinlenme Tesisleri' or a Boztepe dolmuş (from beside the Halkbank on the northern side of Atatürk Alanı). The route goes uphill 1.5km to the local orthopaedic hospital, then another 700m to the Boztepe park with picnic facilities.

Kaymaklı Manastırı

The former Armenian monastery at Kaymaklı makes an interesting excursion to the semi-rural outskirts of Trabzon. Catch any bus or dolmuş going uphill on Taksim Caddesi just above Atatürk Alanı and headed for Çukurayır; tell the driver you want to get out at the Mısırlı Camii. Keep walking along the same road for 100m, then turn left downhill on a rutted, unpaved, unmarked road. Follow the road for 800m, bearing right at a fork and later turning sharp right at a concreted intersection. Soon you'll see on the left the farm buildings of Mr İdris and Mrs Sevgi Kantekin, overlooking the steep valley up which the Erzurum highway passes.

With your own vehicle, in dry weather, you can drive right to the farm, but you could get trapped if the road is muddy.

İdris Bey and Sevgi Hanım are used to visitors, but during the busy farming season it may be one of their children who shows you the fine fresoes (in better condition than most of those at Sumela) in the *katholikon* (monastery church), now used as a barn. Government archaeologists have apparently studied the building, but have allotted no money for its preservation.

To return to Trabzon, the best way is to retrace your steps uphill, although you can continue following the very rough, stony track downhill for almost 1km to the highway, and hope to catch a bus or dolmuş for the 4.5km ride back to Atatürk Alanı.

Aya Sofya Müzesi

Aya Sofya Müzesi (Hagia Sophia or Church of the Divine Wisdom) is 4km west of the centre on a terrace which once held a pagan temple. The site is above the coastal highway, reachable by city bus or dolmuş from Atatürk Alanı – look for a 'Hat C' (Route C) dolmuş on the square's northern side.

Built between 1238 and 1263, the church was clearly influenced by Eastern Anatolian and Seljuk design, though the excellent wall paintings and mosaic floors follow the style of Constantinople. Tombs were built into the northern and southern walls. Next to the church, the gloomy bell tower was finished much later, in 1427. Nothing remains of the monastery that once stood here.

The church is now a museum, open from 8.30 am to 5 pm (closed on Monday in winter); admission costs US$1.

In the museum's garden is a cafe set up as a traditional half-timbered Black Sea coast farmhouse with a raised *serander* (granary)

The Natasha Syndrome

Until 1990, Turkey's borders with the Soviet Union were sealed. Then with the collapse of the Union and the liberation of the ethnic nation-states of Georgia, Armenia and Azerbaijan along the borders, there was a sudden influx of 'Russians' into north-eastern Turkey. First came the traders with an eye to a bargain, but they were soon followed by a flood of women who saw the potential for enriching themselves in Turkey's sexually conservative society.

Of course there's nothing new about prostitution in Turkey. Almost every town of any size has a *genelev* (brothel) on the outskirts where many a Turkish male has received his sexual initiation. It's a testimony to the popularity of these places that throughout the 1980s and early 1990s Turkey's single highest tax payer was Matild Manukyan, a Turkish-Armenian entrepreneur who, along with her fashion apparel enterprises, is also madam of a string of 32 brothels.

But brothels were always limited and tended to be contained to ghettos. The Russian women, in contrast, operate quite openly in the centre of towns, to such an extent, in fact, that it's increasingly hard to find a legitimate hotel in Trabzon, Rize, Pazar, Ardeşen, Hopa or Artvin.

With their bleach-blonde hair, halter-neck tops and mini skirts, the 'Natashas' – as they have been dubbed for obvious reasons – are virtual parodies of themselves. Venture into a *gazino* (nightclub) in any of the aforementioned towns and you'll see them in action, but don't expect to get away with your curiosity free of charge, especially if you're male.

Old-style Turkish brothels are controlled by the government and women working in them are required to undergo regular health checks. With the new-style arrangements, however, anything goes. Reliable *prezervatif* (condoms) are readily available in pharmacies but the Turkish male is no better known for his readiness to wear one than his counterparts elsewhere. The 'Natashas' therefore represent a very obvious way for AIDS to get its teeth into Turkey.

Apparently some 'Natashas' look upon their young and attractive years as the time to make good money and save it up for later. One such immigrant told a Turkish newspaper reporter that she had a husband and children back home, and when she saved up enough capital she'd return and open a shop.

The influx of the 'Natashas' has caused consternation among Turkish call girls who work (illegally) outside the brothels. In 1995 a Turkish newspaper ran a story on two Turkish prostitutes who had been arrested in İstanbul. They had bleached their hair and learned a few words of Russian. When asked why, they answered, 'Are you kidding? We can charge three or four times as much! Turkish men think Natashas are "exotic" and think they know how to do different things than we do.'

from Of county, set on wheel-like blocks to prevent mice from entering.

Atatürk Köşkü

The Atatürk Köşkü or Atatürk Villa ('Atatürk Pavilion' on some signs), accessible by city bus or dolmuş, is 5km south-west of Atatürk Alanı, above the town with a fine view and lovely gardens. The white villa was designed in a Black Sea style popular in the Crimea, and built between 1890 and 1903 for the wealthy Trabzon banking family, the Karayannidis.

The family gave it up when Atatürk visited the city in 1924 although he only actually visited Trabzon and stayed here on three brief occasions, the last time in 1937. When he died in 1938 the villa, and the rest of his estate, became national property. It's now a museum with bits of Atatürk memorabilia, primarily photos of the great man in his plus-fours. There is a nice tea garden surrounded by hydrangeas at the back.

The villa and its well-kept gardens are open every day from 9 am to 5 pm (7 pm in summer) for US$0.50. Take a city bus (US$0.30) or dolmuş from the lower (northern) side of Atatürk Alanı. Buses depart at 20 minutes past the hour, passing the Gülbahar Hatun Camii along the way, and arriving at the villa 25 minutes later.

Avrasya Pazarı

At Çömlekçi, due east of Atatürk Alanı at the bottom of the hill on the main highway, a line of bus shelters has been turned into an open-air market. Formerly known as the Russian Bazaar, it was founded years ago as a way to get peddlers from the former Soviet Union off Trabzon's narrow streets. It once boasted a marvellous array of unlikely items: chandeliers, military inflatable life rafts, decrepit power tools, antique jewellery – anything that could be transported for sale. In recent years, however, rechristened as the Eurasia Market, it has been taken over by local merchants who offer familiar, usual Turkish goods.

Sekiz Direkli Hamamı

The Sekiz Direkli (Eight-Pillared) Hamamı, near the Çarşı Camii off Maraş Caddesi, is among the city's most pleasant Turkish baths. The rough-hewn pillars are said to date from Seljuk times, although the 'rest' area has all mod cons. The bath is open daily for men; women get their turn on Thursday from 8 am to 5 pm. It costs US$3 to use the bath and US$1.50 more to be washed or massaged.

Places to Stay – Budget

Unfortunately, many of Trabzon's cheap hotels are filled with traders and prostitutes from the former Soviet republics, and with so much willing custom, there's little incentive to maintain standards.

Most of the cheapies are in the district called İskender Paşa Mahallesi, off the north-eastern corner of Atatürk Alanı on Güzelhisar Caddesi. Despite the semi-brothels, this area isn't really dangerous or threatening. At the time of writing the following hotels seemed to be 'Natasha'-free zones but the situation can easily change.

Hotel Anıl *(☎ 462-326 7282, Güzelhisar Caddesi 10)*, has a flashy lobby and fairly clean rooms with shower and TV for US$12/18 a single/double.

Hotel Gözde *(☎ 462-321 9579, Salih Yazıcı Sokak 7)*, just off Güzelhisar Caddesi, has a dingy lobby but better rooms for US$12 a double, with shower.

Hotel Toros *(☎ 462-321 1212, Gençoğlu Caddesi 3/A)*, behind the Hotel Horon, has clean if basic waterless rooms for US$5 per bed, or US$6.75 with private shower. If you need a single, have them write down the price so they don't charge for a double.

The aged ***Hotel Benli*** *(☎ 462-321 1022, Cami Çıkmazı 5)*, is just off the eastern end of Atatürk Alanı, uphill behind the Belediye. It's small, old and drab but has clean rooms which go for US$5/10 a single/double with sink, US$2 more with shower. Facing it is the newer ***Hotel Nur*** *(☎ 462-321 2798, fax 321 9576, Cami Sokak 4)*, where clean cell-like rooms cost US$16 with shower; the ones in the eaves have fine views.

Travellers are also welcome at the hostel of the ***Sankta Maria Katolik Kilisesi*** *(☎ 462-321 2192, Sümer Sokak 26)*, a few blocks downhill (north) from Atatürk Alanı. Built by French Capuchins in 1869 when Trabzon was a cosmopolitan trading port, the hostel offers clean simple rooms and the use of hot showers in exchange for a donation. You needn't be Catholic to stay here.

Places to Stay – Mid-Range

The two-star ***Hotel Özgür*** *(☎ 462-326 4703, fax 321 3952, Atatürk Alanı 29)*, has 45 rooms with bath and TV, most of which suffer from traffic noise, for US$30/40/50 a single/double/triple.

The similarly comfortable four-star ***Hotel Usta*** *(☎ 462-326 5700, fax 322 3793, Telgrafhane Sokak 1)*, across from the İskender Paşa Camii on the north-eastern corner of Atatürk Alanı in a fairly quiet yet convenient location, has 76 rooms with bath, TV and minibar for US$44/60 a single/double with

PETER PTSCHELINZEW

PAT YALE

TOM BROSNAHAN

Black Sea Coast Top Left: The Byzantine monastery of Sumela, perched on a sheer rock cliff. **Top Right:** Picturesque humpback bridges arch over the Fırtına Çayı on the way to Ayder in the Kaçkar Dağları. **Bottom:** The magnificent church of Aya Sofya in Trabzon is now a museum.

PETER PTSCHELINZEW

PAT YALE

Eastern Anatolia **Top:** The ruined fortress palace of İshak Paşa, near Doğubeyazıt, retains much of its impressive decoration. **Bottom:** Hosap Kalesi looms over the village of Güzelsu and the surrounding countryside.

breakfast included. If they're not busy, you'll get a discount, perhaps 25% off the posted rates.

Perhaps the best bet is the newly renovated, fairly quiet, two-star ***Otel Horon*** *(☎ 462-326 6455, fax 321 6628, Sıra Mağazalar Caddesi 125)*, with comfortable modern rooms for US$30/40 a single/double.

Places to Stay – Top End

Trabzon's five-star hotel is ***Grand Hotel Zorlu*** *(☎ 462-326 8400, fax 326 8458, Maraş Caddesi 9)*, opened in 1997, charging US$100/130 for a standard room, US$125/155 for an 'executive' room, more for suites. It has all the luxuries, from health club to indoor swimming pool.

Places to Eat

On the southern side of Atatürk Alanı, ***Çınar Lokantası*** is reliably good and cheap, with prices posted prominently and a good selection of ready meals, best eaten fresh at lunch time. The neighbouring ***İnan Kebap Salonu*** is good as well. ***McDonald's*** is here too.

Seyitoğlu Lahmacun, just over a block west of Atatürk Alanı along Uzun Yol, serves good, cheap lahmacun, and is friendly to both men and women. Likewise ***Çardak Pide Salonu*** across the street, directly behind the Turkish Airlines building in a vine-shaded courtyard away from the traffic noise. Freshly baked pide costs US$1.50 to US$2.

Nil Restaurant on the corner of Maraş Caddesi and Gazipaşa Caddesi does good food but without the views.

Ak Piliç Tavuk Bar on the northern side of Atatürk Alanı specialises in grilled chicken. A 100g portion of chicken döner kebap costs US$1.25, a half-chicken costs only US$2.

Derya Restaurant, across from the Belediye on the north-eastern corner of Atatürk Alanı, has a good selection of ready food and serves a tasty İskender kebap (US$2.50). Look also for the ***Volkan 2 Lokantası*** a few steps to the west. Close by is ***Tad Pizza ve Hamburger***, a reasonable approximation to a US-style pizza parlour. Pizzas cost from US$3 to US$6, burgers less than half that, but if you want the bun toasted you may have to ask.

Meydan Kebap Salonu, also nearby, is bright, hectic, crowded, cheap and noisy – a real human fuel-stop – with full meals for less than US$4. The waiters are very tip-hungry, though.

On the eastern side of the square ***Kıbrıs Restaurant*** has a small dining room at street level and a bigger one upstairs. Dishes include the Turkish classics, and a meal with a beer might cost from US$6 or US$8, more if you have fish. Further up this side ***Palmiye Pasta Salonu*** sells excellent *Laz böreği*, flaky pastry sandwiched with confectioner's custard and sprinkled with icing sugar for US$1.

Uzun Yol has a number of shops selling hazelnuts, helva, lokum and pestil for those with a sweet tooth. Try ***Mevlana Kuruyemiş*** at No 31, four shops west of Seyitoğlu Lahmacun.

You can't keep a 'Natasha' from her potatoes and cabbage. Accordingly, down a few steps on the northern side of Güzelhisar Caddesi you'll find ***Hisar Kafeterya*** which serves a range of 'Russian' cuisine at moderate prices.

If you want a beer without a meal, Trabzon boasts a number of basement ***gazinos*** (Turkish nightclubs) of varying degrees of seediness. If you want a glimpse of a side of Turkey the tourist offices keep very quiet about, these could prove illuminating, and sometimes action-packed. Lone women would be unwise to go near them.

Getting There & Away

Transport to and from Trabzon is easy by bus, air and sea.

Air Turkish Airlines has several daily nonstop flights between Trabzon and Ankara and İstanbul. The Turkish Airlines office (☎ 462-321 1680) is on the south-western corner of Atatürk Alanı. Dolmuşes for the airport, 5.5km east of Atatürk Alanı, leave from near the Hotel Toros.

İstanbul Airlines also flies twice daily nonstop between İstanbul and Trabzon for

US$75. Its office (☎ 462-321 1367 or 325 8026, at the airport) is on the north-western corner of Atatürk Alanı at Kazazoğlu Sokak 9, Sanat İş Hanı, above the Mercedes showroom.

Bus Trabzon's otogar, 3km east of the port, is served by buses and dolmuşes running along the coastal road and up to Atatürk Alanı (take the Route 42 dolmuş to 'Garajlar' from opposite the Ulusoy terminal uphill from Atatürk Alanı on Taksim Caddesi.) The otogar has a left-luggage area, post office, restaurant, cafeteria, barber and simple shops.

Details of some daily services follow:

- Ankara – 780km, 12 hours, US$18 to US$20; frequent buses
- Artvin – 255km, 4½ hours, US$10; occasional buses
- Erzurum – 325km, six hours, US$10; several buses
- Hopa – 165km, three hours, US$2.50; half-hourly buses
- İstanbul – 1110km, 18 hours, US$24 to US$32; several buses
- Kars – 525km, 12 hours, US$19; change at Erzurum or Artvin
- Kayseri – 686km, 12 hours, US$22; several buses
- Rize – 75km, one hour, US$2; shuttle dolmuşes
- Samsun – 365km, six hours, US$9; frequent buses
- Van – 745km, 17 hours, US$22; a few buses, direct or via Erzurum

Boat Karden Line (☎ 462-322 5432, fax 326 1401), İskele Caddesi 55, down by the harbour, operates ferries between Trabzon and Sochi in Russia. Boats leave Trabzon on Monday and Thursday at 6 pm and return from Sochi on Tuesday and Friday at 6 pm. Cabin tickets (US$60) are available from Karden, Navi Tour (☎ 462-326 4484), İskele Caddesi Belediye Dükkanları, or from other travel agencies such as Afacan Tur. You probably need a Russian visa obtained in your home country to use this service, however. Check with the Russian Consulate (see Information earlier). For details on the Turkish Maritime Lines' İstanbul-Trabzon-Rize car ferry service, see the Getting Around chapter.

Getting Around

To/From the Airport The airport bus (US$1) leaves the Turkish Airlines office at the south-western corner of Atatürk Alanı for the airport 90 minutes before each scheduled Turkish Airlines flight. You can also take a Havaalanı ('Airport') dolmuş from a side street on the northern side of Atatürk Alanı, near the Toros Hotel.

Bus To reach Atatürk Alanı from the otogar, cross the shore road in front of the terminal, turn left, walk to the bus stop and catch any bus with 'Park' in its name; the dolmuş for Atatürk Alanı is marked 'Garajlar-Meydan'. A taxi between the otogar and Atatürk Alanı costs less than US$4.

Getting to the otogar, the easiest way is to catch a dolmuş marked 'Garajlar' from the north-eastern side of Atatürk Alanı.

Dolmuş The dolmuşes depart from Atatürk Alanı will take you to most sights. Route descriptions are included with the previously mentioned sightseeing information. Regardless of where you're going, the fare should be about US$0.30.

Away from Atatürk Alanı beware of dolmuş drivers who suddenly claim they're driving private taxis. If the vehicle has 'taksi' written on the roof, it's a taxi; if it has a named destination, it's a dolmuş and that should be the end of it.

AROUND TRABZON

Sumela Manastırı

The Greek Orthodox Monastery of the Virgin Mary at Sumela, 46km south of Trabzon, was founded in Byzantine times and abandoned in 1923 after the creation of the Turkish Republic put paid to hopes of creating a new Greek state in this region. The monastery clings to a sheer rock wall high above evergreen forests and a rushing mountain stream. It's a mysterious, eerie place, especially when mists swirl among the tops of the trees in the valley below.

If you want good photographs, come as early in the morning as possible. Note that on Wednesday, when the ferry from İstanbul arrives in Trabzon, Sumela is crowded with cruise passengers. It's very busy over summer weekends too.

You reach Sumela via the Erzurum road. At Maçka, 29km south of Trabzon, turn left for Sumela (16km), also signposted as Meryemana, because the monastery was dedicated to the Virgin Mary.

About 3.5km from Maçka (12.5km from Sumela) is ***Sumela Camping***, a stream-side camping ground. Another 2.5km takes you through Coşandere village, where there's an old Ottoman humpback bridge and more camping possibilities in the grounds of the ***Coşandere Restaurant***. *Canlı alabalık* (live trout) is a popular menu item.

The road then winds into dense evergreen forests, following the course of a rushing mountain stream interrupted by commercial trout pools. Peasant houses looking like those in alpine central Europe are interspersed with more modern brick-built blocks. The road is subject to landslides, and may be impassable after heavy rains.

At the entrance to Altindere National Park you pay an admission fee of US$2 (half price for students) to visit the monastery. Opening hours vary with the amount of daylight, but are generally between 9 am and 6 pm.

At the end of the road you'll find a shady park with picnic tables and fireplaces by a roaring brook, a post office, a ***restaurant*** and several A-frame shelters for rent. (No camping is allowed in the park.)

The head of the trail up to the monastery begins in the picnic area. This trail is steep but easy to follow, and is the one most people use.

A second trail begins further up the valley. To get to it, follow the unpaved road 1km uphill and across two bridges (after the second one turn and look up for a good view of the monastery) until you come to a wooden footbridge over the stream on the right, marked by a sign reading 'Manastıra gider' ('To the Monastery'). This trail cuts straight up through the trees, past another small, abandoned church, and on busy days is likely to be much quieter than the one pointed out by the guides.

If you drive up the road even further, you can ultimately reach a small muddy parking lot from which it's only a five or 10-minute walk to the monastery.

As you climb through forests and alpine meadows, catching occasional glimpses of the monastery above you, the air gets noticeably cooler. In all you'll ascend 250m in about 30 to 45 minutes (if you're in moderately good shape). In autumn just before the snow arrives, a beautiful sort of crocus, called *kar çiçeği* (snowflower) blooms in the meadows.

The various chapels and rooms are mere shells or facades but have a good deal of fine **fresco painting**. The earliest examples of the art are from the 9th century, but virtually all of what you see was done in the 19th century. Many of the paintings are worse for wear, as bored shepherd boys used them as targets for pebble attacks and visitors scratched their names into them. Grafitti identifies many of the vandals, who scratched their names as though proud of their witlessness. In recent years, antiquity thieves have also been a problem.

Restoration work on the monastery will continue for years. A ***teahouse*** provides refreshments.

Places to Stay You can stay in one of the five little A-frame ***bungalows*** above the parking lot at Sumela if you reserve in advance through the Orman Genel Müdürlüğü (Directorate-General of Forests) in Trabzon. They sleep four persons, and rent for US$10 per night.

Getting There & Away In the summer, Ulusoy runs buses from Trabzon to Sumela, departing at 10 am (returning at 3 pm) from the town-centre terminal just uphill from Atatürk Alanı (40 minutes, US$4).

Dolmuşes (US$3) depart from the Çömlekçi dolmuş ranks down on the coastal highway next to the Avrasya Pazarı all day for Coşandere village. They often go as far as Sumela, or you can pay them to do so.

Afacan Tur (☎ 462-321 5804, fax 321 7001), İskele Caddesi 40/C, and other agencies run daily tours to Sumela, departing at 10 am. They charge US$7 per person for transport and a cursory guided tour but tend to hustle visitors back down from the monastery and leave them at the restaurant for two hours. Perhaps the best thing to do is to check the time of the return journey and then let the guide know you can manage without them.

Taxis leaving from opposite the Hotel Özgür in Atatürk Alanı charge US$25 to US$30 for a carload of people there and back, with two hours of waiting time.

TRABZON TO ERZURUM

Heading south into the mountains, you're in for a long (325km) but scenic ride.

Carrying Liquids

The atmospheric pressure at sea level is much greater than it will be in the mountains. If you have a full water bottle in your pack at Trabzon, it will have burst or at least leaked by the time you reach Gümüşhane. If you're descending to Trabzon from Erzurum, your water bottle will collapse and leak due to the increase in pressure as you descend. It's best to carry liquid-filled containers with you as hand luggage and adjust the pressure as you travel.

Sights En Route

Along the highway south, you zoom straight to Maçka, 35km inland from Trabzon. About 1.5km north of Maçka the road tunnels straight through a dramatic rock formation of basaltic columns resembling California's Devil's Postpile or Northern Ireland's Giant's Causeway; you may just catch a glimpse of it before disappearing into the dark. From Maçka, you begin the long, slow climb along a serpentine mountain road through active landslide zones to the breathtaking **Zigana Geçidi** (Zigana Pass) at an altitude of 2030m. The landscape is one of sinuous valleys and cool pine forests with dramatic light. Just before the pass there's a small ***restaurant***, ***grocery*** and holiday village.

The dense, humid air of the coast disappears as you rise and becomes light and dry as you reach the southern side of the **Doğu Karadeniz Dağları** (Eastern Black Sea Mountains). Along with the landscape, the towns and villages change: Black Sea towns look vaguely Balkan, while places higher up appear much more Central Asian. Snow can be seen in all months except perhaps July, August and September.

Gümüşhane, about 125km south of Trabzon, is a small town in a mountain valley with a few simple travellers services, but not much to stop for except the scenery.

By the time you reach the provincial capital of **Bayburt**, 195km from Trabzon, you are well into the rolling steppe and low mountains of the high Anatolian Plateau. A dry, desolate place, Bayburt has a big **medieval fortress** and simple travellers services. The road from Bayburt passes through green, rolling farm country with stands of poplar trees and flocks of brown-fleeced sheep. Wayside stalls sell locally made *pestil*, sun-dried fruit pressed into sheets. In early summer wild flowers are everywhere.

Exactly 80km west of Erzurum is the **Kop Geçidi** (Kop Pass) at an altitude of 2370m. A **monument** here commemorates the countless Turkish soldiers who lost their lives fighting for this pass under the most dire conditions during the War of Independence.

From Kop Pass, the open road to Erzurum offers fast, easy travelling.

EAST FROM TRABZON

Uzungöl

About 56km east of Trabzon is the town called Of. Go south 25km up the Solaklı creek valley past the town of Çaykara, then another 16km along a rough road to Uzungöl (Long Lake, altitude 1100m) to enjoy the mountain air and perhaps hike in the countryside.

Uzungöl is a popular destination for local people on weekend outings, so try and come midweek if you want to stay. In Uzungöl village right beside the lake is ***Özkan Otel ve Restoran*** *(☎ 462-656 6197)*, a simple place with rooms for US$10/18 a single/double. The more basic ***Uzungöl Pansiyon*** *(☎ 462-656 6129)* is even closer to the water. Beyond the actual lake, ***Sezgin Motel*** *(☎ 462-656 6175)* charges US$10 per person for room, breakfast and dinner in pine cabins, with trout from the adjacent fish farm served up in the restaurant. ***İnan Kardeşler Tesisleri*** *(☎ 462-656 6021)* charges much the same and serves simple but delicious meals of local trout for around US$10.

At weekends you may be able to get a dolmuş direct from Trabzon to Uzungöl. Failing that, take a Rize-bound dolmuş to Of and then wait for another heading inland. Afacan Tur (☎ 462-321 5804) at İskele Caddesi 40/C in Trabzon runs tours (US$11) to Uzungöl every Saturday departing at 9 am. They're popular with locals but tend to focus more on lunch at the Sezgin than on seeing the best of the scenery.

Rize

About 75km east of Trabzon, Rize (REE-zeh, population 54,000) is at the heart of Turkey's tea plantation area. Like most Black Sea towns, its architecture is mostly concrete but the steep hillsides above the town are thickly planted with tea bushes. The tea is cured, dried and blended here, then shipped throughout the country.

Arriving by boat in Rize, turn right at the harbour gate to walk into town (about 1km), or flag down a dolmuş.

Rize's main sight is the **Çay Araştırma Enstitüsü** (Tea Research Institute), 800m above town via the steep, sticky road behind the central mosque. Keep walking up until you come to a crossroads, then take the turn to the right that doubles back above you and keep climbing. A taxi from outside the mosque will run you there for US$1. The institute's grounds are a ***tea garden*** set amid hollyhocks, roses and hydrangeas. The views are great, the tea even better. In summer you can sit out here until 10.30 pm.

Places to Stay There are plenty of reasonably priced hotels although many double as brothels.

One of the cheapest is ***Otel Akarsu*** above a kebap shop near the Şehir hamam; clean, simple bathless rooms cost about US$5 per person. Up a notch, ***Otel Efes*** *(☎ 464-214 1111)*, in Atatürk Caddesi, has clean twins with bath for US$30.

For two-star comfort, try ***Hotel Çay*** *(☎ 464-213 1698)* near the Russian bazaar or ***Otel Keleş*** *(☎ 464-217 4612, fax 217 1895)* in Palandöken Caddesi for US$20/30 a single/double.

The four-star, 82 room ***Hotel Dedeman Rize*** *(☎ 464-223 5344, fax 223 5347)*, Alipaşa Köyü, on the western outskirts, has all the usual mod cons and prices to match.

Places to Eat There are plenty of simple kebap and pide places along Cumhuriyet Caddesi. ***Mis Kebap*** and ***Bekiroğlu Pide ve Kebap*** are particularly good, at US$3.50 for a full meal. For something classier try ***Muzë Kafeterya*** in a restored Ottoman building up the hill behind the main post office.

Getting There & Away The bus company ticket offices are on Cumhuriyet Caddesi. Minibuses to Trabzon (one hour, US$2) leave from out on the main highway to the west, those to Hopa (one hour, US$2) further to the east. The harbour for boats to İstanbul is even further west.

KAÇKAR DAĞLARI

The Kaçkar Dağları is a mountain range in the north-east of Turkey with its highest point at **Mt Kaçkar** (3937m). The Kaçkars are increasingly popular for organised trekking trips of anything from one to 10 days. Provided you bring a tent, sleeping bag and good shoes you could even spend a month exploring the mountains and alpine summer villages *(yaylalar)*. If you want to arrange a tour, a good person to talk to would be Adnan Pirikoğlu at the ***Pirikoğlu Aile Lokantası*** in Ayder or you can phone ☎ 464-657 2021 or ☎ 464-655 5084.

The Mountains of Turkey by Karl Smith (Cicerone Press, www.bookweb.co.uk/cicerone/home.html) has detailed information on hiking in the Kaçkar Dağları.

A local trekking company with trips over the top of the Kaçkar Dağları between Erzurum and Trabzon, and into Georgia, is Ritur (☎ 464-217 1484, fax 217 1486, email i.h.yildiz@ihlas.net.tr), Cumhuriyet Caddesi 93, 53100 Rize. Most treks can begin in İstanbul.

Çamlıhemşin

About 40km east of Rize (124km east of Trabzon), just within the western limits of Ardeşen, a road on the right is signposted for Çamlıhemşin (20km), a village deep in the Kaçkar mountains. As you ascend into the mountains, you'll pass several absurdly picturesque ancient humpback bridges across the Fırtına Çayi.

Çamlıhemşin has one basic hotel, ***Otel Hoşdere** (☎ 464-651 7107)*, where the rooms are nothing much to write home about, even for US$5 per person. Still, if you're arriving in Ayder on a summer Saturday it's worth knowing if everything else there is full.

The ***restaurant*** is a much better bet, with a wooden terrace over the river at the back which is popular with tour groups. Here it's worth sampling a Black Sea delicacy, *mıhlama*, a sort of melted cheese soup eaten with thick corn bread. The trout, baked in butter with tomatoes and onions for US$4, is excellent.

Just beyond Çamlıhemşin the road forks and you'll have to decide whether to bear right (signposted 'Zil Kalesi') for Şenyuva or left (signposted 'Ayder Kaplıcaları') for Ayder.

Şenyuva

Şenyuva is beautiful, but has limited public transport. You may have to walk to and from Camlıhemşin, or catch a taxi for about US$4 each way.

About 5km from Camlıhemşin you'll find ***Otel Doğa** (☎ 464-651 7455)* run by İdris Duman who speaks French and English. Some of the simple rooms here have balconies overlooking the river, and there are two suites for up to six people, one with a double balcony. Beds cost US$6 each. Meals are served.

Another 2km along the road, reached by a chairlift across the river, is ***Sisi Pansiyon** (☎ 464-653 3043)*, operated by Doris Güney, who organises treks into the nearby mountains. Beds in A-frame bungalows will set you back US$16, or use your own tent for much less. There are meals here too.

From Şenyuva the road continues past the ruins of Zilkale castle to **Çat** (1250m), a mountain hamlet used as a trekking base. There's one small hotel there, the ***Cancık***.

Ayder

From Camlıhemşin to Ayder (17km), turn left and cross a modern bridge, following the sign for Ayder Kaplıcaları. The road, imperilled by rockslides, winds steadily uphill, crossing and re-crossing the stream, passing small trout farms until finally reaching Ayder (1300m), a high-pasture *yayla* (village) with two *kaplıcalar* (hot springs).

Surrounded by the glory of nature, Ayder was once a picturesque village of farmers, herders and foresters, some of whom tended the hot spring baths. They lived in rustic wood cabins perched on the steep emerald-green mountainside. When tourists arrived in force to enjoy Ayder's natural charms, locals began building hotels to accommodate them. They used concrete, which is cheap, versatile, durable and efficient, and lends itself to the comforts which city folk require. But the locals' fondness for concrete was not shared by the visitors from the city for whom concrete was all too familiar, so now it is forbidden to build city-type structures here. New buildings must be in the 'traditional style', which means sheathed in wood. The lavish new wood villas topped by satellite TV dishes are hardly traditional in Ayder, but they suit city tastes, so no one complains.

Ironically, lots of those building villas are Ayderlis who return for sentimental reasons, having made their fortunes in Ankara, İstanbul and İzmir.

In August the village can hardly cope with the flood of local tourists, especially at weekends when, despite the growing number of hotels, most places will be full by mid-afternoon.

Orientation About 4.5km below Ayder is a gate where you must pay an admission fee of US$1.50.

The village is scattered for 2km on both sides of the road, which is being driven ever further up into the mountains.

Things to See & Do You've come for the wonderful scenery, treks in the mountains and soaks in the **kaplıcalar**. The hot water reaches temperatures of 56°C (133°F) and is said to be good for ulcers, skin complaints, cuts and allergies. There are separate sections for men and women, open daily from 7 am to 6 pm (8 pm in summer). A session in a general bath costs US$2; private family pools cost US$7 per hour; children under seven are allowed to bathe for free.

Hemşin culture is at its height on summer weekends. Wander into the meadow south of Ayder to see groups of Hemşin holidaymakers dancing a conga-like dance to the whining rhythm of the *tulum*, a bagpipe made out of a goatskin. Everywhere you will see women in their splendid head-dresses, incongruously topping off cardigans, long skirts and trainers!

Places to Stay All of Ayder's hotels are pretty basic. Beds in waterless rooms usually cost between US$5 and US$7 in summer but at other times you can virtually name your price.

Coming in from the north, the first place you come to on the left is ***Otel Ayder*** *(☎ 464-657 2039)*, with clean, simple rooms, some with nice views, well away from the village-centre traffic jams. There's a ***restaurant*** downstairs. ***Fora Pansiyon*** uphill behind it, is even quieter, with better views.

Next on the left is ***Otel Pirikoğlu*** *(☎ 464-657 2021)* with pine beds in clean rooms. There's a kitchen for guests to use, and more pleasant mountain views.

A sign on the right points to a brick eyesore which is actually one of the better choices, ***Otel Yeşil Vadi*** *(☎ 464-657 5051)*, where clean, simple rooms are more spacious than usual. The roof terrace is a good vantage point for studying Ayder.

Back on the main street ***Otel Merkez*** *(☎ 464-657 2022)* is as basic (and cheap) as they come but the toilets are smelly and the rooms are like cells.

Ayder's most visually distinguished hotel is ***Hotel Saray*** *(☎ 464-657 2001, fax 657 2002)*, on the left on a bluff. Inside, however, it's not much different from the others and the fact that the rooms open off a central area with TV could mean noisy nights.

Don't let ***Ayder Hilton Hotel's*** *(☎ 464-657 2024)* name fool you. There's nothing remotely luxurious about this place, a large, prominent, ugly but serviceable building.

Turn right behind the Hilton and ascend the steps beside the baths. There are a few more places down here, including ***Hotel Kervansaray*** *(☎ 464-657 2027)*, ***Hotel Altıparmak*** *(☎ 464-657 2052)* and ***Otel Cihan*** (☎ 464-657 2087), but the proximity of the mosque means they're unlikely to be quiet choices.

A path running up beside the Yıldırım Kafeteryası leads to ***Hotel Kaçkar*** *(☎ 464-657 2041)* and yet more clean but simple rooms. The Hemşin women who run this place are a lot of fun but the washing facilities are pretty rudimentary. There are a couple of single rooms if you arrive late and the other places want to charge you for two beds.

Finally, continue past the baths and you'll come to ***Otel Çağlayan*** *(☎ 464-657 2073)*, a family run place in a wooden building on the right. Here, at least, you'll get a quiet night.

Places to Eat Beside the ford are two prominent eating places: ***Nazlı Çiçek*** and ***Otel Saray Et ve Balık Restoran***. The Nazlı specialises in trout and there are big tanks of fish by the entrance; two fish, some rice and a nonalcoholic drink will cost about US$4. For breakfast, they will rustle you up a pair of delicious fried eggs, with bread, cheese and a large tea for about US$1.50. The Saray restaurant serves alcohol and has a central grill where you can watch your köfte being prepared.

Another place to try for breakfast is ***Yıldırım Kafeteryası***, 1700m up the road from the village entrance, which serves bread, honey, olives and vintage cheese at tables enjoying the best views.

Getting There & Away In summer dolmuşes make hourly runs between Pazar on the coast and Çamlıhemşin, in some cases continuing to Ayder. On summer Sundays the trickle of minibuses up to Ayder turns into a flood. Otherwise, passengers are mostly shoppers from the villages, so dolmuşes descend from the mountain villages in the morning and return from Pazar in early afternoon. One bus a day travels direct to Trabzon from Ayder, leaving at 4 pm.

Note that space in the minibuses can be reserved, so if you want to leave on a weekend or on a Monday morning you'd do well to buy your ticket in advance from the Ayder Turizm booth.

HOPA

The easternmost of Turkey's Black Sea ports is Hopa (population 18,000), 165km east of Trabzon. During the Soviet period Hopa was a sleepy backwater, but since the collapse of the Soviet Union and the opening of the Georgian border at Sarp, 30km to the east, Hopa has sprung to life to serve the army of traders and truckers who parade through night and day. The most prominent feature of Hopa's topography is the highway.

Hopa provides what any army needs: places to change money, to sleep, to get fuel, to get food and to get laid. In the budget range, the places to sleep and to get laid are usually the same. Unfortunately sleep tends to suffer. The PTT is at the centre of the town.

Places to Stay & Eat

Most of Hopa's hotels are on the eastern side of the Sundura Çayı stream along the waterfront street called Orta Hopa Caddesi, but they're usually filled with truckers and traders, and suffer from constant truck noise.

The best cheapie that's not a brothel is the drab ***Otel Huzur*** *(☎ 466-351 4095, Cumhuriyet Caddesi 25)* with waterless doubles for US$8, with shower for US$12.

Otel Cihan (jee-HAHN) *(☎ 466-351 4897, fax 351 4898, Orta Hopa Caddesi 5)*, has clean, comfortable modern rooms for US$14/20 a single/double with private shower and TV. Recent refurbishment of the ground floor public rooms may result in a rise in prices.

Just east of the river is ***Otel Ustabaş*** *(☎ 466-351 5784, fax 351 5220)*, with presentable rooms with private facilities for US$18/24 a single/double, breakfast included.

The best in town is actually 700m out of town to the west: the three-star ***Hotel Terzioğlu*** *(☎ 466-351 5111, fax 351 5115)*, charging US$30/40 for comfortable rooms with shower, TV and breakfast. Handy safe deposit boxes right at the reception desk hold your firearms while you're in the building.

For meals, try ***Ustabaş Pide ve Kebap Salonu, Huzur Pide*** and ***Ufuk Lokantası ve Pide Salonu***, all just east of the river near Otel Ustabaş.

Getting There & Away

Direct buses from Hopa to Erzurum depart early in the morning. If you miss the direct bus, you can catch a later one to Artvin (1½ hours, US$2), then an onward bus from Artvin. There are also regular minibuses to Rize and Trabzon (US$2 and US$4 respectively), as well as frequent minibuses for Sarp (US$2) and the Georgian border.

To/From Georgia First, get a Georgian visa from the consulate in Trabzon (see Information in the earlier Trabzon section).

At 7 pm a bus leaves from beside the Avrasya Pazarı in Trabzon to the Georgian seaside resort of Batumi, getting you to your destination in the middle of the night. As the bus is full of Georgian traders with bales of goods, customs inspection can take forever. A cheaper, easier way is to take a minibus to Hopa, then a dolmuş to the border at Sarp. This part of the journey should cost about US$6.

Walk across the border. You can probably ignore half-hearted demands for dollars from the Georgian customs officials; or ask for an official receipt.

On the other side of the border, taxis will be waiting to run you the 15km to Batumi for US$12 to US$15. Ask to be dropped near the train station. There is a small 'hotel' (really a family house with a few spare beds) nearby where you can stay for another US$4.

Only masochists catch the train to Tbilisi (two to three days without electricity for lighting) but there are daily buses which do the run in eight hours for about US$5. Before setting out, though, it would be wise to check the current political situation.

Leaving Georgia to return to Turkey is more tricky. If you take a taxi back to the border and arrive alone you are at the mercy of the avaricious customs officers. On the other hand if you take the bus for collective protection, the bureaucracy involved can result in a four-hour delay.

On the Turkish side of the border they may demand that you buy a new visa. Check to see if 'Multiple Entry' is printed on your visa stamp. If so, you should not have to pay unless you've exceeded your three-month stay.

Eastern Anatolia

Eastern Turkey is a land of adventure where each event of the day seems to take on the character of some fabled happening. You might go to bed at night disappointed because Mt Ararat was covered in cloud. Early next morning the mountain will take you by surprise, intruding into your consciousness, shining in the sun outside your hotel window. Or you might be riding along a rough road and suddenly come upon the ruins of a medieval castle, not marked on any map, not described in any guidebook. Every day reveals some new notion of epic events.

The east is not as well developed as western Turkey. Instead of grain-harvesting machinery, you might come across farmers threshing and winnowing in the ancient manner.

The people are no less friendly than in other parts of Turkey but they are often more reticent and not, generally speaking, used to seeing and dealing with foreigners (except in the hotels and tourist offices). It may take a little more time for the friendliness of the adults to emerge, but not so with the children. Every single one will have to find out where you come from and what language you speak.

When travelling, be prepared for the distances. You may ride for hours to get from one town to the next. When you get to that town, there may not be many hotels to choose from. And the one you want – particularly if it's the best in town – may be fully booked. Travelling in eastern Turkey is certainly not as comfortable as it is in the west. But if you are adaptable and out for adventure, this is the place to find it.

HIGHLIGHTS

- Getting lost in the Ottoman-era bazaars of Şanlıurfa
- Exploring the Seljuk buildings of Sivas, Divriği and Erzurum
- Driving through the Georgian valleys
- White-water rafting out of Yusufeli
- Visiting the İshak Paşa Sarayı in Doğubeyazıt
- Hiking around the ruins of Ani
- Being invited into one of Harran's ancient beehive mud houses
- Gazing at the sunset among the colossal statues atop Nemrut Dağı
- Getting an early morning view of snow-capped Mt Ararat

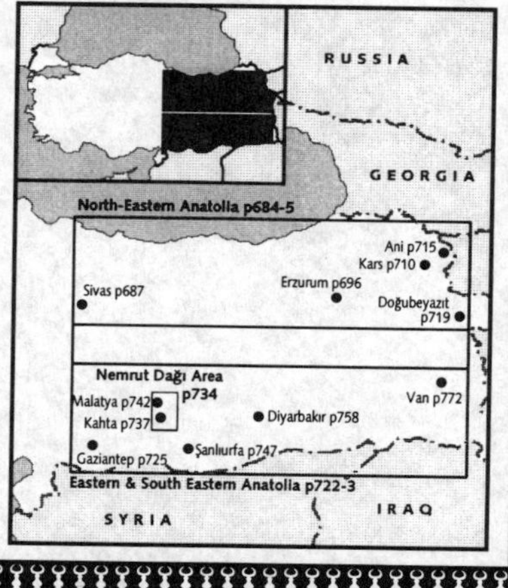

Getting There & Away

Buses, as always, go everywhere; there are even direct buses to İstanbul from most large eastern cities such as Erzurum, Van and Diyarbakır. Though there are some trains, they're usually not as comfortable nor as fast as the buses.

Many visitors spare themselves the agony (and in the case of some smaller and less reliable bus companies, the danger) of a long bus ride to the east by flying to a major eastern city and bussing from there. The flight from İstanbul to Erzurum costs about US$110.

> **WARNING**
>
> When this guidebook went to press, the Kurdish insurgency continued in portions of eastern Turkey. It's still possible to travel to most towns in the region, and as the insurgency dies down (as seems to be happening), more of the region will become safe for travel. The last kidnappings of foreigners occurred in 1994, although it's hard to know whether that's because of better security or because there are fewer travellers about to kidnap. For now, travellers to the east should scrupulously observe the following rules:
>
> - Contact your embassy or consulate in advance, ask about current conditions, tell them your plans and ask their advice. The British Foreign and Commonwealth Office has a hotline for travellers giving their most up-to-date advice. You can access it on ☎ 0171-238 4503, after 22 April 2000 ☎ 020-7238 4503 or on www.fco.gov.uk/travel/countryadvice.asp.
>
> - Travel only during daylight, only on major highways (or preferably by air) and restrict your stops to major cities, towns and sites. Transport stops early in the day in the south-eastern corner bordered by Doğubeyazıt, Elazığ and Diyarbakır.
>
> Frequent military checkpoints are a fact of life east of Malatya. In most cases the soldiers pay little attention to foreigners, although they'll probably want to see your passport and visa.

Air Turkish Airlines (THY) flies between İstanbul/Ankara and Ağrı, Batman, Diyarbakır, Elazığ, Erzincan, Erzurum, Gaziantep, Kahramanmaraş, Kars, Malatya, Muş, Şanlıurfa, Siirt, Sivas, Trabzon and Van, but not every city has daily flights.

İstanbul Airlines has flights from İstanbul to Erzurum, Gaziantep, Kars and Trabzon several times weekly. Check with the airline for schedules.

Bus Services to and from Ankara are frequent. Routes running east-west are generally not a problem, but north-south services can be infrequent, so allow plenty of time and, upon arrival, check schedules for departures to your next destination.

Train From Ankara via Kayseri there are three major eastern rail destinations: Erzurum and Kars, Kurtalan/Diyarbakır and Tatvan/Van. When military and political conditions permit, the Van line goes on to Iran, with a connection to Tabriz and Tehran. South of Elazığ, this line branches for Diyarbakır and Kurtalan.

For information on trains serving these routes, see the earlier Getting Around chapter.

Getting Around

The eastern mountains and high plateau are subject to long and severe winters. We don't recommend travelling in north-eastern and central-eastern Turkey except from May to mid-October and preferably in July and August. (South-eastern Turkey, however, is mild and pleasant in the winter.) If you go in May or September/October, be prepared for some chilly nights. A trip to the summit of Nemrut Dağı (2150m) should not be planned for early morning except in July and August. In other months the summit will be cold at any time and bitterly cold in early morning. There may be snow.

Most visitors touring this part of the country make a loop through it, starting from Amasya, Tokat, Kayseri, Trabzon, Adana or Antakya. Such a trip might follow one of the following itineraries.

From Amasya, Tokat or Kayseri, head via Sivas and Malatya to Adıyaman, then Kahta to see Nemrut Dağı, then either north-east to Erzurum, Doğubeyazıt, Kars and Artvin, or south to Şanlıurfa, and Mardin to Diyarbakır for its ancient walls and mosques.

Starting from Adana or Antakya, go to Adıyaman and Kahta via Gaziantep. After seeing Nemrut Dağı, head south to Şanlıurfa, east to Mardin and north to Diyarbakır.

From Diyarbakır, head east through Bitlis and around the southern shore of Van Gölü (Lake Van), stopping to see the Church of the Holy Cross on the island of Akdamar, before reaching the city of Van. Then head north to Ağrı and east to Doğubeyazıt to see Mt Ararat and also the İshak Paşa Sarayı, the dramatic Palace of İshak Pasha.

From Doğubeyazıt head north to Kars to see the ruins of Ani, then to Erzurum. At Erzurum you can catch a plane westward, or toil through the mountains to Artvin, or head for the Black Sea coast at Trabzon, or start the return journey westward to Sivas and Ankara. This itinerary, from Kayseri or Adana-Van-Kars-Erzurum-Sivas covers about 2500km and would take an absolute minimum of 10 days to complete by bus and/or train. It's better to take two weeks or more.

Car Special warnings are necessary for those driving in the east. Fuel stations are fewer, roads can be significantly worse, and Kurdish separatist activity and the army's reaction to it must be taken into account.

Fill your fuel tank before setting out, carry bottled water and snacks and expect the ride to be longer than you think. Do most of your travelling in the earlier part of the day, reaching your destination by mid-afternoon. Avoid driving in the evening or at night. In some areas curfews are in operation anyway.

Roads in the extreme east of the country and particularly in the north-east, are often riddled with potholes which break tyres and dent rims if hit at speed. When filled with rainwater it is impossible to judge the depth or damage capacity of the potholes. They occur at random in otherwise smooth roads and necessitate slow driving even on good stretches.

The good news is that if you damage a tyre, even to the extent of gashing the sidewall open, a good Turkish *lastikçi* (tyre

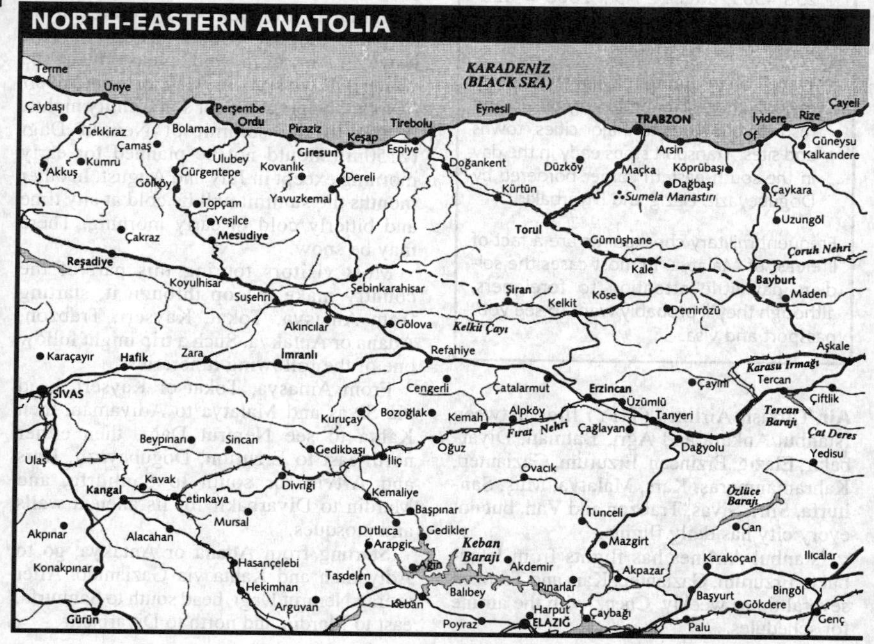

repairer) can probably fix it – unbelievable, but true.

As long as the Kurdish separatist unrest continues in the south-east there will be numerous military and police roadblocks. When you approach a roadblock, slow down and be sure you interpret the soldiers' signals correctly (a red sign reading 'DUR' means stop, a green one reading 'GEÇ' means go). If there's the slightest doubt about the signal, stop. If you misinterpret a signal and unintentionally run a roadblock, there may be serious consequences.

North-Eastern Anatolia

Mountainous and remote from the cosmopolitan atmosphere of Ankara and İstanbul, north-eastern Anatolia is a large slice of the 'real' Turkey, relatively unchanged by the tourist flood which swept over the western and central sections of Anatolia during the past two decades.

As with much of Anatolia, cities and towns here date their existence in millennia rather than centuries. The Hittites, Romans, Persians, Armenians, Georgians, Arabs and Russians have all battled for control of these lands but this is Seljuk country *par excellence*. Sultans of the first Turkic empire in Anatolia (during the mid-1200s) built impressive mosques, medreses, caravanserais and baths in Sivas and Erzurum which shouldn't be missed by anyone interested in architecture. The beautiful mountain scenery and historic Armenian and Georgian churches of extreme north-eastern Anatolia (around Artvin and Kars) are among the most powerful attractions in this region. The mountain trekking in the Kaçkar Range between Erzurum and Artvin is excellent.

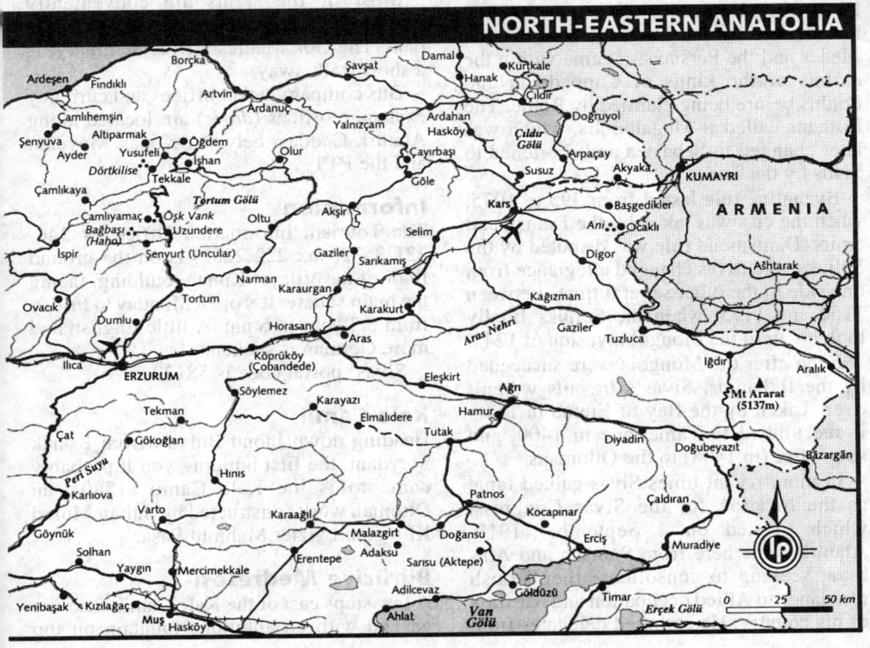

The following description of north-eastern Anatolia moves from west to east, from Sivas via Divriği, Erzincan and Erzurum to Artvin and Kars.

SİVAS

The highway comes through Sivas, the railway comes through Sivas, and over the centuries dozens of invading armies have come through Sivas (population 225,000, altitude 1285m), often leaving the town in ruins in their wake. The Seljuks left perhaps the most obvious mark and the centre of town is liberally sprinkled with some of the finest Seljuk Turkish buildings ever erected.

Nowadays Sivas is fairly modern, with bicycle lanes along its main thoroughfare and even some kerbstone ramps for wheelchairs.

History

The tumulus at Maltepe, near Sivas, shows evidence of settlement as early as 2600 BC. Sivas itself was probably founded by the Hittite King Hattushilish I around 1500 BC. Ruled later by the kings of Assyria, the Medes and the Persians, it came within the realms of the kings of Cappadocia and Pontus before being claimed by Rome. The Romans called it Megalopolis, which was later changed to Sebastea and shortened to Sivas by the Turks.

Byzantine rule lasted from 395 to 1075, when the city was taken by the Danışmend emirs. Danışmend rule was disputed by the Seljuks, and Sivas changed allegiance from one side to the other several times between 1152 and 1175, when the Seljuks finally took it – until the Mongol invasion of 1243.

Even after the Mongols were succeeded by the İlkhanids, Sivas's travails weren't over. Taken by the Bey of Eretna in 1340, it succumbed to Tamerlane in 1400, and soon after (in 1408) to the Ottomans.

In more recent times Sivas gained fame as the location for the Sivas Congress, which opened on 4 September 1919. Atatürk came here from Samsun and Amasya, seeking to consolidate the Turkish resistance to Allied occupation and partition of his country. He gathered delegates from as many parts of the country as possible, and confirmed decisions which had been made at the earlier Erzurum Congress. These two congresses were the first breath of the revolution and heralded the War of Independence.

Orientation

The centre of town is Konak Meydanı, in front of the attractive Vilayet Konağı (Provincial Government Headquarters). Near it are most of Sivas' important sights, hotels and restaurants.

The train station (Sivas Gar) is about 1.5km south-west of Konak Meydanı along İnönü Bulvarı. If arriving by rail, walk out of the station to the bus stop on the station side of İnönü Bulvarı. Any bus running along this major road will trundle you to or from the station. If in doubt, just ask the driver, '*Konak?*'. The bus station (Sivas Otogar) is over 2km south-east of the centre, reachable by dolmuş.

Most of the sights are conveniently grouped in a pleasant park at Konak Meydanı. The Gök Medrese (Blue Seminary) is a short walk away.

Bus company ticket offices and currency exchange offices (*döviz*) are located along Atatürk Caddesi between Konak Meydanı and the PTT.

Information

The Tourism Information Office (☎ 346-221 3535, fax 222 2252) is on the ground floor of the Vilayet Konağı building, facing the main square. It's open Monday to Friday from 8.30 am to 6 pm. A little English and more German is spoken.

Sivas' postal code is 58120.

Kale Camii

Heading down İnönü Bulvarı from Konak Meydanı, the first building you'll probably come to is the Kale Camii (1580), an Ottoman work constructed by Sultan Murad III's grand vizier Mahmut Paşa.

Bürüciye Medresesi

A few steps east of the Kale Camii, near the gazebo with an ablutions fountain on top

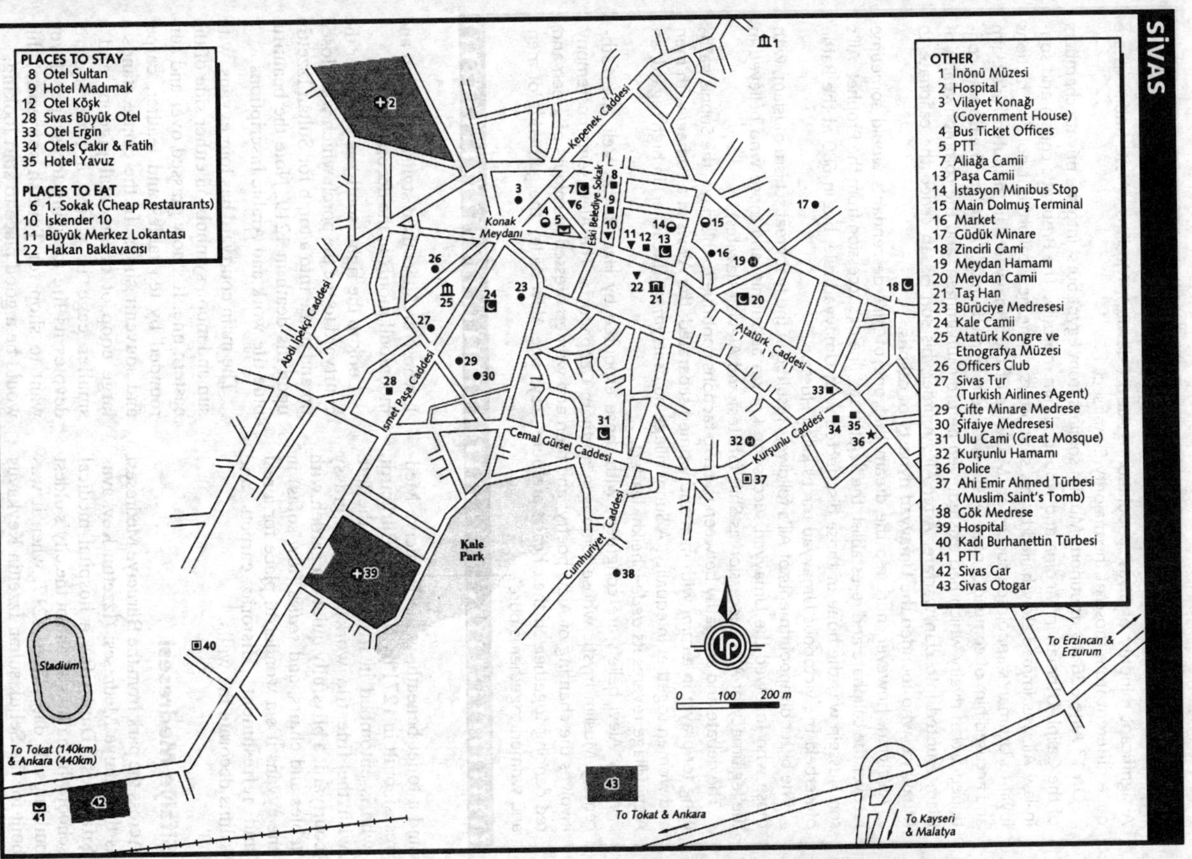
SİVAS
PLACES TO STAY
8 Otel Sultan
9 Hotel Madımak
12 Otel Köşk
28 Sivas Büyük Otel
33 Otel Ergin
34 Otels Çakır & Fatih
35 Hotel Yavuz
PLACES TO EAT
6 1. Sokak (Cheap Restaurants)
10 İskender 10
11 Büyük Merkez Lokantası
22 Hakan Baklavacısı
OTHER
1 İnönü Müzesi
2 Hospital
3 Vilayet Konağı (Government House)
4 Bus Ticket Offices
5 PTT
7 Aliağa Camii
13 Paşa Camii
14 İstasyon Minibus Stop
15 Main Dolmuş Terminal
16 Market
17 Güdük Minare
18 Zincirli Cami
19 Meydan Hamamı
20 Meydan Camii
21 Taş Han
23 Bürüciye Medresesi
24 Kale Camii
25 Atatürk Kongre ve Etnografya Müzesi
26 Officers Club
27 Sivas Tur (Turkish Airlines Agent)
29 Çifte Minare Medrese
30 Şifaiye Medresesi
31 Ulu Cami (Great Mosque)
32 Kurşunlu Hamamı
36 Police
37 Ahi Emir Ahmed Türbesi (Muslim Saint's Tomb)
38 Gök Medrese
39 Hospital
40 Kadı Burhanettin Türbesi
41 PTT
42 Sivas Gar
43 Sivas Otogar
Kepenek Caddesi
Eski Belediye Sokak
Konak Meydanı
Abdi İpekçi Caddesi
Atatürk I. Caddesi
İsmet Paşa Caddesi
Cemal Gürsel Caddesi
Kurşunlu Caddesi
Cumhuriyet Caddesi
Kale Park
Stadium
0 100 200 m
To Erzincan & Erzurum
To Tokat (140km) & Ankara (440km)
To Tokat & Ankara
To Kayseri & Malatya

The Alevis

A significant minority of Sivas' population is Alevi (Alawite), Muslims whose traditions are quite different from those of the majority Sunni sect.

On 17 June 656 AD, mutinous Muslim soldiers from Egypt burst into the private chambers of the Caliph Uthman in Medina and wounded him mortally. The Prophet's cousin and son-in-law Ali was immediately hailed by his supporters as the new caliph, but political factions loyal to Uthman's appointed successor, Muawiya of the Umayyad clan, disputed Ali's claim and accused him of complicity or at least a passive role in Uthman's murder. The dispute continued a clan rivalry which had existed even before Muhammed, and the commonwealth of Islam erupted into clan warfare. After Ali's murder, his son Hasan ceded the caliphate to Muawiya, who founded the Umayyad dynasty of caliphs.

Ali's clan, however, nurtured the dream that one of Ali's descendants would sometime recover the caliphate and re-establish the 'legitimate' line of succession from the Prophet. Ali's son Hussein was the hope of those disaffected with Umayyad rule, but in 680 at the Battle of Kerbela the victorious Umayyad forces killed Hussein.

The bitter disappointments of Ali's followers resulted in the first great schism of Islam, with those who followed the Umayyad succession known as Sunnis, and those who believed in the legitimacy of Ali's succession as Shiis (Shiites) and Alevis (Alawites).

The debate and antipathy between the two factions continue to this day – the Sunnis gathering for prayer in a *cami* with men and women separated; the Alevis in a *cemevi* with men and women together in equality. A Sunni village holds its *imam* (preacher) in high regard; an Alevi village reveres its *dede* (sheikh, leader).

Many Alevi beliefs are congruent with those espoused by Hacı Bektaş Veli, the 13th-century Muslim mystic whose tomb is in northern Cappadocia. The Alevi *semah* ceremony involves the chanting of Alevi poetry; and men and women dressed in colours of green and red dancing together. 'If their hearts are pure', says one Alevi dede, 'the gathering of men and women together is pure'.

and a toilet beneath, is the Bürüciye Medresesi, built in 1271 by Muzaffer Bürücirdi, who is entombed in it (inside, to the left, with the fine tile work). With a grassy courtyard, a blissfully quiet tea garden with tables and chairs, and *sedirs* (low sofas) in the eyvans it's a wonderful place for a rest and refreshment. Historic carpets and kilims decorate the walls.

Şifaiye Medresesi

Across the park from the Bürüciye Medresesi is the Şifaiye Medresesi (İzzettin Keykavus Şifahanesi, Darüşşifa), a hospital medical school which ranks as one of the city's oldest buildings. It dates from 1217, when it was built for the Seljuk sultan İzzettin Keykavus I, whose architect used stylised sun/lion and moon/bull motifs in the decoration.

Look to the right (south) as you enter the courtyard to see the porch which was closed up and made into a tomb for Sultan İzzettin upon his death in 1219. Note the beautiful blue tile work and Arabic inscriptions.

The main courtyard has four eyvans, with sun and moon symbols on either side of the eastern one. It's now grassed over and surrounded by tea tables and leather, carpet and souvenir shops. In the centre stands a large coop of ornamental pigeons and a smaller cage in which a lone squirrel devotes its life to trying to escape. If you want to shop for Turkish souvenirs, this would be a good place to start looking.

Çifte Minare Medrese

Directly opposite the Şifaiye Medresesi, the Çifte Minare Medrese (Seminary of the Twin Minarets) has, as its name states, a *çift* (pair) of minarets. Along with its grand Seljuk-style portal, that's about all it has, as the actual medrese behind the portal has long been ruined. Finished in 1271, it was commissioned by the Mongol-İlkhanid vizier Şemsettin Güveyni who ruled here. If you stand between the two opposing medreseler, you will be able to see clearly what a difference half a century made to the exuberance of Seljuk architecture.

Atatürk Kongre ve Etnografya Müzesi

North-west of the Kale Camii across İnönü Bulvarı is the Ottoman secondary school building which was the site of the Sivas Congress on 4 September 1919. Today it's the Atatürk Congress & Ethnography Museum, open from 8.30 am to noon and 1.30 to 5.30 pm (closed on Monday). Admission is free. The entrance is round the back of the building.

The ethnographical collection is pleasantly displayed on the ground floor and includes a fine selection of kilims and carpets, some magnificent embroideries, the old wooden doors from the Ulu Cami/Darüşşifa complex in Divriği, a 12th-century wooden *mimber* (pulpit) from the Kale Camii in Divriği and relics collected from dervish *tekkes* (monasteries) closed in 1925.

Upstairs, the Congress Hall is preserved as it was when the Sivas Congress met, with photos of the delegates touchingly displayed on old school desks. You can also see Atatürk's bedroom and the cable room which played a more important role in developments than you might imagine. The other displays (mainly photographs and documents) are captioned in Turkish only.

Ulu Cami (Great Mosque)

The town's other sights are south-east of Konak Meydanı along Cemal Gürsel and Cumhuriyet caddesis. To find them, walk to the southern end of the park and turn left (east) onto Cemal Gürsel Caddesi.

The Ulu Cami, or Great Mosque (1197), is Sivas' oldest building of significance. Built during the reign of Kutbettin Melikşah, it's a large, low room with a forest of 50 columns. The brick minaret was added in 1213. Though it's not as grand as the more imposing Seljuk buildings, it has a certain old-Anatolian charm.

Gök Medrese

Just east of the Ulu Cami, turn right (south) on Cumhuriyet Caddesi to reach the Gök Medrese, or Blue Seminary. It was built in 1271 at the behest of Sahip Ata, the grand vizier of Sultan Gıyasettin II Keyhüsrev, who funded the grand Sahip Ata mosque complex in Konya and many other buildings throughout the Seljuk realm.

The building's facade has been decorated with wild exuberance. Although built to the traditional Seljuk medrese plan, here the fancy embellishments of tiles, brickwork designs and carving cover not just the doorway, but the windows and walls as well.

The blue tilework gave the school its name, *gök* (sky) being an old Turkish word for 'blue'.

At the time of writing the medrese was closed for restoration, but you can still enjoy the marvellous facade.

Ahi Emir Ahmed Türbesi & Kurşunlu Hamamı

On Kurşunlu Caddesi just south-west of the budget hotels is the Ahi Emir Ahmed Türbesi, the tomb of a Muslim saint who lived in the late 13th to early 14th centuries. The tomb dates from 1333.

Across the street, the women's section of the Kurşunlu Hamamı Turkish bath is open from 9 am to 5 pm; the men's opens earlier and closes later.

Places to Stay – Budget

Sivas has one or two decent cheap hotels and any number of less decent ones. There are no hotels near the bus or train stations.

The inexpensive hotels in the first 500m south-east of Konak Meydanı along Atatürk Caddesi are uniformly drab and dingy, and expensive for what you get. The better cheap hotels are 700m south-east of Konak Meydanı, at the junction of Atatürk and Kurşunlu caddesis.

Perhaps the best of the newer places in this area is ***Hotel Yavuz*** *(☎ 346-225 0204, Atatürk Caddesi 86)*, south-east of the intersection with Kurşunlu Caddesi. Colourful and friendly, with quiet rooms at the back and a lift to take you there, you pay only US$8/12/16 a single/double/triple with shower; a double with bathtub costs US$19.

Around the corner, ***Otel Çakır*** *(☎ 346-222 4526, fax 224 4753, Kurşunlu Caddesi 20)*, charges US$12/16 for a clean single/double with bath, including breakfast. The nearby ***Otel Fatih*** *(☎ 346-233 4313, Kurşunlu Caddesi 15)*, charges marginally more for similar standards in an atmosphere of Islamic propriety.

Across Kurşunlu Caddesi at Atatürk Caddesi 80 is the friendly, rock-bottom cheap ***Otel Ergin*** *(☎ 346-221 2301)*, formerly the Hotel Evin, offering beds from US$4. The lobby is grubby but the rooms are better; you must look at a room to see what sort of plumbing it has. Single women would probably be better off at the Çakır or Fatih.

Places to Stay – Mid-Range

The two-star ***Hotel Madımak*** *(☎ 346-221 8028, Eski Belediye Sokak 2)* has been completely rebuilt and charges US$22/30 a single/double for quite comfortable rooms with private bath, TV and breakfast.

A few steps further down the same street, ***Otel Sultan*** *(☎ 346-221 2986, fax 221 9346, Eski Belediye Sokak 18)*, across the street from the German consulate, has 30 restored comfortable double rooms. It's good value for US$20/28 a single/double with private shower (copious hot water) and breakfast, and it's quieter than most in Sivas.

Around the corner on the main avenue, the two-star ***Otel Köşk*** (KURSHK) *(☎ 346-221 1150, fax 223 9350, Atatürk Caddesi 7)*, has a restaurant, a lift and 44 fairly noisy, but reasonably modern, double rooms priced at US$22/32 a single/double with private bath, bidet and TV. Buffet breakfast is included. Ask for a room at the back if you're a light sleeper.

The city's newest and most luxurious is the aptly named four-star, 114 room ***Sivas Büyük Otel*** (Grand Hotel) *(☎ 346-225 4762, fax 225 2323)* on İsmet Paşa Caddesi, charging US$45/60 a single/double with all mod cons and buffet breakfast.

Places to Eat

Sivas has plenty of good inexpensive places to eat. For a range of foods at the lowest prices, find 1. Sokak (Birinci Sokak) in Sularbaşı Mahallesi, behind the PTT just off the eastern side of Konak Meydanı. The Aliağa Camii is halfway up the slope, and below it are several small, cheap restaurants good for a quick feed for US$2 to US$4. ***Nimet*** and ***Anadolu*** are the nicest, the Nimet having a particularly inviting upstairs *aile salonu* (room for families and single women). ***Güleryüz Kebap*** is the best for a variety of kebaps, including grills, İskender kebap and spicy-hot Adana kebap.

There are more cheap eating places where Atatürk Caddesi meets Eski Belediye Sokak. The ***İskender 10*** serves İskender kebap later in the day than most other places at US$2.25 per plate; plain döner kebap is even cheaper. Have the *künefe* (shredded wheat cake) for afters. There's also ***Hacı Kasimoğulları***, specialising in *etli pide* (with minced lamb) and *lahmacun*, and ***Özlem***, a men's bar. Have a drink here and you'll probably be the main subject of conversation.

Around the corner on Atatürk Caddesi, near the Otel Köşk and beside the Pamukbank, is the spacious ***Büyük Merkez Lokantası*** serving a wide range of ready meals. If you're very hungry, order their speciality, the *sebzeli Sivas kebabı*, a plate piled high with grilled vegetables and lamb, topped by flaps of soft flat bread, for US$3. The other two restaurants nearby with 'Merkez' in their names – the ***Merkez*** and ***Yeni Merkez*** – are also worth a try.

Across Atatürk Caddesi from the Otel Köşk and down towards the Meydan Camii is ***Hakan Baklavacısı***, where Sivas' youth gather in two upstairs rooms to eye one another warily and consume delicious baklava and other sweets for about US$1 per portion.

Continue south-east along Atatürk Caddesi toward the Paşa Camii and turn left. Walk uphill past a row of *şarküteri's* (delicatessens) to the ***Sivas Pide Fırını*** for good, cheap pide.

For fancy meals with drinks, try the dining rooms of the Otel Köşk and the Sivas Büyük Otel.

Getting There & Away

As Sivas is on Turkey's main east-west highway and is also a north-south transit point, it is well served by rail and bus, and has flights twice a week.

Air Twice-weekly Turkish Airlines flights on Wednesday and Friday connect Sivas with Ankara and, by a connection there, to İstanbul. The ticket agency is Sivas Turizm (☎ 346-221 1147, fax 223 1659), İstasyon Caddesi 50, near the Sivas Büyük Otel. A bus to the airport departs from this office 90 minutes before flight time.

Bus Sivas' otogar is 2.2km south of Konak Meydanı. 'Yenişehir' dolmuşes pass by the otogar and end their run at a stop just uphill from the Paşa Camii near the Sivas Pide Fırını, a five-minute walk from either Konak Meydanı or the budget hotels on Kurşunlu Caddesi.

The otogar has its own PTT branch, a restaurant and pastry shop, a shoe repairs shop and an *emanetçi* (left-luggage room).

The main dolmuş terminal in the centre is behind (north of) the Paşa Camii, just off Atatürk Caddesi.

Bus traffic is intense in all directions, though many of the buses are passing through, so it's hard to know whether seats will be available until they actually arrive. Details of some daily services follow:

Amasya – 225km, 3½ hours, US$6; five buses
Ankara – 450km, six hours, US$10; frequent buses
Divriği – 175km, three hours, US$3; several buses, only one starting in Sivas
Diyarbakır – 500km, eight hours, US$16; several buses
Erzurum – 485km, six hours, US$12; several buses
İstanbul – 900km, 11 hours, US$17 to US$20; several buses
Kayseri – 200km, 3½ hours, US$5; hourly buses
Malatya – 235km, 4½ hours, US$6; several buses
Samsun – 341km, 5½ hours, US$8; several buses
Tokat – 105km, 1½ hours, US$3; hourly buses
Yozgat – 224km, three hours, US$6; frequent buses

Train Sivas is a main rail junction for both east-west and north-south lines. The main east-west expresses such as the *Yeni Doğu Ekspresi*, the *Doğu Ekspresi* and the *Güney/Vangölü Ekspresi*, go through Sivas daily. See the Getting Around chapter at the front of this book for details.

Take an 'İstasyon' dolmuş from the Sivas Gar train station to the city centre dolmuş station by the Paşa Camii.

SİVAS TO DİVRİĞİ

At Divriği, 175km south-east of Sivas, a ruined castle stands guard over two magnificent Seljuk buildings. Along the way at Balıklı Kaplıca is a medical curiosity.

Balıklı Kaplıca

On your way to Divriği, the uninteresting farm town of Kangal, east of the Sivas-Malatya road, offers no reason for you to stop. But 15km east of Kangal at Balıklı Kaplıca (or Çermik), off the Divriği road is a curious – even bizarre – health spa for those with psoriasis. Sufferers from this disease, which causes itchy, unsightly patches on the skin, come to Balıklı Kaplıca (Hot Spring with Fish) to relax in the pools of hot mineral water and let the resident fish nibble their scaly skin. The combination of the water and the fish is said to offer some relief, at least part of which must surely be comic relief.

Divriği

Divriği (DEEV-ree, population 25,000), a town hidden beyond a mountain pass (1970m high) in a fertile valley, is visited by relatively few tourists, foreign or Turkish.

It's a typical old-fashioned Turkish mountain town with an economy based on agriculture. The narrow streets are laced with grapevines and paved in stone blocks, and its houses are still uncrowded by modern construction.

Uphill from the town centre stands the combined complex of the Ulu Cami and Darüşşifa (hospital). Both were founded in 1228 by the local emir Ahmet Şah and his wife, the lady Fatma Turan Melik. Beautifully restored and preserved, these remote buildings have been listed as world heritage sites by UNESCO.

Divriği has a few basic lodging places, some simple restaurants and banks. Given the scarcity of tourists, however, it might be a good idea to change whatever money you'll need in Sivas.

Ulu Cami Say 'Ulu Cami' to anyone in town and they'll point the way 250m up the hill along Ulu Cami Caddesi to the complex.

The northern portal of the Ulu Cami is stupendous, a sort of exuberant rococo Seljuk style, with geometric patterns, medallions, luxuriant stone foliage and intricate Arabic inscriptions bursting free of the facade's flatness in a richness that is simply astonishing. It's the sort of doorway which only a provincial emir, with more money than restraint, would ever dream of building. In a large Seljuk city, this sort of extravagance would have been ridiculed as lacking in taste. In Divriği, it's the wonderful, fanciful whim of a petty potentate shaped in stone.

The northern portal is really what you've come to see, although the north-western one has some fine work as well. The mosque's interior is very simple, with 16 columns and a plain *mihrab*, but you're unlikely to see it as it's kept locked outside prayer times.

Darüşşifa Adjoining the Ulu Cami is the hospital, equally plain and simple outside except for the requisite elaborate portal. Inside, eclecticism and odd ingenuity reigns: the floor plan is asymmetrical, the four columns all dissimilar. The octagonal pool in the court has a spiral runoff, similar to the one in Konya's Karatay Medresesi, which allowed the soothing tinkle of running water to break the silence of the room and soothe the patients' nerves. A platform raised above the main floor may have been for musicians who likewise soothed the patients with pleasant sounds.

The Darüşşifa is open from 8 am to 5 pm Monday to Friday, and is free of charge.

Seljuk Tombs As this was once an important provincial capital, you will notice several drum-like *kümbets* (Seljuk tombs) scattered about town. Ahmet Şah's tomb is near the Ulu Cami, as are several earlier ones dating from 1196 and another from 1240.

Kale Trailing down the sides of the hill dominating Divriği are the ruinous walls of its medieval castle, with the Kale Camii a solid but equally ruinous structure on the summit. Given the difficulty of getting onto a bus out of Divriği, you might want to explore at least some of the kale while you wait.

Places to Stay None of Divriği's three hotels are perfect, but of the three, the best is probably the ***Belediye Oteli*** (☎ *346-418 1825*), which, despite its makeshift air, will suffice for a night. Beds in so-so rooms with showers cost about US$5. Rooms at the back have balconies overlooking the kale ruins. There's a popular ground floor and terrace restaurant, and a large tea garden opposite. The noise from the restaurant and tea garden combined can be deafening but with luck it will stop around 11.30 pm. This hotel is along a side turn-off marked by a broken Pepsi sign on the left, off the main road into town. Ask to be dropped off, otherwise a taxi back from the otogar will cost about US$1.50.

The other two possibilities are on the main commercial street in the centre of town. The ***Otel Ninni*** (☎ *346-418 1239*) charges US$5 for a double room without water; the common shower and toilet, though reasonably clean, are down one floor from some of the rooms. You need to be feeling pretty desperate to go for the ***Hotel Değer*** next door.

Getting There & Away Getting to and from Divriği can be tricky if you don't have a car. Although three or four daily buses run between Sivas and Divriği, all but one of them has come from Ankara or İstanbul, which means they are often already full when they get to Sivas. In the opposite direction, people book days ahead, so this too can be problematic. Only one bus a day actually starts its run in Sivas and that's at 4.30 pm; in the opposite direction it leaves Divriği at 7 am. The journey between Sivas and Divriği takes about 3½ hours and costs US$7. Divriği's otogar is on the highway south-west of the village. If you're driving, note that there is no road onward towards Erzincan from Divriği, forcing you to backtrack.

Given these problems you might prefer to take a train, even though it will take longer than the bus. The rail line from Sivas to Erzurum passes through Divriği and you could continue eastwards to Erzurum (roughly 6½ hours away), though you may have to stay overnight in Divriği and catch a connection the next day. Divriği train station is about 2km south of the Ulu Cami.

Elazığ

Elazığ (EHL-lah-zuh, population 200,000, altitude 1200m) is a new town, only founded in the 19th century at a place called Mezraa.

In 1834 Sultan Mahmut II gave his vizier Reşit Mehmet Paşa the duty of reasserting Ottoman imperial control over the semi-independent provincial lords of the region. The paşa proclaimed Mezraa a provincial capital and installed an army garrison.

During the reign of Sultan Abdül Aziz, its governor gave it the name of Mamuretül Aziz, later shortened to Elaziz and, in republican times, to Elazığ. Today Elazığ is a farming centre and university town, though its importance as an entrepöt ended when the Keban Lake cut it off from main roads to the north and east. Viticulture is important; Tekel, the government spirits company, raises its big dark-red *öküzgözü* (ox-eye) grapes in the region.

If you need to stay for the night, plan to spend some time seeing the Urartian treasures in the archaeological museum and the ruins of ancient, earthquake-ruined Harput, 5km north of Elazığ.

Orientation & Information The city centre is Cumhuriyet Meydanı at the intersection of Bosna-Herzek Bulvarı (shown as İstasyon Caddesi on old maps) and Gazi and Hürriyet caddesis, near the İzzet Paşa Camii; turn left along Gazi Caddesi for Fırat Üniversitesi and right along Hürriyet Caddesi for Harput and the banks.

The Belediye (Municipality) and PTT are here, while the helpful Tourism Information Office (☎ 424-212 3301) is at Bosna-Herzek Bulvarı 35 in the İl Halk Kütüphanesi (Provincial Library) building.

Elazığ's postal code is 23000.

Arkeoloji ve Etnografya Müzesi In the 1960s the creation of the Keban Barajı (Keban Dam) north-west of Elazığ, caused the flooding of the valleys to the north. Before the new lake was created, an archaeological rescue project excavated many likely sites and the artefacts uncovered are displayed in the **Elazığ Arkeoloji ve Etnografya Müzesi** (Elazığ Archaeology & Ethnography Museum) on the campus of Fırat Üniversitesi (Euphrates University) on the outskirts of the city. Among the most valuable finds were Early Bronze Age royal seals, gold jewellery and a cuneiform inscription from the time of Menua, King of Urartu.

You may have to hunt around for someone to open the museum and sell you a ticket for US$1. Given that this is a university museum it's a shame that the labelling is so perfunctory, both in Turkish and in English. Upstairs, carpets to make a Kayseri salesman weep with envy languish unlabelled and poorly lit.

To get to the museum take a bus marked 'Üniversite' from Hürriyet Caddesi. The campus is vast so don't try and walk it.

Places to Stay & Eat Elazığ's places to stay are concentrated in and around Hürriyet Caddesi, which means they're central if not particularly quiet.

On Hürriyet Caddesi, try ***Hotel Divan*** *(☎ 424-218 1103)* or ***Hotel Çinar*** *(☎ 424-218 1811)*, both of which have singles/doubles for US$7/12, slightly more with private baths. If you can afford it, the neighbouring two-star ***Beritan Hotel*** *(☎ 424-218 4484, fax 212 7970, Hürriyet Caddesi 24)*, has 68 comfortable rooms with private baths going for US$23/40 a single/double. The comfortable ***Büyük Elazığ Hotel*** *(☎ 424-212 2001, fax 238 1899, Harput Caddesi 9)*, is the town's other two-star, at similar prices.

In Bakırcılar Sokak, off Bosna-Herzek Bulvarı, the ***Otel Erdem*** *(☎ 424-218 2212)* has bathless rooms for US$9/14 a single/double, but could be quieter than the other cheapies.

If you're just passing through, it's worth noting that the ***Kafeterya*** in the otogar serves better than average food right through from a choice of breakfasts.

Getting There & Away Daily Turkish Airlines flights connect Elazığ with Ankara, and there is at least one nonstop from İstanbul each week. The Turkish Airlines office (☎ 424-218 1576, fax 218 3730), is at Vali Fahri Bey Caddesi 39.

Elazığ's spacious otogar is 3km east of the centre. Dolmuşes will ferry you into the centre for less than US$0.20.

There are fairly frequent services to and from Diyarbakır (151km, two hours, US$5), Erzurum (324km, seven hours, US$12), Malatya (101km, 1½ hours, US$2.50) and Mersin (585km, 10 hours, US$12).

Harput

It was Harput, not Elazığ, which had the long, eventful history, effectively ending in the 19th century when it was ruined by earthquakes. Guarded by its photogenic castle, Harput was an important way-station on the Silk Road to and from China and India, but with the earthquake and the building of Elazığ its importance diminished.

Today, besides the castle, you can visit the Ulu Cami, dating from the 1100s and thus one of the oldest in Anatolia, the **Meryem Ana Kilisesi** (Church of the Virgin Mary), and the **Arap Baba Türbesi**, a Seljuk work. There's also a small, thoroughly dusty museum and assorted other ruins scattered about. Pick up a plan at Elazığ tourist office before you go. Take a minibus from Harput Caddesi (US$0.30) to get to Harput.

ERZİNCAN

Like other north-eastern Anatolian cities, Erzincan (population 100,000, altitude 1185m) is very old. Unlike other cities, however, Erzincan has little to show for its great age, as it lies at the heart of Turkey's earthquake zone.

In 1939 it was devastated by Turkey's worst earthquake this century when almost 33,000 people died. Other quakes, most recently in 1993, have left hardly anything of historical or architectural interest. What you see today is a modern farming town whose people await the next devastation with apparent nonchalance.

Earthquakes have effectively erased Erzincan's old street plan as well. The modern main street is broad and straight, lined with shops, hotels and restaurants. Turn left out of the otogar, then left at the intersection and walk 500m to find hotels and restaurants.

Places to Stay & Eat

Should you need to stop, hotels along the main street can provide basic no-frills lodging. Several of the town's best hotels fell victim to the last quake, and the best is now the brand-new three-star ***Büyük Erzincan Otel*** *(☎ 446-223 7305, fax 223 7309)*, on the eastern outskirts. More convenient for a brief transit stop are the several hotels in the centre within a five-minute walk of the otogar on Fevziaşa Caddesi, Erzincan's main drag.

The fairly basic ***Kılıçlar Oteli*** *(☎ 446-212 1641, Fevzipaşa Caddesi 4)*, has rooms for US$9/16 a single/double with shower, less without the private shower. ***Otel Karakaya*** *(☎ 446-214 3673, fax 214 9322, Fevzipaşa Caddesi 40-B)*, across the street, is a step up in quality for US$13/18. ***Hotel Girne*** *(☎ 446-214 2428, Fevzipaşa Caddesi 58)*, costs the same as the Kılıçlar. ***Hotel Burcu*** *(☎ 446-223 8360, fax 223 5081)*, next to the Halkbank, is the most comfortable of the lot, charging US$22 for a double with private bath and TV.

Given that your stay in Erzincan is likely to be brief, it's good to be able to report a pleasant, shady *çay bahçesi* (tea garden) and the ***Sila Restoran*** right beside the otogar. For spit-roasted chicken, stroll out to the ***Oba Restaurant*** on Fevzipaşa Caddesi.

Getting There & Away

Turkish Airlines has three flights a week between Erzincan and Ankara. Contact Polat Turizm (☎ 446-214 6784, fax 214 8255), Hükümet Caddesi 13.

The otogar is off the western reaches of Fevzipaşa Caddesi not far from the centre. Most buses to and from Erzincan started somewhere else, and are going somewhere else, therefore seat availability is not always predictable.

TERCAN

Midway on the age-old highway between Erzincan and Erzurum stands Tercan (TEHR-jahn, population 10,000, altitude 1475m), yet another ancient settlement with a momentous history. A town of farmers and herders, Tercan is set in a fertile river valley accented by huge rock outcrops to the south. Just west of the town, where the highway and railway cross the river, is an ancient stone bridge with most of its arches fallen.

Tercan houses the **Mama Hatun Türbesi** (Tomb of Mama Hatun), built between 1192 and 1202 and unique in Anatolian architecture. It's uphill through the town 250m off the highway next to the **Mama Hatun Kervansarayı**.

The tomb proper is surrounded by a high, thick wall which you enter through a portal decorated with bands of unusual Kufic script. Inside, the circular wall is pierced by 12 eyvans in which lesser notables could be entombed; several cenotaphs indicate burials below. The south-western mihrab faces Mecca from this easterly location.

If the tomb is unlocked, climb the stairs to the right of the entrance portal to get a view of the tomb and the surrounding cemetery. The eight-lobed tomb proper stands in the centre of the circle, oriented to the points of the compass with the door to the south. Its roof resembles an umbrella. The space above the actual burial chamber is still used for prayers.

The neighbouring caravanserai is topped by a forest of chimneys. The western door, facing the town on the opposite side of the caravanserai from the tomb, is the one most likely to be open.

Though much repaired and rebuilt over the centuries, the caravanserai still exhibits some unusual features. Its long entry hall is lined with eyvans, leading to a singularly large eyvan across the courtyard from the entrance. Conical caps on the bastion tops are an odd feature.

Should you need to stay the night, Tercan has two very small truck-stop hotels, the ***Kervansaray*** and the ***Calışkan***, out on the highway. There are simple restaurants as well.

East and south of Tercan, you pass through dramatic mountain scenery before arriving in Erzurum.

ERZURUM

Erzurum (population 300,000, altitude 1853m) is the largest city on the Eastern Anatolian high plateau. It has always been a transportation centre and military headquarters, and was the command post for the defence of Anatolia from Russian and Persian invasion. Now it's assuming a new role as an eastern cultural and commercial city.

With its severe climate and sparse landscape, Erzurum lacks the colour and complexity of İstanbul or İzmir, but makes up for it with a rough frontier refinement. The orderly, modern, tree-lined boulevards provide a welcome contrast to the arid, almost lifeless appearance of the surrounding expanse of steppe.

It's also a city that seems to face in two directions at once, a town of God-fearing, meat-eating, mosque-going, patriotic, conservative men whose women wear voluminous black drapes or at least headscarves; but also

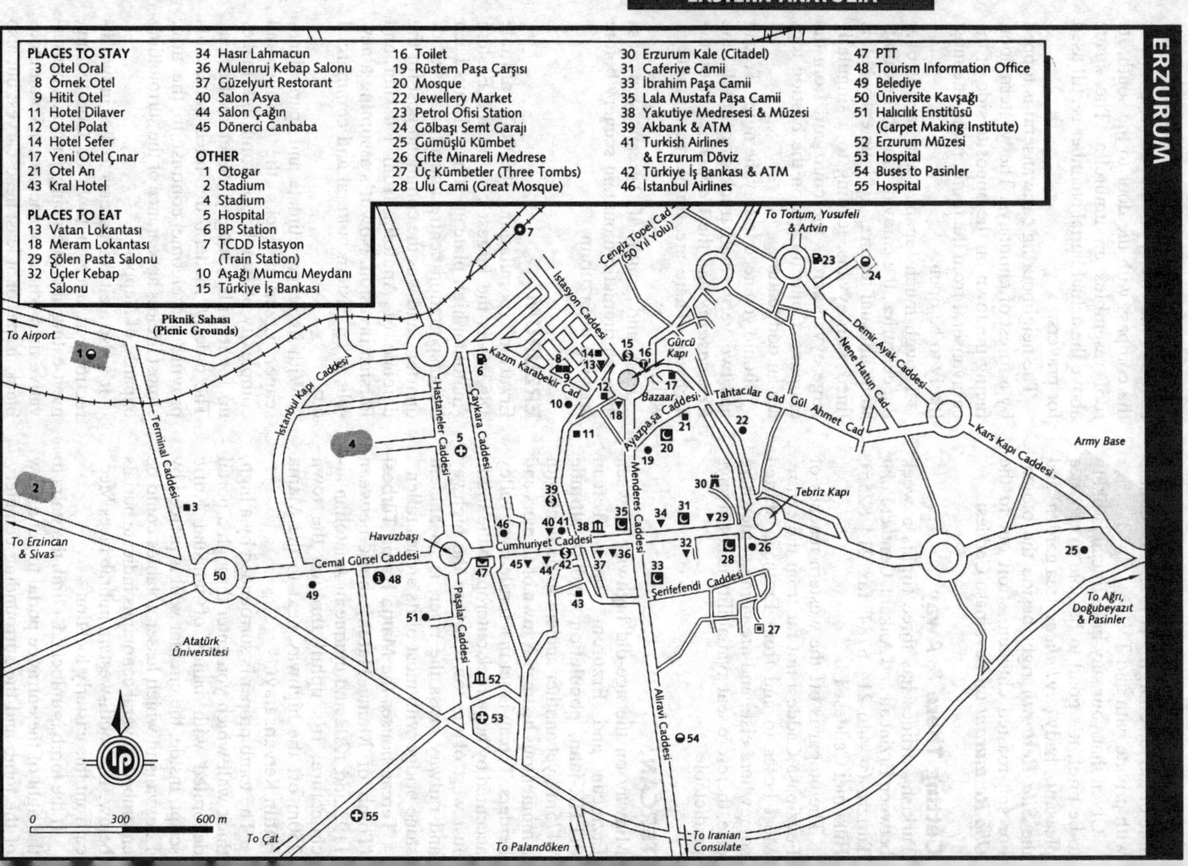

EASTERN ANATOLIA

a university town and an important base for the outspokenly secular military.

For tourists, Erzurum is a transfer point with air, rail and bus connections. But if you stay one or two nights, you'll be able to visit some fine Turkish buildings and a lively market area. You can also take an excursion to the Tortum Valley and the mountain village of Yusufeli on the way to Artvin and, in winter, ski at nearby Palandöken.

History

During the Byzantine era Erzurum was called Theodosiopolis after the emperor who founded it in the late 5th century on the ruins of an earlier settlement. The Byzantine emperors had their hands full defending this town from Arab attack on several occasions. The Seljuk Turks took it after the Battle of Manzikert in 1071, effectively opening Anatolia to Turkish settlement.

Being in a strategic position at the confluence of roads to Constantinople, Russia and Persia, Erzurum was conquered and lost by armies (in alphabetical order) of Arabs, Armenians, Byzantines, Mongols, Persians, Romans, Russians, Saltuk Turks and Seljuk Turks. As for the Ottomans, it was Selim the Grim who conquered the city in 1515. It was captured by Russian troops in 1882 and again in 1916.

In July 1919 Atatürk came to Erzurum to hold the famous congress which, along with the one at Sivas, provided the rallying cry for the independence struggle. The Erzurum Congress is most famous for determining the boundaries of what became known as the territories of the National Pact, those lands which would be part of the foreseen Turkish Republic. Atatürk and the Congress claimed the lands which, in essence, form the present Turkish state and rejected claims to other formerly held Ottoman lands. The phrase at the time was, 'We want no more, we shall accept no less'.

Orientation

Although the old city of Erzurum was huddled beneath the walls of the kale, the new Erzurum, which has grown up around the old, has broad boulevards, traffic roundabouts and an open, airy feeling, part of which is attributed to the constantly dry wind.

You can walk to everything in the centre (Old Erzurum), including the train station, but will need a taxi or bus to get to and from the otogars and the airport.

Besides the main otogar west of the centre, there is the Gölbaşı Semt Garajı on the north-eastern outskirts, with minibus services to points north and east.

In Old Erzurum, a convenient point of reference is **Gürcü Kapı**. Once the 'Georgian gate' in the city walls, it's marked by a chunky stone fountain at a traffic intersection 600m up the hill (south-east) from the train station. The Gürcü Kapı district has hotels, restaurants, banks, shops and bus ticket offices.

Modern Erzurum's main thoroughfare is Cumhuriyet Caddesi, renamed Cemal Gürsel Caddesi along its western reaches. The two parts of the street are divided at the centre by a traffic roundabout bearing a large statue of Atatürk, a pool and fountain and the name Havuzbaşı. It's almost 2km from the otogar to the Havuzbaşı roundabout and 3km from the otogar to the centre of town. The train station is 2.5km north-east of the otogar.

Erzurum's sights are quite conveniently grouped in the old part of town, within easy walking distance of one another.

Information

The Tourism Information Office (☎ 442-218 5697) is inconveniently positioned on the southern side of Cemal Gürsel Caddesi at 9/A, one block west of the Havuzbaşı traffic roundabout. Staff are friendly but speak very little English.

Erzurum's postal code is 25000.

Money Most of the banks and ATMs are clustered around Gürcü Kapı. If you have no ATM card, several banks will change cash but are less keen on travellers cheques. Türkiye İş Bankası changes cheques efficiently and without fuss.

Erzurum Döviz, on Cumhuriyet Caddesi just west of the Yakutiye Medresesi between the Salon Asya and Turkish Airlines, changes cash (deutschmarks and dollars only) daily from 10.30 am to 1 pm and 1.30 to 7.30 pm.

Iranian Consulate Erzurum's Iranian consulate (☎ 442-218 3876), off Aliravi Caddesi across from the Eğitim Fakültesi (Education Faculty), is open every day except Friday from 8 am to 1 pm and 2 to 4 pm.

However, you're better off applying for a visa at the Iranian embassy in your home country. Here, you must pay a nonrefundable application fee of US$50, then wait a month or so and, if your visa is granted, pay a visa fee as well.

Newspapers After 3 pm you can usually get copies of the *Turkish Daily News* in the Kültür Sarayı at Cumhuriyet Caddesi 30, opposite the Yakutiye Medresesi. It's usually kept behind the counter, so if you don't see it, ask.

Çifte Minareli Medrese

At the eastern end of Cumhuriyet Caddesi is the Çifte Minareli Medrese, or Twin Minaret Seminary, open every day from 8.30 am to 6 pm. Admission costs US$0.50.

The Çifte Minareli dates from the 1200s when Erzurum was a wealthy Seljuk city which suffered attack and devastation by the Mongols (1242). It's believed to have been finished in 1253 on orders of Huand Hatun, daughter of Sultan Alaeddin Keykubat.

The facade is a good example of the Seljuk penchant for variation within symmetry: the panels on either side of the portal are identical in size and position, but different in motif. The panel to the right bears the Seljuk eagle, to the left the motif is unfinished.

Enter through the towering limestone portal topped by its twin brick minarets decorated with small blue tiles. The tops of the minarets are gone, having succumbed to the vagaries of Erzurum's violent history even before the Ottomans claimed the town.

The main courtyard, now used by handicraft sellers and a cafe, has four large niches and a double colonnade on the eastern and western sides, though some of the columns were never fully carved. Stairways in each of the corners lead to the students' cells on the upper level. The doorway to each cell is decorated differently, adding a liveliness and interest to the otherwise monumental design.

At the far end of the courtyard is the grand 12-sided domed hall which served as the Hatuniye Türbesi, or Tomb of Huant Hatun, the founder of the medrese. The rich marble decoration was never completed; look inside to the left on the wall for a sample of how it was supposed to have looked, polished and creamy-white.

Beneath the domed hall is a small room with ingenious vents to allow the light and air in. This may have been a *mescit* (prayer room) with a cenotaph, the lady's actual tomb being beneath the floor.

Ulu Cami

Next to the Çifte Minareli is the Ulu Cami (1179). The contrast between the two buildings is striking: unlike the elaborately decorated Çifte Minareli, the Ulu Cami, built almost a century earlier by the Saltuklu Turkish emir of Erzurum, is restrained but elegant, with seven aisles running north-south and six running east-west, resulting in a forest of columns. You enter from the north along the central aisle. Above the fourth east-west aisle a stalactite dome is open to the heavens. At the southern end of the central aisle are a curious wooden dome and a pair of bull's-eye windows.

Üç Kümbetler (Three Tombs)

Scholars believe that the design of Saltuk and Seljuk tombs, or *kümbet*, echoes that of the nomad tents of Central Asia, with a near-conical roof and side panels elaborately decorated as though hung with tapestries. Erzurum has numerous fine kümbets. Walk south between the Çifte Minareli and the Ulu Cami until you come to a T-junction. Turn left then immediately right and walk a short block up the hill to the Üç Kümbetler (Three Tombs), in a fenced enclosure to the right. The best decoration, dating from the

12th century, is on the octagonal Emir Sultan Saltuk Türbesi.

Erzurum Kale (Citadel)

The citadel, or kale, erected by Theodosius around the 5th century, is on the hilltop to the north of the Çifte Minareli and the Ulu Cami. It's open from 8 am to noon and 1.30 to 7.30 pm in summer; admission costs US$0.75.

Walk up the hill towards the curious old clock tower topped by a Turkish flag. The tower was built as a minaret in the time of the Saltuks but was later converted to its current time-keeping function. It stands by the entrance to the kale.

The kale walls harbour a few old cannons with Russian or Ottoman inscriptions, a disused prayer room and a lit-up picture of Atatürk. Steep steps lead up to the rough top of the walls where there's a fine view, especially of the Çifte Minareli huddled beneath the surrounding mountains. This is an especially fine place to be at prayer time, with the call to prayer seemingly coming at you from all sides.

The view from the walls is impressive but this is not an experience for anyone inclined to vertigo. Alternatively you can climb the clock tower, preferably taking a torch with you. Open the cupboard doors at the top of the stairs and you'll find the clock which was made in Croydon, England, and given to the Ottomans by Queen Victoria in 1877.

Every July bouts of wrestling take place in front of appreciative audiences in the grounds of the kale.

Ottoman Mosques

Return to Cumhuriyet Caddesi, then head west and you will pass on the right the small Ottoman **Caferiye Camii**, constructed in 1645 upon the order of Ebubekiroğlu Hacı Cafer.

Cross at the busy intersection and you come to the **Lala Mustafa Paşa Camii** (1563) on the north-western corner. Lala Mustafa Paşa was a grand vizier during the golden age of the Ottoman Empire, and his mosque is a classical Ottoman work of the high period, possibly designed by Sinan or one of his followers.

Yakutiye Medresesi & Müzesi

Just west of the Lala Mustafa Paşa Camii is the Yakutiye Medresesi (Yakutiye Seminary), a Mongol theological seminary dating from 1310, built in the reign of the Mongol Khan Oljaytu for Gazan Khan and his wife Bolugan Hatun by Cemaleddin Hoca Yakut Gazani. In the 1970s and 1980s, encroaching buildings were razed to create the surrounding park, and in 1994 the medrese was opened as Erzurum's **Türk-İslâm Eserleri ve Etnoğrafya Müzesi** (Turkish & Islamic Arts & Ethnography Museum). It's open daily except Monday from 8.30 am to 5 pm for US$0.50. Most labels are in Turkish only.

The Mongol governors borrowed the basics of Seljuk architecture and developed their own variations of it, as is evident in the medrese's portal. Of the two original minarets, only the base of one and the lower part of the second have survived. The türbe at the back was to be used as the emir's tomb.

Inside, the central dome is supported by faceted stalactite work which catches the light from the central opening to make a delightful pattern of light and shadow. The northern eyvan has two levels, which is unusual. The southern eyvan was the mosque, with its mihrab. The room at the south-eastern corner was probably the refectory, the rear (north-eastern) entrance was for traders and artisans. The exhibits include Ottoman jewellery and female ornaments, calligraphy, religious objects, Seljuk ceramics, local embroidery and lace work, and *oltutaşi*, the locally mined black amber.

Erzurum Müzesi

The Erzurum Museum is several long blocks south-west of the Yakutiye Medresesi. Walk west along Cumhuriyet Caddesi to the Havuzbaşı roundabout, then turn left (south) and walk up the hill. The museum is just before the next intersection, on the left (eastern) side of Paşalar Caddesi. It's a 15-minute walk, or you can take any bus climbing the hill from Havuzbaşı. The museum is open from 8 am to noon and 12.30 to 5 pm (closed on Monday); admission costs US$1.

Built as the city's main museum, it suffered when much of its collection was moved to the Yakutiye Medresesi in 1994. It's now mostly an archaeological museum, with finds from digs at Büyüktepe Höyük and Sos Höyük, Urartian and Trans-Caucasian pottery, jewellery from Hellenistic and Roman tombs, and fragments of Seljuk tiles. Many labels are in English.

A few exhibits are dedicated to the massacre and mass burial of Muslim inhabitants of Yeşilyayla and Alaca Köyü by Armenian insurgents at the beginning of the century, but the labelling is only in Turkish.

Bazaars

Erzurum's market areas are scattered throughout the old part of the city and it's easy to get lost in the narrow, winding streets. Start your wanderings at the **Lala Mustafa Paşa Camii**, then walk north along Menderes Caddesi, the street next to the mosque. You will pass the covered **Rüstem Paşa Çarşısı** on the right, which is the centre for the manufacture and sale of black amber prayer beads. For a look at the shops go to the upper floor. Those around the courtyard do a good trade in black amber jewellery too.

Just down the street from the Rüstem Paşa Çarşısı is the small **Pervizoğlu Camii** (1715). Along Kavaflar Çarşısı Sokak you'll find many tinsmiths selling handmade cookers, heaters and samovars – all prized in a town renowned for its snow.

Continuing downhill in the market district will bring you, finally, to İstasyon Caddesi, the street leading to the train station and the numerous hotels in this district.

The **Erzurum Hamamı** at the bazaar end of İstasyon Caddesi has been praised by many male readers of this guide (it's only open to men). Continue along the road winding past the kale, however, and you'll come to two small baths for women: the **Hanım** and the **Kırkçeşme**. Neither is brilliant, although the Hanım may be slightly cleaner.

Palandöken Ski Area

There's skiing from November to mid-May at Palandöken, on the outskirts of Erzurum 8km south-west of the centre. Dedeman Palandöken Ski Center (see later under Places to Stay – Top End) is already in operation with six ski lifts (including two for beginners) and 30km of ski runs on three levels. Other hotels and lifts are under construction, and all come to life especially during April's winter festival. Minibuses run out to Palandöken during the ski season, and you may be lucky and find one on a summer weekend as well.

Places to Stay – Budget

Erzurum is a low-budget traveller's dream, with many cheap places to stay not far from the town centre. As for the upper end, there are several comfortable three-star places but no hotels in the luxury class.

Start your room search in Aşağı Mumcu Meydanı, the little square at the bazaar end of Kazım Karabekir Caddesi. At the 32 room ***Hitit Otel*** *(☎ 442-218 1204, Kazım Karabekir Caddesi 27)*, just off Aşağı Mumcu Meydanı, a room with sink costs US$8/11 a single/double, US$9/12 with private shower. Next door is the similarly priced ***Örnek Otel*** *(☎ 442-218 1203, Kazım Karabekir 8)*, with 35 rooms, all with private showers, and decent value for the price. Beware of noise when you choose a room in either of these places.

Otel Arı *(☎ 442-218 3141, Ayazpaşa Caddesi 22)*, is about average, with rooms for US$7/10 a single/double. Your room may have a sink, or shower, or toilet, or a combination of these; in winter hot water is available on request. The hotel is right next to the Ayazpaşa Camii. From Gürcü Kapı, walk uphill along the street to the left of the Türk Ticaret Bankası ('Türkbank' on the sign) and when it widens into a square go left towards all the 'Avukat' signs.

Nearby is the well-regarded, friendly ***Yeni Otel Çınar*** *(☎ 442-233 9892, fax 233 8963, Ayazpaşa Caddesi 18)*, which is more comfortable for similar prices: US$8 with sink, US$10 with shower for a double room. To find it, look for the Gürpınar Sineması (cinema) in the bazaar. The street opposite leads to the Çınar.

For a step up in quality, the 36 room, two-star ***Hotel Sefer*** (☎ *442-218 6714, fax 212 3775)*, on İstasyon Caddesi near Aşağı Mumcu Meydanı, is the first choice. Convenient, though certainly not fancy, it's a good choice at US$15/20/25 a single/double/triple, breakfast included, for a room with private bath, direct-dial phone and TV.

The one-star, 60 room ***Otel Polat*** (☎ *442-218 1623, fax 234 4598, Kazım Karabekir Caddesi 4)* is also good, with a lift, a business clientele, and double-glazed windows. Posted rates are US$20/30/40, but I was quoted rates of half that much.

Just off Cumhuriyet Caddesi opposite the Yakutiye Medresesi, and so in the heart of things, ***Kral Hotel*** (☎ *442-218 7783, fax 218 6973, Erzincankapı 18)*, has a grubby facade and lobby but surprisingly well-maintained rooms for US$15/21 with sink, US$18/25/30 a single/double/triple with shower and TV. Keep noise in mind when you choose a room.

Places to Stay – Mid-Range

Otel Oral (☎ *442-218 9740, fax 218 9749, Terminal Caddesi 3)* is inconveniently located, noisy, and overpriced at US$35/50 a single/double, and often filled by groups. If you stay here, request a room at the back *(arka tarafta)* to lessen the noise.

Places to Stay – Top End

The three-star ***Hotel Dilaver*** (☎ *422-235 0068, fax 218 1148, Aşağı Mumcu Caddesi, Pelit Meydanı)*, is Erzurum's most comfortable city-centre hotel, with good rooms with breakfast for US$60/85 a single/double, for which you get modern decor and fittings, TV, air-con, a minibar and private bathroom. The top-floor restaurant offers splendid views over Erzurum.

The Palandöken ski area (2450m), 8km south-west of the centre, has the city's most luxurious hotel, the Dedeman. The five-star Polat and three-star Kardelen hotels are under construction at Palandöken, and will probably be open by the time you arrive.

The 186 room ***Dedeman Palandöken Ski Center*** (☎ *442-316 2414, fax 316 3607)*, has all the luxuries for US$90/110 single/double with breakfast, US$10 per person more with breakfast and dinner.

Places to Eat – Budget

As with hotel prices, meal prices in Erzurum are low. ***Salon Çağın***, on Cumhuriyet Caddesi just west of the Yakutiye Medresesi on the southern side of the street, is clean, bright and cheery, with tasty food. On Sunday come for the house speciality, *mantı* (Turkish ravioli, US$2). If you can face it, they'll even do you *işkembe çorbası* (tripe soup) for breakfast.

Across the street is the fancier ***Salon Asya***. The menu includes a large variety of kebaps, including *tereyağlı* (with butter) and Bursa kebap. Meals cost US$3 to US$4.

The place for döner kebap, however, is ***Dönerci Canbaba*** at Cumhuriyet Caddesi 18. Huge vertical spits of succulent lamb are twirling all day long. A portion with salad and soft drink costs US$4 to US$5. They serve Bursa-style İskender kebap as well. ***Dönerci Hacıbey*** on Cumhuriyet Caddesi 38 opposite the Yakutiye Medresesi, is nearly as good: clean, bright and welcoming to female diners.

Just opposite the Akçay Otel on Kamil Ağa Sokak is ***Mulenruj Kebap Salonu*** (that's 'Moulin Rouge'), where the main dining room is decorated with a fine 3D model of a hydroelectric power plant! Döner kebap, along with *kuru fasulye* (beans in tomato sauce), pilav and a soft drink comes to about US$3.50.

Near the Çifte Minareli Medrese and Ulu Cami, try ***Sultan Sekisi Şark Sofrası*** (Sultan's Bench Oriental Dinner Table), Ebuishak Sokak 1, in the narrow street across Cumhuriyet Caddesi from the Çifte Minareli Medrese. Low Ottoman-style tables and folk decoration, traditional Turkish dishes and decent prices make it well worth a try. A full meal might cost US$4 to US$7 per person; no alcohol is served.

Üçler Kebap Salonu, off Cumhuriyet Caddesi on Osmanpaşa Sokak No 2 near the Ulu Cami, serves *kuşbaşı* lamb kebaps (marinated in salt, oil and chili for several days) for US$1.50 as well as the usual range of pides (US$1). There's an unusually attractive *aile salonu* at the back. The lahmacun at ***Hasır*** opposite Osmanpaşa Sokak, is even cheaper.

Several cafes and pastry shops on Cumhuriyet Caddesi are useful for a quick bite or breakfast. Best is ***Kılıçoğlu Baklavaları***, two doors west of the Salon Çağın. Bright and modern, it sells excellent buttery baklava with tea for US$1. ***Patisserie Zirve***, further west down the hill from the Salon Çağın, is good for pastry and tea or breakfast. Further east near the Caferiye Camii is the ***Şeref Pastanesi***, with a fine array of pastries.

Near Aşağı Mumcu Meydanı, try the ***Vatan Lokantası***, opposite the Hotel Polat, a block behind the Hotel Sefer. The Vatan has an excellent selection of *sulu yemek* (ready food, mostly stews) at lunch. Full meals can be had for around US$3. The ***Meram Lokantası***, around the corner on Menderes Caddesi is similar, as is the ***Erdem Lokantası***, opposite the Örnek Otel.

Near the Hotel Dilaver, the ***Rıhtım Restaurant***, at Pelit Meydanı 36, serves good chicken and salads for US$4 or US$5. The ***Dilek Pasta ve Kahvaltı Salonu***, to the left of the Dilaver, serves breakfast, pastries, and *balkaymak* (honey-cream) ice cream.

Places to Eat – Mid-Range

Erzurum's best, since 1928, is the ***Güzelyurt Restorant*** (*☎ 442-218 1514*), directly facing the Yakutiye Medresesi across Cumhuriyet Caddesi. With soft lighting, quiet music, experienced black-clad waiters, alcoholic beverages, and a clientele bonded to their cell phones, the Güzelyurt is the place where westernised businessmen come to dine after a hard day's toil. Have the house speciality, *mantarlı güveç* – a delicious casserole of lamb, pimientos, onions, tomatoes, mushrooms and cheese. It's big enough for two people if you've already had several appetisers. The bill may be US$10 to US$20 per person.

Getting There & Away

As eastern Turkey's main city, Erzurum is well served by all modes of transport.

Air Turkish Airlines (☎ 442-218 1904) at 50. Yıl Caddesi, SSK Rant Tesisleri 24, near the north-western end of Kazım Karabekir Caddesi, has two daily flights to Ankara, with connections to Antalya, İstanbul and İzmir.

Bus The otogar, 3km from the centre along the airport road, handles most of Erzurum's intercity traffic. It has a post office, barber, *emanetçi* (left luggage), shops and a restaurant. City bus No 2 passes the otogar and will take you into town for US$0.30; a taxi costs about US$2.50.

Details of some daily services from Erzurum's otogar follow:

Ankara – 925km, 12 hours, US$18; several buses
Artvin – 215km, four hours, US$7; several buses
Diyarbakır – 485km, eight hours, US$13; several buses
Doğubeyazıt – 285km, four hours, US$7; five buses
Erzincan – 192km, 2½ hours, US$5; frequent buses
İstanbul – 1275km, 18 hours, US$18 to US$30; several buses
Kars – 205km, three hours, US$5; several buses
Sivas – 485km, six hours, US$12; several buses
Tortum – 53km, one hour, US$2; several dolmuşes
Trabzon – 325km, six hours, US$10; several buses
Van – 420km, six hours, US$10; several buses
Yusufeli – 129km, three hours, US$4; several dolmuşes

The Gölbaşı Semt Garajı, about 1km north-east of Gürcü Kapı through the back streets, handles minibuses to towns to the north and east of Erzurum, including Ardanuç, Ardeşen, Arhavi, Çayeli, Fındıklı, Hopa, Pazar, Rize, Şavşat, Şelale, Tortum and Yusufeli. The Gölbaşı Semt Garajı can be difficult to find unless you take a taxi. Look for the Hotel Ersin and a Petrol Ofisi fuel station; it's behind the Petrol Ofisi station.

For Iran (if you already have your visa), take a bus to Doğubeyazıt where you can catch a minibus to the Iranian frontier.

Train The Erzurum Garı (TCDD İstasyon) is at the northern end of İstasyon Caddesi,

600m north of Gürcü Kapı and over 1km from Cumhuriyet Caddesi. You can walk from the station to most hotels except the Oral. City buses depart from the station forecourt every 30 minutes and circulate through the city.

Erzurum has good rail connections with Ankara via Kayseri, Sivas, Divriği and Erzincan. The *Yeni Doğu Ekspresi* covers the distance between Erzurum and Ankara in 21 hours; the *Doğu Ekspresi* takes about 25 hours – if it's on time. For details of these trains, see the Getting Around chapter at the front of this book.

Getting Around

A taxi to or from the airport, 10km from town, costs around US$6. A taxi trip within the city costs US$2 to US$4.

Hat 2 (Route 2), covered by city buses (US$0.30) and minibuses (US$0.30), runs between the district of Yoncalık by the Erzurum Kale (citadel) westward along Cumhuriyet Caddesi as far as the otogar.

GEORGIAN VALLEYS

The mountainous country north of Erzurum towards Artvin was once part of the medieval Kingdom of Georgia, and has numerous churches and castles to show for it. The trouble you take to see this region will be amply rewarded. The mountain scenery is at times spectacular, and the churches, which share many characteristics with Armenian, Seljuk and Persian styles, are interesting and seldom visited. If you happen to be passing in mid-June, the orchards of cherries and apricots should be in bloom – a special treat. Late September and early October can also be fine times to visit (if the rains hold off), with autumn foliage colour.

Getting Around

The small mountain villages in these valleys are a delight to explore, but public transport to and from most of them consists of a single minibus which heads down to Erzurum early in the morning for the market, returning in the afternoon. A rental car, although relatively expensive, is the means by which you'll get to enjoy this beautiful region to the fullest. Try to find other travellers to share the cost.

You can see quite a bit in a one-day excursion, but even more if you plan to spend the night in Yusufeli. If you have another day or two, make the beautiful drive from Yusufeli to Kars; get your permit for visiting Ani, then spend the night in Kars. On the third day, visit Ani, then return to Erzurum by evening.

A taxi for a 12-hour excursion from Erzurum around the churches will cost about US$100, so a rental car is a better choice. If you have time for only one or two churches, head for İşhan or Öşk Vank first.

Most of the villages can rustle up a glass of tea but food is a much taller order. There are a few restaurants along the main highway from Erzurum to Yusufeli and there are plenty of children hawking fruit by the roadside, too. Otherwise, unless you're especially fond of dry biscuits, stock up on picnic foods before leaving Erzurum.

Bağbaşı (Haho)

About 25km north of Tortum is a turn-off on the left (west), near a humpback bridge, to the village called Haho by the Georgians. Go 7.5km up the unpaved road through orchards and fields to the village. Stop at the Belediye and teahouse, and ask for the *kilise anahtarı*, or church key; a guide will probably accompany you for the last 600m up the road to the church, which is now the village mosque. The church, dating from the 10th century, is still in fairly good repair, thanks to its continued use for worship. The guide will show you several reliefs reminiscent of those at Akdamar.

Probably because this church is still in use, albeit as a mosque, it is not signposted as a monument from the highway. No doubt for the same reason, some restoration work has taken place here.

Öşk Vank

Another 15.5km north of the Bağbaşı turn-off, in a wide valley with the river to the left (west) of the highway, is the road to Öşk Vank, 7km off the highway and up into the mountains. In winter, you must ford the river and wind up the road to the village, where you can't miss the big, impressive monastery, built in the 10th century. Most of the roof is gone, but there are still traces of paintings, inscriptions and fine reliefs, both on the outside and on the inside columns. The ***Coşkun Çay Evi*** to the right of the church serves tea.

Tortum Gölü

West of Öşk Vank, the highway skirts the western shore of Tortum Gölü (Tortum Lake), which was formed by a landslide about three centuries ago. Note that the lake is a considerable distance from Tortum village.

The 48m Tortum Şelalesi (Waterfall), in the grounds of the Türkiye Elektrik Kurumu (TEK), is worth seeing in winter when there's plenty of water. In summer, the meagre flow of water is diverted to the hydroelectricity plant. The lake makes a beautiful picnic spot, but if you arrive alone the guard at the gate to the TEK grounds may demand a US$6 admission fee. Accompanied by a Turk you should have no problem getting in for free.

A few kilometres west of the lake at Çamlıyamaç is a lookout across the valley, and the mountains to the Tortum Çayı river gorge cut through the banded rock. Children from the green oasis below will no doubt be on hand to sell you whatever fruit is in season in an area famous for its orchards.

İşhan

Heading north from the lake, take the road on the right marked for Olur and go 6km (exactly 50km from the Vank road) through dramatic scenery to a road on the left for İşhan, marked by a sign reading 'İşhan Kilisesi'. This village is another 6km up a steep, muddy road carved out of the mountainside and probably impassable in bad weather.

The mountain village is spectacularly sited, and the **Church of the Mother of God**, 100m past the village and down the hill, is wonderful. The front faces an open space, while the back nestles into the hillside. The church was built in the 8th century and enlarged in the 11th. There are some traces of fresco inside (vanishing fast – 20 years ago whole walls were covered in them), a horseshoe arcade in the apse and several reliefs on the exterior, including one of a lion battling a snake.

There are several other churches and castles to visit to the east of İşhan along the Olur road. For details, see under Yusufeli to Kars later in this section.

Return to the Olur road, go back the 6km to the highway and then north towards Artvin. In the 8.5km between the Olur and Yusufeli roads, the highway passes through a dramatic gorge, wild and scenic, with striking bands of colour in the tortured rock of the sheer canyon walls. The Yusufeli turn-off is at a place called Su Kavuşumu (Water Confluence), where the waters of the Tortum Çayı and the Oltu Çayı join the Çoruh Nehri (Çoruh River). From here, it's 10km up the Çoruh Valley to the town.

Yusufeli

The swift Barhal Çayı rushes noisily through Yusufeli (population 4000, altitude 1050m) on its way to the Çoruh River nearby. Yusufeli, 80km from Artvin and 129km from Erzurum, is kept neat and tidy in the best tradition of alpine towns. The local people are friendly, and within 15 minutes of your arrival everyone in town will know all about you. If they offer you a cup of tea, try *kuş burnu* ('bird's beak'), a tart-sweet cherry-like herbal tea made from a mountain herb.

Now that they are used to the idea, the locals are warming up to the idea of plunging down the turgid, snowmelt-swollen river in a little rubber boat. White-water rafting is best in May and June; by August the volume of water is insufficient.

Several of the hotels in town can arrange rafting trips for around US$18 for five hours; ask at the Barhal or Çiçek Palas hotels for starters.

Mountain guides Mr Özkan Şahin (☎ 466-811 2187) and Mr Fatih Şahin (☎ 466-811 2150), also contactable through Mr Celal Düz at the Çiçek Palas Oteli, will lead you on customized treks up into the Kaçkar Dağları.

BOTH PHOTOGRAPHS BY PAT YALE

Eastern Anatolia **Top:** Tombstones with Kufic lettering haunt a Seljuk cemetery at Ahlat on the shore of Van Gölü. **Bottom:** The Menüçer Camii at Ani, the abandoned city near the Armenian border.

QUENTIN FRAYNE

PETER PTSCHELINZEW

PAT YALE

Eastern Anatolia **Top Left:** The giant heads of the stone statues atop Nemrut Dağı. **Top Right:** Carvings on a tomb within the İshak Paşa Sarayı in Doğubeyazıt. **Bottom:** Pilgrim crosses adorn the walls of the Akdamar Kilisesi, a 10th century Armenian church built on Akdamar Island, near Van.

A short stroll reveals everything Yusufeli has to offer: Halim Paşa Caddesi, the main street; the Belediye facing the main market street next to the river; the three banks (İş, Ziraat and Halk); and the few small hotels and restaurants. The town hospital (Devlet Hastanesi) is on the road into the village.

Yusufeli's postal code is 08800.

Georgian Churches Yusufeli is a convenient base for visits to the churches at Barhal and Dörtkilise. At the time of writing there was a limited dolmuş service to these villages, but soon, no doubt, the drivers will wise up and offer day-long tours to these and other Georgian churches in the region.

About 32km north-west of Yusufeli, high in the mountains over an unpaved road, **Barhal** (officially called Altıparmak, altitude 1300m), preserves a fine 10th-century Georgian church long used as the village mosque. The church and the village's mountain setting are well worth the bumpy drive or two-hour dolmuş ride. Mehmet Karahan will put you up in his ***Barhal Köyevi*** *(☎ 466-826 2071)*, or Barhan Village House, if you'd like to stay overnight.

About 13km south-west of Yusufeli via Tekkale, **Dörtkilise** (Four Churches) has another ruined 10th-century Georgian church and monastery. On the way there, you'll pass the ruins of another church perched like an eyrie on top of a sheer rock. The main church is similar to, but older and larger than, the one at Barhal, and it takes less time and effort to see it. If you don't have a car, take a dolmuş towards Kılıçkaya or Köprügören and get out at Tekkale, then hike 6km to Dörtkilise, bearing in mind that there is no sign for the church, which is high up amid the vegetation on the left-hand side of the road. If you do have a car, the road is pretty rough from Tekkale onwards.

Places to Stay Cross the footbridge from the town centre and follow the signs to find ***Akın Camping*** and ***Greenpeace Camping***, both very simple and cheap.

The hotels are of the most basic type. The official municipality room rates are US$4/6 a single/double in a waterless room but outside the busiest months of May and June you may get a discount.

The bare white, slot-like rooms at ***Çiçek Palas Oteli*** *(☎ 466-811 2393, fax 811 3393)*, are clean, and the owner talks about putting in some private baths, but the shared ones are okay. The ***Keleş*** is similar. ***Hotel Barhal*** *(☎ 466-811 3151)*, by the rickety suspension bridge over the river, has a room or two with private shower if you must have it, as does the bizarrely named ***Genç Palas*** (Youth Palace) *(☎ 466-811 2102)*. The older ***Hotel Aydın*** *(☎ 466-811 2365)*, is two flights up from the street; opposite is ***Hotel Çoruh*** with smelly toilets.

Hotel Hacıoğlu *(☎ 466-811 2087)*, is apart from these hotels on Mustafa Kemal Caddesi.

Places to Eat ***Saray Lokantası*** on Halim Paşa Caddesi, is the local cheap favourite for ready food at lunch, but can be hot and crowded at this time. ***Yılmaz Pide***, in an alley opposite the Hotel Barhal, is the place for an even cheaper lunch.

Mavi Köşk Et Restaurant, entered via an inconspicuous stairway opposite the Halkbank, is as posh as Yusufeli gets. Satin tablecloths, an elaborate (for Yusufeli) sound system and a TV add to its charm. Prices are about US$4 to US$7 for a meal, and alcoholic beverages are served. The ***Cınar Restaurant***, on the other side of the river, is the next best.

On the far side of the river near the footbridge, the neighbouring ***Mahzen Fıçı Bira*** and ***Kaçkar Fıçı Bira***, are very pleasantly situated for an evening drink. *Fıçı bira* (draught beer) is a strong point, as are the balconies directly over the river.

Getting There & Away Dolmuşes depart from Erzurum's Gölbaşı Semt Garajı several times daily for Yusufeli (130km) and other towns and villages in the Georgian valleys.

Yusufeli to Kars

With your own vehicle, the 3½-hour, 210km drive between Yusufeli and Kars can be among your most enjoyable in Turkey. The natural beauty and dramatic scenery is completely unspoiled, and there is virtually no traffic.

The scenic drive up the valley of the Oltu Çayı from Yusufeli to Olur is along a good paved road. The aptly named Taşlıköy (Stony Village), 22km east of the İşhan turn-off, illustrates the rough living in this harsh if beautiful region: the low stone houses with sod roofs are built half into the earth to escape the rigours of the winter cold.

Just north-east of the Olur road, look over the bridge over the Gölbaşı to see a **ruined Georgian castle** perched on a rock spur, one of many in the region.

Continue south to Yolboyu, the junction with roads east to Bana (Penek) and Göle, and south to Oltu. At Yolboyu, **twin castles** on opposite sides of the stream guard this fertile valley, the eastern gateway to the mountainous region.

There's an even grander **citadel** at Oltu, south-west of Bana and 36km south of the Olur castle.

Bana (Penek), 11km east of Yolboyu, has a fine **7th-century Georgian church** set in a riverside meadow 1km south-east of the road across the Penek Çayı. Though the church is worth a visit, access is difficult and only for the truly devoted Georgian church goer.

From the Bana church it's 7km north-east to the Şenkaya turn-off and another 3km to the village of Akşir. About 17km past Akşir in a particularly lush and narrow valley is Değirmenlidere village, a collection of **low stone houses** with wood portals – an eerie sight when unoccupied – which serve as summer quarters for transhumant herders.

At the upper end of Değirmenlidere, the road emerges from the pine-fringed mountain valleys and the countryside widens out into a vast rolling steppe. The road surface deteriorates markedly soon after, the potholes slowing your vehicle's speed. Göle, 6km past Değirmenlidere, is a desolate village of low stone hovels clustered near a big army base, with two dairies on the outskirts. It doesn't improve until 30km short of Kars. For information on Kars and Ani, see those sections later in this chapter.

ARTVİN

Artvin (ahrt-VEEN, population 20,000, altitude 600m) is the capital of the province bearing the same name. You can approach it from Yusufeli (75km, 1¼ hours) or from Hopa on the Black Sea coast (70km, 1½ hours). Sit on the right-hand side of the bus coming up from Hopa to get the best views.

If you come from Hopa, remember that any liquid-filled containers in your luggage will expand and leak as you ascend into the mountains. Keep these containers with you and open them periodically to adjust the atmospheric pressure.

The ride to Artvin via either route is wonderfully scenic. As you approach the town you will notice ruined medieval castles guarding the steep mountain passes. During the third week in June, the Kafkasör Yaylası, a pasture 7km from Artvin, becomes the scene of an annual festival, the Kafkasör Kültür ve Sanat Festivalı (Caucasus Culture & Arts Festival), with *boğa güreşleri* (bull wrestling) matches as the main event.

Given the town's spectacular mountain setting, it should be a much nicer place to spend a few days than it actually is. In fact Artvin is terribly two-faced, putting on a show of small-town respectability by daylight that rapidly gives way to something raunchier as the sun goes down. Artvin has been dubbed 'one large brothel'. There's a nightlife here to equal Trabzon's but not of a kind that would suit everyone.

Orientation & Information

Artvin is perched on a high hill which snakes its way upwards above a bend in the Çoruh River. It's little more than one steep street (İnönü Caddesi) and is easily negotiated on foot, except for the trip to and from the otogar which lies in the valley below.

İnönü Caddesi is lined with the government offices required of a provincial capital: the Valilik (Provincial Headquarters, also called Hükümet Konağı), the Belediye, and lots of banks. Most hotels are within a block or two of the Valilik.

Artvin's otogar is in Köprübaşı (sometimes called Çarşı), the riverside district at the foot of the hill. Minibuses (Artvin Belediyesi Halk Münübüsü, US$0.30) shuttle passengers between the town centre and the otogar at Köprübaşı. Alternatively, a taxi up will cost you about US$3.

Artvin's postal code is 08000.

Places to Stay

As in Trabzon, most of the cheap hotels have long since given up the unequal battle to make money out of tourism, in favour of the easier pickings from prostitution. At the time of writing the following hotels are legitimate lodging places, but this is subject to change.

Şafak, Konak and ***Trabzon*** are all dispiriting, even at US$2 a bed. Much better is ***Güven*** *(☎/fax 466-211 1118)*, a family run place across İnönü Caddesi from the Valilik and down a few steps on Hamam Sokak behind the PTT and Türk Telekom. The lobby is not inspiring but the rooms, with hospital-style beds, are clean and simple, and cost from US$6 per person, with another US$1 for a shower. Two roof terraces offer mountain views. The Şehir Hamamıı is only a few metres away, guaranteeing a good bath. It's basically for men but women can use it later in the day if they make a prior appointment.

One step up in price and 'comfort' is ***Hotel Kaçkar*** *(☎ 466-212 3397)*, also in Hamam Sokak. The rooms are pretty simple (although some have huge TVs), and a few have wonderful mountain views. A single costs US$7, a double US$12. You may occasionally hear the sounds of nocturnal delight.

Artvin's best hotel is supposedly ***Karahan Otel*** *(☎ 466-212 1802, fax 212 2420, İnönü Caddesi 16)*, although the entrance is actually up the hill on the opposite side of the building. The 48 shower-equipped rooms are pleasant enough, and much better than the old-fashioned lobby and dreary exterior might suggest. However, prices are nothing short of outrageous for what you get at US$24/30 a single/double. It may be booked solid by groups. If so, have a look at ***Özgün Otel*** *(☎ 466-212 5253)* a few steps away toward the Merkez Camii. Passable rooms with shower are US$12 a double.

Kafkasör Tatil Köyü Dağ Evleri (Caucasus Holiday Village Mountain Chalets) *(☎ 466-212 5013)* are simple lodgings near the Kafkasör meadow. Ask at the Karahan Otel about access.

Places to Eat

Efkar Restaurant, at the foot of İnönü Caddesi where it turns to descend the slope, boasts 'million dollar views' from its terrace. It's certainly a good place to take breakfast (US$2), surrounded by signs instructing you not to throw rubbish or cigarette butts over the balcony. It's in hot competition for passing trade with ***Nazar Restoran***.

Hanedan Restorant *(☎ 466-212 7222, İnönü Caddesi 23)*, also has fine views. Get there early as there are only a few tables by the window and big groups like this place.

For cheaper fare, explore the upper reaches of İnönü Caddesi. ***Saray Pide Salonu***, to the left of the Hotel Kaçkar, has good, fresh, cheap pide and fine valley views. ***Birlik Pide ve Lahmacun*** at İnönü 83B, is also good. ***Çınar Lokantası*** has cheap soups and stews.

For tea, pastries and light meals, try the two ***Köşk Pastanesis***, across the street from one another midway along İnönü Caddesi, near the big ***Aile Çay Bahçesi***. ***Cennet Pastanesi***, nearby at İnönü 54, serves luscious puddings in modern surrounds.

The Karahan Otel restaurant is one of Artvin's best but it's not cheap: breakfast costs US$4, a set-menu dinner US$12.

Getting There & Away

The roads from Artvin to Hopa and Erzurum are fairly good, smooth and fast.

A few minibuses depart from Artvin in the morning and early afternoon for Yusufeli, Hopa and Rize, circulating through the upper town looking for passengers before descending to Köprübaşı and the otogar. Metro, Artvin Expres and As Turizm have ticket offices on İnönü Caddesi across from the Valilik as well as at the otogar.

Details of some daily services from Artvin follow:

Erzurum – 215km, four hours, US$7; several buses and dolmuşes

Hopa – 70km, 1½ hours, US$2; frequent dolmuşes
Kars – 270km, five hours, US$8; two buses
Samsun – 577km, eight hours, US$14; one or two buses
Tortum – 91km, 2½ hours, US$4
Trabzon – 255km, 4½ hours, US$10; frequent buses
Yusufeli – 75km, 1¼ hours, US$2.50; several dolmuşes

Some buses coming from Erzurum and heading on to Hopa don't go into the otogar but drop you at the roadside at the very bottom of the hill. Dolmuşes from here take time to fill up, and the taxis waiting will charge about US$4 to run you to the top.

ARTVİN TO KARS

The most direct route between Artvin and Kars, a distance of 205km, is via the old Georgian town of Şavşat. The road deteriorates east of Şavşat, so plan on taking more time for the journey than the distance alone might indicate. The southern road via Ardanuç is little more than a track; go via Şavşat. Both roads meet at Ardahan, then go on via Gölebert and Susuz to Kars.

If you have your own vehicle, start early from Artvin (or Kars) and plan to make an excursion to one of the Georgian churches within easy reach of the main road. Take some water and snacks, whether you go by bus or car. If you have your own car, it's a good idea to fill your fuel tank before setting out on this journey.

Ardanuç, on the southern route, boasts a large **Bagratid fortress**. The village of Bulanık is 14km further on, and the 10th-century **church of Yeni Rabat** is a few kilometres off the main road.

On the road to Şavşat just after passing the Ardanuç turn-off, look for a stone bridge and a sign to Hamamlı. This village, just over 6km off the main road, boasts the fine 10th-century **Georgian church of Dolishane** (now a mosque). Back on the main road, another 12km brings you to Pırnallı village and the trail head for the 30 to 45-minute hike up to the 9th-century **Georgian monastery** and **church of Porta**.

Another **fortress** guards the western approach to Şavşat. From here you can make an excursion north via the Veliköy road for 10km to Cevizli to see the 10th-century **monastery church of Tbeti**, in ruins but still beautiful in its setting.

After traversing the rough road east of Şavşat, the simple town of Ardahan seems an oasis of civilisation. There are a few very basic services, but you'll want to press on to Kars for the night.

ERZURUM TO KARS

East of Erzurum the highway climbs into a landscape of wide vistas, rich irrigated fields and the inevitable flocks of cattle and sheep.

Pasinler

Some 38km east of Erzurum, the **Hasankale fortress** dominates Pasinler (population 22,000, altitude 1656m) from its rock promontory. Much of the triple-walled fortress, reached by a block-paved street on the western side of the highway, is in good repair (some restored). It dates from the 1330s when the İlkhanid emir Hasan had it built. Extensive repairs were made later by the Akkoyunlu leader Uzun Hasan.

The town is conservative in the eastern way, with fiery-eyed, white-bearded men and many women completely enveloped by burlap-coloured chadors. Watch out for shops selling *Hasankale lavaşı,* the village's special metre-long thin loaves of bread.

Pasinler is famous in the region for its *kaplıcalar* (hot springs). From the main intersection next to the Belediye, cross the railway line, turn left and continue 800m to a bridge leading to the Hotel Ter Tur. On either side of the bridge stand bathhouses for men and women. Those for women are open from 10.30 am to 7 pm, those for men for longer. To use them costs about US$1.

To the north-west of the baths is an amusement park with a children's playground and an exhibition steam train (a locomotive and two carriages, but no track) put here no doubt to lure Erzurumlus out to Pasinler on weekends.

The highway and the rail line follow the broad flood plain of the Aras Nehri (Aras River) from Pasinler eastward 43km to Horasan. In Köprüköy just before Horasan you may spot the **Çoban Köprü**, a 16th-century stone bridge designed, it is said, by the great Sinan.

At Karakurt, the road leaves the river valley to climb into the mountains through pine forests, passing one fertile mountain pasture after another on its way to Sarıkamış.

Places to Stay *Hotel Ter Tur (☎ 442-661 3538)* charges US$10/12 a single/double for a quiet but not especially inspiring room with shower. The restaurant is much better than the rooms. A sizeable meal including alcohol costs about US$8. At the back of the hotel are private cabins with their own plunge pools and massage areas. Since the last half-hourly shuttle bus to Pasinler from Erzurum (US$0.50) goes at 10 pm in summer, bath-lovers could consider staying here instead of in Erzurum itself.

For more modest budgets, ***Hotel Park*** *(☎ 442-661 3569)*, a block west of the Belediye in the market, is about the best cheap bet, with clean, simple rooms for US$5 per person. There are some four-bed rooms on the ground floor.

Sarıkamış

Sarıkamış (sah-RUH-kah-mush, population 22,000, altitude 2125m), a lumbering town 152km east of Erzurum, has a small ski resort, a huge army base, a forestry headquarters and, on its eastern outskirts, a big shoe factory.

The army base and a stone monument on the eastern outskirts are poignant reminders of a military disaster. In December 1914, during the early days of WWI, the Ottoman Third Army was encamped for the winter at Sarıkamış, defending this approach to Anatolia against an equal force of Russian troops. The egomaniacal Enver Paşa, effective head of the Ottoman war effort, ordered his troops to attack and push eastward – a disastrous tactic in midwinter. (Mustafa Kemal (Atatürk) was astounded and appalled when he heard of the order.) The Ottomans lost 75,000 troops to cold, hunger and casualties. The Russians counter-attacked and took Erzurum.

Places to Stay Sarıkamış has one hotel better than most hotels in Kars. Since there are frequent buses, you could consider staying here and taking day trips to Kars.

Turistik Hotel Sarıkamış *(☎ 474-413 4176, Halk Caddesi 64)*, is in the centre of town, marked prominently by signs. Although the hotel is not fancy, the lobby is colourfully decorated with local carpets and animal skins, and the rooms are well kept and fairly cheerful. The dining room is quite serviceable. Rooms cost US$7/14 a single/double with bath and breakfast.

Çelik Palas, near where the buses stop, is as basic as they come.

Sarıkamış Kayak Tesisleri *(☎ 474-413 4249)* offers ski facilities 4km west of the town centre. From the Belediye, follow the signs 1.5km to the railway line, cross it and continue past the ghostly shells of crenellated stone warehouse and factory buildings. About 3km from the Belediye turn right by a crude brickyard and walk up the hill to the ski lift. The simple *kayak evi* (ski lodge) has accommodation. You may be able to find lodging here in summer (phone first), and certainly can in winter.

KARS

East of Sarıkamış, the highway climbs out of the lush mountain valleys and away from the evergreen forests to vast rolling steppes with mountains in the distance. It is in this sea-of-grass setting that you'll find Kars (population 80,000, altitude 1768m), a desolate agricultural and garrison town dominated by a permanently lowering sky and fierce, wet weather.

You will see lots of police and soldiers in Kars, and every one of them can tell you without hesitation the precise number of days he has yet to serve in Kars before he can go west to 'civilisation'. As for the locals, a harsh climate and a rough history has made them, for the most part, dour and sombre,

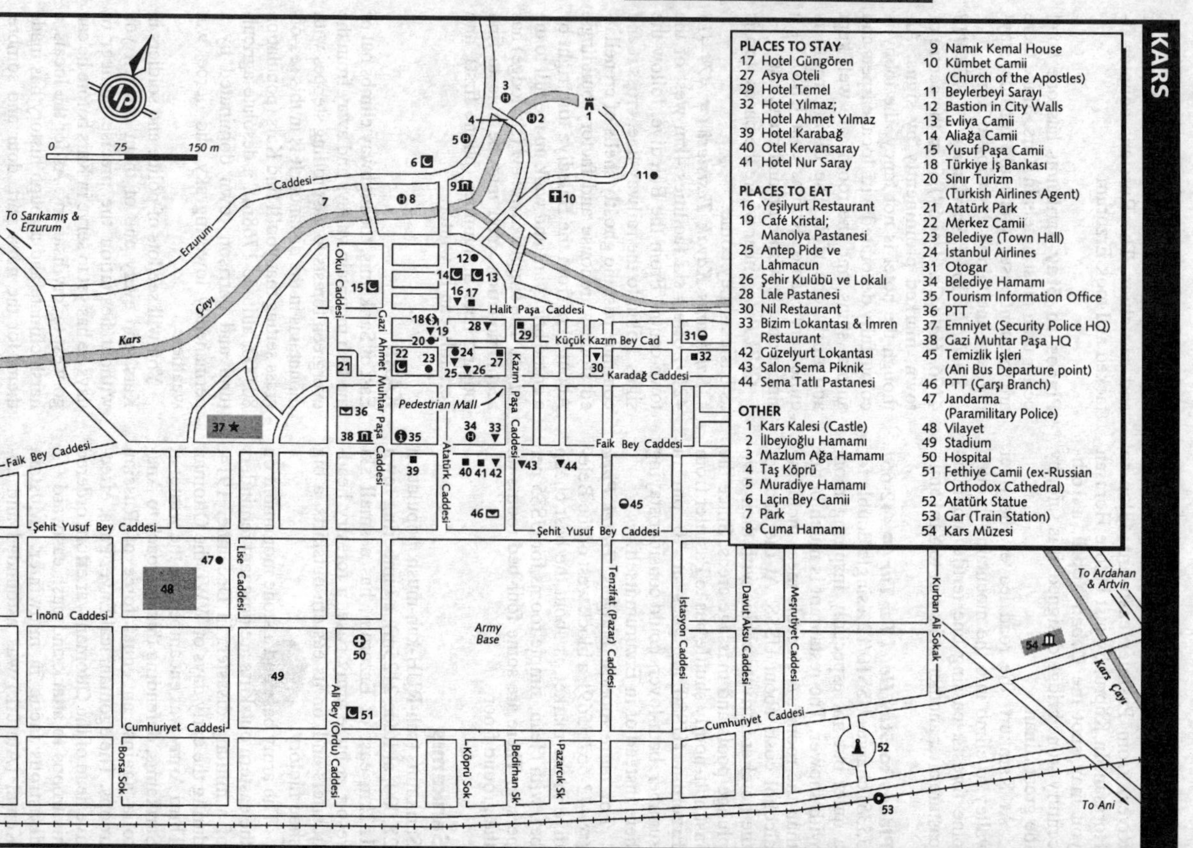
KARS
PLACES TO STAY
17 Hotel Güngören
27 Asya Oteli
29 Hotel Temel
32 Hotel Yılmaz; Hotel Ahmet Yılmaz
39 Hotel Karabağ
40 Otel Kervansaray
41 Hotel Nur Saray
PLACES TO EAT
16 Yeşilyurt Restaurant
19 Café Kristal; Manolya Pastanesi
25 Antep Pide ve Lahmacun
26 Şehir Kulübü ve Lokalı
28 Lale Pastanesi
30 Nil Restaurant
33 Bizim Lokantası & İmren Restaurant
42 Güzelyurt Lokantası
43 Salon Sema Piknik
44 Sema Tatlı Pastanesi
OTHER
1 Kars Kalesi (Castle)
2 İlbeyioğlu Hamamı
3 Mazlum Ağa Hamamı
4 Taş Köprü
5 Muradiye Hamamı
6 Laçin Bey Camii
7 Park
8 Cuma Hamamı
9 Namık Kemal House
10 Kümbet Camii (Church of the Apostles)
11 Beylerbeyi Sarayı
12 Bastion in City Walls
13 Evliya Camii
14 Aliağa Camii
15 Yusuf Paşa Camii
18 Türkiye İş Bankası
20 Sınır Turizm (Turkish Airlines Agent)
21 Atatürk Park
22 Merkez Camii
23 Belediye (Town Hall)
24 İstanbul Airlines
31 Otogar
34 Belediye Hamamı
35 Tourism Information Office
36 PTT
37 Emniyet (Security Police HQ)
38 Gazi Muhtar Paşa HQ
45 Temizlik İşleri (Ani Bus Departure point)
46 PTT (Çarşı Branch)
47 Jandarma (Paramilitary Police)
48 Vilayet
49 Stadium
50 Hospital
51 Fethiye Camii (ex-Russian Orthodox Cathedral)
52 Atatürk Statue
53 Gar (Train Station)
54 Kars Müzesi
0 75 150 m
To Sarıkamış & Erzurum
Erzurum Caddesi
Kars Çayı
Okul Caddesi
Gazi Ahmet Muhtar Paşa Caddesi
Halit Paşa Caddesi
Küçük Kazım Bey Cad
Kazım Paşa Caddesi
Karadağ Caddesi
Pedestrian Mall
Atatürk Caddesi
Faik Bey Caddesi
Şehit Yusuf Bey Caddesi
Lise Caddesi
İnönü Caddesi
Army Base
Tenzifat (Pazar) Caddesi
İstasyon Caddesi
Davut Aksu Caddesi
Meşrutiyet Caddesi
Kurban Ali Sokak
To Ardahan & Artvin
Kars Çayı
Ali Bey (Ordu) Caddesi
Cumhuriyet Caddesi
Borsa Sok
Köprü Sok
Bedirhan Sk
Pazarcık Sk
To Ani

though nonetheless welcoming once you speak to them. They're said to be descended from the Karsaks, a Turkish tribe which came from the Caucasus in the 2nd century BC and who gave their name to the town.

When the sun shines there are hints at what might have been, with fine pastel-coloured stone buildings slowly crumbling to dust. Otherwise Kars has a vaguely Wild West atmosphere, with men on horseback galloping along roads so potholed the taxis have to weave their way along them.

The main reason for coming to Kars is to visit Ani. While you're in Kars, however, there are other things worth seeing.

History

Dominated by a stark medieval fortress, Kars was a pawn in the imperial land-grabbing game played by Turkey and Russia during the 19th century. The Russians captured Kars in 1878, installed a garrison, and held it until 1920 and the Turkish War of Independence, when the republican forces retook it. One of the town's large mosques was obviously built as a Russian Orthodox church and many of the sturdier stone buildings along the main streets date back to the Russian occupation.

Orientation

The Russians must have had great plans for Kars. They laid it out on a grandiose grid plan which, only now over a century later, is being completed. Nonetheless, almost everything in Kars except the train station and the museum is within walking distance. The new otogar is a few hundred metres east of the museum, off the Artvin-Ardahan road on the south-eastern outskirts of the town. Dolmuş minibuses run from the otogar 2km to the town centre.

Information

The Kars Tourism Information Office (☎ 474-223 2300, fax 223 8452), Gazi Ahmet Muhtar Paşa Caddesi 135, at the corner of Faik Bey Caddesi, is open from 8.30 am to 5.30 pm daily in summer, closed weekends in winter. This is where you come to get your permit to visit Ani. Kars' postal code is 36000.

Money Several banks along Atatürk Caddesi advertise exchange facilities, although if you roll up with a travellers cheque they're likely to look at you askance. Persevere and you should manage to cash it. As usual, the Türkiye İş Bankası is a good bet, charging a flat US$3 commission.

Kars Müzesi

Kars Museum is worth seeing. Hours are from 8.30 am to 5.30 pm, except Monday, but with so little to do in Kars, staff are usually on duty on that day too. Admission is US$1.

There are exhibits from the Old Bronze Age, the Roman and Greek periods, and Seljuk and Ottoman times. Photographs show excavations at Ani and there are shots of Armenian churches in Kars province. Look out for a pair of carved doors from the town's main Orthodox church (now a mosque) and a Russian church bell from the time of Tsar Nicholas II (1894-1917).

Don't miss the ethnographic exhibits upstairs, as this area produces some very fine kilims, carpets and *cicims* (embroidered kilims). Costumes, saddlebags, jewellery, samovars and a home carpet loom complete the display. A curiosity designed for local consumption is the Katliam Bölümü (Genocide Section), a showcase displaying photos and documentation (all in Turkish) about the massacre of Muslims by Armenian forces in the early part of the century.

Behind the museum is the railway coach in which representatives of Russia's Bolshevik government and the fledgling Turkish Republic signed the protocol ending the Russian occupation and annexation of Kars in 1920.

Kümbet Camii (Church of the Apostles)

Although called the Drum-Dome Mosque (Kümbet Camii), the Church of the Apostles was actually built between 932 and 937 by the Bagratid King Abas. It was repaired extensively in 1579, when the Ottomans rebuilt much of the city, and the porches were added in the 19th century. The relief carvings on the drum are of the apostles.

Locked and slowly surrendering to weeds, the church would make an excellent museum if Kars ever develops enough of a tourist trade. For now, the only way to see the interior is to peek through the doors on the river side.

Taş Köprü (Stone Bridge)

Near the church is the Taş Köprü which dates from the 15th century. It was repaired in 1579 along with everything else in town, but was later ruined by an earthquake. In 1719 it was rebuilt in its present form by the local Karaoğulları emirs. Ruins of the Ulu Cami and a palace called the **Beylerbeyı Sarayı** nestle beneath the castle (kale) near the bridge.

Kars Kalesi (Castle)

There has probably been a fortress at this strategic spot since earliest times, but records show that one was built by the Saltuk Turks in 1152 and torn down by Tamerlane in 1386. It was rebuilt upon the order of the Ottoman sultan Murat III by his grand vizier Lala Mustafa Paşa in 1579. Further repairs were made in 1616 and 1636, and the entire complex was rebuilt yet again in 1855.

The kale was the scene of bitter fighting during and after WWI. When the Russian armies withdrew in 1920, control of Kars was left in the hands of the Armenian forces which had allied themselves with Russia during the war. Civilians, whether Christian or Muslim, suffered oppression and worse when under the control of irregular troops of the opposing religion. As the slaughter of Christian Armenians occurred in some parts of eastern Turkey, there was also slaughter of Muslim Turks and Kurds around Kars until the republican armies took the kale.

Kars Kalesi is open during daylight hours; there is no admission charge. Take the road which passes the Church of the Apostles and the ruined palace known as the Beylerbeyı Sarayı. The huge sign dominating the kale is a quote from Atatürk: *Vatan Sana Minettardır* ('Your Country is Grateful to You', referring to the armed forces).

Within the kale, besides the ubiquitous boys asking for handouts, is the tomb of Kahraman Celal Baba, the Kale Camii, a 19th-century cannon, and an İç Kale (castle keep) which is off limits. In fine weather, the views of the town amply reward you for the climb.

Historic Houses

The best example of a traditional Kars house is the **Gazi Muhtar Paşa Headquarters** on the corner of Faik Bey and Gazi Ahmet Muhtar Paşa caddesis. This stone house was used as an HQ by Gazi Ahmet Muhtar Paşa, commander of the Ottoman forces during the Russian war in 1877. Later a school, then for a while the tourist office (if only it still were), it's now not open for visits.

The other house with a history is not much to look at, but its former occupant, Namık Kemal (1840-88), played a significant role in the development of modern Turkey. Born in Tekirdağ, the son of the Sultan's court astronomer, he became a government translator. An interest in European society and philosophy led him to translate the works of Rousseau and Montesquieu, and then to expound a similar political philosophy in plays, essays, articles and poems.

Kemal advocated Turkey's adoption of European political, technical, economic and social advances, but did so in the context of devout Islam. He reinterpreted European progress for an Islamic context, adapted it to Islamic traditions, and made it more acceptable to traditional Muslims. Kemal's calls for 'freedom and fatherland' got him into trouble with the sultan. He died in internal exile on Chios, but his ideas were eagerly absorbed by the Young Turks and by Mustafa Kemal (Atatürk).

Hamams

The Belediye Hamamı is on Faik Bey Caddesi, opposite the Otel Kervansaray. The grungy Muradiye Hamamı at the citadel end of the Stone Bridge is for women only.

Perhaps because of its cold climate, Kars has many other warm steamy baths as well.

Places to Stay – Budget

Kars' hotel line-up is as depressing as the town's weather. This is a place where you definitely want to spend a bit more to get decent accommodation.

The best value for money is ***Hotel Temel*** *(☎ 474-223 1376, fax 223 1323, Kazım Paşa Caddesi 4/A)*. Clean and relatively pleasant rooms, some with private shower and wild wallpaper, cost US$12/20 a single/double. Avoid the noisier rooms on the western (kale) side.

Hotel Güngören *(☎ 474-212 0298, fax 223 4821, Halit Paşa Caddesi, Millet Sokak 4)*, is relatively new but reflects hard use. Every room has a private bath with tub and shower, and there's an adjoining hamam and a grill restaurant. Rates are US$15/25 a single/double.

The longtime owner of the Hotel Yılmaz, near the otogar, died in 1997 and upon his death two factions in his family went to war over his estate, which included the hotel. (*Yılmaz* means 'He doesn't give in'.) The Solomonic settlement was to divide the hotel right down the middle. The ***Hotel Yılmaz*** *(☎ 474-223 5174, fax 212 5176, Küçük Kazım Bey Caddesi 146)* occupies the right side of the building. Though the Yılmaz was once the best in town (which wasn't saying much), now even that dubious distinction is long gone.

The left side ***Hotel Ahmet Yılmaz*** *(☎ 474-212 4215, fax 223 1235, Küçük Kazım Bey Caddesi 148)*, however, has been renovated, is better maintained, and charges about half of what the right half charges, so use the door to the left when you enter the building and you'll get a decent place to stay at a decent price.

The 33 room ***Asya Oteli*** *(☎ 474-223 2299, Küçük Kazım Bey Caddesi 50)*, is grubby and run-down, but quiet. Rooms with shower go for US$6/9 a single/double.

If your budget is painfully slim, it may match the 38 room ***Otel Kervansaray*** *(☎ 474-223 1990, Faik Bey Caddesi 124)*. Basic and beat-up, its double rooms come waterless or with sink for US$5, or with shower (but no toilet) for US$7; you can haggle for discounts if it's not busy. Rooms at the back are quieter. The Belediye Hamamı is right across the street. Next door to the Kervansaray, the ***Hotel Nur Saray*** at Faik Bey Caddesi 208, is even more basic, if that's possible.

Places to Stay – Mid-Range

Kars has one reasonably decent modern hotel, the three-star, 50 room ***Hotel Karabağ*** *(☎ 474-212 3480, fax 223 3089, Faik Bey Caddesi 184)*. Rooms with private bath, minibar, TV and (supposedly) air-con cost US$35/50 a single/double. Rooms on the front may be noisy. The restaurant is the most genteel in town.

Groups tend to favour the similarly priced, 96 room ***Anıhan Motel*** *(☎ 474-212 3517, 223 7404)*, but its position 2km south of central Kars detracts from its usefulness unless you have a car.

Places to Eat

Kars is noted for its excellent honey. Look out for ***Lale Pastanesi***, Halit Paşa Caddesi 166. Most of the day it sells just dry cakes and biscuits, but its *kahvaltı* (breakfast) is Kars honey and butter to spread on half a loaf of fresh bread, with tea or hot, sweet milk. Several shops near the Temel and Güngören hotels also sell Kars honey and the local *kaşar peynir* ('kosher' mild yellow cheese). Have a look in Kesgin Ticaret and Sizin Mandıra on Kazım Paşa Caddesi 70 and 72, as well as in Aydar Ticaret, Halit Paşa Caddesi 206, across from the Vakıfbank.

Salon Sema Piknik, Faik Bey Caddesi 204, next to the Kars Şehir Sineması (cinema), is good for light meals and feels comfortable for both genders. ***Sema Tatlı Pastanesi***, Faik Bey Caddesi 238, is the town's fanciest pastry shop.

For cheap ready food, try ***Bizim Lokantasi*** just off Faik Bey on Kazım Paşa Caddesi, and ***İmren*** nearby.

Unexpectedly in a town so full of sheep and horses, the ***Nil Restaurant,*** not far from the Yılmaz hotels, offers several meat-free dishes as well as the usual range of tasty stews.

On Atatürk Caddesi are ***Café Kristal*** and ***Manolya Pastanesi***. The Kristal is the brightest, most cheerful place in Kars and serves a wide range of ready meals: soup, rice, beans and a cold drink for about US$3. 'Saturday is *mantı* (Turkish ravioli) day.' Afterwards you can get a coffee and a pastry in the Manolya. Just up the street, ***Antep Pide ve Lahmacun*** is more traditional but does at least make an effort with its decor.

Perhaps the most decent non-hotel restaurant for a good dinner with drinks is ***Şehir Kulübü ve Lokalı***, Karadağ Caddesi 45 near Atatürk Caddesi. A three-course meal with Efes beer costs US$6 to US$9.

Güzelyurt Lokantası, a few doors down from the Otel Kervansaray on Faik Bey Caddesi, serves all three meals, but in the evenings it tends to attract men who are more interested in drinking than eating. Check prices before ordering as bills have a habit of mounting up apparently by themselves.

For *ocakbaşı* (open-grill) dining, try the restaurant at the Hotel Güngören.

Things to Buy

Kars *halıları* (carpets) are coarse woven with simple but bold patterns and colours. Many of the local yarns used are undyed, retaining the natural colour of the fleece. There are several grades of carpets, and thus several price ranges. Once you've found a carpet you like and have agreed on a price per square metre (haggle!), the carpet is measured, yielding the exact price.

These are not the finest of Turkish carpets but they're sturdy and inexpensive, although heavy and bulky to carry home.

Getting There & Away

Air Turkish Airlines runs a daily nonstop flight to and from Ankara, with connections for İstanbul. The ticket agency is Sınır Turizm (☎ 474-212 3838, fax 212 3841), Atatürk Caddesi 80, next to Café Kristal.

İstanbul Airlines (☎ 474-223 7539, fax 212 5267), Atatürk Caddesi 110, has nonstop flights twice weekly to and from İstanbul.

Bus Kars has two otogars, the new one near the museum 2km from the centre, and the old one near the Hotel Ahmet Yılmaz. Dolmuşes shuttle between the new otogar and the town centre.

The major company here is Doğu Kars, with ticket offices at both otogars and on Faik Bey Caddesi between Atatürk and Kazım Paşa caddesis, near the Otel Kervansaray. For almost all westbound trips you'll take a minibus to Erzurum (205km, 3½ hours, US$5), then board a full-size bus for the onward journey. Here are some distances, journey times and fares:

Ankara – 1100km, 16 hours, US$20; a few buses
Artvin – 270km, five hours, US$8; a few buses
Doğubeyazıt – 240km, three hours, US$6; see following paragraph
Trabzon – 525km, nine hours, US$10; a few direct buses, or change at Erzurum or Artvin

For Ani (45km, 50 minutes), see the transport notes in the following Ani section.

For Doğubeyazıt a special warning is in order. At the time of writing there are very few direct buses from Kars to Doğubayazıt. The usual way to get there is to take one bus to Iğdır then another to Doğubayazıt. The wait in Iğdır varies from minutes to hours which doesn't stop the Kars transport sharks from selling you 'direct' tickets to Doğubayazıt at premium prices. The ticket may indeed take you all the way from Kars to Doğubayazıt, but chances are when you reach Iğdır it will stop like all the rest and you'll have to change.

Train One might hope that the Kars Garı (train station) would be a 19th-century Russian architectural extravagance, but unfortunately it's a crumbling, characterless modern structure. A statue of Atatürk greets you as you approach, and a valiant old steam locomotive, mounted in front of the station, evokes a more romantic age of rail travel.

Three trains – the *Karma* local train, the *Doğu Ekspresi* and the *Yeni Doğu Ekspresi* – shuttle daily between Kars and Erzurum at inconvenient times, taking four to six hours to make the trip (the bus takes 3½ or less).

Returning from Kars to Erzurum the times are more convenient, and you may just want to try the *Yeni Doğu Ekspresi* which departs Kars at 8.30 am on Wednesday, Friday and Sunday, arriving in Erzurum at 12.27 pm on its way to İstanbul (arriving there at 5.30 pm the following day). The *Doğu Ekspresi* departs from Kars daily at 7.10 am and reaches Erzurum at 11.23 am.

A one-way ticket between Kars and Erzurum costs US$3 in 2nd class. Travelling to Ankara costs US$12, İstanbul US$17, with another US$2 for a couchette. Readers have reported waits of several days for booking couchettes.

ANİ

The ruined city at Ani, 45km east of Kars, is striking. Its great walls, over a kilometre in length, rise to challenge you as you drive across the wheat-covered plains and into the poor Turkish village of Ocaklı Köyü. Within the walls is a medieval ghost town set in grassy fields overlooking the deep gorge cut by the Arpa Çayı stream, which forms the boundary between the Turkish and Armenian republics.

During the Soviet period, Ani was within the 700m no-man's-land imposed by Moscow on the Turkish border. Visits to the ruins were governed by the strict terms of a protocol agreed between Moscow and Ankara. Today the mood is much more relaxed – photography, note-taking and picnics are permitted – although remnants of the past linger on in the bureaucracy which must be negotiated to visit the site.

History

Anahid, the Persian equivalent of the Greek goddess Aphrodite, was worshipped by the pagan Urartians and has left her name on this great city as Ani.

On an important east-west trade route and well served by its natural defences, Ani was selected by King Ashot III (952-77) as the site of his new capital in 961, when he moved here from Kars. His successors Smbat II (976-89) and Gagik I (990-1020) reigned over Ani's continued prosperity but after Gagik, internecine feuds and Byzantine encroachment weakened the Armenian state.

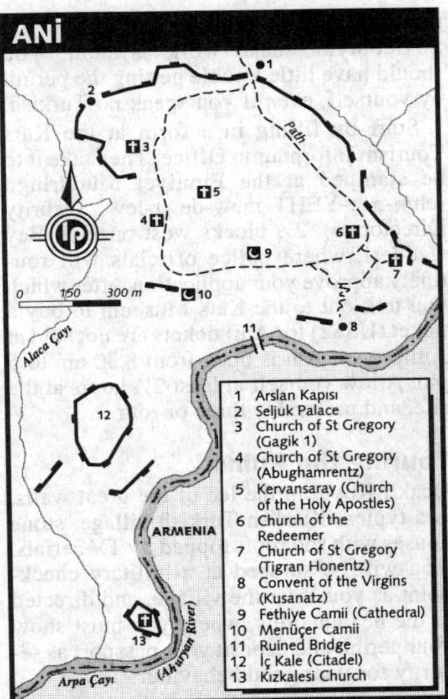

The Byzantines took over the city in 1045, then in 1064 came the Great Seljuks of Iran, then the Kingdom of Georgia and for a time local Kurdish emirs. The struggle for the city went on until the Mongols arrived in 1239 and cleared everybody else out. The nomadic Mongols had no use for city life, so they cared little when the great earthquake of 1319 destroyed much of Ani's beauty – not to mention infrastructure. The depredations of Tamerlane soon after were the last blow: trade routes shifted; Ani lost what revenues it had managed to retain; the city died; and the earthquake-damaged hulks of its great buildings have been slowly crumbling to ruin ever since.

Information

Since Ani stands so near the Armenian border, you must have permission from the Turkish authorities to visit it. The procedure for getting permission takes about 30 minutes, and is reminiscent of the old Soviet-style 'make work' system. You should have little trouble getting the permit by yourself, even if you speak no Turkish.

Start by filling in a form at the Kars Tourism Information Office. Then take it to be stamped at the Emniyet Müdürlüğü (ehm-nee-YEHT mew-dewr-lew, Security Directorate), 2½ blocks west on Faik Bey Caddesi, where police officials will routinely approve your application, after which you trek out to the Kars Museum to buy a ticket (US$2) for Ani; tickets are not sold at Ani proper. Ani is open from 8.30 am to 5 pm. Allow yourself at least 2½ hours at the site, and preferably three or four.

Touring the Ruins

Ocaklı Köyü, in the lee of the great walls, is a typical Kurdish-Turkish village: stone houses with sod roofs topped by TV aerials. You will be stopped at a military checkpoint as you enter the village, and directed to the headquarters, where you must show your permit and deposit your passport as security for your good behaviour.

In the village, you'll smell the distinctive aroma of burning *tezek*, cakes of dried dung used for fuel. The modern 'rest facilities' (restaurant, toilets, shops) built opposite the main gate by the district government may or may not be open and serving. Village children will volunteer to guide you in exchange for tourist treats: coins, sweets, empty plastic water bottles, pens and cigarettes.

Enter the ruined city through the **Arslan Kapısı**, a bent double gate supposedly named for Alp Arslan, the Seljuk sultan who conquered Ani in 1064, but probably also suggested by the lion in relief on the inner wall.

Your first view of Ani is stunning: wrecks of great stone buildings adrift on a sea of undulating grass, landmarks in a ghost city of nearly 100,000 people which once rivalled Constantinople in power and glory. Use your imagination to see the one and two-storey buildings which would have crowded the city's streets, with the great churches looming above them. Today birdsong is almost the only sound carried on the constant breeze, and the tangy scent of mint rises from underfoot as you walk.

The shepherds of Ocaklı Köyü pasture their flocks on the lush grass which grows atop the sprawling field of rubble from Ani's collapsed buildings. During your explorations, you're sure to be approached by someone wanting to sell you *eski para* (old coins) or perhaps a bit of coloured tile unearthed in the ruins.

Follow the path to the left and tour the churches in clockwise order.

Church of the Redeemer The Church of the Redeemer dates from 1034-36, but only half of the ruined structure is still standing, the other half having been destroyed by lightning in 1957.

Church of St Gregory (Tigran Honentz) Beyond the Redeemer church, down by the walls separating Ani from the gorge of the Arpa Çayi, is the Church of St Gregory the Illuminator, called the Resimli Kilise (Church with Pictures) in Turkish. Named for the apostle to the Armenians, it was built by a pious nobleman named Tigran Honentz in 1215, and though exposure and vandalism have done great damage to the interior, it is still in better condition than most other buildings at Ani. Look for the long inscription in Armenian carved on the eastern and southern exterior walls, as well as the frescoes inside depicting scenes from the Bible and Armenian church history.

Convent of the Virgins Follow the paths south-west and down into the Arpa Çayi gorge to visit the Convent of the Virgins (Kusanatz), enclosed by a defensive wall. The scant ruins of a bridge across the river are to the west.

Menüçer Camii The Menüçer Camii is the square building with the tall octagonal minaret. Claimed as the first mosque built by the Seljuk Turks in Anatolia (1072), six vaults remain, each different as was the Seljuk style. Several other vaults have fallen into ruin. This odd but interesting blend of

Armenian and Seljuk design probably resulted from the Seljuks employing Armenian architects, engineers and stonemasons in the work. The structure next to the mosque may have been a Seljuk medrese or palace. Some people climb the minaret, although it's debatable how wise this is.

Fethiye Camii Up on the plateau again, the cathedral (Fethiye Camii) is the largest and most impressive of the churches. Ani cathedral was begun by King Smbat II in 987, and finished under Gagik I in 1010. Trdat Mendet, the cathedral's architect, also oversaw repairs to the dome of Sancta Sophia in Constantinople, brought down in the earthquake of 989. Ani became the seat of the Armenian Catholicos (pontiff). As the grandest religious edifice in the city, it was transformed into a mosque whenever Muslims held Ani, but reverted to a church when the Christians took over. The cathedral demonstrates how Armenian ecclesiastical architecture emphasises height above all else: the churches are not long or wide so much as high – reaching towards heaven. In the case of Ani's cathedral, heaven comes right in – the spacious dome fell down centuries ago.

İç Kale (Citadel) South-west of the mosque across the rolling grass and beyond the ruined walls rises the İç Kale (the keep), which holds within its extensive ruins half of a ruined church. Beyond the İç Kale on a pinnacle of rock in a bend of the Arpa Çayi is the small church called the **Kızkalesi** (Maiden's Castle). If there were a maiden sequestered there, it would take a dedicated swain to reach her.

Church of St Gregory (Abughamrentz) On the western side of the city, the Church of St Gregory (Abughamrentz) dates from the mid-1000s and was built to plans by the same architect as the Church of the Redeemer.

Kervansaray The Church of the Holy Apostles dates from 1031, but the Seljuks added a portal after their conquest of the city in 1064 and used the building as a caravanserai, hence its name.

Church of St Gregory (Gagik I) North-west from the caravanserai, the gigantic Church of St Gregory (Gagik I) was begun in 998 to plans by the same architect as Ani's cathedral. Its ambitious dome, like that of Constantinople's Sancta Sophia, collapsed shortly after being finished, and the rest of the building is now also badly ruined.

Seljuk Palace To the north-west if the Church of St Gregory (Gagik I) is a Seljuk palace, built into the city's defensive walls and recently restored.

Getting There & Away

Transport to Ani has always been a problem but the decline in tourism to the east has made a bad situation even worse.

The cheapest transport (US$1.25) is the municipal bus to Ocaklı which makes one run daily from Kars to Ani at 1 pm, departing from the Temizlik İşleri building on Pazar Caddesi between Faik Bey and Şehit Yusuf Bey caddesis. Unfortunately, this is of little use since there is no return service until the next morning and you're not allowed to stay overnight at the site.

The tourist office attempts to organise taxi dolmuşes to the site for a charge of US$6 or US$7 per person, but if there are no other tourists around you may have to pay the full fare of US$30 for the car. If you do, consider that you'll enjoy having Ani all to yourself. The fare includes waiting time at the site. Make sure that your driver understands that you want a minimum of 2½ hours (*iki buçuk saat*, ee-KEE boo-chook sah-aht) at the site, and preferably three hours (*üç saat*, EWCH sah-aht).

KARS TO IĞDIR & DOĞUBEYAZIT

To reach Doğubeyazıt and Mt Ararat, go south via Kağızman, Tuzluca and Iğdır (UH-duhr), a distance of 240km. The road is badly potholed as far as Tuzluca, then improves considerably.

North of Kağızman, above Çamuşlu Köyü, the villagers can show you 12,000-year-old **rock carvings** *(kaya resimleri)*.

EASTERN ANATOLIA

You'll also get a look at authentic village life. At Tuzluca, there are **salt caves** to visit.

From Tuzluca the road to Iğdır passes very near to the Armenian frontier, and is closed between dusk and sunrise. The army patrols the area to prevent border violations and smuggling, and if you're on that road at night they'll assume you're doing one or the other.

Maps indicate several ruined Armenian churches along this route. However, the authorities are not keen that you explore them and they are not signposted with the usual black-on-yellow signs, making them hard to find. For some, you need advance permission anyway and in the current tense security atmosphere of the east this is unlikely to be forthcoming. You can try approaching the Ministry of Culture in Ankara, but don't hold your breath waiting for the go ahead.

In Iğdır there are two good two-star hotels: the ***Otel Latif*** *(☎ 476-227 7837)*, on Karadağ Caddesi; and the even better ***Otel K Yıldırım*** *(☎ 476-227 9844, fax 227 7429, Hürriyet Caddesi 42)*, in Bağlar Mahallesi next to a Fiat dealer. Both charge around US$10 per person. Coming in from the north you'll pass the cheaper ***Otel Öztürk*** *(☎ 476-227 0099)* at Evrenpaşa Caddesi 172.

AĞRI

The Turkish name for Mt Ararat is Ağrı Dağı, but the town of Ağrı (ah-RUH, population 65,000, altitude 1640m), 100km west of the snow-capped peak, is a strong contender for the title of drabbest town in Turkey. There's a new otogar on the western outskirts with taxis waiting to ferry passengers into town. Once there, however, there's nothing to hold you bar the few very modest emergency-only hotels: the ***Otel Can*** and ***Otel Salman***, within a block of the main crossroads in the town centre. You'd do better to head on to Doğubeyazıt in the east or Erzurum in the west.

DOĞUBEYAZIT

It's only 35km between the Iranian frontier and Doğubeyazıt (doh-OO-bey-yah-zuht, population 36,000, altitude 1950m), a town that is dusty in summer and muddy in winter, and pleasantly quiet after its bigger neighbours. A range of bare, jagged mountains towers above the town, while in front of it stretches a table-flat expanse of wheat fields and grazing land. On the far northern side of this flatness rises Mt Ararat (Ağrı Dağı, 5137m), an enormous volcano capped with ice and often shrouded in dark clouds. The mountain has figured in legends since time began, most notably as the resting place of Noah's Ark.

Doğubeyazıt used to receive a steady stream of western visitors coming to see Mt Ararat (and perhaps look for Noah's Ark) and the İshak Paşa Sarayı, a fortress-palace-mosque complex perched on a terrace 5km east of town. With the security situation in the east improving, there is perhaps reason for optimism that the stream will start again. Besides its own worthy sights, Doğubeyazıt is the starting point for the modern overland trail through Iran and Pakistan to India and thence to China.

Orientation & Information

Called 'Dog Biscuit' by its admirers, it has no Tourism Information Office, but Sanoz Tourism across the road from the otogar will be able to supply you with everything you need to know. Doğubeyazıt is small and easily negotiated on foot. Its markets may have some good bargains in goods smuggled in from neighbouring Iran.

None of the banks in town are currently enthusiastic about changing money, whether cash or travellers cheques. If you run out of liras, you may have to resort to the gold shops or your hotel, where rates will be poor.

Doğubeyazıt's postal code is 04400.

İshak Paşa Sarayı

Head east, 5km from town, to get to İshak Paşa Sarayı. It's a pleasant walk, although you may feel rather isolated. At weekends dolmuşes often pass nearby; otherwise a taxi driver will want about US$5 for a return trip, waiting time included. Admission to the site costs US$2 and it's supposedly open from 8 am to 5 pm, but may close earlier in the winter months.

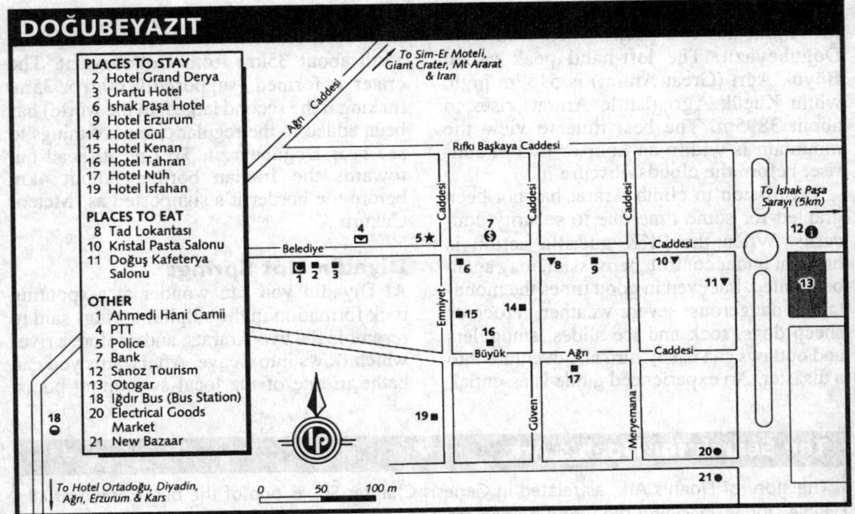

The building was begun in 1685 by Çolak Abdi Paşa and completed in 1784 by his son, a Kurdish chieftain named İshak (Isaac). The architecture is an amalgam of Seljuk, Ottoman, Georgian, Persian and Armenian styles. A grand main portal leads to a large courtyard. The magnificent gold-plated doors, which once hung here, were removed by the Russians and are now proudly displayed in the Hermitage Museum in St Petersburg.

Although ruined, the 366 room fortress-like palace has many elements which are in good condition. The palace was once equipped with central heating and sewerage systems, and with running water. You can visit the mosque (which was used for prayers until the 1980s) and the various palace rooms. You should especially note the little tomb with fine relief work in a corner of the court.

In recent years the palace has been extensively restored (some would say rebuilt) and work will continue for some time. The end results may not please the purists, but the view across the palace at sunset is still spectacular.

Fortress & Mosque

Across the valley are a mosque, a tomb and the ruins of a fortress. The fortress foundations may date from Urartian times (from the 13th to 7th centuries BC), though the walls will have been rebuilt by whoever needed to control this mountain pass.

The mosque is thought to date from the reign of Ottoman sultan Selim I (1512-20), who defeated the Persians decisively near the town of Çaldıran, 70km south of Doğubayazıt, in 1514, thus adding all of Eastern Anatolia to his burgeoning empire. He went on from here and conquered Syria and Palestine.

Nearby stands an 18th-century striped tomb containing the grave of the popular Kurdish writer Ahmedi Hani.

The ruined foundations you see rising in low relief from the dusty plain are of **Eski Beyazıt**. The old city of Eski Beyazıt was probably founded in Urartian times circa 800 BC. Modern Doğubayazit is a still a relative newcomer, the villagers only having moved from the hills to the plain in 1937.

Mt Ararat (Ağrı Dağı)

Mt Ararat has two peaks when seen from Doğubeyazıt. The left-hand peak called Büyük Ağrı (Great Ararat) is 5137m high, while Küçük Ağrı (Little Ararat) rises to about 3895m. The best time to view the mountain is within an hour or two of sunrise, before the clouds obscure it.

Permission to climb Ararat has not been granted for some time due to security concerns. When the PKK guerilla action is brought under control, permission may again be granted, but even in good times the mountain is dangerous: severe weather, ferocious sheep dogs, rock and ice slides, smugglers and outlaws can easily turn an adventure into a disaster. An experienced guide is essential.

Giant Crater

In 1920 a bit of celestial refuse arrived on earth about 35km from Doğubeyazıt. The crater it formed (supposedly 60m x 35m, making it the second largest in the world) has been added to the regular circuit of things to see near Doğubeyazıt. To find it, head out towards the Iranian border. About 4km before the border it's signposted as 'Meteor Çukuru'.

Diyadin Hot Springs

At Diyadin you can wonder at a spouting rock formation in the sulphur springs said to resemble the two Ararats, and explore a river which flows into a cave. Afterwards you can bathe in one of the local swimming pools.

The Search for Noah's Ark

The story of Noah's Ark, as related in Genesis Chapter Six, is one of the best known of all Bible stories. Deciding the world he had created was corrupt, God instructed Noah to build an Ark and fill it with one male and one female of each living animal. A great flood then swept the earth but, after 40 days, the Ark carried Noah and his family to safety. Afterwards the human and animal stock of the Ark repopulated the world. A similar story also appears in the pre-biblical Sumerian *Epic of Gilgamesh*.

In folk memory it has long been believed that the Ark came to rest on Mt Ararat in eastern Turkey.

The Ark Mark One Over the years several people reported sighting a boat shape high up on the mountainside, and in 1955 an expedition brought back what was presumed to be a piece of wood from the Ark, found in a frozen lake. Later radio-carbon dating indicated that the wood dated back only to 450-750 AD. The most famous Ararat Ark-hunting expedition of all was organised by ex-US astronaut James Irwin in 1982 but even he was unable to bring back wholly convincing evidence.

The Ark Mark Two Since Irwin's expedition, the political situation in the east has put Mt Ararat out of bounds to Ark-seekers. Rather conveniently another expedition in 1985 organised by American David Fusold 'discovered' the Ark on Musa Dağı, near the village of Üzengili, east of Doğubeyazıt. The site custodian will point out an elongated oval shape in stone which is supposed to be the boat. He has a sheaf of papers, including a French report setting out at length the 'proof' that this is the true Ark. For those sceptics who are sure that the biblical Ark was wooden, it points out that the meaning of the Hebrew word usually translated as 'cypress wood' is actually uncertain. Whether that convinces you or not, probably depends on your level of cynicism.

Given the current state of security checks in the area, latterday Ark-spotters would probably do well to sign up for a tour out of Doğubeyazıt.

Not all are very clean so it's best to make enquiries first. If you tip the guardian about US$3 you can get a pool to yourself. Security concerns may make it advisable to visit Diyadin on a guided tour.

Tours

Given the security in operation around Doğubeyazıt, you may find it easier to take a tour to the outlying sights. Zafer Önay at Sanoz Tourism (☎ 472-311 5736) opposite the otogar offers tours to İshak Paşa Sarayı, the supposed site of Noah's Ark, the Iranian border and the crater site for US$20 per person. Alternatively he will take you to the hot springs at Diyadin and to some of the Kurdish villages for the same price. These are good tours, and well worth the price for the information you'll pick up along the way.

Places to Stay – Budget

Doğubeyazıt has plenty of cheap hotels considering the shortage of tourists, but many of them are very basic indeed and women travelling alone may not feel comfortable in some of them. On the main street, several blocks from the Hotel İshak Paşa, is ***Hotel Erzurum*** *(☎ 472-312 5080)* on Belediye Caddesi where spartan waterless rooms go for US$9 a double. ***Saruhan Hotel*** *(☎ 472-311 3097)* next door is cheap (US$4 per person) and friendly, and in exchange for very basic accommodation offers good views of Mt Ararat or İshak Paşa Sarayı.

The tidy ***Hotel Tahran*** *(☎ 472-311 2223, Büyük Ağrı Caddesi 86)*, up the street from the big Hotel İsfahan, hosts devout Muslims who delight in simple but clean rooms for US$10 a double with private shower. ***Hotel Gül*** *(☎ 472-311 5176, Güven Caddesi 34)*, behind the Hotel Kenan in the next block, is similarly cheap, and similarly popular with religious Iranian tourists.

Camping Just before you reach İshak Paşa Sarayı, you'll come to ***Murat Camping*** on the left-hand side of the road, where you can pitch a tent for about US$1. There's a tea garden here, and you're within easy walking distance of the palace. If it's open, the ugly ***İshak Paşa Cafeteria***, overlooking the İshak Paşa Sarayı, allows travellers to roll out their sleeping bags in a room off the dining room for US$1.75 per person. Or there's ***İsfahan Camping*** down on the plain.

Places to Stay – Mid-Range

Rising above Doğubeyazıt is the two-star ***Hotel İsfahan*** *(☎ 472-215 5139, fax 215 2044, Emniyet Caddesi 26)*, with five floors of rooms with showers costing US$25/38/46 a single/double/triple. It's comfortable, with lots of kilims and carpets in the lobby and lounge, as well as its own lift and car park.

The three-star, 125 room ***Sim-Er Moteli*** *(☎ 472-215 5601, fax 215 3413)*, on İran Transit Yolu, is 5km east of town on the highway to Iran. This used to be one of Doğubeyazıt's best hotels, but although it's still quiet, with good views of the mountain, it's fallen on hard times since the Ararat trekking trade vanished. Rooms cost US$22/36 a single/double with shower; a set-price meal costs US$18. There's a 30% reduction on room rates for children.

The two-star ***İshak Paşa Hotel*** *(☎ 472-312 7036, fax 312 7644, Emniyet Caddesi 10)*, one block from the Hotel İsfahan at the intersection of Emniyet and Belediye caddesis, is simpler than the aforementioned hotels and lower in price. It has 21 rooms on four floors, each with tiled shower and balcony. There's a restaurant and bar, and rooms cost US$8/12 a single/double.

Places to Stay – Top End

Given the paucity of tourists it's astonishing to find that two new expensive hotels have opened in town. The best is undoubtedly the three-star ***Hotel Grand Derya*** *(☎ 472-312 7531, fax 312 7833)* on Belediye Caddesi, right beside the Ahmedi Hani Camii, with comfortable rooms for US$40 a double.

The three-star ***Hotel Nuh*** *(☎ 472-312 7232, fax 312 6910, Büyük Ağrı Caddesi 65)*, offers panoramic views of Mt Ararat and the palace. There's a private car park, a lift and constant hot water; and the rooms, priced as at the Derya, are clean and comfortable.

Places to Eat

Belediye Caddesi has three or four kebapçıs, including the excellent ***Tad Lokantası***, a bright, cheery place which does good chicken kebaps for US$3. The same people run ***Doğuş Kafeterya Salonu*** near the otogar which makes good fresh pide as well as more substantial meals.

Kristal Pasta Salonu on Belediye Caddesi offers a Turkish breakfast for US$1 and afternoon tea and pastry for about the same price. You can hardly miss the mouthwatering displays of cakes and biscuits in the windows.

For full meals with drinks, the best bets are the top hotels.

Getting There & Away

Doğubeyazıt now has a proper otogar, but bus services are limited and mostly go via Erzurum or Iğdır. Details of (mostly daily) services follow:

Ankara – 1210km, 16 hours, US$22; three buses
Erzurum – 285km, four hours, US$7; three buses
Iğdır – 51km, 45 minutes, US$2; hourly dolmuşes
Kars – 240km, three hours, US$6; a few buses
Van via Ağrı – 315km, 5½ hours, US$6; several buses to Ağrı, change for Van

INTO IRAN

Provided you accept the cultural peculiarities of the Islamic Revolution, travel in Iran can be enjoyable since the people are mostly very friendly and helpful.

To visit or travel through Iran you must have a visa, theoretically obtainable from an Iranian embassy or consulate, but this may depend on the shifting sands of international relations.

It may take anywhere from a week to a month or more to obtain a visa and you may

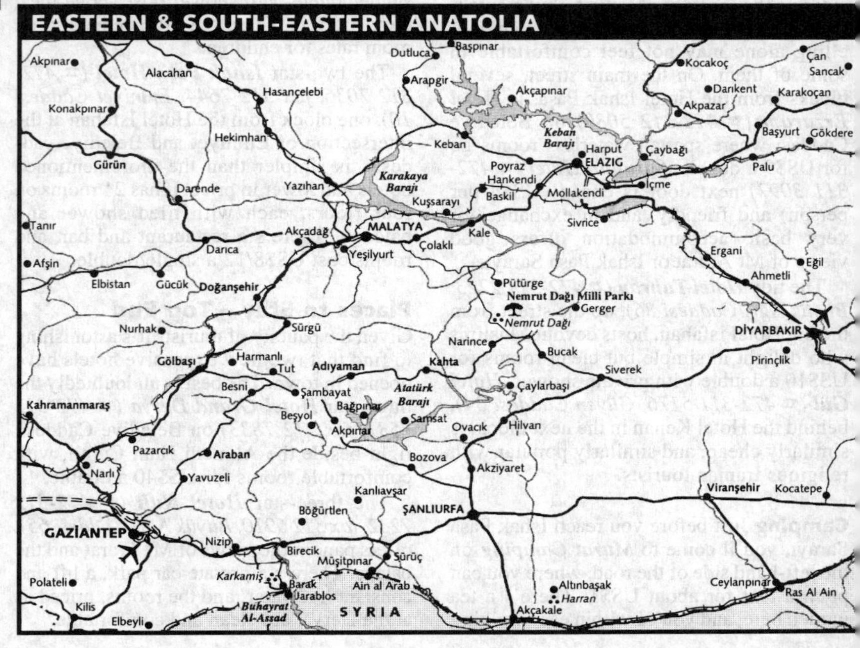

have to show a visa for the country you will enter when you leave Iran as well as a bus or airline ticket out of Iran. Be prepared for some Middle Eastern bureaucratic hassles. See the Visas & Embassies section in the Facts for the Visitor chapter, and contact your embassy in Ankara for details on current availability and requirements for visas.

Women contemplating making the crossing will first need to buy a *chador* (the all-encompassing black robe favoured by the Revolutionary Guards), available in Doğubeyazıt's market for about US$18.

A dolmuş to the border at Gürbulak, 34km east of Doğubeyazıt, should cost about US$1.50. The crossing here may take as little as one hour. You may be asked to pay an unofficial fee (ie a bribe) by the Iranian officials. The Bank Melli branch at the border changes cash (dollars or pounds) or travellers cheques into Iranian rials (tomans). Even if this branch refuses Turkish liras, you may be able to change them at banks further into Iran.

From the border you can take a taxi to Maku, then an Iran Peyma bus from Maku to Tabriz.

There is a post office, a tourist office and a reasonable restaurant on the Turkish side of the border despite its off-putting, shades-of-war-torn-Beirut appearance.

South-Eastern Anatolia

Turkey's south-eastern region shares some characteristics with the north-east: its history is involved and eventful, its landscapes dramatic and its tourist traffic much lighter than that on the congested Aegean and Mediterranean coasts. Other than this, the regions are dramatically different.

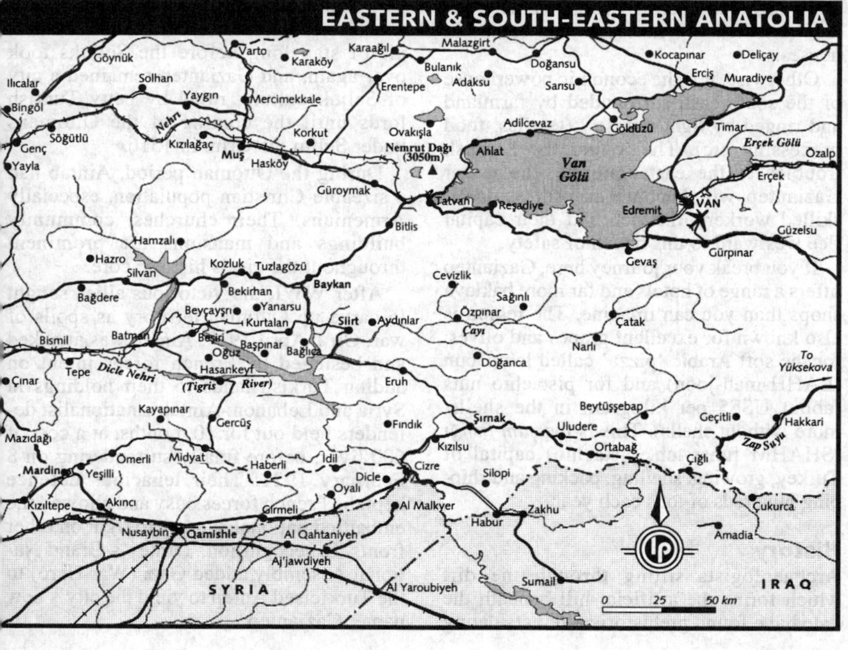

South-eastern Anatolia is mostly hot, dry country with elevations ranging from Şanlıurfa's 540m to Van's 1725m. The people are mostly Kurdish and farming is their principal occupation. With the inauguration in 1992 of the gigantic Atatürk Dam, keystone of the vast South-East Anatolia Project (Güneydoğu Anadolu Projesi, GAP), this poor but fertile land began to get the water it needs to become the country's most abundant producer of crops.

Before travelling in this corner of Turkey, be sure to read the warning at the start of this chapter.

GAZİANTEP (ANTEP)

Known in Ottoman times as Aintab, the city of Gaziantep (population 650,000, altitude 843m) got its modern name from the heroism displayed by its citizens during the War of Independence.

Despite its remarkably long history, Gaziantep today is a large, modern city with only a few sights to interest visitors: namely, the kale (citadel), two museums and some old houses.

Otherwise, it is the economic powerhouse of the south-east, surrounded by farmland and ringed by light industry (textiles, food processing etc). The longer the Kurdish troubles to the east continue, the richer Gaziantep will become as professionals, skilled workers, the rich and their capital flee westward to this haven of safety.

If you break your journey here, Gaziantep offers a range of hotels and far more baklava shops than you can imagine. The region is also known for excellent grapes and olives, for the soft Arabic 'pizza' called lahmacun (LAHH-mah-joon) and for pistachio nuts (about US$5 per kilogram in the shells; more without shells). This is the *şam fıstığı* (SHAHM fuhss-tuh, pistachio) capital of Turkey, growing, shelling, packing and shipping hundreds of tons each year.

History

Archaeologists sifting through the dirt which forms the artificial hill beneath the kale have found prehistoric artefacts dating from Neolithic times (7000-5000 BC), but the town's history really begins when small Proto-Hittite, or Hatti, city-states grew up between 2500 and 1900 BC.

Hittites and Assyrians battled for this region until it was taken by Sargon II, King of Assyria, in 717 BC. The Assyrians ruled for almost a century before being overcome by the Cimmerians, a Crimean people driven from their traditional lands by the Scythians. The Cimmerians swept through Anatolia destroying almost everything that lay in their path, setting an example that would be followed by numerous uncreative hordes which showed up later.

The Cimmerians cleared out and the Persians took over from 612 to 333 BC, only to be followed by Alexander the Great, the Romans and the Byzantines. The Arabs conquered the town in 638 AD and held it until the Seljuk Turks swept in from the east in the 1070s.

With the crusades, Gaziantep's history perks up a bit, but most of the action and romance took place in Urfa. The crusaders didn't stay long before the Seljuks took over again, and Gaziantep remained a city of Seljuk culture, ruled by petty Turkish lords until the coming of the Ottomans under Selim the Grim in 1516.

During the Ottoman period, Aintab had a sizeable Christian population, especially Armenians. Their churches, community buildings and mansions are prominent throughout the city's historic core.

After WWI, the victorious allies sought to carve up Ottoman territory as spoils of war. On 1 April 1920, Aintab was attacked and besieged by French forces intent on adding Turkish lands to their holdings in Syria and Lebanon. Aintab's nationalist defenders held out for 10 months, at a cost of 600 lives, before finally surrendering on 8 February 1921. Their tenacious defence kept the French forces busy and allowed the embattled nationalist army to fight on other fronts. In recognition, Turkey's Grand National Assembly added Gazi (War Hero) to the Turkicised Antep to yield the city's new name: Gaziantep.

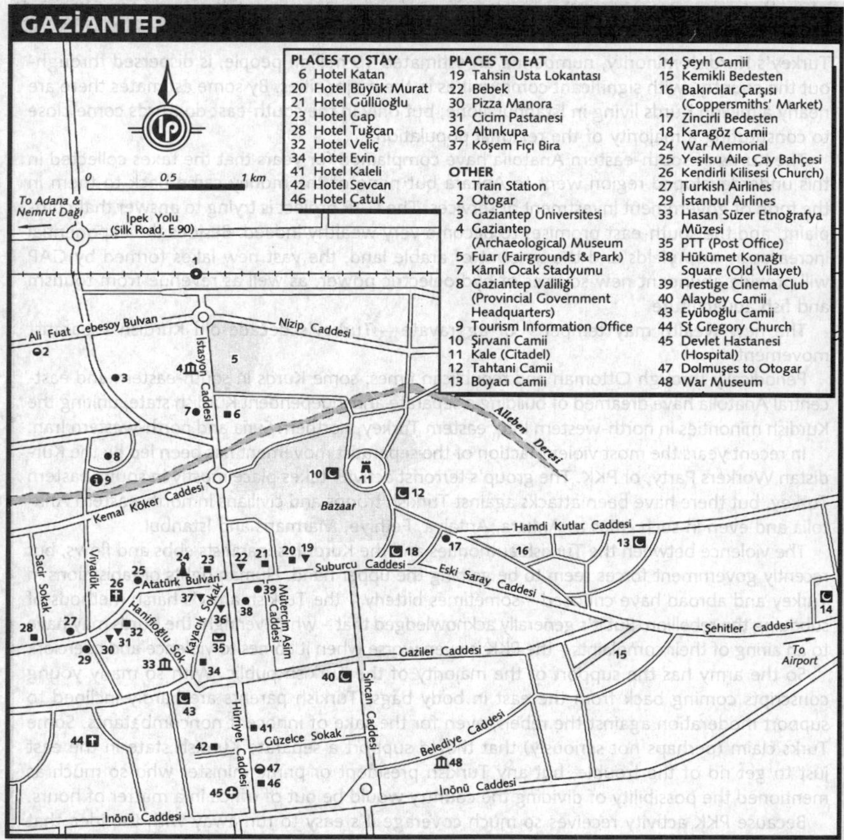

Orientation

The centre of this sprawling and ever-growing city is the intersection of Atatürk Bulvarı/Suburcu Caddesi and Hürriyet/İstasyon caddesis, former site of the Hükümet Konağı (Government Headquarters) and marked by a large equestrian statue of Atatürk. Though the provincial government is now headquartered in a modern building to the north, locals (and, more importantly, dolmuş drivers) still call the place Hükümet Konağı.

The Devlet Hastanesi (State Hospital), another useful landmark, is a few blocks past Hükümet Konağı on Hürriyet Caddesi.

Most hotels and many restaurants are within a block or two of the main intersection. The museum is 500m away. The kale, on the high hill topped by the mosque with twin minarets, is another 500m from the museum.

The otogar is 2km from the main intersection, accessible by frequent minibus (US$0.30) and less frequent city buses; if

Kurdish Separatism

Turkey's Kurdish minority, numbering an estimated 10 million people, is dispersed throughout the country, with significant communities in the major cities. By some estimates there are nearly a million Kurds living in İstanbul alone, but only in the south-east do Kurds come close to constituting a majority of the regional population.

The Kurds of south-eastern Anatolia have complained for years that the taxes collected in this underdeveloped region went to Ankara but none of the money came back to them in the form of government investment or services. The GAP project is trying to answer that complaint, and the south-east promises to become very wealthy indeed. Besides the exponential increases in crop yields and the amount of arable land, the vast new lakes formed by GAP will provide abundant new sources of hydroelectric power, as well as revenue from tourism and fish aquaculture.

The new wealth may temper – or aggravate – Turkey's decade-old Kurdish separatist movement.

Periodically through Ottoman and republican times, some Kurds in south-eastern and east-central Anatolia have dreamed of building a separate and independent Kurdish state, uniting the Kurdish minorities in north-western Iraq, eastern Turkey, northern Syria and north-western Iran.

In recent years the most violent faction of the separatist movement has been led by the Kurdistan Workers Party, or PKK. The group's terrorist activity takes place mostly in south-eastern Turkey, but there have been attacks against Turkish troops and civilians in north-eastern Anatolia and even in such cities as Ankara, Antalya, Fethiye, Marmaris and İstanbul.

The violence between the Turkish authorities and the Kurdish separatists ebbs and flows, but recently government forces seem to be gaining the upper hand. Human rights organisations in Turkey and abroad have criticised – sometimes bitterly – the Turkish army's harsh methods of subduing the rebellion. But it's generally acknowledged that – whatever right the Kurds may have to an airing of their complaints – the PKK is even worse when it comes to violence and coercion.

So the army has the support of the majority of the Turkish public. With so many young conscripts coming back from the east in body bags, Turkish parents are hardly inclined to support moderation against the rebels, even for the sake of innocent noncombatants. Some Turks claim (perhaps not seriously) that they'd support a separate Kurdish state in the east just to get rid of the trouble, but any Turkish president or prime minister who so much as mentioned the possibility of dividing the country would be out of office in a matter of hours.

Because PKK activity receives so much coverage it's easy to run away with the idea that all Turkey's Kurds support its goal of an independent Kurdish state. In fact most Kurds have much more modest wishes: for Kurdish-language newspapers, for Turkey-based Kurdish television programming and for a Kurdish education system.

But, as with other entrenched disputes like those in Northern Ireland and Sri Lanka, the longer the troubles continue, the harder it is to find a solution that will stick.

you want to return to the otogar take a bus or dolmuş from just south of the central Hotel Kaleli. The train station is a short walk east of the otogar. Walk from the station to the first large intersection to catch the 'Devlet Hastanesi' minibus into the centre. A taxi to the centre costs about US$2.50.

Information

Gaziantep's Tourism Information Office (☎ 342-230 5969, fax 234 0603), 100. Yıl

Parkı İçi, Vilayet Konağı Arkası, is behind the new Gaziantep Valiliği (Provincial Government Headquarters) near the fairgrounds. Follow the signs to reach it.

The Akbank opposite the old Hükümet Konağı building in the centre has well-connected ATMs. Should the worst come to the worst while you're in the east, it's worth knowing that Gaziantep has a good, new, modern hospital close to the otogar on Ali Fuat Cebesoy Bulvarı.

Gaziantep's postal code is 27000.

The Kale District

The citadel is thought to have been constructed by the emperor Justinian in the 6th century AD, but was rebuilt extensively by the Seljuks in the 12th and 13th centuries. The massive doors to the fortified enclosure will probably be locked, but at least have a look at them. As you approach the kale bear right around the massive walls. Don't go through what appears to be an enormous stone gateway but is actually the *fosse* (dry moat), straddled in ancient times by a drawbridge high above. Around to the right of the fosse you will come to a small mosque, opposite which is a ramp leading to the citadel doors. If they're open, proceed across the wooden bridge which spans the fosse and into the kale.

At the foot of the kale is an interesting quarter boasting a fruit and vegetable market, workshops where you can see men beating copper into coffee pots and shiny bowls, old stone houses and little neighbourhood mosques. Trucks for hire are gathered at one side of the kale, heirs to the ancient carters and teamsters who may have gathered here in centuries past. You can walk back into town through a partially covered **bazaar** area, looking out for saddlemakers and other artisans at work. If you're unlucky you'll stumble upon the old stone building housing the city's meat market, not a place to explore if you're even slightly squeamish.

Gaziantep Müzesi

The authorities have tried really hard with their local museum. Surrounded by the requisite sculpture garden, Gaziantep Museum, next to the stadium on İstasyon Caddesi, holds something from every period of the province's history, from mastodon bones to Hittite figurines and pottery, Roman mosaics and funeral stones complete with portraits of husband and wife. Unusually it also devotes space to 'nostalgia' with a few cases containing old cameras, radios, children's toys and postcards. There are also cartoons on archaeological themes. In theory there's even wheelchair access although the gradient of the ramps looks alarmingly steep.

The museum is open from 9 am to 4.30 pm except on Monday. Admission costs US$0.75.

Old Mosques & Houses

A few blocks away from bustling Hükümet Konağı are neighbourhoods with old Ottoman houses and mosques of a distinctly Arabic cast.

Walk uphill from the Hükümet Konağı intersection on Kayacık Sokak past the Hotel Evin to the **Eyüboğlu Camii**. This Syrian-style mosque dating from the 14th century was extensively but insensitively restored in 1947, and much of its original character sacrificed.

Walk further uphill along narrow Hanifioğlu Sokak, following the signs for the **Hasan Süzer Etnoğrafya Müzesi**, a two-century-old Gaziantep stone house restored and opened as a museum of local ethnography. It's open daily except Monday from 8 am to noon and 1 to 5 pm. Admission is US$0.75.

A central *hayat* (courtyard) patterned with light and dark stone provides light and access to the rooms. Those on the ground floor were for service; those on the first floor made up the Selamlık, for male family members and their visitors; and those on the second floor made up the Haremlik, for female family members and their visitors. Many of the rooms have been decorated according to their historic function: kitchen, hamam and reception rooms (with bedding stored in the cupboards). Several rooms now hold local historical exhibits, including

EASTERN ANATOLIA

one showing Gaziantep's role in the War of Independence through photographs, documents and artefacts.

On the top floor, one room holds life-size wax figures of the museum's benefactor, Mr Süzer, currently owner of Pera Palas Hotel in İstanbul, and his parents.

The Mesk Odası, a room set apart for the men's games, now holds an exhibit of a *tandır* (charcoal brazier or oven) set under a stone table covered with a *yorgan*, or cotton-filled quilt. This is the traditional means of winter warmth for humble country families: occupants put their legs under the quilt to get the heat, and talk or play games on the quilted table above.

Several rooms also feature striking examples of *sedef*, or furniture worked with mother-of-pearl, a Gaziantep speciality. Don't miss the two-storey Kapadokya-style cellar carved from the rock beneath the house, with a deep well and huge jars to store wine.

Continue following Hanifioğlu Sokak first up and then downhill looking at other old Gaziantep houses on the way. Eventually you'll emerge on Atatürk Bulvarı just east of Hotel Veliç. Turn right and the Hükümet Konağı is 100m away.

Places to Stay – Budget

On a tight budget head straight for Kayacık Sokak, a dingy lane of card rooms, beer halls and billiard saloons just west of the Hükümet Konaği. Bypass the inappropriately named ***Gül Palas*** (Rose Palace) and the ***Emre*** to reach ***Hotel Evin*** *(☎ 342-231 3492)*, which posts rates of US$14/21 for singles/doubles with shower but readily drops them to the US$9/13 of its less enticing neighbours.

Places to Stay – Mid-Range

Three hotels quite close together all charge US$18/25 a single/double with bath and there's not much to choose between them. ***Hotel Güllüoğlu*** *(☎ 342-232 4363, Suburcu Caddesi 1/B)*, has rather cramped rooms but comes attached to a renowned *baklavacı* (see Places to Eat following). Just to the east ***Hotel Büyük Murat*** *(☎ 342-231 8449, fax 231 1658)*, while not overly welcoming, offers slightly more space for the same price. The 35 room ***Hotel Veliç*** *(☎ 342-231 1726, Atatürk Bulvarı 23)*, is further west but all three suffer from traffic noise which their much-touted TVs do little to drown out. Ask for a room at the back.

The 54 room ***Hotel Çatuk*** *(☎ 342-231 9480, fax 233 0043, Hürriyet Caddesi 27)*, just across from the Devlet Hastanesi (hospital), has rooms for US$18/31/42 a single/double/triple with blue-tiled showers. If you could wangle a discount this might make a good choice.

Gaziantep's longtime favourite lodging is the three-star ***Hotel Kaleli*** *(☎ 342-230 9690, fax 230 1597, Hürriyet Caddesi, Güzelce Sokak 50)*, between the main intersection and the Devlet Hastanesi. The 70 rooms (US$23/28 a single/double or US$43 a triple in a suite) are old-fashioned, which means spacious; those at the front have bathtubs and small showers at the back. The rooftop ***restaurant*** is among the city's best.

The three-star ***Hotel Gap*** *(☎ 342-220 3974, 234 2102, Atatürk Bulvarı 10)*, is central, and fancy with huge statues of a *saz* (long-necked lute) player and a *kangol* dog adorning its marble-paved lobby. The spacious modern rooms cost US$33/44 a single/double (breakfast included), good value if you don't mind splashing out a bit. There's a car park as well.

Opposite the Kâlim Ocak Stadyumu is the two-star, 42 room ***Hotel Katan*** *(☎ 342-230 6969, fax 230 8454, İstasyon Caddesi 58)*, charging US$26/39 for cheerful singles/doubles with TV, bath, minibar and balcony – although whether you actually want a balcony when it's overlooking the main road is a moot point.

Places to Stay – Top End

The best place in Gaziantep has to be the five-star, 141 room ***Hotel Tuğcan*** *(☎ 342-220 4323, fax 220 3242, Atatürk Bulvarı 34)*, about 400m west of Hükümet Konağı. A room with all mod cons costs US$150/170/190 a single/double/triple, and there's a swimming pool, sauna and restaurant.

More or less opposite Hotel Kaleli, is the glistening new four-star ***Hotel Sevcan*** *(☎ 342-220 6686, fax 220 8237, Göz Hastanesi Sokak 16)* with 124 modern rooms, some with bath, for US$110/130/150 a single/double/triple.

Places to Eat

Along Suburcu Caddesi and Atatürk Bulvarı banks are interspersed with an incredible number of shops selling baklava, pastries, cakes, kadayıf and other Turkish sweets.

Among the sweets shops, the most famous is ***Güllüoğlu***, in the hotel of the same name (see the earlier Places to Stay – Mid-Range section). Its fame grew because of its *şam fıstıklı baklava* (with pistachios), but the shop serves many other varieties as well, including *kaymaklı* (with clotted cream). A 150g portion costs about US$0.75. You'll see the name Güllüoğlu on other shops, as later generations have taken up the art.

For Turkish treats, the fanciest shop is ***Cicim Pastanesi***, on Atatürk Bulvarı south of the Hotel Veliç, with a little fountain in the centre. The nearby ***Liman*** and ***Kenem*** pastanesis are similar.

For pre-baklava courses, there are many small kebapçıs and restaurants on and off Suburcu Caddesi. A modern choice is ***Tahsin Usta Lokantası*** (closed Sunday), serving a variety of south-eastern kebaps but specialising in oven-baked lahmacun and pide. The dining room is airy and bright. Meals cost US$2 to US$3; no alcohol is served. Nearby is ***Bebek***, which serves a wide variety of stews and kebaps. The *aile salonu* downstairs is decorated with a curious mixture of 3D maritime scenes and pictures of gurgling babies.

Gaziantep's young professionals congregate for pizza and burgers at ***Pizza Manora*** *(☎ 342-233 1045, Atatürk Bulvarı 37/C)*. Though the atmosphere is upmarket (and comfortable for single women travellers), prices are not bad at US$4 for a pizza and soft drink. Afterwards you can take tea in the pleasant ***Yeşilsu Aile Çay Bahçesi*** opposite.

For a more formal dinner with drinks, try the rooftop restaurant at ***Hotel Kaleli*** on Hürriyet Caddesi. Though the setting is genteel, prices are moderate, and a full tuck-in with drinks costs only about US$6 to US$9 per person.

On the corner of Suburcu and Hürriyet caddesis is a shopping complex containing several licensed restaurants, the best of which is the upstairs ***Altınkupa*** with Turkish-style *şantöz* (chanteuse) entertainment some nights.

If you're just after a drink and snacks, ***Köşem Fıçı Bira*** across Kayacık Sokak from the Altınkupa, with its marble counter and well-behaved clientele, is about the most genteel *birahane* in a district awash with them. Along the western reaches of Atatürk Caddesi you'll also find a few cafes where young men congregate to eat burgers and play billiards in more appealing surroundings than the old-fashioned teahouses.

Entertainment

Right in Hükümet Konağı is the ***Prestige Cinema Club***, a state-of-the-art cinema with computerised seating, showing the latest Hollywood blockbusters with Turkish subtitles. The ***cafe*** here sells cappuccino and the sort of boiled sweets you associate with cinema visits at home. Tickets cost US$3 and it's a fun experience.

Getting There & Away

Air Turkish Airlines (☎ 342-230 1565, fax 230 1567), Atatürk Bulvarı 30/B, near Hotel Tuğcan, operates daily nonstop flights between Gaziantep's Oğzeli airport (20km from the centre) and Ankara (one hour) and İstanbul (1¾ hours). An airport bus departs from the downtown office on Atatürk Bulvarı 1½ hours before flight time and costs less than US$2.

İstanbul Airlines (☎ 342-230 0048, fax 230 7866), Atatürk Bulvarı 63, also has flights to İstanbul three times a week.

Bus The modern otogar is 2km from the town centre and the bus service is frequent and far-reaching. If you didn't have time to sample some local baklava in town, don't worry – there are plenty of places to try it here before you leave. Details of some daily services follow:

Adana – 220km, four hours, US$5; several buses
Adıyaman & Kahta (Nemrut Dağı) – 210km, four hours, US$8; several buses
Ankara – 705km, 10 hours, US$15; frequent buses
Antakya – 200km, four hours, US$5; frequent minibuses
Diyarbakır – 330km, five hours, US$8; frequent buses
İstanbul – 1136km, 14 hours, US$21; several buses
Mardin – 330km, 5½ hours, US$8; several buses
Şanlıurfa – 145km, 2½ hours, US$3.50; frequent buses

Train The *Toros Ekspresi* departs daily from İstanbul (8.25 am) and Gaziantep (2.40 pm), arriving in the opposite city about 30 hours later, having made stops in Eskişehir, Afyon, Konya and Adana. A one-way 1st/2nd-class ticket all the way costs US$14/10. The fare in a sleeping car is US$30/52/72 for one/two/three people.

An alternative is to take the overnight *Çukurova Ekspresi* train from Ankara (8.10 pm) to Adana (8.10 am) and then proceed by bus.

GAZİANTEP TO ŞANLIURFA

The road from Gaziantep to Şanlıurfa is very hot in summer, yet the land is fertile, with fig orchards, olive trees, cotton and wheat.

At Nizip, a turn-off heads south for **Karkamış** (Carchemish), a neo-Hittite city which flourished around 850 BC, about the time Akhenaton occupied the throne of Egypt. Though Karkamış assumed the role of Hittite capital after the fall of Hattuşaş, there's little left to see, and what's there you must see with a military escort to avoid getting shot as a smuggler – it's hardly worth the trip.

At Birecik you cross the Euphrates River (Fırat Nehri). The town has a **ruined fortress**, rebuilt and used by the crusaders. In spring (March or April), the town holds a traditional festival in honour of the **bald ibis**, which used to spend winter here, but which may now be extinct.

As you head east, the land becomes rockier and less fertile. By the time you approach Şanlıurfa, the land is parched, rolling steppe roasting in the merciless sun. The landscape is changing, however, as the gigantic South-East Anatolia Project brings irrigation waters to vast tracts of otherwise unarable land.

KAHRAMANMARAŞ

The sonorous new name of this city (population 230,000, altitude 568m) formerly known as Maraş, was given to it in 1973 in honour of its role during the War of Independence. Maraş was occupied by French troops after WWI, and the populace put up such fierce resistance to French rule that parliament added Kahraman (Heroic) to its traditional name half a century later.

The site of the city has moved repeatedly over the centuries, the present site having been chosen by the Dülkadır emirs during the 14th century. Wars and earthquakes have destroyed much of old Maraş, but if you need to stop for a meal or for the night you can spend a few hours pleasantly enough – and you'll see precious few other tourists.

Today Maraş is a modern city set where the agricultural plain meets the slopes of Ahır Dağı (Stable Mountain, 2301m). It's a farming centre with vast, rich crops of cotton, peppers and potatoes in the surrounding countryside. Copper working is also important and the outskirts are filled with textile factories. The Maraşlıs enjoy riding around on motorcycles with sidecars – convenient in this sunny, dry climate.

In 1996 Maraş had a brief moment of notoriety when 13-year-old English schoolgirl Sarah Cook arrived in a city where women in full chadors are not uncommon. She came to live with the waiter she had 'married' after a holiday in Alanya. While recriminations against her parents filled the English newspapers and questions were asked about the legality of their union, the Turks took Sarah to their hearts, dubbing her 'the national bride'. Inevitably it all ended in tears with the husband arrested and Sarah returned to England. In less than a year it was all over bar the baby.

The Decline & Fall of the Bald Ibis

Hot, dusty Birecik, between Gaziantep and Şanlıurfa, was once famous for having the sole nesting place of the eastern population of the bald ibis (*Geronticus eremita*), a chicken-sized, ugly black bird with a crest of black feathers and a curved red beak. The bald ibis was a migratory bird that nested on a ledge cut into a cliff-face at Birecik. Young birds spent six years in the Ethiopian Highlands before flying to Turkey to breed. At one time they were so common that the entire village used to celebrate their return from their winter quarters on the Red Sea in a ceremony beautifully described by the archaeologist Leonard Woolley in his *Dead Towns and Living Men*.

Unfortunately luck seems to have run out for the ibises. 1300 ibises were counted at Birecik in 1953, but between 1956 to 1959 half of them died from organophospate poisoning, as locals sprayed their crops against locusts and the Euphrates against malaria. The surviving birds were often weak and/or infertile and by 1972 only 60 birds remained. Increasingly they were threatened by human interference as houses were built right up against their nesting ledge.

The WWF tried to save the birds by capturing 32 of them and attempting to lure the others to a new site away from town. However, overcrowding of the cages led to the deaths of more birds, while those released from captivity failed to migrate and died of hunger.

By 1989 only three wild birds remained. Two were killed in a freak hailstorm and the third vanished. Unless by some miracle young birds find their way back to Birecik from the Red Sea it looks as if the Last of the Mohicans, as they were so aptly described by the president of the Turkish Society for the Protection of Wildlife, have gone for good.

To end on a more cheerful note, Birecik is still the best place to come to see the rare Pallid Scops Owl, and partridges, eagle owls and rockfinches can still be seen around the cliff-face.

History

Marqasi was the capital of a principality which sprang up after the collapse of the Hittite Empire based at Boğazkale/Hattuşaş in 1200 BC. Destroyed by King Sargon of Assyria in the 8th century BC, it rose again under the Romans, who called it Germaniceia.

The Byzantines employed its citadel as an eastern defence-point against Arab invasion, but the Arabs took it in 637 AD anyway. The Byzantines reclaimed it in later centuries, but while they were dealing with the Seljuk invasion up north, control of Germaniceia passed to an Armenian strongman named Philaterus in 1070. He briefly ruled over a large kingdom until it was conquered by the crusaders and returned to Byzantine control.

A succession of Kurdish, Seljuk and Turcoman emirs and sultans governed the city until it was conquered by the Ottoman sultan Selim in 1515. Maraş had a significant Armenian population until the War of Independence, after which many fled to neighbouring Syria or abroad.

Orientation & Information

The city's otogar is 100m to the west of the main highway on Azerbeycan Bulvarı. This major thoroughfare continues west for 400m to the archaeology museum, and beyond it another 900m to Kıbrıs Meydanı (Cyprus

Square), with its statue of Atatürk, in the heart of the business district. Many hotels are near Kıbrıs Meydanı, or on the 400m stretch of Atatürk Bulvarı which goes west from Kıbrıs Meydanı to the Ulu Cami, an ancient building which marks the city's traditional centre. East of Kıbrıs Meydanı is Trabzon Caddesi dominated by the purple and mustard-coloured Özel İdare İ Merkezi building, a handy, if rather unlikely, landmark.

There are no hotels near the otogar or near the train station which is at the foot of Cumhuriyet Caddesi, just east of the main highway, 2km north-east of Kıbrıs Meydanı.

To get to the centre from the otogar take a dolmuş along Azerbeycan Bulvarı to Kıbrıs Meydanı (US$0.25).

The Tourism Information Office (☎ 344-212 6590, fax 223 0355) is at Trabzon Caddesi, Dedezade Sokak, Özgür Apt, No 6 (2nd floor).

Kahramanmaraş's postal code is 46000.

Kahramanmaraş Müzesi

The Kahramanmaraş Museum, 400m uphill from the otogar on Azerbeycan Bulvarı, is open from 8 am to 5 pm except on Monday. Admission costs US$0.75. Exhibits include dinosaur bones found locally and a dozen fine Hittite stelae covered in lively reliefs. An Assyrian border marker is covered in cuneiform inscriptions. Other exhibits cover every period from the Old Bronze and Hittite to Ottoman. The ethnographic section is rich in textiles, costumes of gold cloth, inlaid woodwork and beautiful local kilims.

Other Things to See

The **Ulu (Acemli) Cami**, on Atatürk Bulvarı, was built in Syrian style in 1502, during the time of the Dülkadır emirate. Note especially its tall and unusual minaret, which has survived the depredations of earthquakes and invaders relatively intact. Across the park to the south-west is the recently restored tomb of the founders. The **Çukur Hamamı** Turkish bath is nearby as well.

A few steps to the north is the **Taş Medrese**, a seminary dating from the 14th century. The **Taş Han** was the city's caravanserai.

The **citadel** (kale) to the south has been repeatedly rebuilt and repaired over the centuries. Inside the walls a pleasant tea garden overlooks fine views of the city.

Parallel with Atatürk Caddesi to the north is Kahramanmaraş's lively **bazaar**. Poke around here and you'll find men making saddles, beating vast copper vats and manufacturing buckets out of old tyres.

Places to Stay & Eat

Because it's an agricultural trading centre, Kahramanmaraş has several comfortable two-star hotels right in the centre off Kıbrıs Meydanı although prices are pretty steep for what you get.

For the time being the best value is offered by ***Hotel Çavuşoğlu*** *(☎ 344-225 3524, fax 214 2303, Şeyhadil Caddesi 50)*, uphill from Kıbrıs Meydanı, where clean simple rooms with light decor cost US$18/30 a single/double with bath and breakfast. Across the road the extremely basic ***Otel Celtik Palas*** is for those on the very tightest budgets.

Otel Kazancı *(☎ 344-223 4462, fax 212 6942)*, just uphill a few steps from Kıbrıs Meydanı near the Hotel Çavuşoğlu, is central, yet fairly quiet, and charges a surprisingly high US$45/70 for a single/double with bath and breakfast.

One block to the north-east is the slightly cheaper ***Otel Büyük Maraş*** *(☎ 344-223 3500, fax 212 8894, Milli Egemenlik Caddesi 7)*, charging US$40/60 for a single/double with bath, breakfast included.

Right next to the Yaşar Pastanesi (mentioned later in this section) is the two-star, 80 room ***Hotel Belli*** *(☎ 344-223 4900, fax 214 8282, Trabzon Caddesi 2)*. Spacious rooms are clean and comfortable and some have little hamam basins and scoops in their bathrooms – a nice touch. Singles/doubles cost US$33/50 with bath and breakfast. Anyone worried about fire will be comforted by the fine array of fire buckets and shovels decorating the corridors.

Maraş is noted for several culinary specialties, among them *saç kavurma*, bits of lamb fried on a convex steel griddle; and *külbastı*, grilled lamb chops with *çemen* (the spice made from ground fenugreek seeds), red pepper and garlic. Finding these in the local restaurants isn't easy and you may have to fall back on the familiar range of kebaps. The bazaar has several small restaurants serving lunch to the local traders. A good place to try is ***Öz Lezzet Kebap ve Döner Salonu*** where Turkish handicrafts adorn the walls alongside pictures of alpine scenery. Soup, salad and a kebap costs just US$1. To find it, at Kösker Çarşısı 24, follow the sounds of copper beating.

Most famous of all local dishes is *hakiki Kahramanmaraş dövme dondurma* (authentic Maraş beaten ice cream), made with so much glue-like binder that it withstands the city's intense summer heat, can be displayed hanging on a hook like meat, and is eaten with knife and fork. For a sample, try the eclectically decorated ***Yaşar Pastanesi*** *(☎ 344-225 0808)*, next to the Hotel Belli, where you can tuck into ice cream and baklava beneath photos of such notables as former prime ministers Çiller, Demirel, Özal and Erbakan doing likewise.

Getting There & Away

Maraş shares the traffic which criss-crosses the region from Kayseri to Gaziantep and Adana to Malatya. Most bus services originate elsewhere, and may or may not have onward seats. Details of some daily services follow:

Adana – 190km, 3½ hours, US$5; frequent buses
Adıyaman – 164km, three hours, US$5; several buses
Antakya – 185km, four hours, US$4; frequent buses
Gaziantep – 80km, one hour, US$2; very frequent dolmuşes from Şeyhadil Caddesi or the otogar
Kayseri – 291km, 5½ hours, US$6; several buses
Malatya – 226km, 4½ hours, US$6; several buses

If you're driving, note that the road from Kahramanmaraş to Adıyaman is narrow and very slow. Between Kahramanmaraş and Gaziantep you'll also pass a reminder of the human consequences of Turkey's appalling road accident rate; a man who lost his entire family in a car crash now devotes his life to standing on a bend warning drivers whether it's safe to proceed or not.

NEMRUT DAĞI

The Commagene Nemrut Dağı (NEHM-root dah-uh) in the Anti-Taurus Range (not to be confused with a mountain of the same name on the shores of Van Gölü) rises to a height of 2150m between the provincial capital of Malatya to the north and Kahta in Adıyaman province to the south.

The summit was formed when a megalomaniac pre-Roman local king cut two ledges in the rock, filled them with colossal statues of himself and the gods (his 'relatives'), then ordered an artificial mountain peak of crushed rock 50m high to be piled between them. The king's tomb and those of three female relatives may well lie beneath those tonnes of rock. Nobody knows for sure.

Earthquakes have toppled the heads from most of the statues. At the time of writing many of the colossal bodies sit silently in rows with the 2m-high heads watching from the ground. But vandals have damaged some of them and work was to begin on replacing the heads on the bodies. Anticipate some disruption at the site for the next few years.

History

Nobody knew anything about Nemrut Dağı until 1881, when an Ottoman geologist was astounded to come across this remote mountaintop covered in statues. Archaeological work didn't begin until 1953, when the American School of Oriental Research undertook the project.

From 250 BC onwards, this region straddled the border between the Seleucid Empire (which followed the empire of Alexander the Great in Anatolia) and the Parthian Empire to the east, also occupying a part of Alexander's lands. A small but strategic area, rich, fertile and covered in forests, it had a history of independent thinking ever since the time of King Samos circa 150 BC.

Under the Seleucid Empire, the governor of Commagene declared his kingdom's independence. In 80 BC, with the Seleucids in

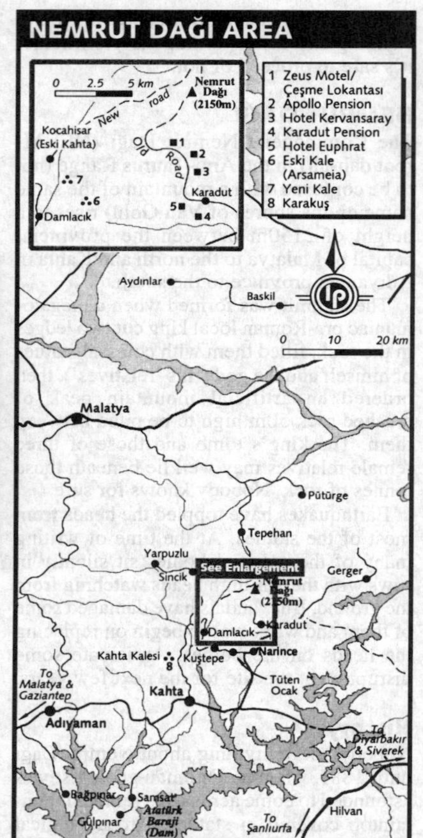

disarray and Roman power spreading into Anatolia, a Roman ally named Mithridates I Callinicus proclaimed himself king and set up his capital at Arsameia, near the modern village of Kahta Kalesi. Mithridates prided himself on his royal ancestry, tracing his forebears back to Seleucus I Nicator, founder of the Seleucid Empire to the west, and to Darius the Great, king of ancient Persia to the east. Thus he saw himself as heir to both glorious traditions. He married a Parthian princess.

Mithridates died in 64 BC and was succeeded by his son Antiochus I Epiphanes (64-38 BC) who consolidated the security of his kingdom by immediately signing a nonaggression treaty with Rome, turning his kingdom into a Roman buffer against attack from the Parthians. His good relations with both sides allowed him to grow rich and revel in delusions of grandeur. As heir to both traditions, he saw himself as equal to the great god-kings of the past. It was Antiochus who ordered the building of the fabulous temples and funerary mound on top of Nemrut.

Antiochus must have come to believe himself immortal, for in the third decade of his reign he sided with the Parthians in a squabble with Rome, and in 38 BC the Romans deposed him. Commagene was alternately ruled directly from Rome or by puppet kings until 72 AD, when Emperor Vespasian incorporated it into Roman Asia. The great days of Commagene were thus limited to the 26-year reign of Antiochus.

In the late 1980s the economy and topography of this area were greatly affected by two developments: the filling of the vast lake behind the GAP project's Atatürk Dam, and the discovery of oil near Kahta. Though the oil is in Kahta, it's Adıyaman, the provincial capital, which has benefited most from the influx of money for building and development.

When to Visit

Plan to visit Nemrut between late May and mid-October, and preferably in July or August; the road to the summit becomes impassable in snow. Remember that at any time of year, even in high summer when the sun bakes the valleys below, it will be chilly and windy on top of the mountain. This is especially true at sunrise, the coldest time of the day. Take warm clothing (gloves, socks, a thick jumper/sweater or jacket and scarf) and a windbreaker on your trek to the top, no matter when you go. Turks in the know will be found swaddled on the summit in their hotel blankets.

Colossal stone heads of up to 2m high are an impressive sight on the summit of Nemrut Dağı, near Malatya

Tour Bases

The traditional bases for ascending the southern slopes of Nemrut Dağı are the provincial capital of Adıyaman and the nearby town of Kahta, both covered in detail later in this section. It costs about the same to use Malatya as a base. There are also tours from Şanlıurfa or even from Cappadocia.

Distances between important points in the region are as follows:

Adıyaman to Kahta – 32km
Adıyaman to Malatya – 190km
Kahta to Nemrut – 52km
Malatya to Nemrut – 110km

Tours from Malatya

The northern road to the summit from Malatya via Tepehan can be covered in a day, or you can stay overnight in the village of Büyüköz near the summit, where there are simple pensions and a basic but adequate hotel. By taking the Malatya route, visitors miss seeing other sites like Arsameia along the Kahta-Nemrut road. For more information, refer to the Malatya section later in this chapter. Be warned that if you are driving yourself, the road can also be very rough.

Tours from Şanlıurfa

One and two-day tours to Nemrut (US$25/35 per person) are also available from Harran-Nemrut Tours in Şanlıurfa (see that section for details). Some of these tours let you see the Atatürk Dam on the way.

Tours from Cappadocia

Several companies in Cappadocia offer minibus tours to Nemrut, despite the distance of almost 600km. Two day tours cost about US$110 to US$120 and involve many hours of breakneck driving. If time allows, it's better to opt for a three-day tour (costing about US$150) which will allow the journey to be broken into more manageable chunks and will also allow you to see the other ancient sites around Nemrut (see below).

Ötüken Turizm (☎ 384-271 2757) has an office opposite the otogar. It does a good three-day tour, leaving Göreme at 9.30 am and stopping at the Karatay Han near Kayseri and in Karamanmaraş for ice cream and a visit to the bazaar before arriving in Kahta at about 8 pm. On the second day you visit Nemrut Dağı for sunrise and then take in the sights at Arsameia, Cendere and Karkuş. Afterwards you continue to Harran, before stopping for the night in Şanlıurfa. On the last day you drive back to Göreme via Gaziantep, following the road through Adana and over the Taurus Mountains to Niğde. Readers have also enjoyed the tours operated by the Kelebek Pension.

Other companies in Göreme offer similar packages but it's worth checking exactly where you'll be stopping.

Adıyaman

The provincial capital of Adıyaman (population 130,000, altitude 669m) is the nearest city to the southern approaches of Nemrut Dağı. Now a booming oil town, Adıyaman is a gritty concrete wasteland stretched along several kilometres of highway D360, known locally as Atatürk Bulvarı.

The Tourism Information Office (☎ 416-216 1008, fax 216 3840), Atatürk Bulvarı 184, is next to the PTT on Atatürk Bulvarı.

Although the **museum** on Atatürk Bulvarı near the Hotel Serdaroğlu contains some of the finds from the local Kommagene sites it has been closed for the past decade. It's possible it will have re-opened by the time you read this. Otherwise Adıyaman has few specific sights other than the **Ulu Cami**, a partially 14th century building buried in the shopping streets to the south of the museum.

Adıyaman's postal code is 02100.

Places to Stay The oil boom has ensured that its a seller's market when it comes to letting hotel rooms. Some hoteliers also have a disappointingly cynical view of their guests – they're only here for one night so why waste money on expensive 'extras' like fans in the bedrooms? When you remember that temperatures around here can soar to more than 40°C in July and August you may want to bear that in mind when picking your room.

Buried in the shopping streets off Atatürk Bulvarı, south of the Vilayet, are two good bets for backpackers, both in Harıkçı Caddesi. ***Otel Yolaç*** *(☎ 416-216 1301, fax 213 5770)* has fairly basic rooms with showers but shared toilets for US$9 per person without breakfast. The ***Ünal*** *(☎ 416-216 1508, fax 213 3344)* has similarly simple rooms with TVs but no toilet for US$9/12 a single/double. Both are likely to be noisy but will suit those who like to be at the heart of the action.

The welcoming ***Beyaz Saray Pansiyon*** *(☎ 416-216 2100, fax 216 1580, Atatürk Bulvarı 136)*, on the highway in the eastern part of town, has reasonable rooms for US$6/10/17 a single/double/triple without bathrooms and US$10/16/23 with bathroom. There's a pool in the garden and a pleasant ***restaurant***, although loud music until midnight might not be what you are after if you are planning for a sunrise trip up Nemrut Dağı.

A short distance further east, along Atatürk Bulvarı at the junction with Turgut Reis Caddesi near the Vilayet and the museum, is the centrally placed two-star ***Hotel Serdaroğlu*** *(☎ 416-216 4841, fax 216 1554)*, offering perhaps the best value in town with singles/doubles for US$15/24 including breakfast. Rooms are reasonably modern and there's a pleasant lobby with TV and a ground-floor ***restaurant***.

At the time of writing, the three-star ***Hotel Antiochos*** *(☎ 416-216 3377, fax 213 8456, Atatürk Bulvarı 141)*, on the main road toward the eastern edge of town, was the newest place, offering clean rooms with TV, fridge, breakfast and modernish decor for US$21/30 a single/double. There's a swimming pool as well. If it's full (which is very likely) the adjacent ***Motel Arsemia*** *(☎ 416-213 4434, fax 214 1010)* is under the same ownership.

The prominent 54-room ***Bozdoğan Hotel*** *(☎ 416-216 3999, fax 216 3630)*, on Atatürk Bulvarı near the western end of town, is very popular with tour groups. For US$30/45 a single/double you get a pleasant room with bath, TV and breakfast but no air-con or fan. If there's a group of you, one four-bedded room offers a good deal at US$47.

Getting There & Away Adıyaman is served by frequent buses, but no flights or trains. Dolmuşes run between Kahta and Adıyaman (35km, 30 minutes, US$0.75) throughout the day.

Kahta

No one could call Kahta (population 75,000) beautiful but it is the most obvious base for trips up Nemrut Dağı. The oil boom is rapidly changing the face of things and the finest building in town is the Turkish petrol company office on Atatürk Bulvarı, not far from the Pension Kommagene. The vast lake formed by the Atatürk Barajı also laps at the edges of Kahta, a good place to come for a meal.

Mr Mahmut Arslan at the Tourism Information Office (☎ 416-725 5007), on Mustafa Kemal Caddesi near the Hotel Kommagene,

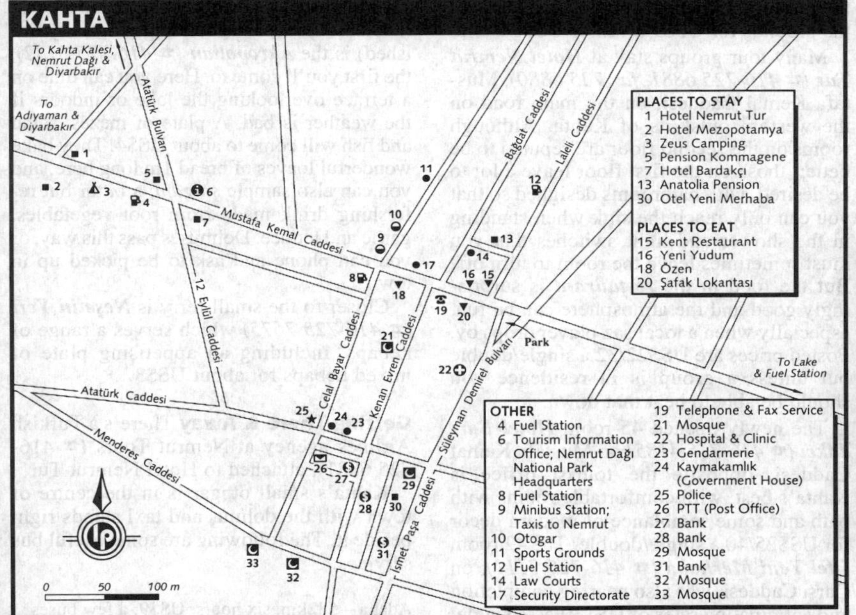

is a mine of useful information not just on Kahta but on other nearby towns too. Come here to check the latest prices for tours.

A good time to visit would be in late June when the **International Kahta Kommagene festival** takes place, with music, folk dancing and all sorts of fun and games.

The town's postal code is 02400.

Places to Stay Basically, you must decide between staying in Kahta itself or on the slopes of Nemrut Dağı. Depending on which you prefer, very different considerations need to be kept in mind. In town, it will be baking hot in high summer but few, if any, of the hotels take account of this by providing air-con or fans. Conversely, on the mountain it will be cold at night even in August so make sure you bring warm clothing and check that adequate blankets are provided.

For details of accommodation on the mountain, see under Mountain Lodgings in the following description of the ascent of Nemrut Dağı from Kahta.

At the time of writing Kahta itself was very short of decent accommodation although things should improve once the new hotels under construction finally open. Sometimes all the hotels are filled with tour groups, so it's wise to phone ahead.

The cheapest backpacker accommodation is at ***Anatolia Pension*** *(☎ 416-715 1774)*, Adliye Karşısı, where extremely basic rooms cost US$3 per person. Breakfast is served in the tea garden or the small ***restaurant*** attached.

At the junction with the Nemrut Dağı road is the pleasant ***Pension Kommagene*** *(☎ 416-715 1092, fax 725 5548)*, which has Turkish carpets dotted about to lend atmosphere. The comfortable rooms on the second floor cost US$7/12 a single/double with bath. More basic first floor rooms are often filled with oil workers. Self-caterers can use

EASTERN ANATOLIA

the restaurant kitchen, and you can camp in the grounds for US$9 a van or US$6 a tent.

Many tour groups stay at ***Hotel Nemrut Tur*** *(☎ 416-725 6881, fax 725 6880)*, Mustafa Kemal Caddesi, on the main road on the western outskirts of Kahta. Although rooms on the second floor are reputed to be better, those on the first floor leave a lot to be desired, with bathrooms designed so that you can only reach the sink when standing in the shower and light switches that you must sometimes leave the room to turn off! But the food in the ***restaurant*** is surprisingly good and the atmosphere can be fun, especially when a local saz player drops by. Posted prices are US$22/32 a single/double but unless a group is in residence you should be able to beat that down.

The newly opened 45-room ***Hotel Bardakçı*** *(☎ 416-715 4185)* on Mustafa Kemal Caddesi, opposite the tourist office is Kahta's best, with comfortable rooms with bath and some semblance of modern decor for US$25/40 a single/double. The 42 room ***Otel Yeni Merhaba*** *(☎ 416-725 7111)*, on Çarşı Caddesi, was also nearing completion and anticipating rates of US$30/50 a single/double with bath.

By the time you read this a new ***Hotel Mezopotamya*** may also have opened across the road from the Nemrut Tur. Beside it ***Zeus Camping*** *(☎ 416-725 5695, fax 725 5696)* charges US$3 per person in a tent.

Places to Eat In the town centre, the best place to eat is the spacious ***Yeni Yudum***, Mustafa Kemal Caddesi 123. All the advertised dishes are unlikely to be available but what remains is excellent. A few doors east the smaller ***Kent Restaurant*** has been open for years and still turns out decent, cheap fare at low prices. Across the road is the friendly ***Şafak Lokantası*** which serves kebaps beneath murals of macaws. Further west is the more isolated ***Özen***. At any of these places, two plates of food and a soft drink costs about US$3.50.

With a car you may prefer to drive along Baraj Yolu, the continuation of Mustafa Kemal Caddesi, to the lake where there are several restaurants to choose from. Nicest (not least because the building is actually finished) is the ***Akropolian*** *(☎ 416-725 5132)*, the first you'll come to. Here you can dine on a terrace overlooking the lake or indoors if the weather is bad. A plate of mezes, salad and fish will come to about US$4. They bake wonderful loaves of bread 1m long here, and you can also sample *şalgam*, a bitter but refreshing drink made from root vegetables, garlic and lettuce. Dolmuşes pass this way, or you can phone and ask to be picked up in town.

Closer to the small ferry is ***Neşetin Yeri*** *(☎ 416-725 7675)* which serves a range of kebaps, including an appetising plate of mixed kebaps for about US$3.

Getting There & Away There's a Turkish Airlines agency at Nemrut Tours (☎ 416-725 6881), attached to Hotel Nemrut Tur.

Kahta's small otogar is in the centre of town with the dolmuş and taxi stands right beside it. The following are some useful bus services:

Adana – 532km, six hours, US$9; a few buses

Adıyaman – 32km, 30 minutes, US$0.75; frequent dolmuşes

Ankara – 807km, 12 hours, US$15; a few buses

Diyarbakır – 482km, three hours, US$6; a few buses

İstanbul – 1352km, 20 hours, US$20; three or fours buses daily

Kayseri – 487km, seven hours, US$10; two buses daily

Malatya – 225km, 3½ hours, US$5; a few buses daily, or change at Adıyaman

Şanlıurfa – 106km, one hour, US$3; frequent dolmuşes

The road east to Diyarbakır was flooded by the lake formed behind the Atatürk Dam. A slow and infrequent car ferry bridges the gap on the road east of Kahta to Siverek, but most buses circumvent the southern shores of the lake on new roads.

Ascending Nemrut Dağı from Kahta

Whichever way you head for the summit, you might want to pack a bottle of water and some dried fruit, biscuits or nuts, as the return journey can take between four and six hours and services along the way are limited. Plan on spending up to two hours driving from Kahta to the summit and back, then add on a good two or three hours for sightseeing at the various sites.

Minibus Tours In the past Kahta had quite a reputation as a rip-off town, but things have calmed down considerably since the troubles in the east reduced the number of visitors. Nowadays you're unlikely to have many problems as prices are more or less set by the Tourism Information Office. Call in there to check the latest prices before booking anything.

Two sorts of minibus tours are available. The short tour (106km, five hours, US$35 per group) takes you from Kahta to the summit and back again, allowing you about an hour for your sightseeing. The long tour (eight hours, 140km, US$45 per group) takes you to the summit, and on the trip down stops at Arsameia, Cendere and Karakuş.

Although it may be more enjoyable to go up the mountain in the middle of the day when it's warmer and you can enjoy the scenery in both directions, most tours are timed to capture the drama of sunrise or sunset; without your own transport or enough people to make your own arrangements you're likely to travel either up or down in darkness.

Private Car These days you can easily make the trip on your own since all the sites are clearly indicated with yellow and black signs. You can either drive up along the old road via Narince and Karadut or by the shorter new route via Karakuş, Cendere, Eski Kahta and Arsameia. Make sure you have fuel for at least 200km or 250km of normal driving. Though the trip to the summit and back is only about 110km by the old road (70km by the new road), much of that will be driven in low gear, which uses more fuel.

Karakuş Highway D360, marked for Nemrut Dağı Milli Parkı (Mt Nimrod National Park, 9km) and Sincik (36km), leaves Kahta next to the Pension Kommagene. Along the way this once agricultural landscape has become a busy oilfield with nodding pumps, storage tanks and earthmoving equipment. More than 100 local oil wells produce around 60% of Turkey's petrol.

You enter the Mt Nimrod National Park at Karakuş, 10km from Kahta, via a road to the left off the highway. Like that on Nemrut, the Karakuş mound is artificial, created to hold the graves of royal ladies of Commagene. An eagle tops one of the columns ringing the site. The summit of Nemrut is clearly, if distantly visible, from Karakuş; it's the highest point on the horizon to the north-east.

Highway D360 descends into the river valley to cross it. Stay on this road marked for Cendere and Kahta Kalesi to see the other sites and for the quickest ascent of the mountain.

Cendere & Kahta Kalesi About 19km from Kahta and 5km before Kahta Kalesi, the road crosses a **Roman bridge** built at Cendere in honour of Emperor Septimius Severus (194-211 AD), his wife and sons, long after Commagene had become part of Roman Asia. Of the four original columns (two at either end), three are still standing. Some historians think that the missing column was removed by one of the sons, Caracalla, when he murdered the other son, Geta, in 212. Unfortunately a heavy petrol truck caused the collapse of the original bridge which was being reconstructed at the time of writing.

As you leave the bridge, a sign points to the right for Nemrut Dağı and Gerger; the road to the left is for Kahta Kalesi.

You approach Kahta Kalesi along the valley of a stream called the Kahta Çayı. Opposite the village are the ruins of a 14th century Mameluke castle, now called **Yeni Kale** (yeh-NEE kah-leh, New Fortress), with some Arabic inscriptions – although originally a Turkic people, the Mamelukes were assimilated into Egyptian society. It's no longer possible to climb up for a close look at the castle though.

Several decades ago the only way to reach the summit of Nemrut Dağı was to walk and it's still possible to engage a guide in Kahta Kalesi to lead you up a trail to the summit.

Eski Kale (Arsameia) About 1km further along the main road, a road to the left takes you the 2km to Eski Kale, the ancient Commagene capital of Arsameia. Admission costs US$1. Walk up the path from the car park and you'll come to a large stele with a figure (maybe female) on it. Further along are two more stelae, a monumental staircase and, behind them, an opening in the rock leading down to a cistern.

Another path leads from the first path to a striking and undamaged stone relief which portrays the founder of Commagene, Mithridates I Callinicus, shaking hands with the god Heracles. Next to it is a long inscription in Greek and to the right is a tunnel descending 158m through the rock. Bring a torch (flashlight) with you if you want to descend the steps to the room at the bottom.

Above the relief on the level top of the hill are the foundations of Mithridates' capital city and a spectacular view, the perfect spot for a picnic.

A new 8km road now makes it possible to drive straight from Arsemeia to Nemrut Dağı.

Eski Kale to Karadut If you're planning to spend the night at one of the hotels or pensions on the mountain before making your ascent you can either take the new road and then drive back down the old road for part of the way or follow the old road up from Eski Kale.

If you choose to do that, 3km up from Eski Kale is Damlacık. The next settlements are Kuştepe (7km), then Tüten Ocak (3km). After Narince the road becomes rougher and steeper. Another 7km east of Narince is a turn-off to the left marked for Nemrut, which you want to take; to continue straight on would take you to the village of Gerger.

Mountain Lodgings Continue up the mountain 5km to the hamlet of Karadut, which has a few small eateries and Mehmet Çınar's ***Karadut Pension*** *(☎ 416-737 2169)*, renting rooms for US$4 and offering home-cooked meals as well. You can camp in the grounds and soak up the wonderful views for US$3. If you stay you'll need to take a minibus on to the summit. A passing minibus may charge US$2 or more; to rent an entire minibus for a trip to the summit and back to Karadut costs about US$13. This is a great place to stay if you want to experience life in a tiny mountain village.

North of Karadut, the last half-hour's travel (12km) to the summit is on a steep road paved with black basalt blocks and still fairly rough. On the left you'll come to the 55 room ***Hotel Euphrat*** *(☎ 416-737 2175, fax 737 2179)*, 9.5km from the summit, which charges US$25 per person for bed, breakfast and dinner; the building's tin roof is a bit of an eyesore but the views are magnificent. A little further up the ***Hotel Kervansaray*** *(☎ 416-737 2090)* has a shady garden with swimming pool and charges US$18 for half-board.

Continuing up the mountain the most basic place is ***Apollo Pension*** *(☎ 416-737 2041)*, a converted village house on the right with a garden ***restaurant***. Bed and breakfast here costs just US$5, with another US$3.50 for dinner. Just 7km from the summit and you'll reach the ugly ***Zeus Motel*** *(☎ 416-737 2089)* where huge but not inspiring rooms cost US$9 per person. You can eat in the eastern-bloc-style ***restaurant*** here (US$3.50 for dinner) or at ***Çesme Lokantası***, a little way back down the road.

All this accommodation is fairly basic, although the stunning views and peaceful settings make up for any lack of mod cons. Note that one dolmuş a day leaves Kahta at about 3 pm to go up the mountain as far as the Zeus Motel, stopping at Karadut village (US$1.50) on the way.

At the Summit By the time you climb the final ridge to the summit you're well above the treeline. Just up from the car park is a cafe for snacks and hot tea, soft drinks and souvenirs. The staff run a basic pansiyon, described by one reader as 'two cement boxes', for US$5 to US$7 per person. Admission to the archaeological site costs US$2.50.

Beyond the building you must hike 500m (15 or 20 minutes) over the broken rock of the stone pyramid to the western temple. Sometimes donkeys are on hand to carry you, but this is not much help since staying on the donkey is almost as difficult as negotiating the rocks on your own. Make sure you're wearing sensible shoes.

Antiochus I Epiphanes ordered the construction of a hierothesium, or combination tomb and temple here:

> I, great King Antiochus, have ordered the construction of these temples, the ceremonial road, and the thrones of the gods, on a foundation which will never be demolished ... I have done this to prove my faith in the gods. At the end of my life I will enter my eternal rest here, and my spirit will join that of Zeus-Ahura Mazda in heaven.

As you approach, the first thing you see is the western temple with the conical funerary mound of fist-sized stones behind it.

At the western temple, Antiochus and his fellow gods sit in state, although the bodies have partly tumbled down along with the heads. But at the eastern temple the bodies are largely intact, except for the fallen heads, which seem more badly weathered than the western heads. On the backs of the eastern statues are inscriptions in Greek.

Both terraces have similar plans, with the syncretistic gods, the 'ancestors' of Antiochus, seated in this order, from left to right: first comes Apollo, the sun god – Mithra to the Persians, Helios or Hermes to the Greeks; next is Fortuna, or Tyche; in the centre is Zeus-Ahura Mazda; to the right is King Antiochus; and at the right end is Heracles, also known as Ares or Artagnes. The seated figures are several metres high, their heads alone about 2m tall.

Low walls at the sides of each temple once held carved reliefs showing processions of ancient Persian and Greek royalty, Antiochus' 'predecessors'. Statues of eagles represent Zeus.

The flat space next to the eastern temple, with an 'H' at its centre, is a helipad to save the rich and important the hassle of walking. It stands on the site of an ancient altar. Look down and you'll see a white building with 'müze' written on its door – this actually serves cups of *çay*! About 3km from the summit in the valley below is the ***Güneş Hotel***, of use mostly to those coming up from Malatya. The Güneş charges US$18 per person for bed and breakfast, with supper and a hot shower (evenings only) included.

MALATYA

Going from Adıyaman via Gölbaşı to Malatya (population 285,000, altitude 964m), the highway crosses the **Reşadiye Pass** (Reşadiye Geçidi; 1510m) and passes through a dramatic rock-bound gorge before descending to Malatya, a bustling modern town grown large and rich on agriculture. This is the *kayısı* (apricot) capital of Turkey, and after the late-June harvest thousands of tonnes of the luscious fruit are shipped throughout the world. Almost as good are Malatya's cherries, which are harvested from early to mid-June. Malatya citizens celebrate the end of harvest with a July apricot festival.

Malatya offers an alternative way of approaching Nemrut Dağı. Otherwise its claim to fame is the birthplace of İsmet İnönü (Atatürk's right-hand man and successor) and Mehmet Ali Ağca (who shot Pope John Paul II).

Very little remains of the Ottoman city although there are some **old wooden houses** in Sinema Caddesi. With the exception of one privately restored building, they're in a miserable state of disrepair.

History

Malatya has stood at the crossroads of major trade routes since Neolithic times. There was an early Assyrian settlement here, and a Hittite one also. After the fall of the Hittite Empire, various city-states emerged, among them Milidia (or Maldia), a name preserved for more than 3000 years and now pronounced Malatya.

EASTERN ANATOLIA

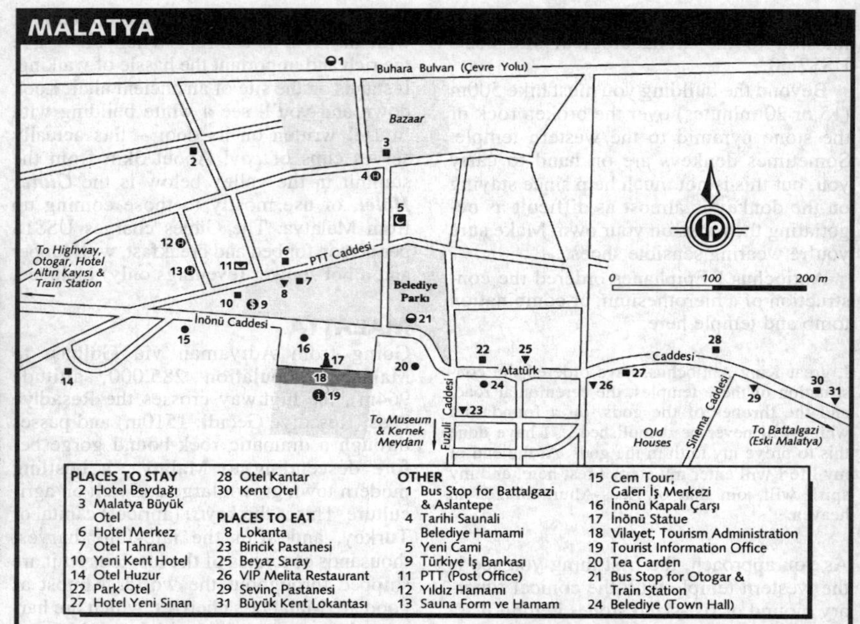

The Assyrians and Persians conquered the city alternately, and later the kings of Cappadocia and Pontus did the same. In 66 BC Pompey defeated Mithridates and took the town, then known as Melita. The Byzantines, Sassanids, Arabs and Danışmend emirs held it for a time until the coming of the Seljuks in 1105. Then came the Ottomans (1399), the armies of Tamerlane (1401), Mamelukes, Dülkadır emirs and Ottomans again (1515).

When the forces of Egypt's Mohammed Ali invaded Anatolia in 1839, the Ottoman forces garrisoned Malatya, leaving it in ruins upon their departure. Later the residents who had fled the war returned and established a new city on the present site.

Orientation & Information

Malatya stretches for many kilometres along İnönü/Atatürk Caddesi, its main street. Hotels, restaurants, banks and other services are near the main square with its ugly statue of İnönü, the Vilayet building and the Belediye nearby. The Belediye Parkı, on the northern side of İnönü Caddesi, is a convenient landmark.

A new otogar about 6km west of the centre, just off the highway, may have come into use by the time you read this. If so, the old otogar will have become a terminal for dolmuş services which, at present, stop and start all over the place.

The train *istasyon* (station) is also on the outskirts, several kilometres west of the centre. City buses and dolmuşes marked 'Vilayet' operate between the station and the centre.

The Tourist Information Office (☎ 422-323 3025) is housed in a booth in a tea garden behind the Vilayet and is open daily from June to November between 8 am and 5 pm. At other times try the administration office on the ground floor of the Vilayet except at weekends.

Old Malatya

About 11km north at Battalgazi are the remains of Old Malatya (Eski Malatya), the walled city inhabited from early times until the 19th century.

As you come into the village from the west you'll see the ruins of the old **city walls** with their 95 towers on the right. They've lost all their facing stone to other building projects, and apricot orchards now fill what were once city blocks, but it's easy to see that this was once a great city. The modern Turkish village (population 14,000) of Battalgazi has grown up in and around the ruins.

The **Ulu Cami** (1224), also on the right as you come in on the bus (look for the broken brick minaret), is a Seljuk work dating from the reign of Alaettin Keykubat I with a fine eyvan with Arabic inscription. Beside it are the ruins of the **Sahabiye-i-Kubra Medrese**, with another broken brick minaret.

The **Silahtar Mustafa Paşa Hanı** (caravanserai) on the main square is an Ottoman work dating from the 17th century. Although it's been restored it is now virtually abandoned and peaceful enjoyment of it is likely to be undermined by persistent small boys in hot pursuit.

Buses to Battalgazi (US$0.25) leave from the northern side of Buhara Bulvarı at the junction with Turgut Temeli Caddesi. This is also where you'd catch a Bahçebaşı bus to the Hittite site at **Aslantepe**, although the scant remains are of specialist interest only.

Malatya Müzesi

The Malatya Museum, is free and is open from 8 am to 5 pm (closed Monday), about 750m from the centre. Walk down Fuzuli Caddesi and cross over the main road. The museum is up a few steps to the left of the big new ice cream garden in Kernek Meydanı.

The dimly lit collection covers everything from the Palaeolithic, Chalcolithic and Old Bronze Age through to Roman and Byzantine times. It also contains finds from the excavations at Arslantepe and also from the Lower Euphrates Project, a rescue mission conducted by the Middle East Technical University (Ankara) and İstanbul University in the Euphrates valley before the Keban Dam flooded it in the 1960s. The ethnography section upstairs contains some fine carpets and embroidery.

Bazaar

Malatya has a particularly vibrant bazaar which sprawls north from PTT Caddesi and the Malatya Büyük Otel. There's a large undercover area which is fascinating provided you're not too squeamish or concerned about fish rights, and an even livelier metal-working area where you must watch out for welders in the middle of the road. You can pick up some fine baskets or packeted *mercimek çorbası* (lentil soup).

Hamams

The men-only Tarihi Saunalı Belediye Hamamı (Historical Municipal Bath with Sauna) faces the Malatya Büyük Otel. The modern Sauna Form ve Hamam and the Yıldız Hamamı are on a side street near the PTT. The small Şifa Hamamı, tucked away behind the Belediye, is open to women on Friday and Saturday afternoons only. A simple bath costs US$2, more if you opt for a washing and massage.

Tours to Nemrut Dağı

For many years the Tourist Information Office has been organising hassle-free minibus tours (daily from April to mid-October) to Nemrut Dağı, leaving from outside the Vilayet. However, a commercial travel agency (Cem Tour – described later in this section) offering tours has now opened and it's not certain that those out of the tourist office will continue, so check before showing up.

Provided the tours continue, the minibus will come and pick you up at noon for the four-hour ride up Nemrut through dramatic scenery. The last 30km of road is unpaved, but it goes right to the summit, closer than the road from Kahta. After enjoying the sunset for two hours, you descend 2km to the ***Güneş Hotel***, where you have dinner and spend the night. In the morning, you take the minibus to the summit for sunrise before returning to the hotel for breakfast, then to Malatya, arriving around 10 am.

The cost per person is US$30, including transport, dinner, bed and breakfast, and you pay another US$2.50 for admission to the national park. Some readers have negotiated a transport-only fare, and taken a sleeping bag and food to the summit with them. If you want to do this, remember that the mornings are freezing cold even in July.

If you prefer to descend via Kahta, hike across the summit to the car park and cafe building, and ask around for a minibus with an empty seat; or hitch a ride with someone going down to Kahta.

The agency offering tours is Cem Tour (☎ 422-322 6666, fax 322 8444) on the first floor of the Galeri İş Merkezi. It'll be some while before it's geared up for the needs of western tourists though.

Places to Stay – Budget

Malatya is doing so well that cheap hotels are being squeezed out. It says everything for the situation that what was once the Mercan Palas Oteli in PTT Caddesi is now a bank. Meanwhile the quieter hotels tend to be the older ones with the least inviting rooms along PTT Caddesi. The better rooms are mainly in the hotels along Atatürk Caddesi, where you'll need one at the back to escape the traffic noise.

For rock-bottom budgets ***Otel Tahran*** *(☎ 422-324 3615)*, on PTT Caddesi, offers basic rooms with sinks for US$5/6 a single/double. It has the smallest, filthiest lift imaginable. The nearby ***Merkez*** and the ***Özen*** are similar.

Noisier but more cheerful is ***Park Otel*** *(☎ 422-321 1691)* on Atatürk Caddesi across from the Belediye. Well-worn doubles are US$8 without shower and US$9 with shower.

A good choice would be the welcoming ***Otel Kantar*** *(☎ 422-321 1510, Atatürk Caddesi 81)*, where a clean if simple double room costs US$6 with sink or US$10 with a shower. There's a good ***restaurant*** with an outside dining area attached.

If you're just passing through, the otogar boasts a basic hotel copiously decorated with pictures of religious and historic sites – ***Otel Pazarbaşı*** *(☎ 422-321 2814)*. A single/double without bath costs US$5/8.

Places to Stay – Mid-Range

Perhaps the best deal in town is the two-star, 52 room ***Malatya Büyük Otel*** *(☎ 422-321 1400, fax 321 5367)*, facing the Yeni Cami, a block north of the Belediye Parkı, which looks more expensive than it actually is. All rooms have baths (with lashings of hot water) and some have TVs but rates can go as low as US$15/19 a single/double, breakfast included, when it's quiet. Despite its position in the bazaar this is likely to be one of the quieter places to stay – except for the morning call to prayer from the Yeni Cami across the road.

One block away is the new ***Hotel Beydağı*** *(☎ 422-322 4611, fax 323 2258)* with a large ***restaurant*** on the ground floor. Pleasingly modern rooms cost US$12/18 a single/double with bath and breakfast; one big family room with a balcony is good value at US$36. You can expect street noise though.

The other star-rated hotels are on Atatürk Caddesi, east of the Vilayet. The one-star, 50 room ***Hotel Yeni Sinan*** *(☎/fax 422-321 2907)* has eight floors, a lift and a bar, and charges US$17/24/34 a single/double/triple including breakfast. Readers have enjoyed staying in its clean, modern rooms which boast TV, minibar and big bathroom.

A bit further east on the opposite side of the road is the one-star, 50 room ***Kent Otel*** *(☎ 422-321 2175, fax 312 3529)* which charges US$14/21/24 a single/double/triple without breakfast, subject to haggling when it's quiet. Rooms are fairly basic but clean, and those on the top floor at the back have pleasant views. The same people also own ***Yeni Kent Otel*** *(☎ 422-321 1053, fax 324 9243)* on PTT Caddesi where newer rooms justify higher prices: US$18 a single and US$25 a double. The decor is pleasingly modern (although the carpet stains are already accumulating), but you'd better ask for a room on the PTT (front) side to escape street noise. Breakfasts here are big enough to suit an apricot trader's stomach ... and include apricots, of course!

Heading west, the new ***Otel Huzur*** *(☎ 422-323 5928, Nasuhi Caddesi 6)* is another good choice on a relatively quiet side street with very reasonably priced singles/doubles/triples for US$9/16/19 without bath.

Places to Stay – Top End

The four-star ***Hotel Altın Kayısı*** *(☎ 422-238 3232, fax 238 0083)*, or 'Golden Apricot', is at the top of İstasyon Caddesi where it meets Buhara Bulvarı. Externally it's nothing to write home about, but inside the rooms are big and modern, with TVs, fridges, air-con and apricot-decorated curtains and bedcovers. There's a ***restaurant*** and ***bar***, and plenty of parking space. The rather remote situation also ensures that it's quieter than other choices in the town centre. Posted prices for singles/doubles/triples are a hefty US$65/100/170 but when it's quiet they drop dramatically.

Places to Eat

At PTT Caddesi 29 next to the Otel Tahran is ***Lokanta***, clean, white and very popular with Malatya's business community. The food is good and moderately priced; no alcohol is served.

On Atatürk Caddesi, near the Park Otel, the popular ***Beyaz Saray*** serves excellent İskender kebap for less than US$2. There's a choice of ready meals as well. A few doors uphill from the Kent Otel at Atatürk Caddesi 137 is the even more popular ***Büyük Kent Lokantası***. Its İskender kebap leaves something to be desired but the soups and stews are excellent. Meals cost between US$3 and US$6.

Malatya has an excellent new restaurant just off Atatürk Caddesi on the first floor of the Turfanda İş Hanı. ***VIP Melita Restaurant*** *(☎ 422-322 4300)* offers a tempting trolley of cold mezes and some beautifully cooked kebaps and other dishes. Despite its size it fills up with courting couples and businessmen any night of the week, and there's music to accompany the delicious food. Of course it depends what you choose to eat but you can have a very good two-course meal with soft drink for less than US$7.

Malatyans seem to have very sweet teeth and the town positively creaks with tempting cake shops. One such place is ***Sevinç Pastanesi***, virtually opposite the Otel Kantar on Atatürk Caddesi, where gleaming showcases are stuffed with all sorts of sweet treats. Another is the ***Biricik Pastanesi*** on Fuzuli Caddesi which does Paris-quality coffee and cake for nothing like Paris-style prices. It's well placed for a stop en route to or from the museum.

Atatürk Caddesi is lined with ***dried-fruit shops*** selling baskets of apricots and other dried fruits with nuts and snacks, both sweet and salty. More dried-fruit shops can be found in the bazaar.

Malatya also has several very pleasant ***tea gardens***. The three most central ones are in the Belediye Parkı, in front of the Vilayet and in the İnönü Kapali Çarşı beneath the main square. Another can be found behind the Vilayet (with the Tourist Information Office) and yet another in Kernek Meydanı in front of the museum; this latter garden is attached to a small fairground.

Getting There & Away

Air Turkish Airlines (☎ 422-321 1922), Kanalboyu Caddesi 10, Orduevi Karşısı, has one nonstop flight daily between Malatya's Erhaç airport and Ankara, with connections to İstanbul and İzmir. There is also a nonstop flight to İstanbul four days per week. The airport bus costs US$1.50 and leaves from the Turkish Airlines office 1½ hours before flight departure time.

Bus Until Malatya's new otogar on the western outskirts of the city finally comes into operation, services will continue to operate from the old otogar closer into town. Dolmuşes (US$0.25) run between the otogar and various points around the town centre.

Malatya bus services include daily trips to the following destinations:

Adana – 425km, eight hours, US$9; a few buses
Adıyaman – 190km, three hours, US$5; frequent buses

EASTERN ANATOLIA

Ankara – 685km, 11 hours, US$13; frequent buses
Diyarbakır – 260km, four hours, US$6; a few buses
Elazığ – 101km, 1½ hours, US$3; a few buses
Gaziantep – 250km, four hours, US$9; a few buses
İstanbul – 1130km, 18 hours, US$21; a few buses
Kahta – 225km, three hours, US$5; two morning buses
Kayseri – 354km, six hours, US$8; several buses
Sivas – 235km, five hours, US$10; several buses

Train Malatya's station can be reached by dolmuş (US$0.25) or by 'İstasyon' city bus from the Belediye Parkı.

The city is served daily by express train from İstanbul (Haydarpaşa; US$11) and Ankara (US$7) via Kayseri (US$3) and Sivas (US$5). On Monday, Wednesday and Friday it's the *Vangölü Ekspresi* to Elazığ (US$6); on other days it's the *Güney Ekspresi*, heading east for Diyarbakır (US$1.50) and Kurtalan (US$4). See the Getting Around chapter in the front of this book for details.

There are also daily services to Elazığ (US$2) but these are likely to be slower than the bus. The 1st-class-only *Mavi Tren* to Ankara (US$9) also passes through Malatya.

ŞANLIURFA (URFA)

The great pilgrimage town of Şanlıurfa (population 295,000, altitude 518m) is a strange mixture of old and new, serene and raucous. In the shadow of a mighty medieval fortress, grey-bearded men and black-chadored women toss food into a pool full of sacred carp or gather at a cave said to be the birthplace of the patriarch Abraham. In the cool darkness of the covered bazaar, shopkeepers sit on low platforms in front of their stores, as was the custom in Ottoman times. Amid the hubbub of Turkish you'll also hear Kurdish and Arabic. But out on the highway the traffic is noisy and unruly and the high-rises as unappealing as anywhere else in the east.

Of all the towns in the south-east, Urfa currently has most to offer tourists. Not only are there several specific sights worth stopping for but much of the town is architecturally interesting as well. Although people are keen to practice their English on you, the level of hassle rarely becomes irksome. You could easily spend four or five days here without getting bored but to get the best out of Urfa allow at least one night and a full day. If you want to make an excursion south to Harran, the biblical town of beehive houses near the Syrian frontier, and to the surrounding archaeological sites, you'll need at least another day. To see the Atatürk Barajı (Atatürk Dam), out on the road to Adıyaman, that is so transforming this corner of Turkey, allow another half day.

History

The mysterious laws of geography ruled that this dusty spot would be where great empires clashed again and again over the centuries. Far from Cairo, Tehran and Constantinople, Urfa was nevertheless where the armies, directed from those distant capitals, would often meet.

The city has been sizzling in the sun for a long time. It's thought that there was a fortress on the hill where the kale now stands more than 3500 years ago. The people built a powerful state (called Hurri (Cave) by the Babylonians) simply because they knew what a chariot was and how to use it in battle when few of their neighbours had heard of such a thing. Although the Hurrites allied themselves with the Egyptian Pharaohs, the Hittites finally got the better of them around 1370 BC. After the fall of Hattuşaş, Urfa came under the domination of Carchemish.

The alliance with Egypt produced an interesting cultural exchange. After Amenhotep IV (Akhenaton) popularised the worship of the sun as the unique and only god, a similar worship of Shemesh (the sun) was taken up here. Sun worship (in this climate one would think it might be shade worship instead!) was not just a religious belief, but a political posture. Thus Urfa defied the cultural, political and religious influence of the nearby Hittites by adopting the customs of the Egyptians, who were a safe distance away.

After a period of Assyrian rule, Alexander the Great came through. He and his Macedonian mates named the town Edessa,

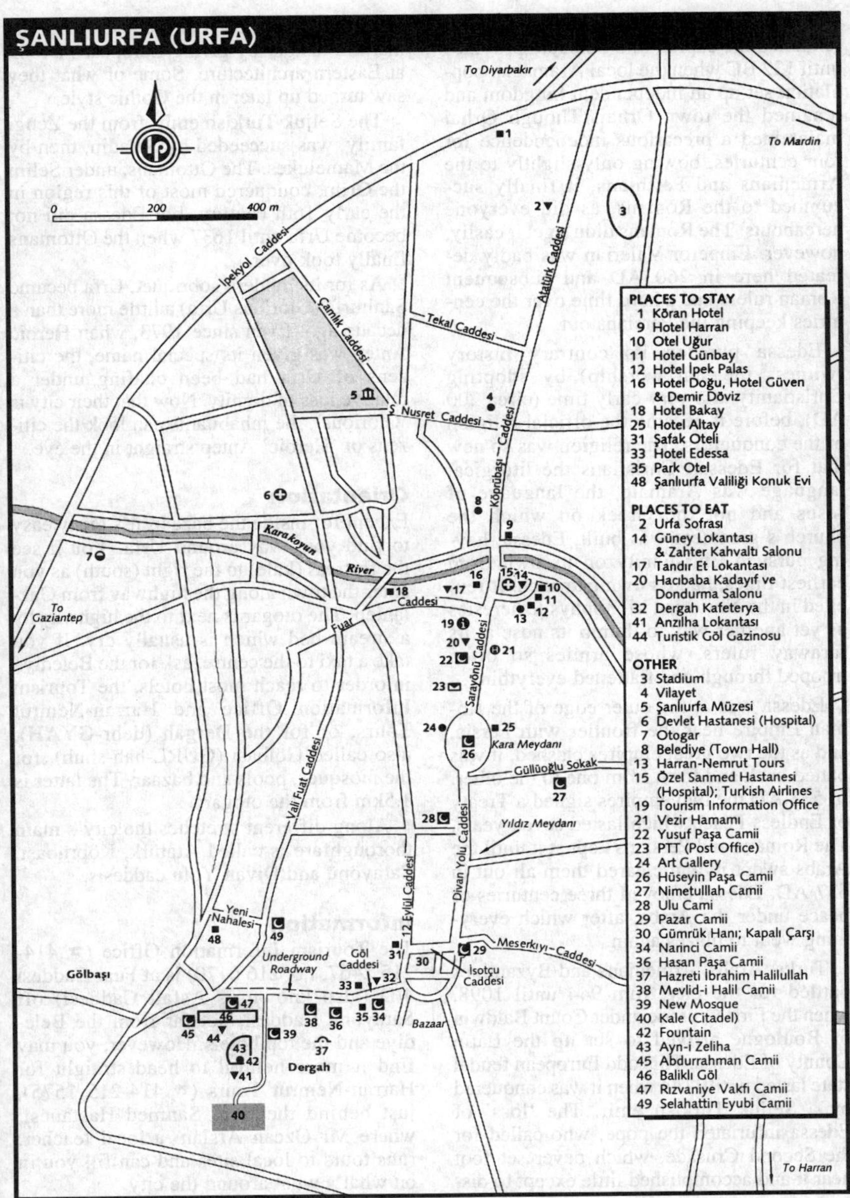
ŞANLIURFA (URFA)
To Diyarbakır
To Mardin
To Gaziantep
To Harran
0
200
400 m
İpekyol Caddesi
Çamlık Caddesi
Atatürk Caddesi
Tekal Caddesi
S Nusret Caddesi
Köprübaşı – Caddesi
Karakoyun
River
Fuar
Caddesi
Vali Fuat Caddesi
Sarayönü Caddesi
Kara Meydanı
Güllüoğlu Sokak
Yıldız Meydanı
Divan Yolu Caddesi
12 Eylül Caddesi
Yeni Nahalesi
Gölbaşı
Underground Roadway
Göl Caddesi
Meserkıyı Caddesi
İsotçu Caddesi
Bazaar
Dergah
PLACES TO STAY
1 Kōran Hotel
9 Hotel Harran
10 Otel Uğur
11 Hotel Günbay
12 Hotel İpek Palas
16 Hotel Doğu, Hotel Güven & Demir Dōviz
18 Hotel Bakay
25 Hotel Altay
31 Şafak Oteli
33 Hotel Edessa
35 Park Otel
48 Şanlıurfa Valiliği Konuk Evi
PLACES TO EAT
2 Urfa Sofrası
14 Güney Lokantası & Zahter Kahvaltı Salonu
17 Tandır Et Lokantası
20 Hacıbaba Kadayıf ve Dondurma Salonu
32 Dergah Kafeterya
41 Anzılha Lokantası
44 Turistik Göl Gazinosu
OTHER
3 Stadium
4 Vilayet
5 Şanlıurfa Müzesi
6 Devlet Hastanesi (Hospital)
7 Otogar
8 Belediye (Town Hall)
13 Harran-Nemrut Tours
15 Özel Sanmed Hastanesi (Hospital); Turkish Airlines
19 Tourism Information Office
21 Vezir Hamamı
22 Yusuf Paşa Camii
23 PTT (Post Office)
24 Art Gallery
26 Hüseyin Paşa Camii
27 Nimetulllah Camii
28 Ulu Cami
29 Pazar Camii
30 Gümrük Hanı; Kapalı Çarşı
34 Narinci Camii
36 Hasan Paşa Camii
37 Hazreti İbrahim Halilullah
38 Mevlid-i Halil Camii
39 New Mosque
40 Kale (Citadel)
42 Fountain
43 Ayn-i Zeliha
45 Abdurrahman Camii
46 Balikli Göl
47 Rızvaniye Vakfı Camii
49 Selahattin Eyubi Camii

after a former capital of Macedonia, and it remained the capital of a Seleucid province until 132 BC when the local Aramaean population set up an independent kingdom and renamed the town Orhai. Though Orhai maintained a precarious independence for four centuries, bowing only slightly to the Armenians and Parthians, it finally succumbed to the Romans, as did everyone hereabouts. The Romans didn't get it easily, however. Emperor Valerian was badly defeated here in 260 AD and subsequent Roman rulers had a hard time over the centuries keeping the Persians out.

Edessa pursued its contrary history (witness the sun worship) by adopting Christianity at a very early time (circa 200 AD), before it became the official religion of the conquerors. The religion was so new that for Edessan Christians the liturgical language was Aramaic, the language of Jesus and not the Greek on which the church's greatness was built. Edessa, having pursued Christianity on its own from earliest times, had its own patriarch. It revelled in the Nestorian Monophysite heresies as yet another way to thumb its nose at its faraway rulers, whose armies so often trooped through and flattened everything.

Edessa was at the outer edge of the Roman Empire near the frontier with Persia, and as the two great empires clashed, it was batted back and forth from one to the other. In 533 AD the two empires signed a Treaty of Endless Peace which lasted seven years. The Romans and Persians kept at it until the Arabs swept in and cleared them all out in 637 AD. Edessa enjoyed three centuries of peace under the Arabs, after which everything went to blazes again.

Turks, Arabs, Armenians and Byzantines battled for the city from 944 until 1098, when the First Crusade under Count Baldwin of Boulogne arrived to set up the Latin County of Edessa. This odd European feudal state lasted until 1144 when it was conquered by a Seljuk Turkish emir. The 'loss' of Edessa infuriated the pope, who called for the Second Crusade, which never set foot near it and accomplished little except to discredit itself. But the Latin county made its mark in history by giving Europeans a look at Eastern architecture. Some of what they saw turned up later in the Gothic style.

The Seljuk Turkish emir, from the Zengi family, was succeeded by Saladin, then by the Mamelukes. The Ottomans, under Selim the Grim, conquered most of this region in the early 16th century, but Edessa did not become Urfa until 1637 when the Ottomans finally took over.

As for its modern sobriquet, Urfa became Şanlıurfa (Glorious Urfa) a little more than a decade ago. Even since 1973, when Heroic Antep was given its special name, the citizens of Urfa had been chafing under a relative loss of dignity. Now that their city is 'Glorious', the inhabitants can look the citizens of 'Heroic' Antep straight in the eye.

Orientation

Except for inside the bazaar, it's fairly easy to find your way around Urfa. You'll see the fortress (kale) to the right (south) as you enter the town along the highway from Gaziantep. The otogar is next to the highway by a stream bed which is usually dry. If you take a taxi to the centre, ask for the Belediye in order to reach most hotels, the Tourism Information Office and Harran-Nemrut Tours; or for the Dergah (dehr-GYAH), also called Gölbaşı (GURL-bah-shuh), for the mosques, pools and bazaar. The latter is 1.5km from the otogar.

Along different stretches the city's main thoroughfare is called Atatürk, Köprübaşı, Sarayönü and Divan Yolu caddesis.

Information

The Tourism Information Office (☎ 414-215 2467, fax 216 0170) is at Fuar Caddesi 4/D (also known as Asfalt Caddesi) off Sarayönü Caddesi, not far from the Belediye and the top hotels. However, you may find it more helpful to head straight for Harran-Nemrut Tours (☎ 414-215 1575), just behind the Özel Sanmed Hastanesi, where Mr Özcan Arslan, a local teacher, runs tours to local sites and can fill you in on what's what around the city.

Urfa's Favourite Son

You won't be in Turkey for long before you hear the dulcet tones of İbrahim Tatlıses, the moustachioed Kurd from Şanlıurfa who was supposedly discovered while singing to himself over a glass of tea during a break from his labouring work and whose tapes and CDs far outsell everybody else's.

Since his chance discovery Tatlıses has gone from strength to strength as the best-known exponent of the style of music known as *arabesk* (see 'Top of the Turkish Pops' boxed text in the Facts About Turkey chapter).

His success has brought him phenomenal wealth which he has ploughed into ventures as varied as the Tatlıses Lahmacun chain of fast-food shops, hotels and his own bus company.

But his career has been no more free of controversy than that of the late lamented Frank Sinatra. Some years ago he was accused of assaulting his partner, and photos of her battered face wound up on the walls of Turkey's first refuge for battered women.

Demir Döviz, on Sarayönü Caddesi between Hotel Güven and Hotel Doğu, and several other banks and exchange offices can change your money. US dollars and deutschmarks are the preferred currencies.

The *Turkish Daily News* and selected foreign newspapers are on sale at Öğrenciler Pazarı in Atatürk Bulvarı, around the corner from the Tourism Information Office.

Gölbaşı

This is the beautiful area to the south of the centre which includes the **pools of sacred carp** (Balıklı Göl), the Rızvaniye and Abdurrahman mosques, and the surrounding park. Gölbaşı means 'at the lakeside', and while the pools hardly constitute a lake, it is easy for Urfa's citizens to amplify the size of these cool, refreshing places in their minds, especially now that a vast rose garden has been planted to make them even more inviting.

On the northern side of the pool is the **Rızvaniye Vakfı Camii and Medresesi**. At the western end of the pool is the **Abdurrahman Camii and Medresesi**, also called the Halil ur-Rahman Camii, a 17th century building with a much older early 13th century Arab-style square minaret which looks suspiciously like a church's bell tower.

Legend had it that Abraham, who is a great prophet in Islamic belief, was in old Urfa destroying pagan gods one day when Nimrod, the local Assyrian king, took offence at this rash behaviour. Nimrod had Abraham immolated on a funeral pyre, but God turned the fire into water (the pool) and the burning coals into fish (the carp). You can sip the sacred water from a subterranean spring within the mosque.

The two pools – this one and the nearby Ayn-i Zeliha (Anzılha) – are fed by a spring at the base of Damlacık hill, on which the kale is built.

Local legend-makers have had a field day with the fish, deciding that they're sacred to Abraham and mustn't be caught lest the catcher go blind. You can buy food for the fish from vendors at the poolside (US$0.30). Most of the time they're so well nourished they can barely muster a feeding frenzy.

After feeding the fish, take a seat at a shady table in one of the tea gardens and have a cool drink or bracing glass of çay to ward off the heat of the day.

Dergah

The area called Dergah, to the south-east of the pools and the park, is a complex of mosques and parks surrounding the **Prophet Abraham's Birth Cave** (Hazreti İbrahim'in Doğum Mağarası) in which, legend has it, the Prophet Abraham was born. There are separate entrances for men and women, as it is a place of pilgrimage and prayer. A large new Ottoman-style mosque stands to the west of the birth cave to supplement the smaller prayer places.

Next door is a complex of mosques and medreses called **Prophet Abraham, Friend of**

God (Hazreti İbrahim Halilullah), built and rebuilt over the centuries as an active place of pilgrimage. To the east, on Göl Caddesi, is the **Hasan Paşa Camii**, an Ottoman work. The **Mevlid-i Halil Camii** holds the tomb of a saint named Dede Osman.

All of these places are open to visitors, but as they are places of prayer and worship, and this is a conservative city, you should be neatly and modestly dressed, and should go quietly and decorously, although you may be surprised at some of the sights you see inside.

EASTERN ANATOLIA

Fortress

Depending upon where you go for your information, the fortress on Damlacık hill was built either during Hellenistic times or by the Byzantines or during the crusades or by the Turks. No doubt all are true, as one could hardly have a settlement here without having a fortress, and it was normal for fortresses to be built and rebuilt over the centuries. In any case, it's vast, looks magnificent when floodlit and can be reached up a cascade of stairs and then down again via a tunnel cut through the rock.

On the top the most interesting things are the pair of columns which local legend has dubbed the Throne of Nemrut after the supposed founder of Urfa, the biblical King Nimrod (Genesis 10: 8-10). Really, you come up here for the spectacular views down over Urfa, worth paying the US$0.75 entrance fee to see.

Bazaar

Urfa's bazaar spreads itself out east of the Hasan Padişah Camii. It's a jumble of streets, some covered, some open, selling everything from sheepskins and saddles to jeans and handmade shoes. Although there are specific highlights to look for, the best idea is just to dive in and take your time exploring. Don't worry too much about getting lost – someone will soon point you in the right direction and the main roads are rarely far away.

One of the most interesting areas is the old **Gümrük Hanı (Bedesten)**, or customs depot, an ancient caravanserai. Here you'll find carpets and secondhand kilims on sale for very reasonable prices, as well as the sort of silk scarves local women tie around their foreheads. Hidden away in the heart of the bedesten is a delightful tea garden shaded with plane trees, where men sit sipping çay and playing cards until summoned by the loudspeaker to attend the mosque upstairs.

To the left (south) of the caravanserai courtyard is the **Kapalı Çarşı**, or covered markey, barely changed over the centuries, except for what's on sale.

Buried in the lanes of the bazaar are several ancient **hamams**, generally open for men from 9 am to 1 pm, for women from 1 to 6 pm, and then for men again in the evening. These are cheap places to while away a few hours and so busy that it takes a bit of confidence to plunge into them.

Mosques

Urfa's Syrian-style **Ulu Cami** on Divan Yolu Caddesi dates from 1170-5. Its 13 eyvans open onto a spacious forecourt with a tall tower topped by a clock with Ottoman numerals.

At Kara Meydanı, the square midway between the Belediye and Dergah, is the **Hüseyin Paşa Camii**, a late-Ottoman work built in 1849.

In Vali Fuat Caddesi which leads up from behind Gölbaşı to the Konuk Evi you'll see the enormous, beautifully restored **Selahattin Eyyubi Camii**, once a church and liberally adorned with Arabic inscriptions.

Old Houses

Delve down Urfa's back streets and you'll find many examples of the city's distinctive stone houses with protruding bays supported on stone corbels. Although many of these houses are falling into decay (and some are far too large for modern families), a few have been restored, most notably the house of Hacı Hafızlar, opposite the Hüseyin Paşa Camii, which has been turned into an **art gallery**. The art is often pretty awful but the courtyards and fine carved stonework are a joy to behold.

You can also wander into the **Şurkav**, a local government building immediately behind the Hotel Edessa where two courtyards are draped with greenery and you can see carvings of dogs wearing chains similar to those in Harran castle.

Şanlıurfa Müzesi

Up the hill to the west of the Vilayet building, off Atatürk Caddesi, is Şanlıurfa's museum.

The gardens contain various sculptures, and on the porch as you enter are several mosaics, the most interesting showing assorted wild animals. Inside, noteworthy artefacts include neolithic implements, Assyrian, Babylonian and Hittite relief stones and other objects from Byzantine, Seljuk and Ottoman times. A downstairs room displays finds from Kurban Höyük, one of the ancient sites that has disappeared beneath the great lake of the Atatürk Dam.

Upstairs, the ethnology section contains some incredibly intricate wooden doors and window shutters from old Urfa houses. There are also fine examples of local calligraphy and statues salvaged from Christian churches as well as the more standard rugs and embroidery.

The museum is open from 8.30 am to noon and 1.30 to 5 pm daily except Monday. Admission costs US$0.75.

Prophet Job's Site

Otherwise known as Eyüp Peygamber Makamı, Prophet Job's Site is marked by signs off the road to Harran; you can visit free at any time. Eyüp (Job), standard-bearer of the Prophet Muhammed, passed through Urfa with the Arab armies riding into Anatolia to attack Constantinople. Local legend holds that he became ill here, but was cured (or at least made to feel a bit better) by drinking water from a spring on the outskirts of town. The spring is now in a grotto next to a mosque within a walled grove of evergreens.

Places to Stay – Budget

Urfa has a wide range of accommodation to suit all tastes and budgets. Most hotels are near the Belediye. There are no places to stay near the otogar.

A real backpackers enclave is growing in Köprübaşı Caddesi behind the Özel Sanmed Hastanesi, a good place to start looking. The popular and recently renovated ***Hotel İpek Palas*** *(☎ 414-215 1546)* has singles/doubles for US$12/17 with private showers. A few doors along and up some steps the very basic ***Otel Günbay*** *(☎ 414-313 9797)* was getting a much-needed facelift at the time of writing. When it's finished, expect prices to rise from the present US$4/6 a waterless single/double. Finally, there's ***Otel Uğur*** *(☎ 414-313 1340)*, up a perilous flight of steps at the end of Köprübaşı Caddesi, opposite the Hotel Harran, where dorm beds in the most basic rooms cost just US$3.

Out on the main road ***Hotel Güven*** *(☎ 414-215 1700, fax 215 9391, Sarayönü Caddesi 133)*, has pleasant enough rooms for US$9/15/23 a single/double/triple with private shower but the welcome may depend on who's staffing the desk. The nearby ***Hotel Doğu*** *(☎ 414-212 1528)* is cheaper at US$5/8/11 a single/double/triple but much more basic.

Around the corner in Fuar Caddesi is the new ***Hotel Bakay*** *(☎ 414-215 2689, fax 215 1156)* where air-con rooms complete with TV and balcony cost US$9/12 a single/double. Readers have enjoyed staying here although you must expect some street noise.

Heading down towards the bazaar you'll find ***Park Otel*** *(☎ 414-216 0500)* upstairs at Göl Caddesi 4. Waterless rooms here are clean but as basic as they come for US$4 per person. The owner, Mustafa Arslan, speaks English.

Hotel Altay *(☎ 414-215 1917, fax 215 9252)*, centrally positioned on Sarayönü Caddesi at Kara Meydanı, offers noisy rooms with bath for US$8 per person but a warm welcome can't be guaranteed.

Places to Stay – Mid-Range

The best place to stay in Urfa is not actually the highest priced although it has only six rooms and tends to get booked up. ***Şanlıurfa Valiliği Konuk Evi*** *(☎ 414-215 9377)* is a delightful 19th century stone building tucked away in Yeni Nahalesi which was turned into the provincial government's guesthouse in 1991. Staff wear Ottoman costume, corridors

EASTERN ANATOLIA

are pleasantly carpeted and filled with huge pieces of wooden furniture and the central courtyard with fountain offers a delightful cafe, so it's slightly disappointing to find the bedrooms furnished in more or less standard Turkish hotel style. Still, the views from the roof more than make up for that and the prices, at US$21/30/45 a single/double/triple, are surprisingly reasonable.

The long-time favourite with tour groups is the three-star ***Hotel Harran*** *(☎ 414-313 2860, fax 313 4918)*, on Köprüboşı Caddesi, directly opposite the Belediye. All the rooms have air-con and private bathrooms, and some have TV and refrigerator. Notices in the bedrooms read 'Turkish Bath is available for the customers', for which read '*male* customers'. The terrace ***restaurant*** overlooking the swimming pool serves good food. Rates are US$20/38 a single/double, or US$50 for a double with bathtub. Be sure to ask for a back room to escape traffic noise. The rooms newly built at the back of the courtyard have come in for particular praise.

Out on a limb at İpekyol Caddesi 13/A-B, the main highway, is the three-star, 54 room ***Köran Hotel*** *(☎ 414-313 1809, fax 312 1737)*. Rooms are comfortable enough, with air-con, minibar and TV, but the dark chocolate decor is depressing and the location inconvenient for walking to town. Rates are US$23/36 a single/double.

Places to Stay – Top End

Urfa now has a top grade hotel perfectly positioned in the new shopping mall overlooking the rose garden by the Dergah. ***Hotel Edessa*** *(☎ 414-215 9911, fax 215 5589)* has lovely bright modern rooms with every comfort: TV, air-con, minibar, comfy armchairs and bathroom with range of toiletries. Secretarial and email services are available and there's a choice of places to eat. For all this luxury you pay a not too alarming US$70/85.

Places to Eat

Warning With the dramatic increase in waterborne pathogens joining the traditional germ-incubating heat, Urfa is a holiday resort for microbes. Indeed, with the coming of large-scale irrigation from the GAP project, professors at Tigris University predict a significant increase in the incidence of dysentery, malaria and other 'tropical' diseases. You must be especially careful with what you eat here. Be sure stews are fresh and hot, or order fully cooked grills or safe foods such as yoghurt or pilav instead.

Specialities Urfa's culinary specialities include *çiğ köfte* (minced uncooked mutton), a sure-fire recipe for gastrointestinal disaster in this hot climate; *içli köfte* (a deep-fried croquette with a mutton filling); and *Urfa kebap* (skewered chunks of lamb or minced lamb meatballs broiled on charcoal and served with tomatoes, sliced onions and hot peppers). Even if you find baklava too sweet, you may enjoy Urfa's *peynirli kadayıf*, cheese-filled shredded wheat doused in honey which you'll see on sale on round metal plates.

Restaurants ***Güney Lokantası*** at Köprübaşı Caddesi 3/D near the Hotel İpek Palas is a popular choice because it's close to many of the cheap hotels. It sells a full range of stews, vegetable dishes, pilavs and soups and a simple meal should cost US$3.

Next door is ***Zahter Kahvaltı Salonu*** where a breakfast of honey and fresh cream mixed together and spread on flat bread, washed down with a large glass of çay, costs less than US$1.

If you don't mind splashing out for the surroundings, a good place to sample içli köfte is ***Urfa Sofrası*** which has two branches: an older, darker place on the Mardin road, a dolmuş ride from the centre, and a brighter, modern and more convenient place on Atatürk Caddesi opposite the stadium. A blowout meal of soup, kebap, cooked meat and lahmacun with soft drink and coffee will come to around US$6.

The food is as good and the bill will probably come to about the same at ***Tandır Et Lokantası*** in Fuar Caddesi, across the road and up from the Tourism Information Office.

South-East Anatolia Project (GAP)

Urfa's character is changing as the South-East Anatolia Project (GAP) comes on line, bringing irrigation waters to large arid regions and generating enormous amounts of hydroelectricity for industry. Parched valleys have become fish-filled lakes and dusty villages are becoming booming market towns, factory cities or lakeside resorts.

The project is truly gigantic, greatly affecting eight provinces and two huge rivers, the Tigris and Euphrates. By the year 2005 when completion of the project is envisioned, 22 dams and 19 hydroelectric power plants will have been built. Three million hectares of land will be newly under irrigation. There will be new employment opportunities for 1.8 million people; per capita income in the region is expected to double.

The Atatürk Baraji (Atatürk Dam), keystone of the project, is capable of generating 8.9 billion kilowatt-hours of electricity annually from the runoff of the vast lake (817 sq km, 162m deep) which its construction created. One element in the project, the Urfa Irrigation Tunnel is, at 26km, the longest such tunnel in the world.

Such a huge project, capable of enormous success, can also generate sizable problems, especially ecological ones. The change from dry agriculture to wet has already caused an explosion of infectious disease. Incidence of malaria has increased tenfold, and it is feared that diarrhoea and dysentery, already on the rise, will follow suit.

The project has also generated political problems, as Syria and Iraq, the countries down-river for whom the waters of the Tigris and Euphrates are also vital, complain bitterly that Turkey is using or keeping a larger share of the water than it should.

You can sample peynirli kadayıf at ***Hacıbaba Kadayıf ve Dondurma Salonu*** on Sarayönü Caddesi next to the Yusuf Paşa Camii. A fair-sized portion costs about US$1.

Perhaps the most pleasant place for an inexpensive meal is in the park at Gölbaşı. At the ***Turistik Göl Gazinosu, Lokanta & Aile Çay Bahçesi***, next to the Balıklı Göl, *domatesli kebap* (köfte grilled with chunks of tomato and served with chopped scallions, grilled hot peppers and huge flaps of flat village bread) with a tankard of cool *ayran* (yoghurt drink) should cost around US$4.

If you feel like enjoying a beer ***Büfe 33***, more or less opposite Hotel İpek Palas, sells canned Efes Pilsen. The restaurant at ***Hotel Harran*** also serves alcohol. Dinner here can be good and not too outrageously priced (assume about US$8 per person for a full meal) but pick a night when it's busy since the empty dining room can seem rather soulless.

Getting There & Away

Air Turkish Airlines (☎ 414-215 3344, fax 216 3245) at Kaliru Turizm Seyahat Acentesi, Sarayönü Caddesi 74/A, Köprübaşı, has nonstop flights to and from Ankara five days a week, with connections to İstanbul and İzmir. There are also two weekly nonstop flights to İstanbul. Service buses to the airport stop outside the office between 9 and 10 am.

Bus The gloomy otogar has a run-of-the-mill restaurant and a left-luggage depot. On the main highway serving the south-east, it receives plenty of traffic, but most buses are passing through, so you must take whatever seats are available. Buses to the otogar are caught on Atatürk Caddesi (US$0.30). If you don't have much luggage it's quicker to walk, but assuming you're laden with baggage note that the circuitous route favoured by the dolmuş takes 20 minutes. A taxi should cost around US$2.

Details of some daily services follow:

Adana – 365km, six hours, US$9; several buses
Ankara – 850km, 13 hours, US$16; several buses
Diyarbakır – 190km, three hours, US$6; frequent buses
Erzurum – 665km, 12 hours, US$23; a few buses
Gaziantep – 145km, 2½ hours, US$4; frequent buses
İstanbul – 1290km, 24 hours, US$22; a few buses
Kahta (for Nemrut Dağı) – 140km, 2½ hours, US$6; a few buses to Adıyaman, change for Kahta
Malatya – 395km, seven hours, US$10; a few buses
Mardin – 175km, three hours, US$6; several buses
Van – 585km, nine hours, US$13; a few buses

Train The nearest station to Urfa is at Akçakale on the Syrian frontier, 50km south of the town from where buses head north to Urfa (around US$1.50).

HARRAN & ENVIRONS

And Terah took Abram his son, and Lot the son of Haran his son's son, and Sarai his daughter-in-law, his son Abram's wife; and they went forth with them from Ur of the Chaldees, to go into the land of Canaan; and they came unto Harran, and dwelt there.

Genesis 11: 31

This is what the Bible has to say about Harran's most famous resident, who stayed here for a few years back in 1900 BC. It seems certain that Harran, now officially called Altınbaşak, is one of the oldest continuously inhabited spots on earth. Its ruined walls and Ulu Cami, its crumbling fortress and beehive houses give it a feeling of deep antiquity.

Of Harran's ancient monuments the most impressive is actually the kale which looms over the modern village. However, most people are more interested in the lifestyle of the local inhabitants even though most have long since abandoned the beehive houses to their livestock in favour of more conventional dwellings. Traditionally they lived by farming and smuggling, but the coming of the Atatürk Dam looks set to change all that as cotton fields sprout all over what was once desert. Many seemingly poor villagers are actually quite comfortably off, with huge TVs and ghettoblasters in their houses.

History

Besides being the place of Abraham's sojourn, Harran is famous as a centre of worship of Sin, god of the moon. Worship of the sun, moon and planets was popular in Harran and at neighbouring Soğmatar, from about 800 BC until 830 AD, although Harran's temple to the moon god was destroyed by the Byzantine emperor Theodosius in 382 AD. Battles between Arabs and Byzantines amused the townsfolk until the coming of the crusaders. The fortress, which some say was built on the ruins of the moon god's temple, was restored when the Frankish crusaders approached. The crusaders won and maintained it for a while before they too moved on.

Beehive Houses

Harran is most famous for its beehive houses, the design of which may date back to the third century BC although the present examples were mostly constructed within the last 200 years. It's thought that the design evolved partly in response to the lack of wood for making roofs and partly because the ruins provided a ready source of reusable bricks. Locals will tell you that the houses stay relatively cool in summer and relatively warm in winter. Although the Harran houses are unique in Turkey, similar buildings can be found in Syria and in Apulia in Italy.

In busier times the **Harran House**, within walking distance of the kale and the Ulu Cami, served as a resting place where tour groups could inspect the architecture at close quarters. Nowadays it's generally kept locked but if you ask, someone will fetch a key and let you look around a series of domed rooms and sell you a cold drink. Conceivably you could also spend the night here although be sure to agree on a price beforehand.

Some villagers will also let you look around their compounds although they usually expect to be paid for doing so.

The Kale

On the far (east) side of the hill, the **kale** stands in the midst of the beehive houses. As soon as you arrive, children will crowd around you demanding coins, sweets, cigarettes, ballpoint pens and 'presents'. Whether you oblige or not, they'll continue their demands and you can expect to have an escort as you pick your way around the crumbling walls.

Although a castle probably already existed on the site from Hittite times what you see now dates mainly from after 1059 when the Fatimids took it over and restored it. Originally there were four multiangular corner towers but only two remain. Once there were also 150 rooms here, but many of these have caved in or are slowly filling up with silt. Make sure you see the **Eastern Gate** adorned with carvings of chained dogs. The guide may also point out extremely worn carvings of angels and assorted inscriptions.

At the time of writing there was no official entrance fee for the kale so beware of anyone claiming to sell tickets. Young men who'd like to guide you wait in the shaded tent that serves as a cafeteria on the summit of the kale. They'll probably want around US$6 for their services.

Other Things to See

The approach road is lined with crumbling stone **walls**, once 4km long and studded with 187 towers and four gates; of these only the restored **Aleppo Gate** remains.

Of the ruins inside the village other than the kale, the **Ulu Cami**, built in the 8th century by Marwan II, last of the Umayyad caliphs, is most prominent – you'll recognise it by its tall, square and very un-Turkish minaret. It's said to be the oldest mosque in Anatolia. Near here stood the first Islamic university (although the precise site has not been discovered), and on the hillside above it you'll see the low-level ruins of ancient Harran dating back some 5000 years.

Han el Ba'rur Caravanserai

About 20km east of Harran are the remains of the Seljuk Han el Ba'rur Caravanserai, built in 1128-9 to service the local trade caravans. Although some restoration work has been done here, there are not enough visitors to justify any services (or tickets for that matter).

Şuayb City

Another 25km north-east of the caravanserai are the extensive remains of Şuayb City, where hefty stone walls and lintels survive above a network of subterranean rooms. One of these contains a mosque on the site of the supposed home of the prophet Jethro. Once again, don't expect to find any services, although villagers will probably be happy to show you around and point out the more accessible cave rooms. Bringing a torch (flashlight) and wearing sturdy shoes will certainly make life easier.

Soğmatar

About 15km north of Şuayb is the isolated, poverty-stricken village of Soğmatar with, at its heart, a cave-temple, the Pagnon Cave, probably constructed around 150-200 AD for the cult of the local moon god Sin. Life-size figures are carved onto the walls on three sides and, although they're extremely worn, two appear to wear crescent headdresses. Inscriptions on the wall are in ancient Syrian.

Soğmatar is surrounded by bare rocks and ledges and on one of these ledges there was once an open-air temple to the sun and moon gods whose effigies can be seen carved into the side. On the top of the rock are assorted inscriptions. Standing on the summit you can see remains of other temples, thought to be linked to other planets, on the surrounding hills.

Most striking of Soğmatar's other ruins is a circular structure on another rocky ledge, with rooms cut underneath it that look as if they may once have contained burials. This is thought to have been a temple to Venus.

Once again there are no services – not even the most basic shop – at Soğmatar, although villagers will no doubt be happy to point out the sites.

Getting There & Away

Getting to Harran is relatively straightforward. The cheapest way is to catch an Akçakale bus south from Urfa and ask to be dropped off at the road junction 10km west of Harran. Here you can wait for whatever transport may appear, bearing in mind that some drivers will expect payment for giving you a lift and that there's little shelter against the boiling sun of high summer.

You may well decide that it's worth paying just a bit more to go on a tour organised by Mr Özcan Arslan at Harran-Nemrut Tours (☎ 414-215 1575) off Köprübaşı Caddesi, Şanlıurfa. Provided there are at least four people, tours depart at 9 am and 4 pm daily and cost US$7 per person. You'll spend two hours in Harran and be back in Urfa by 1 or 8 pm depending which tour you take.

If you're driving to Harran, leave Urfa by the Akçakale road at the south-eastern end of town and go 37km to a turn-off to the left (east). From there, it's another 10km to Harran. While the village is now officially called Altınbaşak, most signs still stick with Harran. As you approach you'll see a *jandarma* (paramilitary police) post, a small restaurant, a camping ground and a souvenir shop.

To get to the sites beyond Harran without your own transport is virtually impossible unless you have limitless time. Even with your own car the roads are not well signed and it would be easy to go astray amid the dusty tracks.

The longer Harran tours offered by Mr Özcan Arslan are therefore particularly well worth considering. For US$15 per person (assuming there are four people) you are taken to Harran, Han el Ba'rur, Şuayb City and Soğmatar, with a chance to take tea with villagers and see the astonishing transformation wrought on the local scenery by the GAP Project – field upon field of cotton where once there was just desert. In high summer tours leave at 6 am and return at 6 pm.

DİYARBAKIR

Of all the towns in the south-east, probably the hardest for an outsider to handle is Diyarbakır (dee-YAHR-bah-kuhr, population two million, altitude 660m). Indeed, many people steer well clear of Diyarbakır because of its reputation as the centre of the Kurdish separatist insurgency.

Life here is particularly hard for the many people who have moved into town from surrounding villages to escape the activities of the PKK and the Turkish army and now find themselves without work. You might be lucky and get away without encountering any kind of trouble but one reader wrote to report that 'within 10 minutes of arriving ... I saw a knife fight and a bomb threat'. Certainly after dark you'd be well advised not to wander about too much. Nor would it be wise to get drawn into political conversations with strangers. That said, your worst problems are likely to be with the ubiquitous street children who can make your life a misery.

The city's claustrophobic feel is amplified by the brooding black basalt walls that ring it. This basalt was thrown out by the Karacadağ volcano, now extinct. The Tigris (Dicle, DEEJ-leh) River flows right by the walls.

As with many Turkish cities, this one has only outgrown its ancient walls in the last few decades but now that it has, it's done it mightily with a satellite town of high-rises encircling the old city. Farming, stock raising, some oil prospecting and light industry fuel the Diyarbakır economy although they can't hope to provide enough work for all the newcomers. Within the walls traditional Kurdish life still continues. Many men still wear the baggy trousers, and older women have black head coverings which they gather in front as veils.

Strangely enough, this city, set in the midst of a vast, rock-strewn plain, prides itself especially on its watermelons grown in pits in the rich soil by the river, with pigeon droppings mixed in for fertiliser. Postcard stands brandish portraits of melons so large babies could easily sit in them.

The narrow alleys and the Arab-style mosques with black and white bands of stone all add to the city's exotic aspect. In summer it's scorching hot, something to bear in mind when choosing a room.

History

Considering that Mesopotamia, the land between the Tigris and Euphrates valleys, saw the dawn of the world's first great empires, it's no surprise that Diyarbakır's history begins with the Hurrian Kingdom of Mitanni circa 1500 BC, and proceeds through domination by the civilisations of Urartu (900 BC), Assyria (1356-612 BC), Persia (600-330 BC), Alexander the Great and his successors the Seleucids.

The Romans took over in 115 AD, but because of its strategic position the city changed hands numerous times until it was conquered by the Arabs in 639 AD. Until then it had been known as Amida, but the Arabs settled it with the tribe of Beni Bakr, who named their new home Diyar Bakr, the Realm of Bakr.

The next few centuries were troubled ones as the city was occupied in turn by obscure Hamdanids, Buweyhids and Marwanids. In 1085 a Seljuk Turkish dynasty, the Cüheyroğulları, took over, only to be overthrown by Syrian Seljuks, Artukids and Ayyubids.

In 1259 the Mongol emperor Hulagu Khan restored the city to the Seljuks. They, in turn, lost it to the Mardin Artukids. In 1394 Tamerlane conquered Diyarbakır and gave it to Akkoyunlu Kara Yülük Osman Bey. The Akkoyunlu (White Sheep Turkoman) ruler formed a pact with the Venetian Empire against the Ottomans, but was defeated by Mehmet the Conqueror in 1473. After 1497, the Safavid Dynasty founded by Shah Ismail took over Iran, putting an end to more than a century of Turkoman rule in this area.

The Ottomans came and conquered in 1515, but even then, Diyarbakır was not to know lasting peace. Because it stands right in the way of invading armies from Anatolia, Persia and Syria, it saw many more tribulations. Now that it's at the centre of the Kurdish insurgency, true peace eludes it even today.

Orientation

Old Diyarbakır has a standard Roman town plan, with the rough circle of walls pierced by four gates at the north, south, east and west. From the gates, avenues travel to a central crossroads. Since Roman times, several sections of wall have been razed and new gates opened. Most recently an area west of the Dağ Kapısı was demolished to ease traffic circulation.

Except for these four major streets, Diyarbakır's street plan within the walls is a maze of narrow, twisting, mostly unmarked alleys, like a Moroccan medina. It's virtually impossible to find your way around this labyrinth without the help of a guide. Nor does it help that most of the mosques have more than one name. Local boys will urge their services upon you, and you may have to use them to find the mosques, museums and churches hidden within the maze which may, in any case, be closed when you find them. Be sure to agree on a price in advance. If you decide you need a more formal guide ask in the Hasan Paşa Hanı or at the Demir Otel and expect to pay up to US$40 a day.

The train station is at the western end of İstasyon Caddesi which heads east to the Urfa Kapısı (OOR-fah kah-puh-suh, Edessa Gate), the city's western gate. Inside the walls, the continuation of İstasyon Caddesi is called Melek Ahmet Caddesi or sometimes Urfa Caddesi. To get to the centre from the train station (about 1.5km), walk out of the front door, go to the first big street and wait on the left (north-east) corner of the far side for a dolmuş going to the Dağ Kapısı (DAAH kah-puh-suh, Mountain Gate).

The otogar is north-west of the city where Elazığ Caddesi (also called Ziya Gökalp Bulvarı) intersects the highway. From the otogar take a dolmuş 3.5km along Elazığ Caddesi to the centre and you'll pass the Turistik Oteli just before penetrating the walls at the Dağ Kapısı, the northern gate, also called Harput Kapısı. From this gate, Gazi Caddesi leads to the centre. Don't let people tell you that there are no dolmuşes and that you must take a taxi; if you do the US$0.25 fare will rocket to around US$6.

Information

The tourism administrative office is on the 6th floor of the Kültür Sarayı in Hindibaba

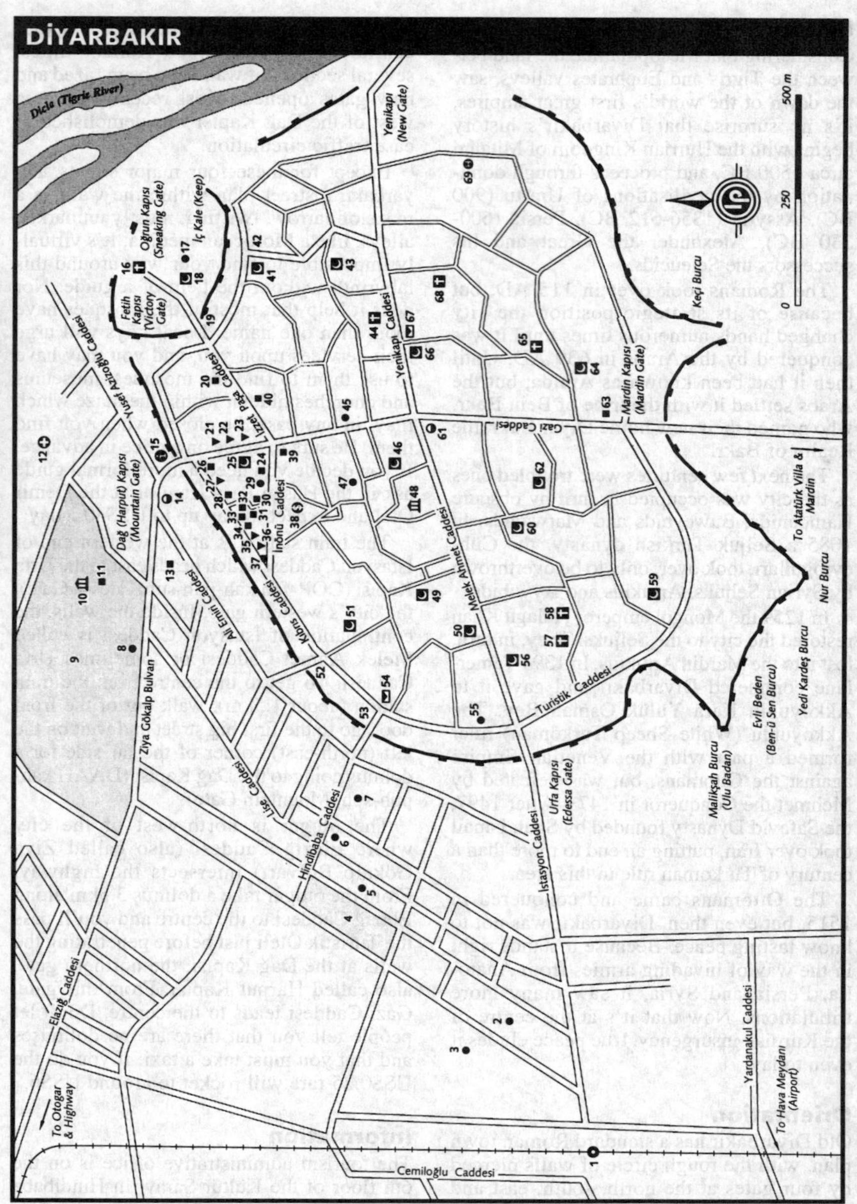
DİYARBAKIR
Dicle (Tigris River)
Yenikapı (New Gate)
Oğrun Kapısı (Sneaking Gate)
İç Kale (Keep)
Fetih Kapısı (Victory Gate)
Yusuf Azizoğlu Caddesi
Dağ (Harput) Kapısı (Mountain Gate)
İzzet Paşa Caddesi
Yenikapı Caddesi
İnönü Caddesi
Kıbrıs Caddesi
Ali Emiri Caddesi
Ziya Gökalp Bulvarı
Melek Ahmet Caddesi
Gazi Caddesi
Mardin Kapısı (Mardin Gate)
Keçi Burcu
To Atatürk Villa & Mardin
Nur Burcu
Yedi Kardeş Burcu
Evli Beden (Ben-ü Sen Burcu)
Malikşah Burcu (Ulu Badan)
Turistik Caddesi
Urfa Kapısı (Edessa Gate)
İstasyon Caddesi
Yardanakul Caddesi
To Hava Meydanı (Airport)
Lise Caddesi
Hindibaba Caddesi
Elazığ Caddesi
To Otogar & Highway
Cemiloğlu Caddesi
0
250
500 m

DİYARBAKIR

PLACES TO STAY
11 Dedeman Hotel
13 Turistik Oteli
20 Hotel Kenan
24 Büyük Otel
26 Hotel Dicle
28 Hotel Güler
30 Hotel Malkoç
31 Hotel Kaplan
32 Hotel Kristal
33 Aslan Palas Oteli
34 Hotel Uçak
37 Otel Balkar
39 Hotel Kervansaray 2
40 Demir Otel
63 Otel Büyük Kervansaray (Deliller Han)

PLACES TO EAT
21 Hanedan Lahmacun ve Pide
22 Antep Baklava ve Pasta
23 Sinan Lokantası
27 Neşem Yemek Salonu
35 Büryan Salonu
36 Sarmaşık Ocakbaşı

OTHER
1 Train Station
2 Radio TRT
3 Şehir Stadı (Stadium)
4 Cumhuriyet Parkı
5 Vilayet Konağı (Government Building)
6 Kültür Sarayı
7 Tea Garden
8 Belediye (Town Hall)
9 Fuar Sahası (Fairgrounds)
10 Archaeology Museum
12 Devlet Hastanesi (Government Hospital)
14 Dolmuş Station & Selahaddin-i Eyubi Çarşısı (Atatürk Statue)
15 Tourism Information Office
16 Church of St George
17 Adliye
18 Hazreti Süleyman Camii (Kale Camii, 1139)
19 Saray Kapısı (Palace Gate)
25 Nebi Camii
29 Turkish Airlines Office
38 Aziz Döviz
41 Nasuh Paşa Camii
42 Dicle Kapısı (Tigris Gate)
43 Fatih Paşa Camii (Arapşeyh Camii)
44 Kaldanı Kilisesi, (Surp) Giragos Church
45 Hasan Paşa Hanı
46 Ulu Cami
47 Mesudiye Medresesi
48 Ziya Gökalp Muzesi
49 Safa Camii (İparlı Camii)
50 Melek Ahmet Paşa Camii
51 İskender Paşa Camii
52 Tek Kapı (Single Gate)
53 Hindibaba Kapısı (Indian Father Gate)
54 PTT (Main Post Office)
55 Balıklı Medresesi (Ayn Zülal)
56 Lala Kasım Bey Camii
57 Mergem Ana Kilisesi (Church of the Virgin Mary)
58 Kozma Greek Orthodox Church
59 Ali Paşa Camii
60 Behram Paşa Camii
61 Minibuses for Mardin
62 Hoca Ahmet Camii
64 Hüsrev Paşa Camii
65 Protestant Church
66 Kasım Padişah Camii (Dört Ayaklı Minare/Şeyh Metar Camii)
67 PTT
68 Armenian Catholic Church
69 Yıkık Hamam

Caddesi but there's also a Tourism Information Office (☎ 412-221 2173, fax 224 1189) right inside the Dağ Kapısı. Neither abounds with useful information. You may have more luck trying Mr Esat Serdar Kahraman at the Bianca travel agency (☎ 412-223 1425), İnönü Caddesi 42.

Most banks have branches on İnönü Caddesi. Aziz Döviz (☎ 412-221 2173) is a convenient currency-exchange house near Hotel Kervansaray 2 (closed Sunday).

Diyarbakır's postal code is 21000.

The Walls & Gates

Diyarbakır's single most astonishing attraction is its great circuit of basalt walls, probably dating back to Roman times, although the present walls date from early Byzantine times (330-500 AD). At almost 6km in length these walls are said to be second in extent only to the Great Wall of China, although a more obvious parallel might be the walls of Derry/Londonderry in Northern Ireland. They make a striking sight whether you're walking along the top or the bottom.

The historic names for the **gates** are the Harput Kapısı (north), Mardin Kapısı (south), Yenikapı (east) and Urfa Kapısı (west). The massive black basalt walls are defended by 72 bastions and towers, many of them clustered around the İç Kale (EECH-kaleh, citadel or keep) on the north-eastern corner, with fine views of the Tigris. Of the gates, the Harput Kapısı or Dağ Kapısı is in the best condition.

Unfortunately, you must be careful during your walks on and along the walls as there have been reports of attempted robberies. Try to go in a group, although until tourism to Diyarbakır picks up again this may be easier said than done.

Perhaps the most rewarding stretch of the walls in terms of inscriptions and decoration is the portion between the İç Kale and the Mardin Kapısı, going westward (away from the river). Start at the Mardin Kapısı near the Deliller Han, a stone caravanserai now restored as the Otel Büyük Kervansaray. Climb up to the path on top of the walls, walk along – dodging the television aerials mounted here for best reception – and you'll pass by the **Yedi Kardeş Burcu** (Tower of Seven Brothers) and **Malikşah Burcu** (Tower of Malikşah, also called Ulu Badan). The bird's-eye vantage point allows you to see a lot of Diyarbakır's street life right below. You must descend at Urfa Kapısı but can climb up again on the opposite side of İstasyon Caddesi.

Mosques

Of Diyarbakır's many mosques, the most interesting is the **Ulu Cami**, built in 1091 by Malik Şah, an early Seljuk sultan, and extensively restored in 1155 after a fire. It's rectangular in plan – Arab-style, rather than Ottoman – with a huge courtyard where, unusually, representatives of all four rites of Sunni Islam (Hanifi, Maliki, Shafii and Hanbali) meet to pray together every Friday.

Across the courtyard from the Ulu Cami is the **Mesudiye Medresesi**, now used as a polyclinic but with revolving columns on either side of its mihrab. Across Gazi Caddesi

Old Diyarbakır Houses

Diyarbakır's long and often violent history, its extremes of climate, and its melange of cultures have produced a distinctive domestic architecture.

Most old Diyarbakır houses are made of the familiar black basalt, sometimes with a wood frame superstructure. 'Female' (the lighter, more porous stone) is used to pave courtyards and build house walls so they remain cool in the heat. 'Male' (dense, fine-grained) stone is used for large public buildings such as mosques, hans and caravanserais.

Rubble walls hide most houses from the narrow passageways which serve as streets in the old quarters. Doorways are marked by neatly cut ashlars, and often sheltered by small roofs from the hot sun and chilly rain.

Within, the traditional house is divided into summer and winter quarters. The centre of the summer house is the eyvan, or arched room open on one side which faces the courtyard. Usually a fountain made of male basalt plays quietly at the centre of the shady eyvan. The sunny courtyard may have a pool and flower boxes. In summer the family moves high wooden platforms called *tahtlar* (thrones) into the courtyard for sleeping, making it possible to catch any wayward zephyr.

The traditional Islamic division into *selamlık* (the men's rooms) and *haremlik* (the women's) is supplemented by a room called the *mabeyn* (interval) which joins the two. Floors may be of basalt or of *horasan*, a traditional mortar developed by the Persians several millennia ago, and used by the Romans and everyone else since.

The *serdap* (larder) is in the basement; the upper floors are known as *çardak* (shelter). Kitchen, toilet, stables and even a private *hamam* (Turkish bath) might complete an elaborate house.

Among decorative elements, the most prominent is *cis* or *kehal*, a stencilled decoration done in colours. The best surviving example is in the Cahit Sıtkı Tarancı Müzesi.

Several traditional houses are open to visit, including the Cahit Sıtkı Tarancı Müzesi in the city proper, the Atatürk Villa, 2.5km to the south, and the Cihannüma Köşk on the eastern bank of the Tigris in Kavs Köyü.

EASTERN ANATOLIA

from these buildings is the **Hasan Paşa Hanı**, a 16th century caravanserai, once busy with carpet sellers and souvenir vendors but now largely deserted.

Black and white stone banding is a characteristic of Diyarbakır's mosques, many of which date from the reign of the Akkoyunlu dynasty. One of these is the **Nebi Camii** (1530) at the main intersection of Gazi and İzzet Paşa/İnönü Caddesis which has a detached minaret.

The spectacular **Behram Paşa Camii** (1572), in a residential area deep in the maze of narrow streets, is Diyarbakır's largest mosque. The **Safa Camii** (1532) is more Persian in style, with a highly decorated minaret with blue tiles incorporated in its design.

The **Kasım Padişah Camii** (1512) is also famous for its minaret, but its engineering is even more interesting – the tower stands on four slender pillars about 2m high, lending it the name Dört Ayaklı Minare or Four-Legged Minaret.

The 12th century **Hazreti Süleyman Camii** beside the İç Kale is particularly revered because it houses the tombs of heroes of past Islamic wars. Local people flock here on Thursdays to pay their respects.

Note that most of these mosques have more than one name. The alternative names are shown on the map key.

Atatürk Köşkü (Villa)

The Atatürk Köşkü or Villa, traditionally known as the Seman Köşkü, dates from the time of the 15th century Akkoyunlu Turcoman dynasty. About 2.5km south of the centre, it's one of Diyarbakır's most beautiful and best-preserved traditional houses.

Alternate courses of light and dark stone banding make for a dramatic effect. Inside, the eyvans on both the ground and upper floors, and its situation overlooking the Tigris, add to its grace and grandeur. The house was given to Atatürk by the city in 1937. It's open from 8 am to noon and 1 to 5 pm, for US$0.75.

To get there, leave the city by the Mardin Kapısı and cross to the eastern side of the Tigris by the historic bridge. It would be wise to take someone with you though.

Arkeoloji Müzesi

Diyarbakır's large Archaeology Museum is near the Fuar Sahası (fairgrounds) off Ziya Gökalp Bulvarı; to get there, leave the old city through the Dağ Kapısı and turn right shortly after the Turistik Oteli. Besides the usual archaeological and classical finds and the obligatory ethnological rooms, it has collections showing the accomplishments of the Karakoyunlu and Akkoyunlu, powerful tribal dynasties which ruled much of Eastern Anatolia and Iran between 1378 and 1502.

It's open daily except Monday from 6.30 am to noon and from 1.30 to 5 pm (US$0.75).

Other Museums

The poet Cahit Sıtkı Tarancı (1910-56) was born in a two-storey black basalt house near the Ulu Cami which is now the **Cahit Sıtkı Tarancı Museum**. The house was built in 1820 and although only the haremlik and the traditional courtyard survive, it's well worth seeing for its architecture and decoration alone.

It's open daily except Monday from 8 am to 5 pm (US$1) and contains some of the poet's personal effects and furnishings, exhibits on his life and work, and standard ethnographic displays.

The **Ziya Gökalp Müzesi** commemorates sociologist Ziya Gökalp (1876-1924), a formative influence on the Turkish movement.

His house in the Tacettin district is open daily except Monday from 8 am to noon and 1.30 to 5 pm for US$0.75. The exhibits dealing with his life and work are of specialist interest, but his graceful old house appeals to all. Hopefully it will have re-opened by the time you read this.

A new museum, the **Esma Ocak Evi** commemorating a female writer, opened recently near the Cahit Sıtkı Tarancı Museum but it's only open on Saturday and Sunday.

Churches

Diyarbakır's population once encompassed many Christians including Armenians and Chaldaeans but most of them are long gone,

EASTERN ANATOLIA

with only their churches left as reminders. The **Kaldanı Kilisesi** (Chaldaean Church) off Yenikapı Caddesi was until recently used by Christians of the Syrian rite (in communion with the Roman Catholic church) although the main building has long been in ruins.

The wonderful **Meryem Ana Kilisesi**, the Church of the Virgin Mary, is an ancient building still in use by Syrian Christians of the Orthodox rite – Jacobites or Monophysites, who refused to accept the doctrines laid down at the Council of Chalcedon in 451 AD (see the Mardin section, following). It's surrounded by its own basalt wall inside which three families live around three courtyards, a garden and the church. The church is immaculately preserved even though only about 15 local families still attend services here. You will have to knock and hope the custodian is prepared to let you in.

Other churches have found new uses: one near the Dört Ayaklı Camii as a PTT, another inside the İç Kale as a prison. The Ulu Cami itself was once a Syrian church.

Places to Stay – Budget

Almost all the hotels are near the Dağ Kapısı on Kıbrıs, İnönü and İzzet Paşa caddesis, or in the narrow alleys connecting them. In summer, avoid hotel rooms just beneath the building's roof or those that receive the wrath of the late-afternoon sun. There are a surprising number of hotels but the collapse of tourism doesn't seem to have led to a commensurate collapse in their prices. It goes more or less without saying that few of these places, especially at the bottom end of the price range, are used to lone female guests. A lot of young men also hang around Kıbrıs Caddesi, ostensibly wanting to practice their English but sometimes trying to lure you into a carpet shop. Some are genuine. You must make up your own mind.

The plain ***Hotel Kenan*** *(☎ 412-221 6614, İzzet Paşa Caddesi 24)* is perhaps the best budget choice, with shower-equipped singles/doubles for US$5/8.

There are three hotels right on Kıbrıs Caddesi. The one-star ***Hotel Dicle*** *(☎ 412-223 5326, Kıbrıs Caddesi 3)*, right at Dağ Kapısı, may be a bit noisy, but is otherwise suitable at US$9/12 a single/double. West of it, the 21 room ***Aslan Palas Oteli*** *(☎ 412-221 1227, Kıbrıs Caddesi 21)* is a bit cheaper, and gives you the choice of rooms without bath (US$9 a double), or with shower and TV (US$15). Finally, ***Hotel Uçak*** *(☎ 412-221 1076, Kıbrıs Caddesi 31)* is cheapest at US$7.50 for a bathless double.

Hotel Güler *(☎/fax 412-224 0294, Kıbrıs Caddesi, Yoğurtçu Sokak 7)* offers excellent value for money: a quiet location, clean, comfortable rooms and bathrooms with lots of hot water for US$18/21 a single/double. If business is slow, they'll drop the price.

Also good is the 44 room ***Hotel Kristal*** *(☎ 412-224 0297, fax 224 0187, Yoğurtçu Sokak 10)*, directly across the street, which charges US$9/15 a single/double.

A couple of real cheapies are squeezed in beside the Otel Kervansaray 2 in İnönü Caddesi. ***Şafak*** *(☎ 412-223 6419)* charges just US$4.50 per person for extremely basic rooms. The ***Van Palas Oteli*** next door is similar.

Places to Stay – Mid-Range

Best in town is the veteran 57-room, three-star ***Turistik Oteli*** *(☎ 412-224 7550, fax 224 4274, Ziya Gökalp Bulvarı 7)*, a block north-west of the Dağ Kapısı. Built in 1953 but exceptionally well maintained, it has spacious public rooms and guest rooms with high ceilings, air-con, refrigerators, TVs, balconies, and bathrooms with tubs. There's a swimming pool and terrace at the back and guarded parking. Posted prices are a steep US$42/70, which, not surprisingly, includes breakfast. Buses to the airport leave here three times a day.

The most atmospheric place to stay is ***Otel Büyük Kervansaray*** *(☎ 412-228 9606, fax 223 7731)*, in the 16th century Delliller Han, a converted caravanserai on Gazi Caddesi next to the Mardin Kapısı. Despite the impressive surroundings, the decor of the rooms is pretty run-of-the-mill (though perfectly comfortable). They cost a reasonable US$30/35 a single/double, breakfast included. There's a beautiful swimming pool in the rear courtyard. Bear in mind that if you're looking forward to an early night or, alternatively, you want to unwind after a long day, then the front court, where the guest rooms are, is used as a nightclub, making sleep difficult, or partying easy – depending on your plans.

The four-star, 58 room ***Demir Otel*** *(☎ 412-228 8800, fax 228 8809, İzzet Paşa Caddesi 8)* is a smart place popular with tour groups and offering rooms for US$40/60 a single/double, including breakfast. Keen readers might find the lighting too dim for comfort.

The nearby 72-room ***Büyük Otel*** *(☎ 412-228 1295, fax 221 2444, İnönü Caddesi 4)* is cheaper and a good choice, with clean, comfortable singles/doubles with bath for US$20/30. Across the road is ***Hotel Kervansaray 2*** *(☎ 412-221 4966, fax 223 5933)*, which, despite its name, doesn't live up to the standards set by its sister company; cluttered rooms with so-so decor cost US$20/34 a single/double.

A newcomer to Kıbrıs Caddesi and a good choice for the time being is the ***Balkar Otel*** *(☎ 412-228 1233, fax 224 6936)* at No 38 where smart, reasonably modern rooms with TV and minibar cost US$18/27.

Place to Stay – Top End

A new ***Dedeman Hotel*** *(☎ 800-211 4444)*, beside the Arkeoloji Müzesi, may be open by the time you arrive, giving Diyarbakır its first top-class hotel.

Places to Eat

A stroll westward along Kıbrıs Caddesi from Dağ Kapısı will reveal several small, cheap places to eat, often featuring goat's head soup as a specialty. One of the best is the clean, proper and popular ***Neşem Yemek Salonu***, just up from the Hotel Dicle. Three-course meals cost from US$2.50 to US$4. It's closed Sunday.

A bit further along is the similar ***Büryan Salonu***, Kıbrıs Caddesi 17 (also closed Sunday). Just beyond it, ***Sarmaşık Ocakbaşı***, has a selection of dishes, but specialises in ocakbaşı grills, where you can sit right at the grill, watch the chef, and eat as he hands you the skewers. It's open on Sunday, and a şiş kebab dinner costs about US$3 to US$5.

In the evenings men set up kebap stands at the Dağ Kapısı end of Kıbrıs Caddesi. The smells are extremely tempting but you probably need a sturdy stomach to tuck in without repercussions.

The air-conditioned ***Sarmaşık Sofra Salonu***, İnönü Caddesi 32/A, is the best place on this street, and convenient to the Derya and Büyük hotels. Near the Demir Otel, ***Şanlı Urfa Kebap Evi*** at İzzet Paşa Caddesi 4 doesn't look much but descend to the basement at lunchtime and you'll find the locals lapping up bowls of ayran and tucking into roast peppers and delicious köfte, always a good sign. You won't pay more than US$3 for your meal.

Few Diyarbakır restaurants serve alcohol with meals, the exception being ***Sinan Lokantası*** *(☎ 412-221 1048)*, not far from Dağ Kapısı. Signs on the facade read (in English) 'Welcome to the best pleace (sic) in down town' and 'Friendly Pleace'. It's not necessarily the best food but in the heat of a Diyarbakır summer the cold Efes beer served on the vine-shaded terrace will go down a treat.

The Dicle, Demir and Büyük hotel restaurants can also do you a meal with wine or beer.

Getting There & Away

Air Turkish Airlines (☎ 412-221 2314, fax 224 3366), İnönü Caddesi 8, next to the Büyük Hotel, serves the city's Kaplaner airport with daily nonstop flights to and from Ankara, İzmir and İstanbul. A taxi to the airport costs about US$4.

Bus Many bus companies, including the large local firms such as Diyarbakır Seyahat and Diyarbakır Sur, have ticket offices in town on Kıbrıs or İnönü caddesis or in other spots near the Dağ Kapısı. Servis minibuses will ferry you to the otogar for free.

Minibuses to Mardin (US$1.50) depart from the junction of Melek Ahmet and Gazi caddesis rather than from the otogar. Other local buses leave from the Selahaddin-i

Eyubi Çarşısı, the modern market complex across from the Dağ Kapısı; come here for dolmuşes to the otogar (US$0.25). Details of daily services on the main routes follow:

Adana – 550km, eight hours, US$12; several buses
Ankara – 945km, 13 hours, US$18; several buses
Erzurum – 485km, eight hours, US$13; several buses
Kahta (Nemrut Dağı) – 192km, three hours, US$6; several buses
Malatya – 260km, five hours, US$5; frequent buses
Şanlıurfa – 190km, three hours, US$5; frequent buses
Sivas – 500km, nine or 10 hours, US$9; several buses
Van – 410km, seven hours, US$9; several buses

Train Train services to the south-east are neither speedy nor reliable. You're probably better off taking a bus. The *Güney Ekspresi* is described in the earlier Getting Around chapter.

MARDİN

About 175km east of Urfa and 100km south of Diyarbakır, Mardin (population 60,000, altitude 1325m) is a scorching hot, ancient town crowned with a castle and a set of immense and jokingly 'camouflaged' radar domes, overlooking the vast, roasted Syrian plains.

In another time and another place travellers would flock to Mardin to explore streets of honey-coloured stone houses that trip down the side of the hillside giving it something of the feel of old Jerusalem. Unfortunately since the Gulf War, tourism to Mardin has virtually dried up. As you stroll in the wonderful bazaar every eye will be upon you. That said, this is not a 'hassley town' – not nearly so bad as Diyarbakır, for example.

There's still a certain amount of smuggling trade with Syria (sheep are much more expensive in Syria than in Turkey) and lots of Kurdish separatist activity, resulting in curfews on all the surrounding roads.

Once the town was home to a large Christian community and there are still a few beleaguered Syrian Christian families to keep the church alive. On the outskirts is the monastery of Deyrul Zafaran where Aramaic, the language of Jesus, is still the liturgical tongue.

Mardin is not well equipped with hotels or restaurants; if you prize your comforts it might make sense to stick with a day trip from Diyarbakır. However, to do that would be to skimp on Mardin's particular beauty. Ultimately you should be guided by the most up-to-date information on the security situation.

History

As with Diyarbakır, Mardin's history is one of disputes by rival armies over dozens and dozens of centuries, though these days the only one that anyone really cares about is the one between the PKK and the government. A castle has stood on this hill from time immemorial and the Turkish army still finds the site useful.

Assyrian Christians settled in this area during the 5th century. The Arabs occupied Mardin between 640 and 1104. After that, it had a succession of Seljuk Turkish, Kurdish, Mongol and Persian overlords until the Ottomans under Sultan Selim the Grim took it in 1517.

Orientation & Information

Perched on a hillside, Mardin has one long main street, Birinci Caddesi ('1st Street'), running for about 2km from the Belediye Garajı at the western end of town and then forking suddenly, after the main square, Cumhuriyet Meydanı. The left fork leads on to Konak, a small square with the Hükümet Konağı and military buildings at the eastern end; the right fork drops steeply to the area where the bus companies have their offices.

Everything you'll need is along Birinci Caddesi (a one-way street) or just off it, and dolmuşes and city buses run along it to save you the effort of walking. If you're driving your own car, you can park in Cumhuriyet Meydanı.

The Tourism Information Office (☎ 482-212 5845, fax 212 1852) is at Cumhuriyet Meydanı 515.

Mardin's postal code is 47000.

Monophysites

In the 6th century, Jacobus Baradeus, bishop of Edessa (Urfa), had a difference of opinion with the patriarch in Constantinople over the divine nature of Christ.

The patriarch and official doctrine held that Christ had both a divine and a human nature. The bishop held that He had only *mono* (one) *physis* (nature), that being divine. The bishop was branded a Monophysite heretic and excommunicated. He promptly founded a church of his own, which came to be called the Jacobite (or Syrian Orthodox) after its founder. During his lifetime he claimed to have consecrated 27 bishops and around 100,000 priests.

At the same time and for the same reason, the Armenian Orthodox Church, the Coptic Church in Egypt and the Ethiopian Church were established as independent churches.

In the case of the Jacobites, control from Constantinople was soon not a problem, as the Arabs swept in and took control, allowing the Monophysites to practice their religion as they chose.

Things to See

Mardin's most obvious attraction is its rambling **bazaar** which runs along the road parallel to Birinci Caddesi one block down the hill. Here donkeys are still the only form of transport and you'll see them decked out in all the finery you sometimes see on sale in carpet shops. Look out also for saddle repairers who seem to be able to restore even the most shabby examples.

Strolling through the bazaar you'll probably spot the secluded **Ulu Cami**, an 11th century Iraqi Seljuk structure. As Mardin's history has been mostly one of warfare, the mosque has suffered considerably over the centuries, particularly during the Kurdish rebellion of 1832.

Mardin Müzesi (☎ 482-212 7797) is prominently positioned in Cumhuriyet Meydanı. It holds bits of statuary, but you've really come to admire the building and the view across the vast plains towards Syria which is just as well since the opening hours – 8.30 am to noon and 1 to 5 pm daily – seem pretty theoretical. Should you catch it open, admission may still be free.

Heading east from the main square, look for steps on the left (north) which lead to the **Sultan İsa Medresesi**, dating from 1385 and the town's prime architectural attraction, with an imposing recessed doorway. Much of the interior now houses local families.

Continuing east you'll come to what must surely be Turkey's most beautiful **post office**, housed in a carefully restored 17th century caravanserai with carvings like frills around the windows and teardrops in stone dripping down the walls.

The **Kasım Paşa Medresesi**, below the main street near the western end of town, was built in the 15th century. You'll probably have to ask for guidance to find it. Look out, too, for the 14th century **Latifiye Camii**.

EASTERN ANATOLIA

Deyrul Zafaran

About 6km along a good but narrow road in the rocky hills east of the town stands the monastery of Mar Hanania, called Deyrul Zafaran (Saffron Monastery in Arabic), supposedly because saffron crocuses were used in the mortar. The monastery was once the seat of the Syrian Orthodoxpatriarchate, and although this has now moved to Damascus, it still has the modest trappings due to the patriarch and continues to act as the local orphanage.

The first sanctuary on this site was dedicated to the worship of the sun. Then in 495 AD the first monastery was built. Destroyed by the Persians in 607, it was rebuilt, only to be looted by Tamerlane six centuries later.

Shortly after you enter the walled enclosure via a portal bearing a Syriac inscription, one of the orphans will volunteer their services as a guide. First they'll show you the **original sanctuary**, an eerie underground chamber with a flat ceiling of huge, closely fitted stones held up as if by magic, without the aid of mortar. This room was allegedly used by sun worshippers, who viewed their god rising through a window at the eastern end. A niche on the southern wall is said to have been for sacrifices.

The guide then leads you through a pair of 300-year-old doors to the **tombs of the patriarchs and metropolitans** who have served here.

In the simple chapel, the **patriarch's throne** is to the left of the altar as you face it and bears the names of all the patriarchs who've served the monastery since it was refounded in 792. To the right of the altar is the **throne of the metropolitan**. The present **stone altar** replaces a wooden one which burnt about half a century ago. The walls may be fairly plain but are adorned with wonderful primitive paintings and wall hangings. Services are held in Aramaic.

The next rooms you'll see hold **litters** used to transport the church dignitaries and a baptismal font. In a small side room is a 300-year-old **wooden throne**. The floor **mosaic** is about 1500 years old.

A flight of stairs leads to a suite of very simple guest rooms for travellers and those coming for meditation. The patriarch's small, simple bedroom and parlour are also up here. On the walls of the parlour are pictures of the patriarch (who lives in Damascus) with Pope John Paul II. An earlier patriarch is cosying up to Atatürk.

As you leave, take a moment to enjoy the fine view of the mountains. Other monasteries, now in ruins, once stood further up the slope. Some of Deyrul Zafaran's water comes from near these ruins, through underground channels excavated many centuries ago. At the end of the tour, be ready to tip the guide.

You can visit the monastery between 8.30 and 11.30 am and between 1.30 and 3.30 pm any day. There's no public transport so you must take a taxi. Hopeful drivers wait outside the bus company offices and will ask US$6. Check that this includes the return journey and an hour's waiting time before setting out.

As you drive to the monastery, you will no doubt notice a hillside on which the motto 'Ne Mutlu Türküm Diyene' (What Joy to the Person Who Says, 'I am a Turk') has been written with white stones. Atatürk originally uttered the phrase as part of his campaign to overcome the Turkish inferiority complex imposed by Europe and the USA. Here, though, it has a different significance, reiterating the government's commitment to the unity of the country against the efforts of Kurdish separatist groups.

Midyat

About 65km east of Mardin is Midyat, a sprawling settlement which has wonderfully carved old houses that make up for the absence of a hillside setting like Mardin's. Dolmuşes will drop you off in the new town (Estel) which is just west of the much more interesting old town, a maze of narrow streets with **honey-coloured houses** with demure doorways that open onto huge courtyards surrounded by intricately carved walls, windows and recesses, a dream of a place if times were more settled. The **church** is kept locked and the key is unlikely to be available.

About 18km east of Midyat, **Mar Gabriel** monastery rises like a mirage from its desert-like surroundings. Though much restored, the monastery dates back to the 5th century and has some fine floor and ceiling mosaics to show for it. Mar Gabriel is home to the archbishop of Tür Abdin (the surrounding plateau), although these days he presides over a diminished and bealeaguered flock. It's worth asking taxi drivers in Midyat whether they'll take you there, although there's no guarantee that you'll still be able to visit by the time this book is published. Make sure you agree on a fare to get you there and back, with a good hour's waiting time thrown in. It's a seller's market, so expect to pay up to US$25.

Places to Stay

In the absence of tourists, Mardin was down to just two hotels at the time of writing. For any semblance of comfort you must head for the three-star, 48 room ***Otel Bilen*** *(☎ 482-212 5568, fax 212 2575)*, 1.5km out on the outskirts near the highway, where spacious if darkly decorated rooms with TV and reasonable bathroom cost US$23/36 a single/double. To get into the centre, cross the highway and flag down any dolmuş.

In the lovely old town centre there's only the poor old ***Hotel Bayraktar*** (☎ *482-212 1338*), on the main street facing Cumhuriyet Meydanı. It would be hard to imagine a hotel that looked more sorry for itself, but if you pick one of the rooms at the back the stunning view down onto the bazaar and out over the plains might just make up for the abject state of the wiring, plumbing and furniture. Singles/doubles cost US$5/8.

Rather surprisingly, Midyat has a better hotel, the ***Yuvam*** (☎ *482-462 2531*), beside the roundabout where the Mardin dolmuşes stop. It charges US$6 per person for a simple room and is worth bearing in mind in case you miss the last dolmuş back to Mardin.

Places to Eat

The restaurant at ***Hotel Bayraktar*** used to be Mardin's best but now looks as sorry as the bedrooms. Local bigwigs seem to frequent the white-tableclothed ***Tüccarlar Kulübü Restaurant*** upstairs in the shopping block to the west of the Bayraktar. Otherwise there are several small, cheap eateries east of the town centre along the main street. Most close early (before 8 pm) although ***Ünsal Yemek Salonu*** hangs on a bit longer and serves pleasant enough spaghetti and a cold drink for less than US$2. The cake shops also continue serving milk puddings until quite late.

East along Birinci Caddesi are three ***tea gardens***, two of them tree-filled, the third with a fine view of the lovely building housing the PTT across the road.

Getting There & Away

Minibuses run every hour between Mardin's Belediye Garajı and the junction of Gazi and Melek Ahmet caddesis in Diyarbakır for US$1.50. The journey takes 1¾ hours.

Most other buses leave from just east of Cumhuriyet Meydanı, at the bottom of the hill east of the centre. Several daily buses connect Mardin with Urfa (US$6, three hours) but, heading west, they're often already full when they arrive in Mardin; you'd be well advised to book a ticket out as soon as you arrive.

Minibuses to Midyat (US$1.50, one hour) and Nusaybin (US$1) also leave from this area. Remember that services stop in late afternoon because of curfews on the roads around Mardin.

While the situation around Mardin/Midyat remains so uncertain you might prefer to travel in an escorted group. It's worth inquiring at Harran-Nemrut Tours in Urfa (for details see Getting Around in that section) since Özcan Aslan occasionally organises two-day tours taking in Harran and the Deyrul-Zafaran and Mar Gabriel monasteries as well as Mar Yakup church near Nusaybin. Tours cost US$50 per person but require a minimum of six people to run.

BİTLİS

About 88km east of Diyarbakır is the town of Silvan from where it's another 22km to Malabadi. Just east of here is the Batman Suyu, a stream spanned by a beautifully restored humpbacked **stone bridge** built by the Artukid Turks in 1146 and thought to have the longest span (37m) of any such bridge in existence. With its engaging kink in the middle, it's truly a work of art.

Another 235km brings you to Bitlis (BEET-leess, population 38,000, altitude 1545m), an interesting but dusty and somewhat chaotic old town squeezed into the narrow valley of a stream. A **castle** dominates the town, and a humpbacked bridge and another old bridge span the stream.

The **Ulu Cami** was built in 1126, while the **Şerefiye Camii** and **Saraf Han** (a caravanserai) date from the 16th century. The town was the capital of a semi-autonomous Kurdish principality in late Ottoman times.

Up the hill at the eastern side of the town, on the left (northern) side of the road, is an old caravanserai, the **Pabsin Hanı**, built by the Seljuks in the 13th century. Often there are nomads camped nearby, their sprawling black tents pitched beneath its crumbling walls.

TATVAN

About 26km from Bitlis is Tatvan, the western port for Lake Van steamers. Now that security problems have written off the *Vangölü Ekspresi* east of Elazığ and reduced the ferry schedule to a shambles, Tatvan (population 54,000) has lost most of its *raison d'être* and its people are, unsurprisingly, gloomy. Several kilometres long and just a few blocks wide, the town itself is not much to look at but its setting on the shores of an inland sea, backed by bare mountains streaked with snow, is magnificent.

Although you'll probably pass through Tatvan on your way east, you're unlikely to want to linger. Fortunately everything you'll need (hotels, restaurants, the PTT and the bus company offices) huddles together in the town centre. The so-called Tourism Information Office (☎ 434-827 6301, fax 827 6300) is at Ziragı Caddesi No 6, beside the Hotel Kardelen, but will not be able to supply any information.

Places to Stay & Eat

Tatvan now has one classy hotel, the ***Kardelen** (☎ 434-827 9500, fax 827 9504)*, next to the Belediye, where spacious singles/doubles cost US$18/30 with bath and breakfast. Some rooms have bathtubs, views are pleasant and it's blissfully quiet. Otherwise, a few basic places cater for budget travellers; among the better ones are ***Otel Trabzon** (☎ 434-817 1044, Ofis Caddesi 18)*, where rooms cost US$4/7 a single/double with washbasin, and the cheerier ***Akgün Otel** (☎ 434-817 2374, Hal Caddesi 51)*. ***Hotel Altılar** (☎ 434-827 4096, fax 827 4098, Cumhuriyet Caddesi 164)* has beds for US$8 per person including breakfast in big if basic rooms. However, it doesn't seem to be anticipating the arrival of any tourists.

Getting There & Away

At the time of writing the *Vangölü Ekspresi* was no longer running east of Elazığ. Should things change Tatvan's train station is about 2km north-east of the centre along the road to Ahlat and Adilcevaz.

Now that there are no trains to tie in with them, the ferries operated by Turkish Maritime Lines cross the lake from Tatvan to Van on a completely erratic schedule; unless you've got endless time for hanging about, forget it. The 156km journey to Van around the southern shore of the lake by bus takes just two hours.

VAN GÖLÜ

On the map of south-eastern Turkey the most conspicuous feature is Van Gölü (Lake Van), formed when the Nemrut Dağı volcano north of Tatvan (not the one with the statues) blocked its natural outflow. The water level is now maintained by evaporation which results in a high mineral concentration and extreme alkalinity: clothes washed in the lake come clean without soap.

In the early 1990s there was insufficient evaporation, and the lake level slowly rose, flooding shoreline villages and bringing a plague of snakes and flies to those slightly higher up. Fortunately the situation seems to have stabilised.

The water near the city of Van at the eastern extremity of the lake is polluted, but the beaches at Gevaş and Edremit are good for a swim. Don't go in if you have sunburn or open cuts or sores, as the alkaline water will burn them intensely.

The South Shore

Travelling south around the lake from Tatvan to Van, the scenery is beautiful, but there's little reason to stop except at a point 8km west of Gevaş, where the 10th century Church of the Holy Cross at Akdamar is a must.

Akdamar Akdamar Kilisesi, or the Church of the Holy Cross, is definitely one of the marvels of Armenian architecture. It is perched on an island 3km out in the lake, and motorboats busily ferry sightseers back and forth.

In 921 AD, Gagik Artzruni, King of Vaspurkan, built a palace, church and monastery on the island. Little remains of the palace and monastery, but the church walls are in superb condition and the wonderful relief carvings on the walls are among the masterworks of Armenian art.

The Van Monster

Van Gölü is too vast not to have spawned a powerful mythology, and one of the most enduring of the myths tells of a Van Gölü Canavarı (Lake Van Monster).

Rumours of the existence of this Nessie lookalike first surfaced in the 1960s when a newspaper article referred to an otter-like animal, perhaps two metres long, spotted swimming in the lake. Since then, of course, the stories have got wilder. Sometimes the monster is said to resemble a horse; at other times it's more like a dinosaur. But the list of sightings gets longer and there have been some tentative – and unsuccessful – attempts to track the beastie to its lair.

In the meantime, Van is dining out on its famous phantom, with shops about town selling Canavar Salam (Monster Salami). The beastie has also acquired a range of fantastic nicknames, amongst them *Bariş* (Peace), *Van Gülü* (the Rose of Van) and *Suların Kralı* (King of the Waters). These days even Van's footballers call themselves the *Canavarlar* (Monsters) and wear a blue and white strip in Vannie's honour.

If you're familiar with biblical stories, you'll immediately recognise Adam and Eve, Jonah and the Whale, David and Goliath, Abraham about to sacrifice Isaac, Daniel in the Lions' Den, Samson etc. The paintings inside the church are rapidly vanishing, but their vagueness and frailty seem in keeping with the shaded, partly ruined interior.

North of Akdamar another even more isolated and forgotten 11th century Armenian church stands on the island of **Çarpanak**.

Gevaş Gevaş has a cemetery full of tombstones dating back to the 14th to 17th centuries, worth a look if you're passing by. Most notable is the polygonal **Halime Hatun Türbesi**, built in 1358 for a female member of the Karakoyunlu dynasty.

Places to Stay & Eat Although there are several basic camping grounds at Edremit on the road from Akdamar to Van, by far your best bet is to head straight for the ***Akdamar Camping ve Restaurant*** immediately opposite the ferry departure point for Akdamar island. Not only is the camp site here raised up, with fine views of the lake, but you'll be in the best position to see when other would-be visitors to Akdamar arrive – vital now that the dearth of tourists makes it hard to get together a boatload of people to share the cost. The restaurant here has a terrace with lake views and an indoor saloon in case of bad weather. A meal of *tava* (a stew made from meat, peppers and tomatoes), rice and salad will cost you about US$3.50.

Getting There & Away Dolmuşes run from near Beş Yol in Van to Akdamar İskelesi (dock) for US$1. If no direct transport is available, take a dolmuş to Gevaş for US$0.75 and get out when it cuts inland from the lake. If it's not too hot you could walk the remaining 8km along the lakeshore to the boat dock. Alternatively, agree on a price all the way to Akdamar İskelesi before you board the dolmuş in Van. In Gevaş itself drivers are likely to demand US$3 for the onward journey.

Boats to the island run as and when traffic warrants it. Gone are the days when so many groups wanted to cross the lake that reservations were necessary. Now the problem is getting together enough people to share the US$18 to US$20 cost of chartering the boat. The voyage takes about 20 minutes.

Getting to Çarpanak is even harder; the boatmen are likely to want US$150 before they'll consider the voyage.

The North Shore

If anything the journey around the north shore of Lake Van from Tatvan to Van, with first Nemrut Dağı and then Suphan Dağı looming beside the road, is more beautiful than going around the south shore. The road is rough in parts, however, so aim to get a seat as far forward in the bus as possible. Security checks become more frequent once you pass Erciş.

Nemrut Dağı The mountain rising to the north of Tatvan is Nemrut Dağı, not to be confused with the one near Adıyaman and Malatya with the statues on top. This Nemrut Dağı (3050m) is an inactive volcano with a beautiful, clear, cold crater lake and hot springs on its peak. Nemrut is the volcano which dammed up the outflow of Lake Van, causing it to cover its present vast area of 3750 sq km and become highly alkaline.

Dolmuşes used to make the run up the mountain whenever there were enough people. However, the tense security situation around the lake has made things more difficult. Some people succeed in getting up the mountain; others are told they need police permission which is not readily forthcoming.

If you have your own transport and want to try it, leave Tatvan by the road around the lake to the north marked for Ahlat and Adilcevaz. On the outskirts of Tatvan, look for a left turn near a Türk Petrol station; this road will take you the 26km all the way up the mountain.

Ahlat Continue northward by car or dolmuş along the lakeshore for 42km and you'll come to the small town of Ahlat, famous for its Seljuk Turkish tombs and graveyard.

History Founded during the reign of Caliph Omar (581-644 AD), Ahlat became a Seljuk stronghold in the 1060s. When the Seljuk sultan Alp Arslan rode out to meet the Byzantine emperor Romanus Diogenes in battle on the field of Manzikert (see the following Malazgirt section), Ahlat was his base.

Later Ahlat had an extraordinarily eventful history even by Anatolian standards, with emir defeating prince and king driving out emir. It's no wonder it's famous for its cemeteries.

Ahlat, and indeed this whole region, was conquered by the Ottomans during the reign of Süleyman the Magnificent in the 16th century which is when the fortress on the shore was built.

The Kümbets, Cemetery & Museum

Just west of Ahlat you'll see the overgrown 13th century polygonal **Usta Şakirt Kümbetı** to the right (south) of the highway, in the midst of a field near some houses and a new mosque.

Across the highway is a little museum, and beyond it a unique **Selçuk cemetery** (Selçuk Mezarlığı) with stele-like headstones of lichen-covered grey or red volcanic tuff with intricate web patterns and bands of Kufic lettering. It's thought that Ahlat stonemasons were employed on other great stoneworking projects, such as the decoration of the great mosque at Divriği, near Sivas.

Over the centuries, earthquake, wind and water have set the stones at all angles, so they stand out like broken teeth. Each and every one has a rook as sentinel, and tortoises cruise amid the ruins.

On the north-western side of the graveyard is the beautiful and unusual **Bayındır Kümbetı ve Camii** (Bayındır Kumbet and Mosque, 1477), with a colonnaded porch and its own small prayer room.

The **museum** has a few archaeological bits and bobs which barely justify even the US$0.30 entry fee. However, it does provide a place to leave your bags while you look around the cemetery provided you arrive during opening hours (9 am to noon and 1 to 5 pm except Monday).

Continue walking towards Ahlat and you will come to a sign on the left pointing to the **Çifte Kümbet** (Twin Tomb), clearly visible across the field.

Malazgirt About 60km north of Ahlat is Malazgirt (Manzikert), which is of immense importance in Turkish history. On 26 August 1071, the Seljuk Turkish sultan Alp Arslan and his armies decisively defeated the Byzantine emperor Romanus Diogenes and took him prisoner, effectively opening Anatolia to Turkish migration and conquest.

The Seljuks established the Sultanate of Rum with its capital at Konya, and other nomadic Turkish tribes came from central Asia and Iran to settle here. A band of Turkish warriors, following a leader named Osman, later spread its influence and founded a state which would become the vast Ottoman Empire. It all started here, in 1071, when the heir of the Caesars lost to a Turkish emir.

Adilcevaz About 25km east of Ahlat is the town of Adilcevaz, once an Urartian town but now dominated by a great Seljuk Turkish fortress, the **Kef Kalesi**, and the even greater bulk of the imposing **Süphan Dağı** (4434m).

Meltwater from the year-round snowfields on Süphan Dağı flows down to Adilcevaz, making its surroundings lush and fertile. As you enter the town along the shore, the highway passes the nice little **Tuğrul Bey Camii**, built in the 13th century and still used for daily prayer. You used to be able to climb Süphan Dağı in summer but these days the security situation has put it out of bounds.

Erciş If you continue around the lake for another 64km, you'll pass through Erciş, a forgettable modern town covering settlements that date back to Urartian times. At this point the roads diverge and you can head south for Van (98km) or you can go north for Doğubeyazıt (137km).

Getting There & Away The big bus companies take the shortest route from Tatvan to Van which goes south of Van Gölü. If you want to travel around the north shore you'll probably have to break your journey into sections. Regular dolmuşes run from opposite the PTT in Tatvan to Ahlat (40km, US$1.25, 45 minutes). From Ahlat to Adilcevaz takes just half an hour and costs US$0.50. From Adilcevaz to Erciş takes one hour and costs US$1.50. Buses run between Erciş and Van, taking 1¼ hours and charging US$2. Most travel in the morning to avoid the 5 pm road closure.

VAN

Almost 100km from Tatvan across vast Van Gölü lies Van (population 160,000, altitude 1727m). Once upon a time this was once the eastern railhead on the line to Iran and the largest Turkish city east of Diyarbakır and south of Erzurum.

Van has several claims to fame. Van Kalesi (Rock of Van) near the lakeshore has several long cuneiform inscriptions from the days when Van was the Urartian capital. Van also acts as a market centre for the Kurdish tribes who live in the mountains of extreme south-eastern Turkey.

The town is also home to a unique breed of white cat with one blue and one yellow eye. These days such cats fetch so high a price tag that their owners tend to keep them locked up indoors; the nearest you're likely to come to seeing one is the absurdly fluffy photographs adorning every carpet shop window. The Van cat is said to be adapted to swimming in the lake – as is a more recent addition to the local fauna, the Van Canavarı, a virtual monster which looks set to give Scotland's Nessie a run for her money.

A day trip to the south-east takes you past the ancient Urartian city at Çavuştepe and the craggy mountain fortress of Hoşap. Beyond them lies troubled Hakkari, deep in the alpine scenery of the Cilo Dağı mountains and likely to be unsuitable for tourism for some years to come.

History

The Kingdom of Urartu, the Biblical Ararat, flourished from the 13th to the 7th centuries

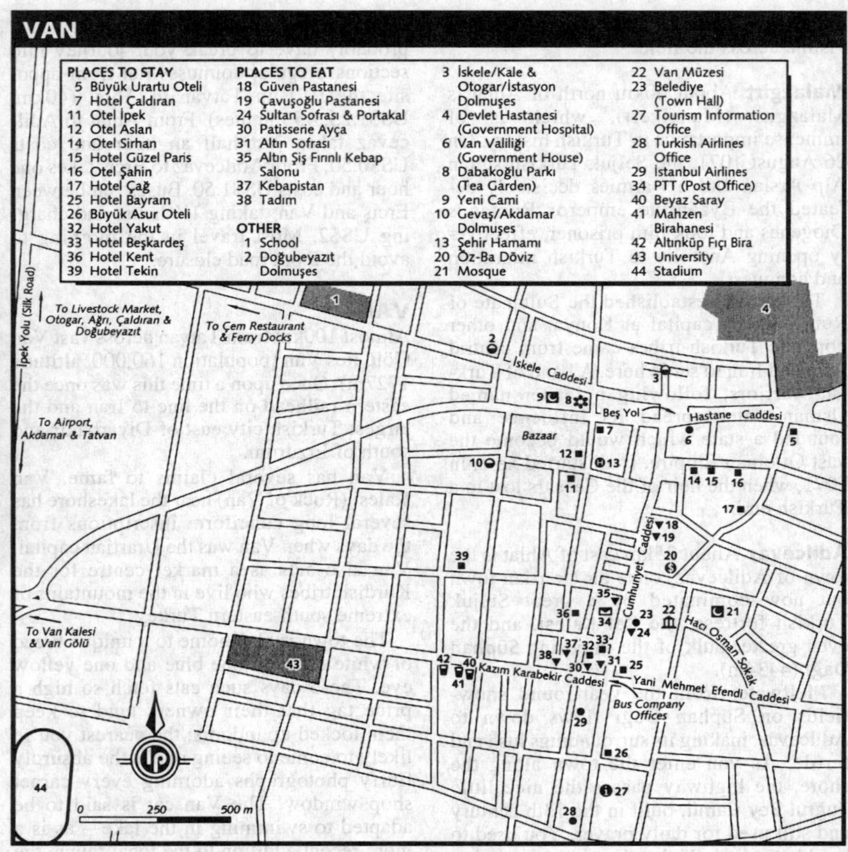

BC. Its capital, Tushpa, was near present-day Van. The Urartians were traders and farmers, highly advanced in the art of metalwork and stone masonry. They borrowed much of their culture, including cuneiform writing, from the neighbouring Assyrians, with whom they were more or less permanently at war. The powerful Assyrians never subdued the Urartians, but when several waves of Cimmerians, Scythians and Medes swept into Urartu and joined in the battle, the kingdom met its downfall.

Later the region was resettled by a people whom the Persians called Armenians. By the 6th century BC it was governed by Persian and Mede satraps.

The history of the Armenians is one of repeated subjugation to other peoples as they occupied a strategic crossroads at the nexus of the three great empires of Syria, Persia and Anatolia. Tigranes the Great succeeded in gaining control of the kingdom from its Parthian overlords in 95 BC, but his short-lived kingdom was soon crushed in the clash of armies from Rome and Parthia.

In the 8th century AD, the Arab armies

flooded through from the south, forcing the Armenian prince to take refuge on Akdamar Island. Unable to fend off the Arabs, he agreed to pay tribute to the Caliph. When the Arabs retreated, the Byzantines and Persians took their place, and overlordship of Armenia see-sawed between them as one or the other gained military advantage.

The next wave of invaders was Turkish. Upon defeating the Byzantines in 1071 at Manzikert, north of Van Gölü, the Seljuk Turks marched in to found the Sultanate of Rum and were followed by a flood of Turkoman nomads. Domination of Eastern Anatolia by the powerful Karakoyunlu (Black Sheep) and Akkoyunlu (White Sheep) Turkish emirs followed, and continued until the coming of the Ottomans in 1468.

During WWI, Armenian guerrilla bands intent on founding an independent Armenian state collaborated with the Russians to defeat the Ottoman armies in the east. From then on the Armenians, formerly loyal subjects of the sultan, were viewed as traitors by the Turks. Bitter fighting between Turkish and Kurdish forces on the one side and Armenian and Russian on the other brought devastation to the entire region and to Van.

The Ottomans destroyed the old city of Van (near Van Kalesi) before the Russians occupied it in 1915. Ottoman forces counterattacked but were unable to drive the invaders out, and Van remained under Russian occupation until the armistice of 1917. After the founding of the Turkish Republic, a new planned city of Van was built 4km east of the old site.

Orientation & Information

Although its present-day appearance hardly matches up to the exotic overtones, the highway passing between the town and the lake was once the ancient Silk Road (İpek Yolu). The city's otogar is on the north-western outskirts, just off the Silk Road, and many bus companies operate servis buses to get you there from the town centre.

In the city itself, the main commercial street is Cumhuriyet Caddesi, where you'll find banks, hotels, restaurants and the Turkish Airlines and tourism offices. At the northern end of Cumhuriyet Caddesi, where it meets five other streets, is Ferit Melen Meydanı, otherwise known as Beş Yol (Five Roads). Here you'll find several dolmuş and bus stops. An imposing landmark around which many hotels are gathered is the barracks-like Van Valiliği government building.

The Şehir İstasyonu (City Station) is north-west of the centre near the otogar, while the İskele İstasyonu (Dock Station) is several kilometres north-west on the shore. At the time of writing no passenger trains were servicing Van.

Van's only significant tourist sight, the Van Kalesi, is about 5km west of the centre. If you're visiting on a Thursday you might want to drop in on the livestock market which takes place from early in the morning just north of the otogar, west of İpek Yolu.

The Tourism Information Office (☎ 432-216 2018, fax 216 3675), is at the southern end of Cumhuriyet Caddesi at No 127 but the most they can rustle up is a street plan.

Van's postal code is 65000.

Van Müzesi

Van Museum sticks with the familiar layout. On the ground floor the museum displays Urartian exhibits including jewellery, some with amber and coloured glass, cylindrical seals and pots from the Old Bronze Age (circa 5000 BC). The Urartu Süsleme Plakaları (Jewellery Breastplates) from the 9th to 7th centuries BC are particularly fine. In the inner courtyard you'll find rock carvings from the Trisin Plateau, 120km away, where thousands of prehistoric carvings of bison, reindeer and other beasts have been found.

The ethnographic exhibits upstairs include local Kurdish and Turcoman kilims and a *sedir* (low couch), such as is found in village houses, covered with traditional crafts. The Katliam Seksiyonu (Genocide Section) is a grisly display of skulls, bones and bits of dress recovered from mass graves left from the massacres of Turks and Kurds by Armenians at Çavuşoğlu and Zeve.

The museum is open from 8 am to noon

and 1 to 5 pm except Monday. Admission costs US$1.25.

Van Kalesi

Van Kalesi (Rock of Van) dominates views of the city across the surrounding plain. It's a wonderful place to come but you should allow plenty of time and bring a drink with you in summer. It's also important to visit in the middle of the day when other people are around and to make sure you're back on the main road by sunset.

On the northern side of the rock is the **tomb** of a Muslim holy man, frequently visited by pilgrims including infertile women who are thought to be helped by coming here.

A stairway from the car park at the north-western corner leads to the top, where you can see the fortifications, including the **Sardur Burcu** (Sarduri Tower, 840-830 BC), which has several cuneiform inscriptions in Assyrian which praise the Urartian King Sarduri I.

On the southern side a narrow walkway with an iron railing leads to several rock-cut **funeral chambers**, including that of King Argishti I (786-764 BC). Before reaching this you pass a long **cuneiform inscription** which recounts the high points of the king's reign.

The view south of the rock reveals a flat space broken by the grass-covered foundations of numerous buildings. Although this was the site of **Tushpa**, an Urartian city which flourished almost 3000 years ago, the foundations you see are those of the **old city of Van**, destroyed during the upheavals of WWI and the futile struggle for an Armenian republic here. The sight is stunning and it's well worth walking around the base of the Van Kalesi afterwards to inspect some of the ruins although you should try and take someone with you.

Of the Seljuk **Ulu Cami** only a broken brick minaret remains, but the **Hüsrev Paşa Külliyesi**, dating back to 1567, is being restored and you may be able to get inside to see the fine brick dome and fragmentary murals; if not, you can still inspect the delicate *kümbet* (vault) attached. The nearby **Kaya Çelebi Camii** (1662) has a similarly striped minaret but is still in use and likely to be locked except at prayer times.

To get to Van Kalesi take a 'Kale' dolmuş from Beş Yol (US$0.75). These are frequent at weekends but if nothing is going, take an 'Iskele' dolmuş and get out at the road junction leading to Van Kalesi (stick with this main road since along the minor roads you may come across stone-throwing children). On a cool day you can easily walk the 5km to the site in less than an hour. Once there go right around the base of Van Kalesi to the entrance; however tempting it may look, if you scramble up the side of the Rock you'll end up stranded outside the walls.

Van Kalesi is open daily from 9 am to 6 pm and admission costs US$0.75.

Çavuştepe & Hoşap

A day excursion south-east of Van along the road to Başkale and Hakkari takes you to the Urartian site at Çavuştepe, 25km from Van, and the Kurdish castle at Hoşap (Güzelsu), another 33km further along.

To get there, catch a bus heading to Başkale (US$5) and say you want to get out at Hoşap. After seeing the castle, catch a bus back to Çavuştepe, 500m off the highway, and then catch a third bus back to Van. Pack a lunch and water, and plan to be gone for most of the day as buses are scarce.

Hoşap Kalesi Hoşap Kalesi perches photogenically on top of a rocky outcrop with the village of Güzelsu and a stream beneath it. On the left side of the road before the village is a badly ruined caravanserai or medrese. Cross the bridge into the village and follow the signs around the far side of the hill to reach the castle entrance.

Built in 1643 by a local Kurdish chieftain, the castle has a very impressive entrance portal in a round tower. The guardian will quickly spot you and rush up to sell you a ticket (US$1). You then enter the fortress via a passage cut through the rock. Many of its hundreds of rooms are still clearly visible and the view is stunning. Across the valley are the remains of badly eroded mud-brick defensive walls, looking disconcertingly like a dinosaur's spine. Soft drinks and simple meals are available in the village.

Çavuştepe The narrow hill on the left side of the highway at Çavuştepe was once crowned with the fortress-palace Sarduri-Hinili, home of the kings of Urartu, built between 764 and 735 BC by King Sardur II, son of Argisti. Climb the hill to the car park, where there is a guardian to keep you from taking photos (excavations are still underway) and perhaps to show you what there is to see. No drinks or refreshments are available.

Climb the rocky hill to the temple ruins, marked by a gate of black basalt blocks polished to a high gloss. A few of the blocks on the left side of the doorway are inscribed in cuneiform. As you walk around, notice the cisterns for water and, at the far end where the palace once stood, the royal Urartian loo.

Places to Stay – Budget

Van is well supplied with cheap hotels although several were undergoing renovation at the time of writing which looked likely to push them up a price category. Those in the bazaar to the west of Cumhuriyet Caddesi tend to be cheapest; those to the east are slightly more expensive, but also cleaner and more comfortable.

Several hotels in the bazaar area serve visiting farmers and traders, charging US$4.50 per person in rooms with sink and/or private shower. Among the better ones are ***Otel İpek*** *(☎ 432-216 3033, Cumhuriyet Caddesi, Sokak No 3)*, with clean, comfortable rooms, and the more basic ***Aslan Oteli*** *(☎ 432-216 2469)*, where the kilim-draped lobby is more inviting than the actual rooms. The Şehir Hamamı is opposite these two hotels. ***Hotel Kent*** *(☎ 432-216 2404)*, Küçük Cami Civarı, charges marginally less but the rooms are extremely basic and the carpets filthy.

Hotel Bayram *(☎ 432-216 1136, fax 214 2668, Cumhuriyet Caddesi 1/A)* is a good choice, with clean, fairly modern rooms with shower and huge sink; some rooms are much larger than others so it's worth looking at several. Singles/doubles cost US$9/15.

Hotel Güzel Paris *(☎ 432-216 3739, fax 216 7897, Hükümet Konağı Binası Yanı 20)*, on the southern side of the Van Valiliği government headquarters, has big, comfortable rooms with shower in an excellent location for US$15/19 a single/double. ***Hotel Çağ*** *(☎ 432-214 5713, Hastane 2 Caddesi 46)* has small but comfortable, if dimly lit, rooms with shower for US$5 per person. Renovations may see prices rise in the near future.

Two short blocks down towards the lake from Beş Yol, ***Hotel Çaldıran*** *(☎ 432-216 2718)*, Sıhke Caddesi, Büyük Cami Karşısı, was charging US$14/20/26 a single/double/triple at the time of writing but once again renovation work in progress looked likely to push prices up for newer, better facilities.

The 52 room ***Hotel Tekin*** *(☎ 432-216 3010, fax 216 1366, Küçük Cami Civarı, Nur Sokak 24)* caters for country-town merchants, charging US$9/13/19 for a simple but spacious single/double/triple with clean bathroom.

Perhaps the best choice is the two-star ***Büyük Asur Oteli*** *(☎ 432-216 8792, fax 216 9461, Cumhuriyet Caddesi, Turizm Sokak 5)*, which has a restaurant, lift and 48 rooms with metal bedframes and well-sprung mattresses. Posted prices are US$18/25 a single/double with shower and plenty of hot water. The lobby has a Turkish corner with big floor cushions. The manager, Remzi Boybağ, speaks English and is a great source of local information.

The two-star ***Hotel Beşkardeş*** *(☎ 432-216 1116, fax 216 6466, Cumhuriyet Caddesi 16)* has 40 cramped rooms with TVs and private showers, priced at US$9 per person including breakfast. Particularly good value is the two-star ***Otel Şahin*** *(☎ 432-216 3062, fax 216 3064, İrfan Baştuğ Caddesi 20)*, which charges US$12 per person for quiet, spacious, modern rooms with bath and breakfast.

Places to Stay – Mid-Range

The best hotel in town is the 75 room, three-star ***Büyük Urartu Oteli*** *(☎ 432-212 0660, fax 212 1610, Cumhuriyet Caddesi, Hastane Caddesi 60)*, across from the Devlet Hastanesi (hospital). Big, comfortable rooms, with private bath and TV, are priced at US$65/78 a single/double, subject to a certain amount of discussion when it's quiet. The decor is undistinguished but some of the rooms have bathtubs.

Hardly in the same league as the Urartu is the three-star, 50 room ***Otel Sirhan*** *(☎ 432-214 3463, fax 216 2867)*, Cumhuriyet Caddesi, Hükümet Konağı Yanı, on the southern side of the Van Valiliği provincial government headquarters. Doubles cost US$28 with breakfast included but some rooms have showers so designed that the water misses the basin and flows onto the floor; if yours does that ask to be shown another. The popular first-floor restaurant-cum-nightclub pumps up the volume until midnight which wouldn't suit everyone but may suit those wishing to unwind from a long day with a drink or two.

The 64 room ***Hotel Yakut*** *(☎ 432-214 2832, fax 216 6351, Kazım Karabekir Caddesi, PTT Sokak 4)*, is cheaper, charging US$30/45/54 a single/double/triple with modern bathrooms and TV. Its central position is an asset.

Places to Eat

Van specialities include *otlu peynir* (cheese mixed with the tangy herb), *geven otu* (gum tragacanth) and *Kürt köftesi* (Kurdish köfte, also called kurutlu köfte – a meatless mixture of bulghur wheat and onions flavoured with mint, formed into balls and cooked). Kürt köftesi can sometimes be found in restaurants, and some of the hotels serve otlu peynir for breakfast; if yours doesn't, try a *bakkaliye* (grocery store) or the bazaar.

An all-round favourite serving good, moderately priced food is ***Altın Sofrası*** on Cumhuriyet Caddesi to the left of the Hotel Beşkardeş. The ground floor houses a supermarket; the 1st floor a restaurant with stews and kebaps; the 2nd floor the aile salonu; the 3rd floor a pastry shop-cafe; and the top floor a women's pastry shop dining room. Soup and a kebap will cost around US$3.

Altın Şiş Fırınlı Kebap Salonu, or Golden Skewer Oven-Equipped Kebap Salon, on Cumhuriyet Caddesi north of the PTT, is typical of the rest with a selection of cheap kebaps, including good döner (US$2) at lunchtime.

On Cumhuriyet Caddesi facing the post office is the big new ***Sultan Sofrası***, open 24 hours a day and serving soups, stews and spit-roasted chicken. ***Portakal*** a few doors down rings the changes with pizzas and burgers.

On Kazım Karabekir Caddesi, ***Tadım*** has a routine choice of kebaps and stews; turn down the lane beside it for ***Kebapistan*** which serves pide on one side of the road and more substantial meals on the other. There are a few outside tables for summer evenings.

If you're prepared to take a dolmuş west along Iskele Caddesi for about 1km you'll come to the deservedly popular ***Çem Restaurant*** *(☎ 432-212 1193)* beside the Türk Petrol station. Here the main draw is a buffet table spread with a vast choice of cold mezes for a set US$3, no matter how high you pile your plate. Cooked food is also available, if a little slow to materialise.

On a sunny summer evening another possibility is to head out along Van Gölü in your own car or by Gevaş dolmuş. The otherwise unexciting town of Edremit, 11km to the south-west,. has several small lakeside restaurants serving fish. Even closer to Van you'll find the ***Yalı Restaurant***, rather ramshackle to look at but with tables right beside the lake for watching the sunset.

Van has a good selection of *pastanes* for cakes and sweet snacks at US$1 per portion. ***Patisserie Ayça*** on Kazım Karabekir Caddesi just west of Cumhuriyet Caddesi is cosy but the ***Güven Pastanesi***, just north of the Vakıfbank on Cumhuriyet Caddesi, is best in terms of space and decor, with floor cushions at the back and tables placed so you can soak up the sun at the front. The nearby ***Çavuşoğlu Pastanesi*** is also nice enough, but its dining room is below street level.

For alcohol with dinner the restaurant in ***Büyük Urartu Oteli*** is good or try ***Beyaz Saray*** (see Entertainment following).

Entertainment

There's precious little nightlife in Van. For a beer, try ***Altınküp Fıçı Bira*** (Golden Mug

Draught Beer), Kazım Karabekir Caddesi 53, or the nearby ***Mahzen Birahanesi***, downstairs at the rear of Kazım Karabekir Caddesi 37. Both are exclusively male hangouts – and even some men might find their atmosphere oppressive. For something more comfortable try the ***Beyaz Saray*** (☎ *432-214 8233*), upstairs at Kazım Karabekır Caddesi, Akdamar Oteli Karşışı. This is a *gazino* serving food and drink, with a floorshow that encompasses singers and a belly dancer. Watch the prices which can mount up quickly – especially if you feel obliged to tip the belly dancer the seemingly standard US$6.

Things to Buy

The collapse of tourism to the east since 1991 has had a disastrous effect on the shopkeepers who used to sell carpets and other handicrafts. A few shops are hanging on, although their atmosphere is subdued. Alongside the usual carpets and kilims they stock more unusual items like the sort of woven backpacks which Kurdish women use to carry their babies.

Getting There & Away

As the 'capital' of the extreme south-east, Van has plenty of transport.

Air Turkish Airlines (☎ 432-216 1241, fax 216 1768), Cumhuriyet Caddesi 196, in the Enver Perihanoğlu İş Merkezi building, has two daily nonstop flights to/from Ankara, and another to/from İstanbul; the Ankara flight meets connections for Antalya, İstanbul and İzmir.

Bus Many bus companies, including Van Gölü, VanTur and Van Seyahat, maintain ticket offices at the intersection of Cumhuriyet and Kazım Karabekir caddesis. They customarily provide şehiriçi servis minibuses to shuttle passengers to and from the bus station. Details of some services follow:

Ağrı – 213km, four hours, US$6; frequent buses
Ankara – 1250km, 22 hours, US$23; frequent buses
Diyarbakır – 385km, seven hours, US$10; several buses
Doğubeyazıt via Çaldıran – 185km, three hours, US$4; frequent morning dolmuşes
Doğubeyazıt via Erciş, Patnos and Ağrı – 315km, 5½ hours, US$8; several to Ağrı, then change for Doğubeyazıt
Erciş – 95km, 1¼ hours, US$2; a few buses
Erzurum – 410km, six hours, US$10; several buses
Hakkari – 205km, four hours, US$5; several morning buses
Malatya – 500km, 10 hours, US$13; several buses
Şanlıurfa – 583km, nine hours, US$13; a few buses
Tatvan – 150km, two hours, US$4; frequent buses
Trabzon – 733km, 15 hours, US$19; a few direct buses, most via Erzurum

Train At the time of writing the *Vangölü Ekspresi* from İstanbul and Ankara was terminating at Elazığ; only freight trains were using Van train station. Should the situation change, you can get to the station by dolmuş from near Beş Yol (US$0.25).

Ferry With no connecting passenger train service to keep it to schedule, the ferry across Van Gölü from Tatvan to Van leaves only when there's enough freight to justify it. 'İskele' dolmuşes ply up and down the main road to the harbour (US$0.30) but unless you're a glutton for punishment, stick with the buses.

Getting Around

An airport bus (US$1) meets each flight, and saves you having to pay a taxi fare of US$5 for the 6km ride. The bus departs the ticket office for the airport 1½ hours before each Turkish Airlines flight.

For dolmuşes to Van Kalesi, the ferry dock (İskele) and the Akdamar boat dock (Gevaş), go to the dolmuş stand near Beş Yol at the northern end of Cumhuriyet Caddesi.

HAKKARİ

Tucked away in Turkey's far south-eastern corner, Hakkari (population 90,000, altitude 1700m) is ringed with mountains, and in good times this was a place people came to for climbing holidays. At the time of writing, however, it was hard to recommend that anyone should go there. Not only is it a centre of the still-smouldering Kurdish insurgency, with the TV reporting almost nightly deaths on both sides of the battle line, but with the Iraqi border just a five-hour walk away and the Iranian border just seven hours walk away, it's also the first port of call for refugees who continue to find their away into Turkey. Not surprisingly the police and army view foreign visitors with suspicion and at the time of writing you were not allowed to go anywhere without a police escort. Partly this is for your own protection but no doubt it's also to prevent you seeing anything they would prefer you didn't.

Hakkari is 210km south of Van via a zigzag road which gets more and more spectacular as you travel along it. Although there are daily buses from Van, the journey takes four hours because of the frequent checkpoints; at some of these your baggage may be searched. The road bypasses Çavuştepe, whips through Hoşap, skirts the Zernik Barajı and, after 112km, arrives at Başkale, notable only for its altitude (2450m).

About 48km further along at Yeni Köprü a road forks left for Yüksekova and the Esendere border post on the road to Iran – an alternative base for climbs into the mountains in better times.

After one more checkpoint you arrive in Hakkari. If things have not changed since the time of writing, you will be escorted from the bus to a hotel by security officers. Hakkari has two hotels: the grungy ***Otel Ümit*** and the nominally three-star ***Şenler Oteli*** (☎ *438-211 5512, fax 211 3809*). It's a seller's market so even the Ümit charges US$9 per person and will try to get away with more even though your shower and toilet are unlikely to function. The better Şenler charges the same price but is often full with builders hard at work expanding Hakkari to take the people who have fled from surrounding villages for the comparative safety of the town. The Ümit is home to many refugee families whose stories and circumstances make a mockery of any idea of visiting Hakkari as a tourist.

When you want to eat, the security officers will lead you to ***Çiçek Kebap Salonu*** near the Ümit which serves everything from *çorba* (soup) at breakfast time to pide in the evening. They will accompany you on a circuit around the town without a single interesting building and will ensure that you don't take any photographs, even of the mountains.

Climbing in the mountains was emphatically out of the question at the time of writing.

NORTH FROM VAN

If you're bound for Doğubeyazıt from Van, you have a choice of routes. Buses go the long way around via Erciş, Patnos and Ağrı, while minibuses travel via Bendimahi, Muradiye, Çaldıra and Ortadirek, a more scenic and considerably shorter 185km run. Keep your passport handy for the army checkpoints and bear in mind that the road officially closes at 5 pm, partly for security reasons and partly so that the army can keep an eye out for smugglers.

Turkish Language Guide

Turkish is the dominant language in the Turkic language group which also includes such less-than-famous tongues as Kirghiz, Kazakh and Azerbaijani. Once thought to be related to Finnish and Hungarian, the Turkic languages are now seen as comprising their own unique language group. You can find people who speak Turkish, in one form or another, from Belgrade all the way to Xinjiang in China.

In 1928, Atatürk did away with the Arabic alphabet and adopted a Latin-based alphabet much better suited to easy learning and correct pronunciation. He also instituted a language reform to purge Turkish of abstruse Arabic and Persian borrowings, in order to rationalise and simplify it. The result is a logical, systematic and expressive language which has only one irregular noun (*su*, 'water'), one irregular verb (*etmek*, 'to be') and no genders. It is so logical, in fact, that Turkish grammar formed the basis for the development of Esperanto, an artificial international language.

This language guide should help you in your travels around Turkey. For the meanings of common terms used through out this book, and Turkish words and phrases you might encounter on signs, please refer to the Glossary at the end of this book.

For a much more comprehensive guide to the Turkish language, get Lonely Planet's *Turkish Phrasebook*.

Turkish Language Cassettes

For a useful aid to learning correct pronunciation, and getting started with speaking a bit of Turkish, we can recommend a 90-minute audio cassette keyed to the words and phrases in this language guide. Send a cheque or money order payable to Tom Brosnahan for US$12 or UK£8 to *Turkish Cassette*, c/o Tom Brosnahan, PO Box 563, Concord, MA 01742-0563 USA. Mention that you'd like Cassette TSK06. Fast letter-mail ('1st-class') postage is included in the price. (This address is for audio cassette orders *only*. Please send all other correspondence to Tom Brosnahan via a Lonely Planet office; for addresses, see the back of the title page at the front of this book.)

Grammar

Word order and verb formation in Turkish are very different from what you'll find in Indo-European languages like English. This makes it somewhat difficult to learn at first, despite its elegant simplicity. A few hints will help you comprehend road and shop signs, schedules and menus.

Suffixes

A Turkish word consists of a root and one or more suffixes added to it. Though in English we have only a few suffixes ('-'s' for possessive, '-s' or '-es' for plural), Turkish has lots and lots of suffixes. Not only that, these suffixes are subject to an unusual system of 'vowel harmony' whereby most of the vowel sounds in a word are made in a similar manner. What this means is that the suffix might be *-lar* when attached to one word, but *-ler* when attached to another; it's the same suffix, though. Sometimes these suffixes are preceded by a 'buffer letter', a 'y' or an 'n'.

Here are some of the noun suffixes you'll encounter most frequently:

-a, -e	'to'
-dan, -den	'from'
-dır, -dir, -dur, -dür	emphatic (ignore it!)
-(s)ı, -(s)i, -(s)u, -(s)ü	object-nouns (ignore it!)
-(n)ın, -(n)in	possessive
-lar, -ler	plural
-lı, -li, -lu, -lü	'with'
-sız, -siz, -suz, -süz	'without'

Here are some of the common verb suffixes:

-ar, -er, -ır, -ir, -ur, -ür	simple present tense
-acak, -ecek, -acağ-, -eceğ	future tense
-dı, -di, -du, -dü	simple past tense
-ıyor-, -iyor-	continuous (like English '-ing', eg '... is eating')
-mak, -mek	infinitive ending

Nouns

Suffixes can be added to nouns to modify them. The two you'll come across most frequently are *-ler* and *-lar*, which form the plural: *otel* (hotel), *oteller* (hotels); *araba* (car), *arabalar* (cars).

Other suffixes modify in other ways: *ev* (house), *Ahmet* (Ahmet) but *Ahmet'in evi* (Ahmet's house). Similarly with *İstanbul* and *banka*: it's *İstanbul Bankası* when the two are used together. You may see *-i, -ı, -u* or *-ü, -si, -sı, -su* or *-sü* added to any noun. A *cami* is a mosque; but the *cami* built by Mehmet Pasha is the *Mehmet Paşa Camii*, with a double 'i'. Ask for a *bira* and the waiter will bring you a bottle of whatever type is available; ask for an *Efes Birası* and that's the brand you'll get.

Yet other suffixes on nouns tell you about direction: *-a* or *-e* means 'to': *otobüs* (bus), *otobüse* (to the bus) and *Bodrum'a* (to Bodrum). The suffix *-dan* or *-den* means 'from': *Ankara'dan* (from Ankara), *köprüden*, (from the bridge). Stress is on these final syllables *(-a* or *-dan)* whenever they are used.

Verbs

Verbs consist of a root plus any number of modifying suffixes. Verbs can be so complex that they constitute whole sentences in themselves, although this is rare. The standard example for blowing your mind is *Afyonkarahisarlılaştıramadıklarımızdanmısınız?* (Aren't you one of those people whom we tried, unsuccessfully, to make resemble the citizens of Afyonkarahisar?). It's not the sort of word you see every day!

The infinitive verb form is with *-mak* or *-mek*, as in *gitmek* (to go) or *almak* (to take). The stress in the infinitive is always on the last syllable ('geet-MEHK', 'ahl-MAHK').

The simple present form is with *-r*, as in *gider* (he/she/it goes), *giderim* (I go). The suffix *-iyor* has a similar meaning: *gidiyorum* (I'm going). For the future, there's *-ecek* or *-acak*, as in *alacak* (ah-lah-JAHK), he will take (it).

Word Order

The nouns and adjectives usually come first, then the verb; the final suffix on the verb is the subject of the sentence:

I'll go to Istanbul.	*İstanbul'a gideceğim.*
I want to buy (take) a carpet.	*Halı almak istiyorum.* (lit: Carpet to buy want I)

Pronunciation

Once you learn a few basic rules, you'll find Turkish pronunciation quite simple to master. Despite oddities such as the soft 'g' (ğ) and undotted 'i' (ı), it's a phonetically consistent language – there's generally a clear one-letter/one-sound relationship.

It's important to remember that each letter is pronounced; vowels don't combine to form diphthongs and consonants don't combine to form other sounds (such as 'th', 'gh' or 'sh' in English). Watch out for this! Your eye will keep seeing familiar English double-letter sounds in Turkish – where they don't exist. It therefore follows that **h** in Turkish is always pronounced as a separate letter; in English, we're used to pronouncing it when it's at the beginnings of words, but in Turkish it can appear in the middle or at the end of a word as well. *Always* pronounce it! Your Turkish friend *Ahmet* is 'ahh-MEHT' not 'aa-meht', and the word *rehber* (guide) is pronounced 'rehh-BEHR' not 're-ber'.

Here are some of the letters in Turkish which may cause initial confusion:

A, a	as in 'art' or 'bar'
â	a faint 'y' sound in preceding consonant, eg *Kâhta* (kih-YAHH-tah)

E, e as in 'fell' or as the first vowel in 'ever'
İ, i a short 'ee' sound; as in 'hit', 'sit'
I, ı a neutral vowel; as the 'e' in 'glasses' or the 'a' in 'about'
O, o between the 'o' in 'hot' and the 'aw' in 'awe'
Ö, ö as the 'e' in 'her'; say it with pursed lips
U, u as the 'oo' in 'moo'
Ü, ü an exaggerated rounded-lip 'yoo'
C, c as the 'j' in 'jet'
Ç, ç as the 'ch' in 'church'
G, g always hard as in 'get' (not as in 'gentle')
ğ silent; lengthens preceding vowel
H, h always pronounced; a weak 'h' as in 'half'
J, j as the 'z' in 'azure'
S, s always as in 'stress' (not as in 'ease')
Ş, ş as the 'sh' in 'show'
V, v soft, almost like a 'w'
W, w same as Turkish 'v' (only found in foreign words)

USEFUL WORDS & PHRASES

Greetings & Civilities

Hello.
Merhaba.
MEHR-hah-bah
Good morning/Good day.
Günaydın.
gew-nahy-DUHN
Good evening.
İyi akşamlar.
EE ahk-shahm-LAHR
Good night.
İyi geceler.
EE geh-jeh-LEHR
Goodbye. (said only by one departing)
Allaha ısmarladık.
ah-LAHS-mahr-lah-duhk
Bon voyage. (said only by one staying ; lit: 'Go smiling')
Güle güle.
gew-LEH gew-LEH
Stay happy. (alternative to goodbye)
Hoşça kalın.
HOSH-cha KAH-luhn
May it contribute to your health! (said to one sitting down to a meal)
Afiyet olsun!
ah-fee-EHT ohl-soon
In your honour!/To your health!
Şerefinize!
sheh-rehf-ee-neez-EH

What's your name?
Adınız ne?
AH-duh-NUHZ neh
How are you?
Nasılsınız?
NAHS-suhl-suh-nuhz
I'm fine, thank you.
İyiyim, teşekkür ederim.
ee-YEE-yihm, tesh-ek-KEWR eh-dehr-eem
Very well.
Çok iyiyim.
CHOHK ee-YEE-yeem

Basics

Yes.
Evet.
eh-VEHT
No.
Hayır.
HAH-yuhr
Please.
Lütfen.
LEWT-fehn
Thanks.
Teşekkürler.
teh-sheh-kewr-LEHR
Thank you very much.
Çok teşekkür ederim.
CHOHK teh-sheh-KEWR eh-deh-reem
You're welcome.
Bir şey değil.
beer SHEHY deh-YEEL
Pardon me.
Affedersiniz.
AHF-feh-DEHR-see-neez
Help yourself.
Buyurun(uz).
BOOY-roon-(ooz)

What?
Ne? NEH
How?
Nasıl? NAH-suhl
Who?
Kim? KEEM
Why?
Niçin, neden? NEE-cheen, NEH-dehn
When?
Ne zaman? NEH zah-mahn
Which one?
Hangisi? HAHN-gee-see
What's this?
Bu ne? BOO neh
Where is ...?
... nerede? NEH-reh-deh
At what time?
Saat kaçta? saht-KAHCH-tah
How much/many?
Kaç/Kaç tane? KAHCH/tah-neh
How many liras?
Kaç lira? KAHCH lee-rah
How many hours?
Kaç saat? KAHCH sah-aht
What does it mean?
Ne demek? NEH deh-mehk
Give me ...
... bana verin ... bah-NAH veh-reen
I want ...
... istiyorum ... ees-tee-YOH-room
this
bu(nu) boo(NOO)
that
şu(nu) shoo(NOO)
the other
o(nu) oh(NOO)
hot
sıcak suh-JAHK
cold
soğuk soh-OOK
big
büyük bew-YEWK
small
küçük kew-CHEWK
new/old
yeni/eski yeh-NEE/ehss-KEE
open
açık ah-CHUHK
closed
kapalı kah-pah-LUH
not ...
... değil ... deh-YEEL
and
ve VEH
or
veya veh-YAH
good
iyi EE
bad
fenah feh-NAH
beautiful
güzel gew-ZEHL

Countries (Informal Names)

Australia
Avustralya AH-voo-STRAHL-yah
Austria
Avusturya AH-voo-STOOR-yah
Belgium
Belçika BEL-chee-kah
Canada
Kanada KAH-nah-dah
Denmark
Danimarka DAH-nee-MAR-kah
France
Fransa FRAHN-sah
Germany
Almanya ahl-MAHN-yah
Greece
Yunanistan yoo-NAH-nee-stahn
India
Hindistan HEEN-dee-stahn
Israel
İsrail EESS-rah-yeel
Italy
Italya ee-TAHL-yah
Japan
Japonya zhah-POHN-yah
Netherlands
Holanda ho-LAHN-dah
New Zealand
Yeni Zelanda YEH-nee zeh-LAHN-dah
Norway
Norveç nohr-VECH
South Africa
Güney Afrika gur-NEY AH-free-kah
Sweden
İsveç eess-VECH
Switzerland
İsviçre eess-VEECH-reh

UK
İngiltere EEN-geel-TEH-reh
USA
Amerika ah-MEH-ree-kah

Accommodation

Where is ...?
... nerede?
NEH-reh-deh
Where is a hotel?
Bir otel nerede?
BEER oh-TEHL NEH-reh-deh?
Where is the toilet?
Tuvalet nerede?
too-vah-LEHT NEH-reh-deh?
Where is the manager?
Patron nerede?
pah-TROHN NEH-reh-deh?
Where is someone who understands English?
İngilizce bilen bir kimse nerede?
EEN-geh-LEEZ-jeh bee-lehn beer KEEM-seh NEH-reh-deh?

To request a room, say:

I want ...
... istiyorum.
ees-tee-YOH-room

a double room
İki kişilik oda
ee-KEE kee-shee-leek OH-dah
a twin-bedded room
Çift yataklı oda
CHEEFT yah-tahk-LUH OH-dah
room
oda
OH-dah
single room
bir kişilik oda
BEER kee-shee-leek OH-dah
double room
iki kişilik oda
ee-KEE kee-shee-leek OH-dah
room with one bed
tek yataklı oda
TEHK yah-tahk-LUH OH-dah
room with two beds
iki yataklı oda
ee-KEEyah-tahk-LUH OH-dah
room with bath
banyolu oda
BAHN-yoh-LOO OH-dah
a quiet room
sakin bir oda
sah-KEEN beer oh-dah

It's very noisy.
Çok gürültülü.
CHOHK gew-rewl-tew-lew
What does it cost?
Kaç lira?
KAHCH lee-rah

cheaper
daha ucuz dah-HAH oo-jooz
better
daha iyi dah-HAH ee
very expensive
çok pahalı CHOHK pah-hah-luh

bath
banyo BAHN-yoh
Turkish bath
hamam hah-MAHM
shower
duş DOOSH
soap
sabun sah-BOON
shampoo
şampuan SHAHM-poo-AHN
towel
havlu hahv-LOO
toilet paper
tuvalet kağıdı too-vah-leht kyah-uh-duh

hot water
sıcak su suh-JAHK soo
cold water
soğuk su soh-OOH soo
clean
temiz teh-MEEZ
not clean
temiz değil teh-MEEZ deh-YEEL
air-conditioning
klima KLEE-mah
light(s)
ışık(lar) uh-SHUHK(-LAHR)
light bulb
ampül ahm-PEWL

Getting Around

Where is a/the ...?
... nerede?
NEH-reh-deh

railway station
gar/istasyon
GAHR, ees-tah-SYOHN
bus station
otogar
OH-toh-gahr
toilet
tuvalet
too-vah-LEHT
restaurant
lokanta
loh-KAHN-tah
post office
postane
POHSS-tah-neh
policeman
polis memuru
poh-LEES meh-moo-roo
left luggage/checkroom
emanetçi
EH-mah-NEHT-chee
luggage
bagaj
bah-GAHZH
street/avenue
sokak/cadde(si)
soh-KAHK/JAHD-deh(see)

left
sol SOHL
right
sağ SAH
straight on
doğru doh-ROO
here
burada BOO-rah-dah
there
şurada SHOO-rah-dah
over there
orada OH-rah-dah
near
yakın yah-KUHN
far
uzak oo-ZAHK

a ticket to (Istanbul)
(Istanbul'a) bir bilet
(ih-STAHN-bool-AH) BEER bee-LEHT
map
harita
HAH-ree-TAH
timetable
tarife
tah-ree-FEH
ticket
bilet
bee-LEHT
reserved seat
numaralı yer
noo-MAH-rah-LUH yehr
1st class
birinci sınıf
beer-EEN-jee mehv-kee
2nd class
ikinci sınıf
ee-KEEN-jee mehv-kee
for today
bugün için
BOO-gewn ee-cheen
for tomorrow
yarın için
yah-ruhn ee-cheen
one-way trip
gidiş
gee-DEESH
round-trip
gidiş-dönüş
gee-DEESH-dew-NURSH
student (ticket)
öğrenci (bileti)
tah-leh-BEH
full-fare (ticket)
tam (bileti)
TAHM
daily
hergün
HEHR-gurn
today
bugün
BOO-gurn
tomorrow
yarın
YAHR-uhn

Arrivals & Departures

When does it ...?
Ne zaman ...? NEH zah-mahn

depart
kalkar *kahl-KAHR*
arrive
gelir *geh-LEER*

early/late
erken/geç ehr-KEHN/GECH
fast
çabuk chah-BOOK
slow
yavaş yah-VAHSH
next/last
gelecek/son geh-leh-JEHK/SOHN

Air

aeroplane
uçak oo-CHAHK
airport
havaalanı hah-VAH-ah-lah-nuh
flight
uçuş oo-CHOOSH
gate
kapı kah-PUH

Boat

ship
gemi geh-MEE
boat
tekne, motor TEK-neh, moh-TOHR
rowboat
sandal sahn-DAHL
ferry
feribot FEH-ree-boht
dock
iskele ees-KEH-leh
cabin
kamara KAH-mah-rah
berth
yatak yah-TAHK
class
mevki, sınıf MEHV-kee, suh-nuhf

Bus

bus
otobüs, araba oh-toh-BEWSS
bus terminal
otogar OH-toh-gahr
direct (bus)
direk(t) dee-REK
indirect
aktarmalı ahk-tahr-mah-LUH

Car

air (tyres)
hava (lâstik)
hah-VAH (lyaass-TEEK)
brake(s)
fren
FREHN
car, truck
araba, kamyon
ah-rah-BAH, kahm-YOHN
diesel fuel
mazot, motorin
mah-SOHT, MOH-toh-reen
auto-electrician
oto elektrikçi
oh-TOH ee-lehk-TREEK-chee
exhaust (system)
egzos(t)
ehk-ZOHSS
headlamp
far
FAHR
highway
karayolu
kah-RAH-yoh-loo
hitchhike
otostop
OH-toh-stohp
motor oil
motor yağı
moh-TOHR yah-uh
petrol, gasoline
benzin
behn-ZEEN
regular
normal
nohr-MAHL
steering (-wheel)
direksiyon
dee-REHK-see-YOHN
super
süper
seur-PEHR

Highway Signs

GİRİLMEZ	No Entry
GİŞELER	Toll Booths
KATOTOPARK	Parking Garage
OTOYOL	Motorway/ Expressway
PARALI GEÇİŞ	Toll Highway
PARK ALANI	Rest Stop
PARK YERİ	Car Park/ Parking Lot
SERVİS ALANI	Service Area
ŞEHİR MERKEZİ	City Centre
TIRMANMA ŞERİDİ	Overtaking/ Passing Lane
ÜCRET ÖDEME	Toll Collection
ÜCRETLİ GEÇİŞ	Toll Highway
VERGİ KONTROLÜ	Tax Checkpoint (for trucks & buses)
YAĞIŞTA KAYGAN YOL	Slippery When Wet
YAVAŞLA	Slow Down

Note Motorway signs are green with white lettering; town signs are blue with white lettering; village signs are white with black lettering. Yellow signs with black lettering mark sights of touristic interest. Yellow signs with blue lettering mark village development projects.

tyre repairman
oto lâstikçi
oh-TOH lyass-TEEK-chee

Train

railway
demiryolu
deh-MEER-yoh-loo

train
tren
tee-REHN

railway station
gar, istasyon
GAHR, ees-tahs-YOHN

couchette
kuşet
koo-SHEHT

sleeping car
yataklı vagon
yah-tahk-LUH vah-gohn

dining car
yemekli vagon
yeh-mehk-LEE vah-gohn

no-smoking car
sigara içilmeyen vagon
see-GAH-rah eech-EEL- mee-yehn

Around Town

Post Office

post office (PTT)
postane, postahane
POHSS-tah-NEH

postage stamp
pul
POOL

by air mail
uçakla, uçak ile
oo-CHAHK-lah, oo-CHAHK-ee-leh

money order
havale
hah-vah-LEH

poste restante
postrestant
pohst-rehs-TAHNT

customs
gümrük
gewm-REWK

inspection (prior to mailing)
kontrol
kohn-TROHL

telephone token (large, medium, small)
jeton (büyük, orta, küçük)
zheh-TOHN (bew-YEWK, ohr-TAH, kew-CHEWK)

Bank

money
para PAH-rah

Turkish liras
lira LEE-rah

dollars
dolar doh-LAHR

foreign currency
döviz durr-VEEZ

cash
efektif eh-fehk-TEEF
cheque
çek CHEK
exchange
kambiyo KAHM-bee-yoh
exchange rate
kur KOOR
commission
komisyon koh-mees-YOHN
identification
kimlik KEEM-leek
cashier
kasa, vezne KAH-sah, VEHZ-neh
working hours
çalışma saatleri chal-ush-MAH sah-aht-leh-ree

Days of the Week

day
gün GEWN
week
hafta hahf-TAH

Sunday
Pazar pah-ZAHR
Monday
Pazartesi pah-ZAHR-teh-see
Tuesday
Salı sah-LUH
Wednesday
Çarşamba char-shahm-BAH
Thursday
Perşembe pehr-shehm-BEH
Friday
Cuma joo-MAH
Saturday
Cumartesi joo-MAHR-teh-see

Months of the Year

month
ay AHY
year
sene, yıl SEH-neh, YUHL

January	*Ocak*	oh-JAHK
February	*Şubat*	shoo-BAHT
March	*Mart*	MAHRT
April	*Nisan*	nee-SAHN
May	*Mayıs*	mah-YUSS
June	*Haziran*	HAH-zee-RAHN
July	*Temmuz*	teh-MOOZ
August	*Ağustos*	AH-oo-STOHSS
September	*Eylül*	ehy-LEWL
October	*Ekim*	eh-KEEM
November	*Kasım*	kah-SUHM
December	*Aralık*	AH-rah-LUHK

Health

handicapped
özürlü/ sakat ur-zuhr-LUR/ sah-KAHT
hospital
hastane hahss-tah-NEH
dispensary
sağlık ocağı saah-LUHK oh-jah-uh

I'm ill.
Hastayım. hahss-TAH-yuhm
My stomach hurts.
Karnım ağrıyor. kahr-NUHM aah-ruh-yohr

Help me.
Yardım edin. yahr-DUHM eh-den

Shopping

shop
dükkan dyook-KAHN
market
çarşı chahr-SHUH
price
fiyat fee-YAHT
service charge
servis ücreti sehr-VEES ewj-reh-tee
tax
vergi VEHR-gee
cheap
ucuz oo-JOOZ
expensive
pahalı pah-hah-LUH
very expensive
çok pahalı CHOHK pah-hah-luh
Which?
Hangi? HAHN-gee
this one
bunu boo-NOO
Do you have ...?
... var mı? VAHR muh
We don't have ...
... yok YOHK
I'll give you ...
... vereceğim VEH-reh-JEH-yeem

Children

child(ren)
çocuk(lar) CHO-jook-(LAHR)
baby
bebek beh-BEHK
diaper (nappy)
bebek bezi beh-BEHK beh-zee
nursery
kreş KRESH

Numbers

-½ *yarım* YAH-ruhm
(used alone, as in 'I want half')
-½ *buçuk* boo-CHOOK
(always used with a whole number, eg '1-½', *bir buçuk*)

0	*sıfır*	SUH-fuhr
1	*bir*	BEER
2	*iki*	ee-KEE
3	*üç*	EWCH
4	*dört*	DURRT
5	*beş*	BEHSH
6	*altı*	ahl-TUH
7	*yedi*	yeh-DEE
8	*sekiz*	seh-KEEZ
9	*dokuz*	doh-KOOZ
10	*on*	OHN
11	*on bir*	ohn BEER
12	*on iki*	ohn ee-KEE
13	*on üç*	ohn EWCH
20	*yirmi*	yeer-MEE
30	*otuz*	oh-TOOZ
40	*kırk*	KUHRK
50	*elli*	ehl-LEE
60	*altmış*	ahlt-MUSH
70	*yetmiş*	yeht-MEESH
80	*seksen*	sehk-SEHN
90	*doksan*	dohk-SAHN
100	*yüz*	YEWZ
200	*iki yüz*	ee-KEE yewz
1000	*bin*	BEEN
2000	*iki bin*	ee-KEE been
10,000	*on bin*	OHN been

one million
milyon meel-YOHN

Ordinal numbers consist of the number plus the suffix *-inci, -ıncı, -uncu* or *-üncü*, depending upon 'vowel harmony'.

first
birinci beer-EEN-jee
second
ikinci ee-KEEN-jee
sixth
altıncı ahl-TUHN-juh
13th
onüçüncü ohn-ew-CHEWN-jew

Emergencies

Help!
İmdat!
eem-daht
It's an emergency.
Acil durum.
ah-jeel doo-room
I'm ill.
Rahatsızım.
rah-haht-sih-zihm
Call the police!
Polisi çağırın!
poh-lee-see chah-ihr-rihn
Find a doctor!
Doktoru arayın (pol)/ara! (inf)
dohk-toh-roo ah-rah-yihn/ah-rah
(There's a) fire!
Yangın var!
yahn-gihn vahr
There's been an accident.
Bir kaza oldu.
beer kah-zah ohl-doo
Go away!
Gidin (pol)/Git! (inf)
gee-deen/geet
I've been raped/assaulted.
Tecavüze/Saldırıya uğradım.
teh-jah-vyu-zeh/sahl-dih-rih-yah oo-rah-dihm
I've been robbed.
Soyuldum.
sohy-ool-doom
I'm lost.
Kayboldum.
kahy-bohl-doom
Where are the toilets?
Tuvalet nerede?
too-vah-leht neh-reh-deh

FOOD

Basics

restaurant
  lokanta loh-KAHN-tah
pastry-shop
  pastane PAHSS-tah-neh
'oven' (bakery)
  fırın FUH-ruhn
'pizza' place
  pideci PEE-deh-jee
köfte restaurant
  köfteci KURF-teh-jee
kebap restaurant
  kebapçı keh-BAHP-chuh
snack shop
  büfe bew-FEH

alcohol served
  içkili
  eech-kee-LEE
no alcohol served
  içkisiz
  eech-kee-SEEZ
family (ladies') dining room
  aile salonu
  ah-yee-LEH sah-loh-noo
no single men allowed
  aileye mahsustur
  ah-yee-LEH mah-SOOS-tuhr

breakfast
  kahvaltı
  KAHH-vahl-TUH
lunch
  öğle yemeği ury-LEH yeh-meh-yee
supper
  akşam yemeği ahk-SHAHM yeh-meh-yee
to eat; meal, dish
  yemek yeh-MEHK
portion, serving
  porsyon pohr-SYOHN
fork
  çatal chah-TAHL
knife
  bıçak buh-CHAHK
spoon
  kaşık kah-SHUHK
plate
  tabak tah-BAHK
glass
  bardak bahr-DAHK
bill, cheque
  hesap heh-SAHP
service charge
  servis ücreti sehr-VEES ewj-reh-tee
tax
  vergi VEHR-gee
tip
  bahşiş bah-SHEESH
error
  yanlış yahn-LUSH
small change
  bozuk para boh-ZOOK pah-rah

The Menu

This guide to restaurant words is arranged (more or less) in the order of a Turkish menu and a Turkish meal. Courses (*çorba, et* etc) are listed in the singular form; you may see them in the plural *(çorbalar, etler* etc).

Soup

balık çorbası fish soup
  bah-LUHK
  chor-bah-suh
corba soup
  CHOHR-bah
domates çorbası tomato soup
  doh-MAH-tess
  chor-bah-suh
düğün çorbası egg & lemon soup
  dew-EWN
  chor-bah-suh
et suyu (yumurtalı) mutton broth with egg
  EHT soo-yoo,
  yoo-moor-tah-LUH
ezo gelin çorbası lentil & rice soup
  EH-zoh GEH-leen
  chor-bah-suh
haşlama broth with mutton
  hahsh-lah-MAH
işkembe çorbası tripe soup
  eesh-KEHM-beh
  chor-bah-suh
mercimek çorbası lentil soup
  mehr-jee-MEHK
  chor-bah-suh
paça trotter soup
  PAH-chah

sebze çorbası SEHB-zeh chor-bah-suh	vegetable soup
şehriye çorbası shehh-ree-YEH chor-bah-suh	vermicelli soup
tavuk çorbası tah-VOOK chor-bah-suh	chicken soup
yayla çorbası YAHY-lah chor-bah-suh	yoghurt & barley soup

Hors d'Oeuvres

Meze (MEH-zeh), or hors d'oeuvres, can include almost anything, and you can easily – and delightfully – make an entire meal of meze. Often you'll be brought a tray from which you can choose those you want.

beyaz peynir bey-AHZ pehy-neer	white cheese
börek bur-REHK	flaky pastry
etli eht-LEE	stuffed with lamb (hot)
kabak dolması kah-BAHK dohl-mah-suh	stuffed squash/marrow
patlıcan salatası paht-luh-JAHN sah-lah-tah-suh	aubergine or eggplant puree
pilaki, piyaz pee-LAH-kee	cold white beans vinaigrette
tarama salatası tah-rah-MAH sah-lah-tah-suh	red caviar in mayonnaise
yalancı dolması yah-LAHN-juh dohl-mah-suh	stuffed vine leaves
yaprak dolması yah-PRAHK dohl-mah-suh	stuffed vine leaves
zeytinyağlı zehy-teen-yah-LUH	stuffed with rice (cold)

Salads

Each of the following Turkish names would be followed by the word *salata* (sah-LAH-tah) or *salatası*. You may be asked if you prefer it *sirkeli* (SEER-keh-LEE), with vinegar or *limonlu* (LEE-mohn-LOO), with lemon juice; most salads (except *söğüş)* come with olive oil. If you don't like hot peppers, say *bibersiz* (BEE-behr-SEEZ), though this often doesn't work.

Amerikan/Rus ah-meh-ree-KAHN/ROOSS	mayonnaise, peas & carrots
beyin behy-EEN	sheep's brain
domates salatalık doh-MAH-tess sah-LAH-tah-luhk	tomato & cucumber salad
karışık (çoban) kah-ruh-SHUHK (choh-BAHN)	chopped mixed salad
marul mah-ROOL	romaine lettuce
patlıcan paht-luh-JAHN	roast aubergine/ eggplant puree
söğüş sur-EWSH	sliced vegetables, no sauce
turşu toor-SHOO	pickled vegetables
yeşil yeh-SHEEL	green salad

Fish

A menu is of no use when ordering fish (*balık*, bah-LUHK). You'll have to ask the waiter what's fresh, and then ask for the approximate price. The fish will then be weighed, and the price computed at the day's per-kg rate. Sometimes you can haggle. Buy fish in season (*mevsimli*, mehv-seem-LEE), as fish out of season are very expensive. From March to the end of June is a good time to order *kalkan* (turbot), *uskumru* (mackerel), and *hamsi* (fresh anchovies), but from July to mid-August is spawning season for many species, and fishing them is prohibited. In high summer, the following are the easiest to find in the markets and on the restaurant tables: *çinakop* (a small bluefish), *lüfer* (medium-size bluefish), *palamut* (bonito), *tekir* (striped goatfish: *Mullus surmuletus*), *barbunya* (red mullet: *Mullus barbatus*), and *istavrit* (scad, horse mackerel).

alabalık ah-LAH-bah-luhk — trout
barbunya bahr-BOON-yah — red mullet
dil balığı DEEL bah-luh — sole
hamsi HAHM-see — anchovy (fresh)
havyar hahv-YAHR — caviar
istakoz uhss-tah-KOHZ — lobster
kalkan kahl-KAHN — turbot
karagöz kah-rah-GURZ — black bream
karides kah-REE-dess — shrimp
kefal keh-FAHL — grey mullet
kılıç kuh-LUHCH — swordfish
levrek lehv-REHK — sea bass
lüfer lew-FEHR — bluefish
mercan mehr-JAHN — red coralfish
midye MEED-yeh — mussels
palamut PAH-lah-moot — tunny, bonito
pisi PEE-see — plaice
sardalya sahr-DAHL-yah — sardine (fresh)
tarama tah-rah-MAH — roe, red caviar
trança TRAHN-chah — Aegean tuna
uskumru oos-KOOM-roo — mackerel
yengeç yehn-GECH — crab

Meat & Kebap

In *kebap* (keh-BAHP), the meat (*et*, EHT) is always lamb, ground or in chunks; preparation, spices and extras (onions, peppers, bread) make the difference among the kebaps. Some may be ordered *yoğurtlu* (yoh-oort-LOO), with a side-serving of yoghurt.

If you don't eat meat, ask *Etsiz yemek var mı?* (eht-SEEZ yeh-mehk VAHR muh, Have you any meatless dishes?), or say *Hiç et yiyemem* (HEECH eht yee-YEH-mehm, I can't eat any meat). The word *vejeteryan* (vegetarian) is slowly gaining currency.

Adana kebap ah-DAH-nah keh-bahp — spicy-hot roast köfte
böbrek bur-BREHK — kidney
bonfile bohn-fee-LEH — small fillet beefsteak
bursa kebap BOOR-sah keh-bahp — döner with tomato sauce
çerkez tavuğu cher-KEHZ tah-voo — chicken in walnut sauce
ciğer jee-EHR — liver
çöp kebap CHURP keh-bahp — tiny bits of skewered lamb
dana DAH-nah — veal
domuz doh-MOOZ — pork (forbidden to Muslims)
döner kebap dur-NEHR keh-bahp — spit-roasted lamb slices
etli pide/ekmek eht-LEE PEE-deh, ehk-MEHK — flat bread with minced lamb
güveç gew-VECH — meat & vegetable stew

kağıt kebap kyah-UHT keh-bahp — lamb & vegetables in paper
karışık ızgara kah-ruh-shuk uhz-gah-rah — mixed grill (lamb)
koç yumurtası KOHCH yoo-moor-tah-suh — ram's 'eggs' (testicles)
köfte KURF-teh — grilled minced lamb patties
mantı mahn-TUH — ravioli (Turkish-style)
orman kebap ohr-MAHN keh-bahp — roast lamb with onions
pastırma pahss-TUHR-mah — sun-dried, spiced beef
patlıcan kebap paht-luh-JAHN keh-bahp — aubergine/eggplant & meat
piliç pee-LEECH — roasting chicken
pirzola peer-ZOH-lah — cutlet (usually lamb)
saç kavurma SAHTCH kah-voor-mah — wok-fried lamb
şatobriyan sha-TOH-bree-YAHN — chateaubriand
sığır suh-UHR — beef
şinitzel shee-NEET-zehl — wienerschnitzel
şiş kebap SHEESH keh-bahp — roast skewered lamb
(süt) kuzu (sewt) koo-ZOO — milk-fed lamb
tandır kebap tahn-DUHR keh-bahp — pit-roasted lamb
tas kebap TAHSS keh-bahp — lamb stew
tavuk tah-VOOK — boiling chicken
tavuk/piliç döner tah-VOOK/pee-LEECH dur-NEHR — spit-roasted chicken slices
tavuk/piliç şiş tah-VOOK/pee-LEECH sheesh — roast skewered chicken

There are numerous fancy kebaps, often named for the places where they originated. Best is *Bursa kebap* (BOOR-sah), also called *İskender kebap*, since it was invented in the city of Bursa by a chef named Iskender (Alexander). Of the other fancy kebaps, *Urfa kebap* comes with lots of onions and black pepper; *Adana kebap* is spicy hot, with red pepper the way the Arabs like it.

Sweets

aşure ah-shoo-REH — walnut, raisin & pea pudding
baklava bahk-lah-VAH — layered pastry with honey, nuts
burma kadayıf boor-MAH kah-dah-yuhf — shredded wheat with pistachios & honey
dondurma dohn-DOOR-mah — ice cream
ekmek kadayıf ehk-MEHK kah-dah-yuhf — crumpet in syrup
fırın sütlaç foo-roon SEWT-lach — baked rice pudding (cold)
güllaç gewl-LACH — flaky pastry, nuts & milk
helva hehl-VAH — semolina sweet
hurma tatlısı hoor-MAH — semolina cake in syrup
kabak tatlısı kah-BAHK TAHT-luh-suh — candied marrow/squash

kadın göbeği kah-DUHN gur-beh-yee	'Lady's navel', doughnut in syrup
kazandibi kah-ZAHN-dee-bee	'bottom of the pot' (cold baked pudding)
kek KEHK	cake
keşkül kehsh-KEWL	milk & nut pudding
komposto kohm-POHSS-toh	stewed fruit
krem karamel KREHM kah-rah-MEHL	baked caramel custard
krem şokolada KREHM shoh-koh-LAH-dah	chocolate pudding
lokum loh-KOOM	Turkish delight
meyve mehy-VEH	fruit
muhallebi moo-HAH-leh-bee	rice flour & rosewater pudding
pasta PAHSS-tah	pastry
peynir tatlısı pehy-NEER TAHT-luh-suh	cheese cake
sütlaç sewt-LAHCH	rice pudding
tatlı taht-LUH	sweet, dessert
tavuk göğsü tah-VOOK gur-sew	sweet of milk, rice & chicken
tel kadayıf TEHL kah-dah-yuhf	shredded wheat in syrup
yoğurt tatlısı yoh-OORT taht-luh-suh	yoghurt & egg pudding
zerde zehr-DEH	saffron & rice sweet

Other Dishes & Condiments

bal BAHL	honey
beyaz peynir bey-AHZ pey-neer	white (sheep's) cheese
biber bee-BEHR	green pepper
bisküvi BEES-koo-VEE	biscuits
börek (-ği) bur-REHK	flaky or fried pastry
buz BOOZ	ice
cacık jah-JUHK	yoghurt & grated cucumber
dolma(sı) lahana DOHL-mah(-suh) lah-HAH-nah	stuffed (vegetable) cabbage leaves
ekmek ehk-MEHK	bread
hardal hahr-DAHL	mustard
imam bayıldı ee-MAHM bah-yuhl-duh	aubergine baked with onions & tomatoes
kabak kah-BAHK	marrow/squash
kara/siyah biber kah-RAH/ see-YAH bee-behr	black pepper
karnıyarık KAHR-nuh-yah-RUHK	aubergine & lamb (hot)
kaşar peynir kah-SHAHR pey-neer	mild yellow cheese
limon lee-MOHN	lemon
makarna mah-KAHR-nah	macaroni, noodles
musakka moo-sah-KAH	aubergine & lamb pie
pasta PAHSS-tah	pastry (not noodles)
peynir pehy-NEER	cheese
pide PEE-deh	pizza, flat bread

reçel fruit jam
reh-CHEHL
sarmısak garlic
SAHR-muh-SAHK
şeker sugar, candy, sweets
sheh-KEHR
sigara 'cigarette' fritters
see-GAH-rah
sirke vinegar
SEER-keh
spaket spaghetti
spah-KEHT
su water
SOO
tereyağı butter
TEH-reh-yah
tuz salt
TOOZ
yağ oil, fat
YAH
yalancı vine leaves
yah-LAHN-juh
yaprak vine leaves
yah-PRAHK
yoğurt yoghurt
yoh-OORT
zeytin olives
zehy-TEEN
zeytinyağı olive oil
zehy-TEEN-yah-uh

Cooking Terms

buğlama steamed, poached
BOO-lah-MAH
ezme(si) puree
ehz-MEH(-see)
fırın baked, oven-roasted
fuh-RUHN
haşlama boiled, stewed
hahsh-lah-MAH
iyi pişmiş well-done
ee-YEE peesh-meesh
ızgara charcoal grilled
uhz-GAH-rah
kızartma broiled
kuh-ZAHRT-mah
rosto roasted
ROHSS-toh
sıcak hot, warm
suh-JAHK
soğuk cold
soh-OOK
etli with meat
eht-LEE
kıymalı with ground lamb
kuhy-mah-LUH
peynirli with cheese
pehy-neer-LEE
salçalı with savoury tomato sauce
sahl-chah-LUH
soslu, terbiyeli with sauce
sohss-LOO, TEHR-bee-yeh-LEE
yoğurtlu with yoghurt
YOH-oort-LOO
yumurtalı with egg
yoo-moor-tah-LUH

Street Food

dürüm grilled lamb roll-up
dur-RURM
gözleme Turkish crêpe
GURZ-leh-meh
kuru yemiş dried fruits
koo-ROO yeh-MEESH
peynirli sandviç grilled cheese sandwich
pehy-neer-LEE sahn-dveech
simit sesame-covered circle roll
see-MEET

Fruit

Turkish fruits are superb, especially in mid-summer when the melon season starts, and early in winter when the first citrus crops start to come in.

armut pear
ahr-MOOT
ayva quince
ahy-VAH
çilek strawberries
chee-LEHK
elma apple
ehl-MAH

greyfurut grapefruit
GREY-foo-root
incir fig
een-JEER
karpuz watermelon
kahr-POOZ
kavun yellow melon
kah-VOON
kayısı apricot
kahy-SUH
kiraz cherry
kee-RAHZ
mandalin tangerine, mandarin
mahn-dah-LEEN
meyva, meyve fruit
mehy-VAH
muz banana
MOOZ
nar pomegranate
NAHR
portakal orange
pohr-tah-KAHL
şeftali peach
shef-tah-LEE
üzüm grapes
ew-ZEWM
vişne morello (sour cherry)
VEESH-neh

Vegetables

bamya okra
BAHM-yah
barbunye red beans
bahr-BOON-yeh
bezelye peas
beh-ZEHL-yeh
biber peppers
bee-BEHR
domates tomato
doh-MAH-tess
havuç carrot
hah-VOOCH
ıspınak spinach
uhs-spuh-NAHK
kabak marrow/squash
kah-BAHK
karnabahar cauliflower
kahr-NAH-bah-hahr
kuru fasulye white beans
koo-ROO fah-sool-yah
lahana cabbage
lah-HAH-nah
patates potato
pah-TAH-tess
salatalık cucumber
sah-LAH-tah-luhk
sebze vegetable
sehb-ZEH
soğan onion
soh-AHN
taze fasulye green beans
tah-ZEH fah-sool-yah
turp radish
TOORP

Cheese

Although there are some interesting peasant cheeses – such as *tulum peynir* (a salty, dry, crumbly goats' milk cheese cured in a goatskin bag) and a dried cheese which looks just like twine – they rarely make it to the cities and almost never to restaurant tables. What you'll find is the ubiquitous *beyaz peynir* (bey-AHZ pey-neer), white sheep's milk cheese. To be really good, it must be full-cream *(tam yağlı)* cheese, not dry and crumbly and not too salty or sour. You may also find *kaşar peynir* (kah-SHAHR pey-neer), a firm, mild yellow cheese, either fresh (*taze,* tah-ZEH) or aged (*eski,* ess-KEE).

DRINKS

İçki (eech-KEE) usually refers to alcoholic beverages, *meşrubat* (mehsh-roo-BAHT) to soft drinks. When waiters ask *İçecek?* or *Ne içeceksiniz?*, they're asking what you'd like to drink.

As for Turkish coffee (*kahve*, kahh-VEH) you must order it according to sweetness: the sugar is mixed in during the brewing, not afterwards. You can drink it *sade* (sah-DEH), without sugar; *az* (AHZ), if you want just a bit of sugar; *orta* (ohr-TAH), with a middling amount; *çok* or *şekerli* or even *çok şekerli* (CHOHK sheh-kehr-LEE), with lots of sugar. When the coffee arrives, the waiter may well have confused the cups, and you may find yourself exchanging with your dinnermates.

Nescafé is readily found throughout Turkey but tends to be expensive, often around 70c per cup.

Nonalcoholic Drinks

su SOO	water
maden suyu mah-DEHN soo-yoo	mineral water
maden sodası mah-DEHN soh-dah-suh	fizzy mineral water
menba suyu mehn-BAH soo-yoo	spring water
limonata lee-moh-NAH-tah	lemonade
meyva suyu mey-VAH soo-yoo	fruit juice
süt SEWT	milk
ayran AH-yee-RAHN	yoghurt drink
boza BOH-zah	thick millet drink
çay CHAH-yee	tea
çay bahçesi CHAH-yee bahh-cheh-see	tea garden
kahve(si) kah-VEH(-see)	coffee
Fransız frahn-SUHZ	coffee & milk
Amerikan ah-meh-ree-KAHN	American coffee
neskafe NEHSS-kah-feh	instant coffee
Türk kahvesi TEWRK kahh-veh-see	Turkish coffee
sahlep sah-LEHP	hot milk & tapioca root

Alcoholic Drinks

bira BEE-rah	beer
beyaz bey-AHZ	light
fıçı bira fuh-CHUH bee-rah	draught ('keg')
siyah see-YAH	dark
şarap shah-RAHP	wine
beyaz bey-AHZ	white
kırmızı kuhr-muh-ZUH	red
köpüklü kur-pewk-LEW	sparkling
roze roh-ZEH	rose
cin JEEN	gin
rakı rah-KUH	aniseed-flavoured brandy
viski VEE-skee	whisky
vermut vehr-MOOT	vermouth
votka VOHT-kah	vodka

Glossary

Here, with definitions, are some unfamiliar words and abbreviations you might meet in the text or on the road in Turkey:

acropolis – high city, hilltop citadel and temples of a classic Hellenic city
adliye – court house
agora – open space for commerce and politics in a classic Hellenic city
aile salonu – room for couples, families and single women in a Turkish restaurant
akaryakıt – liquid fuel, petrol (gasoline), diesel etc
Allah korusun – God protect me!
apse – semicircular recess for the altar in a church
araç çıkabılır – vehicles entering
arasta – row of shops near a mosque, the rent from which supports the mosque
askeri araç – military vehicle
attar – rose oil

banliyö – suburb(an)
bedesten – vaulted, fireproof market enclosure where valuable goods are kept
Belediye – municipality/town hall
bouleuterion – place of assemby, council meeting-place in a classic Hellenic city

cami(i) – mosque
caravanserai – caravan palace, large fortified way-station for caravans
çarşı(sı) – market, bazaar
çeşme – spring, fountain
çevreyolu – ring road, bypass
cuneiform – wedge-shaped characters used in several ancient languages

dağ(ı) – mountain
Damsız Girilmez – 'No single males admitted' (Turkish nightclubs)
DDY – Devlet Demiryolları (Turkish State Railways)
deniz – sea
deniz otobüsü – hydrofoil
Denizyolları – Turkish Maritime Lines
deresi – stream
dervish – member of mystic brotherhood, some (whirling) noted for frenzied dance
Dikkat! Yavaş! – Careful! Slow!
dinlenme parkı – (highway) rest area
dolmuş – minibus or sedan

eczane – chemist/pharmacy
eski – old (thing, not person)
eyvan – large recess, vaulted or domed, open to a courtyard
ezan – the Muslim call to prayer

figure malzeme – gravel mound at roadside

gazino – Turkish nightclub (not for gambling)
geçenek – aisle
geçit, -di – mountain pass
geniş araç – wide vehicle

hamam(ı) – Turkish steam bath
han(ı) – inn or caravanserai in a town or city
harabe(ler) – ruin(s)
harem – family/women's quarters of a residence (see also *selamlık)*
hazır yemek – food prepared and kept hot on a steam table
heyelan (bölgesi) – landslide (zone)
heykel – statue
hisar(ı) – see *kale*
hükümet konağı – government house
Hünkar Mahfili – sultan's special prayer-place in a mosque

ilkokul – primary school
imam – prayer leader, Muslim cleric
imaret(i) – soup kitchen for the poor
İşhanı – office building
iskele(si) – landing-place, wharf, quay
ispirto – ethyl alcohol, methylated spirits

jandarma – gendarme, paramilitary police force/officer

kale(si) – fortress, citadel
kapı(sı) – door, gate

kaplıca – thermal spring or baths
karayolları – highways
kat – storey (of a building)
Katma Değer Vergisi – Value Added Tax
kat oto parkı – multi-level parking garage
kervansaray(ı) – Turkish for caravanserai
kilim – napless woven wool mat
kilise(si) – church
konak, konağı – mansion, government headquarters
köprü (sü) – bridge
köşk(ü) – pavilion, villa
köy(ü) – village
kule(si) – tower
külliye(si) – mosque complex including seminary, hospital, soup kitchen etc
kümbet – vault, cupola, dome; tomb topped by this
küşet(li) – (train carriage containing) couchette(s), shelf-like beds

liman(ı) – harbour

Maaşallah – Wonder of God! (said in admiration or to avert the evil eye)
mağara(sı) – cave
mahalle(si) – neighbourhood, district of a city
medrese(si) – Muslim theological seminary
mescit, -di – prayer room, small mosque
meydan(ı) – public square, open place
meyhane – wine shop, tavern
mihrab – niche in a mosque indicating the direction of Mecca
mimber – pulpit in a mosque
minare(si) – minaret, tower from which Muslims are called to prayer
müezzin – cantor who sings the *ezan*, or call to prayer

narthex – enclosed porch or vestibule at the entrance to a church
nave – middle aisle of a church
necropolis – city of the dead, cemetery
nufüs – population

oda(sı) – room
odeon – odeum, small classical theatre for musical performances
okul taşıtı – school bus
otogar – bus station
otoyol – motorway, limited-access divided highway

pansiyon – pension, B&B, guesthouse
park yeri – car park
patika – trail, footpath
pazar(ı) – weekly market, bazaar
pencere – window
PTT – Posta, Telefon, Telğraf: post, telephone and telegraph office

rakım – altitude above sea level
Ramazan – Muslim lunar holy month

şadırvan – fountain where Muslims perform ritual ablutions
saray(ı) – palace
sarcophagus – a stone or marble coffin or tomb, especially one with inscription
sebil – public fountain or water kiosk
şehir – city; municipal
selamlık – public/male quarters of a residence (see also *harem*)
Seljuk – of or pertaining to the Seljuk Turks
sufi – Muslim mystic, member of a mystic (dervish) brotherhood
sürücü adayı – student (learner) driver

tabhane – hostel for travellers
tatil köyü – holiday village
TC – Türkiye Cumhuriyeti (Turkish Republic), which designates an official office or organisation
TCDD – Türkiye Cumhuriyeti Devlet Demiryolları, see *DDY*
tehlikeli madde – dangerous cargo
Tekel – government alcoholic beverage and tobacco company
tekke(si) – dervish lodge
TEM – Trans-European Motorway
THY – Türk Hava Yolları, Turkish Airlines
tırmanma şeridi – overtaking lane
TML – Turkish Maritime Lines, Denizyolları
TRT – Türkiye Radyo ve Televizyon, Turkish broadcasting corporation
tuff, tufa – soft stone laid down as volcanic ash

tuğra – sultan's monogram, imperial signature
türbe(si) – tomb, grave, mausoleum

uzun araç – long vehicle

valilik, valiliği, vilayet – provincial government headquarters
vizier – high official

yalı – waterside residence
yasak bölge – forbidden zone
yayla – mountain pasture, usually used in summer only
yol(u) – road, way
yol onarımı – road repairs
yol yapımı – road construction

zaviye – dervish hostel

Acknowledgments

THANKS

Many thanks to the travellers who used the last edition and wrote to us with helpful hints, useful advice and interesting anecdotes:

Aliel, Angela, Beytullah & Joanna, Iramage, Jocasta & Trent, Marian, Paul & Emily, Sandra-Lee, M M Addy, Paul Adrian, Helen Akers, Riccardo Alessi, Geoff Alexander, Mark Alexander, Vera Alexander, Jodie Allison, Helen Allmark, AR Alsford, Roberto E Paolo Amore, Fiona Anderson, Kim Anderson, Matthew Anderson, Horace & Katherine Andrews, Angela Archer, Glenn Arendts, Gwen Armstrong, Lene Aronsen, Ian Ashbridge, Kynelle Athorn, Stacey Bailey, Vito Balciunas, Daniel Bampton, Dave Barnett, Lance Bartholomeusz, Kyle Battisti, David & Stewart Bell, Marnie Bender, Joe Bergen, Peter Berger, Diana Berman, Delfine Bermijn, AC Berridge, Lynn Berry, Fabrizio Beverina, Pete Bickford, Paul Bietz, Genc Bilgisayar, George Biro, Therese Bismire, F Blackwood, Andrea Blake, Lindsay Bligh, Jeff Bloom, Nina Blusse, Dilia & Dirk Boag, Roberto Bocchi, Michael Body, Conrad & Dorinda Boerman, Brett Bogie, Sally Bothroyd, Eric Boudin, Armel Boueyguet, H Boverman, Carl Bowden, Alan Bowtell, Joanne Boyer, Phil Bradshaw, Janet Breines, John & Louise Brekelmans, Andra Brill, Manmus van der Brink, James Broadbent, David Broom, Ian Brown, Michael Brown, Rosemary Brown, Marjade Bruin, Karl Buchanan, Rowan & Marleende Buisson, M Burnett, Tamsin & Patrick Bynne, Joan & Guy Caethoven, Kevin Callaghan, Tina Calov, Corinne Campbell, John Campbell, Ronald Campbell, Tanya Campbell, Sebastien Canderle, Jonathon Carapetis, Charles Carbone, JE Challender, Benjamin Cher, Philip Chilvers, Belinda Clapperton, John P Clark, Hilary Clarkson, Deirdre Coleman, Marina Comelli, Alice Cook, Sue & Anthony Cook, Jill Coombs, Amanda Cork, Simon Cornell, Glen Cornwell, Katerina Cosgrove, Helen Coutts, Gabrielle Cramp & Co, Ann & Lindsay Crawford, Bob Creed, M Creighton Scott, Michelle Cresp, Charles Croll, Joe Crouier, Chantal Daniels-Batt, Ren David, Sophie Davoine, JB Dawson, Matt & Christina Delcousay, Fatma Demirel, Suresh Dhargalkar, Rachel Diaz, Bart Diepenbroek, Peter Dietrich, Gigi Dingler, Ian Dobson, Lucy Donovan, Dominic D'Orazi, Benjamin Douglas, Mark Doupe, Ellen Doyle, D Drengubiak, Vicki Dubury, Gillian Dugmore, Tracey Duigan, Caroline Dunn, Cindy Dyball, Dyan Eastman, Nigel Easton, Michael Eckert, Sharon Ede, Ursula Egger, Hansen Egle, Elescia Eisler, Suanne Ekdahl, Ahmet Ektem, Dianne & Colin Elliott, Nalan Erem, Zeyda Erol, Bryan Everts, S Yesin Evrensel, Diane Ezer, Ian Fegent, Ryan Fennell, Stephen Ferguson, Rona Ferguson, Deborah Filcoff, D Finch, Ian Finlay, Anthony Finocchiaro, Ari & Ayelet Fleischer, Phyl Foley, PKae Forbes, Rick Fordyce, John & Emiko Foster, M Foster, Ronald Frank, Mike Frost, Barbara Fudge, Matteo Fumagalli, Suzanne Galler, Belinda Gaskell, Piotr Gaszynski, J Gates, Kathryn Gauci, Matthias Gede, Michele Genovese, David Gibson, Mark Gilchrist, David Gill, Susan Gill, Andrew Gillies, Mihai Gireada, Eric C Glatfelter, Kirby Go, Elizabeth Godfrey, Hilde Goedertier, Howard Goldberg, Lisa Marie Gonzales, Janet & Peter Goodman, Michael Gore, Jan Grant, Paul Gray, Barbara Griffith, Jackie Griffith, Marcel Groeneweg, Peter De Groot, Carol Gross, Sarah Grover, Michael Gubzburg, T Gudgeon, James Guest, Martin Gutjahr, Guy Hagan, Altan Halici, Tarnya Hall, Frank Hansen, Jean L Hardy, Chris & Carol Harman, J Harris, Amanda Harvey, Mr & Mrs Hatvany, Craig Hensberg, Warrick Hewitt, Brian Heyton, Iain Hill, Rich Hill, George R Hoffmann, Amanda Honey, Erik Hoogcarspel, Chris Horan, Mildred Howard, Petr Hruska, Douglas Hunt, Natalka Husar, Mike Inkson, Chris Jackson, Susie Jardine, Marek Jarocinski, Jennifer, Pedro Jorge, Norman Kan, Claire Kanganas, Sandra Kaplan, Ari Katz, Kadir Kaya, Kim Keller-Rakochy, Mary N Kennedy, Duncan Kerr, Michael Kersey, Bari Khan, Christine Kimbrough, Mathias Kindbom, Ian & Tracey Kirkland, Frits Klijn, Emily Kline, Jneke Knol, Jody Marie Kodish, Ferdinand Koldewee, Gali Kolt, Agnieszka Koltonik, Rose Koopman-Damen, Robin Kortright, Meredith Kraike, Elliott & Theodora Krause, Blaz Krhin, Mike Krosin, Jane Lane, Kelly Langdon, Tone Larssen, Joanne Last, DF Latchford, Suzanne

Leak, Cis Lebour, George Lechner, Evelyn C Leeper, Caroline Lees, Hannah Leiterman, Lois Lemehens, Rob Leutheuser, Ray Lidgard, Carol & Brian Little, Jos & Ellen Lommerse, Pietranera Luca, David & Elizabeth Luke, Natalie Lysenko, Sarah MacArtain, Vivian Mackereth, Jo Mackintosh, Laura E Madonna, Linda Main, J Mall, A Mango, Sarah Mankawa, Tracey Maree, Sarah Marsh, Ray Marshall, L Massey, Shoshanna Matney, Celia Mattaloni, P Mattinson, Matthew Mattiske, Laura Mattos, M Mazrui, Kathryn McClurg, Ian & June McCormack, Graham McKenzie, Robert McLeman, Marianthe McLiesh, Simon McPherson, Allard Mees, Bob Meller, Dick Van Mersbergen, Stuart Michael, Kylie Michalski, Jan Miller, Justine Miller, Graham & Susan Mills, Kate Minett, B Mohabir, Seval Molenaar-Denirel, Karen Moore, Angus Morrison, Ari Mosenzon, Dave Mountain, Rowena Mular, Ann Mullen, R Murray, Nick Nasev, Jason Nash, Maya Naunton, Carol Nelson, Lucienne van der Netz, Nevit, Stewart Nicolson, Zoe Nielsen, Nicholas C O'Brian, John O'Brian, Bernadine O'Brien, Rachel Odell, Alisha Oku, Douglas Oles, Jessica O'Neill, Kelly O'Neill, Paula Orbea, Jane O'Riley, Maeve O'Sullivan, Beytullah Ozyurt, Isobel Palson, Santosa Pansiyon, Alan Parkes, Roger J Van Parys, Alex Passerini, Pallab Paul, Ben Peacock, Frank Pears, Scott Penhaligon, Daniel Perry, Michelle Plozza, Fransoise Pohu, Jane Poirrier, Pat Powell, Robert Powell, Darren Pratt, Morten & Oliver Pritzkow, Eugeniodel Punta, Tere Ramos, Rebecca, David E Reibscheid, Hayley Reilly, Jan Rensen, C Reyner, Sam Richard, Terry Richardson, Liesbeth van Riessen, Annamaria & Michael Roberts, Betty Robinson, K Robinson, Terry Robinson, Anthony Roediger, Alexander Ron, Rudiger Rossiy, Michael Rowell, Chester & Linda Rowland, Ian Russell, J Russian, James Ryan, Sezgin Saglam, Judith A Sanderman, Shelley Sanders, Paul Sargent, HU Uli Schlapfer, Urs Schmid, Jann & Kerri Schweusey, Heinz & Sarah Seeberg, Mehmet Semih, Elaine & Doug Senior, Arco Seton, David Sharratt, Fiona Shaw, Stacey Sheridan, Bohdan A Shulakewych, Gemmade Shulbh, Mary Shyng, Russ Siddall, Wlodek Sidorczuk, Cynthia Sim, Sheila Sim, Rochelle Sjolseth, Margaret Skoog, Karolina Skowronek, Sue Skull, Sonia Slawuta, David Hugh Smith, Jean Smith, Stephen Smith, Tracey Smith, Joanna Snowdon, Carolyn Squirrell, Siri Srensen, Anne Stanley, Ken Steele, Mark Stephens, Fam Stoelwinder, Joan Stokes, Saleem Taibjee, Brendan Tate & Friends, Caroline Taylor, A Templeton, Daniel Theil, P & E Theunisz, Merryn Thomae, G Thomas, Amber Thomas, Janni Thomsen, Priscilla Thorley, Georgina Thornson, Judyvan Tijn, Tony Titchener, Gabriele Tognacci, Margaret Toms, Sururi Tosun, Brenda Townes, Stale Bakke Trodahl, KJ Troy, Steven Tuch, Maria Tuchy, Katrina Turner, BM Turner, Peggy & John Tyler, Korcan Unsal, H Yusuf Usul, Marie-Laure Vacher, Eddy & Francois Van Giel, Bernard Van Cuylenburg, Willy Vandewephe, Elina Varmola, George Vasilev, Kari Vaughan, Sara Vega, Konstantinos Velegrinos, John Vezeau, Marco Vink, Karen Visser, Martine Vogels, Simon Wake, J Walker, Carmen & Hilton Ward, Prof & Mrs R Ward, Chern Siang Wei, Philip Weld, Sico van der Werf, Paul Werny, Renate Weyers, Saly Whitney, Teresa Whitt, G Whittle, Jason Williams, Pam Williams, Trevor Williams, Les Winberg, Jenny & Eric Wong, Rhona Woodbury, Louise Woollett, Julian Wright, Liz Wright, Mark Wright, Sarah Wright, Amelia Wu, William Wutka, Jennier Yankoviak, Michael Yeoh, Kamil Yildirim, Robert Youker, Kym Young, Matthew Yovich, Genevieve Zaltatorius, Michael Ziser, Margot Zoeteman.

LONELY PLANET

Phrasebooks

Lonely Planet phrasebooks are packed with essential words and phrases to help travellers communicate with the locals. With colour tabs for quick reference, an extensive vocabulary and use of script, these handy pocket-sized language guides cover day-to-day travel situations.

- handy pocket-sized books
- easy to understand Pronunciation chapter
- clear & comprehensive Grammar chapter
- romanisation alongside script to allow ease of pronunciation
- script throughout so users can point to phrases for every situation
- full of cultural information and tips for the traveller

'...vital for a real DIY spirit and attitude in language learning'

– Backpacker

'the phrasebooks have good cultural backgrounders and offer solid advice for challenging situations in remote locations'

– San Francisco Examiner

Arabic (Egyptian) • Arabic (Moroccan) • Australian *(Australian English, Aboriginal and Torres Strait languages)* • Baltic States *(Estonian, Latvian, Lithuanian)* • Bengali • Brazilian • Burmese • Cantonese • Central Asia • Central Europe *(Czech, French, German, Hungarian, Italian, Slovak)* • Eastern Europe *(Bulgarian, Czech, Hungarian, Polish, Romanian, Slovak)* • Ethiopian (Amharic) • Fijian • French • German • Greek • Hill Tribes • Hindi/Urdu • Indonesian • Italian • Japanese • Korean • Lao • Latin American Spanish • Malay • Mandarin • Mediterranean Europe *(Albanian, Croatian, Greek, Italian, Macedonian, Maltese, Serbian, Slovene)* • Mongolian • Nepali • Papua New Guinea • Pilipino (Tagalog) • Quechua • Russian • Scandinavian Europe *(Danish, Finnish, Icelandic, Norwegian, Swedish)* • South-East Asia *(Burmese, Indonesian, Khmer, Lao, Malay, Tagalog Pilipino, Thai, Vietnamese)* • Spanish (Castilian) *(also includes Catalan, Galician and Basque)* • Sri Lanka • Swahili • Thai • Tibetan • Turkish • Ukrainian • USA *(US English, Vernacular, Native American languages, Hawaiian)* • Vietnamese • Western Europe *(Basque, Catalan, Dutch, French, German, Greek, Irish)*

LONELY PLANET

Lonely Planet Journeys

JOURNEYS is a unique collection of travel writing – published by the company that understands travel better than anyone else. It is a series for anyone who has ever experienced – or dreamed of – the magical moment when they encountered a strange culture or saw a place for the first time. They are tales to read while you're planning a trip, while you're on the road or while you're in an armchair in front of a fire.

These outstanding titles explore our planet through the eyes of a diverse group of international writers. JOURNEYS books catch the spirit of a place, illuminate a culture, recount a crazy adventure or introduce a fascinating way of life. They always entertain, and always enrich the experience of travel.

MALI BLUES
Traveling to an African Beat
Lieve Joris (translated by Sam Garrett)

Drought, rebel uprisings, ethnic conflict: these are the predominant images of West Africa. But as Lieve Joris travels in Senegal, Mauritania and Mali, she meets survivors, fascinating individuals charting new ways of living between tradition and modernity. With her remarkable gift for drawing out people's stories, Joris brilliantly captures the rhythms of a world that refuses to give in.

THE GATES OF DAMASCUS
Lieve Joris (translated by Sam Garrett)

This best-selling book is a beautifully drawn portrait of day-to-day life in modern Syria. Through her intimate contact with local people, Lieve Joris draws us into the fascinating world that lies behind the gates of Damascus. Hala's husband is a political prisoner, jailed for his opposition to the Assad regime; through the author's friendship with Hala we see how Syrian politics impacts on the lives of ordinary people.

THE OLIVE GROVE
Travels in Greece
Katherine Kizilos

Katherine Kizilos travels to fabled islands, troubled border zones and her family's village deep in the mountains. She vividly evokes breathtaking landscapes, generous people and passionate politics, capturing the complexities of a country she loves.

'beautifully captures the real tensions of Greece' – *Sunday Times*

KINGDOM OF THE FILM STARS
Journey into Jordan
Annie Caulfield

Kingdom of the Film Stars is a travel book and a love story. With honesty and humour, Annie Caulfield writes of travelling in Jordan and falling in love with a Bedouin with film-star looks.

She offers fascinating insights into the country – from the tent life of traditional women to the hustle of downtown Amman – and unpicks tight-woven western myths about the Arab world.

LONELY PLANET

Lonely Planet Travel Atlases

Lonely Planet has long been famous for the number and quality of its guidebook maps. Now we've gone one step further and produced a handy companion series: Lonely Planet travel atlases – maps of a country produced in book form.

Unlike other maps, which look good but lead travellers astray, our travel atlases have been researched on the road by Lonely Planet's experienced team of writers. All details are carefully checked to ensure the atlas corresponds with the equivalent Lonely Planet guidebook.

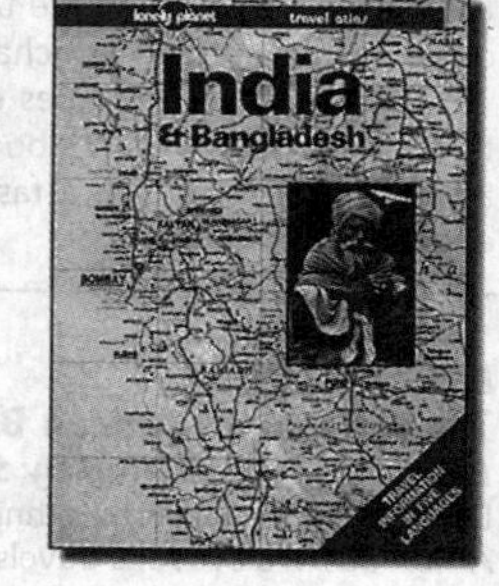

- full-colour throughout
- maps researched and checked by Lonely Planet authors
- place names correspond with Lonely Planet guidebooks
- no confusing spelling differences
- legend and travelling information in English, French, German, Japanese and Spanish
- size: 230 x 160 mm

Available now: Chile & Easter Island • Egypt • India & Bangladesh • Israel & the Palestinian Territories • Jordan, Syria & Lebanon • Kenya • Laos • Portugal • South Africa, Lesotho & Swaziland • Thailand • Turkey • Vietnam • Zimbabwe, Botswana & Namibia

---

Lonely Planet TV Series & Videos

Lonely Planet travel guides have been brought to life on television screens around the world. Like our guides, the programs are based on the joy of independent travel, and look honestly at some of the most exciting, picturesque and frustrating places in the world. Each show is presented by one of three travellers from Australia, England or the USA and combines an innovative mixture of video, Super-8 film, atmospheric soundscapes and original music.

Videos of each episode – containing additional footage not shown on television – are available from good book and video shops, but the availability of individual videos varies with regional screening schedules.

Video destinations include: Alaska • American Rockies • Australia – The South-East • Baja California & the Copper Canyon • Brazil • Central Asia • Chile & Easter Island • Corsica, Sicily & Sardinia – The Mediterranean Islands • East Africa (Tanzania & Zanzibar) • Ecuador & the Galapagos Islands • Greenland & Iceland • Indonesia • Israel & the Sinai Desert • Jamaica • Japan • La Ruta Maya • Morocco • New York • North India • Pacific Islands (Fiji, Solomon Islands & Vanuatu) • South India • South West China • Turkey • Vietnam • West Africa • Zimbabwe, Botswana & Namibia

The Lonely Planet TV series is produced by: Pilot Productions
The Old Studio
18 Middle Row
London W10 5AT, UK

Lonely Planet On-line

www.lonelyplanet.com *or* AOL keyword: lp

Whether you've just begun planning your next trip, or you're chasing down specific info on currency regulations or visa requirements, check out Lonely Planet On-line for up-to-the minute travel information.

As well as mini guides to more than 250 destinations, you'll find maps, photos, travel news, health and visa updates, travel advisories, and discussion of the ecological and political issues you need to be aware of as you travel. You'll also find timely upgrades to popular guidebooks which you can print out and stick in the back of your book.

There's also an on-line travellers' forum where you can share your experience of life on the road, meet travel companions and ask other travellers for their recommendations and advice.

And of course we have a complete and up-to-date list of all Lonely Planet travel products including travel guides, diving and snorkeling guides, phrasebooks, atlases, travel literature and videos, and a simple on-line ordering facility if you can't find the book you want elsewhere.

Lonely Planet Diving & Snorkeling Guides

Known for indispensible guidebooks to destinations all over the world, Lonely Planet's Pisces Books are the most popular series of diving and snorkeling titles available.

There are three series: **Diving & Snorkeling Guides**, **Shipwreck Diving** series and **Dive Into History**. Full colour throughout, the **Diving & Snorkeling Guides** combine quality photographs with detailed descriptions of the best dive sites for each location, giving divers a glimpse of what they can expect both on land and in water. The **Dive Into History** series is perfect for the adventure diver or armchair traveller. The **Shipwreck Diving** series provides all the details for exploring the most interesting wrecks in the Atlantic and Pacific oceans. The list also includes underwater nature and technical guides.

FREE Lonely Planet Newsletters

We love hearing from you and think you'd like to hear from us.

Planet Talk

Our FREE quarterly printed newsletter is full of tips from travellers and anecdotes from Lonely Planet guidebook authors. Every issue is packed with up-to-date travel news and advice, and includes:

- a postcard from Lonely Planet co-founder Tony Wheeler
- a swag of mail from travellers
- a look at life on the road through the eyes of a Lonely Planet author
- topical health advice
- prizes for the best travel yarn
- news about forthcoming Lonely Planet events
- a complete list of Lonely Planet books and other titles

To join our mailing list, residents of the UK, Europe and Africa can email us at go@lonelyplanet.co.uk; residents of North and South America can email us at info@lonelyplanet.com; the rest of the world can email us at talk2us@lonelyplanet.com.au, or contact any Lonely Planet office.

Comet

Our FREE monthly email newsletter brings you all the latest travel news, features, interviews, competitions, destination ideas, travellers' tips & tales, Q&As, raging debates and related links. Find out what's new on the Lonely Planet Web site and which books are about to hit the shelves.

Subscribe from your desktop: www.lonelyplanet.com/comet

Index

Text

Bold indicates maps.
Italics indicates boxed text.

Bold indicates maps.
Italics indicates boxed text.

Bold indicates maps.
Italics indicates boxed text.

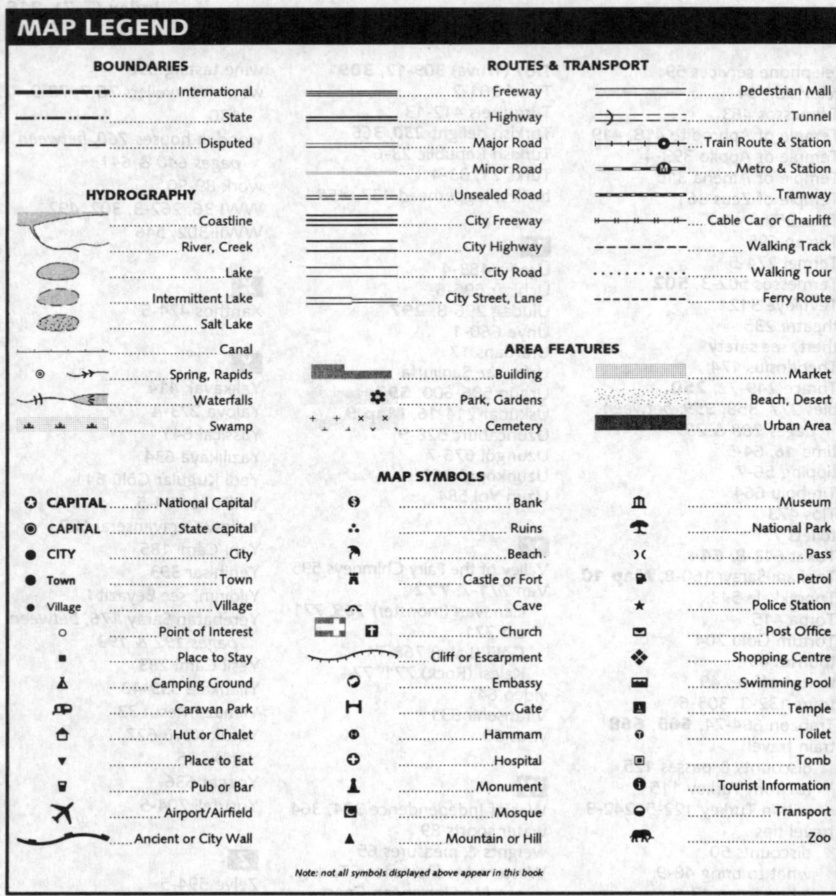

LONELY PLANET OFFICES

Australia
PO Box 617, Hawthorn, Victoria 3122
☎ (03) 9819 1877 fax (03) 9819 6459
email: talk2us@lonelyplanet.com.au

UK
10a Spring Place, London NW5 3BH
☎ (0171) 428 4800 fax (0171) 428 4828
email: go@lonelyplanet.co.uk

USA
150 Linden St, Oakland, CA 94607
☎ (510) 893 8555 TOLL FREE: 800 275 8555
fax (510) 893 8572
email: info@lonelyplanet.com

France
1 rue du Dahomey, 75011 Paris
☎ 01 55 25 33 00 fax 01 55 25 33 01
email: bip@lonelyplanet.fr
minitel: 3615 lonelyplanet *(1,29 F TTC/min)*

World Wide Web: www.lonelyplanet.com *or* AOL keyword: lp
Lonely Planet Images: lpi@lonelyplanet.com.au